HAYDN:
CHRONICLE AND WORKS

HAYDN: CHRONICLE AND WORKS
in five volumes by
H. C. ROBBINS LANDON

Haydn: the Early Years 1732–1765
Haydn at Eszterháza 1766–1790
Haydn in England 1791–1795
Haydn: the Years of 'The Creation' 1796–1800
Haydn: the Late Years 1801–1809

HAYDN:
THE EARLY YEARS
1732–1765

For
Ian M. Bruce
great teacher,
great connoisseur

Haydn: Chronicle and Works

VOLUME I

HAYDN

THE EARLY YEARS
1732–1765

H. C. ROBBINS LANDON

INDIANA UNIVERSITY PRESS

BLOOMINGTON   LONDON

ML
410
·H4
·L26
vol. 1

First American edition 1980 by Indiana University Press

Copyright © 1980 by H. C. Robbins Landon

All rights reserved

No part of this book may be reproduced or utilized in
any form or by any means, electronic or mechanical,
including photocopying and recording, or by any
information storage and retrieval system, without
permission in writing from the publisher. The
Association of American University Presses' Resolution
on Permissions constitutes the only exception to this prohibition.

Library of Congress Cataloging in Publication Data

Landon, Howard Chandler Robbins, 1926–
    Haydn: chronicle and works.

    Includes bibliographies and indexes.
    CONTENTS
  v. 1. Haydn: the Early Years 1732–1765
    1. Haydn, Joseph, 1732–1809.
ML410.H4L26   780'.92'4[B]   76–14630
ISBN 0–253–37001–9   1 2 3 4 5 84 83 82 81 80

Printed in Great Britain

Contents

LIST OF ILLUSTRATIONS

Preface

THIS BIOGRAPHY traces the life of a boy who began in abject poverty, half-trained and largely self-educated, who rose to be the leading musical figure of Europe in the 1790s and achieved greater popularity in his own lifetime than any composer before him. Handel, when he died in 1759, was popular to the point of idolatry in England but was largely unknown in Prague, St Petersburg, Laibach, Venice and Bordeaux. Within two decades, Haydn's music would be adored in all those places, and even in the New World. Haydn died a wealthy man – not quite as wealthy as Handel, with his beautiful old masters on the wall of his Brook Street house, but nevertheless wealthier than his predecessors Gluck or Mozart, or subsequently Beethoven, Schubert and Weber at their respective deaths. The wheelwright's lad from Rohrau also became a markedly successful courtier, gently manipulating princes of the Holy Roman Empire. The present, first volume of this biography tells the story of Haydn's obscure beginnings and the establishment, by 1765, of his fame within the Austrian monarchy as well as the first evidences of his international reputation in France, Holland, Germany, and England. Such a rise was possible in eighteenth-century Austria not only for a penniless choir-boy, but it could also happen in other spheres. The mighty Princes of Grassalkovicz (whose lovely castle, at Gödöllö in Hungary, was later the favourite resort of the tragic Empress Elisabeth of Austria) began with a farmer boy, Anton (1694–1771), who grew rich as a lawyer and, later, Hungarian *Cammer Praesident*, and whose descendants married into the Esterházy family; and in this present volume, we shall mention briefly another spectacular career, that of Franz, later Ritter von Heintl, whose unpublished diaries were discovered by my wife in Florence a few years ago.[1]

The period under present consideration saw the reigns, in Austria, of Charles VI (died 1740) and his daughter, Maria Theresa, with her consort, Francis Stephen of Lorraine. At her accession, Austria was surrounded by potential enemies, her finances and governmental structure in urgent need of reform, and Europe's balance of power – always a delicate matter – in danger of collapse. In the ensuing wars with Prussia, Austria's financial, military, and moral resources were strained to breaking point. As always in this biography, I have tried to sketch in the historical background, without which one is hardly in a position to see Haydn in the round. Actually, one can not provide more than, Michelin-like, 'un peu d'histoire', but to have omitted that 'peu' would surely have been a mistake.

... If, by venturing so rashly into social, political and intellectual history, I have trespassed against the increasingly rigorous demarcations which separate

---

1 *Infra*, pp. 75f. On the incredible story of the Grassalkovicz (Grassalkovitsch, etc.) family, see W. Kisch, *Die alten Strassen und Plaetze von Wien's Vorstädten*, vol. I, Vienna 1883 (reprint: Cosenza 1967), pp. 179ff. The Esterházy family was at first wildly jealous of this upstart: Khevenhüller II (1745–9), pp. 221f.

historians from one another, it is a sin to which I willingly own. We are too overcrowded a profession to entrench ourselves in pedantic specialisations, the cliometricians despising the innumerate, the intellectual historians disdaining the artificers of political history. It is time, perhaps, to poke our heads above our several molehills and to take in a view, however nervous and blinking, of the broader historical landscape.

[Simon Schama, *Patriots and Liberators: Revolution in the Netherlands 1780–1813*, New York 1977, p. xiii]

How did Haydn manage to survive during those terrible years of near-starvation in Vienna? In the authentic biographies, we learn of his various church positions (leader in the orchestra of the Hospitallers, organist in the Haugwitz chapel, *supernumerarius* in the *Capelle* of St Stephen's, where he had been a choir-boy), and also of his first operatic assignment for the Kärntnerthortheater. It has been suggested that Haydn wrote more than the one opera (*Der[neue]krumme Teufel*), and for this volume I have re-examined the anonymous music to several Hanswurst and similar pieces which are preserved in two MS volumes in the Österreichische Nationalbibliothek, and have come to the conclusion that several are indubitably the work of the young Haydn. If confronted with the low literary standard of these plays-with-music, Haydn would, no doubt, have smiled but one doubts if he would have repented. Like Dryden, he could have said, 'I confess my chief endeavours are to delight the Age in which I live. If the humour of this, be for low Comedy, small Accidents, and Raillery, I will force my Genius to obey it.'[1] It was a precept to which both men adhered all their lives.

With the arrival of the Fürnberg family in Haydn's life, one is fortunate to have the great Fürnberg-Morzin archives now in the Hungarian Castle of Keszthely. This major source of information about Haydn's early music will be the subject of detailed analysis (*infra*, pp. 239ff.). I first examined this collection in 1958 and 1959 when it was on loan to the Music Department of the Országos Széchényi Könyvtár, and again in 1978 when it was back *in situ*. For the first time, reproductions of all the handwritings involved in this collection are given in this volume so that my colleagues may have them at their ready disposition.

Haydn was, in May 1761, engaged by the Esterházy family. In an effort to provide this volume with appropriate background material, I went yet again to Budapest in June 1978 and worked not only in the aforementioned Music Department but also in the Hungarian State Archives (Magyar Országos Levéltár), with results which may be seen in the relevant places. In describing the life of Eisenstadt Castle, I was fortunate enough to discover an important and extensive unpublished entry in the famous *Journal* of Count von Zinzendorf, who also provided, in another entry, an answer to the hitherto unsolved problem of clarinets in the Esterházy orchestra of this period.

If the reader notices that there is *on the whole* less material from the Esterházy Archives dealing with the period 1761–5, it is because less material has survived. The now retired former Archivist, Dr Janos Harich, in a letter of 25 May 1979, referring to this problem, writes: 'As early as the 1930s I looked in vain for records of the first years after Haydn's engagement. They seem to have disappeared, perhaps because the bureaucratic organization of the estate was not as severe as it was in later years.' Nevertheless, the occasional document, especially from Forchtenstein Castle (Austria) does turn up. As many as appeared pertinent have been included here.

---

1 'A Defence of an Essay of Dramatique Poesie', 1688. *Works*, IX, ed. John Loftis and Vinton A. Dearing, Berkeley, Cal. 1966, p. 7.

Haydn came from the people; he always felt himself to be in close touch with the people, though at the same time he was a firm believer that 'extra ecclesiam nulla salvus'. Like Dickens, 'his outlook was, in many ways, that of the Common Man writ large and writ brilliant'.[1] Haydn was perhaps the last great composer to be at one with European society, but that was possible because the eighteenth century was the last in which there was usually a quietly integrated oneness between society, music, literature and architecture. This was particularly true of Austria, and it can not be an accident that the French Revolution, despite strenuous efforts by the Jacobins and their sympathisers, was never able to establish itself in the Austrian monarchy. If we examine the organization of a typical town in what is now Burgenland, the border country where Haydn grew up and later worked, we note the extraordinary harmony of the village's overall construction. On this point, we read:

> Why do these villages, constructed with surprisingly similar methods and with the simplest materials in the simplest fashion, exert such a lasting impression and produce such a curious attraction, especially for city dwellers? Why do these villages, with their very severely ordered, low white houses on wide, clearly arranged streets, appear to be so self-evidently a part of the landscape, as if they were symbols of their sunny surroundings? . . . Compared to the oppressive effects of a world dominated by mass values, mechanization and haste, this breadth, peace and simplicity, this synoptical and clearly recognized conformity, the comfortingly human proportions of the villages between the Neusiedlersee and the Leitha Mountains – all this acts like a release, a liberation. . . . Yet all the important conceptual elements and laws of orderliness were immediately determined by the common way of life: the great and generous barns that mark the villages' borders against the fields, the small, low-lying houses, increase the effect of the church which, situated across the village green, forms the end and central point, its shining tower visible from afar, across the quiet, horizontal ridges of barn and house – a beckoning symbol.
> [Roland Rainer, 'Masstab und Ordnung', *Anonymes Bauen: Nordburgenland*, Salzburg 1961, pp. 5, 7]

Not only the French Revolution but even more the coming Industrial Revolution, which may be said to have started in later eighteenth-century England, began to destroy for ever this harmony between man and his surroundings, whether buildings, books or musical scores.

We would like to close this Preface with a quotation from that most civilized of men, Denys Sutton. He writes:

> It has been claimed that Rubens is an artist without any particular appeal to our age. From one point of view, this is perhaps true; he is the very opposite of a *fin de siècle* artist, a man of sunshine not of the shades. He has a cohesive view of life, celebrating the pleasures of existence . . . and he rejoiced in the consolations of the Christian faith. What went on behind his polite and dignified mask is a matter of speculation, but however much he must have been sickened by the intrigues and the failure of his own hopes for peace, his enthusiasm never dimmed for the refreshment of his senses by the contemplation of beauty in humans, Nature or ideas . . . His art is an art of affirmation, a call for hope. That is why it should have a tonic effect and help us to continue to believe in values and quality and to struggle

---

1 Philip Collins, 'Dickens in 1870', *The Times Literary Supplement*, 4 July 1970, p. 606.

for independence, now that the destroyers of civilization move closer to their objective.[1]

If we substitute the Silesian and Napoleonic Wars, all that is said above, and said so beautifully, could apply to the art of Joseph Haydn.

ACKNOWLEDGMENTS

I have once again to thank my friends at the Országos Széchényi Könyvtár in Budapest for their kindnesses to my wife and myself during a visit in June 1978, and also to the courteous and helpful staff of the Magyar Országos Levéltár (Budapest) and the Helikon Library at Keszthely Castle (Lake Balaton). Without their infinite patience and generous assistance, this book would, quite simply, not exist. I also owe a special word of thanks not only to the management and staff of my joint publishers, Thames & Hudson, Ltd (London) and Indiana University Press (Bloomington, Indiana), but especially to my two editors, Messrs Charles Ford and Mark Trowbridge, who fulfilled their tiresome and exceedingly complicated tasks with affection and humour. The following persons and institutions were my hosts on numerous occasions and/or answered questions and supplied photographs of source material:

AUSTRIA: Haus-, Hof- und Staatsarchiv, Vienna (Dr Clemens Höslinger); the Gesellschaft der Musikfreunde, Vienna (Dr Otto Biba, who was also of great assistance in the vexing questions of the organs at Eisenstadt, on which subject he is the leading expert; and Dr Peter Riethus); the Österreichische Nationalbibliothek, Vienna (Hofrat Dr Franz Grasberger and Dr Günter Brosche of the Musikabteilung); the Diözesanarchiv, Graz; the Institut für Aufführungspraxis, Graz (Frau Professor Vera Schwarz, Frau Dr Roswitha Karp, Frau Dr Lilian Putz), the Musikwissenschaftliches Seminar der Universität Graz (Professor Rudolph Flotzinger, Frau Dr Ingrid Schubert, who went to immense pains for me on two trips to Graz in the Spring of 1979); the Landeshochschule für Musik, Graz (Professor Ferdinand Bogner); the Stadtbibliothek, Vienna; the Benedictine Monasteries of Göttweig (Lower Austria), Melk (Lower Austria), Lambach (Upper Austria; and Professor Hermann Lang), and Kremsmünster (Upper Austria); the Premonstratensian Monastery of Schlägl (Upper Austria); the Burgenländisches Landesmuseum, Eisenstadt (Hofrat Dr Ohrenberger and Herr Anton Hahn); the Österreichisches Institut für Kulturgeschichte, Eisenstadt (Frau Dr Gerda Mraz, for numerous acts of kindness, and to her husband, Dr Gottfried Mraz, for answering many complex questions concerning Austrian politics and religion); the Augustinian Monastery of St Florian (Upper Austria); the late Count Niklas Salm-Reifferscheidt, Schloß Steyregg (Upper Austria), and his son, the present Altgraf Salm; as always, to Dr Janos Harich, Eisenstadt; Dr Alexander Weinmann, Vienna, for giving me his as yet unpublished archive material on Albrechtsberger's brother; and to the Library of the Universitätsbibliothek, Vienna.

CZECHOSLOVAKIA: the Národni Museum, Prague; the Schwarzenberg Central Archives, Český Krumlov; the Museum (containing the Archives of the Prince-Archbishops of Olmütz) at Kroměříž (Kremsier); Slovakian Academy of Sciences, Bratislava (Pressburg); National Janáček Museum, Brno (Brünn).

FRANCE: Bibliothèque Nationale, Paris (now incorporating Bibliothèque du Conservatoire de Musique), and M. François Lesure; M. Marc Vignal, Paris; Fondation Ephrussi de Rothschild, St-Jean-Cap-Ferrat.

---

1 *Apollo*, March 1977, p. 158; quoted by permission.

GERMANY: the Fürstlich Oettingen-Wallersteinsches Schloßarchiv, Harburg (Bavaria); the Fürstliches Thurn-und-Taxisches Hofarchiv, Regensburg (Bavaria); the former Preußische Staatsbibliothek, Berlin (which was partly housed, when I studied the MSS., in Tübingen and Marburg/Lahn); the Fürstlich Fürstenbergsches Hofarchiv, Donaueschingen (Baden); Herr Hans Schneider, Tutzing über München, who very kindly photographed various sources in his possession.

GREAT BRITAIN: British Museum (British Library); the Royal College of Music, London; Mr Hermann Baron, for help with complicated technical terms concerning violins in German, and for finding for me some valuable authentic sources of Haydn's early string trios and Opus 1 Quartets; Mr Albi Rosenthal, London and Oxford, for sending me xerox copies of a little-known Italian book with interesting references to Haydn; Dr Roger Hellyer, Oxford; Dr Susan Wollenberg, Oxford; the many friends and strangers who have sent in *corrigenda* and *addenda* are mentioned in the appropriate places. Ian M. Bruce, to whom this volume is dedicated, was kind enough to read the galley proofs and to make useful suggestions.

HUNGARY: Apart from the Budapest libraries, also the Benedictine Monastery of St Martinsberg (Pannonhalma) and the Archives of St Michael's Church, Sopron (Oedenburg).

U.S.A.: the Pierpont Morgan Library, New York; the Library of Congress, Washington, D.C. (Mr Donald Leavitt); Professor A. Peter Brown, Bloomington, Ind., for various kindnesses when he went to Kremsier Castle (tracing watermarks, photographing sources, and providing large amounts of accurate and speedy information).

As before, I owe a special debt of thanks to the many individuals and institutions who supplied the illustrations, the details of which may be seen on pp. 9 and 10. In many cases, it required a great effort to organize the services of a photographer.

Hirschbach im Waldviertel, 28 August 1979.   H.C.R.L.

AUTHOR'S NOTE

Haydn's music

VOCAL MUSIC is identified by title and, on the occasion of the first or major reference, by its number in Hoboken's *Haydn Verzeichnis* (vol. II, Vocal Works), Mainz, 1971. INSTRUMENTAL MUSIC is identified as follows:

Symphonies are referred to by their number in Mandyczewski's list for the publishers Breitkopf & Härtel, which numbering was taken over by Hoboken in his *Haydn Verzeichnis* (vol. I), Mainz, 1955. Symphony No. 95, for example, is I:95 in Hoboken's list.

String Quartets are identified by their opus number and, like all instrumental pieces, by the Hoboken number at the first and/or major reference.

Piano Sonatas are listed by their chronological numbering in the *Wiener Urtext Ausgabe*, edited by C. Landon.

Piano Trios are identified by the new chronological numbering in the *Complete Edition of Haydn's Piano Trios*, edited by H. C. Robbins Landon and published by Verlag Doblinger.

Baryton Trios are identified by their numbers as listed in Hoboken, but the String Trios are identified by the numbering in the new complete, critical edition (H. C. Robbins Landon) published by Verlag Doblinger; in Hoboken these trios are listed in such a way that no clear differentiation between genuine and spurious works is possible.

Other instrumental works are identified by their customary title (e.g. 'London Trios' and 'Overture to an English Opera') and by their Hoboken number.

The system of pitch notation used is based on middle C being represented by the symbol *c'*.

Instruments (in order of their customary appearance in the orchestral score) are abbreviated thus: Fl. – flute; Ob. – oboe; Cor ang. – cor anglais; Clar. – clarinet; Bsn. (Fag.) – bassoon; Hn. (Cor.) – horn; Trbe. (Trpt) – trumpet; Trbn. – trombone; Timp. – timpani (kettledrums); V. – violin; Va. viola; Vc. – violoncello; Cb. (B) – contrabasso (double bass); Cemb. – cembalo (harpsichord); Bar. – baryton.

Documents

In all documents cited in the text the original orthography – whether in English, German, French or Italian – has been retained. Thus, accents have not been inserted where they were omitted in the original document, notably in passages from the Zinzendorf Diaries. The language of the original document is indicated only in those cases which require clarification. Bibliographical references will be found in an abbreviated form in the text, at the end of quotations and in the footnotes; the full titles of works cited are given on pp. 20–22.

The abbreviations 'k.k.' and 'I.R.' (meaning '*kaiserlich-königlich*'/'Imperial Royal') are used interchangeably. Austrian money is abbreviated thus: Gulden (gulden) = 'f.' or 'fl.' (or 'F.', 'Fl.'); Kreuzer = 'k.' or 'kr.' or 'xr.' ('K.', 'Kr.', 'Xr.'); 'd.' or '$\mathcal{A}$' = Denar (see p. 339 for an explanation of the differences between Austrian und Hungarian use of gulden, Kreuzer and Denar). Other abbreviations in general European use: pound ($\mathcal{L}$) = livre = ₶; shilling (*s.*) = sol (sou) = ϒ; penny (*d.*) = denier = denar (see above). For a valuable conversion table and diverse European weights, measures, etc., see de la Porte's *La science des négocians et teneurs de livres, ou Instruction générale Pour tout ce qui se pratique dans les Comptoirs des Négocians, tant pour les Affairs de Banque, que pour les Marchandises, & chez les Financiers pour les Comptes* ... Nouvelle Édition, Amsterdam, Aux Dépens de la Compagnie, M.DCC.LXXXIII.' The livre was also abbreviated by the simpler sign ₶ or ₶. Various kinds of gold and silver ducats were in use; in Venice alone there were three silver ducats of varying value ($8\frac{1}{2}$ lire; 9 lire, 12 soldi; and $6\frac{1}{5}$ lire or 124 soldi). The gold ducat in Frankfurt was exchanged at three florins (gulden), the florin being worth sixty Kreuzer; but in Danzig the ducat was worth six florins and in Königsberg seven florins, twelve Groschen; in Hamburg the gold ducat was traded at six marcs 9 r lubs (lubs = marcs of Lübeck, where the money was physically minted); in Holland, the gold ducat was worth five florins, the silver three. Further conversion tables will be offered *infra* and in the other volumes of this biography, as is found necessary.

1 Haydn's birthplace in Rohrau, anonymous sketch formerly owned by Johann Nepomuk Hummel and inscribed (by Ed. Hummel) 'In diesem Hause zu Rohrau ward Haydn am 31. März 1732 geboren'. This may be the picture of Haydn's birthplace given to Beethoven on his deathbed, on which occasion he exclaimed, 'It has given me a childish pleasure, the cradle of such a great man.' Hummel, who witnessed this scene, may have acquired the picture from among Beethoven's effects after he died (a fortnight later).

II The Cathedral of St Stephen (Stephansdom), Vienna; coloured engraving by Carl Schütz, 1792. Here Haydn was a choir-boy, and he lived in a small building (the Capellhaus, since demolished) located on the other side of the Cathedral.

III The Kärntnerthortheater (right) and the Bürgerspitalskirche, Vienna; coloured engraving (1853) by Jacob Hyrtl after C. Pfeffel (1724). In this theatre Haydn's first Opera, *Der krumme Teufel*, and its successor (*Der neue krumme Teufel*) were performed in the 1750s by the Kurz–Bernadon troupe.

IV, V   The Benedictine Monasteries of Melk (*top*) and Göttweig, two of the great monastic houses in
Austria where Haydn's music was played and collected. Together with others, these monasteries played
an important part in the dissemination of music in the eighteenth century, and notably of Haydn's
(Göttweig began collecting music of Johann Michael Haydn in 1759, and of Joseph in 1762; Melk began
collecting Joseph's music in 1765).

ABBREVIATIONS OF
BIBLIOGRAPHICAL SOURCES

A.M.	Acta Musicalia (from the Esterházy Archives; now Országos Széchényi Könyvtár, Budapest).
AMZ	*Allgemeine Musikalische Zeitung*, Leipzig, 1798 *et seq.*
A.T.	Acta Theatralia (from the Esterházy Archives, now Országos Széchényi Könyvtár, Budapest).
Bartha	*Joseph Haydn, Gesammelte Briefe und Aufzeichnungen*, herausgegeben und erläutert von Dénes Bartha, Budapest-Kassel, 1965.
Bartha-Somfai	Dénes Bartha and László Somfai, *Haydn als Opernkapellmeister*, Budapest, 1960.
Brand *Messen*	Carl Maria Brand, *Die Messen von Joseph Haydn*, Würzburg, 1941 (since reprinted).
Carpani	Giuseppe Carpani, *Le Haydine*, Milan, 1812.
CCLN	*Collected Correspondence and London Notebooks of Joseph Haydn*, translated and edited by H. C. Robbins Landon, London, 1959.
Copyists	In references to MS. copies of scores, individual hands are identified by name (if known) or 'Anon.' with numbers/letters (see Landon, *SYM*, 611, and Bartha-Somfai, 404ff.).
Deutsch *Mozart, Dokumente*	Otto Erich Deutsch, *W. A. Mozart – Die Dokumente seines Lebens*, Kassel-Basel, 1961.
Dies	A. C. Dies, *Biographische Nachrichten von Joseph Haydn*, Vienna, 1810; new ed. Horst Seeger, Berlin, n.d. [1959].
DTB	*Denkmäler der Tonkunst in Bayern.*
DTÖ	*Denkmäler der Tonkunst in Österreich.*
ECP	*Eisenstädter Comissions Prothocoll ... 1777 bis 1790* (in EH, Budapest).
EH	Esterházy Archives (now Budapest, Forchtenstein or Eisenstadt).
EK	*Entwurf-Katalog* (Haydn's draft catalogue of his compositions, *c.* 1765 *et seq.*; Staatsbibliothek, Berlin).
Enciclopedia dello spettacolo	*Enciclopedia dello spettacolo* (11 vols.), Rome, 1954 *et seq.*
Fitzpatrick	Horace Fitzpatrick, *The Horn and Horn-playing, and the Austro-Bohemian Tradition 1680–1830*, London and New York, 1970.
F–M	Copyists found in the Fürnberg-Morzin Collection (see table, *infra*, p. 251).
GdM	Gesellschaft der Musikfreunde, Vienna.
Geiringer 1932, 1947, 1959 and 1963	Karl Geiringer, *Joseph Haydn*: Potsdam, 1932; New York, 1947; Mainz, 1959; Garden City, N.Y., 1963.

Bibliographical sources

Gericke	H. Gericke, *Der Wiener Musikhandel von 1700 bis 1778*, Vienna 1960.
Griesinger	G. A. Griesinger, *Biographische Notizen über Joseph Haydn*, Leipzig, 1810; new ed. Franz Grasberger, Vienna, 1954.
Grove, I, II, III, IV, V	Grove's *Dictionary of Music and Musicians*, first, second, third, fourth and fifth editions.
Harich *Musikgeschichte*	Janos Harich, 'Esterházy-Musikgeschichte im Spiegel der zeitgenössischen Textbücher', in (special number of) *Burgenländische Forschungen*, Heft 39, Eisenstadt, 1959.
Hase	H. von Hase, *Joseph Haydn und Breitkopf & Härtel*, Leipzig, 1909.
HJB	*Haydn Jahrbuch/Haydn Yearbook*, 1962 et seq.
Horányi	Mátyás Horányi, *Das Esterházysche Feenreich*, Budapest, 1959; English edition, *The Magnificence of Esterháza*, London, 1962.
HV	Thematic catalogue ('Haydn Verzeichnis') of Haydn's œuvre (compiled 1805); see Larsen, *HUB*, 53–119; also the final volume of this biography, *Haydn: the Late Years 1801–1809*, 294f.
Jancik	Hans Jancik, *Michael Haydn, ein vergessener Meister*, Vienna, 1952.
JHW	*Joseph Haydn Werke*, the new collected edition of Haydn's works published by the Joseph Haydn Institut, Cologne.
Khevenhüller	*Aus der Zeit Maria Theresias. Tagebuch des Fürsten Johann Josef Khevenhüller-Metsch, kaiserlichen Obersthofmeisters. 1742–1776*, 10 vols., ed. Rudolph, Count Khevenhüller-Metsch and Hanns Schlitter (later, ed. Hans Wagner), Leipzig (later Vienna), 1905 et seq.
Landon *Essays*	H. C. Robbins Landon, *Essays on the Viennese Classical Style*, London, 1970.
Landon *Supplement*	H. C. Robbins Landon, *Supplement to 'The Symphonies of Joseph Haydn'*, London, 1961.
Landon *SYM*	H. C. Robbins Landon, *The Symphonies of Joseph Haydn*, London, 1955.
Larsen *HÜB*	J. P. Larsen, *Die Haydn-Überlieferung*, Copenhagen, 1939.
MGG	*Musik in Geschichte und Gegenwart* (Allgemeine Enzyklopädie der Musik), ed. F. Blume, Kassel, 1947 et seq.
Mozart, *Briefe*	*Mozart Briefe und Aufzeichnungen* (ed. Bauer, Deutsch and Eibl), 6 vols., Kassel, 1962 et seq.
Neukomm	Sigismund (von) Neukomm, *Bemerkungen zu den biogr. Nachrichten von Dies* (MS. in Pohl's hand, owned by Friedrich Matzenauer, Vienna; published 1959).
ÖNB	Österreichische Nationalbibliothek, Vienna.
PCDI	*Prothocoll über verschiedene hochfürstl. Commissiones, Decretationes, Intimata und andere Buchhaltereys Verordnungen de Anno 1734 [et seq.]*, (EH, Budapest).
Pohl I, II, III	C. F. Pohl, *Joseph Haydn* (3 vols.): I, Berlin, 1875; II, Berlin, 1882; III (completed by Hugo Botstiber), Leipzig, 1927. All three vols. since reprinted.
Radant, *Rosenbaum*	'The Diaries of Joseph Carl Rosenbaum 1770–1829' edited by Else Radant, *Haydn Yearbook* V (1968); also as separate publications in the original German.
Rosenbaum	'The Diaries of Joseph Carl Rosenbaum 1770–1829' (MS. in the ÖNB, Vienna); see Radant above.

18

Schmid, 'Eisenstadt'   E. F. Schmid, 'Joseph Haydn in Eisenstadt', in *Burgenländische Heimatblätter* I/1 (1932).

Schmid, *Vorfahren*   E. F. Schmid, *Joseph Haydn. Ein Buch von Vorfahren und Heimat des Meisters*, 2 vols., Kassel 1934.

Somfai   László Somfai, *Joseph Haydn. Sein Leben in zeitgenössischen Bildern*, Budapest and Kassel, 1966; also published in English, London, 1967.

SzM   *Studien zur Musikwissenschaft*, Vienna, 1913 *et seq.*

Valkó I, II   Arisztid Valkó, 'Haydn magyarországi müködése a levéltári akták tükrében', in *Zenetudományi Tanulmányok* VI (1957) = 'I', and VIII (1960) = 'II'.

WD   *Das Wienerische Diarium* (Viennese periodical).

Wirth I   Helmut Wirth, *Joseph Haydn als Dramatiker*, Wolfenbüttel-Berlin, 1941; Kieler Beiträge zur Musikwissenschaft (ed. Friedrich Blume), vol. 7.

Wirth II   Helmut Wirth, 'The Operas of Joseph Haydn before "Orfeo"', in *Joseph Haydn 'Orfeo ed Euridice'*, Haydn Society, Boston, Mass., 1951.

WZ   *Wiener Zeitung.*

Zinzendorf   MS. Diaries of Count Carl von Zinzendorf, in the Haus-, Hof- und Staatsarchiv, Vienna.

CHAPTER ONE

The Austrian Scene before and at the Time of Haydn's Birth

WHEN, ON 12 SEPTEMBER 1683, the Turkish invasion was stopped, at the last minute, before the gates of Vienna, it was obvious to everyone that a European catastrophe had been avoided. But the price had been high: large parts of present-day Hungary, Roumania and Croatia were laid waste, and even today, a traveller through Croatia sees a desolate land ruined by years of Turkish supremacy. When Kara Mustafa and his army left Vienna, they slaughtered their Christian slaves and prisoners of war. In the train of their gigantic army, they had as Christian *impedimenta* 6,000 men, 11,000 women, 14,000 girls and 50,000 children. When they had rolled up to Vienna, they had passed through Hainburg and slaughtered many of the population on 12 July 1683: the small 'Gasse' that goes from the upper part of town to the Danube was thereafter called 'Blutgasse' (bloody street). One of the very few to hide successfully from the screeching invaders was Thomas Haydn (Joseph Haydn's grandfather) and his sister Magdalena, while their brother Hans disappeared for ever in the blood-bath of that July day.

Hainburg was an old border castle on the Danube, and overlooked miles of heath. After the Turks had been forced back into Hungary the population of this part of Austria (through which the River Leitha formed the old border with Hungary – Rohrau being situated on the upper reaches of the river) was found by Emperor Leopold I to have been decimated; he resettled the country with Swabians, who began to cultivate the ruined land, occupying desolate villages such as Pachfurth, Rohrau and Prellenkirchen – where Haydn's ancestors and other German villagers had settled – and prospered there.

In Austria the Turkish trauma continued well into the eighteenth century. 'Turkish' music was a fashionable 'exotic excursion'; both Haydn and Mozart composed many works 'alla turca'. Breakfast croissants were shaped in the form of a Turkish crescent (half-moon); the beautiful paper from the great northern Italian mills of the Veneto had as its principal watermark three crescents of declining size; coffee-drinking became fashionable.

If the Turkish invasion shaped Austrian history in the seventeenth century, Austrian character was even more influenced by the Counter-Reformation. The influx of Lutheran ideas, particularly from Bohemia, had rent the Austrian church and it was no easy task to bring the sheep back to the fold. Schismatical tendencies persisted, and when all else failed, the Protestants went underground. In 1625, the Reformations-Commission in Vienna issued an edict that gave the population two choices: either embrace the Catholic faith or go into exile; many chose to leave the city. The next year, the city was flooded by monks, and the Jesuits ruled supreme in matters of belief and education; but even this Vatican invasion did not cure the population of their Protestantism, and in 1638 a government edict forbade secret meetings, forbade the reading of sermons, forbade offering hospitality to non-Catholic priests, forbade reading non-Catholic literature. It seemed as if another breeding ground for Cathars or Albigensians could be created; but this time the Church was forewarned, and in 1652 the I.R. Government ordered yearly Easter confession and communion for all citizens and strict observance of Sundays and Holy Days – a mockery of the terms of the Westphalian Peace Treaty, which guaranteed religious freedom. Robert Endres writes:

> A severe and thoroughly one-sided censorship forbade any intellectual communication with Protestants abroad. The far-reaching changes that were taking place in northern Germany: the beginning of the Enlightenment, the development of German poetry, the flowering of the natural sciences – of all this Austria felt not a trace. Since the Counter-Reformation was allowed to wither the spiritual life of the Habsburg Monarchy, the creative urges and gifts of its peoples sought other outlets, particularly in the artistic sector, with music and visual arts. Both enjoyed a great flowering in the outgoing seventeenth and early eighteenth centuries, which is called Austrian Baroque. But the Counter-Reformation left deep marks on the Austrian, and especially the Viennese, character. If the late Middle Ages, the period of the crusades, formed the national character of European peoples, this formation was completed during the period 1500–1700. The outcome of the great battle for religious freedom, which turned out so differently in the Germanic and Mediterranean lands, formed the character of the Spanish, French, English, the north and the south Germans. And thereby the Austrians suffered worst of all. The lax religious morality and the outward show of piety; the emnity towards the state, in which every governmental office was regarded as a natural enemy to be avoided; an attitude towards taxation in which cheating the state was not only tolerated but considered clever; the lack of a national consciousness, which appears only as deviated patriotic enthusiasm for a greater Germany – all these unfortunate manifestations were the result of the Counter-Reformation.
>
> ['Türkennot und Glaubenskämpfe', in *Unvergängliches Wien*, Vienna 1964, p. 145]

The Habsburgs themselves were passionately fond of music and many became musicians and composers of professional excellence: Ferdinand III (reigned 1637–57) brought Italian opera to Vienna in the aftermath of the Thirty Years War and was himself an opera composer. His son, Leopold I (reigned 1657–1705), was without any question the most gifted composer of the family, whose operas, ballets and church music show signs of real genius: he played the flute and the harpsichord and had absolute pitch. His son Joseph I (reigned 1705–11) showed even more gifts but his early death from smallpox put the sceptre in the hands of his brother, Charles VI, who was an operatic composer of some stature, and a fine violinist and harpsichord player. He was an excellent *maestro di cappella* and led the Imperial singers and orchestra like any professional. It cannot be said, however, that this musicality progressed beyond Charles VI, for his daughter Maria Theresa was, at best, faintly musical; her prejudices and amateurishness in musical matters were inherited by Joseph II and Leopold II, both of whom displayed conventional, unenlightened musical taste – preferring Florian Leopold Gassmann, Giovanni Paisiello and Domenico Cimarosa to Haydn and Mozart. The last trace of musicality in the Habsburg family resided in Francis II, Leopold II's son; Francis liked church music, was proud of Haydn, but basically preferred the music of Georg Reutter Jr to that of Beethoven.

When the Turkish armies had left the country, there ensued a great period for Austrian architecture. It was during the period 1685–1740 that most of the magnificent Austrian castles, pilgrimage churches and monasteries were rebuilt. When Haydn arrived in Vienna, the city was dominated not only by St Stephen's Cathedral but by the new Karlskirche (begun 1715, consecrated 1737), designed by one of the country's greatest architects, J. E. Fischer von Erlach. It was a daring challenge, and the contorted violence of the huge front pillars ushered in a new era. Fischer von Erlach was also called in to redesign ancient castles such as Riegersburg in Lower Austria, from 1731 in possession of the Khevenhüller family and in 1735 magnificently rebuilt in the grandest Baroque style. A rival in large-scale thinking and the ability to dispose of vast spacial concepts was Jacob Prandtauer, who in the years 1702–36 redesigned the most famous of all Austrian monasteries, the Benedictine Abbey of Melk on the Danube (see pl. IV). Prandtauer also had a decisive influence on the magnificent Augustine Abbey at St Florian and the astonishing pilgrimage church of Maria Taferl above the Danube, where Haydn's friend Albrechtsberger was, from 1757–9, organist (in conjunction with this profusion of rebuilding, new organs were often ordered; for example, the fine organ in Maria Taferl, completed in 1760). Some of the great projects for transforming Renaissance and Gothic monasteries into the Baroque style failed because they were begun too late and funds ran out: with the death of Charles VI in 1740, building on this monumental scale ceased, partly as a result of the financial crisis brought on by the Silesian Wars. Thus the venerable Abbey of Göttweig (pl. V) and even the Monastery of Klosterneuburg, which was intended to be the Austrian equivalent of the Escorial, remained uncompleted. But it was astonishing how many of the great abbeys did complete their vast plans for rebuilding: Altenburg (Benedictine) in Lower Austria, one of the most perfectly proportioned and graceful of them all; Herzogenburg (Augustinian) in Lower Austria, one of the latest in date (the tower was not finished until 1767); Kremsmünster (Benedictine) in Upper Austria, with its famous fish-ponds; Schlierbach (Cistercian) in Upper Austria, surely one of the most perfect of them all, crowned by the Carlone family's breathtakingly lovely church and library; Wilhering (Cistercian) near Linz in Upper Austria, smaller than many of the others but of particularly satisfying proportions (burned almost to the ground in 1733, the rebuilding taking place mostly in the following quarter of a century), and having perhaps the most beautiful Rococo church in Austria.

Europe began to flourish during the eighteenth century. Epidemic diseases were reduced, partly the result of increased Habsburg efficiency in blocking the continual transmission of the plague from the Middle East. It was also the warmest century in eight hundred years, and the population began to rise steadily – in England at the rate of more than one per cent annually from 1750 to 1800. 'Better methods of drainage opened up new lands.

> Increasingly, cultivation of nitrogen-fixing plants replaced traditional systems of fallow on some of the large estates. By growing plants like turnips every few years, all cultivable land could be kept in use, which implied as much as a 33% increase in agricultural production ... The most important new development was a simple one: the introduction of the potato and, in southern Europe, maize from the New World ... Maize also supported population growth in Spain, southern France [and] Hungary ... during the eighteenth century.'
> [Peter N. Stearns, *European Society in Upheaval: Social History since 1750*, 2nd ed., New York and London 1975, pp. 65 and especially 66]

It is now considered possible that the changed climate and favourable living conditions began to alter the psyche of whole nations, as well as individuals, in the second part of the century. How, otherwise, to explain in Italian music the most extraordinary *volte-face* in its history? Italian Renaissance and Baroque music had been grave, moving, powerful and of an irresistible beauty. Suddenly, about the time of Haydn's birth, Italian musical taste changed abruptly, and *opera buffa*, with all its social and musical revolutionary changes, began to reign supreme. Italians could hardly be said, before then, to be famous for their sense of humour: irony, sarcasm, sardonic jocularity – but not *wit* in the sense of British eighteenth-century literature and Pergolesian music. Even *opera seria* began to take on the attributes of its sister form. This craze for *opera buffa*, for light, amusing, superficial, witty, tender situations lasted until the Napoleonic troops invaded the country in the 1790s. Soon thereafter, Italian musical taste changed, and the old love for tragedy returned: Donizetti may have composed delightful comic operas (*Le convenienze ed inconvenienze teatrali; Don Pasquale*) but serious opera was the *genre* in which he and Bellini achieved European fame. And with Verdi, *opera buffa*, except for one youthful experiment which failed (*Un giorno di regno*) ceased to exist until *Falstaff*. *Ottocento* Italian music is essentially tragic, and it is almost impossible for present-day Italian audiences to project themselves into a state of mind capable of understanding and enjoying Paisiello's or Galuppi's or Piccinni's *opere buffe*.

Without the profound influence of *opera buffa* on northern minds, it is doubtful if the second European musical revolution could have occurred – Haydn's introduction of wit and irony into instrumental music. In this, Haydn was taking a single strand of a multiple bushel from his Austrian musical heritage: there had been earlier examples of this transference of popular folk tunes into Austrian 'art music', with genuinely amusing effects; but Haydn made it internationally famous.

The European climate may have induced changes on the widest scale, but when Haydn was born, the social structure, at least in Austria and Hungary, seemed as immovable as the mountains that rose from the plains round Vienna. The great magnates were as far removed from the petty aristocracy as the 'average' aristocracy from the peasants; and Austria was, like all of Europe, completely dominated by its agricultural life. There was a small middle-class society, but only in the major towns and of nothing like the importance and size in England, northern France or Holland; though in Austria it was beginning to emerge and to form, very slowly but nonetheless certainly, a powerful minority.

When Haydn was born, Charles VI was the Austrian emperor. Europe in those days had powerful and traditional alliances: France (and at that period Spain) was the traditional enemy; England, Prussia and Russia were usually in alliance against the Courts of Madrid and Versailles. Charles VI's particular and pressing problem was that he had no male heir, so that on 19 April 1713 he issued the famous 'Pragmatic Sanction', promulgated as a law on 6 December 1713. The document was intended to guarantee the primogeniture of the crown lands even if the heir was a female. The Austrian Estates agreed to the Sanction during the years 1720–3, the Hungarians in their *Reichstag* of 1722 (while demanding that their constitution be confirmed by the Emperor). The rest of Europe gradually agreed, but at a heavy price to Austria, for example the dissolution of the Austrian East India Company in 1731.

When Maria Theresa inherited the Habsburg sceptre upon the death of her father in October 1740, she found herself 'without money, without credit, without any army, without experience, and finally without advice'.[1] It can fairly be said that 1740

---

1 *Maria Theresa*, ed. by Karl A. Roider Jr, Englewood Cliffs, N.J., 1973, p. 3.

was a year of crisis altogether:

31 May: death of Frederick William (Friedrich Wilhelm);
20 October: death of Charles VI;
28 October: death of Anna Ivanovna, Empress of Russia, who was succeeded by the infant Ivan IV.

With Russia immobilized, Prussia's new king, Frederick II considered the situation of the young Empress, some three months pregnant. At the beginnning of December he concentrated a large army on the Silesian border, and sent an offer to Maria Theresa: it was devastatingly simple, the Province of Silesia in exchange for a vote in favour of her husband, Francis Stephen of Lorraine, as future Emperor of the Holy Roman Empire. Prussia had a very tenuous claim to certain (very small) parts of Silesia, but these old feudal rights had been renounced in 1686 and Frederick's action reminds one uncomfortably of similar German procedures in our time. 'Our cause is just', said Frederick as he ordered his troops to advance without waiting for an answer from the Court of Vienna. On 16 December, a Prussian army of 40,000 swept into Silesia and within six weeks it had conquered the entire territory except for some isolated fortresses. The proclamations posted in the towns occupied by Prussian troops assured the population that Frederick II was protecting Maria Theresa from her numerous enemies.

> Maria Theresa had no intention of bargaining with Frederick: 'We shall have no words to exchange with your master so long as a single Prussian soldier remains on the soil of Silesia', she induced her consort Francis, to say on her behalf to Frederick's envoy, excusing herself from personally receiving him because of her advanced pregnancy. [Alan Palmer, *Frederick the Great*, London 1974, pp. 76f.]

As a result of the action of *le monstre* (as Frederick was soon referred to by the furious Austrian Empress), Austria was plunged into the first of a series of wars. Maria Theresa's defensive wars were:

1740–2 First Silesian War
1741–8 War of the Austrian Succession
1744–5 Second Silesian War
1756–63 Seven Years' War (Third Silesian War).

In the War of the Austrian Succession, a formidable coalition faced Vienna, for against her were ranged many nations anxious to confound, if at all possible, the Pragmatic Sanction: Spain, France, the Elector Carl Albrecht of Bavaria (who had allied himself with Prussia in the Nymphenburg Treaty of 28 May 1741 and the Breslau Contract of 4 June 1741) to which Saxony, Sweden, Sardinia, Naples, the Palatine Electorate and the Electorate of Cologne joined. England had meanwhile signed a neutrality agreement with France (27 September 1741), but in the long run, Austria received some assistance from England and Russia. The parallel Silesian Wars did not exactly help Austria's position. The fortunes of the huge coalition waxed and waned. Russian intervention, in the form of an army sent to the Rhine, brought to pass the treaty of Aix-la-Chapelle on 18 October 1748. Although Austria lost large parts of Silesia, she did not fare too badly in other respects: she lost the Duchies of Parma, Piacenza and Guastalla, but the Pragmatic Sanction was now generally recognized and Maria Theresa's husband, Francis Stephen, was meanwhile elected Holy Roman Emperor of the German Nations at Frankfurt-on-Main on 13 September 1745 (Brandenburg and the Palatine Electorate refused to agree to the choice).

The Empress had almost equally pressing domestic problems to settle. On 15 January 1749, with the help of the great statesman, Chancellor Kaunitz, and his ministers, the Justice and Administrative Reforms were promulgated, followed by a thorough reorganization of the army. These reforms had been preceded by careful, well-considered restructuring in the fields of mercantilism, education (foundation of the Theresianum, the Eton of Austrian education to this day), relations between church and state, finances and – negatively – censorship. The Church may have had its holidays reduced (twenty-four abolished in 1745) but a few years later Maria Theresa established state censorship over all printed matter, local and imported from abroad. She was also a prude. The Austrians are an extremely sensuous people, and Maria Theresa fought an uphill battle to curb their old and well-established licentious habits, particularly among the aristocracy. In the end, this was one battle which she had to abandon.

The huge expenses of running these wars reached a climax in the Seven Years' War which, involving North America (French-Indian Wars), became a global conflict. Frederick II began it by invading Saxony (an Austrian ally) with 66,000 men on 29 August 1756. A new constellation of Allies was now to be observed: ranged against Austria were England, Prussia, the Princes of Hanover, Brunswick, Hesse-Cassel and Gotha. On Austria's side were now France(!), Russia, Sweden, and most of the German princes. Frederick II, despite brilliant successes (e.g. Roßbach, 5 November 1757), suffered serious losses at Kolin (18 June 1757), Hochkirch (14 October 1758) and Kunersdorf (12 August 1759).

On 5 January 1762, Tsarina Elisabeth of Russia died and was succeeded by Peter III, a fervent admirer of Frederick's. Russia immediately withdrew from the Austrian alliance. Peter was deposed on 9 July 1762 by his wife, Catherine ('The Great'), but it was too late to prevent a grave Austrian defeat, under Leopold Joseph, Count (Prince) von Daun, at Burkersdorf on 21 July.

Austria's resources were stretched to the utmost, and the government began to take desperate measures. The young men had no taste for the war, and a decree of 24 July 1758 orders the churches

> to announce to the people from the pulpit that one has remarked with displeasure that many of the young unmarried men in the country, from fear of being drafted as soldiers, have inflicted bodily injuries to their members or even mutilated themselves. It must be explained to them how irresponsible this is.
> [Hannelore Fielhauer, 'Eine kurze Geschichte der Gersthofer Johanneskapelle [in Währing]', *Unser Währing*, Vierteljahreschrift des Museumsvereins Währing, 14. Jahrgang, 1979, Heft 2, p. 32]

The clerics were not permitted to give anti-war sermons, but on the other hand, the aristocracy in charge of recruiting the soldiers was not permitted on pain of

> severe punishment, also banishment to the galleys, to impress anyone going to church on Sundays or Holidays, much less to take them from the church itself . . .
> [Fielhauer, op. cit., p. 32]

The churches were issued with a sinister *Fragebogen* in 1758 so that the populace could be better disciplined and 'organized', this time by the Archbishop's *consistorium* in Vienna. This *Fragebogen* or questionnaire contained 121 points which were to be answered and returned to the authorities, including whether the subject was suspected of heretical teaching, of owning forbidden books, if he or she had taken Easter communion, if he or she had committed adultery, if a couple were separated, whether there were enmities within a given apartment house, who were the school-masters and if they fulfilled their duties satisfactorily, how many midwives there were and if they were religious, etc.

On 25 September 1756, a decree arrived whereby the clergy were

> earnestly recommended to educate the people in sermons and catechisms that it is a heavy sin to receive money for superstitious prayers or incantations. This is because from several places we have received notice of such occurrences.
>
> [Fielhauer, 32]

Abandoned first by Russia and Sweden, then by France (November 1762), Austria had to sue for peace (Treaty of Hubertusburg, 15 February 1763): the people were tired of the war, of the heavy taxes, of the lack of food – Lenten restrictions on the consumption of milk and meat were silently overlooked by the clergy – and of the officious prying into their private lives; individuals had taken to mutilating themselves to avoid military service and went to witches instead of to the Church. Austria, by the terms of the peace treaty, had to renounce the unhappy province of Silesia, while France had to admit to English naval supremacy in international waters. Not only was Prussia now a major European power, but Russia began to assume a position of ever increasing importance.

Austrian Life

Travel was difficult and slow. On 15 June 1765 the Nachtrag to the *Wienerisches Diarium* No. 48 gave a list of 'stations' or journey stages for a huge train of carriages arranged to bring the Spanish Infanta, the Archduchess Maria Luisa, from Vienna to Genoa. The train was organized in four sections: (I) 96 carriages and three riding horses; (II) 76 carriages and one riding horse; (III) 60 carriages and one riding horse; (IV) 48 carriages and one riding horse. The 'Stations-lista' was as follows:

> First day: Vienna to Merzuschlag (Mürzzuschlag), 9 hours.
> Second day: Merzuschlag to Judenburg, $11\frac{1}{2}$ hours.
> Third day: Judenburg to Clagenfurth (Klagenfurt), $10\frac{3}{4}$ hours.
> Fourth day: Clagenfurth to Sachsenburg, $10\frac{1}{2}$ hours.
> Fifth day: Sachsenburg to Brunecken (Bruneck, South Tyrol, now Brunico, Italy),[1] $12\frac{1}{4}$ hours.
> Sixth day: Brunecken to Botzen (South Tyrol, now Bolzano, Italy), $8\frac{3}{4}$ hours.
> Seventh day: Botzen to Roveredo (Rovereto), $9\frac{3}{4}$ hours.
> Eighth day: Roveredo to Mantua, $11\frac{1}{2}$ hours.
> Ninth day: Mantua to Cremona, $9\frac{1}{2}$ hours.
> Tenth day: Cremona to Meyland (Milan), $8\frac{1}{2}$ hours.
> Eleventh day: Meyland to Tortona, $7\frac{1}{2}$ hours.
> Twelfth day: Tortona to Genua, $9\frac{3}{4}$ hours.

Some idea of what travel involved is revealed in an entertaining letter by Sir William Hamilton, British Minister to the Court of Naples, written from Rome on 5 November 1777.[2] He writes of the 'uncommon inundations' that have befallen the 'Venetian, Modenise and Tuscan states,

> thro' which we passed at last with great difficulty and hazard, but within these last few days we have met with singular alarms – at Redicofani [*sic*], between Florence & Rome, when we arrived at Night, we found the Inn much damaged by a violent

1 A large part of northern Italy belonged to Austria in those days.
2 Autograph in the Else Radant Landon Collection, Music Library, University College, Cardiff.

earthquake that happend a month ago & the people still in alarm as they had felt a shock the Night before, we were obliged however to shelter there as the road will not allow you to travel by night & we had several slight shocks during the night, one of which opened our door which was bolted. Lady Hamilton's nerves being naturally weak you may imagine sufferd by this allarm, then we found all the Post Horses vicious for want of work as few Travellers have passed of late. On Sunday Evening as we set out from the Post at Montefiascone in an open four wheeld chaise in which we have alway's travell'd (except in the mornings & late in the Evenings when we get into our Post chaise), our Postilion stopt to unlock the wheel having dragged down a hill, we ordered him upon no account to quit his horses but wait for the other chaise that our Servant might do it, he obstinately persisted & having unlocked it went & talk'd to the other Postillions during which time the horses set off full speed[.] Our Courier, a Swiss, as good a Servant as ever was, being just before & seeing our situation, calmly jumped off his horse, quitted his Jack Boots & seized the off-horse just as we were on the top of a steep hill, but as there was no curb to the bit he could not stop them, however he seem'd to resolve either to stop them or perish in the attempt, he ran violently with us holding the horse till he was knock'd down & the carriage went over him, we soon met with his horse on the road [&] went over him also, with great danger of overturning, three Peasants seeing our distress with shouting & holding up their hats turn'd the horses from the road, they leaped a ditch with such velocity that we were not overturnd, tho' violently shook, & we found ourselves in a plough'd field where, after galoping some time[,] were stopped by the three Peasants – Our Courier is greatly cut & bruised, his collar bone bent, he does not appear to be much inwardly bruised, so that we left this brave felow (who shew'd that he woud sacrifice his life to save us) yesterday, at Montefiascone, as the Phisician assured, out of all danger & we shall, as you may well imagine, reward him with a lasting proof of our gratitude, Lady Hamilton was blooded immediately but can not yet recover her allarm. We arrived here last night & I am under the necessity of delaying my journey to Naples for a few days that Lady H. may recover from the violent agitation in which she is at present. . . .

Excuse my giving you the trouble of so long a detail, but upon such occasions so many false accounts are dispersed, that I wished, by your means, to lodge a true one at the fountain head.

I am Dear Sir,
with great regard
your most obedient
humble Servant.
W^{m}. Hamilton.

Some idea of daily life in Vienna may be gained from an interesting little book entitled *Sicheres Adress= u. Reisebuch oder Archiv der nötigsten Kenntnisse von Wien für reisende Fremde und Inländer. Wien 1792 bey Joseph Gerold*[1] which partly refers back to 1785 and earlier. From the book we learn (p. 24) that a gentleman's house (*Herrschaftshaus*) cost about 100,000–200,000 gulden, and a large middle-class (*bürgerliches*) house 50,000–60,000 gulden. Large middle-class apartment houses (on the Graben, the Hof, etc.) brought an income of 6,000–8,000 gulden p.a. A shop (on the Graben, in the Kohlmarkt) cost 600–700 gulden. A nice flat for a family (who also keep a carriage and two horses) on the first or second (U.S.A.: second or third) floor cost 800–1,000 gulden.

1 Copy in the Kartensammlung of the ÖNB (A 9928).

At that time London had 120,000 houses (average number of occupants 4–5) and a birth rate of 18,000–20,000; Vienna (together with its suburbs) had 6,500 dwelling-houses (average 40–50 occupants) and a birthrate of 10,000–11,000. Since the time of Joseph II there had been no payment demanded for entry into the city of Vienna, the gates of which were open.

Later in the same book (p. 64) we have some useful statistics for the year 1785:

Vienna	Berlin	Paris	
11,603	4,961	20,365	births
10,969	4,951	19,919	deaths
2,488	865	5,234	marriages
270,000	140,000	700,000	total inhabitants

Living conditions in Berlin were considerably more precarious than those in Paris or Vienna: in Berlin the birth rate exceeded the death rate by only ten; and Vienna was also much healthier in this respect than the much larger city of Paris, with its 700,000 inhabitants – in Paris in 1785 there was a net increase in population of only 446, while Vienna, with a population of 270,000, showed an increase of 634.

Vienna, according to the *Reisebuch*, had: 3,000 gentlemen's carriages; 648 Fiaker (hackney-carriages) and 300 drivers; 300 stage-coach drivers; 400 chaises belonging to private individuals; 9,500 horses within the outer walls and 24,000 dogs. Here is the city schedule for Vienna (pp. 83–8):

a.m.	6:00–6:30	servant-girls go to church and then to a coffee-house for breakfast; then the women who sell vegetables and the cooks do their shopping.
	8:00–10:00	the wives of clerks, artisans, etc. come to shop. No coach of distinction shows itself on the streets before nine o'clock.
	8:30	Ministry clerks go to their offices.
	10:00	the coffee-houses begin to fill; people drive out in their carriages.
	11:30–12:30	the *haut monde* goes to church.
noon	12:00	Ministry clerks have their break; lunch for the common people.
	11:30–1:00	the *haut monde* of the middle classes promenade on the bastions.
	12:00–1:00	the aristocracy drive out.
p.m.	1:00	lunch for officials.
	2:00	lunch for the nobility; magnates (the highest nobility) take lunch even later.
	3:00	Ministry clerks return to their offices.
	4:30	work or pleasure.
	6:00	the busiest hour – workers go home, offices ditto, businesses close.
	7:00	theatres open.
	twilight–10:00	prostitutes at work.
	9:00	theatres finish, also social gatherings (which last from 7:00 to 10:00 in winter, and from 8:00 to 10:00 in summer).
	9:30	cavalry patrols in the streets.
	10:00	closing hour.
a.m.	3:00	the lanterns in the city are extinguished.

Among its treasures the Albertina in Vienna has a series of exquisite watercolours depicting the Austrian towns, castles, monasteries and countryside, prepared in two groups, *c.* 1785 and *c.* 1795–1800. It would seem that these were in part the sources from which Artaria & Co. in Vienna issued their engravings. They show a kind of earthly paradise, a rich, prosperous and extremely beautiful country: we have gratefully used two of them as illustrations for this volume (plates 2, 3). On looking through the portfolio which houses these lovely views of a long-lost eighteenth-century world, one is filled with a feeling of nostalgia. But there was another side to Austria on which the history books do not dwell: the poor. Unfortunately, we do not have, for Austria-Hungary, anything comparable to the great and humane book by

Olwen H. Hufton, *The Poor of Eighteenth-Century France* (Oxford 1974), but we believe that the definition of poverty by the French writer, Marie Jean Antoine Nicolas Caritat, Marquis de Condorcet (b. 1743, poisoned 1794), which Professor Hufton quotes (p. 19) – 'Celui qui ne possède ni biens ni mobilier est destiné à tomber dans la misère au moindre accident'[1] – applies as much to Austria as it does to France. And we believe that the following description that the Curé d'Athis sent to his bishop in 1774 as an answer to a questionnaire must apply to Austrian villages of the period, too:

> Les journaliers, les manœuvres, les compagnons de métier et tous ceux dont la profession ne fournit pas beaucoup plus que le vivre et le vêtement sont ceux qui produisent les mendiants. Étant garçons, ils travaillent et lorsque par leur travail ils se sont procurés un bon vêtement et de quoi faire les frais d'une noce, ils se marient. Ils nourrissent un premier enfant, ils ont beaucoup de peine à en nourrir deux et s'il en survient un troisième leur travail n'est plus suffisant à la dépense.
>
> [Hufton, op. cit., p. 11]

The poor of Austria were well known to Haydn: he started life outside the choir-school as one of them, without means, without future, with only aspirations and a few friends: those two last factors enabled him to survive, but the line between success/comfort and failure/poverty was thin throughout the century, even for successful young musicians, even for the greatest musical genius that the world has ever known – Mozart. Haydn was, throughout his life, aware not only of mankind's frailty in general but of that of the Austrian *Musikant* in particular. When looking at the ravishing Austrian countryside depicted in the Albertina engravings, with its wealthy monasteries, its splendid castles and neat, thriving towns, we should never forget that behind this beauty lay a life of hopeless poverty for many, in city and country alike.[2]

---

1 *Sur les assemblées provinciales*, 1788, p. 453.

2 Apart from the monumental biography of A. von Arneth (10 vols., Vienna 1863–79), the best short summary of Maria Theresa's life and work is C. A. Macartney's *Maria Theresa and The House of Austria*, London 1969. A very useful book, with personal documents by Maria Theresa and Frederick II, is Hans Jessen's *Friedrich der Große und Maria Theresia in Augenzeugenberichten*, Düsseldorf 1965. An indispensable survey of Austrian history is the recent *Österreich: Daten zur Geschichte und Kultur*, by Walter Keindel, Vienna 1978. It was not considered necessary to list the enormous literature on Frederick II. Of recent books, however, one might, apart from the survey by Alan Palmer (London 1974), mention *The Habsburg and Hohenzollern Dynasties in the Seventeenth and Eighteenth Centuries* (ed. C. A. Macartney, New York 1970) and the intelligent biography by Nancy Mitford, *Frederick the Great* (London 1970).

   The bicentenary of the death of Maria Theresa has been the occasion for the publication in 1980 of five important new works dealing with the history of Austria in Haydn's lifetime. These are: (1) *Österreich zur Zeit Kaiser Joseph II.*, a 750-page catalogue of the exhibition held at Melk Abbey, including many valuable articles; (2) Gerda and Gottfried Mraz, *Maria Theresia* ..., Munich – the best documentary biography of the Empress in our time; (3) Walter Koschatzky (ed.), *Maria Theresia* ..., Salzburg – a symposium; (4) the catalogue of the special Maria Theresa exhibition held at Schönbrunn; and (5) the catalogue of the exhibition 'Maria Theresia als Königin von Ungarn, Schloß Halbthurn' (Burgenland).

CHAPTER TWO

The Haydn Family's Background; Haydn's Birth

IN 1934 A PROMISING young German musicologist, E. F. Schmid, published a massive documentation on Haydn's family, on the population of his native Rohrau, on the division of the local population (German, Croatian, Hungarian), and finally on the influence of various European folk music on Haydn. It was, from any standpoint, a staggering achievement and consisted largely of completely original research, mostly conducted in church and town archives. Curiously, the resulting book, *Joseph Haydn, Ein Buch von Vorfahren und Heimat des Meisters* (Kassel 1934; abbreviated when referred to in this biography as 'Schmid, *Vorfahren*'), although highly regarded in Austria and Germany, received little notice abroad; and this was not simply because it was written in German – Geiringer's Haydn biography of 1932 and Larsen's monumental *Die Haydn-Überlieferung* of 1939 immediately penetrated into the otherwise far-away world of Anglo-Saxon scholarship.

Schmid's fruity, *Biedermeier* style was perhaps not to everyone's taste, and the whole subject was not one of immediate fascination for musicians – indeed, the larger part of the book has nothing to do with music at all. But it was a subject that badly required the serious, systematic kind of research for which German scholarship was deservedly famous. One of the purposes of Schmid's book was, of course, negative: namely, to disprove for all time the hints, suppositions and statements regarding Haydn's supposed Croatian origin in a Croatian town. Haydn's Croatian birth and background were first proposed by Franjo Šaver Kuhač as part of that author's systematic investigation into southern Slavonic (Croatian) folk melodies[1] and later[2] in a separate study. Kuhač's studies aroused intense effort, even in Britain, where a summary was published in 1897 by Hadow.[3] That little book had an influence out of all relation to its size, and even forty-two years after the publication of Schmid's study, we can read (1976): 'Joseph Haydn was born in 1732 in the village of Trstnik on the river Leitha.'[4] (Trstnik is the Slav name for Rohrau).

Schmid's foreword began by quoting one of the three authentic biographies of Haydn, that by Giuseppe Carpani (p. 14), wherein we read his dismissal of Haydn's forebears: 'Gli antenati ... non mi daran molto da fare. Nacquero, vissero e morirono: eccovi la loro biografia.' (they were born, they lived and died, that is their biography). 'Also concerning the brothers and sisters of the master he had nothing to say,' continued Schmid, 'with the explanation that he is not a fly-catcher: "non sono stato mai cacciatore di mosche."' Schmid then continues:

---

1 The invaluable documentation, a kind of Croatian *Denkmäler* series, was published as follows: *Južno-Slovjenske Narodne Popievke* (*Chansons Nationales des Slaves du Sud*), ed. F. S. Kuhač, I. Knjiga, Zagreb 1878; II. Knjiga, Zagreb 1879; III. Knjiga, Zagreb 1880; IV. Knjiga, Zagreb 1881; V. Knjiga, completed by B. Širola and V. Dukat, Zagreb 1941.
2 *Josip Haydn i Hrvatscke Narodne Popievke*, Zagreb 1880.
3 Sir W. H. Hadow, *A Croatian Composer. Notes towards the study of Joseph Haydn*, London 1897 (reprinted in W.H.H.'s 'Collected Essays', London 1928).
4 Antony Hodgson, *The Music of Joseph Haydn – The Symphonies*, London 1976, p. 23.

The author of this book will now attempt to undertake this despised role of a 'fly-catcher' at the risk of bringing down on his head the grim curse of the good old Carpani and those who share his opinion, of whom there live some even today. The times have changed; and nowadays, especially, there may be registered greatly increased interest in the studies of the genealogical and ethnological as well as that of local background, also on the part of the public. The heritage that the great spirits of humanity receive from the blood of their forebears, from the heaven and earth of their countryside – all this is now recognized as an important component, the research into which lays bare the deep roots of genius, as far as human research is capable of so doing.

And so there came into being E. F. Schmid's astonishing book of 355 + xiv pages, followed by a second volume consisting entirely of gigantic genealogical tables, some of them five feet long. As far as pure archival research is concerned, Haydn had received nothing like it ever before. The book's reception was curious. Carpani's 'Gesinnungsgenossen' pounced on the book:

> Giuseppe Haydn è tedesco. Tedeschi tutti i suoi avi paterni e materni risalendo per quattro generazioni. Tedesco il suolo su qui nacquero e vissero, tedesche le loro abitudini e le loro tradizioni.
>
> Questo è, per così dire, il 'basso ostinato' del lavoro in esame e questo è quanto l'autore ci vuole dimostrare, documenti allo mano.
>
> E, senza perdersi in chiacchere, inizia subito un'esplorazione metodica e scrupolosa dei registri parrocchiali più vetusti di Tadten, Hainburg[,] Rohrau, di testamenti, atti di matrimonio, battesimo e morte, di inventari e di lettere; esplorazione che si allarga a ventaglio, di paese in paese, di famiglia in famiglia, insinuandosi in ogni ramo laterale e soffermandosi su tutti i più minuti particolari senza arrestarsi che quando ne è costretta dalla mancanza di documenti.
>
> Di modo che, riuscendo ad eliminare generazione per generazione, tutto quanto possa esser sospetto di croato[,] ungherese o boemo, arriva in poco meno di trecento pagine fitte, a darci un Haydn tedesco al 100%, o, per usare un termine d'attualità, 'arina puro.'
>
> Documentario esaurientissimo, diremmo quasi, prodigioso.
>
> Ma, per conto nostro, non essenziale. . . .

[Translation:]
Joseph Haydn is German. German all his paternal and maternal ancestors for four generations. German the ground on which they were born and lived, German their customs and traditions.

This is, as it were, the 'basso ostinato' of the work under examination and that which the author wishes to demonstrate, using the documents.

And without getting lost in gossip, he begins a methodical and scrupulous exploration of ancient parochial registers in Tadten, Hainburg and Rohrau, of Wills, marriage contracts, baptismal and death certificates, of inventories and of letters; an exploration which spreads itself out like a fan, from country to country, from family to family, insinuating itself in every collateral branch and a dwelling on the most minute particulars, stopping only when so forced by a lack of documents.

In such wise that, being able to eliminate generation by generation all that might be suspected of being Croatian, Hungarian or Bohemian, he arrives after slightly less than 300 closely argued pages at a Haydn 100 per cent. German, or to use the term at present in favour, 'pure Aryan'.

A most exhaustive documentation, indeed we would say prodigious. But as far as we are concerned, not essential. . . .

Later, to close the review, it is noted that Schmid regrets that due to the destruction of the villages in the Turkish invasions, the archives were not able to supply information further back than the fourth generation before Haydn. It was not, concluded the reviewer tartly, 'an opinion which we are able to share'. The review, signed 'c. pi.', appeared in *Rivistá Musicale Italiana*, Anno XL, Fascicolo 3°–4° (1936), pp. 339f.

Schmid's research was carefully summarized in tabular form by Leopold Nowak in his Haydn biography of 1951,[1] which we have gratefully followed, adding certain data which might be of interest to the reader:

HAYDN'S FOREBEARS

PATERNAL GREAT-GRANDPARENTS

Caspar Haydn, born *c.* 1630 in Tadten, died before 1687; 1657 castle bondman (casual labourer) in Hainburg. Married, in February 1675.

Elisabeth Schalck, born ?, died before 1687. Their eldest son was Thomas, grandfather of Joseph Haydn.

Anton Blaiminger, born ?, died *c.* 1687; married one **Barbara** (her family name is not known), who was buried on Christmas Day 1687 in Hainburg. Their daughter was Catharina, Thomas Haydn's wife.

MATERNAL GREAT-GRANDPARENTS

Philipp Koller, born before 1669, died 1688; citizen and juryman of the court at Pachfurt. Married another **Barbara** (family name likewise not known), who died before 1688. Their second child was Lorenz, grandfather of Joseph Haydn.

Martin Siebel, born ?, buried on 11 August 1710 at Prellenkirchen and described as a master miller. His second wife was a widow.

Barbara (family name not known, born 1652, who was buried at Prellenkirchen on 15 April 1696. Their first child was Susanna, second wife of Lorenz Koller.

PATERNAL GRANDPARENTS

Thomas Haydn, born after 1657, buried on 4 September 1701; was wheelwright in Hainburg. Married on 23 November 1687 in Hainburg.

Catharina Blaiminger, born 1671, died at Hainburg on 17 May 1739. After Thomas Haydn's death she married on 8 January 1702 Matthias Seefranz, wheelwright in Hainburg. The sixth child of her first marriage was Mathias Haydn, father of the composer.

The fourth and last child of her second marriage was Juliane Rosina, baptized on 15 February 1711; she married on 6 September 1733 the Hainburg School Rector and *Regens chori* Johann Mathias Franck, Haydn's first teacher.

MATERNAL GRANDPARENTS

Lorenz Koller, born 1675 in Pachfurt, buried on 21 May 1718 in Rohrau, citizen and village magistrate. His second wife, whom he married on 4 July 1702, was

Susanna Siebel, born at Prellenkirchen in 1685 and buried on 19 August 1756 at Rohrau. Their second child was Anna Maria Koller, the composer's mother. When Haydn's grandmother Susanna Siebel died, she left a respectable sum of money (3,231 fl. 57 kr.), of which 1,475 fl. 32 kr.

went to her heirs. Her estate also included '1 old mail coach' (*1 altes Post Calles*) and '1 old iron wall clock'. This comfortable fortune came after Lorenz Koller had died and Susanna had married Michael Crems, a wealthy peasant and church father; he lived on to the then incredible age of eighty-five, and died on 28 May 1783. In Susanna's Will, she left the '6 surviving children by the name of Francisca, Joseph, Michaël, Anna Maria, Catharina et Johannes, from the late Anna Maria's first marriage with Mathias Hayden of Rohrau ... 368 fl. 53 kr.' (Schmid, 176 and esp. 177). The 61 gulden that Haydn inherited as a budding young composer in Vienna in 1756 will have been more than welcome; indeed, they may have been crucial (enabling him to engage copyists and sell 'authentic' MS. concertos, string trios, or piano sonatas to patrons).

THE PARENTS

Mathias Haydn, baptized on 31 January 1699 in Hainburg, died at Rohrau on 12 September 1763 at Rohrau, where he was Citizen Wheelwright and Village Magistrate (*Marktrichter*). Married on 24 November 1728, in Rohrau.

Anna Maria Koller, baptized on 10 November 1707 in Rohrau, died there on 23 February 1754. Before she married Mathias Haydn, Anna Maria had been a cook at Rohrau Castle and, as it happens, Schmid was able to locate some interesting documents, which shed a sudden ray of light on the domestic affairs of Schloß Rohrau in 1728. Rohrau Castle in that year contained the following officials and employees:

1 Secretary
1 Major Domo
1 Abbate
1 Master of the Stable
1 House Physician
2 Valets [*Kammerdiener*]
1 Page
2 Ladies in Waiting [*Kammerjungfern*]
1 Major Domo for the Count's Children
2 Nurses for the Children
1 Cook from Aschach [Harrach estate] for the Young Counts and Countesses
2 Hungarian Heyducks [*Heiducken*]
6 Lackeys
4 Coachman with Outriders
1 Horse-trainer [*Bereiter*]
5 Grooms and Stable Boys
2 Chamber Maids [*Stubenmenscher*]
4 Under-Footmen [*Hausknechte*]
2 Vassals as Hunting-Horn-Players
1 Mathias, bass singer [servant in livrée]

1 *Joseph Haydn: Leben, Bedeutung und Werk*, Zurich/Vienna/Leipzig 1951, pp. 78ff.

33

To the above list may be added details of the actual kitchen personnel (with annual salaries, totalling 948 fl., as follows:

1 Chef Cook 'Zacharias'	300 fl.	1 Female Cook for the Officers	
1 Cook 'Hans Jürg'	200 —	[officer Köchin]	40 —
1 Pastry Cook	150 —	1 Kitchen Secretary	30 —
1 Table Setter	130 —	2 Scullery Servants, together	48 —
1 Female Kitchen Goods' Purchaser	50 —		

[Schmid, *Vorfahren*, 205]

Schmid believes 'Mother Haydn' was the '1 Female Cook for the Officers', unless 'we wish to seek her under the "2 Scullery Servants"'. The most entertaining document that Schmid (206) discovered in the Harrach Archives is a list of kitchen provisions for four days in 1728, which gives us an idea of the astonishing menues prepared for the *Herrschaft* and their guests at Schloß Rohrau; like most food north of the Alps in those days, the items listed represent a pure invitation to gout. In the original the symbols for pounds (lb) and denar (d.) – see p. 16 – are used:

24 lb beef à 3 kr. 3 d.	1 fl.	30 kr.	For yeast	— „	3 „
14 lb veal à 5 kr.	1 „	9 „	12 chickens à 4 kr. 2 d.	— „	54 „
1 offal [*Beischl*]	— „	15 „	150 eggs [*Ayr*]	— „	25 „
1 stomach [*greß* = tripe]	— „	7 „	200 tortoises [*Schülgrotten =*		
12 lb mutton à 3 kr. 3 d.	— „	45 „	*Schildkröten*]	24 „	— „
1 spring lamb [*Lambl*]	— „	30 „	4 goslings	— „	48 „
13½lb pike à 3 kr. 3 d.	2 „	42 „			
11½lb white fish à 6 kr.	1 „	9 „		35 fl.	59 kr.
1 crate of crabs	— „	30 „	['Kuchelzettel Von 20ten bis 23. Juny gelt auß gaab',		
4 lb palm oil à 18 kr.	1 „	12 „	1728]		

The above list shows just how cheap such foods as chickens and eggs were at that time; also delivered were the following:

1 crate of salt	5 wild ducks from the Pheasant Hunter
39 lb beef lard	2 turtle doves from the Hunter of Haßlau
9 hens from the castle farmyard	Estate
20 young pigeons	

[Schmid, 206]

THE CHILDREN OF MATHIAS HAYDN

The discrepancy between the number of Joseph Haydn's brothers and sisters as given by Dies, Griesinger, Carpani, and that shown by the birth/baptismal records is, *inter alia*, because Haydn himself counted only the surviving children (he was probably in total ignorance of those who had died in infancy). And Joseph was not, as Griesinger and Carpani assert, the eldest child.

First marriage, to Anna Maria Koller (twelve children):

Anna Maria Franziska – baptized 19 September 1730 at Rohrau; died 29 July 1781 at Fertöszentmiklós in Hungary. First marriage to Vieltzwieser, Rohrau 1750 (three children, of whom only one survived); second marriage to Jakob Traumbauer, Fertöszentmiklós 1771 (no children).

Franz Joseph – baptized 1 April 1732 at Rohrau; died 31 May 1809 at Vienna. Married Maria Anna Keller, 9 November 1760 at Vienna (no children).

Mathias III[1] – baptized 1733 at Rohrau; died 1734 Rohrau.

Mathias IV – baptized 21 February 1735 at Rohrau; buried there on 7 September 1735.

Anna Katharina – baptized 7 October 1734 at Rohrau; buried there on 13 October 1736.

Johann Michael – baptized 14 September 1737 at Rohrau; died 10 August 1806, Salzburg, was *Konzertmeister* and Court Organist to the Prince-Archbishop of Salzburg. Married court singer Maria Magdalena Lipp, 17 August 1768, at Salzburg (one child, Aloisia Josepha, born Salzburg 31 January 1770, died 27 January 1771).

Anna Maria II – baptized 6 March 1739 at Rohrau; died 27 August 1802. First marriage to Johann Philipp Frölich (Fröhlich), Rohrau 1757 (fifteen children, of whom seven died in infancy); second marriage to Ignaz Rafler, Rohrau 1777 (one child).

1 Numbering from E. F. Schmid, *Vorfahren*.

Anna Katharina (twin) – baptized 6 January 1741 at Rohrau; date of death not known. Married Christoph Näher, Rohrau 1763 (three children, all of whom died in infancy).

Johann Kaspar (twin) – baptized 6 January 1741 at Rohrau; buried there 3 September 1741.

Philipp – born (date not known) in Gättendorf; buried at Rohrau 2 May 1752.

Johann Evangelist – baptized 23 December 1743 at Rohrau; died 16 May 1805, Eisenstadt; was Princely Esterházy Chapel Singer.

Maria Theresia – baptized 22 March 1745 at Rohrau; died there 17 August 1745.

Second marriage, to Maria Anna Seeder, 1755 (five children):

Mathaeus – born and died Rohrau 1755.

Maria Franziska – born 1757 at Rohrau; died there 1758.

Franz Xaver II – born and died Rohrau 1759.

Joseph II (twin) – born and died Rohrau 1761.

Bartholomaeus (twin) – born and died Rohrau 1761.

(After Mathias Haydn's death in 1763, his widow married Franz Michael Ponnath in 1764.)

In the baptismal register of the Rohrau Parish Church, here is what we read of Joseph Haydn's birth (of which it is not quite certain whether the usually accepted date of 31 March, or another, 1 April, is correct: see Neukomm's notes, *infra*, p. 44; Rosenbaum's *Diary*, p. 149, adds that 'The hour of [Haydn's] birth was 4 o'clock in the afternoon', probably information from Haydn's servant, Johann Elssler, and no doubt authentic):

Dies et mensis	Infantes	Parentes	Patrini	Baptizans	Locus
den 1. April	Franciscus Josephus fil: legit:	Mathias Haiden bürgl. Wagner-maister / zu Rohrau Vnd / Anna Maria uxor / ejus	Herr Josephus Hoffmann Herr-schaftl. bestand Müllner zu Gerhaus et Catharina D[omi]na uxor ejus	ego q:[ui] supra	Rohrau

Notes: under 'Parentes' Mathias 'Haiden' is listed as Citizen Wheelwright. The godparents were the Estate's Master Miller Johann Joseph Hoffmann from the nearby town of Gerhaus and his wife; the couple were evidently close friends of Haydn's parents and often acted as godparents. It was customary in those days to make general use of only the second Christian name, i.e. 'Joseph Haydn' and 'Michael Haydn'. Facsimile of entry in Schmid, XIX (where Michael's entry may be also seen). See also Schmid, 217f.

The village of Rohrau has changed somewhat, but not in a very basic sense, from its physical shape of 1732. The church remains; the pious statue that Mathias Haydn erected; the great Castle, now with the magnificent picture gallery from the Harrach Palace in Vienna; and Haydn's house, which has some vague resemblance to Haydn's birthplace; it burned down in 1899 and before that had been subjected to floods which twice (1813, 1834) almost totally destroyed everything except the outside walls. Haydn's birthplace is therefore more a 'remembrance' than an actual relic of his youth.

But that which has changed hardly at all is the mysterious, age-old countryside around Rohrau, with its ancient history of Roman legionaries, migratory peoples from the east, invading Turkish troops and revered Christian traditions, binding people to the Cross and to their country in such ceremonies as Corpus Christi (where Mother Earth was gently combined with Mother Church). And hard by there was the Danube, one of Europe's great rivers, whose endless and swift waters brought ships and men from Germany, Austria and Hungary, to faraway lands at its mouth in the Black Sea. The Danube countryside exerts a peculiar fascination: its surrounding vegetation, the great vineyards which the first Roman settlers had lovingly planted, the texture of the hills and plains through which the river runs, are quite different from those of any other part of Austria. And as the great river debouches on to the great plains, we find ourselves in the former Roman province of Pannonia, on the borders of which Haydn would spend most of his adult life.

It was a good country in which to be born, and Haydn was deeply attached to it and to its people. He was to be their greatest representative. There is, nowadays (1979), a poster that The Museum of Freemasonry at Schloß Rosenau puts out. It shows the magnificent castle, with its traditional 'Schönbrunn yellow' and white walls, against a deep blue, almost Mediterranean, sky, and below are the words 'Natur, Kunst, Humanität' ('nature, art, humanity'), the three most important components of Haydn's music, which, we believe, were the great heritage of his country and its peoples.

CHAPTER THREE

Chronicle 1732–1756

Part I: Chronicle 1732–1749

The Documents
(for numbered notes see end of relevant document)

(1) AUTOBIOGRAPHY 1776:

... I was born on the last day of March 1733,[1] in the market town of Rohrau, Lower Austria, near Prugg on the Leythä.[2] My late father was a wheelwright by profession, and served Count Harrach, a great lover of music by nature. He [my father] played the harp without knowing a note of music, and as a boy of 5, I correctly sang all his simple little pieces: this induced my father to entrust me to the care of my relative, the schoolmaster in Haimburg,[3] in order that I might learn the rudiments of music and the other juvenile acquirements. Almighty God (to Whom alone I owe the most profound gratitude) endowed me, especially in music, with such proficiency that even in my 6th year I was able to sing some Masses in the choir-loft, and to play a little on the harpsichord and violin.

When I was 7, the late *Capellmeister* von Reutter[4] passed through Haimburg and quite by chance heard my weak but pleasant voice. He forthwith took me to the choir house [of St Stephen's Cathedral in Vienna] where, apart from my studies, I learned the art of singing, the harpsichord, and the violin, from very good masters. Until my 18th year I sang soprano with great success, not only at St Stephen's but also at the Court. ...

Notes:
1 *Recte* 1732.
2 In modern orthography 'Bruck an der Leitha'.
3 *Recte* Hainburg. The school rector was Johann Mathias Franck, about whom *vide infra, passim.*
4 Georg, Jr., about whom *vide infra, passim.*

(2) Griesinger:

... Joseph Haydn was born on 31 March 1732 at Rohrau, a village in Lower Austria, in the district Unter-Wiener-Wald hard by the Hungarian border, not far from the little town of Bruk [*sic*] an der Leitha. Of the twenty children from two marriages of his father Mathias, a wheelwright by profession, Joseph was the eldest. As was customary in his trade, the father had seen a little of the world, and during his sojourn in Frankfurt am Mayn he had learned to strum the harp. As a master of his trade at Rohrau, he continued to practise this instrument for pleasure, after work; nature had also endowed him with a good tenor voice, and his wife, Anne Marie,[1] accompanied his playing with her singing. The tunes of these songs were so deeply imprinted in Joseph Haydn's memory that he could recall them even in advanced old age.[2] – One day the school rector from the neighbouring little town of Haimburg [*sic*], a distant relative of the Haydn family, came to Rohrau. Master Mathias and his wife gave their usual little concert, and five-year-old Joseph sat near his parents and sawed at his left arm with a stick, as if he were accompanying on the violin. The schoolteacher noted that the boy marked the time accurately; he inferred from this a natural talent for music, and he advised the parents to send their Sepperl [an Austrian diminutive for Joseph] to Haimburg in order to help acquire an art which in time would without fail open to him the prospect 'of becoming a clergyman'. As ardent admirers of the clergy, the parents jumped at this proposal, and in his sixth year Joseph Haydn went to the school rector at Haimburg. Here he received lessons in reading and writing, in catechism, in singing, and in almost all wind and string instruments, even in playing the timpani. 'I shall owe it to that man even in my grave', Haydn used to say frequently, 'that he taught me so many things, though in the process I received more thrashings than food.'

Haydn, who even then wore a wig for the sake of cleanliness, had been about three years in Haimburg when the Court Chapel Master Reutter from Vienna, who directed the music at St Stephen's Cathedral, came to visit his friend the dean in Haimburg. Reutter told the dean that his older choir-boys, whose voices were beginning to break, were about to become useless, and that he would have to replace them with younger substitutes. The dean proposed the eight-year-old Haydn, and both he and the schoolmaster were at once called for. The badly nourished Sepperl cast hungry glances at the cherries that were sitting on the dean's table; Reutter tossed a few handfuls into his hat, and he seemed quite satisfied with the Latin and Italian strophes that Haydn had to sing. 'Can you also make a trill?' asked Reutter. 'No', said Haydn, 'for even my cousin [*Herr Vetter*] can't do that.' This answer greatly embarrassed the schoolteacher, and Reutter laughed heartily. He showed the mechanical means by which a trill could be produced. Haydn imitated him, and succeeded at the third attempt. 'You shall stay with me', said Reutter. The departure from Haimburg was soon arranged, and Haydn came as a pupil to the Choir School at St Stephen's Cathedral in Vienna, where he remained until he was in his sixteenth year.

Apart from the scanty instruction customary at that time in Latin, religion, arithmetic and writing, Haydn had in the Choir School very capable instructors on several instruments, and particularly in the art of singing. Among the latter were Gegenbauer,[3] a member of the court choir, and an elegant tenor, Finsterbusch.[4] In the Choir School there was no instruction in musical theory, and Haydn recalled having received only two such lessons from the worthy Reutter. But Reutter did encourage him to make whatever variations he liked on the motets and Salves that he had to sing in church, and this discipline soon led him to ideas of his own which Reutter corrected. He also came to know Mattheson's [*Der*] *vollkommene Kapellmeister*,[5] and Fux's *Gradus ad Parnassum*[6] in German and Latin – a book he still in his old age praised as a classic and of which he kept a well-used copy. With tireless exertion Haydn tried to understand Fux's theory; he worked his way right through the whole school, wrote out the exercises, put them by for several weeks and then took them up again, polishing them till he considered them perfect. 'Of course the talent was latent in me: as a result of it, and with great diligence, I made progress.' In his fevered imagination he even ventured into compositions in eight and sixteen parts. 'In those days I used to think everything is fine so long as the paper was well covered. Reutter laughed about my immature products, about movements which no throat and no instrument could have executed, and he scolded me for composing in sixteen parts before I had learned how to write in two.'

At that time many *castrati* were employed at court and in the Viennese churches, and the director of the Choir School no doubt considered that he was about to make the young Haydn's fortune when he brought forth the plan to turn him into a permanent soprano [*ihn sopranisieren zu lassen*], and actually asked the father for his permission. The father, who totally disapproved of this proposal, set forth at once for Vienna and, thinking that the operation might already have been performed, entered the room where his son was and asked, 'Sepperl, does anything hurt you? Can you still walk?' Delighted to find his son unharmed, he protested against any further proposals of this kind, and a *castrato* who happened to be there even strengthened him in his resolve.

The truth of this anecdote was attested by persons to whom Haydn often related it. [Griesinger, pp. 8–11]

Notes:
1 *Recte* Anna Maria.
2 This is confirmed in yet another source, Carl Bertuch's *Bemerkungen auf einer Reise aus Thüringen nach Wien in Winter 1805 bis 1806*, Weimar, im Verlage des Landes-Industrie-Comptoirs 1810, p. 181 (15 April 1805): 'On Sundays he [Mathias Haydn] played his songs, and Haydn's mother sang with him. Even today Haydn knows all those songs by heart. As a lad of five years our Sepperl sat next to his parents, took a piece of wood in his right hand and sawed with it against his left arm, as if he were playing the violin ...'. This raises a rather interesting question: can Griesinger (and Dies?) have garnered this information from Bertuch? It seems possible until we consider that Griesinger was clearly the first to publish, not as a book, but in the *AMZ*: the passage in question appears in the issue of 12 July 1809. Once again the whole problem of authenticity is raised, and once we know the chronological order, one begins to doubt Bertuch's 'original interview'. Of course, Haydn may well have repeated the story to each of the interviewers.
3 Adam Gegenbauer, died 1753.
4 Ignaz Finsterbusch, also died 1753.
5 It appeared in 1739.
6 It appeared earlier, in 1725. Haydn's copy was seen by C. F. Pohl, who transcribed all the supplementary Latin notes. See A. Mann: 'Haydn as a Student and Critic of Fux', in *Studies in Eighteenth Century Music: A Tribute to Karl Geiringer on his Seventieth Birthday* (ed. H. C. R. Landon and R. E. Chapman), London 1970, pp. 323ff. It was hitherto considered that the many additional notes and commentary in Haydn's copy were made by Haydn himself. But this theory is undermined by the presence of another copy, in the Library of Smith College, which we were shown in 1975, wherein there are almost the identical supplementary MS. comments. Perhaps a revised edition of Fux was in circulation. It is, of course, possible that the Smith copy represents another version of Haydn's own *corrigenda*.

(3) Dies, 15 April 1805:[1]

The grace of the Almighty not infrequently compensates for a lack of worldly good by gifts of the spirit. It is everywhere; it was present in the little cottage wherein Joseph Haydn saw the light of day on 30 [*sic*] March 1732; it bestowed on him a rare musical talent.

The father, an ordinary wheelwright and village magistrate in Rohrau,* was married to a woman who had been in service as a cook with the local gentry. She was used to neatness, diligence and order, which qualities she sternly required of her children at a tender age, thereby being the first to pave the way in an efficacious

*[Original footnote:] The market town of Rohrau, from which the whole county takes its name, is not very important and comprises not more than some 65 houses. Rohrau lies on the River Laytha on the Hungarian border downstream from Bruck, which little town would be some $\frac{3}{4}$ of a mile [four English miles] distant.

The family of the Counts von Harrach comes from Bohemia and purchased the estate [*Herrschaft*] in ancient times and inhabits the castle, which stands somewhat apart and has been almost entirely rebuilt. – In the year 1732, Karl Anton C[ount] v. Harrach, Imperial Royal Chamberlain and Privy Councillor, Chief Master of the Hunt for Court and County, Royal Master of the Imperial House, held the fiefdom of Rohrau. His consort Katharina, *née* Countess v[on] Bouquoy, was served by Haydn's mother as cook.

manner for the further development of her six† boys' talents, of whom our Joseph was the eldest.

In his youth the father made a journey, as is the custom of his trade, and reached Frankfurt am Mayn, where he learned to play the harp a little and, because he liked to sing, to accompany himself on the harp as best he could. After he was married he continued to sing. All the children had to join in his concerts, to learn the *Lieder*, and to develop their singing voices. When the father sang, the five-year-old Joseph used to accompany him, as children will, by playing with a stick on a piece of wood; his childish imagination transformed this into a violin.

Haydn still remembers those *Lieder* and innocent scenes of his youth with pleasure. His face is unusually brightened when he tells about them; this time he told it so that I might make use of it. 'Young people', he said, 'can see from my example that something can still come from nothing; but what I am, is the result of dire necessity.'

No doubt one may consider his father's love of singing as the first opportunity for Haydn's spirit, even at this stage of his earliest youth, to enter its proper sphere. How easy it would have been for his father to set him to his own trade. Or, and this was both his father's and his mother's heart's desire, to dedicate him to the cloth. This did not happen, thanks in no small part to the reputation which these concerts made among the neighbours, even the whole village including the schoolmaster; so that when the subject fell on singing, all the inhabitants unanimously praised the wheelwright's son and could not praise highly enough his pleasant voice.

The father and the schoolmaster were firm friends, and it was therefore natural for the latter to be consulted about Joseph's future fate. The deliberations lasted for a long time. The father could not easily forget the priesthood. Finally, however, the moment of decision came; the various opinions converged; it was decided: – Joseph could stay with music and today or tomorrow, somewhere, he would earn an honest living as *Regens chori* or even as *Kapellmeister*.

Joseph had passed the age of six, when he had to leave his birthplace and travel to Haymburg [*sic*], a little town hard by. He was commended to the care of the *Regens chori*, who undertook to put the young lad on the virtuoso's course.

This worthy man was named Frank and was a distant cousin of Haydn's. It was just then Rogation Week, and many processions were held. Frank was in great difficulty because his kettledrummer had died. He cast an eye on Joseph; he ought to learn the kettledrums quickly and resolve the difficulty. He showed Joseph the mechanics of drumming and then left him alone. Joseph took a little basket of the kind country folk use to bake bread, covered it with a cloth, put his invention on an upholstered armchair and drummed with such enthusiasm that he never noticed how the flour in the basket came out as dust and ruined the chair. He received a rebuke for this, but his teacher was easily calmed when he saw with astonishment that Joseph had rapidly become a perfect kettledrummer; a circumstance, moreover, that contributed not a little to the decision that music should be his future career. Since Joseph was so small, he could not possibly reach the drum-carrier used hitherto in processions; so they chose a little man who, alas, was a hunchback and caused laughter among the spectators.

'From that time on (Haydn's words) I have worn a wig. The first one I received from my parents for cleanliness's sake; but when I came under the care of

† [Original footnote:] Three died in childhood. – Michael Haydn, *Kapellmeister* in Salzburg, is the author of many oratorios and other church music, in which field he is unique. Herr Neukomm [Sigismund, later von Neukomm] is one of his pupils but completed his studies with Joseph Haydn. The second brother, Johann, was a tenor in the service of Prince Esterházy in Eisenstadt, and died there on 10 May 1805 at the age of sixty-three. [For a correct list of Mathias Haydn's children, *vide supra*, pp. 34f.]

others, my few articles of clothing and one wig were not sufficient. It pained me to see that uncleanliness was getting the upper hand and although I took great pride in my small person, I still could not prevent my clothes from showing occasional signs of uncleanliness, which shamed my sensitivity no little.'

Joseph learned all the instruments then in use from his masters and to play several suitable to his age. His pleasant voice was a great recommendation. He was praised for his studious diligence. The parish priest knew him; the acquaintance soon proved important for Joseph, as I shall proceed to tell. – The parish priest was a close friend of the Imperial & Royal Court Kapellmeister Reutern [*sic*]; they were cousins. It happened that Reutern travelled on business from Vienna through Haynburg and paid a short visit to the parish priest. On this occasion Reutern discussed the reason for his trip, namely, to find boys with good voices and the ability to serve as choir-boys. The priest at once thought of Joseph and praised his voice and other musical abilities. Joseph was called for. He appeared. Reutern asked him: 'Boy [Büberl],★ can you sing a trill?' – Joseph was under the impression that one shouldn't know more than other honest folk and he therefore answered: 'The schoolmaster can't do that either.'

'Look', answered Reutern, 'I will show you how to trill; pay close attention how I do it! Open your mouth just a little, hold your tongue still, don't move it; sing a note slowly and then without stopping the one next to it; then again the first, and then the second; alternate the two notes, speeding up each time. Watch how I do it.' Reutern then sang a trill. Hardly had he finished when Joseph with the greatest impunity placed himself in front and, after two attempts at the most, brought forth such a perfect trill that Reutern cried Bravo! in appreciation, reached in his pocket and give the little virtuoso a 17 kr. coin.

[Dies 16–22; letterspaced words ignored]

[24 April 1805:] ... After *Kapellmeister* Reutern had given Joseph the 17 kr. coin, he was desirous of speaking to Joseph's father. The meeting was arranged as quickly as possible. Reutern gave the father this comforting assurance: 'he would care for the boy's progress, but he was still too young for it; he must wait till he has completed his eighth year; until then he must diligently practise scales to cultivate a pure, firm and flexible voice.'

Joseph followed that advice. But neither his schoolmaster nor anyone else in the little town was familiar with the *do, re, mi* &c. *solfeggio* method of the Italians, and therefore there was no one to give instructions to the eager boy. What does a genius do in such a case? In these straits, it breaks forth and levels the most untrammelled paths. Joseph discovered the most natural method; he was his own teacher and simply sang, every day, *c, d, e, f, g* &c.,★★ observing all the rules of *solfeggio* without knowing it; and he made such great progress that at the end of the appointed time Reutern was astonished.

Joseph had only his own self-instruction to thank when Reutern declared him entirely ready for the position and took him without delay as a choir-boy into the Choir School of St Stephen's in Vienna.

The reader will perhaps be inclined to accord Reutern's behaviour towards

[Original footnotes:]
★ In what follows Reuter kept using this expression.
★★ I refuse to allow the German method to have its say, for there are important reasons why the Italian method of teaching is better. What is the use of having the pupil sing dry letters incapable of incorporating any kind of expression? At best the pupil learns to find the notes and the letters but not to articulate any syllable. In words, it is not letters that sound but syllables. No song is spelled. In comic singing a very rapid articulation of syllables is required. We admire the Italians for their *rapid* articulation, and cannot imitate them for the simple reason that in our youth we did not practice articulating a series of syllables following one another rapidly.

Joseph that praise which a patron of talent deserves. But that which follows could somewhat dim the fine light in which the man now appears. I had, however, to guess at the circumstances, for Haydn spoke of his teacher with a care and respect which did honour to his heart. All that I could draw from him on this point was that the chapter of St Stephen's paid the *Kapellmeister* for the board and instruction of each choir-boy 700 gulden each year. There were six choir-boys; thus he collected 2,400 fl.

As soon as Joseph in his newly appointed status had received as much instruction as was required to fulfil the duties of a choir-boy, the instruction came to a sudden standstill; this was perhaps because of the *Kapellmeister*'s very pressing affairs.

Joseph was too young to understand that he would learn but little from the abandoned instructions. If matters stood thus with his principal occupation, can one not guess how little opportunity he was given to acquire, apart from the musical, the other required knowledge?

Joseph's great bent for music would not have been lessened through the acquisition of a few languages on the side. He learned some Latin, but everything else went by the board; one might say that he lost ten of his youthful years best suited to intellectual pursuits. Yet in this very neglect and non-development of several gifts, we may, perhaps, seek an explanation for the fact that his musical genius arrogated to itself all this collected power, which was able to flourish to that gigantic stature which we shall, in the event, remark in him.

In the *Biographische Skizze von Michael Haydn*,[2] his intellectual development was placed in a good light. If one were to take literally everything said in that respect, one would be inclined to think that Michael enjoyed an intellectual development more profound in everything, except in music, than that of Joseph. The latter had uncommon capabilities; but in particular he developed a natural judgment which he began to use as soon as he left the Choir School, *but always in his own particular way*; i.e. he easily and swiftly acquainted himself with several branches of learning; he never boasted of his accomplishments and entirely eschewed the wordy pomp of learned phrases. That may be the reason why in general he suffered Mozart's fate and, like him, was taken for an empiricist. Even if this word is taken in its noblest sense, it is still not appropriate. Haydn and Mozart are extraordinary phenomena; it will always be difficult to express the worth of these extraordinary men in ordinary terms.

Meanwhile our Joseph was satisfied with his position at that time. This satisfaction derived from the following circumstances. Reutern was so impressed by the boy's talents that he declared to the father that 'even if he had twelve sons, he would take care of them all'. The father saw himself freed of a great onus by this offer and agreed to it, so that about five years later Joseph's brother Michael, and still later Johann[3] were dedicated to the muse. Both were engaged as choir-boys, and to Joseph's unending joy, both were entrusted to him to be taught.

Joseph even then occupied himself with compositions in his spare time. Reutern surprised him once just as he had spread out a *Salve regina* in twelve parts on a sheet of paper more than an ell long. 'Hey, boy, what are you doing?' Reutern looked over the long sheet, laughed heartily at the copious repetitions of the word 'Salve', and still more at the preposterous notion that he could compose in twelve parts. He added: 'You silly boy, aren't two parts enough for you?'

From such comments, lightly tossed off, Joseph knew how to profit. His compositions took on a less Gargantuan appearance, and that was no small gain for a genius who, left to himself and tempted by the forceful powers of youth, could kick over the traces and thrash about like an untamed stallion until he collapsed on the ground. Naturally, one refers only to the youthful age from ten to fifteen, when no masterpieces are brought forth. But I am of the opinion that the more creative talent a lad shows, the more he should learn that there is an intelligence that informs the *mathematical principles* on which art is based and that a structure not raised on these principles must soon fall.

Joseph had to content himself, until he was eighteen, with the tossed-off comments, of which the one above serves as an example; his spirit received no nourishment. That which was most embarrassing to him, however, and at his age must have been painful, was the fact that they seemed set on a campaign to starve the body along with the mind. Joseph's stomach had to accustom itself to a perpetual fast, which for a time he attempted to improve by the occasional musical academies [concerts], for which the choir-boys were given refreshments.

As soon as Joseph had made this discovery, so important for his stomach, he developed an insatiable appetite for these musical academies. He concentrated on singing as well as possible so as to become known as a clever singer and – this was his secret motive – would be everywhere in demand, thus finding opportunities to satisfy his nagging hunger. Who would have thought that the old saying, 'Make a virtue of necessity', would have to apply even to a genius? – But what am I saying? Does not everyday experience show that the goddess of hunger seeks out genius everywhere and, unbidden, thrusts herself on him as a companion throughout youth, and often throughout life?

As a choir-boy Haydn had many amusing adventures. Once, when the Court was building the summer castle at Schönbrunn, Haydn had to sing there in the choir during Whitsuntide. Except for the church services, he used to play with the other boys, climbing the scaffolding round the construction and making a terrible racket on the staging. What happened? The boys suddenly beheld a lady. It was the Empress Maria Theresa herself, who ordered someone to get the noisy boys off the scaffolding and to threaten them with a thrashing if they dare to be caught there again. The next day Haydn, driven by curiosity, climbed the scaffolding alone, was caught and collected the promised thrashing [*Schilling*].

Many years later, when Haydn was in the service of Prince Esterházy, the Empress came once to Esterhaz [Eszterháza, 1773]. Haydn presented himself before her and thanked her most humbly for the reward he had received. – He had to tell the whole story, which occasioned much merriment.

In nature there is no standing still. Haydn now had to discover that he was not destined to remain a choir-boy for ever. His beautiful voice, with which he had so often sung for his supper, suddenly betrayed him. It broke, and wavered between two whole notes [*zwischen Doppeltönen*].

The following anecdote Haydn told me at a later time, but it belongs to this period in which his voice broke. At the ceremony performed every year at Klosterneuburg[4] in honour of St Leopold, the Empress Maria Theresa usually appeared. The Empress had already let it be said in jest to *Kapellmeister* Reutern, 'Joseph Haydn doesn't sing any more; he crows.' So Reutern had to replace Joseph with another soprano for the ceremony. His choice fell on Joseph's brother, Michael, who sang so beautifully that the Empress had him called before her and presented him with 24 ducats.

'Michael,' Reutern asked him, 'now what will you do with all that money?' Michael thought for a short moment and answered: 'One of our father's animals has just died, so I shall send him 12 ducats; I would ask you to keep the other 12 for me until *my* voice breaks, too.' Reutern took the money but forgot to give it back again.

Since Haydn, with his cracked voice, was unfit to be a choir-boy any more and thus had no monetary value for *Kapellmeister* Reutern, the latter found it only quite fair to discharge him.

A piece of mischief on Haydn's part hastened his dismissal. One of the other choir-boys, contrary to the usual custom of a choir-boy at that time, wore his long hair in a pigtail, and Haydn, just for the fun of it, cut it off. Reutern called him to account and sentenced him to a caning on the palm of the hand. The moment of punishment arrived. Haydn tried every way to escape it and finally declared he would rather not be a choir-boy any more and would leave at once rather than be punished. 'That won't help,' answered Reutern, 'first you'll be caned and then march!'*

Reutern kept his word, and so it was that the cashiered choir-boy, helpless, without money, with three mean shirts and a worn coat, stepped into the great world that he knew nothing about. His parents were very upset. Especially the tender motherly heart showed her anxiety with tears in her eyes. She implored her son that 'he might yet accede to the parental desires and prayers and dedicate himself to the priesthood'. This wish had lain slumbering for ten years, and it now awoke, its force undiminished. The parents gave their son no peace; they were sure that they must impose their will on him, but Haydn remained unswerving in his purpose and paid no attention. It is true that he could not provide any reasons for opposing his parents' wishes; he considered that he had explained things clearly enough when he squeezed the force of genius, mysterious even to himself, into the few words, 'I don't want to be a priest'. But how could this answer satisfy his parents? How could they imagine the development of their son's talents, or the future, so fortunate and so full of fame, when Haydn himself entertained no such thoughts, and when he understood just as little as did his parents what genius was, knew nothing of the pride that usually conquers the youthful genius, and was himself blessed with no insight whatever?

[Dies 24–32; letterspaced names of persons ignored]

* [Original footnote:] Both Joseph and Michael Haydn appear to have vexed *Kapellmeister* Reutern quite often, who punished them frequently. When Michael was in Vienna in 1801, he once passed the Choir School in company with intimate friends. Here he stopped and, with a smile, said: 'in that dear house for many a year I collected a thrashing [*Schilling*] every week.'

Notes:
1 Dies based his biography on a series of interviews with Haydn, beginning in 1805.
2 Published anonymously at Salzburg, in 1808, but actually written by G. Schinn and F. J. Otter and 'published for the benefit of his [Michael's] widow'.
3 There is no evidence that Johann actually studied with Reutter at the Choir School.
4 Augustinian Monastery on the Danube, three miles upstream from the Viennese suburb of Nussdorf.

(4) Neukomm's Corrections and Additions to Dies:

p. 12 [of Dies in the original edition] H. said to me: I was born on 1 April, and that is the date found in my father's *Hausbuch* – but my brother Michael maintains I was born on the 31st (not the 30th) of March because he doesn't want it said that I came into the world as an April Fool.   [Neukomm, p. 29]

(5) Framery, 1810, pp. 2ff.:

JOSEPH HAYDN naquit en 1730, au village de Rohrau, sur les confins de l'Autriche et de Hongrie; son père était charron, et savait passablement la musique, ce qui n'est pas rare en Allemagne parmi le peuple, et même les paysans; il jouait assez bien de la harpe: c'est de lui seul que Joseph apprit à pincer les cordes de cet instrument, ainsi que la lecture de la musique; c'est là ce qui développa dans cet enfant ce goût exclusif et passionné, le germe de ce talent qui devait être un jour incomparable.

Le père d'Haydn, qui avait assez d'aisance pour désirer que son fils reçût une éducation que lui-même n'avait point eue, le fit entrer comme enfant de chœur à Saint-Stéphann, (Saint-Etienne) église cathédrale de Vienne, pour y cultiver la musique, et y faire les études qu'on nomme huma- [p. 3] nités. Joseph, qui avait une voix charmante, et qui, sans autre guide que son goût naturel, chantait d'une manière délicieuse, se fit bientôt une grande réputation. Tout jeune qu'il était, il fut admis dans plusieurs concerts particuliers, où il eut des succès de diverses espèces: dans sa maîtrise il s'était exercé sur le violon, et il en jouait très-bien; il était assez fort sur le clavecin, et, à l'aide de cet instrument et de son oreille, il composait de petits airs et de jolies sonatines, dont il donnait des copies aux amateurs qui les désiraient.

Mais s'il excellait dans tout ce qui concerne la musique, il n'en était pas de même dans l'étude des langues savantes, pour laquelle il avait du dégoût; dans la crainte cependant que ses maîtres ne lui en fissent des reproches, il employait l'argent qu'il gagnait dans les concerts à payer ses camarades, qui faisaient pour lui ses devoirs.

Déjà s'approchait cette crise de la nature où l'enfant passe à l'adolescence, et où sa voix, auparavant aiguë et claire, prend le caractère mâle et grave qu'elle doit conserver à l'avenir; crise toujours redoutable pour ceux dont toutes les espérances consistent dans la beauté de leur voix. Reitter, maître de chapelle de la cathédrale, craignant que son jeune enfant de chœur ne vînt à [p. 4] perdre ce beau DESSUS, l'honneur de son église, résolut de le fixer par cette opération que la barbarie inventa, et que des prêtres du culte de Jésus osèrent tolérer à l'imitation des prêtres du culte de Cybèle. Il en fit la proposition à Joseph en la lui présentant sous le rapport avantageux, et sans lui en faire connaître toutes les conséquences: le jeune innocent, qui n'aimait encore que la musique, qui n'avait de désirs que celui de conserver sa voix, y consentit de très-grand cœur. Le jour et l'heure sont convenus; le chirurgien est averti; tous les préparatifs sont faits; c'est demain à dix heures du matin que l'opération sera faite! ... Par hasard une affaire appelle à Vienne le père d'Haydn; il y arrive à huit heures; son premier soin est d'aller voir son fils: l'enfant se jette dans ses bras, et lui annonce avec une joie naïve que sa voix dont il attend sa fortune, va être encore embellie, et qu'au moyen d'une opération légère elle le sera pour toujours. Le père, qui se fait expliquer la nature de cette opération, est indigné; il détaille à son fils les dangers qui en résulteraient, et ne le trouve sensible qu'à douleur physique qu'il lui fait appréhender; puis sur-le-champ il court [p. 5] chez Reitter, l'accable de reproches, le menace d'aller le dénoncer aux magistrats comme coupable d'avoir abusé de l'innocence d'un enfant pour compromettre sa virilité, même sa vie, à l'insu de son père; d'avoir enfin voulu violer les lois de l'état, de la nature et de la religion: Reitter, confus, et redoutant un éclat qui pouvait le perdre, s'excusa le mieux qu'il lui fut possible, et promit de n'y plus songer. Deux heures plus tard l'Allemagne, l'Italie, l'Europe auraient eu un chanteur qui sans doute se serait distingué; mais, en acquérant ce talent éphémère, la république musicale aurait perdu un compositeur vigoureux, noble, fier et toujours aimable, qu'une imagination brûlante, inépuisable et variée a élevé au-dessus de tous ses rivaux: deux heures plus tard Haydn eût continué d'être un enfant; il lui fut permis de devenir homme, et ce fut un homme en effet!

De ce moment Reitter, humilié, conçut une haine implacable contre celui qui naguère était l'objet de toute sa faveur; il chercha toutes les occasions de lui donner des marques de son animosité, surtout en le privant de ces concerts qui avaient jusque là procuré à cet enfant tant d'agrément et d'aisance, et, pour y mettre le comble, aussitôt que la mue de sa voix fut déclarée il [p. 6] le renvoya inhumainement de la maîtrise, sans argent, et avec vêtemens les plus usés.

(6) Carpani, 1812.

[Credentials:] Di questo prediletto sacerdote dell'armonia [Haydn] io vi andrò tessendo per via di lettere le memorie, quali ho potuto raccoglierle da lui stesso, e dalle persone che più lo frequentarono in diverse epoche della sua vita, come sono il barone *Van-Swieten*,[1] il maestro *Fribert*,[2] la bravissima scolara ed amica d'*Haydn* madamigella di *Kutzbec*,[3] il maestro *Pichl*,[4] il violoncellista *Bertoja*,[5] il consigliere *Griesinger*,[6] il maestro *Weigl*,[7] le Signore *Martinez*,[8] il suo fido copista,[9] ed altri molti che per brevità non vi nomino'   [Carpani, 3]

Notes:
1 Gottfried van Swieten, later to fashion the libretti of Haydn's *The Creation* and *The Seasons*.
2 Carl Friberth, Haydn's principal tenor in the 1760s and the first part of the 1770s. He was still alive when the first edition of Carpani appeared (he died on 6 August 1816; Pohl I, 271).
3 Madelaine (Magdalene) von Kurzbeck (Kurzböck), a brilliant pianist and friend of Haydn's to whom he dedicated the Artaria edition of Piano Sonata No, 62 in E flat. She was the daughter of a well-known Viennese publisher and writer, Joseph, whom Empress Maria Theresa raised to the nobility.
4 The composer Wenzel Pichl (1741–1805), who composed music for Prince Nicolaus Esterházy.
5 Valentino Bertoja, 'cellist at Eszterháza 1780–8; Carpani probably met him in Venice, where he was living about 1800.
6 Carpani and Griesinger knew each other quite well in Vienna.
7 Joseph Weigl, Haydn's principal 'cellist 1761–9; Haydn was an intimate friend of the whole Weigl family; Joseph Sen. was alive when Carpani was writing and did not die until 25 January 1820 in Vienna (Pohl I, 265).
8 Anna Katharina ('Marianne') von Martinez (Martines) (1744–1812) who as a girl (*vide infra*, p. 61) had studied with Haydn, was a singer, harpsichord player and a successful composer. *MGG* 8 (1960), 1716–8 (Helene Wessely).
9 Johann Elssler, Haydn's copyist and valet in the last two decades of the master's life.

Carpani, 1812 [Narrative:]

I genitori d'*Haydn* erano cattolici, e tale visse e morì l'*Haydn*, esattissimo osservatore dei doveri della sua religione. Padrino suo fu il mugnajo della villa, e madrina la mugnaja. Mi dispenserò dall'addurvene i nomi. Il battesimo si fece il primo d'aprile, che da molti poi fu preso pel giorno suo natalizio, e il curioso si è che l'*Haydn* stesso così credeva, non essendosi mai dato la briga di vedere la su fede di battesimo.

Tale si fu l'origine del nostro *Francesco Giuseppe* il quale, no so perchè, chiamossi di poi col solo nome di *Giuseppe Haydn*. Cresciuto in fama e distinto dai grandi, non occultava punto li suoi natali; godeva anzi di dovere a se stesso tutta la sua gloria, come *Orazio* e *l'Arpinate oratore*, e ripeteva a' suoi detrattori il = *quantum generi demas virtutibus addas* = del primo, e come lui protestava che non avrebbe cambiati i suoi parenti, qualora fosse stato in sua balìa di farlo: che anzi soleva ogni anno recarsi a *Pruk* [*sic*], e tutti colà raccoltili dalle vicine ville dava loro da pranzo nella miglior osteria del luogo, e ben pasciuti e dissetati li rimandava ai loro casolari con un piccolo presente in danaro, rinnovando fra i rustici sinceri abbraci l'invito per l'anno susseguente. *Haydn* chiamava questo suo famigliare simposio = il giorno delle sue grandezze = e ne andava lieto e fastoso.

Varj fratelli e sorelle ebbe l'*Haydn*. Suo padre ebbe due mogli e venti figli da esse. *Giuseppe* fu il primo di tutti. I suoi fratelli del primo letto che furono due, Michele e Giovanni, sortirono come lui dalla nascita un deciso genio per la musica; e Michele, divenuto uno de'più profondi scrittori di musica da chiesa, visse e morì al servizio del principe Vescovo di Salisburgo. L'altro divenne musico di camera del principe *Esterhazy*. Le sorelle furono tutte accasate con artigiani di *Pruk*. Una sposò un falegname, un'altra un maniscalco, ed ebbero figli abbastanza. . . .

[pp. 14f.]

Il padre di *Haydn* univa al mestiere di fabbricator di carri due delle prime cariche del villaggio: era giudice del luogo ed insieme sagrestano dalla chiesa parrocchiale; aveva una bella voce di *tenore*; amava il suo Organo, e la musica qualunque si fosse. In uno di quei viaggi che fanno in Germania gli artigiani, aveva appreso in Francfort a sonare un pochino d'arpa. Non era un *Krumpholz*[1] nè un *Delvimar*,[2] ma era il primo sonatore di casa, e si trastulava ne' giorni festivi a cantare e sonare colla moglie, ancor essa amica di quel passatempo . . .

Avvenne che un cugino degli *Haydn*, di nome *Frank*, maestro di scuola ad Haimburg [*sic*], capitò per caso a Rohrau e si trovò presente a questo *Trio*. Notò egli che il fanciullo di sei anni appena, con franchezza mirabile batteva esattamente la musica, e non menava mai a contrattempo il suo supposto arco sul muto suo violino. Questo maestro era buon professore di musica, e qual nuovo Ulisse scoprì a dirittura il musico Achille. Sembrandogli talento da non disprezzare questo che mostrava il fanciullo, chiese ai genitori che a lui l'affidassero, onde ammaestrarlo nell'arte per cui sì chiaramente si vedeva nato. La proposizione fu accolta a pieni voti per la lusinga che concepirono i genitori di poterlo, qualore avesse imparata la musica, più facilmente far prete; e l'Achillino di sei anni partì col suo Chirone per Haimburg. . . .

Di poche settimane soggiornato aveva in Haimburg il nostro Giuseppino, che, scoperti avendo in casa del cugino maestro due timpani che servivano a un lieto romoreggiare da festa nelle solennità del paese, si fece a battocchiarli da sè, e segnando con precisione la misura, e variandone il moto, a forza di battere e tentare, riuscì, all'età di sette anni, a formare su quello strumento a due soli tuoni una specie de cantilena ossia sonata in *ombra* ch'era la maraviglia di chiunque l'udiva. Egli è di questa fatta, che lungo Posilipo il brioso *Lazzarone* ne' giorni di festa, non avendo stromenti, affronta due ciottoli battendoli l'uno contro l'altro, e conservando la misura e il moto della *Tarantella*. . . .

La natura aveva provveduto l'*Haydn* d'una voce sonora insieme e delicata. . . . Il cugino maestro adoprando molta attenzione, e dando al fanciullo, (per servirmi della espressione stessa dell'*Haydn*,) più scappellotti che bocconi, portò ben presto il giovane timpanista in istato, non solo di sonare il violino ed altri strumenti, ma di capire il latino, e di salire in su le cantorìe, e farsi ammirare dalle rustiche orecchie siccome cantante; il che gli acquistò della celebrità per tutto il vicinato. O ne giungesse la voce sino al maestro *Reüter*, o l'accidente portasse questo maestro a Haimburg, nel girare che faceva ogn'anno per trovare fanciulli per la sua cappella di s. Stefano, il fatto si è che il *Reüter* si rivolse al precettore dell'*Haydn* per le sue ricerche, sendo facile che fra i molti ragazzi della sua scuola potessero trovarsi le migliori voci del contorno. Questi gli propose tosto il suo cugino e discepolo. Fattoselo venire innanzi, gli diè il *Reüter* a cantare di slancio *un canone* a prima vista. La precisione, la franchezza, il brio del giovinetto lo sorpresero, ma più di tutto la bellezza della voce. Solo trovò che non trillava, e ne lo rimproverò con grazia. Al che il fanciullo, colla ingenuità propria dell'età sua, ripose = come volete che lo sappia io, se no lo sa nemmeno mio cugino? = *Haydn* diceva il vero: fosse difetto d'organo, o mancanza d'arte, il sig. cugino maestro non aveva mai trillato in vita sua. *Reüter* rivolto al fanciullo gli disse = vieni qua che ti faccio trillare io subito, = e presosi il ragazzo tra le gambe, gli indicò come si dovessero avvicendare velocemente i tuoni vicini, come spingere e ritenere il fiato, e batter l'ugola, onde il trillo ne uscisse, e il fanciullo trillò subito, e bene. Sorpreso di ciò il *Reüter* ed oltremodo pago, diè di piglio a un piatto di belle ciliegie che il cugino

47

aveva fatte apprestare per lui, e tutte le versò in tasca al fanciullo, del che se rimanesse contento il musichetto, ognuno potrà indovinarlo, che sappia essere stato questi ghiottissimo di tal frutta, ed altrettanto avaro il cugino nel dargliene. L'*Haydn*, fatto adulto, non dimenticò mai quelle ciliegie, e mi diceva scherzando, che gli sembrava d'aversele sempre in bocca ogni volta che gli occorreva di trillare.

Ben capirete da questo aneddoto, che il *Reüter* non partì solo per Vienna, ma menò seco il nuovo trillatore che di poco passava allora gli otto anni, e che da quel giorno fu alloggiato in s. Stefano fra li sei giovanetti del coro. Così passò l'*Haydn* dalla natìa campagna alla capitale dell'Austria, dalla semplicità dei villerecci trionfi agli applausi d'una grande metropoli ed alla celebrità, per cui era nato.

Nessuno fra i memorabili ingegni riunì mai più dell'*Haydn* due qualità ben lodevoli, e ben nemiche per lo più l'una dell'altra: una gran sete di gloria ed una vera modestia; è madre la prima delle grandi imprese, ma lo suol essere altresì della vanagloria. Così non avvenne nel nostro *Haydn*. Egli non conobbe altra superbia, che quella consigliata da Orazio = *sume superbiam quaesitam meritis* = L'amore della gloria destò in lui quello dell'applicazione. Mi ha confessato egli stesso, quando era già pieno d'anni e di nome, che non si ricordava d'aver passato un giorno senza avere travagliato sedici ore e talora diciotto. Queste due passioni gli procurarono de' momenti ben felici. Si suol dire, che l'eroe gode più nell'immaginare le imprese, che nell'eseguirle. ... [pp. 16–21]

Notes: Composers and harp players:
1 J. B. Krumpholtz (d. Paris, 1790) or possibly his wife, with both of whom Haydn was on friendly terms; Johann Baptist was a member of the Eszterháza band in the 1770s, and his wife was a regular guest soloist at the Haydn–Salomon concerts in London.
2 P. A. d'Alvimâre, a harp virtuoso who settled in Paris at the end of the eighteenth century. Gerber *NTL* 1, 82f.

Pascal a quattro anni e senza maestro, vedeva da Geometra; di otto disegnava l'Euclide prima d'averlo letto; *Mozart* di dodici anni componeva un'opera ... Men felici di essi, l'*Haydn* all'età stessa, senza guida e senza dottrina, scrisse una Messa a quattro, con sedici parti d'orchestra, e mi diceva egli medesimo, che di quel tempo non sapeva nemmeno scrivere a due, e che di tanto assicurato lo aveva, burlandosi di lui, il buon *Reüter* cui aveva osato mostrare il suo lavoro. Ma la forza inventrice del genio non potè starsene sotto corteccia: la ruppe, e ne uscirono precocemente que' rami che, regolati poi dallo studio ed innaffiati dalla scienza, dovevano arricchire di sì squisite frutta il giardino dell'armonia.

Convintosi il giovane compositore, nel confrontare colle partiture di altri quel suo primo lavoro, che il *Reüter* aveva ragione, e che la natura senz'arte è un'aquila a cui non sono ancora venute le ali, si diede a cercare chi gl'insegnasse il contrappunto e le regole della melodìa. Inutili sforzi! O diciam meglio: rarissima fortuna! Il *Mozart* aveva potuto imparare da suo padre, buon violinista e teorico, il contrappunto; ma l'*Haydn*, non avendo un contrappuntista in familigia, non poteva trovar lezione che pagandole, e per fatalità non aveva quattrini. La sua casa era sì povera in allora che, essendogli stati rubati i suoi abiti ed avendone informato suo padre, questi facendo uno sforzo, gli mandò sei fiorini per rivestirsi. ... [pp. 24f.]

Summary of Carpani in translation:

Carpani lists his sources, Haydn himself, and the list of friends and patrons given in the first paragraph of (5).

[Narrative:] Haydn's parents were Catholics and Haydn grew up a faithful son of the Church. His godfather was the town miller [*sic*]. Haydn was baptized on 1 April and many thought this to be his birth date, also Haydn himself, since he never took the trouble to consult his baptismal certificate.

Haydn, when he was famous, made no secret of his origins and each year he collected his relatives from near and far and gave them lunch at the best restaurant in Bruck, sending them home afterwards with a small present in money for each one, and extending another invitation for the coming year.

Haydn had various brothers and sisters, both of his father's two wives. Joseph was the first, followed by Michael, who later became a leading church composer in the service of the Archbishop of Salzburg, while the other brother was chamber musician to Prince Esterházy. The sisters married local men of Bruck, one a carpenter, the other a blacksmith, and they had many children. . . .

Haydn's father united the professions of wheelwright, village magistrate and sacristan of the local parish church; he had a fine tenor voice. On his journeyman trip to Frankfurt he learned how to play the harp a little. Although not a Krumpholz or a Delvimar, he was the leading player of his own house, assisted on holidays by his wife's singing.

Franck, a cousin from Hainburg [*recte*], came to Rohrau and heard the family making music and noted that boy beat the time exactly with a pretended violin. It was proposed to send the boy to Hainburg, where the boy discovered two timpani in his cousin's house, and although there were only two notes to be played on them, he was able to make a 'sonata of shadows' which was generally admired. Thus do the *lazzaroni* of Naples create a *tarantella* by using two paving stones.

Nature provided Haydn with a sonorous and delicate voice . . . The schoolmaster-cousin, to use Haydn's own words, gave me more thrashings than meals, but taught him the violin and other instruments, a little Latin, and had him sing in the choir-loft, which made him famous in the vicinity. His name was given to Reutter, who was by chance in Hainburg on an annual trip to look for choir-boys for his chapel at St Stephen's. Reutter had Haydn sing a song at sight, and the precision, openness and spirit of the boy surprised, but especially the beauty of the voice. But he knew not how to trill, and on being reproved, said: 'how can you expect me to know if even my cousin doesn't know?' Haydn was speaking the truth, for whether on account of a physical defect, or lack of study, his cousin never produced a trill in all his life. Reutter turned to the boy, 'come here, I'll have you trilling in no time', stood the boy between his legs and showed him the technical details how to produce a trill. He was surprised when the boy produced one, and well. Reutter grasped a plate full of cherries which the cousin had intended for him and poured them into the boy's pocket, who was pleased about the fruit, of which he was inordinately fond and which his cousin was too mean to give him. When Haydn was grown up he never forgot those cherries, and he told me jokingly that he seemed to have them yet in his mouth every time he had to trill.

You will of course understand that Reutter did not leave for Vienna alone, and the new triller remained for the next eight years as a new member of the six choir-boys lodged at St Stephen's. Thus Haydn passed from his native countryside to the capital of Austria, from the simplicity of rustic triumphs to the applause of a great metropolis and to that celebrity for which he was born.

Haydn combined two traits inimical to each other, a great thirst for glory and a genuine modesty. He knew no other pride except for that sung by Horace, 'sume superbiam quaesitam meritis'. Love of glory awakened in him that of application. He himself confessed to me, when he was full of years and reputation, that he could not remember a day passing when he did not work sixteen hours, and sometimes eighteen. These two passions produced some very happy moments. One might say that the hero enjoys more the imagination of the operation than its execution. . . .

Pascal at the age of four, without a master, perceived geometry; at eight, he devised Euclid before having read him; Mozart composed an opera at the age of twelve . . . Less fortunate than them, Haydn at the same age was without guide and without teaching, and wrote a mass for four voices and sixteen orchestral parts; he told me himself that in those days he could not even write in two parts, and the good Reutter, to whom he dared show the work, ridiculed it.

The young composer, comparing his own first effort with the scores of other masters, became persuaded that Reutter was right, and that nature without art is like an eagle without wings. He looked around for someone who would teach him counterpoint and the rules of melody. Useless efforts! Or let us say: rarest fortune! Mozart had his father, good violinist and theoretician, to teach him counterpoint; but Haydn, not having a contrapuntist in the family could only learn lessons by paying for them, and alas, he had no money. His parental house was so poor that, having been robbed of all his worldly goods and upon relating this to his father, he made a great effort and sent six florins to purchase new clothes. . . .

(7) Farington's *Diary* of 30 September 1798 (I, 238):

Hayden told [the artist George] Dance that He was born in Hungary, the Son of a Wheelwright, who, at his business hours amused himself with playing on the Harp. This caused the Son to attempt music, and an Organist from Vienna happening to come that way He was induced to take young Hayden back with him to Vienna. – Dance was surprised at Hayden not knowing or affecting to know anything of Tartini, the celebrated Violin [*sic*] of Italy.

Two groups of principal sources combine to provide the important facts about Haydn's youth: (a) the documents above, all containing information, sometimes *verbatim*, provided by the composer himself or (as in the case of Framery) by Haydn's pupil Ignaz Pleyel, but sometimes, as in the case of Carpani, displaying aspects of bowdlerization; and (b) archive documents connected with Haydn's parents, his house in Rohrau, his stay with cousin Franck in Hainburg, and St Stephen's Cathedral and life in Vienna. As this biography will show, Griesinger, Dies, Framery and Carpani are – in that order – very often the only preserved sources dealing with an event or events in Haydn's life. The biography by Georg August Griesinger (1769–1845) is slightly dry but by far the most accurate of the three; sometimes the *Legationsrath* not only allows Haydn's humorous view of life to colour the pages of his biography in a refreshing way, but we have glimpses of Griesinger's pleasant personality, itself by no means devoid of a sense of humour. Readers may refer to the last two volumes of the present biography[1] and see for themselves that he was a reliable, accurate go-between between Breitkopf & Härtel and Haydn, and as such in a uniquely advantageous position to write Haydn's biography; though for the years before *The Creation*, he had to rely on Haydn's information and such *documenta* as the London Notebooks. Albert Christoph Dies (1755–1822) is garrulous, sympathetic and had the disadvantage of arriving on the scene very late, in 1805, when Haydn's memory was failing. A degree further removed from the truth than Griesinger in many cases, the differences in their approach were in large measure dictated by the difference in their professions. Griesinger came to Vienna as a tutor to children in a noble house and ended as a Secretary of Legation for the Saxonian Embassy. Framery (via Pleyel) often provides confirmation of a tale (proposed castration of Haydn) or a new detail. Dies was a landscape artist who had studied in Rome, had married a Roman girl and ended as Director of Prince Nicolaus II Esterházy's art gallery. Thieme-Becker (IX, 248) describe his works as 'hardly surpassing the mediocre landscape painting characteristic of the period'; and his writing cannot be said to represent a great improvement on his artistic merits. Better, one feels, the dry and prosaic Griesinger to the kind-hearted, talkative Dies.

Whereas neither Griesinger's nor Dies's biographies were reprinted until the second half of the twentieth century, Giuseppe Carpani's (1752–1825) *Le Haydine* (Milan, 1812) was brought out in a revised second edition at Padua in 1823 which, curiously, is much more rarely encountered on the antiquarian market than the first. But what made Carpani's biography world-famous was its being used, illegally and without the author's knowledge, as the basis of Stendhal's *Lettres écrites de Vienne, en Autriche, sur le célèbre compositeur Joseph Haydn suivies d'une vie de Mozart et de considérations sur Métastase et l'état présent de la musique en France et en Italie*, Paris 1814. Of course Stendhal (Henri Beyle), who signed himself Louis-Alexandre César Bombet, plagiarized only the Haydn from Carpani, he used another source for the Mozart (which had appeared in Paris in 1801). But Stendhal's clever adaptation was at once translated into English, where it was edited by William Gardiner (London, John Murray, 1817) and subsequently reprinted at regular intervals. It was also translated into German and other languages.

Carpani, a trained lawyer with the soul of an Italian *uomo di lettere*, is urbane, civilized, humane – and inaccurate. His biography cannot be dismissed because he did know Haydn and certainly interviewed the men listed at the beginning of our

---

1 *Haydn: The Years of 'The Creation' 1796–1800* and *The Late Years 1801–1809*.

quotation, but one has the distinct impression that some of his information comes, mistranslated (his German was probably never very brilliant) from Griesinger and Dies. We have therefore allowed ourselves to shorten the English translation of those parts which we judge to be based on second-hand information. However, since we doubt if those passages 'as Haydn himself told me' are literary licences, we have included all those parts which suggest that the information given came from the composer himself.

There are, moreover, problems in chronology. It is difficult enough to subject these early biographies to a more or less arbitrary chronological division such as we have adopted here: 1732–49 (Haydn's dismissal from St Stephen's) and 1750–56 (one presumes that he was engaged by Count Morzin in 1757); but it is clear that the final paragraph in Carpani describes an event partly when Haydn was still a choir-boy, and able to consult Reutter without undue difficulty, and partly when Haydn was on his own in Vienna (the robbery can have taken place only after he left the Choir School). It seemed unscholarly, however, to break off Carpani in the middle of a thought: Haydn was so poor that he could not afford counterpoint lessons, and his family was so poor that when Joseph was robbed they could afford to pay only six gulden.

Carpani describes the work in question submitted to Reutter as a Mass for four voices with a sixteen-part orchestra; the other biographies report either (Dies) a *Salve Regina* in twelve parts or (Griesinger) an unnamed piece in sixteen. Since it is unlikely that we shall ever recover the work, further speculation seems idle. It does appear quite clear, however, that this piece must have been composed when Haydn was still, officially, Reutter's 'composition pupil'.

It must, from the slightly vague information of the biographies, have been in 1737 or 1738 that Haydn followed his cousin, Johann Mathias Franck, to Hainburg and moved into the house at what is now Ungargasse 3, the management of which was the responsibility of Frau Juliana Rosina Franck, *née* Seefranz. It was Franck's second marriage, which had taken place on 6 September 1733. When Joseph Haydn came to Hainburg, his cousin by marriage (born on 15 May 1708 in Ketzelsdorf, Lower Austria) must have been about fifty, and had been *Schulrektor* there since 1732. His contract specified that he was to instruct the boys not only in the usual disciplines but also in music; thus he was schoolmaster, and *Chorregent* of the Church of SS. Philip and James, the first of Haydn's many relatives to choose an intellectual profession. In his duties as schoolmaster, he was assisted by two preceptors; as choir director he was in charge of the music and was also the sacristan; he was responsible for the clock in the church choir and for the ringing of the bells 'not only in winter but also in summer at seven o'clock in the morning, as well as noontime with the bells of middle size, and with the great bells for prayer service . . .'. The bells were to be rung as a warning of a thunderstorm, for which emergency two assistant bell-ringers were provided. Apart from his modest salary, he was paid additional fees for winding the clock (5 fl. p.a.), half a taler for funeral bells, as well as wood and grain in kind.

The organ had been replaced in 1695 by a new one constructed by the Viennese master Hans Ulrich Römer; it comprised one manual and pedal with Principal, Koppel, Flöte, Oktav, Quint, Mixtur, Corpo (Koppel = gedeckt or covered; Corpo = pedal register), which was presumably[1] Prinzipal 4′, Koppel 8′, Flöte 4′, Oktav 2′, Quint $1\frac{1}{3}$′. This instrument was renovated in 1719–20, at a cost of 200 gulden, by the Master Organ Builder Eberhard Heinrich who was then living at

1 Oskar Eberstaller, *Die Haydn-Gedächtnisorgel in Hainburg a. d. Donau*, Hainburg 1932, p. 3.

Hainburg (since at least 1712); the 'renovation' meant, to all intents and purposes, a new organ, of which the disposition has not survived; neither has the organ or its case.

Perhaps the first large-scale procession at Hainburg in which Haydn was present and played the kettledrums was Rogation week, which in 1738 fell between 11 and 18 May (see the account in Dies).

In Cousin Franck's house, the cleanliness of which left something to be desired (Haydn told Bertuch [183] that 'I was a little porcupine'), the mistress of the house had two children of her own, Anna Katharina (born 24 November 1735) and Anna Theresia (born 19 October 1737), and their brother Johann Leopold was born on 15 November 1739. The two praeceptors also had board and lodging with the Francks, and E. F. Schmid discovered an 'Inventar ab intestato der Schulrektorin Franck' of 28 January 1760 in which a debt of 30 gulden owed by Mathias Haydn is registered, no doubt money for Joseph's tuition, board and lodging with the Francks at Hainburg that Master Mathias had not paid. In this house Franck and his family not only lived but also managed the school itself; and there was a beer house on the ground floor; in its present form, it shows a restoration, with the addition of a second (American: third) floor, of the year 1783, and is no longer the schoolhouse. How many students did the building usually contain? In an undated document by Franck of the 1730s, we read:

> Annually some 70 to 80 children attend the school; they arrive at seven o'clock in the morning, at ten they attend Holy Mass, and after Mass they go home. At noon, twelve o'clock, they return to school and leave school at three o'clock. [Schmid, 99]

Apart from the Scriptures, books for the Catechism and extracts from Ecclesiastes (by Jesus Sirach, 2nd century AD), they learned to write by copying Sirach and the writings of Thomas à Kempis (*De imitatione Christi*). Music was taught, as Franck tells us in a document of 19 September 1770 in the Town Archives of Hainburg, 'in the afternoon, after they have finished school classes'. As we have seen, Griesinger reports that Haydn learned almost all the known instruments, and Bertuch (1805, ibid., 182) says, 'Here Haydn learned to read and write, he was given instruction in Religion, and was taught singing, the violin, the timpani and other instruments.'[1] The Town Archives of Hainburg own a document entitled 'Instruction für den Schulmeister oder rectore' of the year 1734. In it, Franck is told to keep, at his own expense, and to provide lodging, food and drink for two praeceptors who are expected to be proficient at reading, arithmetic and to have a clear hand, as has been the custom from time immemorial. He will have chosen such persons as may be put to good use in the church music. He is to instruct the children in good behaviour and rectitude by giving them good lessons every day, and also in declamation, dictation, and written exercises which are to be corrected, so that the 'few hours for schooling are not wasted, and ... their punishments are to be meted out justly (as is appropriate to small children by birching and caning) and not by pulling their hair and other improper forms of hard beatings, and on no account is he to allow such action by the praeceptors under him or other persons ...'. Every six weeks there were examinations and reports. On Sundays, Mondays, Wednesdays and Fridays the Headmaster (*Rector*) himself or his praeceptors

---

1 Again we note the curious parallel to Griesinger, which is even more apparent if we compare Bertuch's 'Ich verdanke es diesem Manne noch im Grabe, daß er mich zu so vierlerley angehalten hat, wenn ich gleich dabey mehr Prügel als zu essen bekam' (p. 183) with Griesinger's 'Ich verdanke es diesem Manne noch im Grabe, sagte Haydn öfters, daß er mich zu so vierlerley angehalten hat, wenn ich gleich dabey mehr Prügel als zu essen bekam' (p. 9). Here it is quite obvious that Bertuch simply lifted the passage in question from Griesinger, which is why we have refused to consider Bertuch one of the primary biographical sources for this period (or indeed any other).

were to take the schoolchildren to church, where they were to behave themselves and not to chatter or turn round when seated in the pews. Franck was to keep the church music in the same good condition as that of his predecessors, and to perform 'on ordinary Sundays and Holy Day Masses with four vocal parts, viz. bass, tenor, alto and discant with two violins', but on great feast days and the first Sunday of the month 'apart from those four vocal parts and violins, there are to be provided for the choir trumpets and kettledrums and hunting horns together with Violon [double bass] and Passetl ['cello]'. Also,

> Eleventh: It is strictly forbidden for him to employ any church and choir violins, and any of the other instruments, whatever they may be, which were purchased for the choir-loft, for *extra* private music; and they are only for use in the choir-loft and for rehearsals in the school; and since their acquisition was very expensive for the town, if the said rector should refuse to accede to this prohibition [*Verbot*], he must not only make up any losses thus incurred but shall be punished *extra*, according to the circumstances ... Given at this Imperial Border Town of Hainburg This First Day of January ao: 1734. Judiciary and Council Therefor'.
>
> [Schmid, 103]

An inventory of the year 1762 listing the musical instruments found in the parish church's choir-loft, includes:

> 8 trumpets very bad 2 ditto rods [for lengthening the instrument and pitching it a tone, a half-tone, 1½ tones or two tones lower] and 3 brass mouthpieces
> 2 bad brass crooks [presumably for use with the horns]
> 2 useless hunting horns
> 6 old violins, 2 ditto Viennese
> a new Bassetl ['cello]
> a very old useless Violon [double bass]
> 3 carrying-cases for the trumpets
> a pair of new kettledrums
> a pair of old bad ditto
> a pair of leather covers for them
> an old Positiv [organ]
> an old large breviary with red letters in large 4°.   [Schmid, 104]

In the twenty-four years since Haydn's period, the instruments had markedly deteriorated, but we can see that the enlarged music for 'festival' performances, with the additional trumpets, horns, drums, 'cello and double bass, could be mounted with instruments in the choir-loft, and that wind instruments were not commonly in use.

Franck's duties included keeping a library of suitable music and procuring new pieces, many of which seemed to have been his personal property. When he left the town's service as schoolmaster in 1762, he wrote, in a letter to his eldest daughter Leonore,

> ... Greiner [one of the praeceptors] should be kind enough to get hold of the music so that nothing gets lost, for I know it cost me a great deal, as much as 100 or 200 fl., which was a lot for a beginner like me thirty years ago ... The viola belongs to me, and so does one violin ... NB. In Preßpurg [*sic*] there are in the tower six printed vespers that the Cantor has, they cost me 3 fl.; also don't forget the six Masses at H. Philipp Michl's, the schoolmaster, on the [castle] stairs. ...

Schmid, from whom all these documents are taken, imagines that the repertoire consisted principally of works of the Viennese (or Viennese adopted) school

– Antonio Caldara, J. J. Fux, Georg Reutter, his son of the same name, and certainly a number of works by local *Regentes chori* at Pressburg and the Lower Austrian monasteries.

Mathias Haydn, as a Master Wheelwright, belonged to the Hainburg Wheelwright's Guild, which celebrated its highest holiday on the Feast of Corpus Christi. It was a great festival altogether in Hainburg, with the town crowded with the members of the various guilds in their holiday attire. The six town pipers and the schoolmaster received together 3 gulden 30 kreuzer for their participation. In the guilds themselves, masters were solemnly received, journeymen freed and apprentices bound; the farriers expected a new master to offer a meal for thirty-six with music. The Hainburg Wheelwright's Book tells of the Corpus Christi events:

> [28 May 1738:] ... Master Mathiaß Haytn [*sic*] from Rohrau bound his apprentice for four years to learn the trade of making wheels and waggons.

Corpus Christi lasted for several days, at the end of which the individual guilds assembled in the parish church for a solemn service: 'Feria sexta post festum Corporis Christi singuli opificum tribus solent curare celebrari sacrum, sub quo qualibet tribus ad offertorium accedit.'[1]

The year 1738 in Hainburg also saw a fortnight's celebration, *Jubilaeum Universale*, to commemorate victory 'over Turk and Heathen'. There were, in 1738, many people, including Joseph Haydn's grandmother, Catharina Haydn *née* Blaiminger (who was still living in Hainburg and whose daughter from a second marriage, Juliana Rosina Seefranz, had married Franck), who remembered the massacre by the Turks at Hainburg, where the 'Blutgasse' survives as a reminder that the streets of the town, and in particular the one bearing the name, literally ran inches deep in the blood of the Christian victims. On the first day of the celebrations in 1738, the Holy of Holies was taken outside the church and exposed to the populace, and after the solemn procession the choir sang the Antiphon 'Da pacem Domine' with organ accompaniment. On the final day, the procession made its way to the Franciscan Church, where the Holy of Holies was exposed outside; there the choir, with Joseph among the sopranos, participated: 'donec chorus in organo cantando Antiphonam seu cantilenam brevem finierit.'[2]

On 2 and 3 May 1739, the Imperial Commissioner, Cetto von Cronstorff, made his solemn entry into the I.R. Border Town of Hainburg. At the gate he was met by the village judges and councillors, 'nigris pallijs contectis'. Drawn up on the market place were the town trumpeters and kettledrummers in red capes, and the town militia with standard-bearer in their dress uniforms; when the Commissioner and his party approached, the standard was displayed to the fanfares of trumpets and drums.

> stabant in foro extra Ecclesiae portam tubicines et tympanistae suis ad hoc deputatis rubis togis induti, ex altera vero fori parte ... stabant cives gladeati et Sclopis armati cum suo vexillifero, qui sub adventu Domini Electionis Commissarij vexilla solito more rotabat per aerem sonante semper tympano militari: tubicines vero civitatensis inflabant tubas et tympana musicalia pulsabantur. ...[3]

1 Wheelwright's Book: *Wagner: Maister Undt Gesellen Buech in der Kay: Lanndts Fürstlichen Gränitz Statt Hainburg in Österreich. auf Ein Neyes Ist auf Gericht und Connfir Mirdt wordten alß In Jahr Anno 1710: den 6. Juny [et seq.*], Museum of the Town of Hainburg (Schmid, 108). Church ceremony: *Notata Miscellanea* of the Town Curate Anton Johann Palmb in the 'Matrikelbuch 1715–35', Town Archives, Hainburg (Schmid, 108).

2 *Notata Miscellanea*, ibid.; Schmid 106.

3 *Notata Miscellanea*, ibid.

The next day was marked for the election of the town councillors. It began with a solemn procession to and ceremony in the church during which all the bells were rung; after the sermon, fanfares were sounded from the organ-loft:

> Commissarius ... quem Senatores et cives bini et bini sequebantur, sub pulsu omnium campanarum ivit ad Parochialem Ecclesiam ... finita oratione inflabantur tubae in choro. [*Notata Miscellanea,* ibid.]

Before the sermon, the choir sang the Motet 'Veni Sancte Spiritus', and after the solemn Mass the great *Te Deum* was sung. Among the councillors was Haydn's step-grandfather, Mathias Seefranz. Although Hainburg could not boast of a Johann Sebastian Bach to compose the music for the *Rathswahl* (Cantata 'Lobe den Herrn', BWV 137, composed in the year Haydn was born), we may be sure that the Mass and *Te Deum* were selected from 'the best Austrian masters' and that the festival orchestra, with its horns, trumpets and kettledrums, provided that C major brilliance which would remain in Haydn's mind, and appear in his scores, throughout his life – the key of solemn Mass, and works for great occasions.

Our Parish Priest, Anton Johann Palmb, who was responsible for the documents which inform us of life, spiritual and temporal, in Hainburg, was Reutter's friend; and it was to Palmb's quarters that Haydn and Franck were summoned, perhaps (as far as the rather imprecise indications in the authentic biographies allow us to specify a date) in the early summer of 1739. Reutter had, barely a year before, suddenly become Cathedral Chapel Master of St Stephen's in Vienna as a result of his father's death on 29 August 1738. Our sources tell us that Reutter left young Joseph in the care of his cousin until 1740, so that the boy was certainly a witness of the ceremonies at Hainburg attending the peace between Emperor Charles VI of Austria and His Most Christian Majesty of France, Louis XV:

> Anno 1739 ex mandato Aulico celebravimus hic Hainburgi Solemne Te DEUM laudamus 5ta July ob pacis foedus inter nostrum Augustissimum Imperatorem et Galliarum Regem hoc anno initum et conclusum. Sub cantata hymno Ambrosiano cives in foro ante majorem templi portam, id est ad D[omi]ni Comitis de Gaissrugg domum stantes gladijs et sclopetis armati, suos Sclopos exploserunt.[1] [*Notata Miscellanea,* ibid.]

To mark the solemnity of the occasion, the parish church received a splinter of the True Cross.[2]

---

1 'Domum', the house of the Lord of the Castle and Town of Hainburg, Anton Count Gaisruck (*recte*); 'exploserunt', fired a salute of honour. Schmid 106f.

2 The literature on Haydn and Hainburg is, basically, the result of two pieces of scholarly research: Joseph Maurer's *Geschichte der landesfürstlichen Stadt Hainburg*, Vienna 1894, and Schmid's monumental *Joseph Haydn* ..., Kassel 1934, esp. pp. 89ff., from which book we learn the details of Franck's life after Haydn left for Vienna. The next year, Franck was caught cheating at dice (he had thrown the loaded dice out of the window and into the water, but not quickly enough): he was fined three gold ducats. In January 1760, Franck's wife, *Tante* Juliana, died, having borne her husband eleven children, of whom only four survived infancy. The only surviving son, Johann Leopold, entered the Piarists under the name of P. Athanasius; he was a boy chorister in the Piarist Convent in Vienna, with which Haydn would later be associated (*Missa in tempore belli, 1796*: see *Haydn: The Years of 'The Creation' 1796–1800*, pp. 120f.). From a document of 1760 (the year Juliana Franck died), it can be seen that Franck had a comfortable capital of 912 gulden and had been able to help out his father-in-law, Mathias Seefranz, who was in straitened circumstances, with a loan of 140 gulden. But Franck himself soon lost the confidence of the Town Council, and was dismissed in 1762. Franck protested (the letter has survived: Schmid, 114) and was reinstated for a year on probation. He remained for more than twenty years, receiving at the end a salary of 240 fl., with an additional 10 fl. expenses from the church. In 1780, when Franck was seventy, he appeared before the Town Council and asked to be given a pension since he wished to resign. The Council asked him to remain, which he did until his death on 8 May 1783. Schmid 116; Pohl I, 23.

In 1740 the young Joseph Haydn went to Vienna, there to become a member of the choir school at the Cathedral of St Stephen (Stephansdom). Like many European cathedrals, St Stephen's was long in the building; it has a formidable west façade in Romanesque style, while the rest of the edifice ranges from early to late Gothic. There were various buildings outside, but attached to the Cathedral, including the 'Cantorei' or 'Capellhaus' (demolished in 1803), where Haydn and his fellow choristers lived. Apart from him, the musicians at St Stephen's included five boy choristers, nine other vocalists and three 'Extra-Vocalisten', one 'Subcantor', an organist (Anton Reckh), eleven string players (including 'Accessisten' and private substitutes), one cornet player (Andreas Wittmann), and one bassoon player (Jacob Payer). The trumpets, trombones and kettledrums were recruited from the Imperial Trumpeters and the *Thurnermeister* with his apprentices. Anton Reckh was also a composer; his salary was 150 fl., plus nearly as much in kind (*Deputat*). One of the violin players was Georg Ignaz Keller, later a member of the *Hofcapelle*, through whom it is believed Haydn first met his future wife's relatives. In the biographies, we have seen that the boy was instructed by various members of this group of thirty-one individuals, singers included. As in Hainburg, there were basically two types of Mass, one with the full orchestra, *missa solemnis* (especially with trombones, trumpets and timpani) and another, *missa brevis*, with telescoped texts – the words of the Gloria and the Credo apportioned in such a way that usually the four soloists or choir members (S-A-T-B) were each declaiming separate texts at the same time – and a small orchestra known as the 'Vienna church trio', i.e. two violins and *basso continuo* (organ, double bass and perhaps 'cello and/or bassoon). The solemn Masses were reserved, as at Hainburg, for feast days and special occasions, the short Masses for normal, daily use and (without the Gloria in some cases) during Advent.

This was the principal *Capelle* in use, but there was a second, smaller group known as the 'Music-Capelle beim Marianischen Gnadenbild', which was independent and supported by a trust fund. The miraculous portrait of the Virgin, housed on a silver tabernacle, was on the High Altar. At 11 a.m. on Sundays, holidays and feast days, as well as on normal weekdays, there was a sung Mass and at 5 p.m. the Laurentian Litany with music. There was a *Capellmeister* (Georg Reutter from 1740 'provisionally' and from 1743 Ferdinand Schmidt), three choir-boys, and one alto, one tenor, one bass, an organist, a first and a second violin, a 'cellist and a double-bass player, as well as wind instruments – two cornets, one bassoon and three trombones. The trumpets and drums were recruited, as in the case of the large orchestra, from the Imperial Orchestra or the *Thurnereister*. The *Capellmeister* received 300 fl., 50fl. 'adjutum' and 600 fl. for the expenses and education of the boys. The *Capelle*'s yearly cost was 2,800 fl. Schmidt was expected to provide most of the new music; it has only survived in MS. copies outside the Music Archives of the Cathedral which, with some exceptions (some manuscripts now in the Gesellschaft der Musikfreunde, some sheets of Haydn and other composers in Klosterneuburg Abbey), was completely destroyed in 1945. When Schmidt died on 11 August 1756, at the age of sixty-two, there was not enough money at home even to pay for the burial costs – one of the first of that horrifying list of musicians who died in abject poverty of which this present biography contains many examples. It is probable that Haydn's *Missa brevis alla cappella* 'Rorate coeli desuper' was written for the *Gnadenbild Capelle*, as the words 'alla cappella' on the Göttweig MS. suggest.

The collection at the Gesellschaft der Musikfreunde in Vienna enables us to have a comprehensive, if not by any means complete, picture of the repertoire of St Stephen's in Haydn's period (1740–9). The works are primarily by local composers, and in particular those in Imperial-Royal service (which included several Italians such as Giuseppe Bonno, Antonio Caldara, Matteo Palotta and Antonio Ziani. Haydn grew up on the solid, contrapuntally efficient music of J. J. Fux, Francesco Tuma, Georg Christoph Wagenseil, the two Reutters and a score of lesser names. When a particularly magnificent *Te Deum* was given, there were sometimes two and three choirs of trumpets and timpani – an old Venetian custom which we sometimes find even in instrumental music of the period (Georg Reutter Jr., Carlos d'Ordoñez). Later (1754), a Papal decree would ban the use of trumpets and timpani, which the people adored, and we shall see that their return in 1767 was joyfully acclaimed.[1]

The great organ in the west choir had been completely rebuilt in 1730 by Gottfried Sonnholtzer, the expense being borne by the former sacristan of the Cathedral who had later made a fortune in the liquor trade. This enormous organ was used only on special occasions, for example on the arrival and departure of the Court and on the anniversary of the donor's death. There were three other organs, situated in various parts of the Cathedral, all of which (insofar as they survived until then) were destroyed in 1945.

Haydn now became a minute cog in the ponderous, complex machinery of a great European cathedral. He took part in solemn Masses, short Masses, requiems, Te Deums, *rorate* ceremonies for Advent, great processions – all the busy life of a metropolitan church which was also the parish church for many in the neighbourhood. We have seen that soon Haydn began to participate in ceremonies outside the cathedral that required the members of Reutter's *Capelle*, at Schönbrunn Castle, Klosterneuburg Abbey, and at the palaces of the nobility. The following Chronicle attempts to give a limited selection of events that took place in Vienna during the years when Haydn was a boy chorister.

———

The fifty-fifth birthday of the Emperor Charles VI was celebrated at the New Favorita, an Imperial conceit near Vienna, on 1 October 1740. Five days later he suffered an attack of the 'flying gout', but he nevertheless went to a shooting party at Halbthurn, an estate now within Austria on the Hungarian border (it later belonged to the Archduchess Marie Christine and her consort, who used to visit Eszterháza from there). On the evening of 9 October Charles VI, who had caught a cold while stalking a deer, ate three helpings of a favourite dish, mushrooms stewed in Catalan oil. He was taken ill in the night, and it was decided to move him to Vienna. The Emperor, however, wanted to be taken to his beloved New Favorita. At dawn on 20 October he died. Voltaire referred to the event as the 'pot of mushrooms [*'plat de champignons'*] that changed the history of Europe'. The historian Robert Pick closes the account with the words 'Maria Theresa, four months gone with child, was twenty-three years old. She was wholly ignorant of the affairs of the dominions to which she had fallen heir.'[2]

Haydn, newly arrived from Hainburg, will have been witness to the commemorative ceremony at St Stephen's – the Emperor was buried in the Capuchin Church on the Neue Markt, and his heart was deposited in the Loretto Chapel of the Augustinian Church (opposite the great Lobkowitz Palace), while St Stephen's received the monarch's entrails in a silver container. The funeral of an Austrian emperor was always an occasion of awesome ceremony, and it is certain that Haydn

1 *Haydn at Eszterháza 1766–1790*, pp. 137f.
2 *Empress Maria Theresa*, New York 1966, pp. 54–6.

never forgot the huge requiem service in the Cathedral to which he was now bound. Although he never composed music for a requiem service himself, some faint echoes of the impersonal mourning, and the personal comfort of the beautiful words, may be felt in the *Libera* that he was to write for a great-hearted Italian lady (who was his princess) half a century later.

Twelve hours later, Charles VI's daughter, the beautiful Archduchess Maria Theresa, in deep mourning, with a veil over her hair and a fan tightly clutched in her hands, addressed her ministers. Her consort, Francis Stephen, was beside her. The future Queen of Hungary and Bohemia and Archduchess of Austria instantly won the hearts of her kneeling ministers; she was soon to bind to her Imperial heart even the recalcitrant Hungarians when, mounted upon a magnificent coal-black stallion, and wearing the trappings of her coronation ceremony, she galloped up a hill outside Pressburg and brandished her sword toward the four quarters of the globe.[1]

On 13 February 1741 died the *doyen* of Austrian music, the great theorist and composer Johann Joseph Fux, Imperial Court Chapel Master, at the age of eighty. He was buried at St Stephen's next to his wife who had predeceased him by ten years; and on this occasion, too, Haydn participated in the great requiem service.

On 24 February 1741 Mathias Haydn became village magistrate (*Marktrichter*) of Rohrau and retained this position until his death. His duties, which basically consisted in his acting as a go-between between the Harrachs and the town, required him to make fairly frequent trips to Vienna, beginning in 1741, when he will have had the chance to see his son in the *Capellhaus*.

On 13 March there was great rejoicing in Vienna: to Maria Theresa was born a healthy boy-child who would become the Emperor Joseph II. The streets of Vienna were illuminated, and also on 23/24 April when she, accompanied by the Papal Nuncio Paolucci and the Archduchesses Maria Anna and Maria Magdalena, appeared in public for the first time after the birth, driving in an open carriage through the streets of Vienna to the joyous shouts of the populace. St Stephen's participated with a grand *Te Deum*, with trumpets and kettledrums.

No one knows why Antonio Vivaldi was in Vienna, where he arrived shortly before Charles VI died. Perhaps he had hoped for further signs of Imperial favour (Charles liked Vivaldi and his music and in 1728 the Emperor, while in Trieste, 'talked to Vivaldi a long time about music, they say that he has said more to him alone in a fortnight than he says to his ministers in two years').[2] Now he died in extreme poverty and was buried on 28 July in the cemetery of the Bürgerspital.

> Only nineteen florins and forty-five kreuzer were spent on the funeral, and he was ... entitled [merely] to the *Kleingeläut* or pauper's peals of bells, which ... cost [but] two florins and thirty-six kreuzer. He had six pall-bears and six choirboys, too, but one sees how mean ... [it] was when same records reveal that a nobleman's funeral might cost at least one hundred florins. Vivaldi, to die in this way, who had known the splendour of Venice in its prime!
>
> [Alan Kendall, op. cit., p. 93]

Six choir-boys ... The records of St Stephen's include the account-book in use at the time of Vivaldi's death (facsimile in Kendall, 93). Is it perhaps far-fetched to imagine young Joseph Haydn and his five fellow members of the *Cantorei* as the six choir-boys who gave Vivaldi's remains their last musical blessing? It seems almost certain. Here

---

1 Pick, op. cit., pp. 57, 85.
2 Alan Kendall, *Vivaldi*, London 1978, p. 73.

was the first great musician, the beginning of a long line, who died in shameful poverty before, as it were, Haydn's very eyes – Haydn,

> Whose Eyes have wept o'er every Friend laid low;
> Drag'd lingering on from partial Death to Death,
> Till dying all he can resign is Breath.[1]

It was during the Pentecost services at Schönbrunn in the year 1745 that the Empress caught the young Haydn climbing on the scaffolding and had him soundly thrashed (*supra*, p. 43); it was in this year, too, that Haydn's younger brother Johann Michael arrived in Vienna to become a choir-boy at the *Cantorei*.

The feast day (15 November) of the patron saint of Lower Austria – St Leopold – is still celebrated with great style at Klosterneuburg Abbey; on this occasion in 1748, the Empress and her suite were, as usual, honoured guests of the venerable monastery. The young Empress, with her consort Francis Stephen, arrived on Thursday 14 November; also in attendance were Duke Charles and Princess Charlotte of Lorraine. That evening the Court heard Vespers in the abbey church; the next day – 'Leopoldi-Tag' – the Empress paid her respects at the saint's tomb in the abbey. High Mass was celebrated, at which she noted with pleasure the performance of a new boy soloist (soprano) – Michael Haydn, who shone especially by comparison with his brother Joseph ('er krähe', he crowed), and whose performance brought him a reward of 24 ducats, as we have seen from Dies's account, *supra*. In the *Biographische Skizze* (Schinn-Otter, p. 6) of Michael Haydn, the same story is related independently (*Skizze* 1808; Dies 1810) but slightly differently: Michael receives the twenty-four ducats with the proviso 'to ask for a favour' ('eine Gnade auszubitten'), whereupon the boy asked for permission to send half the money to his 'poor, good father'.

On 22 October 1749 there was celebrated the fiftieth anniversary of priesthood by the Cardinal Archbishop Sigismund Count von Kollonicz. All the bells of every church in Vienna joyously greeted the great prince of the church in the morning, whose honour was celebrated in a gigantic procession with two choirs of trumpets and kettledrums. Joseph Haydn was (though he knew it not) singing for the last time in the beautiful 'Asperges me' and (perhaps one of the greatest of all Gregorian chants) 'Veni, sancte Spiritus'. Archduke Joseph, aged eight, Archduchess Maria Anna (the Empress's sister) and Princess Charlotte of Lorraine (Francis's sister) were at High Mass. Thereupon the Cardinal himself intoned the words of the Te Deum, and afterwards went to the Imperial Oratory of the Cathedral to bless the assembled all-highest members of the Court.

Haydn himself gave the date of the MS. parts of his *Missa brevis in F a due soprani* now in the Esterházy Archives as 1749, and we see no reason to doubt the dating, even if it was added by the composer towards the end of his life, when he had 'rediscovered' the work. And we believe, moreover, that it was composed especially for Joseph himself and his brother Michael as the two soprano soloists. It must have been about the same time, too, that Joseph composed his *Missa brevis* in G 'alla cappella' ('Rorate coeli desuper'), for the *Gnadenbild Capelle* of the Cathedral. For the musical aspects of these two youthful Masses, *vide infra*, pp. 139ff. and 145ff.

It was, insofar as the sources allow a precise dating, in November 1749 that Haydn was cast into the friendless streets of Vienna to earn his bread as best he could. In summing up this period of Haydn's life, we prefer to use the composer's own words.

---

1 James Thomson, autograph. Lyttleton Papers, Sotheby's sale catalogue of 12 December 1978, item 133 (facsimile, p. 159).

On 22 May 1808, the Esterházy *Capelle* in Eisenstadt made a guest appearance in Vienna, performing a Mass by Hummel and a vesper by Fuchs in the Chapel of the Ursuline Sisters in the Johannesgasse. The performance was repeated on 29 May. The visit itself falls into the last period of Haydn's life and is treated in this biography in the appropriate place;[1] but one quotation has been reserved for this early period.[2] Haydn made the following address to the princely choir-boys:

> I was once a choir-boy, Reutter took me from Hainburg to St Stephen's in Vienna. I was diligent. When my comrades went to play, I took my little *Clavierl* [portable clavichord without legs] under my arm and went up to the attic, where I could practice on it undisturbed. When I sang solo, the baker next to St Stephen's always gave me a bun [*Kipfel*] as a present. Go on being good and diligent, and never forget about God. [Pohl I, 68]

> I never had real teachers. My beginning was always with the practical – first in singing and playing instruments, after that in composition. In the latter I listened to the works of others rather than studied: but I also heard the most beautiful and finest in every *genre* that existed in those days. And in those days there were many such in Vienna, so many! I remembered and sought to put to good use those things that appeared particularly excellent and to have a special effect on me. But I never merely imitated! And so it happened that what I knew and what I could accomplish grew gradually.
>
> [J. F. Rochlitz, *Für Freunde der Tonkunst*, Leipzig 1832, vol. IV, p. 274]

1 *Haydn: the Late Years 1801–1809*, p. 366.
2 For this period, Pohl (I, pp. 27–78) is still not only invaluable but is also our principal source for the organization of the Cathedral and for the Chronicle as well. The destruction of the Cathedral in 1945 has possibly inhibited any further research in its music history, though many records, and some of the music, survive.

Part II: Chronicle 1750–1756

The Documents
(for numbered notes see end of relevant document)

(1) Autobiography 1776:

... Finally I lost my voice, and then had to eke out a wretched existence for eight whole years, by teaching young pupils (many geniuses are ruined by their having to earn their daily bread, because they have no time to study): I experienced this, too, and would have never learnt what little I did, had I not, in my zeal for composition, composed well into the night; I wrote diligently, but not quite correctly, until at last I had the good fortune to learn the true fundamentals of composition from the celebrated Herr Porpora[1](who was at that time in Vienna).

Note:
1   Nicola Antonio Porpora (1686–1768), a celebrated composer, especially of vocal music.

(2) Griesinger:

... Soon after his departure from the Choir School, Haydn made a pilgrimage to Mariazell.[1] In his pocket he had several motets which he had composed and asked the *Regens chori* there for permission to put out the parts in the church and sing them. This request was refused, and in order to gain a hearing he had recourse to a trick on the following day. He put himself behind the boy who was to sing the alto part and offered him a seventeen-kreuzer piece to give up his place to him; but the boy, fearing the director, did not dare make the bargain, whereupon Haydn reached swiftly over the boy's head, seized the music from the stand and sang to general satisfaction. The *Regens chori* made a collection of sixteen gulden and sent the optimistic lad back to Vienna with the sum in his pocket.

Haydn was dismissed from the Choir School in his sixteenth year[2] because his voice had broken; he could not hope for the least support from his poor parents and thus was obliged to make his own way simply by his talents. He took lodgings in a wretched garret (in the house No. 1220 in the Michaelerplatz)[3] in Vienna, without a stove, and where he was barely protected from the rain. Deprived of life's comforts, he divided his whole time among giving lessons, studying his art and performing. He played for money in evening serenades and in the orchestras, and studied composition diligently, for 'when I was sitting at my old, worm-eaten spinet [*Klavier*] I envied no king his lot'. About this time Haydn came upon the first six sonatas of Emanuel Bach;[4] 'I did not leave my clavier until I had played them through, and whoever knows me thoroughly must discover that I owe a great deal to Emanuel Bach, that I understood him and have studied him with diligence. Emanuel Bach once paid me a compliment on that score himself.'

In the same house wherein Joseph Haydn was quartered there also lived the famous poet Metastasio.[5] He was educating a Fräulein Martinez. Haydn had to give her singing and harpsichord lessons, in return for which he received free board for three years. At Metastasio's Haydn was also introduced to the then aged *Kapellmeister* Porpora. Porpora gave voice lessons to the mistress of the Venetian ambassador, Correr, and since Porpora was too grand and too fond of his ease to accompany her on the fortepiano himself, he entrusted this business to our Giuseppe. 'There was no want of *Asino*, *Coglione*, *Birbante* and pokes in the ribs; but I put up with all of it because I greatly profited from Porpora in singing, in composition and in the Italian language.' Correr went in the summer with the lady to the then much frequented baths at Mannersdorf,[6] not far from Bruk [*sic*]; Porpora also went there to continue the lessons and took Haydn with him. For three months Haydn acted as Porpora's servant, eating at Correr's officers' table and receiving six ducats a month. Here he sometimes had to accompany on the keyboard [*Klavier*] for Porpora at a Prince von Hildburghausen's,[7] in the presence of Gluck, Wagenseil and other celebrated masters; and the approval of such connoisseurs was a special encouragement to him.

The author was told by a very reliable source that the violinist Misliwezech,[8] a Bohemian by birth, had heard some quartets performed during his stay in Milan; and when they told him that the composer was Johann Baptista Sammartini,[9] then a man of seventy, he had cried out in utter astonishment, 'At last I know Haydn's precursor, and the model on which he patterned himself!' It seemed to me worthwhile to investigate this statement more closely, since I had never heard Haydn's originality doubted, especially in his quartets. So I enquired of Haydn if he had known Sammartini's works in his youth, and what he thought of that *compositeur*. Haydn told me that he had in fact heard Sammartini's music but he had never valued it, 'for Sammartini was a scribbler [*Schmierer*]'. He laughed heartily when I produced Misliwezech's supposed discovery, and said he recognized only Emanuel Bach as his prototype ... [pp. 11f.]

In the beginning Haydn received only two gulden a month for giving lessons, but gradually the price rose to five gulden, so that he was able to look about for more suitable quarters. When he was living in the Seilerstadt [Seilerstätte], all his few possessions were stolen. Haydn wrote to his parents, asking them to send some linen to make a few shirts; his father came to Vienna, brought his son a seventeen-kreuzer coin and the advice, 'Fear God, and love thy neighbour!' Haydn soon saw his loss restored by the generosity of good friends; one had a dark suit made for him, another gave him shirts [*Wäsche*, also underclothing] etc., and Haydn recovered through a stay of two months with Baron Fürnberg that cost him nothing. In this period Haydn was also leader of the orchestra in the Convent of the Hospitallers [*Barmherzige Brüder*][10] in the Leopoldstadt, at sixty gulden a year. Here he had to be in the church at eight o'clock in the morning on Sundays and feast days, and at ten o'clock he played the organ in what was then the chapel of Count Haugwitz,[11] and at eleven o'clock he sang at St Stephen's. He was paid seventeen kreuzer for each service. In the evenings, Haydn often went 'gassatim'[12] with his musical comrades, when one of his compositions was usually performed, and he recalled having composed a quintet[13] for that purpose in the year 1753.

Once he went to serenade the wife of Kurz,[14] a comic actor very popular at that time and usually called 'Bernadon'. Kurz came into the street and asked for the *compositeur* of the music just performed. Hardly had Haydn, who was then about nineteen, identified himself when Kurz urged him to write an opera for him. In vain Haydn pleaded his youth; Kurz encouraged him, and Haydn actually composed the Opera, *Der krumme Teufel* – a satire on the lame theatre director Affligio,[15] on whose account it was banned after the third performance.

Haydn liked to linger over the history of his first operatic composition, because it reminded him of Bernadon's many comic traits. Harlequin fled from the waves in *Der krumme Teufel*; to illustrate this, Bernadon lay down at full length across several chairs and imitated all the movements of a swimmer. 'See me swimming! See me swimming!', cried Kurz to Haydn, sitting at the keyboard [*Klavier*], who immediately fell into six-eight time, to the poet's great satisfaction. – When Haydn had finished his Opera, he brought it to Kurz. The maid wanted to send him away because her master was at his studies. But through a window in the door Haydn, to his astonishment, saw Bernadon standing before a large mirror, grimacing and performing the most ridiculous contortions with his hands and feet. Those were the studies of Herr Bernadon. – Haydn received four and twenty ducats for the Opera, a sum which at that time he considered made him a rich man.

Apart from performing and teaching, Haydn was indefatigable in his composing. Many of his easy harpsichord lessons [*Klaviersonaten*], trios, and so on belong to this period, and he generally took into consideration the needs and capacities of his pupils. Only a few of the originals remained in his possession: he gave them away and considered it an honour when they were accepted; he was not aware of the fact that the music dealers were doing a good business with them, and he loitered with pleasure in front of the shops where the one or the other of his works in print were displayed. . . .[16]   [pp. 13f.]

Notes:

1 The vast pilgrimage church in Styria, dedicated to Our Lady, is still Austria's most popular. For Haydn's private thank-offerings to the friendly monks at Mariazell, and Our Lady (for Whom the church is named, 'Maria Zell'), see *Haydn at Eszterháza 1766–1790*, pp. 120ff., 467. The *Regens chori* at that time was P. Florian Wrastil (Pohl I, 121).

2 Surely too early (1757/8).

3 The house, next to St Michael's Church, still exists, but has been slightly altered since then.

4 Rochlitz (op. cit.) quotes Haydn as saying, 'I played them over for my own pleasure countless times, especially when I was burdened by cares or discouraged, and they always cheered me up and I left the instrument in a good mood.' In 1742, C. P. E. Bach's so-called 'Prussian' Sonatas, *Sei Sonate per cembalo*, dedicated to Frederick the Great, were published in Nuremberg.

5 Pietro Metastasio (1698–1782), Imperial Court Poet, who lived for fifty-three years in the house and died there. In 1779 Haydn would set to music his text of *L'isola disabitata*. About Martinez, *vide supra*, p.46.

6 Bad Mannersdorf is still a modest but successful spa.

7 Joseph Friedrich, Prince von Sachsen-Hildburghausen (1702–87), who befriended Dittersdorf

and was himself a well-known general and man-of-politics. See Chapter II of Dittersdorf's *Lebensbeschreibung*.

8 Joseph Misliweczek (Mislivicek, 1737–81), whose operas were performed successfully in Italy and who was a friend of the Mozart family.

9 Giovanni Battista Sammartini (1701–75), about whom *vide infra*, p. 69.

10 The Church and Hospital still flourish.

11 Friedrich Wilhelm, Count Haugwitz, who held a ministerial position at Court.

12 'gassatim' is believed to have its origin in the word 'Gasse' (little street) and to have been manipulated into the piece of music, 'Gassatio' = 'Cassatio'. The term's origin has been the subject of much speculation, largely idle.

13 Believed to be the Quintet in G (II:2), of which there is a Berlin MS. dated 1754; *vide infra*, p. 180.

14 Johann Joseph Felix Kurz (theatrical name: Bernadon; 1717–84), *vide infra*, pp. 67, 69, 72. His first wife was Franziska (died 1755).

15 Giuseppe Afflisio (*recte*; *c.* 1720–1787); vide infra, pp. 77f.

16 Haydn's works were not printed until 1764 – and then, moreover, by publishers in Paris. Perhaps Griesinger means that handwritten copies were placed on display.

(3) Dies, 24 April 1805:

... My readers recognize how little Haydn dared to exploit his own knowledge. When, sometimes in company with his two musical brothers, he visited their parents in Rohrau, they would sing just as they had ten or twelve years before. The father did not allow them to rob him of his right to accompany his favourite songs. It was just like old times, but with one exception, in that the sons often thought their father made mistakes and sought to correct him accordingly. Usually little arguments ensued, wherein the father always cited someone who had taught him this or that song in his youth; and every time he most firmly declared that there was a man who really knew. On the other hand, the sons always cited *Kapellmeister* Reutern [*sic*]: 'He said so, and he ought to know.' Neither party would concede, each repeating his proof until the father, annoyed, ended the dispute with the firm words, 'You're all asses.'

Joseph was silent not merely to honour his father but because he mistrusted his own knowledge. This tormenting mistrust arose from Haydn's new situation. He saw himself sunk in misery; he found it difficult to procure even the barest necessities. Thus he cast searching glances at other young musicians and asked himself, 'Why the great difference between them and me?' It could not take long for such a youth, endowed as he was with so great a musical instinct and in possession, moreover, of natural common-sense, to find the answer to that question. Pride was a stranger to him; it had never allowed him to dream of imagined merits, and so he was in no danger of being disappointed. Blinded neither by self-love, by pride, nor by prejudice, he – seeking the truth – was enabled to make an important discovery:

> Beharrlichkeit im Fleiß führt zu der Weisen Ziel,
> Wo endlich wir uns selbst erkennen müssen.
> O! herrlich ist der Lohn. Glaubt, wir erlernten Viel,
> Wenn wir bemerken: daß wir gar Nichts wissen.

Haydn made this important discovery in a small, dark garret under the eaves on the fifth floor of the Michaelerhaus on the Kohlmarkt. The total loneliness of the place, the complete lack of anything to encourage a spirit unemployed, and his altogether desperate situation led him to speculation of such a serious nature that he felt obliged to take refuge in his worm-ridden spinet [*Klavier*] or his violin to play away his cares. Once these speculations were so serious, or rather his hunger so strongly plagued him, that against all inclination he decided to enter the Servite Order[1] simply in order to eat his fill. But this was just his first impulse which, considering his disposition, could hardly be translated into reality. Only melancholy minds, crushed by the confluence of outward events, can become the unhappy victims of their irritated senses. Haydn's happy and naturally optimistic temperament saved him from the worst fits of melancholy. If the rain in summer, and the snow in winter, entered the chinks in his garret and he awoke soaked through or covered with snow, he found such occurrences quite natural and made a cheerful joke of everything.

The following merry scenes belong approximately to the period shortly before or after Haydn's departure from the Choir School. The episode will acquaint my readers even more with Haydn's youthful, cheery humour.

For some time after his departure Haydn knew not which way to turn; he planned a thousand projects which he discarded at their inception. If he occasionally made a sudden resolve, the motive was hunger, and one time he decided to make a pilgrimage to Maria Zell. As soon as he had arrived, Haydn sent to the chorus master, announced himself as a pupil from the Choir School, produced a few compositions he had brought with him, and offered his services as. singer. The chorus master did not believe him, refused his offer, and when Haydn persisted, dismissed him with these words: 'All kinds of riffraff from Vienna show up here pretending to be discharged choir-boys, and when the time comes they can't sing a single note properly.'

There was, then, nothing to be done along those lines. Therefore the next day Haydn went into the church, went up to the choir-loft with the singers, struck up an acquaintance with one of them, looked through the sheet of music in his hand, and asked to retain it so he could sing it. The young man apologized, saying that he didn't dare. Haydn made another attempt, pressing a coin into his hand, and continued standing near him until the music began and the young singer was supposed to sing. Suddenly Haydn tore the music from his hands and sang so beautifully that the chorus master was astonished and, after the music was over, apologized to Haydn. The clergy sent to enquire after the name of that clever singer, and to invite him to dine. Haydn was right pleased to accept the invitation, which he stretched to eight days and – as he said – filled his stomach for some time to come.

Haydn once took it into his head to invite a number of musicians for an evening serenade [*Nachtmusik*]. The rendezvous was in the Tiefer Graben,[2] where the musicians were to place themselves, some in front of houses and some in corners. There was even a kettledrummer on the high bridge. Most of the players had no idea why they had been summoned, and each had been told to play whatever he wanted. Hardly had this hideous concert begun when the astonished residents of the Tiefer Graben opened their windows and began to scold, to hiss and to whistle at the accursed music from hell. Meanwhile the watchmen, or as they were then called, the *Rumorknechte*,[3] appeared. The players escaped in time, except the kettledrummer and a violinist, both of whom were led away under arrest; however, they were set at liberty after a few days since they could not name the ringleader.

The well-known Ditters[4] and Haydn were youthful friends. Once the two were roaming the streets at night and stopped in front of a common beer hall in which half drunken and sleepy musicians were miserably fiddling away at a Haydn minuet. In those days Haydn composed pieces for the dance halls that, because of their originality, were much in favour.

'Hey, let's go in!', said Haydn.

'In we go!', Ditters agreed.

Into the beer hall they go. Haydn places himself next to the first violinist and asks off-handedly, 'Who wrote that minuet?' The latter answers, still more drily, indeed sharply. 'By Haydn!' Haydn goes and stands in front of him says with feigned wrath, 'That's a pig of a minuet!' – 'What, what, what?' yells the violinist, now in a rage himself, jumping out of his seat, followed by the other players, who are about to break their instruments over Haydn's head; and they would have, too, if Ditters, who was a big man, had not put up his arms to shield Haydn and shoved him out the door.'   [Dies, pp. 32–7]

[9 May 1805:] I reminded Haydn of the garret and asked him to tell me how he escaped from it.

'It happened', Haydn began, 'that I made the acquaintance of the celebrated *Kapellmeister* Porpora, who was much in demand as a teacher, but who, perhaps because of his age, was looking for a young assistant and found one in me. Among Porpora's pupils was a young girl between seven and nine years old. The famous Metastasio was the benefactor of this girl[5] and her mother; he was educating her at his own expense, and Porpora gave her singing lessons.'

The old Porpora made use of young Haydn at these lessons, and Haydn was glad to undertake the task, regardless of the distance; he was now lucky enough to earn two gulden a month. While Porpora taught the girl singing, Haydn, who had to accompany on the keyboard [*Klavier*], found it a useful opportunity to gain a perfect knowledge of, and practice in, the Italian method of singing and accompanying.

Porpora was a man who was severe with Haydn who, for his part, was happy to put up with it all and bore the pokes in the ribs and the epithets 'Bestia! – C[oglione]!' with submission; he even cleaned the shoes when he had to accompany Porpora to the country during the summer months. Haydn was glad to suffer all this because he learned so much from the man.

Haydn's fortunes now seemed to be taking a turn for the better. He was introduced to Metastasio, who gave him much useful advice and in whose house he soon learned the Italian language. About this time he also made the acquaintance of an honest *bourgeois* family[6] in the stocking business who, without being well-to-do or even protected from want themselves, nevertheless did their best to help Haydn. Haydn told the mother about the holes in the roof under which he slept and joked about the snow on his bedclothes. But although he had only intended to laugh at his troubles, the good woman took a more serious view; she was touched, and offered the young Haydn her own bedroom to sleep in during the winters. Haydn was pleased to accept, with the secret hope that he would soon be in a position to return this great service.*

Since the poor woman had only the most essential furnishings, however, the floor had to take the place of a bed; and thus it was that Haydn found at least a warm place ready for him on any winter evening.

Haydn watched with pleasure the improvement in his situation. That which lay closest to his heart, however, was to make use of the important discovery I have mentioned earlier, and by a serious study of theory to enable him to bring order (which, as we know, he loved above all else) into the products of his mind. He decided to buy a good book; but which? That he could not answer: he also had his reasons why he asked no one for advice. Since he was unable to choose, he left it almost to chance, planning at first to leaf through the book a little so as to judge it before perhaps uselessly spending the income of an entire month for it. Haydn ventured to walk into a bookshop to ask for a good theoretical textbook. The bookseller named the writings of Carl Philipp Emanuel Bach as the newest and

---

* [Original footnote:] Haydn's wish was soon realized. The woman grew poor; he helped her and settled on her a monthly pension which, even after her death, was transferred to her daughter for some thirty years, until her own death. Not Haydn, but his servant [Johann Elssler], furnished this information.

best.[7] Haydn wanted to see it, to persuade himself; he began to read, understood, found that which he had sought, paid for the book, and took it away with great delight.

That Haydn sought to make Bach's principles his own, that he studied them untiringly, can be seen even in his youthful works of that period. Haydn wrote in his nineteenth year quartets[8] that made him known to connoisseurs of music as a genius with knowledge of composition: Haydn had understood *that* quickly. As time went on, he produced Bach's later writings. In his opinion Bach's writings are the best, most thorough and most useful textbook ever published.

As soon as Haydn's musical products became known in print, Bach noted with pleasure that he could number Haydn among his pupils; afterwards he paid the latter the flattering compliment that he was the only one completely to understand his writings and to know how to put them to use.

Haydn had left a great deal to chance in the purchase of the work. Fortune smiled at him broadly; she placed in his hands the highest trump card among so many deuces. But this kind of procedure is not to be recommended and in the majority of cases is likely to cancel out the advantages one hoped for. Haydn's action was not, however, altogether blindly undertaken; he did not purchase before he had inspected; he could already trust his common sense to make the right decision. Still, his common sense could have led him astray if he had happened to come upon works like Kirnberger's[9] rather than Bach's, for they might have pleased him and yet in a certain fashion harm him. But far from finding fault with Kirnberger's writings in general, I shall cite Haydn's own opinion. He described them as 'a thorough and strict piece of work; but too timid, too confining, far too many little restrictions for a free spirit.' – I said, 'Like tight clothes and shoes, in which a man can't move, can't walk.' 'That's it exactly', was Haydn's answer.

The second textbook that Haydn later bought was Mattheson's[10] [*Der*] *vollkommene Kapellmeister*. He found that the principles in this work were no longer new to him but that they were good; the written-out examples, however, were dry and tasteless. Haydn set himself the task of rewriting all the examples in this book. He retained the whole framework, even the identical number of notes, and invented new melodies for it.

Haydn now added to his library the textbook by Fux.[11] He found nothing in it to enlarge the scope of his knowledge; but he liked the method and the approach, and made use of it with his pupils at that time.

The reader can easily imagine that our Haydn now had but little spare time. His hours passed with giving lessons and studying. Everything had to be connected with music, and that is why no other book came into his hands in those days; the only exception was Metastasio's poems. And even they cannot be called an exception, for Metastasio always wrote with music in mind; his works were epochal, and any *Kapellmeister* who intended to try his hand at an opera would have to know them.

It is quite natural that in a country bordering on Italy, Italian opera flourished, while no care was taken with the German language. North Germany certainly wrote a purer language and had great poets, but did it not take a long while until its southern parts took cognizance, recognized, and followed suit? Thus one can hardly wonder that Haydn was not quick to acquaint himself with the German poets and writers of that period. But that he possesses a sense and intuition for the qualities of seriousness, greatness, beauty, wit and the naïve in German poetry can be seen in his choice of the German *Lieder* he later set to music.

Haydn was about in his twenty-first year when he set to music a German comic opera. This first product for the stage was entitled *Der krumme Teufel* and came to pass in a curious fashion. Kurz, a genius in the field of German theatre, was then performing in the old theatre at the Carinthian Gate [Kärntnerthortheater]; in his role as Bernadon he delighted the public. He had heard the young Haydn spoken of with great praise, and that incited him to get an introduction. A happy accident soon gave him the opportunity he was looking for. Kurz had a beautiful wife who condescended to receive nocturnal serenades from young musicians. Haydn, too, waited on her with his serenade, which not only she but Kurz considered an honour. He sought a better acquaintance with Haydn. The two came together; Haydn had to go to Kurz's home. 'Sit down at the harpsichord [*Flügel*] and accompany the pantomime that I shall now act for you with some suitable music. Imagine that Bernadon has fallen into the water and is trying to save himself by swimming.' He then called his servant, throws himself on his stomach across the chair, made the servant pull the chair to and fro round the room while he [Kurz] made swimming motions with arms and legs, all the while Haydn was miming the waves and the swimming in six-eight time. Suddenly Bernadon jumps up, embraces Haydn and nearly smothers him with kisses. 'Haydn! You're the man for me! You've got to write an opera for me!' And in this fashion *Der krumme Teufel* came into being. Haydn received 25 ducats for it and considered himself rich.

This Opera was performed twice with great success, and thereafter it was forbidden because of offensive and libellous references in the text.

[11 May 1805:] ... The reader is already acquainted with Haydn's mode of living and day-to-day affairs up to now. He gave music lessons and devoted the rest of his time to his own studies, also giving special attention to perfecting his instrumental technique. He studied under a famous virtuoso whose name escapes me, and became a good violin player; for some time he filled the post of organist in some church in the suburbs; he wrote quartets and other pieces that won him increasing favour with the connoisseurs, and soon he was everywhere recognized as a genius. ...   [Dies, pp. 32–44; letterspaced words ignored]

Notes:
1 Haydn nevertheless remained attached to the Servite Order: it was in the Vienna Chapter of the Order that his *Missa brevis* in F was 'rediscovered' in 1805. See also *Haydn: the Late Years 1801–1809*, pp. 338f., 335.
2 Tiefer Graben is in the old part (inner city) of Vienna and the high bridge still exists.
3 A kind of police force – in modern parlance, 'riot squad'.
4 Carl Ditters, later von Dittersdorf, about whom *vide infra*, p. 388.
5 Martinez, *vide supra*,
6 The Buchhol(t)z family: Haydn left 100 gulden to the granddaughter: *The Late Years 1801–1809*. p. 53, no. 58. p. 46, n. 1.
7 C. P. E. Bach's famous *Versuch über die wahre Art das Clavier zu spielen*, Berlin 1753 (facsimile reprint, edited by L. Hoffmann-Erbrecht, Leipzig 1957. The second part (*Zweyter Theil*) came out in 1762 (also Berlin, and also included in the 1957 facsimile).
8 It is, as shall be demonstrated below, very doubtful if Haydn was writing quartets so early (1751).
9 J. P. Kirnberger (1721–83). Haydn might have been referring to *Die Kunst des reinen Satzes in der Musik ...*, Berlin 1771.
10 *Vide supra*, p. 38 and p. 39, note 5.
11 *Supra*, p. 38.

(4) Extracts[1] from Carpani:

Fra i maestri di Vienna non v'era pel nostro giovinetto l'uomo sì generoso che volesse coltivare gratuitamente quest' ingegno sconosciuto. Doveva dunque

1 In order to reduce the tiresomely verbose Carpani to manageable size, we have here omitted (1) those sections where he digresses completely; (2) those many sections when it seems that Carpani's information is taken straight from Dies or Griesinger.

rimanere incolto? Oh deplorabile disgrazia! No amico: chè anzi fortuna fu questa di non trovar maestri, e fortuna, vi replico, da benedire. ... *Haydn*, con un maestro, avrebbe evitato alcuni errori ne' quali cadde poi scrivendo per la chiesa e pel teatro; ma replico, sarebbe riuscito meno originale nel tutto. ...   [pp. 25f.]

... Che poi non fosse scolare del *Porpora*, lo mostrano li suoi *recitativi* parlanti, i quali sono di tanto inferiori a quelli di quel padre del *recitativo*. Apprese però dal *Porpora* la buona ed italiana maniera di cantare e quella pure d'accompagnare a cembalo, mestiere molto più scabroso di quello che si crede, e che pochi fra i maestri medesimi possedono perfettamente. ...

[Porpora, Haydn e l'amica del Ambasciatore Correr andavano ai bagni di Mannersdorf] ... che godevano allora di qualche voga. Il nostro Giuseppe, la cui bella era quel lurido napoletano stizzoso, si mise a far di tutto per entrargli in grazia ed ottenerne i sospirati armonici favori. La mattina per tempo *Haydn* balzava dal letto e spazzava l'abito, puliva le scarpe del *Porpora* e gli raffazzonava la decrepita parrucca; in una parola egli era il *jaquet* [*sc.* lacchè] del *Porpora*. Questi, uomo poco socievole ed oltremodo rozzo di maniere, gli regalava in premio qualche *ciuccio*; ma vendendosi servito per nulla, e conoscendo nel povero giovinetto molta disposizione e gran brama d'istruirsi, si lasciava commovere a sbalzi, e gli dava qualche buon lume e precetto, sia pel canto, sia per l'accompagnamento, massimamente che doveva accompagnare spesso le difficili sue composizioni, piene di modulazione dotte e di *bassi* non facili a indovinarsi. Di questa fatta, siccome i scavatori delle miniere non isdegnano d'andar curvi e di lordarsi per entro alle viscere della terra onde scoprire le gemme e l'oro, il tante volte battezzato per *ciuccio* [*sc.* ciuco] s'arricchì del sapere del *Porpora*, ed a forza di pazienza e di strapazzi ben impiegati, imparò il buon metodo del cantare italiano. La casa di Venezia non gli recò questo solo vantaggio della conoscenza del *Porpora*; ma un altro glie ne diede opportunissimo nelle circonstanze in cui si trovava. Quell'ambasciatore gli assegnò sei zecchini al mese e la tavola. Oltre di ciò l'*Haydn* destinato a combattere contro la miseria e l'ignoranza, avendo la mattina libera, si procacciava altri guadagni. Suonava cioè il *violino primo* [etc.]. ...

[pp. 28–30]

L'*Haydn* non contento di quanto aveva imparato nel suo *Fux* e nelle partiture del *Bach*, si era posto di buon'ora ad osservare attentissimamente l'effetto de'tuoni, e secondando i consigli sempre sicuri del suo perfettissimo orecchio, aveva trovato, per servirmi della sua frase, *ciò che fa bene, ciò che fa meglio, e ciò che fa male*: e qui dirò di passaggio che quando gli si domandava ragione di un accordo, di una passata, di un passo piuttosto assegnato ad uno stromento che all'altro, o d'altri simili stratagemmi felici, egli non soleva addurne altra che la succitata. = L'ho fatto perchè fa bene = Ma ciò che parrà strano, ed è verissimo, si è ch'egli, erigendo queste sue osservazioni in regole, ne aveva, per via di certi suoi calcoli numerici, stabilito un metodo con cui reggeva l'artificio della sua composizione. Il valente maestro Giuseppe *Weigl*, stato per qualche tempo suo scolare, mi assicurò più volte che l'*Haydn* non volle mai comunicar ad alcuno questo suo magico ritrovato, e quando ne veniva pregato, rispondeva sorridendo = provatevi e trovatelo. = ...[1]   [p. 38f.]

Haydn era tanto avvezzo a questo uso dei numeri e vi aveva tanto di genio che immaginò, oltre varj canoni e minuetti capricciosissimi de' quali parleremo a suo luogo, quel giuoco filharmonico, mercè di cui, traendo a sorte i numeri a cui corrispondono diversi passi, si può anche, da chi non ha idea di contrappunto, formare una serie infinita di minuetti col loro *secondo* e *basso* ...   [p. 40]

[Parlando di Sammartini] ... più volte mi disse di non dover nulla al [Sammartini], aggiungendo di più *ch'egli era un imbroglione*. Io però ne appello a chiunque vorrà imparzialmente esaminare le prime composizioni dell'*Haydn*, e confrontarle con quelle del *Sammartini*. Vedrà egli di quante idee, di quante bizzarrie e di quante invenzioni di questo rinomato scrittore si giovasse l'*Haydn*, non già da vile plagiario ma da maestro. ... Osservate nel primo *quartetto* d'*Haydn* in *Beffà*,[2] al principio della seconda parte del primo tempo, quel movimento di *secondo* e *viola*, e voi che conoscete lo stile del *Sammartini* dite se quello non gli rassomiglia; ma l'*Haydn* era troppo buon contrappuntista e troppo amico dell'ordine e di quella regolata condotta che si trova in uno stile puro e ragionato, per imitare di proposito quel capricciosissimo milanese che nel creare non badava più che tanto alla tessitura, ma seguitava all'impazzata gli impeti della sua fervida fantasia, e quindi aveva qua e là de' lampi bellissimi, contigui a masse tenebrose di nubi. ...   [pp. 56–8]

Mi resta a spiegarvi come l'*Haydn* di Vienna potesse trar profitto dai parti originali e numerosi del *Sammartini* di Milano. ... Prima del *Pallavicini*,[3] era stato governatore della Lombardía Austriaca il conte d'*Harrach*.[4] Questi aveva il primo portata a Vienna la musica del *Sammartini*, la quale subito ottenne applausi ... Il conte *Palfi*[5] gran cancelliere d'Ungheria, il conte *Schönborn*[6] e il conte di *Mortzin*,[7] facevano a gara in procurarsene della nuova, e la sfoggiavano in que' loro concerti quasi giornalieri. L'*Haydn*, giovinetto e studioso, potè e dovette udirla più volte, e più ancora quando passò dal servizio del conte di *Motzin* [*sic*] a quello del principe Niccola *Esterhazy*, dove se ne aveva di nuova ogni mese, attesochè il principe fissato aveva al suo servizio, siccome il conte *Palfi*, anche la lontana penna del *Sammartini*. Sino allo spirare di questo maestro vi fu in Milano un banchiere per nome *Castelli*, destinato dal principe a pagargli otto zecchini d'oro per qualunque composizione gli desse per sua Altezza. *Sammartini* doveva darne almen due al mese; ma era in sua balìa il fornirne di più al prezzo indicato. Io mi sovvengo benissimo d'aver udito nella mia gioventù il banchiere lagnarsi col *Sammartini*, già fatto vecchio e pigro nello scrivere, che da gran tempo non gli avesse dato nulla per Vienna, da dove gli venivano fatte continue ricerche: al che il *Sammartini* sogghignando soleva rispondere = farò, farò, ma il cembalo m'ammazza = ciò non ostante il solo archivio musicale di casa *Palfi* vanta più di mille composizioni di questo autore. ...   [pp. 61f.]

Fatto adulto il nostro *Haydn*, e colla pubertà avendo acquistata la voce virile, uscì dalla classe dei *soprani*, e lasciò in età d'anni 19 la cappella di s. Stefano ... Le prime produzioni dell'*Haydn* furono alcune sonatine di cembalo, ch'egli per poco vendeva alle sue scolare, ad alcuni *minuetti*, e delle *allemande*, ed *arie de Waltzer* peí festini del ridotto. Avvenne ch'egli scrivesse per suo divertimento una serenata a tre strumenti, la quale egli stesso con due compagni andava nelle notti d'estate sonando qua e là per le strade di Vienna. Viveva di quel tempo un certo *Bernadone Curtz*, attore comico di molto grido per la piacevolezza de' suoi motti improvvisi, e che dal carattere arlechinesco che rappresentava sulle scene, fu soprannominato l'*Hanswurst*. ... I nostri notturni avventurieri si portarono a sonare la loro serenata sotto le finestre del *Bernadone* che aveva una bella moglie. La novità e la grazia della musica colpirono per modo *Bernadone*, che calato nella strada domandò di chi fosse quella composizione = mia, rispose l'*Haydn*; = tua? = sì, mia = così giovinetto? = bisogna ben cominciare una volta: mi son provato = bravo! vuoi farmi un opera? = perchè no? ... ma io non ne ho mai fatte = t'insegnerò io = bene mi proverò = vieni sopra = *Haydn* lo segue e ne scende col libretto intitolata *il Diavolo zoppo*. La musica fu composta a volo, gli fu pagata ventiquattro zecchini, ed ebbe il più felice successo; ma dicono che, essendo creduta una satira del famoso conte *Afflisio* (direttore allora degli spettacoli di Vienna, e che finì poi miserabilmente i suoi giorni nell'ergastolo di Pisa, per delitto di falsificazioni), quell'opera venisse per ordine superiore tolta dalle scene; nel che la colpa non potè essere che del poeta. *Haydn* mi diceva che gli era costato più fatica il trovare il su e giù delle onde in una burasca di quell'opera, che il comporre dappoi delle *fughe a doppio soggetto*. *Bernadone*, che aveva genio e gusto, era difficile a contentare, ma questa non era la massima delle difficoltà. Nessuno dei due aveva mai visto nè mare, nè tempeste. Come dipingere ciò che non si conosce? = Vedi, diceva *Bernadone* sbracciato, saltando per la camera d'attorno al maestro seduto al cembalo, tu devi`figurarti una montagna che va su su, e poi una valle che va giù giù; poi torna montagna, poi valle, e le montagne e le valli si corrono dietro, e si succedono rapidamente alpi ed abissi. Il tuono, le folgori e i venti infuriati vi giuocano per entro e fanno una casa del diavolo. Animo! fammi sentire una casa del diavolo; ma ben distinto quel su, e giù. = *Haydn* menava le mani sul cembalo; scorreva per semituoni, versava le settime a battaglioni, saltava dai bassi agli acuti, da questi a quelli come un gatto che piglia sorci, e *Bernadone* non era contento. Alla fine, non sapendo più che farsi, *Haydn* rivolta le mani, stringe le dita, ed a guisa di due scope, le fa scorrere velocemente sui tasti in ragione opposta, ed al modo di chi fa delle volate. *Bernadone*, acceso di maraviglia e di contento, grida: bravissimo! e salta al collo del suo maestrino, lo stringe e lo baciucchia esclamando: = così, così! = e così sia, rispose *Haydn*; ma tu mi strozzi, lasciami scrivere. = La tempestà riuscì come meglio poteasi desiderare. Due volte fu l'*Haydn* in Inghilterra fatto già vecchio, ed amendue le volte, nel passare lo stretto di Calais a mare agitato, diceva d'aver riso invece di vomitare, rammentandosi la tempesta di *Bernadone*. Aveva diciannove anni l'*Haydn* quando compose quella sua prima opera teatrale. . . .

Un anno dopo uscì l'*Haydn* in campo con sei *trio*,[8] che subito per la singolarità dello stile ed il lecco che li condiva, corsero per le mani di tutti, e diedero motivo a fervorosi discorsi fra quelli della professione. Prima di questi *trio* gli scrittori Tedeschi componevano per lo più le musiche da camera a tutto rigore di contrappunto *fugato*, nè la musica piacevolmente scritta dal *Sammartini*, e da altri Italiani aveva potuto smoverli dal metodo dell'antica scuola. . . . Le belle ideine dell'*Haydn*, il suo brio, le sue veneri, le licenze che si prendeva, gli eccitarono contro tutti i Pacomii dell'armonico deserto. Furono trovati o si credette trovare in quelle composizioni errori di contrappunto, modulazioni ereticali, e mosse troppo ardite. Poco mancò che il giovin padre della musica instrumentale non rimanesse schiacciato sotto il peso e la tempesta delle critiche. . . .

. . . [Haydn], fornito di nome ma tuttor povero di sostanze, andò a ricoverarsi in casa del sig. *Martinez*, alle cui figlie egli diede lezioni di cembalo e di canto, e n'ebbe in ricompensa la tavola e l'alloggio. È noto che il *Martinez* era il grande amico di *Metastasio*, e che suo figlio ne fu perfino l'erede. Egli fu allora che una stessa casa, posta vicino alla chiesa dei *Micheli*, accolse in due camere, situate al terzo e quarto piano, l'una sopra l'altra, il primo poeta del secolo, ed il primo sinfonista del mondo. Ma l'*Haydn* che non era al servizio di un Carlo VI, nè d'altro signore, trovava la sua cameruccia freddissima, e non aveva modi bene spesso di comperarsi la legna per riscaldarla, onde era costretto passare disperato dal cembalo alle coperte, e giacersi ozioso nel letto . . . Di gran vantaggio però si fu all'*Haydn* questa sua convivenza coll'unico fra i poeti, che mancasse agli antichi. Il *Metastasio* era nato col buon gusto nelle vene: ogni suo detto lo spirava. Amante e intelligentissima di musica, quell'anima sovranamente armonica gustava i talenti del giovane tedesco, e gli dava coraggio e precetti, oltre all'insegnargli, conversando, la lingua italiana. *Haydn* l'apprese sì bene, che nelle sue composizione italiane non isbagliò mai un accento; errore, dal quale non vanno esenti talvolta i più vantati fra i maestri d'Italia. . . .   [pp. 79–87]

Notes:

1 That Haydn was interested in the mathematical possibilities inherent in music is a supposition quite easily taken; but it is to be doubted whether he made these mathematical operations (golden rule, etc.?) into a 'secret rule' for composing. The Italians were interested in Haydn's role in all this through the 'Gioco Filharmonico, ossia maniera facile di comporre un infinito numero di Minuetti, e Trio anche senza sapere il contrapunto del Sig. Giuseppe Haydn, Napoli presso Luigi Marescalchi...', the authenticity of which is dubious. There is a curious and interesting pamphlet which Carpani perhaps knew: 'Lettera / del Maestro / Innocenzio Filomelo / con una risposta del celebre / Maestro di Capella / D. Gennaro Beccalocchi / sopra il gioco pittagorico / musicale / pubblicato dal sig. / Antonio Calegari / primo organista del santo in Padova / ... / in Padova 1802. / Si vende da Pietro Brandolese Librajo al Bò'. We owe our knowledge of this very rare pamphlet to the generosity of Mr Albi Rosenthal, London/Oxford, who was kind enough to furnish a complete photocopy. Basically, the argument is whether to take this kind of 'aleatoric music' – the precursor of Stockhausen, etc. – seriously. Beccalocchi sums it all up when he writes (p. xi): 'Il Sig. *Haydn* che ha fortito dalla madre Natura quell'intelletto, che tutto il Mondo riconosce, ed ammira ha saputo ben conoscere, che questa barzelletta Musicale non poteva servire per altro, che per divertire una mezz'ora un' oziosa Brigata a combinare in tal modo una qualche Composizioncella Instrumentale breve, e semplicissima, come un Minuetto col solo accompagnamento di un Piano-forte ...'. See Marion M. Scott, 'Fresh facts and old fancies', *Proceedings of the Royal Music Association* LXVIII (1941/2), pp. 87ff.

2 The Quartet Op. 1, No. 1 (III:1).

3 Field Marshal Giovanni Luca, Count Pallavicini-Centurioni (1697–1773), in whose beautiful villa 'Alla croce del Biacco' near Bologna the Mozarts stayed in 1770. Leopold Mozart to his wife, Bologna, 27 March 1770. *The Letters of Mozart and his Family*, ed. Emily Anderson, 2nd ed. London 1966, I, 122f. Erich Schenk, *W. A. Mozart*, Vienna 1955, pp. 247 and ill. f.p. 264.

4 Franz Xaver, Count von Harrach (1732–81) of the cadet branch zu Bruck an der Leitha; commanding general of an infantry regiment in Lombardy, married (1761) to Maria Rebecca, Countess von Wagensberg. Ignaz von Schönfeld, *Adels-Schematismus des österreichischen Kaiserstaates*, Zweyter Jahrgang, Vienna 1825, p. 84.

5 Presumably Carpani means Niclas Count von Pállfy ab Erdöd, Count von Blasenstein (1710–73), Erbobergespann of the Pressburg Comitat and *inter alia* Judex curiae of the Kingdom of Hungary. Schönfeld, ibid., Erster Jahrgang, Vienna 1824, p. 24.

6 One presumes Carpani means Joseph Franz Bonaventura, Count von Schönborn zu Wiesentheid (1708–72), married to Bernhardine Maria Therese, Countess von Plettenberg. Schönfeld 1824, p. 105.

7 Presumably Haydn's patron Ferdinand Maximilian Franz, Count von Morzin; *vide infra*, chapter V.

8 Carpani records that Haydn wrote string trios *before* he wrote string quartets, an opinion now shared by most modern Haydn scholars.

Summary of Carpani in translation:

No one in Vienna was willing to teach Haydn counterpoint, etc., for nothing. But this did not turn out to be a disaster, for Haydn, with a proper teacher, might have avoided some errors but would have turned out to be less original. . . .

. . . That he was not Porpora's pupil can be seen from Haydn's recitatives, much inferior to those of the father of recitative. But he learned the good Italian school of singing and accompanying on the harpsichord from Porpora, and this is much more difficult than one would think. . . .

[Porpora, Haydn and Correr's mistress proceed to Mannersdorf], where Haydn acted as valet to Porpora, cleaning his shoes and putting in order his scruffy wig. Porpora boxed his ears but also gave him good advice, not least on how to play P's difficult works with their learned modulations and bass lines difficult to follow; Haydn earned ten *zecchini* a month and free board from Correr. Haydn had the mornings free and played first violin [etc.]. . . .

Haydn was not content merely to learn from Fux's book and Bach's scores, but he relied on his perfect ear and, to use his own words, to ascertain 'what was good, what was better and what was bad'. If one asked him why he had written this or that chord or modulation he would answer, 'I've done so because it goes well.' Using a system of numbers, Haydn established a structure on which to construct his compositions. Joseph Weigl, his pupil for some time, assured me that Haydn never wanted to communicate his magic formula to anyone, and if you asked, he would answer, smiling, 'try to find it'. . . .

Apart from various canons and highly eccentric minuets of which we will speak later, Haydn put this particular use of numbers to work in his *giuoco filharmonico*, through which a chance combination of numbers corresponding with certain musical phrases enables one to compose an infinite number of minuets with second violin and basso, even without having the least idea of counterpoint . . .

[Speaking of Sammartini], Haydn said he owed nothing to him, adding that he was a trickster. But if one examines impartially Haydn's earliest works and compares them to Sammartini, the latter's bizzare passages and invention were put to good use, not in low plagiary but in masterly fashion. . . . Consider Haydn's First Quartet in B flat, opening movement, beginning of the second part, and in the way that the second violin and viola are used, you will recognize Sammartini's style even though Haydn was far too adept a contrapuntist and too much a friend of order and pure style to imitate on purpose that wayward Milanese with his fervid fantasy. . . .

It remains to explain how Haydn in Vienna could lay his hands on, and profit by, the numerous and original works by Sammartini in Milan. . . . Before Pallavicini, Count Harrach was Governor of Austrian Lombardy; they were the first to import Sammartini's music into Austria, and it was at once successful . . . Count Palfi [Pálffy], Grand Chancellor of Hungary, Count Schönborn and Count Mortzin [sic] hastened to procure this new music, which was given almost daily in their concerts. Haydn, young and intellectual, could hear it often, even more when he entered the services of Count Motzin [sic] and Prince Nicolaus Esterházy, who like Count Palfi, received a new shipment each month from the fertile if distant pen of Sammartini. The go-between was the Milanese banker Castelli, who was commissioned to pay eight golden *zecchini* for each new piece. I can remember in my youth hearing the banker protesting to Sammartini, who had grown old and lazy, that he hadn't sent anything to Vienna for a long time. 'I'll do it, I'll do it', said Sammartini, grinning, 'but the harpsichord is killing me.' Despite that the musical archives of the house of Palfi contain more than 1,000 compositions by him. . . .

Haydn was now an adult, his voice changed from having been a soprano, and at the age of nineteen, he left St Stephen's . . . His first productions were some sonatinas for harpsichord, which he sold to his pupils for a pittance, some minuets, allemandes and waltz tunes for masked balls. He wrote a serenade for three instruments which he and friends played on the streets of Vienna at night, also using it to serenade Curtz [sic], known as Bernadon, who had a beautiful wife. Bernadon asks the composer's name [exchange of dialogue] and commissions H. to write an Opera, *The limping Devil* [*Der krumme Teufel*] which, having been hurriedly composed, is a great success and brings H. 24 *zecchini* [which Carpani uses to mean ducats]. Because it was a persiflage on the famous Afflisio (then theatre director in Vienna, later to perish miserably in the Pisa prison for forgery), the authorities banned the Opera, and that can only be the poet's fault. Haydn told me that it cost him more trouble to find music appropriate to the rising and falling waves of a storm described in the Opera than later to write fugues with two subjects. After many unsuccessful attempts to write this descriptive storm music, Haydn was desperate and banged his hands on the keyboard in the middle and moved them rapidly in opposite directions, *glissando*. Bernardon was delighted and embraced him, 'That's it, that's it'; 'and that's the way it shall be', said Haydn, 'but you are crushing me, let me get on with writing it.' The tempest proved to be a great success. Twice Haydn as an old gentleman went to England, and twice he had to cross the Dover Straits in rough water, but he said he laughed instead of vomiting, thinking on Bernardon's tempest. He was nineteen when he wrote his first Opera. . . .

A year later Haydn brought out six trios which from their singularity of style and seductiveness of manner made them a success everywhere, and the subject of discussion in the profession. Before these trios, German composers wrote chamber music in the strict, contrapuntal or fugue style, and neither the attractively written music by Sammartini and the other Italians would move them from their antique style. This parched harmonic desert was soon watered by the beautiful ideas of Haydn, his verve, his grace, the licences he allowed himself. There were discovered, or thought to be discovered, in these works errors of counterpoint, heretical modulations and too-abrupt transitions. It appeared that the young father of instrumental music would be swamped under the weight of critical opinion. . . .

Haydn, still without money although now possessed of a name, went to recover in the house of sig. Martinez, to whose daughters he taught singing and the harpsichord. Martinez was a great friend of Metastasio, and it happened that near St Michael's Church there was a house containing two rooms situated on the third and fourth floors, one above the other, lodging respectively the first poet of the century and the first symphonist of the world. But Haydn, who was neither in the service of Charles VI nor any other lord, found his room freezing and had not money to buy wood, and was to go from the harpsichord to his blankets and to shiver in his cold bed. . . . It was useful for Haydn to know Metastasio, who was born with good taste, was highly intelligent about and fond of music. He appreciated the young man's talents and gave him the courage to continue, good advice, and lessons in Italian conversation. Haydn learned it so well that in his Italian compositions you will never find a misplaced accent – a mistake from which some of Italy's most vaunted masters are not free. . . .

(5) Framery (Carpani precedes Framery here because in this instance we believe Carpani's report to be more complete and more important):

[p. 6] Le malheureux Joseph ne sut d'abord que devenir, ni à qui s'adresser pour obtenir un asile; il fut forcé de passer la première nuit dans la rue, où un banc de pierre lui servit de lit; le lendemain un pauvre musicien de sa connaissance, nommé *Spangler*,[1] passant dans cette rue, le reconnut.(★) Haydn lui raconta de point en point sa douloureuse aventure: le bon homme en eut pitié, 'Mon ami, lui dit-il, tu sais comme je suis logé: je ne puis t'admettre dans ma chambre où couchent ma femme et mes enfans; mais je t'offre, dans un coin de mon grenier, un matelas, un lit de sangle, une table, une chaise, et de plus une nourriture très-frugale, tant que mes facultés me le permettront.' Joseph [p. 7] accepte avec la plus vive reconnaissance; il se regarde comme trop heureux d'être libre, et à l'abri des mauvais traitemens de Reitter; son imprévoyante jeunesse négligea même pendant quelque temps d'informer son père de l'affreux dénuement dans lequel il se trouvait: cependant il venait enfin de lui écrire, pour céder aux remontrances de son ami, lorsqu'il reçut une visite à laquelle il ne s'attendait guère.

Le repos dont il commencait à jouir avit permis à son génie de se réveiller: tourmenté du besoin de produire, il s'était remis à composer de ces petites sonates qui lui avaient si bien réussi autrefois; la plus jolie etait tombée par hasard entre les mains de la comtesse de Thun,[2] femme de la cour, passionnée pour la musique; elle l'avait trouvée charmante, et voulut en connaître l'auteur. Elle s'informe à tous ceux qu'elle rencontre d'un compositeur portant le nom de Joseph Haydn, écrit au bas de la sonate: aucun n'en a la moindre idée; seulement elle apprend que ce petit Joseph, cet enfant de choeur que son chant avait rend si célèbre, portait aussi ce nom. Mais un enfant pouvait-il etre l'auteur d'une pièce aussi agréable? N'importe, il faut s'en assurer; elle envoie à la cathédrale dire qu'on lui amène le jeune Joseph Haydn: le maître répond 'que ce mauvais sujet n'est plus à la [p. 8] maîtrise, qu'il l'en a chassé pour ses déportemens, et qu'il ignore ce qu'il est devenue.'

Une femme de qualité ne renonce pas facilement à un projet qu'elle s'est mis fortement dans la tête: la comtesse ne cherchait que l'auteur de sa sonate; c'est de ses talens qu'elle voulait etre certaine, plutôt que de ses mœurs: elle continue donc ses recherches, et finit par découvrir le trop modeste réduit où notre jeune compositeur s'est réfugié. Un valet de chambre s'y présente de sa part: on se fait monter au grenier, où le pauvre Joseph, honteux du triste équipage dans lequel on le surprend, se donne pour son propre laquais. 'Vous annoncerez à votre maître, dit l'envoyé, que Mme la comtesse de Thun désire le voir, et qu'il ne doit pas manquer de se rendre demain matin chez elle.' Joseph le promet. Mais comment tenir sa parole? Des lambeaux pour habits, des guenilles pour chaussure, osera-t-il paraître en cet état devant une dame de ce rang? Spangler, son hôte, presque aussi pauvre que lui, n'a pas le moyen de lui faire la moindre avance; il ne peut même, à cause de l'énorme différence de taille, lui prêter de sa garde-robe les choses de première nécessité: cependant l'ordre est précis; sa fortune peut dépendre de cette visite: il se détermine; il ira. Le [p. 9] lendemain il ajuste le mieux possible ce qu'il peut rassembler de vêtemens, en couvre tant bien que mal sa presque nudité, s'arme de courage, et arrive chez la comtesse; il est reçu par ce même valet de chambre qui l'avait vu la veille, et qui, le toisant des pieds à la tête, s'étonne de le trouver si mal vêtu, même pour le laquais d'un musicien, et finit par lui demander s'il va bientôt voir son maître. 'Je n'ai point de maître, dit le jeune homme; c'est moi qui suis Haydn; veuillez m'annoncer.' Le valet hésite s'il doit le croire; mais sa maîtresse l'a voulu: Joseph est introduit. Mme de Thun n'est pas moins surprise de voir dans cet état un homme de cette profession; elle se croit trompée. 'C'est M.

★ [original footnote:] Ce Spangler était alors simple directeur de musique à l'église Saint-Michel, place très-secondaire, qui, avec les leçons qu'il donnait en ville, fournissait à peine de quoi vivre à sa nombreuse famille. Depuis, Haydn par reconnaissance le fit entrer comme premier ténore au service du prince d'Esthérazy: c'était un homme de beaucoup de talent et d'instruction; sa fille ainée a épousé M. Fribert, maître de chapelle d'une des églises de Vienne.

Haydn, dit-elle, que j'avais demandé.—'C'est moi, Madame.—Mais c'est l'auteur de cette sonate, que je voulais voir.' (Elle était sur le pupitre de son clavecin.)—'C'est moi, Madame.—Quel âge avez-vous donc?—Madame, j'ai seize ans.'³— Elle examine alors avec plus d'attention cette figure chétive et pâle annonçant la misère, et peut-être quelque chose de pis. On a eu raison, pensait-elle en elle-même; c'est sans doute le libertinage qui l'a réduit dans cet état. 'Avez-vous fait, ajouta-t-elle, d'autres sonates de ce genre?—Oui, Madame, j'en ai fait un certain nombre pour des amateurs qui ont la bonté [p. 10] de les rechercher; celle-ci est ma dernière.—Et les présens qu'elles vous ont valur ne vous ont pas mis à portée de vous habiller plus décemment?—Quand j'ai fait les premières, Madame, j'étais enfant de chœur à Saint-Etienne, où l'on m'entretenait de tout; les présens que je recevais alors ne servaient qu'à mes amusemens; celle-ci, que j'ai faite depuis que j'en suis sorti . . .—Vous en avez été chassé.—Oui, Madame, à sept heures du soir, en automne.—Comme un mauvais sujet, pour votre inconduite.—Il est vrai, Madame, qu'on m'a traité comme tel; mais il ne l'est pas moins que je ne méritais pas un pareil procédé.—Enfin, celle-ci, vous l'avez faite pour quelqu'un qui sans doute ne l'a pas reçue gratuitement—Non, Madame, elle m'a valu quelques florins, que j'ai donnés au bienfaiteur qui m'accueillit dans ma détresse, et qui se prive à sa table pour me nourrir: comme je ne sors point, je n'ai pas besoin d'habits; mais j'ai besoin de témoigner à mon ami ma reconnaissance; je ne puis rien avoir qui ne soit à lui.'

Malgré ses préventions, la comtesse parut touchée de ces sentimens; elle voulut savoir comment et pourquoi il était sorti de la cathédrale. Avec toute la décence possible Joseph lui fit le récit de sa disgrace, naïvement, [p. 11] tel qu'on vient de l'entendre. L'injustice et la cruauté dont Reitter avit usé envers lui avaient été portées à un excès peu croyable; aussi Mme de Thun les crut-elle exagérées; mais comme le fait était possible, elle voulut au moins suspendre son jugement. 'Voici 25 ducats, lui dit-elle; employez-les à vous faire habiller d'une manière plus présentable; à choisir un logement modeste, mais commode, et achevez de vous acquitter envers votre ami. Si tout ce que vous m'avez dit est vrai, et si vous vous conduisez toujours bien, c'est moi qui serai désormais votre protectrice; vous me donnerez tous les jours des leçons de clavecin et de chant, et je ne vous laisserai manquer de rien; mais si j'apprends que vous vous livrez au libertinage, je vous ferai fermer ma porte, et vous retirerai mes bienfaits.'

Haydn prouva combien cette menace était inutile; tout entier à son art, il ne'eut jamais de passion vive pour autre chose: Mme de Thun eut dans tous les temps à s'applaudir de la confiance qu'elle lui accordait. Elle ne s'en tint pas a ces premières faveurs; comme les sonates que composait son jeune protégé ne prouvaient pas une profonde connaissance de l'harmonie, elle lui fit présent, pour l'étudier, du traité de Fuchs,⁴ alors célèbre, et ce qu'on connaissait de mieux [p. 12] en Allemagne à cette époque: Haydn n'eut jamais d'autre maître de composition. Ce fut elle encore qui le plaça chez le comte de★★★,⁵ riche seigneur de la cour: c'est là qu'il fit les premiers ouvrages qui lui procurèrent une reputation si brillante, et qui le firent placer comme maître de chapelle dans la maison du prince d'Esthérazy.

Notes:

1 Johann Michael Spangler (*c.* 1721–94), tenor at St Michael's Church in Vienna and later *Regens chori* (from 1775). We will see that he was involved in a very early copy of Haydn's *Salve Regina* in E. It is not true that Haydn engaged him but correct that Spangler's daughter, Magdalena Rosalie, would be engaged by Haydn in 1768. This story of Spangler's befriending Haydn is also in Le Breton's early Haydn biography of 1810 (*Notice historique sue la vie et les ouvrages de Haydn*). It was attacked, along with other details of Framery, in Carpani (278), where the Italian maintains that 'Sprangler' (no German name or word was safe in Carpani's tender hands) was 'più giovane di lui' (Haydn), and was not yet thirteen. Carpani got his information from a note by Griesinger in the

AMZ XIII (1810), No. 8: 'Spangler was younger than Haydn and at the time when the latter left the Choir School was certainly not married ...'. In fact Spangler married Maria Theresia Kürner (widow) on 12 February 1748, and one agrees with Pohl (I, 118) that the story seems entirely plausible. Spangler's daughter, Magdalena, did marry Carl Friberth.

2 It is difficult to identify this Countess Thun who figures in this anecdote about 1750 (see note 3): possibly Maria Christine, *née* Countess Hohenzollern-Hechingen, married to Johann Joseph, Count von Thun; they had a daughter, also named Maria Christine (b. 25 April 1738), and a son, Franz Joseph (b. 1734), who later married the famous Marie Wilhelmine (1734–1800), *née* Countess Uhlfeld, who was a friend and patron of Mozart's and Beethoven's and the mother of the 'three graces', who married into the highest society and were famous Viennese beauties. Previously it was thought that Marie Wilhelmine was the lady described here, but she was two years younger than Haydn; she was later acquainted with Haydn, who gave her a MS. copy of the Oratorio, *Il ritorno di Tobia*; see *Haydn: the Years of 'The Creation' 1796–1800*, p. 25. Khevenhüller Diaries (indexes to volumes up to 1759). Notice that here, too, Haydn's short, early keyboard sonatas are discussed.

3 Haydn at sixteen = *c*.1748, perhaps a year or two earlier than the event.

4 J.J. Fux.

5 Morzin?

It would seem an unlikely accident to be able to find archival evidence to assist us in dating these accounts, which were mostly written in the early nineteenth century; but research by Austrian theatrical historians has actually enabled us to establish at least one known performance of *Der krumme Teufel*, and other cross-references are possible.[1] We propose to deal, first, with the material given in the sources, its dating (as far as possible) and the other known events on Haydn's life up to the episode of Haydn's first love. Then, at the end of this chapter, we shall list the archival evidence of Therese Keller's entering a nunnery (1755–6).

Haydn hardly provided the details of these 'years of starvation', but although it is peripheral to our story, some similar details may be gleaned from an unpublished Austrian MS. diary[2] of the period which Else Radant discovered in Florence a few years ago.

[Title:] Die merkwürdigen Begebenheiten / meines Lebens / von mir / Franz Ritter von Heintl / selbst beschrieben / für meine Kinder und Nachkomen. / I Band / geschrieben im Jahr 1818 und 1819. / Von meiner Kindheit bis zum Ankauf meiner / Güter Nexing und Raspach: daher von / meiner Geburth am 29 October 1769, bis zum / Jahre 1802: nemlich bis zu meinem 33igst / Lebensjahre. / Eingebunden den 29 Merz 1823 / Ostersamstag / durch den Buchbinder Lenhardt in meinem Tafelzimer unter meinen Augen zu Wien.

[Summary of contents:] Heintl was the child of poor mountain farmers from the border country of Moravia; he was the eldest son, and there were another ten brothers and one sister. They all rose from grim poverty to be comfortably situated members of the middle class. In 1818 there were still alive Joseph, First Magistrate's Councillor in Stockerau; Jakob, *Oberbeamter* in Würmitz and working for his elder brother Franz, who also had the care of

another brother, Karl, who lived in Altstadt. Their father was a carpenter; his frugality enabled him to buy a small farm at Altstadt in Moravia. In the Bavarian Wars of Succession, the troops maraud in that part of Moravia, and the Austrians (pursuing the defeated Bavarians) nail the peasants' ears to their doors to learn where their valuables are hidden. At the age of four, Franz begins school, and at twelve he enters Latin School. In 1779 he visits a relative who is priest in Pausram. A Capuchin monk, begging, is given a place in the guest room where Franz is also sleeping, and the monk promptly rapes the boy. In 1781 Franz attends the lyceum at Olmütz. His parents provide him with underclothes, an old coat, linen, a pound of butter and 2 kreuzer a day. He finds lodgings with five other students at a Vinegar-seller. He pays 7 kreuzer a year, and the landlady will cook whatever he brings home. The boy goes through his money in a week and faces starvation. He goes to the Capuchin Monastery, where a convent soup

---

1 For example, the pilgrimages to Mariazell, which seem to have been organized by the Franciscan fathers, whose church is located in the inner city, not far from the Cathedral. In the local newspapers, these pilgrimages were regularly announced, e.g. in the *WD* No. 69, 29 Aug. 1759: 'Tuesday, 4th Sept. ... the regular yearly pilgrimage to Maria = zell departs from the P. P. Franciscans ...'.

2 Four volumes, all bound in leather. Private possession, Florence. Vol. I, 418 pp., table of contents numbered separately. Vol. II, 552 pp. Vol. III, 573 pp. Vol. IV consists of remarks by the writer's son, Franz Jr.

is served if you bring your own spoon: all the remains of food on the plates are thrown into a huge cauldron and then warmed up, 'sweet and sour together'. When he finally receives a scholarship he helps his brother to follow him and enter the school. Franz plays violin in the church. The boy wins the national lottery and secures a capital of 23 gulden. In his first year of studies he hires himself out as a scribe: '6 x per Bogen were paid. I went there early, in the summer as early as 5 o'clock and wrote till it was time to go to College ...'. He attends the University in Vienna, now supporting his brothers Joseph and Jakob, 'until I could raise the necessary funds in Vienna, by acquaintances and other sources of income, to have them follow me ...'.

[p. 55:] 'On 24 August 1789 I arrived in Vienna.... My entire capital consisted of 12 gulden. My first quarters were in the rooms of a master tailor ... for which I had to pay 2 F in advance monthly. My shoes and boots had to be put in good order and that cost 6 F 30 x, thus I had only 3 F 30 x for the rest of life's necessities.... [p. 56:] I never had any breakfast, for lunch I went with several other students to a *Traiteur* ... where the portions were small – a small bowl of soup, a tiny piece of beef with vegetables and a quarter of a Groschen-loaf of bread. That cost 6 x daily ... My evening meal was dry bread. The loaf of bread at 6 x weighed in those days 1 ℔ 17 Loth. A third of that was my evening meal.' He finds children to tutor, two hours daily, an income of 4 F 30 x in the month. But since Latin is not his major attraction, he loses the job, but finds other pupils. They live so far apart that he has to run between the jobs to make it in time; he now teaches nine hours daily and that gives him a monthly income of 24 F. With this he supports the two brothers in College in Olmütz, while he studies at night. In 1791 he is very ill, hopes for a scholarship but is not awarded one. He turns to Baron Gottfried van Swieten, who was on the Court Commission for Education (*Studienhofkommission*). [pp. 75ff.:] 'In a frightened mood I went to Hr. Baron van Swieten's quarters, which were in the I.R. Castle on the Josephsplatz [2 April 1791, 4 p.m.]. At this unusual hour of the day, I was let into the antechamber, announced and at once admitted to His Excellency's study. Upon entering I started, "Your Excellency ordered that ...", he interrupted me. He was holding my petition in his hand

and had written my name on the outside in red ink; he addressed me in the following words, which I shall never forget: "I have read your petition, I have found it good and I was touched by it. Take this as the first sign of my sympathy towards you" (and he handed me a banknote for 5 Fl); "there is not very much that I can do to help, but come and pick up the money every month." That was quite beyond my wildest hopes. The sudden change in my soul from the fear, with which I entered, to this joy resulted in my beginning to cry and sob aloud. I bent down to kiss the benefactor's green silk dressing gown with which, adorned by the Commander's Cross of the Order of St Stephen, he had received me. But that noble friend of the young took me in his arms, embraced and kissed me warmly, crying "No, my dear Heintl, not that" (meaning not to kiss the dressing gown); "you must have a noble heart. Now we shall see if we can't get a scholarship out of the Moravian Gubernium, and if we don't get it, you'll see what I can do" (here he embraced and kissed me again). "If, when the time comes I will have made you happy, then you can remember I'm the one responsible. I must tell you, however, to cheer you up that you have only yourself to thank: I found in your *pro memoria* a great deal of healthy common sense; and if I had already read it when you were here yesterday, I would not have sent you away without consoling you. Continue with your studies and come to see me every month." During this whole scene I could not utter a word, and there was nothing but tears of joy, tears of gratitude....

[p. 77:] B: Swieten was the same in the coming months. After the first month had passed I found it difficult to go to him to get the 5 F: I was afraid he wouldn't remember me, and since I was no longer in an emergency, I found it hard to remind him of his promise. On the other hand it would be unseemly, indeed ungrateful, not to accept such a philanthropic invitation. And the noble Swieten had not forgotten me: he recognized me as soon as I entered, asked me how I did, and pressed the 5 F into my hand; he had already prepared them, without [my] having to mention them specifically ...'.

Swieten continued to help Heintl and when the young man became a doctor of law, Swieten visited him in his quarters in the Stoß im Himmel and even entrusted the affairs of his niece, Countess Rosetti, to Heintl.

Obviously we cannot proceed further here with these Diaries, which show how Heintl became a rich and successful man of jurisprudence; there is a particularly striking list of his income, beginning from December 1793 to December 1794 (500 F), and ending in 1818 (18,069 F 6 x), which shows graphically how his life continued to change. It was, then, possible not only for Haydn but for other talented boys to 'begin from nothing' and to make a spectacular career in eighteenth-century Austria. And the reader acquainted with the rest of this long biography of Haydn will not wish to forgo this new insight into the stiff, dry Baron van Swieten who (through the documents) is presented to us as the years go by. Heintl's statement reveals another side of the editor of the libretti of *The Creation* and *The Seasons*.

There are some discrepancies between the three authentic biographies that cannot be resolved at all; for example, the question of Haydn's study of C. P. E. Bach. Griesinger assures us that Haydn studied the 'Prussian' Sonatas, while Dies specifies Bach's theoretical writings. We believe that both are true.[1]

The problem of Haydn and Sammartini will be discussed elsewhere (*infra*, p. 84). The chronology of the events discussed in the earliest biographies is, as one might expect, not entirely accurate: it is now thought that the quartets (as mentioned earlier) were composed later, but that which remains valuable is the list, even if very approximate, of the music Haydn wrote in the 1750s: the two Masses in F and G, some serenades or cassatios (one, in G [II:2], seems to be referred to), some of the early keyboard sonatas, string trios and dance music (e.g. the 'Seitenstetten' Minuets IX:1). We shall discuss these and other works of this era in Chapter Four. And this brings us to the date of *Der krumme Teufel* (XXIXb: 1a), Haydn's first Opera.

If we are to believe the biographies, when Haydn composed this piece for Kurz, he was 'about in his twenty-first year' (Dies) or he 'was ninteen' (Carpani) – which suggests a date between 1751 and 1753. The latest expert on the subject, Ulf Birbaumer, suggests that if there was a performance in 1751/2, it must have been before Easter 1752, because otherwise it would appear in the booklet, 'Répertoire des Théâtres de la Ville de Vienne depuis l'année 1752 jusqu'à l'année 1757' (Vienna 1757), which it does not. In the new standard work by Gustav Zechmeister on the two Viennese theatres from 1747 to 1776, the suggested date for Haydn's Opera is Carnival 1751. Unfortunately, the records for the theatres at this period are very incomplete, especially the German-language repertoire with their in part semi-improvised (*Stegreif*) comedies and *Hanswurstiada*. Thus it was a great surprise when Franz Hadamowsky, in 1959, was able to present documentary evidence for at least one, and possibly the first, performance of *Der krumme Teufel*: at the Kärntnerthortheater on 29 May 1753. The new document also gives us all the box-office receipts for the years 1753/4, and Haydn's Opera can be seen to have earned Kurz a relatively high return (only four other performances in May brought in more money). The music is, alas, entirely lost. The work was revived in or after 1758 as *Der neue krumme Teufel* and for that occasion, at least, a libretto was printed; another was printed when Kurz revived the work at Vienna in 1770. Therefore, we propose to discuss the libretto of the 1758 version in its proper place (*infra*, pp. 232ff.), where the entire literature on the subject – with the exception of the reference to Afflisio – will be listed.

The early accounts suggest that the work was banned because of its pointed references to Giuseppe d'Afflisio, who in fact was in Vienna as early as 1753 (our source is Casanova), but did not direct the Opera until 16 May 1767. Later the Mozarts would have difficulty with this incredible man – swindler, lecher, gambler and opera director. In 1779, Afflisio was condemned for forgery to lifelong penal servitude in the quarries of Leghorn (Livorno), where he died in 1787. Now if all this appears to throw doubt on the connection of *Der krumme Teufel* and the Italian swindler, we propose a different solution to the problem. It was noted that Haydn's Opera was revived in 1770, and as it happens we know the precise date (24 November) and also the fact that in May 1770, Giuseppe d'Afflisio left Vienna for the last time (leaving poor Gluck to wrestle with the debts that Afflisio had incurred in the theatre, with which Gluck was now officially involved). We propose that it was this revival that was brought into

1 For a discussion of the subject, including Bettina Wackernagel's *Joseph Haydns frühe Klaviersonaten* (Tutzing 1975), see *Haydn at Eszterháza 1766–1790*, pp. 337ff. Our colleague, Dr A. Peter Brown, who is at present writing a comprehensive book on Haydn's keyboard music, is working on the influence of C. P. E. Bach on Haydn – a subject on which the last word definitely remains to be said.

connection with Afflisio, and that Kurz on the stage may have imitated the Italian, whose dangerous influence had been removed (as it happened) to Milan.[1]

It has been suggested, first by Robert Haas (1925), that Haydn continued to collaborate with Kurz, and that two volumes of anonymous arias and other vocal numbers entitled 'Teutsche Comoedie Arien'[2] – which constitute extracts from the sung parts of Kurz's many German comedies with music – contain a considerable amount of music by Haydn. We shall discuss this theory, too, together with the music of the period in Chapter Four.

On 21 February 1754, Haydn's mother died in Rohrau, aged forty-seven, 'provisa a me Parocho sacris necessariis omnibus Sacramentis', and was buried on the 25th. We shall see that Joseph received his part of the mother's legacy in 1762 and 1764.[3]

Johann Michael (known to his family as 'Hansmichl') was seventeen in the middle of September 1754. He must have been a brilliant and precocious young man; although he had at first the same schooling as Joseph, in 1753–4 Michael attended the Jesuit Seminary in Vienna, which was of inestimable value to his early career. Michael was always of a more scholarly bent (a trait also displayed in his careful, curving hand) and as one might expect from the Jesuits, he appears to have been in general much better educated. Certainly the music of Hansmichl's earliest period far surpasses that of his brother's of the 1750s in *panache*, flair and a certain external brilliance. Joseph's is tauter, more pithy; Michael's is by contrast discursive. Yet Michael's Double Concerto in C for viola, organ and strings (Großwardein, *c.*1760 – the autograph has the place but the date is erased; Perger 55) is a more daring and original work than his brother's Organ Concerto in C of 1756 (XVIII:1); and Michael's first known work, the scintillating *Missa in honorem Sanctissimae Trinitatis* (1754), with its high trumpets and kettledrums, by far outshines the attractive but modest *missae breves* in F and G of his brother's youth.

Before we proceed to a short but necessary diversion to Hungary, where we must follow Michael Haydn's first engagements, we would draw attention to a document first discovered by Hans Jancik and published in his Michael Haydn biography of 1952. It is a letter from Mathias Haydn to his son and reads as follows:

[Mathias Haydn to Johann Michael Haydn. *German*]
Jesus Christ be praised!
My very dearest Hanßmichl, I am herewith sending you a carriage from Rohrau which can bring you and perhaps a good friend back and forth, and the driver will spend the night in the Landstraß[4] at the Falkon or the Angel;[5] you can talk to him and arrange that you and Joseph and perhaps Ehrrath,[6] all three of you, can get on the road early on Saturday. Mistress Nänerl and Mistress Loßl[7] and another young lady will also receive a carriage, but only very early because it's so pitch dark at night, so heartfelt greetings to all of you, and in God's name
Mathias Haydn

Amid the gloom of Joseph's (and presumably Michael's) youthful poverty, it is nice to think of a weekend party to Rohrau for the two Haydn brothers, their friend

1 On Afflisio see *Enciclopedia dello spettacolo* I (1954), 151–3 (Joseph Gregor); H. Abert, *W. A. Mozart*, 7th ed., Leipzig 1955, vol. I, 98, 101f; Helmut Watzlawick, 'Giuseppe d'Afflisio – Gastrollen eines Falschspielers', *Neue Zürcher Zeitung*, 8/9 April 1978.
2 Musiksammlung, ÖNB, S. m. 19062/3.
3 *Infra*, p. 378. Documentation. Schmid, *Vorfahren*, 236ff.
4 The Viennese suburb of the Landstraße.
5 Inns in the Landstraße. The 'summer palace' of the Counts Harrach was on the 'Hungargasse' (now 'Ungargasse').
6 In the original, 'EhrRath', a friend of Michael's.
7 The diverse young ladies (all referred to as 'Jungfrau' in the original) cannot be identified. The autograph, of which a facsimile is in Jancik (after p. 24), is listed as being in the Museum Carolino Augusteum, Salzburg, but the original can not be located there.

'Ehrrath' and three young ladies. In view of the fact that Michael seems to have left Vienna for a long period in 1754, we may date this letter *c.*1745–54; but we rather imagine it was written in the latter part of this period, i.e. *c.*1753–4.

Until rather recently, no one has pursued Michael Haydn's career in Hungary with much scholarly diligence. The section of Hungary to which Michael was called was Transylvania, and is now in Roumania; to facilitate present-day orientation, we cite each name first in German, then in Hungarian/Latin, then in Roumanian. The Roumanian scholar, Romeo Ghircoiaşiu, has recently summed up the newly discovered facts (*HJB* X [1978], pp. 46ff.):

In 1754, a new leader ('violinista primario') was engaged for the orchestra of Paulus, Count Forgács (reigned 1747–57), Bishop of Großwardein (Lat., Magnum Varadinum; Hungarian, Nagyvárad; Roumanian, Oradea Mare); and it is thought that this might have been Michael's first position on Hungarian territory. 'This "violinista primario" is, however, only mentioned once in the accounts' (p. 46), whereas Michael is mentioned by name first in the book-keeping accounts of 1757: this does not mean much, for the musicians are usually referred to by their function, not by their name (they being, as it were, faceless servants). Michael's *Missa in honorem S[anc]t[issi]mae Trinitatis* (Klafsky I, 1) is dated 1754 on the autograph (ÖNB, S. m. 15589), and on a now lost set of MS. parts in St Peter, Salzburg (Pohl I, 190), the work was called 'Temesvar', which has led Pohl and, after him, many other scholars to suppose that Michael wrote this Mass for Temeschburg (Hungarian, Temesvár; Roumanian, Timişoara) in 1754. Temeschburg, the seat of a bishopric, was the head of the geographical 'Comitat' called the 'Banat' (which, then as now, also includes many Hungarians, Croatians, Roumanians, etc.). Formerly, it was thought that Count Firmian was Haydn's patron; Firmian's name was proposed in the anonymous 1808 biography (as 'Bishop of Großwardein') and, while Jancik is in error when he maintains (p. 29) that no Firmian was ever a bishop – Schönfeld's *Adels-Schematismus* II (1825) lists several, including two Prince-Bishops – no one has yet been able to place a Firmian either in Großwardein or in Temeschburg. Bishop T. A. Count Engl resided as bishop in Temeschburg from 1750 to 1777, and was known as a patron of music. It is thought that he might have been Haydn's patron (perhaps he started out as leader in Großwardein, transferred to Temeschburg and returned to Großwardein in 1757). On 5 September 1757 Michael copied the *Missa canonica* by J. J. Fux (Michael's autograph is in the Musiksammlung of the ÖNB), probably for use in Großwardein. It is interesting to see Michael, like Joseph, studying Fux as the great Austrian contrapuntal master of the preceding era.

The earliest known dated autographs that Michael wrote in Großwardein all come from the year 1760:

1 April:	Te Deum (Klafky V, 1); autograph Bayerische Staatsbibliothek, Munich.
11–16 Aug.:	Part of six *Salve* settings, composed in Belényes, a country seat of the Großwardein bishops located twelve hours' drive south, in the western part of Transylvania (= Belencze = Belincz-Kiszetó = Belint).
11, 13 Sept.:	Rest of *Salve* settings (Klafsky XII, 13), Großwardein. All six autographs Bayerische Staatsbibliothek, Munich.
20 Nov.:	Partita 5ta (Perger 1): the fifth of a set of Symphonies, discussed *infra*, p. 242. Autograph, EH, Budapest.
20 Dec.:	Violin Concerto in B flat; autograph, EH, Budapest.

The last known autograph from the Großwardein period is that of the *Missa Dolorum B.V.M* (Klafsky I, 3), dated 3 April 1762. At the end of the year we find Michael in Pressburg (*vide infra*, p. 381); and new evidence of the brothers' connection during this period has been uncovered in the Fürnberg/Morzin sources which are discussed *infra* (p. 242).

Admittedly, there is much evidence that is lacking in this Chronicle of Michael Haydn's first appointment or appointments in Hungary; but that he was in Transylvanian Hungary probably as early as 1754 and certainly in 1757, and composing large-scale works, is clearly attested by autographs and local documents (the two not always yet in co-ordination). And we shall see that the dissemination of his works began at least in the late 1750s, with a Mass copied for Göttweig Abbey, a long distance from Transylvania (*infra*, p. 586).[1]

It was an auspicious beginning of a career that, in the end, was to prove a disappointment.[2]

Mathias Haydn in Rohrau, having become a widower, proceeded in age-old custom to seduce, and to get with child, his serving-maid, then aged nineteen. Maria Anna Seeder was born at Rohrau on 23 March 1736, of a poor shepherd's family; even before the girl's condition became noticeable someone must have reported Mathias to the authorities for, in a 'Restantien-Specification' of 31 December 1755, the county court of the Harrachs condemned the fifty-six-year-old Mathias Haydn to a 10 gulden fine ('Fornications Straff'). He was obliged to marry the girl, which took place after a special dispensation from the Archiepiscopal Consistory in Vienna, on 19 July 1755. The child, Mathaeus, was born in September (baptized on the 19th) and died seventeen days later. There followed four other children, all of whom died in infancy.[3]

We now arrive at the relationship between the Keller family and Joseph Haydn, or at least the 'opening chapter' thereof, as recounted by the authentic biographers.

(1) Griesinger (15):

Haydn had often received assistance in the home of a hairdresser in Vienna (in the Landstraße) named Keller; he also gave music lessons to their eldest daughter, and with closer acquaintance he grew increasingly fond of her. But she entered a nunnery. ....'

(2) Dies, 11 May 1805 (45):

... the younger [daughter of the Keller family] was the real object of his [Haydn's] love ...

(3) Carpani (80):

Ma la fortuna gli fece trovar ricovero [dopo suo espulso della cappella di s. Stefano] presso un parrucchiere, di nome *Keller*, il quale aveva più volte ammirato nella Cattedrale la bella voce e il bel canto del giovenetto. Questi fu che lo raccolse, e lo trattò da indi in poi come figlio, dividendo con lui la scarsa mensa, ed addossando alla moglie la cura di vegliare sul di vestario. *Haydn* esente per essi da ogni molestia e distrazione potè attendere in quella fortunata casuccia a' suoi studj con gratissimo abbandono, e farvi i più rapidi progressi. Aggiungerò qui una circonstanza che influì molto su quasi tutta la vita del nostro maestro. Il *Keller*

1 Equally interesting: in 1759 the Mariazell Church acquired and performed Michael's *Ave Regina* in A (Klafsky *deest*: Ms. 258 (now Graz, Diözesanarchiv), 'Ave Regina in A / a / Soprano solo / Violinis 2^bus / Organo / cum / Violone / Auth^re Sig^re Giov. Michaele Haydn/ Part . 5 / Ex voto 1759'; perf. dates 1759–1818. Does the 'Ex voto' mean, as we interpret it, that, following in Joseph's footsteps, Michael also made the pilgrimage to Mariazell, in 1759? We believe this to be new and important evidence.

2 Temeschburg and Michael 1754: O. L. Cosma: *Hronicul Muzicii Românesti*, 1, Bucharest 1973, p. 433. Bishop Engl and music: F. Griselini, *Versuch einer politischen und natürlichen Geschichte des temesvarer Bamats*, Vienna 1780, pp. 179ff. Jancik, 29ff., 34.

3 Schmid, *Vorfahren*, 242ff., with complete documentation. Cf. p. 35.

aveva due figlie, una delle quali era piuttosto avvenente. Avvisarono in segreto fin di buon'ora i genitori di farla moglie del loro ospite, ed avendogliene fatto cenno qualche tempo dopo, egli, più per riconoscenza che per genio, non vi si mostrò alieno e, come udirete a suo luogo, tenne parola da qual galantuomo che era e fu tutta la sua vita.

[Summary in translation:]
[After Haydn was expelled from St Stephen's] fate directed his footsteps to a wig-maker named Keller, who had admired the young man's fine voice in the Cathedral. He was taken in and treated like a son, the family sharing their meagre meals with him, and the wife seeing that he was decently dressed. Haydn could now pursue his studies without distractions, and made rapid progress. I will add a circumstance that changed our maestro's whole life. Keller had two daughters, one of whom [Therese] was rather attractive. The parents had intended that their young guest marry into the family, and you shall hear in good time how Haydn kept his word like the gentleman he was and would remain all his life.

E. F. Schmid devoted a whole study to this unfortunate and blighted love affair between Haydn and Therese Keller and her entry into the Nunnery of the Poor Clares (Ordo sanctae Clarae).[1] In fact, Therese was not the elder but the younger of the two daughters; she was born in 1733 and lived to the ripe old age of eighty-six. The eldest, Maria Anna Aloysia Apollonia, was baptized at St Stephen's Cathedral on 9 February 1729 and would later become Haydn's wife (*infra*, pp. 245ff.). As we have seen, one of the violinists in the *Capelle* of St Stephen's was Georg Ignaz Keller, the younger brother of our wig-maker, and it is thought that he acted as go-between. Haydn's 'patron' was Johann Peter Keller, who was born at Chlumetz in Bohemia about 1691, married Maria Elisabeth Sailler at St Michael's Church in Vienna on 12 November 1722; at the time Haydn was taken into their house, they lived on the Ungargasse in the suburb of Landstraße (a pretty old street still filled with eighteenth-century houses, including one where Beethoven wrote part of the Ninth Symphony).

The Kellers were apparently very religious, and nothing would prevent them from forcing Therese to take the veil: she entered the Nunnery see pl. 14) as a Novice on 8 April 1755. In a document dated a few weeks after her entry, the parents professed that their daughter's vows were the result of their expressed wishes 'and for their spiritual comfort'. This document was accompanied by two very large sums of money, 500 gulden before and 500 gulden after Therese entered the Nunnery.

On 12 May 1756 two novices took their solemn vows: Sister Josepha (her new name) Keller and Sister Maria Xaveria Mayr. Apparently Haydn directed the music for the ceremony, which must have taken place in the Convent Church; and here our interest in the whole affair quickens. In 1803, Haydn was trying to persuade Griesinger (as go-between for Breitkopf & Härtel) to accept some old compositions for his Leipzig publishers, and in the process we read, 'Recently he [Haydn] found a concerto for the organ and one violin which he wrote fifty years ago for his sister-in-law when she took the veil.'[2] Haydn seems to be talking of the Double Concerto for Organ, Violin and Orchestra in F (xviii:6), but the work he actually found in autograph was the Organ Concerto in C (xviii:1) – the work will be discussed *infra*, p. 209 – which Haydn proceeded to date '$\overline{756}$'. Another work which turned up in his papers and was also post-dated 1756 was the *Salve Regina* in E (xxiiib:1). The fact that Haydn took the trouble to keep these two very old autographs for very nearly half a century suggests that they had great sentimental value.

1 'Josef Haydns Jugendliebe', in *Festschrift Wilhelm Fischer*, Innsbruck 1956, pp. 109–22.
2 *Haydn: the Late Years 1801–1809*, p. 266.

There are two highly important traits of Haydn's personality which were, it would seem, evolved in these bitter years of starvation. The first is in the emotional quality of the music written for the ceremony of May 1756 – or rather the total *lack* of such emotions. All three works, the two concertos and the Salve, are bright, winning pieces without a single hint of the tragedy that presumably fathered them. And with them we establish one of the principal traits of Haydn's style which would be a permanent one until the middle of the 1760s: to show no deeper emotions of any kind, to avoid any question of personal involvement with the music he was writing. We may find majesty, subtlety of compositional technique, gentleness, gaiety, and so on; but it seems clear that these are various cloaks that Haydn deliberately wears, and which totally conceal the real person beneath them. This philosophy does not change until Haydn becomes full *Capellmeister* to Prince Nicolaus Esterházy in 1766: perhaps it was not until then that Haydn really felt the necessary confidence to enable him to display some of his personal emotions, beliefs and innermost secrets.

Perhaps this deliberate and long-term disguise of his real feelings was somehow bound up with his poverty and his lowly position in society. At any rate the other fact to emerge from Haydn's life in the 1750s in Vienna is his near-fanatical obsession with money – a trait which we shall follow constantly throughout this biography, and which led Haydn to superhuman (and sometimes less than human) manipulations to secure money from patrons and publishers. This biography will see a sorry procession of starving musicians, many of whom died (as we shall have occasion to say, almost with the same obsession as Haydn's, throughout these and future pages) in abject poverty, leaving starving widows and emaciated children – and they include composers, copyists, publishers, violinists, trumpeters, singers: it is a disgraceful and shaming list that (like Haydn) we must never forget when we read of the great banquets, festivities, balls and firework displays with which *Capellmeister* would soon be in intimate and permanent contact.

CHAPTER FOUR

The Viennese Musical Situation, c. 1750, and Haydn's Works, c. 1749–1756 (and partly beyond)

I   The Viennese Musical Situation, c. 1750

'D'OÙ VIENT L'ART DE MOZART?' asked our late and much-lamented friend, Jean Witold, in his provocative little book, *Mozart méconnu* (Paris 1955). We propose to devote a few pages to a subject that deserves an entire well-considered book, 'D'où vient l'art d'Haydn?'. And although it is a subject of essential importance to the history of music, it is one to which hardly more than the occasional specialized article has been devoted.[1]

THE ITALIAN INFLUENCE

We must be careful in our choice of the kind of 'foreign' music Haydn might have heard or studied: consider, for example, that he said in London that Tartini's music was not known to him (*vide aupra*, p. 49). We always imagined that Vivaldi, and especially *Le quattro stagioni*, must have been behind the style of Haydn's Symphonies Nos. 6–8; but it was not until the publication (in *HJB* IX) of the 1759 Catalogue of Prince Paul Anton Esterházy that we knew positively that Vivaldi's great work had been part of the Eisenstadt repertoire. Therefore, if we now propose a Galuppi cantata or a Caldara Mass, we do so to illuminate a general stylistic trait and not to suggest necessarily that Haydn actually knew (or studied) the work in question. But we believe that the works here chosen are sufficiently representative to serve our present purpose.

---

1 A good example is the series of studies on Porpora by Akio Mayeda, especially 'Nicola Antonio Porpora und der junge Haydn', in *Der junge Haydn*, Graz 1972, pp. 41ff. Another is the background to the string quartet in L. Finscher's *Studien zur Geschichte des Streichquartetts* (first volume: Haydn, 1974), 'Erster Teil' (pp. 21–126). There was, at the beginning of the twentieth century, an interesting argument between the Austrian (*DTÖ*) and the German, or rather Bavarian (*DTB*), *Denkmäler*, in which the Germans, headed by Hugo Riemann, tried to promote the Mannheim school and especially its founder, Johann Stamitz (1717–57), as Haydn's true precursors. The Austrians retorted with the publication of several local works, including a since famous D major Symphony of 1740 by Mathias Georg Monn (1717–50) which contained four movements and a minuet; to this work they added others, and also a thematic catalogue. Under the name of 'Monn' or 'Mann', however, there was also a composer and 'Claviermeister' named Johann Christoph Mann or Monn who lived much later, and whose presence causes the same confusion as exists in the Mitscha (Miča) family (see Landon, *SYM*, 3n). It would have been convenient for the Austrians to attribute all the forward-looking 'Monn' or 'Mann' music to Mathias Georg, just as it was enticing to Czechoslovak scholars to try to attribute to Franz Wenzel Mitcha (František Václav, Miča; 1694–1744) all the modern-sounding music by 'Sig. Mitscha', especially the Symphony in D published in Prague in 1946. One of these later 'Mann' symphonies was published in *DTÖ* – cited it in *Haydn at Eszterháza 1766–1790*, p. 276 – but has turned out to be the work of a minor Regensburg composer, F. X. T. Pokorny. See J. LaRue, 'Major and Minor Mysteries of Identification in the 18th Century Symphony', *Journal of the American Musicological Society*, vol. 13/14, pp. 181–91 (191). *DTB*: 3. Jg., Bd. 1 (1902, H. Riemann); 7. Jg., Bd. 2 (1906, H. Riemann); 8. Jg., Bd. 2 (1907, H. Riemann). *DTÖ*: XV/2 (1908, K. Horwitz and K. Riedl), XIX/2 (1912, W. Fischer). Nowadays it is considered that the Austrians were, basically, correct in their argument and that the Mannheim influence on Viennese composers of the period was of fleeting importance only. *Vide infra*, p. 112.

Haydn went through two basic phases as a student of composition, and these are delineated clearly in the autobiographical sketch of 1776: the first period as a choir-boy under Reutter and later as a starving freelance musician in Vienna; and the second period, when he was Porpora's amanuensis, *c.* 1753–5 (Pohl I, 165f.), and for the first time studying the Italian style from an acknowledged master. In his investigation of Porpora's influence on Haydn, Akio Mayeda was puzzled by a lack of Porporan traits in Haydn's music; however, Haydn never said he learned *style* from Porpora, but rather *method*, which means quite clearly (1) composing Italian texts, which he had probably no reason or incentive to do before 1753; (2) teaching the Italian singing method, in this case Porpora's method, using the Italian's own solfeggi exercises, of which a great many have survived;[1] and (3) composing in the strict, or old-fashioned 'correct' style. Haydn's first Masses (in G and F) are in the local *missa brevis* tradition and not in the 'a cappella' style, while his other early compositions were piano sonatas, divertimenti, string trios, etc., all in the local 'divertimento' style where one could get away with writing (as Haydn himself described it) 'diligently, but not quite correctly' (autobiographical sketch, 1776).

The Italian influence on music north of the Alps was still profound, and in Vienna there was not only Porpora but the much greater Italian master, Antonio Caldara (who died in Vienna in 1736), the former a visitor but the latter a permanent fixture, at least in the later years of his life. The Italian influence, as far as Austria was concerned, was chiefly in the field of opera, and both *opera seria* and *opera buffa* continued to be imported from Italy with great success throughout the century and beyond. In instrumental music, however, the Austrians had developed their own style which, while it had many roots in Italian music, was by 1750 a flourishing and independent school of its own. The Sammartini instrumental style has been mentioned, and no doubt his works were known and appreciated in Austria; but there is no reason to doubt Haydn's firm assertion that he was not a *seguace* of Sammartini's. The various modern attempts to resurrect the idea of Sammartini's influence on Haydn are neither convincing musically nor supportable historically. Although we must continue to be careful in our analysis of what foreign music Haydn knew during this period, some hints are forthcoming: if he knew and particularly admired a Galuppi opera (*infra*, p. 98), perhaps he admired Galuppi's harpsichord concertos, too (which might easily have reached Vienna in MS. copies). We may imagine that Haydn knew little of Domenico Scarlatti's piquant and atypical keyboard sonatas; but in Zinzendorf's Diary of 10 March 1762, we read of Giuseppe Scarlatti (who died on 17 August 1777 in Vienna), who (according to Burney) was 'the nephew to Domenico Scarlatti' and had arrived in the Austrian capital to produce his new work, *Il mercato di Malmantile* (Goldoni), in 1757:[2]

> Nous allons ensemble chez le duc de Braganz, qui accompagna du violoncelle un certain Hofmann, puis Scarlatti arrive et joua tout de suite une Sonate nouvelle aiant arrivée du Portugal et très difficile. Hofmann la joua divinement du violoncelle... [Zinzendorf MS.]

This was possibly not so rare an occurrence and may have introduced names like Domenico Scarlatti to Haydn through similarly obscure princely, ducal, ecclesiastic or diplomatic channels (i.e. not in the usual way, via the professional copyist or printed page).

---

1 A selection in facsimile may be seen in Kurt Wichmann, *Der Ziergesang*, Leipzig 1966, which includes a useful chapter on Porpora.
2 *MGG* 11 (1963), 'Scarlatti (Familie)', 1518ff. (H. Hucke).

VOCAL MUSIC
THE CANTATA

The interesting way in which the Italian tradition penetrated the Austrian style may be seen in several examples, of which some are very close to Haydn. Consider the following Motet by J. G. Reutter, Jr.[1] (?), entitled '# /Mottetta/ Della Modona [*sic*], ô qualis /voglio Sancto/ â /Duoi Soprani, Violone et/ Organo /Sgre Reütter/ R: Maÿr.' The work consists of several movements:

I 'Laudentes, plaudentes' (Duetto) – basic key, G major;
II 'Admiramini' (with solo 'Cembalo', range to b'') for Canto 1mo;
III 'Si vita misera' (solo for Canto 2do in E minor);
IV 'Cum $\begin{Bmatrix} \text{matre} \\ \text{Sanctis} \end{Bmatrix}$' (Duetto in C major);
V 'Sola laetitia' (Duetto in G).

The first movement has the strongest Italian flavour, and in the antique manner at that, returning almost to the grey Monteverdian tradition:

[Mottetto: 'Laudentes, plaudentes']

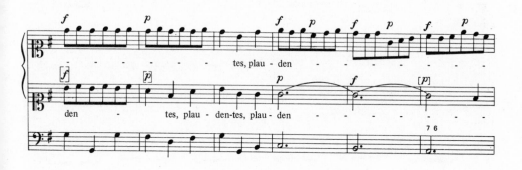

---

1 There is no little confusion regarding the authorship of many pieces attributed simply to 'Reutter' and which might be by the father (1656–1738) or son (1708–72). For example, the two attractive pieces discussed in Leopold Schmidt's *Joseph Haydn*, Berlin 1898, pp. 8–10 (long music example, p. 9) seem to be clearly by Reutter, Sen. The pieces are from a MS. in the Staatsbibliothek, Berlin. Sometimes a MS. of 'Sig. Reutter' is so dated that an attribution to the father is certain, e.g. the *Dixit Dominus* from the Archives of St Stephen's (GdM I. 21561) with performance dates from 1710–23. Our Motet (GdM I. 5295) is on paper with the watermarks: crossed keys, fleur-de-lys, letters 'FPM' in frame. The Venetian style of the opening suggests Georg, Sen., while the harpsichord(?) solo suggests Georg, Jr. In this particular case, the authorship is unimportant to the point we are attempting to establish, viz. the introduction of Italian ideas into Austrian music of Haydn's childhood years (or earlier).

We are drawn to the presence of the two solo soprano parts in a Reutter piece: if not composed for the two Haydn 'Buben' (Joseph and Michael) – and if the piece is by Georg, Sen., it cannot have been – perhaps it was the kind of music they sang, and was the inspiration for the two soprano solo sections of J. Haydn's *Missa brevis* in F. Now in the second movement, we suddenly come upon what is marked, quite clearly and more than once, 'Cemb:S:' ('Cembalo Solo'); what is a harpsichord solo doing in this religious piece, otherwise scored for 'Organo'? Perhaps 'Cemb: S:' was a generic description for organ (keyboard) solo; or can we imagine the Haydn brothers singing it in Klosterneuburg Abbey, with both organ and harpsichord? We give an example of this solo harpsichord section, which meshes into the elaborate and florid soprano solo (the original clefs have been preserved in most of the examples in this section, so that the reader may see some of the problems raised by the sources).

This kind of harpsichord or organ solo, whether in motet, secular cantata or Mass, has always been regarded as something of an Austrian speciality; and certainly there are many examples in Haydn's music that come to mind: the organ solo parts in his Masses,[1] as well as in the Esterházy Cantatas of 1763 and 1764, discussed *infra* (pp. 464ff.), where there are elaborate harpsichord solos. This tradition continues in *Applausus* (XXIVa:6) of 1768. There are, of course, many such examples in other Austrian composers such as Mozart (*Missa brevis*, K.259; *Vesperae de Dominica*, K.321; *Missa solemnis*, K.337, etc.). It is easily demonstrated that this use of the solo organ was prevalent in the Masses of Haydn's precursors, for example, the *Missa* in B flat[2] by Reutter, Jr., where there is a typical organ solo at the very beginning.

We show further examples from the Sanctus and Benedictus: the alternations of triplets, dotted passages, 'sighing' series of (in this case) semiquavers up or down stepwise, scales with trills on alternate notes. These are typical keyboard devices, also found in concertos, sonatas, etc., as we propose to show below.

---

1 Especially in the *Missa in honorem B.V.M.* ('Great Organ Mass') and the *Missa brevis S. Joannis de Deo* ('Little Organ Mass'), but also in the *Salve Regina* in G minor (XXIIIb:2) and, towards the end of his life, in the *Missa in angustiis* ('Nelson' Mass).

2 We used MS. parts in GdM I. 2816, probably material from St Stephen's. Scoring: Org. Solo, S.A.T.B. (soli and tutti), V.I, II, Violoncello, Fagotto Rip:no, Cornetto Rip:no, Trombone I:mo Rip:no, Trombone II:do Rip:no. 4° paper (watermarks: elaborate coat-of-arms with fleur-de-lys on two parts of edge, and letter 'A' beneath). There are organ solo sections in the Kyrie (see example), end of the Sanctus (see example), Benedictus and also Agnus, the latter with trills and the usual Austrian graces (Andante).

The scale in the opening bar of the Kyrie is typically Reutterian (though not restricted to him). However, our calculations are somewhat upset if we realize that exactly this type of frilly keyboard solo appears in Baldassare Galuppi's (1706–85) Cantata, 'Rapida cerva',[1] where in the middle of the first aria, 'Rapida cerva', we are surprisingly confronted with a keyboard solo –

– with the same kind of triplet pattern as Reutter's first organ solo in the Sanctus (see example). Reutter had been in Venice and Rome in 1730, and had been able to study the 'licenciöse Schreibart' (J. J. Fux's ambivalent term).[2] Yet another example of this interchange between Italy and Austria is the case of the Austrian composer F. L. Gassmann (1723–74) producing the three-movement Overture (*sinfonia*) to his Opera, *L'Issipile*, in Venice in 1758; this is the work most similar to Haydn's Symphony No. 1 (1759?) in general form and style, even to the (rare) opening Mannheim crescendo.

1 For Sop. Solo, strings and continuo, e.g. organo or clavicembalo. In the third aria, 'Alleluja', the organ (harpsichord) solo is even more elaborate and extensive, with real concerto-like interpolations.
2 L. von Köichel, *Johann Fux*, Vienna 1872, p.45 (no. 250).

CHURCH MUSIC

The Austrian school, *c.* 1750, was on the whole more conservative than its Italian sister school and also Mannheim, though in all three it is not unusual to find sudden turns of phrase from the Baroque, either in a single passage or in a whole movement. There was always a tendency in Austrian church music to compose in several styles, sometimes even in one and the same work: the 'old' church style ('stylo a cappella') and the modern manner (such as we have just noted in Reutter's Mass in B flat, with its homophonic style and the solo organ taken from the contemporary concerto or sonata). The old (pseudo) Palestrina-style was called not only 'alla cappella' (nowadays we say: 'a cappella') but also 'alla Romana'. We have seen that Pope Benedict XIV issued an Encyclical, 'Annus qui', forbidding all the theatrical instruments in church (1751). Finally, in 1754, it was suggested to Reutter that this 'alla Romana' style be introduced into St Stephen's and the Court Chapel; the orchestra, apart from the organ, was to include only strings and bassoon. Reutter worked out a compromise to avoid having to engage a whole group of newly trained voices, especially castrati. It saved the Court a great deal of money in instrumental players (the budget sank from 20,000 gulden p.a. to 12,000); but the size and standards of the orchestra were gradually reduced, so that at Reutter's death in 1772, the Chapel (*Hofburgcapelle*) consisted of only twenty members. Apart from that, however, the continued presence of this 'alla cappella' or 'alla Romana' style may be attributed to the Papal Encyclical 'Annus qui'.[1]

Haydn must have participated frequently in the real *a cappella* music of the previous era, or at any rate music in the 'old' style – J. J. Fux and probably many of the actual Italians. But he can have heard it at much closer quarters, in the music by his teacher at St Stephen's. From the many examples, we might select a *Libera* by Georg Reutter, Jr.[2]

Libera

J.G. Reutter, Jr.

---

1 Reutter's church music in *DTÖ*, Band 88 (P. Norbert Hofer, 1952), p. xi. Reutter's position included not only the directorship of music at the Cathedral, but also: (a) after 1756 being second Maestro di cappella at St Stephen's, viz. the Gnadenbildcapelle (*supra*, p. 56); (b) from 1741 (death of J. J. Fux) Reutter had assisted the musical services at the Court Chapel (Hofburgcapelle), and from 1747 he was officially listed as Second Capellmeister of the Chapel (Reutter had previously written many operatic works, but from 1740 he found that he had to devote his full attention to these various ecclesiastic positions); finally (c), he also directed the church music at St Augustine's and the Jesuit church.
2 GdM I. 11766 (Q 357) on 'KIESLING' paper: 'Libera / Del Sig: Giorggio Reütter.' For another composition in this same general style, see 'Ecco quomodo moritur justus' in the Reutter Volume (Band 88) of *DTÖ*, pp. 100f.

Here is the essence of the 'Palestrina' style to which Haydn would have recourse in his own *Libera* (*Responsorium ad absolutionem*, XXIIb:1) and in the Offertorium, 'Non nobis, Domine' (XXIIIa:1), which is described in the *Entwurf-Katalog* as 'in Stillo a Capella'.[1]

This *a cappella* style, though it continued to be cultivated throughout the century, was always something of an 'exotic excursion' (to misquote the late Bence Szabolcsi). That which the Austrian composers rather preferred was the mixture of old and new: fugues brought 'up to date' but using all the old Fuxian principles, sometimes flanked by movements in the most modern, almost secular, style. There were, basically, three kinds of Mass (we do not discuss the Requiem here, since Haydn never composed one): the so-called 'cantata' Mass, a very large-scale work in which the Gloria in particular (but sometimes Kyrie and Credo as well) would be subdivided into a great many individual movements. This was the species of work produced for the St Cecilia's Day celebrations at St Stephen's, and which we discuss briefly in connection with Haydn's cantata Mass of 1766.[2] They were usually in C major and scored *inter alia* for prominent high trumpets (*clarini*) and kettledrums – sometimes with four trumpets, two high and two low (this was a Salzburg tradition, too). Then there were the less lengthy, 'ordinary' kind of *missa solemnis* with or without trumpets and timpani and, depending on the work's date and circumstances, with or without other

---

1 *Haydn at Eszterháza 1766–1790*, p. 738 (*Libera*) and *Haydn: the Years of 'The Creation' 1796–1800*, pp. 77ff. (Offertorium and *Libera*, with musical examples).
2 *Haydn at Eszterháza 1766–1790*, pp. 228ff.

wind instruments: the typical key of this festival Mass was also C major, but as the century progressed other keys, especially D major, but also B flat, G, A, F and E flat became equally popular. The third type was the *missa brevis*, a typical composition in use during Advent (when the Gloria was omitted).[1] Haydn could have heard many such *missae breves*, also works by Reutter, Jr., and Arbesser (Cathedral organist), with the characteristic small orchestra usually known as the Viennese 'church trio' (two violins and *basso continuo*). In Salzburg and elsewhere, there was a singular attempt to create a hybrid short Mass but with full orchestra (the texts not usually 'telescoped', one over another, as in the dubious Viennese tradition of Gloria and Credo).

There was also a vast amount of 'smaller' church music, motets, graduals, offertories, hymns, responses – the list is endless. Joseph Haydn wrote relatively few works of those kinds, whereas his brother Michael cultivated this overall *genre* with great success. As a small footnote, we might cite a work from the Cathedral Archives dated 23 March 1752, by Reutter, Jr., in this mixed 'alla Romana' style. Joseph Haydn had already left the Cathedral but was singing there on Sundays as a supernumerary, and his brother Michael might just have still been a member (he left about this time). This performance material, now in the Gesellschaft der Musikfreunde in Vienna, might therefore have been actually used by the Haydn brothers.[2] The title reads: '23 Marti 752 /Antiphona/ Pro Feria quinta post Dominicam /Passionis/ Ad 12. Conciones /Partes. 24. et Spart:/ [later: "Reutter"].' There are two settings, one for boys' voices and one for the full choir. The first setting –

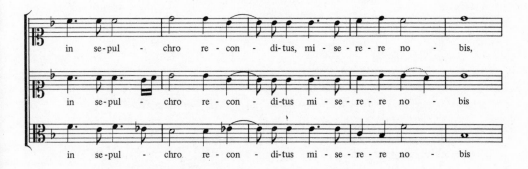

---

1 Sometimes in the *a cappella* style, too, e.g. Reutter, Jr.'s 'Missa Brevis / senza gloria / ... / à 4. Voci capella ...', GdM I.28475 (Q 362).
2 I.2812. Watermarks of the 4° paper: coat-of-arms with three fleurs-de-lys, ornament with fleur-de-lys and letters 'HA'.

mi - se-re-re nos-tri Do - mi - ne, mi - se - re - re nos - tri

mi - se-re-re nos-tri Do - mi - ne mi - se - re - re nos - tri

mi - se - re-re nos-tri Do - mi - ne mi - se - re - re nos - tri

– includes a kind of short score ('Spartita à 3') and parts for six sopranos six altos – large enough forces, but the second setting (of which we quote the *incipit*) was sung by a vast choir.[1]

[Another setting]

T.

Je - su, Je - su dul - cis - si - me

B.

One of the characteristic features of Haydn's style was always his use of Gregorian chants,[2] and not only in his church music (*Te Deum* for the Empress) but in his secular music as well, and as early as *c.* 1760 in a wind-band divertimento (*infra*, p. 273). We would like to show an interesting case of Gregorian chant used *in just the same way* (with a violin part wreathing the melody in Baroque garlands) by Reutter, Jr., who was, we ought constantly to recall, not only Joseph's but also Michael Haydn's teacher. There are several points about the work in question, the *Missa Sancti Placidi* (alternative title: *Missa Sancti Georgi*; Hofer 33).[3] Some features of the Mass lead us to Joseph, others to Michael. A peculiarity of the work is an interesting device to link the various movements of the work by a kind of *Leitmotif*:

We notice in the string writing

Missa Sancti Placidi:
Quoniam (Un poco allegro)

V. I

etc.

---

1 There are *in toto*: 6 T., 6 B., Sop. I Concerto, Sop. II Concerto, Alto Concerto, 3 S. Ripieni, 5 A. Rip., 6 Ten. Rip., 6 Basso Rip. Probably more than two (small) boys were expected to sing from one part, perhaps three.
2 See our article, 'Die Verwendung gregorianischer Melodien in Haydns Frühsymphonien', *Österreichische Musik-Zeitschrift* IX (1954).
3 The score was kindly lent to us by Dr Otto Biba.

details which remind us of Joseph's *Missa brevis* 'Rorate coeli', but both brothers never forgot the ascending and descending scales of the Sanctus.[1]

The *Tonus Pellegrinus* which we find in the Benedictus

is the very Gregorian melody that Michael would use in his *Requiem* of 1771, and at the very same place ('Te decet hymnus') that it would be later used by Mozart in his *Requiem* of 1791 (K.626). The tune is very similar to the Passion sequence used by

1 Joseph: *Missa Cellensis in honorem B.V.M.*, 1766–Credo (bars 7ff., 21ff.); *Te Deum* for Prince Nicolaus Esterházy (bars 2, 4, 6, etc.). Michael: Sinfonia in B flat (Perger 18), 1784 (1st movt., bars 9, 11).

Haydn in Symphony No. 26/I[1] and Mozart in his *Maurerische Trauermusik* (K.477; 1785) – a great and, to use the old Berensonian phrase, life-enhancing tradition which we may trace directly to the Haydn brothers' first teacher.

One aspect of Reutter's writing taken over by Michael but never by Joseph is the curiously stiff, 'fifthy' trumpet writing:

it is precisely the kind of antique and angular writing that we find in the first two trumpet parts – there are four – of Michael's *Requiem* of 1771. One final, interesting detail of Reutter's trumpet style which hardly reappears at all in either of the young Haydns is the clever use of the rare seventh harmonic (written *b flat'*) found repeatedly in Reutter's *Requiem* (of which we show the beginning)

of which a typical specimen may be seen in our next example:

(We recall the stupendous passage in the Finale of Beethoven's Eighth Symphony where the trumpets have this seventh harmonic, together with the horns, at bars 451ff.)

There was a special tradition of German-language (in other parts of the Monarchy, the local vernacular was also used, e.g. Bohemia) songs, with modest orchestral accompaniment (usually strings, organ and perhaps two horns), for the Advent and Christmas seasons. Some of these songs made use of local folk-song idioms, and this was especially true of the *pastorelle* used at Christmas-tide. There, we find music imitating bagpipes, or copying the *tuba pastoralis*, and with melodic patterns of thirds and sixths so dear to the international Christian pastoral tradition. It is hard to date many of these *pastorelle*, but here again the chronological sequence is not the main point. A recent Czech publication[2] gives us a selection of Bohemian *pastorelle* from which we may cite some characteristic melodic patterns (see examples opposite). In his *Cantilena pro Adventu* (XXIIId:3, *vide infra*, p. 275), Haydn wrote a genuine *pastorella*, wherein we may recognize the old tradition (*g sharp* in a D major context)

1 About which, see *Haydn at Eszterháza 1766–1790*, p. 292.
2 *Musica Antiqua Bohemica*, vol. 23: 'České Vánoční Pastoreky' (J. Berkovec), Prague 1955.

94

[Bohemian *pastorelle*:]

which continued to the Piano Trio No. 31 (XV:32) that Haydn brought to England in 1794 and first published there.

Applausus cantatas

There was a similarly flourishing local tradition of Latin *Applausus* cantatas, written for the celebration of some feast or person at one of the great Austrian abbeys: there is a catalogue at Herzogenburg Abbey wherein are listed dozens of these *Applausus* cantatas, all of the period shortly before or after 1750. Johann Georg Zechner (1715–78), a lay priest who had close connections with Göttweig Abbey, composed an *Applausus* for the golden anniversary of the ordination as priest of the Göttweig Abbot Gottfried Bessel (1746), 'Vota quinquaegenalia R. R. P. Ampl. D. D: Godefridi Gottw[icensis] anno professi Jubileo deposita'. Another occasion for an *Applausus* cantata by Zechner was the birthday of the Göttweig *Regens chori*, P. Joseph: 'Plausus ad Natalitia R. P. Josephi'. Haydn's *Applausus* (XXIVa:6) was composed for a seventieth-birthday celebration at Zwettl Abbey in 1768.[1] The texts to these *Applausus* cantatas were often written by local monks or scholars.

---

1 *MGG* 5 (1956), article 'Göttweig' (Landon), p. 467. *Haydn at Eszterháza 1766–1790*, pp. 145–8.

ITALIAN OPERA

It is particularly constricting to have to deal with the whole problem of Italian opera within this limited space, and we have adopted a policy of choosing, here and in similar forms, one or two works to act as representatives for all the others.

Haydn lived a floor above the famous poet Metastasio, who had made Vienna his home. It is nowadays as difficult to understand Metastasio's universal appeal throughout the eighteenth century as it is for us to appreciate the qualities that made Johann Adam Hasse (Metastasio's most successful partner, musically) the most popular mid-eighteenth-century composer of *opere serie*. Part of the reason for this present-day lack of comprehension is that our concept of opera has been radically and permanently altered by the passage of time, always more cruel to operas than to instrumental music, as witness the fate of Antonio Vivaldi, whose operas are now regarded as historical curiosities but whose instrumental works, and especially *Le quattro stagioni*, are among the most popular music in the Western world.

The distinguished Hasse scholar, Professor Sven H. Hansell, has helped us to understand and appreciate the attitude of eighteenth-century audiences to the Hasse/Metastasio team. In a brilliant paper, *Melody Types of Mid-18th Century Neapolitan Arias*, given at Santa Barbara (California) in December 1967, Professor Hansell explained some of the now forgotten principles which guided composers of serious opera in 1750. He notes:

> The melodies of mid-eighteenth century Italian arias were remarkably well suited to serve the exigencies of their poetic texts. At this time composers seem to have been particularly concerned ... with producing clear and balanced settings of texts that observed correct word accentuation; thus, a simple classification of arias according to the poetic metres of their texts can be made. ...
>
> For example, the line of seven syllables, the *settenario*, normally produced a three-bar phrase when set to music in a triple metre. Similarly, when set in six-eight or twelve-eight time, or other compound metres, the musical phrases of *settenarii* were usually three-fourths of a bar, one-and-one-half bars or, again, three bars in length. The musical phrases produced by triple metre settings of the *settenario* and *endecasillabo* will be seen to differ markedly from those of five, six and eight syllable lines, the *quinario*, *senario* and *ottonario* which, as a rule, consist of two or four bar phrases.
>
> Although such [duple metre] phrases are generally two or four bars long, certain differences can be noted among them. For instance, when the *settenario* ... has an accent on the first syllable, many syncopations result. When, however, an accent comes on the second syllable, few if any syncopations generally occur. ...
>
> ... The metre of a text is easily perceived because the opening lines of an aria were normally set in an essentially syllabic manner. If, for example, the first strophe of an aria had four lines of text, the first three lines were usually set with a fairly consistent number of syllables per bar while the last line was permitted to culminate in a melisma. But even the melismatic expansion of the vocal line always preserved some characteristic features of the musical phrases that preceded it, permitting its association with a particular *ritmica* of prosody. ...
>
> The arias of the 1720s, '30s and '40s should be taken to represent a general reaction to the Baroque art of the preceding century. Composers not only eschewed captivating dance rhythms that obscure the length and accentuation of verse lines, but avoided the multiplicity of forms, the variety of orchestrations, the thicker harmonic textures and the counterpoint [of Baroque music]. By the second quarter of the eighteenth century, opera composers had imposed on themselves a restraint – one is tempted to say a 'classical restraint' – which

paralleled a certain self-discipline that poets of the same time also exercized. A librettist like ... Metastasio practised an astonishing self-control by limiting his vocabulary drastically in order to communicate with the greatest possible accuracy and consistency concepts and feelings. In his theoretical writings and letters he called foreign terms undesirable, obscure metaphors objectionable and *ornamenti ambiziosi*, that is, words serving merely decoratively, distasteful. In his hands and those of his contemporaries, Italian emerged as a renovated language.

.... When setting a poem to music, Italian composers [of the period] fostered a musical style characterized, above all, by a relative simplicity and clarity of texture as well as a homogeneity and balance of elements .... the *da capo* form was selected for use by composers who did know others, including [the *durchkomponierte* forms of their religious music, such as their Marian antiphons], but preferred the *da capo* as the most ingenious means of allowing music and poetry to interact. ...

... The classification [here] proposed ... differentiates early, middle and late eighteenth-century Italian attitudes towards texts ... In the second half of the century, infusing music with dramatic implications, composers modified the *da capo* aria by abridging it, enlarging its orchestrations, and introducing contrasting motives or themes with the result that poetic texts were threatened with complications that would obscure them. Musical phrases were no longer homogeneous in character or length ... Irregular in length and accentuation, the melodies of these later arias generally do *not* suggest a classification according to particular poetic metres. ...

... The majority of masters of the Neapolitan School like Leo, Vinci, Jommelli and Hasse can be considered more predictable in their handling of texts than a few like Porpora or Pergolesi. ...

... [This was a] period ... at least as literarily oriented as it was musically.

Recently there have been serious attempts to reconsider the importance of Metastasio from the literary standpoint.[1] As far as Hasse is concerned, we would draw attention to a volume of interesting cantatas of the period 1760–2, where one feels that Hasse's musical language is closest to that of Haydn.[2] There is no fall more dramatic than that of the Hasse/Metastasio team, from their exalted position in 1750 to their total neglect today. Burney writes of them:

> ... This poet and musician are the *two halves* of what, like Plato's *Androgyne*, once constituted a *whole*; for as they are equally possessed of the same characteristic marks of true genius, taste, and judgement; so propriety, consistency, clearness, and precision, are alike the inseparable companions of both ... he [Hasse] may, without injury to his brethren, be allowed to be as superior to all other lyric composers, as Metastasio is to all other lyric poets.
> [*The Present State of Music in Germany, the Netherlands, and United Provinces*, 2nd corrected ed., London 1775, vol. I, pp. 240f.]

The reform poet, Ranieri de Calzabigi (Calsabigi), writing in 1755, considered that

> The force, variety, and beauty of our [Italian] music proceeds, in my opinion, from the majesty, energy, and brilliant images of the poetry of Signor Metastasio. The music of his verses which one can discover simply in their reading impresses itself quickly upon the minds of our composers and provides them all these

---

1 Walter Binni, *L'Arcadia e il Metastasio*, Florence 1963, also his *Classicismo e Neoclassicismo nella letteratura del settecento*, Florence 1954.
2 J. A. Hasse: *Cantates pour une voix de femme et orchestre*, 'le pupitre' (LP 11, S. H. Hansell), Paris 1968.

musical splendours which demand admiration and respect from knowledgeable minds.

[R. de' Calzabigi, 'Dissertazione sulle poesie drammatiche del Metastasio', in *Poesie del Signor Abate Pietro Metastasio*, Paris 1755, vol. I, p. clxxxviii; translation from S. H. Hansell, op. cit. p. vii]

It was, interestingly enough, not the famous team of Calzabigi/Gluck that undermined the then much more celebrated duo, Metastasio/Hasse, but the efforts of the Italians in another form, *opera buffa*. By the time a work like Piccinni's *La buona figliuola* (Rome, 1760), with its delightful text by Goldoni, had conquered Europe, the Hasse tradition began to seem stale and infinitely unprofitable. Haydn was never attracted to *opera seria* except tangentially, though he found the technical aspects of recitative in Metastasian opera provocative (*L'isola disabitata*, 1779).

By 1750, not only the shorter Italian *intermezzi*, of which the famous prototype was Pergolesi's *La serva padrona* (1733), but *opere buffe* on the larger scale, were well established throughout Europe. In 1750, Baldassare Galuppi composed two famous Goldoni texts which had a decisive influence on Haydn: *Il mondo della luna* (Venice, January 1750) and *Il mondo alla roversa o sia Le donne che comandono* (Venice, November 1750), both of which were given all over Italy and at Dresden, Hamburg and Prague. The latter work was even published in piano score by J. G. I. Breitkopf (Leipzig, 1758), and we have concrete evidence that Haydn not only knew the work but admired it to the extent of recommending it especially to pupils. In the 1750s, one of Haydn's pupils was Robert Kimmerling (Kymmerling), later *Regens chori* at Melk Abbey, where the Breitkopf print of this Opera is preserved with the following note on it: 'NB Haec operetta placuit Josepho Haydn, magistro meo. Recommendavit mihi, suo discipulo ut sapius persolvam, propter bonum Cantabile.'[1]

Galuppi's Opera is, of course, as forgotten as anything by Hasse; by contrast, however, Galuppi's style lived on, becoming a foundation of the Mozartian comic opera style – Galuppi was one of many – and has thus, in its modest way, passed into the mainstream of our musical consciousness. Haydn liked it 'because of its good cantabile', by which he meant, presumably, such passages as the following *messa di voce* in Tullia's Aria (Atto I°, Sc. 3):

The thematic type of the moderately slow (Andante) Aria, in 2/4 time, especially for soprano, 'Quegl'occhietti' (Atto I°, Sc. 4),

will pass directly into Haydn's own operas and the kind of insertion aria he would write for Luigia Polzelli, his mistress (with a range surprisingly like that of Aurora in Galuppi's *dramma giocoso*). One thinks of Haydn's insertion, 'Vada adagio'

---

1 *Barockausstellung: Jakob Prandtauer und sein Kunstkreis*, Melk Abbey 1960, Catalogue, p. 258, item 512. We used the copy of the Breitkopf print in GdM IV.7132.

(XXIVb:12), for the Eszterháza performance of Guglielmi's *La Quaquera spiritosa* (1787),[1] or Balkis's Aria, 'Siam femmine buonine', in Haydn's *L'incontro improvviso* (Atto I°, Sc. 8):

In Graziosino's Aria in Galuppi's work (Atto I°, Sc. 5, 'Quando gl'augelli cantano'), we have another prototype for Haydn, the six-eight metre etc., and the evocation of different birds must have quickened Haydn's pulse.

We look forward not only to Buonafede's Aria, 'Che mondo amabile', from Haydn's *Il mondo della luna* of 1777 (Atto II°, Sc. 7), where the words 'Gl'augelli cantano' induce Buonafede to whistle; we also recall the (in)famous word – painting (*Thonmahlerey*) of *The Creation* and *The Seasons*. In Galuppi's Aria by Giacinto (Atto I°, Sc. 7: 'In quel volto'), the constant shifts from Sostenuto to Allegro and the 'patter' in the latter tempo –

ed un uo-mo si ben fat-to con-tra-fat-to mo-ri-rà

– presage Haydnesque techniques (alternating slow and fast tempi in Lisetta's Aria, 'Una donna come me' from *Il mondo della luna*, Atto I°, Sc. 9, and in many other Haydn arias). In the Finale to Atto I° of Goldoni/Galuppi, the pacing and structure remind us of Haydn's own finales, e.g. *L'infedeltà delusa* of 1773, and not only the main segment

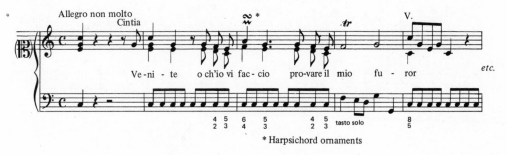

1 *Haydn at Eszterháza 1766–1790*, pp. 683f. and 649.

but in particular the 'follow up' by Giacinto:

We notice, too, the pounding bass rhythm in quavers which will soon become such an essential part of Haydn's style: it is clearly a straight derivative from the Italian operatic tradition. The shifting metres in, let us say, the Finales of Haydn's *Lo speziale* (1768) or *L'infedeltà delusa* also derive from Italian *opera buffa*: in the Finale to Atto I° of *Il mondo alla roversa*, the 4/4 changes to 3/8 and back to 4/4, later to 6/8, and the movement ends in 4/4.

Most of the arias are in the usual *da capo* form with a shorter 'B' section; this was to be Haydn's procedure in the operas of 1762 and 1763 (examined later in this volume). But we also note the encouraging presence of what would later be the 'cavatina' form (a famous example occurs in *The Seasons*:[1] Lucas's *Cavatine* [Germanized form] 'Dem Druck erlieget die Natur'): a slow, very concise Aria, Giacinto's 'Madre natura' (Atto I°, Sc. 6, Largo, C minor). We also register a typical *siciliano* in Ferramonte's Aria, 'Quando le donne' (Atto II°, Sc. 6), which Haydn would remember when composing Nencio's Aria, 'Chi s'impaccia di moglie cittadina' from *L'infedeltà delusa* (Atto I°, Sc. 6). And Haydn must have been irresistibly drawn to the odd shape of the following Aria by Ferramonte, 'Al bello delle feminine' (Atto II°, Sc. 8), where we find the scheme $5 + 5 + 4 + 3 + 4 + 5$ in the opening ritornello:

---

1 *Haydn: the Late Years 1801–1809*, p. 157.

We shall encounter similar eccentricities even in Haydn's arias of 1762–3, and once again they are derived from Galuppi and his compatriots, e.g. Piccinni. An interesting recitative breaks suddenly into Graziosino's Aria, 'Son di corraggio armato' (Atto II°, Sc. 11), and the progress of the piece is several times so interrupted – also a Haydnesque feature, particularly in dramatic situations such as Zelmira's Aria, 'Torna pure al caro bene' from *Armida* (Atto III°, Sc. 2), 1784.

One final detail in Galuppi's Opera was at once taken up by Haydn: the overall tonal scheme. The work is in what is called progressive tonality, as are many Haydn operas (also *The Creation*). It begins (incidentally with a characteristic three-movement *sinfonia*) in G and Atto I° ends in C. Atto II° moves from B flat to E, an interesting relationship by a third which strongly presages Haydn's later fascination with *Terzverwandschaft*, or the relation of keys by thirds. Act III begins and ends in B flat (again a third-related key to G).

Galuppi's *Il mondo alla roversa* is an attractive Opera based upon one of Goldoni's sparkling texts. For Haydn, however, it had no doubt lost much of its appeal by 1800, for (about that date) he confessed to Carpani that he could no longer generate the same enthusiasm for the pieces that had enchanted him in his youth. *Il mondo alla roversa* is one of those many sterling Italian operas which have been permanently and irreversibly removed from circulation by Mozart (and also Rossini), but at the time it reached Haydn's impressionable ears, not only the music but the libretto obviously fascinated him; we must recall that he owned many volumes of Goldoni's collected works (they are listed summarily in the catalogue of Haydn's library in 1809).

GERMAN OPERA (*Singspiel*)

There are, as noted earlier, two volumes of music to the German comedies given by Kurz-Bernadon at the Kärntnerthortheater in the 1750s. They are all anonymous. Robert Haas, and after him Eva Badura-Skoda, have wished to attribute much of this winning and spirited music to Haydn.[1] Although it must sound odd to say so in a Haydn biography, in fact for the purposes of this survey, it matters very little whether Haydn wrote the music attributed to him or not. If he did, we shall rejoice in some extracts from his earliest operatic scores; if he did not, we have a remarkably Haydnesque series of numbers which show us with brilliant clarity, if not 'd'où vient l'art d'Haydn', at least 'd'où vient le style théâtral d'Haydn'. It is precisely the kind of music we know from *Die Feuersbrunst*. The reader may examine all this music in the *DTÖ* volumes listed below (see note 1), but the most spectacularly Haydnesque Aria is Colombina's in E major (one thinks of Colombina's Aria, 'Wie wallet mein Herze', in the second act of *Die Feuersbrunst*,[2] in the same key) which was also published by Frau Dr Badura-Skoda in her article, 'Teutsche Comoedie-Arien und Joseph Haydn' (*Der*

1 The reader may like to know something of this unique source. The two volumes (Österreichische Nationalbibliothek, Musiksammlung, Codex 14062 and 14063) are each entitled 'Teütsche/Comedie Arien' and were written on oblong Italian paper by professional Viennese copyists. As the *DTÖ*'s co-editor, Herbert Zeman, notes in the second selection of these pieces (p. x of Foreword, *DTÖ* Band 121, Graz 1971), this is not just an idle selection but, from all appearances, two operatic entities, each based on selections from the Kärntnerthortheater repertoire of the 1750s, by Kurz-Bernadon and others. The pieces have been selected carefully, the big 'set piece' ensemble numbers being placed at the end, and so constructed that each codex could be performed as an operatic evening. It is not clear for what purpose such a selection was made. It is almost as if someone in the twenty-first century made two operatic evenings, one from Mozart's *Ascanio in Alba, Mitridate* and *Lucio Silla* dealing vaguely with the difficulties of ancient heroes and the wiles of their slave women; and one on the foibles of men and women, based on *Entführung, Le nozze di Figaro* and *Così fan tutte*. Now the watermarks of the two codices suggest strongly that the MSS. were *not* drawn up in the late 1750s but rather about 1770: the Italian paper includes the letter 'w' by itself, three half moons of decreasing size alone or with letters 'REAL/A'. It is thus doubly curious that Haydn's name, if he were the composer of one or more of the numbers, be suppressed. We believe that these two volumes were put together by a clever impresario to make two operatic entertainments, and that the music is partly by Haydn and partly by other composers such as Joseph Ziegler (1722–67), Ignaz Ulbrich (1706?–96), as well as Adalbert Fauner, the violinist Eder and the ominous name of Joseph Hayda – about which *vide infra*, p. 234. In 14062, No. 4, 'Mir ist die Welt zu klein' (*DTÖ* 64, p. 63), we note the presence of the dynamic mark *mf* as part of a crescendo from *p* to *ff* (with interruptions; *DTÖ* 64, p. 64): now *mf* appears in no work of the young Haydn for which we have authentic sources. We believe that the most Haydnesque pieces all come in Codex 14063, the second of the two. Taking the music in its appearance in *DTÖ*, the first series to engage our interest is from Johann Georg Heubel's *Der Triumph der Freundschaft*, 1755, *DTÖ* 64. First a Presto Aria for Bernadon (= Kurz), 'Zurück! ich sage euch', with that springy writing for strings that we admire in Haydn's early symphonies and, of course, the rhythmic fingerprints in the horns. On p. 51 at 'Un poco più' we note a technique of filling in the rests by means of repeated figures ♪ ♫ ♩, as seen in Vespina's accompanied recitative prior to her Aria, 'Ho un tumore' in Atto II⁰ of Haydn's *L'infedeltà delusa* (1773). There follows (p. 53) a slow Aria by Mirile, 'Du könntest zwar vor allen', where the use of triplets is typically Haydnesque, as are the sequential patterns. Also typical is the introduction of Italian into the German text ('la sorte mia crudele läßt mir das bonheur nicht'), also French ('Pardonnez, schönste Seele, ne pensez pas, mein Licht, daß ich dich kann verschmähen, ach, könntest du doch sehen dentro il mio cuore, mia pena ed' amore'. Also the use of *pp* is Haydnesque. In No. 6, Duetto Mirile/Bernadon (p. 58), it is the approach of the trill figure (bars 5f.) which is strikingly like Haydn, also the use of *ff-p*. As stated, the great revelation is Colombina's Aria, 'Wurstl mein Schaz'rl wo wirst du wohl seyn!' from *Leopoldel Der teutsche Robinson* by J. G. Heubel, after Easter 1754, the first of four numbers. We believe all four to be Haydn (and we doubt if Haydn often contributed to plays in which other composers collaborated). No. 2 (*DTÖ* 121, p. 23) is a slow E flat Duetto for Rosaura-Leopoldel, for two flutes, two horns and strings. It, too, is full of characteristic Haydniana almost too numerous to mention singly; there is not one unconvincing detail. Another Aria, No. 3 (Allegro molto, p. 30), for Leopoldel, is in the 'rage' aria manner that we know well in *Applausus* (1768) and other, Esterházy, cantatas examined in this volume. The broken semiquaver violin II accompaniment leaps out of the page, as do the pounding repeated bass quavers. The *piano* interlude (bars 11ff.), with its typically Haydnesque rhythms, and the syncopations at bar 14 are totally convincing; also the final ritornello with its moving up the triad in repeated semiquavers (*à la* 'L'ours', Symphony 82/I) and the attached phrase down to the note of departure, this last section being dramatically extended – all this has every Morellian earmark that one could wish for. Colombina's next Aria, No. 4 (p. 37), 'Schazerl bleib hier', is Andante grazioso in G, 3/8, and its inner construction – we have not the space for the details, alas – reveals Haydn's craftsmanship, and also that certain involvement with the text that we will note in Haydn's operas. Here, we see him lovingly carving out the music, *pp*, to 'Denk an die Schwüre, bezeuge dich treu, wenn ich dich verliere, so sterb ich aufs neu.' Of the remaining music in Codex 19063, the only number which stands head and shoulders above the rather good and capable *gros* is No. 15, Bernadon's Aria, 'Poz tausend, wie will ich mich raufen' from *Hans Wurst Der Stumme in der Einbildung Und Bernadon, Der gezwungene Rauber* by J. G. Heubel, after Easter 1756 (coincidence that so many of the most Haydnesque musical pieces occur in works by Heubel, who was obviously a *poeta locum tenens* for the Kärntnerthortheater?). Here is one of the bright D major pieces with many convincing details, e.g. the running violin II part in semiquavers at bar 1, also repeated when the voice enters, a specialized technique which we also find at the outset of the Overture to *Lo speziale* (1768). There is a curious little middle section, very brief, in D minor ('ach, laßt mich doch leben'). Whoever the composer is, the final ritornello explains the semiquaver technique at the beginning, for the text being described is 'izt laufe davon', the 'running away' being precisely those 'running' semiquavers. It is all in the Haydn technique that we will come to know intimately as the years go by and as opera gains the upper hand in the Esterházy establishment.

It seems unlikely, if not impossible, that we will discover new sources, but Dr Zeman (and we) hope for that stroke of luck which has so often brought to light Haydniana hitherto given up for lost. In particular, we may hope for some forthcoming bills from the archives of the Kärntnerthortheater which will shed much-needed light on the 'house composers' of the 1750s, among which it is entirely possible that we may count Joseph Haydn.

2 *Haydn at Eszterháza 1766–1790*, p. 521.

junge Haydn, Graz 1972, pp. 69–72). In this Aria, there are even direct quotations from other works by Haydn of this early period, the most striking being the beginning of the *Salve Regina* in E (XXIIIb:1) of 1756, quoted in bars 4/5. The interested reader may play the Aria (and sing it): it is printed in a pretty piano score. It is surely the most interesting discovery of its kind in many years.

ORCHESTRAL MUSIC: THE SYMPHONY

In recent years, considerable research has been made into the Austrian symphonic form of *c.* 1750, and although we still await specialized studies about the works of many individual composers (such as Schlöger, M. G. Monn, the Reutters, etc.), we are today in a position to make certain generalizations that no one would have dared to make twenty-five years ago. Some of these summaries have been written with great perspicacity by J. P. Larsen, among which we might single out a recent publication which arrived too late for inclusion in our General Bibliography (*Haydn: the Late Years 1801–1809*): 'Zur Enstehung der österreichischen Symphonietradition' (*HJB* X [1978], pp. 72ff.).

The Austrian symphony developed from its Italian prototype; and like its sister-form south of the Alps, it was in two somewhat similar basic forms, the operatic overture and the concert symphony, though both were usually in three movements. The newly emerging Italian concert symphony may now be studied through the early works of its leading exponent, G. B. Sammartini.[1] Alfred Einstein has summed up this Italian symphony with his usual brilliance:[2]

> It is the spirit of *opera buffa*. The change to this spirit from the early classic *sinfonia* or *overtura*, with its solemnity and *grandezza*, its pathos, its elegiac greatness in the slow movements, its contrapuntal dignity, its *soli obbligati*, is as complete as possible. Music history moves from one extreme to another. When a Neapolitan symphony begins importantly, it does so with chords repeated rhythmically, but it continues with charming little bird-like motives and rhythmic piquancies, and when it reaches the dominant (in major) or the mediant (in minor) there comes a bit of nothingness still more charming, if possible, though perhaps at the same time more lyric. . . . The tension, if any, between these two little figures can never be very tragic, and the solution of the conflict – the so-called reprise – can hardly be anything but light, playful, and conventional. The second movement is usually a serenade, the third a gay farewell or a graceful dance.

One of the first representatives of the Austrian variety of this three-movement operatic overture was Georg Christoph Wagenseil, who by 1740, in his *I lamenti d'Orfeo*, had imported the new form to Vienna. He continued to write successful overtures in three movements which were, however, also circulated to the Austrian monasteries (Lambach, Göttweig, Kremsmünster, etc.) as concert symphonies. Two such works, of particular interest to us, were published in the *DTÖ* XV. Jahrgang ('Wiener Instrumentalmusik im 18. Jahrhundert I'). One is a large-scale Overture to *La clemenza di Tito* of 1746, with flutes (slow movement only), oboes, trumpets, timpani and strings. When the work was marketed as a concert symphony, the

---

1 *The Symphonies of G. B. Sammartini*: vol. 1. 'The Early Symphonies' (Bathia Churgin), Cambridge, Mass., 1968.
2 *Mozart, His Character, His Work*, London 1946, p. 217.

timpani were dropped (as would often happen to Haydn symphonies in the hands of professional copyists) and the trumpets replaced by horns with slightly different notes now and then. There are three movements, the second (Andantino, B minor) being scored for flutes and strings and the third, a 'Tempo di Menuetto' (Austrian spelling) with the orchestration of the first movement. The reduction or total omission of the winds in the slow movement is a typical feature of Italian symphonies, too.

Now there are several details of this Wagenseil Overture that must concern us here. One is the frequent appearance of the trumpet rhythm ♫♫ ♫ , which in the first movement of Wagenseil's music appears no less than a dozen times, at first in a melodic pattern but later in just the same wise as Haydn would later use it, i.e. on one repeated note. The timpani, however, are used in the old-fashioned manner (e.g. ♩ ♫♫ ♩) – and do not double the above trumpet rhythm. This rhythmic tag is so striking that one can only presume that Haydn must have remembered it from this or a similar Wagenseil symphony (there are others using this same 'fingerprint'). A second interesting point: the subsidiary subject is in the dominant *minor* and contains the kind of unison rhythmic theme *forte*, contrasting with a more lyric answer, harmonized and *piano* – all this, *in toto*, is designed to set off the pompous opening theme. This beginning –

– is conventional and very Italian, but the second subject group is much more Austrian and even sounds (as the editors of the *DTÖ* point out) like Haydn:

Although the work was circulated as a concert symphony, there are aspects of it that constantly remind us of its origins in the opera pit, e.g. this is the type of passage work:

This is the kind of figuration that presages Haydn's early operatic overtures, *Acide* and Symphony No. 9 (both 1762). In Wagenseil, there is no development section, simply a middle 'block' which, however, contains one characteristic detail: it begins with the main subject in the dominant and then uses the second subject group in B minor. The whole middle section consists of ten bars. Another operatic practice: there are no double bars in any of the movements except the third (in the middle): the same applies to Haydn's *Acide* Overture, first two movements.

   Wagenseil's slow movement: Andante (other sources: Andantino), 3/8, B minor, with two flutes. Form: basically binary, A and A' (A with modulation to D major, cadence in D, modulation back to B minor; A' remains in B minor and has a little coda). The instrumentation is pretty (ethereal flutes) and the principal theme is a legato line over a sharply etched lower part; when repeated in D, the orchestration is gracefully enhanced by the flutes and 'basso' (hitherto absent). It is all a bit of 'nothingness', as Einstein would say, but deftly organized and possessing real charm.

   Tempo di Menuetto: typical 'sighing' passages in quavers; dotted pattern in the theme; introduction of triplet quavers towards the end of the first part. One is especially struck by the economy and brevity of the whole.

———————

Various kinds of symphonies existed. There was a great tradition of large-scale C major 'Parthien' or symphonies with as many as four trumpets and kettledrums. Reutter, Jr. composed a 'Servizio di Tavola' in 1757 which was published in the *DTÖ* volume containing the above-mentioned Wagenseil work. Except for a wildly eccentric slow movement, which we shall mention later in another connection, this Reutter work is very much like a concert symphony, with double bars (as opposed to operatic overtures) in all sections except the slow movement. The title of the first part is significant: 'Intrada', reflecting a church tradition of pieces that were often in C major and with three movements. Larsen (op. cit., p. 76) draws attention to two such *intrade* by Antonio Caldara in the Austrian National Library (S.m. 3616/7), both in C and one with a typical fugal movement. It should not astonish us that Reutter's earlier (1745) 'Servizio di Tavola' was also played in St Stephen's, as parts from the Cathedral Archives, now in the GdM (XIII. 8093), show. Reutter also composed multi-choired works of this kind, with separate choirs of trumpets and kettledrums which were probably placed antiphonally in the old Venetian tradition of St Mark's Cathedral (Reutter's autographs in Heiligenkreuz Abbey, where they were collected by his son, who was a monk there). This multi-choired tradition was carried on *inter alia* by Carlos d'Ordoñez, in a three-choired Symphony in C (choirs I & II, each with pairs of trumpets and timpani, choir III being the main orchestra; new edition, Universal Edition, edited by the present writer).

   The church tradition also included the old *sonata da chiesa* of Corellian fame, which began with a whole slow movement and continued with a fugal allegro, the whole then being repeated (with or without emendations) to make the customary slow-fast-slow-fast pattern. These sonatas, generally for three instruments with *basso continuo*, could be shortened to a kind of prelude–fugue, of which we have many specimens by Austrian Baroque composers such as J.J. Fux. Haydn's predecessor at Eisenstadt, Gregor Joseph Werner, wrote many church pieces in this prelude–fugue form. As we shall see, there was an Austrian derivative of this *sonata da chiesa* in symphonic form which Haydn was to cultivate; and he also wrote trios for strings and other chamber works in which the old church sonata form prevailed.

Before we leave Reutter's 'Servizio di Tavola' of 1757, we might pause for a moment over the Minuet & Trio. Wagenseil's Overture to *La clemenza di Tito* of 1746 contained a 'Tempo di Menuetto' with many features that would reappear in Haydn; but Reutter's work, being closer to Haydn not only chronologically but also because of the personal relationship between the two men, is even more obviously the kind of model Haydn studied and copied: the combination of trills (in two different rhythms), triplets and straight quavers, dotted patterns, and so on, is precisely Haydn's (cf. Haydn's Minuets in Symphonies Nos. 25, 32, 33, 37, etc.).

The Trio in Reutter has an interplay between violins and divided violas that puts one in mind of Haydn's Symphony No. 15, Trio (where, instead of divided violas, we have viola and 'cello).

The trio sonata of Italian tradition was not only transported to Austria as a *sonata da chiesa*, but it also developed into a hybrid 'Parthia'. Sometimes these 'Parthien' or symphonies were simply reduced versions of an Italian overture, but even then we find the kind of imitational work between the violins that shows the continuing emergence of an Austrian concert symphony. A typical example is Wagenseil's Symphony in G for two violins and 'Basso' (we follow a facsimile of an eighteenth-century score published by Hans Schneider, Tutzing).

The second movement, in G minor (6/8), has that old-fashioned flavour that Haydn would gladly adopt in his early slow movements –

– the dotted rhythms attached to trills, the sequences with tied notes to make syncopations, the imitation between the violins, and so on. The Finale is in 3/8 but is not a disguised minuet or 'Tempo di Menuetto', though it borrows the A-B-A form of the minuet.

We note, in this work, the same kind of impersonal efficiency, a complete lack of dramatic tension, and the same rhythmic vitality that characterize much of early Haydn. All this is nicely balanced by the quiet, rather Venetian 'light melancholy' (*tristezza*) of the slow movement, where we have a rather pretty sequence at the beginning of the second part:

Sometimes such a 'Partita' is nearer the chamber music tradition, for example, those of Franz Tuma (1704–74), of which one may be studied in a convenient modern edition by E. Schenk (*Partita a tre ... No. 7*, Österreichischer Bundesverlag, Hausmusik 6781, 155, now in Diletto Musicale, Verlag Doblinger), based on a set of MS. parts in GdM. Here we encounter, in the 'Intrada', another venerable tradition: the music begins with the first violin and 'Basso'; after three bars, the second violin enters with the same subject in the dominant. We shall see precisely this same procedure in Haydn's String Trios Nos. 6/III (V:6), 21/I (V:G1) and 26/I (V:G4), and in a slightly different fashion in Quartet, Op. 1, No. 3/I. But the remainder of Tuma's Partita No. 7 reflects the old suite tradition: II. Gavotte polonese; III. Menuet (with the violins in unison throughout) and Trio; IV. Gigue. An equally atypical sequence of movements may be found in the first of Five Symphonies for strings by Jan Zach (1699–1773), published as No. 43 in the *Musica Antiqua Bohemica* (Prague 1960) from a MS. in the Grand Ducal Library, Darmstadt (sign. mus. 3889). We have: I. Allegro; II. Polonese; III. Minuetto/Trio; IV. Finale (Allegro, 2/4).

The Minuet/Trio entered the Austrian symphony as early as 24 May 1740, when Monn wrote his now famous Symphony in D (autograph in the Austrian National Library, S.m. 18334) published in the *DTÖ* volume containing the Wagenseil and Reutter works discussed above. The most interesting feature of that 'Menuetto' (no Trio) is the idiomatic use of the horns: the ♩ ♫♫ cadential rhythm will become an integral part of Haydn's style (Symphony No. 5, Minuet, bar 11, same pattern in horn II, cadential context); while in the same movement there is a real solo passage –

– which reminds one that in Vienna, the Bohemian horn tradition was already a flourishing operation as early as 1740. Visitors to Vienna certainly came under the 'horn spell'. Henry Swinburne,[1] visiting Vienna in the summer of 1780, noted, 'There is a heronry here, and much hawking. We heard two French horns in the woods. They also make that instrument too fine, and unnaturally learned.' In Symphony No. 5 by Haydn, we will find such a 'learned' horn trio, the first, perhaps, of many such extravagances which we shall be discussing in more detail elsewhere.

Another curious and rather unusual work in this same crucial *DTÖ* volume is a 'Partitta' by Matthäus Schlöger (c. 1722–1766), I.R. Master of the Clavier, whose symphonies are included in the 1759 Catalogue of Bishop Leopold Egk (*infra*, p. 584). This 'Partitta' comes from a set of contemporary MS. parts in GdM (IX 1083 [Q 16758]) entitled 'Partitta / a / Violino Primo / Violino Secondo / e / Basso / Del Sigre: Matteo Schlöger / [*incipit*]' on Italian paper with the watermark of three crescents. It is a symphony and was certainly intended to be performed either as a solo trio or with several instruments on each part. This is a genuine Austrian 'Partitta', a chamber symphony if one will, which is already a step away from the operatic overture. We include here part of the first movement.

1 *Secret Memoirs of the Courts of Europe. Letters Written at the End of the Eighteenth Century*, Philadelphia, n.d., vol. I, p. 335.

Partitta

Matthäus Schlöger

One notes the second subject group again in the dominant *minor*; one also sees a certain 'open' writing of the various parts, and not just the scales, fanfares, trill figures, etc., of the operatic overture. A typical earmark taken over by Haydn: at the outset of the second part, we have the main theme in the dominant, then almost immediately repeated in the tonic as the springboard to the 'development' (cf. Haydn's Symphonies Nos. 17/I, 19/I). In the Finale, the second subject is also in the dominant minor. There are four movements, of which the second is a rather original Largo:

The muted violins were to become an obsession with Haydn in the early 1770s (slow movements of symphonies) but we find the device even in the slow movement of Symphony No. 4. Note, in the Schlöger Largo, the independent part writing, almost a blueprint for Haydn's largos and adagios of the early trios and quartets. At the end of the exposition: shifting between *a* flat and *a* natural over V, another harmonic cast much appreciated by Haydn. The dynamic marks of this Largo are freer than is usual at this period. The only crescendo in the whole work appears here; in many Haydn symphonies of the early 1770s, the only crescendo marks appear in the slow movements.

And what of the Mannheim school and their famous 'road rollers', 'rockets', crescendos and decrescendos, their rich orchestration? As Einstein says, 'Haydn and Mozart adopted [these very considerable and varied dynamic shadings] with so much hesitation and reserve that they may almost be said to have rejected them' (*Mozart*, 217). It was therefore something of a gigantic red herring that Haydn's Symphony No. 1 began with a fully fledged Mannheim crescendo over a long D major pedal point and that, moreover, Gassmann's *sinfonia* to *L'Issipile* (Venice 1758) begins in an uncannily similar way.[1] Both are exceptions in their respective composer's *œuvre* – another exotic excursion. The Mannheim style was regarded, on the whole, with scepticism by the Austrian school, whose branches were by now (1750) different, even if many of the roots had been the same. There were, too, Mannheim composers whose style was much closer to the conservative Viennese tradition, e.g. Ignaz Holzbauer (1711–83) and Franz Xaver Richter (1709–89), both Mannheim composers by adoption. Such a work as the *Sinfonia* in G minor with the elaborate fugal movements by Richter (MS., Thurn und Taxis Archives, Regensburg) is much closer to the Fuxian *intrada* tradition than to the 'rockets' and 'road rollers' of Johann Stamitz (1717–57). And Franz Beck (1723–1809) was an equally atypical product of the Mannheim tradition, as we shall shortly see.

The difficulty of discussing the origins of the cassatio or divertimento as it was practised in the Austrian Monarchy is the chronological uncertainty of most MS. sources. Both Richter's and Holzbauer's musical origins appear to have been Viennese.[2] Holzbauer was born in Vienna. Richter was born in Moravia but it is thought likely that he was educated in the Austrian capital. Willi Gässler uncovered twelve early symphonies by Richter in the Darmstadt Court Library not known to Riemann (*DTB*), wherein their 'melodic, harmonic and formal structure ... clearly point to Vienna ...'. But of Richter's divertimenti and other forms of chamber music, it is almost impossible to state with confidence which are pre-Mannheim, and the same applies to Holzbauer's various divertimenti and partitas. Some of the Holzbauer chamber music in *Erbe* appears to have distinctive Mannheim features, i.e. to have been composed after 1751 when he left Vienna, whereas other works may have been composed in the early period. There is a three-'voiced' *Sinfonia* in G (MS. parts, Badische Landesbibliothek, Karlsruhe) similar in style to the Wagenseil G major *Sinfonia* discussed above, but which concludes with a distinctive 'Fuga Villanesca', a

1 Gassmann's Symphony edited by the present writer, Diletto Musicale, Verlag Doblinger. For musical examples of the similarity, see our B.B.C. Music Guide, *Haydn's Symphonies*, London 1966, p. 8.
2 Willi Gässler, *Die Sinfonien von Franz Xaver Richter und ihre Stellung in der vorklassischen Sinfonik*, Dissertation, Munich 1941. Hildegard Werner, *Die Sinfonien von Ignaz Holzbauer*, Dissertation, Munich 1942. Holzbauer's chamber music is now available in a volume of the *Erbe deutscher Musik*, Band 24 (Ursula Lehmann), Kassel 1953.

rustic fugue (or rather fugato) on what appears to be a folk tune (upbeat to 5–8, etc.) or series of folk tunes. This work, with its old-fashioned middle movement (Larghetto. Gustoso), seems to date from *c.* 1750. Of particular interest to this investigation is the series of Divertimenti scored, in one version, for two violins, two violas and 'Basso' and in another for flute, oboe, violin, viola, bassoon or 'cello, and Basso; both exist in what are purported to be autographs in GdM;[1] both are prototypes of Haydn works, Cassatios for strings in G (II:2) and A (II:A1), or the pair of works for flute, oboe, two violins, 'cello and bass (II:1 and 11). The Holzbauer works may be later than 1751 but nevertheless they contain points that concern us. All three works in *Erbe* begin with an entire opening slow movement, and this seems to have been something of a speciality with Holzbauer, for in the list of further chamber musical works not included in the *Erbe* volume, one notes three more works (out of five extant) beginning with slow movements or extended introductions. One of the slow movements in *Erbe*, that which opens Divertimento IV, actually turns out to be a huge introduction to an Allegro. One immediately thinks of Haydn's Symphony No. 25, where one believes that the work is in *sonata da chiesa* form but of which the opening Adagio turns out to be one of the longest of slow introductions (a precursor, in turn, of Mozart's 'Prague' Symphony, K.504). Apart from the general form, there are certain ways of scoring for the strings that appear to have been coin of the realm in mid-century Austria and southern Germany, such as these two figures from Divertimento III by Holzbauer (*Erbe*, p. 34), viola parts:

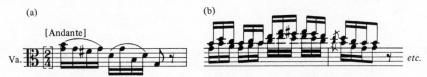

It is the sort of Austrian-Bavarian sound that places the divertimento and cassatio far away from the Italian opera symphony. While at times Holzbauer writes quite a Haydnesque theme – it is no accident that many Holzbauer works were wrongly attributed to Haydn – as in the following passage from Divertimento IV (*Erbe*, p. 48), even here the syncopated figure at bar 56 *in its particular context* is more like Mannheim or J. C. Bach than Haydn.

But in general, Holzbauer is softer, the contours more rounded, than Haydn: not for nothing do we find a Holzbauer slow movement in a *Sinfonia a tre* (Karlsruhe, ms. 211) marked 'Largo ed amoroso'. Something of this languid, Boccherini-like elegance is often part of Holzbauer's melodic constructions; and in this he is less close to early Haydn than, let us say, Reutter or Schlöger.

———

This survey will have shown that the lines of demarcation between trio and symphony, divertimento and quartet, cassatio and partita, are often nebulous. A

---

1 We examined these sources in the Spring of 1979, and we seriously doubt if they are autographs; we believe, rather, that they are copyists' transcriptions of parts into score.

similar overlapping occurs within the keyboard style, concertos, concertini, trios, divertimenti and sonatas. Let us start with the general concerto form, of which those for the keyboard were particularly cultivated in Austria.

On the whole, it cannot be said that the Austrians excelled in the concerto form. There is something more flaccid in their approach to the concerto than to symphony, partita or trio. The same will apply to Haydn's full concertos (as opposed to concertini or smaller concertos); they reveal the same structural and inspirational *lacunae*. Let us take as a characteristic example a 'Concerto per il violino' in D by Wagenseil (GdM, IX. 1446):

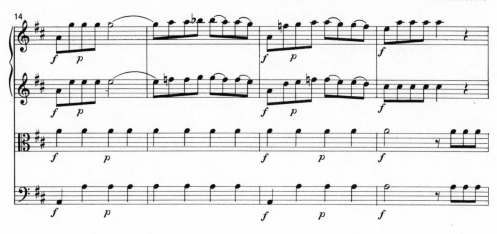

Notice in the opening ritornello the curious practice, to which Haydn often adheres, of writing the violins in unison and giving the only 'filling' part of the viola, thus creating a three- rather than four-part texture (see example). There is a curiously laming habit in this work of literal and sequential repetition which create an oddly disjointed and untaut texture. In the rather perfunctory working-out passage (the wrong term, of course; what we have is simply an extension), the scheme is V (Tutti, Solo), leading to

which will show the type of violin figurations used. One is reminded of Haydn's Concerto in G for violin and orchestra (VIIa:4) which, if genuine (*vide infra*, p. 517), will illustrate how Haydn adopted existing form and patterns to his purposes; if not genuine, we have yet another example of an Austrian pre-classical concerto. We now illustrate another rather conventional series of violin sequences from this section.

Formally, we continue to VI♮ (Tutti, Solo) and back to the tonic and recapitulation.

The opening of the slow movement is shown below; the scheme is the customary one of modulation to the mediant and back to the tonic minor.

Hardly anything in the solo part goes beyond the second position. We show two extensions for the solo violin, with their typical sequential patterns.

The principal subject of the Finale is given below, together with a sample of the violin's solo.

The form is what one would expect: Tutti/Solo in I, modulating to V (Tutti/Solo), and back to I (Tutti/Solo).

Lest this Wagenseil Concerto be considered an anomaly, let us turn to a Harpsichord Concerto by Schlöger, who was a rather good composer of symphonies but whose inspiration flags when faced with a concerto. The same endless repetitions and sequences, sometimes framed by dynamic contrasts, confront us (see example).

Yet the language is surprisingly like much of early Haydn in its detail, of which an extract from within the movement –

– will illustrate the point. Here and in the slow movement –

– there is a precise difference between trills, mordents and turns. The mordent on the off-beat

will later be a speciality of Haydn's. The Finale is illustrated by the opening solo (top range of the harpsichord throughout is *c′′′*):

One again notes the careful differentiation made between the various ornaments and the extreme simplicity of language. The chain trills are also typical. It is hardly an inspiring language and we believe that a case can be made for a general Austrian inability to write great concertos at this period, though they always tended to do better in the shorter kind of concerto to which we may now turn our attention.[1]

We now come to an interesting pair of concertos by Georg Reutter, Jr., in the GdM.[2] Dr Otto Biba believes that in these Reutter concertos, and especially in that in C major, we may have what were originally organ concertos which, as the copyists were to do with Haydn's (probably with his approval), were marketed as harpsichord concertos. There is no difference in technique between these pedal-less (*Positiv*) organ concertos and real harpsichord music in the Vienna of the 1750s and 1760s. Reutter's organs at the Salvator Chapel (still extant) and at St Stephen's did not exceed d''',[3] and none of these concertos exceeds that range. Our C major work is interesting in that it eschews all the cadenzas (perhaps because of its original function as part of a religious

1 Schlöger: GdM VII. 13014 (Q 16301). 'In A♯ / Concerto / Per il Clavi Cembalo / 2: Violini / e / Basso / Del Sig.RE Matteo Schlöger' on oblong paper (watermarks: vertical chain lines, three crescents of decreasing size with letters 'M' or 'W' (latter harpsichord part), fleur-de-lys with a long 'tail'.

2 C major: VII. 12991 'Concerto / per il clavicembalo / à / 2 Violini / e / Contra Basso / Del Sig :re Giorgio Reutter, Maestro di / Capella di S: M: R: è di S; Steffano'. Oblong paper (watermarks: three crescents of decreasing size, alone or with letter 'M'; letters 'AS'; title page on other paper: handsome stag, letter 'W' and another title: 'Concerto / â / Clavicembalo Principale / Violino Primo / Violino 2do : / con Basso / [*incipit* for harpsichord on two staves] / Authore / Reitter').

3 Information generously supplied by Dr Biba in April, 1979. The Salvator Chapel, with a Gothic exterior and 'one of the oldest examples of Renaissance architecture on German soil (second half of the 16th century)' (K. Baedeker, *Austria-Hungary*, 11th ed., Leipzig 1911, p. 41), was in Reutter's (and Haydn's) time the Chapel of the Rathaus and Reutter had charge of its musical activities.

ceremony?) and is in a kind of reduced concerto form. For some reason, this contraction of the concerto form produces a better organization; but in any case the language of this Reutter Organ Concerto is much closer to Haydn's in every way. We observe that the theme is so constructed that it can begin as well in the middle of the bar, which occurs when the solo begins: everything is displaced half a bar to the right.

Concerto

Georg Reutter, Jr.

The absence of a viola part in these keyboard concertos will be noted; this seems to have been a Viennese tradition which Haydn partially adopted, as he also did the overall formal scheme.[1] The language of the slow movement is very close to Haydn's

1 After our example, there is a ritornello in G, followed by a modulation to A minor, then back to the tonic and recapitulation, which differs from the exposition in that the organ has the theme and then the music is marked 'Da capo al Segno'. Thus, the fermata is simply an indication of the first movement's conclusion and is not an agogic indication. Second movement: after

etc. close in E flat and double bar. Second part also framed by double bar: E flat → F minor I_4^6 → recapitulation C minor.

Piano Sonata No. 13's Adagio (XVI:6) (identical with Piano Trio No. 3's Adagio [XVI:6]), while the Finale (Allegro, 3/8) is equally close to many Haydn keyboard concerto and sonata/trio finales. One is also reminded of the proximity of the various keyboard forms, one with the other.

The other Reutter Concerto[1] is also in this shortened form, i.e. without cadenzas and with two sets of double bars, in the middle and at the end of the second and final movements. We show the beginning of the opening Allegro, with its many 'Haydnesque' details, not least the Reutterian scales in the first violin part (bars 9ff.) – see musical example overleaf.

[footnote – *cont.*]

Finale: after

close in G major and double bar; second section also with double bars; 2 bars of Tutti, organ solo in G, modulation to E minor, then to C and reprise with 2 bars of solo, 2 bars of orchestra plus solo and 6-bar closing ritornello.

1 GdM VII. 12992: 'Concerto / Per il Clavi Cembalo con / 2. Violini, e / Basso / Del Sig.ʳ Giorgio Reütter Maestro di Cappella / I: R: M: C: e C:ᵃ' on oblong paper (watermarks: 'ɪɢs' in frame, illegible coat-of-arms).

[J. G. Reutter, Jr.: Organ Concerto – opening]

The second movement is a derivative of the *siciliano* transferred, without much loss of the blue skies, to a northern clime and very prettily done:

while the final Allegro, of which we illustrate the harpsichord's entrance, is in the light-metred two-four time, one of the popular quick metres of the period.

We may now return to Wagenseil and to a curious hybrid form. These works – three are in the GdM[1] – are each entitled 'Concert / pour le / Clavecin / Par M.ᵣ [or "Mons.ᵣ"] Cristoffe Wagenseil'. It is unclear if there was supposed to be an orchestral accompaniment (strings?) or if, as in Bach's 'Italian Concerto', the harpsichord is a solo in the concerto style. In any event they are not real concertos at all but concertini, even smaller in scale than Reutter's pair of works. We show part of the first movement of that in G, and again we are at one remove only from Haydn's very first piano sonatas (Nos. 1–7 of the Wiener Urtext-Ausgabe, XVI:8, 7, 9, GI, 11, 10, DI). The same applies to the second movement (see example), which is couched in the language of Haydn's more extended sonata slow movements, such as those of Nos. 10 and 11 (XVI:1, 2). The tiny last movement is the kind of model Haydn took not only for his early sonatas and trios but also for the concertini and divertimenti with harpsichord and strings which he was writing at least by 1760 for Count Morzin.

1 In C, VII. 13039 (Q 15858). In G, VII. 13038 (Q 15857). In F, VII. 13037 (Q 15850). All on Italian paper (watermarks: three crescents of declining size, with letters 'AZ', the one in C with a large coat-of-arms).

[G. C. Wagenseil: 'Concert pour le Clavecin' in G]

Our final examples[1] are from 'Concerto in C: à / Clavicembalo I[mo] ed II[do.] / Due Violini, / Due oboi, / è / Basso. Del Sigre: Cristofero Wagenseil',[2] which is again astonishingly close to the style of Haydn's early keyboard music: the accompaniment figure (bars 1/2 when the harpsichord enters) may be compared, in Haydn to Sonata No. 1, bars 2/3. As for the broken chords in the right hand (Wagenseil, bars 2/3, 4/5), we may confront them with Haydn's Sonata No. 1/III, bars 3ff. Wagenseil displays a detailed and almost excessive use of different ornaments, which occur throughout Haydn's early keyboard style.

---

1 Many more may be examined in Bettina Wackernagel's book, *Joseph Haydns frühe Klaviersonaten*, Tutzing 1975, containing many valuable musical examples, mostly facsimiles of early editions.
2 GdM VII. 1423 (Q 16321) on oblong Italian paper (watermarks: three crescents of declining size, letters 'PS', 'CS' over 'C'.

In Wagenseil's second movement, the same attention to ornamental detail may be observed:

In Haydn, there is a similar pattern in the heavily ornamented Menuet/Trio in Piano Trio No. 16 (XIV:C1), where we also find a similar differentiation between trills, mordents (crossed turns), etc. In Wagenseil's first movement (opposite), we see a note followed by a pattern of downward-moving notes of quicker value (in bars 1 and 7); compare Haydn's Trio from the Menuet of Piano Trio No. 16, bars 38, 40. A similar correspondence between Wagenseil and Haydn was observed (*SYM*, 199f.) between the elder's Violoncello Concerto in C of 1763 and Haydn's Organ Concerto (XVIII:1) of 1756. A more curious and significant fact is that one MS. of Haydn's Organ Concerto in C (XVIII:8) is given to Leopold Hofmann, one (XVIII:2) to Galuppi, the Organ Concerto in C (XVIII:5) to Wagenseil (*infra*, p. 208), and one of the Organ Concertos in C (XVIII:1) was originally attributed to Joseph Haydn but later to Johann Michael Haydn (*infra*, p. 213).

Running behind this elegant and rather superficial façade was always a vein of what we call, after Bence Szabolcsi, exotic excursions, or a touch of madness. It was something one finds throughout Viennese music from 1750 to 1800. This eccentricity takes various forms. One is the extravagant use of a solo instrument in a capacity for which it was not, strictly speaking, intended. We take note of a wildly improbable trumpet (*clarino*) solo in Reutter's 'Servizio di Tavola' of 1757 (second movement: Larghetto, cantabile) which – at a time when the great *clarino* tradition was supposedly dying out – takes the solo instrument up to sounding *f'''*. Although Haydn never had a trumpeter of such brilliance (until Anton Weidinger in 1796, but that is another story), Michael Haydn did, and we presume that the lunatic trumpet solo in his Serenade in B flat (another version from Lambach Abbey of Perger 52), which rises to sounding *a'''*, is the god-child of Reutter's conceit. But if Joseph Haydn never expected his trumpeters to perform operations of this magnitude, he had horn players who must be counted among the greatest virtuosi of their instrument ever to have lived. Haydn expected them to be able to negotiate sounding *a''* and even on occasion *b flat''*. In this tradition, too, Haydn had a distinguished predecessor in the Bohemian composer Jan Dismas Zelenka (1679–1745), who composed several Capriccios for chamber orchestra with horn parts that are fully the equal of Haydn's for sheer technical difficulty (No. 4 in A requires sounding *a''* and *b''* for the first horn.[1]

Apart from these extravagances, there is yet another aspect of the *settecento* spirit that must not be overlooked. Behind this predominantly gay and unheroic music, there lurked quite another spirit which was at violent odds with itself: the deliberate

1 Issued by the *Musica Antiqua Bohemica*, vol. 61 (C. Schoenbaum), Prague 1963.

cultivation of the minor as a vehicle of passion. We will later mention one such work, Gluck's *Don Juan*, in the Chronicle of 1761 (p. 363), but it was not entirely isolated. Anton Filtz (*c.* 1730–60) was the composer of 'Six / Symphonies, / A Quatre Parties obligées, / avec Cors de Chasse ad libitum', Oeuvre II, published at Paris in 1761,[1] of which No. 2 is an extraordinary work in G minor, with all the paraphernalia that we later associate with the 'Sturm und Drang' style of the late 1760s; yet the work must have been composed in the 1750s. Its rushing semiquavers, pounding bass quavers, and its violence of expression are the kind of thing we associate at this period with the north Germans, and C. P. E. Bach in particular. But here we have the same sort of intensive and disruptive use of the minor key in a Bohemian who died at Mannheim. Nor is this an isolated symphony: we have equally powerful works in G minor (two) and D minor by Franz Beck, several of which were published in Paris in the 1750s and go beyond the G minor work of Filtz in concentration of energy and power of expression.

Was all this eruptive violence a characteristic of the unruly Bohemians and Germans? It was generally considered to be; yet we believe that this theory is mistaken. The lunatic fringe extended even to Italy, to which country we return at the end of this all too brief survey. There we find a most unusual Concerto for Harpsichord and Orchestra in C minor by Galuppi, for which nothing else in Galuppi's *œuvre* quite prepares us: in it, we find the same earnestness of expression, the same relentless repeated notes in the bass line, the jagged syncopations, and so on, that we associate with C. P. E. Bach's Harpsichord Concerto in D minor. Of course, we cannot date this C minor Concerto, and it is just possible that Galuppi composed it under the temporary influence of the northern 'Sturm und Drang'; but it remains a stylistic mystery and is perhaps not so unique as we now imagine. To fix the dates: there was surely a strong minor-key style at great variance with the current musical language, and this 'new' manner was flourishing in various parts of Europe by the mid 1750s (Beck's symphonies were all published in Paris and thus gained the same diffusion as Filtz's). It flared up in Vienna in 1761 with Gluck's *Don Juan*, and was cultivated by many Austrian composers in the middle of the 1760s. Although we can chart its course, albeit somewhat diffidently (for lack of complete information), this stern writing in the minor nevertheless represents an unexplained phenomenon. Why did these composers, including Galuppi, feel the need to explore this violence? It is another warning that our conventional view of the eighteenth century is not only incomplete but in some respects mistaken.[2]

---

1 Cari Johansson, *French Music Publishers' Catalogues of the Second Half of the Eighteenth Century*, Stockholm 1955, facs. 46. New edition of Filtz Symphonies: *Musica Antique Bohemica*, vol. 44 (Jaroslav Pohanka), Prague 1960.

2 Literature: The fundamental study on this subject is Wilhelm Fischer's 'Zur Entwicklungsgeschichte des Wiener klassischen Stils', in *Studien zur Musikwissenschaft*, Drittes Heft (1915), pp. 24ff. Another little known but brilliant study by Fischer is the 'Stilkritischer Anhang' (pp. 225ff.) in Alfred Schnerich's *Joseph Haydn und seine Sendung*, 2nd ed., Vienna 1926. Recently, J. P. Larsen has devoted much attention to the problem; for a list of literature by Larsen prior to 1977, see *Haydn: the Late Years 1801–1809*, pp. 455f. As for specialized studies, for Wagenseil see the indispensable work by Helga Scholz-Michelitsch, *Das Orchester- und Kammermusikwerk von Georg Christoph Wagenseil*, Thematischer Katalog, Vienna 1972. A useful guide is *Der junge Haydn* (Graz Congress, 1970), Graz 1972, ed. by Vera Schwarz, containing essays, many of which have been cited separately in the appropriate place. John Vinton, 'The Development Section in early Viennese Symphonies: a Re-evaluation', *Music Review* XXIV/1 (1963), pp. 13ff.

II Haydn's works, c. 1749–1756

(and partly beyond)

CHURCH MUSIC

(I) THE MASSES

Missa brevis alla cappella: 'Rorate coeli desuper'

(XXII:3; c. 1748–9)

Scoring: Choir (S-A-T-B). 2 v., vc.-b., org.

Principal sources: I. as Haydn: (1) MS. parts of local origin, Göttweig Abbey, discovered by the present writer in March 1957: 'Missa, / à / Canto, Alto, / Tenore, Basso, / Violinis 2^{bus} / Con / Organo, / Del Sig^{re} Josepho Hayden [last two words later cancelled] / F: G:' on 4° paper (watermarks: large crowned ornament with a springing horse in middle; smaller coat-of-arms, like a crown, with the letter 'G' in the middle). Later under anonymous works in Göttweig Catalogue. (2) Entries in *EK* and *HV*, the former in Haydn's own hand, *vide infra*. (3) In Aloys Fuchs's Thematic Catalogue of 1839 (*Thematisches Verzeichnis der sämtlichen Kompositionen von Joseph Haydn zusammengestellt von Alois Fuchs 1839*, Faksimile-Nachdruck, Herausgegeben von Richard Schall, Wilhelmshaven 1968, p. 175), the work is listed as 'Missa brevis / a 4 Voci con strom / Aus der frühesten Zeit. / seine 1. Messe.' (from the earliest time / his first Mass).

II. as Georg Reutter, Jr.: (1) MS. parts, Schlierbach Abbey, Upper Austria. (2) MS. parts, St Paul Abbey (Carinthia). (3) MS. parts, Kremsier (Kroměříž), ČSSR. (4) MS. catalogue, Benedictine Monastery of Herzogenburg. The principal part of the catalogue is dated 1751, one with trumpets and timpani, and one 'Missae: sine Clarinis & Tymp:', of which No. 121 is listed as our Mass (see facsimile). (5) MS. catalogue, Raigern (Rajhrad) Abbey, ČSSR, 1771: No. 115: 'N^{ro} 115 Missa in G Auth: Reutter / Andante [*incipit*] Voc: 4: Violin 2: procuravit R: P: Alexnis [?] Habrier [?].'

III. as Ferdinand Arbesser: (1) MS. Catalogue of 1768, Lambach Abbey (Upper Austria), also the actual MS. parts (facsimile of catalogue entry overleaf). (2) MS. parts from the S. J. in Györ (Raab), Benedictine Abbey of St Martinsberg (Pannonhalma), Hungary, with old cat. no. 29: 'Missa in G / a / 4 Voci / 2 Violini / Con / Organo / et Violone. / Del Sign: Ferd: Arbesser / Chori Jaurinensis Collegy S:J:'.

Critical edition: Haydn-Mozart Presse, London, 23 (Landon, 1957).

First performance in modern times: Trinity Sunday 1957, Göttweig Abbey, conducted by Hans Gillesberger (Anton Heiller, organ). A complete recording of this performance was issued by a Swiss record club (Disco Club, DC 11).

Literature: J. Hofer, *Die beiden Reutter als Kirchenkomponisten*, Dissertation, Vienna University 1915; also *Thematisches Verzeichnis der Werke Georg Reutter jun.*, MS., Vienna 1947 (Österreichische Nationalbibliothek S.m. 28992). E. Schenk, 'Ist die Göttweiger Rorate-Messe ein Werk Joseph Haydns?', *Studien zur Musikwissenschaft*, Bd. 25 (1960), pp. 87ff. K. Pfannhauser, 'Mozarts Kirchenmusikalische Studien im Spiegel seiner Zeit und Nachwelt', *Kirchenmusikalisches Jahrbuch 1959*, p. 167. H. C. Robbins Landon in *HJB* IV (1968), pp. 199f. I. Becker-Glauch in *Haydn-Studien* II/3 (1970), 172. J. P. Larsen in *Der junge Haydn*, Graz 1972, pp. 84f.

On 7 March 1957, the present writer discovered the theme of the present Mass listed under the 'Incogniti' of the Göttweig Catalogue, as '25 Missa a 4 voc 2 Violinis / et / Organo / prod. 1779'. Subsequently we could discover the actual MS. parts, which showed that the work was at first attributed to Joseph Haydn. The cancellation probably occurred at the beginning of the nineteenth century, when the Mass was no longer generally known; for that reason, it was then placed under 'uncertain authors.' The parts themselves bear the title 'Alla Capella', which we have taken to mean that Haydn wrote the work for the *Gnadenbildcapelle* of St Stephen's Cathedral (*supra*, p. 56) rather than the 'big' *Capelle* itself. The title page is signed 'F:G:', the initials of Franz Leopold Graff (1716–79), organist and *ludimagister* at the Abbey of Göttweig. Graff was a prolific composer, and his works were performed at Göttweig as early as 1744; the archives there have several Graff autographs by which his handwriting could be identified. The Haydn Mass may have been acquired by Göttweig from Graff's legacy (he was buried in the chapel of Klein-Wien, at the foot of the hill on which the Monastery stands, on 16 March 1779): the reverse sheet of the title page lists fifteen performances of the Mass at Göttweig, from 5 April 1779 to 15 February 1786. Graff may therefore have copied the work much earlier than 1779.

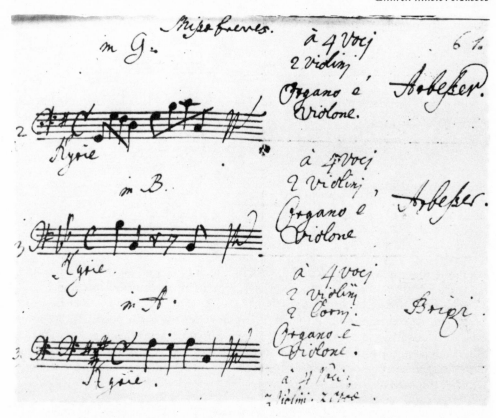

Three facsimilies concerning Haydn's *Missa brevis alla cappella* in G, 'Rorate coeli desuper' (XXII:3): (*opposite, above*) the opening of the first violin part in the Göttweig MS. attributed to Haydn; (*opposite, below*) the entry in the Herzogenburg 'Quartkatalog', under the name of Haydn's teacher, Georg Reutter, Jr., Chapel-Master at St Stephen's Cathedral, Vienna; (*above*) the entry in the Lambach Catalogue (begun 1768), as the first of two Masses by Ferdinand Arbesser, organist at St Stephen's when Haydn was a choir-boy there.

Of Haydn's fourteen Masses listed in *HV*, these two early works, in G and F, had both been forgotten by Haydn and were late discoveries. About that in F, we have considerable documentation (*infra*, p. 145), but about that in G, we have only the entry in the *Entwurf-Katalog* (*EK*). The *incipit* appears on page 15: 'Missa Rorate coeli desuper / in g' with the following identification:

In *HV*, the entry by Elssler is longer. It is slightly faulty and suggests that the extension was made by Haydn from memory (he appears to have confused in his mind the end of the first bar with the beginning of the second):

whereas the actual theme of our Mass is as follows:

A similar case, the *Missa brevis S. Joannis de Deo* (XXII:7), which Haydn quoted in *EK* as follows:

where the actual autograph has:

As a result, there are two *incipits* of the work in *HV*, as No. 4 and No. 15, one the faulty theme from *EK* and the other a more or less accurate listing of the proper line.

The title 'Rorate coeli desuper' (Isaiah xlv, 8: 'Drop down, ye heavens, from above, and let the skies pour down righteousness: let the earth open, and let them bring forth salvation, and let righteousness spring up together; I the Lord have created it') is taken from the Introitus for the Fourth Sunday in Advent, and indeed the theme of the soprano entry in the Kyrie is possibly based on a part of the Gregorian melody (which transposed into modern notation reads

Haydn may have intended the work to serve as a so-called 'Rorate' Mass, a service sung in German-speaking countries on Saturdays during Advent. In this case, however, there would be no Credo; if, on the other hand, the Mass were sung on an Advent Sunday, there would be a Credo but no Gloria. Haydn has allowed for these two eventualities by composing both sections. Those who have worked in Austrian archives will know that there is a substantial 'Rorate' music literature[1] of the period; we have noted in the next volume of this biography (*Haydn at Eszterháza 1766–1790*) the frequent Rorate services in which Haydn and the *Capelle* participated, of which the first not managed by Gregor Werner are mentioned in the ensuing Chronicle of the present volume (*infra*, p. 392).

The *missa brevis* form is a very popular one in Austria, as the Chronicle has several times showed, but the radically 'telescoped' texts are nowhere more devastatingly revealed than in the present Gloria, which is actually contained in $8\frac{1}{4}$ bars in two pages of printed score, and where the congregation cannot possibly meditate upon, and indeed can scarcely perceive, the text of the Mass as it is lustily sung simultaneously by the four sections of the choir. The whole Gloria lasts about sixty seconds.

It appears from the sources that the Viennese copyists marketed Haydn's early *Missa brevis* in G under the names of his teacher, Reutter, and his organist, Arbesser. It will be noted, however, that the Reutter parts which have survived or are known to us

1 For instance, the pretty but anonymous settings of the Rorate Introitus of *c.* 1750–60 from the Piarist Monastery of Gleisdorf (Styria), now in the Musikwissenschaftliche Institut of Graz University (on local paper, watermarks 'THALBERG' and figure of bishop, also wild man).

from catalogues are located in places geographically rather remote from Vienna (St Paul, Schlierbach, Kremsier, etc.) and the same is true of the Arbesser attributions (Lambach, Hungary). It is curious that there are no Reutter/Arbesser attributions nearer to the source. Obviously the copyists considered it more profitable to sell the Mass as if it were by the well-known Reutter or by the fairly well-known Arbesser rather than the totally unknown Haydn. We are sure that further sources will come to light, perhaps even more copies under Haydn's name, which may help to clarify the source situation. A few points may be noted briefly here: (1) support for the authenticity of the work as Haydn is based principally upon the Göttweig source corresponding with the holograph entry in *EK* (p. 15), which was made *c.* 1799, and includes several works, as follows:

Missa brevis in F./ a due Soprani;
Missa in Tempore belli;
Missa Sti Ofridi [Sancti Bernardi de Offida];
Missa in Angustiis ['Nelson' Mass]
Missa Rorate [etc., as above]

The handwriting and other factors suggest the period 1799–1800: the 'Nelson' Mass of 1798 is included, but not the Mass of 1799, nor the Masses of 1801 and 1802 (respectively: *Theresienmesse, Schöpfungsmesse, Harmoniemesse*). It is reported to us that Haydn rediscovered his *Missa brevis in F* much later than this, *c.* 1805;[1] but it is clear that he already remembered its existence, and the fact that it was scored for two soprano soloists (perhaps the main factor in his recollection) as early as 1799–1800. To this was added the three new Masses of 1796–8 and the *Missa brevis alla cappella* to which he provided the hint 'Rorate coeli' *and* the *incipit*. It is unlikely that this was actually a Reutter Mass. If the work be not genuine, it is the only such case in the whole of *EK*. (2) It is impossible to believe that the mature Reutter, careful craftsman that he was, could have written the many mistakes in part writing (Kyrie, bar 5, octaves between soprano and tenor; bar 9, fifths between tenor and bass). E. Schenk has pointed to a long list of typically Reutterian elements in the Mass, but being a pupil of Reutter, it is obvious that Haydn would base his first efforts on his immediate master.

As to the misattributions, we shall see not only Haydn's genuine organ concertos attributed to Galuppi, Wagenseil and Michael Haydn, but also his *Missa brevis* in F attributed, in another thematic catalogue at Herzogenburg Monastery, to Franz Aumon (or Aumann), *Regens chori* of the great Augustinian Abbey at St Florian.[2] Conversely, many of Aumon's chamber works were later distributed under Haydn's name. We believe that the evidence for Haydn's authorship is convincing.

There are three points about this youthful Mass which might be pointed out: one is the perhaps subconscious way in which the little violin figure that opens the Kyrie recurs throughout the work. We have derivations of it throughout the Kyrie and Gloria (Gloria, bar 1, second half = bars 1/2). Not only that: the Gregorian chant theme that opens the Kyrie is clearly 'manipulated' as the entrances of Gloria and Credo; and what is more, these similarities are *aural* in nature and not 'on paper' and extend, particularly in the upward line to e'', to all the movements of the Mass.

There are three such entities, of which the progression from d'' to e'' is matched immediately by the downward progression e'' to d''. The last two sections, on the

1 Letter of G. A. Griesinger to Breitkopf & Härtel of 26 October 1805; *Haydn: the Late Years 1801–1809*, p. 339.
2 The so-called *Quartkatalog* (small format) in two volumes, entry 152 ('Missa in F ... Del Sig: Aumann').

other hand, begin with similar progressions, but down a third. It is all a rather impressive demonstration of that organizational sense for which its composer would one day create a new standard of excellence.

The second impressive moment is the sudden slowing of pace from Andante to Adagio in the centre of the Credo, to introduce 'Et incarnatus est'. This is always a position where the Austrian composers stopped 'telescoping' the texts (the others were the Kyrie, Sanctus, Benedictus, Agnus), but even though we are historically prepared for the act, its arrival is surprising for the power of its language: unity with the rest of the movement is achieved by continuing the same partly syncopated pattern in the violins, diversity by the massive modulation into D minor and even more by the unexpected enharmonic modulation to A minor (middle parts: *a* flat = *g* sharp).

The Benedictus is conventional Austrian music of the period, with typical triplet motion in the violins; and the most striking part of Sanctus and Benedictus is the way in which the Kyrie's violin figure unexpectedly recurs (Sanctus, bars 6, 8, 9, 10; Benedictus, bar 10). This use of a small motif for the purpose of formal unification is, of course, a very Reutterian trait, which we have noted above (*supra*, p. 88).

But surely the one really great movement of this apprentice Mass is the Agnus. Brilliant the way in which Haydn unifies the movement with the 'sighing' pattern in the violins; but totally unexpected, and gripping, the drop into *piano* (strings 'sempre piano') and G minor, which continues to astound our ear until just before the very end. It is music that suddenly presages a great spirit, as does the great-hearted plagal cadence with which the (probably) earliest known work by Joseph Haydn unexpectedly and with marvellous dignity concludes. *Finis origine pendet.*

Missa brevis in F a due Soprani
(XXII:I; *c.* 1749)

Scoring: S–S Soli; Choir (S–A–T–B). 2 v., vc.-b., org.

Principal sources: (1) MS. score, EH, Eisenstadt, by Johann Elssler with title: 'Missa in F' to which Haydn himself added the word 'brevis' underneath; 14-stave oblong paper, of which only the lower nine staves are used: S. I / S. II / A. / T. / B. / V.I / V.II / Vc. [*basso continuo*] / Org. The top five lines are filled in by Fl. / Clar. I / Clar. II / Bsn. I / Bsn. II. These supplementary instruments are said to be in the hand of Antonio Polzelli (Pohl I, 125n.). (2) MS. parts by Johann Elssler and his assistants, EH, Eisenstadt, with title: 'Missa ex F à 2 Canto Conc^do Alto, Tenore, Basso Ripp: 2 Violini, Flauto, 2 Fagotti, 2 Clarinetti, 2 Clarini, Timpano con Organo Violoncello è Basso Del Sig^re Haydn'; each part has its individual title on the right-hand top part of the first page, 'Missa'; on organ part Haydn added holograph note, 'Brevis di me Giuseppe Haydn $\overline{749}$'. (3) MS. parts, EH, Eisenstadt, with title: 'Missa in F (19 Partes) a 5 Voci (2. Canti Concti) 2 Violini in dupli 2 Tromboni Organo con Violone. Del Sig^re Giuseppe Haydn f. 2. 41' – a commercial Viennese copy. Sources (1), (2) were acquired by the Archives after 1800, source (3) even later. When we studied the EH Archives at Eisenstadt, these three sources were missing, and our information is entirely from Hoboken, vol. II, p. 71. (4) MS. score by the copyist of the so-called Keeß Catalogue, ÖNB, Vienna, Codex 15804 (details in *Gesamtausgabe* Series XXIII/1, ed. C. M. Brand, 1951, p. 332), *c.* 1795. Keeß was a patron of Haydn's (*Haydn at Eszterháza 1766–1790*, pp. 503, 663 etc.) and owned a large collection of Haydn's symphonies which were put into a thematic catalogue. It is in a certain chronological order; it gives the scoring, usually with an enlarged orchestration (trumpets and drums, which Haydn seems to have added later to many of his works, both sacred and secular); and it was probably compiled in the 1780s (two final additions were Symphonies Nos. 95 and 96 which Haydn sent from London to Keeß); Princely

Thurn und Taxis Archives, Regensburg; facsimile in J. P. Larsen, *Drei Haydn-Kataloge*, Copenhagen 1941 (new ed., New York 1979). Another copy of the catalogue was owned by Haydn and a fragment of it was attached to the *Entwurf-Katalog* (Staatsbibliothek, Berlin). Thus the copyist of the Keeß Catalogue had a certain connection with Haydn; his score contains the original version (without the added instruments) and was made *c.* 1795. (5) MS. parts of original scoring, Göttweig Abbey, 'Missa Ex F brevis … Comparavit R: P: Marianus A° 1785'. (6) MS. score, made by Aloys Fuchs in 1852 (full scoring of 1805, with the timpani), Göttweig Abbey. (7) MS. parts from the former Augustinian Abbey at Rottenmann in Styria (now Diözesanarchiv, Graz): 'Missa ferialis brevis, Benedicte aquae omnes super caelos sunt, Domine'; local source (watermarks: three acorns, letters 'IM') of the original scoring. (8) MS. parts, Seckau Abbey (formerly Augustinian, now Benedictine) of the original scoring. (9) MS. score, Conservatoire de Musique, Brussels, with added orchestration of fl., clar., bsn., trpt., timp. with note: 'These instruments were added at the request of the Compositeur by H^r Heidenreich, who subjoined them later.' Joseph Heidenreich was a successful arranger and copyist, as well as composer, in Vienna. (10) MS. parts, Benedictine Monastery of Lambach (Upper Austria): 'Missa. in F: Stae Bibianae' (feast day: 2 December) – the source listed in the Lambach Catalogue of 1768 but as a later addition. There are many other MS. sources in Austria and Bohemia, but none even faintly contemporary with the actual work (*c.* 1749), e.g. Břevnov Abbey, now National Museum, Prague.

Critical edition: Haydn Society Gesamt-Ausgabe (Brand) XXIII/1, 1951, of the original scoring. Practical edition: Doblinger (R. Moder).

Literature: Brand, *Die Messen*, 6–16. Geiringer 1932, 123f. D. McCaldin, 'Haydn's First and Last Work: The "Missa Brevis" in F major', *Music Review* 28/3 (1967).

In the legacy of Haydn's music, we read:[1] '356. Missa brevis in F. in score. This was the first Mass that Herr Haydn wrote while still a student.' Whether this honour should really go to the present F major work is doubtful, for it is in all respects a more polished work than the G major Mass; as readers of this biography will see for themselves, however, this is a slippery path and many a Haydn scholar has misdated a work by trying to equate progress with chronology. Both works are unquestionably from his student years, and we have suggested in the Chronicle that Joseph may have designed the unusual layout of the work (only two solo parts, and both sopranos) as a virtuoso vehicle for his brother (first soprano) and himself (second soprano). Both works have the typical 1750 *missa brevis* orchestration: the so-called 'Vienna church trio', which means two violins and *basso continuo* (violone, bassoon, violoncello and, of course, organ). Haydn was to write three Masses in this particular style, the latest being the

---

1 *Haydn: the Late Years 1801–1809*, p. 398, where the original German may be consulted.

beautiful *Missa brevis S. Joannis de Deo* (XXII:7) of *c.* 1777.[1] As a present for Prince Nicolaus II Esterházy, Haydn intended to bring the little Mass 'up to date', which meant adding a huge orchestration. It is a superstructure which the delicate structure of the original neither requires nor is in any way improved by: it was exactly the same misguided principle that encouraged Mozart to dress up *Messiah* by Handel in Rococo orchestration. In the event, Haydn was too old to do the work himself and entrusted it to other(s); and fortunately, too, no one has considered it necessary to perform or record[2] the work in this 1805 + version.

It is well known that Haydn's late Masses (from the 'Mariazellermesse' of 1782 to the 'Harmoniemesse' of 1802) are strongly symphonic, not only in orchestration but in formal structure and general style as well. Haydn's Mass in F is organized along entirely different principles. The shape of the *missa brevis* form dictated the same 'telescoped' texts in Gloria and Credo as in the 'Rorate' Mass, but in the F major work Haydn has matters better in hand: in the Gloria, it is not until we reach the section, 'Qui tollis', that Haydn begins, slightly to overlap the texts, introducing in the midst 'qui sedes' (tenor), and the overlapping continues, but on a small scale, until 'cum Sancto Spiritu'. Altogether the movement is twice the length of the Gloria in the 'Rorate' Mass. The textual overlapping in the Credo is also better organized in the F major Mass; in the traditional way, there is a long middle section, marked Adagio, for the section 'Et incarnatus est' to the 'Et resurrexit', which coincides with a return to the original Allegro tempo. We notice, in the Gloria, the swiftly moving series of Reutterian violin figures. But undoubtedly the real innovation is not only that Haydn uses two solo sopranos but how he is influenced, formally, by their presence. If Haydn's late Masses are symphonic, here the guiding instrumental presence is undoubtedly the Italian concerto. If we assign, in our minds, two solo instruments instead of the sopranos and remove the chorus, the beginning of the Kyrie is like the ritornello and entrance of the soli in a concerto by Vivaldi. It was a very novel, and secular, idea, and once he had started to compose in this fashion, Haydn continued to allow the solo voices to reshape the traditional form. In the Gloria, they are at first given only minor roles ('Laudamus . . .', 'gratias . . .'); but when the text is, as it were, officially finished, at bar 19, Haydn soars away in a virtuoso burst of music on the words 'amen' which continues for another $10\frac{1}{2}$ bars (one-third of the whole movement). At first the solo voices gaily alternate with the choir, but then they continue for several bars until they are once again interrupted by a choral 'ritornello' (bars 24–6), out of which the two sopranos stubbornly emerge in a particularly difficult passage which leads us to one last 'amen' from the chorus. If our theory is correct and the solo parts were composed for Michael and Joseph Haydn themselves, they must have been formidable virtuosi; and the tale of Reutter wanting them (or at least Joseph) to pursue castrato careers may have been purely and simply to preserve what were a pair of glorious soprano voices. (What did Reutter think of the two *missae breves* of his pupil? He must surely have heard them.)

The Credo is, as we say, divided into the three traditional sections, and once again, we have an astonishing formal operation that rivets our musical attention. We note, for the first time, a total absence of the soprano soloists: we reach the fine Adagio with its perceptive setting of the Crucifixion; we proceed to the rest of the Credo and come to the words 'et vitam venturi saeculi', which is then concluded by the word 'amen'.

1 *Haydn at Eszterháza 1766–1790*, p. 554; *Haydn: the Late Years 1801–1809*, pp. 338–40.
2 The first recording was made by Hedda Heusser (S), Anni Berger (S), Akademie Kammerchor, Vienna Symphony Orchestra, Anton Heiller, organ (on a 17th cent. *Positiv*), conducted by Hans Gillesberger, producer: H.C.R.L. Lyrichord, 1952.

Suddenly, in come the two soprani. But what are they singing: we can hardly believe our ears, for they proceed, with the chorus, to *repeat the entire conclusion of the Gloria all over again*. If Haydn had to choose any single thing in 1805 that made him decide to resuscitate this work of his student days, this glorious burst of inspiration must have been it. It is the most original feature of the whole Mass, and also one that utilizes a formal innovation to draw special, indeed redoubled, attention to the two soloists around whom the work was quite patently composed: it is perhaps naïve but it is also a stroke of genius (the two not being, and certainly not in Haydn, mutually exclusive).

In the two-part Sanctus (slow-fast, the latter introducing 'Pleni sunt coeli', as would be the case in many later masses by Haydn), the role of the soloists is reduced, but not totally missing. One notices a plagal cadence at the end, as in the conclusion of the 'Rorate' Mass. The Benedictus has been called Neapolitan by Geiringer; but it is Naples imported and adapted to Viennese standards and already sounds Austrian: this time it is a very long ritornello (14 bars), very secular, almost operatic (of the kind of music found, for instance, in Pergolesi's *La serva padrona* or other Italian *intermezzi/opere buffe*), a perfect match for the resplendent Baroque churches in which it was sung all over Austria (Göttweig, Lambach, Herzogenburg . . .). We register that a *permanent* feature of Haydn's style at this period is his use of syncopations: they dominated every single bar, except for the last, of the violin parts of the G major Mass's Credo, and they are the central rhythmic element in the violins' parts of this Benedictus: a trait that began (in this particular fashion) in Italian comic opera, but was already a firm part of Reutter's style, too.

In the Agnus, the shifting tonality of the beginning is original and professional: we think we are in D minor, but move at once into F, only to slide back to a non-root position in D minor a few bars later. We finally come to a half-close in F *minor*. All this is very sophisticated for a teenage composer, and his solution of how to complete the Mass is at once traditional and effective: the Vienna score by the Keeß copyist describes the process succinctly, 'Dona nobis–cum–Kyrie'. The words of the 'Dona' are to be fitted to the music of the Kyrie, a procedure that we find in many Austrian Masses, also in Haydn's own *Missa Sancti Nicolai* of 1772. In those days, the choir simply performed the task 'all'improvviso'; later, Haydn thought he had to write out the 'Dona' for the *Missa Sancti Nicolai*; and had he actually performed the editing task for the F major *Missa brevis* in 1805, no doubt he would have done the adaptation himself: as it is, several local MSS. have a written-out 'Dona' which takes considerable liberties with the note values of the vocal parts, which motivated the late Carl Maria Brand to produce his own version, 'which adheres, as much as possible, to the original Kyrie . . .' (p. 338 of Haydn Society *Complete Edition*).

(2) SMALLER CHURCH MUSIC

Mottetto I, II, III, IV de Venerabili Sacramento
(*Quatuor Hymni de Venerabili*; XXIIIc:5a–d; *c.* 1750–5)

Scoring: S–A–B Soli; Choir (S–A–T–B). 2 ob., 2 trpt., str., org.

Principal source: MS. parts, Országos Széchényi Könyvtár, Budapest, IV, 71, from the Servite Monastery in Pest. Title of the 4° paper (watermarks: chain-lines 2·5 cm. apart; coat-of-arms with crenellated gate in middle): 'Mottetto Et Salve / Regina: / Mottetto [last word cancelled] I II / de Venerabili Sacramento / à / 4 Voc: / 2 Violinis / Alto Viola oblig: / 2 oboe conc / 2 Clarinis / Organo con Violone / Pro Choro ord. Servor: B: M: V: Pestini / ad Sanctam Annam / 1776 / Auth Sig: Haiden' (for the first two, and:) 'Mottetto Et Salve [insert: "Regina"] III IV / de Venerabili Sacramento / à / 4 Vocibus / 2 Violinis / alto Viola conc / 2 obois / 2 clarinis / Organo con Violone / Pro choro Ord: Servorum B: Mrae Virag Pesti / ad S: Annam 1776 / Auth: Sig Heyden' (for the last

147

two). A substitute 'Salve Regina' text was later added so that the music could be used for services other than Corpus Christi.
Critical edition: Verlag Doblinger (Landon), in preparation.

Literature: I. Becker-Glauch in *Haydn-Studien* II/3 (1970), pp. 172–4. J. T. Berkenstock, 'The Smaller Sacred Compositions of Joseph Haydn', doctoral thesis, Northwestern University, 1975, I, 1ff.

This is the great discovery made in the Budapest Archives, and was presented to an astonished and delighted scholarly world in 1959, when the Catalogue of the collection was published. Frau Dr Becker-Glauch, who was the first to write about the works, also pointed out that there are two sets of entries in *EK* relating to Corpus Christi music, one on page 8 (which, with an *incipit*, refers to the four *Responsoria de Venerabili* [XXIIc: 4a–d] discussed in *Haydn at Eszterháza 1766–1790*, pp. 245f.), and another on page 21, which read (before Haydn cancelled it to make room for more harpsichord sonatas): 'Hymnus de Venerabili / 1^{mus} / 2^{dus} / 3 / 4' which may, unless it be a repetition of the other entry, refer to these works: lacking an *incipit*, we cannot be sure.

This is Haydn's first music for the Feast of Corpus Christi, and that it is from his earliest period is clearly shown by the many consecutive octaves, and so on, that we also find in the two early masses. We must now turn to a brief history of the Corpus Christi ceremonies in Austria which may not be familiar to Anglo-Saxon readers.

> Corpus Christi, a festival of the Western Christian Church in honour of the Real Presence of Christ in the Eucharist, observed on the Thursday after Trinity Sunday. The institution of this feast is due to Blessed Juliana, prioress of Mont Cornillon near Liège, whose veneration for the Blessed Sacrament was intensified by a vision, and who persuaded the bishop of Liège to order the festival for the diocese in 1246. It did not spread, however, until 1264, when Pope Urban IV ordered the whole church to observe the feast, for which a new office (still in use) was written by St Thomas Aquinas. ... By the middle of the 14th century the festival had found general acceptance, and in the 15th century, it became in effect the principal feast of the church. The procession of the Host, its most prominent feature (though not part of the original ritual), became a gorgeous pageant in which sovereigns and princes took part, as well as magistrates and members of the trade and craft guilds, and was followed by miracle plays and mysteries performed by members of the guilds.   [*Encyclopaedia Britannica*, 1967 ed., vol. 6, p. 542]

The tradition of this Corpus Christi Feast in Austria included a procession that halted in front of four Stations, the number four having a symbolic reference, first to the four quarters of globe to which the blessing was directed, and to the recitation from the four Evangelists that accompanied it. Whereas the later Corpus Christi music by Haydn (1768 or thereabouts) has an organ throughout, and was probably performed *within* four different churches in Eisenstadt, our present work has an interesting and characteristic detail which suggests that at least the Budapest version started in church and then proceeded outside, because after No. I the organ has no more figures (except for bar 9 in No. II). As to the Corpus Christi procession, with special reference to Austria and Catholic Germany, one specialist writes as follows:

> ... Once the custom of carrying the Host in procession began, it rapidly spread and developed into a most splendid affair. All over Europe it was treated as a veritable triumph of Christ the King. The whole community from highest to lowest took part enthusiastically in this manifestation of faith and devotion. It was not confined to the church building or even to the churchyard but wended its way through the town and even into the open country. In Germany and Austria it became associated with the processions for good weather, which explains the

practice of celebratory benediction four times en route, given towards corners of the earth. . . .

[W. J. O'Shea, 'Corpus Christi', *New Catholic Encyclopedia* IV, 347]

The beautiful text of the sequence, complete, reads as follows:

(1) Lauda Sion salvatorem, Lauda ducem et pastorem. In hymnis et canticis. (2) Quantum potes, tantum aude: Quia major omni laude, Nec laudare sufficis. (3) Laudis thema specialis, Panis vivus et vitalis Hodie proponitur. (4) Quem in sacrae mensa coenae, Turbae fratrum duodenae. Datum non ambigitur. (5) Sit laus plena, sit sonora, Sit jucundus, sit decora Mentis jubilatio. (6) Dies enim solemnis agitur, In qua mensae prima recolitur Hujus institutio. (7) In hoc mensa novi Regis, Novum Pascha novae legis, Phase vetus terminat. (8) Vetu statem novitas, Umbram fugat veritas, Noctem lux eliminat. (9) Quod in coena Christus gessit, Faciendum hoc expressit In sui memoriam. (10) Docti sacris institutis, Panem, vinum in salutis Consecramus hostiam. (11) Dogma datur christianis, Quod in carnem transit panis, Et vinum in sanguinem. (12) Quod non capis, quod non vides, Animosa firmat fides. Praeter rerum ordinem. (13) Sub diversis speciebus, Signis tantum, et non rebus, Latent res eximiae. (14) Caro cibus, sanguis potus: Manet tamen Christus totus Sub utraque specie. (15) Asumente non concisus, Non confractus, non divisus: Integer accipitur. (16) Sumit unus, sumunt mille: Quantum isti, tantum ille: Nec sumptus consumitur. (17) Sumunt boni, sumunt mali: Sorte tamen inaequali, Vitae vel interitus. (18) Mors est malis, vita bonis: Vide paris sumptionis Quam sit dispar exitus. (19) Fracto demum sacramento, Ne vacilles, sed memento Tantum esse sub fragmento, Quantum toto tegitur. (20) Nulla rei fit scissura: Signi tantum fit fractura, Qua nec status, nec statura Signati minuitur. †(21) ECCE PANIS ANGELORUM, Factis cibus viatorum: Vere panis filiorum, Non mittendus canibus. (22) In figuris praesignatur, Cum Isaac immolatur. Agnus Paschae deputatur, Datur manna patribus. (23) Bone pastor, panis vere, Jesu, nostri miserere: Tu nos pasce, nos tuere, Tu nos bona fac vedere In terra viventium. (24) Tu qui cuncta scis et vales, Qui nos pascis hic mortales: Tuos ibi commensales, Coheredes et sodales Fac sanctorum cirium. Amen. (Alleluia ad Missam tantum)

[*Liber Usualis Missae et Officii pro dominicis et festis* . . . Typis Societatis S. Joannis Evangelistae . . . Parisiis, Tornaci, Romae, 1954, pp. 945–9]

Here was a text to stir the heart of any true son of the Church; and who was a more faithful and devoted son than Haydn? Probably again following a local tradition, he took the first three strophes for No. I, and the twenty-first, twenty-second and twenty-third for, respectively, Nos. II, III and IV. J. T. Berkenstock (I, 40) believes that Haydn also incorporated elements of the 'Lauda Sion' plainchant, as he had done with the 'Rorate' Mass.

It is said that Haydn developed slowly. That is perhaps an inaccurate description: Haydn's style changed, in some respects, several times during his life; but in other respects, and disregarding the technical imperfections of which we have spoken, his style was totally formed by about 1750–5, when these four pieces were composed. Here is already the popular church style, and there is not *basically* much difference between this work and the 'Mariazellermesse' of 1782 except in refinement: the elements are all here. G. Feder pointed out long ago that there is an almost uncanny reference, in No. IV, to the great Emperor's Hymn 'Gott erhalte' of 1797 (*Haydn-Studien* I, 1965, p. 16), and we shall quote the passage in question *infra*.

As far as the orchestration is concerned, it is partly of such typically Haydnesque brilliance that one is reminded of works composed many years later:

[Mottetto I de Venerabili Sacramento]

Here the semiquavers of the violins at bars 9ff. look forward to a similar pattern in
Symphony No. 41/I –

– and the only substantial difference is that in the Symphony the bass line is moving in the famous Haydnesque repeated quavers, while in the sacred piece, the bass line is in crotchets (see example). In all four sacred works, the only feature of the orchestration which strikes one as unlike the Haydn of later years is the use of the trumpets: the cadential figure of ♩ ♪♫ ♪♫ and the frequent use of dotted patterns altogether are not elements of Haydn's mature writing. Indeed, we shall have evidence that such a linking passage as that provided by the trumpets

is a hallmark of Haydn's early trumpet style altogether; we shall encounter it in a newly-discovered sacred *contrafactum* (*infra*, p. 170).

The sound of the chorus is already very characteristic; but there is one technical aspect of the choral layout which is typical of Haydn's early style: the low position of the tenor line (this can be seen to some extent in our first quotation), which continues to be part of the composer's language even in the *Salve Regina* in E of 1756.

All four pieces are organized in the same way, which suggests that this was a firm Austrian tradition. Each of the works begins at once, without any ritornello, and using the upper solo voices (there is a bass solo occasionally, but none for the tenor, which is probably because Haydn lacked one in the vocalists for which he was composing at the time). There is then a choral tutti, and the usual modulation to the dominant; then we have a rather lengthy ritornello. It will be noted, moreover, that all four pieces are in C major, marked 'Vivace' and – most important – are in 3/4 time. Now Haydn was, his whole life through, to have a peculiar predilection for 3/4; and if we examine the Haydn symphonies for opening quick movements in 3/4, we shall see that no less than thirty-three begin in this fashion (slow introductions not, of course, counted). There is, also in this respect, a direct link to the popular, singing theme as exemplified in these Corpus Christi works, and the Kyrie (after the slow introduction) of the 1782 'Mariazellermesse': the same 3/4 tempo and the same kind of theme.

Finally, we would mention an indefinable stylistic, or one might say spiritual, characteristic that informs this music – a certain ecstatic quality, a genuinely deep and loving regard for this central mystery of the church. Of course, Haydn wrote in the warm-hearted, open fashion of his period; but that should not blind us to the music's spiritual qualities, which are manifest in the very popularity of the thematic material and the brilliance of the orchestration (*soli Deo gloria . . .*). To close our brief survey of this remarkable quartet of Corpus Christi music, we would follow G. Feder in drawing special attention to the fourth, whose principal melody looks forward with radiant clarity to what is perhaps Haydn's greatest melody: the *Volckslied*, or Emperor's Hymn, 'Gott erhalte' of 1797. Notice, in our example overleaf, how at bars 17ff. Haydn imitates Gregorian chant in the soprano line – something to which he will return with joy even after 'Gott erhalte' ('et in Spiritum sanctum' from the Credo of the 'Nelson' Mass, 1798).

[*Mottetto IV de Venerabili Sacramento*]

Before leaving our Corpus Christi music, we must add a word about the Budapest copy, since it raises problems common to many non-authentic copies of Haydn made in the eighteenth century. It was made, as the title informs us, for the Feast of St Anne in 1776; but the supplementary 'Salve Regina' text suggests that it was probably performed later as well, on other occasions. Therefore one is fascinated to note that there are grave mistakes in the parts which have not been corrected. A bar is missing (31) in No. III's organ part: since there is no figuring, perhaps, for the Corpus Christi Feast in 1776, this number was performed outside the church (no organ); perhaps, later, they also omitted the organ. Let us hope so. In No. II there are serious mistakes in the violin II and viola at bar 16, which are uncorrected; and what did they do about the violin I part at bar 39, which is totally missing in the Budapest copy? In No. IV, bar 51 of trumpet II is omitted. What did the musicians do in places like this? One hopes that the *maestro di cappella* corrected the mistakes and the musicians played the corrected parts by heart; but there remains the lingering doubt that they were *not* corrected by anybody. It is a fundamental problem for which these Budapest parts, at least, give us no convincing answer at all.

We have seen that the copyists preferred to market as Reutter the 'Rorate' Mass which is probably a student work by Reutter's pupil. A few years later, Reutter (even during his lifetime) was overshadowed completely by Haydn, and a 'Lauda Sion' Sequence by Reutter was being marketed under the name, 'Del Sig^r M[aestro] Gius. Haydn': one such copy has survived, and is in the Conservatorio di Musica at Florence.[1]

1 Hoboken, vol. II, p. 169, XXIIIc:G3. The list of spurious vocal works is very incomplete in Hoboken, who has omitted a whole series of works attributed to 'D^{no} Haydn' (no Christian name) from the important Archives of the Hospitallers (Barmherzige Brüder) in Graz, which collection will figure often in these pages: (1) *Salve Regina* in C, 100 Gbb ♯2: Michael Haydn, Klafsky 13. 6. No. 6 of 1760. (2) *Salve Regina* in D, 100 Gbb ♯3: Michael Haydn, Klafsky 13. 6. No. 5 of 1760. (3) *Salve Regina* in G, 100 Gbb ♯1: Klafsky 13. 6. No. 4 of 1760. Another copy of the latter, 'Del Sig: Haÿdn' from Eibiswald's Parish Church (Diözesanarchiv, Graz). *Salve Regina* in C 'Del Sig: Haÿdn' from Eibiswald: Michael Haydn, Klafsky 13. 6. No. 1 of 1760. The material from the Graz Hospitallers is, at the moment, in the Musikwissenschaftliches Institut in Graz, where we were able to study the MSS., first in the early 1950s, and then again on two trips in 1979.

It is not the purpose of this biography to discuss doubtful and spurious works except in special contexts. In the case of the sacred music of this period, however, Hoboken's Catalogue (vol. II) has included as genuine many works which are probably or certainly spurious (see also *HJB* IX, 363f.), and which therefore would seem to require a brief listing.

XXIIIa:5, the Offertorium 'Ad aras convolate' is considered doubtful by I. Becker-Glauch (*Haydn-Studien* II/3, 213f.), and we concur entirely. XXIIIa:6 is a work by Leopold Hofmann (Becker-Glauch, 213), the Motet 'Salus et gloria'. XXIIIa:7, the *Mottetto de Tempore* 'Super flumina Babylonis', is a work by J. B. Vanhal (Becker-Glauch, 169). The Offertorium 'Ardentes seraphini' (XXIIIa:8), the Oedenburg (Sopron) MS. of which the late Dr A. Csatkai showed us at the Museum there in 1958 is considered a genuine work by G. Feder (*HJB* IV 114 and *Haydn-Studien* I, 17) but spurious by Becker-Glauch. There is also reference to the work in the Göttweig Catalogue, where it is dated 9 December 1765 as 'Haydn, Josephus'. The Oedenburg source reads: 'N° ["14" in red pencil] / Offertorium Te [*sic*] Tempore / a / Canto 1mo / Canto 2do / 2. Violini / Alto Viola / Con / Basso / Auth: Sig^l Haydn / al uso di / Jeann Lehner' on 4° paper (watermarks: fleur-de-lys and 'FCP'). We consider that Michael Haydn may be the correct author of this rather interesting work.

Of the Marian Antiphons, many of those listed as genuine by Hoboken must, we believe, be eliminated. We emphatically do not concur with Frau Dr Becker-Glauch in considering the weak and (as far as sources are concerned) poorly represented *Salve Regina* in E flat (XXIIIb:4) to be a work of Haydn's. On the other hand, we agree with her in dismissing the *Salve Regina* in G (XXIIIb:5), which is known to us under Joseph Hayda's name in Göttweig ('Del Sig^{re} Giuseppe Heyda 766'). Karl Geiringer (*Musical Quarterly* 1959, p. 471) and Becker-Glauch (op. cit., 219) doubt, and we agree with them, the authenticity of the *Ave Regina* in F (XXIIIb:6). The outwardly interesting *Salve Regina* in C (XXIIIb:C7) would seem to merit attention because it is known to us, firstly, from a MS. formerly belonging to the Hospitallers in Graz: 'Salve Tutti in C / a / 4 Vocc / 2 Violini / Clarini 2 / Tympano / Organo Concto / Del Jo. Heyden / Pro Choro Frum: Misericordiae Graecii', and another title page on the organ part: 'Ave Maria / Salve Regina Ex C / a / Canto, Alto / Tenore, Basso / Violino Primo / Violino Secundo / Obois 2 / Clarini 2 / Tympano / Organo Concerto / et / Violone / Del Sig: Giuseppe Hayden / Partes XV.' Another set of parts, from the Monastery of St Lambrecht, is dated 1771 and gives us the probable identity of the rather attractive piece: on the title page, we can see that the name of the composer originally read 'Del Sig:^{re} Giuseppe Heyda' ('Heyder'?). The style, and especially the solo organ writing, remind us of the Litany in C (XXIIIc:c2) which is really by Hayda: *Haydn at Eszterháza 1766–1790*, p. 666. In Eisenstadt there is an 'Aria de Venera[bili] for alto solo, two flutes, strings and organ (XXIIIc:6), with the pencilled remark on the title page, 'Tomasini Pepi / die Solo' (Tomasini's daughter, Josepha, born 1773, engaged from 1807). Originally there was no author, but later someone added a note in red crayon, 'Giosp:Haydn'. A late copy: Italian paper: bow and arrow with 'A M', Andrea Mattizzolli; three stars in ornament with a half-moon; three crescents of decreasing size). Haydn cannot be the author of this pretty but saccharine music.

Salve Regina in E (XXIIIb:1; 1756)

Scoring: S Solo; Choir (S-A-T-B). 2 v., basso continuo, org.

Principal sources: (1) Autograph, Hessische Landesbibliothek, Darmstadt, from the Archives of Breitkopf & Härtel, to which firm Haydn had sent the autograph in 1806 (*Haydn: the Late Years 1801–1809*, p. 342). It is on oblong Italian paper and, as with the Organ Concerto XVIII:1, the first page of music was originally headed: 'In Nomine Domini' (middle) and 'Giuseppe Haydn' (on the right). Later, perhaps as late as *c.*1800, Haydn added 'mpria' to his signature and, underneath it, the date '756'. (2) MS. parts, EH, Eisenstadt, on rather late paper ('1 HELLER' and eagle); cover on different paper. (3) MS. parts, Göttweig Abbey: 'Motetto De B: V: M: ... Del Sig: Hayden ... Comparavit R: P: Josephus die 18ᵗᵉⁿ Aprilis an. 765.' (4) MS. parts from the Hospitallers, Graz cat. H5: 'N° 5 / Ave Maria / Ex E♯ / Salve Regina / a / Soprano Concᵗᵒ / Canto, Alto. Tenore. Basso. Rip: / Violino Primo / Violino Secondo / con / Organo et Violone / Authore D: Joseph Haÿden. / Partes XI / Sub Regente Chori / Fr. Abundio Micksh /

772 / Pro Choro Frum: Misericordiae Graecii' on local 4° paper (title: longer letter 's' in coat-of-arms, otherwise letters 'IK' and man with hammer and coat-of-arms). On the title page, the words 'Sub ... Graecii' were added later. (5) MS. parts, Cathedral Archives, Passau, signed 'Cultui B. V. M. Auxili: Passavi: ad Montem dicata à Vincentio Schmid, Vice M. d. C. & p. t. Chori Regente 1769' (Hoboken, vol. II, 148). (6) MS. parts from Admont Abbey, now Diözesanarchiv, Graz: 'Salve Regina incomparabilis harmoniae et gratiae ... Authore ornatissimo Dⁿᵒ Joseph Hayden ...' on 4° local paper (watermarks: lion in ornament with crown, letters 'IK'). (7) MS. parts 'Chori S. Nicolai / Soc JESU Prague / minoris', National Museum, Prague X.A. 66.

Critical edition: Verlag Doblinger (Landon), in preparation.

Literature: Brand, *Messen*, 16–29. I. Becker-Glauch in *Haydn-Studien* II/3 (1970), 174f. A. Mayeda in *Der junge Haydn*, Graz 1972, pp. 54f. E. Badura-Skoda, ibid., pp. 62f.

The late Dr Carl Maria Brand referred to this *Salve*, to which he devoted an entire chapter in his great book on Haydn's Masses, as 'Haydn's Italian period'. The astonishing polish of this work, compared with the previous works analyzed, must be due to Haydn's fruitful years of study with Porpora; we can see that the young Austrian really learned a great deal in the way of part-writing, handling of the vocal line and, most of all, in sophistication from the crotchety old Italian master. It was the first of many strokes of luck which were to befall Haydn, throughout his life; and they range from his studies with Porpora to Johann Peter Salomon walking into Haydn's quarters in 1790.

The 'Salve Regina' text obviously had a very special attraction for Haydn, devoted as he was to Our Lady. In the Catholic liturgy, it is used from the Feast of Holy Trinity (Sunday after Whitsunday) up to the beginning of Advent. There must have been a very urgent and probably private reason why Haydn kept these two old autographs of 1756, the only pre-1760 autographs which he seems to have kept: if he thought the Organ Concerto in C was composed for the ceremony at which his future sister-in-law took the veil, in 1756, it is obvious that the *Salve Regina* must have been part of the same ceremony, and perhaps even the Double Concerto for Organ and Violin as well. The two autographs (*Salve* and Concerto) were the only relics of Haydn's lost first love, and he treasured them carefully until he was an old man. If, as we assume, the *Salve Regina* was part of this heartbreaking ceremony in 1756, it shows that Haydn had already learned completely and totally to divide his personal emotions from those with which he chose to imbue his music; for both *Salve*, and of course even more astonishingly the gay Organ Concerto in C, bear no witness that they served as the cornerstones of a ceremony which removed from secular circulation, and Haydn's orbit, the first great love of his life. Even more appalling if we imagine that Haydn actually conducted the music and probably played the organ part himself. It is a chilling example of that self-discipline which would enable him to tolerate a lifetime as a courtier.

Forgetting its connection with Therese Keller, however, we find much of the greatest interest in this touchstone of Haydn's early sacred style; for against it must be judged, stylistically, all those myriad numbers of Marian Antiphons attributed to Haydn and nowadays almost all rejected (see the previous footnote, p. 157). There are five movements, which may be summarized as follows:

I. 'Salve Regina', Adagio, 3/4, for soprano solo, strings, organ, E.
II. 'Ad te clamamus', Allegro, 3/4, for choir (S–A–T–B), A; leading to Adagio, 3/4, 'ad te suspiramus' for solo soprano, then with choir. Orch. and organ as before.
III. 'Eja ergo', Allegro moderato, 2/4, for solo soprano, strings, organ, E.
IV. 'Et Jesum benedictum', Adagio, 4/4, for choir (S–A–T–B), E minor, leading to
V. 'O clemens, o pia', Andante un poco, for solo soprano, alternating with choir. Orch. and organ as before.

We show in the example below the striking beginning of this beautiful movement. From it the reader will see for himself the two features which undoubtedly impressed Haydn's contemporaries: the huge swoops in the violins at the beginning, made even more impressive by the double change in dynamic marks; and the *messa di voce* with which the soprano enters the scene after eight bars of ritornello.

Here we see the young composer successfully combining the new orchestral language of northern Europe, with its expressive dynamic marks and range, with the traditionally beautiful exploitation of a trained voice, singing, literally, 'bel canto' at its most Italian, most melting. The encouraging, professional hand of Porpora is over this music: Haydn has learned his lesson well, and quickly. In the middle we have the vocal coloratura for which Naples was always famous; it fascinates us less than it did audiences of 1756, but there, too, Haydn has learned how to write such music as if it had always been second nature to him (which, if we think of the first three vocal works discussed in this volume, it was assuredly not):

The next movement starts rather like the Scherzando No. 6 in A, with the strings striding up the A major scale:

It marks (bar 2) the choir's entrance, and shows that Haydn has now also learned how to 'space' his vocal writing far more concisely and efficiently than in the first Masses. But we are totally unprepared for the sudden move into A minor and a new Adagio, which returns the solo soprano to us after a very brief choral section. After eight bars of this Adagio, we find ourselves in C minor, at the beginning of an extraordinary passage describing 'gementes et flentes in hac lachrymarum valle', where the soprano slides down the scale, bar after bar, in one of the first of Haydn's 'tone painting' episodes (*Thonmahlerey*) – see below; this is then 'commented on', as it were, by the chorus. A movement of brilliant individuality and scope.

The very Neapolitan Aria, 'Eja ergo', with its huge ritornello and endless coloratura, is less interesting to twentieth-century ears and far more ephemeral, curiously, for all its 1756 modernity, than the more old-fashioned sounding parts of the work.

There then succeeds a very old-fashioned choral section, with slow-moving vocal lines ('Et Jesum benedictum') and an old, Baroque-sounding ostinato figure in the strings, which leads us to the final section of the work: yet another movement in 3/4, the metre that dominates this *Salve Regina* in two whole movements. In this radiant concluding music, soprano solo and choir alternate but, as in other of the previous movements, Haydn takes care to leave room for the inevitable cadenza. We have a look forward to the great G minor *Salve Regina* of 1771 (XXIIIb:2) in the sudden *piano* ending, and a plagal cadence such as closed the 'Rorate' Mass – farewell to Haydn's youth, for plagal cadences gradually disappear almost completely. We give the beginning of the movement which shows the popular kind of vocal melody, well organized, however, in its motivic structure (note the recurring figure of bars 2, 4, 6, 7, etc.), and leading to the first choral entry.

Haydn has, with this *Salve*, placed himself in the front rank of vocal composers in Vienna, and it is no accident that whoever imitated the beginning in one of the 'Comoedien-Arien' for Kurz (*vide supra*, p. 102) – Haydn, Hayda or one of the other 'house' composers – was borrowing a leaf from something out of the ordinary. The very fact that none of the individual numbers is in the traditional da capo form shows how early Haydn emancipated himself from the constricting aspects of Porporan or Hassean formal patterns.

Ave Regina in A (XXIIIb:3; *c.* 1755)

Scoring: S Solo; Choir (S-A-T-B). 2 v., basso continuo, org.

Principal sources: (1) MS. parts, Benedictine Priory of Mariazell (Ms. 300): 'Salve / vel / Ave regina / in A / a / Canto conc. / 4 Ripienis / Violino primo / Violino secondo / con Organo / Del Sig. Giuseppe Hayden / Obtulit Don[um] Tenorista / R: R: P: P: Michaelensiu[m] Vienna, / et filia ejusde[m] 11 annoru[m]/belle decantavit. 763.' Performance dates legible from 1766. I. Becker-Glauch (see Literature) has shown that the actual MS. was written earlier than 1763, probably in the first half of the 1750s. Two trombones were added on paper which can be dated *c.* 1754, supporting alto and tenor parts. (2) MS. parts, GdM I. 7841: 'Ave Regina / â / Canto Conc^to / Alto, Tenore, Basso / Violinis 2.^bus / Con / Organo / Del Sig^re Giuseppe Haÿdn / Ex Rebus / Joseph Kraus 3 X' on 4° Austrian paper (watermarks: '1K' and man with hammer for title page; parts: letter 'P' within ornament including pagoda-like roof and circle beneath). (3) Incomplete MS. parts, Országos Széchényi Könyvtár, Budapest, IV, 74, from the Servite Monastery in Pest. Title of the 4° paper (watermarks: chain lines, vertical, 2,4 cm. apart; letters 'HR' in frame): 'N: 52 [crossed out] N° : 4 / N. 63 [crossed out] / Ave † Mra / Salve Regina ex A. / â / Canto Solo / Alto Tenore Basso / Violino

Primo / Violino 2do / Con / Organo. / Authore Signore Hayden. / [later:] Pro Choro Pesth. ord. serv. B. M. V.' The 'Ave' text was added later. (4) MS. parts, 'Salve' text, Augustine Monastery of St Florian on local Upper Austrian paper; (5) MS. parts, Premonstratensian Monastery of Geras (Lower Austria), dated 1773 as 'Salve Regina' (first section of solo part missing). (6) MS. parts, Cistercian Monastery of Lilienfeld (Lower Austria), 'Comparavit S: Andreas Valento pro Choro Campililius', with 'Salve' text. (7) MS. parts (lacking original title page), Melk Abbey, with 'Ave text'. (8) MS. parts, University Library, Laibach (Ljubljana, Yugoslavia), N.794, with 'Salve' text. (9) MS. parts, Kremsmünster Abbey, F5.143, a local copy with 'Salve' text. (10) MS. parts with both 'Ave' and 'Salve' texts, ÖNB, Vienna, S.m. 23 108 (a late copy, *c.* 1800). (11) MS. score, same library, S.m. 15 785 of *Salve Regina* in E, XXIIIb:1, in G minor, XXIIIb:2, and the present work, nineteenth-century copies of little textual value; with 'Salve' text.

Critical edition: Henle Verlag, in preparation (I. Becker-Glauch).

Literature: I. Becker-Glauch: 'Joseph Haydn's *Ave Regina* in A' in *Studies in Eighteenth-Century Music* (Geiringer *Festschrift*), London 1970, pp. 68–73; also in *Haydn-Studien* II/3 (1970), pp. 175f.

Frau Dr Becker-Glauch's thorough studies have clarified the sources and established that the 'Ave' text, not the 'Salve' (which was forced under the original 'Ave' text with not always happy results), was the one Haydn actually composed. As can be seen, the very early Mariazell text is the most interesting; can it have been the 'Motet' that Haydn brought with him to show the *Regens chori* there (*supra*, p. 60), and of which the monks later received a copy? Our date of *c.* 1755 is only intended to be very approximate, and to show that we think it was composed before the *Salve Regina* in E, but we cannot be sure. According to the MS. at Mariazell, writes Frau Dr Becker-Glauch,

> the owner of the manuscript received it in the year 1763 as a present from a tenor who was associated with St Michael's – or more clearly with the Barnabites at St Michael's – in Vienna and whose 11-year-old daughter sang this *Ave Regina* beautifully.

The tenor, whose name is not mentioned, was in all likelihood Johann Michael Spangler who on Haydn's sudden expulsion from the Vienna Cantorei, offered him shelter [*vide supra*, p. 73]. Spangler was from 1749 to about 1764 tenorist at St Michael's in Vienna next to which stands the Michaelerhaus in which Haydn resided for some time in the seventeen-fifties. Spangler's oldest daughter, Maria Magdalena Rosalie, was born on September 4, 1750. The performance of the *Ave Regina* by the 11-year-old girl which is mentioned with such praise in the entry referring to the donation of 1763, must therefore have taken place around 1761–1762. We know that Joseph Haydn engaged in 1768 this daughter of his benefactor as third descantist for the Esterházy court musicians. In the same year the 17-year-old [girl] sang at the première of Haydn's *dramma giocoso, Lo speziale* . . .

> [*Studies . . . (Geiringer Festschrift)*, p. 71]

The three movements of this *Ave* are as follows:

   I 'Ave Regina', Andante, 2/4, for solo soprano, strings, organ, A.
  II 'Gaude virgo', Allegro, 4/4, for choir (S–A–T–B), strings, organ, D.
 III 'Vale o valde decora', Adagio, 3/4, soprano solo alternating with choir, strings, organ, A.

Haydn has once again planned well. The writing suggests that he wrote the piece for the same soprano voice that was the inspiration for the E major *Salve Regina*. Perhaps both were written for service at the Vienna church of the Hospitallers, where Haydn was leader of the violins in the 1750s. The first movement of the *Ave* is similar in structure to that of the *Salve*, a long soprano aria, with florid vocal writing, in the new-fashioned Neapolitan style, with a place for no less than two cadenzas. At this stage in his career, Haydn was fascinated with unison passages in the orchestra, and we find them in concerto, string trio, quartet and in crucial parts of these Marian compositions (e.g., leading up to the final cadenza). We even find one modest crescendo (leading up to the first cadenza). A broad contrast is provided by the middle movement: increased tempo, entrance of choir. The finest and most individual of the three parts is the final movement in Haydn's favourite 3/4: it looks forward to the Agnus Dei of the *Missa brevis S. Joannis de Deo*. One is slightly surprised to find, even here, an indication of a cadenza just before the last choral statement:

This concludes beautifully, with the plagal cadence that Haydn now favours, and pianissimo. In some respects, the whole *Ave* strikes one as being a study for the more polished and more affecting *Salve Regina* in E.

The Eibiswald *Contrafactum*
[Motet:] Duetto ('Jam cordi') and Chorus ('Sit laus plena')
(Hoboken XXIVa: 2c and *deest*; *c*. 1763 and 1755)

Scoring: I. Duet. S Solo, T Solo. 2 ob., 2 cor., str., organ *continuo*. II. Chorus. Choir (S-A-T-B). 2 ob., 2 trpt., timp., str., organ *continuo*.
Principal source: MS. parts by Haydn's pupil, Abundio Micksh, originally from the Graz Order of the Hospitallers, later Parish Church of Eibiswald (Styria), now Diözesanarchiv, Graz. 'N.º 22 [crossed out] / N 1 / 5 / Duetto in D / Canto et Tenore / 2 Violini / 2 oboe oblig: / 2 Cornuj / Alto Viola / Organo / Del Sigl: Jiosepe Heÿden /

[at left:] Chorus in D: / a 4 Voc: / con clarinj / Tympano.' To right: 'Sub Regentre Chori / Fr: Abundio Micksh / 1773.' On 4° paper; title page on blue-toned paper (watermark illegible if any present), rest on paper with a watermark which is so faint as to be almost illegible (perhaps two angels, 14·1 cm. high). The alto, basso and timpani part are missing.
Critical edition: Verlag Doblinger, in preparation (Landon).

The bulk of the Micksh copies of Haydn's music, largely interesting *contrafacta* and at least one a unique copy, is discussed *infra*, pp. 499ff. in the works of the first Eisenstadt period. We have, however, placed this work here, because we believe that certainly the chorus, though not the Duet, belongs to this earliest period, that is, in its lost original form. Because there is no doubt that we are dealing with (1) authentic music by Haydn and (2) *contrafacta*. The transcription is self-revealing: the curious repetitions and interpolations of the Latin words in the Duet reveal that they have been superimposed on the Esterházy Cantata's Duet (*vide infra*, p. 468). The same applies to the Chorus, where the doubling instrumental parts often show us what is undoubtedly the original version. The first interesting stylistic peculiarity of the Duet concerns the use of the horns, which limits the chronological boundaries of the work to within the early 1760s:

(1) In Symphony No. 1, at bars 32–4, we find a peculiar kind of horn writing, whereby Haydn writes for a D-horn as if it were an A-horn.

It was a procedure that he hardly used after the Morzin symphonies. In the present Duet, we find at bars 23–4 a similar procedure, wherein this time Haydn pretends he is using D-horns as if they were G-horns:

Perhaps he later abandoned this kind of writing because there are too many impure notes (this was before the era of hand-stopping): the sounding a'' is particularly unpleasant, and in our Duet, both first notes of bar 24 were impure on natural horns. Haydn continues to use these notes, but he approaches them differently, e.g. in Symphonies 34/IV, bars 5f., and 48, bars 186–90:

169

(2) The chorus has trumpets and timpani (the latter lost but easily reconstructed, as has been done in our edition). Since Haydn had no chorus for Italian works, no trumpets and, until *c.* 1770, no timpani (and none regularly until 1773) in the Esterházy band, it is difficult to imagine the original having been part of an Esterházy cantata or one of the lost comedies of 1762–3. (A single exception to Haydn having a chorus, trumpets, and drums, is the *Te Deum* for Prince Nicolaus, *c.* 1762–4. They must have been the church music choir, and the trumpets and kettledrums hired specially for the occasion, as we shall see; *vide infra*, p. 383.)

(3) The use of the trumpets, with their dotted fanfares to 'fill in' empty gaps between sections, is precisely the way in which we noted their being used in the very early Corpus Christi music. Haydn *never* used them in this fashion after he began to write for trumpets in 1774 (Symphony No. 56; but he may have added the trumpet parts of some earlier works before that date); this is a distinguishing feature of his earliest style, for the trumpet writing in the Morzin symphonies (Nos. 32 and 33) is also different. (See the example, p. 176, for the beginning of the Chorus.) Therefore, we assume that the Chorus was composed *c.* 1755.

But what can the original of this second *contrafactum* have been? We offer a bold suggestion: *Der (neue) krumme Teufel.* In the 1758 libretto we have duets and choruses, and if one wants to amuse oneself by attempting to match texts, one might point to the final Chorus in Act II, 'Wahre Lieb sucht alle Gänge / Alle Vortheil, alle List, / Bis der Gegner in die Länge, / Endlich doch betrogen ist.' This text, with minor rhythmic changes in bars 4–6, can be fitted to the *contrafactum*'s chorus. In the Opera, there are then interpolations by Bernadon and Fiametta, 'Gleich und gleich gehört zusammen', Fiametta then adding 'O das sind die schönsten Flammen, / Die die Tugend zündet an', after which the Chorus repeats 'Wahre Lieb'. In the 1770 version of Haydn's Opera, there are many more choruses (did Haydn compose them? and when? were they adaptations of some of the 1758 music?), including one in Act II, sung by wild men, 'Alle sollt ihr itzt verderben / Fort du schöner Herr Regent'; and with minor rhythmic changes to repeated 'Fort du schöner Herr Regent' in bars 4–6, this Chorus can be made to fit. Similarly, the last two lines of the Opera's Chorus, 'Ihr Betrüger! Ihr sollt sterben. Kommet nur zu eurem End', exactly fit bars 8/9 of the *contrafactum*'s Chorus (beginning of bar 11, changed from two quavers to one crotchet, 'End', as the viola part suggests was Haydn's original anyway).

In the Chorus, as we have noted, the alto, basso and timpani parts are missing from the Eibiswald parts but are easily reconstructed for the main sections of the chorus on the basis of the instrumental parts (see example). Where the orchestral parts suggest a solo interlude (see footnote to bar 6, p. 178), the reconstruction is more problematical, unless one assumes – as one must, apparently – that these solo sections can have occurred only in the lost alto and basso parts. The musical example shows the first of these presumed solo interludes and our reconstruction.

The opening Duet is in that stately, measured Allegretto tempo that we find in many of Haydn's vocal works of this period, and especially in his early operas. Of course, the joints of the translation – adaptation – creak somewhat compared to the smooth Italian original, 'Mai per te, stella rubata'; but we must be grateful to Frater Micksh for having put together Duet and Chorus and thus giving us one lost Haydn work. The text of the Duet reads as follows:

> Jam cordi tuo amando praelucet nobis.
> Sed etiam vis belle laborat
> Pro nobis praestat hoc amoris vis.
> En praelucet amor noster.

> [Variants:]
> En ter amandus praelucet nobis,
> Amor noster hoc praestat amoris vis.

[Duetto, 'Jam cordi' (*contrafactum* of Esterházy Cantata 'Destatevi, o miei fidi', XXIVa:2)]

Again, this is no *da capo* aria form, but with a written-out recapitulation. Formally, here is what we have:

Ritornello – Related music with soprano solo – Related music with tenor solo
I–V–I   I–V –   I   – V

joined by soprano and leading to – Ritornello in dominant – Tenor Solo –
                                                    V   V

Sop Solo Duet modulating back to I – Recapitulation Duet using material
    I   I–IV–V–   I

of opening Ritornello – Cadenza – Final Ritornello
                            I$^6_4$ (21 bars)
                                            I

One of the really haunting passages of this Duet is effected by the use made of the pedal point – later a great speciality of Haydn's, and not of course just in fugues, wherein the device had its origin. We show the opening ritornello, which provides the stuff of the

whole Duet, and the clever way in which, during the recapitulation, Haydn fits the ritornello to the vocal line (where we see the purpose of the alternations between violins and oboes; the one doubles the soprano, the other the tenor – see example overleaf).

The Chorus's text is as follows:

> Sit laus plena, sit sonora,
> Sit jucunda, sit decora,
> Mentis jubilatio, alleluja.

We note, in further stylistic relationships to Haydn's early vocal music, the combination of triplets and 'straight' semiquavers, and the syncopations (violin II, bars 2ff.) as in the 'Rorate Mass' and *Missa brevis* in F. It is another valuable contribution to our scanty knowledge of Haydn's earliest vocal music. And once more, the world must be eternally grateful to Professor Helmut Federhofer, who persuaded the ecclesiastical authorities of Styria to centralize their musical manuscripts in the Graz Diocesan Archives, and thus prevented what would surely have been their almost total dispersal in the chaotic events following the Second World War.

[*Chorus:* '*Sit laus plena*']

* 'molto' = Sop., otherwise 'Allegro'   ** MS. = V. I (cf. 11)

* MS. 'So:[li]'

INSTRUMENTAL MUSIC
DIVERTIMENTI AND CASSATIOS (STRINGS; STRINGS AND WIND INSTRUMENTS)

I. Cassatios for String Quintet (*c.* 1750–3):
No. 1 in A (II: A1); No. 2 in G (II:2) for 2 v., 2 ve., basso

No. 1

Principal source: MS. parts from Raigern (Rajhrad) Abbey, Janáček Museum, Brno, ČSSR. [Various numbers, including the following, not cancelled: 'N⁰ 1326', 'L M 46'] / Cassatio Ex A. # / a / Violino Primo / Violino Secondo / 2^bus [2^dus ?] Viola Obligl / è / Basso. / Del Sig Giuseppe Haydn. / Matth. Bened. Rutka / Org. Raydhradensis.' 4° paper of local origin. A.12.501.
Critical edition: Verlag Doblinger (Landon), withheld until now because it was hoped to find additional source matter (*vide infra*).

No. 2

Principal sources: (1) MS. parts, in the order II, IV, I, III, V, VI, Benedictine Abbey of Kremsmünster, entitled 'Symphonia . . . ad usum P. Henrici Pichler 1763', a local copy. (2) MS. parts by J. Michael Planck, Augustinian Abbey of St Florian; title page lost; parts of local origin. (3) MS. parts, 'Divertimento', Benedictine Abbey of Melk (contrary to Hoboken, vol. I, p. 299: in correct order). (4) MS. parts, Staatsbibliothek, Berlin 10,029/2, entitled 'Cassatio Ex: G:'. (5) MS. parts, same library, 10,029/1 entitled 'Quintetto' (later: 'Notturno'), with 'Flauto ad libitum'[1] (= V.I part) . . . 'di Giuseppe Haÿdn – 1754', but the copy does

not appear to be of 1754 but much later. (6) MS. parts, Diözesanarchiv, Graz entitled 'Scherzo in G'. (7) MS. parts, Mecklenburgische Landesbibliothek, Schwerin. (8) MS. parts from Raigern (Rajhrad) of local origin. A.12.500. Other MSS. have not been listed here. (9) First edition by Simrock, *c.* 1833, 'Quintetto Cassatio in G ... (composto per il Elettore Palatino) / da / Giuseppe Haydn. / Stampato dopo il manoscritto originale ...' In the order I, II, III, IV, VI. It is unlikely that Haydn composed the work for Elector Carl Theodor, and textually very unlikely that Simrock used the original manuscript. Hoboken quotes a weekly magazine, *Iris im Gebiete der Tonkunst*, No. 45 of 11 Nov. 1831 in which chamber musician Friedel received the manuscript of this work from his father [Sebastian Ludwig? see Pohl I, 252] and urgently requested publishers such as Schott and Simrock to issue the work.
Critical edition: Verlag Doblinger (Landon), in preparation.
Literature: Pohl I, 141, 258, 317f. E. F. Schmid, *Vorfahren*, 311. Landon *SYM.*, 176–80.

1 With flute part also in the Archives of Counts Clam-Gallas, Friedland (Frýdlant) Castle, now National Museum, Prague: 'Quintetto'.

When we first uncovered the Raigern MS. at Brno some twenty years ago, we at once realized that we had before us a lost work by a very young Haydn. We had known the *incipit* from the Göttweig Catalogue, where it is listed as having been copied by 'P. Leandri' in 1762, one of the earliest Haydn works to arrive at the Monastery. Curiously, it is missing in *EK*. When we scored the work from the Brno parts, however, we saw that: (1) it was full of the same kind of schoolboy mistakes in part-writing as in the 'Rorate' Mass or the Corpus Christi music, but worse; (2) the Brno copy was full of hideous mistakes. We therefore withheld publication (Doblinger has long since engraved the work) in the hopes of finding another copy, but as it appears very unlikely that another will turn up, we shall, shortly, issue it from the, textually, most unsatisfactory Brno MS.

The work is in the usual four movements, with the minuet coming second. We offer, as an example, the beginning of the Finale, which is perhaps the most forward-looking of the four movements. In the opening and slow movements, we note the constant interplay of triplets and even semiquavers and, as the scoring inherently suggests, the interplay of the two violins with the two violas. Although another example would show the textual difficulties of the Brno source to more advantage, the reader will observe in the passage shown opposite two sets of consecutive fifths (violas 9/10, viola II and bass 11/12) which must surely be attributed not to the Raigern copyist and organist but to the inexperienced Haydn. Interested musicians will shortly be able to judge the whole piece, which in our opinion may be the earliest surviving piece of chamber music by Haydn, 'warts and all'.

[Cassatio for String Quintet, No. 1 in A – Finale]

It is inevitable to think that many of these youthful instrumental works were written in groups of two or three; certainly the next group of works, with their curious orchestration, was conceived as a unity. Haydn never wrote any other quintets, and one automatically places these two works together; but the G major Cassatio is a much more sophisticated work altogether, although it, too, contains its grammatical errors (consecutive fifths, second movement, 72/3, viola II and bass), and awkward, rather pianistic writing (music example: *SYM*, 180). As the list of sources shows, one of the Berlin MSS. is (post-?) dated 1754. Our Chronicle contains Griesinger's report that Haydn wrote a quintet in 1753 for a street-serenading concert (*supra*, p. 62), and the present work appears to be the most likely candidate. It is listed in *EK* (copied by Joseph Elssler).

W. H. Hadow, basing his study on research by F. Kuhač, suggested that the fetching tune of the opening movement was based on a Croatian drinking-song, 'Nikaj na svetu', whereas E. F. Schmid[1] suggests a German folk-song, 'Es trieb ein Schäfer den Berg hinan':

Whatever the origin of the tune, we believe that the important fact is the melody's innate folk-song character. Nowadays we are perhaps even reminded of the *Loreley* ('Ich weiß nicht, was soll es bedeuten, daß ich so traurig bin; Ein Märchen aus alten Zeiten, das kommt mir nicht aus dem Sinn'). This kind of scherzo, often in another position in the work, is frequently encountered in Haydn's early music.[2] Here it is a small, tripartite Presto (middle section G minor). In the next Allegro moderato, the two groups of upper strings are, as in the Cassatio in A, set off against each other very prettily. The minuets (flanking the slow movement) are already in the popular vein that Europe would soon find irresistible, particularly the second:

Both trios are in the tonic minor, and the structure of the second is very close to Haydn's early quartets: gruff unison in G minor, *piano* answer in B flat (interplay violins with violas) (music example in *SYM*, 178): it is only a short step to the Trio of

---

1 W. H. Hadow, *A Croatian Composer, Notes towards the study of Joseph Haydn*, London 1897, p. 41. E. F. Schmid *Vorfahren*, 310f.
2 E.g. Quartet, Op. I, No. 3; *Divertimento* II: D18 for wind band; Quartet, Op. II, No. 6.

Minuet I in the G major Quartet, Op. I, No. 4. The slow movement (Adagio), too is close to other Adagios of the early quartets, and also the Violin Concerto in C (VIIa:1). There is a kind of framing 'introduction' (music example in *SYM*, 178) of two bars, which also close the movement (similar procedure in Quartet, Op. I, No. 1) – here pizzicato. There follows one of those fabulously lyrical, concerto/serenade/Italian aria melodies for the first violin, accompanied by running quavers in the bass line, ♪ 𝄾 ♪ 𝄾 ♪ 𝄾 ♪ 𝄾 in second violin and second viola, and a steady murmur of ♫♫ in first viola. It reminds us poignantly that the starving young Haydn was playing in his own street serenades ('gassatim gehen') of this kind on a warm, summery night in Vienna. Perhaps it was this entrancing movement that tempted the beautiful Frau Kurz to call her husband who, in turn, engaged its composer to write *Der krumme Teufel*.

The racy Finale (Presto), with its saucy themes and brilliant instrumentation, is already the blueprint for the type of popular finale of which Haydn would write hundreds.

Haydn had found his style.

II. Cassatios (Divertimenti) for Flute, Oboe, Two Violins, Violoncello and Bass (*c.* 1755–60): No. 1 in G (II:1) and No. 2 in C (II:11; 'Der Geburtstag') with Andante 'Mann und Weib'

No. 1 in G (II:1)
Principal sources: (1) MS. parts, Mecklenburgische Landesbibliothek, Schwerin (DDR): 'Cassatio ex G♯ [changed at first to 'Noturno', then to 'Divertimento'] / à / Flauto Traverso / Oboe / 2. Violini / Viola ôvero [word subsequently cancelled] Violoncello / et / Basso. / Del Sig Haÿden' on 4° paper. Last movement marked 'Thema La Fantasÿ' (or 'Fandasia', or, correctly, 'Fantasia'). With a substitute viola part for the vc. (2) MS. parts, Christian-Weise-Bibliothek, Zittau (DDR), 'Cassatio in G ...'. Finale marked 'Thema La Fantasÿ'. (3) Arranged for fl., v., va., basso as 'Six / Quatuor / a / flute, violon, / alto & basse. / composés / par / Giuseppe Haydn. / opera quinta / .... / A Amsterdam chez J.J. Hummel, / Marchand & Imprimeur de Musique. / N° 70 – Prix d.5.–'. Announced on 16 Nov. 1768 in the *Haagsche Courant*. Copy in the Hoboken Collection, ÖNB, Vienna. (4) Arranged for fl., v., va., basso as 'Sei / Quartetti / Concertante ... Del Sig^re. Hayden / Maestro di Capella del Principe / Esterhasi. / Opera 16^a. / Prezo 9. di Francia / Mis au Jour par M^r. Huberty / ... / Gravés par Melle. Laurencin. / ... / À Paris / chez l'editeur, rue des deux écus, au pigeon blanc. / ... / A. P. D. R. / Écrit par Ribière.' Announced on 29 May 1773 in the *Catalogue hebdomadaire*. Copy in the Bibliothèque Nationale, Paris. Reprint of Hummel. Another reprint of Hummel by Bremner in London (British Museum), of Huberty by Le Duc (taking over Huberty's plates) (Bib. Nat., Paris). The prints include, in various succession (we show Hummel's as the earliest), II:D9 (D major), II:G4 (G major), II:D10 (D major), the present work, II:D11 (D major) and II:11 (the companion piece, discussed immediately below). There is no evi-

dence that the arrangements were made by Haydn, and no guarantee that the other works have anything to do with Haydn at all: like the spurious Quartets Op. 3, they distinguish themselves by not existing in a single contemporary manuscript and are known to us only by the Hummel edition and the various other prints. We can not believe that they can be by Haydn, even though they are in part very attractive.
Critical edition: Verlag Doblinger (Landon), in preparation.
Literature: Pohl I, 258, 324f.

No. 2 in C (II:11)
Principal sources: (1) MS. parts from the Archives of the Counts Pachta, National Museum, Prague, XXII D 113: 'Der Geburts Tag ...' (exact title of this and other sources, see Doblinger edition, *infra*). (2) MS. parts from Osek Abbey, now National Museum, Prague, 430-A: 'Der Geburts Tag ... 1765 / Prag'. (3) MS. parts from Archives of Counts Chotek, Kačina Castle, now National Museum, Prague, III A 13–750: 'Der Geburtstag', a Viennese source on oblong paper. (4) MS. parts, Kremsmünster Abbey: '... Cassatio in C ... NB: Mann und Weib / ad Usum P. Henrici / Pichler Prof. Cremif. 1765 ...'. (5) MS. parts, Archives of the Princes von Thurn und Taxis, Regensburg, J. Haydn 91: 'Le Mari et la Feme [*sic*] / Sinfonia ...'. (6) MS. parts, St Florian Abbey, 'Der Geburtstag'. Fl. part now wanting and there is a substitute va. part for the vc. (7) MS. parts, 'Der Geburtstag in C', Archives of Princes Schwarzenberg, Krumau (Český Krumlov), ČSSR. (8) MS. parts, Conservatoire de Musique, Brussels: 'Divertimento'. (9) MS. parts, Städtische Musikbibliothek, from the Tonkünstlerverein, Dresden. (10) MS. parts, arrang-

ed as a string quartet: 'Nr. 59 Quartetto in C', GdM, Vienna; signed 'N H 798'. (11) Printed parts, arranged for fl., v., va., basso, Hummel, Amsterdam, 1768: see previous work, source 3. (12) Printed parts, arranged for fl., v., va., basso, Huberty, Paris, 1773: see previous work, source 4. Reprints of Hummel by Bremner in London

(British Museum) and of Huberty (taking over Huberty's plates) by Le Duc (Bib. Nat., Paris). *Critical edition*: Verlag Doblinger, Diletto Musicale 57 (Landon, 1960), also miniature score (Stp. 286, 1978). *Literature*: Pohl I, 193, 321–3. Geiringer 1932, p. 67. Landon *SYM.*, 180ff. with musical illustrations.

The almost identical form (Finale as theme and variations) and orchestration (the use of violoncello, and no viola) make it certain that Haydn, as we have said earlier, conceived them as a pair of works. But for some reason their entry in *EK* is puzzling: No. 2 comes on page four, together with many other divertimenti (many lost), in a block prepared by Joseph Elssler about 1765, when the catalogue was drawn up. No. 1 was entered by Haydn himself on page five, as one of four *incipits* added after the last Elssler entry (which as it happens was the wind-band Divertimento in F, II:15 of 1760):

> Divertimento a quatro [Quartet, Op. II, No. 1]
> Divertimento a quatro [Quartet, Op. II, No. 2]
> Divertimento a Cinque [present work]
> Divertimento a Sei [later 'con 2 flauti'; II:8]

Now it happens that Op. II, No. 1, is part of a now famous manuscript from Lt-Col. von Fürnberg's collection entitled 'VI. / Notturni' which, as we shall see, must be dated *c.* 1757–60. Op. II, No. 2, exists in a copy by Fürnberg-Morzin Copyist No. 3 (Radenín Castle, now National Museum, Prague) made *c.* 1757–60. However, the fourth work we believe to have been composed by Haydn during his early service with the Esterházy family (*infra*, 529). All this does not help at all in dating our No. 1: we assume that the pair was composed later than the Quintets but before Haydn was engaged by Prince Paul Anton Esterházy in May 1761. Another most mysterious fact is that for No. 1, contrary to the many Austro-Bohemian sources for No. 2, we have *no* Austrian sources at all. Breitkopf announced both works separately: in 1767 he offered for sale MS. parts of No. 2, a year later No. 1. Presumably the two German sources – our only sources – have something to do with the Leipzig announcement. But there must be another reason for the popularity of No. 2, and we believe it is because of the slow movement, 'Mann und Weib', which seems to have caught the imagination of Haydn's contemporaries: the dancing melody is presented to us throughout in octaves, man and wife joined together and let no man come between them! It was an enchanting idea and ensured the work's immediate popularity. The last movement of No. 2 (music example in *SYM*, 182) was used as the basis for the slow movement of Symphony No. 14 (musical example in *SYM*, 183), which again suggests that the original was a favourite, perhaps with Nicolaus Esterházy, for whom Symphony No. 14 was presumably written in the early 1760s.

There is another feature of both works that suggests their being treated as a pair: in both trios of the minuets there is a solo for the violoncello. All this makes one think of another much more famous pair which is analyzed later in this volume (pp. 571f. and 564f.): Symphonies Nos. 31 and 72, with their shining four horns. One of them, too, has always been the favourite (No. 31).

Since No. 2 has been long available in print and is, moreover, recorded,[1] while No. 1 is about to be published and is already published and recorded in its flute quartet adaptation, we shall confine ourself to one illustration from No. 1, surely its most

---

1 No. 2 recorded by Nederlands Radio Barok Ensemble on Telefunken A WT 9410-C, No. 1 as a flute quartet recorded by Camillo Wanausek (flute) and Members of the Europa Quartet on Vox-Turnabout TV 34007S. In the flute quartet arrangement, there is a good modern edition by W. Upmeyer (Nagel's series, 1937, now Bärenreiter-Verlag).

striking moment and perhaps the most original music in the whole Cassatio. It is the middle of the second movement, of which the theme is as follows:

The mood that Haydn engenders in the very large middle section (see example) is as surprising – in view of the amiable character of the beginning and whole first part – as it is moving; it is like a piece of improvisation, a 'fantasy' – a much more accurate description of this piece of soaring imagination than the finale which is literally entitled 'La fantasia' (whatever reference was intended, the meaning is now totally lost). What are we to make of this lonely, disturbing music, which looks unwaveringly forward to the *Sturm und Drang* pages of 1772: that duet between the violins of bars 38ff., with its unsettling dissonances at bar 52, its broken melodic lines and syncopations?

Despite this interlude for the connoisseur, however, it was No. 2 that captured the public's fancy, and like all waves of popularity, there is nothing that succeeds like success; so we are not surprised to find selections of the Cassatio (leaving out, strangely, 'Mann und Weib') arranged for harpsichord solo or harpsichord and violin (list: see Hoboken, vol. I, p. 745), certainly not by Haydn. The finale was also printed in a piano reduction of the symphony version in Hiller's *Wöchentliche Nachrichten*, 1767; and, final indignity, arranged as a song, 'Elegy: "Thousands would seek the lasting peace of death"', in 'Twelve / English / Ballads / The Music / the undoubted Composition of / Haydn / The Words selected and adapted to his works / by / Dʳ. Arnold', printed by Longman and Broderip in January 1787. One could hardly say that Haydn's later friend, Dr Samuel Arnold, had performed a miracle in matching that text to Haydn's sturdy and cheerful tune. . . .

III. Cassatios (Divertimenti) for Two Oboes (in No. 1 Two Flutes?), Two Horns, Two Violins, Two Violas and Basso (Violoncello, Bassoon, Double bass) No. 1 in G (II:9); No. 2 in F (II:20); No. 3 in G (II:G1); *c.* 1755–60

No. 1 in G

Principal sources: (1) MS. parts, Premonstratensian Abbey of Schlägl (Upper Austria), of local origin, dated 1775. (2) MS. parts, Staatsbibliothek, Berlin, entitled 'Cassacion', from Artaria & Co., Vienna; with parts for 2 flutes rather than oboes; perhaps this was one of the MSS. that Haydn gave to Artaria for 'un piccolo regalo' (*Haydn: the Late Years 1801–1809*, p. 336) in August 1805. (3) Printed parts, without the wind instruments, de la Chevardière, Paris, April 1768 (announced that month in the *Mercure de France*): 'Six / Simphonies / ou / Quatuors dialogués / .... / Œuvre IV. / .... / A Paris / Chez M. de la Chevardière Md. de Musique du Roi, Rue du Roule à la Croix d'Or ...'. Copy: British Museum. Contains Symphony 33, II:9, Symphonies 32, 15, 'B' and 25. It was later reprinted from the original plates by Le Duc (1785). (4) Printed parts of movements III, II and I for flute, violin and violoncello, by J.J. Hummel, Amsterdam (announced 24 March 1773 in the *Haagsche Courant*): 'Six / Sonates / a flute, violon / & violoncello. / composées / par / Giuseppe Haydn. / œuvre xi. / ... / A Amsterdam chez J.J. Hummel, / au grand magazin / de musique. / Nᵒ. 248. Prix f 3. = '. Copy: Hoboken Collection, ÖNB. The print includes arrangements of baryton trios and our work in penultimate place. For details, see Hoboken, vol. I, p. 599.
Critical edition: Verlag Doblinger (Landon), in preparation.
Literature: Pohl I, 258, 324. Landon *SYM*, 184–6 (with three musical examples).

No. 2 in F (II:20)

Principal sources: (1) MS. parts, Göttweig Abbey, P. Leander, 1763 as 'Gaßatio' (for details of this and other sources, see Doblinger edition). (2) MS. parts, Archives of Princes von Oettingen-Wallerstein, with vc. for viola I, Harburg Castle (Germany), perhaps a Viennese source, with the title 'Sinfonia'. (3) MS. parts, St Florian Abbey, 'Notturno ... pro usu J: / Mich: Planck. (4) MS. parts from the Archives of the Counts Pachta, National Museum, Prague, XXII D 111: 'Concertino'. (5) MS. parts Melk Abbey, 'Notturno', no wind instruments. (6) MS. parts, Stadt- und Universitätsbibliothek, Frankfurt-am-Main, with one viola and one 'cello parts for the two violas. (7) MS. parts, Archives of the Princes von Thurn und Taxis, Regensburg, entitled 'Le Mattin'. (8) Printed parts, with the Minuet No. 1 as 3rd movt.; 2nd Minuet lacking. Madame Berault, Paris

(announced in the *Affiches, Annonces & Avis divers* on 7 May 1772): 'Six / Sinfonie / a grand orchestre / composée / par / Gᵖᵉ. Hayden / .... / œuvre xiv / prix 12 [livres]. / ... / A Paris / chez Madame Berault Marchande de Musique rue de la comédie françoise faubourg Sᵗ. Germain au Dieu de l'Hⁿⁱᵉ. / .... / A. P. D. R.' Copy in Hoboken Collection, ÖNB. Includes Symphony 11, our work, spurious Symphony I:c26 (in other sources variously attributed to 'Mischa' and 'Bach'), Symphonies 59, 34 and I:A5 (actually by Dittersdorf).
Critical edition: Verlag Doblinger, Diletto musicale 56 (Landon, 1962). Misprints: p. 7, viola II, bar 1, first note *a*, not *b* flat; p. 15, bar 18, violin I, first note *g''* (not *f''*).
Literature: Pohl 1, 193, 319f., where he notes that the Archives of Breitkopf & Härtel owned a copy of the work ('Concertante') – they had offered it for sale in 1767 – which was to be placed among the works composed before 1757 (one of the periods Haydn dictated to Griesinger when he was the go-between and Breitkopf & Härtel were preparing the *Œuvres complettes* and questioning Haydn about several of his youthful works of which they had MS. copies). Naturally this authentic information was one of the principal criteria in our proposed dating.

No. 3 in G (II:G1)

Principal sources: (1) MS. parts as 'Cassatio', Lambach Abbey (description of this and other sources, see Doblinger edition). (2) MS. parts as 'Concertino', Archives of Counts Pachta, now National Museum, Prague, XXII D 110. (3) MS. parts from the Archives of Counts von Clam-Gallas, Friedland (Frýdlant) Castle; as 'Sinfonia in G' (listed as 'Nʳᵒ 18') 'Del Sigl Giuseppe Hayden' on 4° Italian paper (watermarks: three crescents of declining size, fleur-de-lys with letters 'GB'), possibly a Viennese source. (4) MS. parts, Mecklenburgische Landesbibliothek, Schwerin, as 'Divertimento'. (5) MS. parts, königliche Hausbibliothek, Berlin (score from this source: J.P. Larsen, Copenhagen). (6) MS. parts, Stadtbibliothek, Leipzig. Other MSS. are not listed here, including some German MSS. (Rheda) and a Viennese source (GdM, IX 29474/9, dated 1798 and signed 'N H', arranged for str. quintet – see Doblinger's Source C).
Critical edition: Verlag Doblinger, Diletto musicale 47 (Landon, 1959), also as miniature score (Stp 287, 1978).
Literature: none (!).

The fact that Haydn included this second work among the music he composed before 1757 has suggested the dating *c.* 1755–60 for all three. In *EK*, No. 3 is entirely wanting. No. 1 was entered about 1765 by Joseph Elssler as the first of the divertimento/cassatio group: 'Divertimento Ex G.' with the *incipit*, to which Haydn has added the words 'a nove Stromenti'. No. 2 appears two numbers later (in between is the 'Divertimento

Ex C', II:17) as 'Divertimento Ex F' with the *incipit* in Elssler's hand and Haydn's addition, 'a 9ᵛᵉ Stromenti'.

As for the orchestration, we have no sure way of knowing whether Haydn wanted two flutes (Berlin) or two oboes; but most of the sources favour oboes, and the music looks more suited to the latter (see music examples in *SYM*, 184f.). Haydn expected a bassoon to be part of the *basso continuo*: this is made clear by the Trio of Minuet I in No. 2, where after the first double bar, the sources specify 'Fagotto': this is the bass line of a wind-band solo, and the same procedure occurs in the Trio of Symphony No. 9 (1762). (In neither work is the bassoon part even mentioned in Hoboken, incidentally.)

Haydn started writing symphonies relatively late in his career, and in some respects these cassatios are the proving ground for his symphonic style. And yet, Haydn is clearly not writing symphonies but open-air serenade music. The differences between Haydn's early symphonies and these works are revealing. The use of the two violas in contrast to the violins is an old Austrian cassatio tradition. Then there is the obvious divertimento/cassatio layout with five movements: quick – minuet/trio – slow – minuet – trio – very quick. The use of the 'quick metres' for the opening movement (in these three cases two-four and six-eight) is also part of the general style, and also the light substance of the themes: to see the difference between a typically symphonic theme and one of these, one only has to compare either the 'learned' thematic material of Haydn's Symphony No. 2/I (much more formal and Baroque than anything in these works), or the dashing Italian overture quality of No. 4/I, or the heavily symphonic language of No. 10/I, not to mention the big Mannheim crescendo that opens No. 1/I.

The developments are less weighty, too: examine the opening Allegro molto of No. 3 and the cassatio style, in this respect, is clear: 62 bars total; 26 bars to double bar, 'development' section 16 bars. 'Development' is a term which applies to much later music, of course; here it is simply a brief contrast, with a pretty 'echo' effect in the I⁶₄–V minor, to reintroduce the main subject.

The movements that strike one as being most like their well-known counterparts in early quartets and symphonies are the minuets. Here Haydn has completely found the popular style: the tunes have that sturdy, driving force and the folk-like quality and already sound thoroughly like Haydn. The trios are full of instrumental delights, and one of the details that spring to eye and ear is the extraordinary tessitura expected of the horns: of course, high *f″* in No. 2, but *g″* several times in No. 3 (Trio of Minuet II). We know that the Morzin horn players must have been among the greatest in the Monarchy (sounding *a″* is required several times in Symphony No. 5): are the exceedingly difficult horn parts of these cassatios evidence that they were composed for Morzin (as we also believe that Divertimenti II:21 and 22, with their difficult horn parts, are Morzin works because of the authentic Fürnberg-Morzin sources, *vide infra*, p. 258)? Or was Haydn able to count on such horn players even for his street serenades?

In the Adagio of No. 2, some of the sources include two elaborate cadenzas (other sources have only the longer of the two, that occurring at bars 33ff., which is certainly original, i.e. by Haydn himself). If the first one, at bar 15, is not actually by Haydn, it is a very useful contemporary 'realization' of that which the composer, at this stage, likes to call a 'Ferma'. These cadenzas, taken over from the concerto, are very much in the Austrian cassatio tradition. In studying the differences between Haydn's symphonies and cassatios, we find the composer immediately beginning to mix the two styles: there are many symphonic elements in these three cassatios, especially in the orchestration. And Haydn's early symphonies partake heavily of the divertimento/ cassatio tradition, borrowing many of the typical devices: elaborate cadenzas and use of solo instruments (Symphony No. 7), and so on.

And yet, there is something very serenade-like, open-airish, about these cassatios; and something magical, too, like the warm summer wind that Italy sends to its northern neighbour. One only need examine the slow movements (wind instruments always dropped) to hear this indefinable but very distinctly felt element, and a part of the peculiarly moving quality is, literally, its pulsating accompaniment, which seems to rustle like the Prater trees on an August night: technically, one notes the exchanges of murmuring demisemiquavers in the violas (No. 1) over a long held cantabile theme; while in No. 2, this same undulating background is provided by the lower strings, especially the bass line in repeated semiquavers. The interludes for pizzicato strings in this same movement look forward to similar effects in the early string quartets. This is the charm and novelty of the Haydn cassatio style, and it is easy to see why his countrymen adored this music at first sight (or sound), but also why it seemed typically flippant and unserious to someone raised in the north-German tradition. What would the average Saxon *Capellmeister* have made of the pert, eight-bar theme of the Finale in No. 3, with its total foreshadowing of the later Viennese classical style (note the delicate symmetry of the 'end' figures, the first rising, the second falling)?

Finale: Presto

He would also have found annoying the unison passages that led to many syncopations, and the repeated semiquavers which, he might have said, 'are a nasty imitation of the Filtz style'. But there were many, even in Germany, that fell at once under the spell of this new music. If there is one word to sum it up, the word is 'wit'; and this was in general the one thing that Baroque music, and certainly Renaissance music, had totally lacked.

It may interest our readers to learn that the first 'publication' of No. 3 came, not by the printed page, but by the gramophone record: as a part of a Decca recording (with works by J. C. Bach, Mozart and Dittersdorf) which Mogens Wöldike made in the early 1950s with the Danish State Radio Chamber Orchestra. Professor Jens Peter Larsen furnished the score (*vide supra*). Despite this, the work was put into the list of doubtful and spurious works by A. van Hoboken. It was not printed until several years after the recording had appeared, and is now again part of the repertoire.

DANCE MUSIC

(1) Twelve 'Seitenstetten' Minuets: *Minuetti* (IX:1; *c.* 1752–5)

Scoring: 2 ob., 2 cor., 2 v., basso (violoncello, bassoon).

Principal source: Autograph, Benedictine Monastery of Seitenstetten (Lower Austria), on permanent loan to the Musiksammlung of the ÖNB. At the top of the first page of music: 'Minuetti [middle:] In Nomine Domini [right:] Giuseppe Haydn.' Oblong Italian paper (watermark: three crescents of equal size). We believe that this and the autograph of Piano Sonata No. 13 (XVI:6) are the oldest Haydn autographs to have survived. They are all undated. We doubt if Haydn began dating his autographs until *c.* 1760: none before that date was originally dated (the date '1756' was added much later to the *Salve Regina* in E and the Organ Concerto in C, XVIII:1).

Critical edition: Verlag Doblinger (Landon, in preparation).

Literature: Landon, *SYM*, 43f., 58n., 59n., 143. G. Thomas in *Haydn-Studien* III/1 (1973).

(2) Sixteen (Twelve) Minuets: *Minuetti* (IX:3; c.1760–5?)
Scoring: Nos. 1–16, as listed in the Breitkopf Catalogue of 1767, for 2 piccolo flutes, 1 fl., 2 bsn., 2 hns., 2 v., basso (violoncello, bassoon).
Principal source: None of the orchestral version has survived. Nos. 1–12: Autograph of the keyboard reduction, prepared *c.* 1762–7, entitled 'Minuetti', EH, Budapest, Ms. mus. I. 53. Oblong Italian (three crescent) paper.
Critical edition: Universal Edition (Franz Eibner, in preparation).
Literature: Pohl I, 103, 259, 327, G. Feder, 'Zur Datierung Haydnscher Werke', in *Festschrift* A.

van Hoboken, Mainz 1962, pp. 53f. G. Thomas in *Haydn-Studien* III/1 (1973).

(3) Twenty-four Minuets (IX:23; *c.* 1765–70)
Scoring (of No. 24): 2 fl. (originally 2 ob.), 2 hns., 2 v., basso (violoncello, bassoon).
Principal source: Autograph of Menuetto and Trio, numbered Nos. 23 and 24, EH, Budapest, Ms. mus. I. 50b. One sheet, signed at the end 'Fine/Laus Deo'.
Critical edition: none (work unprinted).
Literature: G. Thomas in *Haydn-Studien* III/1 (1973), pp. 5ff.

In the *Entwurf-Katalog*, page 11, there was originally a place reserved for dance music, to wit four series of minuets, which Haydn himself entered, alas without the *incipit*, as 'Menuetti / item / item / item' about 1765 or slightly later. Dance music was the most expendable of all music (together with wind-band partitas): nothing is older than yesterday's minuet. It is, therefore, something of a miracle that as much of Haydn's dance music has survived, often in a single copy. Since, in Hoboken's Catalogue, the authentic and doubtful dances are all included *en suite* as if they were authentic, we shall analyze (in the Addenda and Corrigenda to this volume), and cause to fall by the wayside, a whole series of dances listed as authentic, from the period 1766–1809. Concerning the works listed in Hoboken as from 1750 to 1765, the lost group of *Six Menuetti* (IX:2) are known to us only from the Sigmaringen Catalogue, which contains many spurious works. The curious and interesting group of *Twelve Minuetti da ballo* (IX:4), which have come down to us in one single printed source, must concern us next. They are scored for flute, 2 horns, 2 violins and bass, and J. J. Hummel in Amsterdam published them in 1766 (pub. no. 97, announced on 8 September 1766 in the *Haagsche Courant*, copy of the print in the Kungl. Musikaliska Akademiens Bibliotek, Stockholm). One of the pieces (No. 7) is entitled 'Laudon', after the famous Austrian Field-Marshal to whom Haydn later dedicated a symphony (No. 69). But there is no other reference to this work in any Austrian source, and the content of the music is not such that one would be willing on its strength alone to assume that Haydn was really the composer. Until we gather further evidence, they must be regarded as doubtful works. The Benedictine Abbey of St Peter in Salzburg owns another set of Thirteen *Menuetti* (IX:19) for 2 violins and basso; in Hoboken (vol. I, p. 572) they are listed as lost, but we studied them in 1956. They are pretty little works and apart from two quotations, the rest might be by Haydn, and if so they can only be of this early period. The MS. is signed by 'P. Michael Nagnzaun' and is clearly attributed to 'Sige Giuseppe Hayden'; perhaps it arrived in Salzburg via Michael Haydn.[1] The evidence for the music's authenticity is, however, far too slender. We have therefore concentrated on those known pieces, and especially the only complete set of orchestral minuets of this period, viz. the 'Seitenstetten' Minuets.

The Chronicle has provided us with evidence of Haydn's minuets being warmly received in the taverns of Vienna in the 1750s. The accidental presence of this unique autograph source gives us the possibility of studying such pre-1760 minuets at first hand. The handwriting is rather more round, less angular, than the composer's later

---

1 'Menuetti: / a Violino: 1 :mo / Violino 2 :do / e / Basso: / Del Sige Giuseppe: Hayden', a local copy. Minuet No. 11 uses material from a string duo (VI:6, 3rd movt.), while No. 1 seems to have been adapted from String Duo, VI:3, 1st movt. See H. Walter, *Haydn-Studien* III/1 (1973), 16.

hand: the manuscript is neat, careful, well organized. There are hardly any corrections, but one is significant and worth recording: in Minuet No. 2, the last five bars were originally four (fully orchestrated) – see opposite.

In Haydn's first draft, there are ten bars in part one of the minuet and nine in part two; and while Haydn was very fond of these asymmetrical patterns, presumably a real minuet for formal dancing was one place where it was quite impossible; yet if we consider Minuet No. 3, its first part contains eight bars but its second part ten. Yet perhaps combinations of even numbered patterns were acceptable. But apart from the structure of the minuet for dancing, Haydn's second thought grows more organically out of the foregoing material, and by lengthening the ♩ ♫ figure for another bar, Haydn is able, moreover, to create a better ending: the sequence in the third last bar is better in the final version because the subdominant at the beginning of the penultimate bar is better prepared.

Only three of the minuets have trios (Nos. 1, 5, 12), and all are in the tonic minor: this was an Austrian conventionality, perhaps, but Haydn writes serious music. As our final music example, we include the whole of Minuet and Trio No. 5 (see overleaf). Connoisseurs who followed Haydn's career in Vienna and heard both these minuets and the first symphonies for Prince Paul Anton Esterházy will have noted some stylistic 'fingerprints' of Haydn's early style: the dotted figures with trills (bars 5f., 8, 12f.) reappear in the Minuet of Symphony No. 7 and are 'positioned' in a similar way. The rhythmic ♩ ♫♫ of the horn (which we also have elsewhere in the minuets, e.g. at the beginning of No. 1) is also typical of Haydn's early minuet writing for horn. The dynamic writing in the Trio is typical of the unconventional way in which Haydn writes these minuets. In No. 10, both the first and second parts end with several *pp* bars, which give a delicate, almost fastidious flavour: for all Haydn's sturdy masculinity, there was always, even in his music of the 1750s, a delicate and subtle side to the man which is doubly surprising considering his rough education and taking into account the robust nature which is so starkly reflected in his music.

There was always a great tradition of music, and a special veneration for Haydn, at Seitenstetten Monastery; but in point of fact, these Minuets were not part of the original abbey archives but were acquired in the nineteenth century. It would be instructive to know where the manuscript was uncovered, and when.

The keyboard reduction that Haydn made of the Minuets (IX:3) is, as it happens, the only known source, but it gives us, alas, a very pale idea of what the original orchestration must have been, with its entrancing listing of two *flauti piccoli*. Interested readers may study the music shortly in a critical edition by Professor Franz Eibner. Perhaps one day we shall uncover a German manuscript (via the Breitkopf announcement of 1767) of the complete orchestration.

[Minuet and Trio No. 5 from the 'Seitenstetten' Minuets (IX:1)]

TRIO

2 Oboi

*Third ♭ missing in autograph.

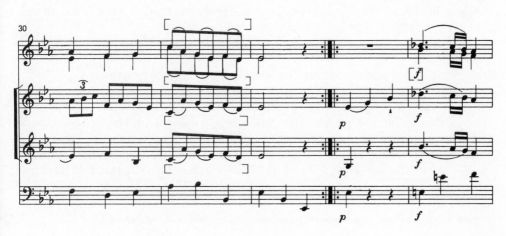

Menuet da Capo

Haydn remembered having composed four sets of minuets by 1765 (perhaps four Esterházy suites of minuets? he must have composed dozens in the 1750s as a student). Perhaps the fragment of Minuet/Trio Nos. 23 and 24 in Budapest was the conclusion of one such set, for some ball at Eisenstadt or Kittsee, of which the Chronicle will supply many occasions. (We have preferred not to split up the dance music, but to treat it all in one group.)

CONCERTOS FOR ORGAN (HARPSICHORD) AND ORCHESTRA

Georg Feder, in a very interesting article,[1] shows that from the tonal range, in which the right hand does not exceed c''', most of Haydn's early keyboard concertos were conceived for organ and not for harpsichord (where the range in Haydn's own works was always greater, at least d''' and slightly later f'''), although the professional copyists, and probably Haydn himself, were glad to offer copies 'per il clavicembalo'. In *EK* one of the concertos is listed as 'Per il clavicembalo' in Haydn's hand and underneath 'Conc per L'organo' in crayon (XVIII:1). We have only one autograph of

---

1 'Wieviel Orgelkonzerte hat Haydn geschrieben?', *Musikforschung*, Jahrgang XXIII (1970), Heft 4, pp. 440ff.

these works: XVIII:1, and that is marked 'per l'organo'. But the real hint that Haydn indeed wrote several concertos for the organ is on page 20 of *EK*, where he lists 'Concerto p[er] violino e Cembalo In F' (which, as it happens, has, in its keyboard part, the range of Haydn's organ and was undoubtedly written for that instrument); to the right is Haydn's supplementary note, 'e ancora altri Due Concerti p[er] l'organo in C'; we have, in fact, another three (not two) additional organ concertos in C. Haydn was leader at the Viennese Convent of the Hospitallers and also organist at the Haugwitz Chapel; no doubt there were many opportunities to compose and perform organ concertos. Although it is not really possible to create a chronological list of these early organ concertos, some attempt had to be made, and here, the central points were the (posthumously) dated Organ Concerto (XVIII:1) of 1756 and the fact that, later, Haydn also believed that the Double Concerto (XVIII:6) had been written for the same event in 1756. It is very much to be doubted if these concertos were the first of their kind: next year (1757) Haydn began to compose quartets for Fürnberg and in 1758 at the latest he was composing symphonies and other works for Count Morzin. Therefore it is to be presumed that these other organ concertos must *predate* the 1756 work(s); and the style of the works in question suggests that, indeed, they are less assured, less polished, than that (those?) of 1756.

We have therefore created a new list of the approximate order in which we presume these six extant concertos were composed:[1]

No. 1 in D (XVIII:2); No. 2 in C (XVIII:10); No. 3 in C (XVIII:8); No. 4 in C (XVIII:5); No. 5 in C (XVIII:1; 1756?); No. 6 in F for organ, solo violin and orchestra (XVIII:6; 1756?).

No. 1. Concerto for Organ (Harpsichord) and Orchestra in D
(XVIII:2; *c.* 1752–5)

Scoring: (1) presumably original version: org. (cemb.) solo, str. (2) with wind instruments and timpani, presumably not by Haydn since the timp. is in transposing C-G notation, quite against Haydn's usual practice: cemb. solo, 2 ob., 2 clarini (trpt.), timp., str. This is the scoring of Berlin, mus. ms. 10067 (*infra*). In one of the thematic catalogues by Aloys Fuchs (Vienna 1840) the scoring is for 2 ob., 2 hns., str. None of the now known MSS. suggests that combination.

Principal sources: I. With strings only. (1) MS. parts, Schlägl Abbey on 4° paper partly from Kremsmünster (crown, within a star, beneath the letters 'FAW', mill of Wurm family; 'w' in ornate design; posthorn) and partly from another mill (coat-of-arms, letters 'IHIM'). (2) MS. parts, Seitenstetten Abbey, '♯ / Concerto ex D♯ / .... / Del: Sigl:

giusephe [*sic*] Haydn / [monogram: "JCH"(?)] / [later:] Comparavit / Ambrosius Abbas / Seitenstetten. / 792.' (3) MS. parts, Göttweig Abbey, 'Comparavit / R:P: Marianus / 774'. (4) MS. parts, Archbishop's Library, Kremsier (Kroměříž), II F.46. (5) MS. parts, ÖNB, Vienna, 5. m. 22 892: 'Concerto per Cimbalo Con Violini, Viola, e Basso Del Sig^{re} Hayden' (only Cemb., V.I., Basso survive). In these incomplete and contradictory parts, V.I contains a Largo and Allegro which belong to another work and are inserted between II and III (*incipits*: Hoboken, vol. I, 816). (6) MS. parts erroneously ascribed to Baldassare Galuppi: Preußische Staatsbibliothek, Berlin, mus. ms. 6995. 'Concerto per il Cembalo concertato, Violino Primo e Secondo, Alto Viola e Violoncello del Signore Galuppi'. II. With the additional

1 We exclude, of course, doubtful works. (1) Concerto in F from the Nunnery at Alžbětinky, now National Museum, Prague, Alž 86: 'Concerto in F. / per il Organo / â / Violino Primo. / Violino Secundo. / Corni Due. / Alto viola / con / Basso / Del: Sig^{re} Hayden [below, to the right:] Ex Musica[libus]: / Joannis P: Slavik mpria' on tall 4° paper (watermarks: title page, sun with letters 'HS' within; parts, circle with anchor-like form; horn parts have eagle and three hearts). The actual part is entitled 'Clavecin'. Critical edition: Breitkopf & Härtel, Leipzig, 1964 (No. 3910), ed. Vratislav Belsky and Vladimir Srámek. Dr A. Peter Brown has meanwhile identified the work as being by Leopold Hofmann: Breitkopf Catalogue 1770, and MS. copies in Kremsier, Staatsbibliothek, Berlin, and ÖNB, Vienna. (2) MS. parts of a Concerto in C by 'Hayden', Academy of Sciences (Marianka), Bratislava, ČSSR, for organ, 2 clarini (trpt.), 2 v., basso 'Possidet Carolus Heninger mpria Leibnitsensis ... 823 die 12th Aprilis' on 4° Slovakian paper. Both these MSS. were consulted in 1959.

instruments. (7) MS. parts, Preußische Staatsbib-
liothek, Berlin, mus. ms. 10067: 'Concerto per
Cembalo 2 Violini, Viola (2 Oboe, Clarini,
Timpani ad libitum) e Basso di Giusep. Hayden'.

Critical edition: Verlag Doblinger, Diletto Musicale
78 (Landon).
Literature: Larsen, *HÜB*, 233f., 294ff.

In *EK* this Concerto is entered in Haydn's hand at the bottom of page 19; as with most of the other concertos for various instruments on the same page, the *incipit* is not that of the opening tutti but of the solo part's first entrance (which, incidentally, establishes that the ornament of bar 22, and thus of the same passage in the violins at bars 1ff., is a crossed turn and not the trill given in the secondary MS. sources). Larsen (*HÜB*, 233) thinks all the works on p. 19 were extant by 1765. Otherwise, the earliest recorded notice of the work comes from the Breitkopf Catalogue of 1767, where the accompaniment is for strings only.

One presumes that the work is in some way connected with one of Haydn's many Sunday jobs in Vienna. It was a typically Austro-Bohemian-Bavarian tradition to perform organ concertos in the middle of Mass. The organs were usually without (or at most with very rudimentary) pedals and known in German countries as *Positiv* organs.

And what are we to make of the attribution to Baldassare Galuppi? Actually, it is not as fantastic as might at first seem. We have seen that Haydn thought highly of the Venetian master and there are surely many elements of Galuppi's style that influenced the young Viennese. We know from Haydn's private thematic catalogue (*EK*) that it is a genuine concerto. The misattribution probably happened in a place geographically far removed both from Venice and Vienna, in this case somewhere in Germany. It may have resulted from two factors: first that the Concerto does not – with a few exceptions (the Finale as a whole is a major one) – reveal Haydn's personal style to anything like the extent of the early cassatios, string trios, quartet-divertimenti and symphonies; the Concerto is also much earlier than even Haydn scholars used to think (surely a decade earlier than its entry in *EK*); thus, secondly, this lack of a stylistic profile, especially the curious slow movement, made it easier to think of a contemporary like Galuppi, whose harpsichord style was greatly admired, and whose harpsichord concertos and sonatas were not so very different in general approach from some sections of Haydn's work.

As a model, as it were, for the puzzled German copyist (who, we may assume, knew enough early Haydn to realize that this Concerto was at best very atypical), we might select by way of illustration a two-movement Sonata by Galuppi (Adagio, Spiritoso)[1] such as circulated in MS. north of the Alps. Our generation, with all its historical hindsight, sees all the Galuppi 'fingerprints' (those dotted chain scales downwards in bars 6ff. of the opening Adagio and bars 7 and 10 of the Spiritoso), which we also find in Hasse and early Mozart, such as *Lucio Silla*; but it is never a Haydnesque feature; and if not a scribal error, the octaves between top line and middle line across the bar-line of 2/3 are not the kind of mistake Haydn usually makes in his keyboard music. (If we find an inept grammatical error in Haydn, it is more likely to be in one of the early vocal pieces.) On the other hand, some of the broken arpeggio writing, the introduction of chain sextuplets, and the running scales in the Galuppi are not wholly removed from the keyboard writing of Haydn's Concerto.

---

1 MS. from the editor's library, of Scottish provenance.

Sonata da Camera Cimbalo Solo del Sig: Baldassar Galuppi·

* Original 𝄢

[etc.]

Neither the opening of Haydn's first movement (we quote the opening of the solo) nor the continuation is more than mediocre:

[Haydn: Organ Concerto in D/I – opening of solo]

and what are we to make of the endless 'chain' sequences,

that type of mechanical keyboard writing to which Haydn all too frequently has recourse in these early concertos (for a similar 'chain' sequence, see bars 118ff. of the Organ Concerto in C [XVIII:1] of *c.* 1756, Breitkopf score, pp. 10f., first movement)?

If one felt that the first movement was somewhat lacking in profile, the Adagio is even more impersonal. When one compares its stiff, old-fashioned style with the slow movements of the cassatios analyzed briefly *supra*, it is hard to believe that this concerto movement is by the same composer. It is not until the Finale that Haydn's personality reasserts itself, and here we feel we are back on firm stylistic ground again. From the delicate imitational opening we arrive at a brilliant tutti with Haydn's usual repeated semiquavers (see overleaf).

The Berlin trumpets and timpani, though a later and almost certainly 'foreign' addition, are spectacular here, with audacious soli and one passage that actually rises at this point, and also in the same place at the end of the movement, to sounding *d'''*. The harpsichord writing is felicitous and reminds one in many sections of the harpsichord sonatas being composed much later. Compare the following passage in the Concerto's Finale

with one from Sonata No. 42 (XVI:27, part of a set assembled in 1776), first movement, beginning of the development section:

203

The Sonatas's language and technique clearly reflect the relevant passage of the Concerto.

Despite its generally undistinguished character, it was seen that – although never printed, like all these organ concertos – this D major Concerto achieved a certain amount of popularity in its day, circulating among the Austrian monasteries and being offered for sale by Breitkopf in Leipzig. If it is rather conventional to our ears, it is a fault shared not only by most of Haydn's early keyboard concertos but also by those of his contemporaries working in Vienna. One must, however, stress the paucity of these Haydn concerto sources, except for the Organ Concerto in C (XVIII:1), compared to other *genres* of Haydn's art; and perhaps this paucity was not entirely due to the fact that most of Haydn's concertos were probably written for a specific player (sometimes himself), who may have wished to keep the new work for his own personal use.

The *continuo* part is actually written out in some sources. If perhaps not by Haydn (for there are sources with figured bass; and who would go to the trouble of rewriting a written-out keyboard part in figures?), it is nevertheless a useful contemporary piece of evidence that shows with what simplicity the figured bass was 'realized' by professional organists and clavecinists in mid-century Austria.

[Organ Concerto in D/III]

No. 2. Concerto for Organ (Harpsichord), two Violins and Basso (Violoncello) in C
(XVIII:10; *c.* 1752–5)

Scoring: Organ (harpsichord), 2 v., basso (vc.). The keyboard part does not exceed *c'''*, and therefore it is, no doubt rightly, presumed that this is one of the early organ concertos.

Principal source: MS. parts, GdM, VII 100 (Q 13142): [upper right corner:] 'Concert N⁰ 4 / Concertino â 4ᵗᵒ: / Clavi Cembalo / Violino Primo / Violino Secundo / e / Basso / [lower left: *incipit* keyboard, two staves; right:] Del: Siegl: Heÿden / Johannes Carolis Müller mpria [left:] Hendel. /

1.7.9.3.' Oblong paper of Austrian origin (watermarks: crown with fleur-de-lys over letters 'NH / CANDER', and a cross over a coat-of-arms with fleur-de-lys within). On reverse side is the beginning of 'Sonata pour Violoncello di Hensel' (*incipit*, see Literature, Weinmann).

Critical edition: G. Henle Verlag, Munich, ed. Horst Walter (1969).

Literature: A. Weinmann in *Haydn-Studien* I/3 (1966), pp. 201f.

The first dated reference is in the Breitkopf Catalogue of 1771. The source in GdM is unique, and it was for many years mislaid; it was found by Dr Alexander Weinmann (*supra*), and is without question a lost organ concerto of this early period. It is more concise than that in D discussed above and, as always with early Haydn, brevity brings with it a better sense of organization, a pithiness that perhaps suits this early keyboard style better than the discursive manner of the Concerto in D. The slow movement is in three-four time. We have spoken about Haydn's fondness for this metre; it appears in no less than four of the six slow movements in the concertos under consideration. In this Adagio (F major), Haydn is closer to his own later style than he was in the particularly 'foreign' sounding G major movement in Concerto No. 1 in D.

Three-eight was, of course, a favourite metre for Austrian finales of this period, and five of the six finales in these concertos use it; thus it was a constricting convention, and with the metre often went, in contemporary organ concertos, a unison opening, followed by a harmonized 'answer'. This procedure is followed here. Recently, listeners at the 'Haydn Tage' in Eisenstadt, 1978, had a unique opportunity to hear this Concerto on Haydn's own organ in the Bergkirche at Eisenstadt, performed by Martin Haselböck and the Niederösterreichisches Kammerorchester, and introduced by Otto Biba, a leading expert on organs and their repertoire in mid-eighteenth-century Austria. It showed – if any further proof were required – how much more attractive these early keyboard concertos sound on the instrument for which they were undoubtedly written, the organ. (They all sound particularly incongruous on the modern piano which, interestingly, most Haydn sonatas and keyboard trios, even the earliest ones, do not.)

No. 3. Concerto for Organ (Harpsichord), two Trumpets or Horns, Timpani, two
Violins and Basso (Bassoon, Violoncello) in C (XVIII:8; *c.* 1752–5)

Scoring: Organ (harpsichord), 2 v., basso. There is considerable confusion in the sources about the horns, trumpets and timpani. In the Breitkopf Catalogue of 1766, the work is scored for horns and strings, in the Berlin source for horns or trumpets and timpani ad lib., in the Raigern source for different trumpets and timpani, in the Kremsier source for the same brass parts as in Raigern (no timpani), in Melk for strings only.

Principal sources: (1) MS. parts, Staatsbibliothek, Berlin, Mus. Ms. 10.064; 'Concerto ... Par Monsieur Hofman' perhaps dated 1771 and with

performance dates from 1772–6; 'Hofman' cancelled and replaced by 'Haiden'; for exact titles of this and other sources, see Doblinger edition. (2) MS. parts, Kremsier (Kroměříž). (3) MS. parts from Raigern (Rajhrad) Abbey, now Janaček Museum, Brno, ČSSR. (4) MS. parts, Melk Abbey.

Critical edition: Verlag Doblinger, Diletto musicale 80 (Landon, 1960), also pocket score (Stp 96).

Literature: Larsen *HÜB* 295. Landon: 'Haydn and Authenticity: Some new Facts', *Music Review* 16/2 (1955), 119ff. *SYM* 43, 231.

The fact that the one authentic source of all these concertos – the autograph of XVIII:1 – originally required trumpets (the stave was, in the event, left blank) suggests that sometimes Haydn had available horns or trumpets; and we believe that some of the horn and trumpet parts for these works may be either original to the work or possibly added later by Haydn; whereas some, like the Bohemian parts to this Concerto, are patently spurious additions. Again, we have sources with figured bass and at least one cleverly 'realized' one from Kremsier, which the interested reader may consult in the Doblinger edition. The realization is, once more, of great simplicity and, if anything, rather prim: we mention this because it becomes a growing fashion to provide these works with very elaborate continuo realizations which we do not believe to have been common at that time in the Austro-Bohemian-Bavarian area.

This is another of the early C major organ concertos, wherein the keyboard part does not exceed c''' at the top. Although more concise than No. 1 in D, it is not as tightly organized as No. 2. There is a very long sequence in the middle of the first movement which seems to have been regarded as almost obligatory in those days (bars 49–63).

The slow movement has an interesting innovation. There is no opening ritornello (as there was in No. 1 to a highly developed extent), and the solo part begins at once, as if we were in the 'concertino' form; we modulate to the dominant, as expected, and still there is only a minute orchestral conclusion (bars 21–3); solo than has the subject in the dominant, and there is a varied middle section, leading us back to the tonic. Now, and only now, do we get a real (albeit short) ritornello, to begin the recapitulation (bars 46–9). At the end there is also a proper closing ritornello. We see that Haydn has already begun to tighten and alter the form bequeathed to him by his precursors.

The same applies to the Finale: the opening ritornello is very short and, interestingly, consists of *nine* bars, while the solo answer is nine bars, too. The next section combines solo-tutti and is *seven* bars long (bars 19–25). All this is unconventional to the point of eccentricity.

The Berlin trumpets and drums are attractively fashioned and, whether genuine or no, contribute materially to the work's success; they certainly do not stand out as incongruous, which those of the Berlin MS. to No. 1 in D surely do.

The attribution to Leopold Hofmann (*c.* 1730–93) is also by no means far-fetched, for Hofmann, later Cathedral Chapel Master at St Stephen's, was particularly successful in harpsichord (and presumably organ) concertos, of which a great many have survived. Being in the general style, and considering that Haydn's language is as yet unformed, it was easy to confuse the two men's styles. Later, a large number of symphonies and other works, including a spurious Flute Concerto in D (VIIf:D1), really composed by Hofmann, was wrongly marketed as Haydn (who, incidentally, had a rather poor opinion of his clever contemporary).[1] Leopold Hofmann was also a prolific and successful composer of symphonies and was instrumental in solidifying the four-movement form as early as 1760, i.e. at the same period as Haydn's own formal experiments.

No. 4. Concerto for Organ (Harpsichord), two Trumpets or Horns, two Violins and Basso (Bassoon, Violoncello) in C (XVIII:5; *c.* 1752–5)

Scoring: In the announcement in the Breitkopf Catalogue of 1763, our work is listed together with XVIII:1 as for cemb., 2 v., va., basso. The viola part applies only to XVIII:1. In Eisenstadt, the title page lists two horns but the actual parts are for trumpets. In Raigern, there are dubious parts for oboes and horns, as well as the str. In Marburg, the parts are for strings. It seems to us that only the

---

1 *Haydn at Eszterháza 1766–1790*, p. 449.

supplementary instruments of the Eisenstadt MS. could be considered as by Haydn, possibly a later addition.

Principal sources: (1) MS. parts, Burgenländisches Landesmuseum, Eisenstadt (*ex coll.* Landon), formerly in the Collection of Alfred Cortot, to whom it was given by Hans Schneider in May 1954. The parts, written *c.* 1770, are on 10-stave German paper in oblong format from the mill of Johann Anton Unold in Wolfegg with the watermarks 'IAV / A [?] WOLFEG' and a coat-of-arms. Title page: 'Concerto in C / per il / Clavi = Cembalo / Violino Primo / Violino 2do / Corno Primo / Corno 2do / con / Basso / Del Sig: Haÿden.' Later Haydn's name was cancelled and 'Wagenseil' substituted in a second hand; in this same, second hand, 'No 14' (underlined) added to right-hand top corner. The parts themselves are all written by the same (third) hand. The brass parts were originally for trumpets, 'Clarino Primo [right:] in C' and 'Clarino Secondo [right:] In C'. Copyist No. 1 (the one who wrote the title page) later added 'Corno ò' in front of the word 'Clarino' in trpt. I. He also added 'In C:' after 'Primo' and 'Ex C' after 'Secondo'. The 'No 14' of copyist No. 2 ('Wagenseil' of the title page) was added to all the individual parts. A player added some pencilled figured basses; in the 3rd movt. the $^6_4$ $^4_2$ of bar 117 is authentic and part of the original

MS. (2) MS. parts about 1770 from the Monastery of Raigern (Rajhrad), now Janáček Museum, Brno on local 4° paper. Title (minus various numbers) 'Concerto In C / per il / Clavicembalo / Violinis 2bus / Obois 2bus / Cornuis 2bus / e / Basso / Del Sigre Giuseppe Haydn / Pat [?] Lang mpria / Chori Rayhradensis.' The MS. contains a great many local additions, even to dynamic marks which differ radically from those of the other two sources. The solo part also shows widespread alterations. (3) MS. parts, discovered by Horst Heussner (place never revealed) from the Archives of the Princes of Hessen-Philippsthal-Barchfeld and now in the Musikwissenschaftliches Institut of the University, Marburg/Lahn: 'Concerto / per il Clavi Cembalo obligato / Con / Violino Primo / Violino Secondo / e Basso / Del Signore Giuseppe Hayden.'

Critical edition: Nagels-Musik-Archiv 200, ed. by H. Heussner from (3) only, and lacking the evidence of (1) and (2); Kassel, 1959. Verlag Doblinger (Landon), in preparation.

Literature: H. Heussner, 'Zwei neue Haydn-Funde' in *Musikforschung* XIII/4 (1960). H. Heussner, 'Joseph Haydns Konzert (Hoboken XVIII:5) ...', in *Musikforschung* XXIII/4 (1969). G. Feder in *Haydn-Studien* I (1968), 29, and *HJB* IV (1968), 124 and n. 108; also *Musikforschung* XXIII/4 (1970), 440.

Here is yet another C major Organ Concerto, which Haydn and the other copyists distributed as 'per il clavicembalo' (note, however, that there is one interesting remark in the keyboard part of source 2 as 'pleno Choro': third movement, bar 117, violins at 118 have 'fortiss'). The whole concerto is laid out very much like the other previous works in C, and it, too, is shorter and more compressed than the earliest, as we presume, in D (also earliest because Haydn still has formal difficulties with dealing in a very large-scale concerto language). We note, in our present work (No. 4), the same rather attractive sequences (e.g. first movement, bars 27ff.), the profuse use of triplets, of chain dotted scales (ditto, 34f.) and of that apparently absolutely necessary gigantic sequence in the central part of the first Moderato, or (in other MSS.) Allegro (moderato), bars 53–64. We also have, as a gradually ever firmer detail, Haydn's choice of one particularly striking passage, which is usually repeated at crucial intervals. In No. 4's first movement, it is the little figure

which really has a kind of hypnotic charm (on its small scale, of course); we first meet it at bar 10 (upbeat), and later at bars 32ff. (in G), 65ff. (A minor), 94ff. (C major), in other words in the form's crucial places – opening ritornello, close of exposition, middle of 'development' (middle section), recapitulation. Apart from being a very useful technical device to give unity to a form which, in those days, was characterized by diversity, 'Fortspinning', the spinning-out of motifs, it also gives the idea a prominence that Haydn reckoned it could easily withstand. Those familiar with Haydn's later music will know that this procedure would be put to superb use in countless works.

In the slow movement (Adagio or Andante, depending on the source; we believe the former to be correct), we notice that Haydn has again followed the procedure of Concerto No. 3 in starting without a ritornello, directly with the solo. The first proper ritornello (as opposed to an occasional bar of orchestral 'fill-up') comes at the end of the first section: ritornello in C. To begin the third part – all these slow movements are in the usual ternary form except where noted – there is a small ($3\frac{1}{4}$ bar) ritornello, and one (6 bars) to conclude. A further characteristic detail: in all these smaller organ concertos, there is no place allotted to a cadenza (in contradistinction to the D major No. 1). We return to the larger form, which automatically includes cadenzas in the first two movements.

The three-eight Finale (Allegro, or Tempo di Giusto; former must be Haydn's designation) is again in the style of a reduced concerto, with very small ritornelli (to open, there is one of ten bars) and the usual array of attractive conventionalities that in no way distinguish it from the equally conventional works of his contemporaries – except for one thing: the precise and (compared to Concerto No. 1 in D) strongly reduced formal structure makes it easier to support the thin fabric that covers it. It was thus easy for a German musician to imagine that 'Haÿden' was a misattribution and the real author one of Haydn's principal precursors in the field of harpsichord music at the Viennese court, J. G. Wagenseil – in 1760, Haydn was probably considered a *seguace* of Wagenseil – see XVIII:1, *infra*.

No. 5. Concerto for Organ (Harpsichord), two Oboes, two Trumpets (Horns?), Str. (with Viola) in C (XVIII:1; 1756)

Scoring: Autograph has, at the beginning, two staves for 'Clarino / 1mo. and 'Clarino / 2do,^ which were never filled out. Since the number of horns, trumpets and timpani in the secondary sources is particularly large, and many have not been seriously investigated, a short survey may be welcome:

(a) trumpets and timpani in source 2, by Viennese professional Copyist No. 2 (= Fürnberg/Morzin Copyist No. 4). The trumpets are stylistically possible and we reproduce them, courtesy of Professor A. Peter Brown, for the first time. The timpani part, on the other hand, is a crude forgery, with extraordinary rhythms quite foreign to Haydn. Scholars may see this, too, courtesy of Professor Brown. Were it not for the undoubted presence of this authentic copyist, these trumpets would be judged, perhaps, as a clever addition. It is always possible that Haydn wrote the trumpet parts straight on the parts for the players and never bothered to enter them later in the autograph.

(b) horn parts in source 4, possibly copies of lost trumpet parts, possibly real C *alto* parts or C *basso* parts; they are neatly made. We include them here in facsimile (they are unpublished). We incline to the belief that they may be lost trumpet parts.

(c) horn parts in source 8, ditto.

(d) trumpet and timpani in source 10, from Olmütz (Olomouc), are local additions, dated 1801, and not very professionally done.

Principal sources: (1) Autograph, Hessische Landes-bibliothek, Darmstadt, from the Archives of Breitkopf & Härtel, to which firm Haydn sent the MS. in 1806 (*Haydn: the Late Years 1801–1809*, p. 342). It is on oblong Italian paper, and as with the *Salve Regina* in E, XXIIIb:1, the 'mpria' and, underneath the signature, the date '756' were added by Haydn later, perhaps as late as *c.* 1800. At the head of the first page of music is the original title: [left:] 'Concerto per l'Organo [right:] Giuseppe Haydn.' (facsimile of first page in Somfai, p. 23 of German ed.). As noted above, at the top of the 10-stave paper of page one were two staves for trumpets, not filled in. (2) MS. parts, Kremsier (Kroměříž) II-G-21 (A 3215): '† / Concerto Ex: C: / à / Cembalo Concerto [later: "o Organo"] / Violino Primo / Violino Secondo / Haubois Prim / Haubois Second: / Alto Viola / e / Basso [right:] Autore Sig^re^ Haÿden / [middle:] H:' on oblong Italian paper (watermarks: three crescents of declining size: 'BT' under crown, ornament with star and, beneath, half-moon; string parts: elaborate ornament with five stars above, coat-of-arms with a hammer within; the trumpet and timpani parts on different paper, fleur-de-lys with letters 'AS', three crescents of declining size and letter 'A'). We are indebted to Professor A. Peter Brown for organizing photographs and for his transcription of the watermarks. The principal copyist made everything except the trumpets and drums; there is a second title at the top of page one of the cemb.: 'Concert pour le Clavecin p^r Mr Joseff Haÿden', which someone later changed by crossing out 'Joseff' and, beneath, writing 'Michael'. But by far the most astonishing feature of this source is that the trumpets ('Clarino Primo In C:' etc.) and timpani (*infra*) are copied by the authentic copyist Fürnberg-Morzin No. 4 (Viennese professional No. 2), who delivered many works to Kremsier. Now it is obvious that, when Haydn was away from Vienna at Lukavec or Eisenstadt, this professional scribe had to make a living and was possibly – though the evidence is not complete – a member of a Vienna scriptorium. Therefore it is entirely possible that he sometimes sold copies of Haydn works in which changelings had been introduced – possibly the case with the trumpets, certainly the case with the kettledrums. (3) MS. parts, Göttweig Abbey, on local paper 'per il Clavicembalo' (orch. oboes, strings). (4) MS. parts, Melk Abbey V 796. Original title page lost. Parts on 4° paper for 'Cembalo', str., 2 ob. and 2 cor., latter shown in facsimile (pp. 214–5). (5) MS. parts, St Lambrecht Abbey (Styria), 'Concerto / per il / Clavicembalo ... / Del Sgre Giuseppe Heyden' on 4° paper (oboe I missing) (water-

marks: title page: crown with letters 'SAJB' [?]; pts. ditto or 's' in coat-of-arms). (6) MS. parts from Raigern Abbey, now Janáček Museum, Brno, A. 12. 505, 2 ob., str., 'Clavecin'. (7) MS. parts, Staatsbibliothek, Berlin, 'Concerto per il Clavicembalo' with str. and 'Due Oboe ad libitum'. (8) MS. parts, GdM, with str., 2 ob., 2 cor., cemb. (9) MS. parts, GdM, for cemb. and str. (10) MS. parts from Olmütz (Olomouc), now Janáček Museum, Brno A. 14.561: 'Concerto in C / per il / Clavi Cembalo / Violino Primo / Violino Secundo / Viola / Oboe Primo / Oboe Secondo [*sic*] / Clarino Primo / Clarino Secundo / Tympani / et / Basso. / [left:] Authore Hayden [at bottom right:] Antonii Plachy / mpria'. Three copyists, some parts signed 'one 26. [27.] czerwna 1801' ('day 26th [27th] June 1801'). The trumpets and drums, as said, are uninteresting local additions. (11) MS. parts, City Archives, Preßburg (Bratislava, ČSSR), with trumpets and timpani added by a local music master; we have not seen this source, which is described by G. Feder in *HJB* IV, 126. In the Catalogue of music from Zeil Castle of 1767, the work is listed, also in the Breitkopf Catalogue of 1763 (cemb., str. only).

Critical edition: none. There is a poor practical edition, Breitkopf & Härtel, Wiesbaden, ed. (1953) by Michael Schneider.

Literature: Pohl I, 355f., III, 222. Larsen, *HÜB*, 48. Geiringer 1932, p. 90. Landon, *SYM*, 58n., 121, 199f., 231.

[Kremsier MS. parts]

II.

LARGO TACET

III. Allegro molto

Clarino 2do

I. [Allegro moderato]

II.
LARGO TACET

III.   Allegro molto

Timpani

I.   Allegro moderato

II.
LARGO TACET

Yet another work attributed to someone else: in this case to Haydn's brother, Johann Michael; and that, too, was not so obscure a (mis)attribution at the time, and for someone in Kremsier. Michael Haydn had composed a brilliant Double Concerto in Großwardein (Perger 55) for viola, organ and strings in C (first edition: Doblinger, ed. P. Angerer), which dates from, at most, a year or two after the present work of his brother's. Michael's highly interesting and sophisticated work suffers from the national sickness: it is too long, and the attractive, deftly composed music is stretched very thin on a frame far too large for its own good. But recently yet another, hitherto unknown Organ Concerto by (Michael?) Haydn in G (see *incipits* below) has been discovered.[1]

1 In November 1975, it was offered for sale to Doblinger and was subsequently purchased by the Österreichische Nationalbibliothek, Vienna. It is on 4° paper of the Austrian monarchy *c.* 1770–80 Cat. Mus. Hs. 34. 905. Title: 'Concerto / Organo vel Forte Piano / [pencil: "Haydn"] / [*incipit*] / 27'. The only attribution, then, is Haydn's name in a later pencilled addition. Parts for organ or fortepiano, V.I, V.II, Va., Basso. The right hand of the organ is in the G-clef. The watermarks show that the paper comes from Eger (Cheb) in the former Sudetenland, now ČSSR (man holding lance over 'EGER', letters 'INS'). The work is now catalogued under Michael Haydn, but we can in fact see no reason for preferring to list it under doubtful Michael rather than doubtful Joseph. Perhaps the style is closer to Großwardein than to St Ulrich's in Vienna (i.e. Joseph Haydn and his 1756 Concerto, XVIII:1).

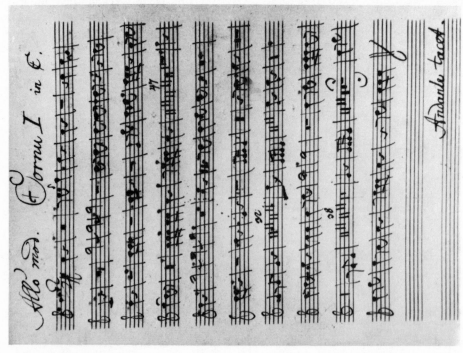

The MS. horn parts for Haydn's Organ Concerto (XVIII:1), from Melk Abbey.

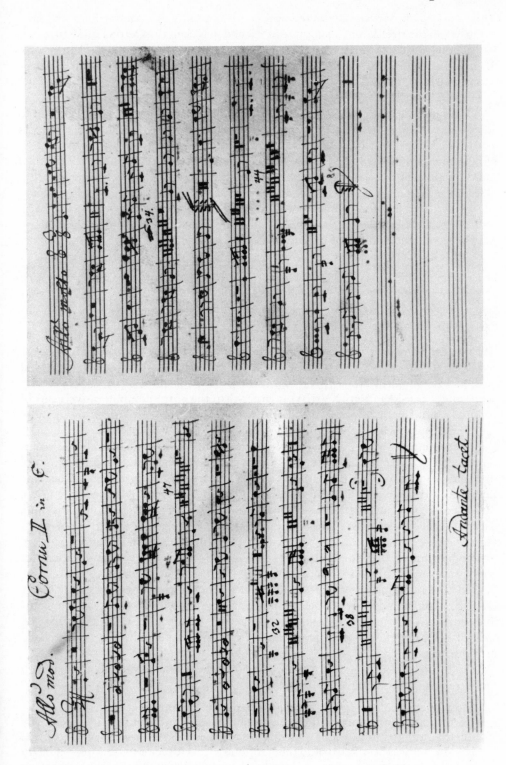

This work is, however, attributed, probably correctly, to Pietro Pompeo Sales (1729–97) in the Breitkopf Catalogue of 1775 and in MS. in the Oettingen-Wallerstein Collection at Schloß Harburg (III 4½ 4° paper 358: Gertraut Haberkamp: *Die Musikhandschriften der Fürstlich Oettingen-Wallerstein Bibliothek Schloß Harburg*, Munich 1976, p. 178).

The fact that there was someone at Kremsier who mistrusted the attribution to Joseph Haydn only shows once again that these organ concertos lack those decisive and persuasive elements of Haydn's early style found in his other works. An even more striking similarity is between Haydn's 1756 piece and a 'Cello Concerto by Wagenseil (autograph dated 1763), mentioned above (example in *SYM* 199f.), although in this case (a) the Wagenseil is later and (b) they both partake of the same stylistic fountain.

Unlike the previous three works in C, XVIII:1 is a 'large' concerto, with indications for a cadenza in the slow movement. Some idea of the comparative size may be seen in the number of bars involved:

FIRST MOVEMENTS
No. 1 (4/4) (XVIII:2): 154 bars. No. 5 (2/4) (XVIII:1): 260 bars. These are the large organ concertos. The small ones are considerably less extended, e.g. 99 bars (No. 3, XVIII:8), or 106 bars (No. 4, XVIII:5), both in 4/4 time.

FINAL MOVEMENTS
No. 1 (2/4) (XVIII:2): 386 bars. No. 5 (3/8) (XVIII:1): 229 bars. The small concertos show: 114 bars (No. 3) or 120 bars (No. 4).

The slow movements of the small concertos, on the other hand, do not show a similar reduction to that extent (though we find, in No. 3, XVIII:8, 66 bars in 3/4, compared with 86 bars in 3/4 in No. 1, XVIII:2). It shows that the 44 bars (Largo, 4/4) of the work under consideration (XVIII:1) is larger than the corresponding movements of Nos. 2–5 principally because the soloist was expected to provide a presumably substantial cadenza.

Everything about this work, written (as one believes) for a nun taking the veil, is on a much grander scale; hence, no doubt, the idea of including trumpets in the orchestra. As in No. 1 (XVIII:2), the scale is far too large for the insubstantial thematic material. When we arrive at the middle section, the *obbligato* (which we use in the eighteenth-century manner) series of sequences outdoes anything else along those lines except for the similar passages in Nos. 1 (XVIII:2, 15 bars) and 3 (XVIII:8, 14½ bars). Here, we have a double sequence, the first one beginning at bar 118 (duration: 19 bars), to which is immediately added another one beginning at bar 137 (duration: 13 bars). It is a classic example of over-extended material.

The last movement is twice as long as any other in the series except for No. 1 (XVIII:2); but in our work of 1756, the Finale (Allegro molto, 3/8) has two double bar lines, and *both* sections were expected to be repeated, which makes the rather daunting total of 458 bars; even at a relatively fast tempo, this makes another over-extended movement.

On the subject of this elaboration, Peter J. Pirie has some pertinent remarks to make (referring to Concerto No. 3, XVIII:8).

> Most of Haydn's concerti, except perhaps the succinct and brilliant Trumpet Concerto, are long and vague works, and it may be said that Haydn never made the transition from Baroque *concerto grosso* to the eighteenth-century concerto as convincingly as he made that to the symphony.... He seems to be improvising, in an effort to find the answer.... Haydn's texture is plain, and for that very reason perhaps is the matrix for mighty things.... Rather dull as music, Haydn's concerti

are a source of infinite speculation and conjecture; they might almost be described as a cul-de-sac, one of the few of his experiments that were fulfilled in a general manner much later, without themselves developing to fruition. . . .

[*HJB* II (1963/4), 101]

No. 6. Concerto for Organ (Harpsichord), Violin Solo and Strings in F
(XVIII:6; *c*. 1756)

Scoring: The keyboard part, in the earliest sources, does not exceed *c'''*, and it is thus presumed that the work was originally written for organ and not harpsichord.

Principal sources: (1) MS. parts, Kremsier (Kroměříž), for cemb. (2) MS. parts, Schlägl Abbey (only cemb., v. solo extant) on local oblong paper. (3) MS. parts, Staatsbibliothek, Berlin, Mus. ms. 10.061, on oblong and 4° (str.) formats, for cemb. (4) MS. score, Sächsische Landesbibliothek, Dresden, Musica 3356/0/16a, on 4° paper, for cemb. Local copyist transcribed part of solo v. for 'Cembalo 2do'. (4a) A single MS. part of v. I (orchestral part), same library, 2256/0/16b. (5) MS. parts, Conservatorio di Musica, Genoa. (6) MS. parts, cemb. only, Janáček Museum, Brno. (7) MS. parts, Library of publisher C. F. Peters, Leipzig, with 'Cadences pour le Concert de Heyden … avec le Violon principal', from which a score was made for the Reichsender, Leipzig; the Peters source was once owned by Joseph Liebeskind. Cadenzas: It seems possible that Haydn actually wrote at least one of the three sets of cadenzas transmitted to us in the various MSS. (see Schultz edition). In Albrechtsberger's *Concerto per l'Arpa* of 1773 (EH, Budapest, Ms. Mus. 2404) we find 'Zum Concert in F // Ferma del Signor Hayden'; the *incipit* of the *Ferma* for the Andante (*sc.* Largo) is shown in the example below. Probably the cadenzas in this MS. are by Albrechtsberger

himself, but the situation needs to be examined critically. In any case, the various cadenzas are most useful in giving us a contemporary view of what their length and general content should be.

Critical edition: Musikwissenschaftlicher Verlag, Leipzig-Vienna, 1937 (Helmut Schultz). Meticulously prepared, like everything Dr Schultz ever did, we have nevertheless many new sources which alter some of the passages, particularly as regards the *top range of the instrument*; Dr Schultz, of course, took the work to be for harpsichord and thus he never worried about adding a *tr* on *c'''* (which, the upper note being *d'''*, Haydn's organ could not have played): II, bar 20. The sources divide here, some adhering to the organ notation (upper range *c'''*), others – Schlägl, Berlin – reaching *d'''* and thus assuming a harpsichord would be used: the passage is II, bar 27, penultimate note (see Feder, 442, *infra*), where the bulk of MSS. have *b''*, Schlägl/Berlin *d'''*. This is a particularly brilliant piece of deduction on Dr Feder's part and taken as a whole it has revolutionized our knowledge of Haydn's early keyboard concertos and his use of the organ *Positiv*.

Literature: G. Feder, 'Wieviel Orgelkonzerte hat Haydn geschrieben?', *Musikforschung* XIII/4 (1970), 442f. *Haydn: the Late Years 1801–1809*, p. 266.

Catalogue references (all for cemb.): Breitkopf Catalogue 1766; Zeil Castle 1767.

Haydn thought at one point, when he was an old man, that he had written this 'Organ Concerto with one violin' for the ceremony at which his later sister-in-law took the veil in 1756. As we have suggested, perhaps he performed all three works: *Salve Regina* in E, Organ Concerto in C (XVIII:1) and Double Concerto in F (XVIII:6). There are two factors that suggest that it was written for some special occasion: first, the presence of the viola, which is the exception rather than the rule in these works; secondly, the Concerto's exceptional length: I (213 bars) in 2/4; II (53 bars) Largo in 4/4; III (279 bars) Allegro, 3/8. There are cadenzas, as noted, expected for both first and second movement. As far as Haydn is concerned, we might postulate that the viola is *only* used in these large-scale works for organ and orchestra; also, that it so happens to agree with the string orchestra used in the *Salve* and the other Concerto in C; so perhaps Haydn really did compose it for the sad ceremony of 1756. Once again, if this be true, there is no trace of emotion in this conventional and, if anything, pleasantly sprightly Concerto. We find many of the early Haydnesque fingerprints: scales in dotted rhythms (I, bar 4; never repeated), frequent introduction of triplets and sextuplets, the chain syncopations in the orchestra of the Largo (very reminiscent in technique of the 'Rorate' Mass), the cadential figures that end the ritornello of the Largo (syncopations against long-held line, resolving in four semiquavers and a crotchet):

(The four semiquavers and a crotchet also appear at similar place in Concerto No. 5 (XVIII:1), bar 10; but for an even more extraordinarily similar passage, cf. Symphony No. 36/II, a concerto movement with solo violin and solo 'cello, bars 15–7, 38–40, where there is the *pp*, the broken syncopated accompaniment, the bass quavers on the beat and the melodic line above. The unison conclusion of the opening ritornello in the Finale, which recurs in the dominant and at the end of the work, is also characteristic of the general style (i.e. not only Haydn's) of the period.

Being a large work rather than a kind of 'concertino', there are complete ritornelli in all three movements, and double expositions of the solo material because of there being two solo instruments. The syncopations in the Finale (first announced at bars 14ff.), which go across the bar-line ♩♩♩ | ♩♩♩ | ♩♩♩ | ♩♩♩, remind us of the Finale of the Violin Concerto in C major 'fatto per il Luigi' (VIIa:1), where there are similar syncopations in a similar place. As far as the fatal series of sequences in the middle of the first movement, Haydn does not disappoint us (or his listeners in the Viennese church of 1756) and gives us a monstrous example that covers nearly two dozen bars (98–120).

In sum: well-knit, dexterous, but hardly memorable – a typical keyboard concerto of the Vienna area in the middle of the 1750s.

———————

Two matters remain to be clarified. The first is perhaps the result of the second, and concerns the extraordinary popularity that Haydn's organ concertos have enjoyed for nearly a quarter of a century. It is inexplicable that these frail works should be vastly more popular than the great string quartets, and so on; and this is especially true in France, for reasons that we cannot fathom.[1] We believe, however, that their fantastic

1 See Marc Vignal in *HJB* II (1963/4), pp. 121 *passim* on this point.

success in our age must depend partly on the reflected glory of witless Baroque concertos, which have swamped our eyes and ears in recent decades, and partly on the gramophone record. All these works have now been recorded, and many times. It is yet another example of the fearsome power of the gramophone record, for good and for less-than-good.[1]

THE EARLY STRING TRIOS

'Haydn, the Inaccessible' was Sir Donald Tovey's description of that which one might call 'the state of Haydn research'; that was some forty years ago, when barely one-tenth of Haydn's music, according to a survey by Karl Geiringer,[2] was printed; and when the *Gesamtausgabe* of Breitkopf & Härtel had, after thirty years, scarcely managed to issue a dozen volumes; and when only a handful of Haydn's works was ever performed.

Nowadays, thanks principally to the new Collected Edition (of the Joseph Haydn Institut, Cologne) and to the efforts of a group of European publishers (principally Universal Edition and Verlag Doblinger), but above all to the gramophone companies, Haydn is no longer inaccessible.

There is, however, one strange exception to this fortunate state of affairs – Haydn's string trios. Even in the otherwise admirable survey of string trios as a *genre* – we refer to Hubert Unverricht's *Geschichte des Streichtrios* (Tutzing, 1969) – Haydn's string trios (we do not refer to the baryton trios, which are analyzed in some detail) are hardly discussed.

The reason for this situation was that there has never been a detailed study of these trios, which are exclusively early works, beginning in the early 1750s and running, at most, to the 1760s. In category V of the Hoboken Catalogue, there are listed twenty-one works of undisputed authenticity (viz., from *EK* and *HV*), but no less than fifty-nine works of dubious genuineness: a formidable total of seventy-eight works, a figure which used to be the nightmare of Haydn research in the 1930s, because it was the number of newly discovered symphonies announced to the astonished scholarly and musical world by the German scholar Adolf Sandberger, and the reason for J. P. Larsen's epochal book, *Die Haydn-Überlieferung* (Copenhagen 1939), in which Sandberger's tenets were categorically refuted. (Subsequently, we have actually found the right composers for most of these spurious symphonies.)

In the years since the Second World War, however, a great deal of evidence on these string trios has come to light, none of which is incorporated in Hoboken's Catalogue. In 1975, therefore, the writer of this biography and Verlag Doblinger, in co-operation with French Decca (which firm is preparing a collected edition of these trios for the gramophone with Jacques-Francis Manzone, violin), decided to issue the first critical and collected edition of Haydn's string trios. At this point in our

---

1 The first recording of any Haydn organ concertos was the now famous record by the Haydn Society of XVIII:1 (with the Melk horn parts played by trumpets) and XVIII:8 (with the Berlin trumpets and timpani), recorded by Anton Heiller on the Baroque organ of the Franziskanerkirche Vienna, with the Vienna Symphony conducted by Hans Gillesberger (1950). A subsequent record of historical importance was made by CBS in 1962 of Concertos XVIII:1, 5 and 8 on the organ of the parish church St Martin (now Cathedral), Eisenstadt, with E. Power Biggs and the Columbia Symphony Orchestra conducted by Zoltan Rosznyai (now reissued as 61 675. Producer of the latter, John McClure; of the former, H.C.R.L. Recently (1978), the first recording of the Double Concerto with an organ was made (reverse side: Double Concerto in C for viola and organ by Michael Haydn), which demonstrated that the work actually sounds far more interesting and attractive in its original clothing: Martin Haselböck (Org.), Siegfried Führlinger (va.). Errst Kovacic (v.), Niederösterreichisches Kammerorchester, cond. by Erwin Ortner, ÖRF (Austrian Radio), PAN 0120 220.
2 'The operas of Haydn', *Musical America*, 1940. Tovey: *Essays in Musical Analysis* (volume on the symphonies).

biography, we propose to present the contents of this new edition and to provide a brief survey of the music – for more detailed analysis, space is simply not available – as a *genre* in Haydn's early years.

The following list is based, primarily, on Haydn's *Entwurf-Katalog* (also the basis of *HV*, the Elssler list of 1805), to which we have appended those other works which inner and outer criteria suggest are indubitably genuine.

HAYDN'S STRING TRIOS

for 2 v. and basso (except where otherwise noted); or v., va., basso

Our no.	Hoboken no.	Key	EK	HV	Authentic sources (if any)
1	V:1	E	13 (Joseph Elssler)	1	None known.
2	V:2	F	ditto	2	None known.
3	V:3	B minor	ditto	3	None known.
4	V:4	E flat	ditto	4	None known.
5	V:5	B	ditto	5	Work lost.
6	V:6	E flat	ditto	6	Wrong order of movements in Hoboken (corrected in vol. III, 1979); the proper order is III–II–I (*incipit* in *EK* is III); V:6 *bis* was supposed to incorporate this order, which is the only one supported by authentic evidence (*EK*).
7	V:7	A	ditto	7	None known.
8	V:8	B flat	ditto	8	None known; for v., va., basso.
9	V:9	E flat	ditto	9	Work lost.
10	V:10	F	ditto	10	None known.

(At this point in *EK*, Haydn added the *incipit* of Trio No. 23; this occurred at the bottom of the page [13]; and on the top left-hand side of the same page Haydn had added the pencilled *incipit* of Trio No. 22. Both these later additions concern works which we believe were composed *c.* 1765 or later and we have therefore placed them at the end of the list of works entered in *EK* by Joseph Elssler.)

Our no.	Hoboken no.	Key	EK	HV	Authentic sources (if any)
11	V:12	E	14 (Joseph Elssler)	12	Authentic parts from the Esterházy Archives, Budapest (Ms. mus. I.105).
12	V:13	B flat	ditto	13	None known.
13	V:14	B minor	ditto	14	Work lost.
14	V:15	D	ditto	15	Viennese Professional Copyist No. 2 (= Fürnberg-Morzin No. 4), Collection Else Radant Landon, Music Library, University College, Cardiff: 'Trio I'.
15	V:16	C	ditto	16	Ditto: 'Trio II'. Both MSS. on 4° paper of the Austrian monarchy, *c.* 1760 or later.
16	V:17	E flat	ditto	17	None known.
17	V:18	B flat	ditto	18	None known.
18	V:19	E	ditto	19	None known.
19	V:20	G	ditto	20	None known.
20	V:D3	D	missing	missing	Authentic source by Fürnberg-Morzin Copyist No. 1, Keszthely Castle (Hungary), with corrections in Haydn's hand, K 1137; with the stamp of 'Fürnberg Obrest Lieut.'.
21	V:G1	G	missing	missing	Ditto, K 1137.
22	V:21	D	13 (in Haydn's hand)	21	None known.
23	V:11	E flat	13 (in Haydn's hand)	11	None known.
24	V:D1	D	missing	missing	Pachta Archives, Prague: Viennese Professional Copyist No. 2 (= Fürnberg-Morzin

Our no.	Hoboken no.	Key	EK	HV	Authentic sources (if any)
					No. 4), in a series with holograph corrections by Haydn.
25	V:C3	C	missing	missing	Ditto.
26	V:G4	G	missing	missing	Ditto.
27	V:B1	B flat	missing	missing	Pachta Archives, Prague: Fürnberg-Morzin Copyists Nos. 6, 8.
28	V:F1	F	missing	missing	*Quartbuch* (*vide infra*, p. 588) and Lambach Cat. 1768 as Haydn; MS., GdM, by Anton Saarschmidt 1765 as 'Geuseppe Hayden', and MSS. Kremsmünster, Berlin Staatsbibliothek (*ex coll.* Artaria, Vienna), Melk, Seitenstetten as 'Giuseppe Haydn' ('Haiden'); Chevardière's printed edition (*infra*, p. 597) of *c.* 1764 as No. 1; remaining works V:19, D2 (autograph GdM = Michael Haydn), 18, 15 and 16; the whole reprinted by J. J. Hummel. Haydn's authorship has strong support from early sources and also from internal evidence.
29	V:C4	C	missing	missing	*Quartbuch* (first of three in this *genre*) and Sigmaringen Cat. 1766 as Haydn; MS. 'Comparavit / Maria Ludovica / Saillerin' (variants, see Hoboken, vol. I, p. 490), Berlin Staatsbibliothek (*ex coll.* Artaria, Vienna; Haydn's mother-in-law was born Sailler; MS. parts, Pachta Archives, Prague (a better piece of evidence, because Frau Sailler also copied one work as Haydn, V:Es 9, which is undoubtedly by Leopold Hofmann; she also copied V:D3, of which we have an authentic source: see our No. 20, *supra*); MS. parts, Berlin Staatsbibliothek, also *ex coll.* Artaria: 'Tre Divertimenti ... Del Sign Giuseppe Haydn' (with No. 7 and XI:11, the latter for v., va., basso). Scoring: 2 v., basso (no authentic alternative for v., va., basso as suggested by Hoboken, vol. I, 489).
30	V:C5	C	missing	missing	*Quartbuch* (second of three in this *genre*); MS. parts, Pachta Archives, Prague: 'Divertimento / A Tree [*sic*] / Del Sigr Giuseppe Hayden'; MS. parts of Finale, GdM, 'Del Sig. Geuseppe Hayden 1766' by Anton Saarschmidt; MS. parts, Seitenstetten, 'Notturno in C / Violin 2 / e / Basso / [*incipit*] / Par Monsieur Joseph Hayden'; MS. parts, Berlin Staatsbibliothek (*ex coll.* Artaria).
31	V:C2	C	missing	missing	*Quartbuch* (third of three in this *genre*); MS. parts, Pachta Archives, Prague: 'Divertimento / à tre / Due Violini / con / Basso. / Basso. / Del Sigl:re Haÿdn.' MS. parts, Monastery of Neuburg im Mürztal (now secularized): 'Trio ... Dell Sign. Giuseppe Hayden Ex Rebus Francis Xav. Rigler Philos: et Math: Stud:', now incomplete.
32	V:C1	C	missing	missing	Göttweig Catalogue (as Joseph Haydn); MS. parts, Pachta Archives, Prague; MS. parts by Anton Saarschmidt, 1765, GdM, 'Del Sigl: Haÿdn'; MS. parts by a Viennese professional copyist, GdM, 'Divertimento ... Del Signore Giuseppe Haÿdn'; MS. parts, Melk; MS. parts, Berlin Staatsbibliothek (*ex coll.* Artaria).
33	V:G3	G	missing	missing	*Quartbuch* as Haydn. MS. parts, Pachta Archives, Prague: 'Divertimento / à tre / Due

Our no.	Hoboken no.	Key	EK	HV	Authentic sources (if any)
					Violini / con / Basso. / Del Sigl.^{re} Haÿdn.' MS. parts, Berlin Staatsbibliothek (*ex coll.* Artaria). Printed parts by Simrock, Bonn, 1796: 'Six Trios / à l'usage des commençans / pour / deux violons & basse …', with two 'livres' making a total of twelve works (V:G1, D1, 7, G3, B1 and 11).
34	V:A2	A	missing	missing	*Quartbuch* as Haydn. MS. parts, Pachta Archives, Prague: 'Divertimento / à / Tre Voci / Del Sig: Giuseppe Haydn'; MS. parts, GdM: 'Divertimento: Ex A: / Violino Primo / Violino Secundo / Viola / Cornu 1$^{mo:}$ } tacent [these two lines cancelled, cancellation possibly applies to viola as well] / con: / Basso: / Del Sigl Geusephe Haÿden. / [*incipit*]. In Raigern Monastery Catalogue as Michael Haydn, in which catalogue, however, the genuine V:11, V:16, V:18, V:D2 [= really Michael], V: Es1 [= really Michael], V:F8, V:G1 are all listed under Michael. V:B2 is, however, listed as Joseph Haydn.

Notes: This is not, of course, a chronological list, which it will never be possible to draw up for the string trios, since we lack too many early dated sources. The information (sources, etc.) provided in the right-hand column is primarily to establish the credibility/authenticity of the piece and is not intended to be regarded as a list of sources. The more we progress numerically, the more information we have been obliged to give, as positive evidence of a given work's authenticity is increasingly lacking (Nos. 28–34). Concerning the identification of 'Fürnberg-Morzin' copyists, *vide infra*, pp. 250ff. The list was prepared in the following order of credibility: first, all the works entered by Joseph Elssler in *EK* (basis for *HV*); then the two works by a Fürnberg-Morzin copyist with corrections by Haydn; then the two works Haydn himself added in *EK* (Nos. 22, 23) which seem to be 1765 or later and are probably later than two works (Nos. 20, 21) prepared by a Fürnberg-Morzin copyist in which we find the spelling 'Minuet' that Haydn used only prior to 1761; we then proceeded to four works (Nos. 24–7) in the Pachta Archives, three by one of Fürnberg-Morzin copyists, with holograph corrections by Haydn (Nos. 24–6), one (No. 27) by two Fürnberg-Morzin copyists with no holograph corrections by Haydn. Nos. 28–34 survive in a series of reliable early sources (e.g. Pachta) and appear from all the evidence at our disposal to be genuine. Concerning the other works in Hoboken's group of spurious and doubtful section (vol. I, pp. 489–507), we provide here a few supplementary notes as an aid to establishing the identity of the true authors. V:Es1 – Michael Haydn also in Kremsmünster, H 120,20. V:Es2 second *incipit*: this version also Helikon Library of Festetics family, Keszthely Castle, K 1159 'Ex Rebus Ignatii Ranson [Ranzen?]' (watermarks of MS.: Austrian double eagle without crown, letters 'H L' [?]). Naturally, this MS. has nothing to do with the authentic MSS. at the Castle; Count Festetics acquired the MS. from some unknown source (Ignaz Ranson or Ranzen), and we could not persuade ourselves that the work was genuine. V:F4: there are other sources as Bach, e.g. Kremsmünster (as quartet) and Breitkopf Catalogue 1772 (citing a French edition). V:G6: National Museum, Prague, XXVII B 60 (Zámek Castle) and Horešovsky Castle (Tyn): Hoffmann. V:G7: Breitkopf Cat. 1771: II Trii by 'Anonymo' No. 2 for v., vc., b., V:A7: Breitkopf Cat. 1767: 'Hoffmann' No. 10 of fol. 34. Horešovsky Castle, now Prague XXVII B 63: Hoffmann. In preparing this new list of Haydn's trios, we have preferred to be conservative, and to omit from the group a rather large number of works for which the evidence of authenticity is not sufficiently positive, either from the standpoint of the sources or from internal evidence.

Haydn's early string trios are valuable to us, and were useful to him, as proving ground for the first string quartets: the firm hand, the assured manner, of the quartets is largely the result of experimentation within the string trio form. It is difficult to say why Haydn preferred, with one exception (as far as we can tell) the scoring of two violins and basso (not necessarily violoncello; Haydn might have considered a small double-bass as equally valid) rather than violin, viola and basso; but possibly Haydn was quite simply bowing to tradition. In many chamber groups, it was obviously easier to organize two violins than a violin and viola.

Chronologically, we have seen in the Chronicle that among Haydn's very first efforts at composition were string trios, which created a *furore* among Viennese amateurs in the 1750s. It is unfortunate that there are so few authentic sources among the first group of trios, that is, those which Joseph Elssler entered in *EK* about 1765. The two authentic MSS. of Trios Nos. 20 and 21 are, however, very useful in establishing that at least those two particular works were probably composed before 1761: Haydn's spelling of 'Minuet', as we noted in the above list, occurs only in works known from other evidence to have been composed prior to that date. We doubt whether Haydn composed any string trios after he again took up the string quartet (Op. 9, written at the end of the 1760s); the reason for this neglect is, we believe, twofold: first, because he soon had a new form of trio which was to occupy his talents for some ten years, viz. the baryton trios (almost all composed between about 1765 and 1775); and secondly, because Haydn was soon to devote his detailed attention to the string quartet during the years 1768–72 (eighteen works).

Formally, the most striking feature of these trios is the preponderance of the old *sonata da chiesa* form, that is, works beginning in the Corellian tradition of an entire slow movement. There are several variants of the basic form, of which the favourite is a three-movement version wherein the second movement is an Allegro and the third a Tempo di Minuetto. This is precisely the form that Haydn used in Symphony No. 18. A second possibility is Adagio – Allegro – Allegro (only one work: No. 10). A third is Adagio – Minuet/Trio – Presto (two works: Nos. 8, 20). Two lost works suggest, by their *incipits* in *EK* that they are in church sonata form but we can not tell of which variety (Nos. 9, 13). Of thirty-four works, fifteen are in some kind of *sonata da chiesa* form, and the opening Adagio became something of a Haydnesque speciality – the long, flowing melody, the gentle repeated quavers of the accompaniment, the obligatory tripartite form (the middle section being a kind of 'varied exposition' and not a 'development' in the later classical style). To offset this, the following Allegro displayed a certain rhythmic tension, and the acceleration of the quaver accompaniment changed the mood enormously.

Another favourite form (which persisted in the baryton trios, too) was that of two movements, an opening Moderato followed by a Tempo di Minuetto (or more rarely, a straight Minuet/Trio); we have half-a-dozen works in this form (Nos. 7, 23, 24, 27, 31, 33). As we examine these trios, a curious fact seems gradually to emerge, namely that Haydn seems to have written them in series; if *EK* presents the works as they were written, and the authentic copies of Nos. 14 and 15 as 'Trio I' and 'Trio II' would seem to support this theory, then the fact that Nos. 1, 2 and 3 are *sonata da chiesa* works in the identical formal pattern (Adagio – Allegro – Tempo di Minuetto) may not be accidental. We will see that in 1764 Haydn certainly wrote two symphonies in the identical church sonata form (Nos. 21, 22), and Symphonies Nos. 31 and 72, despite the apparent chronological disparity, were obviously conceived as a pair.

The other popular form is the more normal one (Allegro, Minuet/Trio, Presto), in which some half-a-dozen works were written. In fact the only form in which no works were composed is the 'straight' four-movement classical pattern (Allegro – Adagio – Minuet/Trio – Presto, with the two inner movements being, at least in the early stages, interchangeable). Haydn uses a variety of other three-movement forms (e.g. Allegro – Adagio – Presto; or Allegro – Minuet/Trio – Theme and Variations on a slow theme; or Allegro – Andante – Theme and Variations on a slow theme).

For whom were these works written? There is a certain correspondence between these string trios and the early piano sonatas, which like the trios fall into two basic patterns of large and small works. In the case of the trios, the *sonata da chiesa* works are, relatively, large-scale works. This can be seen graphically if we compare such a work with, let us say, the really minute Trio No. 21 (Allegro molto – Minuet/Trio – Presto), the small size of which is compounded by the absence of any slow movement. There will be, as we shall shortly see, the same grouping in the early keyboard sonatas, and we suggest that Haydn had in mind the same basic kind of audience: (1) the professionals and amateurs, or the public at large (the difference between professional and amateur not being an essential one); (2) Haydn's pupils, perhaps that category described in the Simrock print as 'à l'usage des commençans'. We would say that the larger *sonata da chiesa* works were intended for the first, and the small trios (such as No. 21) for the second. There are even church sonata works composed on a deliberately small scale, such as No. 20 (opening Adagio with three variations; Minuet/Trio; Allegro), which might be for educational purposes.

We cannot approach these works with the sound or concept of Haydn's late quartets in our ears and minds. The early trios are warm-hearted, formally impeccable and more intended for the player than the public (not the case in late 'public' Quartets such as Op. 71 and 74, 1793). They are in many cases genuine apprentice works, but we believe that once they are known, they will be as popular as the early quartets, which no amount of adverse criticism – of which there has been an endless quantity, mostly because the works were judged on the basis of the later Viennese classical style and obviously found wanting – has ever succeeded in removing from the permanent performing and recorded repertoire.

THE EARLY KEYBOARD SONATAS (PARTITAS, DIVERTIMENTI)
listed in the order of the *Wiener Urtext-Ausgabe*

No.	Hoboken no.	Comments
1	XVI:8	
2	XVI:7	
3	XVI:9	
4	XVI:G1	
5	XVI:11	
6	XVI:10	
7	XVI:D1	
8	XVI:5	Breitkopf Catalogue 1763; authenticity, despite this very early reference, doubtful; *Menuet* possibly genuine. See Foreword to the *Ausgabe*, pp. X, XX.
9	XVI:4	
10	XVI:1	
11	XVI:2	
12	XVI:12	
13	XVI:6	Autograph: (1) first movement, now Royal College of Music, London (facsimile of first page, p. 226); (2) second and third movements, formerly Sándor Wolf, Eisenstadt, now Niederösterreichisches Landesmuseum, Vienna (photograph: Hoboken Photogrammarchiv, ÖNB, Vienna).
14	XVI:3	
15	XVI:13	
16	XVI:14	
17	*deest*	Discovered by G. Feder in a MS. from Raigern Abbey (Janáček-Museum, Brno, ČSSR) together with No. 18. There is no evidence that Haydn had anything to do with this work, which appears to us to be the typical product of a *seguace*.
18	*deest*	Discovered by G. Feder in a MS. from Raigern Abbey (Janáček-Museum, Brno, ČSSR), together with No. 17. It has now been identified as a work by Kayser (Kaiser). See C. E. Hatting: 'Haydn oder Kayser? – Eine Echtheitsfrage', *Musikforschung* XXV (1972), Heft 2.
19	earlier version of Sonata No. 57 (XVI:47)	

Critical editions: *Wiener Urtext-Ausgabe* (C. Landon, 1966), vol. I. G. Henle Verlag, Munich (G. Feder, 1966). The old standard edition by Carl Päsler in the Breitkopf & Härtel *Gesamtausgabe* (Series XIV, vols. 1/3), Leipzig 1914, which was a model of its kind, has now been of necessity superseded because many new sources, including autographs, have meanwhile been discovered; it can be conveniently consulted in a reprint by LEA Pocket Scores, four volumes, New York 1959.

Literature: H. Abert, 'Joseph Haydns Klavierwerke', *Zeitschrift für Musikwissenschaft* II, 1919/20. Landon: *Essays*, 44ff. B. Wackernagel, *Joseph Haydns frühe Klaviersonaten. Ihre Beziehung zur Klaviermusik des 18. Jahrhundert*, Tutzing 1974 (summing up previous literature such as Pohl, Geiringer, etc., which has therefore been omitted here).

It is likely that some of these early keyboard sonatas, which seem to have been written with either the clavichord or harpsichord in mind, are among the first compositions of Haydn. Like the string trios, they were probably written first and foremost for Haydn's pupils. There are short works, such as Nos. 1–9, and more ambitious ones, of which No. 11, with its G minor Largo, is remarkable. Although the sonatas make widespread use of the technical and musical devices of Haydn's precursors – the reader is referred to the first part of this chapter for many examples – nevertheless we can see many of the traits with which his own early music is filled: in the Largo of No. 11, for instance, the chains of syncopations are familiar to us from many other works examined in this chapter. The lean, two-part writing of bars 33ff. is slightly reminiscent of C. P. E. Bach, whose influence on the short divertimenti is negligible. Haydn's fondness for series of triplets is displayed in the opening movement of No. 12 and in the attractive G minor Adagio of No. 13.

Chronologically, it is almost impossible to suggest any kind of order within this group, but if we examine the radiant E major Sonata No. 15, it seems evident that it is much later than Nos. 1–9 and indeed belongs to the early Eisenstadt years: it shares not only the key, but the sunny atmosphere and taut form of Symphony No. 12 (1763). For some reason, there are hardly any works in minor keys among this *genre* before about 1765, but No. 19 is an interesting exception; it is in the *sonata da chiesa* form, with a whole opening Adagio in a kind of *siciliano* rhythm (six-eight), and it breaks off in a held V chord and leads into the ensuing Allegro. Many years later, in the piano trios composed in and after the second London trip, Haydn would return to such slow movements leading to (in those cases final) allegros.

In many respects, the lost sonatas (see *Wiener Urtext-Ausgabe*, I, pp. 132f.), with their tantalizing beginnings – including two works in the minor and one in B major – form a watershed. In the fragment of the otherwise lost Sonata No. 28, we can see Haydn working towards an entirely new keyboard technique: see the extraordinary Trio with its exploitation of the keyboard's bottom range (*F*) and the entirely novel way in which the minor key is approached. The only other work of Haydn's youth with which this may profitably be compared is the equally unique F minor Piano Trio No. 14. After about 1765, and rising to an overwhelming climax in 1771 with the great Sonata No. 33 in C minor, Haydn began to view the keyboard sonatas not primarily as teaching vehicles but as artistic forms to be developed on their own terms.

It is likely that many keyboard sonatas of Haydn's youth have not survived. There may also be some works that have survived in transcriptions or pasticcios. Professor A.

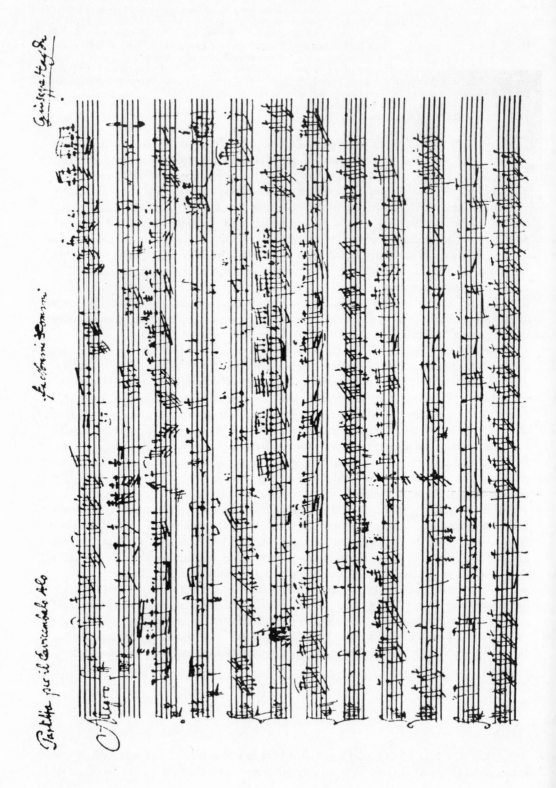

Peter Brown has kindly drawn our attention to a MS. in Kremsier (Kroměříž), A 3001, which consists of

Nʳᵒ Iᵐᵒ Variaziones a Clavi Cembalo Haydn; and
Nro IIᵈᵒ Concertino del Sig:ʳᵉ Haÿden –

of which we give the *incipits* (Hoboken *deest* except as shown):

From information provided by Professor Brown, one sees that the Variations end with a Minuet/Trio. The Concertino has three miniature movements, of which the Finale, curiously, has a middle section in the minor entitled 'Trio'. The Concerto is followed by two minuets, the first with a trio, in what is purported to be Haydn's autograph. The hand is not Haydn's but it may perhaps be the actual composer's autograph: no author is listed. Despite the manuscript's rather odd appearance, it may be that some of the movements are actually by Haydn; perhaps they originally served another purpose, and the 'Concertino' may once have been differently entitled. It is, of course, difficult to assert these pieces' authenticity on the basis of their affinity to Haydn's early style; a *seguace* would write in the Haydn manner, too. We list them only because so much early Haydn keyboard music has survived only in Kremsier and some in authentic copies by Fürnberg–Morzin copyists (see the Piano Trios, Chapter VI).

Our greatest hope for unknown Haydn works is in the Slovakian, Bohemian and Moravian parish churches, the investigation of which is still, at the present time of writing (1979), proceeding. Thus the final chapter on the studies of Haydn sources is not yet quite completed, and we may hope for a few new discoveries from that quarter.

Opposite
The first page of the autograph of Haydn's very early (*c.* 1755?) Keyboard Sonata No. 13 in G (XVI:6), entitled 'Partita per il Clavicembalo Solo'; the piece also bears the composer's familiar dedication 'In Nomine Domini' and his signature 'Giuseppe Haydn'.

CHAPTER FIVE

Chronicle 1757–1760

I. Fürnberg and Weinzierl

THE DOCUMENTS

(for numbered footnotes see end of relevant document)

(1) Autobiography 1776:

... finally, by the recommendation of the late Herr von Fürnberg (from whom I received many marks of favour), I was engaged as *Directeur* at Herr Count von Morzin's ...

(2) Griesinger:

... the following, purely coincidental circumstance led him to try his hand at the composition of quartets. A Baron Fürnberg[1] had an estate in Weinzierl,[2] several stages from Vienna; and from time to time he invited his parish priest, his estates' manager, Haydn and Albrechtsberger (a brother of the well-known contrapuntist,[3] who played the violoncello) in order to have a little music. Fürnberg asked Haydn to write something that could be played by these four friends of the Art. Haydn, who was then eighteen[4] years old, accepted the proposal, and so originated his first Quartet[5]

which, immediately upon its appearance, received such uncommon applause as to encourage him to continue in this *genre*.   [Griesinger, 12f.]

Notes:
1 Carl Joseph, Edler von Fürnberg, *Regierungsrath* in the Lower Austrian Government and I.R. *Truchseß* (which means, in effect, head of the Imperial Household), who died on 21 March 1767 at the age of forty-seven. His second wife, who was the hostess at Weinzierl in the 1750s, was Marie Antonie, *née* von Germetten; she died on 19 December 1779 at the age of fifty-two. Pohl I, 181.
2 Weinzierl Castle, which still survives more or less intact, is some distance from Melk Abbey and a few miles from the pretty old town of Wieselburg, in Lower Austria. It is now an agricultural school.
3 The question of the two Albrechtsbergers will be discussed *infra*. The contrapuntist and teacher of Beethoven was Johann Georg (Klosterneuburg 1732, Vienna 1809); his brother was Antonius Joannes, born at Klosterneuburg on 20 November 1729. The parents were Jacobus and Maria. Anton Johann was also a composer, like his younger brother. On the libretto of his *Singspiel über das Leben des ... Joseph vom Copertin* (National Museum, Prague), 1768, he is listed as *Kapellmeister* to the Bishop of Wiener Neustadt. Melk Abbey owns two divertimenti; the Gesellschaft der Musikfreunde owns two autographs, a *Lied* in Upper Austrian dialect and an Aria, 'Kein lustiges

'Leben'. For details of Anton Johann's life we are indebted to the extraordinary generosity of Dr Alexander Weinmann, who very kindly furnished information from a forthcoming article in the *Studien zur Musikwissenschaft*.

4 It is now generally believed that Haydn was not eighteen but about twenty-five when he wrote these works.

5 Opus 1, no. 1.

(3) Carpani:

Devesi al barone di *Füremberg* [*sic*] il primo *quartetto* dell' *Haydn*. Quel signore amantissimo della musica dimorava per lo più a *Burckersdorff*,[1] e vi sonava de'*quartetti* coll'*Haydn*, col parroco della villa, buon violoncellista, e col suo *Verwalter*.[2] Un giorno il barone disse all'*Haydn* i cui sei *trio* si sonavano ogni sera = dovresti farmi un *quartetto* = mi proverò, = risponde Giuseppe. Impugna la penna, e n'esce quel suo primo *quartetto* a *sestupla* in *befà*, che tutt'i dilettanti di musica impararono subito a memoria. Aveva allora l'*Haydn* poco più di vent'anni.

[Carpani, 85]

Notes:

1 Purkersdorf (*recte*) was the residence of Lt-Col. Joseph von Fürnberg, eldest son of our Carl Joseph, who in the 1750s was living with his younger brother and sister in nearby Wieselburg. Joseph became an army man, but was obviously a passionate music-lover; for it was he who kept the Fürnberg/Morzin collection intact. We shall discuss the collection in detail *infra*; here we may say briefly that it consists of chamber music written for the Fürnbergs and symphonies written for Morzin, as well as some transcriptions of baryton trios and other pieces; many of these MSS. were supervised and corrected by Haydn himself.

2 Estates' manager.

[Summary in translation:]

Baron Füremberg [*sic*] was responsible for Haydn's first quartet. This passionate music-lover lived mostly in Burckersdorff [*sic*] and played quartets with Haydn, the other members being the priest, a good 'cellist, and his estates' manager. One day the Baron said to Haydn, whose trios were played every evening, 'you ought to write a quartet'. 'I'll try'. The result was the First Quartet in B flat (six-eight), which all music lovers immediately learned by heart. Haydn was then a little over twenty.

In 1932, a distinguished Austrian art historian, Fritz Dworschak, published a highly important article[1] which did not receive the attention it deserved. In it, Dworschak was able to show that Johann Georg Albrechtsberger was a fellow student of Michael Haydn's in the Jesuit Seminary in Vienna (1753–4). From 1755–6 (or perhaps to 1757) Albrechtsberger was in Raab (Györ, Hungary), but from September 1757 to April 1759 he was organist at Maria Taferl, about a dozen kilometres from Weinzierl Castle, and later he occupied this post at Melk Abbey. Dworschak suggests that the estates' manager was the 'Pfleger' Matthias Leonhard Penzinger and the priest Johann Joseph Fromiller, 'Benefiziat an der Josephskapelle im Schlosse' (St Joseph's Chapel, which still exists). The commemorative tablet that records Haydn's presence in Weinzierl also suggests 1757–9 as the period in question.

Abbé Stadler, Haydn's friend, writes in his MS. memoirs:

> Joseph Haydn, who at this time composed his first divertimenti near Melk at Freyherr v. Firmberg's [*sic*] – at which Albrechtsberger played violoncello – heard him [Albrechtsberger], admired his artistry, and assured him that he had never heard such perfection on an organ.

1 'Joseph Haydn und Karl Joseph Weber von Fürnberg', *Unsere Heimat*, Jg. 5, July 1932, pp. 190ff. Abbé Stadler's *Materialien zur Geschichte der Musik unter den österreichischen Regenten*, MS. in the ÖNB, Codex S.N. 4310; our quotations from fol. 104v. and 105r. Georg Feder's excellent summing-up of the source situation in his Foreword (1972) to *JHW*, Reihe XII, Band 1 (Early Quartets), does not take into consideration the new material concerning Albrechtsberger's brother.

[Later, we hear of another group including the composer Florian Leopold] Gaßmann, in whose fugal quartets he [Albrechtsberger] often played the violoncello ...

Obviously we cannot solve the problem of the Albrechtsberger brothers with the evidence at our disposal, but if we accept Griesinger's statement that the 'cellist was Anton Johann, then the chronological postulate involving Johann Georg must be dismissed. Nevertheless, we believe that *c.*1757 is the correct date for the first string quartets. First, the Fürnberg/Morzin sources of Op. 1, Nos. 1, 2, 4 and 6 use the spelling 'Minuet', which Haydn writes only up to (and including) 1760, whereas in the authentic sources of Op. 2, Nos. 1, 2 and 6, we find 'Menuet', which suggests a slightly later date (1760–2?). Secondly, we have some very early works by Haydn, such as the *Missa brevis alla cappella* in G, 'Rorate coeli desuper' or the Cassatio in A (II:A1), where there are really serious problems in faulty composition. The quartets, on the other hand, are of flawless construction and cannot be the work of the eighteen-year-old Haydn (1750). Thirdly, there are no dated MS. copies earlier than 1762 (see Chapter Ten, *infra*) and no prints earlier than 1764; it is unlikely that works written in 1750 and achieving instant popularity would have to wait twelve years before circulating to Göttweig and Melk and fourteen years to reach the Paris presses. Finally, we adduce a bit of evidence connected with the Seven Years' War, which was raging in 1757 (Battle of Kolin) and 1758 (Battle of Hochkirch). The Austrians took a number of Prussian prisoners; the officers, considered gentlemen and men of their word, were quartered 'on good behaviour' throughout the estates of the Lower Austrian nobility. One such prisoner was a Prussian major named Weirach, who was paroled to the nobleman on whose estates Haydn was born,' i.e. Rohrau Castle. Weirach told the German composer and writer Johann Friedrich Reichardt 'that during the Seven Years' War he was taken prisoner by the Imperial troops and was quartered with the nobleman on whose estates Haydn was born, and he heard that artist, as modest as his genius was great, himself playing his first quartets. Haydn called them Cassatios – a word that means the same as Notturno or Serenada, altogether a "piece of music" that at the same time is suitable for performance outside. The man was modest to the point of timidity, despite the fact that everybody present was enchanted [*entzückt*] by these compositions, and he was not to be persuaded that his works were worthy of being presented to the musical world. ...'[1]

Apart from the interesting fact that Haydn was now (1757–8) being invited to musical parties at the Castle of his former Lord[2] – which must have been a welcome improvement for his hungry and penniless condition – the story confirms the date of 1757–8 for the performances of Haydn's obviously new quartets, albeit at Rohrau and not at Weinzierl.

---

1 H. M. Schletterer, *Johann Friedrich Reichardt* ..., Augsburg 1865, p. 61. See also Otto Biba, 'Nachrichten zur Musikpflege in der gräflichen Familie Harrach', *HJB* X (1978), pp. 36ff., esp. 38f.

2 There seem to be two possibilities for the *raison d'être* of Haydn's autograph of the Divertimento for 2 oboes, 2 horns and 2 bassoons (II:15) in the Harrach Archives in Vienna. The MS. is dated 1760 (facsimile in *HJB* I, 1962): (1) Haydn wrote it for Count Franz Anton in 1760, which presupposes that he had a wind band either at Rohrau or Vienna or both. Dr Biba (ibid., p. 39) subscribes to this interesting theory. (2) Haydn gave it, when he was an old man and after Count Carl Leonhard had in 1793 erected the Haydn Monument in Rohrau Castle's garden, as a 'keepsake' and a sample of his handwriting, to the family. We believe the work must have been written in 1760 for Count Morzin (it survives in two other sources from Friedland Castle as well) and came into the Harrach's possession much later.

II. The Viennese Musical Scene

In December 1757, Vienna's musical life was greatly enriched by the arrival of two musicians from Lucca, the double-bass player Leopoldo Boccherini and his son Luigi, 'cellist and composer. They were engaged that month in the 'French' (= Burgtheater, as opposed to the 'German' = Karntnerthortheater) Court Orchestra, receiving jointly a quarterly salary of 113 fl. 7½ kr. In the next years, their movements can be traced by letters in the Archivio di Stato (Lucca) and by the listings of their salaries in the Viennese records (Haus-, Hof- und Staatsarchiv, Vienna). In October 1758 they left (possibly for Rome, in any case for Italy), returning in 1760, in which year Luigi composed his first 'opus', a set of six string trios (Gérard 77–82). At this point our knowledge of Boccherini's music and its correct chronology is immeasurably assisted by an autograph catalogue begun, as Boccherini himself tells us, in 'the year 1760, in which I began to compose'.

Meanwhile, the Boccherinis had taken steps, in characteristic Italian fashion, to move numerous members of their family to Vienna. These included a brother named Luigi, a dancer, engaged for the season 1759–60; and another, Giovanni Gastone, who began his career in Vienna as a *figurant* in the Court Ballet, and later became a well-known *littérateur* in court circles, writing *inter alia* the libretto for Haydn's *Il ritorno di Tobia* in 1774 (performed 1775). Maria Ester, his sister, was in Vienna from the season of 1760, earning by 1761 the large salary of 1,652 fl. p.a. as a *prima ballerina*; she later married Onorato Viganó, the famous dancer. Yet another sister, Anna Matilda, was imported to Vienna in 1763, also in the *corps de ballet*. Perhaps this was the girl about whom Zinzendorf wrote on 12 May 1763, '. . . Le Soir au Spectacle. On donna l'Isola abandonnata [*sic*] de Metastasio [= Giuseppe Scarlatti, *L'isola disabitata*]. Il y eut une petite figurante nommée Bocherini [*sic*] qui fit le role de Sylvia, et qui n'avoit point de voix . . .' (Diary, MS.) A third sister, Ricciarda, is mentioned by Zechmeister (331).

Flitting back and forth between Italy and Vienna, Luigi Boccherini now wrote his historic first set of string quartets. While he himself described his first trios as 'Opera piccola', the 'Sei quartetti, Opera 2' of 1761, he describes as 'Opera grande'. This was followed the same year by 'Opera 3. Sei duetti per due violini',[1] also 'Opera piccola'.

It would be pleasant to imagine Haydn and Luigi Boccherini discussing the theory of the string quartet; but alas, there is no evidence that they knew each other more than very fleetingly, if at all: the letter from Boccherini to Artaria, asking the publishers to present his compliments to Haydn and to say how much he admired the Austrian composer's work (February 1781) does not sound at all as if he were renewing an old acquaintance – quite the contrary.[2] But if we cannot arrange such a happy meeting between the two composers, we can be sure that Luigi studied the new quartet-divertimenti by his Austrian compatriot, and of course Haydn's early string trios, as well, many of which existed all over Vienna by 1757.

Boccherini's Trios (1760) and Quartets (1761) are astonishing operations on a number of levels. The most interesting aspect of these twelve works is their total independence from Haydn's style: it was quite another way in which to write

1 Biographical information: G. de Rothschild, *Luigi Boccherini*, London 1965, pp. 9ff. R. Haas, *Gluck und Durazzo im Burgtheater*, Vienna 1925, pp. 56 ('Bogerini'), 59. Yves Gérard, *Thematic, Bibliographical and Critical Catalogue of the Works of Luigi Boccherini*, London 1969; catalogue by Boccherini discussed on p. 683. G. Zechmeister, *Die Wiener Theater . . .*, Vienna 1971, pp. 229, 233, *passim*. A convenient modern transcription of the catalogue in Arnaldo Bonaventura, *Boccherini*, Milan–Rome 1931, pp. 197ff. The 1761 Quartets are Nos. 159–64, the Duos Nos. 56–61. The Boccherini gentlemen gave a benefit concert in Vienna in 1764, at which were played works for one and two 'cellos.
2 *Haydn at Eszterhaza 1766–1790*, p. 447n; also for Giovanni Gastone, op. cit., pp. 214f.

chamber music, and judged from the long historical standpoint, Boccherini's are the first real quartets composed in Vienna (in the sense that Haydn's are divertimenti and he dropped the style in quartet-writing after this series of experiments). Now that Boccherini's chamber music is currently being subjected to serious study, the forward-looking qualities of these 1760–1 works are rightly being stressed – and forward-looking, too, even from the Viennese classical standpoint. Of course, Boccherini's style is much slower paced than Haydn's, and the languid, fastidious lines of his slow movements (including, though not as it happens in these particular works, the tempo marking 'amoroso' – unthinkable in Haydn) are in stark contrast to Haydn's taut style. Boccherini's music has a discursive quality quite different from Haydn's nervous and edgily rhythmic manner. Despite these great differences, however, Boccherini's music of 1760–1 embraces many of the aesthetic principles that we do not find in Haydn until the late 1760s. A few points must suffice. The Op. 2 Quartets begin with a powerful work in C minor: there is no Quartet by Haydn in the minor (and no Trio) until about 1768–9 – his Op. 9, No. 4, in D minor. Boccherini was, like his Austrian colleagues of the late 1760s, preoccupied with the specific gravity of the finale, and we note final fugues in several trio and quartet movements: Haydn uses fugal movements in some early symphonies, but not in quartets until Op. 20 of 1772. A notable difference between Boccherini and Haydn at this period: the Italian adheres strictly to three movement forms, ending with a minuet (or Tempo di Minuetto) or with a straight, non-dance finale. Haydn varies between three and five movements (the latter a characteristic of the divertimento), and at this juncture Haydn, especially in the trio, was very drawn to the *sonata da chiesa* form – something we find in striking profusion in the Italian's trio schemes (Trio 79, Trio 80, Trio 81, Trio 82) but, unlike Haydn, never in the 1761 Quartets. One final, and typical point: in Boccherini's works of 1760–1 we find, as we do in almost all quick movements throughout Europe of the era, the famous repeated quavers (or depending on the time, crotchets) that weld an allegro into a tight dynamic whole; but, whereas in Haydn these repeated bass notes begin at once to exert an almost hypnotic effect of their own, constituting a reservoir of nervous energy on which the composer may draw in unlimited fashion, in Boccherini the repeated notes lose their violence, their tension, and ultimately therefore their importance. It is a small but characteristic difference in the two men's thinking.

We have no evidence as to whether Haydn knew and studied Boccherini's early Trios and Quartets, but certainly MS. copies of both survive in Austrian libraries (e.g. Quartets in the ÖNB, 'Concertino del Signor Boccariny', the Trios in Stams Abbey, Prague, Vienna, and so on) which suggest that they were being circulated by the professional Austrian copyists. In the late 1750s and early 1760s, Haydn was often away from the capital, but it is not impossible, and indeed quite likely, that his attention will have been drawn to these talented works by his young Italian contemporary (Boccherini was seventeen in 1760).

Der neue krumme Teufel (XXIXb:1b)

Libretto: Der neue / Krumme Teufel. / Eine / OPERA-COMIQUE / von zwey Aufzügen; / Nebst einer / Kinder-Pantomime, / Betitult: / ARLEQUIN / der neue Abgott Ram / in America. / Alles componiret / Von Joseph Kurz. The cast ('Agirende Personen in der / Comedie') is listed but not the singers who participated. At the end of Act I followed 'Die Pantomime, / Betitelt: / ARLEQUIN / Der neue / Abgott Ram in Amerika.' A list of persons followed. Next comes: 'INTERMEZZO, / INTITOLATO: / IL VECCHIO / INGANNATO. / [——] / ATTORI. / PANCRAZIO, Giuseppe Kurz. / PANDORA, Cattarina Meyrin. / BETTINA, Theresa Kurzin.' There then follows the rest of the (German) Opera, which was very short and included a final Chorus. At the end of the print: 'NB. Die

Musique sowohl von der Oper-Comique als auch der Pantomime ist componiret Von Herrn Joseph Heyden.' Copies: Stadtbibliothek, Vienna 22.200A; Radenín Coll., now National Museum Prague, 2041. Contents: 78 pp., containing 32 Arias, 2 Duets, 1 Trio, 3 Choruses (including a Finale).

Music: lost.

Revivals: Pressburg, 29 Oct. 1764 (with a new intermezzo entitled 'L'avventure di Lesbina'), Kurz; Heitersheim (Breisgau), Carnival 1765 (Felix Berner and his famous children's troupe; they were primarily attracted to the piece because of the Pantomime of the 1758 version, written with Kurz's own children in mind; F. X. Garnier: *Nachricht von der im Jahre 1758 von Herrn Felix Berner errichteten jungen Schauspieler-Gesellschaft*, Vienna 1786, p. 36; Garnier was a pupil of Berner's; he continues: '[the troupe] made its début in Heitersheim with *der krumme Teufel*, the music by Herr Haiden. This was the first opera that Herr Berner and his children performed.'); Nuremberg, 12 August 1766 (lacking Pantomime & intermezzo), Kurz; Vienna, 24 Nov. 1770 with a new libretto (Kurz):

Asmodeus / der / krumme Teufel / Ein / OPERA COMIQUE / von drey Aufzügen / [ornament] / WIEN, / gedruckt bey Johann Thomas Edlen von Trattnern, / kaiserl. königl. / Hofbuchdruckern und Buchhändlern. / 1770. [The 'Zweyter Aufzug' is numbered separately and has, curiously, a separate title page:] Zweyter Aufzug / Asmodeus zeiget Durch Bernadon und / Fiametta dem Doktor Arnoldus, um ihm sei- / ne heftige Liebe gegen Fiametta zu beneh- / men, dieses pantomimische Singspiel, / genannt: / die Insul der Wilden, / oder die / wankelmütige Insulanerinn / mit Arlequin, / dem durch einen Zauberer zum Abgott Ram / gemachten König von der Insul Tschaleley. / [ornament] / WIEN, / gedruckt bey Johann Thomas Edlen v. Trattnern, / k. k. Hofbuchdruckern und Buchhändlern. / 1770. [pp. 1–18; there then follows 'Dritter Auftritt', pp. 33–44, intended to continue from the beginning, 'Erster Auftritt', pp. 1–32. There is no intermezzo but, in Act III Sc. 3, Fiametta, Kurz's second (Italian) wife, has a series of four Italian Arias, (1) 'A Bologna nò se da'; (2) 'Si è da Napoli Bene mio'; (3) 'Via Seior alloccio'; (4) 'Caro mio bel tesoro'. The first three are in Bolognese, Neapolitan and Venetian dialects; these come from the 1758 version. In the Pantomime the 1770 version has ten new numbers, including three choruses, not in the 1758 libretto.] Copies of the 1770 libretto: ONB, 392/620-A/25; Radenín Coll., now National Museum, Prague, 4126; Library of Congress (from Schatz Coll.).

Also Prague, 17 and 27 Nov. 1771 and 11 Oct. 1772 (Troupe of Johann Baptist Bergobzoomer); Berlin, 12 Feb. 1774 (Koch Gesellschaft; repeated 27 times within one year), as *Der hinkende Teufel* and with some of the roles altered; Warsaw, 1774 (Kurz); Donaueschingen, 1778–9 season (Franz Grimmer Gesellschaft); Dresden, June 1782; Munich, 7 Jan. 1783; Theater 'Zum Fasan', suburb of Neustift (now called Neubau), Vienna, 28 Sept. 1783; Guest Tour of the Franz Huber Company in Upper Saxony, 1796–8: Altenburg, Eisleben, Querfurt, Zeitz, Erfurt.

Literature: Pohl I, 141–60. V. Helfert, 'Zur Geschichte des Wiener Singspiels', *Zeitschrift für Musikwissenschaft*, 5. Jg. (1923), Heft 4/5. R. Haas, 'Die Musik in der Wiener deutschen Stegreifkomödie', *Studien zur Musikwissenschaft* XII (1925), pp. 1ff., and esp. 54ff. *Deutsche Komödienarien 1754–1758* (R. Haas), *DTÖ* XXXIII, Band 64 (1926). *Teutsche Arien, Welche auf dem Kayserlich-privilegirten Wienerischen Theatro in unterschiedlich producirten Comoedien, deren Titul hier jedesmahl beygerucket, gesungen worden, ed. Max Pirker, Vienna 1926 (1927). Alfred Löwenberg, *Annals of Opera*, Cambridge 1943, p. 110. Otto Rommel, *Die alt-Wiener Volkskomödie*, Vienna 1952. F. Hadamowsky, 'Das Spieljahr 1753/54 des Theaters nächst dem Kärntnerthor und des Theaters nächst der k. k. Burg', *Jahrbuch der Gesellschaft für Wiener Theaterforschung* XI (1959), pp. 3ff., esp. p. 8, item for 29 May. H.C.R.L. in *HJB* I (1962), p. 145n. (Donaueschingen). E. Badura-Skoda, 'Teutsche Comoedie-Arien und Joseph Haydn', *Der junge Haydn, Kongressbericht Graz 1970* (Graz 1972, pp. 59ff.). Ulf Birbaumer, *Das Werk des Joseph Felix von Kurz-Bernadon und seine szenische Realisierung*, 2 vols., Dissertationen der Universität Wien, Vienna 1971. Camillo Schoenbaum and Herbert Zeman, *Deutsche Komödiearien 1754–1758*, 2. Teil (see Haas 1926), *DTÖ* 121 (1971). Gustav Zechmeister, *Die Wiener Theater nächst der Burg und nächst dem Kärntnerthor von 1747 bis 1776*, Vienna 1971. Herbert Zeman, 'Das Theaterlied zur Zeit Joseph Haydns, seine theatralische Gestaltung und seine gattungsgeschichtliche Entwicklung', in *Joseph Haydn und die Literatur seiner Zeit*, Eisenstadt 1976, pp. 35–60. For some additional literature, see *Haydn at Eszterháza 1766–1790*, p. 521n. (not specifically dealing with *Der [neue] krumme Teufel*), also pp. 517ff. for general problems of the *commedia dell'arte* and Hanswurstiada.

In view of the extensive literature on this (incredibly) lost Haydn Opera, we propose to omit the usual synopsis of the plot, which in any case is given in Pohl and Birbaumer (II, 591–3), and also an analysis of the sources from which Kurz took his libretto–

F. C. Dancourt: *Le diable boiteux* (1707);

Pantomime: *Arlequin, Roi des ogres ou les bottes de sept lieues* (1720);

Der krumme Teufel (1738).

On 14 July 1755, Kurz's first wife, Franziska, died. On 15 April 1758, Kurz married again, this time a Tuscan ballerina and singer named Teresina (Teresa) Morelli – the date from Birbaumer (I, 16) – and if Birbaumer is correct, we have authentic evidence from other (Viennese) sources that on that same day she appeared at the Kärntnerthortheater where, reports the *WD* No. 31 (Pohl I, 149), '... [she] was highly successful as singer and actress.' She soon learned German, and helped to run the company, which included Bergobzoomer, who in turn formed his own troupe and gave Haydn's Opera in Prague (1771); but one of her great specialities was the performance of ariettas in various Italian dialects, and as soon as we open the printed libretto of *Der neue krumme Teufel*, we find several dialect arias (Bolognese, Neapolitan, Venetian and 'normal') in Italian, and also a whole intermezzo designed especially for her. Robert Haas examined the texts of these Italian arias, and was able to show that one, 'Quanti so gl'anni' comes from *Il viaggiatore ridicolo* which, Haas asserted, was not composed (produced) until 1757. Modern research has absolutely confirmed this date: in the *Enciclopedia dello spettacolo* (vol. V, 1958, article 'Goldoni' by Corrado Pavolini, p. 1441), *Il viaggiatore ridicolo* (or *I viaggiatori ridicoli*), with music by Antonio Maria Mazzoni (Bolognese, 1717–85) was first given in the Carnival season of 1757 at the Teatro Ducale in Parma (see also ibid., vol. VII, article 'Mazzoni' by L. F. Tagliavini). Signorina Morelli may even have been involved with the Parma production; but in any case she brought it to Vienna and introduced one aria (recomposed by Haydn, 1758?) which gives us an accurate *terminus post quem* – 15 April 1758 – for the revival of Haydn's Opera. Since all the music is lost, we can not know if the various new numbers (e.g. the intermezzo *L'avventure di Lesbina* [Pressburg 1764] or the additional arias in the Pantomime for the Vienna revival of 1770) were also composed by Haydn.

But if all the music for *Der neue krumme Teufel* is lost, R. Haas made quite a convincing argument that many of the numbers contained in the anonymous collection, 'Teutsche Comoedie Arien' (ÖNB, S.m. 19062, 19053), which were written for Kurz's plays in Vienna in the 1750s, must have been composed by Haydn. Haas presumes that after the success of *Der krumme Teufel* (1751? certainly done in 1753), Haydn continued to work for Kurz as a 'house composer', at least until the revival of *Der neue krumme Teufel* in 1758. Shortly thereafter, the Kurz Troupe left Vienna (1759) and Haydn was engaged by Count Morzin (1758?; possibly 1757 or 1759). The point was discussed from the musical standpoint *supra*, p. 102, n. 1.

Apart from Haydn, other local composers wrote music for the Kärntnerthortheater. Zechmeister (137) lists Adalbert Fauner, the composer of *Bernadon, der verliebte Weiber-Feind* (1752); Joseph Ziegler, *Leopolden in Africa, Die zaubernde Circe* and *Ramildo und Egissa* (all 1754) and, in collaboration with the violinist Eder, *Leopold, der aus dem Mond gefallene Sclav* (1754).[1] Perhaps the most intriguing name appears in the following context: Kurz performed the Pantomime, *Der Zauberbrunn*, at Nuremberg in 1766, and the libretto, which Frau Badura-Skoda (66) quotes, contains the note: 'NB. die Music ist von Herrn Joseph Hayda, Compositeur und Claviermeister', by which the composer Hayda, organist at the parish church of the Trinity Order in Vienna, is meant.[2] It is startling that Adalbert Fauner, who is listed on the libretto of

---

1 The sources for these composers is in the valuable 1753–4 document published by Hadamowsky, op. cit., pp. 5f. It may be seen that composers were paid one gulden per aria, so that Haydn, with the 32 arias and six other numbers of *Der neue krumme Teufel*, was being extremely handsomely rewarded with 24 or 25 ducats which it is reported Kurz paid him. Fauner: Haas, p. 58.
2 *Haydn at Eszterháza 1766–1790*, pp. 665f.

Bernadon, der verliebte Weiberfeind as the composer, was *Regens chori* of the Trinity Order in Vienna (he died in 1769): the proximity of Fauner, Hayda and Kurz is hardly, in the circumstances, accidental.

So we leave, regretfully, the Faust-like Dr Arnoldus, the ghosts, the Italian ladies, magician, the *commedia dell'arte* figures and the swaggering Bernadon of *Der neue krumme Teufel*, with the hope that this once so popular music will one day be rediscovered for our amusement and edification.

III. Morzin and Lukavec

THE DOCUMENTS

(for numbered footnotes see end of relevant document)

(1) Griesinger:

In the year 1759 Haydn was engaged as Music Director to Count Morzin[1] in Vienna at a salary of two hundred gulden, free lodging and board at the officers' table. Here he was finally able to enjoy the happiness of a carefree existence; he was quite contented. He spent the winter in Vienna and the summer in Bohemia near Pilsen.[2] He used to like to relate, in later years, how one day he was sitting at the harpsichord [*Klavier*], and the beautiful Countess Morzin leaned over him in order to see the notes, when her neckerchief came undone. 'It was the first time I had ever seen such a sight; I became confused, my playing faltered, my fingers became glued to the keys. – What is that, Haydn, what are you doing? cried the Countess; most respectfully I answered: But, Countess, your grace, who would not be undone at such a sight?'

... As Music Director in the service of Count Morzin Haydn composed his First Symphony:[3]

[14f.]

Notes:
1 The head of the house at this time was Ferdinand Maximilian Franz (1693–1763) who on 22 Nov. 1714 had married Anna Catherina *née* Countess Kolowrat-Nowohradsky (died 1736). Eldest son: Carl Joseph Franz (1717–83), married on 4 Feb. 1749 to Wilhelmine *Freiin* von Reisky, who bore him twenty-two children including eleven sons. *Deutsche Grafen-Häuser der Gegenwart in herald., histor. und genealog. Beziehung*, Band 2, Leipzig 1853, pp. 132ff. The list in Wurzbach's *Lexicon* (XIX, 112) is inaccurate – it is said, there, that Countess Wilhelmine died young after bearing ten children. Although we presume Haydn's Countess with the 'Busentuch' (neckerchief) was Wilhelmine, it might have been one of the other members of the family, such as Countess Maria Philippina (b. 1738 as Countess von Weißenwolf) who married a Franz Joseph Count Morzin; the *Wiener Diarium* reports on 9 May 1759 that she had become a Lady of the Stern-Kreuz Order; a portrait of her is owned by Altgraf Salm; her elder sister was Count Durazzo's wife, Ernestine Aloisia.
2 In Unter-Lukavec (Dolní Lukavice), usually referred to simply as Lukavec. The Castle is still standing today, and is used as an agricultural school; we visited it in 1959.
3 We propose to show that Griesinger was quite right, and that Haydn's First Symphony really was the work cited, though it was probably composed earlier than 1759. For a further quotation of the Morzin period from Griesinger's account, see *Haydn at Eszterháza 1766–1790*, p. 117.

(2) Dies, 11 May 1805:

Finally the time arrived when Haydn's fortunes would improve. He was about twenty-seven years of age when the goddess of Fortune for once decided to reward the deserving. A Bohemian Count v. Morzin, a passionate music lover, maintained a number of bachelor musicians. The post of Chamber *Compositeur* was free, and Haydn received it in the year 1759 with a salary of 600 fl. 'My good mother', said Haydn, 'who had always entertained the tenderest concern for my welfare, was no longer living; but my father had the pleasure of seeing me as *Kapellmeister.*' These chance words allowed me to see deep into Haydn's heart and showed it from a very lovable side.   [Dies, 45]

(3) Carpani:

Finalmente anche l'*Haydn* trovò miglior sorte; ed all'età di circa 26 anni, cresciuto essendo in sapere ed in fama, entrò nel 1758[1] al servizio del conte di *Mortzin*, e lasciò la cameruccia ospitale in casa *Martinez*. Avvenne che in case del conte si recasse ... [etc.; for continuation, *vide infra*, p. 245].   [87]

Note:
1 Carpani has already moved the date back to 1758; in view of the MS. of Symphony No. 37 dated 1758 (about which *infra*, pp. 280 and 281), this date is more likely than 1759. Translation: 'Finally Haydn encountered better times; and at the age of about twenty-six, having grown in knowledge and wisdom, in 1758 he entered the service of Count Mortzin and left the hospitable little room in the Martinez house.' (continuation, *infra*, p. 245).

It is not quite clear which Count Morzin engaged Haydn; probably the father (Ferdinand Maximilian Franz) but possibly the son (Carl Joseph Franz), who may have run Lukavec by 1758, especially since the father was now a widower. We presume, too, that the beautiful Countess was the lady of the house (young Morzin's wife). Here Haydn composed his first symphonies, and that which we presume is a large number of the Morzin orchestral parts of Haydn's early symphonies has survived and is discussed later in this chapter. Apart from symphonies, the extant autographs show that Haydn now wrote music for wind band (oboes, bassoons, horns) for his new Bohemian *Feldmusique*, and at least one very eccentrically-scored Divertimento (autograph 1760; II:16, for two cors anglais, two bassoons, two horns and two violins). The story of Haydn at the harpsichord suggests, and confirming evidence is provided by dated autographs, that Haydn wrote for Morzin's entertainment (and perhaps for teaching, as well) harpsichord trios, concertini (divertimenti) for harpsichord and strings, and probably some solo sonatas as well.

Dies's figure of 600 fl. is probably a mistake (and would have meant, moreover, that in 1761 Haydn took a reduction in salary when joining the Esterházy *Capelle*); Griesinger's 200 fl. is probably the correct figure. It was, as salaries for musicians went, a good sum. Since we analyze the value of money at considerable length in *Haydn at Eszterháza*, we mention only a few objects here for purposes of comparison. Living in Vienna was dear, by which we speak of comfortable flats in acceptable districts, not the flats of Haydn's poor friends. The *Wiener Diarium* of the period provides some interesting announcements of flats for rent:

[*WD* No. 10, 2 February 1759:] In the new princely Passau House at the Maria Steps; a whole first floor with 5 rooms, kitchen, cellar, woodshed [in the courtyard, for storage], attic, 225 fl. *per annum*.

In the great Passau House at the Salz-Gries, a small apartment, 2 rooms, 1 chamber [*Kammer*], kitchen, attic, cellar and large shed [*Schupfen*], 170 fl. *p.a.*

And to conclude our brief survey of money values in 1758–9, the *Diarium* also informs us as to the price of new printed music:

Augustin Bernardi, Book-seller in the Obere Jesuiten-pforten . . . Sei divertimenti da Cimbalo Scritti da Giuseppe Steffan,[1] for 1 fl. 30 Kr. and bound 1 Fl. 42 kr.

[*WD* No. 26, 31 March 1759]

Since this was the first orchestra for which Haydn wrote purely instrumental works on a large scale (we are, then, excepting accompaniments of Masses and other church music), it is a particular pity that no lists and no details of any kind survive – except that the authentic MS. orchestral parts, the duplicate string parts of which, violins I, II and 'Basso', suggest that there were at least three (four) first violins, three (or four) second violins, and a 'Basso' section of two desks, with, perhaps, a bassoon, a 'cello and a double bass. Was there a harpsichord *continuo*? Or did Haydn direct from the first violin? In recent years, this subject has been hotly debated. It said that no figured bass for any symphonies of this period has survived, and this is adduced as conclusive evidence that Haydn did not use a *continuo* harpsichord, because in all works of the period where he does expect a *continuo* (cantatas, church music, organ and harpsichord concertos, keyboard trios) we find figures. Unfortunately, this is no argument at all: in Symphony No. 98 (London 1792) where Haydn played a difficult harpsichord solo and also *continuo* throughout this and all the other 'Salomon' Symphonies (Nos. 93–104), there is not one single figure in the autographs. Certainly, in Symphony No. 7, the autograph specifies 'Basso Continuo' (1761 and since all the other 'Basso' instruments – bassoon, violoncello and 'Violone' (double bass) – are carefully specified, the 'Continuo' can only mean harpsichord. Possibly, however, these very eccentric and individual concerto-grosso-like works (Nos. 6–8) – being deliberate throw-backs to the Italian Baroque – require a *continuo* harpsichord as a sort of stylistic 'historicism'; which might mean that the modern, Morzin symphonies, though composed earlier, do not really require a harpsichord. It is certainly not wrong to perform these Morzin symphonies with a keyboard *continuo*, and it is essential to perform at least Nos. 6–8 ('Le Matin', 'Le Midi', 'Le Soir') with one. More than that cannot be said here (we leave the problem of *alto* or *basso* horns to the next chapter). As for the bassoon, it is never mentioned in any known Morzin symphony; but since Morzin's *Feldharmonie* had two bassoons, and the Divertimento (II:16) of 1760 specifies two bassoons, we may imagine that they were automatically considered to be part of the *continuo*. The Morzin band contained no flute, as far as we know.

Did the orchestra play standing, as in the Bach period? Or were they disposed sitting on a low bench, as in the opera? Through the kindness of M. Antonio de Almeida, who is currently (1979) editing the complete, critical edition of Boccherini's symphonies for Doblinger, we can provide an authentic diagram of what Boccherini thought ideal for the performance of a *Sinfonia à grande orchestra*. The work in question is Op. 21, No. 3 (Gérard 495), and is part of a set of autograph parts to a collection of symphonies (Bibliothèque de l'Opéra, Paris, Res. 510) of which the general title page reads as follows:

---

1 Joseph Steffan, the well-known Court harpsichordist and composer whose music was immensely popular and influential; we shall note a concerto by Steffan wrongly attributed to Haydn (*vide infra*, p. 522).

Sinfonia à grande orchestra
Con due Violini Principale, due di Ripieno, oboe
chitarra, Viola, Corni, Fagotto, Violoncello, [*sic*]
obligati, e Basso, da Luigi Boccherini, Compositore di camera che fù dal S S. Inf.^te Dr Luigi Borbon.
è della Maestà di Guillelmo 2.° Rè di Prussia.
Per il Sig.^re Marchese di Benavent[e?].

[Individual title page:]
Sinfonia
Violino Principale obligato.
Boccherini.
collocazione del orchestra per l'esecuzione di questo Sinfonia

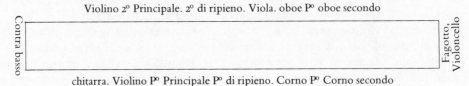

Violino 2° Principale. 2° di ripieno. Viola. oboe P° oboe secondo

Contra basso

Fagotto, Violoncello

chitarra. Violino P° Principale P° di ripieno. Corno P° Corno secondo

Now this arrangement bears a certain resemblance to that of a painting of what is (wrongly) purported to be a performance of Haydn's *L'incontro improvviso* at Eszterháza:[1] the long 'table' or 'bench' with the musicians' stands. Perhaps Boccherini's suggestion was a modification, because of the many odd instruments (two solo violins, guitar), of a typical chamber orchestra. There were, in any case, four violins, one viola, one 'cello and one double bass, with two oboes and two horns; the bassoon sits next to the 'cello (both being part of the *continuo*). There is no harpsichord, but Boccherini's Symphonies Op. 21 were composed in 1775, when a harpsichord *continuo* was generally considered superfluous in most of Europe (except in opera generally and odd cases, such as public concerts in London, where Haydn appeared as pianoforte *continuo* as late as 1795 in his own symphonies). And possibly, the guitar might be considered a kind of *continuo Ersatz*. Apart from the seating arrangements (first and second violins facing each other, in other words separated from each other, also visually), the most interesting fact is the exceedingly small size of the orchestra as a whole: only the violins are doubled. Probably this was the average constitution of a private (court) orchestra, and not only in Spain. Large orchestras were the exception, not the rule. The bass 'weight' has been divided on each end of the orchestra, and this to some extent reproduces the two harpsichords of the larger theatre orchestra (e.g. in the Turin Theatre as represented in the famous painting of *c.*1740, reproduced countless times, *inter alia* in *Enciclopedia dello Spettacolo* IX [1962], facing p. 991),[2] which were often placed at opposite ends of the pit, together with two sets of double basses). So in its basic design, the Boccherini proposal may have a certain international validity.

1 See *Haydn at Eszterháza*, p. 28.
2 This superb and realistic view of the Teatro Regio – with its guard watching the stage with his back to the audience, with its orange- and chocolate-sellers – is thought to show *Arsace* by Francesco Feo, with the stage set by Giuseppe Bibbiena. Painting in oils by D. Olivero with the assistance of an anonymous hand for the 'parte prospettiva'. Museo Civico, Turin.

IV. The Fürnberg–Morzin Legacy

Count Morzin's *Capelle* no longer existed. In Pohl's time no trace of the Morzin family records[1] or musical archives could be found. Then, after the Second World War, a collection of music was discovered in a remote Hungarian castle, and in 1959 (when the collection was housed in Budapest for cataloguing) the present writer saw that Haydn himself had made many – and in some cases very important – holograph additions (dynamic marks, phrasing, even actual notes)[2] to these sets of parts, which were the work of Viennese professional copyists, one of whom ('No. 2') was already well known to us as a man closely connected with Haydn up to (at least) 1776. Until now, it was thought that the symphonies in this collection represented copies of the Morzin parts that Haydn had supervised but we now propose that these MSS. may represent the actual, original Morzin parts of the works concerned. If this is true, the fact that these MSS. usually include two violin I and two violin II parts, as well as two 'Basso' parts, may suggest that the Morzin, or as it may be the Fürnberg, *Capelle* boasted at least six violins (possibly eight) and at least, for the bass part, one violoncello, one bassoon and one *violone* (perhaps more: two 'celli?). In Symphony No. 5, we can see the copying procedure: the copyist prepared one violin I part: Haydn corrected it; the copyist then prepared the duplicate violin I part incorporating these corrections. Sometimes the duplicate parts were already finished and Haydn corrected both: this is the case in Symphony 'A', where Haydn made corrections on both violin I, both violin II and both basso parts. In Symphony No. 11, there are holograph corrections by Haydn on only one of the violin II parts (there are, however, corrections to both violin I parts).

The Morzin *Capelle* having been disbanded, then, there was no reason for the Count to keep large numbers of orchestral parts for which he now had no use whatever; and we believe that about 1761 Haydn persuaded his former patron to arrange a sale of these superfluous parts to the eldest son of another Haydn patron, Lt.-Col. Joseph von Fürnberg.

Before we examine these MSS., we must relate the extraordinary history of the collection as a whole (or rather that part of it which survives). Lt.-Col. Joseph finally retired from the army and returned to manage his many estates, becoming deeply involved in forestry. His principal place of residence was at Purkersdorf, one post station west of Vienna on the great road to Salzburg; there at Purkersdorf he controlled the mails and lived in a beautiful palace which still survives. (Carpani, when he wrote of Carl Joseph von Fürnberg that he 'dimorava per lo più a Burckersdorff' [p. 85], confused the residences of father and son.) Joseph was created a count in 1796 but lost the title because he refused to pay the costs connected with the honour. He died at the age of 58 on 13 September 1799, in his house in the Viennese suburb of Wieden, Hauptstraße No. 3.[3] We have been able to locate an interesting portrait of Joseph, which is published here for the first time (pl. 9).

Now it happened that in the Hungarian castle of Keszthely on Lake Balaton there lived a most original and far-sighted aristocrat named Georg, Count Festetics (a descendent of an old and respected noble Hungarian family). He had followed in Joseph II's footsteps and was an ardent humanist, reformer and idealist; he was also a

---

1 Meanwhile a large part of the Morzin Archives has been located in Prague, but unfortunately not that of the Lukavec estates nor of its owner in the 1750s, Count Maximilian Franz.
2 Symphony No. 11: *vide infra*, p. 282.
3 Pohl I, 182f.

Freemason. As a suspected sympathizer of the Jacobin conspiracy of the early 1790s in Vienna (where he had studied), Count Georg was confined to his estates and contrived to make Keszthely Castle, which he proceeded to enlarge, a centre of learning and culture. In 1799 he sent his music master to Vienna to purchase music for the beautiful new library called Helikon (which was opened in 1801). In this way, the death of Joseph Fürnberg enabled Count Festetics's music master (perhaps with Haydn himself as the go-between) to purchase the Fürnberg music collection together with several others – including a fine collection of wind-band music by Druschetzky acquired in what is now Yugoslavia – and to bring them back to Keszthely, where it was after 1801 housed in a special section of the library planned for music (Count Georg's catalogue labels are still extant). There it reposed quietly, its value unknown to the many descendants of the family who lived in the Castle in regal splendour until the end of the Second World War.

In the Spring of 1945, the Russians arrived at Keszthely, led by a Ukrainian officer who was a teacher in civilian life. He at once realized the library's unique importance (the music, which was concealed behind a façade at one end, was not in direct evidence) – and it was indeed one of the finest in Hungary – and forthwith posted two armed guards at the doors. When his unit had to move on, this officer actually walled up the staircase that led from the ground floor of that wing to the library, and thus saved the collection for posterity.[1] And so it is to this unknown Russian officer that we owe the *only* authentic sources for Haydn's early symphonies, authentic sources of six early quartets, the *only* genuine sources (and the only proofs of authenticity) of two string trios, a unique reference to a Symphony by Michael Haydn, and two authentic sources for the Divertimentos (II:21 and 22) for two horns and strings.[2]

The collection of symphonies, apart from the many holograph additions, is of decisive importance for another reason: on the title page, Haydn himself added numbers which appear from every standpoint to be chronological. This numbering was taken over, continued, and the missing numbers[3] filled in with newer works, when the collection was incorporated into the Helikon Library at Keszthely. But as far as the first sixteen numbers survive, they are clearly numbered by Haydn himself. The principal fact that catches the eye in the list opposite is that Haydn numbered as 'I' the work he described to Griesinger as his First Symphony (giving the *incipit*). Now let us attack the problem of dating. Haydn told Griesinger that this symphony had been composed in 1759, but there are three major reasons for back-dating it by about two years, to *c*.1757:

(1) No. 2 of the series, Symphony No. 37, exists in a dated manuscript of 1758 in the Archives of the Princes Schwarzenberg in Český-Krumlov (Krumau).

(2) When Haydn was helping Breitkopf & Härtel in the preparation of the *Oeuvres complettes*, the firm submitted to him a whole series of *incipits* which he examined and returned via Griesinger. The earliest group of symphonies and trios was dated from 1757. For correspondence on the subject, see *Haydn: the Years of 'The Creation' 1796–1800*, pp. 466ff.

(3) It will be seen (*infra*, pp. 280ff.) that Haydn composed some nineteen symphonies (and possibly six *scherzandi* which, however, for a variety of reasons we have tentatively assigned to the early Esterházy period) for Count Morzin, and also a

---

1 Information from the courteous staff of Keszthely Castle, now immaculately restored and one of Hungary's great tourist attractions, where my wife and I were guests in June 1978. I would like once again to thank our colleagues there for many favours.
2 The existence of the collection was first revealed to us in a letter by Professor Dénes Bartha, Budapest, 25 November 1957.
3 When Festetics acquired the MSS., some were already missing. See list, p. 241.

THE FESTETICS COLLECTION: HAYDN SYMPHONIES

Haydn's no.	Work	Comments
1	1	
2	37	
3	18	
4	[missing]	Festetics substituted Symphony No. 71 (a Viennese professional copy on Italian paper with watermarks of three crescents of declining size and 'REAL' and 'FV').
5	2	
6	[missing]	Festetics substituted a work which can no longer be found.
7	[missing]	Festetics substituted Symphony No. 63 (scoring: 1 fl. obl., 2 ob., 1 bsn obl., 2 hns, strings) in a Viennese professional copy on Italian paper (watermarks: 'FV', three crescents of declining size, and 'REAL').
8	[missing]	Festetics substituted Symphony No. 38 in an early (1760s) Viennese professional copy on oblong Italian paper (watermarks: three crescents of declining size, 'A' and, under canopy, 'AS').
9	15	
10	4	
11	10	
12	32	
13	5	
14	11	
15	33	
16	27	
17	'A'	'Nᵣₒ 17' added by Festetics, but the (originally unnumbered) work bears the stamp of Lt-Col. von Fürnberg, as well as holograph corrections by Haydn.
18	Symphony in F by Michael Haydn (Perger *deest*)	*Incipit:*

'Nᵣₒ 18 / Sinfonia ex F / à / 2 Violini / 2 Oboe / 2 Corni. / Viola oblig: / col / Basso / Del Sigl: Giov. Mich: Hayden. / [stamp: Fürnberg / Obrist Lieut].' On 4° paper as used for copies of works by Joseph Haydn (watermarks: castle in ornament and 'LDF'; cf. Joseph's Symphony No. 18). The number, added by Festetics, was not part of the original copy.

19	Symphony No. 74	Added by Festetics, this is a Viennese professional copy on Italian paper (watermark: canopy with half-moon and 'GFA').
20	Symphony No. 60	Added by Festetics, this is an authentic copy (by Viennese Professional Copyist No. 2) from the library of Franz Gotthárd: 'Nᵣₒ 20 / 38 In C / Sinfonia / à / più stromenti / Par la comedia intitolata / Il Distrato / Del Sigᵣˢ Giuseppe Haydn. [later: "Gotthárd mpria"]'. On 4° Italian paper (watermarks: three crescents of declining size and, in an ornate frame, 'W'). With parts for 'Corno o Clarino Primo [Secondo] / in C Alto è g'. Lacking oboes and timpani. The number 'Nᵣₒ 20' added by Festetics.
21	3	'Nᵣₒ 21' added by Festetics, but the (originally unnumbered) work bears the stamp of Lt-Col. von Fürnberg.

whole series of wind-band divertimentos (*Feld Parthien*); the Divertimentos II:16, 21 and 22; and many early harpsichord trios which have survived in authentic copies of the Morzin–Fürnberg circle in Kremsier. If we consider that Haydn wrote twenty symphonies (and possibly the six *scherzandi*) for the Esterházy house from 1761 to 1765 inclusive, it seems most unlikely that he composed nineteen between 1 January 1759 and May 1761, as well as all the other works just mentioned.

The following Haydn works form the Fürnberg collection:

Symphonies

Nos. 1, 2, 3, 4, 5, 10, 11, 15, 18, 27, 32, 33, 37 and 'A' (several more missing)

Divertimentos (Cassations)

II:21 and 22, for two horns and strings

String Quartets

A set of six: Op. 1, Nos. 6, 2, 4, 1 and Op. 2, Nos. 1 and 6 (III:6, 2, 3, 1, 7, 12)

String Trios

V:G1 and D3 and

'Sei / Divertimenti / a / Violino Primo / Violino Secondo / e / Basso / Del Sigre Giuseppe Haydn', Cat. 1139, with the stamp of Lt-Col. von Fürnberg. 4° Italian paper (watermarks: three crescents of declining size, with 'REAL'; letters 'GFA' [Galvani Fratelli, Pordenone]). Substitute local pages in 'Basso' part on local paper (with eagle as watermark).

The final works for string trios turn out to contain at least one holograph correction in the Trio of No. 4 (XI:35), first violin part. They are transcribed baryton trios (showing that Haydn authorized such transcriptions) XI:39, 34, 38, 35, 37 and 36, composed *c*.1767. Their presence shows that Haydn kept up with Fürnberg at least until that date. It also suggests that not all symphonies – at least not those lacking the Haydn numberings – are necessarily pre-May 1761; perhaps No. 3 is actually an early Esterházy work (though it was in Göttweig as early as 1762, which points to a date earlier than May 1761, since Göttweig always took at least two years, and usually three, to secure a new work by Michael or Joseph Haydn).

The hitherto unrecorded Symphony in F by Michael Haydn is interesting because it is touching evidence that Joseph was looking after the interests of his younger brother. It was drawn up by one of the Morzin (Fürnberg) group of copyists and is written on paper also used for the Joseph Haydn series (e.g. Symphony No. 18). We presume it is one of the six symphonies that Michael composed in 1760–1 for the Bishop of Großwardein.[1]

Other scholars may like to learn of some other interesting MSS. in the Helikon Library at Keszthely[2] which have a bearing on our period. Apart from the works listed above and in the footnote, there is a good contemporary MS. of Haydn's Quartet, Op. 2, No. 4, marked 'Cassatio'.[3] Other details on these sources (watermarks) will be found in the appropriate place: Divertimentos II:21 and 22, the early quartets, early string trios and early symphonies in Chapter Seven; the Quartets, Op. 20 (p. 628), Duets for violin and viola (p. 629); also good MSS. of Pleyel's Sixteen Minuets (composed at Eszterháza) with the typical C *alto* horns; and Ordoñez's Symphony in A (Brown I:A9), using the so-called 'Haydn ornament' (*infra*, p. 557).

1 Perger 1 has survived in autograph and gives us the essential details (EH, Budapest): 'Partitta 5ta in E mol 2 Corni, 2 Oboe, 2 Violini, Viola, è Violone. / di Michele Hayden'. At the end of the MS.: 'M. Varadini 20ma 9bris 760.' (for a long time Michael spelled his name with an 'e'.) The words 'Partita' and 'Sinfonia' were interchangeable, even as late as the Göttweig Catalogue of 1830. Also attributed to Joseph Haydn: see SYM 812, No. 75, and Hoboken I:Es4. Now it was always considered that the other (previous) four works for Großwardein were lost, but we believe they can be reconstructed at least in part: (1) Symphony in F (Perger *deest*), *c*.1760 in Morzin Coll. (2) Perger 35, known to us from Göttweig 1761 (2 ob., 2 clarini, str.). (3) Perger *deest*: Symphony in G (SYM 818, No. 108; Hoboken I:G2), Göttweig 1763 ('Comp. P. Leander.'). (4) possibly Perger 36 (correct scoring to include 2 oboes); SYM 810, No. 62; Hoboken I:D21; Göttweig Catalogue 1747 (*sic*); or Perger 37 (to scoring add 'Flauto' and v. I, II *concertante* from Göttweig); SYM 806, No. 39; Hoboken I:D26; Göttweig 'Comp. P. Odo 1770'. A sixth work may be Perger 2, composed at Großwardein on 16 February 1761.

2 (1) Contemporary Viennese professional copy (parts in all cases unless listed to the contrary) of Haydn's Quartets, Op. 17 (III:25–30), Cat. 0/3a with a different order, starting with III:30 and ending with III:25. French title patterned after a typical print. Basso part: 'Six

INTERLUDE

We have not, in the Chronicle for this volume, listed many of the operas being given as Haydn grew up in the Cathedral Choir School: it is doubtful if Haydn saw any of them. When he was working for Kurz-Bernadon, he might have organized the occasional free ticket; but the works which he might have seen have almost entirely disappeared. It is doubtful if he was rich or influential enough to pay for, or to get a free ticket to, the Italian operas and French *opéras* done at the Burgtheater. So until 1761 and Gluck's *Don Juan,* our theatrical chronicle has been, deliberately, sparse. If we now break that rule, it is because the year is 1760 and Haydn was by then well enough known, and friendly enough with the theatrical authorities, to have been able easily to

---

[footnote 2 – *cont.*]

Quatuors / Pour Deux Violons, Alto et Basse. / Composées par / Joseph Haÿdn / Maitre de Chapelle de S: A: Monsgr. / Le Prince Estherhazÿ ec:'. Italian paper (watermarks: three crescents of declining size, letters 'A / HF / REAL'. (2) Late (*c.*1790) MS. by a Viennese professional copyist of Quartets Op. 9 (III:19–24), with a locally added French title. Cat. 0/3b. (3) MS. parts of the Divertimento for baryton *a otto voci* in A minor (X:3), here arranged for ob. or fl., v., 2 viole, vc. Cat. 868/VIII with old 'Nᵣₒ II'. Italian paper (watermark: three crescents of declining size with letters 'CS'; ornament with star and moon, letters 'VG'). (4) MS. parts of 'VI. / Quintetti / Violino Primo / Del Sigl: Mich: Haydn'. Cat. 0/28. Perger 108, 109, 112, 92, 93 ('Flauto'), 110. Viennese professional copy. (5) MS. parts formerly belonging to Mozart's friend, Sigismund von Barisani of Michael Haydn's 'Menuetti 6 / a / 2. Violini. / 2 oboe / 2. Corni. / Fagotto. / e / Basso. / Del Sigl: Michele Haydn / Maestro di Concerto. [another hand: "1783 / Salzburgo / Per il Sigr. Sigismondo di Barisani"]. Cat. 1081/IX. There are two sets of minuets included: Perger 69 (7 Feb. 1783, autograph EH, Budapest) and 70 (23 Jan. 1784). Italian paper (watermarks: three crescents of declining size, 'REAL' 'W' in ornate frame). (6) MS. of a Symphony by Leopold Mozart, Cat. 945 / VIII. 'Divertimento [another hand "in D"] / 2 Violj / e / Basso / Del Sigʳᵉ Mozarth'. At head of parts: 'Sinfonia'

Allegro moderato

(7) Autograph score, dated 'Composui 2 april 1770' but not signed, of an *Offertorium / de / B: V: Maria* 'Quae est ista'. Cat. 2045/IX. (8) MS. parts of *24 Minuetti de ballo* for 2 fl., 2 ob., bsn., 2 Corni e Trombe, timp., 2 v., basso by Joseph Bengraf on Italian crescent paper.

Cat. 0/34. (9) Autograph score dated 11 April 1779 but not signed for *6 / Allemandes* (2 ob., 2 hns., 2 v., b.)

on Italian paper ('GF' under canopy). Cat. 0/90. (10 *XII/Minuetti de Ballo / a più Stromenti. / da G.* in autograph score for a large orch. (incl. flauto piccolo, trpts., timp.)

p

on Italian crescent paper (also with 'AS' and fleur-de-lys; 'CM' or WG'). Cat. 2094/IX. (11) 'Notturno / a / 2. Violini / Viola / e / Basso / del Sig. G.'

Allegro

Cat. 1187/IX. Austrian paper (watermarks: unicorn and letters 'FD' [?]; eagle with letters 'IEI'[?]). We provide these rather mysterious MSS. in the hopes that they may help to identify the provenance of the non-Fürnberg material. We believe that this modest composer was perhaps the Festetics family's music master at that period.

3 'Cassatio Ex F / a / 2 Violini / Viola / con / Basso / del Sig.ʳᵉ Giuseppe Haydn.', Cat. 2066/II. Italian paper with watermarks: three crescents of declining size; letter 'F'; schematic crown (pagoda?). An early MS. Can it, despite lack of stamp, nevertheless have belonged to Fürnberg? Or is it simply a good Viennese professional copy. There are no corrections in Haydn's hand.

see the following anonymous preview of Gluck's great ballet. The title page of the libretto reads:

> Arien, / Welche in der Comödie, / betitelt: / Das steinerne Gastmahl / gesungen werden, / nebst denen / Verzweiflungs-Versen / des / DON JUANS. / [emblem] / Wien, / Gedruckt mit von Ghelischen Schriften, 1760.

[Radenín Coll., National Museum, Prague, 4126]

The essence of this curious Don Juan parody is its typically Viennese contrast between slapstick Hanswurstiada and high tragedy – in other words, the essence of Haydn's style, and the trait of his character most misunderstood, especially in Germany. In three Arias, Hanns-Wurst parodies, in his usual rough language, the happenings; the first two 'Arias' end

> Ha! ha! ha!
> Was ist das für Narredey.
> (How's that for madness)

and the third

> Ha! ha! ha!
> Schade für die Narredey.
> (Pity about the madness)

As a typical 'Aria' we may select the second (end 'couplet' omitted):

> Aria II
> Dieser schwärmt mit den Gespenstern,
>   Ganze Nächte um die Wett,
> Jener schreyt vors Schatzerls Fenstern
>   Wie die Sau im Todtenbeth,
> Dieser patscht und pfeift,
>   Bis das liebe Stubenmädel
> Nach den Scherberl greift,
>   Und dem Hasen wascht den Schedel;
> Gleichwohl danket der Phantast für die Schopperey,
>   [couplet]

The next extract is the 'Vers / Des / Eremiten' (The Hermit's Verses) in Act II, and this is a serious, introverted piece. But the strange climax of the libretto is the 'Verzweiflungs-Verse / des / DON JUANS', in which we are suddenly in the world of German tragic theatre,

> Nunmehr verruchter Mensch! wach auf von Lasterthaten,
> Du hast die Kindespflicht, und die Natur verrathen,
> Verletzt, beschämt, verfolgt, gehasset, und beraubt . . .

– a huge final scene before Don Juan is dragged into the flames of hell. Hanswurst is, apparently, Don Juan's servant. The crass contrast in tone and message is almost like the style of a Haydn symphony in the 1780s, and we believe that this 'Interlude' shows this to be a thoroughly Viennese trait; though we believe that the Viennese changed enormously in the second half of the eighteenth century, and that now (1979) the people have almost nothing in common with their forebears (1760), except perhaps for their underdeveloped literary sense and their love of extravagant parties (Carnival in Vienna is still a time for endless private parties) and the men's general adoration of, and easy relationship to, the fair sex.

V. Haydn's Marriage

THE DOCUMENTS

(1) Griesinger: (continued from p. 235)

... and Haydn now decided, since his future was, on the whole, established by a fixed salary, to marry the hairdresser's second daughter, especially as the latter (to whom Haydn felt beholden) kept pressing the matter.

Haydn had no children by this marriage. 'My wife was incapable of having children, and thus I was less indifferent to the charms of other women.' Altogether his choice was not a happy one, for his wife had a domineering, unfriendly character; and he had carefully to hide his income from her since she was a spendthrift. She was also bigoted, and was always inviting clergymen to dinner; she had many Masses said and was rather more liberal in her support of charity than her financial situation allowed. Once, when Haydn had done someone a favour for which he would take no recompense, it was suggested that I [Griesinger] offer something to his wife instead; he answered me: 'She doesn't deserve anything, for it is a matter of indifference to her whether her husband is a cobbler or an artist.' She died in the Summer of 1800 at Baden, near Vienna.

[15]

(2) Dies, 11 May 1805 (45f.):

Haydn was now *Kapellmeister*, he had a certain income and was satisfied with his life with one exception, that he was still unmarried. It was not to be expected of a fiery young man that he would continue to heed the ban [on marriage, imposed by Count Morzin on his musicians] for very long. His natural urges only grew stronger because of the ban, and Haydn could withstand it no longer. Since he lived with a wig-maker in his home where there were two daughters, and this man had said jokingly to him: 'Haydn, you ought to marry my eldest daughter,' Haydn did so (against his instincts, in fact, for the younger was the real object of his love), just to get a wife for himself quickly. But in the following years he lived to regret the ill-considered step, as we may presuppose from Haydn's words – 'We became fond of each other, but all the same I soon discovered that my wife was very scatterbrained'★ – and his subsequent silence.

I am no friend of 'they say', and will not introduce into this account any unauthenticated rumour that cannot be verified at the source itself. It seemed to me that Haydn considered the tale of his domestic woes unworthy or too commonplace to enter into his biography; therefore I asked no further and resolved to await further clarification from Haydn's own volition to speak on the subject ... The Count found himself obliged to cut down his hitherto large expenses. He dismissed his virtuosi, and in this fashion Haydn lost his position as *Kapellmeister*.

★ [Original footnote]: The word scatterbrained [*Leichtsinn*] is capable of various meanings, some of them wounding, and these hardly obtain here. According to the most reputable witnesses, Madame H. was a domineering and jealous woman, incapable of making a decision and deserving the name of spendthrift.

(3) Carpani:

... Voglio dire delle sue nozze colla signora Annuccia *Keller*, figlia del già nominato parrucchiere. Memore di quanto aveva promesso, e di quanto doveva a quella famiglia, il nostro signor Giuseppe, trovandosi provvisto di sussistenza onorevole e sicura, passò a quelle nozze, le quali per qualche tempo lo resero felice; ma in seguito i capricci della Signora trasformarono il nodo in catena, il piacere in tormento, e la cosa andò tant'oltre, che dopo aver sofferto molti anni, questo Socrate novello finì per separarsi dalla sua Santippe. Per non tornare su questo articolo, ve ne dirò ora tutta la storia. La signora *Anna* non era bella; ma neppur brutta. I suoi costumi erano illibati, ma aveva una testina di bosso, e quando la si metteva giù, non v'era moda di farla rimovere da un capriccio. Questa donna amava il marito e n'era corrisposta. Un eccesso di religiosa pietà mal diretta venne a sturbare questa beata armonia. La signora *Anna* voleva sempre la casa piena di ecclesiastici, ai quali forniva de' buoni pranzi e cene e merende ad ogni tratto. *Haydn* piuttosto economo, ma più per ragione che per natura, mentre aveva appena di che vivere discretamente, cominciò a vedere di mal occhio queste processioni continue di sante locuste che davano il guasto alla sua dispensa. Non era nemmen compatibile colla casa di un uomo studioso il chiasso indivisibile dalle numerose società geniali e contente; per quanto foss' egli sodamente religioso e dabbene non potè a meno di non sentir noja di questi sacri simposj, e di chiuder la porta al refettorio. Amico: *Inde irae*. La signora *Anna* aveva un fratello religioso. A questi non si poteva nè si voleva impedire di visitare la sorella. I frati sono come le ciliegie. Se una ne levi dal paniere, dieci le tengon dietro. Il convento d'*Haydn* non diminuiva. Nè qui terminava la faccenda. Ogni tratto la signora *Anna* aveva nuove pretese. Oggi un responsorio, domani un mottetto, l'altro una Messa, poi inni, poi salmi, poi antifone; e tuto *gratis*. Se il marito ricusava di farli, venivano in iscena i grandi alleati delle donne capricciose, gli effetti isterici, gli insulti di stomacho, le convulsioni; poi strilli, poi rifiuti, pianti, querele e mal umore continuo. *Haydn* finiva col dover appagare la signora, guadagnar nulla, e pagar per giunta medico e speziale, ed aver sempre la borsa in asciutto e l'animo sossopra. È un vero prodigio che un uomo di genio posto in tale contrasto, potesse creare i mirabili lavori che tutto il Mondo conosce. Fu di quest'epocha che, cercando sollievo nell'amicizia, contrasse quel legame di sentimento che durò sino alla morte colla *Boselli* [sc. Polzelli] cantatrice al servizio del principe *Esterhazy*. Quest'amicizia destando de' gelosi sospetti nell'animo della signora *Anna* finì di renderla insopportabile. Volla la nemica sorte, che dal matrimonio d'*Haydn* nessun frutto ne nascesse. Mancando quindi l'anello più saldo che abbiasi la maritale catena, questa non potè resistere a tanti urti, e s'allentò fatalmente. Cessarono i conjugi di viver insieme, e solo restò indissolubile e fermo il nodo sacramentale, che contratto aveva l'*Haydn* all'età di 27 [28] anni. La signora *Anna* visse oltre li 70 anni, d'una sufficiente pensione che fedelmente il marito le corrispondeva, e morì in Baaden [*sic*] l'anno 1800. Queste vicende furono in gran parte la cagione per la quale *Haydn*, sebbene guadagnasse molto, non potè che ben tardi cominciare a metter da parte un po' di denaro e farsi un piccolo stato.

[Carpani, 81–3]

[Summary in translation:]
Carpani relates the story of Haydn's marriage with Annucia [*sic*] Keller, the daughter of the wig-maker mentioned above, to whom he was indebted, and whom he could now marry, having a fixed income. For a time all went well, but later the relationship was one of Socrates and Xanthippe. Signora Anna was neither beautiful nor ugly, but she was exceedingly stubborn and given to excesses of religious fervour, which manifested itself in luncheons, dinners and teas given to the clergy. Haydn, frugal by circumstances rather than by nature, began to view with alarm this drain on his modest income; nor did the noise of these gatherings encourage a man of scholarly pursuits. Signora Anna had a brother in orders,[1] and one didn't wish to prevent him visiting his sisters, but the monks are like cherries: you take one from the basket and ten others are attached. Not only that: Anna expected Haydn to provide, *gratis*, church music of all kinds, and if he refused, there were great scenes – tears, recriminations, and Haydn could pay the doctors' and apothecaries' bills too. It is a miracle that in these circumstances he could produce the works that all the world admires. In his

attempt to find solace, Haydn made a life-long attachment with Boselli [Polzelli],[2] a singer in the service of Prince Esterházy: a friendship which filled Anna with jealous suspicions. Haydn's marriage was childless, and this was the final unhappiness that fatally damaged the relationship: the partners ceased to live together, but their marriage ties (contracted when Haydn was [28]) remained inviolate. Anna lived to be over seventy, living from a pension her husband had loyally provided her, and died in Baaden [*sic*] in the year 1800. This was why Haydn, even though he earned well, could not begin until later in life to put any money aside.

Notes:

1 Maria Anna's clerical brother was P. Eduard (his religious name) in the Barefoot Augustine Order of Graz. E. F. Schmid, 'Josef Haydns Jugendliebe' (op. cit.), p. 117.

2 Luigia Polzelli, Haydn's mistress from about 1780 to 1790.

(4) Marriage contract between Joseph Haydn and Maria Anna Aloysia Apollonia Keller (usually referred to as 'Maria Anna' or [codicil to Will, 12 March 1800] 'Anna'), Vienna, 9 November 1760:

In the name of the most Holy Trinity, God the Father, Son and Holy Ghost. Amen.

Today, on the date hereto appended, the following marriage contract between the well-born Herr Josepho Heiden [*sic*], party of the first part, and the most honourable and virtuous maid, Anna Maria Keller, party of the second part, has been agreed upon, established and concluded.

First, the above-mentioned maid, Anna Maria Keller, in the presence and with the permission of, respectively, both parents and parents-in-law, gives intent of being engaged to Josepho Haydn [*sic*], with the expectation and promise from both parties of a marriage contracted by a priest.

Secondly, the maid and bride will bring to her bridegroom a dowry in accordance with her rank of goods and chattels valued at the sum of three hundred and fifty gulden (*id est*, 350 fr:) and in addition a true marriage dowry in cash of 500 fr (in words five hundred gulden Rhl: each valued at 60 kr.); which sum is matched [on Haydn's part] by 1,000 fr: (in words one thousand gulden of the same value); and it is understood that dowry and matching sum of fifteen hundred gulden are to be deposited according to the custom of the Lower Austrian courts for the lifetime of each party.[1]

Thirdly it is agreed that whatever during the period of marriage shall, in God's infinite grace, be earned, inherited or purchased will be treated as a single, indivisible capital, equally valid for both parties,

So that

Fourthly, each party reserves the power and free decision to apportion by Will, Deed of Donation or other means, to third parties, his or her resp. portion of the capital sums enumerated above. In witness whereof this marriage contract has been prepared in two identical original copies, signed by both fiancés and also their witnesses, each to be given one copy of the document. Given at Vienna, this Ninth Day of November, 1760.

[seal]	Joseph Häydn as Bridegroom	[seal]	Maria Anna Kellerin as Bride
[seal]	Carl Schunckhe as Witness	[seal]	Antonius Buchholtz Citizen Market Judge as Witness

[Archiv für Niederösterreich, Hinterlassenschaft-Akt 'Maria Anna Haydn'; R. F. Müller, 'Heiratsbrief, Testament und Hinterlassenschaft der Gattin Joseph Haydns', *Die Musik* XXII/2 (Nov. 1929), pp. 93f. Facsimile of first and last pages in R. Tenschert, *Joseph Haydn . . . Sein Leben in Bildern*, Leipzig 1935, doc. 15; and R. Petzoldt and E. Crass, *Joseph Haydn Sein Leben in Bildern*, Leipzig 1959, doc. 24.]

Notes:
1 R. F. Müller (pp. 94f.), to whom we owe the first publication of this document, provides some useful information. The dowry terms were those customary in bourgeois circles at the time. The dowry suggests (as we have seen, too, in the money provided for the sister's entry into the nunnery) a certain financial independence on the part of the bride's family, although Maria Anna's father was to die in poverty eleven years later. The so-called 'Wiederlage' ('Matching Sum') that the bridegroom was expected to provide was generally a cash sum twice that provided by the bride in cash; this 'matched' her cash sum plus her dowry in kind (linen, kitchen equipment, etc.). Müller is, rightly, puzzled about this huge sum of 1,000 gulden that Haydn had to deposit in cash (or papers): he wonders if Buchholtz, who (as we have seen) helped Haydn in his worst days of penury, may have lent him the money on a short-term basis, perhaps only to satisfy the letter of the contract. We doubt this. If Haydn promised to pay 1,000 gulden, he must have had the money to do so, and this sum represents about $2\frac{1}{2}$ years service with the Morzins. We can only repeat our theory that this 1,000 gulden was largely collected from aristocratic and well-off bourgeois clients of Haydn's as fees for new compositions – symphonies, trios, concertos, divertimenti, etc. – which Haydn could now afford to have copied at his own expense: see Chapter Ten, *infra*, p. 575.

(5) From the Parish Register of St Stephen's Cathedral:

1760, 26. Novembris. cop. sunt: The most respected Hr. Joseph Hayden [*sic*], Music-Director at titl. Hrn. Count v. Morzin, single, born at Rohrau near Brugg [*sic*], son[1] of Hrn Mathias Hayden, Wheelwright and late Anna Maria ux:. With the most respected, virtuous maid Maria Anna Keller, born in this town, daughter of Johann Peter Keller, I.R. freed wig-maker and Elisabeth ux. Testes: Hr. Carl Schuncko [*sic*], Citizen Master Stonecutter of this town, and Hr. Anton Buchholtz, Citizen Market Judge.

Dispensati in tribus denuntiationibus Authoritate Ordinaria, deposito utrinque Libertatis juramento.   [Pohl I, 380, doc. 12]

Haydn's marriage was not a success, but as we have had occasion to note (and as the reader will see for himself), Maria Anna had many grounds for protesting against her husband's conduct in the marriage, at least as far as his fidelity to her bed was concerned; and no doubt the black picture of Frau Haydn is a very one-sided one; but that she was incapable, at least during the last years of their life together, of understanding her husband's genius is vouched for by a staggering document provided by a visiting Swede (see *Haydn: the Years of ' The Creation' 1796–1800*, p. 456). There is no evidence, as Carpani suggests, that the Haydns ever separated officially; on the contrary, even the apartment at Eszterháza (Musicians' House) is clearly designed for, and was used by, both Haydns.

There is a touching piece of evidence that Haydn was rather fond of his wife's family (and not just the 'ex nun'), which we reproduce in the Addenda and Errata at the end of this volume (see pp. 641f.).

---

1 The document has, wrongly, 'daughter'.

By the end of November 1760, when Haydn married, we have seen that his fortunes had changed for the better. It must have been in the previous seven or eight years that Haydn gradually began to collect a small library, which of course he slowly enlarged during the course of his long life. This library was dispersed after his death in 1809, but the present writer was fortunate enough to see at least one book with a signature 'Ex libris / Josephus Haydn' which must be c.1760 or before; it was a book owned by the late Erwin Major, who showed it to us at Budapest in 1958. We thought to write down the details,[1] but soon thereafter Dr Major died and no trace of these items can be found in his legacy, which is now in the Library of the Bartók Archives; and although we searched hard on our last visit to Budapest (1978), we could not find Haydn's book, or the *Armida* engraving (see footnote).

A list of Haydn's library in the year 1809 exists, and allowing for what were probably many losses *en route*, a part of Haydn's library of the year 1760 can be reconstructed by using the available sources.[2]

It may be that Morzin (like Prince Nicolaus Esterházy) expected his musicians to remain unmarried; but the fact that Haydn signs himself boldly on the register of St Stephen's (acting, this time, as the local parish church) as 'Music-Director at titl. [Herrn] Count v. Morzin', must mean (1) that he was still in Morzin's service on 26 November 1760, and (2) that the marriage was not at all a secret one, done (as it were) behind the back of the Count. In any event, Haydn had only a few months to wait for a new and even better position; but before turning to that Chapter (which is, in the nature of things, more extensively documented than the present one) we must examine the new music produced in these important interim years.

1 Dr Major also owned what we believe to be the only known copy of the Pressburg engraving from the Erdödy Almanach (*Hochgräflich Erdödischer Theaterallmanach auf das Jahr 1787*) showing a scene from Haydn's *Armida*. It is reproduced as Abb. 25 in Géza Staud, *Adelstheater in Ungarn*, Vienna 1977. We apologize for the vague information about the book from Haydn's library which reminds us of the frank footnotes in Braudel's *The Mediterranean*, where he engagingly admits to forgetting some source or reference.
2 For the musical-theoretical books, see *Haydn: the Late Years 1801–1809*, pp. 402f.; for the rest, see M. Hörwarthner. 'Joseph Haydns Bibliothek – Versuch einer literarhistorischen Rekonstruktion', *Joseph Haydn und die Literatur seiner Zeit*, Jahrbuch für Österreichische Kulturgeschichte, VI. Band, Eisenstadt 1976, pp. 157ff.

CHAPTER SIX

Haydn's Works 1757–1760
(and beyond)

I. THE MUSIC FOR THE FÜRNBERG FAMILY

The Authentic Copyists.
The String Quartets.
The Divertimenti (Cassatios) for Two Horns and Strings (II:21, 22).
String Trios – *vide supra*, pp. 219ff.

II. THE MUSIC FOR THE MORZIN FAMILY

Piano (Harpsichord) Trios.
Divertimenti (Concertini) for Harpsichord and Strings; Divertimento for Harpsichord, Two Horns, Violin and Bass (XIV:1).
Divertimenti:
(a) for Wind Band; (b) Divertimento for Two Cors Anglais, Two Bassoons, Two Horns and Two Violins (II:16).
Pastorella, 'Eÿ, wer hat ihn das Ding gedenkt' (XXIIId:G1).
Symphonies.

III. THE FIRST HAYDN SCHOOL

I. The Music for the Fürnberg Family

THE AUTHENTIC COPYISTS

In the Chronicle, we have seen that, together with Haydn's first modest prosperity, the composer had, in the late 1750s, the first opportunity to establish his own scriptorium. There are perhaps two groups of copies prepared by this scriptorium: (1) the copies made directly under Haydn's supervision and with his corrections; presumably these were the first copies, parts destined for a work's first performance, or they might incorporate the kind of compositional revisions and additions which we have seen that Haydn made in the 'Seitenstetten Minuets'; (2) copies made either after this first step, and therefore needing no revisions by Haydn, or copies which the scribes were allowed to make and sell commercially; we may regard these copies as 'probably authentic'.

250

It was therefore essential, at this point in our biography, to identify presumed members of this scriptorium, which we shall refer to collectively as 'Fürnberg-Morzin Copyists' (see the facsimiles on pp. 576ff.).[1]

No. 1 : At first, it would seem that this man was the principal copyist; we find him as the writer of many MSS., with and without holograph additions by Haydn, of symphonies, piano trios, string trios, symphonies and a divertimento.

No. 2 : A scribe only used occasionally, perhaps a musician who assisted (as would often happen in the Esterházy *Capelle*) in the preparation of parts; he is the second copyist of the Keszthely Castle authentic group of Haydn's Quartets (*infra*). There are Haydn's holograph corrections in his parts.

No. 3 : Another such scribe, known to us from the Keszthely Castle parts of Cassatio (Divertimento) II:22 (*infra*, p. 258). There are Haydn's holograph corrections in his parts.

No. 4 : Known to us from earlier research (*SYM*, 611) as 'Viennese professional copyist No. 2', we now know that he was part of the Fürnberg-Morzin group. There are Haydn's holograph corrections in his parts. He became, it would seem, Haydn's principal copyist, when the composer was in Vienna, *c*. 1760–77; no known copies of works later than 1778 in this hand are extant, which suggests that the scribe may have died in 1778. It is possible that this reliable scribe was the head of his own Viennese scriptorium, and that he was allowed to sell MS. copies of Haydn's works.

No. 5 : The scribe (not, as was previously asserted, Joseph Elssler) who copied the harpsichord part of Piano Trio No. 10 (XV:35) ('Capriccio') in the MS. from Haydn's own library, now EH, Budapest, Ms. mus. I.149. The violin and 'cello parts of this important piece of evidence are by Copyist No. 4.

No. 6 : The copyist of the title page of Quartet Op. I/3 from the Else Radant Landon Collection (Cardiff): *vide infra*. We must reckon this scribe to have been closely associated with Copyist No. 4 and probably a member of Haydn's scriptorium. He is also known to us from one of the string trios (No. 27, V:B1) in the important Archives of the Counts Pachta, National Museum, Prague. The shaky hand suggests old age.

No. 7 : The copyist of the violin II and viola parts of Quartet Op. I/3 from the Else Radant Landon Collection (Cardiff). As the second copyist of this source, we must reckon him, too, as closely associated with Copyist No. 4 and probably a member of Haydn's scriptorium.

No. 8 : The copyist of the violin parts of Trio No. 27 (V:B1) from the Pachta MS. (see No. 6). Certainly associated with Copyist No. 6, and also with Copyist No. 9, one assumes that this scribe was part of Copyist No. 4's, and probably also Haydn's, scriptorium.

No. 9 : The copyist of the actual music of the basso part in the Cardiff MS. of Op. I/3. Probably a musician, not a professional copyist, used by Copyist No. 4, and probably a member of Haydn's scriptorium.

No. 10 : The copyist of Fürnberg-Morzin's MS. of Symphony No. 3.

Copyists Nos. 1–5 may with complete certainly be reckoned among the absolutely authentic Fürnberg-Morzin copyists, while for Nos. 6–9, there is a strong probability that they were members of Haydn's scribal circle. For the details of No. 10, *vide infra* (p. 282).

THE STRING QUARTETS

We shall refer to these early string quartets by the traditional numbers in Opp. I and II, with which Haydn had no connection: they were the numbers assigned to them in the first collected edition of all Haydn's quartets by his pupil Ignaz Pleyel (1801 +). Here is the manner in which Pleyel came to his decision. Haydn's quartets first appeared in 1764 (the famous edition, by M. de la Chevardière, is discussed *infra*, pp. 595f.): the earliest print included four (Op. I/1–4) and was later expanded to six (Op. I/1–6), with No. 5 being a Symphony (as indeed the title also stated). The E flat work which we know as Op. 'O' was first issued in France as a single work, but was then included by

1 Nos. 1–3 (from *JHW* XII, 1) and XVII:1.

Hummel in *his* Op. I (Nos. 'O', 6, 1–4). Pleyel followed the Chevardière gathering, however, and that is why, in the traditional numbering, Opus I/5 (Symphony 'A', as it is now known) was included as a quartet, and 'Opus O' omitted; and this omission caused someone, as we shall see, to refer to it in *EK* as 'a not engraved quartet' (that someone was not aware of the Huberty edition of 1764!). The actual title, 'Opus I', was added by Hummel.

Op. II began its life with M. de la Chevardière as 'Six Sinfonies ou Quatuor [*sic*] dialogués' but was called 'œuvre iii', since 'œuvre ii' – that title, too, was added later, when Haydn's French editions started to proliferate – had meanwhile been issued and contained six string trios (also Chevardière). The 'œuvre iii' which in Pleyel's hands became 'œuvre ii' contained the following works: (1) the Cassatio (Divertimento) for horns and strings (II:21) in E flat; (2) a spurious work, the Divertimento in F for two hours, violin, viola and basso (II:F5), actually by Carlos d'Ordoñez (Göttweig Abbey, 1763); (3) the Cassatio (Divertimento) for horns and strings (II:22); (4) Quartet, Op. II/4; (5) Quartet, Op. II/1; (6) Quartet, Op. II/2. Now Chevardière issued horn parts to the first three works, but shortly afterwards, Hummel made a different collation: his Op. II contained what we know as the whole of Op. II (Nos. 1–6), which means that apart from four real Quartets (Nos. 1, 2, 4, 6), there were two – Nos. 3 and 5 – which were for two horns and strings and had been printed as such by Chevardière in his 'œuvre iii' (the Cassatios/Divertimenti in E flat and D, II:21, 22). It was not just a question of dropping the horns of these Cassatios/Divertimenti to turn them into string quartets; the horn parts were often composed as soli and had to be completely rewritten into the string parts. There is no evidence whatever that Hummel's arrangement of these two works is genuine; and Hummel's is not the only known arrangement, either. The genuine and original versions are attested by Haydn in *EK*, who added the words 'A Sei Stromenti' to the *incipit* of II:21 and 'a Sei' to that of II:22. In the first recording of the complete Op. 1,[1] these sextets were recorded in their original form, using a MS. prepared from a number of old sources by Karlheinz Füssl.

A tabular collation will show the Hoboken numbers:

Opus I

No. 1 (III:1); No. 2 (III:2); No. 3 (III:3); No. 4 (III:4); No. 5 (III:5, in reality a Symphony, 'A', I:107); No. 6 (III:6).

Opus II

No. 1 (III:7); No. 2 (III:8); No. 3 (III:9, in reality a Cassatio or Divertimento for horns and strings II:21); No. 4 (III:10); No. 5 (III:11, in reality a Cassatio or Divertimento for horns and strings II:22); No. 6 (III:12).

In the *Entwurf-Katalog*, all these authentic quartets (except Op. I/6 – and that work is confirmed by another authentic source) are listed with *incipits*:

Haydn's Early Quartets in EK

Work	Entered by	Description
		[*EK*, page 3]
Op. I/3	Joseph Elssler	'Cassatio à 4^{tro} Ex D' [Haydn crossed out 'Cassatio' and changed title to 'Divertimento'; still later, Haydn(?): 'quartet'].
Op. I/4	Joseph Elssler	'Cassatio à 4^{tro} Ex G' [Haydn later: 'Divert.'].
Op. I/2	Joseph Elssler	'Cassatio à 4^{tro} Ex E mol' [Haydn later: 'Divert:'].
Op. O	Joseph Elssler	'Cassatio à 4^{tro} Ex E mol' [Haydn later: 'Divertim'; still later, Haydn(?): 'ein nicht gestochenes quartett']

1 Haydn Society: Op. I (HSQ 1–3), 1952. Op. II (HSQ 3–5), 1954. The Schneider Quartet with Weldon Wilber and Kathleen Wilber, horns. Op. I was recorded with the Symphony 'A' (Op. I/5) dropped and 'Op. O' substituted.

| Op. I/1 | Joseph Elssler | 'Cassatio Ex b Fa' [Haydn later: 'Divertim' and, beneath, 'a quatro']. |
| Op. II/4 | Joseph Elssler | 'Divertimento à 4^{tro} Ex F'. |

[*EK*, page 4]

| Op. II/6 | Joseph Elssler | 'Divertimento Ex b Fa' [Haydn later, beneath, 'a quatro'; still later, in another hand(?), 'quartett']. |

[*EK*, page 5]

| Op. II/1 | Haydn | 'Divertimento a quatro'. |
| Op. II/2 | Haydn | 'Divertimento a quatro'. |

THE AUTHENTIC SOURCES

(1) A collection of 'VI. / Notturni. / per due Violini Violae e Basso. / Composti dal Sigl: Joseph Haydn', a pretty Rococo etiquette pasted as title on the covers of the six parts: Op. I/6, I/2, I/4, I/1, II/1 and II/6, numbered 'N.^{ro} 1' to 'N.^{ro} 6', with the stamp 'Fürnberg / Obrest Lieut', Keszthely Castle, Hungary (0/44). The individual title is in three cases (Op. I, Nos. 1, 2, 6) 'Notturno', in one case (Op. I/4) 'Cassatio'; the others have no individual title. There are two copyists: Fürnberg-Morzin Nos. 1 (first four of set) and 2 (last two). The paper is 4° and there are two types: (a) Italian, with three crescents and letter 'F'; or letters 'AS' in frame; (b) paper from a mill in the Austrian monarchy, used for Op. I/1 (watermarks: 'IGS', crowned eagle. With many additions or corrections in Haydn's hand, mostly added dynamic marks (facsimile of two pages, both copyists, with such additions in *JHW* XII/1, G. Feder & G. Greiner, frontispiece). (2) A set of two Quartets (Op. I/2 and 6), ÖNB, Vienna, S. m. 16932 with the title 'II. Divertimento [changed to "Divertimenti"] à quatro[.] Violino Primo, Violino Secundo, Viola e Basso. Del Giuseppe Haydn.' on 4° Italian paper of exactly the same kind as that used for the Hungarian source, i.e. three crescents with 'F' and 'AS' in frame, and written by Fürnberg-Morzin Copyist No. 1. (3) MS. parts, Archives of Counts von Kolovrat-Krakovský, Radenín Castle, National Museum, Prague, v 530: 'Ex E ♯ / Divertimento a quatro / à / Violino Primo / Violino 2do / Viola / è / Basso / Del Sig^{re} Giuseppe Haydn' (Op. II/2) on 4° Italian paper (watermarks: letters 'AS' under a crowned canopy, three crescents of decreasing size) by Fürnberg-Morzin Copyist No. 3, who copied the Cassatio/Divertimento for horns and strings in D (II:22) in Keszthely Castle (*vide infra*, p. 258), wherein are contained many additions in Haydn's hand. (4) MS. of the viola part of Op. I/6, Collection Else Radant Landon, University College, Cardiff, copied by Fürnberg-Morzin Copyist No. 4 on paper from a mill in the Austrian monarchy (watermarks: letters 'IGS' and star within coat-of-arms, at the top of which is a fleur-de-lys); discovered with (5) in France by Mr Hermann Baron, London, to whom we are indebted for these and the new authentic MSS. of String Trios Nos. 14 (V:15) and 15 (V:16). (5) MS. of Op. I/3 (lacking v.I), Collection Else Radant Landon, University College of Cardiff, copied by Fürnberg-Morzin Copyists Nos. 6, 7 and 9 on

paper identical to that used by Copyist No. 4 in source (4) *supra*. In view of the critical editions – which appeared before sources (4) and (5) were discovered, however – we have listed the authentic sources, but not the secondary MSS. and prints.

Critical editions: *JHW*, Reihe XII, Band 1 (G. Feder, G. Greiner) with Kritischer Bericht, 1973. Verlag Doblinger, Complete String Quartets (Opp. I and II edited by R. Barrett-Ayres, 1968), 1977, 1979.

Literature: R. Sondheimer, *Haydn. A historical and psychological study based on his quartets*, London 1951. L. Finscher, *Studien zur Geschichte des Streichquartetts. I. Die Entstehung des klassischen Streichquartetts. Von den Vorformen zur Grundlegung durch Joseph Haydn*. Kassel 1974. R. Barrett-Ayres, *Haydn and the String Quartet*, London 1974.

Some single studies: Landon, 'On Haydn's Quartets of *Opera* 1 and 2', *Music Review* XIII (1952), 181–6, with *errata* in next issue. James Webster, 'Towards a History of Viennese Chamber Music in the Early Classical Period', *Journal of the American Musicological Society* (*JAMS*), XXVII/2 (1974) with immense subsidiary literature. J. Webster, 'Haydn's String Quartets', in *Haydnfest*, Washington, D.C., 1975. J. Webster, 'The Chronology of Haydn's String Quartets', *Musical Quarterly* LXI (1975), 17–46. J. Webster, 'The Bass part in Haydn's early string quartets, *Musical Quarterly* LXIII/3 (July 1977), 390ff. J. Webster, review of Finscher's book in *JAMS* XXX, 543ff. with valuable subsidiary literature (which we have therefore omitted here).

Literature on Opus 3 (spurious Quartets attributed to Haydn in a print by Bailleux, Paris [1777?] where some of the plates were, however, originally ascribed to P. Roman Hofstetter): A. Tyson and H. C. R. Landon, 'Who composed Haydn's Op. 3?', *Musical Times* No. 1457, vol. 105 (July 1964), 506ff. H. Unverricht (with A. Gottron and A. Tyson), *Die beiden Hoffstetter*, Mainz 1968. L. Somfai, 'Zur Echtheitsfrage des Haydn'schen "Opus 3"', in *HJB* III (1965), 155–165. A brilliant summary, in which it is proposed that there are two, non-Haydn, composers of Op. 3, one for Op. III/5 and one for the rest, is contained in the latest study Øivind Eckhoff, 'The Enigma of "Haydn's Opus 3"', *Studia musicologica norvegica* No. 4 (1978), pp. 9–43. Op. 3 is not discussed in this biography since there is no persuasive evidence that Haydn had anything to do with it.

The Music

We now have superb critical editions, and many specialized studies, of Haydn's ten early quartets. Therefore, the following notes may serve as a summary of the latest scholarly opinion, to which we add some notes and queries of our own.

Haydn was very irritated when it was suggested to him that he was indebted to Sammartini; Haydn then went on to say that he invented the form by accident. There have been endless attempts to trace the real origins of Haydn's early quartets, but in most cases the arguments and illustrations remain, basically, unconvincing (e.g. Guido Adler's proposal that the string works of the German–Austrian Renaissance are the forerunners of the later quartet style, or, *pace* Geiringer 1932, pp. 35f., that a Paul Peuerl *Padouan* prepares us for Haydn's Op. I). At the time when Haydn was refuting the Sammartini influence, the Austrian master was at the pinnacle of his fame, and we believe that essentially Haydn's version, whereby (to quote the Griesinger version), there happened to be four 'friends of the art' and Haydn adapted the form for them or, if one prefers Carpani, that out of the early string trios of Haydn evolved the quartet. No doubt Fürnberg did cultivate Haydn's string trios, but it is not quite true that the early quartets come from the trios. Finscher invented the clever term, 'quartet-divertimenti' for these first ten quartets, and that is precisely what they are: quartets composed in the five-movement cassatio/divertimento form. The string trio, on the other hand, in Haydn's hands was generally in two or three movements and the trio form (unlike the quartet) was being widely practised not only in Austria but in Germany, Italy and England.

To sum up, then, Haydn remembered that the quartet originated by accident. Haydn never said that there were not precursors who wrote in four parts for strings in the division violins I, II, viola and basso (violoncello); but there is no historical evidence that there were any cassatios/divertimenti for that combination before Haydn began to compose his series.

Formally, we may sum up these ten quartet-divertimenti as follows:

> (1) Fast – Minuet/Trio – Slow – Minuet/Trio – Fast: Opus O; Op. I/1, 2, 4, 6; Op. II/1, 2, 4 – the vast majority, eight out of ten works; and
> (2) Slow – Minuet/Trio – Scherzo in 2/4 – Minuet/Trio – Fast – two works (Op. I/3, II/6) in this derivative of the *sonata da chiesa*.

Of the latter pair, one (II/6) begins with a theme and variations, while the other is in the regular tripartite adagio that we know from the string trios (here is a real derivative of that form). Clearly Haydn wrote the two works as a pair, perhaps even with a conterminous performance in mind (the concept of all these early Haydnesque pairs?).

When were the ten composed? The available evidence, despite the confusion of the Albrechtsberger 'cellist (or brother?), tends more and more to suggest that some six (Op. O; I/1, 4, 6) of these ten works were composed *c*. 1757–8 (one summer? two summers?) in Weinzierl Castle, and the others slightly later (1759–61?). That would explain their general polish and self-confidence (compared to the grammatical errors of the really early works discussed *supra*), and in turn these two elements, to which we must add the two principal ingredients – charm and wit – turned them into best-sellers overnight. More than any other category of works, these ten quartet-divertimenti established Haydn as the most popular composer of the 'new' cassatio style. Haydn no doubt called them 'cassatio' or 'notturno'; later he tried to bring some kind of order into the nomenclatural chaos of his early quartets and renamed them all 'divertimento': simpler, more orderly (the age of reason already manifesting itself in

Haydn's head?). The number of MSS. and early editions is phenomenal, and what is particularly interesting, even when Haydn had begun to write quartets in quite a different and far more intellectual manner, these early quartet-divertimenti continued to flourish; and despite all the adverse criticism, they are still very popular.

Indeed, their charm is irresistible. It is, of course, fatal to compare them to Haydn's Op. 20 or Op. 76. It is no accident that Haydn dropped the quartet-divertimento form after these ten efforts and never took it up again. It had served its purpose and been a brilliant success. Even in a remote German town like Königsberg, these quartets were played, admired and discussed, as the famous critic (and composer), J. F. Reichardt informs us in his autobiography.[1] People smiled and were amused; others, especially in the north, began to be increasingly irritated by this general style and by Haydn in particular. It is essential to remember that these quartets do not really lead anywhere; they are a cul-de-sac. Boccherini's Viennese quartets of 1761 are much more the real precursors of, say, Haydn's Op. 9.

This famous charm manifests itself in several ways. First, there are the pert, dancing melodies of the outer movements. The lightness is achieved partly by using quick metres – six eight, three-eight, two-four, never four-four or even barred C. The Italianate, singing charm of the adagios has often been remarked on. Sometimes they are 'framed' on the outside, sometimes 'framed' on the inside, as it were: an outside frame is the slow-moving four bars at the beginning of the Adagio in Op. I/1, repeated with extension at the end of the movement; a frame from within the pizzicato section that ends both the first and second parts of the Adagio in Op. I/2. Haydn achieves a murmuring, undulating background to these cantabile melodies in the adagios by repeated semiquavers (Op. I/1), by broken groups of semiquavers ♩ ♫♫ (Op. I/2) or broken groups of quavers (Op. O), by a swarming procession of triplet semiquavers (Op. II/1), by repeated quavers in three-four (Op. I/3). In Op. I/4 there is an echo effect (the authentic Hungarian source is careful to mark v.II 'con sordino Echo') in the Adagio ma non tanto between first and second violins, the second being with mute (this was an old Baroque device). Perhaps the most devastatingly charming Adagio is that to Op. I/6, which seems to presage the delightfully spurious Op. III/5 ('Serenade') Quartet as well as hosts of Boccherini, Cambini, etc.: the lower three strings are pizzicato, the first violin is muted; it is almost a movement that requires that sub-title 'amoroso'. These quartets were particularly popular in Italy, and we have MSS. in Milan, Genoa, Venice, Bologna, Rome and Naples, something that does emphatically not occur in the case of many much greater works of the 1770s. The Moravian composer Johann Friedrich Peter (1746–1813) copied a whole series of them in 1767 and 1769 and took them in 1770 to America, along with Symphony No. 17 in F, where they were among Haydn's first works to sound in the New World.

To continue, for a moment, with the slow movements, it is possible that a certain morphological progress may be observed if we compare some of the adagios in Op. II with those of Op. I: the solemn F minor Adagio of Op. II/4 is really the gateway to Haydn at Eisenstadt: although it uses precisely the same technique as the opening Adagio of Op. I/3 (three-four time, with constantly repeated quavers in the accompaniment), the melodic lines of Op. II/4 are less 'busy' and the whole is more concentrated, more quietly impressive; and the frame, this time, is the *pianissimo* close at the end of both sections, which is a device we shall encounter frequently in Haydn's music for the court at Eisenstadt in the early 1760s.

---

1 *Selbstbiographie* (ed. W. Zentner), Regensburg 1940, p. 62.

Perhaps Haydn's contemporaries believed the minuets and trios to be the most original movements of the ten quartets: they had twenty to choose from, and in which to admire the quality which was perhaps – after the gift of wit to music – the most outstanding of his long career: the ability to write new and fresh music using old moulds, in other words his prodigious source of melodic, harmonic and formal inspiration. Throughout this biography, we shall encounter minuets with that which is basically the same language as in these twenty dance movements: that sturdy sense of rhythm, that joyous sense of forward movement, and the endless variety of the trios. Some examples of the latter: v.I starts all by itself, plucking its own accompaniment and playing above it the melody (Minuet I in Op. I/3). Trio II in Op. I/3 looks forward to the 'singing lesson' in Symphony No. 6, and is equally original: the first violin and viola in octaves walk up the D minor scale in slow procession, their movement being laced with comments from second violin and 'cello. Now this procedure, one might think, would be repeated at the end of the second part: not at all, however. The middle section is the scale *downwards* on the F major scale, and the recapitulation starts on *f sharp* and reaches its top point on *b flat*. This is brilliant originality; it was not lost on Haydn's European and American contemporaries.

Fingerprints: one will serve for many. One of Haydn's innermost thoughts – it haunted him and it haunts the listener – is the way in which a pedal point is introduced, let us say, in the second part of a minuet, with the pedal point pulsating quietly (whole section marked *piano*) in repeated crotchets from the 'cello. The whole of Haydn resounds with this – not always, but always returning. Here, among these early quartets, we find it beginning the second parts of Minuet II in Op. I/3 and Minuet I in Op. II/4 (there not *p*). Another interesting, and rather obscure, 'earmark' (to use the term in the fashion of the great art historian, Giovanni Morelli)[1] is Haydn's fascination with *bariolage*, the same note being alternated on two adjacent strings: Minuet II of Op. II/2, where the *bariolage* effect is enhanced by starting *p* on the one string and 'pushing' into a *forz(ato)* for the switch-over to the next. In the second part of this 'Menuet', v. II's accompaniment is *en bariolage*. This is typical of that buffonnery in which the Viennese school excelled, and which we have touched upon in connection of Haydn's teacher, Reutter, and the mad excursion with the high trumpet in one of the *Servizio di tavola* pieces (*supra*, p. 137). We shall find the *bariolage* at crucial points in Haydn's career, in Symphony No. 28's Minuet (1765), in the 'Farewell' Symphony No. 45 (1772), and at its funniest and most eccentric in the Finale of the Quartet, Op. 50, No. 6 (1787).

The brilliant young Haydn scholar, James Webster, has written an article (see Literature), in which he suggests most persuasively that although all the authentic sources specify 'basso' for these quartets, a violoncello was nevertheless intended. On the whole, we must accept this traditional method of 'filling' the bass line, but we must, nevertheless, raise one serious doubt; and the doubt is in fact raised in the authentic notation of the music. We refer to 'Opus O',[2] in which the principal subject of the opening movement is announced in imitation, instrument by instrument, starting with the first violin,

---

1 Ernest Samuels, *Bernard Berenson, The Making of a Connoisseur*, Cambridge, Mass., 1979, *passim*.
2 This crucial point is only included in the two new authentic editions; it is found wrongly in the old editions by Marion M. Scott (Oxford University Press) and Karl Geiringer (Nagels Musikarchiv).

continuing through second violin and viola and introducing the 'cello at bar 7:

But is it the 'cello? The sources, as we say, specify 'basso', and the earliest and most reliable are quite clear in requiring this variant *every time the figure enters*, viz., also at bars 37 and 39. Now those familiar with Haydn's scores will at once realize that this curious and otherwise inexplicable phenomenon has every mark of being a simplification for the unwieldy *violone* (double bass). Haydn was meticulous in such simplifications, and one of the most spectacular occurs as late as Symphony No. 97 in C (London, 1792).[1] Otherwise the passage in the 'Opus O' Quartet makes no sense whatever.

To close this remarkable chapter in Haydn's career – his first international success – we would like to remind readers that the composer was shy and hesitant about the reception these works would have (for an eye-witness account of a Prussian officer at Rohrau Castle, *vide supra*, p. 230). It seems incredible to us in the twentieth century, but we are wise with hindsight, viewing the dozens of manuscripts that have survived – from Naples to Zagreb and from Schwerin to Paris – and the prints made in Paris, Amsterdam and London. We may reflect on Bernard van Dieren's intelligent words to Cecil Gray:

> I should think that every talented person is at first somewhat shy and suspicious of his own originality. He is inclined to believe, to fear, that the striking difference between his creations and those of others is the consequence of his technical shortcomings, and his insufficient grasp of the medium in, say, music, that serves him as a means of expression. Later, if he has overcome this, he makes the agreeable discovery that what he feared to be his insipid outlook, his clumsy and childish idiom, was nothing else but the manifestation of his individuality.
>
> [Cecil Gray, *Musical Chairs*, London 1948, p. 110]

THE DIVERTIMENTI (CASSATIOS) FOR TWO HORNS AND STRINGS
(II:21, 22)

Divertimento No. 1 in E flat (II:21)

Authentic source: MS. parts by Fürnberg-Morzin Copyist No. 1, Keszthely Castle, K 1146, with additions and corrections in Haydn's own hand. With the stamp of Lt-Col. von Fürnberg. Title: 'Divertimento / a / Violino Primo / Violino 2do / Viola / 2 Corni / e / Basso / Del Sig^re Giuseppe Haydn.' 4° Italian paper (watermarks: three crescents of declining size, letters 'AS' under crowned canopy).

Some secondary sources: (1) MS. parts, Göttweig Abbey 'Gassatio X^ma' and 'P. Leandri Staininger Professi Göttw: ao. 7̄6̄3̄'. (2) MS. parts, Melk Abbey, 'Divertimento a 6'. (3) MS. parts, Seiten-stetten Abbey. (4) MS. parts from Admont Abbey, 'Notturno festivo', now Diözesanarchiv, Graz. (5) MS. parts, Princely Archives of Oettingen-Wallerstein family, Harburg Castle (Bavaria). (6) MS. parts, Princely Archives of Thurn und Taxis family, Regensburg. (7) MS. parts, Mecklenburgische Landesbibliothek, Schwerin. (8) and (9) Two sets of Ms. parts in the Christian-Weise-Bibliothek, Zittau, both entitled 'Cassatio', one dated 24 Oct. 1781. (10) First edition, M. de la Chevardière, Paris (discussed *supra*, p. 252), announced in the *Mercure de France* in March 1766. Copy of print: Bibliothèque Nationale, Paris; Library of Congress, Washington, D.C. Later reprinted by Le Duc, Paris.

---

1 Haydn-Mozart Presse (Philharmonia) score (Landon), edited from the autograph and other authentic parts corrected by Haydn, I, bars 94ff. This passage was bowdlerized in most editions commonly used.

Critical edition: none. The edition by Vieweg Verlag, Berlin (ed. Anton Egidi, 1936) is unsatisfactory.
Literature: Landon SYM, 187f. G. Feder in *JHW* XII/1 (1973) Kritischer Bericht, esp. 65f.

Divertimento No. 2 in D (II:22)
Authentic sources: (1) MS. parts by Fürnberg-Morzin Copyist No. 3, Keszthely Castle, κ 1163, with additions and corrections in Haydn's hand (for facsimile see p. 578). With the stamp of Lt.-Col. von Fürnberg. Title: 'Divertimento / ã / Violino Primo / Violino 2ᵈᵒ / Viola / 2 Corni / e / Basso / Del Sigʳᵉ Giuseppe Haydn.' 4° Italian paper (watermarks: three crescents of decreasing size, letters 'AS' under crowned canopy). (2) MS. parts by Fürnberg-Morzin Copyist No. 1, Wallenstein Castle at Hirschberg (Doksy), now National

Museum, Prague, with additions and corrections in Haydn's hand (when we examined this source in 1959, we made no notes as to paper and watermarks).
Some secondary sources: (1) MS. parts, Admont Abbey, now Diözesanarchiv, Graz. (2) MS. parts, GdM, 'Cassatio ... P: C: H: 772'. (3) & (4) Two sets of MS. parts, Princely Archives of Oettingen-Wallerstein family, Harburg Castle, one marked 'Sinfonia' and one 'Quattro o Notturno ... P.K.H.P.M. 1773' (a similar source for Quartet, Op. II/1, also in Melk, marked 'P.K.H.P.M.'). (5) MS. parts, Mecklenburgische Landesbibliothek, Schwerin. (6) First edition, see previous work, source 10.
Critical edition: none. There is a good practical edition by Edition Peters (Ewald Lassen, 1958).
Literature: Landon, SYM, 187f. G. Feder: see previous work.

In *EK*, we find the two works on pages 3f., first No. 1: Joseph Elssler entered the work with the title 'Cassatio Ex E mol'; Haydn changed the 'Cassatio' to 'Divertim[ento]' and added beneath, 'a Sei Stromenti'; underneath is an anonymous note, 'als quartett'. No. 2 was entered by Joseph Elssler on page 4: 'Divertimento Ex D', to which Haydn added the words 'a Sei'. Later is the note, 'Bald quartet', which refers, as did the 'quartett' notice for No. 1, to the fact that Ignaz Pleyel, in his Collected Edition of Haydn's Quartets (1801 and later), included these works in the spurious arrangement of J. J. Hummel.

The pair of works is in the usual five-movement cassatio form, with the opening movements in quick metre (two-four and three-eight), and with the horns absent in the slow movements. It is, of course, impossible to date the works exactly, but the fact that both survive in MSS. from Lt-Col. von Fürnberg's collection – he was the eldest son of the gentleman for whom Haydn wrote his first quartets – with the same watermarks as on the paper of many of the early quartets in the same collection suggests that this pair of works was also written for the Fürnberg family. The corrections/additions in Haydn's hand are almost certainly before 1760, or at the latest *c*. 1760. This is not to say that Haydn will not have performed these new works for Count Morzin. The authentic copy in Hirschberg (Doksy) Castle, now ČSSR, suggests a connection with Haydn's sojourn at Lukavec Castle, as indeed do all the valuable sources owned by Count Pachta and other members of the Austro-Bohemian nobility.

Among the many interesting features of this pair of cassatios – we now take for granted Haydn's idiomatic use of the horns, both as virtuoso soloists and as harmonic 'filling' instruments – we must mention one of the most famous of Haydnesque 'fingerprints': the leading note rhythm of 𝄽 ♪♪♪ | ♩ ♪ 𝄽 which is introduced to us at bars 13f. of Cassatio No. 1 and which, in Haydn's later manner, simply takes over the middle (later development) section, dominating the proceedings for a dozen straight bars (36–47). But what is more surprising is that Haydn introduces it rather unexpectedly in the middle part of the Finale (𝄽 ♪♪♪ | ♪♪♪♪ ♪ 𝄽). Now, as it happens, there is a Viennese precedent for this 'fingerprint', and in no less a master than Gottlieb Muffat (1690–1770), whom Haydn might easily have met. Muffat was court and chamber-organist to Charles VI as well as music master to the royal children.

Consider the following extract from a *Fantasie* (MS., Österreichische Nationalbibliothek):[1]

Fantasie

Allegro

Gottlieb Muffat

[etc.]

In the slow movement of No. 1 we find a pattern very similar to that of comparable adagios in the early quartets: a lyrical melody in violin I, broken semiquaver accompaniment in the inner parts, and a pizzicato bass line. In the middle section, for a time we have another formula known to us from Opp. I and II; long melodic line over unbroken repeated semiquavers. One can see how close in style this music is to the quartet-divertimenti. There is a special surprise in store for us when we reach Minuet II, first in the extraordinary Trio with its odd melodic components (is Haydn quoting traditional folk-melodies? Balkan references?), but when the Trio is finished, we are astonished to find not the traditional *da capo* of the minuet but three variations (including one with an exceedingly difficult horn solo) which interpose themselves before the minuet is, finally, repeated.

In No. 2, there is a delightful episode in the first Presto. Just when the movement seems to be coming to a close, there is a pause and Haydn introduces three bars of Adagio, with a frilly cadence in the first violin. It is at the same time laughable and touching, and we are uncannily reminded of the antics of a *commedia dell'arte* clown: Watteau, 'tendre et peut-être un peu berger', seems to be almost foretold.

Even at this early stage in his career, Haydn had the *Ländler*, precursor of the waltz, in his blood; and we hear it, as we will in the Trio of Symphony No. 9 (1762), in Minuet I's accompaniment (⅜ ♩ ♩). This is a minuet totally different from such a movement composed by a Frenchman, German or J. C. Bach living in England: this truism has to be stated because it is the essence of this minuet that made Haydn's contemporaries sit up and take notice. (And once again: the V pedal point in part two, with gently insistent crotchets in the bass line.)

The accompaniment in this slow movement, over the now expected cantabile violin I line, features Haydn's favourite chain syncopations (middle voices); but the composer has learned since the early vocal music, and at bar 18, when we slide into a beautiful and unexpected modulation (a D major cadence is interrupted to favour a B flat followed by a six chord in E flat), these chain syncopations stop instantly, shifting unobtrusively into repeated quavers. This is already the master craftsman at work.

STRING TRIOS

The two known string trios in the collection of Lt-Col. von Fürnberg, Nos. 20 (V:D3) and 21 (V:G1), have been mentioned above. Apart from establishing the two works' authenticity – there are copious holograph corrections by Haydn in each, and both were copied by Fürnberg-Morzin No. 1 – they show that: (1) we must expect that *EK*

---

1 Dr Susan Wollenberg (University of Oxford) kindly pointed out this reference and also sent a xerox copy of the work in question.

cannot, in the nature of things, be complete (by 1765, Haydn and Joseph Elssler cannot have had to hand all the works written as long as a decade previously; (2) at least these two extremely simple works were composed presumably for the Fürnberg family, perhaps even for the children themselves (it is possible that they were performed *inter alia* by Joseph, the eldest son, later the Lieutenant-Colonel and owner of our collection, who inhabited the beautiful summer castle of Gutenbrunn in Lower Austria, built in 1771;[1] he later lived in Purkersdorf, near Vienna).

II. The Music for the Morzin Family

PIANO (HARPSICHORD) TRIOS

If the music for the Fürnberg family was primarily for strings, Count Morzin not only maintained a large (by contemporary standards) orchestra, but also a wind band (oboes or cors anglais, horns and bassoons). Apart from music composed for that group, or sections of it, we also note that Haydn suddenly began to take a renewed interest in keyboard music, presumably in this case the harpsichord (range F' to d''', perhaps a second instrument with a top of e'''), and the reason is documented for us in the Chronicle: Haydn taught harpsichord to the beautiful Countess. Although none of the autographs of the piano (harpsichord) trios has survived, we have one Concertino for harpsichord and strings (XIV:11, discussed *infra*) of which the autograph is dated 1760, a date when Haydn was in the middle of his service with the Morzin family. There is every reason, therefore, to believe that most of these early keyboard trios were composed in the Morzin period, and the fact that the principal (in some cases, *only*) MSS. are located in the Bohemian Castle of Kremsier (Kroměříž) again suggests that the Bishop Leopold Egk was a friend of the Morzins and procured copies of these trios after having heard them at Lukavec.

There are two *Urtext* editions of these early Trios, one by the present writer (Doblinger) and one by Wolfgang Stockmeier for *JHW*. Since the contents of these editions differ – ours includes several arrangements, etc., not in the edition of *JHW* – we propose to list them:

The early Trios in the edition of *JHW*

Trio in E flat	XV:36	Trio in G minor	XV:1
Trio in C	XV:C1	Trio in A	XV:35
Trio in F	XV:37	Trio in F	XV:2
Trio in B flat	XV:38	Quintet (Divertimento) for harpsichord, horns,	
Trio in E	XV:34	violin and basso (XIV:1) is discussed *infra*	
Trio in F minor	XV:f1	Trio in D	XV:33
Trio in G	XV:41	Trio in D	XV:D1
Trio in F	XV:40		

The early Trios in the edition of Doblinger

[The following notes are taken from the Preface to the new edition:]

Although our knowledge of Haydn's early keyboard trios has increased greatly in the past ten years – and in particular with the discovery of a collection of authentic sources in the Archbishop's Archives at Kremsier (Kroměříž) – much remains doubtful. We believe that the sixteen works which

---

1 Georg Dehio, *Handbuch der deutschen Kunstdenkmäler* – 'Wien, Niederösterreich und Burgenland' (Dagobert Frey and Karl Ginhart), Vienna-Berlin, 1935, p. 182. See also our pl. O. We do not know if Haydn kept up with the Fürnberg family after 1770, but very likely; he may have been a guest at the elegant Schloß Gutenbrunn, famous for its glass-blowing works. The Castle, beautifully restored, is still extant.

represent the beginning of our collected edition of Haydn's trios are all genuine works; but it is not certain that Haydn composed all of them originally as piano trios. Nos. 3, 4, the second movement of 15, and 16 all exist in early MSS. for keyboard alone, one (No. 3) in Haydn's autograph. On the other hand, the first movement of No. 15 exists only in our version, for piano trio, in a MS. at Kroměříž Castle; and it seemed only right to present it in the only form in which it has come down to us, together with the well-known variations (XVII:7).

As far as authenticity *per se* is concerned, Haydn – as is well known – was in 1803 shown a list of keyboard works prepared by Breitkopf & Härtel for their forthcoming *Oeuvres Complettes*; and Breitkopf's middleman, G. A. Griesinger, was able to transmit Haydn's opinion on each work, not only as to its authenticity but also as to its approximate date.[1] Neither Breitkopf & Härtel nor Haydn owned copies of some works which have since been, as it were, rediscovered (e.g. the great F minor Trio No. 14, which happens to exist in an authentic MS. at Kroměříž Castle). The following table may be of interest to students of these interesting early works, till recently unknown, in many cases, even to Haydn scholars.

Trio No. 1 in F	XV:37
Trio No. 2 in C	XV:CI
Trio No. 3 in G	XIV:6 and XVI:6
Trio No. 4 in F	XV:39
Trio No. 5 in G minor	XV:1
Trio No. 6 in F	XV:40
Trio No. 7 in G	XV:41
Trio No. 8 in D	XV:33 lost
Trio No. 9 in D	XV:DI lost
Trio No. 10 in A	XV:35
Trio No. 11 in E	XV:34
Trio No. 12 in E flat	XV:36
Trio No. 13 in B flat	XV:38
Trio No. 14 in F minor	XV:f1
Trio No. 15 in D	Hoboken *deest* and XVIII:7 (for trio)
Trio No. 16 in C	XIV:CI (for trio)

Nos. 1–5 are part of Hummel's Op. IV, of which Hummel's No. 6 is a work (XIV:1) with two horns which we have omitted. No. 1: recognized as genuine by Haydn. No. 2: not recognized as genuine, but in this isolated case we believe Haydn's memory was at fault; we have MS. sources just as reliable as for the other early trios, and especially that in Kroměříž Castle. No. 3: recognized as genuine by Haydn; in the *Entwurf-Katalog*; undated autograph (all these statements and documents refer to the version for

piano alone, but the trio version may be earlier or later; there is no evidence apart from the Hummel print, and the reprints by Chevardière, etc.); No. 4: consists of movements (except for the second) known to us from Haydn's sonatas for keyboard solo, viz. XVI:9^{I}; II = a 'new' movement; III = XVI:8^{I}; IV = XVI:9^{II} with XVI:5^{II} as Trio; V = XVI:9^{III}. Haydn recognized as genuine the piano sonatas XVI:5, 8 and 9. It is not known whether our No. 4 precedes, or is an arrangement of, these various movements. No. 5: recognized as genuine by Haydn; the principal MS. in the Kroměříž.

No. 6: the earliest dated reference is the Breitkopf Catalogue of 1766, where the concerto version (XVIII:7) is listed; the concerto version is probably an arrangement of the trio version. This was one of the works that neither Breitkopf & Härtel nor Haydn owned, and thus he could not give any opinion as to its authenticity. The presence of the crossed turn ('Haydn ornament') is a characteristic stylistic trait, however, and there are several good, early MSS. In one German MS. there is a doubtful additional Adagio (this movement has been printed in the Doblinger series, Diletto musicale 4) which we have omitted in our edition, since it does not appear in the other sources.

No. 7: apparently Haydn did not recognize this work (see Hoboken I, 723, but also G. Feder, *Haydn-Studien* II/4, 302n.); but we have what is patently an authentic copy by Viennese Professional Copyist No. 2 (= Fürnberg-Morzin No. 4).

No. 8: lost. Recognized as genuine by Haydn.

No. 9: lost. Not recognized as genuine by Haydn.

No. 10: recognized as genuine by Haydn. An authentic MS., from Haydn's Library is in the Esterházy Archives, Budapest; it was written by Fürnberg-Morzin Copyists Nos. 4 & 5.

No. 11: recognized as genuine by Haydn. An authentic MS. by Fürnberg-Morzin Copyist No. 1 is in Kremsier Castle (Kroměříž).

No. 12: recognized as genuine by Haydn.

No. 13: recognized as genuine by Haydn. Earliest reference: Breitkopf Catalogue of 1769 ('Terzetto di Hayden, a Cembalo, Violino e Basso'). Again, the principal MS. is in Kroměříž Castle.

No. 14: another work owned neither by B. & H. nor by Haydn; thus no opinion as to its authenticity; but an authentic copy, in Kroměříž Castle, was made by Fürnberg-Morzin Copyist No. 1. The first performance in modern times of this astonishing work took place in connection with a lecture on Haydn's trios given by the present writer for the British Broadcasting Corporation in 1967 (with the Virginia Pleasants Trio).

No. 15: in this form, the work exists only in the Kroměříž MS. The first movement was unpublished and totally unknown (Hoboken *deest*), while the second movement (XVII:7), which was recognized as genuine by Haydn, is otherwise known in a version for keyboard solo (announced in the Breitkopf Catalogue of 1766).

---

1 Pohl's MS. copy of the last letter is quoted in *JHW* XVII/1, Kritischer Bericht, p. 8 (Stockmeier, 1971).

No. 16: recognized as genuine by Haydn. The trio version is only in the MS. at Kroměříž Castle. In the Breitkopf Catalogue of 1772, the work is listed as 'I. Divertim. di Gius. Hayden, a Cemb. 2 Viol. e B.' There are two copies of the work for solo keyboard in the Österreichische Nationalbibliothek. We cannot determine whether the work was originally a piece for keyboard solo, or a piece with two violins and bass, or a piano trio; we present, as it were, the Kroměříž evidence for discussion.

In view of the existence of the two critical editions, we may dispense with a list of sources: the authentic MSS. are listed in the notes above.

Literature: G. Feder, 'Haydns frühe Klaviertrios', *Haydn-Studien* II (1970)/4. Landon, *Die Klaviertrios von Joseph Haydn* (German-English brochure), Verlag Doblinger, Vienna-Munich 1970. Since the previous belletristic and analytical literature (e.g. Cecil Gray 1940) was forced to operate in almost complete ignorance of these early trios and their sources, we have omitted it from this list. For the range of Haydn's early keyboard music, see G. Feder, 'Wieviel Orgelkonzerte hat Haydn geschrieben?', *Musikforschung* XXIII/4 (1970), 440–4.

What kind of harpsichords did the Morzin family own? Alas, the evidence of Austrian harpsichords is woefully inadequate; the rapid rise of the new fortepiano rendered the harpsichord obsolete even in the 1780s, and hardly any have survived. In fact, the only mid-eighteenth-century instrument to survive is in Graz, and even there, the evidence is inconclusive. From all the available sources, however, one may state with some confidence that Austrian harpsichords, if many existed, were built on the Italian pattern; that is, they were simple instruments of one manual with, at most, a four-foot stop (and probably that was the exception: two eight-foot stops were more usual). In their simplicity, Italian harpsichords of the period have a warm, attractive sound and were expertly built, the heirs of a long and distinguished Mediterranean tradition which was quite different from Flemish, French, British and German harpsichords in both construction and sound. The elaborate, two manual instruments of the Ruckers tradition were very little known in the Austrian monarchy.

We have suggested that Countess Morzin may have owned two instruments, perhaps one in Lukavec and one in Vienna. The usual range of Haydn's harpsichord pieces composed up to 1765 is at the upper end d''', but there are significant exceptions: the unusual Trio No. 14 reaches $d\,flat'''$, but No. 10, with its interesting opening 'Capriccio', reaches e'''. That is why, earlier, we suggested that the Countess's usual instrument reached d''' but that she owned, or perhaps specially purchased at Haydn's instigation, another instrument that went up to e''' (which she would also need for the Divertimento, XIV:1, where we find $e\,flat'''$). It was not until 1767 or thereafter that Prince Nicolaus Esterházy seems to have purchased a harpsichord (fortepiano?) that reached f''', which we find in Piano Sonata No. 20 (XVI:18). The first known Piano Trio of the middle period, No. 17 (XV:2), although arranged from an earlier baryton piece (Baryton Trio No. 103, XI:103, 1772?), makes use of the keyboard's top note f''', which automatically separates it from the earlier works. It is uncertain how these harpsichords were arranged in the bass, but they might have had what is known as a 'short octave', which meant omitting some of the lower notes. The early piano sonatas proceed down to F', but using B', B flat', A' and G'. It is curious that G sharp' (A flat') appears only in the F minor Trio No. 14.

Now Italian harpsichords of this period were generally C-oriented, i.e. with (at first) C' as the bottom note. We own a harpsichord from Castrocaro (Romagna) of the mid-eighteenth century with C' as the bottom note and e''' as the top, but there are many Italian harpsichords with: (a) that range but the bass limited by 'short octave'; (b) the bass extended downward to F', either with short octave or, more rarely, with all the notes of the scale represented. Almost all such instruments have one manual with two eight-foot registers, often coupled together forcibly in the eighteenth century.

We imagine, though without any proof, that it may have been the appearance of a new instrument that inspired Haydn to write some of these piano trios which, in expression, depth and technique go considerably beyond anything in the keyboard sonatas of the period. We shall, in the long course of this biography, find Haydn deeply involved with a form for a short period, only to drop it completely for several, even many, years. This will occur with the string quartet, which did not occupy him again until the late 1760s. It also occurs with these piano trios: the form seems to have fascinated him in the 1750s, and he wrote at least a dozen works in the form (we discount here possible arrangements, and so on).

The form that Haydn took up, in these piano trios, was that bequeathed to him in generous numbers by his Italian, German and Austrian precursors and con-temporaries. Curiously, the flourishing violin technique we find here requires better playing than in many late trios, when Haydn and his brother-composers imagined that the violin part would be played by an amateur. Perhaps the harpsichord part was for Countess Morzin and the violin for Haydn. The violoncello is always used as part of the *basso continuo* and was never expected to indulge in any solo passages at all, a role to which Haydn restricts it, with minor exceptions, throughout his piano trios, even in the 1790s.

Sometimes the harpsichord is divided into *continuo* and solo functions; when playing *continuo*, we even find, on occasion, figured bass parts (No. 1, XV:37, bars 20f., 29f., etc.; No. 13, XV:38, bar 7) in the old tradition. In other cases, even where there is no figuring, it is presumed that the harpsichord player would fill in continuo-like passages (Trio No. 7, XV:41, bars 7–12 of first movement). This retention of the old Baroque continuo is typical of the conservative tendencies not only in the young Haydn but in his Austrian contemporaries. The old trio sonata exerts a strong influence throughout, both outwardly (*sonata da chiesa*, with opening slow movement, in No. 1, XV:37) but also in the construction, say, of the first movements. In works like the Tuma trio sonatas, one noted a tendency for melody instrument I to announce the theme (II silent), and after it had been displayed, it was taken up by melody instrument II, perhaps in the dominant. We find a variant of this principle in the way the melody of Trio No. 7 (XV:41), or No. 11 (XV:34), is laid out: it is first given to the harpsichord (with or without 'cello) and then repeated by the violin, the harpsichord acting as *continuo* (not filled in for No. 7, filled in for No. 11); in these two works, the dualistic principle is continued. The outward formal pattern varies enormously. By far the most common form – in Nos. 5, 6, 10, 11, 13 and 14 – is:

Allegro moderato	Minuet/Trio	Allegro
or Allegretto		or Presto
or Moderato		(quick metre).

There are two works in church sonata form; one (No. 1) in the usual fashion of string trios of Adagio – Allegro – Minuet/Trio, and one (No. 16) in four movements, with Adagio – Presto 3/8 – Minuet/Trio – Allegro 2/4. Of the three-movement types, we have

No. 2 (XV:C1): Allegro – Minuet/Trio – Slow variations
No. 3 (XV:6): Allegro – Adagio – Minuet/Trio
No. 12 (XV:36): Allegro moderato – Polones(e) – Allegro molto 3/4

The first of the two hybrid works is:

> No. 4 (XV:39) with five movements: Allegro – Andante – Allegro – Minuet/Trio – Scherzo

(It is a curious fact this pasticcio uses movements from works otherwise known as Piano Sonatas, Nos. 1 [XVI:8], 2 [XVI:7] and 8 [XVI:5], but it is by no means certain if the keyboard solo versions are authentic, especially No. 8, which is also very like a pasticcio itself: the individual movements of all these works all appear to be genuine Haydn, but we would like to propose that some of them may have originated as single movements, 'lessons', for pupils and have been put together as sonatas or trios, sometimes by Haydn, sometimes by friends, pupils or, indeed, the clever Viennese copyists. We cannot know the role of Haydn's scriptorium in all these matters, but the composer may have allowed them a certain artistic licence in preparing such works for commercial purposes.)

The second hybrid work is:

> No. 15: Allegro molto leading into – Slow variations

(Again, the individual works appear to be genuine, and as we have seen, the variations are known for harpsichord solo as XVII:7; the opening movement, or glorified swift introduction, is quite an original and quixotic piece, but we shall never know its original purpose.)

There is no doubt that Haydn was not only entranced by the keyboard trio but that he seems to have regarded it as a *weightier* form than the current cassatio-divertimento form, in which most of his other works of this period – except, of course, symphonies, concertos and works for the church – were written. The way in which Haydn attempts to make the trio more solid may be seen in several technical devices, of which the first is the use of a 'larger' metre for the opening movements (four-four and three-four as opposed to two-four, six-eight, three-eight); now this is not to accuse Haydn of formalism, and both here and in the symphonies, he also uses, and to great effect, the more traditional quicker metres for first movements; but the sudden shift to common time and three-four strikes one immediately. Leaving aside entire opening slow movements, we note:

> Common time (4/4): Nos. 2, 3, 5, 13, 14.
> Three-four: No. 10.

To show the change, one need only compare the beginnings of the quartets of this period, where (again apart from opening slow movements) there are only quick metres. Side by side with this increased metrical weight, we may observe that Haydn has also begun to break away from the double thematic announcement which we described above (that is, first harpsichord, then violin); and in these very works with the heavier metre, there is occasionally no strict division between the harpsichord's right hand and the violin: both share the proceedings (cf. especially Nos. 5, 10).

Haydn is never at a loss for variety, either in formal construction or in exotic importations, such as the *polonese* which he unexpectedly introduces into No. 12 (XV:36): when we first encountered one of the principal manuscripts of this (then unpublished) work at Göttweig, shortly after the Second World War, we wondered what the monks must have thought of this new and rhythmically eccentric movement; it is, however, not unique in Haydn's *œuvre*, and we shall meet the Polish dance again in the 'Twelve Cassationsstücke' (XII:19) which Haydn composed to amuse Prince Nicolaus Esterházy in the 1760s.

Perhaps the most original and intellectually stimulating movement of these early trios is the dazzling Allegretto of No. 10 (XV:35), which is marked 'Capriccio'. Haydn retained a manuscript of this work – partly written by Fürnberg-Morzin Copyist No. 4 – all his life; perhaps the work's inception, or first performance, was a turning-point in its composer's career (consider that Haydn also kept the epochal autograph *and* a complete set of parts of Symphony 'Le Midi' No. 7, 1761). Certainly the use of the word 'Capriccio' always meant a movement of the highest inspiration for Haydn: we think of the greatest movement of the 'Paris' Symphonies, the slow movement ('Capriccio') of No. 86; and nearer to hand, we recall the most daring and technically brilliant of Haydn's youthful keyboard works, the *Capriccio* 'Acht Sauschneider' (discussed later in this volume, p. 549). Here note that, as in the other two cases mentioned above, Haydn chooses the three-four metre: this cannot be accidental, and its application here, coupled with the slowish tempo 'Allegretto', must have come as a revelation to Countess Morzin and her cultivated circle. 'Capriccio' seems to have meant, for Haydn, a kind of C. P. E. Bach rondo or ritornello form, which Haydn adapted and transformed for his purposes. One at once sees a new harpsichord technique, quite different from that found in the other trios (cf. the dazzling use of the old Baroque violin 'broken chords', which we all adore in J. S. Bach and Vivaldi, here applied to the harpsichord's right hand, bars 78ff., ♪♪♪ ♪♪♪ ♪♪♪ ; anyone familiar with Bach's transcriptions of Vivaldi for the keyboard will know that the technique works equally well for the harpsichord). We are on entirely new ground here. Part of the movement's hypnotic fascination is the relentless forward drive in a tempo which is deliberately slower than allegro, so that the repeated quavers in the harpsichord's left hand, which begin at bars 10ff. and are used with near-maniacal intensity without a break in bars 40–54, appear to burst the frame of the music in one incredible block during the development (bars 74–98): we are close to the great *Fandango* by Soler, which Haydn certainly did not know (unless by a very freakish accident). There is also a careful attempt, in Trio No. 10, to link the structure, spirit and motivic pattern of the Finale to this opening Capriccio, and also to the central Minuet/Trio.

The most immediately compelling works of the series are the two in minor keys, the first (as it would seem) works in the minor that Haydn ever composed. The very presence of these two unusual pieces serves to confirm Haydn's serious view of the form as a whole. Until the end of the 1760s, Haydn's taking a work particularly seriously often meant composing it in old-fashioned language – hence the sudden proliferation of fugues (in minor keys, sometimes) in Op. 20, the great Quartets of 1772, and before them, in the *Missa Cellensis* of 1766. The G minor Trio No. 5 (XV:1) was known in the nineteenth century because Breitkopf & Härtel was able to procure a copy and include it in the *Oeuvres Complettes*. It begins for all the world like a dignified Baroque trio sonata, with its 'sighing' motifs in the violin and stiff, dotted patterns in the harpsichord; and the rapid scales preceded by ♪ ♪♪ ♪ (bars 8f.) take us back to Caldara or Tuma. Now that he is involved in this antiquated Baroque language, Haydn soon finds a formula which particularly attracts him and which we can trace in many works of this period, the combination of chain dotted passages and trills:

[Moderato]

[etc.]

We also note those Haydnesque syncopations (bars 67, 69, etc.) which have haunted him since his days as a choir-boy and will appear with almost eerie regularity in his music throughout the 1760s.

In all Haydn's minor works of the 1750s and 1760s, one notes a unity of purpose which he will later gladly abandon (for a typical 'abandoned' work in the minor, see Symphony No. 83, of which only the first movement is in G minor). This means not only the unity of key but also the unity of movements in themselves (Symphony No. 49, 'La Passione' is one of the great cases in point): as a small but characteristic example of this, the Trio of this work, in B flat (all the other movements, including the Minuet, are in G minor), which is a lyrical violin solo, has a harpsichord accompaniment in which at some 'level' there are three crotchets, usually repeated, and the pattern ♪♩♫ throughout the entire movement. The Finale is another case in point: Haydn takes the typical cassatio metre of three-eight and turns it into a powerful, restless and compelling Finale, which in some details, such as that grimly repetitious pattern at bars 20ff.,

Cemb. r.h.

takes us without regard to chronology straight into the world of the *Sturm und Drang* a dozen years later. (The passage is, of course, repeated in the tonic at the end of the movement.) The secret of this sense of power is the way in which Haydn uses repetitions, and it is one of the central pillars of his style in the 1760s; first in an ebullient, exhilarating fashion (as in the fabulously repetitive development section in Symphony No. 24/I, *infra*, p. 568) and later in a more sinister context (Symphony No. 26/I, 'Lamentatione', Finales to Symphonies Nos. 49 and 52). Here we have it presented, fully-fledged.

The other work in minor was first presented in modern times – perhaps for the first time in about two hundred years – on a Third Programme concert of the British Broadcasting Corporation in 1967, and people wondered how a piece of this strength and (in the composer's *œuvre*) importance could have been hidden from us all these years. It, too, is in the severe, 'strenge Styl' (as Haydn would have said), with the dotted rhythms, scales upwards, syncopations in huge chains (bars 12–14, the pattern presented six times in a row), syncopations attached to triplet figures – all the Morellian 'earmarks' of Haydn's new Morzin style. His keyboard technique has become immeasurably more sophisticated, and his formal grasp is impeccable; but more important, here again we have that unity of purpose that distinguishes this F minor Trio from the early piano sonatas. Both Minuet and Trio are in F minor, and Haydn uses a simple but devastatingly effective way to bind both into a whole; the pattern of four semiquavers. We find it moving downwards in six bars of the Minuet and in no less than nineteen bars of the Trio (note the acceleration of use). All three movements are inexorably linked together by the similar pattern of their principal themes (*c* to *f*, *f* to *e* natural being the two central pinions of operation).

Allegro moderato

(In the example, the reverse of *c* to *f*, viz. *f* to *c*, is simply shown by bracketing the sign involved.) Similar to the Trio of the work in G minor No. 5, the Finale of No. 14 contains a long violin solo in both exposition and recapitulation – but also in the development – where the right hand of the harpsichord continues throughout in this fashion: ♪ ♫♫ ♪ ♫♫ . This occurs during 13 + 9 = 13 bars and is symmetrically matched by another pattern that also occurs at strategic places, as follows

♩. ♫ | ♩. ♫ (bars 5f., 10f., 28–31 :‖: 45f., 49f., 77f., 95–8).

This is sometimes counterbalanced by a figure in contrary motion in the violin: ♪ ♫ ♩ – and it all goes to show that Haydn has swiftly grasped the unifying power of rhythmic-melodic figures. It was to be the basis of his style and the foundation of his intellectual approach to sonata form. We see it displayed for the first time in a wholly serious manner in these fine piano trios. Before proceeding to the logical continuation of Haydn's music for the Morzin family, the symphony, we must make a brief excursion (as we have every reason to believe Haydn did, in the midst of trio and symphony) to (1) some different types of keyboard works, and (2) some interesting divertimenti in which we may see Haydn raising to a new level of beauty a form of music which was designed, also no doubt for the Morzins, as, literally, *Tafelmusik*.

DIVERTIMENTI (CONCERTINI) FOR HARPSICHORD AND STRINGS (TWO VIOLINS AND BASS)

XIV:11 in C
Principal sources: (1) Autograph, formerly EH, Eisenstadt (now lost); title: 'Concertino per il Cembalo [middle:] In Nomine Domini [right:] Giuseppe Haydn 7̄6̄0̄'. An accurate copy of the autograph made by C. F. Pohl, GdM VII 41 012. (2) MS. parts, Staatsbibliothek, Berlin, Mus. ms. 10.069; 'Concertino in C . . . Par Monsieur Joseph Haydn.' (3) MS. parts, Göttweig Abbey, at present lost. (4) MS. parts, Archbishops' Library, Kremsier (Kroměříž), II F44: 'Concerto'.
Critical editions: G. Henle Verlag, Munich (H. Walter, 1970). Verlag Doblinger, Diletto Musicale 21 (Landon, 1959).

XIV:12 in C
Principal sources: (1) MS. parts, Staatsbibliothek, Berlin, Mus. ms. 10.070; 'Concerto / per il Cembalo / 2 Violini / e / Basso / Del Sig: Haydn. /

[First bar of harpsichord part].' (2) MS. parts, Mecklenburgische Landesbibliothek, Schwerin: 'Concerto in C . . . del Sig.ᵉ Giusep: Haidn.' (3) MS. parts, Archbishops' Library, Kremsier (Kroměříž), II F22: 'Partitta'.
Critical editions: G. Henle Verlag, Munich (H. Walter, 1970). Verlag Doblinger, Diletto Musicale 323 (Landon, 1969).

XIV:13 in G
Principal sources: A manuscript was formerly in Göttweig Abbey but no longer exists. (1) MS. parts, Princely Archives of the Fürstenberg family, Donaueschingen Castle (Germany): 'Concerto à Cembalo conc: Violino 1ᵐᵒ, Violino 2ᵈᵒ e Basso Del Sig: Giuseppe Hayden.'
Critical editions: G. Henle Verlag, Munich (H. Walter, 1970). Schott, Mainz (Ewald Lassen, 1955).

XIV:C2 in C

Principal source: MS. parts, Archbishops' Library, Kremsier (Kroměříž), II F31: 'Divertimento. / Per il Clavicembalo. / con / Due Violini / e / Basso. / Di Giuseppo Haÿdn. / [*incipit*]'

Critical editions: G. Henle Verlag, Munich (H. Walter, 1970). Verlag Doblinger, Diletto Musicale 325 (Landon, 1969).

Clavicembalo. / Violino Primo. / Violino Secondo. / Con / Basso. / Del Signore Giuseppe Haÿdn.'

Critical editions: G. Henle Verlag, Munich (H. Walter, 1970). Verlag Doblinger, Diletto Musicale 324 (Landon, 1969).

XVIII:F2 in F

Principal source: MS. parts, Archbishops' Library, Kremsier (Kroměříž), II F43: 'Concerto / Per Il /

Hoboken *deest* in D

For a description of this work, Kremsier II F14 (A3001), *vide supra*, p. 227.

One of these pieces is dated 1760 and is therefore, one presumes, composed for the Morzin family. Probably these were the kind of attractive pieces for Countess Morzin that Haydn could compose of a morning, give to the copyists in the afternoon, and play with the Countess in the evening. If the whole orchestra was not, shall we say, at Lukavec Castle, two violins and a small 'chamber' *violone* (double bass) could establish a group capable of accompanying dozens of smaller concertos by Haydn and others. The one autograph is entitled 'Concertino'; we have used the title generically for all these works. They are all in three movements and are miniature concertos: we have seen that Haydn's precursors also made a distinction between large and small keyboard concertos. Actually, Haydn has even managed to subdivide the concept, for among these concertini are both small and smaller works: the small are simply miniature concertos in the conventional order of moderately quick/quick (Moderato, Allegro moderato, Allegro) – Adagio – Allegro (Allegro assai, Presto). In this form are cast all except one (XIV:C2). Usually Haydn does not have time to create ritornelli but in the slow movements he sometimes manages to create the illusion of a miniature concerto movement, complete with tiny ritornelli (XIV:11). Unlike the piano trios, which are major works (albeit on a small scale), these concertini are intended to delight and are, like the early piano sonatas, 'lessons' in the old sense of the British title page. XIV:C2 is, as we say, a further subdivision, in that there are only two movements, Allegro moderato and Minuet only. With all repeats, the whole piece lasts $2\frac{1}{2}$ minutes, and we believe that this was not intended for the Countess Morzin but perhaps for one of the children – and what a delight for a child to be playing a genuine miniature concertino with *Capellmeister* Haydn and the other musicians in their elegant *livrée*. The technique necessary is so absurdly simple that there is almost no other possible explanation. In view of the alacrity with which Haydn composed real concertos for his brother musicians in the Esterházy *Capelle*, we believe it to have been in his character to provide the 'Mitzi', 'Sepperl' or 'Mariedl' among the *gräfliche Kinder* with such a surprise offering. Of course, we cannot date any except one of these pieces, but the division we have made between Morzin and Esterházy concertini is according to the sources in the Esterházy Archives (one work dated 1764). The present works do not exist in the Budapest collection (XIV:11 was at Eisenstadt Castle but it was dated 1760 and Haydn obviously took it with him when he left Morzin service); the others, examined *infra* (pp. 544ff.) do. It is an arbitrary division, but such a division existed and we have adhered to it, too.

DIVERTIMENTO IN E FLAT FOR HARPSICHORD, TWO HORNS, VIOLIN AND BASS (XIV:1)

Principal sources: (1) Authentic MS. parts by Fürnberg-Morzin Copyist No. 4, Archbishops' Library, Kremsier (Kroměříž), II G. 18. 'In Dis /

Divertimento / per il / Clavi Cembalo / Violino / 2 Corni oblig. / e / Basso / Del Sigre Giuseppe Haydn' on 4° Italian paper (watermarks: three crescents of decreasing size and comet for cemb., for rest three crescents of decreasing size over 'M', letters 'AS' under a crowned canopy. (2) MS. parts, Schlägl Abbey (Upper Austria): 'Divertimento / di / Clavicembalo / a / Violino Solo / due Corni In Eb / e / Basso / Del Sig^re: Hayden' on 4° Italian paper (watermarks: three crescents of declining size with letters 'REAL', latter 'w' in elaborate frame. (3) MS. parts, St Peter's Abbey, Salzburg, with the horn soli worked into the violin parts. (4) MS. parts, Sächsische Landesbibliothek, Dresden, Mus. 3356/Q/23 with substitute parts in alto clef for viola or horn. (5) MS. parts, Staatsbibliothek, Berlin, Mus. ms. 10.062, also with substitute parts in alto clef for viola or horn. (6) First edition by J.J. Hummel, Amsterdam, November 1767:[1] 'Six / Sonates / pour le / clavecin / avec l'accompagnement / d'un violon & violoncelle / composées / par / Giuseppe Haydn / à Vienne /

Opera Quatrième / ... / A Amsterdam chez J.J. Hummel, / Marchand & Imprimeur de Musique / N°. 89 – Prix f 5.' Copy in the Hoboken Coll., ÖNB, Vienna. Includes Trios Nos. 1 (XV:37), No. 2 (XV:C1), No. 3 (XIV:6; XVI:6), No. 4 (XV:39), No. 5 (XV:1) and the present work, for which there are parts for viola I, II and horns I, II. Reprints by Chevardière, Paris, c. 1771 (copy: Bib. Nat., Paris), Bremner, London, 1772 (announced 13 Feb. 1772, *Public Advertiser*; copies British Museum, Burgenländisches Landesmuseum).
Critical edition: *JHW*, Reihe XVII, Band 1 and Kritischer Bericht (W. Stockmeier, 1971).

1 Cari Johannson, *J. J. & B. Hummel Music-Publishing and Thematic Catalogues*, Stockholm 1972, vol. I, p. 24 – announced in the *Haagsche Courant*, 11 November 1767.

It is presumed that this original and lambent music was composed c. 1760 for Count Morzin: the authentic source by the fourth Fürnberg-Morzin copyist in the Kremsier Archives suggests, as before, a connection with Lukavec Castle. It was, indeed, a stroke of brilliant imagination to use the horns in this chamber musical fashion, just as they are sometimes shown in eighteenth-century drawings, beside a harpsichord and a couple of string players, with perhaps a singer. The players of Count Morzin's horns, as we know from the music Haydn composed for them, were among the greatest of their age, and indeed among the greatest, perhaps, of all time. Here they are used in that dual fashion for which they were admirably suited, as harmonic fillers and as virtuoso soloists. Haydn cleverly avoided a slow movement to avoid tiring the players' lips (similarly, we shall see how he solves this problem in the wind band music), and the three movements are Moderato – Minuet/Trio – Finale: Presto, with a finely shaped C minor Trio for contrast. The first movement is in square eight-eight time, and the interplay between strings/horns/harpsichord is delightful throughout; while in the Finale we have a characteristic rhythmic motif at the beginning that provides the movement's thrusting forward drive (♪ | ♪♪♪♪ | ♪♪). It is the first, perhaps, of a long series of sophisticated and unconventional chamber pieces with horn, of which we shall be examining many in the 1760s and 1770s, but no longer with a keyboard instrument. In the future, much of the horns' brightest music for the chamber will be with baryton; thus, the presence of the horns together with the harpsichord once again suggests the beautiful Countess Morzin.

DIVERTIMENTI FOR WIND BAND

II:15 in F

Scoring: 2 ob., 2 bsn., 2 hns.
Principal sources: (1) Autograph (breaks off in 5th movt., bar 18),[1] Archives of the Counts Harrach, Vienna (cat. 784) with title at head of first page of music: 'Divertimento [middle:] In Nomine Domini [right:] Giuseppe / Haydn / 760' (later '1' added, not by Haydn, making '1760'). On oblong Italian paper (watermark: three crescents of declining size, vertical lines). (2) MS. parts from

1 Complete facsimile in *HJB* I (1962).

the Archives of the Counts von Clam Gallas, National Museum, Prague, cat. 423 (formerly Friedland Castle), No. 3 of 6 divertimenti for wind band. Title: [later: 'N.° 3 Clam Gallas'] 'Divertimento: In: F: / Oboe: Primo: Oboe: 2do: / Cornuo: Primo: Cornuo: 2do / Fagotto: Primo: / Fagotto: 2do: / Del: Sig Josephi: Haydn:'. (3) MS. parts, same archives, cat. 369. 'Parthia in F / 2 oboe / 2 Corni / con / 2 Fagotti / [*incipit*] Del Sigl: Haydn.' Both these sources on local paper (watermarks of source 2, on small, thickish paper of oblong format, 21·5 × 17 cm.: coat-of-arms, crown, letters 'GM' [?]). There are corrections showing that the parts were used in performance. *Critical edition*: Verlag Doblinger, Diletto Musicale 29 (Landon, 1959), also in collected edition: Divertimenti (Feld-Parthien) in pocket score Stp. 180.

II:23 in F

Scoring: 2 ob., 2 bsn., 2 hns.
Principal sources: (1) Fragment of the autograph, Staatsbibliothek, Berlin, Mus. ms. autogr. Jos. Haydn 8, from Artaria & Co., containing movements IV (under ob. I 'Incipit lamentatio' in Haydn's hand) and V, on oblong Italian paper (watermarks: three crescents of declining size, vertical lines). (2) MS. parts from the Archbishops' Archives, Kremsier (Kroměříž), IV B39: 'Parthia in F: / â / Oboa ... 2 / Corni ... 2 / Fagoti [*sic*] ... 2 / Del: Sigl: Haydn.' (3) MS. parts, Clam Gallas Archives, Prague, 423, No. 4 of 6 divertimenti. Title: [later: 'N.º 4 Clam Gallas'] 'Divertimento: In: F: / Oboe: Primo: oboe: 2do: / Fagotto: Primo: Fagotto: 2do: Corno: Primo: Corno 2do: / Del: Sigl: Josephi: Haydn.' Paper etc., *vide supra*. (4) MS. parts, same archives, 371, where the whole work is in G major: 'Parthia in G: / a / oboa Primo / oboa 2do / 2 Corni / 2 Fagotti: / [*incipit*] del Sigl Haÿden:'. Between the 4th and 5th movements is inserted an additional Allegro which is probably a local interpolation; it is printed as an Appendix to the Doblinger edition (pocket score, p. 18). (5) MS. parts, Melk Abbey, where the work was arranged for string quartet. On the cover: 'Francisci Helm Rhetoris 1765' (about whom, *vide infra*, p. 588). *Critical edition*: Doblinger, Diletto Musicale 30 (for details, see II:15).

II:7 in C

Scoring: 2 ob., 2 bsn., 2 hns.
Principal sources: (1) MS. parts, Clam Gallas Archives, Prague, 423, No. 1 of 6 divertimenti. Title: [later: 'N.º 1 Clam Gallas'] 'Diverdimento [*sic*] In: C: / 2: oboe: / 2: Fagotto: / 2: Corni: / Del: Sigl Josephi: Haydn.' Paper &c., *vide supra*. (2) MS. parts, Archives of the Princes von Thurn und Taxis, Regensburg, J. Haydn 90: 'Divertimento Ex C / a / 6 Vocibus / Oboe 1mo / Oboe 2do / Cornu Primo. Cornu Secondo. / Fagotto Primo: Fagotto Secondo: / Authore: Haydn.' Local paper. *Critical edition*: Doblinger, Diletto Musicale 31 (for details, see II:15).

II:14 in C

Scoring: 2 clarinets in C, 2 horns in C (*basso*?).
Principal sources: (1) Autograph, State Library, Leningrad (for history, see Doblinger edition): 'Divertimento [right:] Giuseppe Haydn 761' (2) MS. parts from the 19th century, perhaps copied from the autograph, GdM VIII. 23.669. *Critical edition*: Doblinger, Diletto Musicale 32 (for details, see II:15).

II:D18 in D

Scoring: 2 oboes (2 clarinets?), 2 bsn., 2 hns.
Principal sources: (1) MS. parts, Kremsier, 'N°: 3

Parthia Del Sigⁿᵒʳ Haydn', No. 3 of 6 divertimenti, IV B198; each part dated '1766'. Parts marked 'Oboe Primo ed Clarinetto' (I, II), but at head of parts 'Oboe Primo', 'Oboe Secondo'. Between 5th and 6th movements is an interpolated Allegro, not by Haydn, reproduced in Doblinger ed. as Appendix (pocket score, p. 32). (2) MS. parts, Melk Abbey, where the work was arranged for string quartet. On the cover: 'Francisci Helm, Rhetoris 1765.' (3) MS. parts were formerly in Göttweig Abbey, dated 'P: Leandri 1765', arranged for 2 v., 2 vc. (not 1 as in Hoboken I, 342) and 2 hns. *Critical edition*: Doblinger, Diletto Musicale 33 (for details, see II:15).

II:3 in G

Scoring: 2 ob., 2 bsn., 2 hns.
Principal sources: (1) MS. parts, Clam Gallas Archives, Prague, 423, No. 5 of 6 divertimenti. Title: [later: 'N.º 5 Clam Gallas'] 'Diverdimento: [*sic*]" [later: "in G."] / 2: Cornui: " / 2: oboe: " / 2: Fagotto: " / ♯ / Del: Sigᶫᵒ: Josepho: Haÿden: '". (2) MS. parts, 1766, Kremsier (see II:D18, source 1). Title (ob. I): '[No.] 6 Parthia del Sigⁿᵒʳ Haydn.' *Critical edition*: Doblinger, Diletto Musicale 84 (for details, see II:15).

In G major (Hoboken *deest*)

Scoring: 2 ob., 2 bsn., 2 hns.
Principal sources: MS. parts, Clam Gallas Archives, Prague, 423, No. 6 of 6 divertimenti. Title: [later: N.º 6 Clam Gallas] 'Parttia [*sic*]: Ex: G: / oboe: Primo: / oboe: 2do: / Corno: Primo: / Corno: 2do: / 2: Fagotto: / Del: Sigᶫ.ʳᵉ Josepho: Haÿdn: '". (2) MS. parts, 1766, Kremsier (see II:D18, source 1). Title: 'N°: 2: Parthia: Del Signor Haydn.' Here, the work is in C major; from various technical aspects, it would appear that G is the original key: there would be no point in transposing such a work from C to G, but every reason to rewrite a G major work, with its fearfully high horns, into C. Since II:3 was entered in *EK* by Joseph Elssler in G, we know that Haydn actually wrote such fearful horn parts in G; therefore we presume the present work was also composed in G. *Critical edition*: Doblinger, Diletto Musicale 85 (for details, see II:15).

In D major (Hoboken *deest*)

Scoring: 2 ob., 2 bsn., 2 hns.
Source: MS. parts, Clam Gallas Archives, Prague, 423, No. 2 of 6 divertimenti. Title: [later: 'N.º 2 Clam Gallas'] 'Divertimento: Ex: D: / 2: oboe Primo: 2do: / 2: Cornui: " / 2: Fagotto: " / Del: Sigl: Josepho: Haÿdn: '". *Critical edition*: Doblinger, Diletto Musicale 66 (for details, see II:15).

Literature for series: Pohl I, 326. Landon, *SYM*, 188–91.

DOUBTFUL AND SPURIOUS WORKS

It will not be within the scope of this biography to treat of the many doubtful and spurious works attributed to Haydn except in certain specific instances. There is a substantial body of such wind-band music, including the six *Feldparthien*, II:41–6 (with the 'Chorale St. Antoni' which Johannes Brahms used for his 'Variations on a Theme by Haydn', Op. 56a), for which there is no satisfactory evidence whatever of Haydn's authorship: the stylistic content of II:41–6 is totally foreign to Haydn's wind-band writing, and the only source – from which all others derive – is the set of parts in Zittau, a notoriously unreliable archive as far as Haydn is concerned. Zittau probably acquired their copies from Breitkopf, which announced the works in their catalogue of 1782–4. The other spurious wind-band pieces are gradually being identified: the rather well-known *Parthia*, II:F7, is by one of the Wranizkys, while II:B7, which is of course in E flat (one of Hoboken's specialities is confusing transposing notation of cors anglais and clarinet), has been attributed to both Mozart and the Bath clarinettist Joseph Morris (Roger Hellyer

in *HJB* IX, 354). There is one much more interesting work which we would like to mention here. It is the following Divertimento in F (Hoboken *deest*) which we found, together with all the other wind-band works here mentioned, in the National Museum, Prague, in the former Clam Gallas Archives, Schloß Friedland (Frýdlant):

There is no title page, and on the last page of the horn part is the curt note, 'Nº 9 Hayden'. The MS. is written on Italian paper in oblong format (watermarks: three crescents of declining size with letter 'F', jagged vertical chain lines, ornament with fleur-de-lys); cat. 566. We cannot see that there are either persuasive stylistic characteristics, or satisfactory source material, sufficient to warrant this pretty piece to be considered as Haydn's.

The Bohemians were famous, in the 1750s, not only for the superb standard of their horn playing but also for their virtuoso command of wind instruments altogether; and one of the great Bohemian specialities was wind-band music, to which the present Czechoslovakian archives bear eloquent testimony.[1] There seems little doubt that Haydn came into direct contact with this *genre* as a result of his stay in Lukavec. We have no information about Haydn's movements in Bohemia: was he taken to the great castles of Morzin's friends, such as Kremsier and Friedland (of Bishop Egk and Count Clam Gallas, respectively)? Did he go to Prague? At any rate, Haydn suddenly began to compose wind-band divertimenti: some are listed in *EK*, of which not all survive. Until recently, the only known works of this kind were II:7 (which Adolf Sandberger issued in 1935) and II:14 (which Hermann Reichenbach issued in 1932). The opening of the Bohemian and Moravian archives in the late 1950s completely revolutionized our knowledge of these works and changed our knowledge of Haydn's activities for Count Morzin.

It is difficult to date these works. The fact that II:15's autograph of 1760 was in the Archives of the Counts Harrach does not necessarily mean that Haydn composed it in 1760 for the then reigning Count, Franz Anton (1720–68); on the contrary, we believe that Haydn gave this early autograph as a keepsake to Carl Leonhard, Count von Harrach (1765–1831), with whom he was on friendly terms (the Count had erected a monument to Rohrau's greatest son in 1793; perhaps when Haydn went to see it, he returned the compliment by presenting the family with a keepsake of his early handwriting). There is no record that in 1760, Franz Anton had a wind band; only that Haydn performed quartets at Schloß Rohrau about 1757 at which the Prussian Major Weirach (*supra*, p. 230) was present as a prisoner of war. On the evidence of the date, 1760, it is much more likely that Haydn composed it for his patron, Count Morzin; and the fact that almost all these *Feld-Parthien* in their original scoring (i.e. not in the arrangements of Melk and Göttweig, which suggest that the two monasteries found

1 The principal sources for the wind-band *Parthien* (divertimenti) of Haydn's Bohemian and Moravian precursors are to be found in the National Museum, Prague; in Kremsier (Kroměříž); in the Janáček Museum in Brno; in the Schwarzenberg Archives at Krumau (Český-Krumlov); and in the Archives of the Princes von Fürstenberg, Donaueschingen (the two latter libraries being primarily of interest for wind-band music of a slightly later date). For interesting and accurate information about the Kremsier band in the late 1750s, see J. Sehnal, 'Das Musikinventar des Olmützer Bischofs Leopold Egk aus dem Jahre 1760 als Quelle vorklassischer Instrumentalmusik', *Archiv für Musikwissenschaft* XIX (1972).

difficulty in mounting works for wind band alone) have survived only in Bohemian/Moravian sources, would seem to indicate that they circulated from Lukavec rather than Vienna (no known copies by professional Viennese scribes are known).

Some of the entries of these works in *EK*, such as II:7, are in Haydn's own hand: forgotten by Joseph Elssler? Or composed while Haydn was in Eisenstadt? We have learned that Prince Paul Anton Esterházy could give a concert in his Viennese palace in 1761 using clarinets (*infra*, p. 362): that might be the origin of II:14 which is scored for clarinets. It might also be the origin of the lost Divertimento, II:4, and also II:5 (originally a lost wind-band piece with clarinets, it has survived in an arrangement for baryton as a 'Quintetto'),[1] in which – as *EK* informs us, both entries being in Haydn's own hand – clarinets figured. There was certainly no problem for Haydn to perform wind-band divertimenti at Vienna or Eisenstadt for the normal sextet of oboes (or cors anglais), bassoons and horns, but it seems possible that it was Haydn who (a) suggested to Prince Paul Anton to engage the necessary players to allow for this possibility; (b) introduced the *genre* to the Esterházy Court. In the 1759 Catalogue[2] of the Esterházy Archives, there is no mention whatever of wind-band music. This in itself does not preclude the existence of such music, which would perhaps have been kept in a separate archive by the princely grenadiers; but the pay lists, etc., make it difficult to think that, prior to the Spring of 1761, Werner could organize players – for two oboes, two bassoons and two horns – of sufficient ability to master this exceedingly difficult music: otherwise, why did Haydn at once replace the Eisenstadt bassoon players? And why were two new oboists engaged in April 1761? And two horn players in June 1761? The evidence is overwhelming that 'Feld-Harmonie', or the cultivation of wind-band music, was one of the many innovations that Haydn brought to Prince Paul Anton Esterházy's Court at Vienna and, later, Eisenstadt.

We have thus grouped all this wind-band music together, and the reader will have to imagine that it was first composed for Lukavec, probably quite literally 'pour la table', and later imported to Vienna and Eisenstadt. Probably Haydn ceased writing on a large scale for the *genre* about 1765, when the Court, under Nicolaus 'The Magnificent', began to move to Eszterháza; though there is some evidence that he composed the occasional march for the grenadiers at Eszterháza. Most of the extant pieces are in conservative keys, i.e. C, F, G and D; but in *EK* we have lost works in A (no *incipit* in this case; II:20*bis*) and E flat (II:12; *EK* says specifically 'Ex E mol'. and above *incipit*, 'Corno Inglese'; probably also II:4, if the theme is for B-flat clarinet; if for A-clarinet, the work is in D major; II:5 was probably noted down, in its original state, for A-clarinet, because the transcription is in D major; the entry in *EK* on p. 2, in Haydn's hand, is in F major, but Haydn notes, to the left, that the instruments included '2 Clarinetti 2 Corni' and, presumably, bassoon[s]).

Haydn uses the five-movement divertimento form – allegro, minuet/trio, adagio, minuet/trio, presto. Because of the *genre*'s scoring, i.e. wind instruments unsupported, Haydn takes care not to write long movements: there are great technical difficulties, especially for the horns, which were expected to play exposed *g″*, but always within short movements. The Adagio of II:15 consists of twice eight bars (both repeated). Haydn is extremely adept with the scoring, and the pieces sound magnificent. One feature which must have struck the contemporary listener is the curious sense of poignancy engendered by the adagios: the broken ♪ ♫ figure of the Adagio in II:7

1 *Haydn at Eszterháza 1766–1790*, pp. 355f. For the Harrach family, see Otto Biba in *HJB* X (1978), pp. 36–44.
2 Published by J. Harich in *HJB* IX, 67ff.

begins to haunt the imagination because of its very repetition. One is also intrigued by the many unusual dynamic marks in these slow movements, including crescendi and many contrasts of *f–p*. Some idea of Haydn's innate grasp of the instruments at his disposal may be seen in the Trio of the fourth movement in II:7, where the horns are dropped and the gaunt texture is grotesquely underlined by tall staccati. In II:D18 we have an additional 'Scherzo', such as we know from the early quartets, inserted after the first movement, raising the total to six movements. In the G major Divertimento missing in Hoboken, there is another bizarre and original Trio (of the fourth movement): this time the oboes are silent, and we are given a rich, and yet thinly scored, sound of two bassoons and two horns – a typically Haydnesque tautology. In the D major Divertimento also missing in Hoboken, we have a new sequence: Allegro di molto, Menuet (Allegretto) & Trio, Polonese (Adagio), Presto. The stiff, rhythmically quirky, Polonaise (to use the modern spelling) is eccentric. Altogether, one cannot escape the strong feeling that Haydn deliberately experimented far beyond that which the form usually contained, both in formal scope and in particular regarding the actual sound.

We have saved the greatest eccentricity for the last. Divertimento II:23 in F, of which we have part of the autograph, has as the fourth movement a 'Menuet'. The autograph even tells us what is happening: 'Incipit lamentatio'. What Haydn has, incredibly, done is to take as the melodic basis of this minuet the old Gregorian chant for Holy Week, the setting of the Lamentations of Jeremiah. Haydn was fascinated with this mystical melody, and was to use it many times: in the Trio of Symphony No. 45 ('Farewell', 1772) – the musicians' lament? – and as the basis of the slow movement in Symphony No. 26 (*Sinfonia Lamentatione*); the reader may find the original Gregorian chant in *Haydn at Eszterháza 1766–1790*, p. 293.

This is a Goya-like touch. What did the dinner guests of Count Morzin think when, from the wind band at the end of the room, floated over the dining table at Lukavec Castle the ghostly sounds of Good Friday or Maundy Thursday, recalling penitent processions and monkish prayers? It is the first hint on this scale that Haydn's future will be quite different than that for which the bulk of his early music spiritually prepares one.

Divertimento (Feld-Parthie) in F (II:16; 1760)

Scoring: 2 cors angl., 2 hns., 2 v., 2 bsn.
Principal sources: (1) Autograph, EH, Budapest, Ms. mus. I. 47. Title: 'Divertimento [middle:] In Nomine Domini [right:] Giuseppe Haydn 760' on oblong Italian paper (watermarks: three crescents of declining size over 'P', horizontal chain lines, letters 'AS'). There are sketches on the blank last sheet (ff. 16r. and v.) for Quartet, Op. 20/3 in G minor, about which see *Haydn at Eszterháza 1766–1790*, pp. 332–4 (based on the researches of L. Somfai). At end of MS.: 'Fine'. (2) MS. parts as 'Concertino', Archives of the Princes von Thurn und Taxis, Regensburg.
Critical editions: Score, printed in the appendix of August Reissmann's *Joseph Haydn*, Berlin 1880 (apparently using the autograph). A useful practical edition: VEB Friedrich Hofmeister, Leipzig (Kurt Janetzky, 1954).
Literature: Pohl I, 193, 320f. Geiringer 1932, p. 66. Landon, *SYM*, III, 179f.

When Joseph Elssler entered this unique work into *EK* about 1765, he added, perhaps later, the explanation 'Feld Part:' (literally 'field part[hia]', wind-band music for open-air performance). Perhaps the Eisenstadt grenadiers paraded with it. At any rate, Haydn thought he could use this Divertimento, composed for Morzin, for Prince Paul Anton Esterházy as well. The autograph was among Haydn's effects and after his death came to the Esterházy Archives. We believe that there was always some special significance attached to these youthful works that Haydn kept throughout his life: the

Salve Regina in E and Organ Concerto in C (XVIII:1) reminded him of the sad little ceremony when he lost his first love; Symphony No. 7 (score and parts) for, perhaps, his first triumph with Prince Paul Anton in 1761; we imagine that this work, with its incredibly unconventional scoring, may have been a particular success with the Morzin family. Haydn was fast making a speciality of these 'Feld-Parthien', infusing into this *Tafelmusique* emotions and forms hitherto undreamed of.

Here, Haydn has combined a string cassatio with a wind-band divertimento. The beginning sounds like a *Feld-Parthie*, with the violins taking the role of supporting the wind band, but as soon as the middle section begins, we have the opposite – a pretty flourish from the violins, with the wind instruments providing a discreet background. A typical look into the future, but with the formal attributes of 1760: this little escapade on the violins' part is eight bars long, but the eighth bar is interrupted by the recapitulation (bar 34). Now we see that we are in 1760 because of the middle section's great brevity (also the result of the medium being used, as we noted with Haydn's purely wind-band music *supra*); whereas the fusion of the last bar also serving as the beginning of a new phrase looks forward to late Haydn. Readers may like an example: a famous one in Symphony No. 97, development section of the first movement, after the greatest wind-band solo in Haydn's career up to that time (greater to come in the revised *Seven Words* of 1796): the music moves in slow curves to a cadence, but the cadence's final bar = the beginning of a gigantic tutti (bar 143) marked in the basses *ff*, and our astonishment is compounded when the main theme, which strode down the scale in the exposition like the conquering music of Haydn's greatest pupil, now ends not C–G–E–C but (the ears scarcely believe what they are hearing) C–G–E–C sharp, the C sharp being driven home with *fz*.

Another look forward, this time to the Esterházy years: this is the earliest work of Haydn's with cors anglais. They were, then, available, to the Morzin's oboe players and we doubt whether it is the only work Haydn composed for the instruments at Lukavec (wind-band divertimenti? perhaps some listed in *EK* such as II:12, 'Corno Inglese'). They were to become special favourites of his, assuming a similar role to that of clarinets in Mozart's life. In Haydn of the 1760, we find cors anglais in church music, chamber music, symphony and even opera.

In the slow movement (Adagio) one observes a delicacy of scoring and a profundity of instrumental knowledge that make one realize that Haydn has imperceptibly become one of the world's great orchestrators. Of course he uses his four groups of instruments like multi-choired church music of the Venetian school, imported into Austria *inter alia* for instrumental music alone by Reutter, Jr., and Ordoñez. The syncopations that are so much a part of Haydn's early style colour this music, too (note their subtle use in the horns almost throughout). The second part again gives us that curious sense of poignancy, of *Wehmuth* (as Haydn would have described it), that we find in many of these early wind-band adagios – we conjure up this music floating quietly across the castle lake at Lukavec of a summer evening. Here, the principal subject is used so much that Haydn cuts it out of the reprise entirely. Instead, the brief middle section winds up in a dominant pause; whereupon the two violins have an exquisite four-bar solo, which (by using double stopping in the second violins) Haydn has contrived to sound like a string trio: over the measured quavers of the seconds, the first violins wave a beautiful series of arabesques (musical example in *SYM*, 180) which is, surprisingly, almost like a keyboard sonata on paper (it was one of those passages that we often find in J. S. Bach that sound equally well for the bowed as well as the mechanically plucked string).

In the second 'Menuet poco vivace' we observe yet another look into the future: the attempt, successfully realized, to speed up and at the same time to lighten the texture of the minuet form; hand in hand with this, we find an almost symphonic texture at the beginning of the second part:

In the Finale, Haydn reintroduces the long violin solo that we remember from the Adagio, now, as befits the Presto tempo, lengthened to eight bars.

We assume that the Morzin family (who after all 'passed' Haydn on to the Esterházys) realized that this was entertainment music on a wholly new level of sophistication, beauty and formal efficiency.

PASTORELLA, 'EŸ, WER HAT IHN DAS DING GEDENKT'
(XXIIId:G1 ; *c.* 1760–1 ?)

Scoring: S. Solo, Str. Va. part lost, parts for fl. and 2 hns., noted in one source, questionable but, since lost, the problem is rhetorical.

Principal sources: (1) MS. parts, parish church of Gröbming (MS. 16), now Diözesanarchiv, Graz. Title: 'Pastorella 2. [beneath, a bracket] / à / Soprano Solo / 2 Violini / Viola obligl: / Organo. / Del Sigl: Haÿdn. / 1: Eÿ wer hat ihn das Ding gedenkt. / 2:te 'Herst Nachbä hä sag mir was heut / [lower right:] Ex Rebus " / Raÿ Schörckmaÿr.' 4° paper (watermarks: title page '4' over heart-shaped ornament; rest: bishop with mitre and letter 'A' beneath). No. 1 is our work; No. 2 is the *Cantilena pro adventu* (XXIIId:3), also known under the Latin text 'Jesu Redemptor' and listed briefly in *Haydn at Eszterháza 1766–1790*, p. 245. In the Gröbming MS., the vocal part of No. 2 is lost. (2) MS. parts from the Hospitallers, Kuks (ČSSR), now National Museum, Prague, on local paper and including parts for flute and two horns 'non obligato'; with title 'Pastorella in G ... Giuseppe Haydn ... Pro Choro Fr[atr]um Misericordiae Kukus[i] Sub Regente Chori Fr: Caecilio Wagner [later hand:] Gestorben 21. Jänner 1784 in Graz.' The copyist also prepared the vitally important four *Responsoria de Venerabili* (XXIIIc:4a-d), also from Kuks. See *Haydn at Eszterháza*, pp. 245f. Only the title page and the violone part have survived. (3) MS. parts, GdM, 'Pastorella germanica ... Haydn', on paper from the mill of I. M. Purtscher in Weitra an der Lainsitz, *c.* 1770. (4) Göttweig Abbey. lists the work as 'Pastorella germanica' (with va.) in its Catalogue (actual parts lost) under 'Ignotor Author' No. 3, 'comp. R. P. Josephus 1764.'

Literature: I. Becker-Glauch in *Haydn-Studien* II/3 (1970), pp. 194ff., where news of this interesting work was presented for the first time.

Frau Dr Becker-Glauch, who first assembled the source material (which is only very fragmentarily given in Hoboken II, 173), believes the work to be genuine. There are several factors that support her theory. The presence of a source among the Hospitallers is convincing, and we shall see that the Graz Order plays a vital role in our knowledge of Haydn's early works; the Kuks (Kukus in German) Order has already given us the hitherto lost, and very beautiful, *Responsoria da Venerabili*. And in the Gröbming MS., the second work is a German dialect version of the authentic *Cantilena pro adventu* which Haydn himself entered in *EK* with a slightly different bass part, and which suggests that there were possibly two authentic sets of texts, one in German (Lower Austrian) dialect and one in Latin. Even if the German 'pastorella' version is original, perhaps Haydn himself had a hand in the adaptation with Latin text, or at least gave his seal of approval to it.

The texts themselves are in local dialect, and show Haydn's affection for, and understanding of, the folk-idiom; for the music is full of folk reminiscences such as have been discussed in the music of Haydn's precursors (supra, p. 182). It is the 'low' literary idiom that annoyed north German critics of Haydn (said Griesinger, many years later, 'H. seems predestined for bad texts'). Mozart might have set some such text when he was living at Salzburg, but hardly when he was living in Vienna; and Beethoven would have been appalled both at these 'pastorelle' and at a libretto such as that to Haydn's *Die Feuersbrunst*. Naturally, they would have found Haydn the victim of his 'low' upbringing. There is every evidence that Haydn loved this folk-idiom and revelled in its lusty cadences: in Lower Austrian churches, the Madonna often has the round, slightly double-chinned facial features of a local *Bauernmädel*, and there is every reason to think the population's reverence for their peasant concept of Our Lady was every bit as genuine and profound as the nobility's worship of a great Gothic Madonna with aesthetic, indrawn features.

Our readers may be interested to see this *Pastorella* in G, which we herewith present from the Gröbming manuscript (see example below) as a 'first edition'.

When did Haydn compose these pieces? The more one considers the matter, the more unlikely it seems that Haydn would have tried to compose even German-language (Advent) church music at Eisenstadt so long as Werner was alive and still full *Capellmeister*. The Eisenstadt Advent pieces, as far as they are datable at all, seem to be 1765 or later (such as 'Ein' Magd, ein' Dienerin', XXIIId:1). We wonder if this pair of 'pastorelle', Advent arias, such as the Gröbming MS. presents to us as a unity, was not composed for the Advent services at Lukavec, for the Castle Chapel. We have therefore tentatively dated them *c.* 1760–1: more evidence may come to light.

** MS. corrupted here

* MS 'for' and the next two lines corrupted.

da capo al segno
[= *da capo dal segno al fine*]

[text as in example]

[Translation]

Ah, who would have thought such a thing,
That He should be a god?
He who lies here, sick with cold,
Nestling in the hay.
Ye angels, hasten, fly to rock him!

Ich mein, ich muß schon selbst hingeh'n
und ihme wiegen ein,
doch schauts, das Ding { thuet ganz fest stehn,
                        { thut
es muß
    kan kein wiegen { sein
                    { seÿn.
Ich glaub es ist ein Krippen gar,
worinen sonst das Heu,
Ja, ja, ich trif es auf ein Har [Haar],
das etwas solches seÿ:
dort seind ja schon all' Beede Thier,
die sonst gezehret hier.

I thought I myself must go,
To rock Him a while,
But lo! that thing stands firm:
It cannot be a cradle.
I think it is a manger,
Where the hay is usually kept.
Yes, I've hit the nail on the head,
That's what it must be.
The two animals are yonder
That used to feed here.

Mein Gott, wie weit hat dich gebracht,
die Lieb von unser G'schlecht,
O wens nur war [wäre] in meiner Macht,
dir auch zu danken recht.
Ich neig mich halt und danke dir,
sonst weiß ich nichts darfür.

My God! Love of mankind
Has brought you to this.
If it were only in my power
To thank you rightly.
Therefore I bow my head and offer thanks;
I am unable to do more.

Note: This is the version of the Gröbming MS.; in other MS. sources, there are four verses.

SYMPHONIES

In the previous chapter, it was seen that Haydn assigned numbers to his early symphonies, and that his No. 1 was in fact the No. 1 as we now know it (following the *incipit*, and information, given in Griesinger's biography). We now propose to provide that list once again, but substituting for the missing numbers those early works which are known to us from contemporary sources but which happen not to exist any longer in the Fürnberg-Morzin collection at Keszthely Castle.[1] (It will be recalled that Count Festetics's music master assigned to these missing numbers a random selection of Haydn symphonies in MS. copies which he had also acquired in Vienna *c.* 1801. For that list, *vide supra*, p. 241.) In selecting such a work for one of these missing numbers, we have been guided, as well, by inner stylistic criteria. As an example, for missing No. 4 of the Fürnberg-Morzin series, we have assigned No. 19, a symphony close to No. 1 in stylistic details; while the *Scherzandi* have been assigned later numbers. We have also provided information about the copyists and type of paper used by the Fürnberg-Morzin series at Keszthely Castle and added other authentic sources and information that might prove useful to other scholars working in the field. It was seen that the watermarks/copyists are of vital importance in matters of authenticity and chronology, and as our knowledge of the paper mills of the Austrian monarchy *c.* 1750–70 grows beyond the boundaries established in G. Eineder's great and pioneering book,[2] we may expect confidently that the papers used by the authentic copyists will be able to be classified into much more precise chronological categories than is now possible.

The following list shows in the first column the numbering of the Festetics Collection of the Fürnberg-Morzin MSS. in Keszthely Castle (Hungary), and in the second column the numbering established by E. Mandyczewski in 1907 (these numbers were taken over by Hoboken and used in his series I); information about copyists and watermarks of the Festetics MSS., together with any other information on individual works, is given in the right-hand column:

Symphony No.		*Comments*
F-M MSS.	*Mandyczewski*	
1	1	MS. by F-M No. 4 (the previous designation 'Viennese Professional Copyist No. 2' is omitted from now on) on oblong Italian paper (watermark: vertical lines of chains, three crescents of declining size); copyist writes 'Heÿdn', which was later to become 'Haÿdn' and still later – as on the String Trios Nos. 14 (V:15) and 15 (V:16) – 'Haÿdn mpria', perhaps unconsciously imitating Haydn's autograph signature. Griesinger gives 1759 as the date of composition; perhaps it was 1758. Bishop Leopold Egk acquired this work for Kremsier Castle in 1759. It also appears as No. 1 in the Lambach Catalogue (1768) of Haydn's symphonies.
2	37	MS. by F-M No. 4 on 4° Austrian paper (watermarks: letters 'LDF', coat-of-arms with crown and crenellated tower in middle). In the Schwarzenberg Archives at Krumau, MS. dated 1758 (see opposite).
3	18	MS. by F-M No. 4 on same paper as that of Sym. 37 *supra*.
4	[19]	Number missing in series; we have assigned to it the very early Sym. No. 19, which is the fifth work by Haydn in the Lambach Cat. of 1768. Breitkopf Cat. 1766.

1   As this volume goes to press, Saga Records of London are planning to issue the complete early symphonies of Haydn in a sequence based on the chronological listing given here; the recordings will be made by L'Estro armonico, conducted by Derek Solomons, using instruments of the period.

2   *The Ancient Paper-Mills of the former Austro-Hungarian Empire and their Watermarks*, Hilversum 1960. It was due to the initiative of Jan LaRue that this great work of scholarship reached the printed page.

Symphony No.		Comments
F-M MSS.	*Mandyczewski*	
5	2	MS. by F-M No. 1 on oblong Italian paper (watermark: vertical lines of chain, three crescents of declining size with letter 'c' or 'G'). Printed by Venier in Paris, 1764.
6	['B']	Hob. I:108. Number missing in series. Our 'B' exists in an authentic source by F-M No. 4, Archives of Counts Pachta, National Museum, Prague, cat. XXII D.118, on thickish yellow paper in 4° format from an Austrian mill. The bassoon part is written into the basso part, and the solo passage in the Trio is marked 'Fagotto ô Violonzello Solo.' Göttweig 1765. The second work in the Haydn series of Lambach Cat. 1768.
7	[16]	Number missing in series. Göttweig 1766.
8	[17]	Number missing in series. Breitkopf Cat. 1766.
9	15	MS. in part by F-M No. 2 (title page, Basso, ob. I, II, cor. I, II, v.I, va.) and No. 1 (rest) on 4° Italian paper (watermarks: three very large crescents of declining size placed in the middle of a sheet [4 pp.] in vertical fashion; largest moon measures 3·7 cm. at largest point, smallest 2 cm. at largest point; horizontal lines of chains; letter 'P'). Göttweig Cat. 1764 (parts lost).
10	4	MS. by F-M No. 1. Title page on thick, brownish paper (4°). Rest 4° Italian paper (watermarks: three large crescents in middle of sheet with letter 'F'; letters 'AS / C' under crown). Göttweig Cat. 1762 (parts lost).
11	10	MS. by F-M No. 1 on 4° Italian paper (watermarks as in Sym. 4's MS., *supra*). With 2 v. I, 2 v. II, 2 Basso parts. Holograph corr. by Haydn on both Basso parts.

Title page of the earliest recorded MS. of a Haydn Symphony – No. 37 – dated 1758; Schwarzenberg Archives, Krumau (Český-Krumlov).

Symphony No.		Comments
F-M MSS.	*Mandyczewski*	
12	32	MS. by F-M No. 1 on 4° Austrian paper (watermarks: angel 9 cm. high and with half-moon in middle; wild man with letter 'R' beneath).
13	5	MS. by F-M No. 1 on 4° Austrian paper (cover: rampant horse in circle, with crown and fleur-de-lys above, and on top of that, letter 'P'; parts: angel and wild man as on pts. of Sym. 32, *supra*). Holograph corr. by Haydn (additional *f* and *p*) on one v.I part, already incorporated by the copyist on the duplicate v.I part; also Haydn corr. on both Basso parts. Another authentic source by F-M No. 4 in Kremsier Castle. Göttweig Cat. 1762 (parts lost).
14	11	MS. by F-M No. 1 on 4° Austrian paper (watermarks: eagle with crown 7 cm. high, letters 'IGS', lines of chains 1·4 cm. apart). Holograph corr. by Haydn to both horn parts, changing actual notes by scratching out original version (one such page reproduced in Philharmonia Complete Symphonies, Vol. I, frontispiece; not bound into all copies); also into both v.I parts, and into one of the two v.II parts (the other v.II part remained uncorrected!). In a list submitted by Breitkopf & Härtel to Haydn, the composer referred to this work as 'one of the earliest' (*SYM*, 632).
15	33	MS. by F-M No. 1 on 4° Austrian paper (watermarks: cover has an angel standing in a circle, the whole 10·5 cm. high; the actual parts: angel and wild man with 'R' as in paper of Sym. No. 32, *supra*). Parts for 2 v.I, 2 v.II, 2 Basso.
16	27	MS. by F-M No. 1 on 4° Austrian paper (watermarks: eagle and 'IGS' as in paper of Sym. No. 11, *supra*; wild man with 'R' and angel as in paper of Sym. No. 32, *supra*). No horns in this source. On the title page, Haydn's numbering, 'N: 16' is a correction from another number. 2nd authentic source, Count Sporck Archives, National Museum, Prague (from Kuks Castle),[1] by F-M No. 4.
17	('A')	MS. by F-M No. 1 on 4° Italian paper (watermarks: horizontal chain lines, letters 'AS' in an elaborate coat-of-arms, large sized three crescents of decreasing size in the middle of the sheet and letter 'F'). Holograph corr. by Haydn on both v.I parts (Finale), both v.II parts (Finale), both Basso parts (Finale). The 2nd Basso part contains the whole title page all over again. N.B.: The numbering on the cover, 'N^ro 17' is *not* in Haydn's hand but was added by Festetics's music master; nevertheless we have retained it, because it is obvious that this authentic set of parts belongs to the series, and this is as good a place as any to include it.
18–20	[*Scherzandi* Nos. 1–3 (II:33–5)]	Numbers missing in series, and the *Scherzandi* were part of the symphony list in *EK* prepared by Joseph Elssler, for *EK* begins with the *incipit* of No. 6 (earlier pages of *EK* are now missing).
21	3	MS. by F-M No. 10 on 4° Italian paper (watermarks: three crescents of declining size in the middle of the sheet; the cover of thick local paper, 4°). 2 v.I, 2 v.II, 2 Basso. It is not certain if the 'N^ro 21' on the cover is in Haydn's hand or that of the hand responsible for the later insertions of works when the series was acquired by Count Festetics. But we are inclined to think that the MS. *is* numbered by Haydn and belongs to the series. Here is a sample of this copyist's writing:

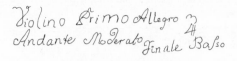

Göttweig Cat. 1762 (parts lost).

1 Wenzel, Count von Sporck (1724–1806), whose Stammschloß at Kukus (Kuks) was adjacent to a Hospitallers' Convent, became on 13 April 1764 I.R. Court & Chamber Music Director and General Director of Spectacles. He was probably one of the Morzin circle that witnessed Haydn's first symphonic successes at Lukavec, and Haydn probably supplied him with this authentic copy. Feder in *HJB* IV, 116.

Symphony No. *F-M MSS.*	*Mandyczewski*	*Comments*
[22–4]	[Scherzandi Nos. 4–6 (II:36–8)]	We have continued the series, which breaks off here in the Festetics MSS., to complete the *Scherzandi*, begun above. The *Scherzandi* were announced in the Breitkopf Catalogue of 1765. They are borderline works, composed between 1757 and 1764, and we have preferred to discuss them briefly in connection with the works of the first Eisenstadt period, *infra*, p. 554.
[25]	[20]	We have completed our hypothetical continuation of the Fürnberg-Morzin series with Symphony No. 20, an early work of which the first dated reference is Breitkopf Cat. 1766. There is a MS. by F-M No. 4 in the Archives of the Princes Thurn und Taxis in Regensburg (title page etc.: *SYM*, 645) on 4° Austrian paper (watermarks: letters 'IGS', crowned heart enclosing a star) which is of this early period. Another, only partly by the same copyist, is from the Keeß Coll., GdM XIII, 19067, and is of a later date, when this scribe was perhaps the head of his own scriptorium. This makes a total, then, of twenty-five symphonic works belonging to this early period, of which (as we said) the *Scherzandi* are borderline cases.

Notes on the Symphonies

Symphony No. 1 in D

Scoring: 2 oboes, 2 horns, strings and *continuo* [bassoon, harpsichord].

'Les commencements obscurs d'un talent célèbre sont toujours un spectacle attachant', wrote La Harpe in the *Correspondance Littéraire*. There is no composer in the history of music who achieved the astonishing progression that we may observe in Haydn's music from the *Missa brevis* in F of *c.* 1749 to the *Harmoniemesse* of 1802. There have been, of course, many composers who went through a similar development in their artistic careers – Monteverdi, Domenico Scarlatti, Gluck and Beethoven are names that spring to mind. But the road that Haydn had to travel is longer than that taken by any of his predecessors, contemporaries or successors. From Symphony No. 1 to Symphony No. 104, or from the *Salve Regina* in E (1756) to the *Te Deum* for the Empress Marie Therese (1799–1800), Haydn's style underwent a metamorphosis almost unparalleled in any of the arts, let alone in music. It is actually difficult to realize that the same man composed the late Baroque music of the *Missa brevis* in F and the prelude to 'Winter' from *The Seasons* (1801). And not only was it composed by the same man, but that creator, starting as an almost anonymous figure in the galaxy of Viennese music *c.* 1750, invented the string quartet as we know it today, became the Father of the Symphony – the Germans called him by that name in 1800, even knowing that there were many predecessors in the symphonic field before Haydn – and the founder of what may be called the greatest school in the history of music. Nowadays Haydn's name is inseparably, and rightly, connected with those of Mozart and Beethoven, the one Haydn's most perceptive musical friend, the other his most talented pupil.

Haydn's Symphony No. 1 begins with a musical red herring – namely, a fully-fledged Mannheim crescendo:

Now, as we have observed above, these Mannheim effects were not wildly successful in Austria; but as it happens, another Austrian composer, Florian Leopold Gassmann (later to become a well-known operatic writer and the producer of some widely admired fugal quartets) was in 1758 – the probable year of Haydn's work, too – in Venice to compose a new opera entitled *L'Issipile*. The three-movement Overture to this opera is preserved in a Viennese manuscript and was thus known to the Viennese as well as the Venetians.[1] The work is scored for the same orchestra as Haydn's except that Gassmann's also has trumpets and timpani (which Haydn's No. 1 does not). Gassmann's work begins:

1 Jan LaRue kindly drew our attention to this interesting work. The first performance in modern times was conducted by Colin Davis in a series devised by us for the B.B.C. in 1957, entitled 'The Pre-Classical Symphony'. The work is published by Verlag Doblinger, in our edition.

But apart from this crescendo, which was apparently the *dernier cri* in those days, Haydn's No. 1 is astonishingly free of Mannheim effects. It is, on the contrary, a thoroughly Austrian symphony. Of course, the differences between this work and Haydn's mature style are enormous. Perhaps the most striking of these differences is the very wealth of material that Haydn displays. In No. 1 we note: first subject (the famous crescendo), bars 1–9 (ending on V); second subject, still in D major, bars 10–14; transitional material (bars 14–22) with chain syncopations, antiphonal effects between violins I & II, with great nervous tension being generated through repeated quavers in the bass line and repeated semiquavers in the violins; third subject (bars 23–8), *p* leading to *f* (in the *p* section, the figure will be important later: ♩♩ ⅄ ♪ ♩♩) and at first ambiguously, then surely, landing in dominant by means of another nervous tutti. Now comes the real subsidiary subject', the fourth, and it is *p* and in the dominant *minor*, a characteristic feature of Haydn's precursors and contemporaries and a Haydnesque trait of this period. Fifth subject is the *forte* conclusion to the exposition (bars 32–9). Now five subjects are a luxury that the mature Haydn would never have permitted himself, but nevertheless one must admire how deftly this exposition is put together.

As to the development, it cannot compare to a stupendous operation such as that of No. 104, which can be regarded as one enormous psychological crescendo leading to the recapitulation in a blaze of glory. But it is undoubtedly unfair to make comparisons of this sort; for seen in historical context, it cannot have been an accident that this very work, No. 1, created an unprecedented *furore* among the *cognoscenti* of the Austrian public, aristocratic and professional. In a brilliant article on the subject,[1] John Vinton praises the development sections of Monn, who 'at his most sophisticated, could write highly organized development sections, even if short motives and undifferentiated rhythms continued to betray his Baroque upbringing'. After examining some developments in unpublished Wagenseil symphonies ('unfortunately these subtleties are neither as frequent nor as well co-ordinated with other elements in the Wagenseil works as they are in the D major Monn *Symphonia*'), he goes on to assert that

> The early works of Haydn present a spectacular contrast to the fore-going symphonies. Apparently Haydn's skills for organization far surpassed anything Monn or Wagenseil could muster, while his imagination produced a variety of musical development, the extent of which they might have found unbelievable. . . .
> [No. 1's development section] contains many features in common with symphonies by Monn and Wagenseil. The section is rather short (26 percent of the movement) and opens

with four bars of fiddling on a triad and scale in the dominant key. The next six bars contain material based on [material from the exposition, including a *forte* derived from the figure ♩♩ ⅄ ♪ ♩♩] out of which a sequence grows. This leads to a further alteration of the [subsidiary] theme, a melodic and textural climax, and a [semiquaver] flourish, ending in a strongly articulated cadence. Although the outward appearance of sequences, melodic peak, and closing flourish may resemble the symphonies [of Monn or Wagenseil], some of the inner details reveal a superior intellect. . . . The derivation of material [– intervallic, rhythmic and harmonic –] is far more complex than any found in Monn or Wagenseil.

> Likewise, the climactic point (bars 54–56) contain a complex rhythmic structure, a relatively long motive size, a long-anticipated melodic peak, and a sudden burst of wind sound. The harmony underscores the climax by landing on a tonic pedal. Wagenseil may have anticipated the use of the increased rhythmic complexity, and Monn the climactic use of a melodic peak, but neither achieved so grandly co-ordinated an effort as this.

Those who will follow Haydn's symphonic career from this beginning to its glorious end may be interested to see, in plentiful numbers, one of the most characteristic of all Haydn's fingerprints, the ♫ ♩ ♫ rhythm that cuts sharply through the texture at bar 6, when the crescendo has reached its full climax. The figure is repeated in the horns at bars 9, 18f., 28, 39, 54–6, 58, 64, 67, 75, 79–81 and 86 – it was well and truly established in everyone's mind, and in the next forty years, Haydn was to see that his public would always, if they were musical, associate his grand tuttis with this unmistakable mason's mark. And as we move into the great and humanistic Allegro of Haydn's Symphony No. 104, the firm tread of ♩ ♫ ♩ ♩ greets us in horn, trumpet and kettledrum at bars 40ff. (the rhythm being, of course, the augmentation of the figure used in No. 1) and will accompany us as the last cadence in the movement thunders in our ears (bars 290–2):

finis origine pendet.

Following the local tradition, the wind instruments are not used in the Andante, which is a light, dance-like movement in 2/4 metre; the alternation of triplets, dotted patterns, series of syncopations and supple dynamic contrasts are all typical of Haydn's early style. At the beginning of the development section, says the astute John Vinton,

> Haydn usually followed the custom of his time and stated [the principal theme] in the dominant at the start of a development section. One of his greatest skills, however, was his ability to extend or contract a phrase. Such alterations in phrase length at the beginnings of his developments often prevent abrupt articulations or

---

1 'The Development Section in early Viennese Symphonies: a Re-valuation', *Music Review* XXIV/1 (1963), pp. 13–22.

bland repetitions. The Andante of Symphony No. 1 contains an excellent illustration:

Haydn: Symphony No. 1/II, violins I & II
(a) bars 1–4 (principal theme)

(b) bars 29–34 (development)

The fact that no modulation occurs in the second version of this phrase proves that Haydn made the extension purely to intensify the upward climb of the melody and thus inject an old theme with new interest.

The Finale (Presto) is in the favourite light 3/8 metre and is in the usual three sections, with a small middle part (bars 33–48) constituting a fifth of the total. It is principally interesting for its rhythmic vitality and the sure organization with which it is constructed.

Symphony No. 37 in C

Scoring: Haydn's original score was for 2 oboes, 2 horns, strings and *continuo* [bassoon, harpsichord]. A MS. by the so-called 'Keeß copyist' (*supra*, p. 145), Thurn und Taxis Archives, Regensburg, calls instead of horns for trumpets and provides a timpani part (added in small print to the Philharmonia/Haydn-Mozart Presse score). It is possible that Haydn added the timpani part for a performance at the house of his friend, Ritter von Keeß: it is neatly made.

Although Haydn uses a 'light' metre (2/4) and very quick tempo (Presto) for the opening, it is

nonetheless a tightly organized and motivically taut movement, which has drawn especial praise in Geiringer's survey of 1932 (p. 72, music ex.). The opening theme contains a central phrase (♩ ♫ | ♩ ♩ ♩ | ♩) which seizes the music instantly, filtering down the strings in fast imitation; and we see it enclosing the transition to the dominant (bars 18ff.) and then completely taking over the final cadential passage (bars 32ff.) before the second subject, as usual in the dominant minor, appears. Our – and no doubt the Lukavec guests' – astonishment grows as we see the little phrase again dominating the entire closing passage, even to the imitations between violins I & II, up to the double bar. The development section is much longer than that in No. 1 and the central phrase continues to operate. At bar 82 we have the first example of a sham recapitulation, a device in which the composer starts what appears to be the reprise but then veers off and continues the development: here in No. 37 we have a classic example, and all this in a work of 1758! Because of the undue attention to the opening subject, Haydn cuts it out of the recapitulation in direct quotation but continues to exploit the crucial pattern in a dense passage of considerable rhythmical complexity (bars 121ff.): here is another splendid climax – one which was artfully worked out, not least by means of a long *piano* section based on the second subject. And the ♩ ♩ ♩ ♩ of Morellian/Berensonian fame, in itself a derivative of the main theme's pivotal kern, is used here with just as much effect as in No. 1, but quite differently. The rhythm – which of course is intended for horns (or *pace* Regensburg, trumpets and timpani) – does not start to appear until within the development; but it is an essential part of the climax (bars 127ff.) referred to above, appearing four times in succession. Haydn is moving, and moving quickly, to the kind of motivic concentration for which his music was soon to be famous.

No. 1 had three movements, No. 37 four; the Minuet is in *second* place and of immaculate construction (beautiful two-part violin interlude in the middle, *piano*). The Trio is in C minor (no wind instruments) with strong Baroque overtones: how could it be otherwise? Haydn has now become thoroughly involved in rhythmic figures capable of welding together whole movements, and here it is ♩ ♩ ♩ ♩ ♩ which figures in some two-thirds of the whole section. It is a clear link, moreover, to the ensuing slow movement which is in the same key (C minor) and is also scored for strings only; but there is more – we find the same Baroque flavour, the upper string parts answering each other (bars 9ff. with upbeat) in Corellian fashion. A passage of haunting beauty and so typical, even now, of Haydn: bars 15(2nd half)ff., long dominant pedal point (bass line, repeated semiquavers), violins tentatively thrusting their phrases at us. It is, of course, deeply satisfying when it returns in C minor, its colour delicately darkened and the bass line's dynamic level lowered to a whispered *pp*. The organizational ability, of which John Vinton has written so well, is here in full evidence.

The Finale is in the usual Presto 3/8. Interesting change to record *vis-à-vis* No. 1's Finale: in the latter there was one sequence of alternating (*f*)–*p*–*f*–*p*–*f* in the exposition which was, naturally, repeated in the recapitulation; otherwise there was an eight-bar *piano* in the middle of the development section. In No. 37, by contrast, we have a constant procession of dynamic contrasts which serve to enliven the textural fabric of the music.

Symphony No. 18 in G

Scoring: 2 oboes, 2 horns, strings and *continuo* [bassoon, harpsichord].

We must assume that Haydn was composing symphonies in intoxicating series, one after the other; so great attention to variety had to be paid to the form *within* and the form *without*. Let us say that in No. 1 Haydn showed that he could marshal Mannheim-like sounds into cohesive patterns and could paint with a broad brush on a generous scale (five subjects). In No. 37 he broadened the form to four movements but subjected the first movement to rigorous intellectual discipline.

Now, in No. 18, we have the first of a special series of works close to Haydn's heart and to lovers of his art ever since: the symphony in *sonata da chiesa* style, that is, with an entire opening slow movement. And Haydn even copies a stylistic feature of the old church sonata, wherein the second violin starts with its highly dotted, Baroque theme, ceding to the first violin at bar 5. The dotted aspect derives from the old French overture, while the entrance of the violins *en suite* also reminds one of another great Baroque form, the fugue, with its *dux* and *comes*; for once the first violin enters, the second violin provides a running counterpoint. Next innovation: the wind instruments are retained, unusual in a slow movement, but as we shall see, standard procedure in the adagios (in this case Andante moderato) of church sonata symphonies.

The second movement (Allegro molto) has tremendous rhythmic drive, as if to release all the tensions gathered by the tautly formal dotted patterns of the opening Andante moderato; it proceeds with the explosive force that characterizes all these follow-ups to church sonata adagios. This is already highly personal music; it uses the conventional clichés of the period but the drive and the sharply etched rhythms make it the most individual of all the allegros so far. And what do we find at the first melodic/structural climax, bar 5? The ♪♪♪ rhythm in the horns (in a double dose, too). And at *exactly* the same climactic point three-quarters of the way through the movement that we have observed in

Nos. 1 and 37, we have the same pattern in No. 18, with the horns biting through the densely exciting rhythmic pattern (marching basses in quavers, middle strings in repeated semiquavers, violins in a taut motivic ♪♪♪♪ and the oboes sustaining long chords) in their 'fingerprinted' contribution. The principal subsidiary theme is in the tonic minor, but given a curiously unsettling, transitional feeling by being formed over a V of V pedal point that only half-heartedly resolves into the proper dominant, only to fall (via B flat) into V of V again.

For the concluding movement, Haydn had another surprise in store for his no doubt enthralled audience at Lukavec Castle: the favourite hybrid form of the string trio, a 'Tempo di Menuet': an overall A–B–A form, of which the 'A' section is in three subsections (*a–b–a*). 'B' is almost like the middle part of the Gavotte in the Ballet Music to Mozart's *Idomeneo* (K.367) – Mozart could have seen or heard Haydn's No. 18 in Lambach Monastery where he sometimes spent the night, and for the friendly monks of which Wolfgang and his father each composed a symphony.

With these three works, the internal chronological order of which we do not for a moment doubt, Haydn had established himself as one of the leading symphonic composers in the Monarchy. He was twenty-seven.

Symphony No. 19 in D

Scoring: 2 oboes, 2 horns, strings and *continuo* [bassoon, harpsichord].

Although not among the Fürnberg-Morzin MSS. at Keszthely Castle, No. 19 is very much of the period and we doubt not that it was composed for Lukavec (rather than Eisenstadt). It is in the three movement form of No. 1, the second in the tonic minor (2/4), Andante, and the third a Presto in the usual 3/8. One's admiration for the formal and motivic efficiency of the opening Allegro molto (again with impeccable use of small motifs) is only equalled by one's delight in the finely wrought Andante. Here we find great rhythmic variety, including several bars of those typically Haydnesque syncopations in the top line over a steady quaver bass line marked, one is sure, by tall staccato marks in the autograph (these were later watered down to normal staccati, but their purpose is as much to *accent* as to be played short: bars 33ff.). The jaunty Finale is equally well composed and on a bigger scale than those of Nos. 1 or 37: when the first part of theme (*f*, shifting at once to *p*) leads to the second (bars 5ff.), we note how the long-held wind instruments and upper strings are the foil for the thrusting lower strings, whose bouncy ♪♪♪, forward-carrying force appears with brilliant panache in a *pp* context in the development (bars 69ff.) where it is, in an act of unsurpassed prestidigitation, lengthened by one bar. This is miniature art of the finest calibre.

Symphony No. 2 in C

Scoring: 2 oboes, 2 horns, strings and *continuo* [bassoon, harpsichord].

Yet another side to the young symphonist: this is a much more learned work than No. 1. The Baroque dotted theme of the first movement lends itself to contrapuntal extension and development. An interesting innovation is that there are no repeat signs in any of the movements, and the whole of each is 'durchkomponiert'. The second subject of the Allegro is, as usual, in the dominant minor and is connected to the first by the dotted lead given to the first violin (bars 41, 43, but even the horns at 40). In the middle of the development there is a most beautiful *pianissimo* passage (bars 86ff.) which leads us to a kind of *fausse reprise*, where we may admire how undramatically but no less efficiently Haydn is suddenly combining the elements of his previous material into four-part counterpoint (bars 94ff.). The real recapitulation is introduced after still another lengthy *pianissimo* which also contains the (for Haydn) rather rare marking, 'dolce'.

The second movement (Andante, 2/4) is without wind instruments. Here we have another experiment: a kind of *perpetuum mobile* in which the violins play in semiquavers from the first to the last note (both are quavers!), the pattern being constantly broken by the use of trills. The whole has a kind of hideous fascination, like the painted grin of a Harlequin in one of those open-air Punch & Judy shows that used to be a feature of the Roman parks in summer.

The Finale (Presto, 3/8) is one of the very first of Haydn's clear-cut rondos. The initial 'A' section is broken into *a–b–a*, and a similar tripartite division may be observed in the 'B' and 'C' sections which are, respectively, in the tonic minor and the subdominant (the latter marked *pp*). Whereas Symphony No. 1 was largely constructed of many small motifs, No. 2 is on the whole based upon single motifs; and with hindsight, we know that it is No. 2's, and No. 37's method that will very soon become the hallmark of the composer.

Symphony 'B' (I:108)

Scoring: 2 oboes, 1 bassoon, 2 horns in B flat [*alto*], strings and *continuo* [harpsichord].

This is the first of three works which we have fitted into a gap in the original numbering with which Haydn supplied his first twenty-one, and presumably, twenty-five works composed up to *c.* 1761.

This four-movement work was included by Haydn as No. 7 of his symphonies in the (Johann) Elssler Catalogue of 1805. While Symphony 'A' (I:107) was hardly circulated in its original symphonic state outside Austria and Hungary, 'B' penetrated even to Venice. It was printed, shorn of its non-*obbligato* – we use the word in the eighteenth-century sense which is the opposite of that in present-day terminology – wind parts, by M. de la Chevardière in Paris (announced in the *Mercure de France*, April 1768) as Oeuvre IV, No. 5. Actually, this constant publication of Haydn's works without their wind instruments – the same happened with Symphony 'A' and two Divertimenti for horns and strings, all three of which became false string quartets – robbed the music of many pretty details (in our first movement, oboe soli at bars 5–7, etc.). Solo wind passages (such as those of the Minuet) had to be rewritten into the strings; but since these presumably Parisian arrangements appeared in print, they achieved the wide circulation that the originals did not, so that in the end such a work as Quartet, Op. 1, No. 5, removed the authentic Symphony 'A' from circulation entirely (first restored in *SYM*, 1955, as a pocket score in the back flap of the book).

Although the solo bassoon passage seems to mark this Symphony as one composed for the Esterházy *Capelle* – no known Morzin symphony[1] employs a bassoon at all – it is nevertheless a more old-fashioned work, and in fact much more like a Morzin piece, than the other known symphonies of the early Esterházy period. The Minuet comes second, and it is in the Trio that the bassoon makes its single appearance: it was, of course, expected to double the bass line even if it was not specifically mentioned; indeed, its sudden appearance as a soloist only confirms that Haydn expected it to double the bass in the other quick movements.

Consider the bass line that opens the Allegro molto:

It could be the fundament of an Austrian Mass, even the beginning of a late Haydn Credo, and is essentially in the purely Baroque style. This 'walking bass', as it is often called, is at the opposite end of the scale from the modern, repeated quavers on a single note ('drum bass', the Germans call it) which was the bass part of No. 1. For the modern reader (listener), the effortless way in which Haydn manages to blend Baroque and Mannheim is one of the intriguing aspects of these early symphonies. Following hard on this old-fashioned opening on the top of which the upper voices give us a principal subject of which the characteristic feature is a trill at the end of each bar, almost purely Baroque in spirit we are suddenly jolted into 1758 at bars 5ff.; here, the strings subside into repeated semiquavers, *fp*, ♩♩♩♩ ♪ ♪ ♪ , while the *fp* wind instruments continue with a derivative of the trill figure, still at the end of each bar. It sounds like an Italian opera aria. A few bars later we slide back into the Baroque with 'walking bass' and the trill figure (bars 12ff.) which, we soon realize, is the essential motivic element of the movement (appearing, with its derivative, in bars 1–3, 5–7, 12f., 18–24, 25–7, 33–5, 37f., 43f.).

---

1 We have seen, however, that the Morzin *Capelle* included two bassoons.

The slow movement (Andante) comes third. This displacement of the minuet and slow movement is rare, but not unique, in the symphonies of this period (others are Nos. 32 and 37 Morzin works, and 44, an Esterházy work); it is much more prevalent in the quartets. In its style and structure (no winds), this G minor movement is the most old-fashioned of this group, starting like a trio sonata without the first violin, and introducing the first violin at bar 4 in the dominant. With its stiff sequences, it looks back to the world of J. J. Fux, whose theoretical work Haydn so much admired.

The most modern-sounding movement is the Finale (Presto), with its characteristic passage for the two violins (bars 17ff., 79ff.) all by themselves. The first subject is also used in an up-to-date way, as motivic material, in the middle section (later called the development, here a kind of varied exposition). Haydn tacks on a racy fanfare in the first violins (bars 36f., 40f., 44f., 48f.) which gives the first subject an entirely new twist in this middle section

Symphony No. 16 in B flat

Scoring: 2 oboes, 2 horns, strings and *continuo* [bassoon, harpsichord].

This is perhaps the most perfect three-movement symphony thus far examined, and so marvellously fashioned that it might actually be an early work for Prince Paul Anton Esterházy. The opening Allegro is composed in double counterpoint at the octave, as the listener can hear all during the main subject (the top and bottom lines being reversible). The part of the theme first given out by the violas and bass line is an old tune used by Mozart and others as a kind of *cantus firmus*. Because the theme and its countersubjects are so rich and also so self-containing, Haydn has no need of any other material and the movement is solidly monothematic. This is the essence of the new Austrian chamber symphony, fastidiously scored, with tight motivic and thematic concentration firmly interlaced with solid contrapuntal knowledge. In the development, Haydn darkens the texture and increases the dramatic power by several factors: he provides the highest point in the first violins' *tessitura* right at the outset (bar 56); but the tension is already greater because unlike the beginning, where we had only two-part counterpoint, we now start at once with the theme and *two* countersubjects. The next method Haydn uses to increase the pace psychologically is to start *piano* and not only to move into *forte* – an obvious move – but within this *forte* to introduce a chain series of syncopations. The last time a similar passage of this kind was presented (bars 34ff.) it was with the imitations between upper and lower voices but without the syncopations. Having reached a climax with this passage in the development (bars· 62ff.), and finding ourselves in G minor, we then find that Haydn abruptly moves his whole string section into quavers which continue for a full nine bars (bars 66ff.). The craftsmanship is here

harnessed to hitherto undreamed-of levels of sophistication.

C. F. Pohl, in his Haydn biography, printed the entire slow movement as an Appendix to Volume I. Several features of this Andante are worth investigation, of which the most obvious is the new way in which the strings (winds are, as usual, dropped) are deployed: the melody is given to unison violins doubled an octave lower by a solo 'cello, and this is followed throughout the movement. The second feature that springs to eye and ear is the total absence of any dynamic marks except that indicated at the beginning, *piano*. Now the reason for this is obvious if we consider the textural complexities and dynamic involvement within the previous Allegro. Our ear and mind must have a release, and here such a release is provided by the entire movement. The melody itself starts with a kind of question mark, i.e. the music stops at the end of bar 2 (the cadence unresolved); the resolution thereafter is all the more satisfactory.

The Finale is a Presto in 6/8, the classic hunting metre. But this is no hunting movement, rather an exhilarating and particularly brilliant conclusion, intended once again to act as a violent contrast to the placid Andante. Who could resist it when the lower strings dance down the scale with a derivative of the main subject (bars 20ff.) with the upper strings rushing headlong in series of repeated semiquavers. It all moves in an impetuous way to the double bar, and not a single bar of *piano* contrast. Then the middle section begins, and we have our *piano*, finely articulated by violins and violas only, launching us into a G minor which – so typically Haydnesque – never appears in root position. When the recapitulation arrives, the theme is suddenly presented as a caricature of itself, *piano* instead of *forte*, with just two violins which split up the bare melodic bones between each other:

As we noted before, wit has entered music. Haydn saw to it that it would continue to be a part of the language for the next forty years.

Symphony No. 17 in F

Scoring: 2 oboes, 2 horns, strings and *continuo* [bassoon, harpsichord].

One of the earliest known sources of this work is a manuscript copied by the German-American composer J. F. Peter on 12 December 1766 and taken with him to the New World, where it now resides in the Moravian Archives of Winston-Salem, North Carolina. It is thus one of the earliest works by Haydn to be heard in the United States. No. 17 has one of the most solidly symphonic first movements of all Haydn's early works in the *genre*. Here we may witness the breaking-down of the themes into small segments which are used like mosaics to create the rest of the movement. Rhythmically the whole Allegro is held together by the bass line in marching quavers – Haydn's call to the symphonic flag in these years, when anything seemed possible and the future lay ahead like a rolling vista. These quavers, which get into the blood of players and listeners alike, only very occasionally cease and are often transferred to another line, as in bars 34ff., where the two violins play alone, the second violin taking over the quavers formerly confined to the bass. The contrasts of *f–p* are beautifully worked out. One example: after a monumental tutti in the development section, we slowly work round to the recapitulation, and to prepare it (the main subject is *forte*), Haydn moves into a gigantic pedal point on V, drops the music to *piano*, drops the oboes and retains the horns only to punctuate with a single crotchet the beginning of each bar. But then he drops the dynamic level still more, to *pp*. It is so simple. It is so magical. When it is over and we sweep into the recapitulation, that previous section sounded absolutely inevitable; that it does so is, simply, the hand of the master.

The second movement (Andante, ma non troppo, 2/4) omits the wind instruments – this convention, by the way, had its origin in the simple and kindly desire to give the men a rest between movements – and is in the tonic minor. It has that typically Italian sense of *tristezza* which we find in most of the minor-key movements of Haydn's early symphonies: a gently sad music without grief. The Finale is a very concise Allegro molto in 3/8. It is, incidentally, typical of almost all these early Haydn symphonies that the first movements are the most interesting, formally and musically, while the last two movements *together* may be said to round out the opening. We would draw attention to a trenchant *ff* which increases the power of the last seven bars; Haydn is thinking in big terms, and his fastidious but telling use of dynamic marks serves a structural purpose: here to end the symphony and to underline the 'peak' which is being carved by the violins as they move steadily upwards in repeated semiquavers, reaching their top notes (*b flat″*) just before the final three cadential bars.

Symphony No. 15 in D

Scoring: 2 oboes, 2 horns, strings and *continuo* [bassoon, harpsichord].

The first movement is formally the most original and interesting of all the Morzin symphonies. It is in the French overture style, with a Presto flanked on either side by an Adagio of substantial proportions. In the first of these adagios, the oboes are not used at all, and in the final part they appear only at the end. We also feel the enlivening influence of the divertimento-cassatio in these adagios, both in the horn soli and in the pizzicato string accompaniments; and there is a strongly Austrian feeling about the music, not least in its winning charm. The Presto section is *durchkomponiert* and without the customary double bar. There are two features to which one might draw special attention. The first is at bars 37ff., where there is a little passage which in the event will provide the principal subject for the next symphony Haydn wrote (at least the one he placed afterwards, i.e. he certainly considered the two works as adjacent): No. 4. The second point we would make concerning this dashing Presto is about the second subject: it starts in the dominant major with a dialogue between the two violins, *pp*; but then it swiftly and unexpectedly drops into A minor, the usual key for second subjects at this period in Austrian music. But it is not just the drop into A minor that is remarkable, but the ominous way in which the music is laid out: that mysterious series of repeated tremolos in the violin, the long-held notes in the wind instruments, and finally, the way in which the whole 'fabric' is geared to repeated semiquavers in the upper voices of the strings and those famous knocking quavers in the bass (bars 49ff.). And all this is without any question several years *before* the chilling D minor accents of Gluck's *Don Juan* (1761) made this kind of sound a household word. Hardly necessary to add that at the climax of the stirring development section, we find the horns suddenly and for the first time slicing the texture with their inevitable fingerprints ♪♫♫ | ♩ (bars 70f.); and that immediately thereafter Haydn again throws into the turbulent texture that final ounce of drama – the introduction of a short *ff*. This is the declared climax, and Haydn 'builds it down' as cleverly as he raised it up: first by a silence, and how intimately shall we come to know those famous silences in the next forty years; and then by a wisp of a *pp* which slides elegantly into *piano* and the less emotionally driven rest of the development.

The second movement is a Menuet characterized by dotted rhythms *à la françoise* and by something that singles out the whole course of this original score: the increased use of strong dynamic contrasts, in this case a sudden *pp*. The Trio again returns to the Austrian divertimento tradition, with contrasting groups of the two violins / viola sola and violoncello solo. The third movement is an utterly charming Andante in 2/4. Students of Haydn's style will note with interest the syncopated passages at bars 22ff. and 68ff: the whole (yet again) marked *pp*, with the violins on the off-beat, the lower strings playing equal quavers marked staccato. As we have hinted before, this Morellian 'ear-mark' will soon become an integral part of Haydn's style in the 1760s, where we find it in work after work, even in the vocal works. For some of these derivatives, see *Haydn at Eszterháza 1766–1790*, p. 274. Here the upper voices are in straight chain syncopations.

The Finale (Presto, 3/8) is again much larger in scope, and thus in size, than Haydn's first symphonic efforts in this direction. It is a large A-B-A form, with 'B' being an intriguing exercise in concentration. The whole is couched in a *piano* context, the wind instruments are silent, and the second violin provides a chattering commentary in running semiquavers which continues without stopping for the whole section (bars 45–103) except for the last bar (104). In the first violin, Haydn is meanwhile experimenting with huge gaps in the melodic line, plunging from *d'''* to *c sharp''*, or from *b flat''* to the open g string (*g*). The whole is full of ingenuity and is, technically a *tour-de-force* of the first magnitude.

Symphony No. 4 in D

Scoring: 2 oboes, 2 horns, strings and *continuo* [bassoon, harpsichord].

There has been considerable evidence that Haydn often composed works in pairs. There were various advantages in this situation: two ways to compose a given set form, different approaches to a problem, and so forth. Here we note that the principal subject is built on a small motif from Symphony No. 15 turned upside down. Since Haydn numbered the two works 9 and 10 in the Fürnberg-Morzin series, the least that can be said is that Haydn certainly took no trouble to conceal the relationship; quite the reverse.

Here we have a work which almost seems, in its opening Presto, to be built along the lines of an Italian opera overture: in other words, a 'modern' symphony, quite different from Symphony 'B', with its Fuxian conservatism, discussed above. Among the many interesting details, we may single out a few. When Haydn reaches the first climactic dominant cadence (bars 19f.), the sudden density of texture is marked by syncopations in the upper strings, sharply etched rhythms in the lower strings (octave jumps deriving from bar 3 and the extension thereof in bars 9f. with the 'lead-in'), and the horns' fingerprint ♩♫♩♫ (twice, but the *only* time it is used in this movement). The second subject is much enlarged. We can see that it is a 1758-ish affair because it is in the dominant minor, but its long lines are new, and also the long legato slurs that point this out to the players (pretty interplay of the main theme, first with the upper three strings sections, then with a grand entry in the 'celli-bassi). End of the first section: deliberate introduction of the main theme in 'codetta' function: this, too, is new.

The development is the finest and most dramatic of any thus far examined. We first note a brilliantly modern crescendo which is used twice, each time rising to *ff* and each time marking a passing dissonance. The tension is increased by moving the whole passage up one half-step the second time; and from the violins's top note of *e'''* (the extent of comfortable orchestral soprano in those days, *f'''* was already problematical) Haydn now begins to de-accentuate the whole development section so that he can present the recapitulation as a conqueror. John Vinton writes sensitively on this process:

Occasionally, these long curves are complemented by harmonic, rhythmic, or textural changes, as in the Symphony No. 1. In at least one case, the first movement of the Symphony No. 4, these elements do not join together but pull apart so that a double peak results. Haydn reaches his first melodic peak at bars 40–50 [discussed above] after a steady rise over the first half of the development section. Dynamics and an unstable harmonic situation in this half support the tension. Immediately thereafter, the melody begins rising again to a lower peak through a sequence built on short motives. Here it is rhythm – an increased use of small note values – that supports the climax and continues to control the rest of the section. While abruptly lowering the dynamic level and reining in on the harmonic movement with a dominant pedal [bars 57ff.], Haydn slackens the rhythmic motion only by degrees, first by keeping a semiquaver and quaver motive on one of the inner parts and then by cutting it down in size and interjecting frequent rests. The cadence thereby achieves complete repose and the development section takes on the character of a self-contained unit.

Now this is, as the reader (listener) will have gathered, a spectacular innovation, and to implement this enormous decrescendo, Haydn's dynamic language is no longer sufficient. In those days, the abbreviation *ppp* did not exist, but at bar 57 Haydn already has a complicated dynamic façade in operation: *pp* in the first violins, *p* for the horns and other strings (*inter alia* for the weaving line of the second violin, on whose shoulders the forward thrust is now placed). At bar 59, however, Haydn needs a kind of *pp* and he expresses this by writing 'pianiss.', which, being interpreted, simply means 'softer than *pp*' (for another and equally dramatic use of this 'pianissimo' after *pp* – and at the same de-acceleration of a development just before the recapitulation – see Symphony No. 56/I, bars 159ff.).

The slow movement is another kind of *perpetuum mobile* (cf. No. 2/II, *supra*), this time with the second violin moving in restless syncopations throughout. The muted violins are also to become one of Haydn's best-loved effects, especially in the symphonic slow movements of the early 1770s. The metre is two-four and the tempo Andante: this is not yet the time for soul-searching adagios, and the melancholy of this D minor movement is of an Italianate kind, the quiet winter mist of the Venetian Lagoon which Haydn can have learned at second hand, from Vivaldi. The Finale, entitled 'Tempo di Menuetto', is Haydn's clever combination of the minuet (though in 3/8 rather than 3/4) with the typical finale form. There is a strong spiritual link to the first movement – another gigantic and breathtakingly effective de-accentuation leading back to the recapitulation. It is the pedal point to end all pedal points, and it begins at once on the other side of the double bar and continues through no less than twenty-four bars until the reprise begins. The dynamic level at first sinks to *piano*, and then to *pp*. While the lower strings perpetuate the basic pulse with their endlessly repeated quavers, the upper strings (backed, first, by horn interjections and then, as part of the master scheme, by a huge held octave from the horns) increase the expectation by broken patterns, each phrase leading to silence, to a concentration on triplet 'ends'). It is all fabulously organized.

In the old days, when a critical edition of Haydn's first forty symphonies was first printed in 1907, Breitkopf & Härtel, the publishers, scarcely bothered to issue practical editions of these works. Who would have performed them? One of the very few exceptions was No. 4, of which they issued a separate score and parts (with a neatly fashioned harpsichord continuo by Günther Raphael).

Symphony No. 10 in D

Scoring: 2 oboes, 2 horns, strings and *continuo* [bassoon, harpsichord].

Another brilliant D major Symphony for Count Morzin (the others are Nos. 1, 4 and 15), with a main theme containing strong contrasts between *p* and *f* and big chords in the violins. This is the most outwardly brilliant of these four D major works, with dashing repeated figures in the violins

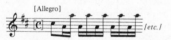

as well as similar patterns in the second violins during massive tuttis. There is a perfect *fausse reprise* a few bars after the development begins – too close to the double bar to make us believe that the real recapitulation is at hand. Actually, this practice comes from another trait entirely, and that is Haydn's habit of modulating immediately back to the tonic at the beginning of the development and thereafter starting the real course of the modulatory pattern. For a classic case, see the first movements of Nos. 17 and 19. There is, however, an innovation which must have struck the attentive listeners of Morzin's circle: the second subject is in the dominant *major* (rather than the customary minor).

Andante, G major, 2/4, strings only: it is based on a classic 'sighing' motif, that is, the stepwise progression downwards:

This chaste and restrained movement is thoroughly dominated by this one idea; there are interesting dynamic contrasts towards the end of both main sections. In the final 3/8 Presto, we are again riveted by the long development section. By now we almost expect the long dominant pedal point with which it opens, but certainly not the

extended section in minor, which is not only *piano* but transforms the little passage of the exposition whence it originates (bars 13ff.) from pert staccato to sinewy legato phrases: as we slowly work round to another dominant pedal point, we realize that we are again witnessing one of Haydn's beautifully constructed psychological decrescendos.

Symphony No. 32 in C

Scoring: 2 oboes, 2 horns, 2 horns in C, 2 *clarini* (trumpets) in C, timpani (C–G), strings and *continuo* [bassoon, harpsichord].

And now the greatest change of all: Haydn's festive orchestra, with trumpets and kettledrums which, at this period, Haydn only uses in C major. C major was no doubt associated in Haydn's, and his listeners' minds, with solemn Masses in that key, featuring trumpets and drums. The Austrians composed hundreds of such festive Masses, and the tradition goes straight to Mozart and even Beethoven, whose first Mass, for Prince Nicolaus II Esterházy, was in C.

We have one serious problem. It is really not certain whether the horns are in C *alto*, i.e. playing at pitch, or C *basso*, i.e. an octave lower. The authentic sources – we have them for all three Fürnberg-Morzin works (Nos. 20, 32, 33) – simply say 'Corno Primo Ex C', with no indication. Now this usually meant C *basso*, but if we begin to examine the Esterházy works, the situation becomes more complicated. One autograph of a C major work with trumpets and timpani survives: No. 56 (1774), where Haydn clearly specifies two horns 'in C hoch' (high C), trumpets and kettledrums. In other C major symphonies (Nos. 38, 41, 48), we have no autographs and it seems that Haydn added the trumpets and timpani for Nos. 38 and 41 later, but at least in the case of No. 41, we have good sources requiring C *alto* horns, trumpets and drums. We therefore consider it possible, even likely, that Haydn's Morzin horn players used C *alto* horns. There is one convincing internal piece of evidence to support this theory, namely that the horns never go higher than written *a″* (which note is required by Haydn in the A major Symphony No. 5 several times), which is also the limit for Esterházy works where we have authentic sources with C *alto* horns, e.g. No. 48 (Joseph Elssler's parts: see *Haydn at Eszterháza 1766–1790*, p. 297). When Haydn is clearly writing for C *basso* horns, e.g. for the early works of the first Esterházy period when he had no trumpets at all in his orchestra, such as Nos. 7 and 9, he has no hesitation in writing for (written) *c‴* (Menuetto of No. 7; Trio in No. 9). Therefore, in our critical edition of these works (Doblinger, also Philharmonia pocket scores) we have opted for C *alto* horns.

The first movement of No. 32 is in quick metre (2/4) and marked, in addition, Allegro molto: it is a large-scale movement and with one crash of the orchestra we are in the blazing world of Haydn's festive C major. This is the first authentic manuscript evidence of Haydn's trumpet writing (we recall that the trumpets for Organ

Concerto, XVIII:1, were called for in the autograph but the staves left blank) in a purely instrumental piece; but we have earlier, authentic trumpet writing with which to compare it: the Corpus Christi music and the Eibiswald *contrafactum*. The trumpet writing of No. 32 is much more modern and looks forward to the trumpet writing of Haydn's maturity. The main difference between the *clarini* of 1758–9 and those of the London period is simply that Haydn still expects his players of the 1750s to negotiate high notes such as *b″* and *c‴* which, in 1791–5, he would not.

In a heavily symphonic movement like this opening Allegro molto, we are not surprised at the brilliance of the orchestration and the masterly way in which it is used for Haydn's grand formal design. The repeated quavers are its mortar. The repeated semiquavers are used to heighten the tension, i.e. before the second subject (still in the dominant minor) and at the end of the exposition. The second subject is intensely rhythmical and deftly orchestrated (note how the bass entry is timed, bars 48ff.) and Haydn has reserved a special entry for it in the development section, so that when we come to the recapitulation, this second subject is simply dropped. The development section is the longest and most tightly organized of any thus far examined. Its predictability is only in the long dominant pedal with which it opens: but this does not lead to a *fausse reprise* and indeed, the tonic is reached obliquely (not in root position) and only as a springboard to further, turbulent development. In the exposition, the repeated semiquavers were used very sparingly, but in the development they are introduced after two bars, in second violins, and then in bars 87–100 in the first violins: all this is Haydn's technical exploitation of the device to lend weight and potency to this by now crucially important part of the formal scheme. The development is now 60 bars long, almost as long as the whole exposition (70 bars): we are in the midst of the most important musical development of these early symphonies. At the end of the exposition, Haydn expands the closing material and starts the end tutti four bars earlier, but because he has now omitted the second subject, the whole recapitulation is put together differently, and in far more complex fashion.

The 'Minuet' (Haydn's pre-1760 spelling, found in the Fürnberg-Morzin parts) comes second and is massively symphonic: Haydn's horn gambit of ♩ ♪♪♪♩ takes on expanded weight when supported by trumpets and timpani. We marvel at the sophistication of Haydn's language: how, for example, the typical triplet rhythm of the violins as they approach the first double bar is at once continued across the double bar in the second violins. In this same four bar phrase, we also marvel how Haydn increases the weight of the repetition simply by increasing the role of the trumpets and timpani – so simple, so effective. The Trio (C minor, strings only) is the strongest possible contrast: old fashioned, with a long glance backwards, it never rises above the *piano* level. The third movement (Adagio, ma non troppo) is also

this kind of contrast and having had two previous movements with the whole weight of Haydn's festive orchestra, the wind instruments and the audience were no doubt relieved to hear the *pp* accents of the strings alone in this Adagio. The Finale (Presto, 3/8) is the kind of movement we have come to expect, but here made heavier and more interesting by the increased weight of the trumpets and drums: the tiny second subject in the usual minor is given a curiously unsettled air by adding repeated semiquaver accompaniment in the first violin (bars 25, 83) – a slight *frisson*. Again, repeated semiquaver patterns, sparingly used in the exposition, are immediately thrown into the texture when the development starts.

Symphony No. 5 in A

Scoring: 2 oboes, 2 horns, strings and *continuo* [bassoon, harpsichord].

Here is another work in the *sonata da chiesa* form, opening with an entire Adagio, ma non troppo (it is a characteristic of these church sonata works that they open with an adagio rather than an andante – the exception, No. 18, was as we have seen marked Andante moderato – so as to give the overall form an increased weight. Here, in No. 5, we have an interesting example of the divertimento-cassatio technique being applied to such a solemn, slow movement: hardly have the strings begun by themselves (leading us to believe that this is a typical wind-less slow movement) than the solo horns enter with a passage of the greatest difficulty. Haydn even witholds the oboes until bar 20. In the recapitulation, the horns are expected to play sounding *a″* in this totally exposed solo section. To balance this fantastic hybrid Adagio, ma non troppo, Haydn writes a very tight second movement, with springy rhythms and wide dynamic contrasts (second subject, beginning with an unsettled harmonic background, veers towards E *major* and is announced only by the two violins, *piano*. The 'Minuet' is even more Austrian than the cassatio-like sounds of the opening movement, and many scholars have commented on its folk-like quality. In the Trio, this atmosphere is, if anything, enhanced by the divertimento-like application of the solo horns (again reaching sounding *a″*) and solo oboes. In such a movement as this Minuet & Trio, Haydn was very far removed from the Mannheim school, and equally far removed from the grave Baroque grandeur of Vivaldi and his Austrian contemporaries. In the Finale to No. 5, Haydn creates a very short but effective conclusion to this church-sonata work: taking a leaf from the second movement, we find wide contrasts between the theme's beginning (two violins alone, *p*) and continuation (a grand tutti, with repeated semiquavers). Being in cut time, it is quite a different kind of finale than the usual 3/8 Presto to which we are accustomed, and it is a clear signpost to the future: this, expanded and developed, will be the language of the great Haydn finales to come.

Symphony No. 11 in E flat

Scoring: 2 oboes, 2 horns, strings and *continuo* [bassoon, harpsichord].

Another work conceived as the second part of a pair? It would seem so, judging from Haydn's consecutive numbering (Nos. 13 and 14 = our Nos. 5 and 11). Perhaps No. 5 was such a success at the Morzin soirée that another in the *sonata da chiesa* form was immediately demanded. Perhaps, indeed, that is the origin of all the pairs in this volume. No. 11 has a gravely beautiful opening in the old *chiesa* formula: first violins silent, theme announced in the tonic by second violins (starting on the 5th of the scale); first violins have the *comes*, starting on the tonic, at bar 5. Haydn made some important revisions in the horn parts of this movement, just before the double bars of both sections (28ff., 75ff.), adding sustained notes throughout rather than a crotchet to reinforce the *f* at bars 28, 30, 75 and 77. He added these personally to the horn parts of the Fürnberg-Morzin manuscript (Keszthely Castle) – one page is reproduced in most copies of the Philharmonia bound score of Vol. 1 of the Critical Edition of the Complete Symphonies (No. 589, 1965). There are no oboes in this whole movement; Haydn has reserved them for the following Allegro, a hard-driven, tightly rhythmic foil to the luxuriant spaciousness of the opening Adagio. The second subject is a contrapuntal variant of the first, but scored only for two violins, *piano*. Throughout we observe that the main theme has been so constructed that it can be exploited contrapuntally (e.g. in canon during the recapitulation, bars 112ff.).

The Minuet is of an irresistible rhythmic drive and also of a rather bizarre construction (the main section's twelve bars may be subdivided into 7 + 5). The Trio, for strings alone, has an oddly syncopated pattern which slides unobtrusively from second to first violin and back again. The racy and rhythmically unconventional Finale is built on the retrograde of the second movement (originally *e flat–f–g–a flat*, but in the Finale *a flat–g–f–e flat*) but employing the syncopated rhythm of the Trio. It is on a larger scale, though in a quick metre (2/4), than the previous Morzin finales; as, indeed, all the church-sonata symphonies exceed in physical size and emotional scope the other, more normal works of the period. Were they, in fact, actually used in the Morzin chapel at Lukavec? Or is the *chiesa* aspect purely on a sublimated level?

Symphony No. 33 in C

Scoring: 2 oboes, 2 horns in C, 2 *clarini* (trumpets) in C, timpani (C–G), strings and *continuo* [bassoon, harpsichord].

If Haydn's numbering is to be believed, Nos. 32 and 33 hardly form a pair of works, but both are similarly scored and are the composer's first symphonies with trumpets and kettledrums. Regardless of these internal numberings, however, and – as so often happens in the case of Haydn's real pairs –

one composition is finer than the other. We have noted all sorts of interesting details in connection with No. 32, including the increased length and weight of the development section in the first movement, as well as Haydn's new way of writing for the trumpets (different from that of the earliest vocal pieces).

Haydn was above all an essentially practical man, and the changes he introduced into his finished works throughout his life show that he relied heavily on his ear for last-minute corrections. The best way for Haydn to learn how to write for this large orchestra with trumpets and timpani was to compose one work after another. Thus there is no question that No. 33 is even finer in overall construction and inner balance than No. 32. The opening Vivace of No. 33 is in Haydn's favourite metre of three-four, and there are several aspects of the movement that compel our interest. By this time, Haydn has rapidly learned how to marshal his four brass instruments and kettledrums, with an experienced ear for the limitations of his (of course) valveless and keyless trumpets/horns. Now on these natural trumpets, the note *g* sharp″ (which can also be *g* natural″) is often – but not always – the better-sounding of the two alternatives for this impure note. The way in which this *g* sharp is introduced in the trumpet parts of No. 33, first movement (bars 29, 31), and later in Symphonies Nos. 41 and 56, suggests that in combination with the horns, and regardless of whether the latter are pitched in *alto* or *basso*, Haydn's sounded particularly splendid when using this *g* sharp″, they rise to their highest register in this fashion; for the *g* sharp is in the *second* trumpet, the first playing *a″–b″*.

The first movement is 149 bars in length (both sections marked with repeats), and the most interesting thing about it structurally is the prominent place assigned to the second subject (in the dominant major, incidentally). It is divided into three sections, no less: a series of syncopated gestures in the violins leading twice to an on-the-beat resolution (bars 27–31), followed by a remarkable passage for the three upper strings (double bass rests), the viola being marked *mezzo forte* to underline its new function as *fondamento*; while the third part also fulfils the function of a closing expositional tutti. This is the longest second subject in any Haydn symphony so far, and Haydn makes prominent use of it in the development, after a classic *fausse reprise*. A few further technical details: Haydn has also become very adept at using his semiquavers to increase tension, as we see at bars 7ff., where the second violins accelerate the pulse of the second part of the first subject. The semiquavers are then transferred to both violins as we move towards a permanent dominant tonal basis (bars 13ff.). The use of syncopations over a steady series of quavers also has the effect of heightening the textural tension (bars 20ff.), and both the syncopations and, alternatively, semiquavers are used adroitly to raise the nervous level of the development (bars 65ff.) which is once again on an unprecedented scale except for No. 32; in No. 33 it is actually the precise equal of the exposition's total length (exposition: 51 bars; development: 51 bars), while the recapitulation is a few bars shorter. Something of the graceful proportions of this Vivace have mirrored themselves in the movement's inner poise.

The slow movement (Andante, 2/4, C minor) is a contrast on every possible level, but mostly in its omission of all the wind instruments and timpani. If in No. 33 the Vivace was extremely forward-looking, this Andante is deliberately old-fashioned in language, with long series of passages in two-part harmony, the violins being in unison and the viola doubling the bass line (bars 27ff., 59ff., 67ff., 93ff.). The frequent use of the triplets almost seems to be schematic, and reminds one of the language used by Wagenseil or Tuma. The 'Minuet' (spelling of our authentic MS.) remind us, in a delightful wash of colour provided by the trumpets and drums *piano* at bars 13–15, that not so long ago these attractive *clarini* and *tympano* parts were not yet discovered. Since then, we found them not only in the authentic Fürnberg-Morzin MS., but also in sources at Prague, Frankfurt-am-Main and (incomplete) in a source in the Gesellschaft der Musikfreunde, Vienna. In the Trio, marked *pp* and for strings only, we note the cat-like syncopations of the violins over the on-the-beat security of the lower strings.

The Finale is on a much larger scale, and is musically more complex than the similar movement in No. 32. No. 33 has a genuine second subject and is in the same kind of sonata form as an opening movement. Several features of note present themselves to eye and ear: the delicate use of *pp* to end the second subject; the use, in the development, of a sudden *ff* which raises to the highest dynamic level a long increase in tension. Here, we may watch Haydn using segments of the main theme in the bass line, a real case of 'motivische Arbeit' (bars 55ff.), with the violins and violas surging forward in repeated semiquavers, rising gradually, in jagged flashes from *d''* to *e* flat'', *e* natural'', *a''*, *b* flat'', *b* natural and, finally *d''*. It is when the violins reach their *d''* that the *fortissimo* is introduced as the climax of a passage lasting from bars 55 to 78 and then dropping away, melodically and in dynamic range to *p* and curving gracefully into the recapitulation.

Symphony No. 27 in G

Scoring: From the Fürnberg-Morzin MS., it would appear that Haydn originally wrote this work for 2 oboes and strings [bassoon and harpsichord *continuo*]. The horns were added at an early date and possibly by Haydn, but there is no authentic evidence for them.

This Haydn Symphony had the distinction of being erroneously 'discovered' in 1946. At Freck Castle near what used to be Hermannstadt in the Austrian Province of Transylvania (now Sibiu in Roumania), this work was discovered in the musical library of Baron Brukenthal. It was quite rightly thought that this was a genuine Haydn

symphony, and on 29 January 1950 the newly resuscitated work was played at Bucharest by the Philharmonic State Orchestra and subsequently recorded as the *Hermannstädter Symphonie*. It was some years before the West could acquire the *incipit* of the work – and some years before Roumania could gather sufficient bibliographical evidence to realize that the work they had found had been codified and published in the Breitkopf & Härtel *Gesamtausgabe* as No. 27 in 1907. In 1960, the present writer was finally able to examine the source: it is a local copy and is dated 1786.

A sturdy and heavily symphonic first movement bursts into immediate energy with repeated semiquavers in the second violins and marching bass quavers. The solid inner parts and the 'rocketing' theme of the violins again show that Haydn was not unacquainted with the techniques of the Mannheim school; but he had not really explored their exaggerated dynamic language since Symphony No. 1's opening crescendo. 'Rocket' in Mannheim language was a theme that moves upwards – in this case a very slow-moving *force de frappe*. Elsewhere the language is massively symphonic too, considering what small forces Haydn was able to muster – at bars 18ff., the weaving of the upper parts from chain syncopations to tight rhythmic figures is set against a procession of accented crotchets in the bass part. For the second subject, we have an interesting hybrid that begins in the dominant major but ends in the dominant minor, truly transitional.

The second movement, without the wind parts, is a *siciliano* in lilting six-eight motion, as Italian an andante as was ever composed in Naples or Palermo: extraordinary how Haydn, whose knowledge of Italy was exclusively at second hand (e.g. via his later mistress, Luigia Polzelli), could so magically recapture the blue skies and dancing waters that he would never see: he provides us with several such Italian serenades, not least in the ravishing Concertos for the King of Naples (1786). The terse Finale (Presto) reminds us yet again that even at this early stage of his symphonic career, Haydn's sense of timing is impeccable. A heavily symphonic first movement leads to an Italian *siciliano* as light as a feather, and the whole work ends with a swift and delicate conclusion in light metre (3/8). A typical pre-1762 work in which the symphonic element decreases as the work continues but whose melodic highpoint is the slow movement: that is why there are hardly any tunes at all in the flanking movements but rather *subjects*.

Symphony 'A' in B flat (I:107)

Scoring: 2 oboes, 2 horns in B flat [*alto*], strings and *continuo* [bassoon, harpsichord].

We have seen that this three-movement work, strongly symphonic in its contours, was inserted into Chevardière's second edition of the Op. I Quartets (where it was never asserted that our work was anything but a symphony, since all six works were entitled as such, also at the head of each work). The wind parts were dropped, which as it happens could be done without having to rewrite the strings. The only authentic source of the work, the Fürnberg-Morzin MS., is as a symphony and was corrected by Haydn who, however, for some reason did not assign it a number; the number was later added by the music master of Count Festetics, but we have retained it. In this authentic copy of our 'Sÿnfonia Ex b Fa', the horns are listed on the title page of the MS. but are missing. Fortunately, another set of parts exists in the Monastery of St Florian in Upper Austria (first recorded performance: November 1767) from which the horn parts could be supplied. Of the Göttweig performance material (which the Catalogue informs us was dated 1762), we were able, many years ago, when assisting the Monastery in putting its scattered collection of music into order, to find the second violin part of the otherwise lost material. The first edition of this recovered work was included as an appendix to *SYM* (1955).

Whatever the proper chronological number of this work should be, we register many 'modern' features: the use of three-four for the opening movement, the prominent second subject in F major (also used in the development), the thoroughly symphonic language (bars 56ff. should have made anyone suspicious that this could have been a string quartet – the semiquaver pattern of the violins is well known to us from all these early orchestral works), the large-scale form of the Finale (using six-eight time). These two, rather intellectual-sounding movements are contrasted by an Andante (no wind instruments) that never once rises above *piano* and moves in a stately pace rather like a gavotte.

Symphony No. 3 in G

Scoring: 2 oboes, 2 horns, strings and *continuo* [bassoon, harpsichord].

It is not certain, as we point out above, that the number '21' is in Haydn's hand, but we are inclined to believe that it is, and that the Fürnberg-Morzin MS. originated contemporaneously with the rest of the series and not later – a theory which is supported by the watermark with its curious position in the middle of the sheet. In any case, and regardless of whether the MS. is part of the series or not, the Symphony was catalogued in Göttweig Abbey by 1762 and is indubitably a part of the Morzin canon. This is altogether, and in many different respects, the most modern and forward-looking of all these early symphonies. The modernity comes, firstly, in the construction of the first movement, with a second subject of great individuality (solo oboes) in the dominant major, but even more in the rich texture that Haydn introduces even as soon as the transition. There is a distinct polyphonic feeling to the music, even in the symphonic way it is orchestrated. As Haydn works into the development, his increased density of thought is matched by a slow piling-up of more countersubjects to the main theme. From the

standpoint of textural density, this development is one of the most significant; but there is more to it, even, than that. The recapitulation continues the development, so that the re-announcement of the principal subject combines the breadth of the very first announcement (bars 1ff.) with the countersubject in the horns with which Haydn adorned the original extension at bars 10ff. (see bars 80ff.). Another aspect of the work's modernity is the use of four movements which, after much wavering and second thoughts on the matter, will be the pattern of the future. And paradoxically, another facet of the work's modernity is its use of the old-fashioned counterpoint throughout. In fact, Haydn's mature style was to include, almost as second nature, a streak of Baroque contrapuntalism which continued through Mozart and was also cultivated by Beethoven, whose 'Große Fuge' carries the art to ultimate splendour and Albrechtsbergian complexity. We may single out, in No. 3, the nature of the theme with which it begins; for it lends itself perfectly to this polyphonic treatment, giving the movement its arresting and multi-voiced richness. On the other hand, the second subject, with its oboe solos, and also the trio of the Minuet, with solo passages for oboes and horns, show their origin in the Austrian cassatio.

The second movement is a fine G minor Andante moderato, very firmly rooted in the Austrian Baroque tradition, where the shifting back and forth of the main theme between first and second violins recalls the old trio sonata. It is a characteristic of Haydn's mentality in this first symphonic era that, when he has created a first movement of startling modernity and complexity, he usually reverts to a slow movement much more old-fashioned and conservative than we might expect from another composer; and in this he reveals, more than in any other single trait, his musical upbringing.

The 'Menuet' (the new spelling Haydn began to adopt about the end of 1760) is if anything even more Baroque in structure, for it turns out to be a canon between top and bottom lines at the interval of one bar: that this created a *furore* at the time may be seen in literal imitations by Johann Michael Haydn, W. A. Mozart and also Haydn himself, in Symphony No. 23 (also in G, about which work *vide infra*, pp. 567f.). The climax of all this preoccupation with contrapuntal forms is the Finale, which is a sturdy fugue with two subjects in the manner of J. J. Fux, the great Austrian contrapuntist whose treatise, *Gradus ad Parnassum*, was Haydn's model and that used for his pupils as well.[1] Haydn's is not, of course, a 'straight' fugue, but is used in conjunction with elements of sonata form, e.g. modulation to the dominant. One particular aspect must be pointed out: the entire 'exposition' of the fugue, up to the first tutti, is announced *pianissimo*, a very outré effect and one that Haydn

---

1 See D. Arnold, 'Haydn's Counterpoint and Fux's "Gradus"', in *Monthly Musical Record* 87, March-April 1957, pp. 52ff.

tends to associate with this Baroque Revival: we will, a dozen years later, find 'sempre piano' in the ghostly F minor Fugue of the famous String Quartet Op. 20, No. 5 (1772) – not ghostly at all unless this strict dynamic requirement is met with. Here, in No. 3, all the entries are carefully marked *pp*, even those of the oboes and horns. There is a stirring middle section, corresponding to the development of sonata form, and of course something that would soon become a great speciality in Haydn's fugal forms, a life-enhancing pedal point, followed by another fingerprint of later Haydn, the final, rousing unison passage (complete contrast to polyphony).

The introduction of the fugue into this Morzin Symphony was, in view of the course that we know the Viennese classical period will take, of crucial importance in the history of music. Thus, this modest Symphony No. 3 certainly deserves the high number 'N^ro 21' in the Fürnberg-Morzin series, for it – of all its sisters – is the one to peer farthest into the future.

Symphony No. 20 in C

Scoring: 2 oboes, 2 horns in C, 2 *clarini* (trumpets) in C, timpani (C-G), strings and *continuo* [bassoon, harpsichord].

We conclude our hypothetical list of Morzin symphonies with No. 20, the third symphony in C with trumpets and timpani, and one added later, in *EK*, in pencil by Haydn and given the relatively high number on *that* list (which is discussed, *infra*, pp. 552f.) of No. 55. When adding up his list of symphonies composed up to *c*. 1770, Haydn seems to have added the *incipits* of two works, Nos. 39 and 20, after he had composed them. But we believe that there are two reasons why the present work must belong to the Morzin period: (1) Haydn had no trumpets and timpani in the Esterházy orchestra before *c*. 1773, and then only the timpani regularly; but we have seen that he did have trumpets and drums in the Morzin *Capelle*. (2) There is one complete copy, with all the instruments, in the handwriting of Fürnberg-Morzin No. 4 (Regensburg), which suggests the work was part of our series. It has been suggested, at one time or another, that it is the kind of work suitable for performance in the great Austrian

monasteries, whose *Prunksäle*, or great halls, glitter with the same slightly impersonal Baroque grandeur as these C major Morzin symphonies with trumpets and kettledrums.

Now there is one feature that all three of these works have in common, namely, the increased weight attached to the development sections. This is also the case with No. 20, whose 2/4 metre and Allegro molto recall the similar outward construction of No. 32. The second subject is another example of the 'pre-classical compromise', starting in G major but ending in G minor. The long development – it is only a few bars shorter than the whole exposition – culminates in one of those quiet pedal points which are fast becoming a regular feature. Here, it serves to reduce the pressure of a long preceding tutti and prepare us for the loud recapitulation. One registers the insistent punctuation of brass and timpani at the beginning of each bar, *piano*: this is soon to become a hallmark of the Viennese classical style whenever trumpets and timpani are being used.

The second movement is much more like an andante from an early quartet, with its running quaver accompaniment in second violin, its pizzicato lower strings and its *pp* melody in first violin. There is a nice surge of feeling at bar 21, marked *poco f(orte)* and led onto the stage by a pretty dialogue between the first and second violins. This 'set piece' appears twice more, in the development and in its proper place in the reprise. This Andante cantabile is for strings only.

This is another four movement work, with the third a Minuet/Trio (the latter for strings only), followed by a Presto Finale in 3/8 which is a very large-scale A-B-A, the 'B' section being in the minor and dropping the trumpets and drums. Contrary to the bolder trumpet writing of Nos. 32 and 33, the trumpets here do not at first exceed the usual *g''*; also that the famous *g sharp''* is here *always* given to the horns (Finale, bars 23'', 25'', 176'', 178''), almost as if Haydn had a different band at his disposal for No. 20. But just before the end, the trumpets suddenly rise to their top *c'''* (bar 243), *not* followed by the C horns: this suggests that the horns really were in C *alto* (otherwise this written top *c''*, sounding an octave lower, would have been easily played and logical) and that, after all, it was Morzin's band for which this work, less interesting than Nos. 32 and 33, was composed.

III. The First Haydn School

Throughout this biography, we shall be noticing Haydn's *seguaci*, some of them forgotten names, almost all of them interesting men and worthy of study. We believe that the study of these various Haydn schools – four are traced in this biography – begins with the swift emergence of Haydn's European fame *c*. 1760, when the quartets began to circulate and his first symphonies were known. Although these earlier symphonies certainly found their admirers and by the second half of the 1760s, a whole group of *seguaci* in the Haydn symphonic style had grown up, it was the quartet-divertimenti which attracted, perhaps, the widest attention. This was because, although there was a flourishing school of Austrian symphonic composers by 1757 – Göttweig acquired a symphony by Ordoñez with a slow introduction in the year preceding – the quartet-divertimenti were something quite new and much easier to perform, because only four instruments were involved, than complicated symphonies, the production of which amateurs could scarcely hope to assail. Therefore, a great many people, amateurs and skilled professionals alike, seized on the style and content of these early Haydn quartet-divertimenti and started to imitate them. Many of these imitations were innocent, along the lines that imitation is the sincerest form of flattery; but possibly others were not so innocent. Sometimes one has the impression that the Viennese agents of Parisian publishers not only scoured the *Kleinmeister* of the Austrian capital and provinces for works that sounded like Haydn, but they actually persuaded (commissioned?) minor composers to turn out works that they could easily market under Haydn's name.

If it was, in fact, J. G. Albrechtsberger who was the 'cellist in the first performances of Haydn's quartet-divertimenti at Weinzierl Castle, he had a perfect opportunity to study the new works at first hand. Being so close, at Maria-Taferl, and later, at Melk Abbey, he was certainly one of the first to try his hand at the form. The Esterházy Archives in Budapest own a series of Albrechtsberger autographs which were acquired by Prince Nicolaus II Esterházy in October 1810, and which include a series[1] of string quartets in Albrechtsberger's autograph, dated Melk. There were, obviously, to be six, for we find 'Divertimento II^{do} a 4^{tro}' ('Composui 20te Feb: / $\overline{760}$ Melcii'), as well as 'Divertimento VI° a 4^{tro} ex B' dated 28 May 1760, and No. IV^{to}, signed 'O A M D G: finivi et composui Melcii Die 23 Julij $\overline{760}$.' The other three of the series do not exist in Budapest. Those three that do are numbered respectively Ms. mus. 2396, 2400, & 2398. No. 3 of another series, also composed at Melk, is dated 1764 (Ms. mus. 2397).

Here, then, are at least three works composed by a friend of Haydn's who was possibly the 'cellist at Weinzierl. What do these works tell us? For one thing, we find all the outward forms of the early Haydn quartets, but also some new ideas by Albrechtsberger. Divertimento II of 1760 has six movements:

I. Andante molto. II. Menuet. III. Allegro, 2/4. IV. Adagio. V. Menuet (Vivace). VI. Finale (Presto), 3/8. E flat major but played in scordatura 'più Basso d'un mezzo tono', i.e. in D major. 4° paper (watermarks: 'FI' in heart, fleur-de-lys in ornament of large size). Ms. mus. 2396.

The Trio of the second movement appears to be original, that of the fifth was added on different paper and probably later. We note that the rare dynamic mark 'mezzo for:' is used in viola and basso. In No. VI we have Albrechtsberger's first innovation: a straight, four-movement quartet:

I. Allegro moderato. II. Menuet/Trio. III. Andante E flat IV. Finale (Presto), 3/8. 4° paper (watermarks: 'FRW', man with club). Ms. mus. 2400.

No. IV has the following arrangement –

I. Andante, F major. II. Menuet/Trio. III. Andantino, C major. IV. Menuet/Trio (the Trio perhaps added later on the last page of the MS.) V. Finale (Allegro molto), 2/4. Ms. mus. 2398.

---

1 L. Somfai, 'Albrechtsberger-Eigenschriften in der Nationalbibliothek Széchényi, Budapest', in *Studia musicologica* I/1–2 (1961), pp. 175ff. We studied the Albrechtsberger MSS. at the Library in Budapest in 1960.

while the 1764 work (on Italian paper, 'AM' with bow-and-arrow, three crescents of declining size) is again in four movements, this time

> I. Moderato, E major. II. Andante con sordino, A major. III. Menuet/Trio. IV. Andante [con variazioni].

Albrechtsberger thus veered to the four-movement form as early as 1760 (with minuet second) and in 1764 with the minuet in third place. Otherwise, we find not only the outward form of Haydn's quartets, but also the tender use of the mute in slow movements – the Italian serenade in six-eight Andante that opens No. IV of 1760 was a feature of Haydn's early quartet style, too. But the movements in which Albrechtsberger most closely imitates Haydn are the minuets, the themes of which are often very like the originals; and the 3/8 finales, if without the frothy effervescence of Haydn's, are extraordinarily good imitations. Like Haydn, Albrechtsberger was also much taken with the *sonata da chiesa* form and some of the best movements are these and other opening adagios or andantes of the period (Divertimento in G for flute, violin, viola, and basso of January 1761). Without exaggeration, these early works by the later teacher of Beethoven may be reckoned to the First Haydn School. It is no accident that one such attractive Albrechtsberger Quartet, in D, the autograph of which is entitled 'Divertimento I^{mo} a 4^{tro}' – the work may even have been part of the 1760 series – was in Göttweig Abbey and falsely attributed to Haydn *as early as 1763* as a sextet with two horns (and later Göttweig also acquired the work as a Haydn string quartet). This false Haydn (Hoboken III:D3), which begins with a beautiful slow variation movement, has movement after movement that sounds amazingly like the Haydn of Opp. I and II. The Minuet No. 1 – the work has five movements – has a theme characterized by that Haydnesque *esprit* and lilt

Menuet

but which is authentic Albrechtsberger. It figures as Haydn in Lambach Abbey and other sources. Here we have the problem of the Haydn *seguaci* at its earliest stage, but also at its most acute. In a word: the cultivated monks at Göttweig Abbey in 1763 were totally unable to differentiate between real Haydn and a work by a talented follower.[1]

The next figure to engage our attention is Franz (František) Xaver Dussek (1731–99), whose early music has recently been catalogued in a useful study by V.J. Sýkora.[2] The scholarly world was particularly interested in Dussek not only on account of his wife, Josepha, who sang in early productions by Mozart and Beethoven, but also because such a large number of string quartets by Dussek had been wrongly attributed to Haydn.[3] Dussek wrote a vast quantity of astonishingly Haydnesque wind-band music – most is preserved in Prague – but also quartets, largely preserved in the Pachta collection, some dating back as far as 1761, including one of the very ones attributed to 'Giorgio Hayden' (Op. 18, No. 2, Pachta XXII C106, dated 1761). The music of all these early Dussek quartets is based on Haydn, but it is very interesting to observe that, like Albrechtsberger, Dussek seems to prefer the four-movement form

1 Landon, 'Doubtful and spurious Quartets and Quintets attributed to Haydn', *Music Review* XVIII/3 (1957), p. 218. Somfai, op. cit., pp. 201f. Albrechtsberger autograph, EH, Budapest, Ms. mus. 2395. As Albrechtsberger also in Melk Abbey. As Haydn, modern edition by Schott (4174, ed. Hans Erdmann).

2 *František Xaver Dušek*, Prague 1958.

3 Including six, 'Del Signore Giorgio Hayden', Op. XVIII, about which see Landon, 'Doubtful...', op. cit., p. 215.

with the minuet coming second, though there are several in the customary five-movement shape as we know it from Haydn. That Dussek literally copied Haydn may be seen in a manuscript prepared by Dussek 'Dermal in Sichelsdorf geschrieben des 1796 Jahres' (description in Sýkora, 201) which includes a Finale by Brixi and as 'Nro I' an Allegro which, though Dussek does not say so, is the Finale of the Divertimento (Concertino) for harpsichord and strings (XIV:4) by Haydn. Dussek was not attempting any mystification; he made this series of copies for himself and entitled it 'Diversae Partes pro Clavicembalo ad usum Franzisco Duschek'. But one can see that from there to attaching a name to such anonymous pieces was a small step (only in this case the anonymous piece was an old Divertimento by Haydn, composed years earlier).

And what of the anonymous *seguaci*? We thought readers might be interested in seeing one of these anonymous copies of Haydn's quartet-divertimenti, which we copied out in 1951. It is the first movement of a MS. from the former Abbey of Rottenmann (Styria) which, when we studied it, was stored in the attic of the parish church in Bad Aussee and is now in the Diözesanarchiv, Graz. In Hoboken it is wrongly listed as II:CI1 among the divertimenti, but it should belong to category III. Now we wonder if we are not dealing in this particular case with a deliberate falsification: what are we to make of 'Giuseppe Hayden. Eisen. AE.' Eisenstadt? It is an almost classic case of a *seguace*'s work: obviously copied from Haydn's quartet-divertimenti; not talented enough to be mistaken for the original by a real connoisseur, but good enough to pass muster at Rottenmann Abbey, and if circulated, it could easily have been marketed as 'Giorgio Hayden' in Paris. There are details directly stolen from Op. I – the tremolo strings at 9ff., the use of the fermata (placed gauchely, of course), and so on. If musical scholars were given to classifying these *seguaci*, one like the author of this quartet might have been called (to borrow the Berensonian 'Amico di Sandro' [Botticelli], which caused such a storm in a teacup years ago) 'Amico di Giuseppe'. We present it overleaf as a symbol of Haydn's growing fame, and as a specimen of the dozens of works, by talented and less talented men, being copied and printed under Haydn's name. Within ten years, they would be printing more spurious Haydn than genuine Haydn in Paris; and this is how it all began, in many cases – in an obscure Austrian town, castle or monastery.[1]

---

1 *Critical editions: Gesamtausgabe*, Breitkopf & Härtel, Series I, vols. 1–3 (E. Mandyczewski, F. von Weingartner), Leipzig 1907, Symphonies Nos. 1–40, textually now out of date. Complete Edition of Haydn's Symphonies (Landon): full scores, Nos. 'A' and 'B' (I:107, 108), Nos. 1–49, Verlag Doblinger. Miniature scores: Vols. 1 ('A', 'B', 1–12), 2 (13–27), 3 (28–40), Philharmonia (Universal Edition), completed 1965. In the B. & H. *Gesamtausgabe*, Ser. I, Vol. 4 (Nos. 1–49) was edited by Helmut Schultz however, authentic sources (Joseph Elssler) have been discovered for Nos. 41 and 48 and better MS. sources for Nos. 43 and 44.

Literature: B. Rywosch, *Beiträge zur Entwicklung in Joseph Haydns Symphonik 1759–1780*, Turbenthal 1934. Landon, *SYM* (1955). J. Vinton, 'The Development Section in early Viennese Symphonies', *Music Review*, XXIV/1 (1963). L. della Croce di Dojola, *Le 107 sinfonie di Haydn*, Turin 1975. A. Hodgson, *The Music of Joseph Haydn – The Symphonies*, London 1976.

Some first recordings: The first attempt to record a large selection of early Haydn symphonies was made by the Haydn Society, Boston–Vienna, 1949–51: Nos. 1, 6–8, 13, 21, 22, 26, 28, 31, 34, 35, 36, 38, 39, 42, 43, 44, 47, 48, mostly by various Viennese orchestras, conducted by Jonathan Sternberg, Anton Heiller, Franz Litschauer and, in No. 43, Mogens Wöldike conducting the Chamber Orchestra of the Danish State Radio. Producer: H.C.R.L. The second attempt: Library of Recorded Masterpieces: Vienna State Opera Orchestra, conducted by Max Goberman, 1960–2: Nos. 'A', 'B', 1–17, 19–24, 26, 27, 32, 34, 35, 37, 40, 41, 48, 49, 51, 52, 55, 56, 57, 60, 65, 92, 96, 98, and Overtures 'Acide', 'Lo speziale', 'L'infedeltà delusa.' Producer: H.C.R.L. Nos. 1–22 later C.B.S. (No. 18 conducted by Charles Mackerras with London Symphony Orch.). First complete recording of all Haydn's symphonies: Antal Dorati conducting Philharmonia Hungarica, Decca (U.S.: London), 1970s. Producer: James Mallinson.

[String Quartet (II:CII), attributed to Haydn – first movement]

*Wrongly ♪ ♪

*Source ♯, wrongly changed on basis of bar 61.   **Wrongly ♩   ***Wrongly ♯

*MS. 𝄽

**MS. 𝄽

It might not be amiss to pause, for a moment, to consider Haydn's musical character on the eve of his new engagement with Prince Paul Anton Esterházy in May 1761. We have seen the composer's secure formal grasp of sonata form and the inherent drama of the development section; his orchestration with its broad brush, underlining big formal concepts. He was adroit at the refurbishing of Italian melodies for cantabile slow movements, in particular the classic siciliano with its six-eight lilt. On the other hand, we have noted strong Baroque influences, especially in the slow movements and trios (where there are no wind parts, usually), where the shape of the melody and inner construction derive from the trio sonata. But we have also seen Haydn emancipating himself from traditional melodic, orchestral and formal influences. His personal style in the early quartet-divertimenti created a new school by 1760, which was informed by its creator's solidity of construction, gaiety, charm and wit.

Taking the wider view, Haydn was fast on the way to displacing the music of his teacher Georg Reutter, Jr., of Wagenseil, Tuma, Caldara, and the older generation. Haydn's sense of musical climax, his grasp of the infinite potentialities of sonata form, far exceeded the limited views and flawed technique of his Austrian precursors in the instrumental field. Like that of all Austrians of the period *c.* 1750, Haydn's music displays no sense of tragedy (but often a quiet *tristezza*), no heroic profundity and no flair for rhetoric (though a strong sense of inner developmental and motivic tension). We have little idea of Haydn's personal involvement in any of this music, and indeed, one is inclined to think that he carefully masked his own aspirations and emotions: starvation was not a fit subject for musical display by a young *compositeur*. In the vocal music that has survived, on the other hand, he reveals a real sense of religious feeling amounting – especially in music for his special protector, Our Lady, – to near ecstasy. All the seeds of later Haydn had been planted, and the soil was rich.

CHAPTER SEVEN

Eisenstadt and the Esterházys:
a short historical survey

THE BURGENLÄNDISCHES LANDESMUSEUM CONTAINS a whole section devoted to the prehistoric era in what is now the Austrian province of Burgenland, of which Eisenstadt is the capital. Eisenstadt itself was a small community in this prehistoric period, as excavations in the section known as Burgstallberg have shown. In the Roman period, the community lay on an old and frequented road between the present Müllendorf and Donnerskirchen. When Charlemagne defeated the Avars for the third time in 796, he afterwards brought the first German-speaking settlers to the western part of Pannonia (which was the more northerly of the two provinces into which Roman Illyricum was divided *c.* AD 10, and which included parts of present-day Austria, Hungary and Yugoslavia). These Germans built a number of churches, chapels and shrines dedicated to St Martin (d.397), to St Stephen the Martyr and to St Radegunde (d.587). The frequency of the chapels dedicated to St Radegunde suggests that these first German settlers came from Franconia and Thuringia, where at this period the cult of this saint was at its height. In the Carolingian period (796–896) a Vice-Domus collected incomes, tithes, etc., for the Church. The present Cathedral of St Martin (formerly the town's parish church) is first mentioned in a document of 1031; it was then a small Romanesque building, remains of which (within the present cathedral) are believed to be this old 'capella S. Martini'. King Stephen (977–1038) – St Stephen of Hungary – incorporated Pannonia as a fiefdom of Hungary, and it was during his reign that ten communities in Pannonia received a mother church, including Eisenstadt.

In those days, the town bore another name, 'De minore Mortin' ('Small Martin', in Hungarian 'Kis Márton' or (modern spelling) 'Kismarton'. We have the first written evidence of 'De minore Mortin' – in Hungarian 'Martin' would be pronounced 'Mortin' – from a document of 1264. The town grew up along the old Roman road which followed the course of the present-day Haydngasse (in Haydn's time it was called the 'Klostergasse' – 'Monastery Street' – since there were two such institutions located on it, a nunnery and the Franciscans). The German inhabitants called the town 'Wenigmertendorf' ('Small Martin Village'). When walls were erected in 1371, a new name for the town began to circulate, 'Eysenstatt' ('iron' or 'strong' town), and in a document of 1388 we read 'Der Statt zu den wenig-Mertendorf anders genannt zu der Eysenstatt'.

The town soon began to receive coveted privileges. In 1372, it was allowed to export wines to Bohemia, Moravia and Poland; and in 1383, it was allowed to hold market days on the feasts of St John the Baptist and St Lambert, with further permission to extend the market for one day in each direction, i.e. to create a three-day market, the central day of which was that of the patron saint. From 1390 the citizens of Eisenstadt could pass through nearby Oedenburg (Sopron) without paying the 'tithe of the thirtieth', and in 1395 they were permitted to sell wine in Oedenburg and Sárvár. Emperor Sigismund issued a privilege in 1397, allowing the Eisenstadt citizens to visit all the markets of Hungary with their wares, wine, etc. In 1414, Sigismund permitted Eisenstadt journeymen freedom from duty on their wares, and in 1429 freedom from tallage (*Mautgebühr*).

In 1371, the Castle was built by the Kanizsai family who at that time moved their *Herrschaft* (domain or estates) from Hornstein to Eisenstadt. It was a building with four sections enclosing a courtyard and was surrounded by a moat; this was to be the basis of the present Esterházy Castle. In the course of six centuries, however, the castle has been almost completely transformed, so frequently and thoroughly has it been altered.

In 1445, the Dowager Queen Elisabeth mortgaged Eisenstadt to the Habsburgs, and as a result of political vacillation, the Kanizsai family lost the *Herrschaft* Eisenstadt, which was given in succession to a number of Austrians, partly as an outright present (grace and favour), partly as a fiefdom on a rental basis (*Pfand*). One such was Johann(es) Siebenhirter (Sybenhirter), Imperial Master of the Kitchen and Grand Master of the Order of St George, who began to rebuild the parish church of St Martin in the Gothic style.

For a while, Eisenstadt was a pawn on the imperial battlefield. The town came under the Hungarian King Matthias Corvinus who, in his third war with the Emperor Frederick III, actually occupied Vienna (1 June 1485) and became the greatest power in central Europe. Matthias Corvinus gave Eisenstadt as a fiefdom to Johann Zápolya. After Corvinus's death in 1490, the Emperor's son Maximilian began to reconquer the lost Habsburg territories, and in the late autumn of 1490 his armies crossed the Leitha Mountains (at the foot of which Eisenstadt stands, overlooking the fertile plains towards Oedenburg) and besieged the town, which resisted for forty-eight hours. If the town suffered in the Corvinus wars, it was wise enough to buy itself free from the enemy when the Turkish armies besieged Vienna. From 1491, the Treaty of Pressburg assured that Eisenstadt belonged to the Austrian Monarchy.

A document of 1296 informs us that Jews lived in Eisenstadt, and by the middle of the sixteenth century they were a powerful faction. At one point, the Eisenstadt citizens protested to the Emperor that the Lord of the *Herrschaft* Eisenstadt, Johann Weisspriach(er) had failed to observe the citizens' ancient rights but had cultivated the Jews, whose protector he had now become. These Protected Jews (*Schutzjuden*) had paid rights to the town, and Weisspriach now organized them into a ghetto and collected those rights for the *Herrschaft* instead of allowing the town to have them. After Weisspriach's death, the Emperor dissolved the fiefdom of Eisenstadt, for which act of grace the town, despite the chaotic times of the Counter-Reformation (the citizenry was mostly Protestant), contributed the huge sum of 4,000 gold gulden. Weisspriach had 'reigned' in Eisenstadt, to the desperation of its citizens, from 1554 to 1572, and after the town had freed itself, the Emperor promised neither to sell nor to mortgage the *Herrschaft*. The institution of the ghetto remained, however, and we shall see that the Esterházys followed the tradition of Weisspriach in protecting the Jews.

The first of several disastrous fires came near to destroying the whole town in August 1589, but despite all this, Eisenstadt prospered and gradually amassed to itself all the privileges that a town could have, including in 1581 the right of judicial execution.

The most important event in the town's history occurred when its fate became linked with that of the Esterházy family. Nicolaus von Esterházy was one of a group of 'new' noblemen[1] who were loyal to the Habsburgs in their fight against the Protestants. Esterházy proved to be not only a loyal liegeman but a vast power in the Counter-Reformation (the Defenestration of Prague had occurred in May 1618, setting off the Thirty Years' War). Ferdinand II (Emperor, 1619–37) rewarded his followers generously: he could distribute the huge estates of the former Bohemian nobility, which had been largely Protestant, to 'foreign' Catholic noblemen. After the Treaty of Nikolsburg, which had been largely the result of Esterházy's clever diplomacy, Emperor Ferdinand II – ignoring the old promise that Maximilian II had given the town in 1572 – gave as a fiefdom (*Pfand*) to Nicolaus Esterházy the *Burgherrschaft* of Eisenstadt, i.e. the 'Castle Fief' which did not include the actual town, by decree of 2 May 1622. In the Nikolsburg Treaty, another Habsburg liegeman, Gabriel Bethlen, Prince of Siebenbürgen, had wanted the Castle and *Herrschaft* of Munkács (eastern Hungary) for his family; and since Munkács belonged to the Esterházys, the Emperor recompensed the loss by giving Eisenstadt to Nicolaus, also conferring on him the title of count. Four years later Esterházy paid 400,000 gulden to the crown and received from the grateful Imperial Royal hand the great fortress and *Herrschaft* of Fraknó (Forchtenstein, now in Austria). Since the fortunes of the Esterházy family will be discussed in a separate section *infra*, we shall now return to our short history of the town, and mention only that the *Burgherrschaft* was conferred as a hereditary estate (and no longer a fiefdom of the Habsburgs) to Count Ladislaus Esterházy on 30 September 1648.

The citizens of Eisenstadt watched with considerable alarm as the two leading 'new' Hungarian counts, Nádasdy and Esterházy, formed a pro-Hungarian faction within the Habsburg circle. They hoped by various means to restore the Austrian parts of Pannonia to Hungary, and gradually the Esterházys acquired all the lands surrounding Eisenstadt, which felt itself (perhaps with some justification) about to be swallowed up by this new and powerful aristocrat.

At an enormous sacrifice, Eisenstadt persuaded the Emperor to allow it to become a royal free town (*königliche Freystadt*). It was on 26 October 1648, not yet a month after the Esterházys had secured the Castle domains as a perpetual *Herrschaft*, that Eisenstadt made a contract with the Imperial House for the purchase of its freedom: 16,000 gulden in cash, 9,000 gulden in wine (a gulden per *Eimer* [keg]), and renunciation of the 4,000 gulden paid in 1572 for the redemption of *Herrschaft* Eisenstadt as a Habsburg fiefdom. The Thirty Years' War had been brought to a close by the Treaty of Westphalia (1648), and Ferdinand III (who had succeeded his father in 1637) was glad to accept any money to replenish the empty imperial coffers. Eisenstadt was made a Royal Free Hungarian Town, and it remained within Hungary until after the Second World War.

It must have been clear to the town's citizenry that its relationship with the Castle *Herrschaft* was, to say the least, ambivalent: like the Vatican and its relationship to Rome, the Esterházy Castle was within the town walls but yet extra-territorial. There were endless possibilities for legal and even personal conflict: repair of the walls, customs (*Maut*), the increasing importance of the Protected Jews, whose ghetto was on land belonging to the Castle. This at times uneasy relationship has continued to the present day, when the Castle occupies a curious role in the town's life: its empty, lifeless windows strike the nocturnal wanderer as slightly sinister.

---

1 The Esterházys were created barons in 1613, counts in 1626.

In this curious relationship, it was, of course, the Esterházy family who was the richer and more powerful of the two partners. The town certainly benefited economically from the family: in 1629, the Esterházys constructed the Franciscan Church and Monastery, in 1678 the Augustine Nunnery (mainly for Prince Paul Esterházy's three daughters, who became nuns there), and in 1663–72 the old medieval castle was transformed into a more comfortable residence by Carlo Martino Carlone, according to whose plans Sebastiano Bartoletto and Carlo Antonio Carlone reconstructed the building. There were four onion towers, one on each corner (see pls. 16, 19). In 1655, a chapel in the west wing was opened, and it was there that Haydn and his *Capelle* performed on high feast days (such as the Prince's name-day, 6 December 1766). In the first storey (American: second floor) there was the great hall, used for banquets and festive occasions, with the musicians in attendance. The ceiling was elaborately decorated (fresco signed 'Tencala Pinxit 1701') and around the walls are portraits of Hungarian kings and generals after the plan outlined in a book, Franz Násady's *Mausoleum regum ac primorum Ungariae ducum* (Nuremberg 1664). Recently Jürgen Meyer[1] has conducted a series of revealing measurements of the acoustical properties of the principal rooms in which Haydn conducted orchestral-vocal music: the great halls at Eisenstadt and Eszterháza, the Hanover Square Rooms and the King's Theatre in London (for the last two rooms, which no longer exist, we possess accurate contemporary measurements). With its exceptional size,[2] Eisenstadt proved to be the largest of the four rooms and also that with the longest echo. It is considered to be very flattering to music, especially with an orchestra of the small size that Haydn used in 1761–5. Dr Meyer believes that the terraced dynamic marks of the early Eisenstadt symphonies, the concerto grosso technique of Nos. 6–8, and especially the heavier scoring with the four horns of Nos. 13, 31, 39 and 72 owe their existence to the acoustical properties of the great hall. The organ-like effect of No. 13/I is enhanced by the long echo. 'One must ... recall that the hall in Eisenstadt, with a small audience, has an echo which is almost like that of a church', writes Dr Meyer. On the other hand, Eszterháza's peculiar acoustical properties are such that 'even orchestral works take on an almost chamber musical character'; special attention is drawn by Dr Meyer to Symphony No. 67's slow movement, wherein 'the energy which is generated [at the *col legno* passage] is so small that for the listener a convincing impression can be achieved only if he can be placed at not too great a distance from the orchestra.' Dr Meyer further thinks that the many Eszterháza symphonies that exist in two orchestrations (one with trumpets and drums) occur because symphonies with heavy orchestration, including trumpets and kettledrums, were 'hardly suited' for performance in the music room, whereas the heavy orchestration would be appropriate in the opera house, marionette theatre, or even the open air.

In Eisenstadt, there are other beautiful rooms on the first floor, facing the front or adjoining it (the so-called 'Empiresaal'), where Haydn and his *Capelle* will have performed chamber and even orchestral and vocal music. In the 'Empiresaal' – so called because of its decorations of the *Empire* period – the very 'live' acoustics enable a chamber orchestra to dominate the room without losing detail.

In its present state, the Castle and gardens are the result of a large-scale (but uncompleted) rebuilding that took place in the 1790s and early 1800s primarily through Charles Moreau. The elegant stables which face the Castle were built in 1793.

---

1 Dr Meyer was kind enough to send us a manuscript of his article, 'Raumakustik und Orchesterklang in den Konzertsälen Joseph Haydns', which will be published in *Acustica* (Mitteilung aus der Physikalisch-Technischen Bundesanstalt Braunschweig).
2 38 m. long, 14·7 m. wide, 12·4 m. high. Volume: 6,800 m³.

To return to the actual town, the next event of great importance was the Plague (Black Death) which decimated the population in 1679: to a superstitious people, it seemed a frightening omen, especially with hindsight. Involved in the Turkish campaign of 1683, Eisenstadt was forced to side with Imre (Emmerich) Thököly, leader of the largely Protestant, anti-Habsburg (and pro-Turkish) faction. The Parish Chronicle records, however, 'how we poor Germans and staunch Catholics felt about this oath of allegiance in our heart of hearts, any good Catholic can imagine'. The Turks nevertheless devastated the countryside. In 1703, Eisenstadt was invaded by Ferenc II, Prince Rákóczy, leader of rebellious Hungarian troops, who dared to begin this insurrection because Austria was heavily involved in the War of the Spanish Succession. Largely Protestant, these rebels robbed the Eisenstadt citizens 'ex puro religionis et nationis odio'. On 22 March 1704, the Imperial General Heister drove the foreign troops out of the town, but two years later the rebels returned, setting Eisenstadt on fire and almost destroying the ghetto. Until 1709, Imperial troops were quartered in the town, which had to pay for that dubious privilege; but at least the population was protected from the invading rebellious Protestant armies.

The worst was now over for Eisenstadt, which had suffered immensely from its geographical position as a border town. As the Turks were pushed steadily back, a long period of peace began which in fact did not end, as far as the town was concerned, until the arrival of French troops during the Napoleonic Wars.

The Esterházy family were staunch Catholics, one of the principal defenders of the faith and spears of the Counter-Reformation in west Hungary. Now that peace had arrived, after the last rebel had been expelled from the town gates in 1704, the Esterházys began to devote their attention to religious buildings and institutions in Eisenstadt. Palatine Nicolaus – we shall encounter him again *infra* – imported Jesuits to re-educate the people, tainted with Protestantism, and apart from the Jewish community in Eisenstadt (Alsókismártonhegy = Unterberg Eisenstadt) whose privileges were retained and whose business dealings were useful to the Esterházys, there was soon not a single non-Catholic town in the family domains. The Palatine's son, Count Paul, continued the missionary work of his father. 'The lowliest servant of Our Dear Lady', as he used to call himself, erected shrines all over his lands; he visited Mariazell fifty-eight times, and the Esterházy chapel there to this day recalls the family's close ties with the great pilgrimage church. With his family and servants, he visited frequently and actively supported another pilgrimage church near Eisenstadt, Loretto. The Esterházys became dedicated upholders of the Marian cult. In 1692, Paul (now Prince and Palatine of Hungary) led a procession to Mariazell in which 11,200 persons took part, and a princely order now required his liegemen to pay an annual visit to the Styrian church. Under Paul's reign, Loretto also became a major religious centre, and during great feast days, 60–65 priests heard confessions and 6,000 persons took Communion. In 1706, 90,000 pilgrims took Communion at Loretto.

In 1674, Count Paul erected in Eisenstadt a chapel dedicated to St Apollonia, on the site of the later Bergkirche; next to it, in the years 1696–9, the Count (from 1687: Prince) built a poor-house. In 1701, Paul visited the pilgrimage church of Maria Lanzendorf near Vienna and was impressed with the Calvary scene incorporated in a specially tall building nearby. He discovered that the architect was a Franciscan monk, Frater Felix Niering (Nierinck), and forthwith secured permission to take Frater Felix to Eisenstadt, there on 22 September 1701 to lay the corner-stone of the new Mount Calvary next to the Apollonia Chapel. The new building was consecrated in a ceremony lasting for a whole week in May 1707. Many years earlier, Palatine Nicolaus had ordered a statue of the Virgin to be placed in the spa of Nagyhöflán (Groß-Höflein), an Esterházy domain. When the rebellious armies sacked the town and burned it, the statue remained unharmed. It proved to have miraculous powers, and on 3 September 1711, in a magnificent procession led by Palatine Paul, who carried the statue in his gala carriage, it was placed in the Bergkirche (Mount Calvary) and became known as the Miraculous Image of Maria-Eisenstadt. Palatine Paul also planned to erect a gigantic pilgrimage church next to the Mount Calvary, but in the event a small Pantheon-shaped church was built which is now the second part of the Bergkirche. When Haydn arrived at Eisenstadt in 1761, he could have seen work proceeding on the former poor-house, now a Franciscan Monastery and in the process of being enlarged. It had been Prince Paul Anton who, in a document of 14 December 1751, had allowed the Order to proceed with the new building, and he also contributed to its construction not only financially but in the form of 100,000 bricks, a quantity of hard wood and lime. The Monastery was completed in 1766 and the ceremonial opening took place on 30 July, at which the key was delivered to Prince Nicolaus.

The new Bergkirche was built between 1770 and 1777. The fresco work inside was allotted to the Princely painter Christian Köpp, who had as assistant his son Wolfgang, 'Academic Painter from Vienna'; the fresco is, however, signed 'W. Köpp 1772'.

With the increasing size of the Calvary Church, Franciscan Monastery (there was, as we have seen, another Franciscan house in the Klostergasse as well) and the new Bergkirche, the poor had to be placed elsewhere. In 1759, a permanent home for them was found in Forchtenau (under Forchtenstein Castle), and a new building for the hospital in Eisenstadt was begun. The hospital and its new chapel were among Prince Paul Anton's many charitable works. The monks who served there were called the Brothers of Mercy (Barmherzige Brüder), with the Viennese chapter of which Haydn, as we have seen, was intimately associated. The new building was opened in 1760 on the Prince's name-day, 14 June, in a fitting ceremony at which the bishop of the diocese presided: during the prayer, 'Miserere', the monks led in the sick and washed their feet.

It is fortunate that the core of eighteenth-century Eisenstadt remains today, though bad town-planning has ruined many details. There still exist in the town a number of authentic eighteenth-century organs, and these alone – if properly restored – should make it a centre for organ studies.[1] Even after two-and-one-half centuries, the force of the Counter-Reformation, and the importance of the Catholic Church for the Esterházys, are strongly felt in Eisenstadt, and this power extended to the population as a whole (except, of course, for the large Jewish community), and not least to Haydn, whose own devotion to Our Lady will have coincided perfectly with

---

1 Chapel at the foot of Mount Calvary: small eighteenth-century organ. Bergkirche: the original organ, which Haydn would have known, was later taken to a nearby parish church; restored by Professor Josef Mertin, it is now in the Burgenländisches Landesmuseum. This organ was replaced in 1797 by one made by J. G. Malleck, who in 1778 had built the magnificent instrument in the parish church of St Martin (recently restored by Schuke, Potsdam, 1942 and 1975). The Positiv in the Chapel of the Brothers of Mercy must have been inherited from the previous chapel, or acquired from elsewhere when the interior fittings were being organized in 1759–60: Dr Otto Biba has identified it as being by Johann Franz Frey and dated 1732.

The organ in the Castle Chapel that Haydn saw when he arrived in 1761 has not survived; the present one is from the period of Nicolaus II Esterházy (perhaps c.1800). The organ in the Franciscan Monastery in the Haydngasse (then Klostergasse) is from the first half of the eighteenth century and badly needs restoring, as do all the other organs in Eisenstadt except that in the Cathedral (then parish church). One of the features of the Haydn-Tage of 1976 and 1978 was the informative tour of these organs organized by Dr Biba.

that of his patrons, the most striking manifestation of which was the miraculous image in the Calvary Church.[1]

———————

The Esterházys had always encouraged music and theatre, beginning modestly with *Tafelmusik* and church music, both of which we know Count Nicolaus (1582–1645) supported. After Eisenstadt became the family's principal seat, he continued to employ musicians, also lending them to the Jesuit College in Oedenburg (Sopron); Nicolaus had been educated by the Jesuits and remained close to them in later years. He also employed a harp player at his court.

Concerning the family's wealth, we read in Horányi:

> The vast estates of Nicolaus Esterházy formed but the foundation of the family's later wealth. Paul Esterházy, the other great maker of the family's fortunes, who succeeded the early-deceased Ladislaus Esterházy ... in 1652, added much further wealth to the riches of the family by the modernization of farming, by large-scale building, and by acquiring additional huge estates, especially in Transdanubia.
>
> By his first marriage to Ursula, the widow of his late brother Stephan, he united the two branches and the wealth of the family, while his second marriage, to Eva Thököly, helped him to acquire a considerable share of the Thökölys' fortunes. Moreover, when Franz (Ferenc) Nádasdy, his brother-in-law, was sentenced to death and to the forfeiture of his property on account of his participation in the Wesselényi Conspiracy, Paul Esterházy acquired – partly by purchase and partly by way of royal grant – the bulk of the wealth of the Nádasdy family. On top of all this the commission entrusted with the redistribution of the country after the expulsion of the Turks allotted 140,000 acres of additional land to Paul Esterházy

[Horányi, English ed., p. 15, with additional material from German ed., pp. 13f.].

Nicolaus's son, Count Paul (1635–1715) was created a prince by Emperor Leopold I on 8 December 1687, and the next day he (as Palatine of Hungary) and the Archbishop of Gran placed the Crown of St Stephen on the Imperial head. Of Paul's religious ardour we have spoken above. He was much drawn to the theatre, and again we read of a performance at the Jesuit College in Oedenburg in 1702, at which the princely musicians from Eisenstadt played. The piece was a Latin panegyric on the ancestors of the Esterházy house, and the bilingual libretto (Latin and German) was printed in Vienna; the music was composed by Franz Rumpelnig. In the great hall at Eisenstadt, plays with music of a popular kind were given at Easter and Christmas. Forchtenstein Castle has a portrait of Paul in the role of Judith in one of the Jesuit plays. Before Franz Rumpelnig (worked 1701–4), Paul employed as choir director Paul Klebovszky (worked 1674–7), later replaced by Franz Schmittbauer. When the Castle at Eisenstadt had been rebuilt (1672), a regular group of singers and instrumentalists was engaged. Palatine Paul was also in touch with the great I.R. 'Music Compositor' Johann Joseph Fux, who according to a contract of 1 June 1707 was expected to train

———

1 Literature on Eisenstadt and this aspect of the Esterházy family: *Die Stadtpfarrkirche in Eisenstadt* (Sonderheft der *Mitteilungen des burgenländischen Heimat- und Naturschutzvereines*), Eisenstadt 1930. *Eisenstadt: 300 Jahre Freistadt* (Sonderheft der *Burgenländischen Heimatblätter*), Eisenstadt 1948 (especially Oskar Gruszecki, 'Die Geschichte Eisenstadts bis 1648'; Josef Karl Homma, 'Eisenstadt – Freistadt'; and Karl Semmelweis, 'Das Esterházysche Schloß in Eisenstadt'). Georg Dehio, *Handbuch der deutschen Kunstdenkmäler* (Zweite Abteilung: Österreich, Zweiter Band), Berlin-Vienna 1935, pp. 640ff. *Geschichte des Calvarienberges und Wallfahrtortes Maria-Eisenstadt*. Von mehreren Priester des Raaber Bisthums, Györ (Raab) 1912. Janos Harich, 'Über das Schloß Esterházy zu Eisenstadt und die Burg Forchtenstein', in *Burgenländische Heimatblätter* 1972, pp. 130ff; also 'Anfänge der Musikpflege in der Residenz des Palatins Nikolaus Esterházy, in *Österreichische Musikzeitschrift*, Jg. 25/4 (1970), pp. 221ff.

two castrated boy singers in music and 'in litteris', obviously for future service at Eisenstadt.

Prince Paul was also a professionally trained musician and composer, and in 1711 he issued in print a set of church music for all the feast days, entitled 'Harmonia caelestis seu Moelodiae Musicae Per Decursum totius Anni adhibendae ad Vsum Musicorum Authore Pavlo sacri Romani Imperÿ Principe Estoras de Galanta regni hungariae Palatino. Anno Domini MDCCXI.'[1] Perhaps one of his *Capellmeister* helped the Prince with the occasional detail, but in their entirety this *Harmonia coelestis* is very attractive music, with adroit vocal writing and deft orchestration (strings, flutes, bassoon, trumpets, kettledrums, organ).

The new Emperor, Charles VI, conferred the hereditary rank of prince on the family in 1712, by which the eldest son inherited the title automatically. Paul's eldest son, Michael, succeeded to the title in 1713; we know that he played the virginals, and inherited his father's love of the stage. Cantatas or operas were now regularly performed to celebrate the birthdays and name-days of the Prince and Princess. In 1715, Prince Michael's birthday was honoured by a Cantata 'Das wahre Ebenbild Eines Vollkommenen Fürsten' with music by Wenzeslaus Franciscus (Venzel Franz) Zivilhoffer, the family *Capellmeister* whose church music has survived in the Esterházy Archives and the Cathedral Archives at Eisenstadt.[2] A curiosity of the Cantata is that it is partly in Latin and partly in German, and since the local forces were insufficient to mount the rather complicated work, 'certain *Comedianten*' were engaged from Vienna – a procedure Haydn was to come to know all too well. These 'Comedianten', who also came in 1716 to sing an opera for the princely name-day, were actors and singers as well, and brought their own costumes (no copy of the libretto, printed in 100 copies at Wiener Neustadt, has survived). Similar appearances with Viennese or Wiener Neustadt guests are known for the years 1717–20. These operas, which were produced in costumes (we have bills for such things as shepherds' staffs) and with scenery (bills in the Esterházy Archives) have not survived, but we know that they occasionally contained ballet insertions, for which a dancing master from Vienna was engaged. Even the printed libretti have all disappeared: for the opera given in 1719 for the princely birthday, 200 copies were printed with some special copies for the high-ranking members of the audience bound in gold brocade, just as would be the case with opera libretti in Haydn's time. From the records, it appears that an Italian *Purlesco* with music was performed in 1720, perhaps an *intermezzo*. Plays were given throughout this period, including a kind of miracle play entitled *Jüngst Gericht Spüll* (Play about the Last Judgment), followed by *Christi Geburt Spüll* (Play about Christ's Birth), both given by a single actor (at least so the records would seem to indicate: perhaps the name was merely an indication of 'Prinzipal' or director of the troupe). Following a Viennese tradition, oratorios began to be performed in Eisenstadt on Good Fridays, for the first time in 1717 (no copy of the printed libretto survives). *Capellmeister* Zivilhoffer wrote the oratorio for 1718 (lost) and probably also for 1719–20.

In a document of 1 January 1720, we note that Prince Michael reorganized the *Capelle*, as a result of which we learn something of its constitution. There were six court and field trumpeters, some of whom were now obliged to sing with the choir instead. Various members of the chorus are listed by name, also a 'lute master' and an alto castrato (H. P. Kniepantl [Kniebandt]) under the direction of Zivilhoffer, who

---

1 Copies in EH, Eisenstadt. A complete recording is now available on Hungaraton (Disco HI1 433/35).
2 Libretto of the Cantata in the Monastery of Klosterneuburg. It was printed by Andreas Heyinger, Printer to the University, Vienna.

received a salary of 320 gulden together with free lodgings, a *Maß* of wine daily, a pair of small loaves of bread (*Semmel*), also daily, and four cords of wood annually as well as the usual *Deputat*. The yearly cost of the *Capelle* (with the *Deputat* translated into money), including three members of the clergy, was 3,058 Fl., 14 Kr.

Prince Michael died on 24 March 1721, and since there was no direct heir, Michael's half-brother, Joseph, succeeded to the title; but he died on 7 June and the title fell to Joseph's son, Paul Anton, who was but ten years of age at the time (b. 22 April 1711). Until he came of age, his mother, Princess Maria Octavia, *née* Baroness Gilleis, and his guardian, Count Georg Erdödy, acted as regents. Meanwhile it was thought necessary to economize, and Zivilhoffer was dismissed (1721). A *Conventional* regulating the musicians was issued by Princess Maria Octavia. The total sum was reduced to 1,479 Fl., 55 Kr., and the *Capelle* consisted of one female discant singer (Antonie Lindt), one male discant singer (Paul Huszár, later tenor), one alto singer (castrato Kniepantl [Kniebandt]), two bass singers (Franz Payr, later organist, and Johann Georg Thonner, who also directed the choir for seven years and worked in the book-keeping department as well), and a small orchestra of two violins, one violone (double bass; this man also played bassoon) and organ, all manned by the children of one family, the Lindts.

Princess Maria Octavia, probably at the instigation of her son Paul Anton, made an important engagement on 10 May 1728: Gregor(ius) Joseph(us) Werner as *Capellmeister*. He received 400 gulden and emoluments (*Deputat*), with 28 Fl. lodging money. The discovery, in an Austrian private library, of Werner's copy of J. J. Fux's *Gradus ad Parnassum* with the Werner family data inscribed on the fly-leaf (much as was done in the family Bible elsewhere) has enabled us for the first time to clear up all sorts of inaccuracies regarding the place and date of Gregor Joseph's birth, the birth dates of his children, and so on. Werner was born at Ybbs an der Donau (Lower Austria) on 28 January 1693. We have no record of where he studied music, but one suspects that it may have been in Vienna, where (at St Stephen's Cathedral) he was married in January 1727, and from which city he was fetched to Eisenstadt. Werner's now well known 'Der Wienerische Tandelmarkt' (The Vienna Flea Market) also suggests an intimate knowledge of the Viennese scene.

The details of Werner's life may be summarized here briefly. He had four children, of which the third, Johann Nepomuk Paul (b. 1734), became a monk in the Cistercian Abbey of Zwettl in Lower Austria (the Abbey Library owns some rare Werner libretti). Werner's wife, Anna Christina, died at Eisenstadt on 22 September 1753, aged forty-eight. Werner thereupon moved from within the town to the princely domains near the Castle (Oberberg), where he took rooms in the lodgings of one Dietzl, probably Joseph Dietzl, the schoolmaster and tenor in the *Capelle*. From the documents, we learn that for a while (until his voice failed, in 1759) Werner sang, in falsetto, alto in the choir at Eisenstadt, collecting the money and the *Deputat* of the vacant position. His relations with Prince Anton were friendly, and we find the Prince acting as godfather to his *Capellmeister*'s first son, born on 11 January 1731. Werner dedicated several works to the Prince, including six symphonies and six sonatas for two violins and *basso continuo*, delivered in 1735 to honour the Prince's return from France with his new bride (*vide infra*). Another time, in November 1738, Werner sent the Prince five symphonies and some other pieces, using the occasion as a pretext for pointing out that the fifteen *Eimer* of wine 'Eisenstädter Hamb' (description of the *Eimer*'s size – there was also a 'Preßburger Hamb') which had been delivered to him turned out to be, 'surely not on purpose, but as an oversight', the new or 'heuriger' wine, whereas all the other court musicians received old wine; he humbly asks for the old wine, too, 'because since much of my work is done while seated, such a young and unprocessed wine is very bad for the health', and to show his thankfulness for such an act of grace, he will continue with indefatigable zeal as 'His Princely Highness' unworthy *Capellmaister* [*sic*]'.

In the obscurity of Eisenstadt, Werner continued to write a large amount of primarily religious music. His arrival signified the beginning of a regular and long-lasting oratorio tradition, in which such works were performed each year on Good Friday from 1729 to (and including) 1762, i.e. for thirty-four consecutive years. They were given in the Castle Chapel, in the Hospital Church (later to be the Church of the Brothers of Mercy), in the chapel of the Augustine Sisters in the Klostergasse and probably in the parish church of St Martin. Haydn was a witness of, and no doubt actively participated in, the last of these oratorio performances in 1762 (*vide infra*, p. 369). Libretti for these oratorios were regularly printed, and apart from those formerly (or currently) in the Esterházy Archives, some have survived in the Monastery libraries of Zwettl and Klosterneuburg. Janos Harich, who is (1979) about to issue the thematic catalogue of Werner's works, has located twenty-two extant oratorios. Apart from them, Werner wrote many Masses, Requiems, Te Deums, Vespers, *Lamentationes*, smaller church music of all kinds, symphonies, concertos, trio sonatas, organ concertos and 'Pastorelle' (both the latter intended for church use), 'parthiae' (mostly for two violins and *basso*), sonatas (including some for flute, violin, lute and *basso continuo*), and many German-language church pieces for Christmas, Advent, etc. Possessing a profound knowledge of the Fuxian contrapuntal tradition, Werner's religious music displays all this learning in a genuinely impressive way. In recent times his music has rightly become an object of scholarly study as well as musical revival. The Mass in C performed at the Haydn Tage in 1978 at Eisenstadt Cathedral, conducted by *Domkapellmeister* Dreo, proved to be a revelation. The fugues were not merely academic exercises but were of great beauty, power and originality. The oratorios, too, contain many moving and effective moments. Naturally, it has been the other side of Werner which has recently appealed to conductors: the 'modern' Werner, who has studied Corelli and Vivaldi but is nevertheless steeped in the local Austrian tradition. Some of Werner's instrumental works have a strong Italianate flavour, but others, such as the Pastorelle and concertos for organ and orchestra or the 'Musikalischer Instrumentalkalender', are typically Austrian of their kind and period. They have a genuine charm and show a strongly developed sense of *Volksmusik*.

Werner's works, most of which have not been printed, survive principally in the Esterházy Archives (Budapest, Eisenstadt), the Cathedral Archives at Eisenstadt, the Burgenländisches Landesmuseum and the Gesellschaft der Musikfreunde, Vienna.

We shall return to Werner several times in this Chronicle, first when (presumably) he met Haydn in Eisenstadt in 1761 (*infra*, p. 347), then when Werner made his first Will (*infra*, p. 386), his codicil (*infra*, p. 415) and lastly when he wrote his famous letter of protest about Haydn (*infra*, p. 418).

Prince Paul Anton and his younger brother Nicolaus continued the long family tradition and studied with the Jesuits (in Vienna), where they were also taught music. Paul Anton played violin, flute and lute, Nicolaus viola da gamba and violoncello. Paul Anton went to study at the University of Leyden, where he was inscribed in the autumn of 1731. He was accompanied, as befitted a Prince of the Holy Roman Empire, by his French instructor, a Hungarian servant-in-waiting and two servants, one Hungarian and one German. These latter were both musicians, Johann Spach and the composer Franz Gletzga, who wrote music for the Prince's amusement. After his studies were completed, he made a long trip through France and Germany, returning home in 1734 with a large collection of books and music – a valuable thematic catalogue of the music was prepared and has recently been published[1] – to take up his duties as head of the great Esterházy estates. Before he returned, however, he married an Italian lady from the highest nobility: Maria Anna (in some sources Marie Louise), Marchesa di Lunati-Visconti. The marriage took place on St Stephen's Day (26 December) 1734 at Lunéville (later famous for the Austro–French Treaty of 1801). The couple had no children. As was the custom in those days, Paul Anton pursued a military career, taking active part in the War of the Austrian Succession (1740–8) and, later, as Colonel of the Cavalry in the Seven Years' War (1756–63). He rose to the rank of Field-Marshal, directing two regiments of hussars which Empress Maria Theresa placed at his disposal. His portrait, in which he wears the Field-Marshal's uniform of his Hungarian hussars, with its blue jacket, heavy lacing and dolman, hangs in Forchtenstein Castle and is reproduced in this book (see pl. 17). Between his duties on the field, he was Austrian Minister Extraordinary at the Court of Naples from 1750–2, and there he lost no opportunity not only to hear, study and come to love Italian opera, but to collect great amounts of Italian music, which was brought back to Austria and later, after the Prince's return from another visit to Naples in 1756, registered in a catalogue. To this end, Prince Paul Anton engaged a musician from the French theatre (the Burgtheater) in Vienna, one Bonifacius Carl Champée, who drew up not only this catalogue but another one in 1759,[2] which Werner continued to keep up to date until 1762. In this latter catalogue is a crucial entry which hangs together with Haydn's engagement (*vide infra*, p. 345).

The *Capelle* in Eisenstadt was still in its reduced state when Werner arrived to become its director, but it soon grew considerably. New musicians were engaged (flute, oboe, trombone and kettledrum players), and any servant who could sing or play an instrument was expected to participate in the performances. When the Prince returned from his diplomatic service in Naples, he ordered a theatre to be constructed in a glass house situated in the garden of Eisenstadt Castle. (The garden itself, previously in the formal Italian manner, was later [1760] transformed in the French style according to plans by Louis Gervais, and space was gained by abolishing the old game reserve.) Even before the Prince left for Naples, G. M. Quaglio (we shall often encounter this family name) notes, on a document of 6 August 1749, expenses for 'theatrical painting' used in connection with the fireworks and illuminations at the Castle on 4 August ('spese della Machina d'illuminazione e Jiuoco artificiato'). While at Naples, Prince Paul Anton arranged to have cantatas composed and performed on Maria Thesesa's birthday (13 May 1751) and on the occasion of his official entrance into Naples (26 June 1750), both on libretti by Metastasio.

The first opera in Paul Anton's reign of which we have some details was given on 22 April 1755, the Prince's birthday; it was entitled 'Ecloga pastorale da Cantarsi in occasione del Giorno Natalizio di Sua Altezza il Sig^r Principe Esterhazi'. The libretto was by Giovanni Claudio Pasquini, the music (lost) by Francesco Maggiore. It is thought that at least part of the ensemble had to be imported from Vienna. For the

1 By J. Harich in *HJB* IX, pp. 31ff.
2 Published by J. Harich in *HJB* IX, 67ff. For Champée (d. 1775), see H. Gericke, p 103.

next year, we have records[1] showing that a guest troupe of eleven persons under the direction of Giovanni Francesco Crosa gave performances at Eisenstadt on 16–23 July 1756. As we shall see, one month after Haydn joined the *Capelle*, Paul Anton gave orders to begin the construction of a new theatre.

It became the rule, then, also in the first years of Haydn's stay, to supplement the modest number of musicians by outside guest artists. This was particularly necessary if opera were to become a permanent fixture of the musical scene in Eisenstadt. Meanwhile, Werner had to make do with not entirely satisfactory substitutes, in the literal sense of the word. In the decade preceding Haydn's engagement, we find that the bassoon players were the schoolmasters of the nearby villages of Groß-Höflein and Klein-Höflein; that the tenor was the Castle schoolmaster Joseph Dietzl (who also

---

1 The document is in German, and often in local dialect; since it is unpublished, we reproduce it here in the original, together with some explanatory notes.

On the cover 'Englwirth' refers to the [Golden] Angel Inn in the upper part of Eisenstadt, where the 'opera people stayed for seven days'. The next page lists in detail what they 'consumed in food and drink'. The various items include: *Brot* – bread; *Suben* = *Suppe* – soup; *Millig* = *Milch* – milk; *Tö/Dö* = *Tee* – tea; *Käse Kipfel* – cheese rolls; *Är* = *Eier* = eggs; *Mittageßen* – lunch; *Nachteßen* – dinner.

The addition of the bill is faulty (to the writer's advantage), which doubtless explains why the (round) sum of 70 Fl. was paid on the instructions of the *Regent*, Count von Herbeviller, and the receipt for this sum 'correctly paid', signed by the innkeeper, Andreas Bettenkhofer.

[cover:]
1756: 23ᵗ Julÿ Eisenstatt / No 27. / Dem Englwirth vor Zehrung davon Operisten durch / 7 Täg. 70 F. —x. / Ad Rub: 8ᵛᵃ Fasc: 1ᵐᵘˢ.

[next page:]
Conto: / Waß vor die Obärristen an Speiß / und Trang erfolgt ist worden — /

	F	6	xr
Den 16ᵗᵉ Julÿ 7̄5̄6̄ Butter und Brot			
Nachteßen	2 „	38	
Wein und Brot	1 „	18	
Vor 3 Zimer	1 „	12	
Den 17ᵗᵉ dito Suben Millig und Dö	„	34	
Mittageßen	4 „	51	
Wein und Brot	1 „	18	
Är und Dö	„	10	
Nachteßen	1 „	49	
Wein und Brot	1 „	18	
Vor Tö	„	18	
Treÿ Zimer	1 „	12	
Den 18 dito Suben Millig und Dö	— „	34	
Mittageßen	5 „	12	
Wein und Brot	1 „	18	
Nachteßen	2 „	18	
Wein und Brot	1 „	18	
3 Zimer	1 „	12	
Den 19 dito Millig, Dö und Suben	— „	36	
1 buch babir [*Papier* = paper]	„	8	
Mittageßen	5 „	12	
Wein und Brot	1 „	18	

Lättus Hinüber [carried forward]   35 F   50 xr

[*continued overleaf*]

played in the *Feldmusique*, or wind band); that Dietzl's wife was a soprano; and one of the violinists a *valet-de-chambre*. In the latter case, the procedure of using servants to assist in the *Capelle* brought forth none other than Luigi Tomasini, who became leader of the orchestra, composer and violin virtuoso.

On 1 January 1759, Paul Anton engaged a capable young man, the tenor Carl Friberth (Frieberth), who spoke fluent Italian and was a modest man of letters as well, later capable of adapting (from a French original) an Italian libretto for Haydn, *L'incontro improvviso* (1775). On 1 January 1760, a fine 'Discantistin', Anna Maria Scheffstoss (see pl. 26) was engaged as 'Choir and Chamber Singer': we shall see that Haydn was soon to compose for her flexible voice.

[new page:]

[*Footnote continued from p. 315*]

		Lättus herüber [brought forward]	35 F	50 xr
	Nachteßen		3 „	12
	Wein und Brot		1 „	18
	¼ lung[?] Zuger [Zucker? = sugar?]		„	10
	3 Zimer		1 „	12
Den 20 dito	Dö Millig und Suben		„	34
	Mittageßen		5 „	36
	Wein und Brot		1 „	18
	Nachteßen		2 „	18
	Wein und Brot		1 „	18
	3 Zimer		1 „	12
Den 21ᵐ dito	Millig, Dö und Suben		„	34
	Mittageßen		4 „	51
	Wein und Brot		1 „	18
	Nachteßen		2 „	12
	Wein und Brot		1 „	18
	3 Zimer		1 „	12
	Vor Dö		„	18
Den 22 dito	Dö Millig Suben		„	34
	Mittageßen		4 „	58
	Wein und Brot		1 „	18
	Nachteßen		2 „	30
	Wein und Brot		1 „	18
	3 Zimer		1 „	12
	Dö		„	8
Den 23 dito	Dö und Käse Kipfel		„	54

Suma   78 F   33 xr:

io dichiaro esser stato per sette giorni nel osteria / con tutti li musici in tutto ondici persone alogiato / li 23 lulio 1756   Giofranco crosa / direttore.

Dieses Tagzetl ist aus den Eisenstadter Ober / Einnehmeramt mit Siebzig Gulden / zu bezahlen. Eisenstadt den 23ᵗᵉ /July 750[!] / Dc ... 70 Fl. Graff v. Herbeviller

Dieser Tag Zetl ist Mir aus den Eysensteter / Einnemeramt mit 70 Fl. Richtig Bezahlt worden / Anteras Bettenkhofer / Wirth beim goltern engl

[A.M. 4291, no. 18.465–7, EH, Budapest]

In July 1759, the Prince sent Luigi Tomasini (whom he had met and engaged at Pesaro in 1757) and Carl Friberth on a study trip to Venice, a generous idea but, in the event, a mistaken one because in that season the nobility was all away on its estates in the country and there were no concerts or opera. The pair also found Venice very dear and wrote to ask for more money, but the Prince obviously considered the trip by then a mistake and had his secretary order them to return.[1]

Fortunately, the princely *Conventionale* of the year 1760 enable us to present a complete list of the musicians, together with details of their salaries and payments in kind (see below).

We shall be examining in more detail those musicians who still remained when Haydn became their *Vice-Capellmeister* in May 1761.

Princely Musicians

Capell Meister Gregorius Werner.

Has in cash	400 f.
For his lodgings	28 f.
Wine *Eisenstäder*[!] *Hämb*.	15 *Emer*
Corn [grain]	15 *Mezen*
For the printing of his oratorio annually allowed in grace	4 ducats

Discantistin Theresia Riedlin.

In cash	60 f.
Wheat	3 ⎫
Corn	8 ⎬ *Mezen*
Barley	2 ⎭
Wine *Eysenstäder*[!] *Hämb*.	9 *Emer*
Lard	50 lb.

Chor-Singerin Eleonora Jägerin.

In cash	62 f.
For poultry	2 f. 30 Xr.
For lodgings	12 f.
Wheat	4 ⎫
Corn	8 ⎬ *Mezen*
Lentils, barley and millet-pap each	1 ⎭
Salt	¼
	30 ⎫
Lard	24 ⎬ lb.
Candles	24 ⎭
Beef	300
Officers' Wine *Eysenstäder*[!] *Hämb*	9 ⎫ *Emer*
Cabbage and beets each	1½ ⎭
Firewood	6 fathom cords

Discantistin Barbara Fuxin.

Has according to Count [von Herbeviller's] intimation à 1 July 1757 a yearly salary of . 20 f.

Item according to princely resolution ddᵒ [*de dato*] 13th August 1758 she is to perfect herself to the best of her abilities in singing and to receive an annual increase, to improve her living expenses, of. 10 f.

Item according to princely intimation ddᵒ 4th January 1759, these 50 f., which used to go to Capell Meister H: Werner for his singing the alto part hitherto, are to be allowed for her better living expenses. 50 f.

Chor und Cameral-Singerin Anna Maria Scheffstoßin.

has from 1 Jan. 1760 in annual cash salary . 100 f.

[*continued overleaf*]

---

1 J. Harich in *HJB* VII, 7f., 75.

[Princely musicians, 1760 – *cont.*]

Tenorista Josephus Diezl.

In cash .	62 f. 30 Xr.
For poultry	2 f. 30 Xr.
Wheat .	4 ⎫
Corn .	8 ⎬ *Mezen*
Lentils, barley and millet-pap each	¼ ⎭
Beef .	300 ⎫
Salt .	30 ⎪
Lard .	24 ⎬ lb.
Candles .	24 ⎭
Wine *Eysenstäder Hämb*	9 ⎫ *Emer*
Cabbage and beets each	½ ⎭
Firewood	6 fathom cords

Franziscus Nigst.

at present cash-keeper in Eisenstadt has à 1 Junÿ 1760, so that he will diligently frequent the princely choir-loft, also the *Tafel Musique*, and to be available for copying music, annually . . . . 50 f.

Bassista Melchior Griessler.

a 1ª Junÿ 761 from this date in cash	200 f.
For a suit of clothes .	60 f.
Wheat .	4 ⎫
Corn .	12 ⎬ *Mezen*
Lentils, barley and millet-pap each	¼ ⎭
Beef .	300 ⎫
Salt .	50 ⎪
Lard .	30 ⎬ lb.
Candles .	30 ⎭
Wine *Eisenstädter Hämb*	9 ⎫
Cabbage and beets each	½ ⎬ *Emer*
Pig. .	1 ⎭
Firewood	6 fathom cords

Organista Joannes Novotni.

in cash together with lodging money .	100 f.
Wheat .	4 ⎫
Corn .	12 ⎬ *Mezen*
Lentils, barley and millet-pap each	¼ ⎭
Beef .	300 ⎫
Salt .	50 ⎪
Lard .	30 ⎬ lb.
Candles .	30 ⎭
Wine *Eisenstädter Hämb*	9 ⎫ *Emer*
Cabbage and beets each	½ ⎬
Pig. .	1 ⎭
Firewood	6 fathom cords

Violinista Tobias Fritsch.

In cash .	50 f.
Annually for a suit of clothes	30 f.
Lodging money	8 f.
Wheat .	4 ⎫
Corn .	12 ⎬ *Mezen*
Lentils, barley and millet-pap each	¼ ⎭
Beef .	300 ⎫
Salt .	40 ⎪
Lard .	30 ⎬ lb.
Candles .	30 ⎭
Wine *Eisenstäder*[!] *Hämb* .	9 ⎫ *Emer*
Cabbage and beets each	½ ⎬
Pig. .	1 ⎭
Firewood	6 fathom cords

Violinista Carolus Lind.

in cash	50 f.	
Lodging money	12 f.	
Wheat	4	
Corn	12	*Mezen*
Lentils, barley *et* millet-pap each	$\frac{1}{4}$	
Beef	300	
Salt	40	lb.
Lard	30	
Candles	30	
Wine *Eisenstädter Hämb*	9	
Cabbage and beets each	$\frac{1}{2}$	*Emer*
Pig	1	
Firewood	6 fathom cords	

Violinista Adamus Sturm.

has in cash annually	50 f.	
Lodging money	12 f.	
Wheat	4	
Corn	12	*Mezen*
Lentils, barley *et* millet-pap	$\frac{1}{4}$	
Beef	300	
Salt	40	lb.
Lard	30	
Candles	30	
Wine *Eisenstäder*[!] *Hämb*	9	
Cabbage and beets each	$\frac{1}{2}$	*Emer*
Pig	1	
Firewood	6 fathom cords	

Violonista Antonius Khünel [*recte*: Kühnel].

In cash	50 f.
Lodging money	12 ,,
Wheat	4 *Mezen*
Corn	12 ,,
Lentils, barley and millet-pap each	$\frac{1}{4}$,,
Beef	300 lb.
Salt	30 ,,
Lard	30 ,,
Candles	30 ,,
Wine *Eisenstäder*[!] *Hämb*	9 *Eimer*
Cabbage and beets each	$\frac{1}{2}$,,
Pig	1
Firewood	6 fathom cords

Violoncelista Sigismundus Gs[t]ettner.

Cash	50 f.	
Lodging money	12 f.	
Wheat	4	
Corn	12	*Mezen*
Lentils, barley *et* millet-pap each	$\frac{1}{4}$	
Beef	300	
Salt	40	lb.
Lard	30	
Candles	30	
Wine *Eisenstädter Hämb*	9	
Cabbage and beets each	$\frac{1}{2}$	*Emer*
Pig	1	
Firewood	6 fathom cords	

Hautboista Carolus Braun.

in cash	144 F.
Lodging money	15 f.
Wine *Eisenstäder*[!] *Hämb*	9 *Emer*
Candles	30 lb.
Firewood	5 fathom cords

[Princely musicians, 1760 – *cont.*]

Chor- und Cameral-Singerin Anna Maria Scheffstossin.
Has à 1ª Jan 1760 in cash annually . . . . 100 f.
Franz Nigst [etc., information repeated as above] . . .
Cash-keeper Franciscus Nigst.

Cash	120 f.
Lodging money	20 f.
Office requirements	8 f.
Wheat	12 *Mezen*
Corn	18 ,,
Lentils, barley *et* millet-pap each	2 ,,
Beef	500 lb.
Salt	60 ,,
Lard	30 ,,
Candles with saucer	100 ,,
Wine *Eisenstäder*[!] *Hämb*	16 *Eimer*
Cabbage and beets each	2 ,,
Pig	1
Firewood	10 fathom cords

Per diem in summer 30, but in winter 45 xr.
Item is to receive half of the bran received.

Cadastre Registrar Johann Michael Hayden.

Cash	120 f.
Lodging money	15 f.
Wheat	6 *Mezen*
Corn	12 ,,
Lentils, barley *et* millet-pap each	$\frac{1}{2}$,,
Beef	300 lb.
Salt	30 ,,
Lard	25 ,,
Candles	20 ,,
Wine *Eisenstädter Hämb*	9 *Eimer*
Cabbage and beets each	1 ,,
Pig	1
Firewood	6 fathom cords

Per diem when he has to register in places from which he cannot return home at
night, for the whole day 30 xr, but if he can get home only at lunchtime 15 xr.,
and he is to explain himself every week about the number of working days, to the
book-keeping administration, and they will decide about the implementation of
this *assignation*.

Buildings Registrar Antonius Kühnel.
According to princely Decretation ddo 28ᵗᵉ August 1758, in recompense for
diligently caring for all princely buildings, for seeing that the workers do their
duty, for having a particularly watchful eye on building materials, and for
entering an accurate bill for all this in the book-keeping department, to receive
annually

In cash	50 f.
Wheat	4 *Mezen*
Corn	6 ,,
Lentils, barley *et* millet-pap each	$\frac{1}{8}$,,
Beef	100 lb.
Salt	25 ,,
Lard	20 ,,
Candles	15 ,,
Wine	3 *Eimer*
Cabbage and beets each	$\frac{1}{2}$,,

Zwey Fagotisten [two bassoon-players] bey der Grenadiers Compagnie.
Each has 50 f. annually, together . . . . 100 f.
to be paid out *quartaliter* at 12 f. 30 xr
In recompense for which they are required to be on parade during the high
presence of his High-Ness [*Durch-Laucht*] and to appear diligently in the *Tafel
Musique*.
Dismissed as of 1ª July 761.

Monsieur Bunon.
According to princely intimation dedato Eisenstadt 14te April 1759, is to receive
from the *General Cassa*, as from 1^a Aprilis 1759 . . . . . . 400 f.

Schullmeister [Joseph Dietzl]

In cash	22 f. 30 xr.
Wheat	2 *Mezen*
Corn	8 ,,
Lentils, barley *et* millet-pap each	$\frac{1}{4}$,,
Beef	250 lb.
Salt	20 ,,
Lard	12 ,,
Candles	8 ,,
Wine *Eisenstädter Hämb*	9 *Emer*
Cabbage and beets each	$\frac{1}{2}$,,
Firewood	3 fathom cords

Buchhalter [Book-keeper] Johann Spach.

Cash salary	400 f.
Lodging money	40 f.
Wheat	20 *Mezen*
Corn	24 ,,
Lentils, barley *et* millet-pap each	$1\frac{1}{2}$,,
Beef	550 lb.
Salt	100 ,,
Lard	50 ,,
Candles	50 ,,
Wine *Eisenstädter Hämb*	22 *Emer*
Cabbage and beets each	2 ,,
Pig	2
Firewood	16 fathom cords
Kindling	200 bundles

According to princely Com[missi]on dd^o 9^t Marty 756 the Herr Buchhalter is
allowed a coachman, for which . . . . 20 f.
then for 2 horses daily $\frac{1}{8}$ oats, hay and straw as necessary.
Item: according to princely Com[missi]on dd^o 20^t Aug. 758 pro melioratione
Salary . . . . 200 f.
Nb. These two written Comm[issi]ons are in the hands of the Herr Buchhalter.

Cancellista [Chancellery Official] Joannes Georgius Thonner.

Cash	170 f.
Lodging money	15 f.
Wheat	8 *Mezen*
Corn	18 ,,
Lentils, barley *et* millet-pap each	1 ,,
Beef	400 lb.
Salt	50 ,,
Lard	35 ,,
Candles	30 ,,
Wine *Eisenstädter Hämb*	12 *Eimer*
Cabbage and beets each	1 ,,
Pig	2
Firewood	8 fathom cords

Then, as long as he remains in this position and also provides service in the choir-
loft, annual increase . . . . 20 f.
Item in regard to his long and faithful service *ad dies vitae titulo pensionis*, from the
General Cassa annually . . . . 60 f.
A[nno]: 1761 died.

[Princely musicians, 1760 – *cont.*]

Cancellista Joannes Novotni.

Cash	170 f.
Lodging money	15 f.
Wheat	8 *Mezen*
Corn	18 ,,
Lentils, barley *et* millet-pap each	1 ,,
Beef	400 lb.
Salt	50 ,,
Lard	35 ,,
Candles	30 ,,
Wine *Eisenstäder*[!] *Hämb*	12 *Emer*
Cabbage and beets each	1 ,,
Pig.	2
Firewood	8 fathom cords

Accessista [Clerk] Franciscus Novotni a 1ª Januar 763.

Valentin Hulpper has a 1ª July 760. [not filled in]
Nb. died at the end of the year 762.

In cash annually	50 f.
Lodging money	15 f.
Wheat	6 *Metz*
Corn	12 ,,
Lentils, barley and millet-pap each	$\frac{1}{2}$,,
Beef	300 pounds
Salt	30 ,,
Lard	25 ,,
Candles	20 ,,
Wine *Eisenstädter Hämb*	9 *Eimer*
Cabbage and beets each	1 ,,
Pig.	1
Firewood	6 fathom cords

Schlos- und Wirthschafts Beamte
[Castle and Economic Officials]

Verwalter [Administrator] Edmundus Schlanstein.

Has in cash plus the increase of [1]756.	230 f.
Lodging money	20 f.
Office requirements	20 f.
Wheat	20 *Mezen*
Corn	24 ,,
Lentils, barley *et* millet-pap each	$1\frac{1}{2}$,,
Oats forage for 3 horses	78 ,,
Beef	550 lb.
Salt	100 ,,
Lard	70 ,,
Candles	70 ,,
Wine *Eisenstädter Hämb*	22 *Emer*
Cabbage and beets each	2 ,,
Pig.	2
Firewood	16 fathom cords
Kindling wood	200 bundles

Hay and straw as necessary for 3 horses.
Except for the above 3 horses no more, also no more cattle (without receiving
express permission from the princely establishment), and the dung to be delivered
to the princely farming department. [There follow rules for the Administrator in
taxing Wills, Birth Certificates, Poaching Fines, etc.]

Rändtmeister Joseph Wilhelm Pohl.
Franciscus Nigst.

Has in cash	150 f.
Lodging money	20 f.
Office requirements	8 f.
Wheat	12 *Mezen*
Corn	18 ,,
Lentils, barley *et* millet-pap each	2 ,,
Beef	500 lb.
Salt	60 ,,
Lard	30 ,,
Candles	60 ,,
Wine *Eisenstädter Hämb*	16 *Eimer*
Cabbage and beets each	2 ,,
Pig	1
Firewood	10 fathom cords

[Prot. No. 4671, EH, Eisenstadt: *Conventionale* 1760, with later additions; J. Harich in *HJB* VII, 50–60]

Notes: Many members of the *Capelle* had two positions, e.g. Anton Kühnel and Franz Nigst, of which the other, non-musical one was the more important and better paid; sometimes these men with two jobs could even collect two *Deputate*, e.g. Kühnel. Single men and women ate at the officers' table, therefore their *Deputat* consisted as a rule only of candles and firewood. The size and constitution of the *Deputat* usually depended on the size of the family. Small or odd-looking *Deputate* (e.g. for Theresia Riedl) probably indicated that the person was living with his or her parents. It could also happen that the single Eleonora Jäger lived with her mother. Persons of female sex were given an '-in' ending to their name, e.g. 'Jägerin' (Jäger). One sees that these *Conventionale* were generally kept up to date with later changes or additions (e.g. 1 June 1761 for Melchior Griessler, 1 July 1761 for the grenadier bassoon players, and even 1 January 1763 for Franz Novotny (usual spelling). Johann Michael Hayden was apparently no relative of Joseph Haydn. *Eimer* (*Emer*) = a liquid measure keg. *Metz* (*Metze, Meze*) = 3·44 litres (miller's dry measure). One pound (*Pfund*[*t*]) = 56 dkg. Johann Spach had been a musician and servant with Prince Paul Anton when he was studying in Leyden, and perhaps an old favourite of the Prince's: that might explain his very high salary. Certainly his large *Deputat* suggests that he had numerous children. Last entry: Pohl's position was taken over by Nigst, who therefore earned 30 Fl. more than he did as Cash-Keeper; in addition, he retained his 50 Fl. as a substitute in the *Capelle*. Schlanstein's entry was retained as a matter of interest. He held a position which made it necessary for Haydn to be in frequent contact with him: Schlanstein had to countersign most of the bills concerning the financial affairs of the *Capelle*.

What kind of patrons were Prince Paul Anton and his wife, the Marchesa Lunati-Visconti (who outlived her husband by two decades, dying on 4 July 1782 at Eisenstadt)? Of the four Esterházy princes under whom Haydn served, Paul Anton and Anton (reigned 1790–4) are the least known, possibly because the former appears in Haydn's life only for some eight-and-a-half months and the latter also rather briefly (and during the time when Haydn was mostly away in England).

The princely couple lived a life of ostentatious magnificence, as might be expected. Their clothes were made in Paris, probably with the aid of dummies (*mannequins*) which the tailors had prepared when the couple visited France, and which could be brought up to date as necessary. The sums for these clothes were astronomical, reaching 11,384 livres – or 4,552 gulden – for the year 1759 alone,[1] which was more than ten times the size of Haydn's salary when he was engaged, and more than one-third of the total budget for the *Herrschaft* Eisenstadt of the year 1763 (*vide infra*, p. 338), 12,939 Fl.

We have seen that the Prince was a great linguist (German, French, Italian), to which must be added his fluent knowledge of Latin, the language used for much of the official correspondence, particularly with Austrian government officials and even with other Hungarian officials[2] (these outgoing letters have been preserved in enormous bound folio volumes (EH, Budapest, Országos Levéltár). The Princess also learned good German (not exactly a habit with Italians, even when they lived for years in a German-speaking country, e.g. Pietro Travaglia, the princely stage designer): the *Prothocollum Missilium* of this period (1758–62) contains a series of German letters dictated by Princess Maria Anna, and they reveal a quick and intelligent mind. She retained her good looks until old age.[3]

Prince Paul Anton, as we have seen, brought back many books from his travels, the catalogue of which filled a large folio volume as early as 1738. It is interesting to see that he ordered from Holland books by Jean-Jacques Rousseau which the Austrian censor would hardly have allowed to pass into Maria Theresa's dominions, but which the Prince (with his diplomatic connections) managed to have conveyed to Eisenstadt without difficulty.[4]

---

1 French currency: livres (cf. p. 16); later francs; sols, later sous; deniers, also in divisions of six. 'Memoire des ouvrages ... pour Monseigneur le Prince d'Esterhassy [*sic*] par moy Veuve Schelling ... Tailleur du Roy ... 25 aout 1761', a total of 4,765 livres 10, with 178 livres 18 'pour les droites du Roy Caisse et Emballage (p. 132.6, fol. 57f.). Fol. 61: 'Memoire des façons et fourniture faittes Pour Madame La Princesse de Strashy [*sic*] par Depuis Maitresse Marchand et Couturiere rue du roule du 1ᵉʳ fevrier 1760'. Fol. 62, another bill, including 'habit d'étoffe d'or Riche nucé lilas olive, et rose, fourni 8 aunes d'étoffe à 140 livres l'aune. 1,120 livres'. Fol. 63, another bill, including 'habit d'etoffe d'argens à Carmetille fond Couleur de Chair, veste et paremens d'Etoffe d'argens, l'habit et la veste brodé en argens, fourni 8 aunes d'étoffe, a 130 livres l'aune 1,040 livres'. Later we note 'pour le transport de paris a vienne 17 [livres] 22', 'payez à la Douane a vienne 86 [livres] 36'. Both the bills of fol. 62 and 63 are undated, and may be approximately allotted to 1760–1. Fol. 62 provides us with an authentic rate of exchange between livres and gulden: the bill totals 2,254 livres, which was exactly 901 Fl. 36 Xr., or roughly 2½ livres = 1 Fl. Fol. 64/5 is Schelling's bill, Paris, 10 Aug. 1760 for 6,745 livres. Fol. 66–8 is Schelling's bill, Paris 20 July 1759 for 8,996 livres. Fol. 70 is Schelling's bill, Paris, 15 December 1759 for 2,388 livres. Total of Schelling's bills for 1759: 11,384 livres or 4,553 Fl. [EH, Budapest, Országos Levéltár, p. 132.6 (formerly fasc. 791)].

The princely administration seems to have used slightly devious channels to avoid local customs checks. In a letter from *Regent* P. L. von Rahier to Prince Nicolaus I of 15 February 1766, Rahier writes that the two crates from Paris are to be sent to Simmering, but he fears 'that these large crates will be noticed by the border customs officials, who are very sharp about inspecting things these days'. It would be better to pack the things in trunks and to give them to the Major Domo, when he has to go to Simmering to receive them. [P. 154 (old Fasc. 1524), fol. 470; EH, Budapest, Országos Levéltár]

2 Empress Maria Theresa corresponded with Prince Grassalkovics (intermarried with the Esterházys), a Hungarian, in Latin rather than German. Letter of 8 July 1762 owned by the present writer.

3 Quotation from Zinzendorf's Diary in *Haydn at Eszterháza 1766–1790*, p. 448, where by an error the entry is listed in July 1781 instead of July 1782 (*recte*: p. 464).

4 The relevant bill in the Esterházy Archives has watermarks 'N V' and coat-of-arms with fleur-de-lys at the foot; the prices listed are shown as 'R' = rijksgulden and 'g' = groschen (24 groschen = 1 rijksgulden or fl.). The document reads:

[on cover:] 1761
Monsieur Jean Charles des Bordes
Secretaire d'Hollande &c &c

le 14 7ᵇʳ September   doit a Arkstée & Merkus

		R		
1	Histoire de Jean Sobieski, Roy de Pologne 3 vol...............	R	4.	—	—
1	Lettres Scamoises Nᵒ		—.	20	g
1	Lettres de deux Amans par Rousseau 6 vol: n ———————————————		6.	—	—
1	Romans trad: de l'Anglois 8ᵒ		1.	—	—
1	Prediction sur la nouvelle Heloïse de Rousseau 8		—.	2	—
1	Contre Prediction au sujet de la Nouv: Heloïse		—.	3	—
		R	12.	1	g

Reçu le payement le meme jour
            Arkstée & Markus   [p. 132.6, fol. 48; EH; Budapest, Országos Levéltár]

Otherwise, apart from the evidence of their education, breeding, high cultural standards in general and their knowledge and appreciation of music, the princely couple remain a rather shadowy pair in the Haydn literature. But we may assume that it was no accident that Haydn wrote one of his most beautiful and successful operas, *L'infedeltà delusa*, to celebrate the (then) Dowager Princess's name-day in 1773.

Paul Anton's younger brother, Count Nicolaus (b. 18 December 1714), who would be Haydn's princely patron from 1762 to 1790, must now demand our attention. Like Paul Anton, Nicolaus was a good musician[1] and became one of the greatest connoisseurs of *settecento* Central Europe. Like his elder brother, Nicolaus pursued a military career with considerable distinction, particularly as Colonel at the Battle of Kolin (1757) in the Seven Years' War where, with great personal courage, he led the wavering cavalry troops to victory. He was later made a Lieutenant Field-Marshal. On 4 March 1737, he had married *Freiin* Marie Elisabeth, daughter of *Reichsgraf* (Count of the Holy Roman Empire) Ferdinand von Weissenwolf. Both Nicolaus and his wife died within a few months of each other in 1790.

Nicolaus returned from the wars to live modestly in a hunting lodge at Süttör on the Neusiedlersee (Lake Neusiedl) in Hungary, on the site of which would later arise the great castle of Eszterháza. The brothers were fond of each other, and Prince Paul Anton took the trouble to write congratulatory letters to his brother (which happen to have survived because, being semi-official, they were entered into the *Prothocollum Missilium*) on the occasion of Nicolaus's birth- or name-day. Here is a specimen:

[Prince Paul Anton Esterházy to Count Nicolaus Esterházy. *German*, 'Sie' form]
To the good Nicolas Esterhazy, Brother of the Prince, from Vienna, 5th Xbris [Dec.] 761 autograph letter of congratulation.
Highly respected *H[er]r Bruder*,
Although you are long assured of my unwavering friendship, brotherly love and devotion, it is nevertheless a particular pleasure for me to confirm them to you in writing on the occasion of your name-day, and especially to add the sincere wish, in which my consort, your Princess, joins me, that my highly respected brother [*Herr Bruder*] may enjoy not only the forthcoming name-day, but many more in years to come, in constant good health, and may continue to live in the present prosperity and in the most pleasant satisfaction. With which I remain for my whole life with deepest esteem, my highly respected *H[err] Bruder*'s
most devoted
brother and servant
Anton *Fürst* Esterhazy.
[P. 131, fol. 1546, EH, Budapest, Országos Levéltár]

Nicolaus engaged strolling players, marionette troupes and Gypsy dance bands in Süttör. He was always devoted to music, and immediately recognized Haydn's talent. The second volume of this biography, *Haydn at Eszterháza 1766–1790*, occupies itself in considerable detail with Prince Nicolaus, and we may thus limit ourselves here to pointing out that, with his military education, he sometimes tended to treat his court employees like foot soldiers, and in this army-like discipline he was materially aided by his Estates Manager (*Gütterregent*), Peter Ludwig von Rahier, also a former military

---

1 Before Werner left Vienna in June 1728 to enter the princely service in Eisenstadt, he was ordered to purchase various items, including a new violoncello for Count Nicolaus, made by the Court Lute Maker Anton Posch, as well as instruments for the *Capelle* and MS. copies of church music by Schmidt, Fux, Oettl, Reinhard, Ziani, Paumann and Caldara. This commission cost nearly 400 gulden. Pohl I, 209f.

man.[1] Nicolaus's love for music amounted almost to an obsession, and there is evidence, especially in the account of him in Framery's *Notice* (1810, based largely on reports from Haydn's pupil Ignaz Pleyel, who was at Eszterháza from 1772–7)[2], that he had serious and perhaps even manic depressions. Nicolaus attempted, with all his military severity, to be scrupulously just. Rahier who, judged only from the evidence of his correspondence with and about this musicians, appears a rather cold, despotic official, was in fact an excellent right-hand man for Nicolaus. We have read through hundreds of letters in the Rahier correspondence files of the Esterházy Archives in Budapest, and there is no doubt that he made every effort to be an impartial judge, scrupulously correct (though formal and, with his inferiors, *de haut en bas*), often taking immense pains over the fate of his and the Prince's *Unterthanen*. Indeed, this volume will show at least one interesting case of his intervening with Prince Nicolaus on behalf of the musicians, in this case Friberth, who must have been a likeable man. To choose a case concerning the Prince's and Rahier's efforts to avoid bribery, corruption and financial inefficiency, we may cite a letter in the period under concern (30 September 1765) from Nicolaus to Rahier. The first part deals with the bassoon player, Georg Schwenda, who had incurred 'passive debts' with the princely cashier's office ('which was hitherto unknown to me') and had petitioned the Prince to change his mind about fining Schwenda 10 ducats (42 Fl. 20 Kr.), which represented more than two months' salary (20 Fl. per month), no doubt for some misdemeanour. The Prince agreed to this and then went on to the next point: the former Administrator of the Castle and lands at Kreutz (now Deutsch-Kreutz), one Tergovihich (Fergovichi) was caught undertaking dubious financial transactions ('malversationes') by his cash-keeper Zöchmeister who, however, did not report them at once 'but waited until they had multiplied'. The Prince made an example of Zöchmeister, too, dismissing him from service, and, furthermore, Rahier was to dismiss 'not only the Judge at Kreutz but also the other members of the Jury, who certainly knew all about the administrator's *maleversationen* and nevertheless said nothing; and to replace them with others . . .'.[3]

1 Basic literature on the Esterházy family of this period, the *Capelle* (Werner, etc.): Pohl I, 199–223. *Geschichte des Calvarienberges . . .* (op. cit.), pp. 107ff. J. Harich in *HJB* I, 9ff., 108f.; in *HJB* IX, 5–88; also his articles: 'Szenische Darstellungen und Oratorien-Aufführungen im 18. Jahrhundert am Esterházy-Hof zu Eisenstadt', in *Burgenländische Heimatblätter*, 38. Jg., Heft 3 (Eisenstadt 1976), pp. 112ff.; 'Die Testamente der Musiker Tobias Fritsch und Gregor Josef Werner', ibid., 39. Jg., Heft 3 (Eisenstadt 1977), pp. 119ff. Oskar Pausch. 'Zwei neue Quellen zur Kulturgeschichte Eisenstadts', ibid., 38. Jg., Heft 1 (1976), pp. 43ff. Horányi (English ed.), pp. 14–28. István Kallay, 'Az Esterhazy hercegi hitbizomány Központirgazgatása a 18. század második féleben', in *Századok* 1976, 5. Szám, pp. 853ff.
2. See Appendix to *Haydn at Eszterháza 1766–1790*.
3. We quote the unpublished letter in its original German. In case it might be thought that Haydn's German syntax and grammar were particularly bad, we offer this extraordinary specimen from a Prince of the Holy Roman Empire:

Wohl Edlgebohrner
Hochgeehrter Herr v. Rahier!

Die bereits / zugeschickte deren Beambten Transposition, und / respective Veränderung schliesse hiermit bey / unterfertiger, ingleichen auch des Georg Schwenda, welcher, waß mir ehedem unbekant / war, seine habende Passiv-schulen selbst er / kennet, und nebst gäntzlichem Relaxirung der an / dictirten Straf von 10 Ducaten solche auß mei / ner Cassa bezahlet zu werden verlanget, Bitt / schrift, wessen Decretation Sie insbesond. zu stellen / verordnen werden. Übrigens, weillen in denen / durch den gewesten Kreutzer Verwalter Tergovihich / Maleversationen umb darümen auch der alldasige / Kastner Zöchmeister interessiret ist, weillen Er nicht alsogleich, da er die erste Maleversation ob / serviret hat, solche angedeutet, sondern biß auf / deren überhäufung gewartet, so werden Sie auch / denenselben alsogleich anderen zum Exempel von seinem / Dienst amoviren, nicht minder sowohl den Kreutzer / Richter, alß auch die übrigen geschworne, so die / gedachte bemelten Kreutzer Verwalters Male / versationen unfehlbar gewust haben, und solche / dannoch nicht deferiret haben, absetzen lassen, / und andere anstatt deren-selben einzusetzen / verordnen. Womit verharre / Euer Wohl Edlgebohrn / Bereitwilliger / Nicolaus Fürst Esterházy.
Süttör den 30᪲ 7bris 765 / P:S: Sie werden den Forstmeister sagen, warumen er / wegen den hiesigen Jäger nichts zu wissen machet, und er / solle alsogleich den neuen anhero schicken.

[On the cover: contents in Latin, file number and date]   [A.M. 4338, No. 18.833–5, EH, Budapest]

While on the subject of discipline, we offer yet another example: the case of the young violinist and composer, Joseph Purksteiner, who was being persecuted by the horn player Franz Stamitz. Haydn was consulted and advised Purksteiner to take the extraordinary step of going over Rahier's head and writing straight to the Prince. Here are the relevant documents:

[Joseph Purksteiner to Prince Nicolaus Esterházy, Eszterháza, *German*]
... Your Serene Princely Highness is asked, in his grace, to forgive me if I, as his liege man, make bold in this case to ask for *refugium* with Your Serene Princely Highness as my gracious Master of the Land [*Landes Vatter*]. I wanted at first to be silent about this unpleasantness that has occurred to me, in order not to awaken the ire of Your Serene Princely Highness by an unfitting act, but the *Capell Meister* informed me how I should comport myself in this regard. Since it was ordered that I reveal the matter, in profoundest submission I present it to Your Highness.

When I had the good fortune to enter this princely house, I asked the hunting horn player Steinmetz [*sic*] (since I knew no one else) to inform me, as a beginner, about the customs of this new and to me unknown house; he promised to do so and I showed myself mindful of this favour; but instead of a reprimand or correction (for which, if it had been proffered in a seemly fashion, I should have been thankful), he treated me almost like a fool, so that when I observed this, I tried to remove myself from his presence, at which he began to maltreat me, but I thought to myself: *omne Initium durum*, and was silent until the 5th week, when one time he proved to be simply too rough, so that I said to him, no one except he says such rude things to me, and then I left him, whereupon he came into my room, called me every insulting name and finally boxed my ears.

Would that Your Serene Princely Highness be minded to act as judge of me and him, otherwise this will be bad for all the other musicians, since this Steinmetz goes about saying that he boxes the ears of your princely musici's, but I ask and hope for no greater grace than to die as Your Serene Princely Highness' true and obedient liege man,

Your Serene Princely Highness'
humble obedient
Joseph Purksteiner

[Eisenstadt, *c.* 25 March 1766] [A. M. 4335, No. 18. 221/3, EH, Budapest]

[Prince Nicolaus Esterházy to P. L. von Rahier, Eisenstadt]
Schloß Eszterház, 6th April 766

Well and nobly born,
Most respected Herr v. Rahier!
... P: S: From the enclosed pro memoria of the newly engaged Musici Joseph Purcksteiner, you will see the general outline of his complaint against hunting horn player Steinmitz, to which may be added that this Steinmitz one time addressed Doctor Vály with the following impolite words, literally: 'Are you a Hungarian?', whereupon he answered, yes, at which he [Stamitz] said, 'I have been long enough in the company of such sons-of-bitches [*Hundesfuthern*]', so in great secrecy you will have 4 grenadiers convey said Steinmitz to the main guard-house and then, as obtains in a regiment, in the presence of the officers and the quartermaster [*Fourier*] have a proper inquest in a case of misconduct. If it turns out that the witnesses, through whose testimony the case must be decided, need to be confronted, prior written permission must be obtained from me. Upon which you will then report to me and send me your opinion.

Nicolaus Fürst Esterházy
[A.M. 4335, No. 18.826, EH, Budapest]

[Eisenstadt Grenadier Officers and Edmund Schlanstein, Administrator, to Prince Nicolaus Esterházy, Eszterháza]

Humble Opinion[1]

Concerning the Hunting Horn Player Frantz Steinmetz

Since in his examination he himself admitted that he boxed the ears of the Musico Pourksteiner [*sic*] in the latter's own living quarters without said Purksteiner having said anything offensive, said Steinmetz would deserve more severe treatment, but if it can be verified that Purksteiner – as said Steinmetz professes – reached for his cane (as must be investigated), the offence were somewhat less, but since physical attack without provocation is forbidden, our humble opinion is that said Steinmetz apologize in the presence of some of the princely musicians for his improper conduct towards Purksteiner and then that he should be arrested for two days.

But as concerns Herr v. Wally [Vály], said Steinmetz denies any improper conduct, and thus his statement would have to be verified by witnesses. Not until then could, in our humble opinion, punishment be meted out.

Eysenstadt, 10 April 766

Josephus Bogus: von Manowsky
First Lieutenant

Joseph Benedictus
Harrich Sequt.
Lieutenant

Jacobus della Wallone
Capitaine

Edmund Schlanstein[2]
Administrator

[A.M. 4335, No. 18.826, EH, Budapest]

We have chosen this one rather interesting example although it slightly exceeds the chronological boundaries of this volume; another case of a disciplinary infraction by a musician (the flautist Franz Sigl) will be found *infra*, p. 412.

------

1 'Ohne maßgebliche' (later, 'ohnmaßgebliche'; 'without prejudice'), a kind of *terminus technicus* also used frequently Haydn's petitions to Prince Nicolaus II in later years (many included in *Haydn: the Late Years 1801–1809*).
2 Stamitz seems to have left the band after this episode. See *Haydn at Eszterháza 1766–1790*, p. 79.

When Haydn was taken into the service of Prince Paul Anton, the contract was signed in Vienna, where the Esterházy Palace is in the Wallnerstraße. Haydn was afterwards a resident in, though not included on the personnel list of, the Domain of Eisenstadt (*Herrschaft* Eisenstadt). The princely domains at the end of the seventeenth century, when the *primo genitur* trust fund had been established in 1696, had consisted of 700,000 *Joch* of land (one *Joch* = 57·546 *ar* in Austria, 43 *ar* in Hungary; one *ar* in Austria = 100 square metres). This was, in Haydn's time, divided into twenty-nine *Herrschaften* (in 1801 thirty, and one 'Gut' or smaller estate), each with a *Verwalter* (Administrator) who, in turn, was responsible to five inspectors-of-estates. The whole pyramid-shaped organization was directed by a *Güterregent* (Estates Director) who, when Haydn joined the organization in May 1761, was Count von Herbeviller and (after his death) from 1763 Peter Ludwig von Rahier.[1]

The *Güterregent*'s salary, like those of several other members of the Esterházy establishment who ranked, as it were, above the individual *Herrschaften* (e.g. the Chief Cashier, Johann Zoller, who disbursed the money for all the estates although he resided, physically, in Eisenstadt), was not debited to, or registered by, any one *Herrschaft*; though the salary in kind (*Deputat*) for Zoller is listed in the budget for the *Herrschaft* Eisenstadt because he was resident there. Since Haydn came to live in Eisenstadt, we have thought it interesting to provide a list of the members of the *Herrschaft* Eisenstadt. It will be noted that only the church choir members' *Deputate* (not their salaries) are listed, as is the case with Chief Cashier Zoller; the other members of the *Capelle* – including Haydn and Werner – do not figure here at all, and this is because the *Capelle*, though in fact they lived with their families in Eisenstadt, were theoretically part of the constantly travelling princely entourage, playing at Vienna, Eisenstadt, Kittsee, Süttör, etc. Since this list of the *Herrschaft* Eisenstadt has never been published, we have given it in German, with all the typical peculiarities of the period ('Eimer' or, incorrectly, 'Emer'; 'jährlich' or, incorrectly, 'jahrlich', and so on). At the conclusion of this 1763 list will be noted some fluctuations as found in the 1764 list (differing meat and lard prices), an English glossary of terms and translation of the essential parts of the document. Some of the least comprehensible words in Austrian dialect or names grossly misspelt have been explained in brackets and, as always, the faulty addition has been indicated by brackets and *recte* indications. The official value of the goods in kind (*Deputate*) in 1761 has been attached to the glossary (see pp. 338f.): it is revealing to see the rise in prices within the next twenty years; for a comparable list during the 1780s, see *Haydn at Eszterháza 1766–1790*, pp. 33f.

---

1 See *Haydn at Eszterháza 1766–1790*, p. 32, n. 1. In the 'Personal und Salarial Stand Numero 1 Anno 1801' (EH, Budapest, Országos Levéltár, P. 156, rkn. 29, 30, 31; old Fasc. 2482–4), the estates are listed as follows:

Herrschaft

Eisenstadt	Kittsee	Buják
Hornstein	Güns	Ipoly-Pászthó
Pöttsching	Lokenhaus	Bittsee
Forchtenstein	Alsó-Lyndva	Sztrencsen
Koberstorf	Nempthy	Wéghles
Schwarzenbach	Gobáncz	Derecske
Süttör	Ozora	Kisvárda
Kapuvár	Dombovár	Szádvár
Kreutz	Kaposvár	(to which was added the 'Gut', or
Lakenbach	Szent-Lörincz	estate, Böke, smaller in size than a
Frau[en]kirchen	Láva	*Herrschaft*)

Extract / Deren in diesem Jahr aus dem Ründt Bezahlten / Solarien Bestallungen / und Pensionen / Dr[?] — 12939 F 65$\frac{3}{12}$ d: / N$\underline{o}$ 104: / Mit 11: Beÿlaagen. / [right, above:] 1763.

[Title:] Extract: / Über die A$\underline{o}$ 1763: Lauth Hoch F$\underline{ln}$ Conventional sowohl der geistlich = / = keit, als auch denen Herren Officieren gebührende, und Be = / = zahlte Solaria, wie auch übrige Bezahlte Bestallungen, / und Pensionen:

Der Geistlichkeit.

Lit: F . di
                                                                                      [denari =
                                                                                      Kreuzer]

Ihro Hochwürden Herr Probst haben jährlich an / Baaren			
Solario	60 F —		
Vor eine Kleydung	40 F —		
Vor 10 St: Gänß 2 F und vor 20 Hüner 3 F F: [facit] .	5 F —		
Vor 300 # [Pfund] Rindfleisch, So lauth Beyligen =			
A: = den auszug Lit: A betraget	19 F 8$\frac{2}{4}$		144:58$\frac{2}{4}$
Vor 30 # Rindschmaltz à 15 xr	7 F 50 d:		
Linß, gerst = und Hierß = prein von jeder			
Sort ein Metzen a 4 F	12 F —		
Vor $\frac{2}{4}$: Emer Rüben	1 F —		
Beede Herren Schloß = Capellani haben jährlich			
jeder besonders Kost = Geld 75 F			
So betraget	— — ,,		150:—:
Schloß = Schullmeister hat jährlich an Baaren-toto .	22 F 50 d:		
Vor 250 # rindfleisch	15 F 90$\frac{5}{12}$,,		
Vor 120 # rindschmaltz	3 F — ,,		45:40$\frac{5}{12}$,,
Linß, gerst = und Hierß = prein jedes $\frac{1}{4}$ Mtz. Facit	3 F — ,,		
Vor $\frac{2}{4}$ Emer Rüben	1 F — ,,		
Schloß = Capelldiener hat jährlich an Baaren .	30 F — ,,		
Vor 300 # rindfleisch	19 F —8$\frac{2}{4}$		
Vor 25 # rindschmaltz	6 F 25 d:		62:33$\frac{2}{4}$,,
Lins, gerst = und Hierß = prein jedes $\frac{2}{4}$ Mtz: macht	6 F — ,,		
Vor $\frac{2}{4}$ Emer Rüben	1 F — ,,		
Die dreÿ Ministranten = Buben haben jeder insonderheit			
jährlich 12 F, in Suṁa also	— — ,,		36:— ,,
Summa	— — ,,		438:32$\frac{5}{12}$,,

Daß unß diese vierhundertdreÿßigacht gulden 32$\frac{5}{12}$ d: aus dem / Ründt = amt bezahlet worden, quittiren wir. Eis: d[en] 31^{tn} xbris $\overline{763}$:

Johann Matthias Knoblauch	Joannes Pauer	Josephus Seitz
Probst in beden Hoflein Undt	p:t: curatus	Joseph Dietzl
Schloß Pfarrer in Eÿsenstatt mpria	Ariendis mpria	Schulmst:
Frantz Pfleÿer [Cappeldiener]		

Der Chor Music:

Discantista Barbara Fuxin hat à 1$\underline{ma}$ Septembris:		
Vor 100 # rindfleisch . . . . . :	6 F —	8:50 ,,
Vor 100 # rindschmaltz . . . . . ,,	2 F 50 d:	
Altista Eleonora Jägerin hat jährlichen:		
Vor 300 # rindfleisch . . . . . ,,	19 F 8$\frac{2}{4}$	
Vor 204 # schmaltz . . . . . ,,	6 F — ,,	29:–8$\frac{2}{4}$,,
Lins, gerst = und Hierß = prein jedes $\frac{1}{4}$ Mtz: . ,,	3 F — ,,	
Vor $\frac{1}{4}$ Eimer rüben . . . . . ,,	1 F — ,,	

Tenorista Herr Joseph Dietzl hat in Baaren eben . . „ 29:–8$\frac{2}{4}$ „
Bassista Herr Melchior grießler hat jährlich:
   Vor 300 ♯ Rindfleisch . . . . : 19 F –8$\frac{2}{4}$ ⎫
   Vor 30 ♯ schmaltz . . . . „ 7 F 50 d: ⎪
   Vor $\frac{2}{4}$ Eimer Rüben. . . . . „ 1 F — „ ⎬ 30:58$\frac{2}{4}$ „
   Lins, gerst = und Hieß = prein jedes $\frac{1}{4}$ Mtz: . „ 3 F — ⎭
Organista Herr Joannes Novotni hat eben so Viel: . . . „ 30:58$\frac{2}{4}$ „
Violinista Herr Tobias Fritsch ingleichen . . . „ 30:58$\frac{2}{4}$ „
Violinista Herr Adam Sturm ebenfahls . . . . „ 30:58$\frac{2}{4}$ "
Violinista Herr Anton Chünel eben . . . . „ 30:58$\frac{2}{4}$ „

                Summa . . „ 219:59$\frac{2}{4}$ „

Daß unß diese zweÿhundert Neunzeten gulden 59$\frac{2}{4}$ d: aus / dem allhiesigen Ränd = amt bezahlet worden, quittiren wir / Eisenstadt den 31$\underline{\text{ten}}$ xbris 1763.

Johann Novotnj mpria   Melch:Grießler mpria
Anton Kühnel mpria   Eleonora Jagerin mpria
Adam Sturm   Joseph Dietzl:
Barbara Füxin

Der Löbl.$\underline{\text{en}}$ Buchhaltereÿ

Herr Buchhalter Paulus Eötvös hat samt Quartier =
   = geld an Baaren . . . . „ 440 F — „ ⎫
   Vor 550 ♯ Rindfleisch . . . „ 34 F 98$\frac{11}{12}$„ ⎪
   Vor 50 ♯ Rindschmaltz . . „ 12 F 50 d: ⎬ 509:48$\frac{11}{12}$„
   Lins, gerst = und Hierß = prein, jedes 1$\frac{2}{4}$ Mtz:Facit „ 18 F — „ ⎪
   Vor 2 Emer Ruben . . „ 4 F — „ ⎭
Herr Buchhalter Joannes Spách hat samt Quartier =
   = geld in Baaren . . . „ 640 F — „ ⎫
   Vor deßen gutscher jährlich . . . „ 20 F — „ ⎬ 729:48$\frac{11}{12}$„
   d[as] übrige, gleich = wie Hr. Buchhalter Eötvös mit . „ 69 F 48$\frac{11}{12}$ ⎭
Cancellista Herr Joannes Novotni hat jahrlich
   samt Quartier = geld an Baarem . „ 185 F —, ⎫
   Vor 400 ♯ Rindfleisch . . „ 25 F 44$\frac{2}{3}$ ⎪
   Vor 35 ♯ Rindschmaltz . . . „ 8 F 75 „ ⎬ 233:19$\frac{2}{3}$ „
   Lins, gerst = Hierß = prein jedes 1 Mtz: . „ 12 F — „ ⎪
   Vor 1 : Emer Ruben . . . „ 2 F ⎭
Cancellista Herr Petrus Voidt hat eben so Viel . . . „ 233:19$\frac{2}{3}$ „
    Herr Franciscus Juház ingleichen . . . „ 233:19$\frac{2}{3}$ „
    Herr Ferdinandus Walch ebenfahls . . „ 233:19$\frac{2}{3}$ „
    Herr Michael Kaufmann auch . . „ 233:19$\frac{2}{3}$ „
    Herr Joseph Zehetner eben . . . „ 233:19$\frac{2}{3}$ „
Accessista Herr Joannes Seitz hat jährlich
   samt quartier = geld in Baaren . . „ 65 F — „ ⎫
   Vor 300 ♯ Rindfleisch . . „ 19 F –8$\frac{2}{4}$ ⎪
   Vor 25 ♯ Rindschmaltz . . „ 6 F 25 d: ⎬ 98:33$\frac{2}{4}$
   Lins, gerst = und Hierßprein, jedes $\frac{2}{4}$ Mtz:. „ 6 F — ⎪
   Vor 1 Emer Ruben . . . „ 2 F — ⎭
Herr Josephus Lex hat eben so Viel . . . „ 98:33$\frac{2}{4}$ „
Herr Franciscus Novotni–ingleichen . . . „ 98:33$\frac{2}{4}$ „

                Summa . . „ 2.933:16$\frac{4}{12}$

Daß wir jeder insonderheit, in Summa aber mit zweÿtau= =send Neunhundertdreÿ ßigdreÿ gulden 16$\frac{4}{12}$d: aus alhiesigen Rändt= =Amt richtig contentiret worden, quittiren wir. / Eisenstadt den 31ten xbris 1763:

Johann Späch	Paul Eötvös mpria
Buchhalter mpria	Buchh[alter]
Johann Novotni mpria	Franciscus Juhárz mpria
Peter Voidt mpria	Ferdinand Walch mpria
Joseph Zechetner	Johann Michael Kauffmann mpria
Franz Novotni	Joseph Lex mpria
Johann Seitz mpria	

Der HochEdßᵉ Registratur.

Herr Registrator Joannes Schmiliar hat samt
Quartier=geld jährlich an Baarem . . . . 380 F — ,, ⎫
Vor 450 ♯ Rindfleisch . . . . . 28 F 62$\frac{3}{4}$ ⎪
Vor 50 ♯ Rindschmaltz . . . . . 12 F 50 d: ⎬ 435:12$\frac{3}{4}$,,
Linß, gerst= und Hiers=prein jedes 1 Mtz: . 12 F — ,, ⎪
Vor 1 Er. Ruben . . . . . . 2 F — ,, ⎭

Cancellista Herr Nicolaus Scheffstos gleich denen Buch=
=haltereÿ=Cancellisten mit . . . . . ,, 233:19$\frac{2}{3}$,,

Herr Franciscus Trimel hat samt Quar=
=tier=geld jährlich . . . . . ,, 125 F — ,, ⎫ 158:33$\frac{2}{4}$,,
d[as] übrige, wie ein Buchhalereÿ Accessist . ,, 33 F 33$\frac{2}{4}$,, ⎭

Herr Josephus Ruehietl hat samt Quar=
=tier=geld in Baaren . . . . . ,, 117 F 50 d: ⎫ 150:83$\frac{2}{4}$,,
d[as] übrige gleich Hr Trimel mit . . . ,, 33 F 33$\frac{2}{4}$,, ⎭

Summa . . . ,, 977:49$\frac{5}{12}$,,

Daß Wir . . . . Eisenstadt den 31ten xbris 1763.

Johann Schmiliar mpria	Nicolaus Schefstos mpria
Franciscus Trimel mpria	Josephus Ruehietl mpria

Vor das Perceptorat: F . d:

Herr Ober Einnehmer Joannes Zoller hat vor die Kuchl=
=Naturalien /: gleichwie die Hr Buchhalters :/ . . . . ,, 69:48$\frac{11}{12}$,,

Daß mir . . . Eisenstadt . den 31ten xbris 1763: Johann Zoller mpria / Ober Einnehmer.

Herren Schloß= und Würthschafts= Beamten

Herr Verwalter Edmundus Schlanstein hat jährlich
Samt Quartier=geld und Cantzleÿ Nothdurft . . 270 F — ,, ⎫
Vor 550 ♯ Rindfleisch . . . . . ,, 34 F 98$\frac{11}{12}$,, ⎪
Vor 70 ♯ Rindschmaltz . . . . . ,, 17 F 50 d: ⎬ 344:48$\frac{11}{12}$
Lins, gerst= und Hierßprein jedes 1$\frac{2}{4}$ Mtz:F: . ,, 18 F — ,, ⎪
Vor 2 Emer ruben . . . . . . ,, 4 F — ,, ⎭

Herr Schloß= Pfleger Franciscus Le gout hat samt
seinem Dienstmensch jährlich . . . . ,, 212 F — ,, ⎫
Vor 700 ♯ Rindfleisch . . . . ,, 44 F 53$\frac{1}{6}$ ⎪
Vor 68 ♯ Rindschmaltz . . . . . ,, 17 F — ,, ⎬ 310:53$\frac{1}{6}$
Vor Linß, Erbsen, gerst= und Hierßprein jedes 2 Mtz: 32 F — ,, ⎪
Vor des Menschens Kuchl= Speiß $\frac{2}{4}$ Mtz : pr. . 1 F — ,, ⎪
Vor 2 Emer ruben . . . . . 4 F — ,, ⎭

Wösch = Aufseherin Frau Catharina Pohse =
= linder hat samt der Dienst = magd.   .   .   . „ 116 F — „
Vor 300 ♯ Rindfleisch . . . . „ 19 F $-8\frac{2}{4}$„
Vor 30 ♯ Rindschmaltz . . . . „ 7 F 50 d:
Lins, Erbsen, gerst = und Hierßprein jedes 1 Mtz: . „ 16 F — „
Vor 1 : Emer Ruben . . . . „ 2 F — „

                    160:$58\frac{2}{4}$

Rändt = meister Franz Nigst samt Quar =
= tier = geld und Cantzleÿ = Tax . . „ 178 F — „
Vor 500 ♯ Rindfleisch . . . . „ 31 F $80\frac{5}{6}$
Vor 30 ♯ Rindschmaltz . . . . „ 7 F 50 d:
Lins, gerst = und Hierßprein jedes 2 Mtz: . . „ 24 F — „
Vor 2 Emer Ruben . . . . . „ 4 F —

                    245:$30\frac{5}{6}$ „

        Latus   „ 1.060.91$\frac{5}{12}$ „

Thonerskürcher [Donnerskirchner] Kellermeister Herr

Josephus Krafft hat an Baaren . . „ 300 F — „
  Vor Kuchl- Naturalien gleichwie Hr. Zoller . „ 67 F $48\frac{11}{12}$
  NB. nach Abzug 2 F ruben = geld

                  367:$48\frac{11}{12}$ „

Kastner Herr Johann Michael Moßer hat samt
Quartier = geld und Cantzleÿ = nothdurft . „ 148 F — „
d[as] übrige gleich dem Rändtmeister mit . . „ 67 F $30\frac{5}{6}$

                  215:$30\frac{5}{6}$ „

Schaffer Herr Franciscus Haÿder hat jährlich . . „ 75 F — „
Vor 300 ♯ Rindfleisch . . . „ 19 F $-8\frac{3}{4}$
Vor 25 ♯ Rindschmaltz . . . „ 6 F 25 d:

                  100:$33\frac{3}{4}$ „

Grund Buch- Schreiber Herr Joh. Michael Haÿden
hat jährlich samt Quartier = geld . . „ 135 F —
Vor die Kuchl = Naturalien gleichwie ein Buch =
= halsterÿ- Accessist . . . 33 F $33\frac{3}{4}$

                  168:$33\frac{3}{4}$ „

Bau = Schreiber Herr Anton Khünel hat jähr =
= lich an Baaren . . . . „ 50 F — „
Vor 100 ♯ Rindfleisch . . . „ 6 F $36\frac{1}{6}$
Vor 20 ♯ Rindschmaltz . . . „ 5 F — „
Linß, gerst = und Hierßprein, jedes $\frac{1}{8}$ Mtz: — . 1 F 50 d:
Vor $\frac{2}{4}$ Emer Ruben . . . . „ 1 F —

                  63:$86\frac{1}{6}$ „

        Latus   1,060:91$\frac{5}{12}$ „

        Summa   1,976:24$\frac{4}{12}$

Daß jeder .... quittiren wir. Eisenstadt. d 30tn xbris $\overline{763}$: / Edmund Schlanstein mpria / Verwalter / Frantz Nigst mpria / Rändtmeister / Anton Kühnelt mpria / Bauschreiber / Frantz Haÿder mpria / Schaffer/.

Les Goutt mpria / Joh: Mich: Moßer mpria / Kast[ner] / chadarinna / boßlinder [Catharina Pohselinder] / Joh: Michael Hayden mpria / Grundbuchschreiber.

Vor die Jägereÿ.   F . d:

Forstmeister Herr Frantz Anton Kandler hat
jährlich an Baaren . . . . „ 500 F —
Vor 500 ♯ Rindfleisch . . . „ 31 F $80\frac{5}{6}$
Vor 50 ♯ Rindschmaltz . . . „ 12 F 50 d:
Linß, gerst = und Hierßprein jedes $1\frac{2}{4}$ Mtz: — „ 18 F — „
Vor 12 Eimer Bier . . . . „ 18 F — „
Vor 2 Emer Ruben . . . . „ 4 F — „

                  584:$30\frac{5}{6}$

Deßen Handjäger hat jahrlich an Baaren . „ 30 F — „
Vor 300 ♯ Rindfleisch . . . „ 19 F $-8\frac{2}{4}$
Vor 25 ♯ Rindschmaltz . . . „ 6 F 25 d:
Linß, gerst = Hiers = prein $\frac{1}{4}$ Mz. davor aber . „ 2 F $31\frac{1}{4}$ d:
Vor $\frac{2}{4}$ Emer Ruben . . . . „ 1 F — „

                  58:$64\frac{3}{4}$ „

Waltmeister Herr Mattaeus Kanhäuser hat

jährlich an baaren	„ 150 F —	
vor 400 # Rindfleisch	„ 25 F 44$\frac{2}{3}$	
vor 50 # Rindschmaltz	„ 12 F 50 d:	203 :94$\frac{2}{3}$
Lins, Gerst = und Hierßprein jedes 1 Mtz:.	„ 12 F —	
Vor 2 Emer Rüben	„ 4 F — „	

Paris = Jäger hat gleich des Hr Forstmeisters Handjäger
jährlich in Sum̄a . . . . „ 58 :64$\frac{3}{4}$ „

St. Geörger Jäger hat eben so viel . . . . „ 58 :64$\frac{3}{4}$ „

Gschießer Jäger ingleichen . . . . . „ 58 :64$\frac{3}{4}$ „

Thonerskürchner [Donnerskirchener] Jäger ...
ebenfahls . . . . „ 58 :64$\frac{3}{4}$ „

Purbacher Jäger ingleichen samt 10 F Quartier = geld . „ 68 :64$\frac{3}{4}$ „

Praittenbruñer [Breitenbrunner] Jäger eben samt 10 F
Quartier = geld . . . . „ 68 :64$\frac{3}{4}$ „

St: Geörger Forster hat an Baaren	20 F — „	26 :36$\frac{1}{6}$ „
Vor 100 # Rindfleisch	6 F 36$\frac{1}{6}$	

Thonerskürchner Forster hat samt 8 F Quartier =

= geld	„ 28 F — „	34 :36$\frac{1}{6}$
Vor 100 # Rindfleisch	„ 6 F 36$\frac{1}{6}$	

Purbacher Forster hat gleich dem Geörger . . . „ 26 :36$\frac{1}{6}$ „

Praittenbruner Forster eben so viel und 6 F quartier =
geld . . . . „ 32 :36$\frac{1}{6}$ „

Latus 1.338 :23$\frac{5}{12}$

Traustorfer Forster hat gleich dem geörger Forster . „ 26 :36$\frac{1}{6}$ „

1ter Gschießer und zugleich Thiergarten = Forster hat an

Baaren	„ 26 F — „	
Quartier = geld	„ 8 F — „	43 :54$\frac{1}{4}$ „
Vor 150 # Rindfleisch	„ 9 F 54$\frac{1}{4}$	

2ter Thiergarten Forster hat an Baaren	„ 26 F — „	35 :54$\frac{1}{4}$ „
Vor 150 # Rindfleisch	„ 9 F 54$\frac{1}{4}$	

3ter Thiergarten Forster hat eben so viel. . . „ 35 :54$\frac{1}{4}$ „

4ter Thiergarten Forster ingleichen . . . „ 35 :54$\frac{1}{4}$ „

Latus 1.338 :23$\frac{5}{12}$ „

Summa . . . 1.514 :76$\frac{7}{12}$

Daß so wohl unß als denen gesam̄ten Jägern und Forstern jedem die ausgesezte gebühr aus dem Ränt-Amt bezahlet worden, wird quittiret. Eisenstadt den 31$^{\underline{ten}}$ xbris $\overline{763}$

Johann Mathes Kanhaußer   Frantz Anton Kandler
Waldmeister mpria   Forstmeister

Vor die gartnereÿ:

Eisenstädter Hofgartner hat Monathlich 17 F So

Vors gantze Jahr betraget.	204 F — „	216 :72$\frac{1}{3}$ „
Vor 200 # Rindfleisch	12 F 72$\frac{1}{3}$	

Der Thiergartner hat Monathlich 12 F So betraget
auf gantzes Jahr . . . . „ 144 :— „

Denen in hiesiger Hofgarten Befündlichen gartner =
gesellen, und Monaths = Knechten seÿnd lauth

B: Beylaâg Lit: B: bezahlet worden . . . . „ 900 :— „

Summa . . . 1.260 :72$\frac{1}{3}$ „

Daß uns das ausgesezte Monath = geld erfolget worden, / quittiren wir. Eysenstadt den 31$^{\underline{ten}}$ xbris $\overline{763}$. / Johann Altwig / Tier gartten garttner.   Caspar Burgerth / Fürstl. Gartner.

Vor die Grenadier = Compagnie:

F . d:

Herr Unter Lieutnant Josephus Harich hat jahrliches

Quar = = tier = Geld . . . . „ 30:— „

Summa per se

Daß Ich diese . . . . . . empfan = gen habe quittire / Jos. Ben. Harrich /
Unt. Lieutnant.

Vor verschiedene Bestallungen.

Rauchfangkehrer- Meister Martin Praetarj hat jahr =
= lich an Baaren . . . . . . „ 40 F — „ } 52:72$\frac{1}{3}$ „
Vor 200 # Rindfleisch . . . . . „ 12 F 72$\frac{1}{3}$. }
Uhrmacher Johann Michael Weltz hat jahrlich
samt Quartier = geld . . . . . „ 65 F — „ }
Vor 250 # Rindfleisch . . . . „ 15 F 90$\frac{5}{12}$„ } 88:21$\frac{8}{12}$„
Vor 24 # Rindschmaltz . . . . „ 6 F — „ }
Linß und Erbsen, jedes $\frac{1}{4}$ Mtz: davor aber . „ 1 F 31$\frac{1}{4}$ }
Bräumeister Paul Maÿr hat an Baâren . . . „ 45 F — „ }
Vor 300 # Rindfleisch . . . . „ 19 F −8$\frac{2}{4}$„ }
Vor 28 # Rindschmaltz . . . . „ 7 F — „ } 74:73$\frac{1}{4}$„
Linß, Gerst = und Hierßprein $\frac{1}{4}$ Mtz: davor aber . „ 1 F 64$\frac{3}{4}$„ }
Vor 1 : Emer Rüben . . . . . 2 F — }
Coṁissions = Köchin hat an Baâren geld . . „ 30 F — }
Vor 200 # rind fleisch . . . . „ 12 F 72$\frac{1}{3}$ } „ 47:47$\frac{1}{3}$ „
Vor 15 # Schmaltz . . . . . „ 3 F 75 „ }
Vor $\frac{2}{4}$ Emer rüben . . . . . . „ 1 F — „ }
Die ordinaire Kuchl = Wäscherin vor 200 # rind Fleisch . „ 12:72$\frac{1}{3}$„
C: Hof Tischler Carl Flach hat lauth Beÿlaâg Lit: C: samt
Seinen gesellen empfangen . . . . „ 893:−3$\frac{1}{3}$„
Hof Binder Jacob Arzt hat jahrlich in Baaren . . . . „ 40:— „
Thonerskürchner Keller Binder hat jährlich . . . . „ 100:— „

Latus 1.308:90$\frac{3}{12}$

F . d:

Thonerkürchner Brandweiner hat an Baaren . . . 40 F — „ } 46:36$\frac{1}{6}$„
Vor 100 # Rindfleisch . . . . . 6 F 36$\frac{1}{6}$ }
Schloß = Schlißer hat samt seinen zweÿen Jungen
an Baaren . . . . . . „ 40 F — „ }
Vor 450 # Rindfleisch . . . . „ 28 F 62$\frac{3}{4}$„ }
Vor 35 # Rindschmaltz . . . . „ 8 F 75 d: }
Ihren Linß, gerst = und Hierßprein jedes $\frac{1}{2}$ Mtz: davor „ 3 F 37$\frac{1}{2}$d:} 86:12$\frac{3}{4}$
Denen 2: Jungen zusaṁen vor $\frac{1}{2}$ Mtz: Linß, und
$\frac{1}{2}$ Mtz: gerstprein . . . . . . „ 2 F 37$\frac{1}{2}$d: }
Vor 1$\frac{1}{2}$ Eimer Ruben . . . . . „ 3 F — }
Hof = Weingart = knecht hat an Baâren . . „ 8 F 25 d:} 16:20$\frac{1}{3}$„
Vor 125 # Rindfleisch . . . . „ 7 F 95$\frac{1}{3}$„ }
Weeg = Nachseher hat jährlichen . . . . . 20:— „
Thorwarther Johann georg Schwab: Seel.[?] [the late]
hatte Bis Ende Junÿ
zu fordern an Baâren . . . . : „ 10 F — „ }
┌ wovon 37$\frac{2}{4}$ # à 4 x ┐ }
vor 75 : # Rindfleisch ┤ 29$\frac{1}{4}$ # à 7 d. ├ NB 5 F 4$\frac{1}{4}$ 5 F 12$\frac{2}{4}$„ } 15:62$\frac{2}{4}$„
└ 8$\frac{1}{4}$ # à 6 d. ┘ }
vor $\frac{1}{4}$ Emer Ruben . . . . . . „ — 50 „ }

335

Neuer Thorwarther Mathias Schwendenwein hat von

1ten Sept.: an baaren	. . . . . .	6 F 66$\frac{2}{3}$	}
vor 50: # Rindfleisch	. . . . .	„ 3 F —„	} 10:— „
vor 1/6 Emer Ruben	. . . . . .	„ — F 33$\frac{1}{3}$„	}

Die fünf Schloß = Trabanten ⊖ hat jeder jahrlich

24 F, in Summa also	. . . . .	„ 120 F —„	}
vor 500 # Rindfleisch insgesamt	. . .	„ 31 F 80$\frac{5}{6}$	} 151:80$\frac{5}{6}$„

Die drey Schloß- wachter haben jeder jährl: 24 F

zusamen aber .	. . . . .	„ 72 F „	}
Holtz = geld jed 3 F facit .	. . . .	„ 9 F —	} 100:—8$\frac{2}{4}$„
vor 300 # Rindfleisch insgesamt	. . .	„ 19 F —8$\frac{3}{4}$	}

Die Eysenstädter drey Maÿr= knechte haben jähr =

= lich insgesamt an Baâren	. . . .	„ 60 F —	}
vor 300 # Rindfleisch	. . . .	19 F —8$\frac{2}{4}$	} 79:—8$\frac{2}{4}$

Der Eysenstädter Maÿrbub hat an Baaren

	. . .	„ 10 F —„	}
vor 50 # Rindfleisch	. . . . .	„ 3 F 18$\frac{1}{12}$	} 13:18$\frac{1}{12}$

Latus	538:47$\frac{8}{12}$

⊖

worunter der Mathias Schwendenwein / bis Ende Aug:,
und der Michael Lind / von 1ten Sept: biß Ende xbris
enthalten ist.

F . d:

Die drey Großhöfleiner Maÿrknecht haben zusam =

= men jährlich	. . . . .	56 F —„	}
vor 150 # Rindfleisch	. . . .	„ 9 F 54$\frac{1}{4}$„	} 65:54$\frac{1}{4}$

Die drey dasigen Maÿrbuben haben zusamen

	. .	„ 30 F —„	}
vor 120 # Rindfleisch	. . . .	„ 7 F 63$\frac{1}{4}$	} 37:63$\frac{1}{4}$„

D: Der Edenburger [Oedenburger] Freÿmann hat Sub Lit:

empfangen	. . . .	„	20:— „

Land = grichts = Diener hat jährlich an Baaren	. .	„ 45 F —„	}
vor 250 # Rindfleisch	. . .	„ 15 F 90$\frac{5}{12}$	}
vor 20 # Rindschmaltz	. . .	„ 5 F —„	} 68:52$\frac{11}{12}$„
Linß und Erbsen jedes $\frac{1}{2}$ Mtz: davor aber	. „	2 F 62$\frac{1}{2}$ d:)	}

Vor das gefligl= mensch im Maÿrhof hat Ihr Schaffer

empfang[en]	. . . . . .		12:— „

Dann seÿnd Nachstehende Stall = knechte anhero
anzuweisen: :

Der Comissions = gutsherr hat Sub N$^{\underline{o}}$ und Zulaag A:
vor dieses Jahr

zu empfangen gehabt	. . . . . .	„	116:— „
E: Ein houssár pro Januario Lauth Lit:	. . . . .	„	10:— „
Der Postilion Pfaltzer Monathlich 10 F .	. . . .	„	120:— „
Jacob Ströckl ... dto	. . . . .	„	120:— „
Paks = Seppl ... dto	. . . . .	„	120:— „
Stroh täglich 12 xr .	. . . . .	„	73:— „
Der Karn =Roß = warther tägl: 15 xr .	. . .	„	91:25 „

Latus . . .	538:47$\frac{8}{12}$„
Item . . .	1.308:90$\frac{3}{12}$„
Summa . . .	2.701:33$\frac{4}{12}$„

Anstatt deren Stallleuthen Trabanten, Wachtern, und Maÿrknechten wird / der Contentirung
halber attestirt. /

Edmund Schlanstein mpria / Verwalt[er]   Martin Antonÿ Pretarÿ
Paul Maÿr / Braumeistr.   Frantz Haÿder mpria /
Jacob Arzd[?]   Schaffer
Ena Maria Stiehaß   Johann Michael
Johannes Kellner   Weltz.

Lit:	Vor gesamte Pensionisten:		F . d:

Herr Johannes Neumann gewester Hauß = Hof Meister

F: hat Sub: Lit: :quartier = geld empfangen . . . . . „ 50:— „

Herr Andreas Vlásics gewester Krenstorfer [?] Pfahrer

    hat an Baâren . . . . . . 25 F — „ ⎫

    vor 200 ♯ Rindfleisch . . . . „ 12 F $72\frac{1}{3}$„ ⎬ 40:$84\frac{5}{6}$

    vor $12\frac{2}{4}$ ♯ Rindschmaltz . . . . . „ 3 F $12\frac{1}{2}$ d:⎭

Die Rosalia Blinde Spittällerin hat jährlich

    vor 100 ♯ Rindfleisch . . . . . „ 6 F $36\frac{1}{6}$„ ⎫ 7:$19\frac{2}{4}$„

    vor 10 ♯ Käß à 5 xr . . . „ — F $83\frac{1}{3}$ ⎭

Frau Heldenreich /: So zu Ende Maii gestorben :/ hat

G: empfangen pro 1tes Quartal vor $78\frac{3}{4}$ ♯

    Rindfleisch à 4 xr . . . . „ 5 F 25 d:⎫

    Bis Ende Maÿ vor $52\frac{1}{2}$ ♯ Rindfleisch à 7 xr . . „ 3 F $67\frac{1}{2}$ ⎪

    Vor Kuchl = speiß auf 5 Monath . . . „ 3 F $33\frac{1}{3}$„ ⎬ 18:$-9\frac{2}{12}$„

    Tisch = geld. dto . . . . „ 2 F 50 „ ⎪

    vor ein Schwein pro 5: Monath . . . „ 3 F $33\frac{1}{3}$ ⎭

Frau Maria Anna Thonerin hat an Baâren . . „ 75 F — „ ⎫ 87:$72\frac{1}{3}$„

    vor 200 ♯ Rindfleisch . . . . „ 12 F $72\frac{1}{3}$ ⎭

H: Eva Jaquetin ebenfahls Lauth Lit:. . . . „ 87:$72\frac{1}{3}$

Carl Tindin vor 300 ♯ Rindfleisch [was listed 1764 as a

violinist] . . . . . „ 19 F $-8\frac{2}{4}$ ⎫

    vor 30 ♯ schmaltz . . . . „ 7 F 50 d: ⎬ 30:$58\frac{2}{4}$

    Linß, gerst = Hierßprein $\frac{1}{4}$ Mz: davor . . „ 3 F — „ ⎪

    vor $\frac{1}{2}$ Emer Ruben . . . . „ 1 F — „ ⎭

Joannes Kozán hat an Baâren samt quartier „ 57 F 50 d: ⎫ 90:$83\frac{2}{4}$„

    d[as] übrige wie ein Buchhalterey Accessist „ 33 F $33\frac{2}{4}$ ⎭

Elisabeth Schaurin Stikherin hat jahrlich samt =

    quartier = geld . . . . „ 40 F — „ ⎫

    vor 200 ♯ Rindfleisch . . . . „ 12 F $72\frac{1}{3}$„ ⎪

    vor 12 ♯ rindschmaltz . . . . „ 3 F — „ ⎬ 59:$22\frac{1}{3}$„

    vor Kuchlspeiß . . . . „ 3 F — „ ⎪

    vor $\frac{1}{4}$ Emer Ruben . . . . — 50 d: ⎭

Oberjägerin Susana geberthin hat jährlich . . . „ 25:— „

Tenoristin Hussarin hat jährlich . . . . „ 10:— „

Leib: houssárin Catharina Sándorin jährlich . . . „ 50:— „

Latus   557:$22\frac{6}{12}$

Postreitherin getzin hat jährlich quartier = geld „ 5 F — „ ⎫

    vor 100 ♯ Rindfleisch . . . . „ 6 F $36\frac{1}{6}$ ⎬ 14:$36\frac{1}{6}$„

    vor 12 ♯ schmaltz . . . . „ 3 F — „ ⎭

Gschießer = Jägerin hat jährlich an Baarem

    samt quartier = geld . . . „ 20 F — „ ⎫

    vor 15 ♯ Rindfleisch . . . . „ 9 F $54\frac{1}{4}$ ⎪

    vor $12\frac{1}{2}$ ♯ schmaltz . . . . „ 3 F $12\frac{1}{2}$ d: ⎬ 34:$32\frac{1}{4}$„

    vor Kuchl = Speiß . . . . „ 1 F $15\frac{1}{2}$ d: ⎪

    vor $\frac{1}{4}$ Emer ruben . . . . „ — 50d. ⎭

Verwittibte Kreibichin hat Monathlich 5 F in Summa . . „ 60:— „

F: Killianische Wittib hat Monathlich 4 F 10 xr in Summa . . „ 50:— „

K: Woffraysche Wittib hat Monathlich 6 F in Summa . . „ 72:— „

Susanna Vlaskin hat jahrlich quartier = geld . „ 5 F — „ ⎫

    vor 100 ♯ Rindfleisch . . . „ 6 F $36\frac{1}{6}$ ⎬ 14:$36\frac{1}{6}$

    vor 12 ♯ schmaltz . . . . 3 F — „ ⎭

Christina Koppin hat jährlich . . . . „ 8:25 „

L: dann seÿnd vor Krauth bezahlt worden. . . . „ 8:— „

Latus   557:$22\frac{6}{12}$„

Summa   818:$52\frac{1}{12}$

anstatt deren ubrigen wird der Zahlung / halber attestiret / Johann Novotni / statt der Fr. Thonerin / Johann Kotzán mpria / Edmund Schlanstein mpria / Verwalt.

	Extract der Betragnuß:		[One year later, 1764]
Von der Geistlichkeit	„	$438:37\frac{5}{12}$ „	$437: 12\frac{11}{12}$
Von dem Chor	„	$219:59\frac{6}{12}$ „	$205: 22\frac{6}{12}$
Von der Lobl.$^{\underline{en}}$ Buchhalterey	„	$2.933:16\frac{4}{12}$ „	$3.716: 69\frac{9}{12}$
Von der Registratur	„	$977:49\frac{5}{12}$ „	$1.083: 37\frac{11}{12}$
Von dem Perceptorat	„	$69:48\frac{11}{12}$ „	$68: 93\frac{9}{12}$
Von denen Würthschafts = officieren	„	$1.976:24\frac{4}{12}$ „	$2.316: 66\frac{2}{12}$
Von der Jägereÿ	„	$1.514:76\frac{7}{12}$ „	$1.502: 72\frac{11}{12}$
Von der gartnereÿ	„	$1.260:72\frac{4}{12}$ „	$1.259: 91\frac{8}{12}$
Von Hrn unter Lieutnant	„	$30:—$ „ Leibgarde	$30: —,,$
Von Verschiedene Bestallungen	„	$2.701:33\frac{4}{12}$ „	$2.545:204\frac{1}{12}$
Auf Pensionen	„	$818:52\frac{1}{12}$ „	$887: —\frac{1}{12}$
In Summa		$12.939:65\frac{3}{12}$	$13.552: 83\frac{1}{12}$

Frantz Nigst
Rändtmstr.

[A.M. 414, EH, Budapest]

Notes:
Partial translation of document: Ecclesiastical Members. The Provost Chaplain has a cash salary annually of . . . / suit of clothes . . . / 10 geese and 20 chickens . . . / 300 lb. beef, see attached docs. Lit: A . . . / 30 # beef lard . . . / lentils, barley & millet-pap each sort a *Metze* . . . / $\frac{2}{4}$ *Eimer* of beetroots . . . / Both Castle Chaplains have each annual money for food, special rate of 75 Fl. which makes . . . / . . . / Castle Chapel Servant has annually in cash . . . / . . . / The three acolytes have each annually 12 Fl., together . . . / [receipts] / Choir Music . . . / The Laudable ['Lobl^{en}' = 'löbliche'] Book-keeping Office / [under Joannes Spach:] For his coachman [*Gutscher*] annually / the same as for the H[er]r Book-keeper Eötvös / *Quartier = geld =* lodging money . . . / The Most Laudable Registry Office / . . . [after 'Trimel'] the same as a book-keeping assistant / For the Receiver [*Perceptorat*] / Herr Chief Collector [Chief Cashier] Joannes Zoller has for goods in kind for the kitchen the same as the H[er]r Book-keeper / Castle and Estate Officials / . . . / . . . / [Schlanstein] has annually together with lodging money and office requirements . . . / . . . / The Castle Guardian Franciscus Le Gout [*recte*] has together with his servant annually . . . / [after 'Lentils' etc.:] For the kitchen servant's needs $\frac{2}{4}$ [*Metze*] / . . . / Mistress of the Linen Frau Catharina Pohselinder has together with her servant . . . / . . . / Rent-Master Franz Nigst together with lodging money and office tax . . . / . . . / The Donnerskirchen Cellar-Master Herr Josephus Krafft has in cash . . . / in kind the same as Hr. Zoller / Nb. after subtraction of 2 Fl. for beetroots . . . / Grain-tither Herr Johann Michael Moßer has together / with lodging money and office requirements / the rest is the same as the Rent-Master at . . . / Farm-Steward [*Schaffer*] Herr Franciscus Hayder . . . / . . . / Cadastre Registrar Herr Joh. Michael Hayden / has annually together with lodging money . . . / for the goods in kind the same as a Book- / keeper Clerk . . . / Buildings Registrar Herr Anton Kühnel . . . / . . . / For the Hunting Office [*Jägerey*] / Forestry-Master Herr Frantz Anton Kandler has / . . . / His Hunting Assistant [*Handjäger*] . . . / . . . / Woodward [*Waltmeister = Waldmeister*] Herr Mattaus Kanhauser . . . / . . . / 'Paris-Jäger': Paris-Hunter receives as much as the Forestry-Master's hunting assistant/ [towns: St Georgen, Gschieß (now Schützen im Gebirge), Donnerskirchen, Purbach, Breitenbrunn] . . . / [town: Trauersdorf] . . . / Ist Gschießer and at the same time Gamekeeper has in / cash . . . / . . . / Gardening Section / The Court Gardener at Eisenstadt has monthly 17 Fl. which / makes for the whole year . . . / The Gamekeeper has monthly 12 Fl. . . . / . . . / The Gardener Apprentices in our Court Garden, and the monthly help are paid according to / attached Document Lit: B . . . / . . . / For the

Grenadier Company / Herr Second Lieutenant Josephus Harich … / … / For the Various Stables / Chimneysweep-Master Martin Pretarj … / Clockmaker Johann Michael Weltz … / For 24 ℔ beef lard … / Lentils and peas, each ½ *Metze* for which, however … / Brewery-Master Paul Maÿr … / … / Commissioned Cook [female] … / … / The ordinary Dish-Washer [female] for 200 ℔ beef … / C: Court Carpenter Carl Flach has according to Document Lit: C together / with his apprentices to receive … / Court Binder Jacob Arzt … / Donnerskirchen Vat Repairer [literally: Tapster-Binder] … / Donnerskirchen Brandymaker … / … / Court Steward has together with his two apprentices … / … / The two apprentices together get ½ *Metze* lentils and / 1½ *Metzen* barley … / … / The Court Vineyard Worker … / The Road-Watcher … / Gatekeeper Georg Schwab has to receive up to the end of June / in cash … / The new gatekeeper Mathias [Schwendenwein] has from / 1st Sept. in cash … / … / The five Castle Guardians [*Schloß-Trabanten*] have each annually … / The three Castle Watchmen [*Schloß-wachter = Schloßwächter*] … / The Eysenstadt three dairy-hands … / … / The Eysenstadt dairy-boy … / … / The three Groß höflein dairy-hands … / … / The three dairy-boys there get together … / … / The freeman at [Oedenburg] has according to doc. to receive [D:] … / … / The steward received for the poultry maid in Mayrhof … / Then there are the stable-boys who / are to receive [left blank] / The Commissioned Estate Director has according to attached document A: to receive / this year … / E: a hussar for January according to doc. … / The Postilion Pfaltzer receives 10 Fl. monthly … / … / [Seppe(r)l = Joseph Paks?] … / Straw daily 12 xr. … / guardian of Dray-horses daily 15 xr. … / … / For all the rentiers / Herr Johannes Neumann, former Major-Domo / … / Herr Andreas Vlásics, former parish priest in [Krensdorf?] / … / Rosalia [who is] blind & in hospital … / … [Käß = cheese] / Frau Heldenreich (who died in May) has / … / For kitchen herbs for 5 months … / money for food 2 Fl. 50[xr.] / for pork for 5 months … / … / Carl Tindin [in 1764 list registered as former violinist] … / … / Elisabeth Schaur, embroideress … / Chief Hunter's Widow Susan[n]a [Geberth] … / Widow of tenor Hussar [Huszár] … / Catharina Sandor, widow of Hussar Bodyguard … / … / Widow of Mailcoach-driver Getz … / … / Widow of Gschießer Hunter … / Widow Kreibich … / Widow Killian … / … / L: then the following was paid for cabbage / Instead of the others the payment is / herewith attested / Johann Novotni / instead of … / … / For the Ecclesiastics … / For the Choir … / For the Laudable Book-keeping Department / For the Registry / For the Receiver / For the Estate [Farm] Officials / For the Hunting Department / For Gardening Department / For the Herr Second Lieutenant / For Various Stables / For Pensions / … / Changes in 1764 show that meat was cheaper but lard more expensive. The Castle Steward receives no cash but the following *Deputat*: same for lentils etc., ²⁄₄ *Eimer* of beetroots, also only 150 lb. beef, 15 lb. lard. Of his two apprentices, one now receives 20 Fl. cash, 150 lb. meat, 10 lb. lard, lentils etc. to the value of 1 Fl., ²⁄₄ *Eimer* of beetroots, while the other receives according to 'Censurresolution' of 1762 half of the first apprentice's salary and goods 'as long as there are still some hunting dogs [*Piquierhund*]'. In 1763, the locksmith received the apprentices' *Deputat*, which is now split into three parts.

Money: Like the British currency until recently, the Austrian gulden had a duodecimal basis: 1 Fl. = 60 Kr., and 1 Kr. = 6 Denar (d.) 1 lb. beef cost 7 xr. (top quality) or 4 xr. (second choice). 1 lb. cheese cost 5 xr. Beef lard cost 15 xr. per lb. 1 chicken 9 xr., 1 goose 12 xr. Lentils, barley and millet-pap cost 4 Fl. per *Metze*. 1 *Eimer* of beetroots cost 2 Fl. 1 *Eimer* of beer 1 Fl. 30 xr. 1 pig cost 7 Fl.

Hungarian money: As a separate crown country, Hungary had a different division, which we herewith present complete, although in our lists, the 'Poltura' and 'Pfennig' do not happen to appear.

Gulden	Poltura	Kreuzer	Denar	Pfennig
1	40	= 60	= 100	= 240
$\frac{1}{40}$	= 1	= $1\frac{1}{2}$	= $2\frac{1}{2}$	6
$\frac{1}{60}$	= $\frac{2}{3}$	= 1	= $1\frac{2}{3}$	= 4
$\frac{1}{100}$	= $\frac{2}{5}$	= $1\frac{2}{3}$	= 1	= $2\frac{2}{5}$
$\frac{1}{240}$	= $\frac{1}{6}$	= $\frac{1}{4}$	= $\frac{5}{12}$	= 1

The Denar coin, which in Hungary was rather rare in 1760 and 1761, was thus worth $2\frac{2}{5}$ Pfennige and was not identical – as it was in the Counties of Siebenbürger (Transylvania), Bohemia and Moravia – with the so-called *Dreipfennigstück* (3 Pfennig coin). The Royal Patent that stabilized this Hungarian conversion was dated 27 March 1761, a couple of months before Haydn became an Esterházy (i.e. Hungarian) 'House Officer'. In 1763 and 1765, a whole series of Denar coins for Hungary were minted to be used as substitutes for the older currency (small *Silberscheidemünze*); these new Denar coins had the Hungarian crown on the obverse.

It has been noted that there was a thriving Jewish community at Eisenstadt, living in a ghetto under princely protection mostly as *Schutzjuden* (protected Jews) and, in constantly fluctuating annual figures, constituting nearly one-quarter of the town's approximate population of 1,500. When Prince Nicolaus I began his reign in 1762, one of his first acts was to establish a commission, of which he was chairman, to settle arguments within the Jewish community and, particularly, with the Christians. There was a constant dearth of living quarters, which persisted throughout the century; in 1800, Prince Nicolaus II issued an edict forbidding Christians to rent accommodation to Jews.[1] The problem, which was rarely settled to the satisfaction of the Jewish party concerned, may be seen in the following extract from a letter addressed to Prince Nicolaus by Rahier:

> ... Eisenstadt, 28th May 766 ... The two Protected Jews David Israel and Lewel Jacob, who, according to all reports, seem to be from Matterstorff, are seeking permission to build an apartment of two rooms (kitchen and chamber) within the walls of Maÿerhoff; I believe their request should be refused, because the Herrschaftliche [i.e. Esterházy property of] Maÿrhoff [*sic*] is not so roomy as to allow space for a proper apartment for two Jewish parties, and apart from that the Jews there are so numerous and are such a burden for the Christians that it is almost impossible for them to increase. ...[2]

A similar lack of space and other factors decided the fate of various other Jews who wished to return to Eisenstadt:

> CASE ONE: Rahier to Prince Nicolaus. The Jew Beer wishes to settle in the ghetto of Eisenstadt, which the Grand Judge of the Jews Abraham Leuberstorfer wants to hinder, because Beer did not register either with him or the Jewish Community. Beer's father-in-law, Josue Camen, was a Protected Jew here, but he left twenty years ago to be a Rabbi in Raab, Semlin and other places, and he died in Raab, moreover. In all these years he never paid his taxes. Rahier is therefore of the opinion that this petition be refused, since the ghetto is small and overflowing, and the Jews themselves do not wish to have Beer. 12 April 1766.
> EH, Budapest, Országos Levéltár, P. 154 (old Fasc. 1524), fol. 544.

> CASE TWO: Title of document – 'Obedient *Relation*. / Concerning the case of the Eisenstadt Jewish Community Contra the Jew Samuel Austerlitz. / Eisenstadt, 19 May 766' signed by Administrator Schlanstein. The Jewish Community asks that the Jew Austerlitz, who has asked to enter the Community once again, be refused permission, since when he left he signed a *Revers* that after three years' absence he would be expelled from the Community. Now Austerlitz has been away for fifteen years, he never paid his taxes, and was never heard from. If he were permitted re-entry, all the economically run-down Jews would come back and be a burden to the others.
> EH, Budapest, Országos Levéltár, P. 154, fol. 560–1.

[Schlanstein's report to Prince Nicolaus, 29 April 1766:] Samuel Hirsch Austerlitz is in fact the son of a Protected Jew, he transferred to Pernitz in Moravia, married there and lived there for seventeen years. He was pushed out of Vienna because the quota is full there. In 1761 he did receive the Protection from Count

---

1 *Geschichte des Calvarienberges* (op. cit.), p. 71. In 1808 Eisenstadt had 1,778 Catholics, 13 Christians of other denominations and 530 Jews; in 1835, 1,770 Catholics, 12 other Christians and 790 Jews. The Jewish community survived in Eisenstadt until the National Socialist era (*post* 13 March 1938). The ghetto buildings still survive and in many cases are intact. The Burgenländisches Landesmuseum contains many interesting and touching relics of this vanished part of Eisenstadt's history.
2 EH. Budapest, Országos Levéltár, P. 154/3, fol. 579r.

Herbeviller, but never paid. The Jews now want him to pay the arrears, which he refuses to do. Therefore the Jews will not meet to discuss Austerlitz's petition. Schlanstein is of the opinion that it would be useful to force the Jews to have a meeting so that a decision can be reached.   [Ibid., fol. 555–6]

[Prince Nicolaus ordered the Jews to convene, following which we have a report from Rahier in Eisenstadt to the Prince of 22 May 1766:] The Jews, upon the Prince's orders, convened and reached the following decision: to adhere to the old custom, that the *Revers* (absence of three years and loss of membership in the Community) is valid, that Austerlitz lived fifteen years in Pernitz and will therefore be expelled. Rahier agrees with this, the more so since the Prince, in a commission held in 1762, gave a decision on such a case, reversing the action of his own late Regent, Count von Herbeviller, who had fined the Jewish Community 100 gulden (this fine was returned to the Jews by Nicolaus at that time, 1762), 'as paragraph 6 of that *Decretation* shows, and so I believe the following decision should be made for this petition: the Jew Samuel Hirsch Austerlitz is to be informed that with his present petition he is no longer to upset and bother the Community, much less the high princely administration, on pain of severe punishment . . .'.   [Ibid., fol. 572–4]

There were always rumours of Jewish children being kidnapped and forcibly baptized into the Catholic Church. That these rumours had a basis in actual fact may be seen from the following extracts of a letter from Rahier to the Prince on 2 May 1766:

A woman from Losing has kidnapped a Jewish girl of eleven or twelve years of age, brought her to the Rector of Kapuvar Church and had her baptized. The Jews want the child returned. Rahier thinks that the girl went of her own free will, and since she has been baptized, one cannot very well return her, otherwise it would be a sacrilege against the Sacrament. He suggests that the Prince take the girl under his protection until she can support herself and enter service. Rahier suggests that the girl might be given to the Farm Warden at Forchtenau, especially since there is no law in Hungary that requires the extradition of abducted or runaway Jewish children.   [Ibid., fol. 560–1]

This extraordinary document shows that the famous Esterházy impartiality had its definite limitations. To close this unhappy series of documents, we might mention a case in which Rahier found a way to levy a new tax on the Jews at Kobersdorf. He discovered that they were making a brandy, 'which is a *regale domini*', and saw no reason why they should not have to pay tax on it, as the Christians do (at $2\frac{1}{2}$ gulden per *Eimer*), 'especially since they only pay 150 Fl. Protection money'.[1]

It is interesting that, in contrast to Beethoven, there is not a single anti-Semitic remark to be found in any of Haydn's letters, London Notebooks (not designed to be read by anyone else), or attributed to him by contemporaries. This is no doubt because, although a fervent Catholic, Haydn thought everyone was entitled to his own beliefs, and he considered all men his brothers (Griesinger, 54).

---

1 EH, Budapest, Országos Levéltár, P. 154 (old Fasc. 1524), fol. 470.

The principal religious edifice in the town was, of course, the Parish Church of St Martin, whose rector was Leopold Hörger. Appointed in 1752 when barely thirty years of age, Hörger was responsible for enlarging the music choir and installing the great organ by Johann Georg Malleck of Vienna in 1778. Hörger died in 1782.

Regular church music at St Martin's had been made possible by the Will of Anna Barbara Kroyer, who in 1753 left a capital of 6,000 gulden, the interest of which was to be used for music at the parish church. The first choir director was Anton Höld, Sen., who was also the town's *Thurnermeister*. In other towns, the *Thurnermeister* and his journeymen were usually trumpeters and kettledrummers, but as the great Baroque tradition of high trumpet (*clarino*) playing slowly died out – Haydn still wrote occasionally for high trumpets at this period – the *Thurnermeister* at Eisenstadt gradually came to be primarily string players (violins and a double bass), supplying dance music for the town's official functions. There was one *Meister* (master) and two or three *Gesellen* (journeymen). The Oedenburg (Sopron) *Thurnermeister* were able to supply Haydn with five trumpeters and kettledrummers for performances on St Anne's Day at Eisenstadt in 1768,[1] which shows that at that date, the Eisenstadt *Thurnermeister* and his journeymen were not primarily (or perhaps not at all) brass and drum players. Höld was master by 1758, and when he died in 1774, his son, Anton Höld Jr, took over his father's position. These *Thurnermeister*, apart from playing string instruments, also formed a *Tafelmusik* of wind instruments; the constitution is not known.

Another friend of Haydn's was Carl Kraus, town schoolmaster and later *Regens chori* of St Martin's. Although under the terms of Haydn's contract he was not allowed to give his music to anyone outside the Esterházy establishment, in the case of church music, an exception does seem to have been made, or tacitly allowed. The Motet S. Thecla (XXIIIa:4), which we discovered in the choir-loft of St Martin's in 1951, is a *contrafactum* of a lost Latin Cantata, probably made by Kraus, but in any case signed by Haydn himself on the double-bass part (*vide infra*, p. 495). There are many other Church pieces by Haydn in St Martin's, and also works by other members of the Esterházy *Capelle*, such as Carl Schiringer. The authentic parts to Haydn's *Libera* (XXIIb:1) were also discovered at St Martin's (1966).[2]

We must now return to the Chronicle, and to Haydn's engagement with the Esterházy family, with whom he was to remain (even nominally, when he was in England in 1791–5) for the rest of his life.

---

1 *Haydn at Eszterhaza 1766–1790*, pp. 149f. G. Feder in *Haydn-Studien* IV (1976), pp. 49ff. About Hörger see Adolf Mohl, 'Die Seelsorger von Eisenstadt', in *Die Standtpfarrkirche in Eisenstadt* (op. cit.), pp. 8f. About the Höld family, J. Harich in *HJB* VIII, 43f.
2 *Haydn at Eszterháza 1766–1790*, p. 738.

CHAPTER EIGHT

Chronicle 1761–1765

Chronicle 1761

THE FIRST FEW MONTHS of the year 1761 are blank ones in our chronicle of the newly married Haydns. We have no knowledge of when Count Morzin was obliged to disband his orchestra, but presumably it occurred in the first part of this year. Just as *Ritter* von Fürnberg handed on Haydn to Count Morzin, it was Morzin who effected the transition to Prince Esterházy.

THE DOCUMENTS

(1) Autobiography 1776:

. . . and from there [Count Morzin] as *Capellmeister* to His Highness the Prince [Esterházy], in whose service I wish to live and die . . .　　　　　　　[CCLN, 19]

(2) Griesinger:

. . . The Count [Morzin] dissipated his substantial fortune in a short time and had therefore to disband his orchestra, and Joseph Haydn came, on 19 March of the year 1760, to the Prince Nikolaus Esterházy, who had liked the afore-mentioned Symphony [*incipit* of Symphony No. 1 cited in connection with Morzin – *vide supra*, p. 235], as *Kapellmeister* with a salary of 400 gulden and other emoluments. Haydn's father was still granted the pleasure of seeing his son in the house uniform of blue with gold trimmings and to hear much praise from the prince about his son's talents. . . .　　　　　　　　　　　　　　　[Griesinger, 15f.]

(3) Dies:

A year passed without Count Morzin's learning of his *Kapellmeister's* marriage; but it happened that Haydn's situation took a different turn. The Count found it necessary to reduce his hitherto great expenses. He dismissed his virtuosi and Haydn thus lost his post as *Kapellmeister*.

　　　Meanwhile, public opinion proved to be a great recommendation for Haydn. His attractive character was known. Count Morzin was at pains to be of service. Three circumstances which fortunately occurred simultaneously enabled Haydn, when he ceased being (in the year 1760) *Kapellmeister* to Count Morzin, to become *Vizekapellmeister*, under the direction of *Kapellmeister* Gregorius Werner, in the service of Prince Anton Esterházy de Galantha at Eisenstadt with a salary of 400 fl. [Original footnote: Apart from the salary, persons in princely service enjoy other advantages, such as free lodgings, firewood, etc.] This gentleman gave Haydn the four periods of the day [morning, noon, evening, night] as the theme of a composition; he wrote them in the form of quartets which are very little known. . . .　　　　　　　　　　　　　　　　　[Dies, 49]

(4) Carpani:

... Avvenne che in casa del conte [Morzin] si recasse un giorno ad udir musica il vecchio principe Antonio *Esterhazy*, appassionato filarmonico, che aveva al suo servizio una scelta e numerosa orchestra, diretta dal maestro *Werner*. Sentita il principe una sinfonía dell' *Haydn* (era quella in *delasolré,* in tempo di *tre quarti*) s'invogliò in maniera di questo compositore, che costrinse il conte a cederglielo. Il conte, che prima di ciò pensava di licenziare, come fece, per oggetto d'economia, la sua orchestra, si arrese ben volentieri alla domanda del principe. Non so per quale indispozione, *Haydn* non fosse quella sera al concerto; so che, udita dal conte la domanda del principe, ne fu oltremodo beato, ed aspettava con impazienza il momento di entrare nel nuovo servizio; ma le cose de'principi vanno d'ordinario in lungo, e forse l'invidia e la gelosia di taluno operava sott'acqua contro del nostro Guiseppe. Fatto è, che già da molti mesi l'*Haydn* era stato ceduto, e mai non si veniva al momento di farlo entrare in casa *Esterhazy*. Vi entrò finalmente nel 1760, e d'una maniera un po' comica. Eccovi come andò la cosa.

Il tuttora vivente maestro *Friedberg*, amico ed ammiratore dell'*Haydn*, e ch'era egli pure allogato presso il principe, dolente quanto l'amico di questo ritardo, eccitò l'*Haydn* a comporre una sinfonía solenne da sonarsi ad Eisenstadt nel giorno natalizio di S. A. *Haydn* la scrisse, e da par suo. Venuto il giorno di eseguirla, standosene il principe in mezzo della sua corte sul suo seggiolone ascoltando al solito la sua musica, il *Friedberg* distribuì le parti della sinfonía convenuta. All'udirla, il principe interrompe i sonatori alla metà del primo *allegro*, e domanda di chi sia sì bella cosa? D'*Haydn*, risponde il *Friedberg*, e fa venire avanti il nostro Giuseppe che tutto tremante stava appiatto in un angola della sala. Il principe al vederlo disse = quel moro? (l'*Haydn* non era certo del colore de'gigli): ebbene, moro, proseguì il principe, tu sei d'ora innanzi al mio servizio. Come ti chiami? = Giuseppe *Haydn* = e il principe = ma tu sei già al mio servizio, e d'onde avviene che non ti ho visto mai? = Il timido maestro non sapeva che rispondere, ma lo tolse d'imbròglio il principe stesso soggiungendo = Va, e vestiti subito da maestro: io non ti voglio vedere in quell'arnese; sei troppo piccolo, hai una figura meschina: no, no; devi avere un abito nuovo, una parrucca con fiocchi, il collare e i talloni rossi; ma li voglio alti, acciò la tua statura corrisponda al tuo sapere. Intendi? Va, e ti sarà dato tutto. = Dovete sapere che così vestivano i maestri di que'tempi, ne'quali la musica era considerata come una scienza e non come un mestiere. *Haydn* baciata la mano al principe, si ritirò nel suo cantone un po'dolente di dover nascondere i suoi capelli, e rinunziare a quella sua giovanile eleganza, alla quale era molto attaccato. Non più tardi dell'indomani bisognò che comparisse davanti a S. A. trasformato nella maniera sovrindicata. Mi diceva il *Friedberg* che il povero maestrino aveva l'aria sì imbarazzata in quel nuovo arredo che moveva alle risa chiunque lo rimirava. In appresso cresciuto in età ed in concetto, e guardandolo sempre più di buon occhio il padrone, egli potè ripigliare per grazia il suo primo modo di vestire; ma gli restò per varj anni quel soprannome di *moro*, che il principe gli aveva dato scherzando. *Haydn* entrò al servizio di S. A. come maestro direttore del concerto, ciò che noi diremmo secondo maestro. Il primo era, come già v'accennai, il *Werner*, uomo di molto merito.

Un anno dopo morì il princ. Antonio, e succedette il princ. Niccola seniore, ancor più intellegente di musica, e più appassionato del suo predecessore.

[Carpani, pp. 87–90]

[Summary in translation:] [Paul] Anton Esterházy, a passionate music-lover who owned a select and numerous band under Werner, hears a Haydn symphony at Morzin's and asks the latter to let him have Haydn. Morzin was thinking of disbanding his orchestra and agreed. Haydn, not present at this concert, looked forward to his new position but for some reason – perhaps intrigue – he could not enter the house of Esterházy; finally in 1760 he did so and in a rather comic manner.

Maestro Friedberg [Friberth?], who is still alive [Friberth d. 6 August 1816] and was a friend and admirer of Haydn's, regretted this delay and had Haydn compose a solemn symphony to be performed on the Prince's birthday at Eisenstadt. When this was done, Paul Anton interrupted in the middle of the first allegro, and asked who wrote such a beautiful thing. 'Haydn', answered Friedberg, and produced the trembling Giuseppe who stood, rooted to the spot, in a corner of the hall. The Prince, seeing him, said: 'That blackamoor?' (Haydn did not in fact exactly have the colour of a lily). 'Well, blackamoor, from this moment you are [*tu* form] in my service. What is your name?' 'Giuseppe Haydn'. 'But you are already in my service, how is it that I've not seen you?' The timid Haydn remained silent, embarrassed. 'Go and get dressed like a *maestro*', said the Prince. 'I won't have you looking like that; you're too small and you look too insignificant; no, no, you must have new clothes, a wig with curls, the collar and red heels, but I want them high, as tall in stature as your knowledge. Do you understand? Go, and all will be provided.' In those days music was considered a science and not a profession. Haydn kissed the princely hand and did as he was bidden, regretting the loss of his youthful elegance and his own hair, to which he was greatly attached. Haydn, said Friedberg, looked most embarrassed in his new uniform ... The name 'blackamoor' stuck to him for many years. ... A year after Prince [Paul] Anton died, to be succeeded by Nicolaus the Elder [by 1812 Nicolaus II had succeeded to the title], even more knowledgeable of music and more passionately attached to it than his predecessor.

The confusion in Griesinger, Dies and Carpani is manifest. In Griesinger, the date of Haydn's contract with the Esterházys is wrong and the surname of the prince as well. But Haydn obviously mentioned 19 March as a date of crucial importance, and perhaps it was (a) the date of the Morzin concert at which Prince Paul Anton heard a Haydn symphony and asked to engage its composer; (b) the date in which Haydn began a 'trial period' with the Esterházys, in this case 1761; (c) the date in which Friberth played the Haydn symphony in Eisenstadt – see the Carpani version. Griesinger specifically says it was Symphony No. 1 that Paul Anton heard at Morzin's; Carpani mentions that the Symphony was in D (*delasolré*) in 3/4 time (No. 1 is in 4/4), but probably means the same work as Dies. Griesinger mentions that Father Haydn came to see his son in the uniform of the Esterházy household; Dies[1] puts this episode in the Morzin period; Griesinger specifically mentions that the event took place shortly before Mathias Haydn's death in 1763 (*infra*, p. 387), and it is probable that this is the case and that Mathias saw his son in the Esterházy blue-and-gold uniform.

From Dies we learn that, as already noted, Morzin insisted that his musicians remain single, probably to save lodging space at Lukavec (just as Prince Nicolaus Esterházy was to do at Eszterháza); and that Haydn's marriage remained a secret. Dies, too, places Haydn's engagement with the Esterházys in 1760, and since that wrong date is in Carpani as well, it would appear to have been fixed wrongly in Haydn's mind (though he still possessed his original contract of 1 May 1761 and could easily have consulted it). In Dies we have the valuable information that it was Paul Anton himself who suggested to Haydn the idea of composing Symphonies Nos. 6–8 ('Le Matin', 'Le Midi', 'Le Soir'): *vide infra*, pp. 555ff.

And garrulous Carpani? Again, we suggest that there is some basis of fact in this apparently unlikely story. Friberth was alive when Carpani published his biography and it is possible, even probable, that Friberth is the 'Friedberg' referred to; Carpani, like most Italians of that day, was incapable of spelling, pronouncing or remembering German names, and we have seen that almost all the names throughout Carpani's account are bowdlerized almost out of recognition. Did Paul Anton at first address Haydn in the 'tu' form? (Dittersdorf asked the Bishop of Großwardein to address him as 'Du' rather than the formal 'Sie', but from other evidence at our disposal it is thought that Haydn was addressed in the third person singular, or 'Er' form.)[2] We

---

1 *Vide supra*, p. 236.
2 Dittersdorf, *Lebensbeschreibung* (ed. Miller), Munich 1967, p. 142.

might certainly see in all this a hint that Friberth, who had been in Paul Anton's service since 1759, was a go-between in negotiations between Haydn and the house of Esterházy.

We have been able to discover some unpublished documents in the Esterházy Archives which show beyond question that Haydn was already part of the Esterházy establishment, though not yet under contract, by 1 April 1761. In the contracts signed with the musicians on that date (*vide infra*) Clause Four contains the explicit rule that the signatory must obey the *Ober-* and *Vice-Capellmeister*. Now on 1 April there was, of course, an *Ober-Capellmeister* (Werner) but no official deputy: therefore Haydn's engagement was taken as a matter of course and the actual contract regarded as a mere formality.

There were certainly concerts at the Esterházy Palais in the Wallnerstraße in March 1761. Our source is the diary of a young man named Carl von Zinzendorf, who was then twenty-two years of age and had arrived at Vienna on Saturday, 7 February 1761, fresh from three years and seven months at the University of Jena. From the 'Journal / de Comte Charles de Zinzendorf et / Pottendorf' we can follow the young man's successful introduction to Viennese society, in which he had the good fortune to be taken up by the childless Prince Paul Anton Esterházy and his Italian-born wife. By the end of March, Zinzendorf and his brother[1] were regular luncheon guests at the Palais:

> [27 March 1761:] ... Apres table Musique, la petite Victoire [one of the guests]. Les C. [Comtes] Stahremberg et Lamberg y vinrent ... [29 March:] Apres table le jeune Lamberg neveu du Prince, Assesseur de Landrecht, agé de 21. ans. ... Il y eut un Concert tres joli, la Chanteuse du Prince y chanta, elle est fille d'un de ses Buch[h]alter [Scheffstoss]. ...

And on 1 April we hear that the health of Prince Paul Anton was not of the best: 'Le Prince Esterhazy étoit encore malade ...'.

It also seems obvious that Haydn was deeply involved in the choice of the new musicians, for the orchestra was to be his responsibility. We propose, therefore, that Haydn's date of '19 March' means that on this date of the year 1761 he began to reorganise the Esterházy musical establishment. But it is significant that no singers except Griessler (1 June), who was also a violinist, were engaged: this was, officially, Werner's responsibility. As soon as Haydn had seen that a number of new players was engaged, the superfluous musicians at Eisenstadt could be dismissed. Since Haydn took care to replace the bassoon players of the Grenadiers, he must have heard them; and this suggests that he must have gone to Eisenstadt to listen to the band as it was constituted in the year 1760 (see our list, *supra*, pp. 317ff.). The Prince must also have seen that Haydn was introduced to Werner and that the latter approved of him.

---

1 Carl, Count Zinzendorf (1739–1813) was the half-brother of Ludwig (1721–80), from 1761 President of the *Hofrechenkammer* (Ministry of Finance) and later Minister of the Interior; Ludwig was one of the first Freemasons in Austria, joining the Viennese Lodge 'Aux trois Canons' on 17 September 1742. He became a Catholic to save the family's Austrian estates (he was born in Saxony), as did Carl, who was called to Vienna by his half-brother. Empress Maria Theresa sent Carl on several long trips through Europe to investigate the possibilities of trade with the Austrian Monarchy. A member of the Order of St John, he visited Malta, and in December 1766 he joined the Freemasons Lodge 'De la Candeur' in Strasbourg. In 1776 he became Governor of Trieste, in 1782 President of the *Hofrechenkammer*, succeeding his brother (who had died in 1780) and becoming the leading financial expert in the Monarchy. He kept a diary from his thirteenth year, and his daily entries, in fifty-six volumes (now Haus-, Hof- und Staatsarchiv, Vienna), are of the greatest value for life at Court as well as the Court Opera (which Zinzendorf regularly attended). The Diaries, except for fragments, are still unpublished. See *Österreichische Freimaurerlogen: Humanität und Toleranz im 18. Jh.*, Schlossmuseum Rosenau bei Zwettl – Katalog, 1976, pp. 71f.; *Wien von Maria Theresia bis zur Franzosenzeit. Aus den Tagebüchern des Grafen Karl von Zinzendorf* (ed. Hans Wagner), Vienna 1972; unfortunately all the entries translated into German.

This brings us to the curious history of Haydn's relationship to his *Ober-Capellmeister*. We know that: (1) Haydn thought highly of Werner's music – Pohl (I, 367f.) tells us that the great Viennese collector Aloys Fuchs owned a Haydn letter in which the composer speaks warmly of some Werner works; (2) Haydn acquired, in some manner, a large quantity of Werner autographs which, after Haydn's death, passed into the Esterházy Archives.[1] When Werner died, his Will showed that he owned no music, and this substantial part of his autographs must have been given to Haydn before Werner died (Dr Harich has shown that the suggestion made by László Somfai, whereby Haydn is supposed to have taken the scores from the Music Archives in the Castle and not returned them, is untenable);[2] (3) Haydn took the trouble in 1804 to issue six fugues by Werner 'Aus besonderer Achtung gegen diesen berühmten Meister'. As for Werner's relations with Haydn, we have the evidence of their nadir in 1765 (*vide infra*), but at the beginning of their acquaintanceship in 1761, things were probably quite different. In Le Breton's *Notice historique sur la vie et les ouvrages de Haydn* (1810), we read that 'Werner prit en affection Jos. Haydn, il lui donna des conseils et des leçons.... enfin, il lui ouvrit le sanctuaire de l'art ...', information which, like that of Framery's *Notice sur Joseph Haydn* (1810), probably derived from Ignaz Pleyel, Haydn's pupil from 1772 to 1777. But Pohl has drawn a convincing picture of the aging Gregor Werner, his position largely taken over by Haydn, who was the fêted darling of Prince Paul Anton and Prince Nicolaus; Werner becomes more and more alone and bitter, sitting as a hopeless invalid in his rooms, writing work after work, his frustration and hate against Haydn growing. Pohl (I, 366) shows that, from 1759 to 1765, Werner wrote numerous religious works: Masses (16), a Requiem, *Salve Regina* (5), *Regina Coelis* (4) and *Alma Redemptoris* (4); these (if they were performed at all) Haydn probably had to conduct and rehearse as well. Musicians in Eisenstadt remembered that Werner had called Haydn a 'Modehansl' ('fashion-monger') and a 'G' sanglmacher' ('cheap tunester') (Pohl I, 211f.). The deterioration in the two composers' relationship is sad but was perhaps unavoidable.

In 1761, however, all this was still in the future. Haydn was now occupied with two full-time operations: learning how to be a courtier, and reorganizing the *Capelle*. The attitudes necessary to become a successful courtier are not given to everyone, and it is difficult to imagine Mozart and Beethoven being good courtiers; but Haydn not only lived in a different age, he had a justified terror of poverty – the automatic fate of most musicians in their old age. Being a successful courtier was the only way to retain a difficult and diplomatically delicate appointment in the service of the Esterházy *Herrschaft*, and Haydn was determined not to fail in these endeavours. When he wrote to his dear brother, Johann Michael, in 1803, on the subject of Michael's accepting a position with Nicolaus II Esterházy or with the Grand Duke of Tuscany, Joseph may have wondered if his rather straightforward, unpolished brother could have coped with life at court.

With the reorganization of the *Capelle*, Haydn could rely on his taste, knowledge and experience. On 1 April the first contracts were ready for signature: Franz Si(e)gl, flautist and oboist; Johann Michael Kapfer, oboist; Johann Georg Kapfer, oboist; Johann Hinterberger, bassoon player; and Johann Georg Schwenda, bassoon and double-bass player. Since we shall be quoting *in extenso*, the contract in German with Joseph Dietzl (*infra*, p. 406), the contract in French with Franz Garnier (p. 349), and a

---

1 For a list, see *Haydn: the Late Years 1801–1809*, pp. 310, 313, 401.
2 Somfai in *HJB* II, 75. Harich, 'Szenische Darstellungen' (op. cit., pp. 122f.). Haydn's 1804 edition: see *Haydn: the Late Years 1801–1809*, pp. 297f.

complete translation of Haydn's contract (pp. 350ff.), it was thought unnecessary to quote all the contracts of 1 April 1761 in full. Where there are differences, however, they will be noted below.

Franz Si(e)gl's contract
This contains nine clauses, as follows:
'1mo ... [He is engaged as flautist and oboist] but he should rather turn to, and thus qualify in, the Houbois. [He] is to conduct himself soberly, modestly, quietly and honestly, and is to appear neatly, in white stockings, white linen, powdered, and with either pigtail or hair-bag ...; 2do ... He shall appear daily in the *antichambre* before and after mid-day, and after his orders have been received he shall appear promptly at the designated time ...; 3^{tio} ... said Frantz Sigl shall be required to appear at the *Herrschaft's* table, there to await the orders of his Serene Princely Highness either during the meal to play music on any of those instruments on which he is skilled or, like the other house officers, not to shirk serving the *Herrschaften*; 4to The *Fleutraversist* shall be required to participate in the *Banda* at Eysenstadt, Kitsee [*sic*], or in other places where the princely Grenadier Company mounts guard, exercises and parades, and likewise to play with the choir Musique at Eysenstadt. [Furthermore, he must follow the orders of the *Ober-* and *Vice-Capel-Meister* and submit petitions only through them.]; 5to Said Frantz Sigl shall not produce any Musique at balls, theatrical representations or at other *Herrschaften* without special permission of the Prince, and 6to said *Fleutraversist* should acquit himself of such duties as are required of him as befits a worthy house officer; and just as the Serene *Herrschaft* does not consider it necessary to put on paper all those his duties, so they are graciously minded to hope that the said Frantz Sigl of his own free will shall observe his duties most exactly, and rely on the ableness and honour of every man; 7mo [salary: 20 gulden Rhenish monthly]; 8to [a suit of clothes or uniform annually which he must care for]; 9mo [contract valid from 1 April[1] for one year] Given at Vienna,

1st April 1761' [Sigl, who is listed as being from Vienna, signs the document]. A.M. 266, No. 1001–3, EH, Budapest. The 'Commission' for Sigl's payment specifies that he also plays the oboe. Sigl was dismissed in 1765 (*vide infra*, p. 412).

Johann Michael Kapfer's contract
The name is spelled 'Capfer' and he is listed as Viennese. The contract is identical to that for Sigl except that from Clause 5 it reads as follows:
'5to Said Huboist [*sic*] will take all possible care and pains that the instruments which the *Herrschaft* have taken over shall not be ruined or made useless through carelessness and negligence. 6to [as Sigl's Clause 5]; 7mo [as Sigl's Clause 6]; 8to [Salary of 20 gulden Rhenish monthly and a suit of clothes or uniform which he must care for]; 10mo [When away from Vienna, he receives 17 xr. *per diem* as 'Kostgeld', i.e. for food; contract for three years] Given at Vienna, 1st April 1761. [Signatures of Kapfer and Secretary Stifftl; it is not clear in all these documents if the signature is 'Stifftl', as in Haydn's, or 'Stiftl' as in most of the others] A.M. 270, No. 1015–9, EH, Budapest.

Johann Georg Kapfer's contract
Identical to that of his brother. The name is also spelled 'Capfer' and is listed as 'Huboist'. A.M. 271, No. 1020–3, EH, Budapest. The Kapfer brothers remained in princely service until 1769 and 1770 respectively; see *Haydn at Eszterháza 1766–1790*, p. 73.

Johann Hinterberger's contract
As for the Kapfers, dated Vienna, 1 April 1761. In this and the other contracts for three years, the players, if they wished to leave the service, are to inform the *Herrschaft* half-a-year beforehand. A.M. 274, No. 1031–5, EH, Budapest. As it happens EH also owns the duplicate contract, signed only by Hinterberger (i.e. the counterpart for the princely administration): A.M. 274, No. 1036–8, EH, Budapest. It is on this second contract that we read the information recorded in the Chronicle for 21 February 1762 (*infra*, p. 366).

Johann Georg Schwenda's contract
As for the Kapfers; dated Vienna, 1 April 1761. A.M. 269, No. 1010–4, EH, Budapest.

1 Not 1 February as stated in *Haydn in Eszterháza 1766–1790*, p. 79. The 'Commission' from the Prince to Chief Receiver (Cashier) Zoller is contained in A.M. 4159, No. 17.663/4. 'Anweisung / Zu folge welcher unser Ober Einnehmer Johann Zoller, dem / als Fleutraversisten, und Houboisten beÿ unserer Hoff / stadt aufgenommenen Franz Sigl, alle monatl zwanzig / gulden Rheinl. entrichten, und solche position, / als eine richtige ausgabe die Buchhalterey angehen solle. / Gegeben Wienn den 1ten April 761 / Antoni Fürst Esterhazy mpria.' Cover: contents.

It was noted that in J. M. Kapfer's contract (Clause 5) he is to protect the instruments 'taken over by the *Herrschaft*'. This at first rather mysterious-sounding phrase refers to an interesting practice of the princely administration. The Prince was in the habit of purchasing, especially from the wind players, the instruments they brought with them. This ensured that the instruments were good (because obviously the new players had to display their ability on them before being engaged) and that the players knew them well. A week after they had been engaged, the Kapfer brothers and the two bassoon players, Hinterberger and Schwenda, signed a document that they had sold their instruments, two bassoons, two oboes and two cors anglais to Prince Paul Anton for 16 ordinary ducats (67 Fl. 5 Kr.); that they renounced their rights to the said instruments which were now princely property; to which they thankfully set their hands.

Das wir endes unterschriebene von Ihro Hochfürstlicher Durch / laucht Herrn Paul Anthon des Heil. Röm. Reichs = Fürsten / von Eszterházy und Galantha Titl. erl. unsern Gnädig Hochge / bittenden Fürsten und Herrn, aus. Handen dero Secretarii, / für unsere mitgebrachten Musicalische Instrumenten, nehm / lich zwey Fagott, zwey Houbois, und zwey Englische Horn, Sech / zehn ordinaire duggaten richtig empfangen haben, solches / bescheinen wir mit unterthänigen Danckh und reversiren / unß hiermit, das wir zu oben benannten Instrumenten / kein- mindesten anspruch weder machen wollen, noch können / sondern stellen, sothane der hohen Herrschaft gehorsamst anheim, als ein Dero Eigenthum. Verbund dessen haben / Wir uns eigenhandig unterschriebn, so geschehen in Wienn / den 8ten April 761. / Johann Michael Kapfer Hoboist / Johan Georg Kapfer Hoboist / Johan Georg

schwenda fagotist / Johannes Hinterberger Fagottist.
[Watermark: a star. A.M. 272, No. 1025–6, EH, Budapest][1]

1 Some further documents (P. 131, fol. 1286; EH, Budapest) may be noted briefly: draft for the above document, with corrections; and the following order from Prince Paul Anton to his Chief Receiver (Cashier) Zoller, recording the salaries to be paid, from 1 April 1761, to Hinterberger, Schwenda and the Kapfer brothers:

Commission / Zu Folge welcher Unser Ober-Einnehmer Johann Zoller unseren dem 1ᵉⁿ April 761 aufgenommenen Musiciis, benanntlich dem Johann Hinterberger, Fagotisten, Johann Georg Schwenda, Fagotisten, dann Johann Michael Kapfer Houboisten, und Johan Georg Kapfer Houboisten ['ihr' deleted] das von uns ['ihren' deleted] einen Jeden accordirtes monath. Geld ['zur' deleted] so 20 Fl. Rhl. alle monath baar und richtig außzahlen auch solche auslage in der Buchhalterey gültig angeschehen werden solle./Ggben Wienn den 18ᵉⁿ April 761. Anthon Fürst Esterhazy m.p.

The next set of contracts date from 1 May 1761. The first is with a French violinist named Franciscus (Franz) Garnier:

Le 1ᵉ May 1761 est entré aux services se Son Altesse Monseigneur le Prince d'Esterhasy, come joueur de violon [addition in Garnier's hand: 'Garnier mpria'] avec les conditions suivantes, savoir que.

1ᵐⁱᵉʳᵉ il s'appliquera de rendre le mieux qu'il lui sera possible son service à l'égard de la musique, soit à table, soit au chœur ou par tout ou luj sera ordoné de jouer le Violon.

2ᵈᵒ toutes les fois qu'il y aura musique, il comparoîtra dans son uniforme proprement peigne, et come il convient pour faire honneur au Service de Son Altesse.

3ᵗⁱᵒ il sera subordonné au Sʳ le vicemaître de Chapelle c'est à dire dans tous les occasions ou il s'agira de musique: il executera avec exactitude, sans opposition et le moindre raisoñement tout ce que ce dit vice = maître de Chapelle luj ordoñera,

parce que Son Altesse prétend, que ses ordres soient considerez, come Les Siens propres.

4ᵗᵒ Comme Son Altesse ne doute pas que le sousigne [later addition, *not* in Garnier's hand: 'Garnier'] observera exactement les points cj- dessus marques
ainsi Elle luj accorde VINGT FLORINS de gage par mois, son quartier franc en campagne, et l'habit uniforme avec ses autres musiciens. À l'exception de toute autre préten [new page] tion qu'il voudroit faire par tout ou il se trouvera. Il s'engage de servir pendant une année complete. En foy de quoi l'on a fait deux contracts semblables, dont celui-cj doit être signé par le susdit joueur de violon
[Garnier's autograph: 'Garnier mpria']
[A.M. 265, No. 998, EH, Budapest]

Franciscus (Franz) Garnier was – it seems – a small man, as we see from a document[1] of 1764 (Rahier's letter to princely archivist Schmiliar). When he left the princely service in 1766, he went to Lyon, where he had, apparently, relatives. In a catalogue of music issued by Guera of Lyon[2] we find compositions by one Lucas Garnier, which explains why Dr Harich confused the two men (*HJB* IV, 15, 32): Lucas was perhaps Franciscus's brother.

1 Well Born, Much Respected Herr Schmiliar. . . . Tell Hr: Heiden [*sic*] to report to me if and for what reason he gave permission for the little French musician to come up here [to Vienna] . . . P. L. Rahier, Vienna, 10th January 764. EH, Budapest, Országos Levéltár P. 154 (old Fasc. 1524), fol. 11.
2 'Six / Duos, / Concertant / pour deux Flutes. . . . / par / L. Demachi / Oeuvre Iʳᵉ. de Duo, de Flutes . . . A LYON Chez Guera . . .'. Signed by Demachi on title page. Cat. = *c.* 1780. Author's collection. Under 'Sonates' we read as the first item, '6. Luc Garnier. Viol.º Op. 1', costing 7 livres 4s.

We now come to Haydn's contract, also signed on 1 May 1761. It has been the subject of widespread comment, as might be expected, but the astonishment as to its language and supposedly debasing contents was perhaps partly because the other contracts with Prince Paul Anton (and later with Prince Nicolaus, where the language was retained) were not known. Many of the 'debasing' clauses were simply standard procedure for all house officers' contracts with the family. It is certainly not true that Haydn was treated like a servant. On the contrary, there was a vast difference between a real servant (and they, too, were subdivided into classes) and a house officer. The language in which a prince of the Holy Roman Empire expected to be addressed, either *viva voce* or in writing, is to be found throughout this biography. The fawning, flattering and demeaning addresses and good wishes for name-days and birthdays strike oddly on the twentieth-century ear, but they were common all over Europe. As a contract, Haydn's was as fair and proper as would have been possible anywhere on the Continent, and there can be no doubt that Haydn signed it with relief, joy and high hopes.

Convention and Rules for Behaviour
of the *Vice-Capel-Meister* [*sic*]

This day, according to the date hereto appended, Joseph Heÿden [*sic*], native of [blank] in Austria, is accepted and appointed a *Vice-Capel-Meister* in the service of his Serene Princely Highness, Herr Paul Anton, Prince of the Holy Roman Empire, of Eszterházÿ and Galantha Tit. etc. etc. in this manner; that whereas

1mo. There is at Eÿsenstadt a *Capel-Meister* named Gregorius Werner, who having devoted many years of true and faithful service to the Princely house is now, on account of his great age and the resulting infirmities that this often entails, unfit to perform the duties incumbent on him, it is hereby declared that said Gregorius Werner, in consideration of his long service, shall continue to retain the post of *Ober-Capel-Meister*, while the said Joseph Heÿden, as *Vice-Capel-Meister* at Eÿsenstadt, shall in regard to the choir music depend upon and be subordinate to said Gregorio[!] Werner, *quà Ober-Capel-Meister*; but in everything else, whenever there shall be a musical performance, and in all required for the same in general and in particular, said *Vice-Capel-Meister* shall be responsible. And whereas

2do. The said Joseph Heÿden shall be considered and treated as a house officer. Therefore his Serene Princely Highness is graciously pleased to place confidence in him [Haydn], that as may be expected from an honourable house officer in a princely court, he will be temperate, and will know that he must treat the musicians placed under him not overbearingly, but with mildness and leniency, modestly, quietly and honestly. This is especially the case when music will be performed before the high *Herrschafft*, at which time said *Vice-Capel-Meister* and his subordinates shall always appear in uniform; and said Joseph Heÿden shall take care that not only he but all those dependent upon him shall follow the instructions which have been given to them, appearing neatly in white stockings, white linen, powdered, and either with pigtail or hair-bag, but otherwise of identical appearance. Therefore

3^{tio}. The other *Musici* are responsible to said *Vice-Capel-Meister*, thus he shall the more take care to conduct himself in an exemplary manner, so that the subordinates may follow the example of his good qualities; consequently said Joseph Heÿden shall abstain from undue familiarity, from eating and drinking, and from other intercourse with them so that they will not lose the respect which is his due but on the contrary preserve it; for these subordinates should the more remember their respectful duties if it be considered how unpleasant to the *Herrschafft* must be the consequences of any discord or dispute.

4to. The said *Vice-Capel-Meister* shall be under permanent obligation to compose such pieces of music as his Serene Princely Highness may command, and neither to communicate such new compositions to anyone, nor to allow them to be copied, but to retain them wholly for the exclusive use of his Highness; nor shall he compose for any other person without the knowledge and gracious permission [of his Highness].

5to. The said Joseph Heÿden shall appear daily (whether here in Vienna or on the estates) in the *antichambre* before and after midday, and inquire whether a high princely *ordre* for a musical performance has been given; to wait for this order and upon its receipt to communicate its contents to the other *Musici*; and not only himself to appear punctually at the required time but to take serious care that the others do as well, specifically noting those who either arrive later or absent themselves entirely. If nevertheless,

6to. Contrary to rightful expectations there should arise between the *Musici* quarrels, disputes or complaints, said *Vice-Capel-Meister* shall endeavour himself to arrange matters, so that the high *Herrschafft* be not incommoded with every trifle and *bagatelle*; but should a more serious matter occur, which the said Joseph Heÿden is not able himself to set right or in which he can not act as intermediary, then his Serene Princely Highness must be respectfully informed.

7mo. The said *Vice-Capel-Meister* shall take careful charge of all the music and musical instruments, and shall be responsible for ensuring that they are not ruined and rendered useless through carelessness or neglect.

8°. The said Joseph Heÿden shall be obliged to instruct the female vocalists, in order that they may not again forget (when staying in the country) that which they have been taught with much effort and at great expense in Vienna, and inasmuch as the said *Vice-Capel-Meister* is proficient on various instruments, he shall take care to practice on all those with which he is acquainted.

9mo. A copy of this *Convention* and Rules for Behaviour shall be given to the said *Vice-Capel-Meister* and to all the *Musiquanten* subordinate to him, in order that he may hold them to all their obligations therein established. Moreover,

10mo. It is considered unnecessary to set forth on paper all the duties required of the said Joseph Heÿden, more particularly since the Serene *Herrschafft* is pleased to hope that he shall of his own free will strictly observe not only the above-mentioned regulations but any others – in whatever circumstances – which the high *Herrschafft* might issue in the future; and that he shall place the *Musique* on such a footing, and in such good order, that he shall bring honour upon himself and thereby deserve further princely favour; to which end his discretion and zeal are relied upon. In confidence of which

11mo. A yearly salary of 400. frn [florins] Rhine value to be received from the Office of the Chief Collector [Cashier] in quarterly payments is hereby agreed. In addition,

12mo. When on the estates, said Joseph Heÿden shall board at the officers' table or receive half-a-gulden in lieu therefor. Finally

13mo. This *Convention* with the said *Vice-Capel-Meister* is agreed to on 1st May 1761 and is to hold good for at least three years, in such manner that if the said Joseph Heÿden at the end of that period wishes to seek his fortune elsewhere, he shall inform the *Herrschafft* of his intention by half-a-year's previous notice. Similarly,

14mo. The *Herrschafft* undertakes not only to retain the said Joseph Heÿden in his service during this period, but should he provide complete satisfaction, he may look forward to the position of *Ober-Capel-Meister*. On the other hand, his

Highness is free at all times to dismiss him from his service, also during the period in question. In witness whereof, two identical copies of this document have been prepared and exchanged. Given at Vienna this 1ˢᵗ of Maÿ 1761.

Joseph Haydn mpria.

Notes:
Two copies of this historical document survive, both written by a princely secretary with calligraphic emphasis placed on certain words (roman instead of the document's gothic script, or larger size) which cannot be reproduced in translation. Copy one was retained by the princely administration and signed by Haydn; it is now part of EH, Budapest, Országos Levéltár (at present [1978] in the exhibition room in the Archives). Facsimile: Somfai (German ed.), pp. 25–33, with accurate transcription. Copy two is the one which was given to Haydn, now A.M. Fasc. I, 88, EH, Budapest. It is signed [left:] 'Ad mandatum Celsissimi Principis' [right] 'Johann Stifftel / Secret.' There are small differences between the two MSS., which may be examined easily in Bartha, 44f. First paragraph: Haydn's birthplace 'Rohrau' inserted in copy two; the word 'Hochfürstlicher' omitted in copy two, also the abbreviation for the many princely titles, 'Tit.' Paragraph 7: in copy two, the text has the following words at the end of the section: '(auch für solche repondiren)', i.e. 'and he is to bear the responsibility' for any ruined instruments.

On 1 June, further contracts followed. The original contracts of the two horn players have not survived, but since they are missing in the 1760 *Conventionale* and also in another list which was apparently made about 1 June (overleaf), we suggest that they were engaged about 10 June, effective retroactively from 1 June; for they appear on the pay list for June made out in July. We shall see that this kind of retroactive pay will often occur in the forthcoming Chronicle.

Melchior Griessler's (Grießler) contract
He was from Nußdorf and his name also spelled 'Greißler'; he was engaged as from 1 June 1761 as violinist and bass singer. Contract as usual.
'№ 3 [He is] to play on all those instruments on which he is skilled at such Musique as may be ordered during table, or like the other house officers he is to serve the *Herrschaft*; and he is to attend the choir music at Eisenstadt; 4ᵉ [He is to be subordinate to the *Ober-* and *Vice-Capel-Meister*.]; 5ᵗᵒ [He is to execute all the required services as a house officer.]; 6ᵗᵒ [He is to receive] every year 200 gulden Rhenish, and quarterly to receive in his capacity as violinist a *Deputat*:

    4 *Metzen* of wheat
    12 *Metzen* of corn
    1 quarter *Metzen* Barley corn
    1 quarter *Metzen* millet pap
    1 quarter *Metzen* lentils
    Beef 300 ℔ [lb.]
    Salt 5 pounds
    Lard 30 pounds
    Candles 30 pounds
    Wine 9 *Eimer*
    Cabbage 1 *Eimer*
    Beetroots ½ *Eimer*
    S: V: pig 1 whole one
    Firewood 6 *Klaftern* [fathom cords].
8ᵗᵒ [every year a uniform or cash in lieu ...]
Therefore after the end of the first year he is not allowed to dispose of clothes received during the first year, but must keep them together with his new clothes, so that he always has two uniforms, the one only for travelling or also in the town, in rain and snow, but the new one for service with the Lords ...; 9ᵗᵒ [Contract for three years; and half-a-year's notice of intention to leave]. Given at Vienna, 1st June 1761. [Signatures of Griessler and Johann Stif(f)tel, Secretary] A.M. 273, No. 1027–30, EH, Budapest.

Joseph Weigl's contract
Form similar to the others. Spelled 'Waigl'. Engaged as violoncellist for three years at 20 gulden Rhenish per month and a new uniform annually or 60 Fl. in lieu. Clause about uniform as in Griessler's contract. Signed and dated 'Vienna, 1st June 1761, Josephus Weigl'. A.M. 267, No. 1004–6, EH, Budapest.

Johann Georg Heger's contract
Form similar to the others. Engaged as 'Geiger' (violinist) for three years at a salary of 150 gulden Rhenish p.a., but without mention of a yearly uniform or 60 Fl. allowance in lieu; otherwise, payments made quarterly. Clause about uniform as before. Signed and dated 'Vienna, 1st June 1761, Heger'. A.M. 258, No. 1007–9, EH, Budapest.

1   Joseph Haydn, portrait in oils *c.*1762–3, probably by Johann Basilius Grundmann (1726–98), who was a painter in Esterházy service. Haydn is depicted wearing the blue uniform with silver trimmings of the *Vice-Capellmeister* in Prince Esterházy's household.

2   View of Hainburg, where Haydn was a pupil at the choir-school of his cousin Johann Mathias Franck in the 1750s (cf. p. 51); watercolour by Ferdinand Runk (1764–1834).

3   View of Böhmisch-Krumau (now Český Krumlov), showing the Schwarzenberg Castle (left background). The castle contains one of the very few eighteenth-century princely theatres in Europe to have survived largely intact; its design and construction have provided invaluable information about contemporary stage production methods, especially important in the case of Haydn's operas written for performance at Eszterháza. Watercolour by Laurenz Janscha (?; 1749–1812).

4 Pietro Metastasio (1698–1782), the great Italian poet, who in the 1750s in Vienna helped Haydn learn the Italian language. Engraving by J. E. Mansfeld after J. N. Steiner.

5 Georg Reutter, Jr. (1708–72), Chapel-Master at St Stephen's Cathedral, Vienna, who taught both Joseph Haydn and his brother Michael; anonymous pastel.

Below
6 Nicola Antonio Porpora (1686–1768), Haydn's employer and teacher in the 1750s; anonymous portrait in oils.

7 Christoph Willibald, *Ritter* von Gluck (1714–90), who was engaged by Count Durazzo (cf. pl. 23) in 1754 as composer to the Burgtheater, Vienna (cf. pp. 243f.); anonymous portrait, chalk on paper.

8   Weinzierl Castle, the country seat of the Fürnberg family (cf. p. 228); detail from a painting by Jakob Alt (1789–1872). Haydn was invited to the castle by Carl Joseph, Edler von Fürnberg (1721–67), and it was at the latter's suggestion that Haydn wrote his first string Quartet, later published as No. 1 of the set known as Op. I.

9, 10   Glass medallion beaker with portrait and coat-of-arms of Lt-Col. Joseph von Fürnberg (1746–99), elder son of Carl Joseph (cf. pl. 8); the beaker, decorated by Johann Joseph Mildner (1764–1808), is inscribed (on the bottom) 'Verfertigt / zu Gutenbrunn / Im Jahre 1789. d. 28 Augusti / von Mildner'; ht $4\frac{3}{4}$ in. (12·1 cm.).

11 Lukavec Castle, the former seat of the Morzin family (cf. p. 235), for whom Haydn wrote orchestral works and pieces for wind band, as well as chamber music, in the years 1759–61, and possibly as early as 1757–8.

12 Kittsee Castle, one of the princely Esterházy estates, with the town of Pressburg (identified in this anonymous eighteenth-century engraving by its Latin name, Posonium) on the opposite bank of the Danube. Prince Paul Anton Esterházy built a new castle c.1740 on the site of a medieval fortress; after entering Esterházy service in 1761 Haydn often led concerts in this castle.

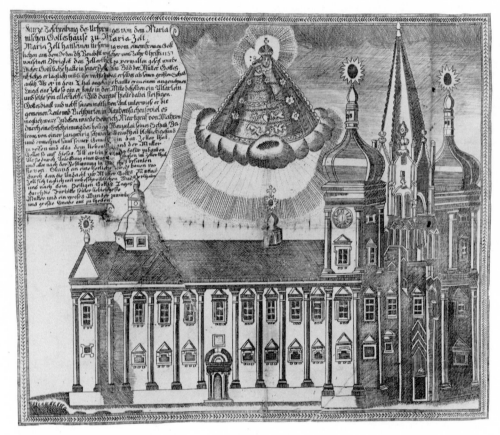

13 The Benedictine pilgrimage church of Our Lady, Mariazell, in Lower Austria; souvenir engraving such as Haydn might have acquired on his journey there in the early 1750s (cf. p. 64).

14   The Nikolaikirche, Vienna, with (right) the Convent of the Poor Clares where Haydn's first love, Therese Keller, took the veil in 1756 (cf. p. 81); Haydn composed his *Salve Regina* in E (XXIIIb: 1) and the Organ Concerto in C (XVIII: 1) for that occasion. Engraving by J. G. Ringlin after Salomon Kleiner (1700 or 1703–61).

15   The Esterházy Palais in the Wallnerstraße, the princely town residence in Vienna. Engraving by J. G. Ringlin after Salomon Kleiner.

16 (a) The Esterházy Castle and park at Eisenstadt as Haydn would have known them when he entered service there in 1761; and (b) the Esterházy family coat-of-arms, together with a hunting scene in which the huntsman is sounding a coiled *cor de chasse* (hunting horn). Details from an engraving by Martin Tyroff (1704–?), Nuremberg, after a drawing executed in 1759 by the Princely Architect (Ingénieur), Nicolaus Jacoby.

Opposite
19 View of Eisenstadt in the third quarter of the eighteenth century; engraving after a pen-and-ink drawing by Leopold Kraus(?), son of Haydn's friend the *Rector*, Carl Kraus (1723–1802), to whom the engraving is dedicated.

17, 18   The two Princes Esterházy–Paul Anton (1711–62) and his younger brother, Nicolaus I (b. 1714) – in whose household Haydn remained in continuous service, first as *Vice-Capellmeister* (1761–65) and subsequently, until the death of Nicolaus in 1790, as *Capellmeister*; anonymous portraits in oils.

20 Haydn's Symphony No. 7 ('Le Midi'), 1761: first page of the autograph score inscribed 'Le Midi In Nomine Domini Giuseppe Haydn 761'. The division of staves reads: 'Corni Ex C'; 'Oboe 1ma'; '[Oboe] 2da'; 'Violino 1mo Concerto'; '[Violino] 2do Concerto'; 'Violino 1mo Rip:'; '[Violino] 2do Rip:'; 'Viola'; 'Violoncello Obligato' and (to the right) 'Fagott'; 'Basso Continuo'; also, underneath the tempo marking 'Adagio', 'Violoncello con Basso continuo'.

21, 22 Symphony No. 7 ('Le Midi'), 1761: two pages from a set of authentic parts (with additions in Haydn's own hand), formerly part of the composer's own library; there are candle-wax stains on the parts, indicating that they were actually used. The copyist is known to us from other early Esterházy copies. Haydn's additions are (p. 1): (top line) 'Violin Principale', and (lines 9, 10) various dynamic marks; (p. 2, bottom line) 'for', 'p.' and 'Adagio'.

23, 24   Giacomo (Jacob), Count Durazzo (1717–94), and his wife Ernestine Aloisia (*née* Ungnad von Weissenwolf; 1732–94); details from a pair of portraits painted in 1756 (badly damaged in the Second World War), formerly in the possession of the Weissenwolf family. From 1749 Durazzo was Genoese ambassador in Vienna; he later managed the Burgtheater in Vienna, and was on excellent terms with Haydn (cf. pp. 361f.).

25   Johann Joseph Felix (later von) Kurz-Bernadon (1717–84), who in the 1750s engaged Haydn to write his first (now lost) opera, *Der krumme Teufel*, for performance in Vienna at the Kärntnerthortheater (cf. pl. III); engraving by Ferdinand Landerer (1730–95).

26 Anna Maria Josepha Weigl (*née* Scheffstoß), who was Haydn's principal soprano in the 1760s, taking a leading role in his opera *Acide* (1763). For the companion piece showing her husband, the 'cellist Joseph Weigl, see *Haydn at Eszterháza*, pl. V; trompe-l'œil collage in watercolour and wash, by J. M. Richter(?), 1772.

27 Carl Ditters (later von Dittersdorf; 1739–99); Haydn and Ditters were friends and they frequently discussed the new music they heard. This anonymous portrait in oils, dated 1764, was discovered (in a badly damaged state) in the cellars of the Gesellschaft der Musikfreunde in Vienna.

28, 29   Haydn's *Acide*. Pages from, respectively: the autograph score of 1762, headed 'Aria In Nomine Domini Giuseppe Haydn 762; and (below) one of the elaborate accompanied recitatives of the 1762–3 version (cf. pp. 439ff).

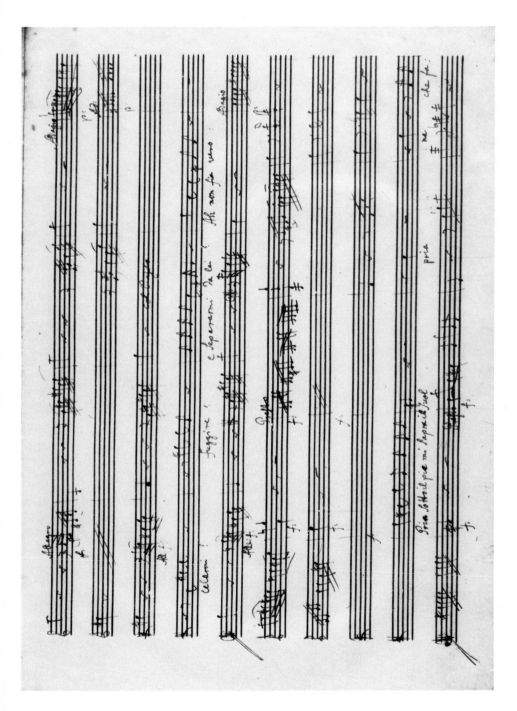

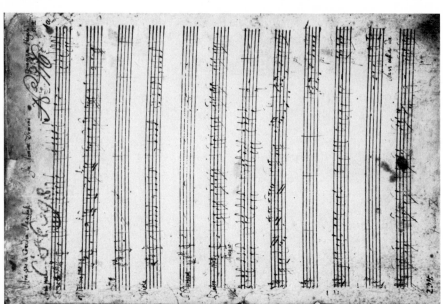

Far left
30 Haydn's Symphony No. 13 (1763): first page of the autograph score, inscribed 'In Nomine Domini / Giuseppe Haydn / 763'. The instrumentation, by staves, reads: 'Flauto'; 'Corno 1mo / et Secondo / Ex D'; 'Corno / 3 4to'; 'Oboe 1ma' and '[Oboe] 2da'; 'Violino / 1mo and '[Violino] 2do'; 'Viola'; 'Basso'. The timpani part was added at the foot of the MS. in an unknown hand.

Left
31 Haydn's *La Marchesa Nespola* (*Il Marchese*; XX:1): first page of the autograph score, inscribed 'Arie per la Comedia *Marchese* In Nomine Domini Giuseppe Haydn 762'; the MS. was at first dated 1761 and the last digit later altered to read '2'.

Meanwhile, it was necessary to 'regulate' these new musicians, and this was done in a list prepared about 1 June 1761, because all the newly engaged musicians except for the horn players are included (see table overleaf).[1] From the notes to this document, provided by Georg Feder and Sonja Gerlach at the time of its first publication, we learn that the 60 Fl. uniform money for Heger was added later. As his contract had shown, he was not paid as much as the others, and it was not intended to give him a uniform. Another interesting fact is that it was generally expected that the *Herrschaft* spend five months on their estates (probably Kittsee and Eisenstadt) and the rest of the year in Vienna. It turns out that Prince Paul Anton spent most of the summer of 1761 in Vienna. The string players were not expected to go to the country estates and that is why no *per diem* is indicated for them, while the wind players (to which we must add the horns) did service with the Grenadiers and could play wind-band sextets for the *Herrschaft* as *Tafel Musique*.

In the pay list for June 1761, we find the following names:

Specification

Of the Musicians for Court and Chamber, who were paid for the Month of June from the General Cassa.

Paid to the Gentlemen by virtue of their Signature	Officia	f	Xr
Joseph Haÿdn mpria	Vice Capellmeister	33	20
Luigi Tomasini [mpria]	First Violinist	12	30
Frantz sigel [mpria]	Flut: Traversist	20	..
Garnier mpria	Other Violinist	20	..
Johann Georg Heger [mpria]	Other Ditto	12	30
Josephus Weigl [mpria]	Violoncellist	20	..
Michael Kapfer	First Hauboist	20	..
Georg Kapfer	Other Hauboist	20	..
Johannes Hinterberger	First Bassoonist	20	..
Georg Schwenda	Other Bassoonist	20	..
Johannes Knoblauch	First Horn Player	20	..
Thadteus Steinmüller	Other Horn Player	20	..
	in Summa	238	20

[EH, Forchtenstein, Generalcassa 1761, Rubr. VIII. Fasc. 3., No. 74. Facsimile in *HJB* IV, 38; J. Harich in *HJB* IV, 42]

In this list we suddenly notice the name of Luigi Tomasini as leader, but with approximately the same poor pay as was given to Heger. Tomasini, though in Paul Anton's service since 1757, was a *valet-de-chambre*, and it was not for some time that he was given the same pay as the other members of the *Capelle*. Perhaps Heger was also a servant and transferred to the *Capelle* in the same manner as Tomasini. When we

---

1 There are two outstanding mathematical errors in this list, the first of which concerns the musicians' uniforms. Ten musicians receive uniforms at 60 fl. each, a total of 600 fl., not 540. The second concerns the players' payments *per diem* on the estates under the column 'Makes for 1 month of 30 days', where the total must be 47, not 49.

TABLE
of the Musicians engaged in the Princely Court and Chamber Musique and their annual Salaries

Name	Cash	Uniform or money	Per diem on estates	Makes for 1 month of 30 days		Makes for 5 summer months		Deputat [in kind]		Total sum		Engaged for years	Month
	flo:	flo:	xr.	flo:	xr.	flo:	xr.	flo:	xr.	flo:	xr.		
Vice-Capell-Meister Joseph Heyden	400.	60.	30.	15.	—	75.	—	—	—	535.	—	3.	From 1 May 1761.
Houboist Johann Michael Kapfer	240.	60.	17.	8.	30.	42.	30.	—	—	342.	30.	3.	From 1 April 1761.
Houboist Johann Georg Kapfer	240.	60.	17.	8.	30.	42.	30.	—	—	342.	30.	3.	From 1 April 1761.
Fagotist Johann Georg Schwenda	240.	60.	17.	8.	30.	42.	30.	—	—	342.	30.	3.	From 1 April 1761.
Fagotist Johann Hinterberger	240.	60.	17.	8.	30.	42.	30.	—	—	342.	30.	3.	From 1 April 1761.
Fleutraversist Franz Sigl	240.	60.	—	—	—	—	—	—	—	300.	—	1.	From 1 April 1761.
Violinist Guarniere	240.	60.	—	—	—	—	—	—	—	300.	—	1.	From 1 May 1761.
Violoncelist Joseph Waigl	240.	60.	—	—	—	—	—	—	—	300.	—	3.	From 1 June 1761.
Bassist und Violinist Melchior Grießler	200.	60.	—	—	—	—	—	119.	6.	379.	6.	3.	From 1 June 1761.
Geiger Johann Georg Heger	150.	60.	—	—	—	—	—	—	—	150.	—	3.	From 1 June 1761.
Summa	2,430.	540.	98.	49.	—	245.	—	119.	6.	3,334.	6.	—	—

[Acta varia, EH, Forchtenstein; after *Haydn-Studien* III/2 (1974), p. 93]

arrive at the pay list for July, we note that the members were numbered 1–15: Haydn as No. 1, and as No. 2 'Maria Anna Scheffstosin Erste Discantista' at 8 Fl. 20 Xr. per month; No. 3 was 'Barbara Fuxin Anderte Discantista' at 6 Fl. 40 Xr.; No. 4 was 'Carl Friberth Tenorista' at 25 Fl. per month.[1] The singers, then, were as of 1 July transferred from the 'Chor Musique' to the 'Cammer Musique', which no doubt meant that they were now singing secular music (arias, cantatas, etc.) as well as church music.

We have violated our chronological method in favour of keeping all the new musicians and their contracts together in one place, but meanwhile the documents in the Esterházy Archives show us other aspects of life at court. The first is a tailor's bill of 15 May:

15 May 7̄6̄1̄ with God. In Vienna

List

What I did, and expended, in the way of tailoring work for the High Serene Prince and Lord Esterhasÿ

First 16 embroidered [*gebrante* = *gebrämte*] uniforms made, for the making with all that belongs to it, 8 f each	128	—
135 ells of half castors for lining a 22 x	39	30
7 ells of material [*schallan*] for vestment of linen 1 f	7	—
For the *Calbel Master* [*sic*] a uniform made with embroidery and with sewing it and for making and with all that belongs to it	9	—
3½ *loth* of fine golden *Palletten*[2] a 2 f	7	—
2 *loth* golden thread a 2 f	4	—
7 ells of material [*schallen*] for lining a 1 f	7	—
The facings instead of being tailored, lined with 9 ells of half castor [a] 22 [x]	3	18

Sum̄a.... 214 48

[*recte* 204 48]

Johann Georg Mösner
Citizen Tailor Maker

[Generalcassa 1761. Rubr. V. No. 7, EH, Forchtenstein; *HJB* IV, 79f.]

With this interesting bill we begin the vexing question of Haydn's uniform. We presume that by *Calbel Master* – the whole bill is in excruciating Viennese dialect – Haydn and not Werner is meant. (Werner was in Eisenstadt anyway, and Haydn had to have a new uniform.) From the bill it is clear that Haydn's uniform (and waistcoat) was embroidered with gold, not silver. Yet Haydn's father saw him in the blue uniform with silver embroidery. At the risk of pursuing a line of total unimportance, we may rapidly state that from the records now at our disposal Haydn started in May 1761 with uniform of unknown colour with gold embroidery; in August 1762 his uniform, and those of the musicians, was of unknown colour and had silver embroidery; in January 1763, the musicians wore dark-red uniforms with gold embroidery; in August 1764, they wore uniforms of unknown colour with silver embroidery; in November 1764, they were grey trimmed with gold.[3] In fact the subject is of vital importance in dating the earliest portrait of Haydn, that painted by Johann Basilius Grundmann showing the subject in a blue uniform with silver embroidery. In view of the bill of August 1762 (silver embroidery), and taking into consideration the fact that Mathias Haydn visited his son before 12 September 1763 († Mathias in Rohrau), we suggest that the portrait might have been commissioned by

1 Complete list in *HJB* IV, 42f., also for August-December, (where we suddenly find Si(e)g(e)l signing himself 'Sigl'; in November Haydn signed for Si(e)gl: 'Francesco Sigl'.
2 *Pallette* = French *paillette*, gold spangles sewed to an elaborate waistcoat.
3 The documents from which this information comes appear *infra*. For further changes in the colour of the uniforms, see *Haydn at Eszterháza 1766–1790*, p. 88.

Prince Nicolaus shortly after Grundmann was engaged on 1 October 1762.[1] The question also arises in connection with the (spurious) painting of Haydn's *L'incontro improvviso*.

On 21 May, Prince Paul Anton issued a decree, of which we have the draft, regulating the superfluous musicians in Eisenstadt.

> An Buchhalter Johann Späch aus Wienn den 21ten Maÿ 761 ergangene Befehlschreiben / Nachdeme Wir in unsere Dienste [words deleted: neue einen Vice Capell Meister dann zwey Houboisten und 2 Fagotisten zu unserer Cammer und Chor Musique aufgenommen haben als bleibt Euch geschrieben wir an Euch, das ihr durch] neue Leüthe / : wie ab der anlage zu ersehen : / zu unserer Cammer- und Chor Musique aufgenommen haben, so [deleted: finden] geruhten wir ein und andere [deleted: Musicus] in unseren Diensten zu Eisenstadt stehende befindliche Musicos [deleted: für über flüssig zu seyn] nehmlich den Violoncelisten Sigmund Gstettner, Violonisten Anton Kühnel, und die zwey Fagotisten überflüssig sey. Darum haben Wir entschlossen, nun eractete 4. Musicos ende dieses quartals ihrer Bishero sowohl in Chor als bey unserer Hofstadt geleisteten Musicalischen Dienstes zu entlassen mithin gesinnen Wir an Euch, das ihr durch den Ober-Capel- Meister Gregorius Werner, ihnen oben benanneten 4 vier Musicis unsere disfällige festgestellte resolution rechter zeit bedeüten lasset. Darin beruhet unsere Willenmeynung, Womit Wir Euch nebst allen guten beygethan verbleiben. Ggben Wienn den 21ten Maÿ 761/Anthon Fürst Esterhazy m.p.
>
> [Protocollum IV. p. 131 (old Fasc. 715), fol. 1350, EH, Budapest, Országos Levéltár; Valkó I, 536; here from original]

[Summary translation: To Book-keeper Johann Späch from Vienna 21 May 1761 – Decree. We have engaged new people (see attached document [not attached]) for our Chamber and Choir Musique [words deleted: a *Vice Capell Meister*, two oboists and 2 bassoon players]; thus we are pleased to find the one or other of the musicians in our service at Eisenstadt superfluous, viz. the violoncellist Sigmund Gstettner, the double-bass player Anton Kühnel and the two bassoon players. Therefore we have decided to dispense with the musical services of said 4 players at the end of this quarter, for both court and choir, and thus we ask you to have *Ober-Capel-Meister* Gregorius Werner inform the 4 musicians of our decision in good time. ...

After 1 June 1761, therefore, Haydn's orchestra in Vienna (for the *Chor Musique* at Eisenstadt had to remain there for the regular church services) consisted of the following members:

Flute: Franz Si(e)gl

Oboes: Johann Michael and Johann Georg Kapfer

Bassoons: Johann Hinterberger and Georg Schwenda (also a double-bass player)

Horns: Johann Knoblauch and Thaddeus Steinmüller

Violins and Violas: Haydn, Luigi Tomasini, Franciscus Garnier, Johann Georg Heger, Melchior Griessler.

Violoncello: Joseph Weigl

Double bass: Georg Schwenda.

Since Haydn's Symphonies Nos. 6–8 ('La Matin', 'Le Midi', 'Le Soir'), the first works he wrote for Prince Paul Anton, never require more than one bassoon, Schwenda probably always played double bass except in the *Feld Harmonie* (wind band). If Griessler was not sent at once to the *Chor Musique* in Eisenstadt, he could have helped out in the violin section; but a number of facts – that he received a *Deputat*, that he is

---

1 Grundmann's date of engagement from Simon Meller: *Az Esterházy-képt története*, Budapest 1915, XXXI, 16 and (index) 261. An undated reference of 1762 to Grundmann's engagement is quoted *infra*, p. 373. Grundmann was born in Germany and it is likely that he was in service at Esterházy, even on a trial basis, before 1762 (therefore, for the date given in *Haydn at Eszterháza 1766–1790*, p. 30, read 'c. 1761'.

missing from the pay list for the *Capelle* in June, and that Haydn had to order him to come from Eisenstadt on 4 March 1762 in a letter wherein we read that Griessler had only performed services at Eisenstadt in the summer of 1761 – suggest that Griessler was not part of the *Capelle* for the first performances of Symphonies Nos. 6–8. But there must have been at least four violinists, because the scores require two solo violins and two *ripieno* violins, which (counting the available players, minus Griessler) leaves no one for the viola part. We must therefore assume that either from the ranks of the servants, or from outside, some violinists and viola players had to be found. Does the tailor's bill for the sixteen (presumably musicians') uniforms on 15 May 1761 – Haydn's was reckoned separately – give us a hint of the size of the *Capelle*? Do the sixteen include the *Chor Musique* at Eisenstadt? Do they already include the musicians engaged on 1 June? It seems idle to continue the speculation.

The beginning of Haydn's musical life with the Esterházys, then, took place in Vienna, where the whole entourage seems to have remained for most of the summer. We have no idea where Haydn and the musicians were lodged, perhaps on the top floor of the great Esterházy Palace in the Wallnerstraße. Haydn began his waiting in the antechamber, and he told Griesinger (58) that the habit of being dressed and ready early in the morning came from the time of his service with the Esterházys, 'when his Prince often called for him unexpectedly'. The new Symphonies (Nos. 6–8) were no doubt first heard in the state room of the Palace in the Wallnerstraße.

We say most of the summer was spent in Vienna; but the princely family was certainly in Eisenstadt for a large part of June. Our source is Count Zinzendorf's Diary, in which he never mentions any music being given; but that does not mean a total absence of concerts, and Haydn and the *Capelle* were probably in attendance at Eisenstadt in this period (for explanatory notes see end of quotation).

[3 June 1761:] ... Diné avec mon frere chez la Princesse Esterhazy ... le Prince m'invita de venir a Eisenstadt. ...

[21 June:] J'avois compté d'aller avec Cassini a Presbourg, mais comme il n'étoit pas de retour d'un tour qu'il a fait a la campagne avec le Prince de Lichtenstein [*sic*], j'allois avec mon frere à Eisenstadt. Il est tout a faire le matin que nous ne partimes qu'apres 10ʰ· nous fimes a trajet de 7 lieues d'allemagne en 3ʰ· et un peu plus. On passe pres de Theresien, meme a Laxenburg reste a droite, on passe Klein Neusiedl, Leopolsdorff[*sic*], Hochau ou on change de chevaux. Nous y trouvons le Duc de Bragance retournant d'Eysenstatt a Vienne. On passe ensuite Minkendorff frontiere d'Hongrie et d'Autriche, au dela de cette riviére est Ungarisch Protterstorff ou commence le territoire de Prince Esterhazy. Le puis est tres beau, on commence a voir une Enfilade de Vignes. De ce dernier endroit il y a 1 poste et demi jusqu'a Eysenstatt. Chateau tres beau situé a un coté. On y étoit a diner dans la grande sale que je juge de 90–100 piés de longueur. Elle seroit magnifique si elle n'etoit gatée par des barbouilleries des peintroits de tous les Rois d'Hongrie peints a la diable. Il y avoit Mᵉˢ d'Esterhazy, la mere du Prince et sa belle soeur, Mᵉˢ le Durazzo, de Windischgraetz, de Sinzendorff, Mᵉˡˡᵉ de Nimptsch, notre parente par le C. [comte] Louis, le Prince de Lowenstein, Keglowitsch, le jeune Lamberg, le C. Erbviller [Herbeviller], M. Molitori, le marquis de Montecuculi[.][1] Apres table les Dames allent se promener, et le Prince aussi tout seul. Mᵉ d'Esterhazy se flatta de me convertir.[2] La Princesse alla aux Vépres, ou j'entend dis jaser quelque chose, apres cela elle alla avec nous 2. au jardin[.] Il est tres vaste, il n'y en a pas si beau a Vienne, on y entre par un pont levis. A chaque poste de la Cour et de la grande Sale il y a une Sentinelle des 120. gards du Prince, habilles en bleu avec des vestes et paremens paille, et des brandebourgs d'or filé. On m'invita d'y venir une autre fois pour y rester quelques jours. La Durazzo et la Wind.[isch-Graetz] me parlerent. Nonobstant l'orage que nous vient s'approcher, nos partimes d'Eysenstatt apres 6^h. La pluye et les orages nous accompagnent toujours, mais a Hochau nous en eumes la plus fortesse, des Eclairs terribles sans fin, et une Ondée copieuse, le Grand chemin et tout le voisinage paroit un Etang, c'est ce qui nous émpecha d'arriver là plutôt qu'a 11^h. A Ung. Prott[ersdorf] il y avoit une jolie fille. ... Le Matin tres chaud, une chaleur étouffante avec beaucoup de Vent. Le Soir des Orages tres forts et une pluye prodigieuse.

[27 June:] ... A 4^h et $\frac{3}{4}$ parti avec M. le Baron d'enzenberg et son fils pour Eisenstadt, nous passerons Schwechat ou est une belle fabrique de toiles, arrivames là avant 9^h ou étoit un jardin. Apres le souper promené au jardin jusqu'a 11^h. avec Me de Durazzo et de Sinzendorff et le C. Keglowitz et Mr Richard. Le tems étoit beau. ...

... Le 28 Juin ... levois a 4^h du matin pour ne sortir qu'a midi. On alla au Couvent des religieuses sous moi, et moi je montois tout seul sur la Galerie et sur un des Clochers d'ou on decouvre toute la contrée, vers le Nord on ne voit que des vignobles, vers le sud et l'Ouest nombre d'endroits, vers l'Est le grand Lac de Neusiedel derrière le parc. Apresmidi on alla tirer feu blanc, Me de Durazzo tira bien, mais la Princesse fit sauter 4. fois la bambe. M. de Keglowitz repartit. On alla apresmidi sur une hauteur voisine, ou de dessous une Tente nous [étions] Spectateurs des Exercises de la Garde du Prince, ils firent nombre d'Evolutions militaires, le Feu de l'attaque, de la Retraite, le Hakefeuer, tantot toute la Ligne, tantot elle decharga par platons, le Duc de Bragance partit avant la fin. Ils jetterent ensuite des Grenades, dont Me de Sinzendorff eut furieusement peur. En allant j'étois en voiture avec le Prince de Lowenstein et M. d'Enzenberg, en retournant, tout seul. Apres le Souper joué aux Echecs avec le petit Enzenberg. Fort beau, le soir un orage qui n'approche pas.

Le 29. Juin. Le matin il y avoit grande Messe. M^e d'Esterhazy la Polonoise[3] m'invita de l'y suivre. Parlé avec la[4] Nicolas Esterhazy [Weissenwolf] de religion. Elle me raccomonda beaucoup le P. Manzador. Pendant le diner M. de Durazzo arriva. Apres diner a 4^h. et $\frac{1}{2}$ nous allames en 3. Voitures, moi avec Mes Nicolas Est. [Weissenwolf] et Enzenbert pere et fils a 1^h et $\frac{1}{2}$ dis[tance] a Traisburg, village Croate appartenant au Prince a 1$\frac{1}{2}$^{h} d'Edenburg [Oedenburg], le Comte d'Erbvillé [Herbeviller] ferme [?], qu'y a une belle maison et un jardin charmant, avec beaucoup d'eaux[,] nous donna du froid [glace], du Lait, des fruits, je fis seul tout le tour du jardin, qui est tout a fait joli. Nous mangeames dans une Grotte. Ce jardin en terrasse a couté de l'argent immense à M. d'Erbvillé, sa femme est une Hongroise. Durazzo, la Princesse. De la retour parlé a M^e d'Esterhazy qui me temoigna beaucoup de politesse. La Nic. Est. [Weissenwolf] me parla en chemin que mon frere avoit voulu se mesallier en epousant Melle de Chotek, qui Taffé[5] a depuis epousé. Enzenb. me parla d'avoir tiré avec beaucoup de permis toutes les preuves de sa famille, ils ont aussi une Cour feodale en Tyrol. Apres le Souper apres avoir deja pris congé du Prince Me de Sinzendorff m'offrit de me ramener en ville en cas que je voulusse rester aussi [?] demain pour voir la chasse. Lu dans les œuvres de Regnard, ses voyages en Flandre, dans les Paÿs bas. ...

Le 30. Juin. Promené a 6^h. et $\frac{1}{2}$ au jardin que j'ai parvenu entierement. La piece a droite du Chateau avec ses petits bosquets me plut davantage, le Vivier est fort joli, aux Espalier il y a une plante comme la fanesse Arasia. Lu les lettres de Voltaire et de Palissot⁶ ou le premier me plait davantage. M. d'Enzenberg repartit avec son fils. Je fus a la messe avec M̲ᵉˢ de Durazzo et de Sinzendorff, ou je n'entendis que sonner et chuchotter. Apres le diñer on alla au Parc pour la chasse du cerf, j'allois moi avec le Comte d'Erbevillers [Herbeviller], qui s'offrit a me procurer du Vins de Tokay pour 18 ou 20. Ducats. La pluye et l'orage nous atteignant a S. George,⁷ nous tous retirammes dans la maison du Chasseur a l'entrée du Parc, apres qu'il fut passé nous continames notre chemin, on s'arreta souvent au son de la quête mais on n'entendit que rompre les chiens, et ils ne parent pas de cerfs. On se ressembla au RendezVous, un tres joli pavillon bien preferable à ceux de Laxenburg, au plafond il y a le tableau charmant d'un paysage. La vue est tout a fait belle, on voit les tours d'Edenburg [Oedenburg] vers le sudouest, on voit le grand Lac de Neusiedel et au dela Frauenkürchen [Frauenkirchen], toutes les belles allées du Parc. Erbville [Herbeviller] et moi étions seuls en Barotshe [barouche], mais en retournantes nous nous mènans en voiture avec M̲ᵉˡˡᵉ Victoire et sa Demoiselle. Erbeville conta le Roman de l'Isle de la Felicité. Au retour le Prince se trouva tres mal, de sorte⁸ qu'il n'osa pas souper avec. nous. Il avoit voulu diner demain au Parc, mais son indisposition l'empecha. Le soir la Durazzo montra ses bruns cheveux longs, qui lui sont jusqu'aux genoux, elle etoit charmante dans cette figure, sans coiffe. . . .⁹

Le 1. Juillet. Joué aux Echecs avec le Prince de Lowenstein[.] le Prince [Esterházy] ayant bien reposé, diné avec nous. apres le diner j'ai fait une bévue,¹⁰ qui tire son origine de mon caractere ambitieux, et de l'impression que sont encore sur moi les vanités de ce monde. <u>Durazzo</u>. <u>Quelles</u> idées! Cela m'enquieta pour plusieurs jours, j'allois avec M. de Durazzo voir la petite machine semblable a celle de Marly. Complimens de la C. Esterhazy, la Polonoise a M̲ᵉ sa mere, du Prince et de M̲ᵉ de Durazzo au jeune Lamberg¹¹ et a M̲ᵉ de Dietrichstein.¹² A 5ʰ· et ½ je partis d'Eisenstadt avec M̲ᵉ la Comtesse de Sinzendorff, une des femmes de la Princesse alla avec nous. . . .

[3 July, Vienna:] . . . Chez la Princesse Esterhazy arrivée ici d'Eisenstadt avec le Prince, Quinquin [Franz, Count von Esterházy] y parla beaucoup de sa perte au Pharaon [faro] a Laxenburg, ou il a perdu 7500. Ducats. . . .

[4 July, Vienna:] . . . Diné avec mon frère chez la Princesse avec le Duc de Bragance et M. d'Enzenberg.¹³ L'Archeveque y étoit avant table. . . .¹⁴

[Zinzendorf MS.]

Notes:

1 'Mesdames d'Esterházy' probably means Princess Maria Anna (Marchesa Lunati-Visconti, wife of Paul Anton) and Maria Elisabeth (wife of Count Nicolaus). Paul Anton's mother: Princess Maria Octavia. Count Jacob Durazzo and his wife. Carl Joseph Windisch-Graetz (*recte*) and his wife, *née* Maria Josepha, Countess Esterházy. Probably Rosine Veremond, Countess von Sinzendorf-Ernstbrunn, niece of the 'Grand Prior' of Hungary (*vide infra*, p. 360n.) and her husband, Count Franz Wenzel. Löwenstein: probably the head of the cadet (Catholic) branch, later Löwenstein-Wertheim-Rosenberg, since 1711 princes of the Holy Roman Empire. Joseph Keglevich (usual spelling), *Obergespan*. Lamberg: son of Prince Paul Anton's sister, Maria Josepha (1712–56) married in 1733 to Franz Anton, Count von Lamberg-Sprinzenstein (the line has since died out). *Regent* Count von Herbeviller managed the Esterházy estates (*vide supra*, p. 329); his wife was Hungarian. Dr von Molitori (= Franz Joseph von Molitor), was the personal physician to Prince Paul Anton. Francesco, Marchese di Montecuccoli (modern spelling).

2 Zinzendorf was actually converted, with many feelings of guilt (these, incidentally written in German, the language of his Protestant faith, in the *Journal*), to Catholicism in May 1764. Zinzendorf's family, and Count Carl, had been staunch supporters of the Moravian Brotherhood, some members of which settled in North America. As late as January 1800, Zinzendorf still had secret guilty feelings about his conversion.

3 Maria Anna, Countess, *née* Princess Lubomirska, married Nicolaus, Count von Esterházy (1711–64), Austrian Ambassador to Russia. His cousin was Franz, Count von Esterházy, known as 'Quinquin' (a variant of 'chienchien', a term of endearment usually given to children). Franz was Hungarian Court Chancellor.

4 The feminine form 'la' denotes the wife of Count Nicolaus, Maria Elisabeth, *née* Weissenwolf.

5 A collateral branch of the Viscounts Taaffe of Corran and Baron of Ballymote, County Sligo (Ireland): the Austrian cadet branch were counts of the Holy Roman Empire and he was Chamberlain to the Emperor Francis Stephen. Edmund Lodge, *The Peerage of the British Empire*, 3rd ed., London 1834, p. 439.

6 Charles Palissot de Montenoy (1730–1814), whose *Lettres sur de grands philosophes* (1757) were a counter-attack on the Encylopédistes, who were up in arms against his earlier barbs aimed at Rousseau in *Le cercle*.

7 St Georgen is a suburb of Eisenstadt, on the far side of which is the (still extant) hunting preserve of the Esterházy family, surrounded by high walls.

8 Prince Paul Anton's illness seems to have been an internal cancer (of the intestinal tract).

9 Jacob Durazzo's attractive wife was Ernestine Aloisia Ungnad von Weissenwolff (1732–94), whom he had married on 17 March 1750. See plates 23, 24.

10 Zinzendorf does not tell us the nature of this *faux-pas* ('bévue').

11 Prince Esterházy's nephew; see note 1.

12 Identity uncertain: probably the wife of Prince Carl Maximilian who was present at Zinzendorf's first audience with the Empress on 2 January 1764.

13 An old established noble family with estates in Swabia and Tyrol. Possibly Cassian Ignatz Bonaventura, Count von Enzenberg (1709–72), *Landeshauptmann* and *Gouverneur* of Tyrol, is referred to here.

14 Zinzendorf (usually with his brother) dined at the Esterházys on 5 July ('Diné avec mon frere chez le Prince et la Princesse Esterhazy, avec le Prince Joseph Wenzel [Liechtenstein], et les Enzenberg pere et fils et le C. Lamberg …'); on 1 Aug. ('Diné avec mon frere chez le Prince Esterhazy, la première fois depuis sa maladie. Il y avoit les Enzenberg, M⸰ d'Esterhazy, le Grand Prieur [Sinzendorf] et le Prince de Loewenstein …'), and, after an interval, on 19 and 23 Sept. ('Le Prince entra un moment dans la chambre, mais je ne l'ai pas vû, étant sur le balcon …'), 26 Sept. ('Diné seul chez la Princesse … La Princesse alla promener en voiture'), 27 Sept., 30 Sept. ('le Prince … me salua fort gracieusement'), 3 Oct., 4 Oct., etc. Later, after the Prince had died, Zinzendorf continued to attend the salon of the (now Dowager) Princess; he seems not to have been so close to Count (later Prince) Nicolaus.

Although much of the year 1761 centred on Vienna, Prince Paul Anton had elaborate plans for a new theatre in Eisenstadt. The new theatre was to be placed in a glass house in the garden behind the Castle, and work on it continued throughout the summer and autumn of 1761.[1] Obviously it was very expensive, as are all theatres, and was intended not only to be the home of the various strolling players who were engaged for regular appearances of both spoken theatre and opera, but also to be a permanent opera house. Alas, it has totally disappeared.

1 For the benefit of theatrical scholars who may wish to consult the accounts in more detail, we herewith provide a list of their contents. They are all part of the Acta Theatralia of the Esterházy Archives, now in the Music Section of the National Széchényi Library (Országos Széchényi Könyvtár), Budapest.

No. 698/9, No. 1: 2 July 1761, Eisenstadt. Paid to the Viennese theatrical painters and carpenters 134 Fl. 34 xr. Frantz Amon and Johannes Vogt, the latter a Master Carpenter in Eisenstadt, acknowledge receipt of 22 Fl. 63 xr. On the other side of the bill, it is noted that Carl Higsch, Frantz Bratfish and Joseph Jung, all carpenters in Eisenstadt, received 30 xr. daily. Amon, who came from Vienna, received an additional 18 xr. allowance *per diem*. The carpenter apprentices receive 15 xr. daily, Summa 22 Fl. 3 xr. The bill is countersigned by Count Durazzo and Count Herbeviller.

No. 700/1. Carlo Quaglio, Frantz Purgauer, Gefall and Wolfgang Kopp [Köpp] sign receipt of a bill for decoration (painting) work: 98 Fl. 45 xr. Eisenstadt, 12 July 1761. 'j'atteste que tout à eté fait par ordre [du] Prince Esterhasi, et accordé par moj. J: Comte Durazzo. Dieser außigab wurde der Herr obereinnehmer Zoller betzahlen welche in seiner Rechnung vor Kiltig acceptiret wurde. Wienn den 19[?] July 1761 [huge ink splash] Graff v. Herbeviller.' One is fascinated by the appalling German written (personally) by Count von Herbeviller.

No. 702/3. Paint-grinder Joseph Stieber and Baul [Paul] Klein acknowledge receipt of 13 Fl. 46 xr. on 12 July 1761. Justina Köppin [Köpp] receives for sewing scenery à 18 xr. for 10 days, 'Summa 13 Fl. 46 xr.' 'J'atteste que les tout à eté fait par ordre [du] Prince et accordé par moj J: Comte Durazzo. Dieses außigab wurde der Herr Obereinnehmer Zoller betzahlen welche aüßigab in seine Rechnüng von kildig acceptiret wurde.' – signed by Herbeviller, Vienna, 12 July 1761.

No. 704/5, No. 3. 1761, 13 July, Eisenstadt: No. 2 The Viennese painters and carpenters, after-payment of 29 Fl. 42 xr. Quaglio, Johann Gfall, Franz Purgau [Purgauer], Franz Amon acknowledge receipt; countersigned by Administrator Schlanstein.

No. 707/6, No. 3. 1761, 22 August, Eisenstadt: No. 3 Theatrical Painters and Carpenters acknowledge pay and *per diem* allowances totalling 124 Fl. 40 xr. Quaglio acknowledges receipt of work and goods.

No. 708/9, No. 4. 1761, 30 August, Eisenstadt: No. 4 Theatrical Painters and Carpenters acknowledge receipt of 92 Fl. 39½ xr. Quaglio acknowledges receipt of work and goods. The journeyman Purgau [Purgauer] and Kopp, Carpenter Amon and Paint-grinder Johann Michael from Vienna acknowledge receipt.

No. 710/11, No. 5. 1761, 12 Sept., Eisenstadt: No. 5 Theatrical Painters and Carpenters 87 Fl. 30 xr. Quaglio signs as

In the organization of this theatrical work, we note the name of Count Giacomo (Jacob) Durazzo, the famous impresario who managed the Vienna Court Theatre (Burgtheater) so brilliantly and was of crucial importance in encouraging Gluck and Calsabigi (Calzabigi) in their collaboration. Durazzo (1717–94) was a Genoese nobleman who in 1749 became his city's Ambassador at the Court of Vienna and soon

[footnote – *cont.*]

before, and the journeymen and Kopp, the Carpenters Amon and Johann Crißler, and the Paint-grinder Paul Klein from Vienna all sign as usual.

No. 712/3, No. 6. 1761, 12 Sept., Eisenstadt: No. 6 Theatrical Painters and Carpenters 72 Fl. 27 xr. Quaglio engages: one journeyman, Carpenter Franz Amon from Vienna, Paint-grinder Paul Klein, Johann Stüber [Stieber] from Eisenstadt, Christian Kopp from Eisenstadt. Helena and Crystina Köschin [Kösch] helped with sewing and various other work. They receive 18 xr. daily, the painters 20 xr. plus 12 xr. *per diem*, Stüber receives 24 xr.

No. 714/5, No. 7. 1761, 17 Sept., Eisenstadt: No. 7 Theatrical Painters and Carpenters 31 Fl. 45 xr. Quaglio signs as before, Schlanstein countersigns. Quaglio engages the same persons as listed in No. 712/3 except that Christian Kopp is not included.

No. 716/7, No. 8. 1761 17 Sept., Eisenstadt: No. 8 Painter Kopp paid, for work in the new and old theatre, 14 Fl. — xr. (his bill of 17 July). 'daß dieße Tagwerk bey ausbesserung des alten Theatri mit wissen meiner verricht worden attestire Anton Kühnelt / Edmund Schlanstein [mppriae]'; Christian Kopp acknowledges receipt as of 17 July.

No. 718, No. 9. 1761, 11 Sept., Eisenstadt: No. 9 Locksmith Kößler for work in new theatre, 41 Fl. 50 xr. Kößler originally asked for 48 Fl. 14 xr., but Schlanstein (Administrator) deducts 6 Fl. 24 xr. 'for deficiency' ('*für abbruch*'). Kühnelt acknowledges work on 11 July, the sum received and signed by 'Käsler Sebastian, Schloßer und großuhrmachermeister' (Locksmith and Tower Clock Master) on 11 July.

[No. 719 missing, but also in the second number, i.e. No. 8, 9, 10 etc.]

No. 720/1, No. 10. 1761, 16 Sept., Eisenstadt: No. 10 Master Turner, for work on the new theatre, 5 Fl. 8 xr. Ignatius Wottowa acknowledges receipt '16. 7bris [Sept.] 761'. Schlanstein deducts 38 xr., Kühnelt and Quaglio acknowledge the work. The bill was originally for 5 Fl. 46 xr.

No. 722/3, No. 11. Rope-maker's bill: 1761. 16ᵗᵉ Sept. Eisenstatt / No. 11 / Master Rope-Maker for work in new theatre 25 Fl. — xr.' Peter Frinsberg [?] asked for 28 Fl., 34 xr., but Schlanstein deducts 3 Fl. 34 xr. 'for deficiency' ('*für abbruch*'). Quaglio and Kühnelt acknowledge the work, the rope-maker acknowledges receipt of 25 Fl. on '16. 7bris 1761'.

No. 724/5, No. 12. 1761, 17 Sept., Eisenstadt. No. 12 for silver fabric [*Silbertock = Silberdocht*] for the new theatre 12 Fl. — xr. 'Daß zum Wassermachen und Muschelgarniren bey dem Teatro durch Hrn. Quaglio 24 Ellen Sielber Tock in Wien gekauft, und zum Theatro geliefert worden attestire hiermit Eisenstadt den 16ᵗᵉ 7bris 761 Idest 24 Ellen sielber Tock à 30 xr. betrag 12 Fl. Anton Kühnelt / Bauschr. / Edmund Schlanstein / Verwalt. / Io ho Ricevuto Giustamente Carlo Quaglio'. The silver fabric was used to create the effect of water and for ornamental shells. This is the first concrete example we have that plans for Haydn's *Acide* perhaps already existed, because the libretto requires a scene (Scena V) on the banks of the sea, 'Spiaggia di mare ingombra[ta] di s[c]oglie', and now we even see, in the same scene, the necessity for a conch. Galatea sings: 'È pronta al Lido / La marina mia conca ...'. The silver fabric was required for all this.

No. 726/7, No. 13. 1761, 17 Sept., Eisenstadt. No. 13 for the purchase of linen canvas for the new theatre 118 Fl. 33 xr. Mathias Heystinger acknowledges receipt of the sum on 17 Oct. 1761. Quaglio, Schlanstein and Nigst countersign on 16 October.

No. 728/9, No. 14. 1761, 17 Sept., Eisenstadt. No. 14 ironware for the new theatre 64 Fl. 5½ xr. Frantz Hias ac-

knowledges receipt, countersigned by Quaglio, Kühnelt and Schlanstein.

No. 730/3, No. 15. 1761, 23 Sept., Eisenstadt. No. 15 Herr Oberauer for supplying paint for the new theatre 185 Fl. 20 xr. Oberauer acknowledges receipt '23. 7bris 1761' in Eisenstadt. Receipt of paint acknowledged by Carlo Quaglio, Schlanstein and Kühnelt. Someone corrected the bill's 'Idest Fl. 183, 33 xr' and wrote beneath it 'Errores 1. 48 und 185. 20.' The quaint title of this bill: 'Laus Deo aug. 76ı Monath July. Berg Calvāry zum Hoch: Fürstl. Schloß Eisenstatt Specification, Waß von die Wienerische Mahler, in Dem Hochfürstl. Glaß = Hauß allhier zu dem Teatro-Mahlen an End Schittlichen[?] Farb Matteriale Erfolget worden', from which we can see specific reference to the theatre's being in a 'Glaß = Hauß'.

No. 734/5, No. 16. 1761, 23 Sept., Eisenstadt. No. 16 Paints for the new theatre 7 Fl. 44 xr. Receipt signed 'Oberauer Franz, Eisenstadt, 23 7bris 1761.' Carlo Quaglio, Schlanstein, Kühnelt and Johann Bobitsch acknowledge receipt of the paints.

No. 736/7, 1761, 8 Oct., Eisenstadt. No. 17 For the Grenadiers for daily work in the new theatre, 17 Fl. 16 xr. Corporal Dräxler, Joseph Arbinger, Jacob Miller, Johannes Oberman work for 148 days on the orders of the Prince 'with the painters in the Eisenstadt Court Garden at the New Theatre'. The bill dated '16. 7bris 1761', receipt 8 Oct. 1761. Chief Receiver Zoller and Dräxler sign the receipt, which was written in Vienna and paid in Eisenstadt.

No. 738/9, No. 18. 1761. Master Potter Ferdinand Rinisch acknowledges receipt of 42 xr. for paint-jars; the bill dated 4 July 1761, the receipt '23. Xbris 76ı [Dec.]'.

No. 740/1, No. 19. 1761, 23 Sept., Eisenstadt. Paints for repairing the decorations for the fireworks, 118 Fl. 15 xr. Frantz[!] Oberauer signs the receipt, Eisenstadt, '23. 7bris 76ı'. The bill was issued in August. Kopp (as the painter), Kühnelt (as Works Director), Schlanstein (Administrator) and Oberauer (as deliverer of paints) acknowledge (in the first three cases) receipt of the goods, Oberauer the cash.

No. 696/7 is a general summary of nineteen bills for work on the new theatre, and reads as follows:
[No. 696/7:] 1761 / No. 20 / Elenchus über vorstehende / 19. Stck. Innlaagen / 1083 Fl. 11 xr. / [overleaf:] Elenchus / Uber die gemacht- und bezahlte ausgaaben wegen dem / Neuen Theatro. / No. 1: Denen Mahlern und Tischlern in 3.

	Auszügen	134.34
2:	detti	29.42
3:	detti	124.40
4:	detti	92.39½
5:	detti	87.30
6:	detti	72.27
7:	detti	31.45
8:	dem Mahler Kopp	14.—
9:	dem Schlossermeister	41.50
10:	dem Traxlermeister	5.8
11:	dem Saillermeister	25.—
12:	vom Silbertock	12.—
13:	von Leinwath	118.33
14:	von Eisenwahren	64. 5½
15:	von Farben	185.20
16:	von Mahler Materialien	7.44
17:	von Tagwerk	17.16
18:	von Farbentögl	— 42
19:	von mehrmahlen Farben	18.15
	Summa	1083.11

[A. T. 108, nos. 694–741, EH, Budapest]

became a protégé of Chancellor Prince Kaunitz. In 1752 Count Durazzo was made 'Cavaliere' to the Chief Intendant of the Court Theatre, and in July 1754 Durazzo himself became Chief Intendant. One of his first acts had been to see that Gluck was engaged 'zur Componierung der Theatral- und Akademiemusik'. In 1760, Durazzo was created 'Cavaliere di musica' at the Viennese Court, which meant that he was now in charge of the *Hofcapelle* (Court orchestra), whose conductor was Haydn's teacher, Georg Reutter, Jr.

When Joseph II (Crown Prince) married Princess Isabella of Parma, Gluck was commissioned to write the opera to celebrate the occasion, which was Giovanni Battista Migliavacca's *Tetide* (8 October 1760, Vienna). It was perhaps on this occasion that Prince Paul Anton became acquainted with the work of the librettist who would be chosen, no doubt with Durazzo's approval, for Haydn's first Italian opera, *Acide*.

When Prince Paul Anton decided to build a new theatre at Eisenstadt, it was natural for him to call on this successful and experienced Genoese nobleman, with whom Haydn was on excellent terms. In a letter to Artaria, his publishers, of 20 March 1783, Haydn writes, '... I value Count Durazzo's house above all others'.[1] Both Haydn and the Esterházys remained firm friends with the Count, who in 1764 became Austrian Ambassador to the *Serenissima* at Venice. It is to this astute connoisseur that we owe the great collection of Vivaldi's music, and especially his church music, which is now in the University Library in Turin.[2]

Prince Paul Anton, by now very ill indeed, was in Vienna during the month of October, and Count Zinzendorf dined with them on the 6th, 7th, 8th, 9th, 12th, 14th, 16th, 18th, 21st, 23rd, 25th, etc. He was by now a regular 'member of the family'. His *Journal* once again provides a fascinating detail which clears up part of a great mystery as far as the musical household of the Palais in the Wallnerstraße is concerned. In the musical section *infra* (pp. 522 and 538) we shall see that Haydn composed at least one and probably two works in 1761 using clarinets, instruments which, however, never figure in the lists of musicians or in the bills of the Esterházy Archives. Yet here is authentic evidence that clarinets were played at Prince Paul Anton's concerts:

> [6 October 1761:] ... Diné chez la Princesse [Esterházy] avec mon frere, l'Eveque de Neytra qui est un vieux C. Esterhazy de 74 ans, le C: Oginsky, Polonois[,] le C: Keglevitch e Mᵉ d'Esterhazy. Apres table le Prince entra tout habillé, cependant extremement défait, il y eut Concert chez lui, Oginsky joua de clarinettes des pièces de sa propre composition. ...

Perhaps, then, these mysterious works for clarinet[3] by Haydn were actually composed for Count Oginsky 'the Pole', who played the instrument. The incident also illustrates an important point: Esterházy's band was sometimes reinforced by players from outside. A further comment on the progress of Paul Anton's ghastly illness occurs ten days later in Zinzendorf's Diary: '[16 October:] ... le Prince sortit après midi, il a l'air d'un mort ...'.

---

1 See *Haydn at Eszterháza 1766–1790*, p. 473.
2 The Durazzo Collection later formed two private collections, one by Mauro Foà and one by Renzo Giordano. For Durazzo, see Robert Haas, *Gluck und Durazzo im Burgtheater*, Potsdam 1925; and Rudolf Gerber, *Christoph Willibald Ritter von Gluck*, Potsdam 1941, pp. 52, 54ff. For the Vivaldi connection, see Alan Kendall, *Vivaldi*, London 1978, pp. 102ff.
3 The clarinet was circulating in the concerts of the Viennese nobility by 1764. Zinzendorf reports on 12 March: '... Diné avec mon frere, Mᵉ de Schoenborn et M. de Belgiojoso chez Mᵉ de Paar, M. etant malade. On joua dans sa chambre des airs d'opera Comique Francois avec les Clarinettes et des Hautbois. Cette musique donc tendre et pathétique qui approchoit si bien de la musique d'eglise de Herrnhuth [seat of the *Herrnhuter*, or Moravian Brotherhood, and its founder, Nicolaus Ludwig, Count Zinzendorf, Carl's uncle and the composer of many hymns for the Congregation] me toucha jusqu'aux larmes et m'attendrit extrémement ...'. 25 March: '... Dela j'allois chez M. de Paar ... Il y eut encore de belle musique des Clarinettes ...'. Paar = Wenzel Johann Joseph, Count (later Prince) and his wife, *née* Countess Esterházy.

In February 1761, Raniero di Calsabigi (1714–95), a fascinating adventurer, operatic reformer and poet, arrived in Vienna. The first result of Calsabigi's collaboration with Gluck occurred when Calsabigi collaborated with composer and choreographer on *Le festin de pierre*, a tragic ballet on the subject of Don Juan. The choreography was by the Florentine, D. M. G. Angiolini (1731–1803), a pupil of the former Ballet Master of the Vienna Court Theatre, Franz Hilverding von Waven (1710–68), who in turn was steeped in the new, dramatic ballet style of the great J. J. Noverre (1727–1810). He officially signed the elaborate foreword to the first libretto (facsimile in new Bärenreiter score). Angiolini was also to do the choreography in *Orfeo* (1762).

Don Juan was first performed on 17 October 1761 at the Burgtheater in Vienna, where it received the title 'Don Juan ou le Festin de Pierre'. It followed a performance of *Le joueur* by Jean François Regnard (1655–1709). A month later, at a subsequent performance at the Kärntnerthortheater, *Don Juan* ended with the whole theatre going up in flames. From the preface that Angiolini wrote to the original libretto, we learn that the décor was by Giovanni Maria ('Giulio III'). Quaglio; Angiolini also has much praise for the music by Gluck. G. M. Quaglio[1] was the father of Carlo, who worked for Prince Paul Anton (*supra*).

Apart from much beautiful, indeed exquisite, music, it is the final Larghetto followed by a Chaconne (Allegro non troppo, in D minor), describing Don Juan's descent into hell, which is the central part of this historically important and musically fascinating score. Gluck later used it as an entr'acte in the Paris version of *Orphée*, and in this slightly different orchestration it became one of its composer's most famous pieces; and rightly so, but we miss in this later version the wonderfully dramatic Larghetto and also the leaner orchestration of the Allegro non troppo in the 1761 score. The Chaconne form, which is characteristically used to end ballets and even operas at this period (see even the Ballet Music to Mozart's *Idomeneo*, K.467), provides the base for what was, for many people in the audience that October night in 1761, the first piece of music to describe real fear.

It is usually difficult to mark the beginning of a new school, or movement, with one specific work; but in the case of *Don Juan*, this final Chaconne is without any question the father of the *Sturm und Drang* movement which in a few years would flood Austrian music.[2] Even the key, D minor, was always to assume special qualities in the *Sturm und Drang*, its predecessors and its successors (e.g. J. S. Bach's Harpsichord Concerto in D minor, Haydn's Symphony No. 26, C. P. E. Bach's Harpsichord Concerto in D minor, Mozart's own *Don Giovanni* as well as other works, e.g. the Quartet, K.421, or the Piano Concerto, K.466). Gluck's music not only started a movement of immense importance, but it was quite literally copied. We find Luigi Boccherini writing as the Finale of his Symphony 'La casa del diavolo' an introduction followed by an allegro that, with some additions and interesting transformations (a description of which space forbids), is lifted straight from *Don Juan*. An even more unlikely tribute comes from Russia, where we find whole passages from Gluck's *Don Juan* (*via* the *Orphée* adaptation of Gluck himself) in a work by Evstignei Ipatovič Fomin (1761–1800) – *Orfeo i Euridica Melo-Dramma: Posto in Musica da E. I. Fomine Acade: Filarmonico à Pietro-borgo* (autograph title), first performed at St Petersburg on 13 January 1792 – thus carrying this symbolic use of demonic D minor to the far north

---

1 On the Quaglio family, see *Enciclopedia dello spettacólo VIII*, 616–22.
2 On *Sturm und Drang*, see *Haydn at Eszterháza 1766–1790*, Chapter Four.

a whole generation later. Fomin (the 'e' was to Italianize his name) was born the year *Don Juan* was composed.[1]

From Zinzendorf's Diary we are informed as follows:

[17 October 1761] ... Au Spectacle on dansa le Joueur, et puis un ballet de Pantómimes, le festin de Pierre. Le sujet en est extremement triste, lugubre et effroyable[.] Don Juan porte une Serenade a sa Maitresse et entre chez elle[.] le Commandeur le trouve sur le fait, se bat avec lui en duel, est blessé mortellement, et tombe sur le théâtre[.] On l'emporte, Don Juan entre avec des dames et danse un ballet, puis on se met a souper, sur ses entrefaites arrive le Commandeur en statüe, tous les convives se sauvant, Don Juan s'en moque, et imite tous les mouvemens du spectre, il monte un cheval molasse sur le théâtre, Don Juan s'en moque encore, le spectre s'en va[?]et tout d'un coup l'enfer paroit, les furies dansent avec des torches allumés et tourmentent Don Juan, dans le fond on voit un beau feu d'artifice, qui represente les feux de l'enfer, on voit voler des Diables, le ballet dure trop longtems, enfin les diables emportent Don Juan et se precipitent avec lui dans un gouffre de feu. Tout cela etoit tres bien executé, la musique fort belle.

[Zinzendorf MS.]

We read of the continued success of the new Ballet in the entry for 2 November: '... tout le monde étant à la Comedie allemande ou on donne le Festin de Pierre ...'; and Zinzendorf reports on the conflagration which the fireworks in the piece caused on the next day, when the Kärntnerthortheater burned down, killing the cashier and his wife: '... on nous dit que le theâtre allemande bruloit. En effet nous vimes le Ciel tout rouge de ce coté.' Later they climbed on the ramparts to see the spectacle and found the Emperor there, too (Zinzendorf MS.).

As might have been expected, there arose considerable opposition to the Durazzo-Calsabigi-Gluck operations, and this opposition was headed by none other than the famous poet Pietro Metastasio and the equally famous composer J. A. Hasse, both now settled in Vienna. The Durazzo faction received support, however, from an unexpected direction: the Italian composer Tommaso Traetta (1727–79), who himself was involved in an operatic reform in Parma. Traetta, whose music made a definite impression on Haydn,[2] now arrived in Vienna and produced *Armida* on 2 January 1761. The libretto had been originally written by Durazzo and was rendered into verse by none other than Migliavacca, whose literary presence in Vienna was thus once again brought to Haydn's and the Esterházy family's notice. (Traetta returned to Vienna two years later to conduct his masterpiece, *Ifigenia in Tauride*. It is entirely possible that Haydn actually met this excellent Italian composer, either in 1761 or in 1763.)

What do we know of Haydn's life as a house officer with Prince Paul Anton, apart from the documents in the Esterházy Archives (which, however revealing in their details, tell us nothing of the composer before the first surviving autograph letter of 1765)? As it happens, we have, probably transmitted by Haydn's pupil Ignaz Pleyel, a curious anecdote from Framery's *Notice sur Joseph Haydn* (Paris 1810). After noting that a 'riche seigneur de la cour' (probably Morzin is meant) assisted the composer in

1 *Don Juan* was first published in *DTÖ*, Band 60 (1923), ed. Robert Haas. A new edition of the work, by Richard Engländer, is included in the new Gluck *Sämtliche Werke*, II, 1 (Bärenreiter Verlag). On Fomin see *MGG* vol. 4, cols. 490–2 (G. Abraham, without any reference to Gluck's influence).
2 For some startling Traetta reminiscences in Haydn's operas, see *Haydn at Eszterháza 1766–1790*, p. 272.

gaining 'une réputation si brillante', and that Haydn entered the service of the Esterházys, Framery continues:

Son entrée chez ce seigneur fut marquée par un trait de caractère qui honore tous ceux qui professent l'art musical. Les premiers jours où il fut admis à la table des officiers du palais le maitre d'hôtel était absent pour cause de maladie; le secrétaire fit mettre Haydn à côté de lui, à la place que ce maître d'hôtel occupait ordinairement. Peu de jours après cet homme, rétabli, vient pour se mettre à table à sa place habituelle; il la trouve occupée par le couvert du nouveau commensal. 'Qui a osé, dit-il, faire placer ici ce jeune homme? – C'est moi, répond le secrétaire. – Vous! est-il possible? Comment, un faiseur de notes, qui arrive à peine dans cette maison, jouirait d'une telle distinction, au détriment de celui qui sert le prince depuis longues années? – Partout, dit Haydn, où il y a un maître de chapelle, il doit occuper la première place: celle-ci m'a été donnée, et je la garderai.' Le maître d'hôtel, très-piqué, prend le couvert du compositeur, va le porter à la dernière extrémité de la table, et revient se mettre à la place qu'il exigeait: le secrétaire, sans dire un mot, va s'asseoir à côté de celle où le couvert d'Haydn vient d'être mis; les autres officiers le suivent, chacun selon son rang, de telle manière que le maître d'hôtel se trouve tout naturellement le dernier; il sort furieux pour aller porter sa plainte au prince.

Cette querelle, qui dut avoir dans un pays aussi esclave de l'étiquette tout autrement d'importance qu'elle n'en aurait eu ici, affligea le prince assez sérieusement. Le lendemain il fait demander notre jeune maître pour lui adresser des reproches. 'Vous avez offensé, lui dit-il, un vieux serviteur que je considère, et qui m'est attaché depuis longtemps; je désire que la concorde règne dans ma maison; vous n'auriez pas dû la troubler dès votre arrivée.' Le maître de chapelle répéta d'abord ce qu'il avait dit la veille des prérogatives et des droits attachés à ce titre; puis il ajouta: 'Mon prince, j'ai eu plus d'une fois l'honneur d'être admis à la table de grands seigneurs; je n'y ai jamais vu de maîtres d'hôtel, si ce n'est pour servir; quelques-uns m'ont servi comme les autres; jamais je ne leur ai rendu la pareille. Je n'ai point eu l'intention d'offenser votre homme; mais sa prétention, et sa manière de la soutenir, étaient une insulte qu'il était impossible à vôtre maître de chapelle de supporter.' Le prince sourit, et promit d'arranger cette affaire: en effet, il fit sans doute entendre raison à son homme; car dès le lendemain il prit une autre place, et il ne fut plus question de rien.

It would appear, then, that Haydn's 'protector' was none other than the man who drew up his contract, Johann Stifftel (Stiftel), who signs himself 'Secretaire'. The Haus-Hofmeister (*Maître d'hôtel*) at the time (May 1761) was one J. Neumann.[1] This episode is revealing in that it shows that the courtier Haydn even at this stage had enough self-confidence to assert his (as he considered) proper position in the *Hofstaat*.

Operatic events in Vienna must be temporarily put aside for life at the Esterházy Court. It was seen that as a result of the engagements, some of the Eisenstadt musicians, including Anton Kühnel, had been dismissed. Now, however, we read:

No. 445 de anno 1761: Princely Decretation ddọ [*de dato*] 15th Juny according to which Anton Khunelt [*sic*] is permitted to retain his Convention [contract] in the Choir and as Building Clerk as before.

[PCDI, EH, Budapest, Országos Levéltár]

---

1 Information kindly provided by Dr Janos Harich in a letter of 8 August 1978. Neumann was also involved in the exequies of Princess Maria Octavia in 1762; little is known about him.

No doubt it was reconsidered because, with the body of the *Capelle* remaining in Vienna, Kühnel as double-bass player was essential for performing church music at Eisenstadt and, if dismissed, would have to be replaced. Two more such entries may be noted:

No. 450 de anno 1761: Gent^le Com[missi]ons Resolution dd^o 28^m 8bris [Oct.] according to which the widow of Tenor Huszar is to be given alms each year.

No. 453 Gent^le Comons decretation dd^o 28^m 8bris 7̄6̄1 according to which the former Choir Violoncellist Schtettner [Gstettner] shall receive the same *Deputat* cabbage, beetroots and pig each year.

No. 454 Gent^le Comons Resolution dd^o 12^m Xbris according to which the widow of Tenor Husar shall be granted *titulo pensionis* 100 bundles of kindling wood annually in quarterly instalments.   [PCDI, ibid.]

The alms for widow Hus(z)ar are also seen in the list of the *Herrschaft* Eisenstadt for 1764 (*vide supra*, p. 337). All these entries show a certain humane treatment of widows and former officials (retired) which was atypical of many great houses and certainly ahead of the age in what we would now call a social conscience.

Chronicle 1762

On 21 February, Paul Anton for some reason demanded to see Haydn's contract. On the contract of the bassoon player Hinterberger we find the following note: 'NB: Des Capel-Meisters Hayden Convention, und Instruction haben des Fürsten Durchl. zu sich genommen in Wienn den 21ten Feby 7̄6̄2.'[1] In view of the fact that one of Prince Nicolaus's first acts was to raise substantially Haydn's salary, perhaps Paul Anton had intended to do this after having heard a whole season of Haydn's compositions, including Symphonies Nos. 6–8; and thus Nicolaus was fulfilling his brother's intention.

We now come to the first extant letter written by Haydn; it was probably also the first official letter sent in his capacity as head of the instrumental players and *Capelle*:

[To Melchior Griessler, Eisenstadt. *German*. From the contemporary copy in the Esterházy Archives]
    Letter which the *Capel-Meister* was ordered to write to Melchior Griessler, bass singer and violinist, sent from Vienna on 4th March 7̄6̄2.

    Most noble,
    respected Sir [2]
    Inasmuch as His Princely Highness was here in Vienna for the whole of the last summer, the services rendered by you, Sir, consisted only in the choir musique there [at Eisenstadt]; but now His Highness, according to a decree [*Convention*]

---

1 'NB: *Capel-Meister* Haydn's Convention and Instruction have been taken by His Princely Highness in Vienna [etc.]'. A.M. 274, No. 1036–8.
2 'Wohl Edler / Geehrter Herr'; 'Edler' (noble) was a polite form of address which did not, of course, imply that the recipient was of noble birth. One feature of this translation must be mentioned: all the 'you', 'you, Sir' were in the original German in the third person singular, i.e. 'the services rendered by the gentleman . . .', '. . . wishes to have the gentleman a part of . . .', 'he' for 'you', and so on. Prince Anton addressed Haydn in the third person, 'He will write to Griessler', and it seems that the Esterházy order of hierarchy required Haydn to address his musicians in the third person, too, at least in an official letter.

issued, wishes to have you as a part of his chamber musique, and thus needs you here [in Vienna]; and therefore I have received the order to write you, Sir, that upon receipt of this letter, you are to come here, also for several months (this is to be understood as meaning the length of time before the high *Herrschaft* departs for Eisenstadt), for which period there will be provided lodging and food.

Which, as a result of the order given to me, I herewith communicate and remain,

Your most obedient Servant,
Heydn *Capell-Meister* [*sic*]

[EH, Budapest, Országos Levéltár, P. 131/5 (old Fasc. 715): 'Prothocollum Missilium . . . de Anno 1758 usqᵘ Messem Martem 1762', f. 1660f. Valkó I, 536; not in CCLN].

We may now follow the final weeks of Prince Paul Anton's life, as described in the Diary of the family's friend, Count Zinzendorf:

[9 March:] . . . Diné avec mon frere chez la Princesse Esterhazy, qui etoit tres triste a cause du Prince. . . .
[11 March:] . . . Le pauvre Prince Esterhazy etant tres mal, nous ne prenons pas diner chez la Princesse. . . .
[12 March:] . . . la Khevenhuller [probably a daughter of Prince Johann Joseph, the major domo at the Court of Vienna] . . . la petite etoit triste au sujet du pauvre Prince, qui se meurt, on s'attend qu'il mourra la nuit. . . .
[18 March:] Le pauvre Prince Esterhazy est mort ce matin a 3ʰ· La Princesse a quitté la maison hier au soir [insertion with caret: 'cela n'est pas rien'] et s'est refugiée chez sa belle mere [Princesse Maria Octavia]. . . .
[23 March:] . . . A 10ʰ· j'allois a S. Michel [parish church of the district where Paul Anton lived] entendre les obsèques du P. Esterhazy, j'y restois jusqu'a 12. a coté de Keglevich, puis entre Czobor et le P. de Deux Ponts [Duke Friedrich, Count Palatine of Zweibrücken-Birkenfeld]. Il y avoit une bière intournée de cierges, et les armes Suspendues dessus devant le Maitre autel, les plus proches parentes a droite, les plus proches parens [*sic*] a gauche, les plus eloignées dans les bancs, en manteau noir et en voiles. . . .
[13 April:] . . . A 8ʰ· j'allois pour la première fois depuis la mort du Prince chez la Princesse Esterhazy douairiere. . . .[1]

[Zinzendorf MS.]

It is not known when Paul Anton's successor, Prince Nicolaus, decided to retain the musicians, but we may assume that he reassured Haydn on this point at an early opportunity. During the period of mourning, nothing except religious music could be played officially.

Nicolaus proved among many other qualities to be an excellent head-of-court. No doubt his military training assisted him in developing the qualities of a leader, but by the time of his death in 1790 he had, by wise financial management, greatly increased the wealth of the family estates. Part of this successful management depended on having scrupulously honest, efficient, humane officials, and it is most

1 Zinzendorf became a kind of legal adviser to the Dowager Princess. He translated into French(!) the marriage contract between her and Prince Paul Anton (it had taken place in Lunéville but was probably written in Latin; Diary entry, 29 April). On 6 Sept. Zinzendorf 'Ecrit pour la Princesse la lettre a Mᵉ d'Herbvillé' (Countess Herbeviller). The following day 'La Princesse me donna encore davantage de ses papiers le contrat de mariage de 1734, la convention de 1737 annulée'. He remained her firm friend until her death in 1782. Prince Paul Anton's sickness is reported at length January and February; we have begun this part of the Diary in March after a slight improvement on the part of the patient (13 Feb.: 'Le Prince se porte un peu mieux mais il est dans un assoupissement terrible'), which proved to be only of a very temporary nature.

revealing to study a printed document on this general subject which Prince Nicolaus issued at Eszterháza in 1777. We quote extracts:

Instructionsmaßige Verordnungen, nach welchen unsere Beamte, und in jährlichen Convention stehende Diener dieses Eisenstadter, und Lendváer Districts sich in Ansehung ihrer allseitig = pflichtmaßigen Verhaltnuß, und anhabender Schuldigkeit ins künftige zu reguliren wissen werden.

[Summary]

1. No official or servant may retain more than the permitted number of cattle, for otherwise the grazing ground of the poor subjects will be reduced.
2. Bills must be dealt with properly and punctually.
3. No official may accept perquisites on earnest-money from subjects, for they as well as the *Herrschaft* would be harmed thereby.
4. Officials should use their own horses and not use or pay the relays, since the officials receive oats for their horses.
5. Firewood and building-wood must be taken from the felled trees of the forestry department, until the supply is used up; not until then should new wood be felled, and for that purpose unfruitful trees should be chosen. Building-wood must be registered, and if more is required, the Chief Hunter will then decide where the new wood is to be felled, taking care that the subjects do not have too great a distance to drive with the horses, and also that the forest is not damaged.
6. Forestry officials must be instructed as to which trees may be felled and which allowed to grow.
7. Locks on the granaries must be subject to control.
8. Intoxication is the greatest vice.
9. Only the hunters may retain hunting dogs, and no one may hunt without permission.
10. Annual closing accounts must be delivered punctually.
11. Neither servants nor officials may remain away overnight without permission.
12. All buildings should be repaired in time, before the damage becomes too costly or is irreparable.
13. Fish and tortoise ponds should be made in view of the growing expenses of the latter. They already cost 30 to 45 xr. a pair.
14. Judges and Church Elders must deliver their accounts in the presence of an administrator, so that the subjects are not treated detrimentally.
15. Officials who think for themselves should be rewarded.
16. Minerals and marble should be looked for in mountainous districts.
17. All farm work must be organized in good time, so that the subjects have enough time to till their own fields.
18. Threshing must be done cleanly so that no grain remains behind.
19. Fruit must be stored properly.
20. Thefts during threshing time must be prevented.
21. Villeinage is not to be wasted, and is to be precisely controlled.
22. All manorial income must be precisely registered and sent to the *Regent*.
23. Rights of pasture must be protected.
24. The bee-hives are to be counted.
25. All contracts are to be registered and reported to the Rental Office.
26. An annual report is to be made on the profit from sheep and cattle.
27. Granaries must be kept clean so that good-quality crops may be sown.
28. Stewards and cash-keepers should control how much is growing in the fields and send in specimens of the fruit.

29. Stewards and cash-keepers should control the income from titheable grain.

30. Stewards must keep the stalls locked until such time as the Rent Master or Administrator comes to organize the sale.

31. The sale of fruit must be supervised and quarterly accounts rendered.

32. Officials must be polite to everyone.

33. The I.R. *Urbarium* (Manurability) must be examined.

34. Officials must lead God-fearing lives.

35. All princely orders in copies are to be read allowed and proclaimed.

Eszterhaz, 3rd Novembris 1777   Nicolaus Fürst Esterházy.

[Copy of this printed pamphlet, 30 × 20 cm., in EH, Budapest, Országos Levéltár: Izemelyzeti ügyer 1767– 1909/Va/727 + 408/a No. 695]

Although far in the future, this remarkable document shows in a vivid way the problems (and the suggested solutions thereof) that any huge estate in those days entailed. It also suggests that by 1762 Nicolaus, who was a mature man in his forties when he succeeded, already had in his mind many of these rules and regulations for his officials. The successful implementation of those thirty-five points – and we may assume that these orders were in large measure followed – certainly contributed to the steadily growing wealth and efficiency of the Esterházy estates.

The first large-scale performance at Eisenstadt during this period of which we have precise record also marks the end of a long tradition: on 9 April, the last of the long series of Good Friday Oratorios by Werner was given, and we must assume that Haydn prepared, or at least participated in, the performance. The libretto reads as follows:

1762. ORATORIUM. Antiochus der wütende Tyrann, und Vorbild des künftigen Antichrist, bestürmet den geheiligsten Tempel Gottes, erwürget auch einen grossen Theil der Israeliten. Judas Machabeus, der Helden-müthige Krieges-Fürst, besieget ihn hingegen durch die mächtige Hand des Herrn. Allen derley stolzirenden Feinden zu einem schröckbaren Beyspiel. Abgesungen in dem Hochfürstl. Estorasischen Schloss bey dem Heil. Grab, durch dero Hof-Capelln zu Eysenstadt den 9. April 1762. Durch Gregorium Josephum Werner, Hochfürstl. Capell-Meistern. Neustadt gedruckt bey Joseph Fritsch.
[Copy formerly in EH, Budapest; Horányi (Ger.), 204f.; J. Harich 'Szenische Darstellungen', op. cit., p. 128]

This is one of the scores that Haydn owned; Werner had composed it in 1757 (signing it 'A.M.D.G. 16 May 757').

We cannot be sure of Haydn's whereabouts at this period, but he may have heard some of the following performances in Vienna, as reported in the *Wienerisches Diarium*:

[No. 30] Vienna, 14 April 1762. The 9th which was Good Friday at the Church of St John [Johannes Kirche] here, there was produced a new Oratorio on Christ's Martyrdom by the composer Cherzelli, executed by good forces in the presence of many of the nobility & gentry.
[No. 34] Vienna, 28 April 1762. . . . Yesterday evening in the presence of the All Highest, both I.R. Majesties and their Royal Highnesses, was produced a new

Opera with the title Il Trionfo di Clelia in the French Theatre next to the Hofburg ... [music by Christoph Georg Wagenseil].

[No. 39] Vienna, 15 May 1762. ... in the usual attendance of our Cardinals and the Papal Monsignor Nuncio, was an excellent *Tafel-music*, at which the famous violinist Herr Pugnani was heard; and there was a public banquet.

Gaetano Pugnani (1731–98), a handsome portrait of whom was recently (1977) sold at Christie's,[1] was the successful violin virtuoso and composer, some of whose works were wrongly attributed to Haydn. We do not know whether the two men met, now or in 1796.

Several months having elapsed since Prince Paul Anton's death in March, Prince Nicolaus now began to reorganize his *Capelle*. In the middle of his plans, however, his (and Paul Anton's) mother, Princess Maria Octavia, died on 24 April. By this time, plans for Nicolaus's official entry as Lord of the *Herrschaft* Eisenstadt had been made, and on 17 May 1762 this great event occurred. It is not known in which particular way this festival was celebrated by the *Capelle*, but it is now considered that the Haydn *Motetto di Sancta Thecla*, the authentic parts of which (signed by the composer himself on the bass part) we were fortunate enough to find in Eisenstadt in the organ-loft of St Martin's (1951), was a re-working of a Latin (or, as we suggest, an Italian) Cantata composed for Prince Nicolaus's entry into Eisenstadt on 17 May 1762. It is also possible that Haydn composed his early *Te Deum* for this occasion, though there are several other events for which this (alas undated) piece of early church music can have been written.

On 12 May, Italian *Komödianten* came to stay at the Inn 'Zum Greifen'. As this is a visit of some importance and is directly connected with Haydn, we must note that the Italian Company came from Pressburg and was under the direction of a talented and versatile man named Girolamo Bon (also: Hieronymus Bon, Le Bon, Buon, Monsieur Bunon, etc.). His career has been summed up in *Haydn at Eszterháza 1766–1790* (pp. 64f.), so that here we may note only that he was a Venetian and married to Rosa, *née* Ruvinetti. Bon was a theatrical jack-of-all-trades, an excellent stage designer and painter, and in addition a composer (*Sei facili Sonate*, Nuremberg 1752) and writer of libretti and impresario. His career had taken him all over Germany and for many years to Russia, where his daughter Anna appears to have been born. Both ladies of the family were singers.

The Bon family's connection with Pressburg seems to date from as early as 1741, when we find him listed as 'Hieronymi Bon, Impresario der Wellischen [Italian] Opera', while in 1759 and 1760 he and his whole family appeared in the cast, as indicated in the libretti of the operas *Leucippo* and *Don Calandrano*, where we find them as 'Anna, Rosa [&] Girolamo Bon'. In the printed libretto of *Don Calandrano*, dedicated to Carl Erdödy-Pálffy, he signs himself as 'Girolamo Bon, pittore Architetto e Direttore dell'Opera'. In the 1759 Opera (*Leucippo*) Carl Friberth was one of the tenors; since he had been engaged by Prince Paul Anton on 1 January 1759, his appearance at Pressburg must have been by special arrangement. In *Don Calandrano* of 1760, Leopold Dichtler appears as one of the two tenors; Dichtler joined the *Capelle* on 1 March 1763. Now it seems that this Italian company at Pressburg was engaged by Prince Nicolaus to come to Eisenstadt, where they settled as 'Welsche Komödianten' at the 'Greifen' (Griffin) Inn, remaining there to the end of June. Apparently they were

---

1 Christie's Catalogue for the Sale of 19 July 1977, item 32, reproduced as the frontispiece. Spurious Haydn actually composed by Pugnani: see Landon, *Supplement*, p. 57. The standard work on Pugnani is Zschinky-Troxler's *Gaetano Pugnani*, Berlin 1939 (Atlantis Verlag). Pugnani was again in Vienna in 1790: see *Haydn: the Years of 'The Creation' 1796–1800*, p.96.

a great success, for on 1 July Prince Nicolaus engaged the Bon family. The contract,[1] which we quote here in its original (unpublished) German, specifies that Bon, his wife and daughter are engaged under the following conditions: (1) He will accomplish painting work, especially for the theatre; (2) his wife will be a member of the chamber and choir music and be subordinate to our Capel-Meister, singing what is given her; further details are not considered necessary, their discipline and diligence are relied upon, and they should conduct themselves honestly, quietly, peacefully and as Christians. (3) For this Le Bon will receive lodgings, 10 fathom cords of wood and (4) 600 gulden p.a. or 50 Fl. Rhenish monthly. (5) They receive 10 *Eimer*, Eisenstädter size, of wine, Eisenstadt 1 July 1762.[2]

Haydn composed his first Italian stage music for this visiting troupe: the autograph is entitled 'Arie per la Comedia <u>Marchese</u> [middle:] In Nomine Domini [right:] Giuseppe Haydn / 7̅6̅2̅' (G. Feder thinks it is unclear whether Haydn wrote '7̅6̅2̅' or '7̅6̅3̅' but while the autograph shows some correction in the last digit, on our most recent visit to Budapest in June 1978 we again examined the autograph and believe that Haydn's first date was '7̅6̅1̅' and the *final* date was, in fact, '7̅6̅2̅'; on the question of the watermarks, *vide infra*, pp. 426ff.) In May 1761, Haydn's own *Capelle* contained

Discant voices: Anna Maria Scheffstos(s) and Barbara Fux.

Alto: Eleonore Jäger (Jaeger).

Tenor: Carl Friberth.

Bass: Melchior Griessler.

Considering that Leopold Dichtler was part of the Pressburg Troupe in 1760, we may assume that he was with them in Eisenstadt in 1761. Otherwise, we have no list of the company when it was at Eisenstadt. However, if we examine Haydn's score, we must come to the same conclusion as Bartha-Somfai, that the titles and roles may in some cases indicate the actual names of the singers.

Aria No. 1: 'S.^{ra} Barbara' (Barbara Fux?), soprano.

Aria No. 2: 'Colombina' (from the traditional *commedia dell'arte*), soprano.

Aria No. 3: 'Leopoldo' (Leopold Dichtler of the Pressburg Troupe?), tenor.

Aria No. 4: 'Scanarello' (*commedia dell'arte*), soprano.

Aria No. 8: 'Pantalone' (*commedia dell'arte*), soprano.

Aria No. 9: 'Sign^{ia} Augusta' (member[3] of Pressburg Troupe?), soprano.

---

1 The original of this contracts reads:

> Im heute unten eingesezten Tag und / Jahr ist der Mahler Le Bon samt seinem / Weib und Tochter auf ein Jahr Lang in / unserem Dienste an- und aufgenommen / worden folgendermassen:
> 1mo Wird seine Schuldigkeit seyn zu allen Mahler / arbeith welche ihme von uns, oder durch / andere, jedoch aus unseren Befehl an / gegeben wird, Besonders was das Theatre / anbelangt, all seinen möglichsten Fleiß / anzuwenden, und weilen sein Weib eine / Singerin ist, als wird Sie gehalten seyn / 2do So wohl zu den Cammer- als Chor Musique / zu erscheinen, und unsern Capel- / Meister alle parition zu Leisten, mit- / hin was von Musicalien ihnen vorge / legt werden, solche abzusingen, und da / all-ihre Schuldigkeiten zu Papiere zu / setzen für uberflüssig erachtet wird, / so überlasset mann sothanen ihrer ge / schicklichkeit, und Diensteifer das / Dieselben nach gestalt deren umbständen / von selbsten dahin Bedacht seyn werden, / alle Satisfaction von sich zu geben, / überhaupt eben sollen Sie sich ehrlich, / Christlich, ruhig und friedig aufführen / Dagegen / 3^tio für solche dienst-Leistung wird ihme le / Bon als Mahlern quartier, und 10. / Klafter Holtz für sich, als auch sein / Weib, und Tochter, welche Leztere zu / all-obigen verbunden ist, Resolviret / 4to An baaren geld für alle jährlich 600 Fl. / oder Monatlich 50 Fl. Reinl. und werden / hiermit an unser Ober Einnehmer- / Amt angewiesen. Nebst und ohnedem / 5to Werden ihnen 10 Eimer Wein Eisenstadter / Hain accordirt. Geben Eisenstadt / den 1ten Julii 7̅6̅2̅. Hieronymus Bon [mpria]
>
> [Cover:] 7̅6̅2̅ Conventio pictoris le Bon et / ejus uxoris ut Cantatricis.
>
> [A.M. 253, No. 960–2, EH, Budapest]

2 Literature: Pohl I, 208, 231; I. Becker-Glauch in *Haydn-Studien* II/3 (1970), pp. 177ff; Horányi (English ed.), pp. 29–30, also the brilliant rediscovery of what are undoubtedly two set-pieces by Bon, unsigned, but dated 1762; Bartha-Somfai, p. 378; G. Feder, 'Zur Datierung Haydnscher Werke', in *Anthony van Hoboken, Festschrift* ..., Mainz 1962, p. 52.

3 Augusta Houdière? See 9 April 1763, *infra*, p. 385.

Apart from this work, which is listed in *EK* as 'La Marchesa Nespola' (not 'Napoli', not 'Nepola'; 'nespola' = pomegranate), and which is discussed in detail in the musical section (*infra*, pp. 425ff.), *EK* lists three other titles: 'La Vedova, Il dottore, Il Scanarello' (p. 17), and later Haydn added the word 'Comedia' to each. Bartha-Somfai consider that the role 'Scanarello' in the *Marchese* (*Marchesa*) is identical with the 'Il Scanarello' of *EK*, but we doubt this. In a catalogue of manuscript music offered for sale by the Viennese Simon Haschka in 1774 (*Wienerisches Diarium*), we find '5 kleine Operetta von Herrn Hayden' (Pohl I, 231f.), of which we have the titles of four from *EK*.

As we shall have occasion to observe *infra*, these arias display an astonishing command of the idiom and seem to have impressed Prince Nicolaus (who can hardly have imagined the abilities of his *Vice-Capellmeister* along these lines) as much as they do in our age. For the first time, Haydn enjoyed a brief exercise in several forms of vocal music (if we allow, on speculation, the Latin [Italian?] Cantata and perhaps the *Te Deum*). Perhaps the little Symphony No. 9 (autograph 1762, seen by Aloys Fuchs at Artaria's; now lost), which is in typically overture-like form (three movements with a closing minuet), was composed as a prelude to one of the operas or the Cantata.

In the middle of the Italian company's guest appearance, Prince Nicolaus performed his first official act for a member of the *Capelle*:

> According to princely Decretation dd⁰̲ 25ᵗᵉⁿ Junÿ (which is attached to the General Cassa Statements of the year 7̄6̄2) [*Vice-Capel-Meister* Haydn] is to receive an annual increase of . . 200 f.
> [This and the other increase of 1 May 1763 are contained in Haydn's *Conventionsblatt* of 1771, EH, Forchtenstein. Facsimile in *HJB* IV, 37; J. Harich in
> *HJB* IV, 11]

In other words, Haydn's salary had been raised by fifty per cent. A more dramatic way of showing princely approbation and encouragement could hardly be imagined.

The next document in our Chronicle provides an interesting and surprising connection between the Haydns and Joseph (not Ignaz) Leutgeb, Mozart's friend who was horn player and cheesemonger:

> Josephus Leüthgeb ein Musicus in der golden[en] Aul [Eule] allhier / Barbara ux[oris]. / Infans: Anna Maria Catharina / 3. julius 1762 / Matr[ina]: Frau Maria Anna Haydenin mar[ita]: H[err]. Joseph, Capell-Mstr. von Fürst Esterhazy, abs[entibus].
> [Parish church of St Ulrich, Vienna, Taufband 30 (1760–2), f. 314 v. Karl Maria Pisarowitz, 'Mozarts Schnorrer Leutgeb', in *Mitteilungen der Internationalen Stiftung Mozarteum*, 18. Jg., Heft 3/4 (1970), pp. 21f.]

Haydn's wife was godmother to Anna Maria Catharina Leutgeb. Haydn, obviously in Eisenstadt, was prevented from attending. It is interesting that Haydn left his wife in Vienna when he was on the *Herrschaft*'s country estates, presumably because there was no room for wives of those musicians who were 'stationed' in Vienna.

Joseph Leutgeb, born in the (then) Viennese suburb of St Ulrich on 8 October 1732, had on 2 November 1760 married Barbara Plazzeriani, daughter of an Italian cheese- and sausage-monger, Blasius, and his wife Catherine, *née* Zehr; this took place in St Ulrich (Church of Maria Trost). The bride came from Alt-Lerchenfeld, a nearby Viennese suburb. It is not known when the Haydns met the Leutgebs, but we wonder if there is not quite a different explanation for the existence of the Horn Concerto in D (VIId:3) than that provided hitherto: it has been assumed that this work was composed for Thaddäus Steinmüller, but our lists show clearly that Steinmüller was a *second* – or 'low range' – horn player, whereas Haydn's Concerto is clearly for a first – or 'high range' – performer. The autograph (Gesellschaft der Musikfreunde) is dated 1762, and this is the work where, towards the end, Haydn mixed up the staves and wrote on the edge of the MS., 'In Schlaff geschrieben' (facsimile in Geiringer 1932, p. 92). Being clearly for a *first* horn player, we wonder if it was not a gift for Joseph Leutgeb on the occasion of his daughter's birth. (There is a lost horn concerto in D of this period, VIId:1, which may have been written for the *Capelle*.)

Leutgeb died a pauper on 27 February 1811, with debts of 1,286 Fl. 28 xr., yet another talented musician who would perish in dire financial circumstances.

Meanwhile, the festivities and the opera company's visit now being terminated, Prince Nicolaus set about regulating his *Capelle*. We have the original draft, with heavy corrections (by Nicolaus? by his secretary?; 'Domasini' corrected to 'Tomasini' and other lapses into Austrian dialect improved), as well as the final document. A summary of the final version is given below in translation, and we also include (overleaf) the text of the draft document, together with a facsimile of the original (pp. 375–7), and finally (p. 378) the full text of the final document in German.[1]

[Summary translation:]
Since we have decided to retain the *Camer Musique* engaged and retained by our late brother, they and the others listed below are to receive the following salary: [list follows]

Apart from the salaries indicated, the *Feld Musique*, consisting of 6 persons, namely 2 oboists, 2 bassoon players and 2 horn players, are to receive a daily payment of 17 xr. when and only when they are in Eisenstadt. And to all this the above-listed musicians should receive a uniform every year or every two years two uniforms but with the expressed proviso: that they should be satisfied with such a salary and not bother us further. (1) They are to appear, not only in Eisenstadt, at the Chamber and Choir *Musique* diligently and as long as the *Herrschaft* orders, whether early or late, also in Vienna and in other places whereto they may be ordered to perform their duties. (2) They are subordinate to the *Vice-Capel-Meister* and to follow his orders without contradiction. (3) Each shall comport himself honestly, quietly and peacefully, as is expected of any honest man in a princely court. (4) They are not to absent themselves without our permission from Eisenstadt, Vienna or wherever the court happens to be, nor to be absent from the Chamber or Choir *Musique*, but to make such a request to the *Capel-Meister* and according to the circumstances our Resolution shall be made. Otherwise all the terms and conventions of my brother in regard of the musicians are hereby confirmed. Given at Eisenstadt, 5th July 1762. [Signatures added]

To this may be added some relevant documents:
[PCDI] No. 464 de Anno 1762. Princely Comons Copia dd⁰ 5ᵗᵉ July: 7̄6̄2̄, according to which the *Feld Music* receive daily 17 xr. for food, over and above their salary, in Eisenstadt and in Kittsee, herewith graciously commanded. N: the original document is with the Chief Receiver (Cashier).

[PCDI] No. 471. Princely Intimat. dd⁰ 1ᵗᵉ July 1762, according to which Painter Le Bon is engaged as painter, his wife and daughter as singers, for 1 year. . . .

[PCDI] No. 472. Princely Comĩssion dd⁰ 14ᵗᵉ Aug. 1762, according to which the musician Aloysio Domasini [*sic*] is to be provided with an increase of 50. to his Convention, violinist Heger also 50., and the singer Barbara Fuxin 20 Fl. Then the painter Le Bon is to be paid a *gratiale* of 82 Fl.

[PCDI] No. 479. Copia of a princely Comĩssion, according to which the Cabinet Painter Basilius Grundman is to receive an additional 100 Cremnitz ducats to his salary for life from the G[ene]ral Cassa.

1 The first document to be given here is the draft. Sections in ( ) were marked later by the Prince or his secretary, those in [ ] were deletions made on the draft. The second document is the corrected, final version, from which we have only omitted the final list of autograph signatures attached to the document after the end date: all the musicians therein listed signed. The document was published in extract in Valkó II, 634f. We have consulted and transcribed the originals: draft, A.M. 252a, No. 955–7; final document, A.M. 252b.

[continued overleaf]

[THE DRAFT:]

[Cover:]
762 / Conventio / Musicorum
[next page:]
Nachdeme Wir die Bishero geweste Cam̄er- Music, und darzu nachgefertigte [word cancelled underneath] Persohnen ebenfalls / zu Behalten Unß entschlossen haben; alß wird derenselben künftiger Gehalt ['und Tractament' cancelled] folgender gestalt ['Specifiziert' cancelled] ausgeworfen / ['alß' cancelled]

Dem Vice = Capel[n] = Meister Joseph[us] Haiden . . . . ,, 600. F
Tenorist(en) Car[o]l[us] Friberth . . . . ,, 300.
Erst(en) Violinist(en) Aloysio[s] Tomasini . . . . ,, 200.
                        [at first: 'Domasini']
Flautroversist Franz(en) Sigl . . . . ,, 240.
[at first: 'Fleutroversisten']
Anderte(n) Violinist(en) Frantz(n) Guarnier[n] . . . . ,, 240.
Anderte(n) deto Johann Georg Heger . . . . ,, 150.
Violoncelist(en) Joseph Weigl . . . . ,, 240.
Erste(rn) Hautboist(en) Johann Michael Kapfer . . . . ,, 240.
Andert(er) deto Johann Georg Kapfer . . . . ,, 240.
Erster(n) Fagotist(en) Johann Hinterberger . . . . ,, 240.
Anderte(n) deto Johann Georg Schwenda
    zugleich Violinist(en) . . . . ,, 240.
Erste (n) Waldhornist (en) Johann Knoblauch . . . . ,, 240.
Anderte(n) deto Thadaeo Steinmüllner . . . . ,, 240.
            [at first: 'Thadaeus']

[passage deleted:] Notandum: von der Banda, welche zugleich, beÿ / der Compagnie die gewöhnliche Dienste beÿ denen / Paraden und Wacht ablesungen zu verrichten ha / ben, wann dieselbe daselbst wirklich occupiret/seÿn oder wann dieselbe mit der Compagnie be/ordered, und comandiret werden, hat ieder Tägl:/Siebenzehn Creüzer, id est 17.xr, ausser der Com/pagnie Dienst aber in Hinkunft dieses Kost/ geld nicht mehr zu empfangen.

[p. 2]
    Dem Bassisten Griessler, welcher zugleich nebst den schon ebenfahls unter die Camer Music zu zehlen ist, / haben Wir 30. F als ein Quartier geld seinen bis / herigen Gehalt zugeworfen.
    Jeder von obbenannten Musicis soll zugleich alle Jahr / die Kleÿdung, oder aber alle zweÿ Jahr zweÿer / leÿ Kleÿdung nach Unserer Verordnung, und dis / position zu empfangen haben / Wir hoffen dahero, daß Sie mit diesen zufriden und / Unß weither nicht incom̄odiren werden. / Dahingegen und eines iedwedren schuldigkeit seÿn: / 1ᵐ nicht allein hier in Eisenstadt die Cam̄er Music / und Kirchen Dienst fleissig, und accurat nach denen / gegebenen Stunden zu frequentiren, und dabeÿ, / so lang der Herrschaft fruhe oder Spat beliebig / seÿn wird, zu verbleiben, sondern auch zu Wienn / und in anderen Orth, wohin dieselbte Breuchen wer / den gegen vorbeschrieben- ausgeworfenen Ge / halt, und Tractament zu erscheinen, und ihre Dien / ste zu praestiren. Ferners / 2ᵈᵒ Dem Vice– Capeln– Meister alle parition zu leisten / und was Er in Herrn– Diensten anordnen, und / befehlen wird, ['accurat auch' cancelled] ohne widerrede zu bewerken, somit sowohl Er Vice– Capeln– Meister / als such die übrige Die von Unsern / Fürstlichen / Herrn Brudern seel.: gedächtnus hinausgegebe / ne Instruction so weith, was hier abgängig / genau zu observiren. / [p. 3] 3ᵗᵒ sich gut, still und from aufzuführen, überhaubt / aber einen iedweren obligen wird die Einig / keit zu lieben, die gute beständus zu hegen, / mithin alle Unordnung, und Ungleichheiten zu / vermeÿden. / 4ᵗᵒ Ohne Unserer Erlaubnus von Eisenstadt, Wienn / oder wo dieselbe einige zeit sich beÿ der Hof / stadt aufhalten werden müssen, nicht zu absen / tiren, noch weniger von der Music ausbleiben / es seÿe dan, Er hätte erhöbliche Ursache, wel / che dem Vice– Capeln-Meister, und durch ihme / Unß sogleich angedeüttet werden sollen. Eisen / stadt den 26ᵗᵉⁿ Junÿ 762.
[In another ink and handwriting:]
Commisssion / Vermög welcher unser Ober- Einnehmer Johann Zoller / denen zur Feld- Musique gehörigen 6. Musicis / ehnlich denen zweÿn Hautboisten zweÿn Fagotisten / und zweÿn Wald-Hornisten, nebst ihren monatlichn / gehalt, all- täglich 17 xr. von den Tag ihrer ankunft aus / Eisenstadt, das ist vom 10ᵗᵉⁿ April laufenden / Jahrs, und künftighin so lang, als dieselben sich / hier in Eisenstadt, oder Kitsee in unseren Diensten befinden werden, entrichten / und solche ausgab, als ein richtige position in der Buch / haltereÿ angesprochen werden sollen. Gegeben Eisenstadt / den 5ᵗᵉⁿ Julii 762 / Nicolaus Fürst Eszterházy / m.p.

[Marginal note, in the same ink as the corrections to the draft:]
Mit diessen zusaz: das die zur Feld-Musique / gehörige oberwehnte 6 Persohnen, Benanntlich die / 2. Hautboisten, 2. Fagotisten, und 2. Waldhornisten zur zeit ihrer Dawesenheit in / Eisenstadt alle Täglich nebst obigen gehalt [n(?)] 17. Xr ['zu empfangen' cancelled] haben sollen.

Opposite and overleaf
The *Conventio Musicorum* of the year 1762, regulating the salaries of musicians in the Esterházy *Capelle*, in draft form; the document, in a copyist's hand, also bears holograph corrections by Prince Nicolaus.

H…

Nachdem Wir die bißhero gewöste Zimmer-Music, und darzu … Vnderhaltung … zu … Uns entschloßen haben; alß wird denenselben Künstlern … und Tractament folgender gestalt … und untergeordnet …

Dem Vice-Capel Meister Joseph Haydn	600 fl
Tenoristen Carolus Friberth	300
Ersten Violinisten Aloysius Tomasini	200
Flautraversisten Franz Sigl	240
Andertem Violinisten Ignatz Marteaux	240
Andertem deto Johann Georg Geyer	150
Violoncellisten Joseph Weigl	240
Ersten Hautboisten Johann Michael Kapfer	240
Andertem deto Johann Georg Kapfer	240
Ersten Fagotisten Johann Hinterberger	240
Andertem deto Johann Georg Schramli	
zugleich Violonisten	240
Ersten Waldhornist Johann Knoblauch	240
Andertem deto Thadäus Steinmüller	240

Notandum: … von der Banda, welche zugleich bey der Compagnie die gewöhnliche … bey … Paraden … abschprüngen zu verrichten haben, wann dieselbe … reluiert … oder wann dieselbe mit der Compagnie … und Commandiret werden, … die künftige Zulage, … daß … wegen ihrer Compagnie Dienst … künftig … bezahlt nicht mehr zu verlangen.

Item

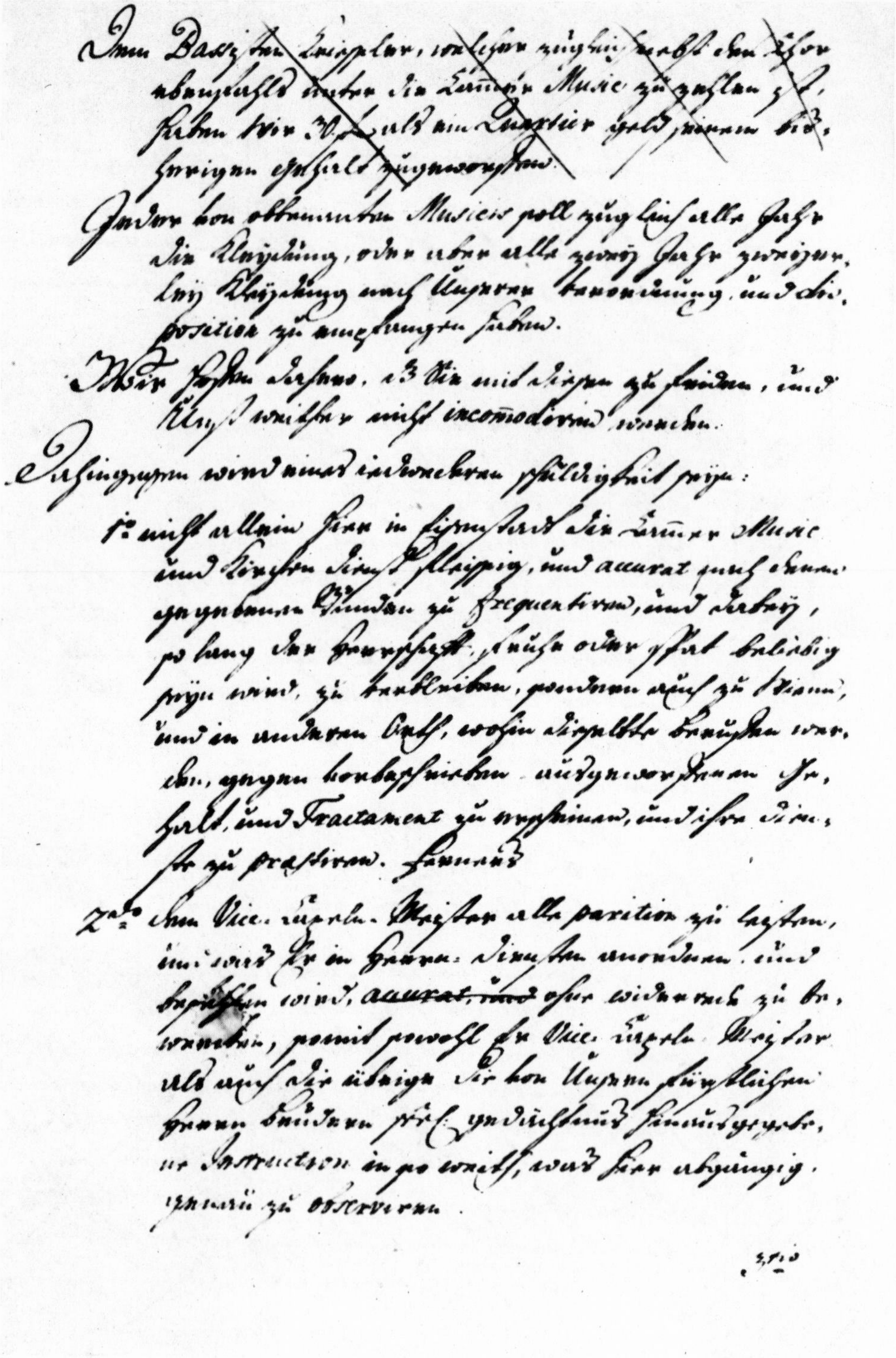

3tis sich gut, still, und einem ordtzüglichen, überhaupt aber einem iedwedern obligen wird die seinige Arbeit zu lieben, die gute Harmonie zu hegen, müssin alle Unordnung, und Ungleichheiten zu vermeiden.

4tes Oher Unseren Anlernstund von Eisenstadt, Wienn, oder wo Dieselbe einige zeit sich bey ehn Hoffstatt aufhalten werden müssen, sich zu absentiren, noch weniger von der Music auszbleiben, ... sehr ... , Er hätte wesentliche Ursachen, wel- che ihm Vice-Capellen Meister, und ... ... aufgehezt eingenommen werden sollen. Eisen- stadt, den 28ten May 1762.

Commission

... welcher auch der Ober-... Johann Tolle, ... zur Feld-Musique ... C gehörige ... Musici, nehmlich denen zweyer Hautboisten, zweyer Fagotisten, und zweyer Feld-Hornist, wohl ... ihre monatliche gehalt, all-täglich 17. ... bey ihnen ... ... Eisenstadt, ... ist von 10ten April ... ... , und künftig hin so lang, ... sich hier in Eisenstadt, oder Kittsee, befinden werden, ... solche ... als ... richtigen position in der Cust. Ledtwig ... werden sollen. Forchen Eisenstadt den 5ten Julii 1762.

Nicolaus fürst Eszerházy
m. p.

[THE FINAL DOCUMENT:]

[Cover:]
7̄62. Reversales / Instructio et Conventio Musicorum.
[next page:]
Nachdeme Wir die von Unserem Herrn Brudern seel. an- und aufgenohmene Camer Musique, und / dazu nachgesetzte Persohnen gleichfahls zu Be / halten Unß entschlossen haben, als wird deren / selben künftiger Gehalt folgendermassen Be / stättigt:

Dem Vice Capeln-Meister Joseph Haydn	600 Fl.
Tenoristen Carl Friberth	300.
Ersten Violinisten Aloysio Tomasini	200.
Fleutraversisten Franz Sigl	240.
Anderten Violinisten Franz Quarnier	240.
Dritten Violinisten Johann Georg Heger	150.
Violoncellisten Joseph Waigl	240.
Ersten Hautboisten Johann Michael Kapfer	240.
Anderten Hautboisten Johan Georg Kapfer	240.
Ersten Fagotisten Johan Hinterberger	240.
Anderten Fagotisten Johan Georg Schwenda	240.
zugleich Violinisten	
Ersten Wald- Hornisten Johan Knoblauch	240.
Anderten Wald- Hornisten Thadæo Steinmüller	240.

Nebst oben angesezten gehalt werden die zur / Feld Musique geh[ö]rigen obenwehnten 6 Persoh / nen, Benamtlich die 2. Hautboisten, 2. Fagotisten, / und 2. Wald- Hornisten, allein nur zur Zeit / ihrer Dawesenheit in Eisenstadt all- Täglich / 17 xr. zu empfangen haben. Zu deme ferner / Solle / Solle ieder von obbenamten Musicis alle Jahr ein / Kleyd, oder aber alle zwey Jahr zweyerley / Kleyder nach Unseren verordnungen bekom̄en, ie / doch mit diesen ausdrücklichen Zusatz: daß die / selbe sich mit solchen Behalt Begnügen, und / Unß nicht mehr Beunruhigen sollen. Dagegen / wird eines ieden schuldigkeit seyn / 1ª nicht allein in Eisenstadt Bey der Cam̄er und Chor / Musique nach denen gegebenen stunden fleisig zu erscheinen, und so lange, als der Herr- / schaft frühe, oder spät Beliebig seyn wird, mitzu- / machen, sondern auch zu Wienn, und in andern Orthen, wohin dieselben Berufen werden, ihre Dienste emsig zu leisten. 2ª Dem Vice- Capel- Meister alle parition zu bezeugen, / und was Er in Herrn- Dienst anordnen wird / ohne widerrede zu befolgen. / 3ª solle sich ieder ehrlich, ruhig und friedig / : wie es von einem ieden ehrliebenden Menschen bey einer / Fürstlichen Hofstadt die Umstände erfordern: / aufführen, und alle Unsinnigkeiten vermeyden. / 4ª Ohne Unsere Erlaubnis von Eisenstadt, Wienn oder wo dieselben eine zeit lang bey der Hof-stadt / sich werden aufhalten müssen, solle sich keiner / absentiren, viell weniger von Cam̄er oder Chor / Musique ausbleiben, sondern ehe, und bevor / dem / Capel- Meister melden, und wann die vor / gewendete Ursachen f[ü]r billich erkant werden, / so dann wird auch nach gestald deren Umstan / den Unsere Resolution erfolgen. Übrigens wird / hiermit die von Unseren Herrn Brudern seel. / ihnen Musicis hinausgegebenen Vorschrift, und / Verhaltungs-Norma durchaus bestättiget. Ge / geben Eisenstadt den 5ᵗᵉⁿ July 1762.
[Followed by all the signatures of the *Capelle*]

Johann Basilius Grundmann, it will be recalled, is believed to have painted the first known portrait of Haydn, *c.* 1762 (pl. 1). In August the musicians, Haydn included, were given summer uniforms:

[Extract]

For the summer uniforms ordered for the musicians, Month of August A° 7̄62
   Capel Meister: Coat, waistcoat, 2 pairs of breeches and a hat trimmed with silver: the coat with small, the waistcoat made with small and broad *bordures* and all with silver *paillettes* [spangles]
   14. Musicÿ, for each a coat, waistcoat, 2 pairs of breeches and hat, the waistcoat with narrow silver trimming, all with silver *paillettes*.
S[umm]a: 15 complete uniforms . . . . to pay 879 gulden 33 xr.
[EH, Forchtenstein, Generalcassa, 1762. Rubr. VIII. Fasc. 4. Nr. 14. J. Harich in *HJB* IV, 80]

Haydn's mother had died at Rohrau on 23 February 1754, aged 47. It took years for the authorities to settle her affairs, but finally, on 15 September 1762, Joseph was in Rohrau Castle to receive official word of his inheritance (total: 77 Fl. 34 xr., 3 Pfennig).[1]

The musical event of the year was certainly the première of Gluck's *Orfeo* (libretto: Calsabigi; choreography; Angiolini; sets: Giovanni Maria Quaglio) with the castrato Gaetano Guadagni (Orfeo), Marianna Bianchi (Euridice) and Lucia Clavareau (Amore), at the Burgtheater on 5 October. The libretto in two languages (Italian-German, later also Italian-French) was announced in the *Wienerisches Diarium* the next day, together with a short but positive criticism of the work ('... which brought much honour not only to its originator, Herr Calcabigi [*sic*] but also to the composer of the music, Herr Cav. Gluck.' Although *Orfeo* created a profound impression, some parts of it – the Overture, 'Che farò' and the closing ballet – came in for criticism, also from the Dowager Princess Esterházy (*née* Lunati-Visconti). Count Zinzendorf reports in his Diary (we include some 'previews' as well):

LE 8. JUILLET. . . . Nous dinames chez M. de Calzapigi [*sic*], sur le Kohlmarkt avec le Duc de Bragance, M. de Durazzo, le C. Philipp qui étoit assi entre nous deux [frères], le Chevalier Gluck et Guadagni. Tout étoit bien apporté, le vin excellent. Apres table Guadagni chanta des airs d'un Opera que Calzapigi a composé sous le nom d'Orphée et d'Euridice. Gluck contrefit les Furies. Le Duc de Bragance me mena a Schönbrunn, le Cour alloit precissément a la Comédie. . . .

LE 6. AOUT: . . . puis chez le Duc de Bragance ou nous dinames avec Calzapigi, Laugier,[1] Guadagni et Lion et M. Chevalier Gluck qui joua des airs de l'opera d'Orphée, et Guadagni chanta. Me de Los Rios[2] et M. De Freyra[3] y vinrent. . . .

LE 5. OCTOBRE. La P^esse Esterhazy n'est pas bien, j'ai été informé hier de son mal, dont je n'avois jamais rien ouï dire. . . . au Théatre, qui etoit rempli, on ne point pas davantage. On donna Orfeo ed Euridice, opera de Calzapigi, la Musique etoit de Gluck. Elle est divine[,] toute pathetique, toute accommodée au sujet, les decorations tres belles. On trouve a redire a la piece, qu'il y manque l'unité du Lieu, que les passions ne sont pas exprimes assez fortement, qu'on passe trop rapidement de l'une a l'autre, qu'a la fin du second acte Orfée s'en va avec Euridice sans qu'on sache ce qu'ils disparoissent de la scene. On trouve a redire dans les Decorations, qu'Euridice quand les ombres l'amenent, n'est past vétüe comme elles en Ombre, ce qui devoit etre puisque elle n'est plus encore sur la terre, que dans les champs Elisées les fleurs, les arbres, les plantes ne sont pas de la couleur de la verdure naissant mais de la couleur de feuille-morte. On repond sur cette derniere objection, ce que Vergile rapporte, que les champs Elisées ont une espece de brillant qui éblouit les yeux, et qu'on a voulu representer par cette couleur. . . .

LE 7. OCTOBRE. Joué du Clavecin. Sorti a 8^h. et ½ le soir pour aller chez Figuerole,[4] dela chez la Princesse Esterhazy, ou on parla beaucoup sur le couleur des champs Elysées, dans l'opera Orféo, les uns dirent que c'est la moyen rouge, les autres gris de lin, d'autres feuille morte, d'autres aurore. L'ambassadrice[5] trouva la musique de l'air Che faro senza Euridice! trop gaie pour un homme qui vient se tuer, elle dit cependant que l'ensemble faisoit un fort beau Spectacle. Me de Sternberg[6] trouva la musique du dernier ballet affreuse, rempli di repétition ennuyantes [*sic*]. M^c. d'E.[sterházy] la Polonoise[7] dit que l'ouverture étoit mauvoise. Tous

---

1 Schmid, 241: 'Ao. 1762 den 15. 7bris he [Joseph] acknowledged, being present in this Office, that some years ago he had received 30 fl.' On 17 January 1764, Haydn's brother-in-law Johann Philipp Frö(h)lich received the remainder. Jancik (p. 37) maintains that Johann Michael Haydn was also present at Rohrau on 15 Sept. 1762. Pfennige (or Groschen) were abbreviated by the old *denar* sign (see p. 16) and were reckoned 6 = 1 Xr.

desapprouvent hautement Euridice. De la chez Colloredo ... Il a plu depuis le matin jusqu'au soir sans cesse. [Zinzendorf MS.]

Notes:
1 Alexandre-Louis Laugier, Physician in Ordinary to the Empress.
2 Antoinette, Marquise de Los Rios, *née* Countess Pálffy.
3 Freyra: the Portuguese Ambassador, Don Ambrosio Freire d'Andrade e Castro. M. Lion can not be identified.
4 Raimond, Count Figuerole; Zinzendorf was an intimate friend, as he was also of Countess Francisca and their daughter 'Nani', to whom a few months earlier (3 July) he had brought a bouquet of carnations from the Botanic Gardens.
5 The wife of 'le C. Esterhazy de Russie ..., il est arrivé hier, c'est un bel homme' (1 Dec. 1761). On 24 May 1761 we read of '... d'Esterhazy, la femme de l'ambassadeur'.
6 Probably Maria Leopoldine, *née* Countess Stahremberg (1712–1800), married on 18 April 1731 Franz Philipp, Count von Sternberg (1708–86), Privy Councillor and *Obersthofmeister* to Empress Maria Theresa.
7 Maria Anna, *née* Princess Lubomirska – *vide supra*, p. 359, note 3.

On 6 October 1762, Leopold Mozart and his two children, Wolfgang and 'Nannerl' arrived in Vienna and apart from playing at Schönbrunn on the 13th, they appeared at various salons. Zinzendorf reports:

LE 9. OCTOBRE: ... Le soir a 8ʰ j'allois prendre Lamberg et nous allions ensemble chez Colalto, ou la Bianchi [Gluck's Euridice] chanta et un petit garzon qu'on dit n'avoit que 5 ans et demi joue du Clavecin. ...

LE 17. OCTOBRE: ... Puis chez Thurn, ou le petit Enfant de Salzbourg et sa soeur jouaient du Clavecin. Le pauvre petit joue a merveille, c'est un Enfant Spirituel, vif, charmant, sa sœur joue en maitre et il lui applaudit. Mˡˡᵉ de Gudenus, qui joue bien du clavecin, lui donna un baiser, il s'essuya le visage. ...

A few days later, we learn of the payments made by the I.R. family – in the person of the Empress herself – to a number of people, including those responsible for *Orfeo*:

LE 21 OCTOBRE: ... L'imp. a fait present de 100 ducats au premier Valet de Chambre, et d'une tabatière d'or avec 100. ducats a M. Kornbeck, Medicin de M. de Kaunitz [the Chancellor] ... Elle a donné une belle bague de la valeur de 300. ducats à Guadagni et l'a arrété ici pour un an, et une tabatiere avec 100 # [ducats] a Gluk. ...

We hear of *Orfeo* and its apparently growing success once more, in Zinzendorf's *Journal* for 9 December:

... Le soir au Théatre. on donna la fille arbitre, suivi de l'opera d'Orphée, qui fut tout applaudie, que Durazzo fut obligé de la [deleted: 'repettre'; insertion with caret:] faire annoncer de nouveaux pour Sammedi. ...

Returning to the affairs of the Esterházy Court at Eisenstadt, and of Johann Michael Haydn's career, we close our Chronicle for 1762.

The future organist of the *Capelle*, Franz Novotni,[1] first comes to our notice when he is engaged as a clerk (*Accessista*):

[PCDI] No. 484. Princely Commissions Decretation, according to which Frantz Novotnj is to be granted the same Convention as that of a Book-keeping clerk [*Accessisten*]. ddᵉ 20ᵐ Xbris [Dec.] 762.

His contract was effective from 1 January 1763.

1 *Haydn at Eszterháza 1766–1790*, p. 75

Michael Haydn's position in Großwardein (Oradea Mare) had now terminated, and we must break this Chronicle for a moment to follow, if briefly, his fortunes. Shortly before Christmas, we find Michael in Pressburg, where on 22 December he completed a *Partita* in F (Perger 107). Can the brothers have met in the Hungarian Coronation Town? Subsequently, Michael found his way to Salzburg, for in the Court Diary of Franz Anton Gilowsky von Urazowa, under date 24 July 1763, we read:

> The high princely table [of the Archbishop] was today in the hall at Mirabell [Castle] on account of the rainy weather. 24 Ordinari [people who usually dined at the court table] and 8 guests and *Tafelmusique*, which today was set forth by a foreign composer from Vienna by the name of Michael Heiden. [Jancik, pp. 37f.]

Michael settled in Salzburg, married the soprano Maria Magdalena Lipp, daughter of the cathedral organist (marriage: 17 August 1768), and died there in 1806, leaving behind him a vast quantity of vocal and instrumental music which is just now receiving the recognition and appreciation it deserves.

Our account for 1762 closes with the first known bill in the Esterházy Archives with which Haydn was involved:

Specification

What I the undersigned delivered and made for the princely choir music in the year 1762, viz.:

	fl	xr
on 5th May a saddle delivered and the fingerboard bound with wire per	—	6
on 11th May 2 saddles delivered per	—	6
and an overspun G per	—	5
then on 18th May again 2 saddles delivered per	—	6
Item the choir violon [double bass] newly strung per	—	12
on 20th July 2 broken bows repaired and new hairs attached per	—	16
on 15th July 1 saddle delivered per	—	3
on 25th July a saddle and a new bow for the violin made per	—	15
In the month of Augusti the new violon [double bass] glued with fish glue [*Hausen blater* = glue made from sturgeon bladder] per	—	6
on 14th November 3 overspun strings delivered per	—	15
Again 10 mutes made â 3 kr. makes	—	30
Suma	2	—

[Haydn's hand:]
Joseph Haydn mpria / Vice Capell Meister
as agreed upon

[First writer's hand:]
I acknowledge receipt of above listed two gulden from the Rental Office.
Eisenstadt, 30th X^bris [Dec.] 762   Carl Braun[1]
                                             Princely Musician

[Third hand:]
To be paid by the Rental Office
Edmund Schlanstein mpria
        Administrator

[Cover: contents, file number & date]
    [A.M. 411, EH, Budapest; Valkó II, 636; here from original]

---

1 Princely oboe player with the *Chor Musique* who occupied himself with the repair and upkeep of the instruments; he died in 1764.

We now come to the first of the great festivals which Prince Nicolaus held between 1763 and 1775, thereby earning for himself the famous title, 'Der Prachtliebende' ('The Magnificent' – not quite the same thing). This *Fest* centred on the marriage of the Prince's eldest son, Count Anton (reigning Prince, 1790–4), with Marie Therese, Countess Erdödy, the daughter of Count Nicolaus. The marriage ceremony took place in the Mirror Room of the Vienna Burg on 10 January 1763, and was performed by the Archbishop of Colossa, Count Bathiany (Batthiany). Thereafter the newly married couple and their parents were invited to the I.R. table, and then set forth for Eisenstadt. Our information about the activities at Eisenstadt comes from the *Wienerisches Diarium*:

> Eisenstadt, 20 January.
> We have never seen so many distinguished guests, and such joyous festivities, as during the last week on the occasion of the marriage of the Lord Son of his Princely Grace, Fürst Niclas [*sic*] Esterhazy of Galantha, our gracious Sire, with the Demoiselle Countess von Erdödy, I.R. Maid of the Chamber. After the noble bridal pair had been joined in matrimony, with the usual ceremonies, on the 10th inst. by the Lord Archbishop of Colocza[1] at the Court in Vienna, they enjoyed the favour of being invited, together with their nearest noble relatives, to lunch at the table of both their Majesties and Serene *Herrschaften*. We then had the pleasure of seeing them here, with a large number of distinguished guests, that very same evening. The road from Windpaßing [Wimpassing] to Eisenstadt, which is a three hours' drive, was illuminated, and the same with our suburb and the ghetto, through which the procession passed. But the magnificent illumination of the princely castle outshone all else and was generally admired. In the middle of the square in front of the castle, a portal of honour had been erected, whereupon trumpets and kettledrums were heard. The Princely Guard, consisting of a Grenadiers' Company of selected men, stood to attention. After the happy arrival of the noble Count and Countess, with their company, the Te Deum was celebrated in the Castle Chapel. Then, at two tables, each containing more than sixty couverts, the evening meal was taken; during which the guns were fired, a well trained exercise performed by the Princely Guard, and grenades were exploded, for the amusement of the spectators.
> The next day, after solemn Mass, His Serene Princely Grace had arranged for a tribune in the manner of a Neapolitan *cocagna* to be put up, on which were roast hams, *Würste*, smoked meats and bread, and these were then distributed to the population which had assembled in very great numbers. Wine flowed from two great vats. And not the least disorder was to be observed. The midday meal in the Castle was most excellent, and afterwards there was a beautiful Italian Opera entitled *Acide*, performed by the virtuosi in the actual service of His Princely Grace: the princely musicians were all in identical, dark-red uniforms trimmed with gold. Thereafter, in the incomparable, and for this purpose marvellously decorated, great hall of the Castle was a masked ball, to which anyone possessing an entrance ticket was freely admitted: the number of masks was exceptionally large, and refreshments of all kinds were provided in abundance.
> On the 12th the midday meal was even more largely attended. In the evening, part of the time was devoted to a pleasant spectacle of tightrope-walkers, acrobats, jugglers and balancing artists; and part to a ball which lasted until the early

---

1 Archi-Episcopus Colocensis = Klausenburg = Kolozsvár = Cluj (Roumania).

morning: 600 masks were counted, and many of them changed costumes several times.

On the third day an *opera buffa* was given with exceptional applause, and afterwards a ball began, during which the entire castle garden was magnificently illuminated and the number of masks even greater than before. And with this, these marvellous three-day festivities were at an end, distinguished not only by their magnificence and opulence, but also by the exceptional hospitality to the many lunch and dinner guests, and also by the excellent taste and the most fitting sense of order that obtained throughout: but most especially by the delightful and condescending[1] fashion which His Princely Grace showed to every man, and which was generally admired. In the reflection of the host's honour, and in a universal enjoyment, the events thus concluded.

It will be noted that there is no particular mention of a ceremony in which Haydn's new Cantata, 'Vivan gl'illustri Sposi' (XXIVa:1), which he describes in the *Entwurf-Katalog* 'Als sich der Fürst Anton vermählte' (when the Prince [*sic*] Anton was married), was performed. The music of this Cantata is unfortunately lost and it is unlikely if anything of it has survived even in *contrafacta* church music. We note that perhaps one of the *Thurnermeister* groups – if not from here, then from Oedenburg or Wiener Neustadt – supplied the trumpets and timpani for the occasion which greeted the bridal pair when they arrived at the Castle. Trumpets were no longer part of the *Capelle* – they had been at one time – but Adam Sturm was alive and could have played the timpani. If in fact Haydn's early *Te Deum* (XXIIIc:1) was composed for this occasion, these trumpeters will have played in the Castle Chapel as well. (In any case, it is unlikely that in 1762, a princely chapel would have performed a Te Deum without trumpets.) The most intriguing problem is the 'opera buffa' performed on the third day. By whom? Perhaps Haydn's *La Marchesa Nespola* (*Il Marchese*) was repeated; or perhaps this is the occasion for the little Italian *Comedie* (*La vedova*, etc.) mentioned in connection with the festivities in May and June 1762. Of the dance music, we know nothing, and it is a pity that all the dance music from all the Esterházy castles has disappeared completely; there must have been an enormous amount, but nothing goes out of fashion more quickly than dance music, and that must explain why all the Esterházy family's eighteenth-century orchestral parts for dances were given away or destroyed.

After the festivities were over, the Kapfer brothers, no doubt at Haydn's suggestion, wrote the following letter to the Prince (for original text see footnote), written at Eisenstadt, *c.* February 1763 : [2]

---

1 Used throughout this biography, of course, in the eighteenth-century, and not its twentieth-century pejorative, sense.

2 Original text: 'An Den Dürchlauchtig- Hochgebohrnen / des Heil. Röm. Reichs Fürsten und Herrn / Herrn Nicolaus Eszterházy von Galantha / Erb Grafen zu Forchtenstein, Rit / tern des goldenen Vließes, Ihro Röm. / Kaiserl. und Königl. Apostol. Maysteten wirckl. / geheimer Rath, Kammerer, Comandeur / des Konigl. Theresianen Militaire / Kreutz- Ordens, im Königreich Hun / garn, Obrist Kammerer, Capitaine / der Adelich Hungar. Leib- Gaarde, Ge / neral Feld-Zeugmeistern, Obristen / und Inhabern eines Hungar. Infante / rie Regiments, wie auch der Lobl. Oeden / burger Gespannschaft Erb- und würkl.en / Obergespann, sp / unterthg. und gehorsamster Bitten / Johanni Georg und Michael Kapfers / Hautboisten / [new page] Durchlauchtigst und Hochgebohrner Reichs-Fürst, / Gnädigster Fürst und Herr Herr! / Es haben Euer Hochfürstl. Durchlaucht nach Antrettung Dero / Regierung, all- und jedes was wie vorhin gehabt, ebenfahls bey / zulassen, in hohen Gnaden zu resolviren geruhet, solches auch bis / her ohngekränkt erhalten: Nun aber leider wurden uns inerst / abgewichenen Monath January o.a. 8 Fl. 47 xr unter dem Vorwand ab / gezogen, als wäre dieses eine Zulaage von wegen der Compagnie / da doch solches nicht an deme ist, sondern es sind uns diese 17 xr. / tägl. als ein Kostgeld in unserem Contract N$^{\underline{ro}}$ 10$^{\underline{mo}}$ ausdrücklich / resolviret worden: Zudeme ist Euer Hochfürstl. Durchlaucht oh / nehin bekannt, daß wir nicht nur in einem, sondern mehreren / Instrumenten bis anhero unseren unermüdeten Fleiß und Dienst / Eifer jederzeit darzuthun auf das genaueste geflossen waren / Als / Gelanget an Euer Hochfürstl. Durchlaucht unser unterthanig / gehorsamstes Bitten Hoch- Dieselbe geruhen, in Ansehung un / serer treu-emsig-leistenden Diensten, uns / :vermög Hoch Dero / eigenen gnädigsten Resolution: / die in unseren Contract enthalte / ne tägl. 17 xr. Kostgeld aus hohen Gnaden beyzulassen, dann in die / Bezahlung deren pro Janu. ruckstandige 8 Fl. 44 xr gnädig zu gewilli / gen, und diesenwegen das Behörige an seine mildest zu verord / nen. Zu gnädigsten Bittsgewehr uns unterthänig gehorsamst empfehlen / Euer Hochfürstl. Durchlaucht / unterthänig- gehorsamste / Johann Georg, und Michael / Kapfer, Hautboisten.   [A.M. 72, No. 211–2]

[Summary translation:] The Prince, upon succeeding to the title, agreed to take over all the conditions that had previously obtained. But in January 8 Fl. 47 xr. was deducted from each of our salaries with the excuse that this must have been an additional sum because of the Compagnie, but in fact it is the 17 xr. daily money for food as in our contract clause 10. Your Highness knows that we play several instruments with diligence and in view of our faithful service, we asked you to make a gracious Resolution to give back to us the 17 xr. per diem in our contract, and the 8 Fl. 44 xr. refunded to us.

The whole affair seems to have been a stupid clerical error, for on the next lists of the musicians (*infra.*, pp. 408–9) the Kapfers' *per diem* allowance, like that of the other members of the *Feld Harmonie* is listed as 103 Fl. 25 xr. p.a.

On 19 February Prince Nicolaus was back in Vienna and gave a large dinner party followed by a grand concert. Our source for this hitherto unrecorded event is once again the *Diary* of Count Zinzendorf:

> ... Diné chez le Prince Eszterhazy a une grande table de 174 [corrected from '176'] couverts. Il y avoit le Comte et la petite Comtesse, M. e M̄ Bathyani, Louis Stahremberg et sa femme, puis M̄ de Walldorf, les deux freres Salm, les deux freres Mac Elligot. M. de Wallis Colonel, M. de Lanuis, Colonel du Régiment de Cuirassiers de l'Archiduc Leopold, M. de Weissenwolf, Colonel, frere de la Princesse.[1] Apres table avec Eszterhazy et Lamberg chez le Grand Chambellan[2] ... Retourné chez le Prince ou il y avoit grand Concert. Descendu chez la Princesse ... Tems triste et couvert.

For this large concert, there are two Haydn symphonies the autographs of which are dated 1763 and each (or even both) of which may have been included in the programme: Nos. 12 and 40. We may note that the Princess Dowager (Marchesa Lunati-Visconti) seems to have had quarters on the ground floor: the great hall and the lovely Chinese Room are next to each other on the first (American: second) floor and thus one 'descended' to the Princess's chambers.

Our attention is now drawn to two items in PCDI:

No. 493 de Anno 1763: Princely Com̄on dd̄ 9ᵐ April 7̄6̄3, on the strength of which the newly engaged hunting-horn player Carl Frantz is committed to sign his drafted contract. [ink spot]
N°. 494 Princely Comon dd̄ 9 Apr: 7̄6̄3, according to which the singer Augusta Houdiere is to receive a Convention of 60 Fl.

Here is official notice of the engagement of a remarkable horn player who was also a baryton player and violinist, for whose fantastic abilities Haydn would write some of

---

1 'le Comte et la petite Comtesse' are the newly wed couple, Count Anton Esterházy and his wife Marie Therese. 'Bathyani' = probably the Palatine of Hungary, Count Louis (Ludwig), who died on 26 October 1765, and his wife Maria Theresia, *née* Countess Kinsky; of him, Prince Khevenhüller (Diaries 1764–7, p. 149) wrote, 'Ce n'étoit pas une aigle, mais il avoit du bon sens' and knew 'Hungary and how to deal with that nation'. The proper spelling is 'Batthyány'. 'Stahremberg' = probably Johann Ernest (1716–86), Count von Starhemberg (*recte*), and his wife, *née* Weissenwolf; perhaps 'Louis' was a nickname, for there is no Ludwig known in any of the Starhemberg genealogies (Schönfeld's *Adels-Schematismus ... Zweyter Jahrgang*, Vienna 1825, pp. 38ff.). Madame von Walldorf can not be identified. Count Salm: probably Carl Anton Joseph (with whom Zinzendorf was friendly) and his wife, Maria Francisca, *née* Countess Esterházy; Carl Anton Joseph, born 1697, was the founder of the princely line of Salm-Reifferscheid zu Krautheim. His brothers included Franz Ernest (1698–1770), Bishop of Tournay, and Leopold (b. 1699), founder of the cadet branch zu Hainspach (Counts) in Bohemia. 'Mac Elligot' (brothers): one of them was an Imperial Captain (Khevenhüller 1758–9, p. 59), perhaps identical with, or the brother of, Freiherr Ulysses Mac Eligot who was created *Kämmerer* in 1770 (Khevenhüller 1770–3, p. 237, document 31). Many members of the Wallis family were in the military profession; possibly our Colonel was one of the sons of the famous *Feld-Marschall* Franz Wenzel (d. 1744). 'Lanuis' = Franz Joseph Lanjus von Wellenburg (1757–80), later *Rittmeister* in the Archduke Leopold's Cuirassier Regiment (*Gothaisches Genealogisches Taschenbuch der Gräflichen Häuser*, 114, Jahrgang, Gotha 1941, p. 263. Lamberg = Anton Franz de Paula, Count von Lamberg, later Ambassador in Turin and Naples.
2 Johann Joseph, Prince von Khevenhüller-Metsch, the author of the invaluable Diaries here often cited.

his most difficult music for the horn.[1] But the more interesting item of the two is that referring to the engagement of Augusta Houdiere (Auguste Houdière). Previously our knowledge of her activity in the *Capelle* was limited to Pohl's mentioning her in connection with the year 1766 (Pohl II, 261). Now we have the date of her engagement and the terms of her contract. From the small salary we may assume that she was a young singer, still learning: Barbara Fux started with but 20 Fl. in 1757, and Theresia Riedl was only earning 60 Fl. in 1760. We believe, as noted before, that she may have belonged to Bon's Pressburg company, and may have been the 'Sign[ia] [Signorina?] Augusta' for whom Haydn wrote an aria in *La Marchesa Nespola* (*Il Marchese*). Possibly she contributed to the 'opera buffa' given at the January festivities and was engaged on the strength of a good performance. Nevertheless she remains an elusive member of our steadily growing *Capelle*: missing on the 1765 list (*infra*, pp. 406ff.), she is reported again (by Pohl) to be included in a 1766 document.

On 1 May, Prince Nicolaus made another financial arrangement for Haydn. In 1761, the *Vice-Capellmeister* had received 30 Kreuzer as a *per diem* allowance for food when he and the *Feld Musique* were on the Esterházy country estates. In Prince Paul Anton's time, this had meant for '5 Sommer Monathe'. Prince Nicolaus, however, obviously intended to spend much more time on the country estates, and therefore granted Haydn the 30 xr. *per diem* for the whole year:

> [PCDI] No. 497. Princely Comission dd[o] 1[m] May, according to which the princely *Capellmeister* Hr. Joseph Haÿden instead of board is to receive at all times a *per diem* of 30 xr. from the Gral [General] Cassa.

This meant that Haydn now received a fixed addition of 15 Fl. 30 Xr. each month. His first receipt in this new capacity is dated 31 May 1763 (Eisenstadt) and the money was paid by Chief Receiver (Cashier) Johann Zoller.[2] This addition meant a total of 182 Fl. 30 Xr. p.a., which, added to his 600 Fl., made the impressive total of 782 gulden 30 Kreuzer p.a.

On 1 August 1763, a fourth horn player was engaged:

> [PCDI] No. 502 Princely Resolution dd[o] 1[m] Aug. 1763, following which the new hunting horn player Franz Reinerd [Reinert; Reiner] is accepted into princely service, and receives a Convention [contract].

> [PCDI] No. 506 Princely Common dd[o] 30 Aug: 763, on the strength of which the hunting-horn player Reinert à 1[m] ult., i.e. July, is graciously granted 17 xr. board money.

For the first time Haydn now had four horn players in the *Capelle*, and there were also sufficient string players to enable the horn players to play their own instruments and not to substitute as string players (e.g. Franz). The horn 'choir' from 1 August to 31 December (when Reiner[t]) left, was therefore as follows:

		[In Haydn's scores]
First (high) Players:	Johann Knoblauch (from 1761)	[I]
	Carl Franz (from April 1763)	[III]
Second (low) Players:	Thaddäus Steinmüller (from 1761)	[II]
	Franz Reiner(t) (from August 1763)	[IV]

Haydn lost no opportunity to show Prince Nicolaus the increased sonority of symphonies with four instead of two horns. Probably the first three of Haydn's several

---

1 See *Haydn at Eszterháza 1766–1790*, p. 71.
2 EH, Forchtenstein, Generalcassa, 1763. Rubr. VIII. No. 128. J. Harich in *HJB* IV, 43.

works with four horns are: (1) Cassatio for four horns and strings in D (Hoboken *deest*; discovered in the Clam Gallas Archives in Prague by the present writer, 1959; Diletto Musicale 66, Verlag Doblinger), which uses the famous 'Posthorn' signal also found in Haydn's Symphony No. 31. (2) Symphony No. 13 in D (autograph EH, Budapest; 1763). (3) Symphony No. 72 in D (no autograph and grossly out of date in the chronological list of 104 symphonies prepared by E. Mandyczewski for the Breitkopf & Härtel *Gesamtausgabe* in 1907; for a discussion of the chronological aspects of this work, *vide* pp. 552, 564, 647). We have indicated, in the list of Haydn's horn players, the probable disposition in Haydn's scores of 1763, where we already find the 'interlocking' pattern of nineteenth-century horn-writing, whereby chords are spaced as follows:

[Symphony No. 13/I, opening:]

4 Corni in D

or in a graphic disposition
$$\begin{bmatrix} I \\ III \\ II \\ IV \end{bmatrix}$$
– yet another of the many pieces of evidence in this

biography illustrating Haydn's uncanny sense of modernity in musical notation (another is his writing for the timpani in real, rather than transposed, notation).[1]

Gregor Werner made his Will on 2 August. It was first published by the indefatigable Janos Harich (loc. cit., 'Die Testamente'), and we give some extracts here. It is the Will of a profoundly religious, modest man. After the usual opening formulas, we read:

1° I leave my poor soul in the hands of God, to Whose boundless mercy I commend myself, in repentance; and my body shall be committed to earth by a priest. Without the previous death knells, and at the service a Requiem shall be sung.

		fl
2° For my poor soul, 20 Holy Masses should be read, facit	. . .	10
3° For the P. Franciscans, and for each one of the musicians a quarter-pound candle, for each of the Petrines a half-pound candle	. .	
4° For the 3rd Order I leave	.	4
For the Franciscan Brotherhood	.	2
For the Order of the Rosary	.	3
For the Order of Children's Teachers	.	2
To be distributed *extra* to the children	.	1
For the Town Hospital	.	2
For the poor Husarin[2]	.	3
For the poor Christina[3]	.	2
For charity money	.	4
For cook Maria Anna for long and faithful service and also my usual bed	.	30
	facit	63

---

1 On the question of range and disposition of Haydn's horn players, see Paul Bryan in *Haydn-Studien* III/1, pp. 53ff.
2 The widow of the tenor Hussar (Huszar, etc.).
3 Probably Christine Kopp.

In the last place, my few worldy goods should be auctioned except for clothes, linen, cane and dagger, which should be left to my profane son Antonio Werner on account of his many children and which should thus be considered *in extra* but with the proviso that their father should be obliged to see that his children diligently pray for me, and as for the remaining furniture and cash, my most respected Herr son who has taken [holy] orders, Nepomuc Werner, should in peace divide these goods with the other brother, but each should obligate himself to pay from this his inheritance the sum of 12 f., from which a gravestone should be made for me as pro memoria. NB. Board and salary, and a Dono gratuito for Marianna [the cook], as well as house rent, should after my death be paid out in full. Given at Eisenstadt this 2nd day of August 1763.

Josephus Gregorius Werner
Hochfürst-Esterhazyscher Capellmeister.[1]

Johann Späch[2] as invited witness.
Franz Nigst[3] as invited witness.

The soprano Barbara Fux was now granted a *Deputat* (payment in kind):

[PCDI] No. 501 Princely Resolution dd̶e̶ 1̱m̱ 7bris [Sept.] 7̄6̄3, on the strength of which the singer Barbara Fuxin is graciously allowed a *Deputat*.

In the late summer, Mathias Haydn suffered an accident in Rohrau. 'As he was working', Griesinger (16) tells us, 'a pile of wood next to him collapsed; some of his ribs were broken, and he died shortly thereafter'. His Last Will reads:

In the name of the Holy Trinity, God the Father, the Son and Holy Ghost, Amen.

I, Mathias Hayden, Wheelwright in Market Rohrau, being sound in mind and body, do hereby make my Last Will,

Firstly, I leave my soul to God, my maker, and my body to be buried according to the Rites of the Holy Catholic Church.

Then I leave for the preservation of the Holy Statue of the Pierced Side	30 Fl.
For 10 Holy Masses to be read here	5 Fl.
For the Brotherhood of the Saint Joann Nepo[mucensis]	5 Fl.
I leave to my wife M; Anna in cash, together with the Marriage Dowry	100 Fl.

Item the Marriage Bed or Canopy Bed
The cupboard in the chamber with its clothes
A cow with the fodder for the current year
She should not be repudiated [cast out] unless she can not get along [with the stepchildren], and from the house she should be left 2 *Metzen* of corn.
Then 2 sheep, 1 billy-goat – the old one.
The house and the trade should go to my daughter Catharina, together with the vineyeard, it and the cellar [outside the house for storing wine] should remain with the house.

My son Johannes should be given in advance	100 Fl.

[for signatures see overleaf:]

---

1 For the codicil to this Will, see 9 October 1765, *infra*.
2 Joannes Spach (Johann Späch), book-keeper in the Eisenstadt Castle Administration.
3 Franz Nigst, Esterházy Rent-Master.

Caspar Gobatsch, Master Tailor from here as witness
Mathias Pimpl [Mathias Haydn's successor as village judge], Co-
citizen, as witness
Liebolt Schnabl, Cobbler Master as witness

Mathias Heyten. [Haydn's seal: oval shield held by two lions, on
top a five-pointed crown]
                [Harrach Archives, now Adelsarchiv, Vienna; Schmid, 249]

Notes:
Haydn's second wife was Maria Anna Seeder, who had been the serving maid in the house before
Haydn's first wife died: *vide supra*, p. 80. Her relationship with her stepchildren was apparently not
the best. It is touching to see Mathias leaving ready cash to the least talented of his sons, Johann, who
later went to Eisenstadt as a tenor under Joseph Haydn's protection. The Statue of the Pierced Side
still exists: the trust fund for it was renewed on 7 November 1804 (document: Schmid, 253); Haydn
considered the Statue in both his Wills (1801, 1809). Gravestone: see Schmid, 252. The Will was
deposited on the day of Mathias's death, 12 September 1763 and probate granted on 10 December.
Mathias Haydn's daughter, Anna Catherina, married Christoph Näher on 20 November 1763 and
therefore had 'no need of the trade' (permission to exercise the trade of wheelwright). It devolved on
the apprentice in the house, Joseph Ammon. The house, valued at 1,600 Fl., was turned over to
Mathias Haydn's son-in-law, the farrier Johann Philipp Frö(h)lich, who in turn accepted the
responsibility of paying all the hereditary portions and settling the trust funds. Contract: 21 April
1764, signed by Frölich, Johann Vieltzwieser, Christoph Näher – Mathias Haydn's sons-in-law –
'Herr Joseph Haydn, also authorized representative of his two younger brothers, Johann Michael
and Johann Hayden [*sic*], present in Rohrau.' Under the terms of the Will, although not mentioned,
Joseph Haydn and his brothers received most of their mother's and grandmother's share in the
worldly assets. Joseph's share was 105 Fl. 43 Xr. 2 d., and after the legal manipulations were
completed, he received, a quarter of a century later(!) 67 Fl. 21 Xr. 3 d. which he generously turned
over to his brother Johann, tenor in Eisenstadt. The protocol of the inventory reads: 'According to
the subjoined declaration ddto Esterhaz the 29th of May 1787 H. Joseph Haiden presents the
inheritance sum per 67 fl. 21 kr. 3 d. to his brother Johann Haiden in Eisenstadt.' Schmid 250f.,
Ferdinand Menčik, 'Einige Beiträge zu Haydns Biographie' in *Musikbuch aus Österreich*, 1909 (many
documents).

On 17 September, the Haydns were godparents to the newly born son of his
oboist, Johann Michael Kapfer, in a ceremony at the Bergkirche:

17. huius Baptizatus est Josephus, Legitimus filius Joannis Michaelis Kapffer [*sic*]
musici Arcensis, ac coniugis eius Elisabethae, Levavit Dominus Josephus Hayden
Vice-Capellae Magister, cum coniuge sua Anna Maria.

The Haydns, together or separately, were soon to be in great demand to act as
godparents of the many children born to members of the *Capelle* and as witnesses of
their marriage. As early as 1763, therefore, we can see the beginning of that special
relationship between Haydn and his musicians which was soon to place him in the
ranks of regular Esterházy diplomacy, acting as go-between in the often difficult
triangle of *Regent* Rahier, the Prince and the supposedly (but not always) submissive
musicians. A few days later, on 23 September, the Haydns again acted as godparents,
this time at the baptism (in the parish church of St Martin) of Joseph Carl Anton, son of
the princely hunting horn player Thaddäus Steinmüller and his wife.[1]

Haydn's relations with his fellow-composers was often equally warm. Carl
Ditters (later von Dittersdorf), in his autobiography,[2] relates:

I spent the rest of the summer and the following winter, apart from my duties,
in the frequent company of the charming Joseph Haydn. Which music friend does

1 André Csatkai, 'Die Beziehungen Gregor Josef Werners, Joseph Haydns und der fürstlichen Musiker zur Eisenstädter Pfarrkirche', in
Burgenländische Heimatblätter, Jg. I/1 (1932), p. 15.
2 *Lebensbeschreibung* (ed. Miller), Munich 1967, pp. 127f. From the detailed circumstances of Dittersdorf's life, we are able to date the
above quotation in the summer of 1763 and autumn/winter 1763–4.

not know the name and the beautiful works of this excellent composer? – About every new piece that we heard by other composers, we made our comments under four eyes, permitted to each that we considered good its just deserts and criticized what there was to criticize.

I advise every budding composer to enter into a similar covenant with one of his colleagues, forsaking envy and ill-will, and to do that which Haydn and I did with our examinations; I assure you that there is nothing which is more suited to educating oneself than such friendly relationships, when all prejudices are removed. It is not only useful for understanding how with certain means many a beautiful passage can be produced, but it will also teach you to avoid those rocks on which this or that composer came to grief. Of course what I am saying is nothing new; for it is well known that criticism – real, unprejudiced criticism by real connoisseurs – has always been of assistance to all the fine arts and sciences, and will always continue to do so.

Haydn was always a good and generous colleague, and as soon as Prince Esterházy began to hold regular operatic seasons at Eszterháza Castle (from 1776), Haydn suggested performing a whole group of operas by his old friend Dittersdorf.[1]

———

Haydn and the musicians lived in the so-called 'Old Apothecary' next to the Bergkirche, and it is with that rather uncomfortable and draughty building that the following document deals:

> ... In the old Apothecary, where the musicians Ludovici [Luigi Tomasini] and Weigl live, it would be very necessary to put down a new floor and also to repair the doors, because the wind blows the dust, the rain and in wintertime the snow right into the middle of the room; if Your Highness would approve this small *reparation*, please graciously approve the enclosed estimate of costs ... Eisenstadt, 21st 8bris [Oct.] 7̄6̄3̄.
> [EH, Budapest, Országos Levéltár P. 154 (old Fasc. 1524), ff. 3 v. and 4r.]

This short description makes it easier to understand why, as soon as Werner died and Haydn was automatically created Head Chapel Master, in 1766, he fled from the Old Apothecary on the hill and purchased a little house in the Klostergasse; the chequered history of Haydn's house belongs to a later volume of this biography.

We now come to a bill for the repair of instruments and purchase of mutes for the violas, new strings, and so on:

Specification
of repairs to the princely choir music instruments and of other things delivered during this current year 1763, as followeth:

	fl	kr
First 2 mutes made for the violas . . . . . . :	—	6
Item 1 new saddle made for the violin . . . . . :	—	3
Then an overspun viola string . . . . :	—	7
Item 11 violins cleaned à 4 kr. makes . . . . . :	—	44
Again 1 new violin bow delivered pr. . . . . . :	—	12
On 12th February the old choir violas glued and repaired, for which . . . . :	—	12
On 1st April a new saddle delivered per . . . . . :	—	3

1 See Chronicle 1776 in *Haydn at Eszterháza 1766–1790*, pp. 394ff.

On 2d April a violin bow delivered per . . . . . : — 12
On 4th Juny 2 fingerboards bound with copper wire, the soundpost
[*Stimholtz*] put right . . . . : — 4
On 17 July 2 overspun string delivered per . . . . : — 12
On 22 July 6 overspun strings delivered per . . . . : — 36
On 10 Augusti a violin glued and a new saddle delivered per : — 7
Then 3 new violin bows delivered à 12 kr., makes . . : — 36
Item 4 pegs for the violin made to order per . . . : — 7
Item a large ruling machine for 6 staves per . . . . : 1 25

Summa : 4 46

Carl Braun
Princely Oboist

[Haydn's hand:]
Josephus Haydn mpria
as agreed

[Schlanstein's hand:]
Edmund Schlanstein mpria
Administrator

Eisenstadt, 29th 8bris 1763
[Receipt; signed by 'Carl Braun / Hoboist']
[Cover: contents, file number & date]
[A.M. 418, EH, Budapest; Valkó II, 637; here from original]

The feast of St Nicholas, patron saint of Nicolaus Esterházy, falls on 6 December. It is thought that the annual name-day was celebrated each year in Eisenstadt, and that Haydn usually contributed by composing a new cantata. That for 1762 has disappeared but relics of it may have survived in a *contrafactum* for the church (*vide infra*, pp. 495ff.). Fortunately the Cantata for 1763 has survived: it is in G, for soli, choir and orchestra, beginning with the words 'Destatevi, o miei fidi' (XXIVa:2). We cannot determine who in Eisenstadt wrote the words for these Latin and Italian cantatas; possibly Carl Friberth was responsible for the Italian cantatas, but we rather imagine that Girolamo Bon, who had fashioned such libretti before, was the author. A complete list of these Cantatas for 1763 and 1764, as given in Hoboken, vol. II (pp. 183ff.), will be found *infra*, pp. 464ff. The autographs of these three Cantatas, formerly in the Preußische Staatsbibliothek Berlin, were taken to Grüssau Monastery in Poland at the end of the Second World War and are now (1978) officially in the safe keeping of the Polish authorities,[1] pending their return to Berlin.

The following bill from the Esterházy Archives is more interesting than it looks, for as a result of its existence, we can establish that Haydn's double bass, or at least his solo or *Cammer Violon* (small bass), was tuned in the following unusual, gamba-like fashion:[2]

---

1 *The Times Literary Supplement*, 26 May 1978.
2 There is a manuscript score, reputedly autograph, by J. B. Vanhal signed 'Divertimento Vanhal Violino, Viola, Violoncello ô Violone' of which the first two pages are in the National Library in Prague and two further pages in the Campori Collection of the Biblioteca Estense, Modena. On page two of the Prague MS., Vanhal (or the copyist) has written the double bass ('Violone') tuning on the right-hand margin, A–F sharp, D–A, i.e. Haydn's tuning. The Vanhal MS. suggests that this tuning was by no means uncommon in Austria at that time. We are indebted to our colleague at the University College, Cardiff, Dr David Wyn Jones, for this valuable information.

– whereas of course our modern tuning is

It is probable that Haydn's large double bass had three strings, either tuned in the old way G-d-a or possibly with Contra C being the lowest note (there are many times when Haydn requires this low C). The technical aspects of this *Cammer* tuning will be discussed in connection with the actual music.

Specification

of strings delivered to the princely chamber musique from 1st April to 9th X^bris 763.

	fl	xr
3 Violoncello [*Passetl*] A	—	,, 12
4 ditto D	—	,, 24
4 ditto overspun G:	-1-	,, 24
2 ditto ditto C:	—	,, 42
1 violon [double bass] A:	—	,, 17
1 ditto f sharp	—	,, 34
1 ditto D:	—	,, 51
1 ditto large A:	-1-	,, 8
2 bundles violin E:	-4-	,, —
1 bundle ditto A	-1-	,, 30
4 overspun viola G. et C:	—	,, 24
3 violoncello [*Passetl*] A:	—	,, 12
more 3 ditto ditto	—	,, 12
1 bundle E:	-2-	,, —
½ ditto A:	—	,, 45
4 violoncello [*Passetl*] A:	—	,, 16
more 2 ditto violin E:	-4-	,, —
1 bundle ditto A:	-1-	,, 30
1 violon [double bass] f sharp:	—	,, 34
1 ditto A:	—	,, 17
20 violin D:	—	,, 30
Summa	21	,, 42

Eisenstadt, 9th X^bris 1763

[Haydn's hand:]
As agreed Joseph Haydn mpria

[Sigl's hand:]
I acknowledge receipt of this sum from the Rental Office in full payment for strings delivered by my father Eisenstadt, 9th Xbris [Dec.] 1763

Frantz Sigl mpria

[Cover: contents, file number & date]
   [A.M. 417 (1,883), EH, Budapest; Valkó II, 636f.; here from original]

In Advent-tide, there was regularly an early Mass, known as the 'Rorate service'. In his youth Haydn had composed a 'Rorate' Mass, the *Missa brevis alla capella* 'Rorate coeli desuper', using a Gregorian melody from the Introitus of the Votive Service for Our Lady. 'Rorate' comes from a passage in Isaiah (xlv, 8): 'Drop down, ye heavens, from above' which has been quoted in full (*supra*, p. 142). In Eisenstadt, the *Capelle* participated in these Advent services in the early morning, and were given a breakfast

'Rorate soup' afterwards in the Inn 'Zum Goldenen Greifen' (where the strolling players were also lodged in 1762). Later, however, the musicians were given 9 gulden in lieu of the soup. Since the *Chor Musique*, at this period, was still under Werner, it was not until Werner was terminally ill (1765) that Haydn was called in about the *Rorate* soup. In 1763, the 9 gulden were accepted in Werner's name by Johann Novotni.[1]

Apart from the Cantata and the performance of *Acide* (composed in 1762), the principal works composed in 1763 are (at least) three Symphonies, all of which survive in dated autographs: Nos. 12, 13 and 40.

Chronicle 1764

Haydn had a brief respite from the daily requirements of his Prince in the first part of 1764, for Nicolaus attended the Coronation of Joseph II as King of the Holy Roman Empire at Frankfurt-am-Main. Nicolaus was sent as the First Ambassador of the Elector of Bohemia. The formal election took place on 27 March, the coronation on 3 April. Among the court musicians from Vienna were Gluck, Dittersdorf, the castrato Guadagni (who had created the role of Orfeo) and twenty members of the *Hofkapelle*. Concerning Prince Nicolaus Esterházy's spectacular appearance at Frankfurt, we have the interesting description by the young Goethe:[2]

> Scarcely had I reached home than my father caused me to be called, and communicated to me that it was now quite certain that the Archduke Joseph would be elected and crowned King of Rome. An event so highly important was not to be expected without preparation, nor allowed to pass with mere gaping and staring. He wished, therefore, he said, to go through with me the election- and coronation-diaries of the two last coronations, as well as through the last capitulations of election, in order to remark what new conditions might be added in the present instance. The diaries were opened, and we occupied ourselves with them the whole day till far into the night. . . .
>
> After the preliminary alteration and arrangement of the rooms in the town-house had seemed to us worth seeing, after the arrival of the ambassadors one after another, and their first solemn ascent in a body, on the 6th of February, had taken place, we admired the coming in of the imperial commissioners, and their ascent also to the *Römer*, which was made with great pomp. The dignified person of the PRINCE of LICHTENSTEIN made a good impression; yet connoisseurs maintained that the showy liveries had already been used on another occasion, and that this election and coronation would hardly equal in brilliancy that of Charles the

---

1 Receipt:
Quittung
Über Neun Gulden, welche ich Endes Unter Schribener, als ein von der gesamelten Music, wegen gehaltene Rorate jährlich aufgeworfenes Contingent von Eisenstädter Rändtmeister Herrn Frantz Nigst richtig eingefangen habe. Eisenstadt, den letztem Decembris 7̄6̄3̄.

Johann Novotnj mpria
Statt Hrn Capellmeis[ter]
Id est 9 fl. — xr.   Werner

[Cover: contents, file number and date]

[A.M. 917, 2nd document of 1.881, EH, Budapest]

2 From *Dichtung und Wahrheit*: we use the pretty translation entitled *The auto-biography of Goethe. Truth and Poetry: From my own Life.* Translated from the German by John Oxenford, Esq. London: Henry G. Bohn, York Street, Covent Garden, 1848, Fifth Book, pp. 147ff. Mr Mark Trowbridge kindly procured this translation for us.

Seventh. We younger folks were content with what was before our eyes; all seemed to us very fine, and much of it perfectly astonishing.

The electoral congress was fixed at last for the 3rd of March. New formalities again set the city in motion, and the alternate visits of ceremony on the part of the ambassadors kept us always on our legs. We were compelled, too, to watch closely, as we were not only to gape about, but to note everything well, in order to give a proper report at home, and even to make out many little memoirs, on which my father and Herr von Königsthal had deliberated, partly for our exercise and partly for their own information. And certainly this was of peculiar advantage to me, as I was enabled very tolerably to keep a living election- and coronation-diary, as far as regarded externals.

The person who first of all made a durable impression upon me was the chief ambassador from the electorate of Mentz [Mainz], BARON VON ERTHAL, afterwards Elector. Without having anything striking in his figure, he was always highly pleasing to me in his black gown trimmed with lace. The second ambassador, BARON VON GROSCHLAG, was a well-formed man of the world, easy in his exterior, but conducting himself with great decorum. He everywhere produced a very agreeable impression. PRINCE ESTERHAZY, the Bohemian envoy, was not tall, though well-formed, lively, and at the same time eminently decorous, without pride or coldness. I had a special liking for him, because he reminded me of MARSHAL DE BROGLIO. Yet the form and dignity of these excellent persons vanished, in a certain degree, before the prejudice that was entertained in favour of BARON VON PLOTHO, the Brandenburg ambassador. This man, who was distinguished by a certain parsimony, both in his own clothes and in his liveries and equipages, had been greatly renowned from the time of the seven years' war, as a diplomatic hero. At Ratisbon, when the Notary April thought, in the presence of witnesses, to serve him with the declaration of outlawry which had been issued against his king, he had, with the laconic exclamation: 'What! you serve?' thrown him, or caused him to be thrown, down stairs. We believed the first, because it pleased us best, and we could readily believe it of the little compact man, with his black, fiery eyes glancing here and there. All eyes were directed towards him, particularly when he alighted. There arose every time a sort of joyous whispering, and but little was wanting to a regular explosion, or a shout of *Vivat! Bravo!* So high did the king, and all who were devoted to him, body and soul, stand in favour with the crowd, among whom, besides the Frankforters, were Germans from all parts.

On the one hand these things gave me much pleasure; as all that took place, no matter of what nature it might be, concealed a certain meaning, indicated some internal relation, and such symbolic ceremonies again, for a moment, represented as living the old Empire of Germany, almost choked to death by so many parchments, papers, and books. But, on the other hand, I could not suppress a secret displeasure, when I was forced, at home, on my father's account, to transcribe the internal transactions, and at the same time to remark that here several powers, which balanced each other, stood in opposition, and only so far agreed, as they designed to limit the new ruler even more than the old one; that every one valued his influence only so far as he hoped to retain or enlarge his privileges, and better to secure his independence. Nay, on this occasion they were more attentive than usual, because they began to fear Joseph the Second, his vehemence and probable plans. . . .

The coronation-day dawned at last, on the 3rd of April, 1764; the weather was favourable, and everybody was in motion. I, with several of my relations and friends, had been provided with a good place in one of the upper stories of the Römer itself, where we might completely survey the whole. We betook ourselves to the spot very early in the morning, and from above, as in a bird's-eye view, contemplated the arrangements which we had inspected more closely the day before. . . .

Neither my years nor the mass of present objects allowed me to make many reflections. I strove to see all as much as possible; and when [at the subsequent banquet] the dessert was brought in and the ambassadors re-entered to pay their court, sought the open air, and contrived to refresh myself with good friends in the neighbourhood, after a day's half-fasting, and to prepare for the illumination in the evening.

This brilliant night I purposed celebrating in a right hearty way; for I had agreed with Gretchen, and Pylades and his mistress, that we should meet somewhere at nightfall. The city was already resplendent at every end and corner when I met my beloved. I offered Gretchen my arm; we went from one quarter to another, and found ourselves very happy in each other's society. The cousins at first were also of our party, but were afterwards lost in the multitude of people. Before the houses of some of the ambassadors, where magnificent illuminations were exhibited (those of the Elector-Palatine were pre-eminently distinguished), it was as clear as day. Lest I should be recognised, I had disguised myself to a certain extent, and Gretchen did not find it amiss. We admired the various brilliant representations and the fairy-like structures of flame by which each ambassador strove to outshine the others. But Prince Esterhazy's arrangements surpassed all the rest. Our little company were in raptures both with the invention and the execution, and we were just about to enjoy this in detail, when the cousins again met us, and spoke to us of the glorious illumination with which the Brandenburg ambassador had adorned his quarters. We were not displeased at taking the long way from the Rossmarkt (Horse-market) to the Saalhof; but found that we had been villanously hoaxed.

The Saalhof is, towards the Maine, a regular and handsome structure, but the part in the direction of the city is exceedingly old, irregular, and unsightly. Small windows, agreeing neither in form nor size, neither in a line nor placed at equal distances, gates and doors arranged without symmetry, a ground-floor mostly turned into shops, – it forms a confused outside, which is never observed by any one. Now here this accidental, irregular, unconnected architecture had been followed, and every window, every door, every opening, was surrounded by lamps; as indeed can be done with a well-built house; but here the most wretched and ill-formed of all façades was thus quite incredibly placed in the clearest light. Did one amuse oneself with this as with the jests of the Pagliasso,* though not without scruple, since everybody must recognise something intentional in it; – just as people had before glossed over the previous external deportment of Von Plotho, so much prized in other respects, and when once inclined towards him, had admired him as a wag, who, like his king, would place himself above all ceremonies – one nevertheless gladly returned to the fairy kingdom of Esterhazy.

This eminent envoy, to honour the day, had quite passed over his own unfavourably situated quarters, and in their stead had caused the great esplanade of linden-trees in the Horse-market to be decorated in the front with a portal illuminated with colours, and at the back with a still more magnificent prospect. The entire enclosure was marked by lamps. Between the trees stood pyramids and spheres of light, upon transparent pedestals; from one tree to another were stretched glittering garlands, on which floated suspended lights. In several places bread and sausages were distributed among the people, and there was no want of wine.

---

* [Original footnote:] A sort of buffoon.

Here now, four abreast, we walked very comfortably up and down, and I, by Gretchen's side, fancied that I really wandered in those happy Elysian fields where they pluck from the trees crystal cups that immediately fill themselves with the wine desired, and shake down fruits that change into every dish at will. At last we also felt such a necessity, and conducted by Pylades, we found a neat, well-arranged eating-house. When we encountered no more guests, since everybody was going about the streets, we were all the better pleased, and passed the greatest part of the night most happily and cheerfully, in the feeling of friendship, love, and attachment.

Pohl and the older generation of Haydn scholars assured us that, before arriving in Frankfurt, Prince Nicolaus had made a trip to Paris (Pohl I, 242). Janos Harich, on the other hand, categorically states that the Prince did not visit France on this occasion, and that the first time he saw Versailles and the French capital was on the occasion of his visit in 1767.[1] Prince Nicolaus also visited Paris in the autumn of 1781. On our most recent trip to the Budapest Archives in 1978, we could find no evidence that Nicolaus was in France in 1764, and the text of the Cantata which Haydn composed on the occasion of the Prince's return mentions the River Main ('. . . il merito lo innalzo la dove bagna il Meno le sue sponde').

The Prince's absence enabled Haydn, as we have seen, to be at Rohrau to attend to the legal work in connection with his father's death the year before. This was on 21 April. Four days later he was in Eisenstadt again, and we have a bill which, insignificant though it first appears, throws light on the above-mentioned Cantata.

[Haydn's hand:] Receipt
For 2 gulden which I the undersigned received, and herewith offer as receipt, from Herr Capel-Meister Haÿdn for tuning, stringing and other repairs done to the princely harpsichord [*Cembalo*]. Eisenstadt, 25th April $\overline{764}$.

Id est 2 Fl.   Joseph Zuerengast
                Organ Builder from
                der Neustadt [Wiener Neustadt]
[Cover: contents, file number and date]
                [A.M. 426, EH, Budapest; Valkó II, 639; here from original]

Presumably Zuerengast (in other documents he is listed as 'Zierengast') was illiterate and Haydn kindly wrote the whole receipt in the organ builder's name. Why this sudden preoccupation with repairing the harpsichord? The answer is provided by the Cantata, 'Da qual gioja improv[v]iso',[2] which in its second movement, an elaborate 'Coro' (really the four vocal soloists: this ensemble was often called 'coro' in Italian operas and cantatas of this period), contains a harpsichord solo. Haydn had used the princely absence to practice the instrument, which he had been forced to neglect because of all his orchestral duties: they consisted of leading from the violin since the violin section was so pitifully small in those days though it was, as we have seen, growing larger and was thus freeing the horns from having to double as string players, apart from enabling Haydn to write for himself a substantial 'Cembalo Solo'.

---

1 Harich, *Musikgeschichte*, p. 29. On the visits of 1767 and 1781 see *Haydn at Eszterháza 1766–1790*, pp. 141f., 452f.
2 XXIVa:3, but not 'al tuo arrivo felice', which Haydn composed, according to an autograph note in *EK* 'bey zurückkunft des Fürst Nicolay von Paris', or (if Harich's statement is correct) in 1767 and probably on 6 December of that year, the princely name-day. The whole problem of these cantatas and Hoboken's listing is discussed *infra*, pp.474ff.

Another bill, equally insignificant, reads as follows:

[Entire document up to and including Rockobauer's signature in Haydn's hand]

Catalogue

What I the undersigned delivered for his princely Highness Esterhasi's Musique and repairing the instruments.

Item Hautbois, bassoon and English horn reeds manufactured

	fl	X:
Sum	–9	7.

Mathias Rockobauer
Instrumentalist mpria

[Rahier's hand:]

The Eisenstadt Rentmaster should pay the above 9 fl. 7 xr. and enter the same in the books.

Eisenstadt, 9th Julÿ 764. P. L. Rahier

[Kapfer's hand:]

These nine gulden 7 xr. have been paid from the Rental Office, 9th Julÿ 764. Johann Georg Kapfer.

[Cover: contents, file number & date]

[A.M. 421, EH, Budapest; Valkó II, 637f.; here from original]

If we examine the autograph score of Symphony No. 22 of 1764 ('Philosopher'), we will see that it requires two cors anglais (English horns), for which, it would seem, new reeds were required.

Meanwhile, the soprano Anna Maria Scheffstoss had married the 'cellist, Joseph Weigl, and she asked to have her meals at the officers' table converted into a *Deputat*. The Prince agreed:

[PCDI] No. 516 de Anno 1764. Hochfürstl. Intimat ddͤ 17ᵐ Junÿ 764, on the strength of which the Court Singer Frau Anna Maria Weiglin instead of eating at the officers' table is granted money instead in the sum of 180 Fl. annually.

Anna Maria Weigl pursued a meteoric, though alas very short, career. She and her husband left Eisenstadt to go to Vienna, where he joined the orchestra of the Italian Opera and she became a member of the Burgtheater. She retired in 1773. The year before, she had been called '... a great musician and actress and equally strong in both *genres* [*opera buffa, opera seria*]'.[1] Although we know of her singing only in Haydn's *Acide* (Galatea), we may be sure that she also participated in the cantatas of this period, e.g. in the Duet 'Mai per te, stella rubella' from the Cantata 'Destatevi, o miei fidi' (XXIVa:2), written for Barbara Fux (Fuchs) and Anna Maria Scheffstoss.

In August, new uniforms for the men and dresses for the ladies were ordered for the Capelle:

Specifica[ti]ion

Of the newly made summer uniforms for the Musicÿ in the month of Augustj 764: what was necessary thereto, and what it cost:

The male uniforms of fine English fustian [*Parcan* = *Barchent*], that of the *Capel Meister* with woven silver loops, the waistcoat with broad and narrow *bordures*; 17 others with silver loops and tassels; for each uniform 2 pairs of breeches, viz.:

Capel Meister Heiden. Luitschi [Luigi Tomasini]. Heger. Nigst. Dichtler. Fribert. Garnie [Garnier]. Carlfranz [*sic*]. Sigl. Grießler. Knoblach [Knoblauch]. Steinmiller [*sic*]. Schwenda. Weigl. Hinterberger. 2. Kapfer. Bonno [Bon].

---

1 Müller's *Genau Nachrichten von beyden k. k. Schaubühnen* (Vienna 1772); Pohl I, 265.

S[umm]a: 18 persons 18 coats, 18 waistcoats, 36 pairs of breeches and 18 hats with silver *bordures*.

Item for the lady singers: 5 dresses *en robe* [*Roberond*] trimmed with silver fringes, and made from prepared [manufactured] cotton [*Groitos* = *coton*] fabric: viz. the Bonnin [Signora Bon], her daughter, Schefstoßin [= Frau Weigl], Barbara Eleonora [Barbara Fux, Eleonora Jäger]. S[umm]a: 5 female persons. 5 dresses. 5 skirts.

[Generalcassa, 1765. Rubr. VIII. Nr. 12½; J. Harich in HJB IV, 80f.]

We may note that the mysterious Augusta (Auguste) Houdière is missing; was she absent, or still a pupil and not yet entitled to an expensive court dress?

On 6 October, Prince Nicolaus made the unusual gesture – later to be repeated many times – of making a present in cash to Haydn:

Commission

According to which our Chief Receiver [Cashier] Johann Zoller is to pay our Capellmeister Joseph Hayden a gratiale pr[per] twelve ducats, and said Johann Zoller is to accept this disbursement as valid in his current accounts.
Schloss Süttör, 6th Octob. 1764.

Nicolaus Fürst Esterhazy (L.S.)

Idest 12. Ducats.

Receipt

Pr: Twelve ducats which I the undersigned have received in cash from the princely Chief Receiver Herr Johann Zoller according to a princely commission of a present for me. For which I hereby acknowledge receipt. Eisenstadt, 8th October 764

Id est 12 ordinary ducats per 49 f 30 Xr

Joseph Haydn mpria.

[EH, Forchtenstein, Generalcassa, 1764. Rubr. VIII. Nr. 105. J. Harich in *HJB* IV, 43]

Now from future 'gratiale' payments of this kind, we shall see that they are usually made after a successful performance or première of a Haydn opera – *La canterina, Lo speziale, Le pescatrici* and *L'infedeltà delusa* all earned substantial cash bonuses not only for Haydn but for Girolamo Bon, the singers and sometimes also the orchestra as well. But an opera performance in 1764? Haydn's last operatic première (as far as we know) was *Acide*, in January 1763, and his next *La Canterina* in July 1766 (later Pressburg, Carnival 1767). Once again, the documents in the Esterházy Archives come to our rescue. We quote this one out of context (it is a summary statement from 12 June 1764 to 16 May 1765):

Anno 1764, month of Juny in Eisenstadt Herr Heyten [*sic*] Kupel Meister [*sic*] should give:

12 d [June]	12 spinet strings [*Spieller Trats* = *Spieler-Draht*, literally players' strings]	. . .	× 2 =		24
8 July	26 ditto	. .	× 2 =		52
16 9ᵇᵉʳ [Nov.]	10 ells of silver fabric [*silber tocht*]	. .	× 16 =		2 44
——	3 ells of blue linen . . .	. .	× 15 =		45
11 January 765	8 [spinet strings] . . .	. .	× 2 =		16
10 May	12 ditto . . .	. .	× 2 =		24
16 d[itto]	6 ditto . .	. .	× 2 =		12

fl 5 37

[Haydn's hand:]

The silver fabric and linen were required for the opera and the 5 fl 37 xr have been paid

Joseph Haydn mpria

[Cover: 'Payment of various necessities for the Chamber Music.' File number and date]

[A.M. 439, EH, Budapest; Valkó II, 639; here from original]

Haydn tells us, in an autograph statement on this bill, that the 'silver fabric and linen were required for the opera'. Which opera? If we examine once again the bills submitted when the Eisenstadt 'glass house' opera was being constructed, we will recall that silver fabric was also then required, and that the 'mussels' (shells) and water effects for which this silver fabric was necessary were part of the scenery for Haydn's *Acide* (*vide supra*, p. 361n.). It is therefore *Acide* which was now being revived. Until quite recently, it was believed that *Acide* was performed in 1763 and then set aside; but contemporary newspaper reports show that it was still in the repertoire as late as 1774 (for the 1773–4 revival Haydn made substantial changes),[1] and here is strong documentary evidence that its first revival on the stage at Eisenstadt[2] took place in the autumn of 1764.

Another bill of the period belongs in this place:

Specification

of strings delivered for the Chamber Music. From 26th Maÿ to the end of October 7̄6̄4.

	[Haydn's hand:]	fl	xr	
Received	One low A violon [double bass]	1	8	——
	2 bundles violin E	4	—	——
	1 bundle A	1	30	——
	1 half bundle D at 15 *Klaffter*[3] [cord measure for string]	1	—	——
	6 violin bows	2	6	——
	8 violin G	—	24	——
	2 bundles E	4	—	——
	4 G for the viola and 2 C	—	35	——
	2 bundles E	4	—	——
	1 bundle E	2	—	——
	1 half bundle A	—	45	——
	2 G for the viola	—	12	——
	2 violon [double bass] A	—	34	——

Summa   22 fl 15 xr.
[22 fl 14 xr.]

Joseph Haydn mpria

[Sigl's hand:]

I acknowledge receipt of these twenty gulden 15 xr. paid by the Rental Office to me instead of my father.

Eisenstadt, 22nd 8bris [Oct.] 7̄6̄4. Frantz Sigl.

[Cover: contents, file number and date]

[A.M. 422, EH, Budapest; Valkó II, 640; here from original]

---

1 *Haydn at Eszterháza 1766–1790*, pp. 210f.
2 Or Kittsee? *Vide infra*.
3 *Clafter* (*Klafter*) or fathom: an old measure = 1·90 metre.

In the autumn, new winter uniforms were prepared for the *Capelle*:

Specification

Of the newly prepared Musicy winter uniforms, ordered in the month of November the 1st d̊ 7̄6̄4̄ and ready this day [not specified], what was required for them and what it cost, viz.:

A coat of pike-greyish fine-quality cloth, also waistcoat and breeches. The *Capel Meister's* made throughout *à la Bourgogne*, the others have the coats with *bordures*, the waistcoats with *bordures* and with broad gold facings.

For 17 persons without Bonno, as said, 17 complete uniforms with hats.

[EH, Forchtenstein, Generalcassa, 1765. Rubr. VIII. Nr. 12½. J. Harich in *HJB* IV, 8of.]

Some time in the summer or autumn, the whole *Capelle* was taken to the beautiful Esterházy Castle of Kittsee (pl. 12). Can it be that the revival of *Acide* took place there, in the great hall, on a temporary stage? It seems unlikely, but one would like to know what the singers performed – perhaps Haydn's cantatas; this latter theory would perhaps explain why the harpsichord at Kittsee required substantial overhauling. To this bill in Haydn's own hand may be added another, rather lengthy one, submitted by the Widow Braun (opposite). The list at the end of this document includes five bills, of which we omit that of the locksmith and that of the merchant with the almost illegible name. The other three, printed in this Chronicle, are: 'C:C:', concerning repairs to musical instruments earlier in the year (*supra*, p. 390); 'D:D:' appears immediately below; and the fifth is Widow Braun's account, brought forward.

Specification

What my late husband Braun brought to, and made, in strings and other appurtenances, for the princely choir. Namely:

Annô 1763

	X
In the month of Novemb: a bridge for the violoncello [*Bassetel*] constructed pr	9 xr
21st Xmb: [Dec.] for the princely choir 6 overspun strings for the violin, brought there per	30—
Together . .	39 xr

Annô 1764

		X
Vide [brought forward]		39
In the month of Januario two books of lined paper pr . . .	„	–8.
In the month of Martio 8 violins cleaned, then a violin glued, supplied 3 pegs, and the fingerboard bound with wire	„	30.
Also the old choir violoncello [*Passetel*] put in order, a hole plugged in the bridge	„	–9.
Then a book of lined paper . . . . :	„	–4.
The 22nd of Martÿ [March] 2 books of lined paper	„	–8.
The 28th ditto 2 books of lined paper	„	–8.
The 8th of Aprill [*sic*] 3 books of lined paper	„	12.
The 30th of Aprill 3 books of lined paper	„	12.
Item 1 peg supplied	„	–1.
The 20th of Maÿ restrung a violoncello [*Passetel*] . . .	„	17.
Then 2 new frogs for a bow	„	–6.
The 22nd of Maÿ an overspun G put on the violoncello [*Passetel*] and 3 pegs on the violin pr	„	18.

In the month of Maÿ 7 books of lined paper . . . . . „ 28.
In the month of Junio 5 books of lined paper . . . . . „ 20.
Then on the Cremona violin a hole plugged and glued with fine fish
   glue [*Hausen Blaterleim* = glue made from sturgeon bladder] . „ –6.
Then on another violin the fingerboard bound with a new copper
   wire . . . . „ –3.
In the month of Julio 12 books of lined paper . . . . „ 48.

Therefore the sum Pro Anno 1763, et 1764, all together . . . 4 f 37.

[new page, new hand:]

List: fl xr
A[:]A: The locksmith according to statement . . . . = —,, 17 ,,
B: B: The merchant Aukerl [?] . . . . . . = —,, 44 ,,
C: C: The organ builder from Neustadt [Wiener Neustadt] . = 2 —,,
D: D: The organ builder in Presburg [*sic*] . . . . = 2 —,,
               The above account thus . . = 4 ,, 37 ,,

                     In Summa = 9 ,, 48 ,,
                     [9 fl 38 xr]

    I acknowledge receipt of these nine gulden, 48 xr
    which were paid to me by the local Rental Office.
               Eisenstadt, 20th 9bris [Nov.] 1764:

         [Haydn's hand:] Joseph Haydn mpria

[Cover: contents, file number and date]
    [A.M. 423, EH, Budapest; Valko II, 637f.; here from original]

[Haydn's hand throughout:]
    I herewith attest that the organ builder from Presburg [*sic*] completely
overhauled the instrument or harpsichord [*Cembalum*] at the time when the whole
music [orchestra and singers] were in Kittsee, and I had to pay him two gulden.
    Eisenstadt, 20th 9bris [Nov.] 1764.

                Joseph Haydn mpria
    [A.M. 418, EH, Budapest; Valkó II, 638; here from original]

Another marriage within the *Capelle* united Barbara Fux (Fuchs) with the tenor
Leopold Dichtler. Joseph Haydn gave away the bride in this service at the parish
church of St Martin, and Georg Spach 'citizen' (*Bürgher*) was Dichtler's 'best man':

28 9ber [Nov.] Nomen et Cognomen Copulatorum:
Leopoldus Dichtler Tenorista sub Arce cum Barbara Fuxin
Nomen et Cognomen Testium:
Ex parte Sponsi Georgius Spach civis
Ex parte Sponsae Josephus Hayden Capelle [*sic*] Magister sub Arce
        [J. Harich in *HJB* VII, 20]

The Prince's name-day on 6 December was celebrated in various ways. From the
I.R. government it was announced this day that Prince Nicolaus was created Captain in
the Noble Hungarian Bodyguard formed in 1760.[1] And Haydn contributed a new

---

1 Pohl I, 244n.

Cantata, 'Qual dubbio' (XXIVa:4). It seems that Haydn's début [1] as a solo harpsichord player, when the Prince had returned from the coronation ceremony at Frankfurt early in the year, had not been unsuccessful; for in 'Qual dubbio' there is a soprano aria 'Se ogni giorno' which includes an elaborate 'Cembalo Solo'. Incidentally, the text of these cantatas – perhaps by Bon, as suggested before – always helps us in identifying the circumstances for which they were written. In this case, it is clear that Prince Nicolaus's name-day (not his birthday, which was on 18 December) was being celebrated: 'celebriamo con pompo del suo Nome il grande'.

Haydn was ill. We know nothing of the details, but the matter was serious enough for the composer to ask for help, as the Prince's reply makes clear:

> Petition of *Capell-Meister* Heyden.
> The subject of this petition is hereby graciously permitted to purchase the necessary medicines at our expense, but without setting a precedent; for the other musicians, since they are in any case well paid, are to secure the necessary medicines on their own.
>
> Vienna, 27th Xber [Dec.] 1764.
Nicolaus Fürst Esterhazy mpria
>
> [EH, Forchtenstein, Acta varia, Fasc. 189; G. Feder and S. Gerlach in *Haydn-Studien* III/2 (1974), p. 94]

Note:
There is the original of this document (signed by the Prince) and a copy (with the title not found in the original). The clause 'but without setting a precedent' is inserted.

Here is one of the many instances of Prince Nicolaus's personal kindnesses to his *Vice-Capellmeister*, of which the Chronicle in the forthcoming quarter-of-a-century will contain other touching examples. It was not only a question of money, although for a variety of reasons – not least, perhaps, Frau Haydn's apparently spendthrift nature, quite the opposite of her husband's – Haydn never seemed to have more than that which his daily needs required: we shall see that when he went to England, he had to his name hardly more than 2,000 gulden capital.[2] Apart from the question of money, we shall see that Prince Nicolaus twice rebuilt at his own expense Haydn's house, destroyed by fire in 1768 and 1776 (the cost of rebuilding the house in 1776 was 450 Fl.). It was, essentially, this princely kindness which kept Haydn part of the *Capelle*.

Our Chronicle closes with a bill from the Esterházy Archives; in it we note repairs for the cor anglais, required in Haydn's Symphony No. 22. In this year, apart from the Cantatas 'Da qual goija improv[v]iso' and 'Qual dubbio', we have dated autographs of Symphonies Nos. 21, 22, 23 and 24 as well as a Divertimento for harpsichord and strings (XIV:4), discussed *infra*.

---

1 A Divertimento for harpsichord and strings (XIV:4) also dates from 1764.
2 *Haydn at Eszterháza 1766–1790*, p. 410, and *Haydn in England 1791–1795*, p. 319. Most of Haydn's capital was, from 1766 to 1778, invested in his little house in Eisenstadt (Klostergasse). When he finally sold the house in 1778, he was paid 2,000 Fl., of which he invested 1,000 Fl. with Prince Esterházy's banking system, using the remaining 1,000 Fl. to pay off his various debts. Another factor in Haydn's penury was his generosity towards his relatives, not least towards Johann, his youngest brother, who was at first an unpaid member of the *Capelle* from 1765. Prince Nicolaus obviously engaged Johann *ex gratia* and Haydn had to support him. See also Johann's engagement, *infra*, p. 424.

[Haydn's hand:]
Specification

What was expended for strings and new oboe reeds sent for and for repairing the English horn and other instruments, viz.:

	F	Xr
First 3 bundles violin E	4	30
1½ bundles A	2	15
40 batches D	—	40
2 *violon* [double bass] A	—	42
For evening up [*abgleichen*] the violoncello and new strings with a new bridge	1	25
6 bundles A at 4 kr makes	—	24
item same amount D at 6 kr makes	—	36
the same 3 of G at 17 kr makes	—	51
item 3 of C each at 24 kr makes	1	12
for a bow to be given new hair	—	24
for 12 oboe reeds à 10 Kr the piece	2	—
for repairing the English horn	1	6
to the organ builder for quilling and tuning the *clavier* 4 times	4	—
item viola, restrung and put in order	—	20
item 3 G for the viola	—	12
Summa	20 fl	37 kr.

[Another hand:] I acknowledge receipt of these twenty gulden 37 xr which were paid to me by the Rental Office. Eisenstadt, 31st Xbris [December] 1764:
[Haydn's hand:] Joseph Haydn mpria

[Cover: contents, file number and date]
[A.M. 428, EH, Budapest; Valkó II, 638f.; here from original]

Chronicle 1765

Dichtler, now a married man, needed a *Deputat* instead of his board at the officers' table:

[PCDI] No. 522. Princely Resolution dd° 16 Jan: 765, according to which the princely Musico Tichtler [Dichtler] is to be granted a *Deputat* instead of his previous board at the officers' table.

Haydn was recovering from his illness in Eisenstadt, and it is not known when and if he joined the Prince in Vienna for the customary annual visit at Christmas and the New Year (which often continued for some weeks). Joseph II, now King of the Romans, had lost his much cherished wife, Princess Isabella of Parma, through a smallpox epidemic on 27 November 1763. But he was expected to marry again, and this time it was with Maria Josepha of Bavaria. The ceremony took place on 25 January 1765, and this second, unhappy, marriage also terminated with smallpox, which killed Maria Josepha at Vienna on 28 May 1767.

We now present a letter (not in CCLN) which was discovered recently in the Esterházy Archives at Forchtenstein:

SERENE HIGHNESS AND NOBLE PRINCE OF THE HOLY ROMAN EMPIRE
GRACIOUS AND DREAD LORD![1]

I have wished to inform Your Serene Highness in profound submission that yesterday one of the hunting-horn players named Knobloch[2] died and will be buried today. And since for the completeness of the *musique* another two hunting-horn players would be necessary, I wished to recommend to Your Serene Highness Anton Reibisch,[3] whose art and deportment I know well and find suitable. He has lately served with His Excellency, Count Frantz Eszterhazy[4] (who has dismissed his *musique*), and will most submissively wait upon Your Serene Highness; and, if considered acceptable, he will also find a suitable partner. But all this is suggested to Your Serene Highness without the least prejudice to your gracious consideration. I have felt badly several times in the past few days, and much worse than before. Thus I take the liberty of submitting, not only for me but in the name of the whole *musique*, a petition,[5] herewith enclosed, whereby medicines would be graciously resolved to be made at princely expense (just as was always done for me in the past); and I console myself in the hopes of high princely favour and in submissive respect, I remain

Your Serene Highness'
Most humble, obedient
Joseph Haydn.

Eisenstad [*sic*], 23rd January 1765.

[G. Feder and S. Gerlach in *Haydn-Studien* III/2 (1974), p. 94]

In the Appendix (*Anhang*) to the *Wienerisches Diarium* No. 9 of 30 January 1765, we read of a performance of Gluck's *Il Parnasso confuso* which must have contained one of the most extraordinary casts ever to grace a Viennese stage. There is a very long (six columns) description of this event; we read:

> ... the music of this piece is by Chevalier Gluck and again received the general applause that is always given to this clever composer. Archduke Leopold played the harpsichord [*continuo*]. Archduchess Amalia sang the role of Apollo, and the other roles (Muses Melpomene, Euterpe and Erato) were sung by Serene Highnesses, Archduchesses Elisabeth, Josepha and Charlotte. [Ballet described, Shepherds and Shepherdesses danced by the young Counts Franz von Clary, Xavier von Auersberg, Johann von Clary, Friedrich von Fürstenberg, Theresa von Clary, Christine von Auersberg, Christiane von Clary and Pauline von Auersberg.][6]

In the same paper, we also read of 'the new Opera by Herr Marco Coltellini: Il Telemaco, with the music by Herr Caval. Christoph Gluck, performed on the stage of the Burgtheater *gratis*, in the presence of the Court.' Here we encounter the name of Marco Coltellini, who wrote the libretto of Haydn's *L'infedeltà delusa*.

---

1 'Durchleuchtig Hochgebohrner Reichs Fürßt / Gnädigst Hochgebiettender Herr Herr!'

2 Johann Knoblauch, who had been with the *Capelle* since 1761. Now that Franz Reiner(t) had also left (December 1763), there were two horn players: Carl Franz and Thaddäus Steinmüller.

3 For some reason unknown to us, Anton Reibisch was not engaged. In May and June 1765, Franz Stamitz (Steinmetz) and Joseph Dietzl were given contracts as horn players – *vide infra*, p. 405.

4 Franz, Count Esterházy (1715–85), for whose funeral ceremonies Mozart wrote the great *Maurerische Trauermusik* (K.477). O. E. Deutsch, *Mozart und die Wiener Logen*, Vienna 1932, pp. 12f., 31; also our edition of the score for the *Neue Mozart Ausgabe* (advance edition by Bärenreiter Verlag, Kassel; also miniature score Tp.18).

5 The petition was certainly refused. It seems that this letter must have crossed that of Prince Nicolaus' dated 27 Dec. 1764, in which it is stated that the musicians have to purchase their own medicines.

6 There is a famous painting of this dazzling occasion; it hangs in the *Arbeitszimmer* (study) of the Austrian President in the Imperial Palace (Hofburg), Vienna, and the faces painted are obviously portraits. The painting is by Johann Franz Greippel (1720–98) and is reproduced in colour in *The Eighteenth Century: Europe in the Age of Enlightenment*, London and New York 1969, p. 26. The seating plan of this orchestra (Schönbrunn, Schloßtheater) is similar to that of the Teatro Regio in Turin (op. cit., p. 27) – two lines of musicians as in the spurious Eszterháza picture of Haydn's *L'incontro improvviso*. It must have been typical.

Prince Nicolaus may have been a witness to all these events, but Haydn, recuperating in Eisenstadt, was not. His name appears on a bill of 28 January:

Extract

What I, Franz Altmann, belt-maker, produced on the orders of the *H: Capel Mayter* [*sic*], as follows.

First, 4 little leather bands for the harpsichord [*Flüg*] which makes: 30 xr.

2nd on the case of the princely violin a catch was placed: 10 xr.

Together 40 xr.

[Haydn's hand:]

I acknowledge receipt of these forty xr. from the Rental Office.

Joseph Haydn mpria.

[Altmann's hand:]

Eisenstadt, 28th January 1765. Frantz Altmann.

[Cover: contents, file number & date]

[A.M. 433, EH, Budapest; Valkó II, 641; here from original]

We next hear that the widow of Carl Braun, oboist, was to receive a pension:

[PCDI] No. 523 Princely Resolution ddᵉ 25 Martÿ, on the strength of which Ursula, the widow of the oboist Praun, is graciously to receive a pension.

For Carnival, Prince Nicolaus now engaged a troupe of players from St Pölten, formerly known as the 'Schultz Compagnie' and now directed by his widow, 'die Schultzin'. The bills (given in extracts in a footnote)[1] show that the Country

1 EH, Budapest: A.T. Nr. 107, No. 669–692:
'*Pro Anno 1765* / EXTRA- AUSGAABEN. / Rubr. VIIIᵃ Fas. IVᵃ / Denen Comedianten ist vermög denen Inlagen bezahlet worden 1036 Fl. 15 Xr. / № 12 ist der Elenchus

Nr. 670/1: 1765. 16. Aprill Eisenstatt / № 1 / Commission von S. Dchl. die Comedianten betreffendt. [next page =] Commission Vermöge welcher unser ober Einnehmer Zoller denen aufgenohmenen, und hier spühlenden Comödianten alle wohnen, solang dieselben Uns mit solchen Bedienen von 9ᵗᵉⁿ April 765 angefangen Ein Hundert Gulden außbezahlen, und in verrechnung bringen solle. Ingleichen die jenige 50 Fl. welche vor die Fuhr umb dise Comödianten von St Pölten bis Eisenstadt zu Transporthieren durch unseren Haus Hofmeister Züsser bezahlet worden, sein demselben ebener Massen zu bonifitiren passiret. Eisenstadt den 16. Apl. 1765. Nicolaus Fürst Esterhazy [mpria]:

No. 672/3: '1765. 16ᵗᵉ Aprill Eisenstatt / No. 2 / Denen Comedianten vor die Fastenwochen laut Contract 100 Fl –xr.' [Principalin Josepha Schultzin acknowledges receipt for the week 9–16 April of 100 gulden and seals the document in red wax; her seal: head and shoulders of a man in armour, underneath oval coat-of-arms with bow-and-arrow, on top of head, a bird.]

No. 674/5: 'Land Kutscher Conto / 1765. / 18ᵗᵉ Aprill / №. 3 / Dem Landkutscher, so die Comedianten auferogeführt 50 Fl. / Elias Stadlinger, Bürgerl. Landg. [acknowledges receipt of the sum in cash, Vienna, 4 April 765, for 31 March 765, when he] 'mit 8 Pferdten 1 Laadtung und 1 Leitterwagen nach St Pölten abgegangen den 1ᵗᵉⁿ Aprill von da mit einer Comique Banda gegen Eisenstadt abgegangen, den 2ᵗᵉⁿ alda eingetroffen, den 3ᵗᵉⁿ von da leer zurückgekehrt'. [Underneath: Züsser acknowledges having received the money for Zoller on 18 April 1765.]

[There follows the list of weekly receipts for the Troupe, each signed by Directrice Josepha Schultz(in)]:

No. 676/7: 1765. 23. Aprill Eisenstat / №. 4 / denen Comedianten vor die zweyte Wochen 100 Fl. —x. Josepha Schultzin Directrice [signs].

No. 678/9: 1765. 30ᵗᵉ Aprill Eisenstatt / № 5 / denen Comedianten vor die 3. Wochen 100 Fl. [Schultzin signs].

No. 680/1: 1765. 7ᵗᵉ May Eisenstatt / № 6 / denen Comedianten vor die 4ᵗᵉ Wochen 100 Fl. [Schultzin signs].

No. 682/3: 1765. 14ᵗᵉ May Eisenstatt / № 7 / denen Comedianten vor die 5ᵗᵉ Wochen 100 Fl. [Schultzin signs].

No. 684/5: 1765 21ᵗᵉ May / № 8 / denen Comedianten vor die 6. Wochen 100 Fl. [Schultzin signs].

No. 686/7: 1765 28ᵗᵉ May Eisenstatt / № 9 / denen Comedianten vor die 7ᵗᵉ Wochen 100 Fl. —x. [Schultzin signs].

No. 688/9: 1765. 3ᵗᵉⁿ Juny Eisenstatt / No. 10 / [8ᵗᵉ Woche] [Schultzin signs].

No. 690/1: 1765 3ᵗᵉⁿ Juni Eisenstatt / Nᵒ 11 / denen Comedianten Ein graziale in 50 Stck. ord: Duc. 206 Fl. 15 xr. zum Abgang. [Prince orders this on 27 May in Eisenstadt. Schultzin signs].

No. 692/3: Pro Anno 1765 / № 12 / Elenchus uber Vorligende / Beylaagen betragendt / 1056 Fl. 15 xr. [other side:] Specification dessen, was denen Comedianten Bezahlet /

No. 1. Die Fürstliche Commission
  2. Vor die Fasten Woche [Shrovetide-week]   100.—
  3. Dem landkutscher [carriage]   50.—
  4. Vor die zweyte Wochen [2nd week]   100.—
  [5–10. 3rd to 8th weeks, 100 fl. six times in six columns]
  11. Für Graziale [tip]   206.15

Suma   1056.15

Coachman (*Land Kutscher*) with two waggons and eight horses left Eisenstadt on 31 March, fetched the 'Comique Banda' from St Pölten on 1 April, arrived there on the 2nd and on the 3rd returned to St Pölten empty. The Troupe received 100 Fl. per week, starting on 9 April, the Country Coachmen 50 Fl. Frau Josepha Schultz and her Troupe seem to have pleased the Prince, for they remained eight weeks. Horányi (German ed., 37), basing his theory on the Troupe's repertoire when in Pressburg, suggests that in Eisenstadt they played popular and partly extemporized pieces (Hanswurstiada). One of the members was Carl Marinelli, later a famous director in his own right. Another member, Menninger, was (according to the testimony of Frau Schultz herself) an excellent Hanswurst; but perhaps she was prejudiced, seeing that she married Menninger and he took over the Schultz Troupe as director. We may assume that Haydn supplied the required overtures, entr'actes, etc., with the *Capelle*.

The following bill now engages our attention:

<u>Received</u>

2 bundles violin E	„	4 fl.	—
ditto 1 bundle A	„	1 „	30
20 batches D	„	— „	30
1 violon [double bass] A	„	— „	17
1 violon f sharp	„	— „	34
1 bundle violin E	„	2 „	—
12 overspun violin G	„	— „	36
2 viola C	„	— „	12
dᵉ 1–G	„	— „	6
2 lengths violoncello [*zwey Claftrige / Bassedl*] A . . .	„	— „	30
1 length violoncello [*zwey Claftrige / Bassedl*] D . . .	„	— „	15

[Sigl's hand:]   10 fl   30x

[Haydn's hand] From 1st January to 10th Aprill [*sic*] the above-listed strings correctly received

Joseph Haydn mpria

[Sigl's hand:]
I acknowledge receipt of these
ten gulden, 30 xr which were paid
to me instead of to my father from
the Rental Office. Ei: 10th April 765
      Frantz Sigl

[Cover: contents, file number and date]
          [A.M. 434, EH, Budapest; Valkó II, 640; here from original]

Finally, Prince Nicolaus began engaging the new horn players, to bring the total number to four:

[PCDI] No. 526. Princely Intimat ddᵉ 1. Ap. 765, according to which Frantz Stainmetz [*sic*] is engaged as hunting-horn player.[1]

Girolamo Bon's contract was now renewed, as we are informed by the following PCDI: 'No. 535½ New original contract, ddᵉ 15ᵐ Apr. 765, of the painter & operisten Le Bon.' Now about this time the name of Signora Bon seems to disappear, and one assumes she died; however, in the forthcoming list of the *Capelle* of 25 April, Bon and daughter are listed. Presumably that is why a new contract had to be issued.

1 Franz Stamitz (Steinmetz, etc.), about whom *vide supra*, pp. 327f. For his salary and *Deputat*, see the forthcoming list.

It was always assumed that the rewards (collectively with the other musicians on 2 March 1767 but individually on 9 December 1766) were for his exquisite stage sets. However, in view of the fact that Bon was well known for his libretti, we wonder if he was not responsible not only for the Italian text of the cantatas (1763, 1764) but possibly also for the arrangements of the Haydn operas from (lost or known) Italian originals, i.e.

La canterina (1766): libretto by? (lost Italian original, arranged by Bon?);

Lo speziale (1768): libretto by Goldoni with various later additions, also adapted for Eszterháza (by Bon?);

Le pescatrici (1769; performed 1770): ditto;

L'infedeltà delusa (1773): libretto by Marco Coltellini with widespread adaptations for Eszterháza (by Bon?). Bon was given an increase on 1 October 1772, and was dead by 1 December 1773. See *Haydn at Eszterháza 1766–1790*, pp. 64f.

Hitherto it was thought that these adaptations were the work of Carl Friberth. It now seems that Bon, with his experience, is the more likely candidate; perhaps Friberth acted as his 'assistant' and learned the trade; at any rate Friberth was doing this kind of arrangement himself by 1775 (*L'incontro improvviso*).

We come now to an important interim list of the *Capelle*, drawn up on 25 April; because it has not hitherto been published in its entirety, it is given (pp. 408–9) complete in the original German,[1] together with a partial translation and glossary (opposite). Here, it will be noticed for the first time that instead of singers being required to serve in the chamber and choir music, they are now obliged to serve chamber and theatre. For the greater part of his life at Eszterháza, Haydn's services were in the opera house, and this list, and the resuscitation of *Acide*, are the first hints of the importance that the stage would come to have in the life of Prince Nicolaus and his *Vice-Capellmeister*.

Two further documents now claim our attention:

[PCDI] No. 525. Princely Intimat dd̥ 15ᵗ May 7̄6̄5̄, on the strength of which the first violinist Aloysio Tomasini is to receive 50 Fl. increase in his salary.

[PCDI] No. 527. Princely Intimat dd̥ 15ᵗ May 7̄5̄6̄ [*sic*], on the strength of which Joseph Dietzl[2] is to be engaged as a hunting-horn player. NB vide 1049 [a later addition, referring to changes in his status].

Haydn now had four horns in his *Capelle* and celebrated the event by writing another work using all four instruments, an even more brilliant conception than the earlier pieces so scored: Symphony No. 31 ('With the horn signal').

---

1 A.M. 154, No. 465–7; extracts in Valkó II, 641f.

2 Dietzl's contract, which we reproduce here for the first time, reads (as can be seen) like those of previous years; but it was thought that students might like to have the original German of such a contract – now that we have given one *in extenso* in French and others summarized in English; Dietzl was also a violinist, as we shall see later.

Nachdeme wir den Joseph Dietzl in / unsere Dienste als Waldhornist auf / und angenohmen, und ihme nachstehenden / jährlichen gehalt, oder Besoldung Gnä / digst ausgeworfen haben. Also / In Baaren jedes Monath ..... 15 Fl. / Wegen Paradirung gleich denen andern täglich ..... 17 xr / Jahrlich Ein, oder alle zwey Jahr / zweyerley Kleyder; / So wird seine Schuldigkeit seyn; / 1° Nicht allein in Eysenstadt Bey der Cam̄er, / und Chor Musique nach denen gegebenen / Stunden fleissig zu erscheinen, und solche / so Lang, als uns freue oder statt Beliebig / seyn wird mit zu machen, sondern auch zu / Wienn, und in Andern orthen wohin der / selbe / Beruffen sein wird, seine Dienste embsig / zu Leisten. / 2ᵈᵒ dem Vice-Capellmeister alle parition / zu Bezeigen, und was Er in Herren Dienst / anordnen wird, ohne wieder- Rede zu / Befolgen; / 3° Solle Er sich ehrlich, ruhig und friedig / wie es von einem jeden ehrliebenden / Menschen bey Einer Fürstl.ᵉⁿ Hofstadt / die umbstände erfordern auffführen, und alle Unsinnigkeizen zu vermeyden. / 4° Ohne Hochfürstl. erlaubniß von Eysenstadt, / Wienn oder wo derselbe eine zeitlang / Bey der Hofstadt sich wird aufhalten / mussen, solle Er sich nicht absentiren, / vill weniger von der Cam̄er, oder Chor / Musique ausbleiben, sondern ehe, und / bevor dem Capellmeister melden, / und / Wann die vorgewendedte Ursachen vor / Billich erkannt werden, so dann wird / auch nach Gestalt deren Umbstanden / die Hochfürstliche Resolution erfolgen. / Gegeben Schloß Eysenstadt / den 15ᵗᵉ Maÿ 7̄6̄5̄ / Nicolaus Fürst Esterhazy [mpria]. [A.M. 4291, No. 18. 465–67, EH, Budapest]

The final bills of the spring season concern strings, repairs to string instruments and supplying reeds for woodwind instruments (for a facsimile of the first see p. 410):

[Sigl's hand:] From 10 Aprill [*sic*] [Haydn's hand:] to 23rd Maÿ
[Sigl's hand:]

	f	xr.
6 mutes	=	36
8 violin bridges	=	32
1 violohn [double bass] bow	=	34
6 violin bows	2	6
1 bundle E	2	—
1 violohn A	=	17
1 violohn D	=	51
1 violohn f sharp	=	34
1 bundle E	2	—
3 Bassetl [violoncello] G	1	3
3 Bassetl C	1	3
2 viola G	=	12
2 viola C	=	12
	12	=

I acknowledge receipt of these twelve gulden from the Rental Office
Eisenstadt, 24th Maÿ $\overline{765}$:   Frantz Sigl

[Haydn's hand:]
These correctly received. Joseph Haydn mpria

[Cover: contents, file number & date]
          [A.M. 443, EH, Budapest; Valkó II, 643; here from original]

Receipt

For six gulden 36 xr. which I the undersigned received in full and in cash from the hands of the Herr Rentmaster Nigst, and for which this is the receipt; in payment for 18 *Huboi* [oboe] reeds, 6 English horn reeds and 12 bassoon reeds.
Eisenstadt, 25th May $\overline{765}$. [Mathias Rockobauer]
     Huboi á 12 xr. – Eng^{ln} C^{ro} á 10 xr. – bassoon á 10 xr.
Id est 6 fl: 36 xr.   [Haydn's hand:] As agreed Joseph Haydn mpria

[Cover: contents, file number and date]
          [A.M. 442, EH, Budapest; Valkó II, 642; here from original]

Notes on the list of the Esterházy *Capelle* given overleaf:

PARTIAL TRANSLATION

Names – Dichtler and Jäger 'who are obliged to participate in both the chamber and theatrical music'; Griessler also obliged to participate in the chamber and theatrical music; Nigst, same remark. After Staimiz: 'The summer uniforms pro 1763 cost ...' / 'The winter uniforms pro 1764 ...'.

At end of names: 'From analysis one year results in' ... 'The theatrical painter, Gierolomo Le Bon, together with his daughter' ... 'Castle and Book-keeping Dept., Eisenstadt ...' etc.

GLOSSARY

Naturalien – goods in kind
Rindtfleisch – beef
Saltz – salt à 4 denar [pfennige]
Schmaltz – lard
Kerzen – candles
Schwein – pig
Brenn Holtz – firewood
Kraut et ruben – cabbage and beets
Nebenstehende [etc.] – these goods in kind reckoned in cash make ...
Die Baare [etc.] – the sum received in cash makes ...
Das Quartier Geldt – lodging money
Das Kost Geld – money for food
Die Kleydung – uniform (or dress)
Summa der völligen Ertragnis – sum in full

1765 Extractus Conventionum Musicos ad N^um 52
Fasc. 27 Miscell. Conventionals Auszug. Was nemblichen die Hochfürstliche
Chor = Cameral & Theatral Music sowohl an baaren Geldes Besoldung als Naturalien,
und Kleydung all Jahrlich zu empfangen haben.

	Wein à 4 Fl.	Weiz à 1 Fl. 15 xr.	Körn. à 51 xr.	Kuchl-Speis à 3 Fl.	Rindt fleisch à 3 xr.
Chor Music					
	Emer		Metzen		♯
Ober Capell Meister Herr Gregorius Werner	15	—	15	—	—
Discantistin, Barbara Dichtlerin } Welche zugleich die Cameral	6	6	10	—	300
Altistin, Eleonora Jagerin } & Theatral Music zu versehen	9	4	8	¾	300
Tenorista, Josephus Diezel } Schuldig seynd	9	4	8	¾	300
Bassista, Melchior Griessler, so auch die Cameral et Theatral Music zu versehen Schuldig ist	9	4	12	¾	300
Organista, Joannes Novothny	9	4	12	¾	300
Violinista, Franciscus Nigst, So zugleich die Cameral Music zu versehen schuldig ist	—	—	—	—	—
Violinista, Adamus Sturm	9	4	12	¾	300
Violinista [Violonista], Antonius Kühnel	9	4	12	¾	300
Summa der Chor Music	75	30	89	4¾	2100
Cameral Music					
Vice Capell Meister Herr Josephus Heiden	—	—	—	—	—
Discantistin, Anna Maria Weiglin	—	—	—	—	—
Erster Tenorist, Carolus Fribert	—	—	—	—	—
Anderter Tenorist, Leopoldus Dichtler	6	6	10	—	300
Erster Violinist, Aloysius Thomasinj	—	—	—	—	—
Anderter Violinist, Franciscus Garnier	—	—	—	—	—
Dritter Violinist, Johann Georg Heger	—	—	—	—	—
Fleutraversist, Franciscus Sigl	—	—	—	—	—
Violoncelist, Josephus Weigl	—	—	—	—	—
Erster Hautboist, Johann Michael Kapffer	—	—	—	—	—
Anderter Hautboist, Johann Georg Kapffer	—	—	—	—	—
Erster Fagotist, Johann Hinterberger	—	—	—	—	—
Anderter Fagotist, zugleich Violonist Johann Georg Schwenda	—	—	—	—	—
Erster Waldhornist, Carolus Franz	—	—	—	—	—
Anderter Waldhornist, Thadaeus Steinmiller	—	—	—	—	—
Dritter Waldhornist, Franciscus Staimiz	—	—	—	—	—
Die Somer Kleydungen pro 1763 haben erfordert 1679 Fl. 56 Xr.					
Die Winter Kleydungen pro 1764 2191 Fl. 34½ Xr.					
Facit 3871 Fl. 30½ Xr.					
Eruirtermaßen fallen auf ein Jahr	6	6	10	—	300
Summa der Cameral Music	6	6	10	—	300
Der Theatral Mahler, Gierolomo Le Bon samt seiner Tochter	7	—	—	—	—
Hierzu die Cameral Music	6	6	10	—	300
Dan die Chor Music	75	30	89	4¾	2100
Summa Sumarum	88	36	99	4¾	2400

Schlos, und Buchhalterey Eisenstadt den 25ᵗᵉⁿ April 1765

tz d.	Schmalz à 15 xr.	Kerzen à 10 xr.	Schwein à 8 Fl.	Brenn Holtz à 2 Fl. 30 xr.	Kraut et Ruben à 2 Fl.	Neben stehende Naturalien ertragen in Geld		Die Baare Geldes Besoldung ertraget		Das Quartier Geld		Das Kost Geld		Die Kleydung		Summa der völligen Ertragnis	
	#	#	Stuck	Klaft[er]	Emer	Fl.	xr.	Fl.	xr.	Fl.	xr.	Fl.	xr.	Fl.	xr.	Fl.	xr.
	—	—	—	—	—	72	45	400	—	28	—	—	—	—		500	45
o	30	30	—	6	—	83	42	100	—	—	—	—	—	—		183	42
o	24	24	—	6	I	93	15	64	30	12	—	—	—	—		169	45
o	24	24	—	6	I	93	15	65	—	—	—	—	—	—		158	15
o	30	30	I	6	I	107	57	200	—	—	—	—	—	in Natura		307	57
o	30	30	I	6	I	107	57	100	—	—	—	—	—	—		207	57
	—	—	—	—	—	—	—	50	—	—	—	—	—	in Natura		50	—
o	30	30	I	6	I	107	33	50	—	12	—	—	—	—		169	33
o	30	30	I	6	I	107	57	50	—	12	—	—	—	—		169	57
o	198	198	4	42	6	774	21	1079	30	64	—	—	—	—		1917	51
	—	—	—	—	—	—	—	600	—	—	—	182	30	in Natura		782	30
	—	—	—	—	—	—	—	100	—	—	—	180	—	—		280	—
	—	—	—	—	—	—	—	300	—	—	—	182	30	in Natura		482	30
o	30	30	—	6	—	83	42	150	—	—	—	—	—	in Natura		233	42
	—	—	—	—	—	—	—	250	—	—	—	182	30	in Natura		432	30
	—	—	—	—	—	—	—	240	—	—	—	—	—	in Natura		240	—
	—	—	—	—	—	—	—	200	—	—	—	—	—	in Natura		200	—
	—	—	—	—	—	—	—	240	—	—	—	—	—	in Natura		240	—
	—	—	—	—	—	—	—	240	—	—	—	—	—	in Natura		240	—
	—	—	—	—	—	—	—	240	—	—	—	103	25	in Natura		343	25
	—	—	—	—	—	—	—	240	—	—	—	103	25	in Natura		343	25
	—	—	—	—	—	—	—	240	—	—	—	103	25	in Natura		343	25
	—	—	—	—	—	—	—	240	—	—	—	103	25	in Natura		343	25
	—	30	—	6	—	20	—	330	—	—	—	—	—	in Natura		350	—
	—	—	—	—	—	—	—	240	—	—	—	103	25	in Natura		343	25
	—	—	—	—	—	—	—	240	—	—	—	103	25	in Natura		343	25
30	30	60	—	12	—	103	42	4090	—	—	—	—	—	1935	45¼	1935	45¼
30	30	60	—	12	—	103	42	4090	—	—	—	1348	—	1935	45¼	7427	27¼
-	—	—	—	7	—	45	30	400	—	30	—	—	—	—		475	30
30	30	60	—	12	—	103	42	4090	—	—	—	1348	—	1935	45¼	7427	27¼
80	198	198	4	42	6	774	21	1079	30	64	—	—	—	—		1917	51
10	228	258	4	61	6	923	33	5569	30	94	—	1348	—	1935	45¼	9870	48¼

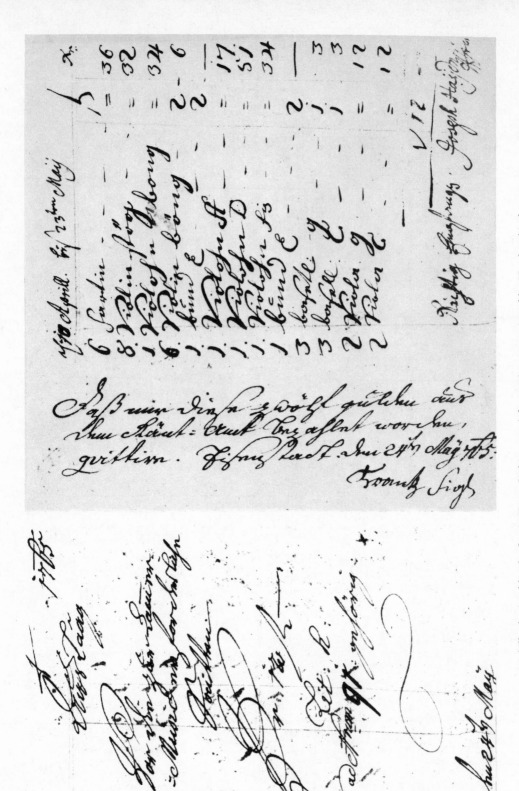

A bill submitted by the flautist Franz Sigl in 1765 (cf. p. 407), countersigned by Haydn; this document establishes the fact that the stringing of the double basses in Haydn's orchestra was different from the method used today.

Prince Nicolaus decided to join the ceremonies at Innsbruck for the forthcoming wedding of Archduke Leopold with the Infanta Maria Luisa of the Spanish Bourbons, which was to take place at St Jakob's parish church on 5 August. Nicolaus ordered a new baryton to be made at Innsbruck, together with a richly ornamented travelling case for it (leather studded with brass ornaments and nails); this is a lost instrument and not the baryton now preserved in the National Museum, Budapest (see *Haydn at Eszterháza, 1766–1790*, p. 90).

The old team of Pietro Metastasio and Johann Adolph Hasse produced the festival opera, *Romolo et Ersilla*, given in the Court Theatre on the Rennplatz the following day, 6 August. But, as the great Austrian historian Adam Wandruszka says, 'a curiously unlucky star shone over the festivities. As far as the Opera is concerned, neither the libretto nor the music nor the ballets by Hilverding pleased, and the fireworks on 13 August were drenched by a thunderstorm.' (It was the first of several ominous warnings for Hasse: his days of serene triumph were numbered, and in the next volume of this biography, we shall see the failure of his last operas. *Romolo et Ersilla* was the third from last of his stage works.) The unlucky star shone over the bridal pair: Leopold, for whom this was an 'arranged marriage', was seriously ill with what we would call a pyschosomatic intestinal ailment. The Spanish contingent quarrelled among themselves.

The Viennese Court had also attended, including the Emperor and the Empress, and when (on 22 July) the news that Don Philip, the bride's uncle and father of Archduke Joseph's first wife, had suddenly died, the Empress tried to keep the news secret; but an indiscretion on the part of her consort prevented circulation of the bad tidings from being postponed until after the ceremony. Then, between the theatre and a *souper* on 18 August, Emperor Francis Stephen died suddenly. Maria Theresa, prostrate with grief, cut off her hair and wore black for the rest of her life.[1]

Joseph II now began the long period of unhappy co-rule with his mother who, after the mourning period, continued to exert great influence almost until her death in 1780, prohibiting her headstrong son from accomplishing many of the reforms to which he was dedicated. The career of Joseph II and his relationship to Haydn in particular and music in general is discussed in the second volume of this biography (*Haydn at Eszterháza 1766–1790*, especially pp. 411ff.).

Meanwhile at Eisenstadt Johann Novotni, who had served faithfully for many years as Castle Organist and Cancellista, now died. Prince Nicolaus gave the position to his son, and also helped the other children who were under age:

[PCDI] No. 531. Intimatum of the Herr Regent v. Rahier to the Princely Book-keeping Dept., according to which ... 'Franz Novatni [*sic*] is to be granted the position of organist with the same salary as that which his father received as organist [as opposed to Cancellista]. Ad. 30ᵐ Aug. 765.

[Conventionale 1769, but with earlier notes:] The two [minor] children of the late Book-keeping Cancellista Joannis Novotni, by name Aloÿsius and Theresia Novotni, are according to princely Decretation ddᵉ Süttör 1ᵗ 8bris [Oct.] 1765, in consideration of the long service of their late father, to receive the following

---

1 A. Wandruszka, *Leopold II*, vol. I, Vienna-Munich 1963, p. 109. Harich, *Musikgeschichte*, 29f. Hasse, not Gassmann, composed the Opera.

pension until they are themselves able to earn their own bread, viz. [long list, including clothes for each, wheat, corn, etc. and 'a little pig' (*Schweindl*)].

[EH, Eisenstadt, Prot. Nr. 4678. J. Harich in *HJB* VII, 75f.]

On 1 September, an interesting new addition to the Esterházy house officers may be registered:

[PCDI] No. 535. Original contract of Hr. Dr. Sonnleithner as newly engaged house inspector in Vienna, together with his Convention for 200 Fl. . . . [orders to collect documents for Dr Sonnleithner] a dato 1. 7bris [Sept.] $\overline{765}$.

Christoph Sonnleithner (1734–86) had studied law and it was in a legal capacity that he was engaged by Prince Nicolaus, first as a 'house inspector' but later as what we would call a 'family lawyer'. In that versatile age, it should perhaps not surprise us that he was also a good composer, several of whose symphonies[1] were attributed to Haydn. It is reported in the Wurzbach *Lexikon* (see entry 'Sonnleithner') that at the sale of Dr Sonnleithner's effects in 1786, Haydn was present and bought all the music.

We now come to the first serious altercation, or rather series of altercations, between Haydn and the *Capelle*, on the one hand, and *Regent* Rahier and the Prince, on the other. The matter happened in this fashion:

[Letter from P. L. Rahier to Dr Christoph Sonnleithner. *German*]
High, well born,
Most respected Herr Doctor!
    In answer to your letter of the 10th instant, I send you the information that the musician Frantz Sigl anno 1765 through an explosion from his flint, when he shot at some birds on the roof, set on fire a princely house next to the castle and that house burned down completely; if swift assistance had not arrived, and if the roof of the neighbouring house had not been removed by a providential foresight, the whole town could have been set on fire and a great catastrophe could have occurred; all of which was a great shock to His Highness the Prince, and which also involved great expenses, so that the subject was dismissed from service, but engaged again anno 1767. . . .
    Eisenstadt, 17th 7ber [Sept.] 1772, P. L. Rahier. . . .[2]

[A.M. 4159, No. 17.663/4, EH, Budapest]

Haydn considered Sigl's arrest and dismissal for this accident wrong and protested to *Regent* Rahier, who (as will be seen) flew into a rage and apparently put the whole matter in the darkest terms to the Prince who, in turn, reprimanded Haydn (in a lost letter dated 8 September). But Haydn himself was by now quite appalled by the whole affair, and especially by the conduct of Rahier who, true to type, started to behave like

---

1 Landon *SYM*, p. 812 (77), 815 (93); Hoboken I: E55, F3.
2 This letter was once of a series collected by Dr Sonnleithner in the context of the lawsuit Sigl *contra* Esterházy, held in the Lower Austrian Court. Prince Paul Anton in his Will had left all the house officers one year's salary as a legacy, but for some obscure reason the princely administration paid out only half a year's salary to Franz Sigl and J. G. Kapfer – possibly because of Sigl's pyromanic efforts and, as far as Kapfer is concerned, for some infraction of which we no longer have the details. Kapfer and Sigl sued Prince Nicolaus, however, for the remaining half-a-year's salary and won.

an army officer whose authority is being threatened by the men. Here is the first preserved letter entirely in Haydn's own hand (the two previous letters in the Esterházy files were copies dictated and only signed by Haydn, if at all):

[To Prince Nicolaus Esterházy. *German*]
SERENE HIGHNESS AND NOBLE PRINCE OF THE HOLY ROMAN EMPIRE, GRACIOUS AND DREAD LORD![1]

I have received with every submissive and dutiful respect YOUR ILLUSTRIOUS AND SERENE HIGHNESS' letter of the 8th inst. addressed to me, and I see from it that your Highness has taken it very amiss that I protested against the detention of the *flauto traverso* player Frantz Sigl to Herr von Rahier, whose commands I am now admonished to follow, in order that I may behave better in the future, on penalty of the dread displeasure of my SERENE HIGHNESS.

MOST SERENE HIGHNESS! GRACIOUS LORD! On behalf of the above-named *flauto traverso* player, because of whom the fire started, I went with the whole band to Herr von Rahier, and it was not on account of the detention, but only on account of the rude detention and the harsh treatment of the subject that I protested, but with all proper respect, to Herr von Rahier. But we could not get anywhere with the administrator, and I even had to put up with his slamming the door in my face, he addressed all the others in the 'Ihr' form[2] and threatened everyone with detention. Similarly, this very day Friberth fled excitedly from the *Regent*'s passion (on account of not doffing his hat, which must have been an oversight), and does not dare to come home, because this same *Regent* pretends that the first-mentioned Friberth was rude to him, and that therefore he will mete out his own punishment. But I testify, as do all the other musicians, that Friberth did nothing else except that, when the *Regent* threatened all of us with detention – and without any reason – he said he had no other master but HIS SERENE HIGHNESS, PRINCE ESTERHAZY. I myself told the *Regent* to complain to YOUR SERENE AND ILLUSTRIOUS HIGHNESS if he felt his own person to have been insulted, but I was given the answer that the *Regent* is his own judge and will meet out the punishment himself. Everyone is very upset on this account, these honourable men find this treatment very unfair and hope that YOUR SERENE AND GRACIOUS HIGHNESS' intentions certainly do not extend this far, and that for this reason you will graciously put a stop to such exercises of power [*Potere*] whereby anyone can be his own judge without differentiating between guilty or not guilty.

The orders of the oft-mentioned *Regent* (as YOUR SERENE AND GRACIOUS HIGHNESS knows anyway) have been correctly carried out at all times, and as often as I receive through him an order of YOUR SERENE AND GRACIOUS HIGHNESS, I shall always execute it to the best of my ability; if therefore the *Regent* has complained in this regard, it must be the result of his angry pen. But moreover YOUR SERENE AND ILLUSTRIOUS HIGHNESS must yourself remember, in your graciousness, that I cannot serve two masters, and cannot accept the commands of, and subordinate myself to, the administrator, for YOUR SERENE AND ILLUSTRIOUS HIGHNESS once said to me: COME FIRST TO ME, BECAUSE I AM HIS[3] MASTER.

---

1 'Durchleuchtig Hochgebohrner Reichsfürst. / Gnädigst Hochgebiettender Herr Herr!'
2 'die übrige gesamte per Ihr tractiret'. Instead of addressing them as 'Sie' (for the plural of 'Er'), Rahier called them 'Ihr', which is the plural of 'Du', used for menial servants, children, dogs (and, in the concentration camps of our own era, by the S.S. when addressing Jews).
3 'His' = 'your'; again, Haydn tells us that Prince Nicolaus referred to *Kapellmeister* in the third person singular, 'Er' form (see note 2).

I am therefore confident that YOUR SERENE AND ILLUSTRIOUS HIGHNESS will not receive ungraciously this my most submissive and obedient letter, but will regard me and the whole *Musique* with gracious eyes, and, since everyone is desirous of this grace, that you will watch over us in fatherly protection. I hope for further marks of favour and grace from YOUR HIGHNESS and I remain ever, with every mark of profound respect,

YOUR SERENE AND GRACIOUS HIGHNESS'
most humble and obedient
Josephus Haydn.

Eisenstadt, 9th September 1765

[On the outside, in another hand, the date of the letter again and the following summary of its contents: 'Excusatio Capellae Magistri Haydn adversus delationem D. Regentis de Rahier'.]

[CCLN, 3f.]

In fact Rahier fully intended to arrest poor Friberth as well, as the following letter shows. But Haydn's intervention on all these levels seems to have had its wished-for effect; perhaps Rahier's anger had died down in the intervening four days, and possibly Prince Nicolaus put in a word to calm the irate spirits, but in any case Rahier's next letter is in a more civilized tone ('as', might have thought Esterházy, 'befits the language of an honourable princely court'). Unfortunately there was no way to save Sigl; but as we have seen, even that part of the story had a happier ending.

[P. L. Rahier to Prince Nicolaus Esterházy, *German*]
Most Serene, Nobly Born Prince of the Holy Roman Empire, Gracious Lord & Sire, etc., etc.

Yesterday *Kapellmeister* Hayden and Friberth were finally here before me; the latter submissively apologized for his recent offensive and improper language which was to lead to his arrest, and has asked that he be forgiven. I answered him that I had already informed Your Highness and that any further decision must be awaited from that source, but since he has submissively apologized, I would ask Your Highness with due respect this time graciously to leave it at the submissive apology; and, with respect, I would also ask for a confirmation of this.

This afternoon, in the presence of all the musicians, as was ordered, I had Siegl [*sic*] arrested and dismissed from service, and ordered the *Kapelmeister* [*sic*] to collect everything in the way of clothes, instruments and music which might belong to Your Highness, and finally that Chief Cashier Zoller pay him [Sigl] his final salary up to and including today.

The two hunting-horn players should have left for Süttör today, as Hayden informs me, but because one of them fell ill this morning and had to take some medicine and was therefore unable to travel, they will leave at daybreak tomorrow morning so as to be there at noon; and with this I remain, in profound respect,

Your Highness' etc.
Most obedient servant
P. L. Rahier mpria

Eisenstadt, 13ᵗʰ 7ᵇʳⁱˢ 765

[Cover: contents, file number & date]
[A.M. 175, EH, Budapest; Valkó II, 540; CCLN, 4f. (extracts); here from original]

Sigl may have been summarily dismissed, but one is interested to see him still in Eisenstadt settling bills two days later:

From 24th May to 15th September $\overline{7}$65

	fl	kr
1½ bundles E	3	—
½ bundle A	—	45
A piece of ivory made for the flute	1	—
One half bundle D	1	—
15 *Claffter* for the Bassetl [violoncello]	1	—
[*Claffter* = cord measure for length of string = 1·90 m.]		
One half bundle A	—	45
One bundle C	2	—
One violohn [double bass] A	1	8
Ditto one D	—	51
Ditto one small A	—	17
Summa	11 fl	46 X

[Haydn's hand:]
These correctly received Joseph Haydn mpria

[Sigl's hand:]
I acknowledge receipt of these eleven gulden, 46 xr from the Rental Office. Eisenstadt, 16th Sept^r $\overline{7}$65

Frantz Sigl

[Cover: contents, file number and date]
            [A.M. 441, EH, Budapest; Valkó II, 642f.; here from original]

We come now to the final chapter of Werner's life. Feeling his end near, on 9 October 1765 he drew up a Codicil to his Will:

Codicil

or addition, which after my death shall be added to the bequests already established *in testamento*, and to be implemented.

1° After my death my body should be clothed in that shroud which has already been prepared.

2° Since at present I live on princely territory, my body, after three death knells have been rung, shall be carried with the whole Castle Personnel, which costs 9 f., into the Castle Chapel, there to hold a Requiem Mass, and then taken to the princely cemetery and buried there.

3° The coffin shall be simple, with a white cross, made by the carpenter in the Mayerhof.

4° The Rosary and Franciscan Brotherhoods should, for the usual payment, attend my funeral.

5° On the *labra* and the banner [on which the coffin rests] the necessary plants should be placed. Item the announcer to receive his fee and a plant, each of the coffin-bearers a plant and 17 X.

6° The children of the Castle, and also the Parish, should accompany and each should be given 1 X. Everyone of the poor who accompany, however, to be given 3 X. alms.

7° Each of the Father Petrines to receive a 2/4 lb. wax candle
    Each Musician 3/8 lb
    Each of the Franciscan Fathers who accompanies 1/4.

8° A gravestone should be set on my grave, which will cost 24f., and on it should be placed the epitaph which I wrote myself. The necessary sum should be divided between my two sons.[1]

9° The two Castle Chaplains should be given a further six gulden together, for Holy Masses to be read, id est . . . . 6 f.
for the Father Franciscans for Holy Masses . . . . . . 6 f.

10° For Maria Anna Plötzpaurin [Plötzpaur], my former cook (since God the Almighty has up to now still given me my life, and she in my long illness served me truly and faithfully) should receive apart from what is in the Will four ducats at least which my two sons should give her. Then she should have the few remaining kitchen utensils (except all the pewter), and the little wine glasses, as well as other minor utensils such as bottles, glasses and other similar items without discussion and disputes, and also the washing kettle and the bed-warmer. She is at present spinning a piece of linen, and if I should live long enough for it to become a real piece of linen, this piece of linen should go to my son Antonio. But if at my death it has not become a piece of linen, all of it, that is the flax and the frame should be given to my cook, if she should remain with me until the hour of my death.

11° My late wife and my children are buried in the Parish Church Cemetery, and thus I have wanted to leave a few keepsakes to that Parish Church consisting of 15 Stations of the Cross, on which the painter Gstöttner [Gestettner] hath begun working. I have agreed with him to pay four gulden for each painting including the frames stained in black with gold edges. Should these 15 Stations be completed within my lifetime, I shall pay for them and see that they are hung in the said Town

---

1 The epitaph (now barely legible) reads:

Alhier ruhet der Wol Edle und Kunstreiche Herr
Gregorius Josephus Werner, Weyland gewester Hoch-
fürstlich Eszterhazyscher Capell = Meister, seines erlebten
mühsamen und kränklichen Alters 71 Jahr: deme Gott
nun wolle zur ewigen Ruhe aufnehmen. Ist gestorben
A. 1766, d. 3 Marty.

EPITAPHIUM
Hier ligt ein Chor-Regent, der ein Groß Fürsten = Haus
sehr viele Jahr bedient, nun ist die Musik aus.
Er hatte große Plag mit Creuzl und B-moll,
wust' endlich nicht, wie, wo Ers resolviren sollt
Bis Er die Kunst erlernt nur in Geduld zu sein,
alsdann gab Er sich willig und ganz bereit darein.
Dich aber großer Gott!
bitt Er in höchster Noth,
Du wollst die Dissonanzen
von Ihm gesetzt zu frey
Verkehren in Consonanten
Durch seine Buß und Reu.
Wil Er die letzt Cadenz sodann ins Grab gemacht,
ist folglich all sein Müh zum guten Schluß gebracht.
O Heiland nehm ihn auf zu deinen Himels-Chor
den nie ein Aug gesehn, noch g'hört ein menschlich Ohr.
Wann dann die groß Posaunen
wird rufen zum Gericht,
Mit aller Welt Erstaunen
alsdann verdam ihn nicht

Dich aber fromer Wanders-
Mann
Ruff ich um ein Gebettlein an.
[Pohl I, 396]

This extraordinary gravestone takes us back, not only to the Baroque but almost to the Renaissance, with its naïve, crude, pious language. There are similar gravestones in good condition (with such Renaissance poetry) at, e.g., the great Gothic parish churches of Steyr and Braunau (Upper Austria).

Parish Church on the side walls, but if my death should intervene, my two sons should from their inheritance pay the agreed sum of 60 f. id est 60 f.

Datum Eisenstadt the 9th 8bris [Oct.] 1765,

Gregorius Werner as the Father

Joseph Seitz curatus arcensis, testis et confessarius.

Franz Nigst as witness.

[J. Harich, 'Die Testamente . . .', 131ff.]

Notes:

The list of the goods, money, etc., in Harich, pp. 133ff. Werner's effects, which included (of musical interest) only a clavichord assessed at 2 Fl. 7 Xr., were valued at 1,019 Fl. 11 Xr. His debts amounted to 100 Fl. 32½ Xr., leaving 918 Fl. 38½, a respectable sum saved by a thrifty, God-fearing man.

Prince Nicolaus was now the recipient of a great honour: he was made Commander of the Order of Maria Theresa, which was bestowed upon him in Vienna. We have two sources describing the event, the first being the official *Wienerisches Diarium* No. 83 (16 October 1765):

Tuesday the 15th, which is the Feast of St Theresa . . . as far as the present mourning period [for Emperor Francis Stephen, d. 18 August] permitted, the Feast was solemnly celebrated. [A new class of the Maria Theresa Order was created, that of Commandeur. Joseph II did the honours. The insignia of the order included a large silver cross on red background with the word 'Fortitudini'; it was worn on the left breast. The first to receive it in the ceremony was, 'General-feld-zeugmeister Niclas[!] Fürst Esterhazy', who knelt on one knee as Joseph placed the sash around the princely neck. Mass and Knight's Table in the Audience Room of the Burg (Castle), while the ladies looked down from a box.]

The second report is from the Diary of Major Domo Prince Khevenhüller, whose description of life at Court is so valuable for historians:

On the 15th, the Feast of St Theresa, the Empress-Queen[1] was unseen and since yesterday she has locked herself in for eight days, but the Gala Day and the Celebration of the Order were conducted in a festive manner. The *pleureures* [mourning dress] were set aside and ornaments could be worn again, though the *dames* could wear only their jewellery and colliers but nothing elaborate on their head-dresses. Before the Emperor [Joseph II] went to church with the knights, there was in the *Rathstube* [Councillors' Room] quite a new and special ceremony: the *Herr Ordens-Canzler* made (as is his wont) a very eloquent *harangue* in which he informed us that H. M. permits the Grand Cross bearers to wear a jewel (or *par sobriquet* what is called a *crachat*) sewn to the coat, then that he was pleased to create a new rank with the title of Commandeur (stolen from the Order of St Stephen), and the list of recipients was read forth. Those present received at once the Order's sash, placed around their necks by the Grand Master, then they received the star and accompanied H. M., according to their rank, into the Chapel. Afterwards they dined, but only the Grand Cross bearers in the great *Anticamera* where the *Herrschaften* are wont to dine *in publico*; for the Commandeurs and the Small Cross bearers, a special table was served in the Knights' Chamber. The present Lord [Joseph II] remained in his previous living quarters, but since they are very narrow and confining, all public functions such as the midday meal, investitures, etc., were

1 Maria Theresa was doing penance on her name-day (she had cut off her hair immediately after the death of her husband). In *WD* No. 85, 23 Oct. 1765, we read that 'on Monday the 21st at 4 o'clock p.m. Widow Empress Maria Theresa . . . received the bearers of the Great Cross, Commandeurs and Knights of the Order of Maria Theresa, who kissed the I.R. hand.'

held on the other side [of the Burg] in the chambers formerly occupied by his Lord
Father, and which in time he [Joseph] will himself occupy.

[Khevenhüller: 1764–1767, Vienna-Leipzig 1917, p. 148]

Towards the end of October, Werner, now a sick and embittered old man, wrote
the following letter:

[Gregor Joseph Werner to Prince Nicolaus Esterházy, Süttör. *German*]
HIGH BORN PRINCE OF THE HOLY ROMAN EMPIRE,
GRACIOUS AND DREAD LORD!

I am forced to draw attention to the gross negligence in the local castle chapel,
the unnecessarily large princely expenses, and the lazy idleness of the whole band,
the principal responsibility for which must be laid at the door of the present
director, who lets them all get away with everything, so as to receive the name of a
good Heyden [*sic*]; for as God is my witness, things are much more disorderly than
if the 7 children were about; it seems that there are only libertines among the
chorus people, who according to their fancy take their recreation for 5 or even 6
weeks at a time: the poor chapel thus has only 5 or six at a pinch, also not one of
them pays attention to what his neighbour is playing. Over half the choir's
instruments are lost, and they were collected only seven years ago, after many
requests, from the late lamented Prince. Apart from all that, now most of the
church music itself goes out to all the world; before, the late organist took good
care of it, but after his death it had to happen that I gave the key to the present
Capell Meister to care for; but with the proviso that he should draw up a proper
catalogue of the items in the choir-loft, and this should have been copied three
times. One for Your Highness; the second for the princely book-keepers; the
third deposited in the actual choir-loft. Herr Heyden most willingly agreed, also
with the preparation of the catalogues, which he was to bring to my sick bed; but
up to now nothing has been done.

The cabinet with the music, however, as true Christian men report to me, has
been considerably depleted, which is the more easily credible if one considers that
on my sick bed I have already had requests from three parties, asking if I could
supply church music for them advantageously, since Vienna at present has a
considerable lack of church composers.

I, however, left such letters unanswered. But it is easy to presume that they
will have addressed their request to Heyden. Thus the church choir will be
meanwhile depleted completely unless Heyden is seriously ordered to prepare a
catalogue at least of what pieces remain.

Incidentally, it is humbly requested: Your Princely Highness should give him
a severe order that he must issue the strictest command to the princely musicians
that they appear in the future, all of them without exception, at their duties. And
because it is likely that he, Heyden, will try to lie his way out of it, the order must
come from on high, that the extant choir instruments be examined, among which
there must be 12 old and new violins.

Of the violas, 2 old and 2 new, but 2 Passetel [violoncellos] and 2 good large
double basses: all too soon it will be seen where the truth lies.

Under the late lamented Prince, apart from the usual summer *fatique*, it was
ordered that in winter time we were to give two academies [concerts] a week in
the princely officers' room, Tuesdays and Thursdays, for which two hours each
was required. If this were to be reinstated now, the injurious laziness would be
removed, and no longer would such bad practices obtain as, alas, experience has
shown to have occurred.

Because today, as a very old man who has borne the title of *Capellmeister* here for 37 years, and because the price of wood has risen considerably, and I as a sick man cannot deal with the heating myself and am forced as a result to get outside people, who do not forget to look after their own interests, to come and do it.

Thus I mòst humbly beg your Princely Highness only out of pity to add two cords of wood to my emoluments [*Deputat*], for my constitution is so weakened by loss-of-weight, that my sick body consists of almost nothing except skin and bones. For such a stroke of generosity I will earnestly pray to God, not only as long as I am alive but also when I am dead, for your long and happy reign and for an increase of your rents and income.

With which I most humbly recommend myself to Your Highness' grace and favour, and remain,

> Your Serene Highness'
> most obedient servant
> Gregorius Werner

1765 in 8^ber [October]

[Cover: contents,[1] file number and date]

[A.M. 84, Valkó I, 537–9; here from original]

How much of this diatribe is true? Surely a part of it. Haydn was clearly easy-going, and discipline was probably comfortable under his sympathetic leadership. Probably, too, the catalogue and condition of the music itself left a good deal to be desired. It is not likely that the Masses, etc., were actually taken out and sold, but it is quite possible that some of the manuscripts were lent and never returned. Obviously it was found that no musical instruments were actually missing.

Prince Esterházy, busy supervising the new Castle of Eszterháza in Süttör, seems to have taken this outburst with a grain of salt, for when he returned it to Rahier, it was accompanied by the following laconic note: 'Moreover, I attach the document of *Kapellmeister* Werner here; as concerns his laments, you will be in the best position to act on them' (Pohl I, 367). Some days went by. Apparently the famous *Regulatio Chori Kissmartoniensis* (cited below) was, in its concept, the work of *Regent* Rahier, which would explain its master-sergeant tone. We suspect that clauses 1–6 were *verbatim* the work of Rahier and that the last paragraph (concerning the lack of baryton trios) preceding 'Formulae' was by Prince Nicolaus himself.

We are able to date this hitherto undated document by two entries in PCDI, of which the first describes the *Regulatio* itself and the second patently sets out the (new) duties of the Castle Schoolmaster Joseph Dietzl who was supposed to be in charge of the cataloguing of, and, generally, the archival work connected with, the actual music itself (see clause 2 of the *Regulatio*):

[PCDI] No. 537. Command and order of His Highness himself dd° 3^m 9bris [Nov.] 7̄65 raone [ratione] concerning the Choir Music instruments and musical inventory, of which the original document was given to Hr. *Capellmeister* Haydn, *in Copia* however, as drawn up by him, attached here [no longer attached, June 1978. H.C.R.L.].

---

1 'Capellae Magister Verner instat pro Lignis, focalibus et conqueritur contra Musicorum Negligentiam et distractionem Musicalium'. Latin was, apart from German, the principal language used by the Esterházy Court and indeed in Hungary altogether; *vide supra*, p. 324.

[PCDI] Princely Mandat dd° 3ᵗⁿ 9bris 7̄6̄5, which contains all the duties of the Castle Schoolmaster Joseph Diezl [*sic*].[1]

[To Haydn. Draft of an Order from Prince Nicolaus Esterházy. *German*]

Regulatio Chori Kissmartoniensis

Inasmuch as the musicians of the Eisenstadt Castle Chapel have produced a great disorder in the choir-loft, because of indolence and carelessness, and have neglected the instruments through poor care and storage, *Capellmeister* Hayden [*sic*] is herewith earnestly enjoined,

First, to prepare an inventory, in three identical copies, of all the instruments and music in the choir-loft, according to the enclosed formulae, with indication of the composers, number of parts, etc., to sign it and within eight days from today to deliver one to us, the second to the book-keeper's office, and the third to the choir-loft:

Secondly, the schoolmaster Joseph Diezl is to collect and distribute the necessary music before each choir service, and after the service to collect it and to see that it is properly returned to the cupboards wherein it belongs, locked, so that nothing will be removed or lost:

Thirdly, to see to it that the schoolmaster keeps all the choir instruments constantly in good repair and in proper order, to which end said schoolmaster is ordered to appear in the choir-loft one quarter of an hour before each service:

Fourthly, to take especial pains that all the members of the chapel appear regularly at the church services and fulfil their duty and obligations in a proper and disciplined fashion:

Fifthly, in our absence to hold two musical academies [concerts] each week in the Officers' Room at Eisenstadt, viz., on Tuesdays and Thursdays from two to four o'clock in the afternoon, which is to be given by all the musicians, and in order that

6thly, to assure that in future no one is absent without permission from the church services or the above-mentioned academies (as was the case hitherto), a written report will be delivered to us every fortnight, with the name of, and reason for, anyone presuming to absent themselves from duty.

[Nicolaus, Prince Esterházy]

Süttör, the [blank = 3 November] 1765

Finally, said *Capelmeister* [*sic*] Haydn is urgently enjoined to apply himself to compostion more diligently than heretofore, and especially to write such pieces as can be played on the gamba [baryton], of which pieces we have seen very few up to now; and to be able to judge his diligence, he shall at all times send us the first copy, cleanly and carefully written, of each and every composition.

---

1 Dietzl had a *Capell-Diener* (servant for the choir-loft) named Christoph Pleyer, who was engaged about this time; according to PCDI No. 552, 'Resolution of Hr. Regent v. Rahier dd° 21ᵗⁿ Feb: 7̄6̄6 by which Christoph Pleÿer is engaged, provided he pay [his predecessor's] widow a pension for life of 30 Fl., see attached revers: Sub. A:' – in truth a tiny enough pension, but sufficient for a single woman living very frugally in the country.

Formulae

Inventarium

Of the music and instruments which are under today's date found in the choir-loft of the Eisenstadt Castle, viz.:

Nro	Musicalien	Stimmen [parts]
1.	Missae Solemniores	
	Missa Primitiva cum Tympanis et Clarinis. Here must follow the *incipit* with 2 or 3 bars of the organ part etc. Auth. Werner. E.g. with . . . . and thus the Masses, Vespers, Litanies, Symphonies, Offertories, etc., whatever is there.	10.

	Instrumenten	Number
	Violins old	
	Violins new	
	Violas old	
	ditto new	
	Bassetlen [violoncellos] old	
	ditto new . . . . etc., etc.	

Eisenstadt the [blank] $\overline{7}65$

[A.M. 346, EH, Budapest; Valkó I, 539f.; CCLN, 5 (extracts); here from original]

It is one of the real tragedies for Haydn scholarship that this thematic catalogue has not survived. However, to redress the balance, it now seems clear that we owe the existence of Haydn's own thematic catalogue known to scholars as *EK* (*Entwurf–Katalog* or Draft Catalogue) to this storm-in-a-teacup. Haydn assembled all the works of which he still owned a copy – perhaps he had made his own lists, too – and had the princely copyist Joseph Elssler draw them up thematically. Haydn himself then added to this *corpus* as time went on, making entries sporadically until after the London journeys. We wonder if in fact *EK* is not Haydn's copy of a similar list presented as part of the (lost) *inventarium* to Prince Nicolaus as a living sign of dutiful and submissive diligence.

A bill for horn repairs now follows:

For repairs to the princely Esterhasi hunting horn, I acknowledge herewith the receipt of six gulden 34 xr. [another hand: 'Sigl']
     Pressburg, 23 Novemb: $\overline{1}765$.
                         Johann Bernhoffer Hunting Horn
                         Maker in Pressburg

[Haydn's hand:]
     Agreed
Joseph Haydn mpria

[Cover: contents, file number & date]
[A.M. 644, EH, Budapest; Valkó II, 644; here from original]

Prince Nicolaus was now back in Vienna for more honours at court. In the *Wienerisches Diarium* No. 96 (30 November 1765) we read that on Friday evening, the

29th, the Knights of the Golden Fleece, with Joseph II, gathered at court, first in the Great Council Chamber (*Große Rathstube*) and then for Vespers in the Court Chapel (*Hofburgcapelle*). A few days later, the *WD* No. 97 (4 December) reports that, on 30 November, at a celebration of the Order, Joseph II (as Grand Master) and two Archdukes presided over thirty robed knights, who dined at a V-shaped table. Her I.R. Majesty and the Archduchesses looked down from a raised tribune. The newly created knights were headed by 'Titel Hr. Franz Fürst [*recte*: 'Graf'] Esterházy, K.K. Feldmarschall-leutnant ... [etc.]'.

On 12 December, the Prince's grandson, Nicolaus (later Prince Nicolaus II), was born to Maria Theresia, wife of Count Anton Esterházy. Although we must break chronology, it is interesting to think that the new Esterházy would later marry a Princess Liechtenstein, one of several very musical children.[1]

The happy occasion prompted Rahier to write the following letter to his Prince:

[P. L. Rahier to Prince Nicolaus Esterházy. *German*]
Serene Highness and Noble Prince of the Holy Roman Empire,
Most Gracious Sire and Lord,
May Your Highness permit me to present my and also my wife's most humble felicitations for your forthcoming high birthday[2] and moreover in submission to hope for ourselves further high favour and grace, and to wish that Providence grant to Your Highness countless years in the happiest prosperity and pleasure.
Since Her Highness the Princess was graciously minded to have me informed that the Lady Countess Antoni v. Esterhazy has been safely delivered of a young sire, I have informed the present Castle Provost Chaplain that there will be held tomorrow a High Mass with all the musicians as a Thanksgiving Service, which all the princely officers and officials (such as are here) will attend; and that the Grenadier Company should assemble for a parade salute, and hope that Your Highness will not disapprove of this ... With which I remain, in profound respect, Your Highness' [signature torn off]
Eißenstadt, 15th xbris [Dec.] 7̄6̄5.
        [EH, Budapest, Országos Levéltár, p. 154 (old Fasc. 1524), fol. 331]

Werner was now too ill to fulfil his duties with the *Chor Musique*, and it was Haydn himself who for the first time collected the annual 9 gulden *Rorate* money on 24 December 1765 [*HJB* IV, 70]. He also countersigned one of the following bills:

---

1 It is a curious coincidence that the *WD* No. 84 of 19 Oct. 1765 reports: 'Last Tuesday [15th], St Theresa's Day, at the Brothers of Mercy [Barmherzige Brüder] in the Landstraße in the Reconvalescence House was there Mass during which the young Leopoldina, daughter of H.H. Grace, Herr Franz Prince von Liechtenstein, played a concerto on the organ, and for the first time, to the admiration of all present. She is still very young. Her playing does no little credit to her teacher, Herr Christoph Stephan [Steffan].' Maria Leopoldina Adelgundis (b. 30 Jan. 1754) was the sister of Nicolaus II's later unhappy wife, Maria Josepha Hermenegild (b. 13 April 1768). Nicolaus II and Maria Josepha Hermenegild married, as child brides in the literal sense, on 15 September 1783. See *Haydn: the Years of 'The Creation' 1796–1800*, pp. 43ff. and *passim*.
2 I.e., 18 December.

List

What I undertook during the year 1765 for the Princely Esterhasi Hof Capelle in Eisenstadt in repairs for musical instruments, and delivered strings, viz.:

	F	xr
Two bundles E	3	—
Bundle A		45
A violon [double bass] newly strung, with new fret, new velvet, pegs repaired, glued, and a new bow	8	30
In addition 2 bundles E	3	—
6 violin saddles [*Sädl*]		18
	15 F	33 xr

[another hand:]
Johann Xtoph Leÿdolf
payment correctly received.

[original hand:]
Johann Christoph Leÿdolf
Burgl. Lautenmacher, his
widow

I hereby acknowledge receipt of fifteen gulden from Herr Räntmeister Frantz Nigst. Received Vienna, 31 Xbris 1765:

[third hand:] NB The signature is above

[Cover: contents, file number and date]

[A.M. 436, EH, Budapest; from original]

Laus Deo. Anno 1765. Eisenstadt.
Herr Joseph Heydn *hochfürstl. Capellenmaister* [*sic*] here is requested to give:

				fl	xr
9bris [Nov.]	15.	6 batches fine Venetian strings	E á. 3 xr.		18
—	20.	3 batches ditto			9
—	30.	10 batches ditto	E á. 3 xr.		30
—	—	6 batches fine ditto	A á. 2 xr.		12
Xbris. [Dec.]	24	30 batches fine ditto	E á. 3 xr.	1	30
—	—	15 batches fine ditto	A á. 2 xr.		30
—	—	7 batches fine ditto	A á. 2 xr.		14
			Summa	3	23

Matthias Stübner

I acknowledge receipt of these three gulden 23 xr. from the Rental Office Eisenstadt, 24th Xbris 1765.

[Haydn's hand:] Joseph Haydn mpria
[Cover: contents, file number and date]

[A.M. 438, EH, Budapest; Valkó II, 644f.; here from original]

We are at the end of our first Chronicle of the Esterházy period. Before proceeding to the actual music of this time, we might remind our readers that while Haydn and the *Capelle* resided at Eisenstadt, Prince Nicolaus was often at Süttör, supervising the building of Eszterháza Castle. There was not yet room for more than a few musicians. Presumably Prince Nicolaus could recruit from among the officials a violin or two, a viola and (if baryton trios were needed), a viola and violoncello. We have noted that the two horn players were sent to Süttör, partly for the hunting season, but perhaps also for chamber music. Haydn wrote some chamber music with baryton and two horns.

We know almost nothing of Haydn's personal life at Eisenstadt. He lived in an apartment in the 'Old Apothecary', and he seems to have employed a boy servant. At least that would seem to be the explanation for an unedifying legal wrangle recorded in the Eisenstadt Town Books, in which Haydn's 'Godless boy' (*gottlosem Buben*) is mentioned, one Ludwig Hänl.[1]

Joseph Haydn, 1762.5.10 / Minute

On the application of the Music Director to the Prince Esterházy, Joseph Haydn, a further examination is to be undertaken of the case of the weaver Mathias Strobel, who is in custody under suspicion of conspiracy [with Ludwig Hähnl in respect of a theft of money]; but since, according to the written report received from Ferdinand Petzelbauer, Master Weaver residing at Wandorf near Ödenburg [Sopron, Hungary], the aforesaid conducts himself at all times with honesty, and since the impious knave ['Godless boy'] Ludwig Hähnl has confessed before a Justice to having withdrawn his previous evidence and has further stated that he did not give any of the stolen money to Strobel, Strobel is not only freed from arrest but it is ordered that a confirmation of his innocence in this instance as well as a judicial attestation shall be made available in the determination of the examination.[2]

Apart from these things, however, which were typical manifestations of life in a small town during the period, Haydn had consolidated his position, both financially and in other ways. Despite the *Regulatio*, Haydn enjoyed the greatest confidence of his patron, and all things considered, the history of Joseph Haydn and Nicolaus Esterházy is one that reflects the greatest credit on both sides. The two (for Esterházy's role cannot be underestimated) made cultural and musical history. Haydn was now sufficiently well situated to ask Prince Nicolaus if Johann Haydn might come to Eisenstadt as an unpaid tenor in the *Chor Musique*. The Prince agreed and in 1765, Johann joined the *Capelle* in an honorary capacity, being supported by his brother. About 1765, Haydn began to use the permanent services of a copyist in princely employ named Joseph Elssler. Haydn became a kind of protector to the whole Elssler family, being present at their marriages and christenings, and finally engaging the son Johann as a permanent valet, factotum and copyist (Johann went with Haydn to England in 1794). Joseph Elssler's hand was clear and precise, and Haydn used him for the most important tasks, though of course there had to be many other copyists as well to cope with the enormous amount of scores and parts being produced. Joseph Elssler, who helped with the *Entwurf–Katalog*, signed himself on a copy of Haydn's *Salve Regina* (XXIIIb:2; the copy owned by the Gesellschaft der Musikfreunde, dated 1771), which enables us to identify his hand.

In 1765, Haydn is known to have composed at least four Symphonies: Nos. 28, 29, 30 'Alleluja') and 31 ('Hornsignal') – not necessarily in that order – and probably many other works as well which cannot be dated precisely. But even these four works reveal a sure hand technically and an inner emotional stability, a maturity, which augured well for the future of the *Capelle*, and the future of music, too, though no one could yet foresee the effect that Haydn would have on that future.

1 G. Feder, 'Haydn und Eisenstadt', in *Österreichische Musikzeitschrift* 25. Jg., Heft 4 (1970), p. 214. The document was discovered by Christina Stadtlaender and is reproduced *in extenso* in her interesting book, *Joseph Haydn of Eisenstadt*, trans. and ed. by Percy M. Young (Dennis Dobson, London 1963), quoted by permission. She writes (p. 37) that in 1762 Haydn was 'angered by a servant of the court who, guilty of many irregularities, finally came before the magistrate of the town on a charge of larceny preferred by a weaver with whom he had been friendly. Haydn's name appeared for the first time on a "charge" in the Minutes of the Eisenstadt Council.'
2 As it was set out in the Minute, Hähnl himself seems to have made an accusation of petty theft. We do not in fact know whether he was convicted or whether the good-natured Music Director managed to shift the blame from him. The case is not mentioned again in the Council Minutes. It is another typical instance of Haydn's interest in the underdog.

CHAPTER NINE

Haydn's Works, 1761–1765

Operas and *Comedie*: *La Marchesa Nespola* (*Il Marchese*; XXX:1; 1762); *Acide* (XXVII: 1; 1762, performed 1763, revised 1773–4); Aria, 'Costretta a piangere' (XXIVb:1).
Italian Cantatas: 'Destatevi, o miei fidi' (XXIVa:2; 1763); 'Da qual gioja improviso' (XXIVa:3; 1764); 'Qual dubbio' (XXIVa:4; 1764).
Church Music: *Te Deum* (XXIIIc:1).
Contrafacta Church music (from other *genres*): *Motetto di Sancta Thecla* (XXIIIa:4) *vel de Tempore* (Hoboken *deest*); 'Ego virtus' (Hoboken *deest*); *Motetto de Beata* (XXIIIa:c7); Aria, 'Maria, Jungfrau rein' (Hoboken *deest*); recitative, 'Quid hostem times', and *Aria de B.V.M.*, 'Verbo fata portalata' (Hoboken *deest*).
CONCERTOS:
Horn and Orchestra in D (VIId:3; 1762);
Violin and Orchestra: in C (VIIa:1); in A (VIIa:3); in G (VIIa:4);
Violoncello and Orchestra in G (VIIb:1);
Lost concertos and some doubtful works (Violoncello Concerto, VIIb:4; Horn Concerto, VIId:4);
Harpsichord and Orchestra: in F (XVIII:3), in G (XVIII:9), and a doubtful work (XVIII:G1).
CHAMBER MUSIC:
Mixed Divertimenti:
Divertimento (Cassatio; II:17); Cassatio in D (Hoboken *deest*); fragment (II:24); Divertimento (II:8); Wind-band *Feldparthien* (II:14, 1761; and lost works); Baryton Divertimenti (Trios; XI:1–12); works for Harpsichord, strings (and sometimes horns) (XIV:3, 4, 7, 8, 9, 10).
Solo Harpsichord music (except Sonatas): 20 Variazioni in G (XVII:2); *Capriccio* 'Acht Sauschneider' (XVII:1, 1765).
Symphonies and *Scherzandi* (II:33–8).

Operas and Comedie

La Marchesa Nespola (Il Marchese; XXX:1, 1762)

The *Entwurf-Katalog* lists the work with the first title, the autograph with the second. This is not necessarily a contradiction, for both roles might have appeared in the original score of which we have only fragments. 'Nespola' means a medlar, and was a typical doggerel title in Venetian operas of the period, for example the *intermezzo*,

Conte Nespola (1746).[1] In view of the fact that no recitatives have survived (nor is it certain that any existed: the Italian troupe from Pressburg may have had spoken dialogue between the numbers), we propose to proceed from number to number, listing the text of each and discussing the musical content. No synopsis of the plot is possible.

Autograph: EH, Budapest, Ms. Mus. I, 9. Title at the top of No. 1: '[left:] Arie per la Comedia <u>Marchese</u> [middle:] In Nomine Domini [right:] Giuseppe Haydn / $\overline{762}$.' For *incipits* see Hoboken, vol. II, pp. 447f. The score comes from Haydn's legacy: *Haydn: the Late Years 1801–1809*, p. 317, item 234, where the date is given as '1763'. Although Haydn made corrections to the last digit, as we have observed before, it seems that the final reading should be 1762 (when the Italian Troupe

from Pressburg was in Eisenstadt; no such troupe was there in 1763). Watermarks: Larsen Nos. 1 and 2 (Bartha-Somfai 188, 189), but Bartha-Somfai 3 (p. 438) requires correction – see Aria No. 3, *infra*. The whole autograph on 4° paper (description of page divisions etc.: Hoboken, vol. II, p. 448).

We have seen that many of the roles may be attached to some singer in the Esterházy or Pressburg companies.

Aria No. 1 'Navicella da vento', Adagio, D, barred C. 2 hns., str. Role: 'S.^{ra} Barbara' (soprano).

> Navicella da vento agitata,
> Se resiste nel lungo camino,
> Spera il porto che vede vicino,
> Ne più teme i perigli del mar.

The text calls forth one of the oldest images in Italian opera: the image of the person as a boat on the agitated waters, hoping for haven in the safe port. The form is as follows:

	A		A′
Ritornello tonic [10 bars]	→ Vocal entry (tonic) same theme [uneven nos. of bars] modulating to dominant	→	Ritornello (dominant) using material → from earlier section.

		A′′′
Vocal entry (dominant) modulating to A → minor → dominant of I (music example, opposite)	Third part omits opening ritornello and opening vocal part, and condenses material used up to (imaginary) double bar; ending with ritornello of the dominant cadence that began A′ (now in tonic) [tonic, with excursion to subdominant]

The simplest of Italian forms, then. Haydn binds it together with steady syncopations (the 'agitated' sea), which begin with the horns and violas at the very opening and continue to underline the music throughout.

The two features which strike us forcefully are (1) the almost incredible self-sufficiency of this music, which shows at no juncture uncertainty, *gauche* transitions, or any other of the traits usually associated with a composer's early vocal works; (2) the uncanny glimpses into Haydn's operatic future which we find all through this operetta. These two statements require, perhaps, some elucidation. This is by no means the first music to an Italian text composed by Haydn, for in *Der (neue) krumme Teufel* there was an entire Italian *intermezzo*; and, as we have observed, Haydn doubtless composed many such Italian operas in the 1750s. But the assuredness of this music is nonetheless unexpected: the glimpses into the future are only another aspect of this

---

1 Robert Haas, *Die Musik in der Wiener deutschen Stegreifkomödie*, Studien zur Musikwissenschaft, Heft 12 (1925), p. 6. Literature on *Marchesa*: Pohl I, 231f. Bartha-Somfai, 379f.

mastery. Haydn has already perfected the language with which he will write operas for the next twenty years; as he grows older, the emotional content will of course broaden and deepen; but the technical devices are all here in this 1762 *Comedia*, and presented to us without a trace of hesitation. Consider the following example, which is the lead–back to the third part.

It looks forward directly to two later operas by Haydn: (1) the first part appears in *La vera costanza* (1778?), Atto II° Finale, also in the same key, 'Ah tutta, tutta tremo':

while the second part rounds out one of Haydn's 'ominous cadences' in *L'anima del filosofo* (1791: see *Haydn in England 1791–1795*, p. 341, last four bars of the bottom example).

In this first Aria from *La Marchesa Nespola*, we might note that the last note of the 'cello-basso part is *D* below the bass clef, which means that the lowest string of the *violone* must have been tuned at least to *D* and probably to *C* below the staff. This again suggests that Haydn used two tunings for his double bass instruments, one for chamber and symphonic music of certain kinds, another for church music and symphonic music of other kinds. We shall return to the problem later.

Aria No. 2, 'Tu mi piaci', Andante, G, 2/4. 2 fl., 2 hns., str. Role: 'Colombina' (soprano).

> Tu mi piaci ed io ti bramo,
> Il mio cor tutto è per te
> Via, rispondimi si t'amo,
> E tu ancor sarai per me,
> Qual diletto, qual piacere,
> Nò ch'al mondo equal non v'è.

The first thing we notice about this pert little theme is (1) that it is written on the kind of text that always amused Haydn and was to become a great speciality of the arias composed for his mistress, Luigia Polzelli, in the 1780s; (2) the extraordinarily asymmetrical cast of the theme itself. The ritornello is 6+4+6 [3+3] (see musical example).

The scheme is different from Aria No, 1. After the ritornello, the vocal entry begins and modulates to the dominant; after the ritornello in the dominant, we are surprised to find ourself modulating straight back to the tonic and the recapitulation. There simply is no middle section at all. Here we find the trend towards brevity which is, of course, typical of Haydn all his later life. In the A″ section we find another glimpse into the future,

where the off-beat comments by woodwind, horns and lower strings sound like music of the 1780s. *In nuce*, we have the whole Polzelli music before our astonished eyes.

Recitativo ed Aria No. 3. Recit: 'Vincesti, empio, vincesti'; Aria: 'Trema, Tÿrran regnante'. Recit.: bar 2: Allegro, bar 26: Adagio. Aria: Allegro. Recit. modulating to Aria in G, 4/4. Scoring: Recit.: 2 ob., str. [harpsichord *continuo*]; Aria: 2 ob., 2 hns., str. Role: 'Leopoldo' (tenor).

Recitativo
Vincesti, empio, vincesti,
Ma non andrano i tuoi falli impuniti.
L'odio già sei del ciel, del mondo tutto,
Ciascun brama fellon la morte tua,
Ogn'un grida vendetta,
E vendetta dal cielo il mondo aspetta.
Torno a miei ceppi, ingrato,
Resta tu intanto col rossor che t'ucide,
Poco godrai d'un dolor che mi svella il cor del seno
Morrò se'l vuoi, ma senza colpa almeno.

Aria
Trema, Tÿrran regnante,
Col tuo rimorso al core
Sazia l'insan furore.
Straggi, vendetta, e morte attendi,
Pur dal ciel attendi, pur dal ciel.

Here we have a text taken straight from the *opera seria* of the Metastasio-Hasse kind, and Haydn sets it with a vengeance, using (in the Recitativo) related motivic fragments in the old Italian tradition. The Aria, too, is in the grand bravura style of the *seria* form, with its typical leaps in the vocal line (to describe rage, etc.). And here, once again, we are immediately in the future with the enormous opening ritornello (see example).

*Autograph ♩ no ♯.

Haydn always sought to combine the new symphonic style with the form of Italian opera, and here we have the kind of example we will find in *La canterina*'s parody of the form, 'Io sposar l'empio tiranno' (note the similarity in the text which calls forth the same kind of music),[1] and in countless other symphonic-like ritornelli in Haydn's operas and cantatas (*vide infra* for some characteristic specimens in the latter form). Now this noble style, reminiscent of Hasse at his grandest, explains why this whole scene was used as a *contrafactum* piece of church music. In the autograph itself, a rather rude, 'Gothick' hand has added the Latin words, which are cleverly adapted (and obviously with Haydn's approval): the Recitativo is in *contrafactum* 'Vicisti, heros, vicisti' and the Aria 'Justus ut palma stabit', and in this form one contemporary MS. has survived in the National Museum, Prague (*ex coll.* Kuks). Everything about this scene differs from the previous soprano arias. Their ritornelli were (as would have been appropriate to slow tempi) short; this one is long. There was hardly any coloratura in

1 *Haydn at Eszterháza 1766–1790*, p. 233.

the soprano arias, but now – when the dominant is reached – there is a fantastic piece of bravura writing:

Haydn's setting of the words, 'Straggi, vendetta, e morte' is also prophetic, looking forward to the Cantata 'Miseri noi' and even to *L'anima del filosofo*.

Later the tenor even ascends to high *b'* :

In this work there is, Hasse-like, a brief middle section with extended coloratura.

There is at this point in the autograph a series of inserted pages (23–6) written on quite a different kind of paper: apart from a new stag paper with the letters 'IGS', there is a coat-of-arms consisting of an eagle with sword and sceptre, with a cross over his head, and the letters 'J. G. MODVB.' (not 'MOLUB' as in Bartha-Somfai, p. 438, No. 3). Now we wonder if these inserted pages do not represent a new ending to replace what was perhaps a much longer lost original version, with a varied repetition of A, lengthened coloratura and perhaps even a cadenza, in the typical *opera seria* pattern of that day. As it stands, the last ritornello is much shorter so that even here, Haydn was already modifying the usual form to avoid a straight *da capo* technique.

Aria No. 4 'Non o [ho] genio con amore', Allegro Molto, B flat. 2 ob., 2 hns., str. Role: Scanarello (soprano).

> Non o genio con amore,
> Non mi voglio maritar;
> Non ò mai donato il core,
> E lo voglio conservar.
> [Adagio:]
> Che n'è dici?
> Non fo bene?
> [Allegro]
> Questo è stato sino ad ora
> Il mio modo di pensar.

The figure of 'Scanarello' (Sganarello), like the others, comes from the *commedia dell'arte* and once more suggests how Venetian are the text and the characters that sing it throughout this 'comedy'. This is the most forward-looking of all the arias: there are only two bars of orchestral introduction and away the 'patter' aria rushes: it is as if we are transported to the Haydn operas of the 1780s. This is true as well of the sudden *adagio* hold-ups, which will become an integral part of the *buffo* style of the typical Polzelli aria (and indeed, long before that). We also note what might be called the 'manipulation' of text, whereby Haydn combines lines that did not belong together originally, e.g.

> Non o genio con amore
> E lo voglio maritar.

A pretty specimen of this may be seen in the following passage, where the music is running towards a pause:

[non fo] be - ne, che nè di- ci non fo   be - ne, be-ne, be-ne be - ne,   be - ne

The end is one of Haydn's famous surprises, here fully-fledged in 1762:

Just before the end Adagio enters again, but instead of continuing in allegro, 'non fo bene' and before we know it, the piece is over. It is the essence of the Haydnesque spirit and wit.

434

[Aria No. 4, 'Non o genio con amore' – opening]

Arias Nos. 5 and 6 are missing.

Aria No. 7 appears to be the 'Poco Adagio' kind of piece. The whole beginning is missing (part of one 'Bogen'; the fragment begins with 'Bogen' No. 2, the number in Haydn's hand). A major, 3/8, 2 ob., 2 hns., str. Soprano.

> Se non mi credi,
> Se non m'intendi,
> Quest'occhi teneri,
> Se non comprendi,
> Tutto è tua colpa.
> Credi al mio labbro,
> Son tutta amore,
> Son fida a te.

A tender Aria for soprano with a lover's text. There is the usual vocal shorthand: in bar two of the fragment the violin has ♪ 𝅘𝅥𝅮 but the soprano ♪♪ ♪; while the soprano, only a few bars later, has correctly ♪♪ ♪ – and this, too, is (alas) prophetic. It is the kind of imprecise notation which disfigures Haydn's vocal scores (and not only them) throughout his life, and its origin comes from having a regular ensemble who understood, without being told a second time, how such imprecisions should be adjusted. Actually, we believe the text to be complete and only the beginning of the ritornello to be wanting, perhaps the outside sheet which 'enclosed' the aria, say two pages. We arrive, it would seem, at the end of the ritornello. Also here, we look forward: the following passage –

quest'occ-hi te - ne - ri,
(*fz* Orch.)

– reminds us of the first aria in *L'infeltà delusa*:

[Allegro Moderato]

Quan-do vie-ne, gli hai da dir [sempre di no].

This present piece, in its curious notation, also contains hints that even within such a piece (i.e., not just in recitatives), appoggiature were sung. Consider this passage:

tutto è tua col - pa   tutto è tua col - pa

the accompaniment of the first violins, (arrow)

presupposes that at '*col-pa*' an appoggiatura at '*col-*' be sung. (Incidentally, at the beginning of the middle section, the soprano has, correctly, ♪♪ ♪ – also the 'cello-

436

bass line again has low D.) In this quietly affectionate piece, we notice the rather unusual dynamic mark, 'poco for:' which we encounter very rarely in Haydn's instrumental music of the period but more often in vocal music (a revealing point).

Aria No. 8, 'Se credesse', Andante, G, 2/4. 2 ob., 2 hns., str. Role: 'Pantalone' (soprano).

> Se credesse che un visetto
> Me volesse contentar,
> Ghè vorria dar un basetto,
> E'l vorrave sempre amar.
> [Allegro]
> Viva i visetti, viva quei occhetti,
> Gusto più bello non posso trovar.

(Pretty detail in the autograph: towards the end, Haydn wrote a bar twice. The first one was crossed out and violin II has a little sour face ⊗ to remind the copyist what is happening.)

'Pantalone' is another famous figure of the *commedia dell'arte*, often reproduced as a porcelain figure north of the Alps. The ritornello –

– is like an Italian theme, but suddenly we realize that the prototype has been strangely warped with the layout of $4+5$ bars. Even stranger, when the vocal part enters the sections are regular: $4+4+4+4$. The Allegro section is in the dominant and it, too, is perfectly regular:

$$2+2 \mid +4 \mid 2+2 \mid +4 \mid 4+4+5$$
$$a+a \quad \ b \ \ a+a \quad \ \ b \ \ c \ \ c' \ \ c''$$

– all except for that wilful five-bar tail. We return to the A section, but this recapitulation is once again eccentrically varied: $4+5+4+5$ (at the beginning of this part, we find a note to the copyist: 'Bleib[t] aus geschr[ieben]', 'must be written out', in case an over-clever scribe might imagine he could simply write, 'Da capo'). The Allegro returns the second time, and by now we realize that Haydn has begun the kind of 'endless variations' for which he would later be famous. It is now, of course, in the tonic (G), but although using the same thematic material as before, it is altered to fit the new key and range: instead of

we have

The layout of the bar lengths has also changed subtly:

8 | +8 | 4 + 4 + 4 + 2 closing bars
  a + a' + 4   [ditto, exact repeat]
                       ↑[here repeat signs :‖ were added later]

There are two things that need to be said about this interesting formal scheme: first, its patent irregularity and secondly, that it is the mother of many such Andante – Allegro – Andante – Allegro movements in Haydn's operas, such as in *Il mondo della luna* (Buonafede's 'Intermezzo' and 'Ho veduto' in Act I, Lisetta's Aria in Act I, 'Una donna come me', Bärenreiter No. 10, piano score, pp. 134–45). Haydn is already fast developing his own personal style, based of course on his Italian predecessors but with many original and atypical features of its own.

Aria No. 9 'Se non son bella tanto', Andante, E, 2 4. 2 hns., str. Role: 'Sign^{ia} Augusta' (soprano).

> Se non son bella tanto,
> Almeno o [ho] il cor sincero,
> Credi! ti dico il vero,
> E ti prometto amore
> E fedeltà risolva.

Another pert soubrette aria, alas only in fragment (it breaks off somewhere in the middle), with a saucy theme looking forward in style, text and treatment to *Le pescatrici* and *L'infedeltà delusa* (in the latter the delicious E major Aria by Vespina, 'Ho tesa la rete'). This piece again shows a peculiar aptitude on Haydn's part for the witty, slightly ironic side of the *commedia dell'arte*; but also to the gently affectionate and (in the eighteenth-century sense) sentimental. We look forward to one of the great *feste* at Eszterháza, in 1772, when (in a special 'small listening hall' in the park) 'sundry female singers' sang only of love: 'From their eyes sad woe, from their singers' tongues lust and melancholy'.[1] Perhaps Haydn often used these attractive numbers from *La Marchese Nespola* in future years.

Marchesa* is a vitally important milestone in Haydn's career: it is his first extant entry in *opera buffa*, a form in which he was to excel and in which he would write his most interesting, beautiful and lasting operatic music. These little 'comedy arias' show complete mastery of the Italian language of the *opera buffa* form as it was bequeathed to him by Galuppi (one of his special favourites), Piccinni (whose epochal *La buona figliuola* coincided with *Marchesa*) or Traetta. Haydn's ease in dealing with the different situations called for by the libretto is as sovereign as his ability to introduce various formal experiments (such as melodies of five bars) to prevent monotony.

There is every reason to believe that Prince Nicolaus encouraged Haydn to continue with his operatic endeavours (although it is probable that *Acide* was already planned before Prince Paul Anton's death). It is to that work – like *La Marchesa Nespola*, unpublished as yet (1978) – that we must now turn our attention.

---

1 *Haydn at Eszterháza 1766–1790*, p. 179.

Acide, festa teatrale in 13 scenes
(XXVIII:1; 1762, performed January 1763)

Scoring: 2 fl., 2 ob., (2 cors. angl.), 2 hns., str. Galatea: sop.; Glauce: sop.; Tetide: contralto; Acide: tenor; Polifemo: bass.

Principal sources: Autograph: (1) Overture, lacking the first 32 bars of the first movt., Conservatoire de Musique (now Bibliothèque Nationale), Paris, on 4° paper from the Esterházy paper-mill in Lockenhaus. (2) EH, Budapest, Ms. Mus. I.8, on Italian paper in oblong format. (a) Sc. I, Acide's. Aria, 'La beltà'. [top left:] 'Aria' [middle:] 'In Nomine Domini' [right:] Giuseppe Haydn / $\overline{762}$'. 2 ob., 2 hns., str. Watermarks: fleur-de-lys. (b) Sc. III, Glauce's Aria, 'Perchè stupisci tanto'. [Top of page, in middle:] 'In Nomine Domini'. 2 ob., 2 hns., str. Watermarks: letters 'FC'; three crescents of declining size. (c) Sc. IV, Polifemo's Aria, 'Se men gentile'. 2 ob., 2 hns., str. Watermarks: ornament, from which hangs a cross; cut-off top part suggests a crown; three crescents of declining size with letter 'M'. (d) Sc. XII, Tetide's Aria, 'Tergi i vezzosi rai' (first version). 2 solo fl., 2 hns., str. Watermarks: canopy with a fleur-de-lys above; three crescents of declining size. (e) Scena ultima. Quartetto, 'Ah vedrai'. 2 ob., 2 hns., str. Watermarks: as in (d). At end 'Fine / Laus Deo'. (3) Bibliothèque de l'Opéra, Paris, cat. Haydn 2. Sc. V, Acide's recitativo acc., 'Misero! che ascolto!' str. only. Watermarks: three crescents of decreasing size (oblong paper). Secondary sources for the Overture: (1) Göttweig Cat., 'Comparavit R. P. Odo ao. 769'. (2) MS. parts from Hirschberg (Doksy) Castle, National Library, Prague, with 2 fl. (3) MS. parts by Viennese copyist No. 3 (*SYM*, 611), St Florian Abbey, from the library of Dr Stocker (who also owned several Joseph Elssler copies of Haydn symphonies). (4) MS. parts, Archbishop's Library, Kremsier (Kroměříž), ČSSR, IV. A.121. All these sources are listed as 'sinfonia' (we have given only the principal MSS.). *Libretto*: Giovanni Battista Migliavacca. Printed libretto for the 1763 première: 'Acide / festa teatrale, / che si / rappresenta in Eisenstadt, / nell'occasione / del felicis[s]imo Imeneo, / degli / illustrissimi ed eccellentissimi / il Signor Conte / ANTONIO D'ESTERHASY / de galantha etc: etc: / e la Signora Contessa / TERESA D'ERDÖDI / de N. etc: etc: / Ai 11, de Gennaro dell'Anno 1763 / [line] / Vienna / nella stamperia di Ghelen. [new page:] Illustrissimi / ed / eccellentissimi / SPOSI, E SPOSA! / Più che mai superba và a comparire su le scene di

questo prencipal Teatro la nostra Teatral Festa, perchè le avviene la fortunata sorte di festeggiare parimente il Vostro Glorioso Imeneo. Effetta della Vostra Clemenza, Eccellentissimi, ed Illustrissimi, sarà il benignissimo aggradimento: dal canto nostro mancato non abbiamo di procurare con tutta la maggior diligenza di rendere questa Festa Teatrale più degna del Vostro umanissimo compatimento. Degnatevi dunque Illustrissimi ed Eccellentissimi j dei accoglierla benignamente sotto l'autorevole Vostro Patrocinio, e seco insieme vi piaccia pur di non sdegnare la tenue divota dedica, che vi consagriamo, e che ci produce la gloria di confermarci con profondissimo inchino / di Voi / illustrissimi et ecclessentissimi [*sic*] [originally:] / Friberth e gl'altri / Attori / [covered by a strip of paper with the following MS., not in Haydn's hand: 'Hayden Con la / Musica'].

Attori

Accide, Carlo Friberth
Galathea, Anna Schefstoss
Polifemo, Melchiore Griessler
Glauce, Barbara Fichsin [*sic*]
Tetide, Eleonora Jegherin [*sic*]

Tutti in attuale Servizio di S. A. S. il Signor Prencipe Nicolà d'Esterhasy de Galantha etc.

Cori di Nereidi

La Scena è in Sicilia alle falde del
    Monte Etna, vicino alla Marina.

La Poesia è del celebre Poeta il Signor
    Giovanni Battista Migliavacca.

La Musica è del Signor Giuseppe Hayden,
    Maestro di Cappella di S. A. S.

[Mutazioni di scena:]
Scena prima: Bosco alle falde del Monte Etna
Scena V: Spiaggia di mare ingombra[ta] di s[c]oglie.
[Copy formerly in the Esterházy Archives, destroyed at Buda in 1945; MS. copy of EH print by C.F. Pohl, Gesellschaft der Musikfreunde, Vienna, 10957/Textb. This is the only source of this otherwise lost printed libretto.]
Critical edition: Overture: Verlag Doblinger, Diletto Musicale 39 (Landon).
Literature: Pohl I, 232–8. Geiringer 1932, pp. 102f. Wirth II, 14f. Bartha-Somfai, 381–4.

Second version of *Acide* (XXVIII:1 *bis*)

See *Haydn at Eszterháza 1766–1790*, pp. 252f. One fragment, (Hoboken, vol. II, p. 346, h), beginning with the words 'Se nol turbasse', must be discussed here because of its involvement with the Aria di Dorina (*infra*). 'Se nol turbasse': autograph, EH, in Ms. Mus. I. 8. 4° paper from the Esterházy mill in Lockenhaus. Watermarks: Larsen 11, 10 (Bartha-

Somfai 194a,b). The watermarks show that this was one of the additions for the second version, 1773–4; this fragment is an insertion in Sc. II, Galatea's Aria, 'Troppo felice'.
Scoring: 2 cors. angl., 2 hns., str. Unpublished.
Literature: Bartha-Somfai, 381.

Aria di Dorina, 'Costretta a piangere' (XXIVb:1).

Scoring: Sop. Solo, 2 cors. angl., 2 hns., str.

Sources: Three autograph fragments: (1) Göttweig Abbey; (2) Conservatoire de Musique (now Bibliothèque Nationale) Paris; (3) Kästner-Museum, Hanover. For details of these sources, see Landon: *Haydn Arien, Kritischer Bericht*, Haydn-Mozart Presse, 192. A nearly complete MS. copy of this Aria: Preußische Staatsbibliothek, Berlin.

Critical edition: Haydn–Mozart Presse, 136–7 (Landon).

Synopsis of the plot: Glauce implores Acide to flee from Polifemo, the 'horrid cyclops'. Acide has no fear and will not leave Galatea, who shortly appears. Glauce warns her to flee. Polifemo appears, enquiring of Glauce after the 'blonde Galatea'. Glauce suggests that it is futile for Polifemo to pursue Galatea, who loathes him. 'You will find another nymph, less proud'. Glauce thereupon pretends to fall in love with the astonished Polifemo. Aria (Glauce): 'Why be astonished if I burn with love for thee?' etc.

Polifemo, alone, considers his fate in an Aria, 'If my exterior is less attractive, I feel a virile heart in my breast', etc. Scene V at the sea: Acide and Galatea exchange vows of love. Galatea suggests that they leave in her shell, moored in readiness. Glauce arrives, exclaiming 'Stop your flight for the moment'. She suggests that Polifemo might be surprised in his sleep and overcome. Acide is not pleased at this prospect and is uncertain whether to stay or to flee. He leaves the scene, presumably to seek Polifemo. Galatea and Glauce are surprised by the cyclops. Both now spurn him, and Polifemo hides. Glauce (who has left the scene meanwhile) returns with Acide. Glauce again warns Acide to flee – in vain: Polifemo rolls a huge rock on the beach, crushing the lover; wherepon a *flebile sinfonia* (a sad symphony) indicates the Nereids' mourning. Tetide arrives on a wave and the *flebile sinfonia* changes to *allegro*. She restores Acide to life and, as the curtain falls, a quartet proclaims a happy end.

Acide's three-movement Overture (*sinfonia*) was circulated as a symphony (see the list of sources, *supra*), and in fact the only outwardly formal trait that distinguishes this overture from a contemporary symphony is that in the former there are no repeat signs (i.e., no intermediary double bars). The fanfare-like material of the first movement, with its scales and repeated semiquavers, shows its relationship to the stage in its avoidance of clearly profiled themes – there is also no real second subject, only a 'section' in the dominant. The middle section begins with the opening material in the dominant, and after a very brief series of modulations and a *piano* interlude, the recapitulation occurs. Like contemporary symphonies, both the next movements are in quick metres (in this case 3/8), and as we have seen in almost all the regular early symphonies (not the *sonata da chiesa* works), the wind parts are dropped from the slow movement. The most characteristic feature of this Andante grazioso is that it is chiefly held together by three different rhythmic features: the trill figure which we hear at once in bar 1; the series of semiquaver triplets, occurring in 56 of the movement's 86 bars; and the dotted 'courtly' rhythm which, as we shall soon see, is a central element in Haydn's works for the Eisenstadt court in the early 1760s. The same fanfares, repeated semiquavers (and chords made out of semiquavers) of the first movement are also found in the final Presto. There is a regularity, one is almost tempted to say 'formalism', even in the way that quite a lengthy *piano* 'second subject' appears not only in the first and third parts but also in the middle (E minor). It is perhaps an error, from the historical standpoint, to talk of sonata form in relation to works of this kind: each of the three movements is in that three-part structure which we know well from the early symphonies. But one cannot escape the feeling that there is less personality in this *sinfonia* to an opera seria than in the other work of this kind and period: the little three-movement Symphony No. 9 (1762), discussed later.

The fragmentary state of *Acide* is probably due to most of it having perished in the great fire at Eszterháza in 1779. The work had been (probably in a revised state) in the repertoire as late as 1774. It is thus idle to speculate on this non-existent revised version, but in the course of this brief summary, we shall have occasion to discuss one number of the 1773–4 version which, as will be seen, is in a curious way connected with an aria composed *c*. 1762 (*vide infra*, pp. 446f.).

The first piece to survive is, as it happens, the first aria of the libretto, Acide's

> La beltà, che m'innamora,
>> Dolce rende il mio periglio;
>> Mi difende, m'avvalora,
>> Non mi lascia paventar.

> [Middle section with faster tempo: Allegro molto]
>> Il rival superbo, e fiero,
>>> Benché opprima il mondo intero,
>>> Non vedrà la mia costanza
>> Un istante [a][1] vacillar.
>>>> La beltà [etc.]

Haydn sets the principal part of this Metastasian text in what we might call the early C major Eisenstadt courtly style, which contains some stylistic traits every bit as clearly defined as those which will mark the C major style of Haydn's symphonies in the 1770s (C *alto* horns, timpani, etc.). In the C major courtly style of the 1760s, we find: (1) a strong dotted rhythm (see the beginning of our musical example); other cases are the beginning of Symphony No. 7 ('Le Midi', 1761) and the 'Cello Concerto (VIIb:1); (2) the use of the Lombard (or reverse dotted) rhythm, as in bars 7ff. of our example; another example in the 'Cello Concerto's opening tutti; (3) the use, generally, of oboes and horns, with bassoon(s) regarded as an automatic part of the *basso continuo*, as the basic orchestration apart from strings. For another interesting case, see the church *contrafactum* 'Ego virtus gratitudo' (*infra*, p. 504), where the presence of this new style is a determining factor of the work's authenticity.

1 The bracketed word is missing in the libretto but appears, correctly, in Haydn's autograph.

[Acide's Aria, 'La beltà che m'innamora' – opening]

We also note that the so-called 'Haydn ornament' is now an essential fingerprint:

In the middle section of this Aria, we find those incredible coloratura passages which, for the average tenor voice of today, are virtually impossible to sing:

[paven] tar - - - - - - - - - - -

pa - ven - tar

etc.

It will be noted, however, that Haydn's sense of motivic unity will not allow him to compose empty *fioriture*: the passage here quoted is based entirely on material placed before us in the exposition – the triplets, the Lombard rhythm, etc. Here is the formal scheme of the first section of this typical *da capo* aria form:

ritornello (key) I	vocal entry I——→	section in V	ritornello V	vocal entry using first subject: modulations	recapitulation with woodwind and horn soli I

Although Haydn was relatively new at this *opera seria* – or rightly considered, pastoral – type of form, he is already starting to 'manipulate' the text; consider the following passage, where the words 'no, no' are not in the libretto at all:

V. I

V. II

Acide [non mi] la - scia pa-ven - tar no no

Va. + Vc., B.

Just before the end, Haydn carries the tenor part up to high *c*, and it even appears that the passage in question

pa - ven - tar — — — — non la - scia pa - ven - tar

was not sung *in falsetto*, as was often the case. There is a place for a cadenza in this recapitulation, and the final ritornello is shortened. Throughout, we find that Haydn's treatment of cool and abstract text is itself rather cool and abstract: we shall see, in the course of this biography, that he is never his best with Rousseauesque or Voltairean rationality. The 'B' section begins in F

and the principal contrasts are that now there are no wind parts (this was a typical feature in Hassean *da capo* arias), but a shift to a much more modern metre (3/4) and rhythmic treatment (instead of dotted and Lombard rhythms, straight quaver plus semiquavers, and so forth. The ending reveals another Hassean feature: the conclusion in E minor. Altogether this middle or 'B' section is in the event much more forward-looking than the Baroque C major splendours of the beginning: the F major part even reminds us of Haydn's later operas, such as the 3/4 section of *L'infedeltà delusa*'s Finale to Atto II° (bars 85ff.; Philharmonia, pp. 415ff.)

The next scene contains Galatea's Aria

Troppo felice	Ad ogni passo
Troppo beato	Trovo un cimento;
di questo cuore	Se crolla un sasso,
Sarìa lo stato,	Se spira un vento,
Se nol turbasse	Mi gela il petto,
Crudel timor.	Mi trema il cuor.

The fragment of the autograph (EH, Budapest) is written on 'IGW' stag paper and belongs to the 1773–4 revision. It begins with the words '[ti-]mor. Se nol turbasse' and therefore places us at the end of the first strophe. In this fragment, it appears that the recapitulation begins at

and at this point we are plunged into a mystery. The orchestration (with two cors anglais and two horns), the key (E flat), the metre (3/8) and the actual theme are the same as the *Aria di Dorina* (XXIVb:1), 'Costretta a piangere'. Now when we issued the first edition of this pretty music many years ago, it was clear to us from the autograph

446

fragments that the music must have been composed about the time of the *Marchesa Nespola* fragments (1762). But how is it possible that Haydn, who almost never borrowed from himself anyway, would borrow (as it seems) this *Aria di Dorina* for insertion in *Acide*. Here is a mystery that cannot yet be explained. The autograph of the 'Troppo felice' shows that it was written as a kind of insertion; at the end of the Budapest MS. is the sign ∮ all the way down the score, which means that the copyist must continue in the (lost) remainder of the Aria where the sign indicates. Another hint how the revision of 1773–4 proceeded: perhaps cadenzas removed, middle sections of *da capo* arias excised, and other 'old fashioned' traits brought up to date. A beautiful extract from this 1773–4 revision may be seen in the musical example shown overleaf. The Berlin State Library insertion (Mus. ms. autogr. Jos. Haydn 55),[1] '[Il] caro tuo tesoro', which is a magnificent accompanied recitative, also reveals to us that at least this particular scene was not only newly composed but since the entire section is missing in the 1763 libretto, newly added by a house poet at Eszterháza (Friberth?). In the original Scena XI of the 1763 libretto, Galatea and Glauce are alone and Polifemo has just murdered Acide. Glauce says:

> Ah (non so dirlo.)
> Fra quei dirupi ascoso . . .
> Il mostro traditor . . . Con quel che vedi, . . .
> Dal monte in un balen svelto macigno,
> Il caro tuo Tesoro . . .
> Sotto l'enorme peso . . .
>
> Gal.   Ah Glauce! Io moro (Sviene.)
>
> Gl.   Soccorso, o Dei!
> [Tetide arrives on a wave, end of Scene]

The Berlin fragment, then, is a whole new insertion, and what we have is the end of the secco ('. . . caro tuo Tesoro . . . peso') and then a *scena* by Galatea:

> Giusti Dei!
> Misericordia!
> A tanto dolor chi può resister mai?
> Io manco, deliro, correi . . .
> Acide!
> Ah si, ombra diletta, ora ti sieguo . . .
> Nò, nò! Vendetta vuoi, vendetta avrai.
> Deità da Caligini, ed furie d'Averno,
> Voi tutte invoco.
> Con voi vengan da neri chiostri tuoni,
> Lampi, stragi e flagelli
> A lacerar il cuore,
> E l'anima di quel perfido mostro
> Strappa tagli e viscere e sangue.
> Non resti in lui parte intera;
> L'indegno perisca,
> Mora il traditor.
> Folle che ragiono; i spiriti infernali
> Non hanno pietà di me.
> Deh, abbiatela voi, Numi celesti!

[*cont.*, p. 449]

1 Hoboken, Vol. II, pp. 346f., item 1.

[Galatea's Aria, 'Troppo felice': 1773–4 version]

Rendetemi l'idol mio o toglietemi questa vita:
Grazie, benigni Dei! Grazie,
E voi alfine sentite pietà di me,
Già si perde il respiro, la luce, e la voce.
Ohime, che martoro!
Assistemi.
Glauce, io moro.

Gl.   Soccorso, oh Dei!

This is followed by 'Vi=[de]'. It is fascinating to think that Haydn must have commissioned this violent textual insertion at this point to heighten the drama, and the music which accompanies it is the only *opera seria* text (in Italian) that Haydn composed between 1762–3 and *L'isola disabitata* of 1779. Its power and Gluckian sense of matching word and music make it a great pity that the majority of this *Acide* revision of 1773–4 has not survived.

To return to the 1762 composition, our next number, chronologically, is Glauce's Aria in Scena III, 'Perchè stupisci tanto', of which the text is:

Perchè stupisci tanto
    S'ardo per te d'amor?
    Quel volto à tale incanto,
    Che come sol risplende,
    Subito accende un cuor.

S'e la rival più bella,
    Son men crudel di quella,
    E te prometto Fede;
[Allegro]
    (E il barbaro lo crede,
    Nè sa, ch'io scherzo ognor.)
            Perchè [etc.]

Another text of the kind that fills the serious operas of Metastasio and Hasse, demanding (and here receiving) a rather impersonal and formal approach. In the opening ritornello, notice after the initial forte the syncopated section:

this kind of cross-rhythmed tension, in which the unsyncopated bass line has staccato accents, is a typical feature of Haydn's 1760 style. Here it forms the basis of the setting of the words 'Quel volto'

providing the music with a springy interest which the libretto hardly contains. The usual coloratura passage appears after the passage quoted above and takes the soprano up to *b flat''*. The E major ritornello is compressed to the typically Haydnesque length of seven bars. The soprano's theme in E major is followed by a short 'extension' (development is the wrong word throughout most of the middle sections of this period), and a lead-back to the tonic via a short instrumental interlude. The recapitulation shows the beginnings of Haydn's formal economy (in a structure which was, by its nature, diffuse): we jump straight to the vocal entry, omitting the ritornello entirely. The disposition of our last example in the tonic is slightly but interestingly varied, with the second violin having the syncopations. The big middle section, 'B' speeds up the tempo; the key is E minor, and the music has much less profile than the 'A' section. The wind instruments are omitted, and the light-textured music is perhaps motivated by the words 'ch'io scherzo ognor'; but the approach, with its antiquated modulation to D major in preparation for the *da capo* in A major, is somehow stiffly conventional.

As if to make up for this Hassean excursion, the third extant Aria, Polifemo's 'Se men gentile' (Scena IV), is completely personal and shows Haydn at his most original.

Se men gentile   Se il crine incolto
    L'aspetto ostento,   Se austero hò il volto;
    Con più virile   Emula al monte
    Nel sen mi sento: Va la mia fronte;
    D'ardir fo pompa   Con lui gareggia
    Non di beltà.   Di maestà.
                                 Se men gentile [etc.]

A very fast-moving (Allegro molto) work in Haydn's favourite 3/4 with the characteristic horn rhythm ♩♪♪ ♪ ♪ ♪ ♪ which will accompany us to 1802 in chamber, church and opera house, while the violin parts abound with those nervous repeated semiquavers ♩♪♪♪ ♬♬ which will also become a hallmark of Haydn's instrumental style, as will the 'leading-note' rhythm ♩♪♪ | ♪♪ ♪ and the *forzato* accents (ritornello as below) —

*At first

All his life, Haydn wrote most idiomatically for the bass voice – it was often said, in the eighteenth century, that his bass arias 'sang themselves'. Here is the first known, recorded example, and even here the result is brilliantly successful. The effective long-held notes for the voice, the syncopations above

and the distillation of the famous 'leading-note phrase'

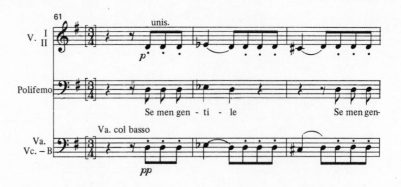

– all are known to us from countless later works. Another pattern which will often recur in the future is the following:

With its broken semiquaver chords in the second violin, the vocal part in tight, rhythmic patterns and syncopations (derived from the previous forte), and the bass nervously repeating quavers for bar after bar, we have here the essence of early Haydn that must have captivated that brilliant first audience in the glass-house theatre. The big middle section is, in this Aria, not in another tempo but continues the pattern of the previous material, now in C major. Here is the new, less conservative type of *da capo* aria in which the flow is less disturbed by the intrusion of a totally foreign 'B' section. The repeated semiquavers carry on the drive of the 'A' section, which is reached by a modulation C major to the dominant of E, of which the root position is reached only just before the modulation back to the *da capo*.

The Bibliothèque de l'Opéra in Paris owns, for some extraordinary reason, the 1762–3 *recitativo accompagnato* 'Misero! che ascolto' (Acide in Scena V), a long and dramatic solo scene that Haydn sets very expertly and with those characteristic changes in tempo (Adagio – Presto, etc.) which, of course, he inherited from the Italians and Hasse but which he very much makes his own. The ensuing Aria 'Ah se ancor soffrir degg'io' is missing: we reproduce (pl. 29) a page of this tautly reasoned recitative from Haydn's manuscript, from which a good idea of the style and content may be seen.

The next section is Tetide's Aria 'Tergi i vezzosi rai':

> Tergi i vezzosi rai,
>> Il tuo martir consola:
>> Ai sospirato assai,
>> Preparati a goder.

> [Middle section:]
> Or sempre al fin serena
>> Sarà per te la sorte:
>> Tutto fin' or fu pena,
>> Tutto or sarà piacer.   Tergi [etc.]

457

When Haydn revised this work, he wrote an entirely new Aria on this text, transferring it from alto (sung by Miss Jäger in 1763) to bass and renaming the role 'Nettuno'. In the 1763 première, this must have been Miss Jäger's star piece. The scoring for 2 transverse flutes instead of oboes seduces Haydn into using them in a J. C. Bach-like fashion as soli, and the style looks forward in a quite uncanny way to the Concertos for the King of Naples (1786). The beginning of this gay and insouciant music is here reproduced from the autograph:

The gigantic size of this ritornello and the extended concertante sections for the flutes may have suggested to Haydn to drop the Aria from the revival of 1773–4. The virtuoso character of these concertante flutes may, too, have suggested that the vocal coloratura of this 1762–3 version be kept to a minimum. The middle section makes use of the same thematic material, starting in C major:

At the words, 'Tutto fin' or fu pena' etc., the words are set by Haydn with a characteristic twist:

The final extant work in *Acide* is, as it happens, the last Quartetto, which Haydn signs 'Laus Deo' with a large flourish.

Gal.   Ah vedrai, bell'idol mio,
        Pria tornar sul monte il rio,
        Che quest' anima infedel!

Acide   Ah vedrai, mia bella speme,
        Pria la notte, e il giorno insieme,
        Che quest' anima infedel!

Gal.   Se il mio cuor dal tuo divido:
        Se a te mai divengo infido:
        a due
      Sempre trovi amor sdegnato,
        Trovi sempre avesso il Ciel!

Tet. e Glauce {   Ah ci sia cortese il fato,
        Quanto già vi fu crudel.

Gal. e Acide {   Ah ci sia cortese il fato
        Quanto già ci fu crudel.

Gal. e Acide   ... Ah ci sia etc.

Tutti: Tet. Gl. e Galat.   ... Ah ci sia [etc.]

This Finale seems to be the most conventional and least inspired of the extant numbers, notwithstanding its pretty moments (in the ritornello a typically well organized pedal point with imitational writing in the upper parts:

The whole is in the original Allegretto tempo, with the plan as shown opposite.

The autograph shows us the manner in which Haydn wrote out the score, and this is particularly clear in 'Perchè stupisci tanto'. The strings were put down first, and the woodwind and brass last (added in much paler ink). This is also the practice of Haydn's maturity (easily seen on such an autograph as Symphony No. 54 of 1774, with at least three sets of instrumental additions).

[*Acide* – plan of Finale:]

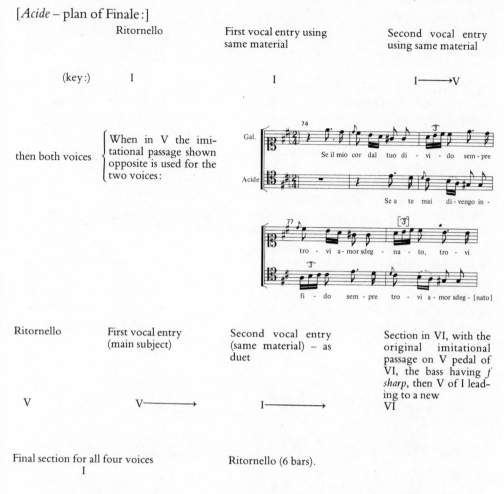

	Ritornello	First vocal entry using same material	Second vocal entry using same material
(key:)	I	I	I——→V

then both voices { When in V the imitational passage shown opposite is used for the two voices:

Ritornello	First vocal entry (main subject)	Second vocal entry (same material) – as duet	Section in VI, with the original imitational passage on V pedal of VI, the bass having *f sharp*, then V of I leading to a new
V	V——→	I——→	VI

Final section for all four voices
I

Ritornello (6 bars).

___

On the whole, Haydn is more successful with his comic opera settings than with this first, interesting attempt at *opera seria* or *opera pastorale* (to coin a term). The enormous strides that he made in this kind of *genre* can, as we have observed above, be studied most dramatically by means of the Berlin fragment, though even in 1762–3, it is clear that Haydn was more comfortable with dramatic *recitativo accompagnato* than with the pale Metastasian aria of vague content.

Italian Cantatas

Cantata, 'Destatevi, o miei fidi' (XXIVa:2; 1763)

Scoring: 2 S., T. Soli; Choir (S–A–T–B). 2 ob., 2 hns. in G, C *basso* and D, str., cemb. [bsn.].
Text: Girolamo Le Bon (?).
Principal sources: (1) Autograph, formerly Preußische Staatsbibliothek, Berlin, Mus. ms. autogr. Jos. Haydn 35, sent during the Second World War to Grüssau Monastery and now (1978) awaiting its return to Berlin. 4° paper from Esterházy mill at Lockenhaus (watermarks: Larsen 1/2 = Bartha-Somfai, 188/9). At the top of the first page: 'Giuseppe Haydn 7̄6̄3' and at the end 'Laus Deo.' (2) Copies of the autograph: Göttweig Abbey (*ex*

463

coll. Aloys Fuchs), and a copy of the Göttweig MS. prepared by C. F. Pohl, GdM, Vienna, III.40865. Another copy: Preußische Staatsbibliothek, Berlin. Only the Viennese MS. is now complete (counting both Cantatas).

Critical edition: none (1978).
Literature: Pohl I, 242ff. Geiringer 1932, 132f. I. Becker-Glauch, 'Neue Forschungen zu Haydns Kirchenmusik', in *Haydn-Studien* II/3 (1970), 183ff.

These three Cantatas of 1763–4 are certainly the most interesting and in many respects original vocal works of this period. The one under consideration was written to celebrate the name-day of Prince Nicolaus and was presumably first performed at Eisenstadt Castle on 6 December 1763. The first movement is a large accompanied recitative that begins with an enormous ritornello – a characteristic not only of the three works composed in 1763–4 but also of *Applausus* (1768). The opening ritornello is on such a large scale that there is room for a large section in the dominant. It is in the modern, 3/4 style, with all the characteristics that we have first encountered in 'Se men gentile' from *Acide* – the pounding repeated quavers in the bass line, the 'leading note' rhythm (here ♪ ♪♪♪ | ♪♪ ♪), the syncopations, the dense compounding of small rhythmic fragments and the lean brilliance of the chamber orchestration. When at last the solo soprano enters, we learn that this is the day set apart to 'celebrate the fine name of our Prince, of which I shall be the messenger'. There then follows a duet for soprano and tenor, with the orchestra consisting of oboes, horns, and a separate 'cello part. Again, we have a classic example of Haydn's early festival writing: C major, with the syncopations, the Lombard rhythm (almost literally, in the beginning, quoting [1] the end of the C major 'Cello Concerto's opening ritornello):

1 See G. Feder, 'Similarities in the works of Haydn', in *Studies in Eighteenth-Century Music* (Geiringer *Festschrift*), London 1970, p. 193.

(cf. V. I, bar 14)

Note, too, the dotted rhythm that predominates towards the ritornello's end. The text tells us of his (Nicolaus's) heroic deeds, 'receive pure homage, grand hero, honour from the world', and the music is of fantastic difficulty for the two soloists:

Haydn has abandoned the *da capo* aria form, and after the cadenza he writes only a shortened final ritornello.

A short *secco* recitative (S.) leads to another Duetto, for 2 soprano solo voices (in this case obviously Scheffstoss and Fux), with the whole orchestra in D: a quiet and attractive Allegretto movement of which the ritornello was quoted in the Eibiswald *contrafactum* (pp. 171ff). We now provide a sample of the pretty vocal writing:

The text is as fulsome as the Metastasio cantatas for the I.R. family: 'Mai per te, stella rubella, splenda in cielo a danni tuoi, ma per te risplenda quella che ti presti il suo favor'. Formally, we have another arrangement similar to that of the first Duetto – a shortened final ritornello which has been preceded by the inescapable cadenza.

If the Cantata has thus far not exceeded the bounds of the conventional name-day panegyric, that which follows is no less than astonishing: the first of Haydn's many D minor *Sturm und Drang* arias based upon the metaphor of the raging sea. Here the text is

> Quanti il mar tesori aduna,
> Quanto dar può la fortuna,
> Non sarà gioja sicura,
> Che il poter a lui servir.

And the opening ritornello and vocal entry will show the stark power that Haydn is able at once to generate (see musical example opposite).

This is the interesting and original way in which Gluck's Finale to *Don Juan* has been subtly altered for Eisenstadt. It is the father of many D minor seascapes of this kind:– 'Si obtrudat' from *Applausus* (1768), 'Varca il mar' from *Le pescatrici* (1769–70), 'Svanisce in un momento' (addition to *Il ritorno di Tobia*, 1784) and *The Storm* ('Madrigal', 1792).[1] The fact that this heroic, totally unexpected piece of musical drama appears in a fashionable name-day Cantata suggests that the recipient must have been interested in, and approved of, this display of *Sturm und Drang* – which was about to colour all Haydn's thinking very shortly. It is typical of the Aria's unconventionality that it ends as unexpectedly as it began: on a pause leading directly

[1] See *Haydn at Eszterháza 1766–1790*, p. 278 etc.

[continued from p. 470]

to the final chorus without break ('Siegue Subito il Coro'). The Chorus itself is in *da capo* form (E minor middle section); its 3/8 metre and general style remind one of the Finale to one of Haydn's operas (e.g. that to *Lo Speziale*, Atto III°).

Cantata 'Da qual gioja improviso' (XXIVa:3 ; 1764)

Scoring: S. Solo; Solo Quartet (or Choir?) (S–S–T–B). 2 fl. (autograph = 'Flauti'), 2 ob., bsn., 2 hns. in C *basso*, str., cembalo solo.
Text: Girolamo Le Bon(?).
Principal sources: (1) Autograph, formerly Preußische Staatsbibliothek, Berlin, Mus. ms. autogr. Jos. Haydn 35, sent during the Second World War to Grüssau Monastery and now (1978) awaiting its return to Berlin. 4° paper from Esterházy mill at Lockenhaus (watermarks: Larsen 1/2 = Bartha-Somfai, 188/9). At the end of the Chorus, 'Laus Deo'. (2) Copies of the autograph: Göttweig Abbey (*ex coll.* Aloys Fuchs), and a copy of the Göttweig MS. prepared by C. F. Pohl, GdM, Vienna, III.40865. Another copy: Preußische Staatsbibliothek, Berlin. Only the Vienna MS. is now complete (counting both Cantatas).
Critical edition: none
Literature: Pohl I, 242ff. Geiringer 1932, 132f. I. Becker-Glauch, op. cit., 183ff.

The text of this Cantata reveals that it must have been composed in celebration of Prince Nicolaus's return from the Frankfurt Coronation in 1764. In the opening recitative, the soprano asks, 'Which day is this?' and answers that Heaven has returned to us, happy mortals, our amiable sovereign, and he has returned from that place where the Main washes its banks ('e il merto lo innalzo là dove bagna il Meno le sue sponde'). Since composing the 1763 Cantata, Haydn has managed to make his opening ritornello even more massively symphonic on the one hand and more cohesive motivically on the other: note how, in bars 15ff., the bass line has taken over the opening phrase of the violins:

The second and closing movement is one of Haydn's first attempts at what would be, in his later operas, a large-scale ensemble. Although the four vocal parts are called 'Coro', we doubt that a chorus is actually intended: the intricate and delicate melodic patterns suggest solo voices. Now it happens that there exist *contrafacta* church music arrangements of all the principal movements of these two Cantatas at present under discussion, and although it is unlikely that Haydn himself was responsible for these *contrafacta*,[1] they are worth examining. Unfortunately, they do not materially aid us in the question of 'Solo' or 'Tutti' for the vocal parts of this ensemble: the *contrafactum* 'Plausus honores date' (MSS. in Göttweig Abbey, ÖNB and Schottenstift, Vienna – all post 1800) starts with solo voices and at bar 26 changes to 'Tutti'; after the harpsichord solo, the *contrafactum* specifies 'Soli' ('Et laudio et amore'), and the last dozen bars before the next harpsichord solo are 'Tutti': this exchanges continues to the end, but there is no hint of such alternating solo and tutti in Haydn's autograph.

Naturally a very large movement (179 bars, Moderato) of this kind requires considerable formal planning. First, let us examine the text:

> Sembra che in questo giorno
> Più chiaro il sol risplenda;
> E a noi ch' egli ti renda
> Equali al suo apparir.
>
> Degl'avi tuoi su l'orme,
> Di merti e gloria adorno,
> A noi tu fai ritorno
> E il mondo fai stupir.

1 See Becker–Glauch, op. cit., pp. 183ff.

Di rare cosi illustri
A tua virtù ed onore,
Prepareranno allori
È regi all'avvenir.

Se a noi ti serba il Cielo,
Lieti saremo, oh come;
Nel mondo il tuo gran Nome
Mai si vedra finir.

Più lode ti darei,
Spirito maggior se avessi,
Ma quanto dir potessi,
Poco sarebbe dir.

Eviva il nostro Prence,
Che il mondo fa stupir.

It is no more revoltingly sycophantic than the endless birthday and name-day cantata texts that, as noted above, Metastasio felt obliged to provide for the Empress, Archdukes and Archduchesses in Vienna, though the Metastasian libretti[1] are, naturally, for more elegant. The movement starts without any introduction (as shown in the musical example opposite). At first there are only two voices involved but, at the end of the first section, all four enter, the top two in pretty imitation (see pp. 481–4). The whole final part of this section has been in the dominant, and now, Haydn himself joins in the proceedings with the first harpsichord solo[2] (at the conclusion of our example). For some reason no longer ascertainable so long after the event, in 1764 Prince Nicolaus took a sudden interest in his *Vice-Capellmeister*'s harpsichord playing, and we find not only the solo sections in this and the 'Qual dubbio' Cantatas, but also an unexpected resuscitation of the 'Concertino' (or, as it was more usually called, 'Divertimento') for solo harpsichord and strings. So 'der grüne Flich' (dialect for 'der grüne Flügel'), the green harpsichord, was carried back and forth from great hall to small hall to glass-house opera.

---

1 An example from 1757 reads:
  All'Augustissima / IMPERATRICE REGINA / Per la compita vittoria riportata a Colin in Boemia dalle armi Austriache, sotto il commando del Maresciallo Conte di DAUN, il giorno 18. Giugno 1757.

SONETTO

Oh qual, Teresa, al suo splendor natío
Nuovo aggiunge splendore oggi il tuo Nome!
Ecco a seconda dell commun desío
Le orgogliose falangi oppresse, e dome.

Di guerra il nembo impetuoso, e rio
   Sveller parea gli allori alle tue chiome:
   Tu in Dio fidasti, Augusta Donna; e Dio
   In favor tuo si dichiarò: ma come?

Il Sol non s'arrestò nel gran cimento:
   Il mar non si divise: il suo favore
   Non costò alla natura alcun portento.

Il Senno, la Costanza, ed il Valore
   Fur suoi ministri; e dell'illustre evento
   Ti diè il vantaggio, e ti lasciò l'onore.

[*Opere*, Venice 1781, Tomo XIV, 291]

2 In the church music *contrafactum*, solo violin.

478

(cf. V.)

The second section of the ensemble begins after a concluding ritornello in G major and presents the whole first section all over again – a straight (though written out) repetition of everything up to the conclusion of the harpsichord solo. The first section set to music the first strophe, the repetition the second. The third section starts with the main theme in the dominant, but there is then a large-scale shift to the subdominant (end of the fourth strophe), in which key (F) the harpsichord solo appears. It contains the same music as in its first two (C major) appearances. Fifth strophe: all four voices in F major, with modulation back to the tonic and the solo harpsichord entry in C, and the setting of the last two lines (with Haydn's usual manipulations: 'che il mondo fa stupir, che fa stupir'). In other words Haydn treats the voices as one block and the solo harpsichord as the second, and writes a kind of Vivaldian ritornello form as if for a double concerto. This is a daring, unconventional ensemble and already reveals Haydn's aptitude for, and fascination with, the large-scale forms that he could not write in sonata, trio or symphony. It is always in the vocal works, particularly those which he could write after Werner died in 1766, that Haydn's unfolding of panoramic, broad formal patterns may be observed. In the very short period between the Finale of *Acide* (probably completed in 1762) and this ensemble two years later, Haydn's grasp of a big ensemble has made astonishing progress.

Cantata 'Qual dubbio' (XXIVa:4; 1764)

Scoring: S. Solo; Choir (S–A–T–B). 2 ob., 2 hns. in A, str. [bsn.], cembalo solo.

Text: Girolamo Le Bon (?).

Principal sources: (1) Autograph, first offered to the antiquarian market in Auktion XCII, C. G. Boerner, Leipzig, 8/9 May 1908, No. 80 (fetched M. 5,680), lacking the final chorus, 'Scenda propizio'; the autograph of that chorus was sold in 1889 by Julian Marshall to W. H. Doane for £20[1] and, if still extant, is probably in American private

1 We are indebted to the conductor, Max Rudolf, for this information (letter of 22 July 1975); Mr Rudolf is at present attempting to trace the chorus's autograph as well as that of the Mozart Fantasia and Sonata in C minor (K.475 and 457), also owned by Doane.

possession. Facsimile of the first page of the autograph: Boerner Cat., Tafel V. On the top of the first page: [middle:] 'In Nomine Domini' [right:] 'Giuseppe Haydn $\overline{764}$'. Formerly owned by the Wittgenstein Family in Vienna, this autograph (minus the chorus) was sold after the Second World War to the Library of Congress, Washington. (2) Complete copy of the autograph, including the missing chorus, by Aloys Fuchs, Burgenländisches Landesmuseum, Eisenstadt (*ex coll.* Landon). (3) Other, incomplete copies of the autograph: Vienna, III.40865; Conservatoire de Musique, Brussels.

Critical edition: Verlag Doblinger, Diletto Musicale 200 (Landon).

Literature: Pohl I, 242ff.

Here, as in the works already discussed, we encounter the same type of opening – a grand ritornello – and one which is orchestrated with particular panache (see overleaf). The text of the *recitativo accompagnato* (soprano, as usual) tells us, as mentioned earlier, that this Cantata is for the name-day (6 December 1764) of Prince Nicolaus. The libretto also informs us that 'il nostro Prence ancora a gradi più sublimi eletto lo vedrem', which Pohl (I, 244n.) rightly considers to be a reference to the forthcoming honours of 1764 and 1765: on this very name-day in 1764, Nicolaus was created Captain of the Noble Hungarian Bodyguard, and on 12 October 1765 he was made a Commander of the Order of Maria Theresa.

The central part of the Cantata is a big Aria, 'Se ogni giorno', in D major (with the oboes and horns). The solo harpsichord is again introduced, but on a much larger scale:

The large scope of this solo harpsichord is made clear to us by the enormous size of its first entry. It is also used in conjunction with the voice as well as being a separate entity. Once again, the technical demands on the soprano are formidable:

The text is as follows:

> Se ogni giorno, Prence, invitto [*sic*]
> A te crescono gl'allori,
> Che Eroi spargere sudori,
> Che vorrà teco pugnar.

At the end of the first section of this *da capo* Aria, there is a double cadenza, one for the soprano and one for the harpsichord: this procedure will be repeated in the *Applausus* Cantata when there are arias with solo harpsichord and solo violin. The middle section, using the solo harpsichord, is much shorter:

> Non vegg'io che i figli tuoi,
> Che del orme all' genitore
> Con virtù parie valore
> Cercheranno te imitar.

A short *secco* recitative leads to the final chorus, also in *da capo* form with a short middle section (though not as short in relation to the main section as was the case with the Aria: 140 to 22 bars, the chorus 69 to 20). Although formally more conventional than the Cantata 'Da qual gioja', 'Qual dubbio' is a bright, attractive work which will always find its admirers. All three Cantatas have far more chance of survival than the huge *Applausus*, the daunting length of which, as well as the Latin text, are almost insuperable hindrances to its present-day appreciation. We will see that the monks at Zwettl prepared handwritten copies for the celebration during which *Applausus* was first performed, and we presume that the same thing happened with the Esterházy Cantatas of 1763 and 1764: there is no record of the libretti being printed and unlikely that this would have occurred for works of such an ephemeral nature. It is, moreover, curious that while there exist many *contrafacta* for the first two Cantatas – a convenient list is on p. 186 of Hoboken, vol. II – none for 'Qual dubbio' has been thus far discovered.

In *EK*, Haydn lists a number of these 'Choruses' (as he entitled them), including one 'bey zurückkunft des Fürst Nicolay von Paris' (the 1767 trip?; probably not the 1781 return), and another, 'Dei Clementi, bey wieder genesung des Furst Nico:

Ester[házy]', in other words to celebrate Nicolaus's recovery from an illness. A third work composed for the wedding of Count Anton in 1763 has been mentioned. Now in *EK* (p. 17) there are listed: 'Coro Primo' ('Vivan gl'illustri sposi'); '[Coro] 2do' ('Al tuo arrivo felice'); '[Coro] 3zo' ('Dei clementi'); '4to', 'quinto' and, on another page (18), 'Coro 6to', the last three without any further identification.[1] The first three 'Choruses' are, as we have seen, lost; this leaves three, and it is tempting to see in these listings the three works here under discussion. It is interesting to note that the autographs of the three extant Cantatas were not in Haydn's library at the time that Johann Elssler drew up his catalogue.[2] Either they were given away, as Haydn often did with his manuscripts, or they had passed out of his (and from the Esterházy library's) possession prior to *c.* 1804–5.

Church Music

Te Deum (XXIIIc:1)

Scoring: S–A–T–B Soli; Choir (S–A–T–B). (2 ob., apparently later additions), 2 trpts., timp., str., organ *continuo*.

Principal sources: (1) MS. parts, erroneously under Michael Haydn's name, Göttweig Abbey, 'R. P. Josephus; die 28 Novemb. 765'. The parts have disappeared but were copied by C. F. Pohl, and his score is now in the GdM, Vienna, I.40970. (2) MS. parts, Seitenstetten Abbey, 'Sub P. M. Hoffmann 785'. (3) MS. parts, Lambach Abbey. (4) MS. parts, as Michael Haydn, Kremsmünster Abbey.

(5) MS. parts, St Florian Abbey. (6) MS. parts, Melk Abbey III.194, with 2 oboes. (7) MS. parts, Zwettl Abbey, with 2 oboes. (8) MS. parts, Burgenländisches Landesmuseum, Eisenstadt (*ex coll.* Landon), with 2 oboes. (10) MS. parts, Janaček Museum, Brno (ČSSR), A4047.

Critical edition: Verlag Doblinger, D.10.476 (Landon).

Literature: Pohl I, 242f. Geiringer 1932, 130f. Brand, 31ff. Becker-Glauch, op. cit., 192ff.

Although once a very popular piece – there are another dozen old copies not included in the above list of sources – Haydn's early *Te Deum* was completely forgotten until its resuscitation at the Holland Festival in 1967. Haydn entered it provisionally, i.e. without the *incipit*, in the *Entwurf-Katalog* (p. 21). There are many occasions for which he can have composed this *Te Deum* at Eisenstadt, beginning with Prince Nicolaus's official entry into Eisenstadt (17 May 1762); continuing with the marriage of Count Paul Anton and Marie Therese von Erdödy in January 1763 (see the article in the *Wienerisches Diarium, supra,* pp. 382f.), when we know a Te Deum was played in the Castle Chapel, and – for an ultimate date – some ceremony in 1764 connected with Prince Nicolaus's return from the Coronation at Frankfurt. This latter was the occasion suggested, without any actual evidence, by C. F. Pohl. It is curious that no parts at Eisenstadt have survived, neither in the Esterházy Archives nor in the Parish Church of St Martin.

Haydn's early *Te Deum* is clearly rooted in the Austrian tradition: the organization of the work in three parts and the key of C are features we find in many such compositions of the 1740s and 1750s, such as may be examined in many Austrian monastery collections (Göttweig, Melk, Kremsmünster). The three parts are as follows: (1) the opening, primarily homophonic choral writing with series of scales, semiquavers, triplets, and in general the use of the violins in the Reutter manner; a long tenor solo ('Tu Rex gloriae, Christe', etc.) leads to a half-cadence on G. (2) The middle section, 'Te ergo quaesumus', with darkly shifting harmonies, pulsating *p* strings, and

---

1 See Larsen, *HÜB*, 236. Titles and explanations were added later.
2 *Haydn: the Late Years 1801–1809*, pp. 299ff.

the oboes, trumpets and kettledrums dropped. (3) The final section, introducing the other solo voices (not, interestingly, the tenor). This third part has, again in the best Austrian tradition, a fugue on the words 'In te Domine speravi'. At the end of this fugal section, Haydn reintroduces the music of the work's beginning (Reutter-like scales, triplets, semiquaver patterns), thus giving the whole a fine sense of unity. Apart from the impressive middle section, which looks forward to the intense Adagio of the late *Te Deum for Empress Marie Therese*,[1] we have many characteristic details (the ♫♫ ♩ rhythm of trumpets and kettledrums, already a firm 'fingerprint') which look forward to later Haydn; but as we might expect, this *Te Deum* relies heavily on the Austrian tradition and there is no gainsaying a certain stiffness and awkwardness in the vocal layout, and a degree of stereotyped writing for the strings which Haydn will very soon outgrow for ever. It was not altogether foolishness on the part of the monks in Göttweig, Kremsmünster and St Peter's in Salzburg that led to the attribution to Michael Haydn – something that could never happen with any church work by Joseph from the *Missa Cellensis in honorem B.V.M.* (1766) onwards.

Contrafacta Church Music
(from other *genres*)

Motetto di Sancta Thecla (XXIIIa:4) *vel de Tempore*
(Hoboken *deest*)

Scoring: S. Solo; Choir (S–A–T–B). Str., organ continuo. Later (?) additions: Aria – 2 fl., 2 hns. (source 6). Chorus – 2 hns. (source 6) and 2 trpts., timp. (Haydn?; source 2 – authenticity very unlikely – but also mentioned in source 6 on title page; parts themselves lost).
Principal sources: (1) Authentic parts, signed by Haydn on the Violone part 'Del Giuseppe Haydn mpria', Parish Church of St Martin (now Cathedral), Eisenstadt, cat. 102 (old No. 3), at present on loan to the ONB, Vienna. There are three types of paper, the first Italian (three crescents of declining size) 4°, the second local (much thicker, watermarks illegible), and the third (title page) from St Pölten ('IAVG', eagle). Four copyists: (a) 'Passo' (Basso), by the copyist of Symphony No. 7 in EH, Budapest; (b) Carl Kraus, at this time 'Rector' at St Martin's, who wrote out the title page and vocal parts; (c) Str. parts, including the 'Violone' signed by Haydn; (d) text of the recitative for the 'Passo' part, which was used by the organist. Title: '† Motetto / de / Sancta Thecla = [later: "Protho Martyr / et aliis Sanctis"] / à / Canto Conc:to / Alto / Tenore / Basso. / ripie: / Violinis 2:bus / Alto Viola oblig. / Con / Organo è Violone. / Del Sigre Gioseppe [*sic*] Hayden'.
(2) MS. parts, Országos Széchényi Könyvtár, Ms. mus. IV. 1.866. Title: ' In F / Motetto de Tpore / a / Canto Solo / Alto Tenore Basso Ripienj / Violinis 2bus / Clarinis 2bus In C / Viola et Organo / Del: Sig Giuseppe Haydn:' with two trumpet parts and a different text for all three numbers (recitative, aria, chorus) – *vide infra*. Parts from an unknown

archives on 4° paper of several types and hands. The trumpets appear to be a later addition and of local origin; the watermark of their paper (kindly traced by the librarians) is an eagle; viola part missing. The watermarks of the other pages are almost entirely illegible. The title page is on yet another kind of (bluish) soft paper. The Library kindly sent a microfilm.
(3) MS. parts of the aria only, Diözesanarchiv, Graz (from the parish church of Göss): 'Aria de Santo in F' with the text as in Budapest.
(4) Catalogue reference, in 'Thematischer Catalog / aller / im königlichen Präemonstratenser Stifte Strahof in Prag vorhandenen / Kirchenstücke / In drey Bänden ... Stift Strahof d 1ten April 833. / Gerlak Steinschtir mpria[?] / Regens chori in Strahof' (National Museum, Prague), to Aria 'de Beata; oder de queris Martyre' with 2 trumpets and timpani.
(5) MS. parts formerly in Klosterneuburg Abbey, with the trumpets and timpani, and with the text as in Budapest.
(6) MS. parts, Order of the Brothers of Mercy (Hospitallers; Barmherzige Brüder), Graz, now Musikwissenschaftliches Institut of Graz University, cat. 100 Gbb H27. This source was discovered in a pile of anonymous MSS. from the Order when the present writer was working at the Institut in March 1979. Frau Dr Ingrid Schubert of the Institut thereupon produced the (up to then unfilled) cover with the title page, and we were thus able to produce this new and interesting MS. title: 'No 3. Ave Maria / Offertorium Pro

---

1 See *Haydn: the Years of 'The Creation' 1796–1800*, pp. 605ff.

Pentecostis / et de Tempore. / Soprano Concerto / Alto. Tenore. Passo. / Violino Primo / Violino Secondo / Flautravers: Prima et Seconda Ad Libt: / [Bracket enclosing 'Cornuis' and 'Clarin':] Cornuis 2 Cum Aria Ex F / Clarin 2 in C / Tympano / Organo et Violine / Del Joseph Haÿdn. / Partes XV.' As far as can now be determined, there are two sets of parts in this folio, both now incomplete. Set one consists of 'Soprano Solo', A., T., B. V.I, V.II and Organo on 4° paper (watermarks: lion rampant in coat-of-arms, letters 'I K' ('L K'?), with the text (Aria) 'Veni creator Spiritus' and (Chorus) 'Deo patri sit gloria'. The title page, because of its orchestration, must belong to the second set. Watermarks of title page: wild man with club, letters 'A' over 'W W'. There is a vocal part which would appear to have been copied later, on paper in oblong format, consisting

of the Aria with the text 'Quem pie laudant populi'. The other parts are: Fl.I, Fl.II, Hn.I, Hn.II, V.I, V.II, Va., Org. Str. 4° paper with watermark: 'HF' in ornament and large star. Wind parts: 4° paper with watermark: three crescents of declining size, letters 'FA' over 'C', the whole of the letter group under a 'canopy'. The trumpet and timpani parts listed on the title page are now missing. The watermarks suggest that the wind parts were, at least, copied separately from the other parts; these wind parts are probably of local origin, though they are rather cleverly fashioned.

Critical edition: Verlag Doblinger, in preparation (Landon).

Literature: Karl Geiringer, 'The small sacred Works by Haydn in the Esterházy Archives at Eisenstadt', *Musical Quarterly* XLV (1959), pp. 467 *passim*. Becker-Glauch, op. cit., 178ff.

(1) *The sources of Eisenstadt and Budapest (etc.)*

In a closely reasoned, well-considered argument, Frau Dr Becker-Glauch of the Joseph Haydn Institut (Cologne) has suggested that this *Motetto di Sancta Thecla* is a *contrafactum* of a Latin Cantata in honour of Prince Nicolaus. Perhaps Carl Kraus was responsible for the necessary textual changes to make it a Motet in honour of Saint Thecla, Virgin and Martyr, whose 'Commemoratio' falls on 23 September. But as we have seen, there exists a set of sources in which an entirely different text for all three sections appears, and at least in the chorus, this second version seems to be much closer to the original. The autograph signature of the Eisenstadt copy may be dated 1765–6: the use of 'Del' as part of the signature is first recorded in two works of 1765, Symphony No. 28 and the *Capriccio* 'Acht Sauschneider' (XVII:1). It is this autograph that tells us (a) that the work is genuine and (b) that Haydn approved of the *contrafactum* as we know it in Eisenstadt. Some curious mistakes in the string parts (violin II's copyist suddenly introducing the appropriate bar from violin I) show that the copyists were working directly from the now lost autograph score.

The text of the Eisenstadt *contrafactum* is as follows:

Recitative (S. Solo)
Quis stellae radius splendore circumdatus
Sub sensus nostros cadens astra illuminat?
Stupenda eius claritas iam pia corda recreat.

Aria (S. Solo)
Aurora ridet post atra nubila.
Fremant iam licet averni monstra
[Variant: Fremat iam licet averni Styx,]
non cura has minas, stat Deus pro te.
[Variant: non cura has minas, si Deus pro te.]

Cor pergit amare perfecto amore,
mens sobria surgit sedato maerore.
Non sentit dolores zelosus ardor,
qui escit in Deo nunc castus amor.

Choir
Sic virtus coronatur lauris decora,
encomium laudis est corona.

We may now compare this with the text of the Budapest MS.:

Recitative (S. Solo)
Quae admiranda lux virtutibus decore
Descendit de caelo, et ornat caelestes
Quos mundus olim oderat coronat Deus gloria.

Aria (S. Solo)
Perge blandire dulcedine vocis.
Freme, Tyranne, tormentis atrocis.
Regis minantis portenta nec mors,
Terrebit victores nec alia sors.

Nam fides pro Sancto et casti amores,
Sunt arma eorum ac Sancti adores.
His vincitur orbis extinguitus fax,
Inferni et flamma fit amoena pax.

Choir
Triumphum cantemus in jubilo,
Victoribus Sanctis in Domino.

The fact that at least the chorus appears much closer to the original in this Budapest version may be seen if we compare musical examples of each:

[Eisenstadt *contrafactum*:]

* Written out only in Graz.

[Chorus text, Budapest (Graz shown in parentheses):]

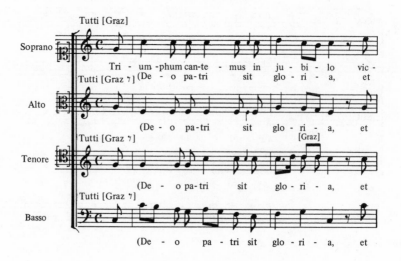

Frau Dr Becker-Glauch did not have at her disposal this vitally important Budapest source when she wrote her article, but she saw from the *incipit* of the lost Klosterneuburg MS. that Haydn's original must have had the latter's rhythm and not the 'chorus parlando' of the Eisenstadt MS. And this leads us to the central question: what evidence is there that the original lost Cantata was actually in Latin? Using the Eisenstadt text, Frau Dr Becker-Glauch reasons that tragic events had occurred, but all will be well 'stat Deus pro te', and she attaches the first part to the deaths of Prince Paul Anton on 18 March 1762 and Princess Maria Octavia on 24 April of the same year, and the second part, as it were, to Prince Nicolaus's installation at Eisenstadt on 17 May 1762. She suggests that the very overture-like Symphony No. 9 (autograph: 1762) might have been used to introduce this Cantata. With all this there can be little argument, but we wonder if the Cantata was not, after all, written to an *Italian* text. All the other extant and lost Cantatas for Prince Nicolaus were in Italian, and in the famous 1768 letter about *Applausus*, Haydn writes explicitly (concerning the correct stress for the word 'metamorphosis' in Latin) that there were very few Latin scholars in Eisenstadt. Then who could have written such a Latin text? The question cannot, of course, be answered.

(2) *The source(s) from the Hospitallers Order, Graz*

We shall see later that there is a direct connection between one of the members of the Graz Order, Frater Micksh, and Haydn. From the watermarks of the Haydn sources of the Order, we may see that all were copied locally. Presumably, someone in Vienna, or Haydn himself, sent the original, or a copy, from which the brothers in Graz worked in each case. The title page informs us that the original cantata has now been transformed into a *contrafactum* for use at Pentecost and 'de Tempore'. This new text, the third in our series of sources, is as follows:

Recitative: here the music was copied but *the text left blank*. Thus we probably have the physical notes of Haydn's cantata just as it was written (bar 3: Graz agrees with Eisenstadt, not Budapest).

Aria (S. Solo)
Veni, creator Spiritus,
mentes tuorum visita,
imple superna gratia
quae tu creasti, pectora.

Accende lumen sensibus,
infunde amorem cordibus,
infirma nostri corporis
virtute firmans perpeti.

Choir
Deo patri sit gloria,
et filio qui a mortuis.
Surrexit ac paraclito
in saeculorum saecula.

The text of the Aria is, of course, one of the most beautiful in the Church's history. It is the first and fourth verses of the 'Hymnus de Spiritu Sancto'.[1]

The Graz text of the Choir fits badly to the music, so that the upbeat had to be omitted (see example); but in its basic shape, Graz is nearer to Budapest than to Eisenstadt. The fourth version of the Aria in *contrafactum*, 'Iste confessor Domini colentes', is probably a local adaptation of the Pentecost version. We show – as Graz I and Graz II – the beginnings of these two texts as footnotes to the musical example (p. 503).

The Aria (Allegro in Eisenstadt and Graz; Allegro moderato in the other sources) once again shows a relationship to other Esterházy Cantatas, in which – a fact that will not have escaped the reader's attention – all the brilliant solo passages are for one or two sopranos, followed by the tenor; but above all, soprano music. There are no solo arias or duets with the alto or bass. We show the opening recitative and beginning of the Aria, with its attractive melodic line.

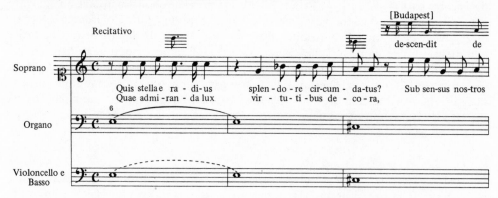

---

1 *Graduale Sacrosanctae Romanae Ecclesiae de Tempore et de Sanctis*, Abbatia Sancti Petri de Solesmis, Tournai, 1974, p. 848.

Aria

* All the appoggiature written ♪ throughout.

* Budapest ♩♪ (♪ changed to ♪ locally)

* Budapest as above, bar 23

As we have come to know in the other Cantatas, there is difficult coloratura. The Aria is in strict *da capo* form and the middle section is, as usual, very short (18 bars, the 'A' section 145 bars. The tiny chorus of 32 bars may in its original form have had a middle section and then a *da capo* of the first part.

'Ego virtus' (Hoboken *deest*)

In *Haydn at Eszterháza 1766–1790* (p. 245), we give a list of the smaller church music presumed to have been composed in the years 1766–1790 – but mostly in the first few years of that period – and including a source of the Motet 'Ens aeternum' from Graz (Barmherzige Brüder, the Order with which Haydn was on friendly terms in both Eisenstadt and Vienna). Now this source requires further elucidation:

Principal source: '№ 1 / Ave Maria / Tutti Ex G / Aria Ex C / ~ / Offertorium / pro / Resurrectio Domini / Sti. P. Joan. de Deo / [later: "Sta–Anna"] / à / Canto Conc.ᵗᵉ / Alto, Tenore, Basso. / 2 Violini / 2 oboe / Alto Viola / 2 Corni / 2 Clarini / Tympano / Organo / Del Sigl Joseph Heyden / Sub Regente Chori / Fr. Abundio Micksh / 772.' All the parts in one hand on 4° paper (watermark: mountain man holding hammer in hand and with coat-of-arms including crossed hammers; letters 'ɪκ' ['ᴊκ'?]). Dup. parts: A., T., B., V.II (2 dup. pts.), V.II (2 dup. pts.) on same kind of paper but of a diff. (later?) date. Order of Hospitallers (Barmherzige Brüder), Graz, now Musikwissenschaftliches Institut of Graz University, cat. 100 Gbb H4. Contents: (1) Motet 'Ens aeternum' minus the middle part (and thus the *da capo*) and with new text, 'Eia venite, estote iam toti'. (2) A hitherto unknown Recitativo and Aria for S. Solo, 'Ego virtus'. (3) *Contrafactum* of the closing chorus of the Cantata 'Destatevi, o miei fidi', with the text 'O sancte Pater'.

Scoring: S. Solo, 2 ob., 2 *clarini* (trpts.), timp., str., org. We suppose the timpani part, marked 'Semper piano', is a local addition (see music ex.). We suggest the oboes are original and the trumpets are literal copies of Haydn's original C *basso* horn parts. (N.B. the trumpets and timpani of 'Ens aeternum' ('Eia venite') are totally different from those of the other known sources, and the horns are known only from this source; on the other hand, the oboes are known from other sources.)

Critical edition: the work is unpublished ('Ego virtus').
Literature: I. Becker-Glauch, op. cit., pp. 186f. It was Frau Dr Becker-Glauch who first drew attention to this important source in Graz.

In the Dlabacž *Lexikon*,[1] Frater Abundio Micksh (Mikysch) is listed as a counterpoint pupil of Haydn's in Vienna, where Micksh was *Regens chori* at the Barmherzige Brüder in the Leopoldstadt, at which institution Haydn was leader of the violins. Later Micksh was transferred to the Order of Graz, where he was *Regens chori*[2] and also composed. He probably added the 'new' horns, trumpets and drums for 'Ens aeternum' and certainly fashioned the recitative 'Concurite et stupete mortales' using quotations from 'Ens aeternum'. Frau Dr Becker-Glauch saw at once that the attractive Aria, with the words

Ego virtus gratitudo   Illi, qui se in labore
inaurata vincla cudo,   fatigavit ex amore,
benefacta non illudo,   ut conservet me in flore
sed rependo gratias.   i [*sic*] et idem facias.

was a hitherto unknown work by Haydn, perhaps part of a lost Esterházy cantata, perhaps from the Italian operas (we recall that *La Marchesa Nespola* is very incomplete, and the others all lost). We cite the beginning of this very typical work, with its C major 'Esterházy' style (the syncopations in the viola, the dotted patterns, etc.).

1 Gottfried Johann Dlabacž, *Allgemeines historisches Künstler-Lexikon für Böhmen und zum Theil auch für Mähren und Schlesien*, vol. II, Prague 1815, p. 320.
2 He also copied Haydn's *Salve Regina* in E (XXIIIb:1), of which the parts (cat. 100 Gbb H5) – not the title page – are on the same 'IK' paper.

* ≡ rubbed out

*Corrected from ♩

cu - do, in   au - ra - ta   vinc - la   cu - do

Motetto de Beata,
'Magna coeli Domina' (XXIIIa:c7)

Scoring: Bass Solo, 2 trpts., timp., str., organ continuo.

Source: 'Motteto [*sic*] [right, above: "Basso Solo"] de Beata / Violino Primo / Violino Second [*sic*] / Viola oblig / Clarino 1mo / Clarino 2do / Tympano / Organo ["è Violone" added later] / Auth. d: Josepho Haÿden / Ex Rebus / Caspari Melchioris Balthasaris / Prantner'. parish church of St Martin (now Cathedral) Eisenstadt, cat. 109 (old No. 49), at present on loan to the Musiksammlung of the ONB, Vienna. There are several different papers and copyists. The 'Violone' part is in Esterházy paper with stag (Larsen, 9; Bartha-Somfai, 193) and 'IGW', which may·be dated *c.* 1769–1773 but possibly as early as 1766. Some of the other parts are signed 'R'; the papers include the watermarks: 'MP'; a crown; a double eagle with sceptre and sword plus the letters 'GMP' (Frau Becker-Glauch reads 'CMP'). The trumpet and drum parts, though also signed 'R', are written on quite different paper but they are listed on the cover and were thus planned *a priori*; they are, however, a local addition. Prandtner wrote the text of the 'Passo Solo' part (the music is in another hand) and provided alternate masculine endings so that the work could be used for the feast days of (male) saints.

Critical edition: none.

Literature: I. Becker-Glauch, op. cit., pp. 189–91.

The text (before changes) reads as follows:

> Magna coeli Domina
> summa orbis gloria!
> Quanto digna es honore,
> quae virtutum plena decore.
> [middle section:]
> Tua semper crescant gaudia,
> nostra augeantur merita.

Frau Becker-Glauch, pointing to the unsatisfactory rhymes, suggests that we have, in this Motet, a *contrafactum* of a secular aria which has survived only in this form. It might have been part of a cantata or one of the arias from the Italian comedies of 1762. Like all Haydn's music for bass solo, this 'aria' is particularly idiomatic in its vocal writing. If

the trumpets and timpani are clearly a local addition, one wonders what the scoring of the lost secular version actually was. We illustrate the opening ritornello with the curious trumpet and kettledrum parts, as well as a specimen of the vocal writing that follows.

Aria 'Maria, Jungfrau rein' (Hoboken *deest*)

Scoring: S. Solo. Str., organ *continuo*.
Source: MS. parts from the Barmherzige Brüder in Kuks (Kukus): 'Aria pro Adventu / ã / Soprano Solo / Due Violini / Organo e Violone / Del Sig. Giuseppe Haydn.' Now National Museum, Prague.

Critical edition: none
Literature: G. Feder in *Haydn-Studien* I/1 (1965), pp. 20f.; G. Feder in *HJB* IV (1968), pp. 116f. l. Becker-Glauch, op cit., pp. 191f.

Georg Feder first drew attention to this piece, which on first sight would appear to be a lost 'Cantilena pro Adventu'. Writing about the collection at Kuks (Kukus), Dr Feder explains that it 'comprises only two groups of works: Symphonies and sacred music.

> The distinct division into two groups is easily explained: attached to Kukus Castle, residence of the Counts von Sporck, was a hospital and monastery of the Hospitallers [Barmherzige Brüder = Brothers of Mercy]. Dlabacž says about Johann Wenzel, Count von Sporck (1724–1804), that he was 'one of the most capable violoncello players'. 'He often gave musical academies ... Many of our Bohemian musicians owe to him their good fortune, particularly after April 13, 1764, on which date he was appointed by the Empress Maria Theresa to be the Imperial and Royal Court and Chamber Music Director and also General Director of Spectacles; in this connection he brought several of our musicians to Vienna as court virtuosos.' Many of the Kukus copies are of local origin, as the watermark 'TRAVTENAV' (a town not far from Kukus [in north-east Bohemia]) reveals. But Viennese copies are also present; for example, we encounter Viennese Copyist No. 2[1] in a copy of Symphony No. 27 and in the arrangement as a sacred piece of an aria from the comedy *La Marchesa Nespola* [*Marchese*[[Aria with Recitative of Leopoldo, here with the text 'Vicisti, heros' and 'Justus ut palma' – *vide supra*, p. 432]. Two of the sacred pieces, which were heretofore considered lost, are especially worthy of mention: four hymns on *Lauda Sion* (p. 8) [XXIIIc:4a–d] and the Advent Cantilena *Jesu redemptor* [XXIIId:3] (here with the later added text 'Ihr Kinderlein kommet'). But one or another of the pieces not listed in the *Entwurf-Katalog*, such as the pretty Advent aria 'Maria Jungfrau rein', is worth closer investigation.

When the present writer examined the sources at Prague, the Kuks collection was not yet available, and one is therefore happy to rely entirely on the Haydn Institut for information on, and the judging of the authenticity of, this Aria. Frau Dr Becker-Glauch and Dr Feder have now scrutinized this Advent Aria and have come to the conclusion that the German text cannot be original, and that the work must be a *contrafactum* of an otherwise lost piece from an Esterházy cantata or one of the 1762 comedies. This is the more likely as an authentic copy of such a *contrafactum* from *La Marchesa Nespola* has, as we have just seen, survived at Kuks. 'Maria, Jungfrau rein' is of the same general type as the 'Aria 8ᵛᵃ' of *La Marchesa Nespola*, with which it shares key, metre and tempo. The beginning of the vocal entry is shown overleaf.

By the time all the evidence on these *contrafacta* has been assembled, and after the completion of the present investigation of the parish churches in Bohemia, Slovakia and Moravia, we shall perhaps find more information to guide us through the labyrinth of those hundreds of smaller church music pieces attributed to Haydn in obscure, and also less obscure but by no means convincing, manuscripts. We believe that among this mass of material we have located another *contrafactum* in the following work.

---

1 For this copyist's connection with Haydn, *vide supra*, pp. 251ff.

[Aria, 'Maria, Jungfrau rein': vocal entry]

Recitative and Aria de B.V.M.,
'Quid hostem times' and 'Verbo fata portalata' (Hoboken *deest*)

Scoring: S. Solo. Str., organ *continuo*.
Source: MS. parts from the Jesuit College in Raab (Györ), Monastery of St Martinsberg (Pannonhalma, Hungary), cat. no. 209: 'Aria a Canto Solo de B V M ... Del Sig: Authore Heyden Descripsit Michael König Discantista Anno 1765.' The *incipit* of the Aria is shown below.

We were fortunate enough to be able to examine all the holdings of St Martinsberg in the autumn of 1960 (see *HJB* IX, 364), including this otherwise unknown MS.
Critical edition: none
Literature: H.C.R.L. in *HJB* IX, 364.

Aria Andante

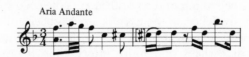

The Jesuit College in Raab (Györ) enjoyed a long and close connection with the Esterházy family, as the previous Chronicle has shown on many occasions. It is not known when the music collection passed to St Martinsberg, but probably after the suppression of the Order by Pope Clement XIV in 1773. This is an early copy of a work which, it would seem, was originally secular in character and possibly from one of the lost Esterházy cantatas or the Italian comedies of 1762.

Concertos

Concerto for Horn and Orchestra in D
(VIId:3; 1762)

Scoring: horn solo, 2 ob., str. [bsn.].

Source: Autograph, GdM, Vienna, VIII.14982. 4°
Italian paper (watermarks: three crescents of
declining size; crown with a very characteristic
cross [counter-mark]). At the head of the first page
of music: [left:] Concerto per il Corno di Caccia
[middle:] In Nomine Domini [right:] Giuseppe
Haydn 7̄6̄2'. At end of MS.: 'Fine' and lower, in
the middle of the page: 'laus Deo'. There are no
other contemporary MSS.

Critical edition: Eulenburg (C. Landon).

Literature: Pohl I, 230. Geiringer 1932, pp. 91f.
(with facsimile of last page of the autograph,
containing the 'NB [right:] im schlaff
geschrieben'.

It is not known for which first horn player (high range) Haydn composed this now
well-known Concerto of 1762, but it was suggested that the recipient might have been
Mozart's and Haydn's friend, Joseph Leutgeb. Haydn cannot, in any case, have kept
the autograph very long, for the work is totally missing in *EK* (which, however,
contains the *incipit* of another, lost Horn Concerto). As with Haydn's most famous
Concerto, that for trumpet, it is something of a miracle that this Horn Concerto has
survived at all, and only in the actual autograph.

This was a period in which very little hand stopping existed, so that most of the
horn notes of this bright, open work are those of the harmonic scale – but not entirely.
As soon as the soloist enters (bar 31) we find the written note *b'* (sounding *c♯'*) at the
end of his first phrase, and at bar 44

which (see arrow) would have to be 'lipped down' from *b flat*. The first hint that
Haydn will exploit the low, so-called pedal notes comes in a striking passage at bars
87ff. (strings *pp*), where the soloist sustains written C below the bass clef for several
bars. The real exploitation of the horn's lowest range comes in the beautiful slow
movement (Adagio). The first thing that strikes us is the enormous length of the
ritornello (27 bars), with the many syncopated patterns typical of Haydn's music in the
early 1760s. Although in A, the horn is retained in D, which is possible but involves
various tricks. The exploitation of the pedal range certainly suggests that even at this
very early, pre-hand-horn stage of the instrument's development, some kind of
stopping was possible by virtuoso artists such as Leutgeb:

This passage is repeated later. In the final Allegro, there is even a modest attempt to
introduce some contrapuntal devices (the lines of violins and bass are in invertible
counterpoint at the octave), which we begin to see taking effect, as it were, at bars 74ff.
The agility which Mozart required of the soloist in his magnificent concertos for
Leutgeb is, of course, legendary; but even in 1762, Haydn expected Leutgeb or his first
horn player in Eisenstadt, Johannes Knoblauch, to negotiate (in this Finale)

On the last page of the autograph, Haydn mixed up the order of the violins and oboes, which is why he explained 'written while asleep'. The composition of this Concerto must have taken place late at night, when all his duties in the Esterházy household had ceased for the day.

CONCERTOS FOR VIOLIN AND ORCHESTRA

(a) in C major (VIIa:1)

Scoring: V. solo, str. [cemb.]
Principal sources: (1) MS. parts, Melk Abbey, v.764. (2) MS. parts from Admont Monastery, now Diözesanarchiv, Graz. (3) MS. parts, Schlägl Abbey (written for violin piccolo in F-notation). (4) MS. parts, 'Ex Rebus Josephi Sternat', Seitenstetten Abbey (with two trumpet parts, dubious). (5) MS. parts, Schwarzenberg Archives, Ceský-Krumlov. (6) MS. parts, Conservatorio di Musica, Genoa. (7) MS. parts, formerly in the Archives of Breitkopf & Härtel, Leipzig. (8) MS. parts, Kremsmünster Abbey.
Critical editions: *JHW* (Reihe III, Band 1; G. Thomas); Eulenburg 1202 (Landon). *Literature*: Pohl I, 262. Geiringer 1932, p. 91. Landon in *HJB* IX, 373f.

This Concerto, as good as unknown when it was first recorded by Michelle Auclair after the Second World War, is now one of Haydn's most popular works. In *EK* we are told that it was 'fatto per il luigi', i.e. for Tomasini, whose brilliant technique and beautiful Italianate tone are suggested, the former in the flanking movements and the latter in the famous Adagio. In the copy of the Breitkopf & Härtel edition of this work in the New York Public Library, the following clipping, presumably from the *Signale* of 1909, is attached:

Haydn's Recently Discovered Violin Concertos

To the recently announced discovery of Haydn's two violin concertos follows an interesting account of the first performance. Carl Tomasini, great-grandson of Luigi Tomasini, the Esterházy first violinist for whom Joseph Haydn in 1769 composed the C major Concerto, is at present a violinist in the court-chapel at Neustrelitz [residence of the grand dukes of Mecklenburg-Strelitz, 107 km. north of Berlin]. He has, however, not only remained faithful to the artistic calling of his progenitors, but he possesses the violin on which Haydn's Concerto was first played, 140 years ago. Now, this precious instrument belongs to the great-grandson of the original owner. It is guarded as a valuable family heirloom and it is the violin for which this resurrected work was written.

The date 1769 was simply attached to the work because of its announcement that year in the Breitkopf Catalogue (the work was for sale in MS. copies). This and the G major Concerto were discovered in one of the old Breitkopf MSS. in the Archives of Breitkopf & Härtel in 1909 and were published that same year by Walther Davisson, both for the first time. As we shall see, it is probable that the G major Concerto was written for someone else, while the A major Concerto seems to have been also composed for Tomasini.

Again we notice the preponderance of dotted figures in the first movement, partly an inheritance from the Baroque but also part and parcel of Haydn's grand C major courtly style. Much of the solo writing is in the Italian tradition, the skips of the tenth, the Vivaldi-like sequences, the chains of triplet figures – all, it would seem, tailor-made for Luigi. The slow movement is, broadly speaking, in three sections: the outer parts are simply a rising scale for the solo violin, with the accompaniment (semiquavers) following the rise with a long crescendo. The middle part, with pizzicato accompaniment in the orchestra, is a lovely solo in the manner of the slow movements of some of the early quartets – a kind of serenade, made to display the soloist's singing tone. It is certainly one of the most winning slow movements of this whole period.

The last movement, in typical three-eight metre, offers a whole variety of technical problems: fingering in tenths (bars 83ff.), spiccato bowing across the strings (bars 192ff.), great dexterity in the left hand (bars 225ff.), and bowing across the strings in chordal style (bars 283ff.).

Contrary to some recent opinions, we can not see how Haydn expected this Concerto to be performed without harpsichord *continuo*: consider bars 71ff. of the finale, where the solo violin is accompanied *only* by the bass line. But it is curious that no authentic figured bass parts for symphonies and concertos survive (though as we shall see, the bass part of Symphony No. 7 is marked 'Basso Continuo'), and possibly the last word as to the question of a harpsichord *continuo* for these works remains to be spoken.

(b) in A major (VIIa:3)

Scoring: V. Solo, [2 ob.?], 2 hns., str. [cemb.]. *Principal sources*: (1) MS. parts, Melk Abbey; ob. listed on the title page, but none present; extant parts for 2 horns, str. (2) MS. parts, Conservatorio Benedetto Marcello, Venice; for strings only.

Critical editions: JHW (Reihe III, Band 1; G. Thomas); Haydn-Mozart Presse (Anton Heiller and Landon), based on Melk only. *Literature*: Landon in *HJB* IX, 373f.

In the *Joseph Haydn Werke*, one is astonished to see the horn parts of Melk simply omitted, probably because the source in Venice does not have them. But these same horn parts were announced in the listing of the work in the Breitkopf Catalogue of 1771 (where, however, the solo instrument is listed as a violoncello, probably a printing error), and there are several other early concertos with wind instruments (Violoncello in C [VIIb:1] and the Göttweig listing of the lost Violin Concerto in D [VIIa:2], both with oboes and horns). There was no reason whatever to omit them from the new critical edition; at least they could have been included in smaller print.

The technique of this Concerto, which is more ambitious and longer than that in C major, is similar, so that we may assume that it, too, was created for Luigi Tomasini. Haydn placed it twice in *EK*, once with the *incipit* (p. 10) and once without (p. 19, 'siehe Vorne'). Of course there is no possible way to date these two Violin Concertos precisely, but we may assume that the C major was composed about 1761 and the A major perhaps a few years later. As in that in C, we note chain passages of dotted rhythms, sequences, echo effects, and the rest of the characteristic paraphernalia of the late Baroque concerto. But although it is a more ambitious work, it lacks (at least in the first two movements) something of the spontaneity and gaiety of the C major work. The slow movement of the A major Concerto (an Adagio [moderato] in D) not only lacks the charm of the famous 'serenade' in the C major work but suffers from a certain total lack of inspiration. The most engaging of the three movements is the Finale, which develops an irresistible drive and is on an impressive scale (238 bars).

The first performance of the Concerto in modern times took place in the Mozart-Saal of the Konzerthaus in Vienna, on 6 October 1950 (soloist: Edith Bertschinger).

(c) in G major (VIIa:4)

Scoring: V. Solo, str. [cemb.]. *Principal sources*: (1) MS. parts signed 'NZ 1777', GdM, Vienna. (2) MS. parts formerly in the Archives of Breitkopf & Härtel, Leipzig.

Critical editions: JHW (Reihe III, Band 1; G. Thomas); Verlag Doblinger, Diletto Musicale 79 (Landon); Eulenburg (C. Landon).

This Concerto was announced, together with that in C (*supra*), in the Breitkopf Catalogue of 1769. The first thing about this G major work that strikes the ear is the totally different technique with which the solo part was composed: it hardly goes beyond the first three positions. The second point is the bad situation of sources and references: not in *EK*, not in *HV*, no evidence of authenticity whatever. There are just enough elements of Haydn's early style in all three movements to allow it to remain in the list of genuine early works, but stylistically it is the most old-fashioned of all three works under discussion. Perhaps the last movement, with its nervous drive, is stylistically the most persuasive, while the slow movement, with its attractive arching lines, is the most beautiful of the three movements. It is very unlikely that this was composed for Luigi Tomasini; perhaps Haydn wrote it for the leader of the Morzin orchestra or for one of the Fürnberg groups (the orchestra of the Lieutenant-Colonel?). We may entertain the (small) hope that more sources for these violin concertos may be uncovered, particularly in Bohemia.

Concerto for Violoncello and Orchestra in C (VIIb:1)

Scoring: 'Cello Solo, 2 ob., 2 hns., str. [bsn.].
Source: MS. parts from the collection of the Counts Kolovrat-Krakovsky, Raděnín Castle, now National Museum, Prague; discovered in 1961 by O. Pulkert. 4° Italian paper, with watermarks ('AS' under fleur-de-lys, three crescents and 'A') that suggest an early (1761–5?) date of origin. The original title disappeared long ago ('Ohne Tittel'). The same hand copied this solo 'cello part and that to another in C under the name of Weigl in the same collection: this suggests a close connection with Haydn's principal 'cellist for whom our work was written.
Critical edition: Export Artia, Prague (O. Pulkert), 1962.
Literature: Foreword to the edition. In the *Revisionsbericht* there are valuable notes on the source (with watermark tracings).

Here is the major discovery of our age, and surely one of the finest works of this period. Unlike the A major Violin Concerto, which although available in print since 1952 has never won the interest of the public or the soloists, the C major 'Cello Concerto instantly became one of the most popular of all Haydn's works,[1] both with the public and with the 'cellists, starved as they are for repertoire. Haydn entered the work in *EK* on p. 19, and Larsen (*HUB*, 233) considers that all the works originally entered on p. 19 'must have been available by about 1765' – which includes the Violin Concerto in C and (lost) D, a number of lost works, and the present C major Concerto for 'Cello (the harpsichord concertos are discussed elsewhere).

The first movement is in Haydn's grand C major style, with all its Lombard rhythms (end of the tutti), dotted patterns, syncopations and courtly atmosphere. The work was probably written for Joseph Weigl, the 'cellist in the Esterházy *Capelle* and a warm personal friend of Haydn's. The technique of the great solo 'cello sections in Symphonies Nos. 6–8, 13/II, 31, 36/II and 72 are all somewhat similar and show Weigl to have possessed a matchless technique and, judging from a slow movement in a symphony especially written for him in 1763 (No. 13/II), a beautiful tone in adagios. The slow movement of the C major Concerto (oboes and horns silent) is indeed very like the mood and compositional technique used in the symphonic movement of 1763. The last movement is a *tour-de-force* of epic proportions, with passages lying very high indeed and difficult even for the greatest soloists of today. Formally, this last movement is brilliantly laid out, the culmination of all the concerto finales of this period and a worthy successor of the great Vivaldian ritornello form. It is sobering to think that this great and noble work was almost lost to us for ever, had not this single set of parts happened to survive the Second World War and its aftermath.

---

1 The *Bielefelder Katalog* lists (in its issue of Autumn 1977) nine recordings. The first performance in our age: 19 May 1962 with Miloš Sádlo and the Czechoslovak Radio Symphony Orch., cond. by Charles Mackerras.

LOST CONCERTOS AND SOME DOUBTFUL WORKS

From *EK* (and in one case from *HV*) we have a long list of lost concertos of this period:

Violin in D (VIIa:2; a copy was in Göttweig Abbey and the listing in the Göttweig Catalogue includes oboes and horns);
Violoncello in C (VIIb:3);
Violone (double bass) in D (VIIc:1);
Flute in D (VIIf:1);
Horn in D (VIId:1);
 Two horns in E flat (VIId:2; probably known to Haydn from its announcement in the Traeg Catalogue of 1799 and thus included in *HV*; not in *EK*; see *Haydn: the Years of 'The Creation' 1796–1800*, p. 226).

The spurious Violin Concertos are now identified:

VIIa:D1 – Carl Stamitz; VIIa:G1 – Michael Haydn; VIIa:A1 – Giornovichi (Jiornovik); VIIa:B1 – Michael Haydn (autograph: Großwardein, 20 Dec. 1760, EH Budapest); VIIa:B2 – Christian Cannabich.

The spurious 'Cello Concertos are as follows:

VIIb:4 – an exceedingly weak work for solo vc. and str., listed in the Breitkopf Catalogue of 1772 and only known in two MS. copies in the Gymnasialbibliothek, Zittau, a notorious place for spurious Haydn concertos. There is no evidence at all that Haydn had anything to do with this conventional and old-fashioned work.

VIIb:5 is a concoction by David Popper in the manner of the Kreisler and Casadesus falsifications.

VIIb:G1 is a G minor Violoncello Concerto, of which no copy exists, attributed to Haydn in the Breitkopf Catalogue of 1773 (vc. solo, str.).

The spurious and doubtful concertos for wind instruments are:

FLUTE

VIIf:D1 – by Leopold Hofmann (many sources)

OBOE

VIIf:C1 – only known to us in one MS. from Zittau where Haydn's name was added later to the (originally anonymous) listing on the title page. A pretty work in the manner of the Bohemians (e.g. Leopold Kŏzeluch's Bassoon Concerto in C, also with trumpets and drums).

HORN

VIId:4 is a Concerto 'per Corno Secondo', i.e. for a second horn player, announced in the Breitkopf Catalogue of 1781 (scoring: solo horn, str.) and existing only in one MS. in the Zittau Collection. The connection between the announcement in the Breitkopf catalogues and the presence of Zittau MSS. is obvious. There is the faint possibility that this old-fashioned, rather stiffly Baroque work, with a slow movement in B minor, is for a second horn player in the Morzin, Fürnberg or Esterházy orchestra (Steinmüller) and is actually by Haydn; but the style is not sharply individual and the source situation very poor. The last movement has a certain flair, but the leading-note rhythm could perfectly well be from the pen of Michael Haydn or a *Kleinmeister*. We can see no justification at present for including this weak work in the list of genuine Haydn compositions. A new edition, edited by H. H. Steves, is available at Messrs. Boosey and Hawkes, London.

BASSOON

The lost Concerto (*Haydn: the Years of ' The Creation' 1796–1800*, p. 226) cannot be dated even approximately.

CONCERTOS FOR HARPSICHORD AND ORCHESTRA

(a) in F (XVIII:3)

Scoring: (1) presumably original version: cemb. solo, str. (2) the same with two hns. 'ad libitum', of which there is no evidence whether original, added later by Haydn, or a spurious addition; the hns. are, however, stylish and possibly genuine.

Principal sources: (1) MS. parts, Mecklenburgische Landesbibliothek, Schwerin: 'Concerto in F per il Clavi Cembalo con 2 Violini, Viola, e Basso del Sig^{re} Giuseppe Haidn'. (2) MS. parts, Preußische Staatsbibliothek, mus. ms. 10.065: 'Concerto per il Cembalo concertato accompagnato da Due Violini, Violetta e Basso, Due Corni ad libitum composto da Giuseppe Haydn'. (3) Printed parts by Le Duc, Paris (announced 28 July 1787 in the *Journal de la Librairie*): 'Troisiéme [*sic*] / Concerto, / pour le clavecin ou piano-forte / avec accompagnement / de deux violins alto et basse / composé / par J. Haydn / Prix 6 #. / Pour Paris et la Province, port franc par la poste. / a Paris / chez Le Duc successeur et propriétaire du fond de M^r. de la Chevardiere Rue du roulle / à la croix d'or N°. 6'. Copy: Hoboken Collection, ONB, Vienna.

Critical edition: Schott 4958 (Ewald Lassen), with the horns, based on (1), (2) and (3), 1958.

Literature: Larsen, *HÜB*, 233, 294ff.

In *EK* this Concerto is entered in Haydn's hand as the second *incipit* of p. 20; as with most of the other concertos for various instruments on pages 19 and 20, this *incipit* is not that of the opening tutti but of the first entry of the solo part (which, incidentally, again establishes – as with that of the D major Organ Concerto XVIII:2 on p. 19 – that the ornament of bar 2, and whenever it recurs, is a crossed turn and not the trill found in the sources). Larsen (*HÜB*, 233f.) thinks the keyboard works on pp. 20ff. were written slightly later than the various concertos on p. 19; but although our F major Concerto is first listed in the Breitkopf Catalogue of 1771 (strings only), it may be presumed that it was composed several years earlier. Perhaps, indeed, it is in some way connected with the sudden revival, in 1764, of Prince Nicolaus's interest in Haydn's harpsichord playing, referred to *supra* (pp. 395 and 401). It is, however, curious that the work seems to have had very limited distribution in the Austrian monarchy: no monastery collection (at least now) includes it, and it is rather surprising that it found its way at a very late date to a French publisher (who tried, it would seem, to capitalize on the success of two previously issued Haydn piano concertos, the famous XVIII:11 and the less famous XVIII:4, in D and G respectively).

The F major Concerto suffers from the conventionality that places it at a lower spiritual level than most of the other works composed about 1764 or 1765 (symphonies, cantatas, the Capriccio for harpsichord 'Acht Sauschneider', etc.). In this respect, Haydn's keyboard concertos until the great D major work (XVIII:11) suffer from a curious lack of profile. There is, for example, nothing really memorable about this F major work: neither the subjects, nor the harpsichord writing (with those 'chain' sequences that we remember to have been a feature of the early organ concertos, too), nor even the rather pretty slow movement can approach the best instrumental music that Haydn was simultaneously composing. It may be an accident that the work hardly achieved any circulation in Austria, but one can not think the cultivated circles, sacred and secular, in which Haydn's sonatas and symphonies were being heard with increasing pleasure, could find anything more than efficiently routine about the present Concerto. And so perhaps the total lack of sources in Austria is not entirely fortuitous. If Haydn's concertos had been, at this period, on the level of his symphonies, some way would have been found to distribute them to court, monastery and home. (In fairness to Haydn, one must of course imagine that Weigl jealously retained the 'Cello Concerto in C [VIIb:1], which disappeared entirely for nearly two hundred years; that work's non-distribution had entirely non-musical reasons. The same probably applied to other concertos, especially those that have disappeared for ever.)

(b) in G (XVIII:9)

Scoring: cemb. solo, str.
Source: MS. parts, Preußische Staatsbibliothek, Berlin, mus. ms. 10.066: 'Concerto per il Cembalo concertato accompagnato da Due Violini, e Basso composto da Giuseppe Haydn' by the same copyist as the previous work.

Critical edition: Schott 5313 (Mizi Brusotti)
Literature: Larsen, *HÜB*, 295. G. Feder, 'Probleme einer Neuordnung der Klaviersonaten Haydns', in *Festschrift Friedrich Blume*, Kassel 1963, p. 102, n. 31.

Our work was registered in the Catalogue of Schloß Zeil of 1767, and in that same year it was offered by Breitkopf in Leipzig (scoring: 'II Conc. di Hayden, a Cemb. conc. 2 Viol. V. B.' [= XVIII:2], No. II marked '2 Viola'). Larsen considers the work genuine, Feder does not. We might sum up the evidence as follows: no authentic sources, no listing in *EK*, and only one, rather remote, MS. has survived; but 1767 is early for the falsification of Haydn keyboard concertos. Stylistically, the second movement sounds slightly old-fashioned and impersonal, but then so does the Adagio of the authentic Organ Concerto (XVIII:2) which was announced in the same Breitkopf listing. The range of the right hand reaches f''', which is high for Haydn *c.* 1765 (Capriccio 'Acht Sauschneider' reaches only d''', but Trio No. 10 (XV:35) reaches e''' and Trio No. 17 (XV:2) f'''; Trio 10 is certainly an early work, of the 1760s at the latest, while Trio 17 dates from *c.* 1771).

The work has a certain genuine charm, but again the music is not so strongly etched that one would wish to assert the work's authenticity on stylistic grounds alone. With the very bad situation of sources, the work rather falls into the category of the G major Violin Concerto (VIIa:4): both may be early works by Haydn. At present, more cannot be said.

(c) Doubtful and spurious works

Of the doubtful and spurious harpsichord concertos (XVIII:ES 1, F1, F3, G1 and G2), the most interesting candidate was always G1, which has survived in a set of MS. parts in the Archives at Kroměříž (Kremsier), one of the most important centres for early Haydn keyboard music in the world.[1] The present writer is collaborating with Dr A. Peter Brown on various matters of Haydniana, and Dr Brown kindly arranged to have this G major Concerto scored. The source is written on Italian paper, partly oblong and partly 4° (watermarks: 'HF/REAL', three stars in an ornament), and apparently by a Viennese copyist: the title reads '♯ In G / Concerto / per il clavicembalo / Due Violini / Due oboi / Due corni / Due Traversi in Andante / è / Basso / Del Sig^re Giuseppe Haÿdn [bottom right-hand corner:] Spect: ad me / J: H:'. The 'J: H:' was the organist Joseph Haroldt from Vienna, who signed his name in full on several MSS. at Kroměříž. The MS. contains many crossed turns, used just as Haydn would have; but otherwise, we are clearly dealing with a well made concerto by an unidentified Austrian composer of the 1760s or 1770s. It shows, among other valuable lessons, that even Haydn's 'fingerprint' (the crossed turn) was used in precisely Haydn's manner by other Austrian composers of the period. Among the many details that make Haydn's authorship quite impossible, we might note the

---

1 See Landon, *Supplement*, 24, for a short description.

tempo of the slow movement 'Andante ma con gusto, e sempre piano'. As such, the piece is in no way inferior to the previous G major Concerto (XVIII:9), which has slightly greater pretensions to Haydn's name. Dr A. Peter Brown has identified the Concerto, XVIII:G2, as being by Joseph Steffan (Stephan; Setkova No. 135), with MS. parts in the Staatsbibliothek, Berlin.

Chamber Music

MIXED DIVERTIMENTI (STRINGS AND WIND INSTRUMENTS)

Divertimento (Cassatio) in C (II:17)

Scoring: 2 clar., 2 hns., 2 v., 2 violas, 'Basso' [Vc., Bsn., Cb.]

Principal sources: (1) MS. parts by Viennese Copyist No. 2 (Fürnberg/Morzin No. 4) from the Library of the Archbishops, Kremsier (Kroměříž) IV A.164. Title (another hand): 'Cassatio in C. / à / Violino Primo / Violino Secondo. / Viola Prima. / Viola Seconda. / Clarinetti Due / Corni Due / et / Basso. / Del Sig̅r̅ Jiuseppe Heyden.' 4° Austro-Bohemian(?) paper: watermarks 'REINFERES' or 'ALLEMODE PAPIR' with coat-of-arms; chain lines (vertical, *c.* 2.5 cm. apart), man with what appears to be club or stick with fleur-de-lys on end. (2) MS. parts, Országos Széchényi Könyvtár, Budapest, Ms. mus. IV.97. No title page extant. Pts. marked 'N: del Sig̅r̅ Hayden'. Beginning and end of 'Basso', which probably included the title page as well, missing. 4° Italian paper (watermarks: 'GF' [Galvani Fratelli, Pordenone] under canopy; half-moon attached to coat-of-arms with three stars and letter 'w'). (3) MS. parts, Schlägl Abbey. Oblong paper from a German paper mill (letters 'SB', large fleur-de-lys as watermark: this same combination found in the German paper used in the otherwise authentic MS. parts of Symphony No. 92 in the Oettingen-Wallerstein Collection, Harburg Castle; see Landon, *SYM*, 744, source 2). (4) MS. parts, Abbey of St Paul in the Lavanttal (Styria): 4° local paper, with parts for two clarinets (no title page of the period has survived, but the MS. may be dated *c.* 1770–80 and is probably a local copy, though other Haydn copies at St Paul show a relationship to St Florian via the copyist J. Michael Planck). (5) MS. parts, Archives of the Princes of Thurn und Taxis, Regensburg, cat. J. Haydn 88: 'Sinfonia o cassatione due Violini, due Viole, due oboe, due corni, Viola e basso del Sig. Giuseppe Haydn'. The transfer from the original clarinets to oboes was easy because the clarinets are written in C (i.e. C-clarinets). (6) MS. parts, Seitenstetten Monastery, dated 1770. (7) MS. parts from the collection of the Counts Pachta, now National Museum, Prague. (8) MS. score, written on nineteenth-century paper from a mill in Alsace, Library of Congress, Washington, M.1045 A2 H3 (watermark: 'J: PASQUAL / EN ALSACE'), with stamp: 'BIBL. MUSICALE DE L. PICQUOT BAR-LE-DUC'.
Critical edition: Verlag Doblinger, Diletto Musicale (Steppan).
Literature: Larsen, *HÜB*, 223, 279. Landon, *SYM*, 232f., 263f., 353. Geoffrey Chew in *Haydn-Studien* III/2 (1974), pp. 106ff. *Haydn at Eszterháza 1766–1790*, pp. 280f.

This is perhaps the most interesting of the divertimento-type works which fall in the period 1761–5. It contains several problems, however, which require elucidation. The first is the clarinets, which are in C and are specified in one probably authentic, and many other good sources. Now the dated autograph of the Divertimento, II:14 (Leningrad), composed in 1761, specifies clarinets. This suggests, at any rate, that our Divertimento (II:17) could have been composed in 1761, also, and this supposition is borne out by yet another detail: in the fourth movement we find a long dramatic 'Recitativo' with the first violin taking the part of the dramatic soprano – exactly the same procedure as in the second movement of Symphony No. 7, the autograph of which is dated 1761. The length and complexity of II:17 suggest that it was probably composed for some special occasion, and we suggest that it is Haydn's first specimen of the cassatio or divertimento form after he was engaged by Prince Paul Anton. But this brings us back to the problem of the clarinets. Who, in the Esterházy band of 1761, played the instruments? And which instruments? In all the bills concerning the purchase of, and repairs to, instruments, clarinets are never mentioned – not once.

However, apart from the period of the Griesbacher brothers (who were with the *Capelle* from December 1775 to 1 March 1778) Haydn did write for clarinets – *EK* lists two lost Divertimenti (II:4 and 5) which are described by Haydn as being 'a cinque stromenti cioè 2 Clarinetti 2 Corni . . .' and which, according to the handwriting of the entry, were composed *after* 1765 (see *Haydn at Eszterháza 1765–1790*, p. 355n.). Or were these works of 1761 composed for the visiting Polish Count Oginsky, who played clarinet at Prince Esterházy's concert of 6 October 1761 (*supra*, p. 362)? In any case, the similarities of the *opera seria* recitative parodies in Symphony No. 7 and in II:17 suggest that Luigi Tomasini was the likely recipient of both works.

There are many other unusual features of this work, the first of which is the opening 'Marcia' – itself a very usual beginning for works in the Salzburgian tradition but almost unique in the whole of Haydn's early divertimenti (Notturno [II:25] for the King of Naples, 1790[?] contains another march opening). Perhaps the dotted rhythms that fill Haydn's courtly C major music of this period have their origins in the 'Marcia' (perhaps even this very one), which is of course full of series of dotted patterns. The second movement is a large (164 bars) Allegro which is laid out quite differently from a symphonic Allegro: quick metre (2/4) and divertimento-like confrontation of blocks of instruments, i.e. clarinets *versus* violins *versus* violas (two, not one, throughout), coupled to a certain lightness of touch and instrumentation. The third movement is a minuet and trio, and it is followed by the unexpected 'Recitativo' which, apart from the delightfully bizarre idea in the first place, is interesting because of the written-out indications for appoggiature (drops of a third changes to drops of a second), such as also occur in the similar movement in Symphony No. 7. The fifth movement is a light-footed Andante in G, showing the same fondness for juxtaposing the various choirs (here violins *versus* violas, because the winds are, characteristically for this period, dropped). Sixth comes another minuet with a trio including a solo section for the horns. Instead of what we would expect, namely a final movement, Haydn gives us three more: the seventh – what looks like a Finale – is an Allegro molto in 2/4; that which follows is another remarkable innovation, the mysterious and slightly sinister 'night watchman' theme first encountered in the Morzin Cassatio (II:21) and now presented in a 'purer' (less altered) state, *pianissimo*. The origin of this Christmas / Advent / night watchman / Hungarian / Moravian / Czech melody is admirably discussed by Geoffrey Chew in the first important article ever to deal seriously, systematically and scientifically with Haydn's use of folk-songs. The exotic nature of this melody is immediately apparent: it arrives like a cloaked gypsy in the dead of night. A further use of it is quoted in connection with Symphony No. 60 (Chew and No. 60 – see literature). After this 'exotic excursion' (Bence Szabolcsi), as the eighth movement, the real Finale (ninth movement), in the then fashionable Presto 3/8, makes a swift and fanfare-like conclusion (only 46 bars) to this interesting and unusual work.

Cassatio in D for 4 Horns and Strings
(Hoboken *deest*)

Scoring: 4 hns., v., va., 'Basso' [with vc.].
Source: MS. parts from the archives of the Counts Clam Gallas, now National Museum, Prague (cat. Clam Gallas, 212) on 4° Italian paper (letters 'OA' under crown; three crescents of decreasing size). Probably a Viennese source by a professional copyist: ('1 No 6 C: / Conte / Clam Gallas' added later) 'Cassatio In D. / á / Violino / Viola [later: "2 oboe"] / 4 corni di Caccia / e / Basso / Del Sig: Giuseppe Haydn.' .Discovered by the present writer at Prague in 1959.
Critical edition: Verlag Doblinger, Diletto Musicale 66 (Landon); also miniature score Stp. 285.

The rich, and for Haydn extremely important, collection made by Count Christian Clam Gallas used to be in Friedland (Frýdlant) Castle. It contained not only this *unicatum* but several others (wind-band divertimenti, discussed *supra*, pp. 269f.). Haydn had four horns in his band in 1763, 1765 and for a time in 1767, but we believe that this Cassatio was first composed in 1763, as soon as there were four players. The disposition of the parts, and the fact that there is only one violin part, suggest that we have before us a piece of chamber music and that the string parts were not reinforced (though in performances nowadays, especially in the concert hall, they will be). The way in which the horns are scored in the opening Allegro moderato (bars 1–8 for I and II, bars 8–12 for III and IV) would seem to indicate that the pairs of horn players sat separately from each other and that this division could thus be heard clearly: we believe that this is also the case with Symphonies Nos. 31 and 72. The second movement is a rhythmically taut minuet, where Haydn's combination of quavers with slower note values produces one of those dancing motions that grace so many of his minuets. In the Trio, the division between horns I–II and III–IV is once again stressed, leading to a run up the D major scale (horn I, bar 47), echoed two bars later by horn III. The slow movement is written round the four horns, which are used almost continually together (only exception: I and II in bar one). We note pedal effects in horn II (bars 9ff.), anticipating Symphonies Nos. 31 and 72, and which almost guarantee the authenticity of this Cassatio: in laying out these four horn parts, horn II (not horn IV) is the lowest of the four, showing that Haydn was, as it were, catering to the player's special facility in the pedal range: *exactly* the same effect is to be noted in similar four-horn, closely worked, passages in the Finales of the Symphonies – Var. 4 of the Finale in No. 31 (Philharmonia, vol. III, p. 86); Var. VI of the Finale in No. 72 (Philharmonia, vol. VII, p. 326). Here is an almost perfect application of the Berensonian 'fingerprint' to the technical aspects of a musical score. As with all the slow movements in works devoted to wind instruments – especially to be noted in the *Feld Parthien* for wind quartet and sextet – Haydn keeps this Adagio short so as not to tire his horn players (total: twenty bars). In the fourth movement, Menuet & Trio, we encounter, at the beginning of the minuet's second section, the posthorn call on which Horst Walter has recently written so brilliantly;[1] here it is given to horns III–IV and in this manner:

[Cor. in D]

Now previously, we were led, as a result of research by Dr Ernst Paul and incorporated in Hoboken, vol. I, p. 35, to believe that this horn signal was a southern-Hungarian / Roumanian / Croatian hunting signal used as late as 1800 for *par force* ceremonious hunts of the Austrian-Hungarian aristocracy. Dr Walter has shown, however, that this signal was much more widely used as a posthorn call, throughout Germany and Austria. We will encounter it in a much more exposed fashion in the famous Symphony No. 31 'mit dem Hornsignal'. Our Cassatio closes with a short Finale where the violin is, for a change, given the centre of the stage: again Luigi Tomasini? It was a very original idea to double, in bars 1f., horn I's run up the scale of D with the 'Basso', another very exotic idea that Haydn takes care never to repeat, so that it happens almost before we are aware of it (the section is repeated, so we do, in

1 *Haydn-Studien* IV/1 (1976), pp. 21ff.

fact, hear the strange sound twice). Haydn not only keeps this Finale simple for the horns but he also keeps it very short: twenty-four bars (each section of twelve bars repeated) and a miniature coda of four bars. We believe that this attractive Hunting Cassatio was Haydn's first virtuoso score in 1763 for the four horn players (in Symphony No. 13 of 1763 they are used more as an orchestral 'choir'). And this is another work – like so many of this period – that has survived, almost by accident, in one single copy.

Divertimento Fragment in E flat (II:24)

Scoring: 1 fl., 2 cors angl., 1 bsn., 2 hns., v. solo, vc. solo, 'Violone Solo' str. (no violas).
Source: Autograph, Lehman Collection (on loan: Pierpont Morgan Library, New York), *ex coll.* Aloys Fuchs⟶Ferdinand Heckel⟶Julius

Lichtenberger. Oblong paper of north Italian origin (watermarks: chain lines, letters 'A' over what appears to be ' PH ' and ♀).
Critical edition: none.

The autograph consists of five variations, at the end of which we read 'Menuet da Capo'; this minuet, the theme (it would seem) of which served as the basis of these variations, is now missing. Contrary to Hoboken (vol. II, pp. 314), who suggests a dating of *c.* 1773–4 (literally: 'before 1775'), the autograph, the watermarks and the style all suggest a period at least ten years earlier, and probably *c.* 1761–3. The form is somewhat similar to the last movements of Symphonies Nos. 72 (1763?) and 31(?). The formal scheme is as follows:

> Var. I: cor angl. I, II, v. I, II, 'Basso'.
> Var. II: fl., str.
> Var. III: bsn., vc. solo, str. with 'Violone'.
> Var. IV: v. solo, str.
> Var. V: 'Corno 1mo Solo', hn. II 'Violone Solo', str.

The keys are E flat, B flat (Var. II), E flat (III), A flat (IV), E flat (V), and the whole way in which the music is written would suggest one of Haydn's enterprising operations to 'illustrate' all his virtuoso players; the lack of four horns suggest a dating of 1761–3 or 1764. (The fourth horn player of 1763 was in service from August to December.) For some curious reason, the work is not in *EK*, not in *HV* and remained unknown to the scholarly world until the late Frank Walker discovered the autograph in Heidelberg (Julius Lichtenberger). We show here the first and fifth variations as characteristic of this attractive fragment.

Variatio 5ta

* Autograph ♪

129

* Autograph ♪

Menuet da Capo

Divertimento (Cassatio) in D (II:8)

Scoring: 2 fl., 2 hns., 2 v., 'Basso' [bsn., vc.]
Principal sources: (1) MS. parts from the library of the Counts Pachta, now National Museum, Prague: 'Divertimento in forma d'una Cassatione'. (2) MS. parts as 'Sinfonia', Melk Abbey. (3) MS. parts, Archives of the Princes of Thurn und Taxis, Regensburg, cat. J. Haydn 92 ('Divertimento'). (4) MS. parts, Städtische Musikbibliothek, Dresden. *Critical edition*: Bärenreiter Verlag, Pro Musica Series, ed. Kurt Janetzky (1953), based on source 4. *Literature*: Pohl I, 193. Larsen, *HÜB*, 223.

In *EK*, Haydn describes this work as 'Divertimento a Sei con 2 flauti', and although there are actually seven parts, the autograph confirmation of the '2 flauti' is important. Haydn uses two flutes in the slow movement of Symphony No. 7 (1761) and in vocal works of the period: the Aria 'Tu mi piaci' from *La Marchesa Nespola* and 'Tergi i vezzosi rai' from *Acide*, both composed in 1762. There is every reason to place this lively and attractive 'Divertimento in forma d'una Cassatione' (as the old and reliable source from Count Pachta calls it) at the beginning of the Eisenstadt period. The Kapfer brothers, who were proficient (as we have seen) on several instruments, probably played not only oboe and cor anglais but also the flute. Together with Sigl, who was a flautist *a priori* (but also played the oboe), Haydn had three potential flutes. Two flutes are required also in 'Che visino delicato' from *La canterina* (1766), when Sigl was in limbo (he was re-engaged on 2 February 1767), and in the first (original) version of 'Caro Volpino' from *Lo speziale* (1768), but since our Divertimento was. announced in the Breitkopf Catalogue of 1767 (as part of six divertimenti: II:20, 16; I:22; II:8, 11 and 2), 1766 is about the latest date possible for its composition since Haydn's works never reached the Breitkopf Catalogue the same year in which they were composed but at least one, and usually two and more years thereafter. As to its being much earlier than May 1761, we would remind our readers that the Morzin orchestra seems to have contained no flutes at all: at least there are no known Morzin symphonies or divertimenti that include flute parts.

Haydn had by now developed a gracious and winning divertimento style, in which the famous early quartet-divertimenti and many other works had been composed prior to this Cassatio or Divertimento in D 'con due flauti'. It is interesting to observe the great difference between Haydn's symphonic works of the same period and such a piece as this one under discussion. We notice at once that the first Allegro is in a 'light' metre, here 2/4: now Haydn wrote symphonies for Morzin that begin with 2/4 allegro movements, such as No. 20; but it is not just the metre that makes our Divertimento's Allegro light, but the texture and the way the music progresses. If we may continue to show the differences between Symphony No. 20's Allegro molto and our Allegro, the actual size turns out to be a major factor: 177 bars for the Symphony and 101 for the Divertimento. The Symphony continues massively, after its proud opening and following the contrasting material in G, we have, at the exposition's end (opposite), the typical nervous orchestral language of Haydn *anno* 1760. This may be placed in vivid contrast if we study the opening (overleaf) of the Divertimento (II:8), where the opening section's continuation at bars 13ff. is firmly in the divertimento, and not the symphonic, tradition. Note the delicately defined scoring of bars 26ff. (the 'second subject', as it were). As opposed to the symphonic style, this divertimento tradition makes a virtue of short phrases, short movements and short 'thinking' altogether. Although Haydn's early symphonies very often incorporate divertimento style, such as the opening of Symphony No. 5 with its elaborate horn writing, the differences are by 1761 firmly established and will grow further apart as the 1760s progress.

[Haydn: Symphony No. 20 – opening]

[Haydn: Divertimento in D (II:8) – opening]

The Menuet has that enticing crotchet rhythm that informs so many of Haydn's minuets of the 1760s, the novelty and freshness of which impressed the musical world of that age. In the Trio, the solo flute has a curious progression that helps us to date the work in the early 1760s:

– not exactly what might be called a characteristically 'flautish' sound. But we find the same kind of awkward skips in the solo flute writing from the Trio of Symphony No. 13 (autograph 1763):

It is a device to which Haydn hardly has recourse after this period, one of those famous experiments in which he could 'observe that which enhanced an effect, and that which weakened it . . .' (into which latter category this pattern of large skips in the flute must be said to belong).[1]

Third movement: a pretty Adagio which sounds like the slow movement of a concerto for two flutes (preview of the celebrated G major Concerto by Domenico Cimarosa of 1793). This is the central section of the work and a clever amalgamation of the divertimento and concerto styles, something that would attract Haydn off and on for many years (e.g. the series of works, in concerto and divertimento form, for the King of Naples, 1786–90); we quote the Adagio's beginning:

1 Quotation: *Haydn at Eszterháza 1766–1790*, p. 117.

Yet another highly original minuet (fourth movement) is dominated by a ♩. ♪ ♩ which slips into the music on the off-beat at bars one and two and becomes part of the melody at bar three on the main beat – a detail that shows its composer's immaculate craftsmanship by this period (see p. 536).

The Trio (see p. 537) is a solo for the horns and strings, of which we note the beginning of the second section, with its felicitous horn writing also for Corno 2do and the lead-back to the main theme.

The Finale, in 3/8 time, is another example of Haydn's ability to write concerto music in divertimento form: sophisticated, light, gay and of astonishing technical assurance, ending with a clear fingerprint:

– a real surprise, even to our jaded ears (and with Symphony No. 94 in our minds).

[Haydn: Divertimento in D (II: 8) – fourth movement]

Menuet da capo

537

WIND-BAND *Feldparthien*

One work, the Divertimento (II:14) for two clarinets and two horns, has survived in dated autograph (1761). The problem of the clarinets and the Esterházy *Capelle* has been mentioned earlier.

Divertimento in C (II:14)

Scoring: 2 clar. in C, 2 hns. in C.
Source: Autograph, Saltikow-Schtschedrin Library, Leningrad, signed on the first page of music 'Giuseppe Haydn 761'.

Critical edition: Verlag Doblinger, Diletto Musicale 32 (Landon); also miniature score Stp. 180.

Apart from this pretty, miniature work (the entire printed score requires three pages for its five movements – Allegro, Menuetto, Adagio, Menuetto, Finale-Presto), there are several others of the same kind listed in the *Entwurf-Katalog* and lost: II:4 and II:5 are listed in *EK* on pp. 5 and 2 as being scored for two clarinets, two horns and one (two?) bassoon(s) – Haydn lists one bassoon but he often did that even when two are required, as in the letter to Boyer of 15 July 1783.[1] Assuming that the two *incipits* quote the clarinet, there would seem to be three possibilities for the proper key (both *incipits* as they now stand are in F major): for clarinets in C, the two pieces are in F; for clarinets in B flat, the pieces are in E flat; and for clarinets in A, the pieces are in D. Considering that the other, extant version of II:5 – for baryton, two horns, a viola and 'Basso' (X:10) – is in D, we may, lacking other evidence, consider that the two *incipits* were for A-clarinets and therefore in D major. As mentioned earlier, both these entries are in Haydn's hand and therefore post-date the original entries of *EK* made *c.* 1765. The other entries in *EK* that might have been wind-band works are: II:10 'Der Schulmeister genannt', 'a Sei', which was entered by Joseph Elssler; II:12 'Divertimento, Feld Parthie, Corno Inglese' (Elssler's *incipit*) is surely noted in cor anglais transposition and is therefore not in B flat but E flat; II:13 (D major) is an Elssler entry and is 'a Sei'; II:20 *bis* is a 'Feld Parthie ex A' listed by Haydn but without *incipit* and in any case lost.

BARYTON DIVERTIMENTI
(for Baryton, Viola and Basso)[2]

Trios (XI:1–12)

These dozen Trios are considered to be Haydn's first efforts in this new form and all probably composed by the end of 1765. The difficulty is that many have survived only in arrangements, the authenticity of which is questionable – as trios for two violins and 'Basso'; as trios for violin, viola and 'Basso'; as trios for flute, violin and 'cello; and

---

1 *Haydn at Eszterháza 1766–1790*, p. 477. *EK*'s entry for II:5 originally read 'a Sei Stromenti'.

2 The baryton as an instrument was always rare and the literature, apart from that written for Prince Nicolaus, scanty. Efrim Fruchtmann wrote a dissertation, *The Baryton Trios of* [Luigi] *Tomasini, Burgsteiner* [Joseph Purksteiner] *and* [Anton] *Neumann*, University of North Carolina, Chapel Hill, 1960, which contains much useful information. For additional baryton literature, see also *Haydn at Eszterháza 1766–1790*, p. 353n. The baryton was known by the end of the seventeenth century. In Daniel Speer's *Grund-richter* ... *Unterricht der Musikalischen Kunst* (Ulm, 1687) we read that 'Very few musicians can be found who can play this instrument. During my travels I met only one, in the Episcopeal See in Freysing [Freising], and I saw only one instrument of this kind in Eperjes in Hungary [now ČSSR], in the possession of the town musician, Adam Bessler, who being a famous violin maker constructed it himself.' For a list of literature on the instrument, see n. 64 on p. 137 of H. Unverricht's *Geschichte des Streichtrios*, Tutzing 1969.
  Oliver Strunk, in his article, 'Haydn's Divertimenti for baryton, viola, and bass' (*Musical Quarterly* XVIII [1932], p. 218) succinctly describes the instrument as follows: 'The extraordinary instrument which finds employment in these pieces is a member of the viol family. In size and shape it corresponds roughly to the tenor gamba, its neck being noticeably longer, its body somewhat smaller in scale. Like the *viola bastarda*, or lyra-viol, and its treble counterpart, the *viola d'amore*, the baryton was fitted with sympathetic strings

transposed into a variety of non-original keys. In some cases, the original baryton versions have survived (XI:4, 7, 8, 12), and in others fragments of the autograph (XI:2, 5, 10). This means that the original scoring no longer exists in many cases and that our knowledge of the music rests entirely on these contemporary but probably non-authentic arrangements. As in all these interesting trios, Haydn uses a large variety of forms. The curious nature of the scoring seems to have encouraged him to use the old *sonata da chiesa* form much more frequently than, say, in quartets or symphonies: four of the works are in three movements with an opening Adagio (XI:6 has 'Più tosto Adagio') followed by a minuet and a Presto or Allegro. A fourth (XI:3) opens with an Allegretto (followed by a minuet and a presto). A fifth and sixth open with an Andante or Allegretto theme and variations (XI:2, 8 – XI:6, listed above, is also a theme with variations). The other regular pattern is a Moderato opening (the kind of 8/8 or 8/4 or slow 3/4 which Haydn prefers, at this juncture, to faster tempi). Rather than transpose the arrangements back to the original keys (simple transposition is in most cases not enough, because the tessitura of the top line[s] has been changed as well), we have preferred to quote from the authentic MSS. available to us.

Principal sources: Autographs in fragmentary form only for XI:2 (3rd and possibly [*vide infra*] 4th movts.), XI:5 (2nd movt.), EH, Budapest, Ms. mus. I.50c; I.50d; for XI:10 (1st and incomplete 2nd movts.), ditto, Ms. mus. I.50a. XI:2, 4, 7, 8 and 12 in the original version (bar., va., basso), Archives of the Counts Pachta, National Museum, Prague. For the numerous arrangements, see Hoboken, vol. I, pp. 593–602. The largest coll. in the Preußische Staatsbibliothek, Berlin. Some early printed collections, see Hoboken, vol. I, 599, esp. Hummel's *oeuvre* xi, 'Six Sonates a Flute, Violin & Violoncelle', 1773 (not 1771).
Critical edition: none (as of 1978). Nos. XI:3, 5, 6,

2*bis*, 7 and 9 may be conveniently studied in arr. for two violins and violoncello in a score edited by Adolf Hoffmann (Möseler Verlag, Wolfenbüttel, 'Deutsche Instrumentalmusik' No. 2, 1939).
Literature: Oliver Strunk: 'Haydn's Divertimenti for Baryton, Viola and Bass', *Musical Quarterly* XVIII/2 (April 1932), pp. 216ff. Béla Csuka, 'Haydn és a baryton', *Zenetudományi Tanulmányok* VI (1957), pp. 669ff. Larsen, *HÜB*, 226f., 282. Hubert Unverricht, *Geschichte des Streichtrios*, Tutzing 1969, pp. 127ff.
Facsimile of autograph fragments from EH (including XII:19, XI:2 and XI:5) in Unverricht, Faksimile 13–16.

Unverricht has devoted a useful section of his book to the baryton trios and, as it happens, to the works with which we are concerned. It is not possible to date early trios exactly, and our listing of Nos. 1–12 as belonging to this period 1761–5 is, at best, hypothesis. From Prince Nicolaus's letter to Haydn of 1765 – which we have now been able to date precisely as 3 November (*vide supra*, p. 420) – we learn that up to that date Haydn had composed 'very few' baryton works. One Trio (XI:24) has survived in autograph and is dated 1766 (Stanford University: Memorial Library), and it may be permissible from this evidence to suggest that the previous twenty-three were composed between 1761 and 1766, and perhaps the first dozen or so before the famous letter of 3 November 1765. The exact division is not important in any case.

[footnote 2, *cont.*]

of metal in addition to the usual complement of gut strings. It differed, however, from these instruments in that the peculiar construction of its neck, which was hollow and open at the back, made it possible for the player to reach the sympathetic strings, which passed beneath the fingerboard, with the thumb of his left hand. These strings could accordingly be used to provide a sort of plucked accompaniment to the bowed melody. Since the baryton was cultivated only in seventeenth- and eighteenth-century Germany and Austria, and there but sparingly, it never became standardized. Instruments with six or seven gut strings were the rule, to judge from the recorded specimens; the number of metal strings, usually ten to fifteen, varies considerably, ranging from eight to as many as thirty. Prince Esterházy's baryton . . . had seven gut . . . and ten metal strings . . .'. For problems arising in the differences between the tuning of Esterházy's instrument and that of Haydn's, see *Haydn at Eszterháza 1766–1790*, p. 354 (citing Riki Gerardy).

It is significant that in all the trios under discussion in this volume – as far as we are able to construct the original text, which is at times no longer possible – there is no evidence that Haydn ever used the sympathetic strings for plucking, as he would do later. Perhaps Prince Nicolaus had not yet mastered this particular technique by 1765.

Prince Esterházy's baryton, by Johann Joseph Stadlmann (1750), is now in the National Museum, Budapest. For notes on other extant barytons, see *Haydn at Eszterháza 1766–1790*, p. 120.

Unverricht was the first critically to examine the curious four pages of autograph containing fragments of various baryton trios of this period (*supra*). If we may summarize Dr Unverricht's findings, they are as follows:

The contents of this curious manuscript suggest an odd compositional procedure, to say the least. Page one contains the end of the Finale of 'Dodeci Divertimenti per il Pariton Primo e Secondo col Basso' (XII:19), that is for two barytons and basso. There then ensues 'Menuet' to which Haydn added, presumably at a later period, 'del 2.do Divertimento', which concludes on page two. The next item is marked 'Finale', with the original tempo marking 'Allegro' to which Haydn later added the words 'di molto'. This continues through the middle of page three, when we find a new movement, 'Menuet', to which Haydn later added 'del 5.to Divertimento'. On page four is the Trio, marked 'canone'.

Unverricht writes as follows (pp. 147f.):

This holograph double sheet contains, then, single movements not belonging together. Haydn later noted in the case of the two minuets to which divertimenti they belong. From the order it is clear that these two minuets ... were written down separately from the movements which they preceded. Thus one may come to the conclusion that the finale movement does not necessarily belong to the preceding minuet, and may be – indeed, must be – considered an isolated movement. The fact that Haydn himself only [with the odd exception] composed three-movement baryton trios may strengthen this supposition. It was the copyist who out of ignorance added to the minuet of Trio No. 2 the unnecessary finale as fourth movement, which perhaps was destined for another trio entirely....

[As a result of the affair with Werner and Prince Nicolaus's letter about the 'very few' trios thus far composed] Haydn had to attempt ... to persuade the Prince of his [Haydn's] abilities and value. He quickly conceived some movements for baryton trios which he later put together in cyclic form. ... There is hardly another autograph score by ... Haydn that reveals so much haste ..., carelessness, oversights and mistakes as these movements for Trios X:2 and 5. Therefore it appears possible, even likely, that at least Baryton Trios Nos. 1–5 were completed by October 1765.

There is no doubt something rather odd about these movements, tacked on to the end of baryton pieces for two barytons and bass (thus written in G clef/G clef/bass clef). When he started to write the first minuet, he forgot that the official trio combination was for baryton, viola and basso; and the viola part started in the G-clef. The most curious fact is the identical key of all the pieces on the autograph, not only the end of the 'Dodeci Divertimenti' but both minuets (not counting the trios, which both happen to be in A minor) and the 'Finale': all are in A major. It certainly appears that Haydn at first intended to continue writing some individual 'pezzi' and later organized them into cohesive series of trios. But we beg leave to doubt that 'the copyist' was responsible for adding the Finale to the Minuet of Trio 2: 'the copyist' must have been Joseph Elssler, working directly under Haydn's supervision. The haphazard order of movements in this odd little autograph does, however, reveal an atypical Haydnesque method of composing and serves to underline the *Gelegenheitsmusik* character of these little trios.

Lacking proper sources – the Pachta MSS. listed above are fortunate exceptions – it will be very difficult to reconstruct the original texts with absolute certainty. Although the situation regarding the sources is not very satisfactory, it is something of a surprise that so many have survived at all, considering the exceedingly recherché instrument, and the 'private' circumstances, for which they were composed. As it happens, we have an interesting passage in Dies, which suggests how at least some of these works survived into the early nineteenth century:

> Seventh Visit, 17 May 1805 ... Haydn was not always the publisher of his own works. Many of his products, not even excepting his earliest, suffered the fate of being subject to all sorts of metamorphoses at the hands of speculators. Even at present Haydn is at odds with a person who shall remain unnamed, into whose hands devolved some works of Haydn's early period. They were composed for the baryton and were favourite pieces of the late Prince Nicolaus Esterházy.
>
> [Dies, 57]

Unverricht rightly puts the story in its proper context by recalling a whole series of such arrangements issued between 1804 and 1808 by the Viennese publisher Joseph Eder,[1] whose shop was on the Graben. Now Eder, having (as it would seem) procured a whole set of the first twenty-four baryton trios, proceeded to make his own order, which was as follows:

VI Trios (pl. no. 334)

Trio	Movement	Hoboken
I	I	XI:19/I transposed to B flat
	II	XI:24/II
	III	XI:19/III transposed to B flat
II	I	XI:20/I
	II	XI:1/II
	III	XI:20/III
III	I	XI:5/I
	II	XI:15/II
	III	XI:15/III
IV	I	XI:17/I
	II	XI:5/II
	III	*deest*
V	I	XI:21/I transposed to B flat
	II	*deest* III/
	III	XI:21/transposed to B flat
VI	I	XI:24/I
	II	XI:19/II
	III	*deest* (also found in a MS. from Tepla, now Prague: G. Feder in *Haydn-Studien* I/1, 23, and *HJB* IV, 118)

[Copy of the print: Stadtbibliothek Vienna, M 15291/c]

Eder then followed this up with two other sets of 'III Trios' (pl. nos. 427, 454) of which the contents – unlike those of the 'VI Trios' – were known to Hoboken and may be omitted here.

Although not composed with the same refinement as some later works, with their haunting slow movements, plucked strings at the back of the instrument, fugues, and so on, there are many works of great interest and beauty among the first dozen baryton trios. As we have seen, Eder published in 'VI Trios' some movements not found in other sources, and in 'III Trios', issued four years later (1808), there are two movements which, although surviving only in this 'metamorphosis', may be considered genuine Haydn; note that one such movement also survives in a Bohemian

---

1 A. Weinmann, *Verzeichnis der Musikalien des Verlages Joseph Eder – Jeremias Bermann* (Beiträge zur Geschichte des Alt-Wiener Musikverlages, Reihe 2, Folge 12), Vienna 1968, pp. 22 (334), 26 (427), 27 (454).

MS. from Tepla. Unverricht (pp. 150f.) has provided a good interim list that revises Hoboken, but we doubt if the last word on the subject has been spoken.

The most characteristic feature of these early baryton trios is their extreme brevity. The opening Allegretto movement of No. 3 contains fifty bars and is in itself a kind of miniature in the same fashion as the *scherzandi*; No. 3 is a miniature trio movement, with pretty imitations between baryton and viola, and the *scherzandi* are miniature symphonies. The first (Moderato) movement of No. 4 contains twenty-five bars, the minuet sixteen and the Finale (Allegro molto) thirty-six. It is known that the opening Moderato of No. 5 is taken from 'Che farò' in Gluck's *Orfeo*, which (as we have seen) was the subject of much discussion in Viennese society, including the Dowager Princess Esterházy (*supra*, p. 379), when it was first performed in 1762. No doubt Prince Nicolaus and Haydn discussed the work's merits, and perhaps this pretty, miniature movement (thirty-six bars) is a result of that discussion. Here is Haydn's adaptation of the famous theme:

*Berlin, Mus. ms. 10043/1, bar 2 has *tr*. We have transposed the only known source of the work (Berlin) from G to A, in which key Haydn entered the work in *EK*.

As if to compensate for all this brevity, Haydn often has recourse to sets of variations – one of his lifelong preoccupations – in these early trios (Nos. 2/I, 6/I, 8/I, 12/I), and these variation movements certainly contributed to the works' distribution in arranged form. Nos. 6, 7, 9, 11 and 17 (the latter begins with a set of variations) were 'metamorphosed' for flute, violin and 'cello (with some transpositions of keys and substitutions of some of the movements) by Hummel in 1773, and Eder issued sections of Nos. 6, 8, 14 and 18 as pl. no. 454 (1808?), as well as sections of Nos. 11, 12, 13, 16 and 17 as pl. no. 427 (1807?). Hummel's edition was imported into England and France (see Hoboken, vol. I, pp. 599f.) and possibly even published in England. An equally interesting way of distributing such a variation movement appears in connection with the beautiful opening Allegretto of No. 2, which was first published in a Viennese musical magazine of 1770 entitled *Der musikalische Dillettante, eine Wochenschrift*,[1] which (like most Viennese musical periodicals of that period) enjoyed a flourishing but very brief existence. There is something quite haunting about the melody

1 We used the copy owned by Miss Noel Seitz (then Vienna, now Mrs. Taishoff, San Francisco). It is curious that the watermarks of the magazine, the number '4' over 'GT', a snake in the 'T', are also found in the so-called 'Keeß Catalogue', the list of Haydn's symphonies drawn up about 1790 by the composer's friend, Franz Bernhard Edler von Keeß – about whom see *Haydn in Eszterháza 1766–1790*, esp. pp. 503, 663.

so that we are not surprised to learn that it circulated as piano variations in manuscript (XVII:8). Whereas the baryton version has five variations (at least in the Berlin MSS. we have examined), certainly one old MS. (Berlin) of the 'Variazioni per Cembalo' has eight variations and there appears no reason to doubt the keyboard version's authenticity. (For some reason, the keyboard version has not yet been printed.) Haydn himself seems to have been slightly mesmerized by this melody, for we find him using its skeleton as the beginning (Moderato) of Trio 9:

A hint of the new thinking which would colour Haydn's style, and change the history of Western music, comes in the Trio of the Menuet in No. 5, marked 'canone'. We give it as the conclusion to this brief survey of Haydn's early baryton trios: a summing-up, and a glance towards the future.

[Trio No. 5; Trio of the Menuet (from the autograph, Esterházy Archives, Budapest, Országos Széchényi Könyvtár)]

DIVERTIMENTI (CONCERTINI) FOR HARPSICHORD, STRINGS AND SOMETIMES HORNS (XIV: 3, 4, 7–10)

XIV:3 in C

Scoring: cemb., 2 v., 'Basso' [vc.].
Principal sources: (1) MS. parts, EH, Budapest, Ms. mus. I.150: 'Sonate / pour Clavecin ou Piano Forte / Del: Sig^re Joseppe Haydn'. Only the keyboard part. (2) MS. parts, Preußische Staatsbibliothek, Berlin: 'Concertino in C per il Clavi Cembalo, Violin 2 al piac. col. Basso'. (3) MS. parts, Archbishop's Library, Kremsier (Kroměříž), II f28. (4) MS. parts, ÖNB, Vienna.
Critical edition: Concertini für Klavier mit Begleitung von zwei Violinen und Violoncello (Horst Walter), G. Henle Verlag.

XIV:4 in C

Scoring: cemb., 2 v., 'Basso', 2 hns. added later (by Haydn?).
Principal sources: (1) Autograph, EH, Budapest, Ms. mus. I.51, with title at the head of page one: 'Divertimento per Cembalo [middle:] In Nomine Domini [right:] Giuseppe Haydn 764; at end 'Laus Deo'. (2) MS. parts by Johann Radnitzky and another copyist, Kremsier (Kroměříž) Castle, ČSSR, II g17 – apparently an authentic source. (3) MS. parts, Preußische Staatsbibliothek, Berlin: 'Concerto in C. o. Partitta Per il Clavi Cembalo, Violin 2, Corni 2 ad lib con Basso par Monsieur [both 'Michael' and 'Joseph'] Haydn.' (4) MS. parts from the collection of Archduke Rudolph, GdM, Vienna: 'Concerto in C per il Clavi Cembalo a 2 Violini, 2 Corni ad lib. con Basso Del Sig. Giuseppe Hayden'. (5) Keyboard part alone, same library. (6) Printed edition by William Forster, London (announced 2 January 1784 in the *Morning Herald*): 'A / Favorite Lesson / for the / Harpsichord, / Composed by / G: Haydn, / of Vienna. / Price 2^s. / London. Printed for W^m. Forster Musical Instrument Maker and Music Seller to their Royal Highnesses / the Prince of Wales and Duke of Cumberland Corner of Dukes Court St Martins Lane'. Copy: Hoboken Collection, ÖNB, Vienna. There are various reprints of this edition (see Hoboken, vol. I, 673).[1]
Critical editions: Henle (Walter): see XIV:3. With the horns: Boosey & Hawkes (Gertrud Wertheim).

XIV:7

Scoring: cemb., 2 v., vc.
Principal sources: (1) MS. parts from Haydn's library, EH, Budapest, Ms. mus. I.146: 'Divertimento in C. / per il / Clavicembalo: / à / Violino Primo / Violino Secondo / e / Violoncello. / Del Sig^re Giuseppe Haydn.' (2) MS. of the keyboard part in 'Divertimenta ac Galantheriae', GdM, Vienna, VII 40623. (3) MS. parts for cemb., 2 v., basso, in G major, Kremsier (Kroměříž) Castle, ČSSR, II f22.
Critical edition: Henle (Walter): see XIV:3.

XIV:8

Scoring: cemb., 2 v., vc.
Source: MS. parts from Haydn's library, EH, Budapest, Ms. mus. I. 145: 'Divertimento: in C. / per il / Clavicembalo / 2 Violini / è / Violoncello: / Del Sig^re Giuseppe Haydn.'
Critical edition: Henle (Walter): see XIV:3.

XIV:9

Scoring: cemb., 2 v., vc.
Source: MS. parts from Haydn's library, EH, Budapest, Ms. mus. I.147: 'Divertimento F. / per il / Clavicembalo / Violino Primo / Violino Secondo / Con / Violoncello: / Del Sig^re Giuseppe Haydn:'.
Critical edition: Henle (Walter): see XIV:3.

XIV:10

Scoring: cemb., 2 v., [basso?].
Source: Harpsichord part only, by Joseph Elssler, Preußische Staatsbibliothek, Berlin, Mus. ms. autogr. Jos. Haydn 32. Haydn later used a spare sheet of this MS. on which to write his *Lied* 'Der schlaue und dienstfertige Pudel' (XXVIa:38). Title in Elssler's hand: 'Divertimento N° 1. con Violini. [above, to right:] Del Sig: Gius: Haydn.' / Clavi Cembalo.' From Artaria & Co.
Critical edition: none.
Note: It would be a rash man who would attempt to place this pretty and inoffensive little work before or after 1761 on the basis of its style; but we think the fact it was copied by Joseph Elssler *might* speak for its having been composed in the service of the Esterházy family. We reproduce in facsimile overleaf the whole work (a total of four pages), which may serve as a characteristic example of Haydn's harpsichord writing for his pupils during this period. Haydn used the Finale in a Piano Sonata in F, where it is marked 'Scherzo': No. 3 (XVI:9); but the Sonata version is slightly different in details and the tiny middle section is quite new (and shorter by four bars) in the Divertimento (Elssler) work.
Literature: Larsen, *HÜB*, 303, where scholarly attention was first drawn to the work, to its authenticity, but not to the identity of its copyist (another confirmation of the work's probable date).

---

1 The present writer owns a curious British edition of this work without *impressum* (watermark date: 1799). Title in an oval 'frame': A Favorite / Lesson / – for the – / Harpsichord or Piano-Forte / in C. – composed by – Pr. 2. 6. / G. Haydn. / – .'

Haydn had started composing these 'concertini' at least in 1760 and probably before that. XIV:11's autograph, formerly in the (apparently private) possession of Prince Esterházy in Eisenstadt, was dated 1760. One may assume that this first group was composed for Count Morzin's entertainment, and for a discussion of those works, *vide supra*, pp. 267ff. The autograph of XIV:4, dated 1764, shows that perhaps in that very year, Haydn and the Prince showed a sudden interest in the harpsichord and Haydn's performances on it. As it happens, a division between the Morzin and Esterházy 'concertini' is to some extent possible because it seems that Haydn kept in his own library the performance material of several which have been listed above. Otherwise it would have been very difficult to divide the works into pre- and post-May 1761 only on the basis of their style, because such a work as XIV:4 of 1764 sounds just as light-hearted and divertimento-like as the work presumed to have been composed for the Morzin family four years earlier (cf. pp. 268f.), but of course XIV:1 – which Haydn himself entered in *EK* on p. 20 and which was announced in the Breitkopf Catalogue of 1766 – may have been written as late as *c.* 1761–65.

Formally, that which strikes one at the outset is the lack of a slow movement in all these Esterházy 'concertini': I Allegro (or Moderato or Allegro moderato). II Minuet & Trio. III Finale: Presto (or Allegro molto). This is part of the light character of the pieces, which may literally have been Prince Nicolaus's *Tafelmusik*. The light, carefree quality of the music is everywhere apparent, in the themes, in the harpsichord writing, in the delicate accompaniments for the strings. In *EK* Haydn specifies the instruments of XIV:1 – 'Divertimento per il Cembalo col Violino 2 Corni e Basso' – which assures us of the horns' authenticity. Although they are not in the autograph of XIV:4, they are very idiomatically written and may be genuine later additions which Haydn wrote straight into the players' parts. Among the many felicities of this winning music, we might draw attention to the Menuet of XIV:4, with the same pre-waltz ⸗ ♩ ♩ rhythm as in the Trio of Symphony No. 9. Another feature which is identical in all the works except XIV:9 is that the Trios are all in the minor key (most complicatedly in XIV:1, which is altogether the most serious and in some respects most thoroughly developed of the series). The easy technical level of all the parts, especially of the harpsichord throughout, make them ideal for beginners; and now that they are all available in good modern editions, one predicts that teachers will find them perfect examples of easily playable and easily comprehensible introductions to Haydn. The same procedure has already occurred with the piano sonatas, which have taken on a whole new lease of life because of the new *Urtext* editions now available.

Overleaf
The only four extant pages of the Divertimento (XIV:10) for harpsichord, two violins (and basso?); the harpsichord part is in Joseph Elssler's hand. Preußische Staatsbibliothek, Berlin (formerly Universitätsbibliothek, Marburg/Lahn)

SOLO HARPSICHORD MUSIC (EXCEPT SONATAS)

20 Variazioni per il cembalo solo in G
(XVII:1, *c.* 1765)

Principal sources: (1) MS. copy in a volume of keyboard music entitled 'Divertimenta ac Galantheriae Variae a Diversis Authoribus conscriptae', GdM, Vienna, VII 40623. This is the only complete copy known. (2) MS. copy, Archbishop's Library, Kremsier (Kroměříž), ČSSR, II A40, containing eleven variations (I, II, IV, V, VIII, XI, XII, XVI, XVII, XVIII, XX). (3) MS. copy transposed into A major (*vide infra*), National Museum, Prague, from Osek Abbey, XXXII A391. 'Variazioni Nᵒ 17 Per Il Clavi Cembalo Del Signore Giuseppo Heyden [*sic*] ad usum P. Jacobi', containing I, II, V, VI, IV, VIII, XII, XI, VII, XIV, XVI, X, XX, XVII, XV, XIX, XIII. (4) Before the Second World War there was a complete copy (20 var.) in A major, Thüringische Landesbibliothek, Weimar (DDR), now lost. It was, however, used for the Peters Edition of this work by Kurt Soldan. (5) In 1788/9, Artaria issued a revised version, much shortened (12 var.), probably using a MS. supplied by Haydn. Title: 'Arietta con 12 Variazioni...Nᵒ. [ink: "2"].' Copy: GdM, Vienna.
Critical editions: Verlag Henle (S. Gerlach). Wiener Urtext-Ausgabe (Franz Eibner).

We are indebted to Franz Eibner for the first critical edition of this G major version, which was patently the original: in *EK* (p. 23) Haydn entered it as the end of a series of harpsichord pieces. He started to write it in G and then corrected it into A, but without adding the two additional sharp signs; and Johann Elssler rather mindlessly entered it into *HV* without the two ♯s. Larsen (*HUB*, 217f.) places these two pages of *EK* 'gegen 1770, oder vielleicht noch um 1767.' The D major Sonata No. 30 (XVI:19), at the top of *EK's* p. 21, was composed in 1767 (dated autograph). Supposing 1770 to be an outside limit, it means that our Variations had been already transposed into A major by that time; and it was in A that Haydn gave it to his publishers Artaria to engrave.

It is a deceptively simple theme, but the variations contain many surprises, harmonic, rhythmic, structural and above all in keyboard technique (crossing the hands in Var. III, the incredible chords with tenths in the left hand in Var. XX). Franz Eibner writes interestingly on the work's character:

> In its complete version, Haydn's work lies firmly within the tradition of the chaconne, which at that time had the same objectives as later led, under utterly different technical conditions, to the composition of études. Great as the demand for variations was in Haydn's day, the market for this kind of variation had probably already declined. So it is not surprising that a revision was made later; even the copyists ... had displayed no interest in it as an entity. Yet today this work seems interesting precisely because of what was, at the time, its all too conservative character.   [Foreword to the Wiener Urtext-Ausgabe, p. xix]

Perhaps both these keyboard solo pieces (i.e., including the *Capriccio*) are part of the 'harpsichord renaissance' at Eisenstadt Castle that we have noticed in connection with the cantatas and concertos (concertini). On the other hand, these Variations almost look as if they had been composed *a priori* for didactic purposes, not like the improvisational *Capriccio* which is really the kind of piece with which Haydn might have chosen to display his abilities as a keyboard player. And if Haydn played these two works, on what instrument? The great green harpsichord? Or a newly imported square fortepiano from London (many were circulating on the Continent by 1765)? Franz Eibner is persuaded that both were especially designed for the new piano, but his opinions were angrily discounted by László Somfai (in a review of Eibner's edition, *Music & Letters*, 1977) who, on the other hand, was not aware that Haydn quite certainly had at his disposal a piano at least as early as 1773[1] and very likely before that

---

1 *Haydn at Eszterháza 1766–1790*, p. 343.

date. Neither *Variazioni* nor *Capriccio* have any dynamic markings at all. But what are we to make of the following passages in the Variations?

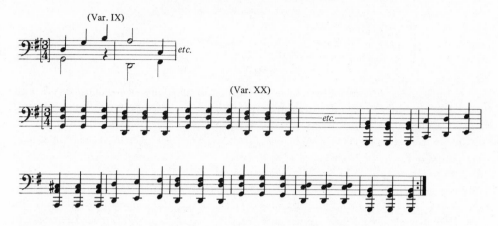

(Var. IX)

(Var. XX)

etc.

There is no hint of an arpeggio sign, but one source simplifies the whole passage

etc.

from Var. XX just quoted. Various improbable suggestions have been made to explain this very bizarre passage: one that appears attractive at the outset is that Haydn was writing for an instrument with a so-called 'short octave' in the bass, i.e. that some of the lower notes were tuned lower than their position would normally suggest; but it is rather unlikely that Haydn could have expected his public to use such an old-fashioned instrument (though he may have had some special keyboard in mind, because this particular variation, and also IX, quoted above, were cancelled for the Artaria print of the late 1780s). A simplistic, but not impossible, explanation is that one of Haydn's pupils (or Haydn himself) had a left hand capable of stretching a tenth. Nor does the range of the pieces help us: G′ in the bass as the lowest note in the Variations and on the top d‴; in the *Capriccio* F′ in the bass (the lowest note on both piano and harpsichord at that time) and again d‴ on the top.

With all their repeats, the *20 Variazioni* are not short; but they are, as we have said, by no means devoid of interest and are excellent teaching material. They sound rather better on the harpsichord than the *Capriccio* and it is certainly no violation of style to use the instrument which Haydn himself specified in his draft catalogue.

Capriccio 'Acht Sauschneider' (XVII:1, 1765)

Principal sources: (1) Autograph, formerly in the Selden-Goth Collection, Florence (where we repeatedly examined it), now in Austrian private possession. Title: 'Capriccio / Acht Sauschneider müßen seÿn / del giuseppe Haydn mpria 765.' At end: 'Fine / Laus Deo'. Oblong Italian paper (watermarks: crown, three crescents of declining size; letters 'ʙᴛ'). Photograph: Hoboken Photogrammarchiv, ONB, Vienna. Facsimile of first page of music: Schmid, Tafel XXIV. (2) First edition, Artaria & Co., Vienna: 'Caprice / pour / le clavecin ou piano-forte / par / Ioseph Haydn / oeuvre 43 / Vienna chez Artaria Comp. / C. P. S. C. M. – 170 – f.1. 30x.' Announced on 19 March 1788 in the *Wiener Zeitung*. Copy: ÖNB, Vienna (Hoboken Collection); another in GdM, Vienna.
Critical edition: Verlag Henle (S. Gerlach). Wiener Urtext-Ausgabe (Franz Eibner).
Literature: Pohl II, 236f. Schmid, 303–7. Geiringer 1932, 99f. Geiringer 1947, 249f. K. M. Klier, 'Das Volksliedthema eines Haydn-Capriccios', *Das Deutsche Volkslied*, Jg. XXXIV, Vienna 1932.

The old folk-song on which Haydn based this *Capriccio* has the following text:

> Eahna achte müassen 's seyn,
> Wann s' an Saubärn wolln schneidn.
> Zwoa voran, zwoa hintn,
> Zwoa schneidn, zwoa bindn,
> Eahna achte müassen 's seyn,
> Wann s' an Saubärn wolln schneidn.[1]

As it happens, the same melody was set by Mozart in his *Gallimathias Musicum* (K.32), first performed at The Hague in March 1766. In the region between Salzburg and Augsburg, the tune was known with a different text, and E. F. Schmid[2] has located this version in the *Ohrenvergnügendes und Gemüthergötzendes Tafelconfect* (Augsburg, 1733–37–46):

---

1 It takes eight of you, / If you want to castrate a boar. / Two in front and two behind, / Two to cut and two to bind. / It takes eight of you, / If you want to castrate a boar. Schmid, 306.

2 'L'héritage Souabe de Mozart', *Les influences étrangères dans l'oeuvre de W. A. Mozart* (lecture given at the Sorbonne in October 1956), Paris [1957]), pp. 70f.

Notice that at the hold, Mozart marks the cadenza that was expected to be improvised as 'Capriccio', which is Haydn's actual title.[1] Mozart, like Haydn, uses the version

with the additional figure in bar 1 (Haydn: 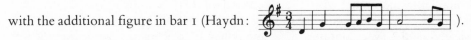).

Until the autograph's rediscovery *c.*1932, it was generally thought that the *Capriccio* had been composed shortly before its publication with Artaria in 1788 (Pohl, for example); it is yet one more, and perhaps the most sensational, case of back-dating in Haydn's works – another is the *Missa Cellensis in honorem B.V.M.* (1766). Based on the characteristic C. P. E. Bach monothematic rondo, Haydn achieves a remarkable, indeed unique, fusion of what *sounds* like a splendidly free 'improvisation' with a strict formal scheme. At this early date one might more profitably speak of a ritornello form, such as we have observed in other works, vocal and instrumental, of this period.

Although there is absolutely no evidence from the Esterházy Archives to support (or indeed negate) the theory, we agree with Professor Eibner that this *Capriccio* appears to have been written with the fortepiano and not the harpsichord or clavichord in mind. The bold formal scheme, which includes the double quotation (at the end, bars 265, 296 and 341, triple quotation) of the *castrator porcorum* theme (in itself suggested by the text's repetition of lines one and two), may be outlined as follows.

Entrance of the theme (ritornello):

Bar	1	24	62	85	114	157	190	233	274	296	341
Key	G	D	A minor	E minor	C	B minor	C	F	G minor	B♭	G

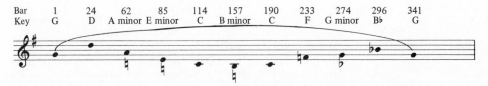

In other words, using the tonic and the appearance of the theme in the tonic, Haydn spans a huge arch between the beginning and the end of the work: all this is musical thought on a very grand scale, and with this *Capriccio* Haydn achieved the finest keyboard work of this early period. It is more subtle, more delicate in its pastel shading, than the equally bold *Fantasia* in C which Artaria published in 1789;[2] but the later work is even more dedicated to the sound of the new fortepiano. One final point to be noted in the *Capriccio* is Haydn's delicate flirtation with third-oriented keys: *e* to

1 Mozart's K.32 in *Neue Ausgabe sämtlicher Werke*, Serie IV, Werkgruppe 12, Band 1 (Günter Hausswald and Wolfgang Plath), 1970.
2 For the work and the resulting correspondence with Artaria, see *Haydn at Eszterháza 1766–1790*, pp. 643ff., 718, 724.

c, g to *b flat* to *g*. Here we have the remote beginnings of a subject which will continue to fascinate Haydn all through his life. Even two years later, in 1767, we find the *Stabat Mater* (XX*bis*) laid out in a central pattern of descending chains of thirds (the descending is typical of Haydn):

| Gmi | E♭ | Cmi | F | B♭ | F | Dmi | B♭ | Gmi | E♭ | Cmi | Cmaj | Gmi | Gmajor |

Altogether this *Capriccio* is one of those many works composed in the early 1760s where one feels strongly that

finis origine pendet.

Symphonies

We may now continue with the discussion of Haydn's early symphonies and *scherzandi* begun in connection with those works composed for Count Morzin (*vide supra*, pp. 280ff.). We continue with our policy of placing the works here under discussion in their probable chronological order, which does not always agree with the old numerical order of Mandyczewski.

Works composed c. May 1761–1765

Symphony No.	Date	Comment
6–8	1761	Trilogy 'Le Matin', 'Le Midi', 'Le Soir'. The autograph of No. 7 ('Le Midi') has survived and is dated 1761. According to Dies (*supra*, p. 343) these were the first works Haydn composed for, and according to a suggestion by, Prince Paul Anton. The titles survive on many contemporary MSS. and prints. Not in surviving part of *EK*.
9	1762	Autograph (Artaria, now lost).
25	*c.* 1762	This is the only one of the 106 Haydn symphonies for which we have no authentic sources, no listing in *EK* and no listing in *HV*. It is listed in the *Quartbuch* (thematic catalogue of an Austrian monastery, perhaps in St Pölten, later owned by Haydn and some misattributions corrected in his hand) as Haydn, and there are many copies under Haydn's name. Breitkopf Catalogue 1767, Sigmaringen Catalogue 1766.
14		Göttweig Cat. 1764. MS. parts, 'Synfonia' (Haydn's spelling of the word until end of 1764), by Joseph Elssler, St Florian Abbey. Unlikely for Haydn/Elssler to be selling MS. copies of symphonies composed in Morzin period. Not in surviving part of *EK*.
36		Breitkopf Cat. 1769. In the third part of *EK* (p. 34) which was compiled later than the first part, otherwise here discussed. Stylistically, use of solo violin and solo violoncello suggest proximity to the other *concertante* works of 1761–5, and certain other stylistic traits indicate *c.* 1761–2 rather than later (*vide infra*, pp. 561f.).
12, 13, 40, 72	1763	Dated autographs of Nos. 12, 13 and 40 (marked 'N° 7') dated 1763. No. 72 with four horns and solo instruments as in No. 31 (1765), but appears to be a study for No. 31 and to be placed here rather than 1765. Nos. 12 and 72 in second (also later) part of *EK*.
21, 22, 23, 24	1764	Dated autographs. Not in surviving part of *EK*.
30, 29, 31, 28	1765	Dated autographs. The order from *EK*, where No. 30 probably contained in lost, opening part.
34	*c.* 1765	Breitkopf Cat. 1767. In second (later) part of *EK*.

If we examine the first two pages of *EK*, we notice that Haydn has added his own numbers to *incipits* of the symphonies up to about 1770, and it now appears that these numbers are even more significant and accurate than was realized. The facsimile of *EK* was published by Larsen in 1941 and pages 1–2 in Landon, *SYM* (Plates II, III), but perhaps a résumé might be welcome. We enter *in medias res* with the last of the six *scherzandi*:

Work	Haydn's no./Comment
Scherzando VI (II:38)	'N:20' but *incipit* in Joseph Elssler's hand, i.e. the last entry of the lost pages including all the earlier, pre-1765 symphonies (and *scherzandi*). The early number shows that the rest of these works may have figured as Nos. 15–20. See also our reconstruction of the Morzin list, *supra*, p. 283.
[Symphony No.] 27	'N:12': *incipit* and No. in Haydn's hand: apparently a work forgotten in the first section of *EK* and therefore added later. This would explain the low numbering. The numbers must have been added after the catalogue had been laid out, because when Elssler entered the last *scherzando*, it contained no such numbering. The fact that 'No. 12' is not that of the Fürnberg series of Morzin Symphonies (there it is No. 16) does not mean much. Haydn liked to 'shuffle' the numbers when offering works to different patrons and/or publishers. The proximity of Nos. 12 and 16 in the two lists only confirms that Symphony 27 must have been an early, Morzin work.
29	'N:40'. Autograph 1765. From here, all *incipits* and numberings autograph.
31	'N:41'. Autograph 1765. The two entries of Nos. 29 and 31 entered about the same time in *EK*.
28	'45': Haydn now drops 'N:'. This entry and the next two are in the same ink. Autograph of No. 28: 1765.
35	'46'. Autograph 1 Dec. 1767.
59	'47'. MSS. (copies): 1769.
38	'48'. Göttweig 1769, Breitkopf Cat. 1769.
49	'49'. Autograph 1768.
58	'50'.
	[*EK*, page two:]
Overture *Lo speziale* (1768)	'51'. Performed at Eszterháza 1768.
26	'52'.
41	'53' MS. Joseph Elssler, Prague, with watermarks which may be dated 1769. Göttweig 1771. Osek Abbey 1771.
	[entries placed on left-hand, otherwise blank, margin:]
39	'54' Obviously some kind of afterthought: entered in pencil.
20	'55' Ditto (pencil).
Overture *Le pescatrici* (1769–70?)	'56' Autograph of actual opera dated 1769, performed 1770.

Now if we take the 25 works presumably composed for Morzin, add to them the list of 10 presumably written for Princes Paul Anton and Nicolaus Esterházy 1761–5, and then add the remaining works listed in pages 1–2 of *EK* (omitting the duplications such as Nos. 20, 27 and the *Scherzando* VI, also Nos. 29, 31 and 28, which have already been covered in the above lists) – Symphonies Nos. 35, 59, 38, 49, 58, Overture *Lo speziale*, 26, 41, 39, Overture *Le pescatrici* (a total of ten) – we arrive at fifty-five works. To this we must certainly add the three-movement Overture to *Acide* which was listed (as we have seen) as a 'sinfonia' in Göttweig and elsewhere, and which Haydn certainly counted, with the Overtures to *Lo speziale* and *Le pescatrici*, as genuine symphonies. That would bring the total to 56, which is precisely Haydn's own reckoning.

There are several reasons why the *scherzandi* might have been composed for Esterházy and not Morzin. In the first place, there is the presence of the flute (always in the trio of each work), and no known Morzin symphony features a flute. Secondly, Haydn seems to have made copies of the *scherzandi* using one of the Esterházy copyists: II:34 and II:35 exist in MSS. by the man who copied Symphony No. 7 ('Le Midi'), formerly in Haydn's own library, now in EH, Budapest (reproduced in pls. 21, 22). The *scherzandi* were announced under that title in the Breitkopf Catalogue of 1765, but whether Haydn called them that, or symphonies, or (as in MSS. in the Biblioteca Estense, Modena) 'Sex Sinfonietti'. A list of the sources may be omitted here, since there are now two critical modern editions.[1] A brief survey of the works' form, instrumentation and character may be given here, since they were analyzed in formal detail in *SYM* (191ff.). All six are scored, as we now know from the number of authentic and good MSS. which have been uncovered in the last twenty years, for one flute (plays in the trio of each work only), two oboes, two horns and strings (bassoon *continuo* advisable, also harpsichord if thought advisable). It seems clear that all six were designed as a series, which perhaps explains their tremendous concentration and distillation (looking forward to Anton von Webern), also their brevity. They are scored in F, C, D, G, E and A and may actually represent Haydn's first attempt at a cycle: all the early quartets, string trios, harpsichord sonatas, harpsichord trios and symphonies appear to have been composed separately. In several libraries (Modena, Hirschberg [Doksy] Castle [now National Museum, Prague], Zittau, etc.) all six have been preserved in one MS. series. The outer scheme is always: I. Allegro. II. Minuet & Trio. III. Adagio (some MSS. Andante). IV. Finale – Presto. There is a clear attempt to wed the lighter divertimento style with the heavier symphonic form: the opening movement of II:35 is like one of Haydn's own cassatio movements, while the allegros of the *scherzandi* in C (II:34) and A (II:38) are more in the 3/4 metre symphonic style of the early 1760s. Some of the trios are in the subdominant, some in the relative minor; all except one (II:38) of the slow movements are in the tonic minor and although outwardly this is a typical feature of Viennese symphonies (Wagenseil, Hofmann, Schmelzer, etc.) of the period, nevertheless these adagios are unexpectedly serious. The alternation of unison openings with 'harmonized' material is found not only in the quick movements (typical opening of II:38 in A, where this alternation is underlined by a change from f to p) but also in the adagios (beginning of II:37). Haydn's professionalism is revealed in the astonishing diversity of detail and construction he is able to instil into a most rigid formal mould which never changes from work to work. He also shows himself to be a master of miniature forms; perhaps this was a natural consequence of his love for brevity and pithiness in his music generally. The Finale of the G major (II:36) is only sixteen bars long, while the longest is that to the A major (II:38) which is the result of the more weighty symphonic style also adopted for the opening movement. It is also a characteristic of these extraordinary – indeed, in eighteenth-century music quite unique – *scherzandi* that every movement (trios included, of course) is divided in two parts, each to be repeated; and of course the music makes no aural sense unless these miniatures are repeated as Haydn instructs.

---

1 Verlag Doblinger, Diletto Musicale 71–6 (Landon). *Joseph Haydn Werke* (Makoto Ohmiya), in preparation.

Notes on the Symphonies

Symphony No. 6 in D ('Le Matin')

Scoring: 1 flute, 2 oboes, 1 bassoon, 2 horns, strings (with *violino concertante, violoncello concertante* and *violone* [double bass] solo) and *continuo* [harpsichord].

If we examine the music that Prince Anton had put together in a thematic catalogue[1] in 1740, we will notice, apart from anonymous works, many works by the Italians, with special emphasis on Antonio Vivaldi (whole series of the printed works, such as *Il cimento dell'armonia e dell'invenzione*, which of course includes *Le quattro stagioni*). There are, as we might expect, many works by Werner; but a fair selection of Albinoni, Valentini, Tartini, and minor masters such as Curcillo, Sozzi, Sasano, Simoni, Zanni, etc. In the Catalogue of 1759, discussed above, where we find one Haydn symphony, there is a large part devoted to Italian instrumental music. (This is not to overlook all the music by local composers, French operas, French ballets, and so on, but it is beside the point we are making.) In the famous trilogy, comprising Symphonies Nos. 6–8, which is so different from the Morzin works, it is probable that the new formal structure was to a large extent a reflection of Prince Paul Anton's taste for the older Italian school and the *concerto grosso* with its division into *concertino* and *ripieno*. In 'Le Midi' we even have, in Corelli fashion, two solo violins and 'cello (the old Roman *concertino*) except that Haydn broadens the basic structure to include (on occasion) the flute, oboes, bassoon, horns and even the double bass in the *concertino* concept. By doing this he was able to display the virtuoso qualities of his new orchestra – which no doubt flattered and delighted the players – and, although retaining the structure of Prince Paul's beloved Italian concerto, dress it in modern clothing. Here we have another example of Haydn's uncanny ability to write music that pleased the patron (or group) for whom it was composed and yet was uncompromising in technical, formal and instrumental level of standards. It is a pattern that will continue throughout his long life and which constitutes a chameleon-like quality that has always slightly puzzled historians. It accounts for the often inexplicable difference in styles and approach between works composed in immediate proximity to each other. Nor was the trilogy entirely an isolated event: we find its style again in several movements of other symphonies composed *c.* 1761–1765, sometimes as episodes from a solo concerto (e.g. No. 13/II for solo 'cello or No. 24/II for solo flute) and at other times as derivatives from the *concerto grosso* (e.g. No. 36/II, with concertante violin and 'cello) or even more *outré* mixtures of divertimento, concerto and suite (e.g. Nos. 31, 72).

No. 6 has another rare feature for this period: a slow introduction. The device is known to us in a different aspect in the Morzin Symphony No. 15

1 J. Harich in *HJB* IX, 35ff.

(there as a French overture), and as a straight (but longish) introduction to No. 25 (a work difficult to date but possibly a transitional work between Morzin and Esterházy, in any case close to No. 6 in dating). Otherwise, at this period Haydn prefers either the *sonata da chiesa* sequence with an opening slow movement, or the normal sequence of three or four movements beginning with allegro and with or without a minuet. It is generally thought that the opening of No. 6 depicts a sunrise, which Haydn was later to repeat on a vast scale in *The Creation* and *The Seasons* many years later. In 'Le Matin', Haydn's modest sunrise requires six bars. We note that the elaborate *concerto grosso* scoring is not yet in effect during this movement, which opens with a gay subject for solo flute, taken up by the oboe and then the whole orchestra. Shortly before the end of the exposition there are the first instances of Haydn's use of chain *forte-piano* effects in the symphonic forms: the effect must have been very new in 1761 and adds a characteristically nervous, forward-driving impetus to the whole movement. The development is notable for the retransition to the recapitulation: here is the first example of such imaginative tapestry-like wood-wind writing over pizzicato strings (bars 76ff.), quite different from the divertimento-like solos of the Morzin symphonies. Otherwise we may note the dotted rhythm of the introduction, derived from the French Overture, and one of the rare uses of *crescendo* in this period (the most famous being that which began Symphony No. 1). The recapitulation begins with a delightful 'preview' of the main theme on the horns.

The second movement is perhaps the crown of the work. There are three sections, an Andante flanked on both sides by an Adagio. The winds are as usual dropped; a *concertante* violin and violoncello are introduced, and this *concertino* is balanced by a *ripieno* of strings (and harpsichord *continuo*). What begins to be an amusing parody of a singing lesson (do-re-mi-fa-sol...) gives Haydn the opportunity of displaying his mastery of polyphonic string writing. Now this use of an upward scale in a slow movement is a device long known and cultivated by the Italians of the Corelli school and his disciples and followers. Here is yet another reminder of Prince Paul Anton's love of the great instrumental tradition south of the Alps. As a typical example to illustrate this use of the do-re-mi-fa progression by one of the Italian masters, we may select the slow movement of Domenico Scarlatti's Sinfonia No. 10 (one of a series of operatic overtures preserved in Paris). In Haydn's movement, the do-re-mi-fa is a kind of slow introduction to the Andante, a stately Baroque dance in 3/4 time (as contrasted with the 4/4 of the flanking Adagio sections). Concluding the Andante are two chords in the style of a closing recitative. The scale parody is then reintroduced, except that we are now given to understand that it is no longer a parody: suddenly we are in the middle of a most heartfelt and moving tribute to

[D. Scarlatti: Sinfonia No. 10]

[Bibliothèque Nationale, Paris, Fonds Général 10.513]

the beauty of Italian Baroque music that was so dear to Prince Paul Anton.

The elegant Minuet – a bit French in its poise – brings back the wind band; and the second part has a passage for unaccompanied wind instruments that reminds us of the work's chronological proximity to the wind-band divertimenti (*Feld Parthien*) for Morzin and for the Grenadiers at Eisenstadt. The astounding Trio, with its grotesque double-bass solo, sets the pattern for all the trios of this set: here, and only here, is the double bass given a solo. J. G. Schwenda, who was hired as a bassoon player, must have been a good enough violonist. Was it actually for him that Haydn wrote the lost 'Concerto per il Violone'? It seems that Schwenda hardly played the bassoon at all except in *Feld Parthien*, because there is *never* a single work, or even a passage, in the symphonic music of 1761–5, requiring two bassoons. (And the *violone* of the Capelle in Eisenstadt was only a part time player, *Bauschreiber* Anton Kühnel.) The extravagantly Baroque language in which this Trio is cast is perhaps part of the whole scenario, which is close to the world of Faustino Bocchi and the Bergamo grotesque school of *settecento* art: the use of D minor is not merely a formal contrast here.

The Finale retains the *concertante* violin and 'cello parts (they had almost disappeared in the Minuet except for a short solo 'cello part in the Trio). The solo violin is required to play a long and technically difficult solo in the middle part of the movement, and one is strangely reminded of the Fourth Brandenburg Concerto (which neither

Tomasini nor Haydn could have heard, the whole Bach cycle being totally unknown in Austria at that date). It is clear that this displaying of Tomasini, Weigl ('cellist) and, to a lesser extent, the flautist Sigl was one way of proving, as it were, their indispensability. It is perhaps the most difficult of the Tomasini solo sections in this trilogy. Even the horns emerge into prominence at the end of this large-scale violin solo. As we listen to this movement, we must remind ourselves that it was a brilliantly original way of pouring new wine into old bottles.

Symphony No. 7 in C ('Le Midi')

Scoring: 2 flutes, 2 oboes, 1 bassoon, 2 horns, strings (with *violino I concertante, violino II concertante, violoncello concertante* and *violone solo* and 'Basso Continuo' (harpsichord). Fortunately, there is now a fine facsimile edition of the autograph available (edited by László Somfai, Editio Musica, Budapest, 1972), from which all Haydn's idiosyncratic notation may be usefully studied.

Again a slow introduction, and with the dotted rhythms and chains of dotted figures which mark Haydn's courtly Eisenstadt C major style (which had, as we now realize, to dispense with trumpets and timpani except on very rare occasions). Haydn's adaptation of this feature from the French Overture is now an essential part of his style: compare this beginning with the C major beginnings of the Violin Concerto in C, 'Cello Concerto in C, or the Aria 'La beltà che m'innamora' from *Acide* and one sees that this has become a personal, strongly profiled language with a whole series of 'fingerprints', some of which have been mentioned. The Allegro has for its main subject just such a fingerprint: repeated violin

semiquavers ♪♪♪ | ♪♪♪ over repeated

quavers in the bass ♪♪♪♪♪♪ line: just what one would expect from a Neapolitan opera overture of the 1740s and 1750s. But as the subject unfolds we notice that the top and bottom lines continue and that a middle line has now been added, showing that Haydn is automatically thinking in terms of double counterpoint at the octave (bars 17ff.). And instead of whirling us away to the dominant, as he and others would do in an overture or normal symphonic movement, we remain in the tonic and the Corelli-derived *concertino* (2 v., vc.) is brought in, as if we were in a multiple concerto. The flutes, interestingly enough, do not play in this movement; and here again, we are seeing before our eyes the birth of a trait which would make later and grander symphonies famous: withholding instruments in the first movement and introducing them in some dramatic and unexpected way in a later section. Here we shall see how Haydn will do this with the flutes; on a larger scale, it is what happens with Symphony No. 88, wherein the trumpets and drums are withheld until the first tutti of the slow movement. As the first movement of 'Le Midi' progresses, we notice that first the oboes, then the bassoon, are used in a *concertante* way, so that we have what is effectively the predecessor of the 'symphonie concertante' later so beloved in Paris. (Curiously, No. 6 was printed in Paris by Anton Huberty in 1773, and No. 8 a few years later by Bailleux; but not No. 7.)

The most remarkable idea in 'Le Midi' is surely the Recitative which constitutes the second movement, and which we have noted in a parallel work, the Divertimento (Cassatio) in C (II:17) of the same period. The solo violin produces a realistic parody of the anguished dramatic soprano of a Metastasian *opera seria*. She is accompanied by strings and sustained oboes, and if we imagine the violin to be a Dido or Cleopatra, we are re-living a *recitativo accompagnato* such as Haydn himself was to compose with the greatest seriousness all his life. There are the sudden changes in tempo – Allegro suddenly sweeps us off, to stop with dramatic suddenness on *fp* and a return to Adagio and solo violin (bar 16). Actually, there is no evidence whatever that this recitative was intended to be humorous: on the contrary, the lonely wanderings of the strings in the final Adagio (bars 20ff.), moving quietly and in stately quavers, are suddenly very touching. All through the music of the Viennese Classical School, this attempt to introduce recitative into purely instrumental music runs like an unbroken thread. Johann Michael Haydn tried the experiment in the great Serenade[1] in D (Perger 87: Salzburg, 1767), seventh movement; Mozart has a recitative in one of his Salzburg divertimenti;[2] the recitative in the final movement of Haydn's *Concertante* (I:105, London 1792) is well known; and of course the culmination of this tradition is the great instrumental recitative in the Finale of Beethoven's Ninth Symphony.

After the angular strength and curiously moving power of the recitative, Haydn adds the prescribed V–I cadence, ending in B minor. In the next movement (Adagio) we are in G major, and in the first bar two flutes, not previously used in this Symphony, suddenly soar over the sustained solo violin and the accompanying strings. The effect of G major after B minor and the soft warmth of the flutes is like the sudden and unexpected release of a damned spirit who is now free, like Orpheus, to walk in the Elysian fields. But the effect is totally Haydn's, because Gluck's *Orfeo* – with its famous flute soli which accompany Atto II°, Sc. 2: 'Deliziosa per i boschetti che vi verdeggiano, i fiori rivertono i prati, i ritiri ombrosi che vi si scuoprono, i fiumi ed i ruscelli che la bagnano' – was not composed (or at least not performed) until 1762. (The most celebrated flute

solo in this section of *Orfeo*, in D minor, was not written until the Paris version.) The atmosphere conjured up by Gluck in 'Che puro ciel', which follows hard on a 'Ballo', is not unlike the ecstasy of Haydn's Adagio. Gluck uses not only 'Flauto solo' but oboe, bassoon and violoncello soli and two horns,[1] apart from the usual strings. Our surprises in the Haydn work are not yet over, however: after approaching the close of the second part in normal fashion, Haydn leads the music to a six-four chord, whereupon the solo violin and solo 'cello are given a long cadenza to themselves, entirely written out in the autograph (and not left to the performers to improvise or compose, as was usually the case in eighteenth-century instrumental cadenzas). In the midst of this section, a few bars of Allegro are introduced, almost as if we were witnessing an improvisation by a soloist during the cadenza of his concerto. Just before, too, Haydn creates an extraordinary atmosphere – the violin accompanying in whispering broken chords and the 'cello, with the melody (bars 41ff.), falling down to the crucial *c sharp* in tentative quavers with a crossed turn: here is yet another 'fingerprint'. The crossed turn, though we find it in an anonymous (spurious Haydn) harpsichord concerto (*vide supra*, p. 521), in Ordoñez (*vide supra*, p. 242) and even in Gluck's *Orfeo*, soon becomes a positive obsession with Haydn. Where another man would have used a trill – just in this very section, for example –

Haydn uses the crisper abbreviation of (bar

42), which creates quite another effect. After the Allegro interruption, the music subsides to Adagio again, and in a carefully prepared conclusion, with a long trill, this highly individual movement ends, just as if it were a concerto, with a two-bar tutti. This influence of the concerto on the symphonic style, and particularly Haydn's, continues well into the late 1770s, where we find many slow movements with cadenza-like insertions, concluding trills, and final tuttis (see Symphonies Nos. 66/II, 68/III, etc.).

The autograph is useful to us in establishing[2] that it really was a 'Violone' that had the solo in the Trio (some of the secondary sources changed it to 'Violoncello' – the scribes not, as it were, believing their eyes). The high range used in these three Trios, and in the solo sections of the Finales in Symphonies Nos. 31 and 72, confirm that the tuning (which we have seen in the bills of the Esterházy Archives) A–d–f♯–a was indeed the Eisenstadt *Kammerstimmung* (literally: 'chamber tuning'). Chords like

$$\left. \begin{matrix} \mathbf{9\!:} \end{matrix} \right.$$

(autograph: Symphony No. 7 Trio, bar 44) and

---

1 Scored for 2 ob., 2 bsn., 2 hns., 2 trpts. and str. with solo violino principale, trombone and violoncello concertante. The autograph is in EH, Budapest, II, 82 and is signed 'Salisburgo, li 10 Agosto 767.'

2 K.287 (K.271b, 271H), *c*. June 1777. *Neue Ausgabe* VII, Werkgruppe 18 (Albert Dunning), 1976, pp. 138f., 152f.: introduction to Finale, later reintroduced; notice, here too, the written-out *appoggiature*.

1 Gluck, *Sämtliche Werke* I/1 (A. A. Abert), Bärenreiter Verlag, pp. 88f. (Ballo), 89ff. 'Che puro ciel'.

2 It also firmly establishes that a harpsichord was required. The two bottom lines read 'Violone Solo' / 'Violoncello e Basso Continuo' (autograph).

the use of the low *A* string as an empty string

(autograph: Symphony No. 31, Finale, Var. 7, bar 115) confirm that which the bills proposed. And this *A* is the lowest note ever found in any of these solo passages. It is thus a perfect combination of archival evidence combined with the musical score (in this case reinforced by two autographs as well).

The Finale of 'Le Midi' again provides Haydn with the structure of the *concerto grosso* (two violins and 'cello *concertino*) which he enlarges to proportions of a *symphonie concertante* by giving almost equal prominence to the solo flute. The scoring is often of divertimento-like transparency (e.g. bars 95ff.), and it is of its time in the form (a kind of presonata, with a sharply etched 'second subject' in the dominant, at bars 38ff.). This material which occupies the place of the second subject in later classical form returns in the development and in the recapitulation. (We do Haydn and his contemporaries of 1760 no justice in forcing their music into sonata form terminology, but the period has been so neglected that no proper terminology for this kind of movement has been invented in the English language.). In many respects this Finale is the most forward-looking part of 'Le Midi'. The 'second subject' with its twittering violin solo and off-beat accompaniment is the basis of Haydn's language for the next forty years, while the rushing semiquaver passages are in the newest Italian opera overture manner (bars 16ff.). But there is always a purposeful hand behind the use of these modish effects. The semiquaver passages started out as the short tutti interjections of bars 4f. and 6f. (the Finale begins with a series of these *concerto grosso*-like alternations of two solo violins with the *ripieno*). The semiquavers are then transferred to the solo flute, and it is not until bars 16ff. that they turn into the rushing pattern of a Neapolitan *sinfonia*.

Symphony No. 8 in G ('Le Soir')

Scoring: 1 flute, 2 oboes, 1 bassoon, 2 horns, strings (with *violino I concertante, violino II concertante, violoncello concertante* and *violone* [double bass] solo) and *continuo* [harpsichord].

'Le Soir' is equally diverse. The opening Allegro molto is in a metre usually reserved for finales, 3/8, and here the *concertino* is not yet used. The first subject begins only with the violins and is *piano*: second innovation (consider the almost omnipresent *forte* openings of Italian operatic symphonies). Third innovation: it is a regular series of four-bar phrases, but at the end of three such periods there is a little 'flourish':

– almost a raising of the eyebrows. Thereupon the first subject is repeated (varied this time by a new flute obbligato). The insertion of this 'raised

eyebrows' phrase creates the kind of limping motion for which Haydn's later quartets are celebrated. The movement is also noteworthy in that there is only one subject: here is one of the first of many such monothematic movements, culminating in the oft-cited Finale to the 'Drum Roll' Symphony (No. 103), composed thirty-four years later in London. Although this is a most modern-sounding and formally up-to-date Allegro molto, Haydn has not forgotten one of the great features of the Vivaldian concerto – the sequence. Here Haydn creates a marvellous sweeping sequence at bars 122ff., forcing our attention to the off-beat second part of each bar by having the bass line spring up the octave at that point

(continued for a total of twenty bars) and the violins execute a similar pattern

Another modern feature is the freedom with which the wind section is used, with constant solo passages in conjunction with the strings and one solo section (bars 173ff.) which – having no strings – sounds like one of Haydn's *Feld Parthien*.

In the Andante, the scoring is bassoon solo, violins I, II and violoncello *concertante*, balanced by a *ripieno* of string orchestra and *basso continuo*. With its series of dotted figures, it is very much of its period. It is also one of those curious movements in Haydn which recall that as soon as he became a courtier he adopted something of a mask to conceal his personal, private emotions. One result of this mask is his extraordinary ability to adopt different attitudes, to compose in various styles; another is that a beautiful movement such as this one contains no clear 'message'. It is neither sad nor happy; it is above emotions (in itself, the courtly dotted figures are in themselves polite masks). We can easily conjure up the atmosphere in which it was first played in one of the halls of Eisenstadt Castle or the Vienna Palace – they are all there for our inspection. But no amount of staring into the past can quite give us an ability to get behind this delicate, subtle, exquisitely scored music which lies before us in all its beauty but whose emotional message we strive in vain to understand.

The 'Menuetto' is perhaps the most popular of those in the trilogy. It has that irresistible rhythmic drive for which Haydn's minuets were soon famous through Europe. This is accomplished by various adroit technical means. One is the constant forward drive of the crotchets which continue except for two crotchet rests (bar 24) throughout the entire minuet. If there is a minim in the bass line, the upper parts have crotchets (bar 6); if there is minim in the top line, the bass has crotchets (bars 9, 11, 13). The juxtaposition of minims with crotchets also add to this infinitely kinetic music:

♩ ♩ | ♩♩♩ | ♩♩♩ | ♩♩♩ |

(bars 9ff.). The connoisseurs (which meant the entire public: Prince Paul Anton, his family and his guests; we hope that Prince Nicolaus was in the audience as well) will have relished the plunge into minor during the second part (bars 21ff.), in the middle of a long wind-band solo to which the viola, after a few bars, adds a delicately poised touch of colour (bars 21ff.). The Trio, although continuing the trilogy's tradition of featuring a double bass (*violone*) solo, is in the same modern style as the Minuet: but with a difference. If we examine the metric division, we shall see that Haydn has returned to the 'raised eyebrows' of the first movement, that is to say the beginning is, here, 6 + 4 + 2 + 6; the second part starts 2 + 2 + 6 (with bar 5 extended by a *fermata*) and finishes like the beginning. For all its outward melodic simplicity, it can be seen that the construction is not without its idiosyncrasies.

The Finale, which the composer entitled 'La tempesta', is a typical Baroque conceit, one that we find in the Italian masters,[1] and in the Finale of Ignaz Holzbauer's Symphony in E flat, Op. IV, No. 3 (Madame Bérault, Paris) we also find a 'tempesta di mare'. The flute is used to depict lightning (bar 14ff.), and curious though this may seem, we must remember that the orchestra Haydn had at his disposal was really a chamber group with no trumpets, trombones or timpani (instruments otherwise available in Vienna in 1761). Even when he had a huge orchestra, as in *Die Jahreszeiten* (1801), when the time came to depict a storm it was still the flute(s) that depicted lightning. The *concertino* of two solo violins and solo 'cello is still retained, and perhaps because it is a piece of straight programme music, this Finale perhaps comes closest in manner (if not, of course, in style) to Vivaldi's *Seasons* – among Prince Paul Anton's favourites, as we have seen.

The trilogy was a great achievement, and it must have been clear to the whole Esterházy family that they had in their *Vice Capellmeister* one of the finest musical minds in Europe. Although a graceful tribute to the music of Corelli, Geminiani, Vivaldi and the Scarlattis, 'Le Matin', 'Le Midi' and 'Le Soir' were nevertheless very up-to-date music, and their scores show us that Haydn's small orchestra must have contained as fine musicians as could be assembled anywhere in Europe. The trilogy was a highly auspicious beginning to Haydn's new career with the greatest Hungarian magnate of the age.

Symphony No. 9 in C

Scoring: 2 flutes, 2 oboes, bassoon, 2 horns, strings [harpsichord *continuo*].

The autograph of this work was formerly owned by Artaria and was dated 1762.[1] Ending as it does with the Menuetto and Trio, we have long suggested that this Symphony might have served originally as the Overture to one of the Italian 'comedie'. Also, the whole thematic material and organization of the opening movement is more that of an overture than a real symphony: the fanfares, runs and roulades remind one of Italian opera overtures and of Haydn's own Overture to *Acide*, discussed above (p. 440). The opening movement is scored for oboes, horns and strings. The Andante which follows introduces two flutes and drops the horns. The use of triplet semiquavers also seems to be bound up in Haydn's mind with the slow movement of opera overtures, for we find them in *Acide*'s middle movement and even as late as the Andante in the Overture to *Lo speziale* (1768). In the Menuetto we return to the scoring of the first movement, except for one surprise in the Trio (a delicious waltz[2] which astonishes because of its early date – then they would have called it a 'Ländler'): in the second part we read, over the bass line 'Fagotto' and later 'Tutti bassi'. The solo bassoon part is the bass line of a charming windband section. It shows, of course, that Haydn expected the bassoon to double the bass line although not specifically required until this tiny solo in the Trio.

Apart from serving as an overture to a 'comedia', Symphony No. 9 can also have had its première as the beginning of one of the Esterházy cantatas, such as the lost original of the *Motetto di Sancta Thecla* (*supra*, p. 496). It has the same rather un-symphonic gestures that we also feel vaguely in Symphony No. 25.

Symphony No. 25 in C

Scoring: 2 oboes, 2 horns, strings [bsn. and harpsichord *continuo*]. The watermarks of the Budapest source (Philharmonia, vol. II, p. xlv), which by the way comes from Tata Castle, seat of a collateral branch of the Esterházys,[3] are: three crescents of decreasing size alone or with the letter 'м'; 'GFA' (Galvani Fratelli, Pordenone) under canopy; large fleur-de-lys; half cup (bow?) with arrow running through it and the cut-off bottom of letters 'AZ'

1 E.g. Vivaldi's Concerto for flute, oboe, violin, bassoon and orchestra (three versions: Ryom 98, 433, 570), entitled *La tempesta di mare*.

1 *Thematisches Verzeichnis der sämtlichen Kompositionen von Joseph Haydn*, zusammengestellt von Alois Fuchs 1839. Faksimile-Nachdruck herausgegeben von Richard Schall. Wilhelmshaven 1968, p. 11: '... Comp. 1762. [theme] Aut. b[ei] Art:[aria]'.
2 The first edition of No. 9 was as No. 4 in Bailleux's œuvre vii (Paris, announced in *L'avantcoureur* on 2 Oct. 1769), of which no copy survives(!). Gerber, in *NTL*, tells us that when the edition appeared, 'the last two [Nos. 9 and 3] were the most successful. Especially that in C because of the winning oboe Trio of the minuet.'
3 Kornél Bárdos, *A tatai Esterházyak zenéje 1727–1846*, Budapest 1978, p. 131, item 330. On Tata Castle, see also K. Bárdos in *HJB* X, pp. 29ff.

(similar to Bartha-Somfai No. 71, 1777). The top of the parts marked 'N^{ro} 10. Sig. G. Hayden'. The source must date from the middle of the 1770s, not earlier. The earliest source is possibly that, now lost, made in the 1760s by P. Joseph, *Regens chori* at Göttweig Abbey.

As we have seen, at this period Haydn uses the slow introduction sparingly, preferring whole opening slow movements in the *sonata da chiesa* tradition. Here we have an interesting compromise: a very extended Adagio introduction which starts out as if it would become an entire movement of its own. But by about bar 12 we see that the music is going to remain in the tonic and that the pedal on V is about to lead us back to C major. The following Allegro molto is of that tight rhythmic structure and nervous forward drive that now mark the Eisenstadt style. There is an almost perfect example of a *fausse reprise* in the middle section (bars 94ff.): a 'false recapitulation' which in fact leads to further development, so that by the time we reach the dominant of A minor we realize that the return was only a sham. The real recapitulation occurs at bar 133. Great is our surprise to hear a Menuet as second movement. Is this to be another work in which the positions of the minuet and slow movement are reversed (as in the Morzin Symphonies 'B' and 32)? The Trio is like a divertimento, with solo horn and solo oboe parts throughout, the strings in pizzicato accompaniment. By the time the third movement (Presto) is under way, we realize to our astonishment that Haydn has simply done away with the slow movement altogether. The Finale turns out to be a terse 2/4 movement in what one might call (for want of a better term) abbreviated sonata form, the 'development' and 'recapitulation' being skilfully merged and the main theme being introduced with itself in canon between the top and bottom lines (bars 67ff.), a small motif from the exposition (♩ ♪ ♪ ♪) serving as a sort of countersubject. The whole Symphony, in its extreme brevity and telescoped form (no slow movement, Finale with merged development and reprise), suggests the theatre or the cantata. As in Symphony No. 9, we suggest that the explanation for No. 25's curious form is that it originally served as the prelude to a piece like *La Marchesa Nespola*, or perhaps even as late as the 'Da qual gioja improviso' Cantata of 1764. The precise chronological placement within a given year of an undated work like No. 25 (earliest reference: 1766) is impossible on stylistic grounds alone.

Symphony No. 14 in A

Scoring: 2 oboes, 2 horns and strings [bsn. and harpsichord *continuo*].

The autograph of this delightful miniature Symphony has not survived. The oldest and textually most reliable copies were made by Joseph Elssler: one is in the University Library of Frankfurt-am-Main and the other was owned by Dr Stocker in Linz and is now in the library of St

Florian Abbey. Haydn was apparently interested in writing compressed symphonies in the early 1760s, for we have not only the *scherzandi* but also works like Symphonies Nos. 12 (1763) and 14. Unlike No. 12, No. 14 includes a minuet and is thus a perfect, if small-sized, specimen of a Haydn symphony composed during this period. There are no particular experiments; yet if one were to choose any single work to illustrate a well-proportioned and sophisticated symphony of the early classical period, this one, just because it indulges in no formal or instrumental experiments, would serve perfectly.

In the first movement we may observe a stylistic trait which is typical of all Haydn's symphonies of the 1760s: the whole structure is held together by the constantly repeated quavers in the bass line.[1] This lends to the music some of that nervous, restless quality which we associate with the young composer, bursting with energy and vitality. It is something particularly Haydnesque, and while all his life he liked to keep the music 'moving forward' by this device, it is especially in these early works that the repeated quaver (or if in barred C, repeated crotchet) assumes such an insistent, driving force. This great unifying factor must have fascinated Haydn's contemporaries, too; for it was just these symphonies of the 1760s that began to circulate in manuscript copies throughout Austria, Bohemia and Hungary and which spread his name throughout Central Europe. It is revealing to see the astuteness with which the monks of the great Austrian and Bohemian monasteries collected Haydn's music. By 1770 such abbeys as Melk, Göttweig and St Florian owned more symphonies and quartets by Haydn than they did by almost any other composer. When one of the monks wrote on the title page of a symphony 'male', there was generally a good reason. Towards the end of the 1760s Haydn was producing such masterpieces as Symphonies 26 ('Lamentatione') and No. 39 in G minor, and when the monks at Lambach Abbey acquired the rather low-pitched Symphony No. 58 they thought it 'schlecht'. No. 14, to return to our work at hand, exists in copies of the period in the following abbeys: Göttweig (1764, lost; another copy, this time in score, survives), St Florian, Melk, Lambach (before 1768 when it was entered in the Lambach Catalogue), Osek, and others known only from catalogues. It was, moreover, printed no less than twice in Paris, once in 1769 by Madame Bérault, as œuvre viii, No. 1 (announced on 11 December 1769 in the *Affiches, Annonces & Avis divers*) and the next year by Simon & Fils in a joint edition of 'Trois Symphonies / a grand et petit / orchestre, / par del Signor Richter, / del Sig. Ginsepp [*sic*] Toeschi, / del Sig. Huyden [*sic*] . . .'. This list, taken all together, meant a wide distribution for Symphony No. 14.

We have said that elements of the concerto, opera (recitative), divertimento and suite – non-symphonic forms, in other words – are occasion-

---

1 For the origins of this device, *vide supra*, p. 100.

ally woven into the fabric of Haydn's symphonies. The second movement of No. 14, an Andante which became very popular and was even printed for keyboard in *Wöchentliche Nachrichten, die Musik betreffend*, 32stes Stück (Leipzig, 3 February 1767), was originally the Finale (a theme and variations) of a very early Divertimento in C (II:11) – *vide supra*, pp. 183ff., where the differences in techniques are explained. Haydn created a whole movement in No. 14 using this obviously successful tune; he changed the original shape, which was symmetrical, making it asymmetrical and adding a 'cello part doubling the melody at the octave. The divertimento technique persists in the Menuetto (note the horns' solo passage at 17ff.) and especially in the Trio, where the viola part is dropped and there is an oboe solo accompanied only by violins and 'cello-bass (tonic minor). In the final movement we anticipate the *cantus firmus* technique of which the Finale of No. 13 (1763) will be a typical example. Here in No. 14 we have a two part subject (only for violins I and II) written in double counterpoint at the octave. The whole movement is a fascinating hybrid; the old 'light' (6/8) metre is combined with the revival of contrapuntal texture which was to play such a significant role in Haydn's hands as the 1760s progressed; we even have little stretti. Thus this miniature Symphony contains a number of revealing stylistic permutations that obviously made it a great success with Haydn's European contemporaries. Something of this universal popularity may be seen in the extant sources of almost every single work now under discussion – monastery, prince, Viennese professional copyist and French publisher all vied with each other to procure copies of these new works.

Symphony No. 36 in E flat

Scoring: 2 oboes, 2 horns, strings (with *violino principale and violoncello solo*) [*continuo*: bsn., harpsichord]

Although the very Baroque organization of the slow movement with its *concertino* (violin & 'cello) and *ripieno* suggests Prince Paul Anton's taste and a chronological proximity to Nos. 6–8, many of the other stylistic features of No. 36 point to the Morzin period: (1) the second subject of the first movement is in the dominant *minor* (rather than major), a trait that Haydn inherited from his Austrian predecessors and which is found in many of the Lukavec works (e.g. Symphonies Nos. 1, 2, 4, etc.) but hardly in those of the Esterházy period; (2) none of the movements in No. 36, with the possible exception of the Trio in the Minuet, employs symmetrical four- or eight-bar periods. Even if we stretch a point and consider the opening subject of the Finale as 4 + 4, it is still very much a pre-classical concept. Despite these reservations, however, we have placed the work where it is on the overwhelming evidence of the solo string writing, which never occurs in this form in any known Morzin symphony.

The sturdy opening Vivace of No. 36 reflects the sunny warmth so characteristic of Haydn's writing in E flat. The theme is one which extends itself in asymmetrical phrase lengths and generates its strength by rhythmic rather than melodic tension. Such phrases as

$$\frac{3}{4} \; \text{♩.} \quad \text{♫♩♫} \; | \; \text{♫♩♫♫♫}$$

accompanied by semiquavers in V.II and by quavers in the lower strings generate a momentum of their own. The second subject in B flat minor is constructed in Baroque imitations, but the rhythmic basis of the first subject returns afterwards to conclude the exposition. The second part is not a development in the later sense of the word: here the material is further extended. There now occurs a device which we know from Symphony No. 17 (another work which cannot be dated precisely): the second part begins with the first theme in the dominant, followed by a rapid transition (simply marching down the interval of the fifth between V and I) to the tonic and a repetition of the theme in the home key. Only *after* this procedure does the extension begin, and also the modulation to remoter keys. Two offshoots of this practice may be observed. (1) It is the basis for what will soon (Symphony No. 25) become the *fausse reprise*; but to create a 'false recapitulation' there must be much more time between the statement of the theme, or whatever, in the dominant and the statement in the tonic, which then turns out to be a springboard for further development rather than a recapitulation. A brilliant early example of such a *fausse reprise* occurs in the first movement of No. 41.[1] (2) This return to the tonic as a beginning of the development section is a feature of Haydn's mature sonata-rondos, usually finales (Symphony No. 85/IV). There is little doubt that this Baroque turn of key (as one might call it) in No. 36, and in many other first movements of the early symphonies, is a device that later became expanded to different and structurally more potent means. Both parts of the movement are to be repeated, as is usually the case in the early symphonies: this in itself presupposes that there will not be a great crisis in the development leading to a dramatically important recapitulation, for such a second section could hardly be repeated. The later Haydn – of the London Symphonies – writes such unrepeatable second sections. But in the early 1760s the symphony was not yet a dramatic form of expression (exceptions: Franz Beck and some of the symphonies by Filtz), nor had it been exposed to the wit of comic opera. Haydn, using these Baroque or pre-classical methods of construction, is nevertheless able to create an interesting and taut piece of music that retains an extraordinary high level of rhythmic tension.

We assume that the string solo parts were intended for Tomasini and Weigl, respectively. As in the first movement of the C major Violin Concerto, the texture and language of this majestic

1 *Haydn at Eszterháza 1766–1790*, p. 296.

561

Adagio are exaggeratedly Baroque. It is written like the slow movement of a double concerto for violin and 'cello with string orchestra and *continuo* harpsichord (no wind parts). There is the clear division of tutti and soli and the piece is written in Vivaldian ritornello form, the ritornello appearing, *forte*, at bars 1ff., 5ff. 14ff. (dominant), 17ff. (dominant), 30f. (tonic), 37f. Sometimes the ritornello is shortened, but it is usually slightly varied. The same general type of dotted figures as in the Violin Concerto strengthen the archaic effect.

As if to offset this nod to the past, the Menuetto is in the newest style, with those Austrian snaps (♪♪♪·) which Haydn so much likes at this period and even retains as late as the Minuet in Symphony No. 87 (1785). The Trio is very original, using the oboe like an organ stop in the first section. In the Finale we note the many imitative effects between top and bottom lines and the way in which the four string parts suddenly broaden into complex polyphonic writing (bars 16ff.); but note, too, that the phrase of bar 3 (♩· ♪ ♪♪♪♪) in the violins is now (bars 17ff.) retained in the second violin and bottom line in contrary motion. The second subject (bars 29ff.) is once again in the dominant *minor* (as was the case in the first movement) and has an intriguing rhythmic pattern – first violin in repeated semiquavers, lower strings entering in curiously unsettling, off-beat quavers. Closing section of part one: return to the phrase of bar 3 (quoted above), which continues to dominate the whole of the middle section up to bar 71. The compulsive use of this little phrase cements the whole movement together and gives it a unity which the symmetrical structure encourages: therefore the subjects can afford to be asymmetrical.

Symphony No. 12 in E

Scoring: 2 oboes, 2 horns, strings [*continuo*: bsn., harpsichord].

The internal chronology of the three Symphonies known to have been composed in 1763 (Nos. 12, 13 and 40) can no longer be established. In the valuable thematic catalogue of Haydn's symphonies up to 1790 prepared by his friend, Ritter von Keeß, the three works are listed as Nos. 12, 15 and 16. Each is an entity and each completely different from each other: the dashing bravura of No. 13, with its four horns and (later) kettledrums; the elegant, suave No. 40, with its pixie-like, wistful slow movement and its concluding fugue; and the present work, radiant, glowing, with something of a fresh Spring day about it.

Like No. 14, No. 12 is a perfect miniature symphony. The miniature quality of No. 12 is reflected not only in the small size of the work as a whole – it lasts little longer than fourteen minutes with all the repeats – but also in the construction of the individual movements. The opening *piano* (as opposed to the *forte* that would of habit, if not

necessity, open a grand symphony 'avec trompettes et timballes'). The warmth of the key, E major, and the brightness of the string sound are well utilized. The second subject, with an imitation between upper and lower strings, continues the intimate tone. In the passage at the end of the second subject, we have a striking preview (bars 44ff.) of the Overture to *Die Zauberflöte* (introduction, bars 10ff.). Mozart of 1791 is rather a long way from Haydn of 1763, but Symphony No. 12 illustrates just in this one interesting relationship that it is the gate to the Viennese classical period: a modest gate but beautifully wrought.

All during these experimental years, Haydn's symphonies weave into their pattern elements of other musical forms: the concerto, *concerto grosso*, divertimento, *Feld Parthie* and (as we have seen) *opera seria*. No. 12's slow movement, an Adagio in 'siciliano', rocking rhythm, also has its roots in the operatic aria – not so much in the actual form but in the underlying spirit. It is a rather serious movement in E minor, and is full of gestures (bar 3, violin I's *forte*) that remind us of Italian opera: the gesture is broadened in the middle section (bars 29f., 33f.). The virility of this music forms (as was clearly intended) an excellent foil to the soft and gracious warmth of the opening Allegro.

There is no minuet. The Finale (marked 'Allegro di molto' on most early MSS. but 'Presto' on the autograph – we believe the former is a change made on the [lost] original parts to warn against too swift a tempo) bubbles over with high spirits. The jaunty opening subject acquires its lilt from the peculiar type of phrasing which accentuates the up-beats. The furious but skilfully controlled energy of this Finale also gives us a clue to the kind of movement that will dominate Haydn's symphonic thought in 1764 and 1765: its culmination, the furthest point to which this energy can be strained, will be seen in the opening movement of Symphony No. 24 and the Finale of No. 29.

Haydn was in such high spirits that he even forgot to add his usual 'laus Deo' at the end of the manuscript.

Symphony No. 13 in D

Scoring: flute, 2 oboes, 4 horns, timpani and strings [*continuo*: bsn. and harpsichord].

Of the three symphonies composed in 1763, No. 13 is the grandest. Part of its immediate effect is the large size of the orchestra, one of the biggest Haydn used until 1774. The orchestra was now enlarged to include four horns, the engagement of which has been registered in the Chronicle (*supra*, pp. 385f.). It is not only that the size of the orchestra is bigger on paper but Haydn knows how to make this large wind band sound new and different. The autograph (EH, Budapest) shows Haydn's high spirits in a touching and graphic way, with elaborate flourishes to conclude each movement. The impressive opening – in which the wind instruments are used in massive blocked chords, holding the harmony over many bars like a sonorous organ while the strings pierce through with their highly rhythmic unison figure – owes, as Dr Jürgen Meyer has conclusively shown, much to the church-like acoustics of the great hall in Eisenstadt (*vide supra*, p. 307). It is a totally different sound than that of Nos. 6–8, composed for the Esterházy Palace in Vienna.

In the autograph, the timpani part was added at the bottom of each page on a free stave; but not in Haydn's hand. The ink suggests, however, that it was added early, possibly by the timpanist Adam Sturm, perhaps under Haydn's supervision (contrary to Haydn's later habit of notation, the drums are in transposing notation, i.e. in C and G; Haydn, at least later, writes for the timpani in sounding notation). It contributes to the dash and vigour of the quick movements. Actually, we have evidence that the timpani part is contemporary, for we find it in several copies: Archives of the Princes of Oettingen-Wallerstein (Harburg Castle); Archives of the Counts of Waldstein in Hirschberg (Doksy) Castle, now National Museum, Prague; and in the music archives of Náměšť Castle (Count Heinrich von Haugwitz).

Unlike its numerical mate, No. 12, the present D major is a festive piece. There is hardly anything of the chamber musical atmosphere of No. 12, and indeed there is something rather operatic about the first movement of No. 13 – the same kind of gesture (in a different context) that we noted in connection with No. 12's Adagio. In No. 13/I, there is no real second subject, and most of the movement is built round the terse pattern of the strings at the beginning. The little figure at bars 15ff. (with upbeat) assumes overriding importance in the development section. The recapitulation brings in the whole first subject *piano* instead of *forte*, reserving the *f* for a dramatic fanfare for the four horns, striding up the open harmonics of their instruments.

The second movement borrows a leaf from the contemporary concerto: it could be the slow movement of one of Haydn's 'cello concertos of the period (scoring: strings only). Here we have *concertante* music in the noblest early classical tradition, an arioso without formal pretentions (no stiff ritornelli, no chains of dotted figures): highly decorated but never overladen, luxuriant but never too long. We have moved a step away from the *concertante* movement of No. 36, and specifically we have moved away from the typical Baroque structure to early classical.

In No. 12 there was no time for a minuet. But No. 13 is on a bigger scale and the *Menuet* is written with the same panache as the rest of the work. There are many strong dynamic contrasts, especially the striking *pianissimo* passage in the second part (strings and horns, bars 23ff.) which sets off the dramatic chordal pattern of the opening and closing sections. The Trio is again a solo – this time for the flute; but whereas the slow movement drew its inspiration from the concerto, the Trio seems to approach the divertimento form, in which the trios were often reserved for a solo

player. The light style and 'Lombard' rhythm[1] when the flute plays without accompaniment take us to the world of *Tafelmusik*.

We have seen in No. 3 how Haydn experimented with the fugue to lend greater power and weight to his finales, a procedure culminating in the famous fugal finales of the Op. 20 Quartets (1772), where the fugue reaches proportions of epic grandeur and noble emotions. Apart from this severe style – Haydn would have perhaps referred to it as 'lo stile antico' – the composer essayed various other methods to make the final movements more weighty in content. Here in No. 13 he uses a Fuxian *cantus firmus* together with a countersubject in third species counterpoint: it is the Gregorian 'Credo' theme of Mozartian fame (Symphonies: K.319 and, of course, K.551's Finale), the history of which has been admirably traced by A. Hyatt King.[2] No. 13's Finale is not a fugue, however, but a deft combination of sonata and fugue (a *stretto* at bars 145ff.); and it was in this hybrid form that the Viennese Classical School was to revive, in a last golden harvesting, the beauty and strength of a vast contrapuntal tradition that stretched back unbroken to the late Middle Ages.

Symphony No. 40 in F

Scoring: 2 oboes, 2 horns, strings [*continuo*: bsn., harpsichord]. In the autograph the Trio is scored for oboes, horns and strings; but in one contemporary MS., a late copy from the library of Archduke Rudolph, it is scored for oboes, horns and bassoon with the strings silent. We have no idea if this charming version is authentic.

The first movement is a breezy Allegro in 3/4, with the same asymmetrical quality and self-propelling motivic continuation that we noticed in No. 36/I. The forward-moving character of the theme, which is clearly felt, is achieved by rhythmic diminution, or to put it in another way by constantly decreasing the lengths of the note values, viz.;

Like so many movements of the early 'sixties, there is no real subject (or rather no real 'tune'); when Haydn reaches the dominant, he pauses a moment and then resumes the spinning out, or extension, of material found in the opening subject.

The slow movement (Andante più tosto allegretto, B flat, 2/4) is one of the most original and delightful of the period. It owes its basic character – a 'quick slow movement', one might term it – and the use of two-part harmony throughout (top line: violins I, II; bottom line:

---

1 *Vide supra*, p. 534.
2 *Mozart in Retrospect*, London 1955 (2nd ed. 1970), pp. 262ff.

viola doubling 'cello-bass at the octave or unison) to the famous 'Mann und Weib' movement of the early C major Divertimento ('Der Geburtstag'; II:11). This was the famous two-part texture that is one of the principal pillars of Haydn's early style. It was, in one sense, a deliberate return to the type of *continuo* writing of the Baroque period, in which the harpsichord filled in all the missing harmonies; but Haydn has brought the device 'up to date', has filled it with his modern rhythms and harmonies, his wit, and his delicately balanced formal sense. If one analyzes this movement, it will be observed that it is executed with the greatest attention to detail, so that (for example) the second part, after the double bar, balances the first without directly repeating the opening material. Only once, in his 106 symphonies, does he treat us to this kind of light, dancing 'Midsummer Night's Dream' music whose subtle, scherzo-like effervescence brings us close to the enchanted world of Mendelssohn.

The *Menuet* is beautifully rounded and sonorous, with a delightful Trio almost like a divertimento of the period. The Finale is a fugue; apart from one more fascinating example (the giant triple fugue at the end of Symphony No. 70 in D composed to honour Prince Nicolaus's birthday, and the laying of the cornerstone of the new theatre at Eszterháza, in 1779), it is the last time in a symphony when Haydn has recourse to an elaborate fugue. As we know, Haydn's contrapuntal education was largely taken from Fux's *Gradus ad Parnassum*, and No. 40's fugue is predictably Fuxian, with the *cantus firmus* melodies that we find in the great textbook. It was Haydn's favourite practice to announce the fugue simultaneously with its countersubject in a kind of third species of counterpoint. Actually, the previous fugues have something slightly schoolmasterish about them: the reek of the classroom (or rather the Fuxian page) rather than the orchestral hall. But in No. 40 Haydn creates a strict fugue along his own lines: the rest at the beginning of bar 3 in the subject provides a typically Haydnesque impetus to the whole contrapuntal texture. Incidentally, one realizes at once what makes this movement such a successful combination of *stile antico* and Haydn: the episodic material, as it is described in theoretical treatises, is textually contrapuntal but has a strong motivic and rhythmical background that brings us forward to 1763. The ends of such episodes will also revert to Haydn's usual orchestral texture, and of course the work must conclude with a rousing pedal point – a tremendous build-up of motion and tension (the syncopated violins are most important here), followed by the kind of unison that Haydn so loved and that his listeners undoubtedly received with the satisfaction of hearing a 1763 sound at the end of a 1663 historical revival. The movement is a brilliant *tour-de-force* but not something Haydn chose to repeat often in a symphonic work. The movement is, apart from its intrinsic interest, one of the blocks with which the composer would one day construct the towering fugual masterpieces of the late Masses and Oratorios.

Symphony No. 72 in D

Scoring: 1 flute, 2 oboes, 1 bassoon, 4 horns, strings (violin solo, 'cello solo, *violone* [double bass] solo), [harpsichord *continuo*]. In one MS. (GdM, Vienna: XIII, 41 540) there is a dubious timpani part which is certainly not original.

We have suggested that this work, with its four horns, belongs to the year 1763 rather than 1765 (when its spiritual partner, No. 31, was composed), and that No. 72 is the first of its kind. If in No. 13 Haydn was at pains to show the effective use of four horns as part of a wind ensemble, in No. 72 we have a display piece similar to the Cassatio in D discussed above (pp. 523ff.), written around the four horn players, whose virtuoso abilities are displayed in a spectacular way. The beginning of the Symphony sounds more like a divertimento, but at bar 8, the four horns suddenly blanket the texture, running up and down scales and arpeggios in the most astonishing operation of its kind Haydn ever undertook. The first horn rises to sounding *f sharp''*. The rest of this extremely original Allegro is Haydn's tightrope walk, formally speaking, between the horns' *concertante* music and the theme with which the movement opened, which when it takes over from the horns in bar 25 develops into a much more symphonic texture than the divertimento-like beginning (and the typical divertimento 'light' 2/4 metre) would have led us to believe. The tension that Haydn manages to create by this juxtaposition is revealing: by using his beginning all through the development, Haydn slides into the recapitulation without using bars 1–8 of the exposition. We are simply led (always with the material of the first subject) into the fantastic horn solo again.

Haydn has reserved the flute for the second movement (Andante), which is in a hybrid mixture of divertimento and concerto. Without any ritornello – just as in No. 13's slow movement for solo 'cello – the music starts with a solo for Tomasini, accompanied by strings only (horns are silent), in the modern symmetrical pattern of four bars, each formed by the identical appearance of

the figure ♩ ♪♪ ♪♪♪♪ . This is then given to the solo flute, and the rest of the movement is a dialogue in the form of a double concerto but presented like a divertimento.

The horns are back in the *Menuet*, and are used in echo fashion, again suggesting that they were separated at the back (front?) of the orchestra, one pair on the left and one on the right. The flute is again silent, and is not used until the Finale. Continuing his series of daring experiments, Haydn scored the Trio for wind band only (2 oboes, 1 bassoon, 4 horns), a larger-than-life *Feld Parthie*, again with echo effects between horns I–II and III–IV which make it essential in modern performance to divide the horns in such a way that the echo effect makes an impact.

The Finale (full orchestra including flute) is a theme and variations of that slowly marching kind (Andante); there are many such movements in the earlier divertimenti and cassations, and they must have struck an instantly responsive chord in Haydn's listeners. (He never repeats an unsuccessful idea.) Variation I is for flute solo and strings; Variation II for solo 'cello and strings; Variation III for solo violin and strings; Variation IV for *violone* solo and strings, the technical aspects of which have been discussed *supra* (p. 557); Variation V for oboes, horns I, II (used quite normally) and strings; Variation VI for flute, oboes, bassoon, all four horns and strings (no particularly difficult music for the horns). We notice that Haydn is now very fastidious about his four virtuoso horn players: they have displayed their fantastic abilities in the first movement, have rested through the slow movement, have had complicated but not extremely difficult solo passages in the Minuet & Trio, and are now given easy music because it is assumed that their lips will be tired from their previous exertions. It is a typical Haydnesque touch: always to consider the needs of his musicians, and we will see evidences of this fatherly care for his orchestra all through his life.

Variation VI ends with a little coda which modulates to a half-close, whereupon there is a gigantic surprise. Having taken the basic structure of the movement hitherto from the divertimento, Haydn now turns to the suite and introduces a Presto in a different metre and with entirely different music. In dance music of the period, this kind of procedure was known as the *Kehraus*, the signal that it is time to go home. Of course, horns were associated with hunting, and to underline the meaning of the hunting metre (6/8), the Symphony ends with a flourish of the four horns. We shall see that Haydn retains this form *in toto*, with minor changes in the details, as the Finale of Symphony No. 31.

Symphony No. 21 in A

Scoring: 2 oboes, 2 horns, strings [*continuo*: bsn., harpsichord]. The internal chronology of Nos. 21–4 (dated autographs of all four: 1764, in EH, Budapest) cannot be established. In the Keeß Catalogue and *HV* they appear as follows:

Work	Keeß	HV
21	17	16
22	21	20
23	19	18
24	20	19

Apart from the autograph of No. 21, old parts by Joseph Elssler also survive (St Florian Abbey), formerly owned by Dr Stocker in Linz.

Yet another *sonata da chiesa* work, probably with No. 22 the first for the Esterházy Court: Nos. 5, 11 and 18 – all in this form – are known to have been Morzin works. But if we compare this Adagio with those of the three previous works, we will notice that Haydn's touch has become more subtle, more refined. In No. 21's Adagio there is no double bar and the whole movement proceeds in a new kind of intense monothematicism. The wind

instruments have suddenly become vitally important, and they are used here not in a divertimento-concerto fashion (as they had been in No. 5) but in the newer symphonic style, dividing the whole opening thematic material with the strings. One notes the rare dynamic mark *mezzo f* which the viola is given when it accompanies the wind instruments (bar 4). The quietly undulating opening figure

carries the whole of this movement, whose remarkable free form approaches that of a capriccio or fantasia. The bracketed section of the main theme is the binding link, used at bars 16ff. in second violins with the first violins proceeding with a derivative of bar 3. In the dominant, the figure appears in a long passage of great intensity and beauty, in which it is given to the 'cellos and basses (bars 29ff., the bass line marked 'tenute'). The 'recapitulation' (the sonata form terms are meaningless in this formal context) introduces the essence of the theme in a breathtaking *pianissimo*, and in *stretto*.

After the melodic and structural intensity of this opening, Haydn needs to provide a wide contrast; he does this by writing a movement in 4/4 in which a very tight rhythmic control is exercized throughout. The very beginning

♩. ♪ ♫♫ | ♩ carries in its shape a sub-sidiary rhythmic pattern which dominates large sections of the movement (bars 10f., 12f., transition to the dominant 17–21, development 43ff., etc.). As this Symphony progresses we observe an interesting fact: that the highpoint of the work was the opening Adagio and that the rest of the work is a gradual descent from that pinnacle; the same may be said to apply to all Haydn's church-sonata symphonies, even to the greatest of them (No. 49) and this, essentially, was probably why he abandoned the form in the symphony after 1768. The symphony as such always tended, even its primitive state as an Italian *sinfonia*, to be head-loaded: that is, the greatest intellectual, or in the case of the Italian overtures the noisiest, parts came at the beginning; the same applied to the Austrian chamber symphony, in which interest centred intellectually around the first two movements, whereas the minuet (if there was one) and the finale tapered off and relaxed the intellectual pressure. In a *sonata da chiesa* this element was even more accentuated, especially when the form was applied to the already top-heavy Austrian chamber symphony. Haydn of course cannot avoid his own trap, but he finds delightful ways of making the let-down a pleasant one.

It will be noted that the first eight notes of the *Menuet* were taken over by Mozart and used *verbatim* in *Eine kleine Nachtmusik* (K.525), another interesting case – we have seen one in Symphony No. 12 – of Mozart's assimilating a piece in his youth and storing it in his unconscious, from which it emerged, unbidden, many years later. (The most famous case of this kind is the *Requiem* [K.626], which utilizes many features of the *Requiem* for Archbishop Schrattenbach composed twenty years earlier at Salzburg by Johann Michael Haydn.) Haydn's Minuet is no longer a dance movement but is slightly quicker: the basic beat is now crotchets, and this basis is only disturbed by a few Lombard quavers ('Scottish snaps') in the central part. The difference between this kind of minuet and the one used for dancing may be seen graphically if we turn to the famous 'Minuet' in *Don Giovanni*, where the opening rhythmic pattern shows us that the basis must be the quaver:

♩ 𝅘𝅥𝅯𝅘𝅥𝅯𝅘𝅥𝅯𝅘𝅥𝅯 | 𝅗𝅥.𝅘𝅥𝅯 .

The Finale of No. 21 is again intensely rhythmic and bolsters up the tapering end of the work. Haydn has composed an Allegro molto which is formally much more like an opening movement than a Finale: though the thematic material, with its syncopations, would not have done for an opening allegro. To emphasize this first-movement feeling – first movement in an ordinary sonata structure, of course – Haydn links the rhythmic structure to his previous quick movement. The bracketed portion of the example of that Presto noted above also dominates large tracts of the Finale.

It is curious to find that Haydn made some rather important changes in this movement after he had completed the autograph; these changes are incorporated in the St Florian parts and mainly concern enlarged oboe parts (bars 76–80), supplementary oboe phrasing and, at the end, different horn notes. Since it is presumed that the orchestral materials of the period 1761–79 were destroyed in the great fire at Eszterháza in 1779, MSS such as St Florian's for this work (and for Nos. 14 and 29 as well) are invaluable since they show that Haydn made many changes in his works *after the autograph had been completed*. We know this to have obtained even in works of the London period (introduction of Symphony No. 102) and thereafter (soprano solo of the *Missa in angustiis* ['Nelson' Mass]). It means that, when we have works only surviving in secondary sources, we must be on the watch for textual operations of this kind: a perennial source of complications is the later addition of trumpets and timpani (positively authentic case: Symphony No. 70).

Symphony No. 22 in E flat
('Philosoph')

Scoring: 2 cors anglais, 2 horns, strings [*continuo*: bsn., harpsichord].

Usually, the names attached to Haydn's symphonies are marks of desperation to distinguish between large numbers of works in C, D and so on; but in the present case, the idea is better than usual. In fact this title was known in Haydn's lifetime: we find it on MS. parts in the Biblioteca

Estense, Modena (cat. D.145): 'Le Philosoph'. Haydn told his biographer Griesinger (62) that

> in his symphonies he often described – moral character. In one of his oldest, which he could not precisely indicate to me, 'the idea predominated of God speaking to an unrepentant sinner, asking him to reform, but the sinner in his rashness heeded not these exhortations.

Can this dialogue be the first movement of No. 22, a supreme example of the *sonata da chiesa* technique? Haydn sets this Adagio, surely one of the *settecento*'s supremely original concepts, as a kind of chorale prelude, in which the French horns intone the first part of chorale *ff* and the cors anglais answer, also *ff*. One may also analyze the formal structure as a sophisticated application of the Vivaldian ritornello: the chorale (or ritornello) returns in several different keys: I (opening), V (strings only, after the double bar, 23ff.), IV with cors anglais (bars 30ff.), II with cors anglais (bars 33f.), III with horns (marvellous climax as horn I rises to sounding *d''*: bars 40f.) and then the recapitulation. By this brief scheme one can see that Haydn has delicately combined an old Baroque tonal and formal scheme with the precursor of sonata form which predominates in this period (by which we mean: basic three parts,

double bar in the dominant ⟶ :||: ⟵

dividing the movement in the middle, and with repeat signs). In this deliberate return to an antique language, we note the beautiful Corelli-like suspensions with the 'walking' bass for just the strings and *continuo* (bars 50ff., just after the return of the first dialogue between French and English horns): as always, the use of this antique pattern from the Roman Baroque constitutes a point of great (if quiet) emotional stress, as it did in the slow movement of 'Le Matin'.

The highpoint of the Symphony is obviously this opening Adagio, round (or following) which the rest of the work was composed. As with No. 21, in the following *Presto* (4/4) we have the strongest contrast, and we note the use of the same

rhythm ♩. 𝅘𝅥𝅮 𝅘𝅥𝅯𝅘𝅥𝅯𝅘𝅥𝅯𝅘𝅥𝅯 | ♩ ♩ as a binding

force. Haydn's sense of tone colour was always aroused when writing for his favourite cors anglais, and they are used in a delightfully comic effect at the end of the exposition and recapitulation. In itself, the introduction of English horns into a symphony was a daring innovation but, interestingly, not one that Haydn chose to repeat: instead they are used increasingly in his vocal music all through the 1760s and the first half of 1770s, after which his interest in them (or Prince Nicolaus's?) seems to die out. In Haydn's mind, the cors anglais are primarily associated with E flat, though he also uses them in F (Divertimento, II:16, *vide supra.* p. 273) and C minor (Gasperina's Aria, 'Non v' è chi mi ajuta', from *La canterina*). The rhythm of this characteristic solo in No. 22/II is once again based on the rhythm of No. 21/II, repeated as the opening of No. 22/II (musical example, *supra*).

The final two movements of No. 22 present the same problem as in all church sonata symphonies: a natural, 'inbuilt' slackening of tension. The *Menuetto* has that same poised, crotchet-dominated rhythm that we noted in No. 21's Minuet. Whereas the Trio of No. 21 was quiet and rather old-fashioned (it recalls the previous generation of Austrian symphonic writers such as Wagenseil, and is intended to be another point of dynamic rest in that it never rises beyond *p*), the Trio of No. 22 is of the divertimento type; or rather a combination of *Feld Parthie* (solo wind writing throughout) and *Ländler* (string accompaniment, often off-beat ♩ ♩ | ♩ ♪ ♪).

In the Finale of No. 22 we see that Haydn's policy of making a virtue out of lightness and thus raising the (automatically falling) level of interest – divertimento and *Ländler* in the Trio – was deliberate. Using the typical finale metre of 6/8, Haydn introduces a new element: the hunt (*la chasse*). Nowadays, it is hard for us to imagine the profound effect that *la chasse* had on the Austrian aristocracy of the period (and not only Austrian, naturally). 'The hunt', writes Horace Fitzpatrick in his brilliant book, *The Horn & Horn-Playing and the Austro-Bohemian tradition 1680–1830* (London 1970, p. 20),

> stood for all that was desirable in wordly virtue, representing a new embodiment of the old *ritterlich-höfisch* (chivalrous-courtly) ideals which were at the centre of aristocratic thought. As the ceremonial and signal instrument of the hunt, the horn in turn became a symbol of these values. To a nobleman of the time the sound of the horn had the power to excite deep feelings, for it called forth those ideals and aspirations which lay at the very heart of the *adeliches Landleben*.

And 'courtly country life' is the essence of this Finale, with its 6/8 hunting metre and its horn calls (also given to the cors anglais). It calls forth the rolling hills of the Austro-Hungarian-Bohemian-Croatian countryside, and all the formal paraphernalia of a ceremonial *battue*. The scene has been depicted by numerous French painters. It is typical of Haydn that although he intends to call up memories of *la grande chasse*, the Finale of No. 22 is not primitive programme music but rather the symphonic application of the *idea* of the hunt (symbolized by the metre and the horn calls). In the remaining volumes of this biography, we shall have ample possibilities to see Haydn's varied treatment of the hunting theme, from Symphony No. 65's Finale, to the famous Overture to *La fedeltà premiata* called 'La Chasse' and later used as the Finale of Symphony No. 73, to the great hunting chorus of *The Seasons* – or a chronological span from 1764 (Symphony No. 22) to 1801.

There was a second version of No. 22 which began with the second movement, continued with a new Andante grazioso in 3/8 (A flat) and

concluded with the fourth movement (omitting the minuet). This version, in which flutes take the place of the cors anglais, was circulated in MS. as far as Spain and possibly South America (see *SYM*, 651), and was printed in 1773 by Venier in Paris (announced in the *Mercure de France*, April, pp. 189f.). The 'new' slow movement, which is pretty but of which there is no evidence of Haydn's authorship, is printed as Appendix I of the Philharmonia score (vol. II, pp. 189ff.) and the flute parts as substitutes for the cors anglais as Appendix II, pp. 191ff. (also, of course, in the full score by Doblinger). What can have been the origin of this curious hybrid? We believe that the original version of No. 22 was regarded as impossible to market (a) because of the strangely original opening Adagio and (b) because of the cors anglais, instruments which were not available in many parts of Europe.[1]

Symphony No. 23 in G

Scoring: 2 oboes, 2 horns, strings [*continuo*: bsn., harpsichord].

No. 23's opening is typical of its period: terse, tense, with an enormous sense of youthful energy. Its forward drive is hardly interrupted by *piano* sections at all (and these are only echo effects, or in passages where the oboe is accompanied). The use of *ff*, on the other hand (bar 10), is like a sudden splash of colour. Contrapuntal or polyphonic effects are gradually becoming more and more important to movements of this kind: consider the sweepingly powerful imitations between violins I & II at bars 65ff. in the development, which added to the omnipresent bass line in quavers and the nervous semiquavers in the violins, lend a kind of explosive high spirits to this music. In fact the level of tension in such opening movements is so breathtaking that the same falling-off occurs as in the *sonata da chiesa* symphonies. The quiet Andante which follows (no wind parts) is bound to be an anticlimax, because Haydn has not yet found (or perhaps even wanted to find) a proper way to balance the last third of the symphony with the first third.

The *Menuet* is an interesting formal experiment which created a profound impression on Haydn's contemporaries: it is a canon between the top (violins I, II, doubled by oboes) and bottom (viola doubling the 'cello and bass) lines at the interval of one bar, with the horns filling in the harmonies. One finds G major canonic minuets of this kind in two works by distinguished Salzburg contemporaries: four years later in Michael

---

1 Symphony No. 22 in its original version was also printed in Paris (with oboes instead of cors anglais) by Borelly (announced by the *Affiches, Annonces & Avis divers* on 7 May 1770, together with new symphonies by 'Vanhall' and 'Ditters'). The Haydn print was marked 'mis au jour par / Mᵉ Hugard de Sᵗ. Guy'. Copy: Grima Collection, Gefle, Sweden (now: Kungl. Musikaliska Akademiens Bibliotek, Stockholm). Title: see Hoboken, vol. I, p. 25. Hugard de St. Guy also issued several other works by Haydn of which no copy has survived and which are known to us only from catalogue notices (see Hoboken, ibid, 'NB').

Haydn's Symphony (Perger 7) made up of incidental music to *Die Hochzeit auf der Alm* (completed: 6 May 1768); and by Mozart in his Symphony, K.110 (75b), of 1771. Here is a clear case, with all the dates verified by autographs, of the manner in which a new Haydn idea travelled westwards. Haydn's Trio is also canonic (strings only, C major).

Symphony No. 23 was printed as part of œuvre viii (No. 6) by Madame Bérault, Paris (*vide supra*, Symphony No. 14), in December 1769.

Symphony No. 24 in D

Scoring: 1 flute (only in slow movt. and Trio), 2 oboes, 2 horns, strings [*continuo*: bsn., harpsichord].

The first movement of this work pushes to its outside limit the nervous, exuberant and exhilarating kind of allegro with which Haydn's music of the 1760s is filled. Of an almost appalling vitality, this music seems to create a new language: what shall we say of that figure at bar 23 which comes *four* times in succession? Or the development section, with those furious semiquavers in the upper strings (the beginning of each bar marked *ff*) and the relentless quavers in the bass line, which continues from bars 44–58 without stopping? It is controlled lunacy and is, naturally, a mannerist stroke that Haydn never repeated. The recapitulation, to reduce the temperature slightly, is *piano* and in the tonic minor. As a *tour-de-force*, however, this movement is unique and its terrifying intensity was not lost on his astute contemporaries: unlike almost all the works of this period, it seems that there is no Parisian print of No. 24 (or is it one of the lost Hugard de St Guy publications?); but it did come out in England, as 'The Favorite / Sinfonie' No. 11, published by John Bland, some time in the 1780s. It was surely works of this kind that led the English to call Haydn's style 'full of . . . phrenzy and fire'.[1]

We have noted the constancy with which Haydn infuses elements of divertimento and concerto into his symphonies, and returning to the kind of slow movement found in No. 13/II, we have in No. 24's Adagio what might have been the slow movement of Haydn's lost Flute Concerto in D. Although taken straight from the concerto form, Haydn follows the procedure of No. 13 by omitting the ritornello and beginning with the solo section: this makes for a less formalistic design. It is known that Haydn played a number of instruments, probably almost all then in general use: he had an immaculate sense of what was appropriate for each and the impeccable flute writing of this movement (accompaniment: strings only) makes us regret the Concerto's loss. There is even a place for a cadenza, and to introduce it we have the Adagio's only ritornello: barely $2\frac{1}{2}$ bars.

The *Menuet* is even more Austrian than those of the other 1764 Symphonies, and one remarks an

1 *Haydn at Eszterháza 1766–1790*, p. 598.

increased amount of dynamic 'tricks' (like the extraordinary *ff* in the horns at bars 40 and 42, sounding like a church bell through the *Kirtag* festivities: and this was preceded by *ff* in the strings but *not* the horns at bar 37). Haydn also takes care to focus attention on the flautist: he does not play in the first movement and is also silent in the *Menuet*, but he is the soloist together with the two horns in the Trio. Here again the *Ländler* predominates, and we can see the composer gradually becoming more and more fascinated with the popular, folk-like aspects of the dance and its popularization as part of the symphonic form. It is in movements such as these that Haydn shows a quite different set of values than, let us say, Boccherini or the elegant and courtly J. C. Bach in London. This Minuet & Trio are the opposite of courtly; they are from and of the people. They did not meet with approval or understanding when they travelled west, as we have seen and will increasingly see from the reviews in German periodicals of *c.* 1766 *et seq.* (Is there some significance to be attached to the print by the Neapolitan publisher Marescalchi, who was one of the few in Italy to produce Haydn editions in a spiritual climate not ideally suited to their reception? In his *Raccolta di ventiquattro Minuetti Composti da varii Autori*, No. 13 includes the Minuet of our No. 24 – but not the Trio.)

The Finale, in 'sonata form' of its period, is one of Haydn's many experiments as to the character of the symphony's last movement. Here, he uses the language of the opening Allegro and even retains a 4/4 (rather than the customary lighter) metre, but the finale character is achieved by other means, e.g. the *pp* opening with its unsettling violin II part in repeated semiquavers for nine bars, introducing a change (*c sharp*) only in the second half of bar 10. Haydn is also now concerned with holding his symphonies together by means of motivic similarities. Here we see that that bar 4 of the first movement's opening

becomes that lunatic phrase introduced four times (see above)

and in turn bar 11 of the Finale:

While on the subjects of borrowings, Haydn was not a composer to lift large movements from one work and use them in another, in the Handelian manner; but in this Finale he wrote a kind of farewell music which significantly turns up in the same key, and as real 'farewell' music, in the last act of *Le pescatrici* (first performed at Eszterháza in 1770; composed the previous year). The orchestration is even the same, too, with the darting strings in semiquavers and the sustained oboes (*legato* oboes against semiquaver or quaver strings are a great speciality in Haydn's scores altogether): [Symphony No. 24, Finale].

'Andiamo, partiamo', sings Mastricco in the opera, 'di cintia allo splendor'.[1] So there is something final in this music, also in Haydn's subconscious, despite the fact that he has turned to the average first movement for melodic shapes and general details (4/4 metre, etc.).

Symphony No. 30 in C ('Alleluja')

Scoring: 1 flute (in 2nd and 3rd movements), 2 oboes, 2 horns [*continuo*: bsn., harpsichord]. This work is listed in the Keeß Catalogue as No. 22 'con Oboe, Corni, Clarini, Flauto, Tympani' and these trumpet and timpani parts are also noted in the Breitkopf Catalogue of 1773. They have not survived but are very likely a later addition of Haydn's (the Keeß Catalogue contains many symphonies with such added parts, and it is quite possible that they were in some cases actually written for the Keeß Academies).

Having turned to divertimento, opera and concerto for his symphonies, Haydn now has recourse to Gregorian Chant, in this case the 'Alleluja' melody for Holy Week. Perhaps Symphony No. 30 was intended for performance on Easter Sunday, 1765. It must be understood that in eighteenth-century Austria the local churches sang all these old chants in versions which are far removed from the original, or at any rate the earliest, forms as found in the 'Liber Usualis'. Modern scholarship returns, of course, to the earliest sources for the definitive critical text of these ancient church melodies, and quite rightly, but we must seek the later, corrupted texts which were the only ones Haydn could have known. The earliest form (a) is taken from the 'Liber Usualis',[2] while (b) is taken from the 'Brixen Compendiosa'.[3] In the latter, the opening note has been characteristically changed from *la* to *sol*, thus creating a tonal concept, while pauses have been added, rendering the old, asymmetrical chant symmetrical: whether the extension of the 'b' section was made by Haydn or whether it, too, may be traced back to some now forgotten text, is not known.

1 Haydn-Mozart Presse (Universal Edition), 1971, p. 319. *Joseph Haydn Werke* XXV/4 (Bartha), Finale, bars 52ff. For 'farewell' harmonic patterns see also *Haydn in England 1791–1795*, p. 576n.
2 *Liber Usualis Missae et Officii*, Ex Editione Vaticana Adamussim Excerpto, Parisiis, Tornaci, Romae (1936; Latin edition), p. 759.
3 *Cantus | Gregorianus | item | Ritus Sacri | Observandi | Praecipuis Functionibus. | Ad Usum | Dioecesis Brixinensis | ...* MDCCCVII (inner title: *Compendiosa | ad | Cantam | Gregorianum | Institutio | ... Brixinae | ...* 1806), p. 309.

Haydn: Symphony No. 30/1

The 'Alleluja' melody has long proved attractive to composers. Mozart wrote a delightful canon on it (K.553), which he entered in his *Verzeichnüß* [*sic*] *aller meiner Werke von Monath Februario 1784* ... on 2 September 1788, just after completing the last three Symphonies (K.543, 550, 551) and when he hardly had any reason to raise his voice in thanks: like Haydn, he used the modernized text with *sol*. One of the finest works to use the melody is the magnificent *Regina Coeli* by Ferdinand Schubert, where the 'Alleluja' – also the *sol* version – enters in syncopation, supported by trumpets and drums.

Whenever he uses Gregorian Chants, Haydn tends to conceal the melody in the second violin and wind parts, overlaying it with an elaborate façade of some kind (Symphony No. 26, the late *Te Deum*). But in No. 30 the second subject, with its trills, is nothing but a derivative of the melody and so is the long sequence in the development section based on the first four notes of the chant. In the recapitulation, the theme is brought out of obscurity and given to the solo wind band, where it is thundered out *forte*.

The slow movement introduces the flute for the first time, just as in No. 24. The melody is of a kind which we shall now encounter frequently, with a dotted upbeat and a certain pert, almost prim melodic line; such melodies are often in 2/4 time and in bare two-part harmony (or with very 'transparent' harmonic support). Perhaps the most famous of these popular melodies is that in Symphony No. 55's slow movement. Here, in No. 30's Andante, the movement is laid out like a miniature concerto movement (the horns, but not the oboes, are dropped). Ritornello, followed by the 'entrance' of the solo flute (same melody). But if up to the middle of bar 12, it all sounds like a concerto, the entrance of the two oboes at this juncture show that the form is not far from a divertimento. By the time we reach the end of the first section and *neither* flute nor oboes are in operation, we realize that Haydn has created a chamber symphonic slow movement of quite a new variety, drawing from elements of concerto and divertimento: the same hybrid style persists to the end of this attractive movement, which is of particular interest because it is the first of its kind.

For the Finale, Haydn writes: 'Tempo di Menuet, più tosto Allegretto', and at first thought (or sight) it would appear that we may expect the kind of pretty 'Tempo di Minuet' known to us from Morzin symphonies (such as Nos. 4 or 18). The flute has also disappeared again. But after the 'A' section (bars 1–32), the flute appears in a solo in F major. We expect a (perhaps shortened) 'da capo', but no: 'C' section is in A minor. Finally we do have a fully-fledged *da capo* section. Throughout this novel Finale, the wind instruments are used with great sophistication and fastidiousness; they are completely integrated into the scheme.

This 'Alleluja' must have been a particular favourite with Prince Nicolaus, because we find it as the basis of Baryton Trio No. 64, where it is in D major and treated differently; the Trio must have been written about four years after the Symphony.

Symphony No. 30 was first published by Madame Bérault in an extraordinary conglomeration of works, all spurious except for No. 30 (last of the set), entitled 'œuvre ix' (announced in the *Affiches, Annonces & Avis divers* on 13 September 1770). Five years after No. 30 had been composed, there was already total confusion among the Paris publishers, where the number of spurious works was seriously threatening to engulf the genuine ones. We shall touch on this problem again in the final chapter of this volume. Copy of Bérault print: British Museum, g.75.

Symphony No. 29 in E

Scoring: 2 oboes, 2 horns, strings [*continuo*: bsn., harpsichord].

E major is always a key of particular radiance when used by Haydn, whether in one of these early symphonies or as the beginning of Part III in *The Creation*. But although there are two symphonies (Nos. 12, 29) and one *scherzando* (II:37) in E, Haydn never wrote another symphonic work in the key. This is especially odd if we consider the many times it was and will be used in vocal works, sacred (*Salve Regina*, XXIIIb:1, 1756(?); 'O pii Patres' from *Applausus*, 1768) and secular ('Voglio

goder contente' and the Chorus 'Soavi zeffiri' from *Le pescatrici*; 'Ho tesa la rete' from *L'infedeltà delusa*; 'Son quest'occhi' from *L'incontro improvviso*; 'Care spiagge' from *La vera costanza*, 'Ah se tu vuoi' from *La fedeltà premiata*; 'La mia bella diceva di no' and 'Miei pensieri' from *Orlando Paladino*; 'Il pensier sta negli oggetti' from *L'anima del filosofo* – just to list those in the operas), not to mention the key's use in string quartets and piano trios.

In the opening Allegro di molto[1] of No. 29, we have a typically sophisticated case of a singing allegro, a great speciality of the Viennese chamber symphony. Haydn has divided up the melody between strings and oboes, which increases the chamber musical (divertimento) quality. This gossamer pattern is worlds away from the big symphonic effects of Mannheim or the brilliant scores of J. C. Bach and C. F. Abel in London which the young Mozart was, just in this year, taking as models for his own first Symphony (K.16). The *piano* opening of No. 29 is also essentially different from Haydn's own courtly C major works and the typical Italian opera overture. It is not just the low dynamic level and the delicate orchestration but also the use of 3/4 metre, which is much more conducive to this chamber orchestral style than 4/4 or barred C and is in any case a special favourite of Haydn's: omitting slow introductions, of the symphonies composed between c. 1761–5, the first movements of Nos. 6, 7, 14, 36, 21, 23, 29, 28 and two of the *scherzandi* are in this metre. The metre itself is not, of course, an automatic guide to a singing allegro, but perhaps Haydn arrived at the concept via his own treatment of No. 21's opening Adagio: namely, the bar-wise crotchet phrasing

♩ ♩ | ♩ ♩ which is, speeded up, the

precise notation of No. 29's first theme (for 'singing' extensions, see the particularly beautiful sequence at bars 63ff. in the development, and the gentle alteration of the main subject at bars 108ff.). Here in No. 29 is an entirely new[2] kind of opening movement which makes an enlarged piece of chamber music out of the symphony; even the *forte* passages are transparently scored. It is the kind of movement in which one of Haydn's greatest *seguaci*, J. B. Vanhal, would excel.

The second movement (no wind parts) divides up the melody (just as, in the previous movement, the first subject had been divided between strings and oboes); but here between the first and second violins, almost phrase by phrase. J. A. Hiller, writing in the Leipzig periodical,

---

1 Haydn originally wrote 'Allegro ma non troppo', which is the tempo marking of the authentic parts by Joseph Elssler for Dr Stocker in Linz (now St Florian Abbey).

2 Of course there are cantabile beginnings even in symphonies of the Mannheim school, such as the Allegro non tanto from Anton Filtz's Symphony in F, Op. 2, No. 4: Anton Huberty, Paris, announced on 30 June 1760 in *Affiches, Annonces et Avis divers*. A. Weinmann, *Kataloge Anton Huberty (Wien) und Christoph Torricella*, Wiener Urtext-Ausgabe, Vienna 1962, p. 15. But the structure of this work, for strings only, is highly symphonic and the orchestration dense rather than open.

Wöchentliche Nachrichten und Anmerkungen, die Musik betreffend, auf das Jahr 1770,[1] calls it 'auf eine lächerliche Art' (in a ridiculous fashion). An interesting and very characteristic passage is the long series of syncopations at the end of both main sections (bars 29ff., 79ff.) and in the middle as well (bars 55ff.). The bass line 'walks' along with the main rhythm while the violins are one quaver 'off' (behind). Here we have another Haydnesque fingerprint of his style in the 1760s and 1770s, and the bass line is often marked with tall staccato strokes to show that it must stay on the beat and accent the basic rhythm.

It is the Trio which provides the surprise in the next movement: it follows a singing minuet where the basic pulse is crotchets but all the melodic work makes use of many quavers (thus it is somewhat slower than, say, that of No. 21 discussed above). It hardly prepares us for the sombre and secretive beauty of the strongly Balkan Trio (note the abrupt modulation from the tonic minor to the dominant *minor*). The weird atmosphere of this little E minor Trio is enhanced by the dark-hued pedal point in the horns and the total absence of any melody whatever.

We have seen that the opening of this Symphony was almost like a piece of chamber music, a 'singing allegro' in the Viennese chamber symphony tradition. The Finale of No. 29 is the highpoint of the work, and thus Haydn has cleverly managed to reverse completely the normal decrescendo pattern of the average symphony. Here is Haydn at his most aggressive and brilliant; there is only one small episode in *piano* (beginning of the middle section, where the viola is marked *poco forte* because it must take over the function of the bass line); otherwise the entire movement is *forte* and the bass line in crotchets hammers away throughout most of the movement. It is a stupendous example of the nervous energy which begins more and more to consume these quick movements. The *forte* unison opening is an effect that Haydn later used frequently in the first movements of the period *c.* 1771–1774 (see Symphonies Nos. 44, 46, 51, 52, 56). We may now observe in retrospect how carefully the composer has worked out the preceding movements so that this Finale will stand out in the listener's mind as the climax of the Symphony.

Apart from the autograph (EH, Budapest), we are fortunate in having an authentic copy to Joseph Elssler, now in St Florian Abbey.[2] This MS. shows some important textual changes made after the autograph's completion, e.g. the new second violin part in the Andante, bars 83ff. The first edition was as No. 2 of Bailleux's œuvre vii (Paris,

1769), of which, incredibly, no copy is known to have survived. J. A. Hiller (whose criticism of the second movement has been quoted above) thought that the 'personal and original manner' of Herr Hayden (*sic*) were not to be found either in this work, nor in Nos. 28 and 9; the composer's style was changing too rapidly and this chameleon-like side of his personality was already causing confusion among the critics; it has done so ever since.

Symphony No. 31 in D ('Hornsignal')

Scoring: 1 flute, 2 oboes, (bassoon, taken from several contemporary MSS. but not in autograph, though clearly an unwritten requirement for the *continuo*), 4 horns, strings (*violino principale, violoncello solo, violone solo*) [*continuo*: harpsichord]. The autograph (EH, Budapest), dated 1765, shows that this work, using four horns, was written to display the abilities of the horn choir now, after a year's interval, reinforced by two new players, Johann May and Franz Stamitz (Steinmetz).

The famous horn signal that opens the work is in two sections, one of the fanfare type but the other a signal which has survived in two groups of sources, (a) as an old hunting signal which announced a ceremonial *battue*, and (b) 'alla Posta' (designation on one MS.), a very widely known posthorn signal which has been discussed in connection with the Cassatio in D (*supra*, p. 524). These striking signals do not appear at the beginning of the recapitulation, which starts (and what a shock that must have been in 1765) in D *minor* and *piano*, returning to the opening material with the *second* part of the horn signal ('alla Posta'); while the fanfares are used to *end* the movement. Sophisticated application of the 'reversed recapitulation' (first and second subjects in reverse order) found in symphonies of the Mannheim school? It is altogether fascinating to observe with what taste and formal judgement Haydn has incorporated the horns and their *battue*/'alla Posta' signals into this movement, which also has another extraordinary feature: in the midst of all these fanfares and *Hornsignale*, and not forgetting the overture-like scales and passages of the strings, the flute suddenly soars away by itself, up the scale from *a'* to *e'''* (bars 41ff.), no less than three times, in the middle of the section in the dominant (first part). In the development section, this concerto-like episode is also introduced, but with a slightly different twist: twice starting on *g'* and twice starting on *a'* (in the middle of a modulatory passage); while in the recapitulation it reappears three times in the tonic (starting point: *d'*).

In the first movement, all four horns were pitched in D; in the Adagio they are separated into two pairs, one in D and one in G, which means that they can play in the tonic (G) as well as the dominant (D). The other wind instruments are, interestingly, marked *tacent*, but in this seductively beautiful 6/8 *siciliano*-type of movement, we are given not only a virtuoso treatment of the horns (also the second, who displays his ability to leap

1 Hiller was reviewing the Bailleux print; see *Haydn at Eszterháza 1766–1790*, p. 169.
2 We identified these Elssler MSS., which also include the *Missa Sancti Nicolai* (all four MSS. on Esterházy stag paper or paper from St Pölten), as well as a presumably authentic MS. by Viennese Professional Copyist No. 2 of the *Missa in honorem B.V.M.* (and also his copy of Symphony No. 52) when preparing the sources for *SYM* in the late 1940s and early 1950s.

571

into the pedal range at the beginning of the second part), but also complex parts for Tomasini and Weigl. Much of the transparent loveliness is Haydn's orchestration, and in particular the shifting from pizzicato to arco string writing. A moment of total emotional involvement: the *pianissimo*[1] at the end of both exposition (bars 27ff. with upbeat) and recapitulation (bars 70ff. with upbeat): an early and thoroughly typical example of the Viennese Classical School's use of exaggerated dynamic marks to serve as a kind of searchlight on some structural, unusual or emotional point that requires isolation. (Therefore such *pp* or *ff* are always of limited duration.)

The third movement is one of those irresistible minuets of which Haydn's music is full, bursting with energy and containing a large measure of that which can only be described as dance-like (an unfortunate word which, like 'painterly', seems unavoidable). It carries the listener as surely as any waltz by Johann Strauss or a Csárdás by a Gypsy *primas*. In the Trio the oboes are used, divertimento-like, in delightful consort with the horns. This Trio might be used as a textbook exercise on the fine art of orchestration. We may select two features: (1) how sparingly Haydn uses the violins here, having them enter three times with great effect after they have paused when the oboes and horns play together; (2) how Haydn uses the flute only to double the first horn and only in two 'entries' (to borrow a term from the language of film music), at the end of each section. It is all immaculately written and with an infallible sense of economy: once when, as an old gentleman, Haydn was examining the first allegro of a pupil's symphony, he found a long section therein during which the wind instruments paused. He said something pleasant to the pupil and then added in a half-joking tone: 'rests are the most difficult thing of all to write; you were right to remember what a big effect longer piano passages can have.'[2]

The Finale is a set of slow (Moderato molto) variations, with the following scheme: the theme (strings in two-part harmony). Var. 1: solo oboes, horns III–IV, strings. Var. 2: solo 'cello, strings. Var. 3: solo flute, strings. Var. 4: four horns soli (of extreme technical difficulty and intricacy, also horn II), strings (marked *pianiβ*:). Some technical aspects of the four horns' layout will be found *supra*, p. 524. Var. 5: solo violin, strings. Var. 6: tutti but softly. Var. 7: *violone* solo: for some technical details as to the double bass's *Kammerstimmung* (*supra*, pp. 557f.). The listener conversant with Symphony No. 72 will, no doubt, be counting the many parallels. There is now a transition in D minor which leads, in near operatic suspense, to a half-cadence and then the *Kehraus*

which we noted as the conclusion of No. 72. Here it is a Presto in 3/4 and has two novel features. In bars 152ff. we have what sounds like a folk-tune. Now the introduction of such popular tunes in circumstances of this kind was quite a well-known tradition and we find it in Mozart (example: the 'Straßburg' tune that is brought in at the end of the Violin Concerto in D, K.218; the tune was also used by Dittersdorf): it seems to have been derived from the *quodlibet* suite. Having been exposed to this contradance-like theme (quotation?), we are totally unprepared for the last seven bars: a literal repetition of the horn call that began and ended the *first* movement. No device could have more effectively cemented the loose construction of the Finale to the rest of the work.

For those who know the rest of Haydn's œuvre, stretching away (as it were) towards the distant horizon, there is something peculiarly poignant about this *Hornsignal* Symphony, whose perfect construction and gay, light-hearted language, as yet untroubled with the ominous accents of *Sturm und Drang*, represent in some indefinable way Haydn's farewell to youth; for in the next decades he was never quite able to recapture the deep-seated joy and innocence of this music.

No. 31 was not published until the middle of the 1780s (by Sieber in Paris and Forster in London). A later edition by Sieber includes two horns, trumpets and timpani and is surely spurious.

Symphony No. 28 in A

Scoring: 2 oboes, 2 horns, strings [*continuo*: bsn., harpsichord].

The main subject is laid out in such a way that until bar 6 the listener without a score cannot tell that the music is not in 6/8 time; in fact it is in 3/4 and in bar 6, Haydn writes an unequivocal 3/4. Apart from this experiment, the whole Allegro di molto is built upon this first subject or its derivatives, melodic and rhythmic. It is one of the most intellectual and 'abstract' of all these opening movements. Possibly Haydn regarded it as the prelude to the unconventional, indeed eccentric, slow movement, which sounds as if it had programmatic connotations. It is another 'dialogue' similar to the opening of *Der Philosoph* (No. 22), but here only for strings. We encounter another fingerprint which will accompany us through symphony after symphony of the late 1760s and 1770s: the use of muted violins (never muted violas or 'cellos). The *conversazione* is between the tutti strings (*pp*) and the violins, who have a spiky little answer, marked *staccato* and with tall staccato dashes as well. And the passage that repeats itself like a musical clock (bars 27–29) sounds like music to some play; it could have been so, for we have seen that in April and May 1765 the Theatrical Company of Madame Schul(t)z was in residence at Eisenstadt as guests of Prince Nicolaus, mostly giving buffooneries and Hanswurstiada. We wonder if this witty and totally

1 A technical point: Haydn writes here 'pianiß:', which is the marking *pp* (also used by Haydn) raised to a higher potential. We can see this because there are cases when Haydn is already in *pp* and then goes into *pianiß*: Nowadays we would write *ppp*. See Symphony No. 56/I, bars 159ff.: Philharmonia, vol. V, p. 237.
2 *Haydn: the Years of 'The Creation' 1796–1800*, p. 335.

uncharacteristic Poco Adagio might not refer to some action in a Hanswurst play as acted by the Schul(t)z Company and of which this movement was one of the entr'actes: we shall see that Haydn, later in his career, put together symphonies from incidental music (certain examples: Nos. 60 and 63), and perhaps this is an early case in point.

Possibly, too, that is the explanation for the even more unconventional *Menuet*, marked Allegro molto and using the device of switching from open to fingered string (such as would be later immortalized in the 'frog' movement of Op. 50, No. 6, the great Quartet in D from the set dedicated to the King of Prussia). The Trio is like a lost Balkan tune sounding from far across the *puszta*; it is Gypsy music and has in it the dark feeling of eastern Europe. The Germans instantly took a dislike to it. J. A. Hiller, from whose criticism of Bailleux's œuvre vii (which included No. 28) we have already quoted, wrote that 'it would have been better to have omitted the silly Trio, together with the Minuet'. Prince Nicolaus was obviously not of this opinion, for we are interested to see that Haydn wrote a 'private' version for him, in the form of a Duet for two barytons and bass,[1] where it is in D minor.

There is some evidence that the Finale was added later; in the autograph (Preußische Staatsbibliothek, Mus. ms. autogr. Jos. Haydn 17) it is missing, as it is in a very early (1766) MS. from Kremsier (Kroměříž) Castle (IV A124). This only increases our suspicion that the work was originally conceived as separate sections before various scenes of a play. The Finale is a spirited gigue-like Presto in 6/8 time, with pretty imitations in the string parts. The typical quaver motion in the violins against series of dotted crotchets in the lower strings is a feature of Haydn's later gigue-inspired movements, as is the pattern of these dotted crotchets *down* the scale (bars 16ff., 78ff.; cf. Symphony No. 41/IV, bars 1ff.). In some respects this Finale is designed to bring down to earth the fancies of the middle movements and especially the Minuet/Trio.

Symphony No. 34 in D minor

Scoring: 2 oboes, 2 horns, strings [*continuo*: bsn., harpsichord].

From all the evidence at our disposal, it would seem that this is Haydn's first symphony in a minor key; the only other candidate, No. 39, would seem to have been written (performed) after 1 March 1767 (the presence of four horns, also possible in 1765, hence the query). For this presumably first excursion into a minor key for a symphony, Haydn again chooses the *sonata da chiesa* form. The opening Adagio suddenly introduces yet another element into Haydn's already varied language: that of tragedy. His symphonies had encompassed

1 *Joseph Haydn Werke*, Reihe XIII (Sonja Gerlach): Duet No. 4 (Finale). Hoboken *deest*.

a wide range of emotions hitherto, but not the lonely voice that we find, totally unexpectedly, in this movement of quiet, profound sadness. The heavy background of the sustained horns makes the beginning, with its long-held violin I, portentous. We note the use of 3/4 again and another striking use of *pp* (bars 23ff., 79ff.). There is a great sense of breadth and spaciousness, and a new use of D minor: not the old stormy associations of the sea, but as the language of drama. In this respect, the Adagio is the forerunner of Symphony No. 26 ('Lamentatione') and to the Mozart of the Quartet in D minor, K.421, and Concerto, K.466 – a proper use for Parry's description 'The Great Precursor'.

The rest of the Symphony is in D major. The Allegro is fiery and heavily symphonic (broken semiquaver chords in the second violin, repeated quavers in the lower strings, long held notes in the oboes and horns), whose passionate language is symbolized by the wide skips in the opening thematic material:

(notice the brilliant compression, whereby the wide intervals are *then repeated in smaller note values*: a similar rhythmic diminution with the appoggiatura in bars 32ff.) – the new language of passion which will be forthwith transmitted to the coming *Sturm und Drang* as an essential stylistic element (Symphony No. 49/II, etc.).

We have mentioned that the church sonata form includes a certain element of psychological diminution. No. 34 is certainly of this type; that is, it cannot escape the potency of its initial movements. Perhaps this was why, in some old sources, the first two movements were reversed. This diminution of power is a typical feature of the Baroque suite form altogether: famous examples are Bach's Overtures (Suites) for Orchestra (BWV 1066–9) wherein the opening movements are by far the weightiest and musically the most substantial. Another point may have suggested itself to Haydn, too: *anno* 1765 or 1766, symphonies in minor keys were as good as unknown in Eisenstadt Castle and Haydn may have been wary as to the reception it would have: so he used the form in which the powerful opening effect would most quickly fade into oblivion. The slow-moving *Menuet*, marked Moderato (as Haydn was to do many years later in the equally slow-paced movement in the 'Military' Symphony [No. 100]) is matched by a leisurely Trio, where the genuine waltz (*Ländler*) accompaniment in the strings (*pp*) is deliberately disturbed by the chain syncopations in the horns. This very Austrian movement will hardly have found favour with the north German critics, brought up on the controlled hysteria of C. P. E. Bach and the sober tradition of his great but by then almost forgotten father. Nor will the critics have thought much of the racy (Presto assai) Finale, which sounds like a perpetuum mobile and is in easy-going tripartite form ('B' being the section in the minor).

The exceedingly rare first edition was issued by Madame Bérault as œuvre xiv (announced on 7 May 1772 in the *Affiches, Annonces et Avis divers*) and included the Divertimento, II:20, a spurious symphony (Mitscha or Bach[1]), Nos. 59, 34 (with I and II reversed) and another spurious symphony (Ditters): the only known copy of this edition is in the Hoboken Collection, ÖNB, Vienna.

1 Hoboken I: c26.

CHAPTER TEN

The Dissemination of
Haydn's early Works

Austria
(1) The Copyists and the Princely Houses:
(2) The Monasteries: Göttweig (from 1762); Kremsmünster (from 1762); Melk;
    Lambach; St Florian and other Monasteries.

Germany
(1) The Breitkopf Offices in Leipzig (from 1763);
(2) Sigmaringen Castle (Bavaria).

The first editions of Haydn's music:
(1) Paris (from 1764);
(2) Amsterdam (from 1765);
(3) England.

Austria
(1) THE COPYISTS AND THE PRINCELY HOUSES

As we have noted in earlier parts of this volume, the first known authentic copies (not autographs) of Haydn's early music were string trios (Keszthely/Prague [Pachta]/Landon), quartets (Keszthely/Prague [Radenín]/Vienna/Landon), divertimenti (Keszthely/Kremsier/Prague, etc.), symphonies (Keszthely and a few isolated copies, e.g. Prague), piano trios (Kremsier/Budapest), some piano sonatas (Kremsier), and some isolated concertos (Kremsier, etc.): all presumably made in the late 1750s or early 1760s, when Haydn was writing quartets for Fürnberg and was then engaged by Count Morzin and (May 1761) Prince Esterházy. Until Haydn was in possession of a certain amount of capital, he could not afford to engage professional copyists to make 'official' manuscript parts of his new works for sale to persons or institutions; but we have seen that by November 1760, when he married, Haydn was able to produce a substantial sum of money to counter his bride's dowry. It must have been clear to Haydn that it was far better for him to organize the sale of his works directly to interested parties; and he must have been painfully aware of the competition being offered by the Viennese copyists in this regard. Once a number of these 'official' copies had been sold by Haydn, it was obvious that further, unauthorized copies were going to be made from them, in turn, and sold; but at least Haydn could have the satisfaction of reaping some of the initial profit to be made from distributing his own works.

In all the known cases in which Haydn himself made corrections and additions to these MSS., particularly the Keszthely symphonies, quartets and trios and the Vienna quartets, the handwriting suggests c. 1760. Perhaps when Morzin closed down musical operations in Lukavec, Haydn was able to start his own copying workshop when he

[continued on p. 584]

THE FÜRNBERG-MORZIN COPYISTS:
EXAMPLES OF INDIVIDUAL COPYIST'S HANDWRITING

COPYIST NO. 1.

Above. Title page of the Piano (harpsichord) Trio No. 11 in E (XV:34). Library of the Archbishops of Olmütz, Kremsier Castle (Kroměříž), ČSSR.

Left. The Violin I part from the String Trio No. 21 in G (V:G1); in lines 4 and 5 there are additions – 'p' and 'for' – in Haydn's own hand. Helikon Library, Festetics Castle, Keszthely, Hungary.

576

COPYIST NO. 2. The Violin I part from the String Quartet, Op. II, No. 6, bearing the stamp of Lt-Col. von Fürnberg. Helikon Library, Festetics Castle, Keszthely, Hungary.

COPYIST NO. 3.
Title page (*left*) and 'Basso' part from the Divertimento for two horns and strings (II:22). Helikon Library, Festetics Castle, Keszthely, Hungary.

COPYIST NO. 4 (=
Viennese professional No.2).
Violin I part (*right*) and title
page (*below*) from the Piano
(harpsichord) Trio No. 7 in G
(XV:41). Library of the
Archbishops of Olmütz,
Kremsier Castle
(Kroměříž), ČSSR.

COPYIST No. 5. Title page ('Capricio') and harpsichord part from the Piano (harpsichord) Trio No. 10 in A (XV:35), formerly in Haydn's own library. Országos Széchényi Könyvtár, Budapest.

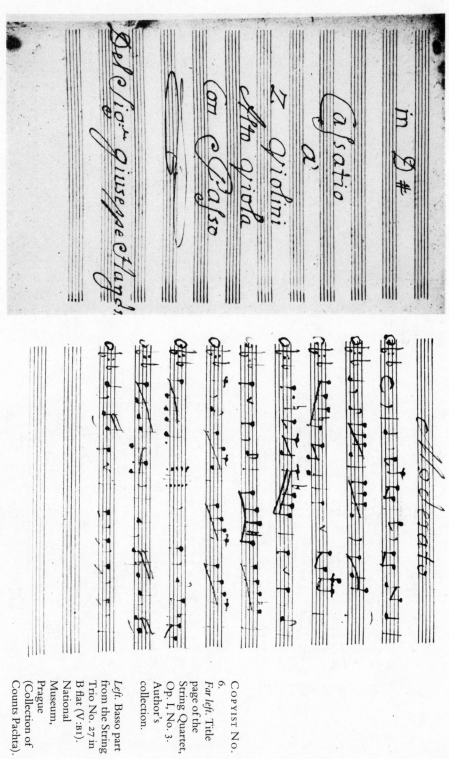

COPYIST NO.
6.
Far left. Title
page of the
String Quartet,
Op. I, No. 3.
Author's
collection.

Left. Basso part
from the String
Trio No. 27 in
B flat (V:BI).
National
Museum,
Prague
(Collection of
Counts Pachta).

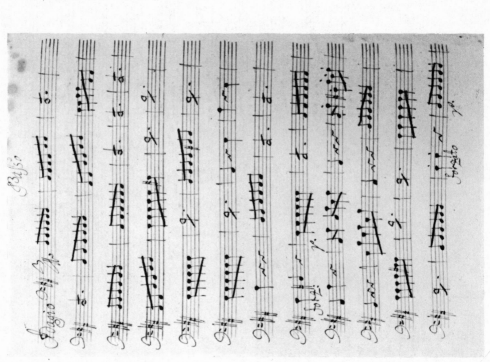

Left. COPYIST NO. 7.
First page of the 'Basso' part from the String Quartet, Op. I, No. 3.
Author's collection.

Opposite, left. COPYIST NO. 8.
First page of the Violin II part from the String Quartet, Op. I, No. 3.
Author's collection.

Opposite, right. COPYIST NO. 9.
A page of the Violin part from the String Trio No. 27 in B flat (V:BI).
National Museum, Prague (Collection of Counts Pachta).

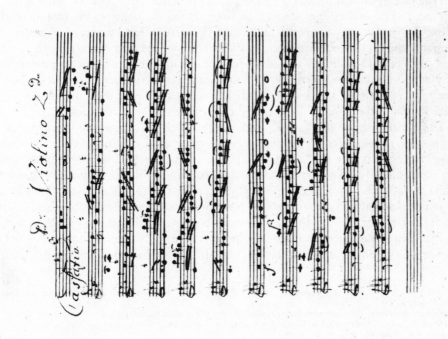

[continued from p. 575]

returned to Vienna, and to continue it on a fairly large scale at least until he was engaged by Prince Paul Anton Esterházy in May 1761.

We may assume that the professional copyists in Vienna began to sell Haydn's music within the Monarchy and possibly even abroad by c. 1760–1. We can give this date with some confidence because we have two spectacularly early dates (1758 and 1759) for copies which were acquired by, respectively, a princely house and a lord of the church.

The Princely Houses

The earliest known dated[1] copy (again, not autograph) of a Haydn work is Symphony No. 37: the Princely Schwarzenberg Archives in Krumau (Český Krumlov) own a set of parts dated '1758' on the cover. The date was written in the same kind of ink, and is contemporaneous with, the actual copying of the music. We include a specimen of the copyist's handwriting (p. 281), from which it will be seen that the scribe is not identical with any of the other Fürnberg/Morzin copyists and that there are no corrections in Haydn's hand; therefore it must be presumed to have been made by a professional scribe.[2]

An equally interesting piece of evidence about the early dissemination of Haydn's music was uncovered by Jiří Sehnal[3] in the form of a 'Cathalogus über die Hochfürstl. Musicalia und Instrumenta' of Bishop Leopold Egk von Hungersbach who, as Bishop of Olmütz (Olomouc) 1758–60, resided briefly at Kremsier (Kroměříž) Castle. The Catalogue contains a list of musical instruments and music, often identified with *incipit*. It seems that Bishop Egk formed his new *Capelle* under the direction of *Capellmeister* Anton Neumann, a prolific composer, in 1758; it consisted, as was so often the case in those days, mainly of servants proficient on one or the other musical instrument. The orchestra is known to have included clarinets; the names of the players, Anton Fernier (Fournier) and Franz Fogenauer, have survived. Apart from Neumann, the most celebrated member of the band would turn out to be Johann Carl Franz, born in 1738 as the son of a textile dealer in Langenbielau bei Schweidnitz, and later Haydn's famous first horn player.[4] Franz joined the Kremsier *Capelle* at the age of twenty, in 1758, with a salary of 156 fl. He was listed, even then, simply as 'Carl Frantz', without the 'Johann'. 'Cammerdiener Neümann' earned 350 fl.

The repertoire of the *Capelle*, according to the 'Cathalogus', included 124 symphonies, 33 wind-band 'Parthien', 8 concertos, 5 oratorios and 56 trios. The price of the copy, 7 Kreuzer per 'Bogen' (4 pages), was registered in some cases, while Neumann cost only 5 Kreuzer per 'Bogen'.[5] That most of the music was purchased in Vienna is made clear by a note at the beginning of the symphonic section, 'Von Wien mitgebracht' and after Symphony No. 50 'Bis anhero alles richtig bezahlt den 25. nov. 1759 70[?] fl. 10 kr.' No. 7 of this list shows by its *incipit* that Haydn's Symphony No. 1 ('12 B[o]g[en]') had been acquired in Vienna before 25 November 1759; it was the only Haydn symphony in the collection. Can the Bishop have heard a performance at

---

1 The Quintet in G (II:2) is dated 1754 on a Berlin MS., but as we have seen, the date refers presumably to the date of composition rather than the actual copy.

2 Attention was first drawn to this copy by G. Feder (*Haydn-Studien* I/1 [1965], p. 25; *HJB* IV, 120).

3 'Das Musikinventar des Olmützer Bischofs Leopold Egk aus dem Jahre 1760 als Quelle vorklassischer Instrumentalmusik', *Archiv für Musikwissenschaft* XXIX/4 (1972), pp. 285ff.

4 *Haydn at Eszterháza 1766–1790*, p. 71.

5 Dr Sehnal presumes that these prices were introduced after the Bishop's death and indicated the value of the music as part of Egk's legacy.

Lukavec in 1758 or 1759? Or was the work already a new and popular 'hit' in Vienna, being marketed by the copyists, in 1759? Since it is the only Haydn symphony in the collection, it is unlikely that Haydn himself was involved, but since the parts do not survive, we cannot tell the manuscript's provenance for certain.

It is interesting that Haydn's wind-band divertimenti (composed, for the most part, when he was in the service of Count Morzin) have survived almost exclusively – autographs apart – in Bohemian and Moravian sources; only one work in the original version has survived in a contemporary copy outside Bohemia – II:7, in the Thurn und Taxis Archives, Regensburg. A few of the others were transcribed as string quartets in Melk (*infra*, p. 588). It would seem, therefore, that the existence of two sets of such sources, one in the Clam Gallas Archives (Friedland Castle, now Prague) and one in Kremsier Castle, may be linked directly to the fact that the works were composed, or at any rate performed, at Lukavec. It is thus fair to suggest that Bishop Egk's Symphony No. 1 was the harbinger of a close contact between Haydn and Kremsier. It does not surprise us that these wind-band 'Parthien' were not yet in the Bishop's 'Cathalogus', because by 15 December, when the Bishop died (at the age of sixty-four), most of these wind-band divertimenti were hardly a few months' old and not yet circulating outside the Morzin *Capelle*. Kremsier had, however, six of Haydn's wind-band works ('Parthia del Signor Haydn') by 1766.[1]

Jiří Sehnal has also informed us about the *Capelle* under the next Bishop, Maximilian Hamilton (1761–76).[2] It was for Hamilton that Haydn delivered most of the authentic copies of his works now in Kremsier, and this includes the wind-band divertimenti, the early piano trios by the various Fürnberg/Morzin copyists, and so on – up to the authentic copies by Viennese copyist No. 2 (= Fürnberg/Morzin copyist No. 4) of the Piano Sonatas 'anno 1776' Nos. 42–47 (XVI:27–32). The presence of an authentic copy of the last Piano Concerto, in D (XVIII:11), by Johann Radnitzky, which must post-date 1776, shows that Haydn continued relations with the next Bishop of Olmütz at Kremsier, Anton Theodor Colloredo-Waldsee (1777–1811).[3]

It is also probable that the early copies (string trios and Symphony 'B' [I:108]) by Viennese Copyist No. 2 (= Fürnberg/Morzin No. 4) in the Archives of the Counts Pachta, now in the Prague National Museum, as well as many unique copies of the baryton trios and duets in their original versions, indicate a connection with Haydn born, perhaps, in the Lukavec years. It would seem that the very extensive Haydn collection of Count Christian von Clam Gallas (1749?–1805), formerly in Friedland (Frýdlant) Castle, also had its origins in the Lukavec period, considering the substantial amount of Haydn's early wind-band music found there and constituting important and rare sources for those works.

It is likely that Haydn, as Morzin's *Capellmeister*, made contact with various Bohemian and Moravian houses and supplied them and their descendants with new music (for example, Johann Rudolph, Count Chotek, 1748–1824, who owned the authentic copy of Symphony No. 41 in Joseph Elssler's hand which we found twenty years ago in the Prague Museum, though this particular Chotek must have appeared on the scene later than the Lukavec period). The number of private orchestras in Bohemia and Moravia declined sharply from 1760 to 1780, and most members of the nobility in the provinces were reduced to keeping a wind band for the 'Tafel', or to cultivating chamber music with family and friends.

---

1 Description: see Divertimento (II:3) in Diletto Musicale No. 84 (Landon, 1960), Verlag Doblinger.
2 'Die Musikkapellen des Olmützer Bischofs Maximilian Hamilton (1761–1776)', *Die Musikforschung* XXIV (1971), pp. 411ff.
3 About whom see the indefatigable Dr Sehnal's article in *HJB* X (1978), pp. 132ff. For the MS. of the Concerto, *vide infra*, p. 634.

(2) THE MONASTERIES

The next group of institutions which must concern us here are the great Austrian monasteries, then much more numerous (before Joseph II's widespread reforms in the decade 1780–90, when many venerable abbeys were closed, often for ever – e.g. Mondsee). The larger, and even some of the more remote and smaller abbeys such as Schlägl in the Mühlviertel (Upper Austria), maintained not only a choir but an orchestra. The selection here presented was made only on the basis of the abbey in question having music by Haydn earlier than 1766.

Göttweig Abbey

Here we have the interesting case whereby it would seem that the first contact with this great and ancient Benedictine Abbey, perched high on a hill overlooking the Danube valley near Krems, was not Joseph but his brother, Johann Michael. In 1759, when Johann Michael was in Großwardein (Oradea Mare), Göttweig acquired his *Missa sub titulo St Michaelis* (Klafsky 27). During our period, the Abbot was Odilio Piazol (he held office 1749–68), who continued the rebuilding of the new Abbey from plans by Johann Lucas Hildebrand (after a disastrous fire on 17 June 1718 had destroyed almost all the old series of buildings) – destined, alas, to remain unfinished. The *Regens chori* at our period was P. Joseph Seneviis (1754–69), but the school rector, Pater Leander Staininger, was also responsible for some of the early Haydn works which suddenly, in 1762, arrived in quantity at the Monastery: Symphonies 'A' (I:107; P. Joseph), 3, 4, 5 (all P. Joseph), Quartets Op. 2, No. 4 (P. Leander), No. 6 (P. Leander), Quintet in A (II:A1; P. Leander), and the String Trio (V:15; P. Leander). From then on, Göttweig acquired vast quantities of Haydn's music, a little each year. Now enough of these copies have survived to enable one to see that not only those of 1762 but the works acquired thereafter were not procured from Vienna but copied locally, on the premises. From which sources? 1762 is really a very early date, and the only explanation that immediately suggests itself is (a) some kind of connection with the Haydn brothers and (b) perhaps a visit in 1762 by Haydn to the Abbey, where he may have allowed the monks to make those many copies. Perhaps Haydn had a spare week or ten days after Prince Paul Anton's death to make such a visit. Otherwise how would two monks acquire the sources from which to copy, at Göttweig itself, at least eight works – perhaps more had disappeared by the time the catalogue in question, wherein these works are listed, was made, in 1830 – in 1762? It seems more likely that, if not Haydn himself, perhaps a friend or colleague made the trip to Göttweig rather than the two monks going to Vienna or Eisenstadt to obtain the sources. Nevertheless, there is something of a mystery here. (Other monasteries in Austria sometimes made their copies locally but also purchased them from the copyists in Vienna: there are Haydn MSS. in Lambach and Stams that originated with the Viennese copyists.)

The actual parts of these works, whether sacred (in Haydn's case, there would be many, but they did not begin to arrive until a few years later) or secular, often tell us where and when they were played within the Abbey, and not just in the church – 'in Crypta', 'ad prandium', 'post cenam', 'in horto', 'in Regenschoriatu', also 'in Refectorio'. The occasional stain of a wine glass put down on a Haydn copy provides a homely touch. Very often all the recorded performances at the Monastery, from the first to the last, are listed.[1]

---

1 Literature: Larsen, *HÜB*, 79f.; Landon *SYM*, 42f. MGG 5 (1956), article Göttweig (461–9, Landon), with specialized literature.

Kremsmünster Abbey

This venerable Benedictine institution has a famous school attached to it. The town which the Abbey dominates is in Upper Austria, not far from Lambach Abbey, off the main road between Linz and Salzburg. The Mozarts, and Michael Haydn, were frequent guests at the Abbey. Joseph Haydn seems to have had some personal connection with the monks there, for in *EK* (p. 18), we find the *incipit* of the 'Applausus' Cantata (1768) with the note, added by the composer many years later (perhaps even as late as 1800 or even thereafter), 'Applauso [this was the original entry, *c.* 1768–70, later changed to "Applausus"] in lateinischer Sprache / bey gelegenheit einer Praelat[en] Wahl / zu Crems Münster' ('in Latin, on the occasion of an Abbot's Election at Kremsmünster'). We know now that the work was in fact written for Zwettl Abbey in Lower Austria,[1] but the entry in *EK* is important in that it shows that Haydn remembered, as an old man, having once had dealings with the cultivated and friendly Benedictine monks. Further proof comes from an authentic copy by Joseph Elssler and Johann Schellinger of Symphony No. 67 in Kremsmünster, which the present writer found there many years ago, on one of his numerous visits to the Monastery (where he remembers, with gratitude, many kindnesses, not least being the spoiled guest of the Abbey for a week in 1956 and sitting next to the late Abbot at high table).[2]

The first, and characteristically early, entry about Joseph Haydn in this great Benedictine centre of culture and learning occurs, as at Göttweig, in 1762: a series of the early String Quartets.

> V Simphoniae auth. Josephe Hayden [later:] de Musica ex S. Scriptura: I. Gremula Carbunculi in ornamento auri ed Comparatio Musicorum in Convivio vini. (Ecclesiastici Cap. 32 V. 7); II. Sicut in Fabricatione auri signum est Smaragdi sic numerum Musicorum in jucundu et moderato Vini. (Ecclesiastici Cap. 32 V. 8); III. Primum verbum diligenti scientis et non impedias Musicam. (Ecclesiastici 32 V. 5) ... ad Usum P. Henrici Pichler 1762 [and another title:] ... V. Sinfonie ... ad usum P. Henrici Pichler Prof. Cremif. 1762.

A year later P. Pichler copied the Cassatio in G (II:2) with the title of 'symphony' ('ad usum P. Henrici Pichler 1763'). As a result of the brilliant research of our old friend and colleague, P. Altman Kellner, O.S.B.,[3] we know something of P. Heinrich Pichler. He was born in the attractive old Upper Austrian town of Wels on 22 February 1722 and entered the Abbey on 13 November 1743. He was a singer and violinist, and kept a diary which is of great importance for the history of the Monastery (and Upper Austrian cultural life altogether). From 1744 to 1747 he studied at the Benedictine University at Salzburg, and even at this time he kept a 'Diarium Salisburgense' which sheds much light on Mozart's birthplace a few years before the composer's birth (extracts in Kellner, 425–8). With a useful and cultivated life behind him, he died a few months after Haydn, on 26 July 1809. Again, we ponder, and can find no likely answer to, the problem: these are local copies and made from some unknown source. (We know they are local copies because of the watermarks, which include 'FAW', paper of the Wurm family at Kremsmünster – see Landon *SYM*, 613f.) Where did P. Pichler find the sources from which to copy these important early MSS. of Haydn's Quartets?

1 *Haydn at Eszterháza 1766–1790*, pp. 236ff.
2 Landon, *SYM*, 41.
3 *Musikgeschichte des Stiftes Kremsmünster*, Kassel/Basel 1956, an 826-page history of the Monastery with the publication of which we were fortunate enough to be intimately involved.

In the following years, Haydn became a major musical factor at Kremsmünster Abbey: they copied and performed with love and reverence symphonies, quartets, trios, Masses, divertimenti and cassations in great number – *ad majorem Dei gloriam*.

Melk Abbey

It was J. P. Larsen who first drew attention to the importance of Melk as a centre of 'Haydnpflege' in the eighteenth century. The actual building, rising spectacularly above the Danube, has always been admired as one of the great examples of *settecento* Baroque architecture. The fortunate combination of the Austrian architect Jakob Prandtauer, working with the wise and well-organized Abbot Berthold von Dietmayr (Abbot, 1700–39), has given us one of Austria's finest monuments. As far as Haydn's music is concerned, the monks at Melk collected some sixty symphonies and eighty quartets and divertimenti. Unfortunately, some well-meaning archivist in the nineteenth century replaced the old title pages with modern substitutes, and the only original title pages to survive were those on which music was copied on the reverse side(s). Thus it is difficult to establish when Haydn's music first arrived at Melk, but certainly by 1765, one Franciscus Helm, 'Rhetoris' was collecting Haydn's wind-band divertimenti arranged as string quartets[1] and also a real String Quartet (Op. 1, No. 3 [III:3; Melk V, 810]). Franz Helm was a boy chorister in Nikolsburg (now Mikulov in Moravia) and came to Melk in 1766, later becoming Pater Rupert, under which name he continued to copy Haydn's compositions: Divertimento, II:2 [Melk V, 77], dated 1773, and three early Quartets [III:7, 10, 12; Melk V, 812, 806b, 778]. But Pater Rupert, ex 'Rhetor Nicolsburgi', was not Haydn's only connection with Melk. The Monastery had among its monks a pupil of Haydn's, Robert Kimmerling (Kymmerling; 1737–90), a nephew of the Abbot of Melk, Thomas Pauer. Kimmerling seems to have been Haydn's pupil in the mid 1750s. On 29 June 1761, Kimmerling was ordained at Melk and became in that same year *Regens chori*, a position which he retained until (and including) 1777. Of his many sacred and secular compositions, at least one Symphony in C, with trumpets and kettledrums, was attributed to Haydn in a Göttweig manuscript of 1772.[2] An even more interesting connection is through Johann Georg Albrechtsberger, who at the time Haydn's quartets were being first played at Weinzierl Castle was organist at Maria Taferl and probably the 'cellist of the Fürnberg quartet. Later, 1760–6, Albrechtsberger became the organist of Melk Abbey; some of his compositions of this period, including some very early string quartets, have been preserved in autograph in the Esterházy Archives.[3] The compiler of the so-called 'Quartbuch',[4] Johann Nepomuk Weigl, was also active at Melk, but at a date slightly later than that at present under discussion. Larsen refuted Sandberger's theory that 'Quartbuch' was a repertory catalogue of

---

1 Details in our editions of Divertimento (Parthia) II:D18, Diletto Musicale 33 (1959), and II:23, Diletto Musicale 30 (1959), Verlag Doblinger. For literature on Melk, see Larsen *HÜ* 80f.; Landon *SYM* 42f.; *MGG* 9 (1961), article 'Melk' on pp. 11–5 (Trittinger); R. Freeman, *Die Musikforschung* XXIII (1970), pp. 183ff. On the 'Quartbuch', see the Larsen-Sandberger controversy in *Acta Musicologica* and *Zeitschrift für Musik* 1935–7, also *Jahrbuch der Musikbibliothek Peters* 1933, pp. 35ff.; Larsen *HÜB* 80f., Landon *SYM* 13ff.; R. Freeman, *The Practice of Music at Melk Monastery in the Eighteenth Century*, Dissertation, University of California, Los Angeles, 1971; Larsen, 'Evidence or Guesswork: The "Quartbuch" Revisited', in *Acta Musicologica* IL/1 (1977), pp. 86ff., attacking A. Peter Brown: 'The Chamber Music with Strings of Carlos d'Ordoñez: A Bibliographical and Stylistic Study', *Acta Musicologica* XLVI/2 (1974), esp. 223f.

2 As Kimmerling in the 'Quartbuch'. Landon *SYM*, 800 (II:10), Hoboken I:C10. *MGG* 7 (1958), article 'Kimmerling', pp. 902f. (Wessely). *Vide supra*, pp. 288ff., for Albrechtsberger and Weinzierl.

3 *MGG* 1 (1949–51), article 'Albrechtsberger', 303–7 (Herta Goos). On the Albrechtsberger Quartets, *vide supra*, pp. 297ff.

4 The 'Quartbuch' is a valuable thematic catalogue formerly in EH, Budapest. A photograph is in the Hoboken Collection, now Österreichische Nationalbibliothek, Musiksammlung. MS. copy, same library, S. m. 9040. Haydn at one time came into possession of the catalogue and made many corrections concerning works falsely attributed to him.

music formerly in the Esterházy Archives and suggested, instead, that it was a list of music at Melk Abbey *c.* 1775. Freeman and Brown (as well as the present author in *SYM*, 1955) suggest that this is extremely unlikely; among the theories propounded, one places 'Quartbuch' as a list of music at one of the secularized abbeys in St Pölten,[1] while another (Freeman) is the most intriguing of all: that 'Quartbuch' was the repertory catalogue of Weinzierl Castle. Perhaps, then, its reappearance *c.* 1800 is connected with the death of Lt-Col. von Fürnberg, discussed *supra*, pp. 239ff., and the transference of the authentic Morzin/Fürnberg collection of divertimenti, trios and symphonies to Keszthely Castle, in which operation Haydn may have been personally involved. Weigl copied sundry MSS. by Haydn at Melk, e.g. the duplicate string parts of Symphony No. 61 (Melk IV, 82) and the early Quartet, Op. 2, No. 2 (III:8; Melk V, 73).

Lambach Abbey

The ancient Benedictine Abbey of Lambach, on the post road between Linz and Salzburg, owns a valuable thematic catalogue dating from 1768.[2] It contains later additions, which are recognizable as such, but the large quantity of Haydn's music that the Abbey owned by 1768 suggests that they must have started collecting his works in the early 1760s. On pp. 273ff. of the catalogue, we find thematic listings of instrumental works by Haydn, as shown in the accompanying table.

CONTENTS OF LAMBACH CATALOGUE

Work	Comments
Symphony No. 1	Significant that here, too, this work opens the list of Haydniana: can the monks at Lambach have known that this was in fact Haydn's First Symphony? It would seem that they did.
Symphony 'B' (I:108)	
Cassatio in F (Quartet, Op. 2, No. 4; III:10)	
Symphony No. 2	Unlike most of these early Haydn copies at Lambach, this one has survived; it is written on paper from the mill at Kremsmünster and *appears* to have been copied from Kremsmünster Abbey's copy of the work, also written on paper from the local mill and copied in part by Friedrich Kramer, a local monk born in 1727 and since 1760 active at the Abbey; see P. Altman Kellner, op. cit., pp. 407ff. for interesting notes on this active musician and composer. Here, then, we have a seemingly clear case of Lambach securing a new Haydn Symphony from its sister monastery a few miles away (Kremsmünster copy: H 38, 34; missing in *SYM*). But it is curious that Kremsmünster owns no copy of Symphonies Nos. 1 or 'B', nor for that matter of Nos. 19, 14 or 18 – the next works in the present list.
Symphony No. 19	
Symphony No. 14	
Symphony No. 18	
Divertimento in D (String Trio, V:21)	
Divertimento in F (String Trio, V:F1)	
Divertimento in D (Quartet, Op. 1, No. 3; III:3)	

1 Augustinian Monastery, suppressed in 1784 by order of Joseph II.
2 See *Haydn: the Late Years 1801–1809*, p. 440.

Work	Comments
Divertimento in B (B♭: Quartet, Op. 1, No. 1; III:1)	
Divertimento in D (spurious work; III:D3)	Actually by J. G. Albrechtsberger, autograph in Budapest, but already attributed to Haydn as a Cassatio with two horns in Göttweig, copied by P. Leander in 1763.
Cassatio in C (Quartet, Op. 1, No. 6; III:6)	
Cassatio in E (Quartet, Op. 2, No. 2; III:8)	
Cassatio in E♭ (Quartet, Op. '0'; II:6)	
Cassatio in E♭ (Quartet, Op. 1, No. 2; III:2)	
Cassatio in D (2 horns, 1 v., va., b.; II:D1)	Disregard the J. C. Bach information in Hoboken I, p. 337; possibly a work by Michael Haydn, though the (extant) Lambach parts, on paper from the Kremsmünster mill, and also the source at Kremsmünster Abbey (also on paper from the local mill, Fasc. 42, No. 112) specify Joseph; another source at St Florian, also on Kremsmünster paper, has lost its title page but is placed among the Haydn sources.
Variatio in B (B♭; String Trio, V:8)	
Variatio in B♭ (String Trio V:ES1)	By Michael Haydn, autograph in the Gesellschaft der Musikfreunde (IX, 36892), probably from the Großwardein years.
Symphony No. 37	

We have seen that *all* the music listed in the Esterházy catalogues compiled prior to Haydn's arrival in 1761 has disappeared. Therefore it is not surprising that most (if not all) of the music listed in the Lambach Catalogue of 1768 has disappeared, too. In fact one can only repeat one's surprise that so many sources from the Austro–Hungarian monasteries – i.e. including those in Bohemia, Moravia, Slovakia and, of course, Hungary itself – have survived, often providing us with unique, or nearly unique, copies of Haydn's music.

St Florian and other Monasteries
Haydn's music was collected by many more monasteries, of course, but from the evidence now available (which must, in the nature of things be incomplete), it appears that the extensive Haydn holdings in St Florian (many authentic sources by Joseph Elssler and Viennese Copyist No. 2), as well as those – some larger, some smaller – at Admont, Herzogenburg, Michaelbeuern, Osegg (Osek; now National Museum, Prague), Raigern (Rajhrad; now Brno), Reichersberg, Rottenmann (secularized under Joseph II; later Bad Aussee, now Graz), St Lambrecht, St Paul in Lavantal, Salzburg (St Peter), Schlägl, Schlierbach, Seckau, Seitenstetten and Wilhering, were all formed somewhat later than 1765, though evidence may come to light that one or the other source is of earlier date. Certainly, as we have seen, the year 1762 saw a sudden proliferation of Haydn sources throughout the monarchy, and not only at the monasteries of Göttweig and Kremsmünster. We also find a manuscript, now in the National Janáček Music Library at Brno (Brünn), of Symphony No. 1 from Lipník in Moravia, inscribed 'Procuravit P. Fr. Georgius / profes. gradie p. t. Regenschori in annu II^do 1762, 10 Januarius' and 'Descripsit Joannes Schultz sintaxus stud. / Anno 1762' (Brno, A 324.; Landon, *Supplement*, 21). We can see that Symphony No. 1 was

considered something new and special; and even from the paltry documents at our disposal over two centuries later, we can see that it was not only eagerly sought after, but was also known to be Haydn's first effort in the form. Clearly, many thousands throughout the length and breadth of the crown lands were initiated into the mysteries of Haydn through the monasteries and their schools. Haydn's reputation among the monks was high as early as the 1760s, and they assiduously cultivated his art throughout the century and beyond.

Germany

We may select two characteristic sources of early Haydn in Germany, first the Breitkopf 'Officinen' in Leipzig and secondly the great Hohenzollern Castle of Sigmaringen, in both of which places Haydn's music was being distributed before 1765.

(I) THE BREITKOPF OFFICES IN LEIPZIG

In the thematic catalogues of Breitkopf, now handsomely reprinted,[1] Haydn's name first appears in the 'Catalogo / de' / Soli, Duetti, / Trii, Terzetti, Quartetti / e / Concerti / per / il cembalo / e / l'harpa. / che / si trovano in manoscritto / nella officina musica di Breitkopf / in Lipsia / Parte IVta. / 1763'. There, on p. 6, we find 'Divertimento di Gius. HAY- / DEN, per il Cemb. Solo', with the *incipit* of Piano Sonata No. 8 (XIV:5), and on p. 134 we note 'II. Concerti di HAYDEN in Vienna, *a Cl. [clavier] ob. / c. [con]* 2 Viol. V. [Viola] B. [Basso]', with the themes of the Organ Concertos, XVIII:1 and 5. Two years later, in *Parte Vta* ('Quadri, Partite, Divertimenti, Cassat.[ioni], Scherz.[andi] ...'), we find eight early quartets by Haydn: I. Op. 1, No. 1 (III:1); II. Op. 2, No. 1 (III:7); III. Op. 1, No. 2 (III:2); IV. Op. 1, No. 6 (III:6); V. Op. 1, No. 3 (III:3). VI. Op. 'o' (II:6); VII. A spurious work (I:F7; III:F4; Landon, *SYM*, 816, No. 97 – variously attributed to Ignaz Holzbauer, F. Schubert and Carlos d'Ordoñez [Raigern Catalogue: Sinf. a 4tro]), of which Breitkopf quotes the slow movement; VIII. Op. 1, No. 4 (III:4). A few pages later, we find a heading 'CASSATIONES / ô NOTTURNI' with 'VI. Cassationes del Sigr. Gius. HAYDEN.': Quartet Op. 2, No. 2 (III:8); II. Quartet Op. 2, No. 4 (III:10); III. Divertimento for 2 horns and strings (II:22); IV. Divertimento for 2 horns and strings (II:21); V. Divertimento (Quintet; II:2); VI. Quartet Op. 2, No. 6 (III:12). These are followed, on the next page, by 'VI. Scherzandi del Sigr. Gius. HAYDEN, *a 2 Corni / 2 Oboi, 1 Flauto, 2 Viol. e Basso.*' (II:33–8).

Haydn's symphonies do not begin to appear until Supplement I of 1766, but at that time Breitkopf was able to announce two sets of six each (first set: Nos. 17, 18, 1, 19, 20, Overture to *Acide*; second set: Nos. 10, 'B' [I:108], 5, 14, 18/II and 32).

It was to be expected that some of these MS. copies would survive, and the Haydn Institut (Cologne) believes it has identified a series of four MSS., in the Berlin Staatsbibliothek, of Op. 1, No. 4, and Op. 2, Nos. 4, 1 and 6, as having originated in the Breitkopf Offices. But against this interesting theory, we would point out that the Berlin MSS. are dated 4 December 1763, 24 January 1764 and 16 February 1764,[2] whereas Breitkopf did not advertise the works until 1765; and we see no reason to

1 *The Breitkopf Thematic Catalogue. The Six Parts and Sixteen Supplements 1762–1787*, ed. and with an Introduction and Indexes by Barry S. Brook, New York 1966.
2 *JHW* XII/1, Kritischer Bericht, Munich 1973, p. 19, source 77.

591

presume that Breitkopf had actually owned the works, and was selling them, since 1763, but did not advertise them until two years later. The matter is of little importance, for one day a serious attempt must be made to identify the handwritings of Breitkopf scribes, and to the best of our knowledge, the only Haydn copies that may with some confidence be traced to Breitkopf are those in the Gymnasialbibliothek in Zittau (concertos).

Breitkopf was certainly the most important source for the diffusion of Haydn's music in Germany at this period. We have no evidence as to how he procured the original sources from which he made his copies; presumably he had an agent in Vienna who purchased the necessary copies from a local scribe. There is no evidence that Haydn personally was in any way involved in these transactions.

(2) SIGMARINGEN CASTLE (BAVARIA)

As we explained in 1955 (*SYM*, 610), the Haydn sources listed in the thematic catalogue from Sigmaringen Castle of 1766 have all disappeared; they may be divided into several groups – the original 1766 entries and three groups of later additions which need not concern us here. It was thought instructive to supply a list of a typical Haydn collection belonging to one distinguished member of the German aristocracy, most of whose noble contemporaries must have collected music in the first half of the 1760s, and which graphically shows how widely Haydn was known in the Bavarian castles at that period.

SIGMARINGEN CASTLE THEMATIC LIST OF WORKS
'Auth.ͤ *Hayden*'

[No. in list]	[Works listed]	[Comments (H.C.R.L.)]
I	Notturno in dis à 2 vv. alto viola. 2 cornj. con Basso —	Divertimento, II:21.
2	Synf.ᵃ in A. à 2 vv. viola, et Basso	Scherzando No. 6, II:38.
3	Synf.ᵃ in B. à 2 vv. con Basso	String Trio, V:18.
4	Serenada in E♭ a. 2. VV. viola oblig.ᵃ et Basso —	Spurious work, II:Es6; in Stams as Aumon; in Göttweig 1764 as (?) Bach
5	Synf.ᵃ in G. à 2. VV. viola oblig.ᵃ con Basso	Symphony No. 27.
6	Quattro ex Dis. à: 2. vv. alto viola. et Basso.	Quartet, Op. 'o'; II:6.
7	Quartetto ex Dis. à: 2: vv. violetta obligᵃ: et Basso:	Quartet, Op. 1, No. 2; III:2.
8	Notturno in C. à: 2. VV. 2. cornj. 1. flauto trav: viola. et Basso —	Spurious work, II:C1; rightly attributed to Dittersdorf in the Pachta Coll., Prague (XXII B289).
9	Synf.ᵃ in D. à. 2 VV. 2: Cornj, viola. con Basso.	Symphony No. 10.
10	Quartetto in E♭ A. 2: vv. viola oblig.ᵃ con Basso —	Spurious work, I:Es5 and III:Es6, variously listed as a symphony, quartet, notturno, etc. and also variously attributed to Christoph Sonnleithner, Rugietz, Michael Haydn and Joseph Haydn. Landon *SYM* 812, No. 77.

[No. in list]	[Works listed]	[Comments (H.C.R.L)]
11	Notturno in Dis à 2: VV. 2: Violae. 2: cornj. Con Basso	Doubtful work, II:Es5, beginning with a march in the Salzburg tradition – Michael Haydn?
12	Notturno in Dis à: 2. VV. 2: Violae. con violoncello.	Spurious work, II:Es8, variously attributed as a Concerto to Wagenseil (Brussels), or to Ignaz Holzbauer (Breitkopf Cat. 1766 and, in the key of D, in Göttweig).
13	VI. Menuetti. à 2: VV. 2 Cornj. con Basso	Lost works, IX:2.
14	Quattro in C. à 2. VV. alto viola oblig.ᵃ con Basso	Quartet, Op. 1, No. 6; III:6.
15	Quattro in Dis. [sic] a. 2: VV. viola obligᵃ: con Basso —	Quartet, Op. 1, No. 1; III:1.
16	Divertimento. a: 2 VV. Viola obl.ᵃ Con Basso [new page begins:]	Otherwise known as String Trio V:c4; listed again in the Sigmaringen Cat. under No. 62, for 2 v. and basso.
17	Quartetto. in E ♯ à 2. VV. viola. con Basso	Quartet, Op. 2, No. 2; III:8.
18	Scherzando. in E ♯ à 2. VV. 2. cornj. viola. et Basso.	II:37.
19	Quartetto. in B. à 2. VV. viola con Basso:	Quartet, Op. 2, No. 6; III:12.
20	Divertimo. con Echo à. 2: violini 1ᵐⁱ 2: violini 2ᵈⁱ et 2. Bassi —	II:39.
21	Quartetto. in F. à 2. VV. Viola. et Basso — —	Quartet, Op. 2, No. 4; III:10.
22	Quartetto in A. à. 2. VV. Viola obl.ᵃ con Basso —	Quartet, Op. 2, No. 1; III:7.
23	Synfo.ᵃ in D ♯. à 2. VV. 2. cornj. viola. et Basso.	Scherzando, II:35.
24	Synf.ᵃ in C. à 2. VV. Viola 2 Cornj. Basso.	Scherzando, II:34.
25	Synfon: in C. à: 2. VV. 2 clarini viola. et Basso. et tympᵃ.	Symphony No. 32.
26	Notturno in D. à. 2: VV. 2. Corn: viola. et Basso.	II:22.
27	Synfon: in F. a 2. VV. 2 Cornj Viola. con Basso.	Scherzando II:33.
28	Synfon. in G. à: 2. VV. 2: Corn: Viola obl.ᵃ Basso.	Scherzando II:36.
29	Serenada. in G. à. 2. VV. 2. Violae. con Basso —	II:2.
30	Notturno in B. à. 2: VV. 2. cornj. violoncello. et Contra = = Basso	II:B3, a lost work.

[*No. in list*]	[*Works listed*]	[*Comments (H.C.R.L)*]
31	Quartetto in A. [*sic*] à. 2. VV. viola con Basso —	Quartet, Op. 1, No. 3; III:3.
32	Quartetto in G. à. 2. VV. viola con Basso —	Quartet Op. 1, No. 4; III:4.
33	Quartetto in Dis. à. 2. vv. viola Con Basso. [new page begins:]	Doubtful work, III:Es7; also attributed as Piano Trio, Op. 1, No. 4, by Joseph Anton Liber, in G.
34	Trio in D.♯ a 2. VV. & Basso	V:15.
35	Trio in C.b. [*sic*] a 2. VV: & Basso	V:B1.
36	Trio. in A: à. 2. VV: et Basso	V:A1; a work by Michael Haydn (autograph in GdM).
37	Trio. in C. à. 2 VV: et Basso	V:C5.
38	Trio in Eb à 2. VV. & Basso	V:Es9, a spurious work rightly attributed to Leopold Hof(f)mann in the Breitkopf Cat. of 1766 and in a Brussels MS.
39	Trio in G à. 2 VV. et Basso	V:G1.
40	Divertimento à. 2. violino Solo Viola Sola. con Basso ——	V:8.
41	Divertimento à. 2. VV. et Basso	V:A2.
42	Trio. in C. à. 2. VV. et Basso —	V:16.
43	Gassatio. A. à. 2. VV. 2 Violae Con Basso —	Spurious work, II:A2, by Franz Aumon.
44	Parthia in G. à 2. VV. 2. Violae Con Basso —	Lost work, II:G3; theme is for Viola I.
45	Trio in G. à. 2: VV. et Basso	Spurious work, V:G6, by Leopold Hof(f)mann, in MS. XXVII B60 Zámek Castle, Tyn, now Prague National Museum; also in Breitkopf Cat. 1766.
46	Quartetto. in D. à. 2. VV. viola. con Basso — —	Spurious Quartet, III:D3, by J. G. Albrechtsberger; autograph in Budapest.
'vide N.º 26'	Notturno in D vide N.º 26	Another copy of II:22, here without the horns, in the quartet version.
	[The next entries possibly later:]	
47	Serenada Eb à. 2: VV. con Basso.	Trio V:17.
48	Sinfonia. F. à' 2. VV. 2. obois 2. Cornj. viola et Basso ——	Symphony No. 17.
49	Sinfonia G. à. 2. VV. 2. obois. 2: côrn.: viol: et Basso. [new page begins:]	Symphony No. 18.
50	Synfonia à 2. V.V. ex G Symphony No. 3. 2. oboe 2 corn: viola con Basso	Symphony No. 3.

[No. in list]	[Works listed]	[Comments (H.C.R.L)]
51	Synfonia Ex C à 2. V.V. 2. Oboe. 2 Corn: et Basso—Viola	Symphony No. 2.
52	Synfonia ex C à 2. V.V. 2. oboe. 2. Corn: et Basso — Viola	Symphony No. 25.
53	Trio ex B. a — 2 V.V. et Basso [possibly later additions:]	V:18.
54	Trio ex G à 2: V. V. et Basso	V:20
55	Trio ex E. dur à 2. V. V. et Basso	V:19.

The first additional group contains the following works: No. 56, Symphony No. 5; No. 57, Gassatio, II:F3 (Purksteiner); No. 58, Gassatio II:F4 (spurious); No. 59, Quintetto, II:F5 (Ordoñez at Göttweig, 1763); No. 60, Quintetto, II:Es9 (Ordoñez in Brtnice [Brno]); No. 61, Quartetto III:B5 (in the Ringmacher Catalogue of 1773, rightly attributed to Gewey); No. 62, a Tre, Trio, V:C4; No. 63, a Tre in B, Trio, V:Es1 (Michael Haydn, autograph in the Gesellschaft der Musikfreunde); No. 64, Notturno in G, II:G2 (Purksteiner); No. 65, Notturno in C. a. 2 VV. 2 Viola. 2 Clarinet e Basso, II:17; No. 66, Quintetto, II:Es10 (spurious).

The second additional group had to be squeezed into the catalogue after Holzbauer, 'vide post Holzbauer': No. 67, Divertim[ento], II:1; No. 68, Divertim[ento] II:D8 (spurious); No. 69, Symphony No. 15; No. 70, Gassatio, II:9; No. 71, a spurious Symphony, I:C29 (lost); No. 72, Variationes di Clavicembalo in A, XVII:A1 (lost). There is no No. 73. The third additional group contains: No. 74, a spurious Symphony, I:D25 (lost); No. 75, Menuett Con variation (2 fl., 2 ob., 1 bsn., 2 hns., str.) –

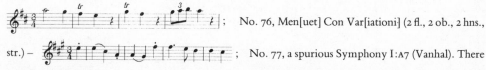

; No. 76, Men[uet] Con Var[iationi] (2 fl., 2 ob., 2 hns.,

str.) – ; No. 77, a spurious Symphony I:A7 (Vanhal). There

was no more room on this page, so the copyist wrote 'vide. I post Jomelli.' No. 78, Symphony No. 38; No. 79, Symphony No. 28; No. 80, Symphony No. 26; No. 81, Symphony No. 34, second movement; No. 82, a spurious Symphony, I:G8 (Michael Haydn); No. 83, Symphony No. 23.

Now the most interesting facts about this collection are (a) its size and (b) the relatively large number of doubtful and spurious works it contained. Obviously the demand for new Haydn was so vigorous that the copyists began, even *c.* 1765, to search for works by other members of the Austrian or south German school whose style was similar enough to that of Haydn to enable the spurious objects to pass, at least superficially, as the real thing. The step from these false manuscripts to the false French prints was merely a different geographical concept and provided a slightly more durable method of falsification.

The first editions of Haydn's music

(I) PARIS

Although Haydn never visited France, his music was very popular there, and in the course of this biography, we shall often register enthusiastic Gallic reaction to Haydn's muse.[1] It was in France that Haydn's music was first published. On 30 January 1764, Louis-Balthasar de la Chevardière, rue de roule à la croix d'or, paid for an

1 *Haydn at Eszterháza 1766–1790*, pp. 590ff.; *Haydn: The Years of 'The Creation' 1796–1800*, pp. 578ff.; *Haydn: the Late Years 1801–1809*. esp. pp. 66ff.

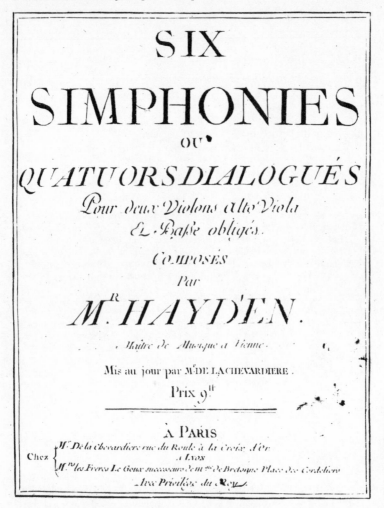

The title page of the first edition of Haydn's String Quartets, Op. I, Nos. 1–4, published in Paris in 1764. This is probably the earliest edition of any music by Haydn.

announcement in the *Affiches, Annonces & Avis divers* which informed the public of 'Six Simphonies ou Quatuors dialogués ... par Mᵣ. Hayd'en'; in fact there were four Haydn Quartets (Op. 1, Nos. 1–4) and two Flute Quartets by Toeschi (see above for a reproduction of the title page). The engraver signed himself 'Ceron' at the foot of the first page of each part. Now we can not tell when Chevardière issued the second edition, but it was certainly by the late autumn of 1768 or early in 1769.[1] The original four Haydn Quartets were now enlarged to six (including Symphony 'A' and Op. 1, No. 6) and the Toeschi Quartets eliminated. The engraver Ceron was replaced by another for these two additions, and the style of engraving is quite different. Although Chevardière dropped the wind parts of the Symphony, he never stated that it was a quartet at all; on the contrary, its own title is 'Sinfonia / V', and it is, moreover, the only one of the six works which is accurately described by the principal title, 'Six Simphonies'.

---

1 Our copy is earlier than that in the Bibliothèque Nationale, Paris (description: *JHW* Reihe XII, Band 1, Kritischer Bericht, Munich 1973, p. 25, source 132, 1770–1). Our copy has the catalogue as in Cari Johannson's *French Music Publishers' Catalogues of the Second Half of the Eighteenth Century*, Stockholm 1955, p. 75 (Haydn's œuvre IV) and it also contains a slip pasted on the blank verso of the title page: 'a Lyon / Chez Serriere Rue / Syrene Vis a Vis la Rue / Milet ou l'on trouve un Grand / Magazin de Musique Moderne.' We owe this interesting (and perhaps the earliest extant) copy of the revised edition to our kind friend, Hermann Baron, in London.

On 12 March 1764, another French publisher, Jean Baptiste Venier (a distinguished old Venetian name), used the *Affiches, Annonces & Avis divers* to announce the publication of what would be Haydn's first published Symphony, No. 2, which was No. 14 in a series of symphonies by various authors. In Venier's own catalogues of the period – for a facsimile see Johansson, op. cit., Facs. 120 – this 'opus' is listed as follows:

> Opera Decima Quarta
> Les Noms inconnus bons à connoitre
> 13. Vanmaldere. 14. Heyden. 15. Back [Bach].
> 16. Pfeiffer. 17. Hchetky. 18. Fränzl.
> Per Due Violini Alto e Basso. ... 9 [livres]

The only surviving copy of Haydn's Symphony is in the Conservatoire de Musique, Paris (now Bibliothèque Nationale, H.118a–d) and contains only the string parts, which is probably all that Venier actually printed (see his listing in the catalogue just cited); but he may have sold the oboe and horn parts separately, in manuscript, because the title page carries the note, 'Les parties de Cors de Chasse, Hautbois, Flutes, et Bassons y seront comprises, mais le plus souvent elles ad Libitum.' Venier issued two other announcements of the new Haydn Symphony, in *L'avant-coureur* (26 March 1764) and the *Mercure de France* (1 April).

The next French publisher to turn his attention to Haydn was Anton Huberty, who in 1764 was in the middle of a series of 'Symphonies Périodiques'. On 18 June (*Annonces ...*) he announced No. 18 of his series, a Symphony by Wagenseil. No. 19 was a Symphony by Stamitz, while Nos. 20 and 21 were by 'Hayden'. No. 20, although its title page[1] lists 'Simphonia / a più Stromenti / obligati' turns out to be the String Quartet known as Opus 'o' (II:6). No. 21, tantalizingly, has never been discovered; no copy has survived.

About 1764 or, at the latest, in 1765, M. de la Chevardière issued his next series of Haydn: 'Six / Sonates / en Trio / pour deux violons & basse' – six String Trios (V:FI, 19, D2, 18, 15, 16).[2] The craze for Haydn in France had begun.[3]

How did Messrs de la Chevardière, Venier and Huberty procure the music for these editions, all of which were presumably undertaken without Haydn's knowledge? As it happens, some new evidence has recently (1979) come to light. Mr Hermann Baron, who has been supplying us with rare Haydn MSS. and editions for many years, discovered in France a small, but complete collection of authentic Haydn MSS. which he was kind enough to pass on to us. A description of the Quartets (Op. 1, Nos. 3 and 6) and Trios (V:15 and 16), by Viennese Professional Copyist No. 2 (= Fürnberg/Morzin No. 4) and Fürnberg/Morzin Nos. 6, 7, 9 will be found *supra*, pp. 251 and 220. All four works were among Chevardière's pre-1766 publications, the Quartets in 1764 and the Trios shortly thereafter. Did Haydn himself sell these copies to someone in France, or to someone who took them to France? Or did the copyists organize the sale? The problem is insoluble, but the very existence of these MSS., by

1 Copies in the Cambridge University Library, Marion Scott Coll., and Conservatoire de Musique, Paris. Johansson, op. cit., p. 46. A. Weinmann, *Kataloge Anton Huberty (Wien) und Christoph Torricella*, Beiträge zur Geschichte des alt-Wiener Musikverlages, Reihe 2, Folge 7, Vienna 1962, p. 19. In Hoboken (I, p. 301), the print was wrongly dated *post* 1768 rather than 1764(?).

2 Dating: Cari Johansson, op. cit., Facs. 50 and pp. 69f. Chevardière soon referred to this publication as Haydn's œuvre 2.

3 La Fondation Ephrussi de Rothschild, St-Jean-Cap-Ferrat, owns a Sèvres service of 402 pieces made, according to the porcelain experts, in 1767 and supposedly containing the themes of Haydn quartets. We have examined that part of the service which is exhibited, but the protecting glass screen prevented our being able to approach the pieces closely enough to identify the music. M. Marc Vignal, who is at present writing a large-scale biography of Haydn, is currently investigating the matter at our request.

the Fürnberg/Morzin copyists, shows how Haydn's earliest works managed to reach the Parisian publishers.

AMSTERDAM

In Holland, there lived two brothers, Johann Julius and Burchard Hummel, horn players, who settled in The Hague in the 1740s. In the 1750s, J. J. Hummel moved to Amsterdam, there to establish what would become the leading Dutch music publisher of the century. On J. J. Hummel's first catalogues, we find him listed in Amsterdam, but with the note: 'NB. on peut avoir la même Musique ci dessus marquée chez B. Hummel Marchand de Musique à la Haye.' In 1770, J. J. Hummel opened a branch in Berlin and moved there himself in 1774, from which city he entered into correspondence with Haydn. But at this period, J. J. Hummel operated only from Amsterdam, where on 13 April 1765, he announced in the *Amsterdamsche Courant* six Haydn Quartets: Op. 'o' and Op. 1, Nos. 6, 1, 2, 3 and 4. The print already states 'opera prima'; presumably Hummel knew more works were to follow shortly.[1]

Hummel, being a musician, allowed himself textual licence with these early quartets. In Op. 1, No. 6, third movement, he cancelled bars 5 and 28 in order to turn Haydn's nine-bar phrases into eight-bar lengths. A similar state of affairs obtains in Op. 'o', where Huberty's text is the original and authentic one. Marion M. Scott, who first drew attention to these differences in her edition for the Oxford University Press (1931), knew none of the manuscript copies (which on the whole agree with Huberty and not Hummel) and thought the Hummel text represented Haydn's own revision. In fact the revisions are clearly Hummel's own, and are poor.

ENGLAND

Readers of the *St James's Chronicle* in London on 25–27 June 1765 could read an announcement of the Hummel edition, 'Printed at Amsterdam and sold by R. Bremner, opposite Somerset House in the Strand' (Hoboken I, p. 302). And with this modest announcement, many people in England will have heard the name of Haydn for the first time. These early products of Haydn's art were as successful in England as they had been on the Continent, for a few years later, Bremner found it worth his while to order a new engraving, using as his text the Hummel edition.[2]

By 1765, then, these pirated editions had circulated Haydn's music over the western parts of Europe, while over the eastern parts, manuscript copies fulfilled the same function. The foundations of Haydn's fame had been well laid.

1 Hoboken I, p. 302. Cari Johansson, *J. J. & B. Hummel Music Publishing and Thematic Catalogues*, 2 vols., Stockholm 1972, pp. 4f. and Facs. 3. G. Feder (*JHW*, Reihe XII/1, Kritischer Bericht, Munich 1973, pp. 26, 29f.) has shown clearly that Hummel's edition is textually independent of Chevardière's, and the same independence was established by R. Barrett-Ayres in his new edition of the early Quartets for Doblinger. Hummel added figured basses and made other changes as well; on the subject of the textual unreliability of Hummel's prints, see also G. Feder, 'Die Eingriffe des Musikverlegers Hummel in Haydns Werken', *Festschrift Karl-Gustav Fellerer zum 70. Geburtstag*, Cologne 1973, an important article which was only recently drawn to our attention and is thus missing in the general bibliography – *Haydn: the Late Years 1801–1809*, add to p. 448.
2 Title: Hoboken, Vol. 1, p. 301; copies: British Museum, Hoboken Collection, Österreichische Nationalbibliothek.

Index

The indexes to all five volumes of this biography were prepared by Else Randant Landon. Principal references are shown in bold type and references to illustrations in italics; references to artists, engravers, etc, in captions to the plates are indicated parenthetically, e.g. (*pl.2*). References to the Addenda and Errata section on pp. 625–44 (concerning the other volumes of this biography) are also included. In documents cited in the text variant forms (and misspellings) of names are frequently found; such variations are shown in parentheses, e.g. 'Buchhol(t)z, 'Mitscha (Miča)' etc., as appropriate. For abbreviations of musical instruments, see p. 16; the abbreviation HDSW refers to the separate index, on p. 622, of doubtful and spurious works attributed to Haydn.

INDEX OF COMPOSITIONS BY HAYDN
(HOBOKEN REFERENCES SHOWN IN PARENTHESES)

DOUBTFUL AND SPURIOUS WORKS
ATTRIBUTED TO JOSEPH HAYDN
(correct authors, as far as can be established, are shown in parentheses)

Aria de Venerabili (XXIIIc:6) 157n.
Ave Regina in F (XXIIIb:6) 157n.

Cassatio in D (II:D1; J. M. Haydn?) 590
Chorale St Antoni (Wind-band Partita in B flat; II:46) 271
CONCERTOS:
— for cemb. and orchestra: — (XVIII:G2; = J. Steffan) 521; — (XVIII:Es1, F1, F3, G1) 521;
— for cor. and orchestra (VIId:4) 519;
— for flute and orchestra (VIIf:D1; = Leopold Hofmann) 207, 519;
— for oboe and orchestra (VIIf:C1) 519;
— for organ (cemb.) and orchestra: — in C (Hoboken *deest*; from Preßburg/Bratislava) and — in F (Hoboken *deest*; = Leopold Hofman) 197n.; — in G (Hoboken *deest*; = P. P. Sales) 213, 216;
— for v. and orchestra 519; — in D (VIIa:D1; = Carl Stamitz) 519; — in G (VIIa:G1; = J. M. Haydn [Perger *deest*]) 519; — in A (VIIa:A1; = G. M. Giornovichj) 519; — in B flat (VIIa:B1; = J. M. Haydn [Perger 53]; and VIIa:B2; = Christian Cannabich) 519;
— for vc. and orchestra: — in C (VIIb:5; = David Popper) 519; — in D (VIIb:4) 425, 519; — in G minor (VIIb:g1) 519

DANCES: for questionable works see index of compositions by Haydn
DIVERTIMENTOS: (see also *Feld Parthien*, below):
— (II:C1; = Carl Ditters [dorf]) 592; — (II:C11) 299ff.; — (III:D3; = J. G. Albrechtsberger; Sextet) 298 (see also Quartet, III:D3, below); — (II:D8) 595; — in D for 2 cor., strings, see Quartet, III:D3, below; — (II:Es5; = J.M. Haydn) 593; — (II:Es6) 592; — (II:Es8; = J. G. Wagenseil and others) 592; — (II:Es9; = Carlos d'Ordoñez) 595; — in E flat (*Feld Parthie*, II:B7; various attributions) 271; — in F (Hoboken *deest*) 271; — (II:F3; Joseph Purksteiner; and II:F4) 595; (II:F5 = Carlos d'Ordoñez) 252, 595; — (II:F7 =Wranizky) 271; — (II:G2), see below under Notturnos: — (II:G3; lost) 594; — (II:A2; = Franz Aumon) 594

Feld Parthien (II:41–6) 271

Gioco filharmonico (IV:Anhang) 71

Litany in C (XXIIIc:C2; = J. Hayda) 157n.

MOTETS: — 'Salus et gloria' (XXIIIa:6; = Leopold Hofmann) and 'Super fluminia' (XXIIIa:7; = J. B. Vanhal) 157n.

NOTTURNOS: — (II:G2; = Joseph Purksteiner) 595; — (II:B3; lost) 593

OFFERTORIES: — 'Ad aras convolate' (XXIIIa:5) and 'Ardentes seraphim' (XXIIIa:8; = J. M. Haydn?) 157n.

QUARTETS (string):
— (III:C13; = J. B. Vanhal) 622;
— (III:D3; = J.G. Albrechtsberger) 298, 590, 594;
— (III:Es6), see below under Symphonies: I:Es5;
— (III:Es7; = J. A. Lieber) 594;
— (III:B5; = Gewey) 595;
— Op. 3 (III:13–18; = Roman Hofstetter) 183, 253, 255;
— Op. XVIII (III:G4; = Franz Dussek) 298n.
Quintet (II:Es10) 595

Salve Regina settings: — (XXXIIIb:4; XXXIIIb:5 and C7 [= Hayda]; and XXXIIIb:6) 157n.
Sextet (III:D3; = Albrechtsberger), see under Divertimentos
SONATAS (pf.): — No. 17 (Hob. *deest*) 224; — No. 18 (Hob. *deest*: = Kayser [Kaiser] 224
SYMPHONIES:
— in C (I:C10; = Robert Kimmerling) 588;
— in C (I:C26; Bach or Miča) 574;
— in C (I:C29; lost) 595;
— in D (I:D21; (= J. M. Haydn [Perger 36]) 242n.;
— in D (I:D25; lost) 595;
— in D (I:D26; = J. M. Haydn [Perger 37]) 242n.;
— in E flat (I:Es4; = J. M. Haydn [Perger 1]) 242n.;
— in E flat (I:Es5; = Christoph Sonnleithner and others) 412, 592;
— in F (I:F3; = Christoph Sonnleithner) 412;
— in F (I:F7; various attributions) 591;
— in G (I:G2; = J.M. Haydn [Perger *deest*]) 242n.;
— in G (I:G8; = J. M. Haydn [Perger 7]) 595;
— in A (I:A5; = Carl Ditters[dorf]) 188;
— in A (I:A7; = J. B. Vanhal) 595;

TRIOS (string; arranged by Hoboken numbering):
— (V:D2; = J. M. Haydn [Perger 101]) 222, 597; — (V:Es1; = J. M. Haydn [Perger *deest*]) 222, 590, 595; — (V:Es2; = ?) 222; — (V:Es9; = Leopold Hofmann) 221, 594; — (V:F4; = Bach) 222; — (V:F8; =J. M. Haydn [Perger *deest*]) 222; —(V:G6; = Leopold Hofman) 222, 594; — (V:G7; = ?) 222; — (V:A1; = J. M. Haydn [Perger *deest*]) 594; — (V:A7; = Leopold Hofmann) 222; — (V:B2; = J. M. Haydn [Perger *deest*]) 222

VARIATIONS: — *Variaziones a Clavicembalo* (XVII:G1) 227; — *Variationes di Clavicembalo* (XVII:A1; lost) 595

NOTES

ADDENDA AND ERRATA

Haydn at Eszterháza 1766–1790

[Plate 12, caption:]
After 'Duke Albert von Sachsen-Teschen' add 'Leopold (later Grand Duke of Tuscany and Emperor Leopold II)'.

[page 11, line 5:]
The last word should read 'Levéltár'.

[page 28, n. 2:]
David Clegg writes (29 Oct. 1978): 'With reference to the picture supposedly but not showing Haydn conducting *L'incontro improvviso*, the engraving by Bellotto of *Le turc généreux* is referred to in S. Kozakiewicz, *Bernardo Bellotto*, vol. II, Catalogue (Elek 1972) pl. 287. *Le turc généreux* was performed in April 1758 (Cat., p. 227).'

[page 53:]
Ullmann: some of the drama behind 'mit halben Junii 769 weggegangen' appears in a petition which she addresses to Prince Nicolaus, *c.* March 1769, wherein she laments being separated from the chamber musicians; i.e. she was assigned to church music duties at Eisenstadt. She asks to be allowed to join the other chamber musicians at Eszterháza, and in view of her meagre salary, on which she cannot live, she asks for an increase of 100 gulden. Here is the document:

> [A.M. 145, EH, Budapest, No. 416–8:]
> [cover:] Francisca Ullmanni bittet nacher / Eszterház mit 100 Fl. Jährl. / Zulaag als Cameral Sängerin zu / kom̄en. [Beneath:] A Son Altesse / Monseigneur le Prince dᵉ Eszterházy.
> [next page:] Durchlauchtig Hochgebohrner Reichs Fürst / Gnädigst Hochgebiettender Herr Herr / Euer Durchlaucht wird ohnehin annoch in Hoher Andächtung seyn, / welcher Gestalten Höchstdieselbe mich mit Anderen vor / ongefehr ¾ᵘ Jahren als Cameral Singerin in Höchst / dero Dienste aufzunehmen, und ein Salarium von Jährl. / 300 Fl. nebst Quartier, Holtz, und Liecht mir zu entwerffen / Aller gnädigst geruhet Zu haben, und gleich wie ich von Jugendt / auf mit grosser Mühe, und Fleis dieser so edlen Kunst sonderbar / zugethan, eben so auch zeit dieser meiner dingfähiegen Dienstleistung, beflüssen ware, Mich nach Möglichkeit alßo / zu qualificiren, daß als Cameral sowohl als Theatral Sing / erin Euer Durchlaucht meine unwürdige Dienste zu / prastiren in Stande zu seyn, gedenke; / Nun Durchlaucht / iger Fürst, und Herr Herr, da ich Zeit meines allhier / seyn fast beständig allhier, und auch ferners von der / Cameral Music anwiderum entfernet seyn solte, ge / folgbar das wenige so ich in dieser Kunst mit

vieler Mühe / erlehrnet, viellmehr vergessete, als das ich mich in selber / qualificirter, und tauglicher machete, Euer Durchlaucht hohes / Vergnügen hindürftig zu verwahren, gleich wie Euer / Durchlaucht, als ein Hocher Kenner dessen, ein solches / ganz wohl einsehen wird; / So dennoch / Gelanget an Euer Durchlaucht meine Unterthanigst / gehorsamstes Anlangen Höchstdieselbste geruhen Mich / Zu der übrigen Cameral Music nacher Eszterház zu / beordern, anbey aber meinen geringen Gehalt deren 300 / Gulden, willen auf solche Arth mit diesem ohnmäglich sub / sistiren könte, annoch jahrlich 100. Gulden Allergnädigst / beyzulegen, vor so Höchste Gnaden, allstäts und sonderheit / lich befließen seyn werde, Euer Durchlaucht hohes Con / tento im̄ermehr zu vermehren in Tiefster Submission / ersterbend / Euer Hochfürstlichen Durchlaucht. / Unterthanigst gehorsamste / Francisca Ullmanin / Hochfürstl. Cameral Singerin, mpria.

[page 65 col. 1, line 18:
For '... finally, "Bonno who is ...' read '... finally, "Bonno" who is ...'.

[page 79:]
Franz Sigl (probably *recte*) was engaged on 1 April 1761, not 1 February.

[page 120:]
In the third line of the Stadlmann bill read '... the bass-bar reinforced'.

[page 126, footnote 1:]
For '... which words ...' read '... which works ...'.

[page 132:]
Details of the Keller loan are given in Christina Stadtlaender, *Joseph Haydn of Eisenstadt*, trans. and ed. Percy M. Young, London 1968, pp. 74f.

[page 135, line 8:]
Delete footnote reference.

[page 149; footnote:]
For '... and two timpani players?' read '... and one timpani player?'.

[page 150, line 26:]
Footnote reference should read '2'.

[page 151, line 30:]
Footnote reference should read '3'.

[page 151f.:]
According to J. Harich (*Musikgeschichte*, p. 32), *Lo speziale* was first performed – perhaps as a kind of

'general rehearsal' – on Princess Maria's name-day, 5 August 1768, for which celebration there were also fireworks, illuminations, spoken theatre, and balls.

Page 152, penultimate paragraph: the details of this entertaining document may now be supplied from Stadtlaender (op cit., quoted by permission, pp. 38f., where however the author wrongly attributes the document to 1762 – many of the musicians named in this document were not engaged until 1768):

List of items of Masque clothing for
the Court Musicians of His Highness

	Fl.	Kr.
To Music Director Haydn: Man's black domino, velvet waistcoat, velvet breeches, and hat with feather; one new lady's domino of glossy taffeta, velvet skirt, and lady's hat of black taffeta	4	0
„ *Herr Friberth*: Green and red Dutch peasant costume;	4	0
similar female costume, with curls;	1	8
One man's black domino with Jabot and breeches	2	0
1 domino curls and beard		51
„ *Herr Franz*: 1 wealthy Milord [costume] and curls	2	34
„ *Herr Kiefel* [Ignaz Küffel]: 1 English peasant [costume];	2	0
curls and gloves	1	8
„ *Herr Loigi* [Tomasini]: 1 domino and fancy waistcoat	2	0
„ *Herr Victorini* [Colombazzo]: 1 domino with fancy waistcoat;	2	0
curls, beard and 1 pair gloves	1	25
„ *Herr Jos. Weigl*: 1 domino and fancy waistcoat;	2	0
curls, beard and 1 pair gloves	1	25
„ *Herr Specht*: 1 domino and fancy waistcoat;	2	0
curls, beard and 1 pair gloves	1	25

[From EH, Forchtenstein Castle; probably only the one page exhibited at Schloß Petronell in 1959; see *Haydn at Eszterháza*, p. 152, n. 2.]

Note: This enchanting document shows that Haydn and the band were dressed, for this occasion, like *commedia dell'arte* musicians. The ladies with Haydn and Friberth were possibly their wives; Magdelena Friberth, *née* Spangler, had been engaged shortly before; or perhaps Haydn's 'lady' was one of the other singers. A Watteau picture springs to mind.

[page 153:]
Letter to Scheffstoss: in line 3 for 'I sent you ...' read 'I send you ...'.

[page 167, line 44:]
Footnote reference should read '2'.

[page 168:]
Footnote 1 should read '*Vide supra*, p. 158.'; footnote 2 should read '3 Jancik, p. 222.'; insert missing footnote: '2 See *Haydn in England 1791–1795*, p. 58.'

[page 199:]
Bill from Fischer, 10 Dec. 1773; after Fischer's signature, next line, for '... ["30 fl. 44 xr." ...' read '["3 fl. 44 xr." ...'.

[page 227, line 10:]
For 'and for the quarters ...' read 'and for the quartets ...'.

[page 236:]
Some comments on the Vanhal entries were kindly provided by our Cardiff colleague, Dr David Wyn Jones. We have preferred to deal with them together.

[Dr Jones writes:] '236: *Applausus*, final Chorus as V. Not an "odd reason" when one considers that from the mid 1770s onwards V's name, within Austria, was associated with church music as much as with symphonies, quartets. In fact, judging by the number of works and extant sources. I am coming to the tentative conclusion that V. was as respected in this genre as Michael Haydn. 308: The Guera print of H., V. and Lochon appeared in 1779. 316 & 319: *Re* the influences of H's opp. I & II on V's opp. I & II. V's opp. I & II seem to me to owe most to Dussek's quartets of the 1760s, especially the use of the four-movement pattern Fast-Slow-Minuet/Trio-Fast. V. ignores the five-movement pattern used by H., and also the three-movement pattern used by Ordoñez, Gassmann, etc. Stylistically, too, the influence of H. is not obvious, e.g. there is no octave doubling in the minuets. 319: V's Quartet in C minor, Op. I, No. 4 and *Sturm und Drang*. This is V's *only* minor key quartet up to the late 1770s. It has none of the power of H's D minor or, indeed, of V's own minor key symphonies; in all respects it is consistent with its major key companions and, in particular, has little counterpoint. In V., and this is again an under-researched theory, *Sturm und Drang* was revealed only in his symphonies. 319: V's C major Quartet is Hoboken III:C13. The Kremsmünster copy has 'Compos 1773' on the title page. Published by Huberty as Op. 13, No. 2. Although in many ways this set of six works does not show the influence of H's Opp. 9, 17 and 20 (no fugues, no minor key works), in other respects it does. V. uses FMSF, the first violin parts are demonstrative, the slow movements are violin concertos (including pauses and opportunities for cadenzas), and there is octave doubling in the minuets. 380: V. died "almost entirely forgotten". What is striking about V's late career is how adept he was at changing from being a successful composer of symphonies, quartets, etc., to being a successful composer of salon music. He remained popular, respected and well-known until his death. There are, for instance, over a dozen reviews of piano pieces in *AMZ* between 1797 and 1813. 380: "Vanhal began composing in the 1760s ...". Possible to refine this to late 1760s. Gerber states that V's first symphony appeared in 1767. As negative evidence, V. is not mentioned in the *Wiener Diarium* article of October 1766 whereas Hofmann, J. Haydn, Dittersdorf, Ordoñez and Gassmann are. 380, n. 3: V. article in *MGG* Vol. 13, not 14. 381: Bailleux Op. 25. Date of publication Oct.–Nov. 1779 (deduced by comparing its catalogues with the catalogues contained and cited in Johansson; her name, by the way, appears as Johannson in Bibliography, *The Late Years*, p. 453). Another copy of the print: British Library, h.1507 j. 381: Many slow movements in V's symphonies have concertante parts including, *inter alia*, parts for flute, oboe and 'cello. 381: Date(s) of compositions for V's G and D minor symphonies is/are still irritatingly vague. I would like to believe that he composed them before going to Italy in 1769. 474: Hummel Op. 10 appeared in 1781. I cannot locate a copy of this print and so cannot comment on Gerber's review. Generally, V's music was being published by Hummel some three or four years after its composition and the text was often taken from a French source. 491: Storace's "quartett party". Date of 13 June 1784 has been proposed for this event. J. H. Eibl, *Mozart. Die Dokumente seines Lebens. Addenda und Corrigenda*, Kassel 1978, p. 44. 591: Most of the spurious publications of music by V. date from the 1770s, but, strangely, no Vanhal was performed at the Concert Spirituel and the only item in the d'Ogny Catalogue is a print of spurious arrangements of wind quintets.'

[page 245:]
IV. Offertorium 'Agite properate ad aras', under *Sources* read: '(2) MS. parts, Pilgrimage Church (Benedictine Priory) of Mariazell, ms. 20: 'Motett / Offertorium de Sc^{to} v: Sc^{ta} in C (Agite, properate ad aras) a / Canto 2, Alto / Tenore, Basso / Violinis 2 / Oboe 2 / Clarinis 2 / Tympano / Viola / con / Organo e Violone / Auth Dno Hayden.' Over twenty performance dates listed, from 1778 to 1822. (3) [add at end of entry:] 'and text, "Animae Deo gratiae".' (4) [add at end of entry:] and text, "Animae Deo gratiae".'

[page 257:]
The *Singspiel* version of *Philemon und Baucis*. As if by a miracle, we have suddenly gained authentic news about this mysterious adaptation of Haydn's marionette opera. The only known copy of this libretto (Stadtbibliothek, Vienna) seems to have been for a performance at Regensburg, whither Pauersbach, as we have seen, proceeded in 1784; from the new document, it seems clear that he had connections with Regensburg before that date – either that, or Haydn sent the music; but we believe the go-between was probably Pauersbach, since his name is specially mentioned in the following report, which we owe to the kindness of our French colleague, M. Marc Vignal. It is from the unpublished Diaries of the Marquis de Bombelles, which M. Vignal procured from the present owner/publisher.

[Ratisbonne, 5 Nov. 1780] Pour célébrer le retour du Prince [Thurn und Taxis] en ville, on a joué un opéra nouveau. Les paroles sont d'un M. Bauersbach, qui a travaillé sur le sujet déjà traité par le frère de M. Pfeffel le jurisconsulte. Ce frère, quoiqu'aveugle, écrit bien et facilement à l'aide d'une plaque de cuivre qu'il pose sur son papier et qui, creusée en intervalles de lignes, sert à lui diriger la main. La pièce dont il s'agit est *Philémon et Baucis*. La musique est de Heyden, bon compositeur allemand et maître de chapelle du prince Esterhazy en Hongrie.

On a supposé que Jupiter, en reconnaissance de l'hospitalité de Philemon et de sa femme, ressuscite son fils Aret et la compagne de ce jeune homme qui, ainsi que lui, avait été frappée par la foudre. Mais M. Bauersbach n'a tiré aucun parti du moment agréable où des deux personnes r'ouvrent les yeux à la lumière. Cependant cette pièce renferme des situations assez touchantes, des vers heureux et un dialogue intéressant.

[Reprinted by permission of M. le Comte Clam Martinic and the Librairie Droz, Geneva]

Among the other entries: 24 June 1794. Bombelles stops at the monastery of Rheinau, between Zurich and Constance. The abbot invites him to dinner ... 'Au dessert, il a fait arriver une douzaine de moines, qui ont joué une symphonie d'un élève de Heyden [Pleyel?]. Cette musique, très belle, a été très bien exécutée.' 14 Sept. 1802. In his castle of Falkenberg (Bohemia) 'le comte de Praschma, aidé du recteur de la paroisse, d'un chapelain et d'un bourgeois de la ville, nous a fait entendre le *Printemps* et l'*Été* du célèbre Haydn.' In 1790, he heard an English girl nicely playing sonatas by Pleyel and 'Haiden' in Venice; in 1803, a Haydn Gloria at Falkenberg, and on 12 April 1811, *The Seven Words* in the oratorio version at Oberglogau (Silesia).

[page 259:]
Il ritorno di Tobia: we have meanwhile located fragments of the original 1784 performance material at the Landesbibliothek für Musik, Graz, cat. 318. There is also a score of *c*. 1800 (cat. 41681); but the parts are much more valuable. We have 'Mademois. Teyber/Sara' (8° paper with watermarks of three crescents, letters 'BV/C' under crown; later additions on paper with 'VG', also 'GFA' under ornament, or three stars under schematic crown; other parts with letters 'CS/C' etc.); 'Mad: Cavaliere/Rafaelle' (paper as before; another later addition has frog as watermark); 'Tobit' (later, red crayon, 'Saal', a later addition). This material was used, it appears, in some revival such as that of 1808; the orchestral parts would seem to be of that later date; bass part (instrumental) has 'Sign: Stadler', viola 'Ruz ... za' in red crayon.

[page 263:]
Length of *L'incontro improvviso*: Antal Dorati (letter of 30 June 1979) gives the overall timing of his new recording of the Opera for Philips as 150 minutes.

[page 264:]
Terzetto 'Mi sembra un sogno che diletta' lasts 8

minutes in the new Philips recording; the timing cited was from the Austrian Radio's broadcast in 1959.

[page 276:]
In musical example a) at bar 5, the last note is c'''.

[page 281, line 18:]
For '... melodies, ...' read '... melodies. ...'.

[page 306; col. 2:]
Minuet/Trio and Finale of a Symphony in C. Another version using these two movements is: I. Overture to *L'infedeltà delusa* (Ia:1), first movement. II. Ditto, 2nd movt., in the shortened version of the autograph (later rejected in favour of a longer one known to us from the Artaria print). III and IV: the Minuet/trio and Finale of our fragment. Scoring: 2 ob., 2 cor., str. Library of Congress, Washington, from Spanish MSS. (Catalán paper with watermark 'R ROMANI'); two copies, M 1004. A2H4 No. 1P and 1PB. The Library of Congress MSS. originated at the Spanish Court and were part of the Library's Martorell Collection. See the important article by Stephen C. Fisher in *Haydn-Studien* IV/2 (1977), pp. 65ff. We had suggested that his combination of Ia:1 and the fragment might have been Haydn's own (*Complete Symphonies*, Philharmonia Vol. VI, lxix-lxx), but at that time (1967), there were no sources to confirm the hypothesis. The Library of Congress/Madrid sources are secondary, but it is nevertheless possible that Haydn, needing new symphonies for Spain, made not only this compilation but also another, combining the Overtures to *L'incontro improvviso* (Ia:6) and *Le pescatrici* (I:106), and sent them to Spain *c.* 1779–81 (Fisher, op. cit., p. 82).

[page 309:]
Musical example: first note g'' not f''.

[pages 315, 325:]
In considering the order of the Op. 20 Quartets, an authentic source partly by Fürnberg-Morzin Copyist No. 4 (ex prof. Viennese copyist No. 2) may be significant: Keszthely Castle, cat. 0/53. The MSS. are: 'Quattro / Quartetti / Per due Violini, Viola & Basso / Composti / dal Sigl: Giuseppe Haydn / Violino Primo / N° I, II, III & IV.' If we examine the individual title pages, we see that at one time all six works must have been present. The numbering 1–4 would seem to have been superimposed when the MSS. were incorporated into the Festetics Coll. 'N^{ro} I' = Op. 20/2 = No. 5 in original. Copyist: F-M No. 4, 'Divertimento 5$^{\underline{to}}$'. The parts were later owned by Franz Gotthard. 4° Italian paper (watermarks: horizontal chain lines, 'REAL', 'GF s[?]'). 'N^{ro} II' = Op. 20/4 = 'Divertimento 4to' by the same copyist, which was later owned by Gotthard (watermarks: horizontal chain lines, fleur-de-lys over 'E' and a reversed 'C'). 'N:° III' = Op. 20/6 = 'Quartetto in A♯' by a second hand, of which we made tracings (here reduced):

No number; no 'Gotthard'. Watermarks: 'GFA' and three crescents, horizontal chain lines. 'N^{ro} IV' = Op. 20/5 = 'Divertimento 3$^{\underline{zo}}$' by F-M No. 4 and later owned by Gotthard (watermarks: 'GF' below crown, three stars in coat-of-arms). We believe that this incomplete MS. series is nevertheless authentic, or probably authentic, evidence of an internal numbering of the set approved by Haydn for the Artaria series of *c.* 1800–01, but which had been established before 1778 (when Copyist F-M No. 4 is presumed to have died) and therefore had a much older claim to authenticity than previously known.

[page 344f.:]
Piano Concerto in G (XVIII:4). Professor A. Peter Brown kindly provided a detailed description of the most important source of this work, a set of MS. parts in Kremsier Castle (II.F.40) by a professional Viennese copyist. Oblong Italian paper (watermarks: three crescents of declining size with 'REAL'; letters 'HF/REAL'; three stars in ornament). Title: 'Concerto [far right: "in G."] / per il / Clavi Cembalo / Violino Primo / Violino Secondo / Viola / Basso / Del Sig:^{re} Gius: Heyden. / [lower right corner: "L'Ambassadeur de Russie"].' The most important contribution that this source makes is the presence therein of a whole series of hitherto unknown cadenzas, of which we give the *incipits*, courtesy of Kremsier Castle and Professor Brown, who will himself publish the cadenzas in full.

[*Incipits* of cadenzas:]

Who wrote them? Dare we hope that they are Haydn's original cadenzas for Mademoiselle Paradis? We have no authentic keyboard cadenzas by Haydn (for one set in GdM, see pp. 571f.). The present ones are far more ambitious and are in any case valuable; perhaps they were written by Mlle Paradis, who was a composer, too. About the Russian Ambassador, Prince Dimitri Galitsin, see G. Feder in *HJB* IV (1968), p. 121.

[page 346:]
Six Duets (VI:1–6). Authentic MS. parts by Fürnberg-Morzin No. 4, Keszthely Castle, o/14, scored for violin and Basso; perhaps Haydn even made this arrangement, or sanctioned it. 'Sei / Sonate / per il / Violino solo con Basso / del Sigl: Giuseppe Haydn / Violino Solo'. Other title on Basso part. Again, the original order differs from that in common use (e.g. in Hoboken).

Hoboken VI	F-M original no.
1 in F	1 in D
2 in A	2 in C
3 in B flat	3 in E flat
4 in D	4 in B flat
5 in E flat	5 in F
6 in C	6 in A

The authentic order of *EK* conflicts with the F-M sequence, but the latter may nevertheless represent one of which Haydn approved: he liked to 'manipulate' the order of his *opera* when selling to new clients. The MS., which was once owned by Franz Gotthard, is written on 4to Italian paper (watermarks: 'w' in ornate frame with crown, three crescents of declining size).

[pages 349ff.:]
Baryton Trios. One has always imagined that Haydn himself made, or at any rate caused to be made and sanctioned, the various arrangements for other groups of instruments more suited to general distribution. In the following authentic source from Keszthely Castle (cat. K.1139), we have such an arrangement, for there are corrections in Haydn's hand in the Trio of No. 4, violin I. $4°$ Italian paper (watermarks: 'GFA' under canopy, three crescents of declining size with 'REAL'); some *Ersatz* paper for Basso part on other, local paper (watermark: eagle). 'Sei / Divertimenti / a / Violino Primo / Violino Secondo / e / Basso / Del Sigre Giuseppe Haÿdn.' Contents: XI:39, 34, 38, 35, 37, 36. Handwriting specimen (here reduced):

This MS. is interesting because it is the latest of the authentic series of MSS. for Fürnberg, and shows that Haydn's association with the family continued after he had become *Capellmeister* to Prince Nicolaus; the Trios were composed *c.* 1767.

[page 394:]
Orfeo, Libretto, line 6: for '... Dr Janos Harich on 26 July 1777 ...' read '... Dr Janos Harich on 26 July 1977 ...'.

[page 406, lines 23–4:]
For '... Schönbrunn ... rewarded ...' read '... Schönbrunn. This time the Imperial House, through the offices of Prince Esterházy, rewarded ...' The relevant documents are important and are given here *in extenso* for the first time:

[EH, Budapest, A.M. 436, Nos. 18.923–930:]
[Nos. 18.923/4–cover:] 1778 / Verzeichniß über die angefange / ne Kays: Regale v. Conthen / des H: Referenten v. Kauffman.
[next page:] Ausweiß / über die von Ihro Durchl. empfangenen 1000 Ducat. / Kays. Regale.

			Ducat.
No. 1.	Den H^n Capellmeister Haÿdn nt. Beylaag N^{ro} 1		641.
	2°	Nacher Wienn dem Inspectori Kleinrath nt. Beylaag N^{ro} 2	102.
	3°	Verschiedenen anderen Partheyen nt. Beylaag N° 3	257.

Facit zusammen 1000.
Jacobus Kaufman mpria

[Nos. 18.925/6–cover:] 1778 / Quittung des H^n Capelln Meister Haÿdn über 641. Ducat. / N° 1.
[next page:] Repartition / Von dem Kays: Regale auf die Hochfürstliche Capelle.

Singerinnen	Ducaten
Poschwa	25.
Puttlerin	25.
Prantnerin	25.
Musici	
Louicy [= Luigi Tomasini]	25.
Drobney	25.
Marteau	25.
Poschwa	25.
Hirsch	25.
Pauer	25.
Oliva	25.
Rosetti	25.
Dichtler	25.
Specht	25.
Ungericht	25.
Hoffman	25.
Schaudig	25.
Hollerieder	25.
Peczival	25.
Schiringer	25.
Purgsteiner	25.
Rupp	25.
Pohl	25.
Dieczel	25.
Griesbacher	25.
Griesbacher	25.

Latus 625. Duc.

[*Ducaten*]

Dem Scolare Koswitz	5.
Dem Scolare Ernst	5.
Dem Copisten	2.
Denen zweÿ Sohnen des Hⁿ Oliva	4.
Summa	641

Welche Sechshundertvierzig Ein Ducaten ich / Endes gefertigter von dem Hⁿ Secretaire Kaufmann / zu meinen Handten empfangen zu haben be / scheine. Eszterhaz den 17ᵗᵉⁿ July 777. / Josephus Haydn mpria.

[Nos. 18.929/30 – cover:] 1778 / N° 3.
[next page:] Repartition. / Des Kaysl. Regale

Ducat.

Mons. Bader & Mad. Bader zusamen richtig empfang.	25.
[signatures:] Mad. et M. Bader	
Hr. Mahler Rodhe	25.
[signature:] Friedrich Rhode	
Decorateur Holzer	20.
[signature:] Holzer	
Acteur Sica	12.
[signature:] Josephus Sicka	
Sica der Sohn	6.
[signature:] Sicha	
Camer Laquey Franz Teiber	12.
[signature:] Franz Teuber	
Acteur Hofmann	10.
[signature:] Hofmann	
Der Fulleres Tochter Catherina	6.
[signature:] Catherina Gubin	
Dem Haus Tischler Mayer	12.
[signature:] Nicolaus Mayer	
Dem Schlossergesellen Martin	3.
[signture:] Martin Rieger	
Denen drey Tischlern jeden 3 Ducaten	9.
[signatures:] Martin Holzl / Antoni Droher / Ferdinand Schatten	
Latus	140.
Denen 3. Zimerleuthen je 3 Duc.	9.
[signatures:] Stefan Berger / Gotlib Dunstner / [?]wineth Gleich	
Denen 16. Grenadiers jeden 3. Ducat.	48.
[signature:] De Pawloski / Lieutn.	

[*Ducaten*]

Denen 17 Stall Leüthen als 11 Postilions 1 Pierutsch / Gutscher / Vorreuther, / Reit Knecht und 3 Strapa / cier Züg jeden 3. Ducat. zusam.	[*sic*] 50.*
[signature:] Jacques Posselinnen Denen Trabanten, und Leüthen, welche zu Eszterhaz / aufladen geholfen zusam.	
[signatures:] Trabant Bender, Hanß und Christl und ebensolche Grenadiers	3.
Denen 9 Buben, als des Satl Knechts Reitknechts / und Ziṁermanns jeden 2. Ducat. zusam.	6.
[signatures:] Joseph Gollnhofer / Michael Duiffner / Joseph Schültdanster	
Suṁa	[*sic*] 257

[Nos. 18.927/8 – cover:] 1778 / N° 2
[next page:] Waß von den Kays: Regale nacher Wienn gehört.

Duct.

Hⁿ Inspectori Kleinrath	40.
Denen Trompettern von 3 Gard. [Pard.?] / zusammen	50.
Denen von Seithen des Hⁿ Schloßhaubtmanns / bey den Theater angestellten N.N.	12.
Summa in Wienn	102.

* The missing 1 gulden was simply added on to the final total – H.C.R.L.

Notes:
Watermarks: stag and letters 'IGW'. The fact that there were three trumpeters present, recruited from the guards, is yet another piece of authentic evidence that Haydn could, if necessary, find a pair of trumpets.

[pages 409f.:]
Re the Sommerfeld claim, see Stadtlaender, op. cit., pp. 76f., for details.

[pages 414f.:]
Newly discovered documents in EH, Forchtenstein Castle, now enable us to give precise dates for the first performances of *La vera costanza*. First perf.: 25 April 1779 (preceded by three full rehearsals on 23 and 24 April); repeated on 29 April, 6, 16, 23 and 30 May, 6, 10 and 24 June, 8 and 22 July, 1, 8 and 22 August, 5 and 19 September, 3 and 14 October, 7 and 24 November (the last, following the fire of 18 Nov., took place in the marionette theatre – see p. 421). A bill for the

original performance material, or rather part of it (for the 1785 revival, the copyists required 477 Bögen), has also come to light.

[Leopold Dichtler's hand:]
>   Copiatur Conto:
>   Dell Opera
>   La vera costanza:
> Orchestra, together with { Follia:
> Study scores, make   { 179

The Bögen ['follium'] reckoned at 5 xr: makes ... 14 fl: 55 xr:
[Haydn's hand:] These 179 written Bögen have been examined and approved. Joseph Haydn mpria

[The following passage, in Bader's hand, later cancelled:]
The above listed fourteen gulden and 55 xr will be paid by our Süttör Administrator Adam Peregrin Stumpf and entered in the books. Eszterház, 5th May 1779.
Above found to be correct / Bader mpria
[Nagy's hand:] Above found to be correct and payment herewith authorized. Eszterház, 7th May 1779.
>   Stephan Nagy / Regent mpria

[Dichtler's hand:] I hereby attest that I have received the above fourteen gulden 55 xr., through the *Herr* Administrator ... from the Eszterháza *Bau Caßa* correctly and in full. / Süttör Office, 8 May 1779 / Id est 14 f 55 Xr. / Leopoldo Dichtler.
[EH, Forchtenstein; Ulrich Tank in *JHW*, Reihe XXV, Band 8 (*La vera costanza* – kritischer Bericht), Munich 1978, pp. 9f.]

[page 421, line 9:]
The date – 18 December – was, of course, also the Prince's birthday.

[page 434, line 3:]
Re the uniforms: we reproduce the document here because it shows that the trumpeters' uniforms were more expensive than those of the other musicians (not counting Haydn's, of course), a tradition that derived from the Baroque, when trumpeters, because of the difficulty of their craft (*clarino* technique), received better pay and enjoyed a better position – also literally, in the way in which they were placed in the orchestra – than their fellow musicians. Unlike the other members of the *Capelle*, the Esterházy trumpeters had a coat with lappets (*revers*) on the tails of their coats, for which a large amount of extra gold braid was required. This was because the trumpeters probably fulfilled other duties outside orchestra pit and chamber, i.e. playing fanfares with and for the military, etc., and perhaps their uniforms were more closely modelled on military uniforms. It is possible, however, that some of this gold braid was not only destined for the 'Rock' (coat) but was intended to be wound around their instruments.

[A.M. 1490/837, EH, Budapest:]
Extract / Wie hoch die Musique Somer Kleyder Anno 1780. zu stehen gekomen sind.
Capelln Meister.

	Fl.	x.	Fl.	x.
Rock:				
7½ Elen Pringer Dreydratt à 30. [symbol = Groschen?]	11.	15		
7¼ Elen Damis à 18 [symbol]	6.	31½		
1¾ Elen weissen Damis à 18 [symbol]	1.	34½		
16⅔ Elen goldene Kettel Schnur mit 4 9/12 Lot à 2 Fl.	9.	35		
Kleyd Macherlohn	5.	56	48.	59
Stig und Nähseiden	—	51		
Sigl Leinwat, sib und Watta	—	40		
1½ Elen ungeblächten Canafas à 24 x	—	36		
6 Elen Croise à 1 Fl. 30 x	9.	—		
2½ Elen goldene Band Knöpf à 24 [symbol]	3.	—		
Weste:				
3⅓ Elen Bonson Koderos à 3½ Fl.	11.	40		
5½ Elen goldene Borten mit 11¾ Lot à 1 Fl. 54 x	22.	19½		
42. Stück goldene Quastln mit 12⅛ Lot à 2 Fl. 6 x	25.	27¾	65.	27¼
für weisse Leinwat	—	27		
für Nähe Gold	—	27		
2 Elen weissen Croise à 1 Fl. 30 xr	3.	—		
3½ Duzent kleine goldene knopf auf Weste & Hoosen à 12 [symbol]	2.	6		
2 Paar Hoosen:				
4 Elen Pringer Dreydratt à 30 [symbol]	6.	—		
1 paar goldenes Kuyr Band mit 1 1/16 lot à 1 Fl. 54 x	2.	1⅛	9.	31⅛
4 Elen weisse Leinwat a 20 x	1.	20		
2 Hoosen Schallen und Schnürren	—	10		

Hut:
2 Elen goldene
Borten mit $3\frac{1}{3}$
Lot à 1 Fl. 54 xr   6.   20
1. goldene Hut
Schlinge mit $\frac{4}{16}$
Lot à 2 Fl.   —   30
1. goldener Hut
Knopf   —   12   }10.   2
1 Hut samt
stolpen und
seidenen
Schnuren   2.   45
für Hut einfassen   —   15

Summa von
Capelln Meist.   138. $59\frac{3}{8}$

1. Camer Musicus

Rok:
$7\frac{3}{8}$ Elen Pringer
Dreydratt à 30
[symbol]   11. $3\frac{3}{4}$
5 Elen Damis à
18 [symbol]   4.   30
$1\frac{3}{8}$ Elen weissen
Damis a 18
[symbol]   1. $14\frac{3}{4}$ }36. $23\frac{1}{2}$
$16\frac{2}{3}$ Elen goldene
Kettel Schnur
mit $4\frac{9\frac{1}{2}}{12}$ Lot à 2 Fl.   9.   35
$3\frac{3}{4}$ Duzent Knopf
à 48 x   3.   —
Kleyd
Macherlohn   7.   —

Weste:
$2\frac{1}{6}$ Elen Bonson
Koderos à $3\frac{1}{2}$ Fl.   7.   35
$5\frac{1}{2}$ Elen goldene
Borten mit $11\frac{3}{4}$
Lot à 1 Fl. 54 x   22. $19\frac{1}{2}$
20 Knöpf à 2 x   —   40 }31. $28\frac{1}{2}$
für Näh Gold   —   24
1 Elen rote
Leinwat   —   15
$\frac{1}{2}$ Elen roten
Canafas   —   15

2 Paar Hoosen:
4. Elen Pringer
Dreydratt à 30   6.   —
[symbol]
1 paar goldene
Kuyr Band mit
$1\frac{1}{16}$ Lot à 1 Fl. 54 x   2. $1\frac{1}{8}$
22 Knöpf à 2 x   —   44
Schneider Arbeit   —   36
Stig und   }10. $19\frac{1}{24}$
Nähseiden   —   12
2 Elen
ungeblächten
Canafas à 20 x   —   40
Sigl Leinwat
zum Bindl   — $1\frac{2}{3}$
Hoosen Schallen   —   3
Knöpf zum
Uberziehen   — $1\frac{1}{4}$

Hut:
2 Elen goldene
Borten mit $3\frac{5}{12}$
Lot à 1 Fl. 54 x   6. $29\frac{1}{2}$
1. goldene Hut
Schlinge mit $\frac{4}{16}$
Lot à 2 Fl.   —   30 }10. $11\frac{1}{2}$
1. goldener Hut
Knopf   —   12
1 Hut samt
stolpen und
seidenen Schnüren   2.   45
Hut einfassen   —   15

Summa von 1.
Camer Musicus   88. $22\frac{6\frac{1}{4}}{12}$
Summa von 18
Camer Musicus   1.590. $45\frac{3}{4}$

[figures cancelled
and corrected:]   88. $54\frac{6\frac{1}{4}}{12}$
              1.601. $15\frac{3}{4}$

1. Trompeter

Rock mit
Flügeln:
$7\frac{3}{8}$ Elen Pringer
Dreydratt à 30
[symbol]   11. $3\frac{3}{4}$
5 Elen Damis à
18 [symbol]   4.   30
$1\frac{3}{8}$ Elen weissen
Damis à 18
[symbol]   1. $14\frac{1}{4}$
$16\frac{2}{3}$ Elen goldene
Kettel Schnur
mit $4\frac{9}{12}$ Lot à 2 Fl.   9.   35 }76.   23
$9\frac{1}{4}$ Elen goldene
Borten mit 20.
Lot à 1 Fl. 54 x   38.   —
$3\frac{3}{4}$ Duzent Knöpf
à 48 xr   3.   —
Kleyders
Macherlohn   7.   —
2 Flugel
Macherlohn und
Seiden   2.   —

Weste:
$2\frac{1}{6}$ Elen Bonson
Koderos à $3\frac{1}{2}$ Fl.   7.   35
$5\frac{1}{2}$ Elen goldene
Borten mit $11\frac{3}{4}$ Lot
à 1 Fl. 54 x   22. $19\frac{1}{2}$
20. Knöpf a 2 xr   —   40 }31. $28\frac{1}{2}$
1 Elen rote
Leinwat   —   15
$\frac{1}{2}$ Elen roten
Canafas   —   15
Nähgold   —   24

2 Paar Hoosen:
4 Elen Pringer
Dreydratt à 30.
[symbol]   6.   —
1 paar goldene
Kuyr Band mit
$\frac{1}{16}$ Lot à 1 Fl. 54 x   2. $1\frac{1}{8}$

22 Knöpf à 2 x	—	44		
Macherlohn	—	36		
Stig und Nähseiden	—	12	10.	$19\frac{1}{2}$
2. Elen ungeblächten Canafas à 20 x	—	40		
Sigl Leinwat zum Bindl	—	$1\frac{2}{3}$		
Hoosen Schnallen	—	3		
Knöpf zum Uberziehen	—	$1\frac{1}{4}$		
Hut:				
2 Elen goldene Borten mit $3\frac{5}{12}$ Lot à 1 Fl. 54 x	6.	$29\frac{1}{2}$		
1. goldene Hut Schlinge mit $\frac{4}{16}$ Lot à 2 Fl.	—	30		
1 goldener Hut Knopf	—	12	10.	$11\frac{1}{2}$
1 Hut samt stolpen und seidenen Schnuren	2.	45		
für Hut einfassen	—	15		
Summa von 1. Trompeter			128.	$22\frac{1}{24}$
Summa von 2. Trompeter			256.	$44\frac{1}{12}$

2 Paar Hoosen:				
4 Elen Pringer Dreydratt à 30 [symbol]	6.	—		
1 paar goldenes Kuyr Band mit $1\frac{1}{16}$ Lot à 1 Fl. 54 xr.	2.	$1\frac{1}{8}$		
22 Knöpf à 2 x	—	44	10.	$15\frac{1}{8}$
4 Elen ungeblächten Canafas à 20 xr.	1.	20		
Schnallen und Schnürren	—	10		
Hut:				
2. Elen goldene Borten mit $3\frac{1}{12}$ Lot à 1 Fl. 54 xr	6.	$29\frac{1}{2}$		
1. goldene Hut Schlinge mit $\frac{4}{16}$ Lot à 2 Fl.	—	30		
1. goldener Hut Knopf	—	12	10.	$11\frac{1}{2}$
1 Hut samt stolpen und seidenen Schnüren	2.	45		
für Hut einfassen	—	15		
Summa von 1. Chor Musicus			76.	$21\frac{1}{8}$
Summa von 2. Chor Musicus			152.	$42\frac{1}{4}$

1. Chor Musicus

Rok:				
$7\frac{3}{8}$ Elen Pringer Dreydratt à 30 [symbol]	11.	$3\frac{3}{4}$		
5 Elen Damis à 18 [symbol]	4.	30		
$1\frac{3}{8}$ Elen weissen Damis à 18 [symbol]	11.	$14\frac{1}{4}$		
$3\frac{3}{4}$ Duzent Knöpf à 48 x.	3.	—	26.	6
Kleyd Macherlohn	4.	30		
Stig und Nähseiden	—	40		
Sib und Watta	—	38		
$1\frac{1}{2}$ Elen ungeblächten Canafas à 20 xr.	—	30		
Weste:				
$2\frac{1}{3}$ Elen Bonson Dreydratt à 2 Fl. 36 xr	6.	4		
$5\frac{1}{8}$ Elen goldene Borten mit $11\frac{3}{4}$ Lot à 1 Fl. 54 xr.	22.	$19\frac{1}{2}$	29.	$48\frac{1}{2}$
20 Knöpf à 2 x	—	40		
für weisse Leinwat	—	27		
Nähe Gold	—	18		

[page 448:]
After line 24 insert reference: 'CCLN, 29f.'. The passage beginning (line 28): 'On 4 July ... Eisenstadt.[4]' and the accompanying footnote relate to the year 1782 and should be transferred to follow the first paragraph on p. 464.

]page 472:]
ITALIAN MARIONETTE OPERA 1783: the last line should read '... Landon in *HJB* I, 192' etc.

[page 517, col. 2:]
Critical edition: in line 2 read '... and parts on hire' etc.

[page 527:]
Principal sources: another authentic MS. score, Landesbibliothek, Graz (Lannoy Collection), 41237, by Copyist Anon. 63 on 8° Italian paper (watermarks: three crescents of declining size, letters 'PS', crown with fleur-de-lys above, letters 'GA' below ornament; and, when paper changes to 12-stave for Finale, 'AM', bow and arrow, crescents).

[page 533:]
In the first musical example, in the second bar of line 3, the last two notes should be quavers, not crotchets.

[page 537:]
Principal sources: for '(5) ... Artaria (pl. no. 1783), 1783: ...' read '(5) ... Artaria (pl. no. 29), 1782: ...'.

[pages 560f.:]
CHRONOLOGY: Symphony No. 53. The version with Finale 'A' was available in 1779 (MS. sent from Vienna to the Court of Oettingen-Wallerstein and signed 'Riersch Kopist'); see Stephen C. Fisher in *Haydn-Studien* IV/2 (1978), p. 76, n. 56. Symphonies Nos. 62, 74: further authentic copies, by Joseph Elssler and others, Palacio Real, Madrid (Fisher, op. cit., pp. 76f.); this is the earliest authentic MS. source for No. 74.

[pages 571f.:]
Sources. Add the only authentic MS. source (another proof of the work's genuineness): MS. parts by Johann Radnitzky (harpsichord part) and another copyist, Kremsier Castle, II G 20. Harpsichord part on oblong paper, orchestral parts on 4° Italian paper (watermarks: letters 'BV' under canopy; letters 'GF' under canopy). Title: 'Concerto / per il / Clavi Cembalo / 2 Violini / Alto Viola / 2 Oboe / 2 Corni / e / Basso / [lower left corner:] Del Sigl Giuseppe / Haydn.' At head of harpsichord part: 'Violini Basso Corni / Alto Viola 2 Oboe [middle:] Clavi Cembalo [right:] Del Sigl:

Giuseppe Haÿdn.' We include specimens of Radnitzky's hand and that of the other copyist.

[Copyist's hand:]

[page 627:]
In the musical example, the bass line in bar 2 should read:

[page 664, line 6]
For 'Gyrowetz ... asked how ...' read 'Gyrowetz, naturally astonished, asked how ...'.

[page 675:]
A newly discovered document in EH, Forchtenstein Castle, provides us with Schellinger's copying bill for 1785:

Copiatur Conto

What was copied, from 1st January 785 to December 785, for the princely theatre, and delivered as agreed, the Bogen for vocal parts à 7 xr., for instruments à 5 xr.

Concerto (XVIII: 11), Radnitzky's copy: the entrance of the keyboard solo in the harpsichord part. Note that the keyboard's right hand uses the G-clef, while the left hand uses the soprano clef; this is a Viennese tradition of Haydn's youth (cf. Reutter's notation, pp. 128, 131, 137 in the present volume).

For operas	Bögen vocal parts	Instruments
Calipso.....................	21	19
Veracostanza [sic].....	279	198.
Contratempi............	87	89
Montezuma.............	216	293
Matrimonio per ing.	148	191
geloso in cimento	279	189
Villanella rapita	48	59
l'astuzie di bettina	169	195
	1,247	1,233

Joan Schiling [sic] Copist / di Theatro Soma 248 fl. 9 xr.   die 20 10bris $\overline{7}85$.

[Haydn's hand:] The above sum for copying has been carefully examined by me, the undersigned, and found to be correct. Estoras, the 30th December $\overline{7}85$.

Josephus Haydn mpria Capell Meister

[Prince Nicolaus's hand:] The above two hundred and forty-eight gulden 9 Xr. have been paid from our princely *Bau Cassa* and correctly delivered in cash by the Administrator, *Herr* Johann Vadász. Süttör Office, the 8th of March 1786. Id est 248 fl 9 xr

Joannes Schilling fürstl. / Theater Copist
[EH, Forchtenstein; Ulrich Tank in *JHW*, Reihe XXV, Band 8, Munich 1978, p. 16]

Notes: The three operas with small numbers of parts – Bologna's *L'isola di Calipso abbandonata*, Sarti's *I contratempi* and Bianchi's *La villanella rapita* – formed part of the 1784 season (cf. p. 499) and the present bill probably indicates new insertion arias or transposed numbers for 1785 revivals. Since the Bologna opera does not figure in Schellinger's 1784 list of copying work, we must presume that it was either placed on a separate bill (cf. p. 482) or was purchased abroad and merely 'improved' by Schellinger. The question is only of theoretical interest, since the entire Bologna opera has disappeared from EH.

[page 692:]
Re Sigmund Barisani (lines 7f.): *vide supra*, p. 243n.

[page 708:]
At top of page, add: 'On 3 April 1788, Maximilian Stadler was at Eszterháza and wrote in Weber's commonplace book: "Erreichen Sie bald Ihren Meister Haydn und Ihren Freund Mozart.'
Note 2: Weber's commonplace-book was sold by J. A. Stargardt, Marburg/Lahn, in 1962.

[page 779:]
Mozart, W. A.: add reference '506'.

[page 782:]
For 'Rahier, Ludwig Peter ...' read 'Rahier, Peter Ludwig ...'.

[page 789:]
As first index entry, add: 'Alleluja' (XXIIIc:3) 236.

[page 790:]
Arietta (XVII:3): add reference '342'.

[page 791:]
OPERAS: *La Circe*. In the third line read 'Lavatevi presto (not 'Levatevi'; also wrong in Hoboken), and correct references on pp. 649, 715. On p. 650, in line 31 the phrase 'no less than 545 bars' should read 'no less that 532 bars'.

[page 792:]
OVERTURES: for '—in D (Ia:7) 567–9;' read '—in D (Ia:4) 567–9;'.

[page 794:]
DOUBTFUL AND SPURIOUS WORKS: TRIOS, for reference '763f.' read '761f.'

Haydn in England 1791–1795

[plates II, III, 16, 20:]
The Times, 26 June 1794: 'PORTRAITS of Mr. W. CRAMER, Dr. HAYDN, Mr. PLEYEL, Mr. SALOMON, Mr. DUSSEK, and Mr. NORRIS, of Oxford, may be had of J. Bland, No. 45, Holborn. They are all esteemed striking likenesses; and Dr. Haydn and Cramer were from Pictures in the Royal Academy, Somerset House.' Thus, the portrait of Dussek (plate 16) is also by Hardy.

[pages 59, 120, 122; also Addenda (*Late Years*, p. 492):]
Concerning Signora Negri: *The Times*, 10 March (see Addenda), states that '... her reception was again most flatteringly favourable.'

[page 88:]
Sheldonian Theatre: the maximum safe capacity is now reckoned to be 1,400 persons (information from the attendants of the Theatre).

[page 133:]
Tassie: We have meanwhile been able to locate the lost Tassie medallion portrait of Haydn (Scottish National Portrait Gallery). See our article in *Soundings* (1980), where the portrait is reproduced for the first time, together with a portrait of James Tassie himself.

[page 171:]
Purcell's 'From rosy bower' is taken from his *Don Quixotte*.

[page 219:]
Mr David Clegg (letter 22 November 1978) points out that Haydn's letter to Polzelli of 20 June 1793 is now in the Bodleian Library, Oxford (*ex coll.* the Deneke sisters). We have since been supplied with a photograph by the Bodleian.

[page 258:]
Morning Chronicle quotation beginning 'The Musical Season' should end '... this country ever witnessed.'

[page 268:]
Rauzzini and Haydn's Canon: it was first printed in Rauzzini's 'A periodical collection of vocal music (never before printed) consisting of Italian and English songs, duetts, terzetts, recitatives, canzonetts, ballads &c. ... dedicated to ... the Duchess of York. In two volumes. Printed for the author by A.C. Farthing and sold by Messrs. Lintern's, Bath and at Messrs. Longman & Broderip ... London. The music engraved by R.B. Whitley (1797).' The two volumes are through-paginated, including a four-page list of subscribers and the first edition (not in Hoboken etc.) of 'Turk was a faithful dog' on page 340, 'ex tempore, when on a visit to the Author.' We are indebted to our kind friend, Mr Hermann Baron, of London, for these details.

[page 280:]
The arrangements between Haydn/Salomon and the Opera Concert must have been made between 29 December 1794 and 12 January 1795 (date of Salomon's letter), for on the former date the *Morning Chronicle* prints an announcement of the forthcoming subscription series of the Opera Concert in which there is no mention of either Haydn or Salomon.

[page 282:]
Concerning the arrival, from Russia, of Vincente Martín y Soler ('Martini'), *The Times* of 30 October 1794 states: 'It is from the works of this master, that of the favourite Airs in the siege of Belgrade and the Pirates are compiled; a stile of composition very popular in this country.'

[page 292:]
Debora and Sisara – announcement in *The True Briton* (20 February 1795):

KING'S THEATRE
... At the Harpsichord, Mr. Federici. ... End of first Act. ... A Grand Overture, MS. by Dr. Haydn, conducted by Himself; [rest, with Handel's 'Angels ever bright and fair' with Banti, etc.] ... under the Direction of Dr. Arnold, who will preside ... at the Organ ...

The True Briton prints the *Sun*'s review verbatim, also on 21 February; and *Sun*'s review of the Third Concert (page 293), also on 24 February.

[page 294:]
Some additional Haydniana from the newspapers:

VOCAL CONCERT / WILLIS'S ROOMS.
MR. HARRISON and MR. KNYVETT most respectfully acquaint the SUBSCRIBERS, / that the FOURTH PERFORMANCE will be on THURSDAY [26 Feb.] NEXT.
To begin at Eight o'Clock
FAVOURITE OVERTURE   HAYDN
· · · ·
Canzonet, Mrs. HARRISON ... HAYDN
[rest: compositions by Handel, Rauzzini, Danby, Stevens, Dr Boyce, Guglielmi, Atterbury, Webber, etc.] [*True Briton*, 24 Feb. 1795]

KING'S THEATRE
ON FRIDAY next, the 27th inst. will be performed a GRAND SELECTION of SACRED MUSIC, chiefly by HANDEL.
... PART II Grand Overture; M.S. Haydn ...
[*The Times*, 26 Feb. 1795]

[page 300:]
The Danby concert also in *True Briton*, 7 April 1795, 'ON FRIDAY Next'. *True Briton* on 10 April, of *Windsor Castle*:
... The Overture, composed expressly for the occasion by
DR. HAYDN
As is the rest of the Music by Mr. SALOMON.

[*re* Danby concert:]
... THIS PRESENT EVENING, April 10th ... [Haydn's Overture] under his immediate Direction.

In all the reviews, also *True Briton* of 13 April 1795, of *Windsor Castle*, it is never stated that Haydn actually conducted his new Overture 'to an English Opera' (Ia:3), whereas it is stated explicitly that he was at Mr Danby's concert.

[page 304:]
True Briton of 22 April 1795, *re* Madame Gillberg's concert: 'Dr Haydn will preside at the Piano Forte.' In a letter printed in that issue, the New Musical Fund Concert thanks '... Dr. Haydn' for participating, with many other artists, in its concert of the 20th.

[page 309:]
Harrison's concert, according to *True Briton* (11 May 1795), also opened with 'Grand Overture, HAYDN.'

[pages 309f., 316, 318n., 452; also *The Years of 'The Creation'*, pages 72–6:]
'Jacob's Dream' has now been discovered: it is the second movement of Piano Trio No. 41 (XV:31) which was *not* (as we had been led to believe by the owners) written in Italian but on British paper of two types, both dated '1794', and the second movement contains a later cancelled title (illegible on the microfilm): 'Sonata, Jacob's Dream by Dr. Haydn 1794'. Alan Tyson in the *Times Literary Supplement*, 26 May 1978, p. 589. Therefore, the Piano Trio, incorporating the 'Sonata Jacob's Dream', was composed in England in 1794 and 1795 (the latter date for the opening movement, written later).

[pages 310f.:]
A revised version of the two additional concerts is given in *True Briton*, 18 May 1795, and obviously represents what was actually played. We therefore give it *in extenso*:

FIRST NIGHT – PART I
Overture, double Orchestra, MS. – BACH. / New Song, Signor BRIDA – MARTINI. / Concerto Bassoon, Mr. HOLMES – HOLMES. / New Song, (Composed for the occasion) Madame BANTI – /

BIANCHI / Concerto upon the Hautboy, (the second time in this country) Signor FERLENDIS – FERLENDIS
PART II
Overture, MS. – HAYDN. / New Duetto, Madame MORICHELLI and MORELLI – / MARTINI. / Concerto Violin, Mr. SALOMON – SALOMON. / New Song, Madame BANTI – HAYDN. / [*Scena di Berenice* (XXIVa:10)] / Concerto on the English Horn (for the first time in this / Country) Signor FERLENDIS – FERLENDIS. / FINALE.

SECOND NIGHT, June 1 – PART I
Overture, Double Orchestra, MS. – BACH. / Song, Signor ROVEDINO – PAISIELLO. / Concerto Double Bass, Signor DRAGONETTI – / DRAGO-NETTI. / New Rondeau, (composed for the occasion) Mad. BANTI – / BIANCHI. / Concerto Hautboy, Signore FERLENDIS – FERLENDIS
PART II.
Overture, MS. – HAYDN / Quartetto, Madame MORICHELLI, Signors [*sic*] BRIDA, / ROVEDINO, and MORELLI – CHERUBINI. / Concerto Violin, Mr. SALOMON – SALOMON. / Song, Madame Banti, accompanied upon the English Horn / (for the first time in this Country), Signor FERLENDIS – / ZINGARELLI. / FINALE. [etc.]

[page 310 (311):]
A hitherto unknown benefit concert given by Salomon must now be added to the exhausting series of concerts for the 1795 season; but we wonder if, in the event, it ever took place. (1) On the same day, 18 May, the Opera Concert's Ninth Subscription performance was given; (2) Salomon played a violin concerto, it would seem, in both additional concerts, 21 May and 1 June. At any rate, the document reads:

NEW ROOMS, OPERA-HOUSE
MR. SALOMON most respectfully acquaints the Nobility[,] Gentry, and his Friends in general, that his BENEFIT CONCERT is fixed for MONDAY the 18th May, at the New Rooms, Opera-house; the Particulars of which will be advertised in due time.
Tickets, at 10s. 6d. each, to be had of Mr. Salomon, Assembly Rooms, Hanover-square.
[*True Briton*, 28 March 1795]

[page 313:]
Ashe's concert was announced in *True Briton* (28 May, 1 June, 6 June); the programme opens not with Clementi's 'Grand Overture, MS.' but with 'Grand Overture, MS – WRANINSKI [Wranizky]' and (*recte*) 'Giordanello'. In *The Times* of 29 May the mis-spelling of Giordanello is corrected but the first item is still listed as by 'Clementi'.

[page 316:]
Re Macartney: possibly Haydn got his information from Aeneas Anderson's *Narrative of the late British Embassy to China*, which was advertised in *True Briton* on 30 April 1795.

[page 358; also Addenda (*The Late Years*, p. 492):]
The autograph sketch of the *Third Commandment*

and the authentic copy of the *First* were purchased not by the Bodleian Library but by a Swiss private collector.

[page 484:]
'The Princess of Wales's Favorite Dance by Dʳ. Haydn' (Hoboken *deest*). We have been fortunate enough to discover yet another of the lost English country dances, again from one of Nathaniel Gow's 'corrections': it comes in a volume of miscellaneous music, bound in Scotland *c.* 1800, which we found in 1978, and is entitled 'The South Fencible's March / As approved of by the / Earl of Hopetoun. Colonel. EDIN.ʳ Printed and Sold by N. STEWART & CO. Music Sellers Nº. 37 South Bridge Street / Where may be had Music & Musical Instruments at the LONDON prices.' The print consists of two pages and, apart from the March, has: 'Miss Murray of Auchtertyre's Strathspey', 'Miss Ann Æmelia Stuarts Strathspey', and as the last item on p. 2, 'Haydn's Strathspey' (see overleaf). At the bottom of page 1, 'Entered at Stationers Hall' and on the right, under the Haydn, 'Corrected by Nath: Gow.' By 'correction', one presumes that Haydn may have found the new Scottish 'snaps' difficult and made small errors in writing them down. Now since the extant country dances are inextricably bound up with Gow, we have done some research on this subject and present the results here. As is well known, Gow was a careful and reputable publisher. On another print in this same bound volume, we read: 'The Author thinks proper to mention, that the Tunes which are not Composed by him are Published by Authority of the Different Composers, which has induced him to secure the Book in Stationers Hall According to Act of Parliament.' There were several active members of the Gow family, including, Niel, Nathaniel and John; and we now have positive and authentic information that the Gows arranged balls at the King's Theatre in 1794 and 1795 and were thus in the immediate proximity of Haydn in 1795. Balls were held not only in the Opera House but even at Hanover Square in 1794, and in *The Times* of 13 February 1794 there is an announcement of subscription balls 'under the Patronage of Ladies of Fashion'; and with the stern war-time note, 'No French Wines.' A few weeks later, *The Times* of 1 March 1794 announces:

KING'S THEATRE
ON MONDAY next, March 3, there will be given at This Theatre A GRAND MASKED BALL, with a SUPPER. . . . Messrs Gows will provide and conduct the band for the Country Dances in the Theatre, and the Band belonging to his Royal Highness the Duke of York's Regiment of Guards will play in the Gallery over the great entrance the fore-part of the night, and afterwards in the New Room during the time of Supper.
. . . The new SUBSCRIPTION ROOM will be opened for the first time.

[Review in *The Times*, 5 March:]
[mentions large crowd; the] Prince of WALES

Haydn's Strathspey (cf. p. 637).

was in a black domino. ... There were about 2,700 persons in the rooms, and among them some of the prettiest women in town.

Next year, the Gows were still organizing the Opera balls, and it is for this 1795 season that we believe Haydn to have been persuaded – no doubt to his financial advantage – to compose the '4 Contrydances' and '2 Contrydances'.

KING'S THEATRE

On THURSDAY NEXT, the 12th instant, / there will be given at this Theatre, / A GRAND MASKED BALL, / (The only one before Easter) / With a Supper, Madeira, Sherry, and Port Wines, of / the first quality. / Messrs. GOWS will provide and conduct the Band for / the Country Dances, in the Theatre.

The Subscribers to the Opera are respectfully acquainted, that their Boxes will be kept, as usual, to such Subscribers as may wish to see the Ball from them.

N.B. The Gallery will be opened for the Spectators at the usual Price of Admission.

The Door to be opened at Ten o'Clock, and the Supper Rooms at one.

For the convenience of the Company, in coming into the Theatre, on that night, the Door in Market-lane will be open for their reception; but Coaches are to go from Pall-Mall only.

Tickets, One Guinea each, to be had at the Office of the Theatre, adjoining Union-court; and at Messrs. Longman and Broderip, Cheapside.   [*True Briton*, 7 and 10 Feb. 1795]

As usual, there must have been pandemonium, and Haydn will not have found amusing 'the frolics of some *drunken Cyprians*' (*True Briton*, 14 Feb. 1795).

[page 487:]
The situation regarding the Redoutensaal Dances of 1792 has meanwhile become vastly more complicated. First, the authentic Dances: *Twelve Minuets* (IX:11). Original performance material: ÖNB, S.m. 15661, from the Pensionsgesellschaft Archives. MS. parts, 4°, by Johann Elssler scriptorium. One v. I, from which the dances were conducted; 5 other v. I; 4 v. II, 2 vc. obl., 4 Bassi and two each (double woodwind!) of fl., ob. I, II, bsn. I, II, cor. I, II, clarinetto I, II, clarino I, II (trpt.), but only one timp. Haydn personally corrected almost all the parts. Second, *Twelve Deutsche Tänze* (IX:12). Original performance material, ÖNB, S.m. 15660. MS. parts, 4°, by Johann Elssler scriptorium. 8 v. I parts; v. II parts all missing; 8 Basso parts; 4 '2 Flauti' and 'Flautino' parts, 4 ob. I, 4 ob. II, 2 clar. I, 2 clar. II, 4 'Due Fagotti' (later: 1 bsn. I, 1 bsn. II), 2 hn. I, 2 hn. II, one each of 'Clarino I:ᵐᵒ' and 'Clarino 2:ᵈᵒ' and one 'Timpano'. Title in Elssler's hand 'Anno 1792'. With Haydn's own corrections on almost all the parts.

Now we come to a fascinating problem. This evening was the first given by the Pensionsgesellschaft (1792), and it apparently became famous overnight. Apart from Haydn's Dances, which were performed in the Great Hall with an orchestra of 47 persons, conducted by Johann Patatschny, there was a smaller orchestra (27 players) in the Small Hall, conducted by Anton

Höllmayr. Hardly had the balls finished when the professional copyists began to market music supposedly played at the occasion. Since many of these sources are new,[1] we present them here:

(1) '12 / deutsche Tänze' (IX:13), MS Donaueschingen (see p. 487), copied partly by J. Schellinger. Professor Franz Eibner and the author of these notes have now played and discussed these Dances, and from inner criteria we may flatly state that they *cannot* be by Haydn. Therefore Schellinger must have been working on his own, and IX:13 must be listed as doubtful.

(2) ÖNB, S.m. 12987. Piano reduction by two copyists of IX:15 *as anonymous*, but with this remarkable title: '6 / Menuetti welche im k: k: kleinen / Redoutten Sall den 25 Novembris producirt worden 1792 / Clavi Cembalo'. None other than an anonymous copy of the GdM parts, xv 40962, where we read: 'Menuetti / Violino Primo / di Hayden'. Now the ÖNB piano reduction was by two copyists, 'A' and 'B'; 'A' did the title page, 'B' the actual music. Great is our surprise, therefore, to find that GdM's parts were copied by 'A' throughout and this time attributed to Haydn. Watermarks: of ÖNB oblong Italian paper – three crescents of declining size, chain lines (1 inch; 2·5 cm.) apart, letters 'cs'; of GdM – three stars in elaborate ornament, chain lines (1⅛ in.; 2·7 cm.) apart, three crescents of declining size, letters 'A / HF / REAL' (4° paper). Both GdM and, it would seem, ÖNB parts come from the Kaiserliche Sammlung in Graz. We have meanwhile put into score GdM's parts, and we may again state flatly that, from a great deal of internal evidence, including transposing timpani parts and B flat trumpet parts without drums, these Dances cannot possibly be by Haydn. Now the fact that the piano reduction was anonymous does not *necessarily* mean that Haydn's name must be ignored, for ÖNB owns an astounding piece of evidence (S.m. 12917), an authentic MS. by Anonymous 63 on oblong Italian paper (watermarks: 'GFA', three crescents of declining size), eight staves, of the genuine Redoutensaal 'Deutsche Tänze' with simply those two words as the title: no composer whatever. One cannot escape thinking that some very murky operations among the copyists, including Schellinger and Anonymous 63, were involved in these Dances.

(3) ÖNB, S.m. 12988, provides yet another surprise: '12 / Menuetti welche im K: K: Redutten / Sal den 25 Novembj: producirt worden / 1792.' These are 'Clavi Cembalo' reductions by Copyist 'A' on oblong Italian paper (watermarks: 'w' in elaborate frame, three crescents of declining size with 'REAL'). The MS. appears to have been part of the Kaiserliche Sammlung, at any rate from Graz. No. 1, *incipit*:

1 For the latest article on the subject, see G. Thomas in *Haydn-Studien* IV/2 (1978), pp. 117f.

No. 2 in B flat, No. 3 in F, No. 4 in D, No. 5 in A, No. 6 in C, No. 7 in G, No. 8 in E, No. 9 in A, No. 10 in F, No. 11 in C, No. 12 in G.

(4) ÖNB, S.m. 12900: '12 / Deutsche welche im K: K: Redutten / Sal den 25 Novembris producirt worden / 1792 / Clavi Cembalo' by Copyist 'A' on oblong Italian paper (watermarks: 'cs' and (separately) 'c', three crescents of declining size) in reduction for 'Clavi Cembalo' (Kaiserliche Sammlung?):

(6) ÖNB, S.m. 11140: 'Deutsche Tänze ... grossen Redouten Saale 1792' by Joseph Heidenreich Lausch (Viennese copyist), MS. parts for large orchestra. Another copy: S.m. 12839 (Sammelband: Heidenreich ff. 34rr.: 'k. k. grossen Redouten Saale von 1792').

(5) ÖNB, S.m. 12899: exact title as in source 4, by Copyist 'A' on oblong Italian paper (watermarks: 'w' in ornate frame, bow and arrow, letters 'FL' and 'REAL', canopy), in reduction for 'Clavi Cembalo' (Kaiserliche Sammlung?):

Notes: The Haus-, Hof und Staatsarchiv have among the bills for 1792 a 'Berechnung / über / Empfang und Ausgabe / Bei den: den Fasching 1792 in den k: k: re- / douten Säälen abgehaltenen 12 / maskirten Bällen', i.e. the bills for Carnival 1792 (Hoftheater, S.R. 46, f. 7), wherein the Minuets and German Dances are listed as being composed by Joseph Heydenreich (Heidenreich), Johann Patatschny (director of the Large Hall in the Redoutensaal) and Anton Höllmayr (director of the Small Hall). Therefore one may presume that source 6 is what it says, 'Deutsche' performed in the Large Hall in 1792, probably at Carnival time. As for the incredible collection, sources 1–5 are all said to have been performed on 25 November 1792, the day that Haydn's works were also first given.

All this gives rise to a fundamental question: when Haydn's Dances were given on 25 November 1792 in the Large Hall, were they given once? Were they repeated? What else did the orchestra play all evening? There seem to be endless possibilities. When the *Wiener Zeitung* announced the new pieces in the Large and Small Halls, did that presuppose that *only* those pieces were given and no others? That it was customary to repeat popular dances in those days may be seen from *The Pembroke Papers* (1734–80), ed. Lord Herbert (London 1939, p. 97):

[Rev. W. Coxe to Lady Pembroke, Mannheim, 3 Feb. 1777:] The masked Bal de nuit was very crowded: they dance here Allemandes, minuets and English country dances. The confusion in the latter is curious enough, the musicians play the same country dance for an hour together, and the couples dance till they are tired.

These are not questions that can be answered easily, and we believe that a great deal of research remains to be done on the whole problem. Possibly the new sources listed above may be of some help in the matter.

Further Dances by Haydn. IX:6: only source, GdM, old MS. parts, of Twelve Minuets: Nos. 1–8 known only here, Nos. 9–12 are authentic dances (Nos. 1–4 of IX:5, autograph 1776). There are two things to be said: in their present orchestration, Nos. 1–8 cannot be by Haydn, and the orchestration of No. 12, with the false timpani part added in the G clef (original form: IX:5, No. 4, has no drums at all), renders the whole (as yet unpublished) manuscript suspect. Written on local Austrian paper ('WEITRA', angel). At best, we suggest that some of the dances Nos. 1–8 may have been composed by Haydn; at worst, they are clever forgeries or works of a *seguace*. IX:14: Thirteen Minuets (unpublished) for Orchestra, known only from one MS. source in GdM ('Del Sigl^re Heyden', later 'Jos.' added), are equally dubious; the strange horn writing, the amateurish basses, the unmotivated syncopations in v. II (No. 5), and the extraordinary two (real) parts of No. 8 which turn into triple upper octaves over the bass line (these curious unisons in the violins occur often) – all this does not inspire confidence. Written on Austrian(?) paper (fleur-de-lys and 'HW'). IX:20 is a set of 'Menuetti per il Cembalo' (Staatsbibliothek, Berlin), issued by O. E. Deutsch (Ed. Strache, Vienna, 1930); one, No. 2 of the set, is a transposition of IX:3/10 (autograph). G. Thomas rightly describes the set as a 'more or less corrupted keyboard arrangement of dances from various cycles' (*Haydn-Studien* III/1, 16). IX:21: Unpublished (except for two small extracts: see Hoboken, vol. I, p. 574), keyboard arrangement(?) of 'Menuetes de la Redoute par Mons: Hayden' on Italian paper (crescents with 'REAL' / A' also 'w'). Contrary to the opinion of G. Thomas (op cit., p. 21), we regard it as possible that these are rather thin arrangements of real Haydn minuets, but the evidence – the MS. is from the Kaiserliche Sammlung in Graz – is thin. The evidence for IX:22 (another set of dances for harpsichord) is even more slender: a MS. in Dresden. IX:24 is *not* autograph at all, but does appear on the reverse side of a real autograph (details in Hoboken, vol. I, pp. 575f.).

In the Musikwissenschaftliches Institut at Graz, there is a volume of miscellaneous music of unknown provenance which contains a series of individual pieces by Haydn, at the end of which, on the bottom part of the page, we read 'Joseph Haydn' and turn over to a whole series of hitherto unknown dances. The MS. is of late eighteenth-century date, and the dances are for harpsichord.

There are three sets:

(1) Deutsche Tänze, Nos. 1–11 (Hoboken *deest*) – beginning

– all with Trios. The set ends with the following Allegretto:

The second set, Nos. 1–8 (Hoboken *deest*), are also *Deutsche* and begin:

The third set, Nos. 1–6 (Hoboken *deest*), are Minuets and begin:

We can give no further information about these attractive German Dances and Minuets, for even the attribution to Haydn is questionable (it may apply to the preceding work and not to these dances).

[pp. 507f.:]
Witt and 'Jena' Symphony: another MS. of this work, marked 'di Witt', is in the Landesarchiv, Rudolstadt. *MGG* 14 (1968), article 'Witt' (Oskar Kaul), p. 741.

[page 511:]
Mayr's treatise had not only *AMZ* (written not by Rochlitz but by Zelter, see *The Years of 'The Creation'*, pp. 585ff.) as a source but also a similar passage from Carpani's *Le Haydine*, pp. 98ff. It was also used in I. F. Arnold's *J. H … Seine kurze Biographie und ästhetische Darstellung seiner Werke*, Erfurt 1810, pp. 77–83.

[page 568, line 9:]
For '… obvious that ♪. of the Adagio …', read '… obvious that ♩ of the Adagio …'.

[page 614:]
'Hot Cross Buns', as in *A Christmas Box containing the following Bagatelles … Set to Music by Mr. Hook … London … A. Bland & Weller …*, is quite another tune than that used by Haydn. Author's collection.

[page 623, col. 1:)
Add: Dussek, Johann Joseph 138.

[page 637, col. 2:]
Under 'Country Dances … *Princess of Wales's Favorite Dance* … 206', page reference should read '484'.

Haydn: the Years of 'The Creation'
1796–1800

[plate 32, caption:]
The portrait of Griesinger is by Leopold Kupel-wieser (1835); *MGG* XVI, pl. 32. Present location not stated.

[plate 35, caption:]
For '1880' read '1800'.

[page 49, line 44:]
For '... Mount of Cavalry ...' read '... Mount of Calvary ...'.

[page 53, lines 10f.:]
Re Gelinek and the Esterházy household, we have now personally examined the important 'Personal and Salarial Stand Numero 1 Anno 1801' (see *Haydn: the Late Years*, p. 64), and nowhere in that document is he listed, in any capacity. The information that he was a part of Nicolaus II's establishment comes from Grove I (C. F. Pohl).

[page 56:]
We have meanwhile, on a trip to Budapest in June 1978, been able to discover a document in EH, Magyar Országos Levéltár, giving us the authentic size of the tiny Esterházy Capelle in 1795–6 (with salaries, *Naturalien*, i.e. payment in kind, etc.), when Haydn returned from England. The list does not include the *Feldharmonie* (two oboes, two clarinets, two bassoons, two horns).

[Varia 2461, now P. 149. 15:]
1796–7 [fol. 83]
Conventionale
der Hochfürstlichen Chor Musique von 1795

Organist Johann Georg Fuchs	[salary
als Tenorist item	etc.]
Discantistin Barbara Pillhofer	,,
Altistin Josepha Griesslerin	,,
Tenorist Johann Haydn	,,
Baßist Christian Specht	,,
Violinist Leopold Dichtler	,,
Violinist Franz Pauer	,,
Violinist Michael Ernst	,,
Violinist Joseph Dietzl	,,
Fagotist Caspar Peczival	,,

Buchhalterey Eisenstadt am 6tn Julÿ 796
Michael Zoller mpria

[On the right, the first column is marked: 'Betrag / als barer / gehalt und in Naturalien' ('Amount in cash and in kind'); column two: 'Besoldung' ('salary').]

[page 99, line 41:]
'Debfitz'. Roger Hellyer, who sent a long list of addenda and corrigenda on 30 July 1977 (here-inafter simply ('Hellyer') writes: 'I have met this signature many times and am almost convinced that the man's name was "Delefils", or "Delifils".' Jakob Eisen in fact died on 9 April 1796 (lines 36, 44).

[page 100, para. 5:]
Another hand: the handwriting is that of Count von Ugarte, *Hofmusikgraf* (Hellyer).

[page 155, musical example:]
Bar 2, B.C. third note = demisemiquaver; bar 3, B.C. ditto; bar 4, v. I fourth note = *a'* natural; bar 8, v. I appogg. a note higher; bar 10, v. I first note, add ♭ (Hellyer).

[page 235, second musical example:]
Bar 8, v. I for 2 quavers read 2 semiquavers (Hellyer).

[pages 238f.: musical examples:]
Add two flats to signature of timpani (as on pp. 236f.).

[page 242:]
Running head should read: 'Chronicle 1797'.

[page 261:]
Haydn had to engage outside musicians for some of the church services held at Eisenstadt in 1797, perhaps for the *Missa in tempore belli*. In a document in EH, Budapest (P. 149. 15, old 2461, now in Országos Levéltár) from Prince Nicolaus II Esterházy (fol. 101) to his *Gral Caßa* (General-Cassa, Chief Cashier's Office), dated Vienna, 3 April 1798, we read, 'There still remains the Specifica[ti]on of Kapellmr Haydn from the preceding year, concerning the individuals then engaged for church services, and which sum, one hundred three gulden 40 x [corrected to '15'], is outstanding and in accordance with the attached document Sub N 1 is to be forwarded to my Chief Cashier's Office for payment ...' (document continues with another payment to Pietro Trava-glia for the illuminations of the Eisenstadt Castle, for which he was responsible); on the left-hand margin at the bottom, the document is signed 'Exp fürst Esterhazy mp'.

[page 267:]
On 22 December 1797, Haydn wrote a letter to the Ministry of Justice:

Most worthy Imperial Privy Court Chancery of the Ministry of Justice:
Since the Imperial Court Chancery Official Joseph Keller, according to attached statements (No. 1) of witnesses, is not insane but only weak of mind [*blödsinnig*], the undersigned asks permission to have him removed from the insane asylum and brought home to his wife in his own apartment; and he [the petitioner] further takes upon himself the responsibility of engaging at his own expense an attendant who shall watch over him [Keller] day and night, until such time as one is persuaded that he is completely freed of his weakness of mind.
I am the most worthy Imperial Privy Court Chancery's Ministry of Justice's
Most obedient servant,
Joseph Haydn mpria [etc.]
[not in CCLN]

Notes: This letter, discovered by Peter Riethus, was published in Anthony van Hoboken's interesting article, 'Joseph Haydns Schwager', *Festschrift Josef Stummvoll*, Vienna 1970, p. 790. Joseph Keller was Haydn's brother-in-law and 'Registrant' in the Imperial Court Chancery. He was married to Maria Anna Eschenbruch who was forty-four years his junior. He owned a large and valuable library which he was forced to pawn; and when unable to repay the debt, he borrowed the sum plus interest from the Vice Chancellor, Prince von Colloredo-Mansfeld. On 1 August 1793 Joseph Haydn lent his brother-in-law 1,000 gulden for a period of four years at 4% annual interest, but Keller never paid the interest, and on 10 August 1797 Haydn joined the other creditors in trying to recoup his losses. At the end of August 1797, Joseph Keller declared himself bankrupt, and in the process of wrangling with the authorities he was declared insane (among other things, he was accused of keeping up to ten dogs 'which are better fed than many middle-class citizens', and also a collection of birds, including pigeons, 'so that his apartment is more like a *cloaca* that a place for human beings'; the doctor also thought it very odd that Keller should have spent 20,000 gulden on books, 'which he cannot possibly read').

Haydn, in his infinite goodness, was now so famous that the authorities at once released Keller and, two days after Haydn had written the letter, he was able to accompany his brother-in-law home. In January 1798 Keller was locked up again, and again Haydn went and had him freed, this time without any written request: Haydn simply went and extracted his brother-in-law from the madhouse without further ceremony. Keller's wife loved her husband to the end, and the authorities received a touching letter from her on 16 November 1801, saying that 'to my great sorrow, my husband Herr Joseph Keller ... died on 10 November of this year without leaving any last will or testament ...'. Meanwhile the Ministry of Justice was able to repay all Keller's creditors, and Haydn received his 1,000 gulden (but without the interest). For other details see Hoboken's article.

[page 271, line 8:]
The proper Croatian form of Kuhač's forenames is Franjo Saver (David Clegg, 29 Oct. 1978).

[pages 271ff.:]
H. Watzlawick, Venier (Switzerland), reminds us of an interesting publication not included in the Bibliography (*Haydn: the Late Years*): Franz Graeffer's 'Ursprung und Sachverhalt des Volksliedes "Gott erhalte Franz den Kaiser"', in *Franciseeische Curiosa*, Vienna 1849. Mr Watzlawick was kind enough to send a photograph of the complete article.

[page 287:]
In line 1 after '1780s', read 'Count Johann Nepomuk owned the ...' etc.; in line four read: '... Traeg, after the Count died in 1788. We suppose ...' etc.

[page 314, para. 2:]
The wind band was dismissed, with effect from 15 March 1798. EH, Budapest, Orszāgos Levéltár (P.149.15, fol. 105ff.), and that same document is a petition from the eight 'Harmonisten' (wind-band players) to the Prince, asking that they be retained, mentioning that they also 'participated in large-scale [*grosser*] music which the *Kapelmeister* [*sic*] Haydn performed to his [the Prince's] satisfaction ...'. The undated letter is filed under 1798.

[pages 421, para. 3, and 425, para. 1:]
The letter from Michael Haydn from which these quotations are taken was written in May 1806; it is cited in the *Biographische Skizze* of 1808 (Schinn, Otter), p. 24.

[page 429, final para., line 8:]
For 'November 1799' read 'November 1800' (Hellyer).

[page 527, third musical example:]
Insert ♭ before last note (= *b flat*).

[page 555, footnote:]
Letter sold at Sotheby's, 23 November 1977, lot 220; now Coll. Else Radant Landon, Library, University College, Cardiff.

[page 557, lines 12ff. and footnote 1:]
Barbara Scheiger (see also Addenda, *The Late Years*, p. 493). Through the kind offices of Otto E. Albrecht and the owners (who wish to remain anonymous), we are able to present this document in translation. It sheds some interesting light on social conditions of the period and shows beyond doubt that Haydn was physically present at the wedding; he probably took two days off from his duties at Eisenstadt.

In the name of the Most Holy Trinity
God the Father, Son and Holy Spirit,
Today on the date given below the following marriage contract – between the well born Herr Franz Xav: Disenni Magistrate Councillor's servant in Vienna as the bridegroom and party of the first part, and the honourable and virtuous maiden, Barbara Schaiger [Schaigerin], daughter of the late Karl Schaiger, citizen wig-maker in Vienna and his lawful wedded wife the late Barbara Keller [Kellerin], as party of the second part, – is herewith agreed and subscribed to as follows.

Firstly, the maiden bride brings to the above bridegroom and future husband apart from the dowry she has gathered a real capital for the marriage portion consisting of one hundred and fifty gulden which

Secondly, the bridegroom matches, as is customary in this land, with a counter sum of three hundred gulden, which marriage portion, that is of the first part and its counter sum, makes together a total of four hundred and fifty gulden, which sum they both

Thirdly, shall be considered to own during the marriage, and shall be entered in a special register, each for itself, to which shall be added any monies inherited or accrued in a legitimate fashion, the total to be considered common property; therefore, in case of death, and if there be children from this marriage, half shall belong to the children from this marriage and the other half the surviving partner; in case there be no children, the surviving partner shall inherit the entire property.

In attestation whereof this contract is drawn up in two identical copies, each of which bears the signatures and seals of both parties and those of the *Herr* witnesses, this First September 1800 at Vienna.

Franz Disenni mpria	Ursula Barbara
Magistrate's servant	Schaiger
as bridegroom	as ['bar' crossed out]
	bride
Paul Johann Siebert	Joseph Haydn
I. R. Office of Prin-	Fürstl. Esterhazischer
cipal Hall,	Capell-Meister
Assistant Clerk as	as witness
witness	

[page 566, line 4:]
Dr Hellyer writes: 'Johann Michel Werlen is surely an error for the bassonist Johann Michl, who should be in this list (see *Late Years*, p. 67). So far as I know, the name of a second clarinettist has not yet been traced for the Eisenstadt *Feldharmonie*.'

[page 620:]
Footnote reference 1 in text is missing: add to line 7, after word 'suspected'.

[page 636:]
Czerwenka: index entry should refer to the oboist Joseph, not the bassoonist Franz (Hellyer).

[page 639:]
For 'Füssel', read 'Füssl'.

[page 643:]
Under 'Krumau' read '(Český Krumlov)'; missing ref. for 'Kunst- und Industrie-Comptoir' is '47'; for 'Leó' read 'Léo'.

[page 648:]
Amend entry 'Scheiger, Barbara' as follows:
Scheiger (Schaiger), Barbara (I) 484
Scheiger (Schaiger), Ursula Barbara (II) 557.
In the case of (II) see also Addenda to page 557 (*supra*).

[page 651:]
Triebenesee: all references should be to Joseph, the son, not to Georg, the father (Hellyer).

Haydn: The Late Years 1801–1809

[pages 64f. and 67, line 14:]
Add to the list two more names which appear at different places in the same volume: (on f. 21v.)

'Klaviermeister Johann Fux [hat vorhin gedient als] Violinist bei W. Sʳ d. Fürsten Nicolaus', i.e. formerly violinist in the service of the late Prince Nicolaus; and (on f 37v.) 'Musik-Ansager Martin Czech' (his name also appears as Zech) who was aged 24 in 1801, spoke German and 'Bohemian' and had been 'Thurner Gesell in Wr. Neustadt dem Insurections Trompeter [beigegeben]', i.e. apprentice trumpeter in the Insurrection-Batallion at Wiener Neustadt. These were trained musicians whom Haydn could use, for example, as kettle-drummers or (in Fux's case) as violinist; the music announcer was hardly needed in the church.

[page 72:]
On 26 July 1801, Haydn signed a receipt at Eisenstadt for 2,000 gulden received from Härtel through Griesinger (autograph, Breitkopf & Härtel, Leipzig, destroyed in the Second World War but reproduced in facsimile in Wolfgang Schmieder, *Musikhandschriften in 3 Jahrhunderten*, Leipzig 1939, pl. 13.

[page 139, first music example:]
In bar 3, add ♭ in front of note.

[page 216, line 31:]
For '... ad graecas latendas!) 'read '... ad Graecas Kalendas!).'. This and other useful corrections were noted by the Rev. Nicolas Jowett, Sheffield.

[page 264:]
Mr J. O. Urmson, Cumnor, Oxfordshire (24 July 1977) writes of the following note by William Stenhouse in the 1839 edition of *Johnson's Museum* (Blackwood): 'This tune ["Galla Water", XXXIa: 15*bis*] was greatly admired by the celebrated Dr. Haydn. ... On the MS. of the music, which I have seen, the Doctor expressed his opinion of the melody, in the best English he was master of, in the following short but emphatic sentence: "This one Dr. Haydn favourite song".' See Hoboken, vol. II, p. 480.

[page 285:]
In their auction on 6–7 June 1978, Messrs. J. A. Stargardt sold an unpublished letter by Michael Haydn to his brother, undated, but which they (we believe rightly) date 1804, written in honour of Joseph's name-day, 19 March. We include here a translation of this previously unpublished letter (now Else Radant Landon Collection, Library, University College, Cardiff); the cover of the letter bears an authentication by Franz Joseph Otter, whose biography of Michael Haydn was published in Salzburg in 1808.

Johann Michael Haydn to Joseph Haydn, Salzburg. Du form]

[c. February 1804]
Once again your name-day is approaching, for which I wish you, without further ado, that which is dear and valuable to you; but for my part I, too, wish for myself that you will continue to remember me in brotherly love. – I have long wanted to write to you about our

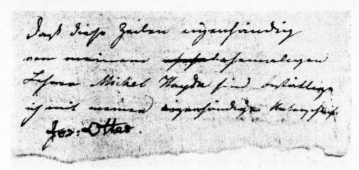

Certificate of authenticity, signed by Joseph Otter, written on the cover of Michael Haydn's letter to his brother (see below).

musical organization (which didn't start life until the second part of January [continued in a note at the bottom of the page:] and which you couldn't describe as jammed full) NB. The whole organization was begun with too much enthusiasm; by the time it arrived here, it had already got stuck. The first ones skimmed the cream off, and all that was left for us was a watery soup. Anyway, I didn't write because I was ashamed of myself. I was astonished when I received my contract – they had always kept me in hopes and in promises, and so time went by. I would rather tell you the naked truth myself, before someone else tells you about it with distortions. My entire increase in salary for the whole year consists of not more than 150 gulden. If I could have foreseen this, I would have accepted with both hands the generous offer of your prince. Why didn't I do so at the first opportunity! Well, *tempi passati*! I must comfort myself with the general consolation: it had to happen that way and not otherwise. But just this one thing: I remain with the innermost respect Your o[ld] b[rother] p.p.

On the cover: various calculations and certificate of authenticity signed 'Jos: Otter', with notes above:
'Berlin L[eo] L[iepmannsohn] / April [18]87', the great Berlin antiquarian.

Concerning the proposed engagement of Michael Haydn at Eisenstadt, see *inter alia*, pp. 252f. and 77.

[page 335:]
Haydn's letter of 6 March 1806 written by Cherubini was offered for sale by the Viennese antiquarian dealer, Wolfdietrich Hassfurther, on 16 December 1978. Several friends made transcriptions of the French original, including Warren Kirkendale and Helmut Watzlawick:
                    Vienne 6 Mars 1806
Messieurs,
M.ʳ Cherubini en me remettant la medaille que vous m'avez envoyée, a été temoin de la vive satisfaction avec la quelle je l'ai reçue. La lettre dont elle etoit accompagnee, en m'apprenant avec des expressions flatteuses pour moi, que les membres du Conservatoire de musique me

regardent desormais comme leur collegue a mis le comble a mes souhaits.

Je vous prie Messieurs à recevoir mes remercimens, et de les faire agréer aux membres du Conservatoire, aux noms des quels vous avez ₁eu la bonté de m'ecrire; ajoutez leur, que tant que Haydn vivre il portera dans son cœur le souvenir de l'interêt et de la consideration qu'ils lui ont temoigné.

J'ai l'honneur de vous saluer, Messieurs
          [Haydn's hand:] Joseph Ḥaydn.

[page 339:]
A letter from Haydn (not in CCLN), possibly to one of his many female admirers, must be inserted:

[To an unknown friend. *German. Sie* form]
– What? is that possible? That you allow your good old friend and servant to sigh so long after your noble presence? To see you for even a quarter of an hour would make me happy.
          Jos: Haydn mpria in his 74ᵗʰ year
          of age / 1805 / 6ᵗʰ 9ᵇᵉʳ [November]

[First published by Karl Scheffler in facsimile in 'Notenhandschriften großer Komponisten', *Kunst und Künstler*, XXIX. Jahrgang, Berlin 1931, p. 405; republished by H. Walter in *Haydn-Studien* III/1 (1973), p. 43]

[page 393:]
The first subheading should read 'KUPFERSTICHE UNTER GLAS UND RAHMEN ...'.

[page 403:]
Under subheading 'EIN LEBENDER PAPAGEY': in line 2 for 'Pagagey's ...' read 'Papagey's ...' (Jowett).

[page 439:]
MS. Catalogues: Clam Gallas Catalogue is in the National Museum, Prague; Dunwalt Catalogue in British Museum (British Library).

[page 455, column two, line 1:]
Read: 'Haydn's Missa Cellensis of 1766 ...'

[page 474:]
For 'Drobnat' read 'Drobnay' (Hellyer).

[page 488:]
Under MASSES: *Missa brevis* in F, for '328f.' read '338f.'

SUMMARY OF DOCUMENTARY EVIDENCE IN THE ESTERHÁZY ARCHIVES
FIRST PUBLISHED IN 'HAYDN-STUDIEN' (MAY 1980)

The publication in *Haydn-Studien* IV (May 1980), pp. 129–333, of documents in the Esterházy Archives (Forchtenstein Castle and Eisenstadt) has enabled us to include a summary of this essential new evidence before the present volume finally goes to press. The documentary material, published in detail by Ulrich Tank in *Haydn-Studien*, relates to the years 1761–1770, and we present it here in two parts – the first covering the period 1761–5, i.e. the years under discussion in the present volume, and the second covering the period 1766–70, which is discussed in the second volume of this biography, *Haydn at Eszterháza 1766–1790* (abbreviated here as *H. at E.*). In the following summary we shall omit all detailed references – these can be consulted in *Haydn-Studien* – and present the newly published documents with appropriate comments, referring – for purposes of identification – to the numbers allocated to individual documents in *Haydn-Studien* and to the page on which each appeared there (shown in square brackets). The relevant page reference in the present volume and (for the years 1766–70) in *H. at E.* is given at the beginning of each new item listed.

I Documents of the period 1761–5
(page numbers refer to the present volume)

1761

[page 349:]
Süttör, 5 May. Receipt signed by Theodor Liebscher, hunting-horn player, who – together with another horn player, Joseph Teucher – received 15 f. monthly; both were engaged as 'liveried servants and stable hands' in the retinue of Count (later Prince) Nicolaus Esterházy [Doc. 4 and 9; pp. 153, 155]. The names Liebscher and Teucher appear for the last time in a document of June 1761, but they may have continued until October (*vide infra*); neither man was a member of the official princely orchestra and the two are thus new to scholars.

[pages 356ff.:]
15 June. In a list of the musicians [Doc. 16, p. 160, with commentary, p. 159], the individuals are graded according to their position in the orchestra – thus confirming our table on p. 356.

[page 363:]
15 October. Receipt for the Oedenburg *Thurnermeister* and his musicians for playing at Süttör for 'His Excell. Hhrn Grafen Nicolao Esterhazy'. Playing dance music was not among the regular assignments of the Esterházy musicians, and balls required the engagement of an outside orchestra – Oedenburg's Town *Thurnermeister* for Süttör and their local counterpart for Eisenstadt. There is no

evidence that Haydn's orchestra ever played at the balls given in the various Esterházy castles, though on one occasion we hear (in 1772) of Haydn's conducting dance music at the Grassalkovic Palace in Pressburg (see *H. at E.*, p. 180). There may well have been exceptions to this rule, however.

[page 366:]
Süttör, 31 October. A new musician is engaged from 16 October to replace Theodor Liebscher and Joseph Teicher, horn players: one Andreas Krämpl (or Krampl), at 10 fl. monthly, again part of Count Nicolaus's retinue [Doc. 28, pp. 162f.].

1 November. Receipt by Haydn (Vienna) for 50 fl. paid as an additional salary for the quarter 1 August–31 October from the privy purse ('Cammer Beutel') of Prince Paul Anton. Is it possible that the Prince was privately paying Haydn more than his official 400 Gulden p.a. (the same as Werner's salary) so as not to offend Werner? Facsimile in Valkó I, after p. 632 [Doc. 31, p. 163] See also our commentary on p. 366 (1762).

1762

[page 366:]
28 February. Receipt by a music copyist, Georg Brenner, for 88 Bogen of music for Count Nicolaus who, as we see, had his own small music establishment in Süttör [Doc. 43, p. 166].

[page 367:]
Süttör, 10 March. Gotthard Carl Sutor (Sütter, Suter) is engaged to replace Andreas Krampl as

Addenda and Errata

part of Count Nicolaus's retinue, and receives 12 f. as a liveried servant [Doc. 48, p. 167]. When Nicolaus becomes Prince, Sutor is included in the princely *Haushofmeister* bills and his name appears next to another liveried servant, Anton Adolph, copyist, who became the official Esterházy copyist until May 1764 and is thus of great importance to us. He receives, like Sutor, 12 f. monthly (liveried servants were paid monthly salaries, the lowest class of servants daily). [Doc. 49, p. 168].

[pages 371f.:]
Haydn did not compose *La Marchesa Nespola* in 1761 or 1762 but more likely in 1763, because it was not copied until the Summer of 1763 (*vide infra*).

[page 372:]
Eisenstadt, 25 June. Haydn's bill [Doc. 53, pp. 170f.]:

Specification

What I the undersigned organized in the way of various musical requirements for His Highness, The Prince, viz.

	f	Xr.
First, on 1st April mouthpieces for the oboe, English horn and bassoon	6	11.
One bundle of E strings	2	—
Item half a bundle A	—	45.
No less, a violin bow 5° makes	2	—
Music paper 4 books	3	12.
The 15th of June 4 more such books	3	12.
The 18th ditto 2½ bundles E	5	—
Item the above d° one bundle A	1	30.
No less, 40 batches D	—	40.
Also 2 'Cello [*Passetl*] C	—	34.
The same 2 *Passetl* G	—	34.
Ditto 2 *Claffter* [denotes size] *Passetl* D	—	12.
No less 3 *Claffter Passetl* A	—	12.
Also 5 overspun Violin G	—	15.
And also 2 Violon [double bass] A	—	42.
Also 4 *Claffter Passetl* D	—	24.
The locksmith for repairing the music cabinets [and] making new keys	1	3.
Summa	28	26.

Joseph Haydn mpria.

These expenses of eight and twenty Gulden 26 x should be paid by our Eysenstadt Disbursement Office.

Nicolas Fürst Esterhazy mpria.
Eysenstadt, 25th Juny 762.

I attest that the above eight and twenty gulden 26 Xr have been paid to me by the local Disbursement Office, for which this is the receipt.
Eisenstadt, 27th June 762:

Joseph Haydn mpria.

1763

[pages 382ff.:]
Eisenstadt, 20 January. Receipt by the local *Thurnermeister*, Anton Höld, and his men, for 16 f. 40 xr., for 'music provided at the marriage of His Excellency Count Anton Esterhazy.' Trumpets and drums were used to accompany fireworks, strings (two violins, double bass) for the dance music [Doc. 70, pp. 175f.].

[page 384:]
Vienna, 20 February. contract with the Impresario-Actor Johann Michael Brenner to go with three other persons on 21 Feb. to Süttör, to take his theatre together with his marionettes and to entertain His Highness daily with German comedies (etc.). It is signed with the additional information '... Brenner, Actor in Vienna in the Landtstrasse living at H[err] Binapfel's in the Gemein Gasse.' It is significant that this previously unknown document shows Prince Nicolaus's interest in marionettes [Doc. 73, pp. 176f.].

[pages 384f.:]
Auguste Houdière. In a newly discovered document [No. 95, pp. 188f.] of August 1763, listing all the musicians, her name is crossed out, so that it is now believed she remained only four months in princely service. Correct *H. at E.*, p. 48. Doc. 80, p. 179 (in the present volume on p. 384).

In a series of bills submitted by the Hospitallers in Eisenstadt, various medicines for Haydn and the musicians are listed. We do not propose to list them all in detail since the information may be found in *Haydn-Studien*, but the evidence seems to point to Haydn suffering from stress (steady stream of laxatives, purgative medicines, medicines for wind in the stomach, *Lattwerg = Electuarium*, a mixture of various pills with dried prunes [and sometimes honey] as a strong laxative, etc.). See Docs. 85, 89, 102, 113, 175, etc.

From 26 April to the end of July, Prince Nicolaus visited Italy [Doc. 80, 2nd part, p. 179].

The most significant document [No. 93, pp. 182f.] in this series is a pathetic letter by the copyist Anton Adolph, which – because of its great interest – we translate in full:

Most Serene Highness and Noble Prince of the Holy Roman Empire Gracious and Dread Lord!

It will be known to Your Serene Princely Highness in your infinite grace that I, a poor copyist, Antonj Adolph, have often submissively requested Your Princely Highness in your gracious mercy to improve my yearly salary; for I, a poor man, who is also married, have no more each month than twelve gulden in cash, together with the livery like other servants, and from this my meagre salary I must not only pay for my lodgings but also for wood, candles, and must support myself, miserably, even though I am crushed with work, so that as copyist I work day and night to supply the operas and comedies, as the enclosed list will attest. And not only must I copy all this but even supply my own ink.

Considering that for all this I receive only 12 fl. and the livery (but without coat), it is difficult especially when it rains or snows, which is bad for the paper I take back and forth; that I have to pay for lodgings, wood and especially candles because I have to write so much at night; that my yearly salary, which is anyway not large, is stretched to the utmost; therefore I beg Your Serene Princely Highness on my knees, in humility and submissiveness, that in your graciousness (known to the whole world) you grant me some improvement in my monthly salary, or something towards lodgings, wood or candles; for which act of grace God the Almighty will reward you richly, but I with my poor wife will pray to God every day in our prayers to grant rich blessings to Your Serene Princely Highness. And so I comfort myself that you will heed this my request, and remain, Your Serene Princely Highness's

Humble and Submissive Servant,
Antonj Adolph

Specification

What was copied for Your Serene Princely Highness for operas and comedies, paper lined, and copied, from 3 May to the month of August this year 1763, viz.

Whole Bogen
[4 pages]

First. Opera Vocal score, together with the Recitatives for Friedberg [Friberth] of L'Mantile	24.
Sinfonia ex D	14.
paper lined with music staves	96.
Opera vocal score for Bon	40.
lined the paper for composing, 6 books, makes	144.
Music ordered by Your Serene Highness and sent to Italy:	
1mo } written	14.
item }	18.
lined	48.
written	34.
Ditto }	71.
item } written	15.
Ditto }	9.
Opera vocal score L'Mantile for the Italian, written	48.
Ditto, lined, 4 books, makes	100.
written	5.
item for the new Comedy L'Marchese, violin & Bass	18.
Parts for a new Sinfonia ex D with all instruments	17.
Ditto a new Concerto for Schwenda on the double bass	13.
item 6 new Trios, written	18.
Lined	72.
item, ditto, lined	14.
Summa	832.

Translation: we have rendered the word 'Auszug' as 'vocal parts', but it may mean – as it certainly does in the case of the Symphony in D – simply 'parts'. The first Opera is probably Domenico

Fischietti's *Il mercato di Malmantile* (Carlo Goldoni), Rome 1757, given in Vienna in 1763, of which Haydn owned the libretto (cf. *Haydn: the Late Years 1801–1809*, p. 323, last entry); Ulrich Tank's notes – but see also *infra*, note concerning p. 392, for another possibility. The first Symphony in D is apparently No. 13, of which the autograph is dated 1763, but in view of the four horns must be *post*-August), while the sensational 'Auszug eine Neüe mit allen Instrumenten ex D: Sinfonia' can only mean the hitherto elusive No. 72 (with its solo violin, solo 'cello, solo double bass, flute, two oboes, bassoon, four horns and strings), which we tentatively dated 1763 (see the present volume, pp. 552, 564), but which may now with confidence be assigned to the months May–August 1763. The Concerto for Double Bass is surely the lost work by Haydn (VIIc:1), which may now also be dated 1763. The other important fact is that the 'Neüe Comedie L'Marchese' – which is of course Haydn's *La Marchesa Nespola* – is now known, on the basis of this document, to have been first copied in the middle of 1763 – which date also coincides with the engagement in that year of Auguste Houdière and with the Aria composed for her. We congratulate Herr Tank on this brilliant discovery. The unfortunate Adolph later (in May 1764 – *vide infra*) ran away from Eisenstadt in desperation.

In a further document [No. 95, pp. 188f.], the range and 'order' of the musicians are given – important in connection with the horn players: '1ter Waldhornist Carl Frantz [*sic*], 2ter ... Frantz Reiner, 3. ... Johann Knoblauch, 4ter ... Thadeus Stein Müller', which means that in our order in the present volume (on p. 385) Franz, not Knoblauch, should appear as first horn.

[page 387:]
Süttör, 19 September. Receipt concerning one of the actors staying for a month. No record of the players, or the additional singers (from an Italian company?) needed to mount *La Marchesa Nespola*, appears in the records [Doc. 101, p. 190].

[page 389:]
Vienna, 20 November. Receipt of organ-builder Johann Fridolin Ferstl for repairs done in the St Leopold Chapel of the Esterházy Palace in Vienna ('Repairung des Positif'), where on St Leopold's Feast-Day (15 Nov.) instrumental and vocal musicians from St Michael's Church under Ferdinand Zängl, *Musices Director*, held a service in memory of Emperor Leopold I, who had conferred the title of Prince on the Esterházy family. [Docs. 107, 108, pp. 191f.]. See also *infra*, note to *H. at E.*, p. 125.

[page 392:]
December. There is a copyist's bill by Champée, who made the catalogues for the Esterházy house discussed in the present volume on p. 314. Now we find him submitting a bill [Doc. 115, p. 193], as follows:

Memoire
de
la Copiature faite pour Son Altesse le Princ [*sic*]
Esterhasi

	feuilles
Airs Francois	18
Le Ballet de Bergers d'arcadie	22
Les Sculpteurs	22
La vengeance de l'amour	39
flore [*sic*]	27
Totale	128

à 25 fl 36 Cr.
recû la dite Somme à 24 fl: — Cr: [*sic*]
Champée Copiste

Noteworthy that Prince Nicolaus's interest in French music continued in the tradition of Prince Paul Anton, and that presumably Haydn conducted all this 'foreign' music as well. In other documents (Vienna, December 1763) we learn of a visit to the Esterházy Court of Georg Noëlli, a famous virtuoso on the 'Pantaleon' (*MGG* 9, Sp. 1547f.). [Docs. 117, 118, p. 194].

1764

[page 392:]
Receipt, Vienna, 2 January 1764, by the famous Giuseppe Scarlatti, who incidentally also composed *Il mercato di Malmantile* (see the present volume, p. 84), and who is therefore a candidate for the Eisenstadt production of that Opera in 1763 (*supra*, 385). Scarlatti received a fee for having 'insegnato á cantare a due Giovane due Mes: . . .' and was thus in close contact with the *Capelle*. [Doc. 124, p. 196].

[page 395:]
May 1764. List of liveried servants at the Eisenstadt Court: '. . . the copyist Adolph has secretly fled, therefore no salary listed', a shameful end to a shameful episode in the Esterházy chronicle; and yet one more ghastly reminder, to Haydn, of the dire poverty in which most musicians lived in those days. *Vide supra*, p. 385. [Doc. 133, p. 199].

[page 398:]
Opera performances. A series of documents, partly to do with wine for the performers in Kittsee Castle and Pressburg, suggests that Haydn gave operas in the summer at both those places: the *Capelle* was at Kittsee from the end of June until 30 September, but there is a document about 'Wine consumed in Kitsee [*sic*] and Brespurg [*sic*] on 14th July 764' [Doc. 140, p. 201]. The *Haushofmeister* bills also inform us that the Emperor himself was at Kittsee on September 1–3 and 26. Another most entertaining document [No. 162, p. 205] Pressburg, 17 December 1764) tells us of wine consumed by the musicians on that day, viz. 6 bottles of white wine, 1 of vermouth, 2 champagne, 1 Cyprus, half a bottle of muscat, 3 of tokay and 26 half-bottles of officers' wine – obviously a reward for a performance of some opera. The most intriguing document (Vienna, 29 Dec. 1764, pp. 206f.) is Prince Nicolaus's own letter to Rahier,

authorizing the printing of two Italian opera libretti in 4to format, with 50 copies 'of each kind'. There is no trace of these libretti anywhere. Could one have been the revised *Acide*?

In August 1764, Joseph Elssler was engaged as music copyist at 12 f. per month (the same sum as that of the departed Adolph) [Doc. 144, p. 202]; correct *H. at E.*, p. 65. He soon became Haydn's principal personal copyist, too, and no doubt earned some welcome extra money in that capacity.

[page 401:]
Medicine bills for musicians (also the present volume, p. 403). Prince Nicolaus relented and, by January 1765, the other musicians were again receiving free medicine from the Hospitallers in Eisenstadt. [Docs. p.206; 175, 176 etc., p.209].

1765

[page 405:]
1 April (Stamitz), correct *H. at E.*, p. 79 (1, not 15, April). On 20 March 1765 we now have the first bill by the famous string-instrument maker, J. J. Stadlmann, for repairs to a baryton. [Doc. 185, p. 211].

[page 411:]
Novotny family: the widow of Johann Novotny, Anna Maria, seems to have lost her sanity and had to be locked up in Landsee. She was later released. [Doc. 206, pp. 215ff.: 20 July *et seq.*].

Innsbruck baryton: we now have a bill, dated Millau (Mühlau), 7 August, in which Nicolaus Esterházy asks that his expenses of 40 ordinary ducats for the purchase of the instrument be entered in the books. Haydn seems to have sent three baryton pieces to the Prince at Innsbruck, to which the following document [No. 210, p. 220] refers:

> . . . The three new pieces for my gamba which were sent to me have been received in time, and I am satisfied with them, which is to be told also to Capelmeister [*sic*] Haydn. / Inspruckh [*sic*] 10th August 765. Nicolaus Fürst Esterhazy mpria.

In a bill submitted by J. J. Stadlmann (undated, but in the *Haushofmeister* papers of September), he refers to various repairs on the baryton and then adds the interesting note, 'Pariton repaired at Insprug', which seems to suggest that Stadlmann was (a) in Innsbruck and (b) intimately connected with the sale of the new instrument to Prince Nicolaus. [Doc. 214, p. 221].

[pages 412ff.:]
Further documents about the fire and Sigl [Docs. 215, 218, pp. 221ff.]. Prince Nicolaus writes to Rahier:

> . . . Moreover, in case such an occurrence should be repeated in my absence at any time in the future, and the musicians should object to your orders, you yourself, should it become neces-

sary, should also have them arrested by the grenadiers, and I shall support you at all times.
. . .

On 15 September Nicolaus, then at Süttör, answered Rahier's letter (present volume, p. 414) by writing that in view of his apologies Friberth was to be retained in princely service,

but he is to be warned not to indulge in any insubordination, bad conduct or to stir up any trouble, as he was hitherto wont to do, otherwise he may be assured that one will not permit his presence in our service for a single moment . . .

[page 417:]
20 October. Haydn countersigns a bill of the paper-seller Franz Oberauer for thick paper for the covers of MS. parts. On 25 October Franz Novotny submitted various expenses for the 'Fürstl: Chor Flich', the harpsichord in the choir at Eisenstadt, also for quilling two instruments in 1765. [Docs. 227, 228, pp. 225f.]. In an earlier bill (1763), Friedrich Schüller, master locksmith, refers to 'den fürstlichen Klavikordi', i.e. the princely clavichord. [Doc. 88, p. 181].

[pages 418ff.:]
Further documents on the lack of order in the choir-loft, etc. [Docs. 230, 233, 237, pp. 226ff.] In one letter, from Rahier to Prince Nicolaus, we read: 'As I learn from outside sources, the musicians like to play, sometimes at Countess Lodron's, sometimes at Countess Amour's; if I knew that Your Highness did not approve, I would forbid it ...'. Nicolaus even occupied himself with the excessive use of wax candles in the Castle Chapel, and suggested that one could have a test case and see how long a wax candle (such as was being used in the Chapel) actually burned, and expected an answer of the subject from Rahier. Süttör, 3 November 1765: this is the document referred to in the present volume at the bottom of p. 419.

[page 422:]
3 December. Bill from J. J. Stadlmann for repairs to a baryton, and also to a 'cello (glued in many sections) [Doc. 243, p. 229]. Interesting that all these early Stadlmann bills, having to do exclusively with Prince Nicolaus's own instruments, were paid by the Cashier without being countersigned by Haydn.

II Documents of the period 1766–70
(page numbers refer to *Haydn at Eszterháza 1766–1790*)

1766

[page 71:]
Carl Franz left service in December 1776 but his salary was paid till the end of January 1777 (*HJB* VII, 94).

[page 118:]
A communication from the Eisenstadt Administration [Doc. 254, p. 233], dated 5 January, reads:

Because Herr Capellmeister Heyden at princely request had to depart at once for Vienna, no *robbath* [= *Robot*, compulsory services (in manorial practice), here used for a kind of waggon] could be organized in time, so a transport]*Fuhr*] had to be ordered in Eisenstadt, which was paid according to agreement by the Rental Office pr 5 f. Eisenst 5th Jan 1766

Edmund Schlanstein
Admin.

I acknowledge receipt of these 5 fl. from the Rental Office, Eisenst 7th Jan 767:

Joseph Haydn mpria

We cannot explain the discrepancy in the dates, but we propose that 1767 may be correct; Haydn was not yet full *Capellmeister* in January 1766, since Werner was still alive.

Undated petition by Hieronymus Le Bon and four singers for new sets of clothes (uniforms for men, dresses for women). Two years ago all the musicians received new clothing, but since then the non-singers have received uniforms several times. [Doc. 250, p. 232].

[page 120:]
Re Stadlmann's bill of 4 April, countersigned by Haydn, note that this relates to general repairs to various instruments used by the *Capelle*. In the *Haushofmeister* bills for February [Doc. 258, pp. 233f.], March [Doc. 267, p. 236] and May [Doc. 277, p. 239], there are other bills submitted by Stadlmann for work on the princely baryton, these not countersigned by Haydn.

In an undated letter (May 1766?), Simon Thaddäus Kölbel (cf. *H. at E.*, p. 201), organist and pupil of Werner, who had earlier (March 1766) applied for further funds for his music studies, now applies for the post of violinist made vacant by Garnier's departure in February 1766, but which in the event was filled by Purksteiner. Kölbel played not only organ and violin but also double bass (*violon*); he says he applied for the post nine weeks earlier and was well known to 'Herrn Capellmeister Heyden'. Kölbel became organist at the Church of St Dorothea in Vienna and later held the prestigious post of Choir Director at the Church of St Charles Borromeo (*Karlskirche*) in Vienna. Haydn was not an admirer of Kölbel. [Doc. 280, pp. 240f.].

[page 123:]
Eisenstadt, 24 July. Melchior Griessler, the singer, applied to the Prince for lodgings or, in lieu, payment; this request was granted, 'thirty gulden for this year' was allowed to the suppliant 'as a special act of grace'; and Griessler is to have the first available lodgings in the Mayrhoff (the Mayerhof, a large building near the Castle which is still [1980] intact, though there are rumours that the town of Eisenstadt intends to demolish it). [Doc. 285, pp. 241f.].

In the monthly bills of the *Haushofmeister* at Eisenstadt Castle [Doc. 289, p. 242] there is a note:

f Xr:

To the musician Hölbl who
composed 2 Parthien for baryton
at princely request 2: Duc: 8   15

U. Tank thinks, no doubt rightly, that the document refers to baryton music composed by Simon Thaddäus Kölbel (*supra*).

[page 125:]
15 November, St Leopold's Day. Another memorial service held in the St Leopold Chapel of the Esterházy Palace in Vienna, with forces from St Michael's Church under Ferdinand Zängl. See also *supra*, Part I; note to p. 389 (1763). [Doc. 300, p. 244].

28 November. Bill for repairs to the seat of the Choir Organ in the Eisenstadt Chapel, signed by Franz Novotny. [Doc. 301, p. 244].

Undated request (among bills of 1766), by the copyist Joseph Elssler, for a new coat [Doc. 305, p. 245; also reproduced in facsimile (p. 333)]:

... Inasmuch as Your Highness has engaged me as part of your Chamber Music as a copyist and has graciously consented to grant to me, as with other servants, livery, a coat was also granted to me two years ago. But since this coat is already falling to pieces, and in this year all the servants received a coat apart from their clothing, whereas I received neither, therefore
my submissive request is extended to Your Highness, that His Grace allow me, a poor man, also to have this coat ... [etc.]
Your most humble
Joseph Elssler, Copyist.

1767
[page 132:]5 January. Bill for various items connected with the princely baryton, submitted by J. J. Stadlmann, without Haydn's countersignature. Refers to the Innsbruck baryton. Also repairs to a viola (part of the Esterházy chamber ensemble for baryton trios) and a 'cello (ditto). [Doc. 317, pp. 247f.]

Vienna, 14 January. A newly discovered document [No. 318, p. 248] regarding the binding of the first 'official' volume of Haydn's baryton trios, twenty-four in number, reads as follows:

Conto
That which was done for bookbindery work on order of Titl: His Princely Highness and Lord von Esterhasj
3 music books with 24. Divert: by Hayden
Red with gilt in a slip cover, as agreed à 10 f —
Paid in full by the Herr Hauß Hofmeister Zisser [Züsser] to the amount of 10 f — Vienna 14th Januarj 767
Josephus Aloy: Maurer mpria
Bibliopeg [*sic*]

See letter in *H. at E.*, p. 126, footnote 1; but according to this new evidence it would seem that the three parts (baryton, viola, violoncello)

included Baryton Trios XI:1–24, the first of five such MS. collections put together by Haydn for Prince Nicolaus. The fourth has survived and is now in EH, Budapest, Mus. Ms. I.110. For the (lost) fifth volume, see *H. at E.*, p. 411.

[pages 134f.:]
February. *Haushofmeister* bills, Eisenstadt, note the following [Doc. 320, p. 249]:

f   Xr

107. To H Heyden, for the
extraordinary engagement
[in Pressburg] of hunting
horns and double-bass
players   22   37½

Haydn, having written horn parts in *La canterina* which were less difficult than (say) those of Symphony No. 72, could afford to use local Pressburg horn parts for the Opera, and use Dietzl and Franz as violinists. We suggested (p. 135) that a double-bass player was engaged locally, and as we see, this was in fact done. Perhaps Haydn used a local first horn for the high (first) part and Steinmüller for the less difficult second horn part. The double-bass player(s?) were required for almost the whole Pressburg sojourn. It is a pretty gesture on the part of Prince Nicolaus to have rewarded not all the playing musicians but also Joseph Elssler, the copyist, whose receipt [Doc. 324, p. 249] reads:

I acknowledge receipt of a present consisting of 1 Duc: which I have received in full and in cash from Titl: Herrn Hauß Hoffmeister Zisser [Züsser]. Preßburg, 28th Febr: 767
Joseph Elssler
Copyist.

Elssler's beautiful and accurate hand was much appreciated by both Esterházy and Haydn.

The lack of a double-bass player no doubt encouraged Haydn to speed the engagement of Carl Schiringer, double-bass and bassoon player, at Pressburg on 1 March (*H. at E.*, p. 78).

[page 137:]
Eszterháza (now used officially instead of 'Süttör'), 15 March. Prince Nicolaus writes to Rahier that the Prince had promised to be godfather to the latest child born to Anna Maria and Joseph Weigl, 'and you will be good enough to do this [i.e. act as proxy] for me'. The couple also received 24 ducats. [Docs. 331, 337, pp. 250–2].

Carl Franz, Eszterháza, 20 March, signs a receipt for travel expenses from Pressburg to Eszterháza, 'Pr six gulden eight Xr ... when I and Zweglin [Frau Zwegl] and the wife of the Pressburg House Inspector and many other princely officers went from Pressburg to Esterhaz ...'. Prince Nicolaus liked to have his horn players at his constant disposition for chamber music and perhaps the hunt and other fanfare-like music. [Doc. 332, p. 251].

Eszterháza, 26 May. In a newly discovered document we now have for the first time authentic information about the theatrical activities at Eszterháza in the early summer of 1767: Lorenz Riersch, 'Principal' of a Theatrical Company, signs a receipt for 48 f. as a fee for his troupe during their stay at Eszterháza Castle from 3 to 26 May. They gave 'comedies' (i.e. plays – which might have included tragedies, too) every day. The agreed fee was 40 f., to which Esterházy added a 'Discretion' (additional fee) of 8 gulden. [Doc. 343, pp. 252f.].

Eisenstadt, 3 June. Letter from Rahier to Prince Nicolaus about Leopold Dichtler and his wife, who would have liked to have had an increase either in cash or of goods in kind. Rahier notes [Doc. 346, p. 253]:

He receives 150 f. in cash and the *Deputat* his job entails; his wife receives 100 f. salary and the same *Deputat* as he; so I don't really see how he can ask for more. At the beginning he dined at the officers' table, but since that's been stopped, he asked Yr. High. that he receive instead 30 xr. *per diem* to be paid out to him together with his salary. But Yr. High. has given him that *Deputat*, as is proper for such a person ...

[page 138:]
3 July. Fireworks-Producer Johann Georg Stuwer (not 'Stuwez') receives 20 f. 37½ Xr., apparently for the celebrations in connection with the birth of Count Anton, son of Count Anton who would later reign as Prince (1790–4). Herr U. Tank thinks that the money paid by Princess Esterházy three days later (see *H. at E.*, p. 138, last two lines) to Haydn and Dr Molitor was in some way connected with the birth. [Doc. 351, p. 254].

11 July. Griessler (*supra*, p. 123, 1766), noting that as yet no lodgings are free in the Mayerhof, requests, also for 1767, thirty gulden lodging money. This was granted. [Doc. 353, pp. 254f.]

[page 141:]
Yet another bill, dated 3 October from Vienna, from J. J. Stadlmann for various items for the princely baryton, not countersigned by Haydn. The inclusion of many bushels of strings suggests that Prince Nicolaus intended to take his baryton to Paris and laid in a good supply of spare strings. This theory is supported by the final note, 'Item for the packing box and for the packing 2 [f.] 30 [Xr.].' [Doc. 362, p. 256].

[page 143:]
After Christmas, 1767: bill from Franz Nigst, *Rentmeister*, summing up the expenses of the Castle Chapel at Eisenstadt and the *Capelle* from 16 March. Many of these bills have been quoted for the year in *H. at E.*, and great is our astonishment to see that in several cases the total sums of the bills *do not agree* with the sums for the same bills found in the Nigst document. Examples: as item 'M' in Nigst we find the bill of 25 September (*H. at E.*, p. 140). Nigst has 60⅔ Xr., the actual bill 40. Item 'N' in Nigst is the bill (*H. at E.*, p. 140) for binding *inter alia* the second volume of Haydn's Baryton Divertimenti, 28 f. 10 Xr.; the actual bill reads 25 f.

15 xr. [Doc. 375, p. 258]. We are, unfortunately, unable to explain these discrepancies, which Herr U. Tank seems not to have noticed (explanation of Austrian dialect words also faulty in Tank's footnotes, e.g. his eccentric transliteration of 'Karmesin' for 'Charmosin', which means, of course, chamois).

1768

[pages 148f.:]
Jacob Wan Week's (Wanweg's) binding bill contains *inter alia* the Third Volume of Haydn's Baryton Trios for Prince Nicolaus. Herr U. Tank thinks that the following document may be a reward for the completion of this Third Volume:

Commission

According to which our Chief Cashier Johann Zoller is to pay against receipt to our Capelnmeister [*sic*] Haÿdn four and twenty Species Ducats and to enter the same in the books, Eszterház, 26th May 1768.

Nicolaus Fürst Esterhazy

Above 99f have been paid to be correctly and in full by the General Cassa through Herrn Johan [*sic*] Zoller

the 19th Junj 768

Josephus Haydn mpria

[*HJB* IV, 46]

In the Eisenstadt *Haushofmeister* accounts for June 1768, there is a hitherto unknown bill from J. J. Stadlmann for items in connection with Prince Nicolaus's baryton [Doc. 400, p. 262].

Oedenburger *Thurnermeister*: A bill [Doc. 403, p. 263] in EH, Eisenstadt, informs us of the unexpected principal duties of the trumpeters and drummers, viz.:

House Expenses July 768

	f	xr:
The 26th dº to the ThurnerMaister Planckh in oedenb: for a choir of trumpets and kettledrums to accompany the fireworks	12	22½

It is nevertheless possible that such choirs of trumpets and drums were used also in church and/or chamber besides accompanying firework displays.

Vienna, 27 July [Doc. 404, p. 263]:

I the undersigned herewith confirm that I have received from *Titul* Herrn Michael Kleinrath [Esterházy's inspector of buildings] for a musical instrument, namely a baryton, correctly and in cash the sum of 4 ducats in gold.

Vienna 27th July 768   Joseph Adam
                          Court Musician

[pages 151f.:]
The visit of Duke Albert von Sachsen-Teschen and Archduchess Marie Christine. In a document of the *Haushofmeisteramt* [No. 410, p. 264], we read:

Extra House Expenses 7ber [September] 768

Nº		f	x
...			
420	the 28th to the man who lends the masks, for the masks for the entourage of the Archduchess at the ball in Esterhas	18	—
421	Item for the masks which at Highest Request were given to the princely musicians	63	—

For further details see *H. at E.*, p. 152, and the present volume, p. 622.

Concerning the first performance of *Lo speziale*, U. Tank says that there is no evidence in EH for Harich's assumption that it was given on 5 August (see the present volume, p. 621, last entry), and that it is more likely that it coincided with the visit of the Duke Albert and Marie Christine, 24–29 September; thus our original assumption that the Opera was given on 28 September (*H. at E.*, p. 152) is probably correct, especially since Magdalena Spangler was engaged on 18 September (retroactive date: 1 Sept., see *H. at E.*, p. 48) and was not a member of the *Capelle* on 5 August.

Some further documents, hitherto unknown: [Doc. 412, p. 265:] 31 [*sic*] September, bill by Castle Innkeeper Ignaz Eigner at Eszterháza Castle for 20 musicians' wine and keep, 6½ days; countersigned by Haydn, Eisenstadt, 8 October 1768. There were not yet quarters at Eszterháza to lodge 20 musicians. For the dance music, for trumpet and kettledrum fanfares (and possibly for use with fireworks), the *Thurnermeister* of both Eisenstadt and Oedenburg were engaged [Doc. 415, p. 266]: Antoni Höldt, 'Thurner / Maister in Eysenstatt', signs a receipt for 12 f. 30 xr., for the ball at Esterhaz; [Doc. 416, p. 266]: Joha: Leopold Planckh, 'Thurnermstr mpria / Oedenburg' signs a receipt for 50f., for the trumpets and kettledrums together with 11 persons for the ball (more than two violins and bass, then).

[page 152:]
19 December. Vittorino Colombazzo, engaged on 1 September 1768, leaves the *Capelle* (correct *H. at E.*, p. 70) [Doc. 438, p. 275]. An interesting new list of the *Capelle* [Doc. 426, pp. 270f.] of 11 December 1768, is also given, together with a whole series of documents specifying the detailed repairs to Haydn's destroyed house, then being rebuilt at princely expense [Docs. 428, 435, 462, 463 (1768, 1769)].

[pages 153f.:]
Actually, the case of Nigst is more complicated, and Haydn's petition was not entirely successful; though in the long run, Nigst was reinstated. On 30 December [Doc. 433, pp. 272f.] Nigst writes:

... I had to learn from the Bookkeeping Department and also from Capellmeister Haydn that not only am I dismissed as violinist with my previously yearly salary of 50 f but also that I am to return the summer uniform, given to me in grace and worn all last summer,

together with the winter uniform, recently given but nonetheless already worn.

I am not aware of having done anything wrong, so that this sad sentence crushes me to the ground, especially as ... I have suffered greatly through the fire and the new rules of the town and, God knows, I am in no condition to buy a suit of clothes out of my present salary ... [He relies on Prince Nicolaus's generosity and goodness.]

The petition was refused.

1769

[page 155:]
29 January. Prince Nicolaus gave a ball in his palace in the Wallnerstraße for the Noble Hungarian Bodyguard, and we are astonished to learn, from newly discovered documents, that there were five trumpeters and a kettledrummer [Doc. 458, p. 281] and also that the dance music was ordered from Pancrazio Huber (about whose dance music, see *H. at E.*, 405, 431 – Haydn's invitation to compose dances for the Redoutensaal as polite answer to Huber's composing dances for Esterházy?); Huber was paid 65 f. Anton Meckel, 'Musician', provided an orchestra of 17 persons, for which he was paid 84 f., 40 xr. [Docs. 444, 445, pp. 277f.]. Question: for the various foreign orchestras that played at the various Esterházy balls, did Haydn compose his dance music? Did the normal Esterházy *Capelle* never play dance music? If so, why did Haydn compose dances with the typical Esterházy orchestral constitution of two *C alto* horns and timpani (see *H. at E.*, p. 575)? Also, Playel wrote dances with that peculiar combination (see the present volume, p. 242), presumably for Eszterháza.

[page 156:]
Eisenstadt, 18 February. In connection with Dietzl's re-engagement, P. L. Rahier writes [Doc. 450, pp. 277f.] to Prince Nicolaus that

it really is the case that our schoolmaster Joseph Dietzl cannot exist just from his schoolmaster's contract, for turned into money it does not consist of more than 83 f. 32 xr.; the school children's fees will bring him in about 40 f. p.a., and the fees from his church duties are very small. It is also true that as Schoolmaster and Market Clerk at Purbach he earns, without church fees and schoolchildren's fees, 184 f. 31 xr. in cash and kind ...; therefore I think that his old contract should be, in grace, confirmed and continued.

On 4 March 1769, Joseph Dietzl (Sen.) was re-engaged as musician in the church choir.

Eisenstadt, 5 March. An unedifying row between the two 'cellists, Ignaz Küffel and Joseph Weigl [Docs. 456, 457, pp. 279ff.]. Küffel submitted a petition to Prince Nicolaus (5 March), in which he says, '... During the return trip from Esterhaz to Eisenstatt, the whole Chamber

Musique had lunch with the *traiteur* at Edenburg [Oedenburg], and at the end of lunch there arose words between me and Weigl, in the end Weigl, without having endured an insult from me, called me a son-of-a-bitch [*Hundtsfutt*] in the presence of the Capellmeister and the whole Musique; Yr. Serene Princ. Highn. cannot allow such a name to stick to me, and I call to witness my superior the Herr CapellMeister, that I am in no way inferior to Weigl ...', etc. To this P. L. Rahier added a long *postscriptum* (also 5 March). Contents: according to Weigl, 'Küffl' while at Esterhaz said in the presence of 'Tomasiny' and the valet-de-chambre Prügel that Weigl plays out of tune and is not capable of accompanying an opera, and that the 'Kapelmstr' himself said that to 'Küffl'; whereupon when Weigl got back to 'Eißenstadt' he asked the 'Kapelmeister, did he say such a thing to Küffl? The Kapelmeister answered him, No, and he should repeat the assertion with Küffl in front of him,' etc. Now when the 'Kapelmeister', Weigl and 'Küffl' were brought together and confronted with all this, Haydn admitted that he had said Weigl sometimes played out of tune, but not that he couldn't accompany an opera, whereupon Küffl said that he had never said the latter, only that he plays out of tune, etc, etc. The Kapelmeister also said that Weigl had called the other one a ... [omission in original] etc. Moreover, they all say that the whole animosity between the two arose because each one wants to be the first and sit at the right hand; but both are sorry that they bothered Yr. Princely Highn. with it all and want to make it up with each other. Prince Nicolaus's answer (Vienna, 6 March) reads *inter alia* that Rahier should 'reprimand Weigl this time and moreover indicate to them both that neither is the first and both are equal'.

[page 157:]
Eisenstadt, 12 April. Rahier on the complicated subject of Leopold Dichtler's contract suggests that since Dichtler has the smallest salary/*Deputat* of the officer/musicians, it would be right that instead of board and *Deputat* he should, in grace, receive half a gulden daily. [Doc. 464, pp. 282f.].

Add to the first bill (p. 157) at the end, 'I hereby acknowledge to have brought the above from Vienna, and have been paid 5 f 21 xr from the Rental Office. Eisenst. 29th April 769 / Christian Specht.' [Doc. 466, p. 283].

Olmütz, 14 May [Doc. 472, p. 284], letter to Prince Nicolaus from the composer Anton Neumann, who also wrote 24 Baryton Divertimenti for Prince Nicolaus. Neumann writes:

... Attached I take the liberty of proffering, in humble submission, the 6 Duets which are missing from the second dozen, and I can only wish that they please Your Highness. The narrow limits of this instrument [the baryton] make many of the pieces sound similar, because not every idea can and should be realized on it. I have taken special efforts with these 6 Duets as an experiment, so that they should have more

harmony in them but at the same time not be difficult ...

Anton Neumann, Capellmeyster
to the Cathedral Church [of Olmütz].

10 June. A newly discovered bill from J. J. Stadlmann, 'What was delivered to the house of Your Serene Prince Highness Fürst von Esterhasy', strings and items for two barytons, a viola and a violin, not countersigned by Haydn so presumably for Prince Nicolaus's private chamber music. [Doc. 479, pp. 285f.].

July, August, September, December. Bills for new uniforms [Docs. 485, 486, 496, 499, 500, 522, pp. 287–300], from which we learn that the basic colour was now 'speckled' grey [Doc. 496, p. 291], and that two 'ordinary Grauen Campagne livere' (livery) suits were delivered – perhaps for someone like Joseph Elssler?

[page 158:]
Eszterháza, 20 July. Document for the *Feldharmonie* (wind band), in which adjustments need to be made (*H. at E.*, p. 72) to the departure dates of the Kapffer brothers: Johann Michael left at the latest on 20 July 1769, Johann Georg at the end of 1770 or the beginning of 1771. [Doc. 487, p. 288].

[page 159:]
Eszterháza, August. During this month there was another visit by the Hungarian Palatine, Duke Albert von Sachsen-Teschen and Archduchess Marie Christine. There is a newly discovered bill [Doc. 489, p. 289], from which we see that there was a masquerade, with masks for the eyes and 'domino masks', some with beards. We read the intriguing note: 'then, for the H: Capell Meister once again 2 domino masks for the Opera' and sixteen masks for the actors and actresses of the Catherina Rössl Troupe. Which Opera? A revival of *Lo speziale*? The new *La contadina in corte*?

Eszterháza, 24 August. On that day was a grand ball at the Castle, for which Prince Nicolaus engaged no less than sixteen musicians of the Oedenburg *Thurnermeister*, Johann Leopold Planckh, who received 40 f. Perhaps this was the last event of the visit by Duke Albert and Marie Christine.

[page 160:]
Eszterháza, 17 September. Engagement of Giacomo Lambertini as bass, needed for Haydn's new Opera, *Le pescatrici*. Add to *H. at E.*, p. 59, the following data: appeared as 'Mastricco' in Haydn's *Le pescatrici* (1770), left Eszterháza some time after 18 September 1770 (given a cash reward: *H. at E.*, p. 166), during his second engagement also appeared as 'Valerio' in Guglielmi's *La sposa fedele* (1778).

Eszterháza, 17 September. Yet another grand ball, for which Planckh supplied sixteen musicians, this time at a fee of 48 f. We also have the detailed bill from the Castle Tavern [Doc. 503, p. 294], showing what the musicians were given to eat, and a very handsome menu it was, the day after (perhaps they were given princely refreshments while they played during the evening of the 17th):

Specification

....

	f	Xr
First, soup for 16 persons	—	32
Beef with red beets	—	48
A dish with vegetables and meat	—	32
6 pairs of frying chickens with salad, 20 Xr the pair	2	—
8 Maß of wine à 16 Xr makes	2	8
Bread for everybody at 1 Xr makes	—	16
Summa	6 f	16 Xr.

Ignati Eigner
schloß wirth in
Esterhas ...

Eszterháza, 15 October. Yet another splendid celebration, with a ball, for which *Thurnermeister* Planckh supplied his sixteen musicians at 48 f., but apart from them 'Extra for the trumpets and timpani during the fireworks', for which 4 fl. were required. Ignaz Eigner, at the Castle Tavern, gave them an evening meal 'auf die Nacht' on the 15th with 'Eingemachtes' (veal in a sauce), geese, wine and bread, for lunch the next day there was soup, beef with horseradish sauce, vegetables and meat, 'Eingemachtes', wine and bread. Again those trumpets and timpani: *only* for the fireworks? [Docs. 506, 507, 508, pp. 294 ff.].

Vienna, 30 November, 1 December. Newly discovered documents show that the musicians, with some exceptions, were not taken to Vienna during the Christmas period and the first months of the new year. Prince Nicolaus arranged to have quarters rented from one Josepha Star for the two horn players (probably Joseph Oliva and Franz Pauer), for Luigi Tomasini, and for Carl Friberth. [Docs. 517, 519, 520, 532]. The winter period in Vienna lasted from 30 November to the end of March 1770 (U. Tank). Interesting that Prince Nicolaus always had the horn players in his vicinity. All this fascination with horns and horn playing is undoubtedly reflected in those exceedingly difficult horn parts in Haydn's music of this period.

1770

[page 161:]
Vienna, 28 March. The whole bill, countersigned this time by Haydn on 6 April, is Stadlmann's list of material for many princely instruments (hence Haydn's countersignature), and herewith [Doc. 537, pp. 305f.] reproduced correctly for the first time. Interesting note on the tuning of the double bass: apart from the usual 'Cammerstimmung', in this case F sharp and A strings, we also find the 'Kirchenstimmung', (low) F 'ibersponen mit Trat', i.e. with metal wire wound round it.

Eisenstadt, 30 April. Robbery in the quarters of Carl Friberth, as reported by Rahier [Doc. 538, p. 306]: the thief stole two gold watches and a purse

with 12 Kremser Ducats, etc., the thief was seen, and had his own hair with a 'bad hat' and a blue coat.

Ditto. bill countersigned by Haydn for 4 dozen oboe reeds and a dozen cor anglais reeds, each 10 Xr., makes 10 f: 'which I have received correctly and in cash from Herrn Rentmayster Nix [Nigst] ...' [Doc. 539, p. 306].

Eisenstadt, 3 May. Bill by master-carpenter Carolus Flach, a new case for a harpsichord 7 feet 8 *zol* (*zoll*) long, 3 feet 4 *zol* wide, 1 foot high, and various repairs, etc. In 1769 Flach had made another harpsichord case (*H. at E.*, p. 160, but correct note 3 to read: 'Flach: A.M. XIII, 739', whereas the document of 3 May 1770 is A.M. XIII, 722).

[page 164:]
Kittsee Castle, 25 July. The mysterious trumpets and timpani and the other additional musicians are now explained in a newly discovered document [No. 546, p. 308] that once again shows how extremely useful Herr Tank's research is for all of us:

To His Highness Prince Esterhasi for 20 music persons in service in Kitse[*sic*], as agreed 3 f. per person with my own person double makes f 63 — / for 1 choir of trpts & timpani [f] 4

f 67

30th July 1770

Paid in cash to me 67 f. by
Herr Hauß HofMeister Züsser
Mathias Azlsberger
Town-*ThurnerMeister*

Extra for the trip 1 f 12 x – paid

No doubt this very large group played the dance music, while the trumpets and drums were used for various fanfares and perhaps for other kinds of music as well. This was the Eisenstadt *Thurnermeister*, and is a new name.

While on the subject of the great *Fest* at Kittsee Castle, the crucial tailor's bill (*H. at E.*, bottom of p. 162, top of p. 163) is now reproduced for the first time complete and accurately [Doc. 559, pp. 311f.].

[page 165:]
Eszterháza, 17 September. For the ball, Prince Nicolaus again engaged the Oedenburg *Thurnermeister*, J. L. Planckh, who brought not only eighteen men for the 'Ball Musiq in Esterhas' but a choir of trumpets and timpani for the fireworks, for all of which Planckh received 48 f. The receipt is signed 'Esterhas, den 18ten 7ber [September] $\overline{770}$' [Doc. 553, p. 309]. Dr Harich had kindly informed us of the existence of this large group of non-*Capelle* musicians (see *H. at E.*, p. 166, also note 1) but it is good to have the precise details.

Vienna, 20 August. Rental of a Viennese flat for two horn players, as before. The flat was in the Naglergasse (the huge Esterházy Palace extends a whole block, its façade facing the Wallnerstraße, its rear entrance on the Naglergasse), a stone's throw from the Palace. *HJB* VIII, 139f.

[page 166:]
Vienna, 25 September, Stadlmann's bill also includes strings for the double bass in the *Cammerstimmung*, 'the weak A string' (i.e. the high *A*), 'One Violon Fis' (*F* sharp) and 'One Violon D', as well as 3½ 'Glaffter' (*Klafter*) 'Violon A for the strong string', i.e. low *A* [Doc. 555, pp. 309f., reproduced complete for the first time].

Vienna, 15 November: Ferdinand Zängl again organized the music for the Feast of St Leopold in the Leopold Chapel in the Esterházy Palace on the Wallnerstraße, Vienna [Doc. 564, p. 313]. Apparently this would now become a regular feature of life in the Vienna Palace.

[page 169:]
Vienna, 31 December: a bill for J. J. Stadlmann for 'What I delivered to His serene Highness Prince von Esterhasy in 7̄7̄0̄ for lutemaker work.' The first half of the bill seems to concern the usual princely instruments for the *Capelle*, hence also the double-bass strings in the *Kammerstimmung* (*A–D–F* sharp–*A*), while the second half is marked: [delivered] 'to the Princely House' and concerns repairs to, and strings for, a violin and a viola. Haydn countersigned the bill on 31 December 1770. [Doc. 569, pp. 314f.].

Eisenstadt, 31 December: a bill from Joseph Dietzl, Sen., listing expenditures for the Castle Chapel music *Capelle* during the year 1770. It includes strings for violins, viola, violoncello ('Bassl') and other items but, curiously, no reference to anything for a double bass. Countersigned by Haydn. [Doc. 571, pp. 315f.].

An interesting list, from the Eisenstadt *Rentamt*, informs us of the musicians' salaries, *per diem* monies and their goods in kind (*Deputat*) for the latter part of the year 1770. It is signed by the individuals concerned, Maddalena Friberth, Barbara Dichtler, Eleonora Jager [Jaeger], [Franz] Novotni [Novotny], Melchior Griessler, Gertrud Cellini, Christian Specht, Joseph Oliva, Frantz Pauer and Carl Franz. [Doc. 576, pp. 316–8.].